THE FIRST EARL OF SHAFTESBURY
From the painting, after J. Greenhill, in the National Portrait Gallery

THE FIRST
EARL OF SHAFTESBURY

BY

K. H. D. HALEY

*Professor of Modern History
in the University of Sheffield*

CLARENDON PRESS . OXFORD
1968

69 953
942.063

THE FIRST
EARL OF SHAFTESBURY

Oxford University Press, Ely House, London W. 1

GLASGOW NEW YORK TORONTO MELBOURNE WELLINGTON
CAPE TOWN SALISBURY IBADAN NAIROBI LUSAKA ADDIS ABABA
BOMBAY CALCUTTA MADRAS KARACHI LAHORE DACCA
KUALA LUMPUR HONG KONG TOKYO

FOR IRIS

PREFACE

IT is now just over twenty years since I first began my attempt to elucidate the personality of 'the false Achitophel' and over such a long period the debts that I have accumulated to fellow-scholars, archivists and others have become considerable. There are those who think that the world of scholarship is a world of intense rivalry and *odium academicum*; but I should like to place it on record that in working on this book I have experienced nothing but co-operation and encouragement. If I have not attempted to repeat my thanks to all those who have helped in various small ways by including a long list of their names, this is not the result of any ingratitude on my part.

Amongst my larger debts I must first acknowledge that to the present Earl of Shaftesbury for permitting me to see the books in the Library and the papers in the Muniment Room at St. Giles House; and to Lady Ashley Cooper for opening these rooms for me. I am equally indebted to the Marquis of Bath for making it possible to see the Coventry and Thynne Papers at Longleat, and to the then librarian, Miss Coates, for her kind assistance. Like many others, I owe much to librarians and assistants in the Bodleian Library, in the British Museum, the Public Record Office and the Sheffield University Library, though it would be impossible for me to name them all.

I owe a more general debt to Mr. C. D. Beatty, to Christopher Hill, and to Sir Keith Feiling for each in their different ways stimulating my interest in the seventeenth century, though I fear that none of the three will be altogether satisfied with the view of Shaftesbury which is presented in this book. Mr. E. S. de Beer has shown a constant kindly interest in its preparation, and finally devoted himself to reading it through in typescript and making some valuable criticisms: I hope that the finished work does not fall too far short of his exacting standards of scholarship and style. More indirectly I owe much to the constant encouragement and friendship of George Potter, under whom it was my good fortune to work at Sheffield for eighteen years. I suspect that secretly he may sometimes have wondered whether the project which was first mentioned to him so long ago would ever be completed. That it has been finished is partly the result of my being able to work in the congenial environment which he provided at Sheffield University.

A tribute is also due to two people whom I have never met, my predecessors as biographers of Shaftesbury: to W. D. Christie, whose book was a considerable achievement when it was published in 1871, and to Miss L. F. Brown, who unfortunately was never able to write the second book which she promised when she concentrated on Shaftesbury's earlier years in 1933. If I mention these writers only where I differ from them this is not from any desire to denigrate their work.

Finally, two acknowledgements which might appear to be formal but are not. One is to the Sheffield University Research Fund and to those administering it, for the grants which have made possible many of my visits to archives. The second is to my typist, Miss Dorothy Kirkland, whose care and accuracy helped to keep me up to the mark.

K. H. D. HALEY

Sheffield, January 1967

CONTENTS

The First Earl of Shaftesbury. From the painting, after
J. Greenhill, in the National Portrait Gallery   *Frontispiece*

CONTENTS

LIST OF ABBREVIATIONS

THE following list is not intended as a bibliography, but only as a guide to the references. The titles of all other manuscripts and books referred to are given in full in the footnotes.

MANUSCRIPTS

1. In the Public Record Office
   Shaftesbury Papers. This refers to the collection of family papers which were deposited in the Public Record Office a century ago. Some accounts and legal documents remain in the Muniment Room at St. Giles House; where these are referred to, their location at St. Giles House is always mentioned.
   C.O. Colonial Office Papers.
   P.C. Reg. Registers of the Privy Council.
   S.P. Charles II. State Papers Domestic of the Reign of Charles II.
   S.P. State Papers Foreign (cf. also Foreign Entry Books).
2. Bodleian Library
   MSS. Ashmole, MSS. Carte, MSS. Clar., MSS. Locke, MSS. Rawl., MSS. Tanner. These refer to the well-known Ashmole, Carte, Clarendon, Locke, Rawlinson and Tanner collections.
3. British Museum
   Add. MSS., Egerton MSS., Lansdowne MSS., refer to the collections of Additional, Egerton, and Lansdowne manuscripts.
4. Longleat
   Coventry Papers and Thynne Papers.
5. Despatches of Foreign Ambassadors
   References to these are by the name of the ambassador and the date of his despatch (given in both styles). The despatches of the French ambassadors may be consulted in the Baschet Transcripts in the Public Record Office; those of the Dutch in transcripts in the British Museum, Add. MSS. 17677, references being given to distinguish between the ordinary and the secret series; those of the Venetians are calendared in *C.S.P. Ven.* (see below) and those of the Brandenburg envoy are printed in L. von Orlich, *Briefe aus England über die Zeit von 1674 bis 1678* (Berlin, 1837). References to Spanish ambassadors are to their correspondence now in the archives at Brussels, from the Ambassade Etrangère de la Haye (A.E.H.). Imperial despatches have been used by O. Klopp, *Der Fall des Hauses Stuart* (Vienna, 1875–88), and Florentine despatches by Anna M. Crinò, *Il Popish Plot* (Rome, 1954).

PRINTED BOOKS

Brown. L. F. Brown, *The First Earl of Shaftesbury* (New York, 1933).
Browning, *Danby*. A. Browning, *Thomas Osborne, Earl of Danby and Duke of Leeds* (1944–51).
Burnet. G. Burnet, *History of My Own Time*, ed. O. Airy (1897–1900).

Burnet, *Supplement*. *A supplement to Burnet's History of My Own Time*, ed. H. C. Foxcroft (1902).

Burton. T. Burton, *Diary of Thomas Burton, Esq., Member in the Parliaments of Oliver and Richard Cromwell* (1818).

Christie. W. D. Christie, *The First Earl of Shaftesbury* (1871).

C.J. Journals of the House of Commons.

Clarendon, *Continuation*. *The Continuation of the Life of Edward Earl of Clarendon* (1827 ed.).

Clarendon, *Rebellion*. Clarendon, *History of the Rebellion* (1888).

C.S.P. Col. *Calendars of State Papers, Colonial series, America and the West Indies.*

C.S.P.D. *Calendars of State Papers, Domestic series.*

C.S.P. Ireland. *Calendar of the state papers relating to Ireland, 1625–1670.*

C.S.P. Ven. *Calendar of State Papers and manuscripts relating to English affairs existing in the archives and collections of Venice.*

C.T.B. *Calendars of Treasury Books.*

D.N.B. *Dictionary of National Biography.*

E.H.R. *English Historical Review.*

Evelyn. *The Diary of John Evelyn*, ed. E. S. de Beer (1955).

Grey. A. Grey, *Debates in the House of Commons* (1763).

Groen van Prinsterer. *Archives ou Correspondance inédite de la maison d'Orange Nassau, Second Series*, ed. G. Groen van Prinsterer (Leiden, 1857–62).

Hatton Corres. *Correspondence of the family of Hatton*, ed. E. M. Thompson (Camden Society, 1878).

H.M.C. *Reports of the Historical Manuscripts Commission.*

L.J. Journals of the House of Lords.

Luttrell. N. Luttrell, *Brief Historical Relation of State Affairs* (1857).

Martyn. B. Martyn and A. Kippis, *The First Earl of Shaftesbury*, ed. G. W. Cooke (1836).

Pepys. *Diary of Samuel Pepys*, ed. H. B. Wheatley (1893–9).

Reresby. J. Reresby, *Memoirs*, ed. A. Browning (1936).

Sidney Diary. H. Sidney, *Diary . . . including his correspondence with the Countess of Sunderland*, ed. R. W. Blencowe (1843).

State Trials. *Collection of State Trials*, ed. W. Cobbett (1809–28).

Temple, *Works*. Sir W. Temple, *Works* (ed. 1754).

Note on Dates. The year has been taken as beginning on 1 January. In the text the day of the month has always been given in the Old Style which was in use in England in the seventeenth century; but in the footnotes, where letters by ambassadors and others were originally dated in the New Style, dates in both styles are given (e.g. 14/24 Aug. 1667).

CHAPTER I

INTRODUCTION

> Of these the false Achitophel was first;
> A name to all succeeding ages curst. . . .

IN these familiar lines Shaftesbury stands pilloried for all time. The couplets follow one another with a measured inevitability which gives the illusion of a carefully considered, objective, judicial sentence. When one thinks of Shaftesbury this description of Achitophel naturally springs first to the mind. 'Not to be familiar with *Absalom and Achitophel* is not to be educated'[1] and it is commonly regarded as the just exposure to permanent public ridicule and scorn of a noted criminal, caught *in flagrante delicto*. It is not easy to escape from this first view.

Yet any student of the seventeenth century knows well that not everyone who was sentenced to the pillory was sentenced justly: that sometimes the rotten vegetables, brickbats and filth which were thrown were undeserved. Sharpness of characterization is not the same thing as accuracy: the Englishman who is being politically educated must include in his education an appreciation of the circumstances in which the poem was written and the purposes for which it was designed. He may compare with the pseudo-moderation of *Absalom and Achitophel* the greater malice of *The Medal* and the crudities of *Albion and Albanus* and wonder whether the one is likely to be more reliable than the others, or whether the identification of Shaftesbury with Achitophel is any more satisfactory than that of Charles II with King David.

It is also true that many of Dryden's attacks on Shaftesbury do not coincide with modern ideas. Whereas the twentieth century probably thinks first of the innocent victims of the Popish Plot scare and the perjuries of Titus Oates whom Shaftesbury patronized, Dryden omitted any reference to the former and cautiously took the view that 'some truth there was, but dash'd and brew'd with lies'. On the other hand, Dryden's definition of Achitophel's purpose,

> That Kingly power, thus ebbing out, might be
> Drawn to the dregs of a Democracy,

though it may have caused the blood of contemporaries to run cold, is hardly likely to have that effect on us today, who do not share Dryden's scorn of 'the Solymaean rout'. As the loyal subjects of a queen who is far

---

[1] C. V. Wedgwood, *Poetry and Politics under the Stuarts* (1960), p. 164.

from being the nearest claimant to the throne by strict hereditary succession
and who bases her title entirely on the Act of Settlement, we cannot but
agree with the words put into Achitophel's mouth as he tempts Absalom,
that

> . . . the People have a Right Supreme
> To make their King; for Kings are made for them.
> All Empire is no more than Pow'r in Trust,
> Which when resum'd, can be no longer Just.
> Succession, for the general Good design'd
> In its own wrong a Nation cannot bind:
> If altering that, the People can relieve,
> Better one Suffer, than a Nation grieve.

After 1688, the argument over the principle of Exclusion was effectively
decided in the Whig favour. In so far as Dryden's satire retains its force,
it depends on the genius with which the poet argues that the discussions
over principle were simply a cover for the 'wilde ambition' of Shaftesbury
and the folly or knavery of a gang of worthless supporters.

It may of course be reasonably argued that ambition is an indispensable
quality in a political leader, and even that unless, like the elder Pitt, he
believes that he can save England and no one else can, he has no right to
aspire to power. But not unnaturally his opponents are apt to believe that
an ambitious politician is concerned rather with the exercise of political
power for its own sake, irrespective of the national good, 'Resolv'd to ruin
or to rule the state.' This is the motivation which Dryden ascribes to
Shaftesbury; as he says at some length,

> Great Wits are sure to Madness near ally'd;
> And thin Partitions do their Bounds divide:
> Else, why should he, with Wealth and Honour blest,
> Refuse his Age the needful hours of Rest?
> Punish a Body which he could not please;
> Bankrupt of Life, yet Prodigal of Ease?

The basic problem is whether the famous statement about great wits and
madness is as clever as it seems to be, or whether it is only a facile remark
betraying the fact that Dryden has failed to find a convincing explanation
for the old man's restless political activities. Is it, for instance, the only
logical conclusion to be reached from the various 'changes of side' commonly
detected in Shaftesbury's career? Looking back with the hindsight of three
centuries, and the attitude of mind of Private Willis, we like to be able to
allocate politicians firmly to one side or the other in a particular dispute;
there is a natural tendency to regard doubts, inconsistencies and changes
of side as the mark of insincerity, self-seeking and downright dishonesty.
But the more we know about a period, the less able we are to regard it in
the tidy categories of a century ago. It may, for instance, be possible to

consider 'changes of side' as only the expression of changes of mind about the best political means to make effective a general outlook that is consistently held. The question is whether this applies to Shaftesbury's case, or whether the simpler explanation of ambitious knavery is adequate.

Shaftesbury's career therefore presents considerable personal and psychological attractions to the biographer. Not only this, but it is one of great importance to the historian, in that it influenced most of the great issues which were being fought out in the seventeenth century.

The year 1621 in which he was born was not one of epoch-making events in English history. Even Macaulay's schoolboy might be forgiven for not having much detailed knowledge of what occurred in it. Yet as we look back on it, we can discern already most of the themes which were to dominate the sixty-two years of Shaftesbury's lifetime.

If we take first of all the most obvious of these, the No-Popery issue with which Shaftesbury was to be associated, we can find first expressed in this year the fears of the parliamentary classes that Roman Catholicism might return to England through the passing of the crown by normal hereditary descent to a Roman Catholic prince. The danger from foreign invasion and the internal rebellion of a Catholic minority which had dominated the second half of Elizabeth's reign and the Gunpowder Plot period was giving way to the new dangers presented by the Spanish match—the danger that the royal family itself would come under Catholic influence until a Catholic monarch appeared who would conduct a Counter-Reformation. On 3 December 1621, the House of Commons drew up a petition to James I in which they objected to the Spanish match and to the other encouragements which they said royal policy was giving to Popery. 'For', they said, '1. The Popish religion is incompatible with ours in respect of their positions. 2. It draweth with it an unavoidable dependency on foreign princes. 3. It openeth too wide a gap for popularity to any who shall draw too great a party. 4. It hath a restless spirit and will strive by these gradations: if it once get but a connivancy, it will press for a toleration; if that should be obtained, they must have an equality; from thence they will aspire to sovereignty, and will never rest till they get a subversion of the true religion.'[1] Here we see stated in terms which would have been regarded as axiomatic by Protestants for the rest of the century the reasons why they felt that Popery should not be encouraged: Roman Catholics would naturally look to the leading Catholic power on the continent, whether Spain at the beginning of it or France at the end; and in addition peaceful co-existence of Catholics and Protestants within the country was impossible because Catholics in the long run would not be satisfied with it. And it must be agreed that in seventeenth-century conditions there was much justification for these arguments, as the history

[1] J. R. Tanner, *Constitutional Documents of the Reign of James I, 1603–1625* (1930), p. 277.

of Belgium, Bohemia and France shows. The dislike of the Spanish Infanta in the 1620s, of Queen Henrietta Maria in the 1630s, and of the Duke of York in the Exclusion crisis was not as irrational as has sometimes been lightly supposed.

This theme, the fear of a possible Popish successor, was linked with others. It is unnecessary to labour the point that this was not purely a religious issue, but concerned everything which the twentieth century has come to sum up under the cliché of 'our way of life'. Englishmen regarded Catholicism as the natural ally of royal absolutism, and therefore also as the normal accompaniment of the subordination of the material prosperity of the subject to the financial needs or caprices of the king; Popery meant 'wooden shoes'. These political and economic themes were also discernible in 1621. In January of that year Parliament met for the first time for seven years, or ten if the brief fiasco of the Addled Parliament is excluded; and in the course of the debates the whole question of the position which Parliament was to occupy in the constitution was raised by implication. When James tried to prevent the House of Commons from discussing foreign policy and the Spanish match, the Commons protested in sweeping terms 'that the arduous and urgent affairs concerning the King, State, and defence of the realm and of the Church of England, and the maintenance and making of laws, and redress of mischiefs and grievances which daily happen within this realm, are proper subjects and matter of counsel and debate in Parliament', and that every member had complete freedom to discuss them.[1] James, arguing that such ambiguous and general words 'might serve for future times to invade most of our inescapable rights and prerogatives'[2] took the famous step of tearing this protestation from the Commons' Journals with his own regal hand; but, notwithstanding this drastic action, the underlying assumptions of the Commons could not be so easily exorcized. They foreshadowed the demands of the Long Parliament for at least triennial parliaments and of Shaftesbury's followers for annual ones, and the insistence of both on pressing upon the King their views on any subject they chose.

Not only that, but the events of 1621 also pointed out a way in which they could make their views felt. Although the medieval weapon of impeachment was certainly not revived as a means of securing the responsibility of ministers to the Commons instead of to the king, the fall of no less a victim than Lord Chancellor Bacon himself was a precedent clearly showing later Parliaments the uses to which this procedure could be put. Implicit already in this impeachment was the possibility of preventing the king from pursuing a policy contrary to the wishes of the parliamentary classes by threatening with ruin or even death the ministers on whom he would have to rely. The attempt to impeach Lord Treasurer Danby and to prevent him from pleading the royal pardon was a logical consequence,

---

[1] Tanner, op. cit. p. 289.   [2] Ibid. p. 294.

revealing the determination of the king's opponents to subject him to the wishes of the nation in Parliament; though as almost always in the century the question whether Parliament really did represent the view of the nation was conveniently begged.

In the economic life of the country dates are naturally of less significance, and although 1621 was a poor year for English trade, which was still suffering the effects of the misguided Cokayne project which James I had adopted, no dramatic events took place. If a symbolic date is wanted here, we must look forward two years to the so-called 'massacre of Amboina'. The English merchants who met their deaths at the hands of the Dutch in the East Indies may be taken to represent both the overseas expansion of English trade which was the most prominent feature of English economic history in the seventeenth century and also the rivalry with the Dutch to which it gave rise. No single event did more to foster anti-Dutch prejudice than this. On this point, curiously enough, Shaftesbury and Dryden came closer together than on most others; while the politician was in three different governments which fought wars with the Dutch, and was responsible for the famous *Carthago delenda est* speech, the poet wrote a propagandist play on the subject of the massacre of Amboina itself.

In another part of the globe also the early 1620s saw important events taking place. From the standpoint of world history there can be no doubt of the immense importance in the long run of the colonization of the eastern seaboard of northern America. Though this had begun earlier in Virginia, when Anthony Ashley Cooper was born the Pilgrim Fathers had spent only one grim winter struggling with hardships and disease on the desolate shore of New England. When he died in 1683 several flourishing colonies had been securely planted across the Atlantic, and his own inspiration had been largely responsible for the beginnings of one of these, in Carolina. But when mention is made of the Pilgrim Fathers, we are reminded also of their determination to worship God in their own way, and consequently of what became (though no one envisaged it quite in that way in 1621) the eventual development of religious toleration for different varieties of Protestant Dissent from the established Church. Here too Shaftesbury and his friend John Locke had their part to play.

Finally one other date may be mentioned. Periods are no more satisfactory in intellectual than in economic life, but still the publication in 1620 of Bacon's most important philosophical work, the *Novum Organum*, remains noteworthy. Bacon's work points not only to the repudiation of traditional Aristotelianism which was going on apace, but to the development of experimental science, the secularization of large areas of thought, and the growth of an empirical approach. It is no accident that the century which began with Bacon ended with Locke, who at an important period of his life was a member of Shaftesbury's household.

No Popish successor; parliamentary sovereignty; overseas economic

expansion and colonization; religious toleration for Dissenters; an intellectual revolution in the direction of rationalism: these were the issues
uppermost in the sixty-two years of Shaftesbury's lifetime. None of them
was to be finally decided before he died, a defeated exile; but on all of
them he had an important influence. The nature of this influence and the
extent to which it was directed by public or personal motives or the result
of accidental circumstances are the subjects of this book.

CHAPTER II

THE BOY AND HIS INHERITANCE (1621–39)

ON 10 December 1616, articles were signed providing for a marriage which would unite the Ashley and Cooper families. In an age when marriages were commonly made not in heaven but in the muniment-room, this was an eminently suitable match. The families were close neighbours: the Ashley seat at Wimborne St. Giles in the north-eastern corner of Dorset lay only six or seven miles across hill and stream from the Cooper house at Rockbourne in the far west of Hampshire. There was no great difference in birth between them. It is true that the Ashleys could lay claim to a longer pedigree, extending back to one Benedict de Ashley of Ashley *juxta* Bradford, Wilts[1]; indeed according to one tradition the family was of Saxon origins. Fortunately the details of such pedigrees are of less importance nowadays than they were to the aspiring gentry of the early seventeenth century, and it is unnecessary for our present purpose to conduct a renewed heraldic visitation to verify them. We may take it that the Ashleys were a gentry family of insufficient distinction to play any part on the national stage before the sixteenth century, but steadily adding to their landed possessions in Wiltshire and Dorset by judicious marriages; and it is likely that the same is true of the Coopers, although in their case we do not possess even the shadowy names of ancestors before the reign of Henry VII.

To many such families of minor gentry the Tudor period presented opportunities, and both Coopers and Ashleys availed themselves of them. Richard Cooper was granted the manor of Paulet in Somersetshire, taken from the Gaunt's Hospital in Bristol, by Henry VIII[2]; and half a century later his son John won both the honour of knighthood and a seat for Whitchurch in Hampshire (where he owned property) in the Parliament of 1586.[3] Whether for lack of opportunity or lack of ambition, he did not follow these successes up by sitting in any further parliaments, but the Coopers had clearly 'arrived'. The Ashleys had done more. Henry Ashley, who was also knighted, sat not for a mere borough seat but for the county of Dorset in the parliaments both of 1554 and 1563.[4] His son, another Henry, married into the aristocracy, his wife being Anne, daughter of

---

[1] See J. Hutchins, *History of the Antiquities of the County of Dorset* (1861–73), iii. 594–5 for this pedigree.   [2] J. Collinson, *History of Somersetshire* (1791), iii. 100.

[3] Miss Brown (p. 5) states wrongly that this was Richard, who died in 1556.

[4] Miss Brown (p. 5) is mistaken in identifying Henry's wife Katherine Ashley with Queen Elizabeth's governess. The latter, born Katherine Champernowne, was often called Katherine Ashley, but her husband was John Astley, Master of the Jewel House (see *D.N.B.*). Henry's wife was born Katherine Basset.

Lord Burgh, and sat in turn for the boroughs of Wareham, Christchurch and Poole in the parliaments of 1572, 1576 and 1589. But the cousin of this latter Henry, Anthony Ashley, drew nearer to the centre of political power at court, and, since he was undoubtedly the relative who had most influence on his grandson, Anthony Ashley Cooper, he deserves fuller treatment.

Anthony Ashley was an interesting person in his own right,[1] with many of the characteristics which we have come to regard as typically Elizabethan. Vigorous, thrusting and versatile, he combined an intense Protestant patriotism with a keen eye for the main chance, and a strong practical sense is evident in everything that he did. The inscription on his tomb declares that in his youth he improved himself by travel and by acquiring a knowledge of 'various languages' and of military matters, but where or when this was done is not known.[2] In about 1572 he first entered the Queen's service in some unknown minor capacity. He was also able to win the patronage of the Queen's favourite and minister, Lord Hatton, and, thanks to this, on 19 March 1587 he was sworn one of the Clerks of the Privy Council.[3]

This post meant that in addition to his formal clerical duties he was on the spot to be given special tasks and commissions; he had a certain standing, familiarity with the great men at Court, and various perquisites and opportunities of personal gain through inside knowledge. When Howard of Effingham drew the Privy Council's attention to the importance of the collection of sea-charts published by the Dutch sailor Lucas J. Wagenaer, it was Ashley who was entrusted with the task of translating Wagenaer's Latin edition. His version appeared in 1588, duly dedicated to Lord Chancellor Hatton, as *The Mariners' Mirrour of Navigation . . . now fitted with necessary additions for the use of Englishmen by Anthony Ashley. Herein also may be understood the exploits lately achieved by the right honourable Lord Admiral of England with Her Majesty's navy, and some former services done by that worthy knight Sir Fra. Drake.* In its preface he excused some delay in its appearance by the need to examine 'by the aid of the best experienced' the true equivalence of the technical terms in the commentary which he had to translate; and, never backward on the subject of his own merits, he claimed to have in many places improved on Wagenaer. His work is both useful and attractive, with its fresh colours, and the ships in full sail, and whales and sea-monsters spouting water, which fill some of the larger expanses of sea in the British Museum's copy.[4]

[1] There is a short article in *D.N.B.*   [2] Hutchins, iii. 604.
[3] Petition of Anthony Ashley, *c.* 1621, in *H.M.C. De La Warr MSS.* (IVth Report), p. 277; Ashley to Sir Robert Cecil and Sir John Fortescue, 26 Sept. 1596, *C.S.P.D. 1595–7*, p. 286; *Arts of the Privy Council, 1586–7*, p. 385.
[4] Cf. D. W. Waters, *The Art of Navigation in England in Elizabethan and Early Stuart Times* (1958), pp. 168–75; G. R. Crone, '*The Mariners' Mirrour, 1588*', in *Geographical Journal*, cxix (1953), 455–8.

As this reference in the title to the defeat of the Armada and the singeing of the King of Spain's beard reminds us, the prime of Ashley's life was that high Elizabethan noonday when the nation stood threatened by foreign invasion and internal plot in aid of a Catholic claimant to the throne. Indeed he travelled on two of the largest expeditions. He was the Queen's special representative on the expedition to Portugal in 1589 which ended in ignominious failure, and among those whose valour he commended was one John Cooper who may have been his neighbour[1]; and later he became secretary to the council of war on Essex's devastating expedition to Cadiz in 1596. On the latter occasion he represented himself to Burghley as having 'received some brushes with stones cast down from the walls, at our first entry, with but few men. . . . God make us all thankful to him. . . .' After this victory he was one of the many who received knighthood at Essex's hands, with prospects of a share in the immense loot at the disposal of the victors. But he and others were too greedy, and in the temptations of the moment they forgot to reckon with the Queen's anger when she discovered what had happened. When Ashley was sent home in advance of the main fleet to report on the position at Cadiz, he did not meet an enthusiastic welcome; instead he had to bear the brunt of the accusations of embezzlement which began to pour in. Colleagues who either had cleaner hands, or were envious of Ashley's greater gains, or who sought to defend themselves from the Queen's displeasure by diverting it against a convenient scapegoat hastened to accuse Ashley. He was accused of ransoming prisoners at £500 or £700 each, removing plate and jewels and the Corregidor's gold chain worth £500, and trying to ship home oil and sugar for his own advantage. Even before the expedition he had been in trouble with the Queen and Sir Robert Cecil over an exceptionally valuable diamond, and they now committed him to the Fleet prison, whence there began to flow a series of agonized letters full of false humility to Cecil. In essence he admitted his fault and sought to free himself by expressions of contrition, offers of restitution and counter-accusations against his associates. Whether he was any worse than others at Cadiz, or whether he only made more skilful use of the opportunities given him by his official position is doubtful; but the remark that he was alleged to have made, that 'I will make this commission worth a good manor to either of us', clearly represents his outlook.[2]

At the beginning of October 1596 he was released from the Fleet prison after only six weeks, and eventually the Queen seems to have forgiven him.[3] He did all he could to recover Cecil's patronage, offering to put him in the

---

[1] *C.S.P.D. 1581–90*, p. 596.

[2] R. Hakluyt, *Voyages* (1904), iv. 241; Ashley to Burghley in J. Strype, *Annals* (1824), iv. 400; *Acts of the Privy Council, 1596–7*, pp. 84–89, 180; *C.S.P.D. Eliz. 1595–7*, pp. 270, 279–80, 283–6; *H.M.C. Salisbury MSS.*, vi. 180–5, 320, 328–32, 346–7, 351, 355, 365, 383, 385–6, 390–1, 399–400, 402, 409–10, 568–9; B.M. MSS Sloane 1303, fo. 6.

[3] *H.M.C. Salisbury MSS.*, vi. 422; *C.S.P.D. 1598–1601*, p. 506.

way of profiting to the tune of £1,000 a year clear from the estate of a lunatic—a suggestion which illuminates the character of both men, and of the age[1]; but he did not recover the ground he had lost. When James I succeeded to the throne Ashley was once again sworn Clerk of the Privy Council, and from the prodigality of the new king he secured a grant of £266 in consideration of thirty-three years' service; but evidently, whatever his abilities, Cecil knew too much about the faults which went with them to entrust him with great responsibilities, and he did not receive the promotion which he might otherwise have expected. Perhaps he was partly consoled for this disappointment when on the death of his childless nephew in 1604 he succeeded to the estates of the elder branch of the Ashley family, including the house of Wimborne St. Giles. Here he could live the life of a country gentleman of greater wealth than the average, and in 1610 he gave up his position as Clerk of the Privy Council, not scorning to receive an annuity of £50 to add to his other sources of income.[2]

Although he was now nearly sixty, he did not retire to vegetate, but rather, like a more famous politician a century later, to grow vegetables. His own interest lay not in turnips but in cabbages. John Evelyn later stated that Ashley was the first to grow cabbages in England, and since he knew Shaftesbury this may even represent the latter's boast about his grandfather.[3]

The cultivation of his vegetable garden, the rebuilding of the parish church (since largely destroyed by fire) close to his park gate, with an almshouse for eleven poor people hard by,[4] did not however absorb all his interests. He had not abandoned his ambitions for the advancement of the Ashley family. Only one child had survived the many hazards of infancy at this period, and this was a daughter, Anne, who was the sole heiress to the extensive properties which her father had purchased or inherited in the last thirty years. For a husband for her he had only to look a few miles to Rockbourne, where, just after he had succeeded to Wimborne St. Giles, the manor had been sold by a previous owner to Sir John Cooper in 1608.[5] When Sir John Cooper died two years later, he left a boy, another John, to succeed to his property. A marriage between Anne and John would unite extensive neighbouring estates in the area where Dorset, Hampshire and Wiltshire meet (with outlying estates in Somerset, Staffordshire, Derbyshire and Middlesex); and there was also the consideration that,

[1] *H.M.C. Salisbury MSS.*, vii. 4–5.

[2] *Acts of the Privy Council, 1601–4*, p. 496; *H.M.C. De La Warr MSS.* (IVth Report), pp. 277, 309; *C.S.P.D. 1603–10*, p. 615.

[3] J. Evelyn, *Acetaria, a Discourse of Sallets*, in *Miscellaneous Writings*, ed. W. Upcott (1825), p. 738; *Notes and Queries*, 3rd ser., xii. 287, 533; 4th ser., i. 156, 228–9, 329–30, 398, 472–3; Brown, p. 6.

[4] *Report of the Charity Commissioners* (1837), xxx. 139–40.

[5] *Victoria County History of Hampshire*, iv (1911), 581–3 (including a plan of the old Rockbourne buildings as standing in 1911, with remnants of fourteenth-century and Elizabethan or Jacobean houses).

since John was still under twenty-one when the marriage took place, he might be amenable to the influence of the dominating old man who was giving him his heiress.

These circumstances are reflected by the marriage articles which were signed by Sir Anthony Ashley and John Cooper's trustees on 10 December 1616.[1] The old man drove a hard bargain. Not only were the trustees to bind themselves to pay Ashley £2,000, but John was to settle and entail all his lands of inheritance on his heirs male by this marriage; the eldest son was to be christened Ashley and to take the title of Lord Ashley 'if the King's Majesty shall think him worthy of that honour' so that the name of Ashley would be perpetuated; and the newly-married couple were to live with Sir Anthony at Wimborne 'as long as it shall like the said Mr. John Cooper and his wife so to continue in the company and for the comfort of the said Sir Anthony Ashley'. They had every reason to humour the old man in this way, because Anne's immediate dowry of two Wiltshire manors was less substantial than her prospects when her father died; for Ashley entered into a £10,000 bond to perform his part of the contract. Clearly, in spite of his servile habit of writing to Cecil in earlier years 'from my poor house at Holborn' or 'my poor house at St. Giles, Wimborne', he was now a very rich man, able to think in terms of a peerage for his grandson; and able to ask that his last years should be spent with his daughter and son-in-law under his own roof.

It was thus in his grandfather's house that Anthony Ashley Cooper was born on 22 July 1621, shortly after 3 a.m. As he describes himself as 'the eldest child then living' of his parents,[2] it is possible that others may have died in infancy. He was baptized on 3 August, with his grandfather and two neighbours who will reappear in his story, Henry Hastings and Lady Honoria Norton, as godparents.[3] Keeping their promise to Sir Anthony, the parents gave the baby not one, but both of his grandfather's names. Two Christian names were something of a novelty in England at this date, and in later days Oliver Cromwell for one spoke disapprovingly of 'Trinomius' or the man with three names, as though there were something vaguely sinister about this.[4]

Reading between the lines of the autobiography which Shaftesbury wrote fifty and more years later, we can easily discern his admiration for the old man whose name he had inherited.[5] Though only six when Sir Anthony died, he did not forget him; when the time came for him to choose a title for his peerage in 1661, he called himself Lord Ashley of his own

---

[1] Copy in Shaftesbury Papers, XXXII, 3. The marriage was fixed for 1 Jan. 1617.

[2] Christie, i, App. II, p. xxv.

[3] Hutchins, iii. 605.

[4] J. Warner, *History of the English Persecution of Catholics and the Presbyterian Plot*, ed. J. A. Birrell for the Catholic Record Society (1953), i. 183.

[5] Christie, i, App. I, pp. iv–v. This fragment of autobiography was written in his last years, and extends to 1639.

volition, not knowing anything of the clause in his parents' marriage
articles, and was delighted afterwards to discover that he had unwittingly
fulfilled it.[1] Precisely what lessons the boy absorbed at his grandfather's
knee it is not easy to say. In his seventies Sir Anthony was still vigorous
in body and alert in mind, and he evidently spoiled his grandson, 'a prating
boy and very observant of him' wrote Shaftesbury with an indulgent smile,
a grandfather himself by that time. It is natural to suppose that the old
man told stories of his youth as grandfathers will, and talked to an admiring
audience about his doings at the Court of Queen Gloriana, about the
Spanish Armada and the exciting expedition to Cadiz—especially when
another expedition to Cadiz in 1625 turned out to be sadly unsuccessful.
Sir Anthony certainly centred all his aspirations on the little boy, and it
would be natural for young Anthony Ashley Cooper to look forward to the
day when he could emulate his grandfather's achievements and even
pursue a more successful career. Equally naturally it fell to Sir Anthony
to choose the boy's first tutor, and shortly before his own death he selected
a noted Puritan, Aaron Guerdon, saying characteristically that 'youth could
not have too deep a dye of religion; business and conversation in the world
would wear it to a just moderation'. To the last the same down-to-earth,
practical spirit remained uppermost in him, even where the kingdom of
heaven was concerned.

The boy's parents made decidedly less impression upon him than his
grandfather. He remembered his mother, who died two days before his
seventh birthday, as being as small of stature as her father, 'of a weaker
mould, and not so stirring a mind' as he. This dim memory is all that has
come down to us. The father was good-looking, of medium height, 'of an
easy and an affable nature, fair and just in all affairs'—not a very much
clearer picture. From what follows, however, we know also that these
graces had another side to them. Sir John Cooper's affability extended to
excessively lavish hospitality, heavy gambling and general extravagance,
which were to make difficulties for young Anthony and perhaps to act as a
warning to him in later years against such wasteful habits. His local
standing was such that in the parliaments of 1625 and 1628 he secured
election for the borough of Poole, some thirteen miles away from his home
at Wimborne; and on 7 February 1629, at a committee on religion with
Pym in the chair, he supported his Puritan friend Sir Daniel Norton in an
attack on the Arminian tendencies of Bishop Neile of Winchester.[2] He
was not very prominent in the House, however; yet the mere fact of his
election was a sign that his son, when he grew to manhood, could expect

---

[1] See Stringer's note in Shaftesbury Papers, XXXII, 3.

[2] *Commons Debates of 1629*, ed. W. Notestein and Frances H. Relf (University of
Minnesota, 1921), pp. 133, 180.

Christie's statement (i. 3 n.) that John Pym was his colleague at Poole was the result of
confusion between the names Pym and Pyne (a local family a member of which later
served in Anthony Ashley Cooper's household, ibid. App. I. xxii). Pym sat for Tavistock.

to follow in his father's footsteps and find a seat in one of the local boroughs. It would be expected of the heir to the Ashley and Cooper fortunes almost as a matter of course.

Anthony also had the unusual experience of growing up with a step-grandmother as well as a stepmother. His grandfather performed the last of his many startling actions early in 1622, when, having been a widower for two years, at the age of seventy he married a girl of nineteen, Philippa Sheldon. This naturally caused great comment at Court, and it is not easy to tell how serious Shaftesbury himself was when in his autobiographical fragment he referred to the old man's hopes of having children, in spite of his advanced age. Probably the second motive which Shaftesbury assigns was more important. For there was some method in the old man's madness; Philippa was related to the Duke of Buckingham, the all-powerful dispenser of the royal patronage, and this was obviously an attempt to get a share of whatever could be had. In the previous year he had sought to curry favour with Buckingham by passing on the stories which reached his London house in Holborn of the activities of the Duke's enemies in the House of Commons. Now the wedding was attended not only by the favourite and his relatives and friends at Court, but by King James I himself, ever ready to take part in any convivial occasion. There were even rumours that Sir Anthony was to be made Secretary. But the only positive gains from all these hopes were the baronetcies which were granted to Sir Anthony Ashley and John Cooper in July 1622, and even these had to be paid for at the market rate; Sir Anthony's title was conferred a day earlier than Sir John's, thus very properly preserving his seniority over his son-in-law.[1] Lady Philippa Ashley's presence in the household does not, however, appear to have led to any discord. Sir Anthony duly provided that his estates should pass first to his daughter and son-in-law for their lives, and then to Anthony Ashley Cooper, while Philippa, when widowed, was quite content to marry again. Her choice of a second husband is of some interest. She married Carew Raleigh, the son of the great Sir Walter. Anthony always remained on good terms with his step-grandmother, and visited the Raleigh household, where he could have seen the family heirloom. After the hero's execution by James I at Spanish and Papist bidding, his head was embalmed, and put into a red leather bag to be kept by his widow and son.[2] If Anthony as a young man saw this grisly relic, he could hardly foresee that his own praises would be sung as *Rawleigh Redivivus*, and that he would enter the gallery of Protestant heroes by the side of Sir Walter, having narrowly escaped a similar fate.

His stepmother, whom Sir John Cooper married within a year of his

---

[1] Ashley to Buckingham, 12 May 1621, *Cabala* (1691), p. 2; *C.S.P.D. 1619–23*, pp. 173, 306, 332, 414; report of the marriage festivities in Shaftesbury Papers II, 14; *Letters of John Chamberlain*, ed. N. E. McClure (American Philosophical Society, Philadelphia, 1939), ii. 419, 437, 446.

[2] A. L. Rowse, *Ralegh and the Throckmortons* (1962), p. 319.

first wife's death, was Mary, widow of Sir Charles Moryson, and, what was more important, one of the daughters of Sir Baptist Hicks and co-heiress to his great commercial fortune. Sir John and his family now divided their time between Wimborne and Lady Mary Cooper's house at Cassiobury in Hertfordshire, and it was thus as a small boy that Anthony Ashley Cooper first went to a house which he was to revisit in later years; for Lady Cooper's grandson by her first marriage was the Earl of Essex who was Shaftesbury's associate in the days of Exclusion, and in September, 1682 when his political position was crumbling round about him, he returned for a last great Whig 'consult' to a new house on the site of the one he had lived in as a boy of eight or nine.

There was one other adult member of the household at Wimborne and Cassiobury who influenced the boy's early years, and indeed his early manhood. This was a German named Dr. Olivian. When Shaftesbury came to write his autobiographical fragment he could not remember whether Dr. Olivian was a native of the Palatinate or of Bohemia, but whichever was correct, the doctor was a Protestant refugee from the successes of the Counter-Reformation in the early years of the Thirty Years War. Besides being a physician he was an astrologer, and, having the fortune-teller's common knack of foretelling a future which would flatter his clients and satisfy their aspirations, he pleased the fond grandparent who gave him asylum by casting Anthony Ashley Cooper's horoscope and prophesying great things for the boy. Young Anthony was himself impressed by these forecasts, which perhaps served to encourage the alleged dotage on astrology on which Burnet later commented. But his attitude to predictions of the stars was rather that of the person who amuses himself by watching to see whether they came true or not than of one who allows them to dictate his actions. Certainly they may have contributed psychologically to strengthen his ambitions to play an important part in political life, but it is at least as important that Dr. Olivian was in his own person a reminder of the danger to Protestantism from the armies of international Catholicism on the continent, and could make European politics real to him.[1]

Finally, the household included a sister, born in 1623 and named Philippa like her step-grandmother, and a brother, two years younger, christened George after the Duke of Buckingham. The curious thing about George and Philippa is how little is known of them. Normally in the seventeenth century the relatives of a rich and successful politician expected to cling to his coat-tails and profit from the family relationship; but unlike the flock of Finches, Berties, Montagus and others, George and Philippa Cooper continued to live their lives in obscurity, whether their famous brother was in power or in disgrace. George married a London heiress, acquired a country seat at Clarendon Park in Wiltshire, sat for Poole in

[1] Christie, i, App. I, pp. iv, n., v; Burnet, i. 172–3.

1654 and was a candidate at a by-election in 1673; Philippa married Sir Adam Browne of Betchworth Castle in Surrey (later a member of Danby's Court Party in the Cavalier Parliament) and outlived both her brothers and the century to die in 1701; and that surprisingly is almost all that is known of either of them.[1]

This was the household in which young Anthony grew up, whether at Wimborne in the Dorsetshire country under Cranborne Chase, where the new almshouses stood by the parish church at his grandfather's gate, or at Cassiobury nearer to the great city of London but still deep in the country-side of Hertfordshire. It was a well-to-do, comfortable, happy household, containing a variety of adults with many different experiences, not the household of a squire whose interests were confined to a narrow circle in his own county; and Anthony was the eldest son and heir, evidently a forward boy, of whom great things were expected.

Before he was ten, however, he was an orphan. His grandfather died on 13 January 1628; his mother died on 20 July 1628 of smallpox, while the children were kept away from Wimborne to escape the contagion; and his father died 'of a consumption' on 23 March 1631 while still in his early thirties. On his deathbed Sir John Cooper suffered what was for people of his class a fate almost worse than death: the knowledge that since he held most of his lands by knight service his heir and estates would pass into the clutching hands of the Court of Wards, and be exploited either in the interests of the King or some favoured courtier. Moreover the inheritance which he left to his son was a particularly difficult one, for by heavy gambling, lavish hospitality and an expensive Jacobean tomb for his father-in-law in the parish church, he had contrived to run up debts which were later calculated at £35,080 'besides a great sum of money for interest'.[2] Only a very rich landowner could pile up debts on this scale, and as it turned out the sale of some of the manors would supply enough to satisfy the creditors. When the *inquisitio post mortem* was held at Basingstoke on 11 May 1631, the list of the deceased's estates was im-pressive: some twenty-one and a half manors in Dorset, Wiltshire, Hamp-shire, and Somerset, besides various tithes, advowsons, water mills and messuages such as that 'in Holborn called the Black Bull'.[3]

The question was which of these lands were to be sold in order to raise the necessary sum, and how they were to be sold in order to obtain the best possible price. There were neighbours on the look-out for bargains from the enforced sales; Shaftesbury writing some fifty years later dipped his pen in vitriol to draw brief portraits of them, with considerable verve and literary skill. There was Sir William Button, 'a miserable wretch';

---

[1] Christie, i, App. I, pp. xliv–xlv.

[2] This and much of what follows is taken from a book in the Shaftesbury Papers, XXXII, 7, containing copies of all the orders of the Court of Wards on the Cooper estates.

[3] M. J. Hawkins, *Sales of Wards in Somerset, 1603–1641* (Somerset Record Society, 1965), pp. 97–101.

'old Mr. Tregonwell, a near neighbour but no good Samaritan, one that never knew generosity or kindness but for himself, his horse, or his dog', who coveted Sir John Cooper's old home at Rockbourne; and, most serious of all, there was his grandfather's younger brother, Sir Francis Ashley, 'one of more elocution, learning and abilities than gratitude or piety to his elder brother's family', who wanted Damerham and Martin, only five miles away from Wimborne St. Giles, and Loders, near Bridport. Sir Francis was an exceptionally dangerous enemy, for he was King's Serjeant-at-Law, had earned the gratitude of influential people at Court by his passionate defence of the royal prerogative at the time of the Petition of Right, and had useful friends like Sir Walter Pye, the Attorney of the Court of Wards, 'a corrupt man' whom Shaftesbury remembered as the effective head of the court. He was evidently cast for the role of wicked uncle.[1]

It is significant that Sir John, who apparently had some warning of his impending death, did not ask Sir Francis Ashley to watch over the boy's interests, as otherwise would have been natural. Nor could young Anthony expect much help from his step-grandmother and stepmother, both of whom married again, and the latter of whom had her own claim on the estate. Instead, on 6 March 1631, a fortnight before his death, Sir John chose three trustees to attend to the payment of his debts and to look after the boy. One of them, a relative, Thomas Hanham, foreseeing the difficulties and inconvenience which would follow, declined to serve, leaving the burden of the trust to Edward Tooker (who had married one of Sir John Cooper's sisters), and still more to Sir Daniel Norton. For the next four years, indeed, the young Sir Anthony Ashley Cooper, baronet (as he became on his father's death), lived with Sir Daniel Norton, either at his London address in Three Cranes Court, Fleet Street, during the legal terms, or at his house at Southwick, near Portsmouth—the house where Charles I had been staying in 1628 when he received the news of Buckingham's murder.

The Nortons were old friends of the family. Lady Norton was the boy's godmother, and, as we have already seen, Sir Daniel had been Sir John's colleague in the House of Commons. In youth he had been a sailor, and now that he had retired from the sea he had, like many sea-captains, developed some strong opinions. He was bitterly opposed to the Arminian party which under Laud was now winning power over the Church; and he married one of his daughters to Sir John Eliot's son, within a few hours of Eliot's death in the Tower,[2] so that young Anthony had an acquaintance with the families of two great men whom the Puritans looked upon as martyrs, Raleigh and Eliot, and would know how the former had been executed by James I's order at the bidding of the Spanish ambassador, and how the latter had been buried, in Charles I's vindictive words, in the church of that parish where he died. This marriage must have further

[1] Christie, i, App. I, pp. vi sqq.   [2] H. Hulme, *The Life of Sir John Eliot* (1957), p. 391.

antagonized people at Court who had noticed Sir Daniel Norton's activities in the Commons in 1629, and cannot have made it easier for him to prosecute his case in the Court of Wards. But an uphill struggle in opposition to authority appealed to Sir Daniel's Puritan spirit, and when writing his memoirs Shaftesbury acknowledged his debt to both the Nortons for their care of him. His debt to Sir Daniel for the formation of his own opinions between his tenth and fourteenth birthdays was less explicit, but may have been more profound.

For £3,000 Norton and Tooker bought the wardship of the boy from the King—but found themselves still under the authority of the Court of Wards when it came to selling land to satisfy the claims of Sir John Cooper's creditors. In addition to the decrees of the Court we possess only Shaftesbury's own memoir, presenting with emphasis his own side of the case. Nevertheless, even with this reservation, his tale of a ward being oppressed by greedy relatives and neighbours who were able to pull strings in the Court of Wards for their own benefit was a plausible one, which certainly accords with the Court's general reputation at this time.[1] Arguing speciously that delay would only harm the boy's own interests because the load of debt would be increased still further by heavy interest charges and legal expenses, Sir Francis Ashley persuaded the Court to press on with the sale of some of the richest parts of the estate. Commissioners, who did not include either of the trustees appointed by Sir John Cooper, conducted sales in January 1632, and it is a suspicious fact that two of the commissioners themselves picked up useful bargains in Somerset. Sir Daniel Norton complained that lands bought by Sir John Cooper's widow were later resold for more than twice the price; the price of £7,000 offered by Sir W. Button for Rockbourne was later superseded by Tregonwell's offer of £8,000, and the property in Holborn now sold for £1,100 was later bought back by Sir Anthony Ashley Cooper for £1,800.[2] There would therefore appear to be substance in the complaint of the boy's trustees that the lands were being sold for less than their true value, and they tried to prevent the sales from being completed by arguing that the boy should be allowed the opportunity to buy some of his father's land for himself at the same prices, using money raised on some property settled on him by his grandfather, which did not come under the jurisdiction of the Court of Wards. Neither Tregonwell nor Sir Francis Ashley was willing to forgo his bargain, and the Court of Wards upheld the sales; so that the two trustees had to fall back on a policy of obstruction, failing to produce the deeds so that the conveyances could be completed. At one point, on 6 November 1632 they were ordered to seal a conveyance by 2 p.m. on the

---

[1] Cf. H. E. Bell, *An Introduction to the History and Records of the Court of Wards and Liveries* (1953), p. 136 for the case of *Harcourt* v. *Roberts*, and p. 148 for the growth of discontent with the Court generally.

[2] Shaftesbury Papers, XXXII, 7; Christie, i, App. II, p. xlvi.

B

following Saturday or go to the Fleet prison, and on 13 May 1633 an attachment was awarded against them for delays in the transfer of Damerham. Puritan as he was, Sir Daniel also did not neglect to make friends of the mammon of unrighteousness. At Lady Day 1635 'a teaser and ewer gilt Nuremberg work worth £100' was presented to Sir Walter Pye, in an attempt to wean the attorney to the Court of Wards from his friendship with Sir Francis Ashley; money was given to Sir Richard Stroud, and there is a note of 'plate to Cottington £105.01.00', but in this case the sum of money is crossed out, and the plate may or may not have been given to the new Master of the Court.[1]

While these proceedings dragged on in term after legal term young Anthony was being made acquainted with the realities of seventeenth-century life. He was not left in the country at Southwick while his trustees fought his battles in his absence; instead he was regularly taken up to London in the hope that his boyish presence would appeal to the better nature of his judges and persuade them to make some arrangement which would allow him to retain, for instance, his father's old home at Rockbourne. And so he walked through the immensity of Westminster Hall, and up to the chamber where the Court of Wards sat, and was certainly intelligent enough to follow something of what was being said and done impressively in the name of the law in his case. He was a witness of the dramatic climax of the case in 1635.[2]

By this time his trustees had admitted that the estates at Damerham and Loders must pass to Sir Francis Ashley, but were trying vainly to establish that Sir Francis had made a verbal promise to reassign them to the ward when he came of age. Sir Francis, on the other hand, tired of these obstructions, retaliated by trying to strike at his opponents' funds, arguing that the separate estate which the boy had inherited from his grandfather ought to come under the Court of Wards as well, because the deed of settlement was invalid. What followed was still vivid in Shaftesbury's mind when he started to write his memoirs over forty years later. He describes with some self-satisfaction how, as a desperate measure, his trustees advised him to make a personal appeal to the King's Attorney-General, William Noy, who, as an intimate friend of his grandfather, had drawn the settlement, but would be reluctant to defend it as being against the King's interests; and how, as a boy of fourteen, he alone paid a visit to Noy 'and performed with that pertness that he told me he would defend my cause though he lost his place'—obviously food for the boy's self-esteem. When the matter was argued in the Court of Wards, Sir Francis began with a 'long and elegant speech' attacking the validity of the deed. Lord Cottington, the Master of the Wards, 'sitting with his hat over his eyes', made his own sympathies clear by remarking openly, 'Sir Francis,

---

[1] Loose note in the trustees' book of accounts, Shaftesbury Papers, XXXIII, 8.
[2] Not 1634 as stated by Christie and Brown, for the reasons given below.

you have spoke like a good uncle', a sentiment which must have been extremely unpalatable to the boy and his trustees as they sat in their place in court, and must have made them fear the worst; so much so that after Noy had replied and when Sir Francis got up to make a rejoinder, the boy had recourse to a short silent prayer to God to deliver him from this oppression. The result, or what appeared to be the result, was startling. Before Sir Francis could utter two words, he collapsed, 'his mouth drawn to his ear; was carried out of the court and never spoke more'. To a boy brought up on Puritan sermon illustrations, the wicked uncle's seizure was an obvious intervention of Divine Providence.[1]

Unfortunately there is a slight difficulty in the way of accepting this story as it stands. Noy died in August 1634, seven months before Cottington became Master of the Wards, and over a year before Sir Francis Ashley's death in November, 1635.[2] The story may however be saved by suggesting that when Shaftesbury wrote his memoirs over forty years later he confused Attorney-General Noy with the Queen's Attorney-General, Sir Edward Herbert, who moreover later became Attorney-General proper and acted in that capacity in the impeachment of the Five Members. Both Noy and Herbert are recorded as appearing on the ward's behalf, but Herbert the more often; and since Herbert at different times sat in parliament for Downton (in south Wiltshire) and Old Sarum, there is a possibility of a local connexion and friendship with old Sir Anthony Ashley. It is likely enough that Shaftesbury's memory of the events of his boyhood deceived him into confusing the two men, and incidentally saved him from acknowledging a debt to the attorney-general of a Popish queen, Henrietta Maria.[3]

In retrospect his uncle's collapse and death marked the end of the greatest difficulties attendant upon his wardship, but litigation continued for several years to fill the pockets of the lawyers without doing very much good to the ward. Indeed Sir Francis Ashley's estates descended to his daughter Dorothy and her husband, who was none other than that Denzil Holles who was to be one of the Five Members and eventually was to share with Anthony Ashley Cooper both service of and opposition to Charles II down to 1680. Always stiff, argumentative and uncompromising in his opinions, Denzil Holles was not the man to abate one jot of his legal rights, and on 13 February 1637 the Court supported his view that he was not legally bound by any promise to reconvey Damerham and Loders to

---

[1] Christie, i, pp. 9–11, App. I, pp. ix–x; Brown, pp. 20–21 and n. It is interesting that Shaftesbury, having written of his prayer, later crossed out this sentence; perhaps the old man's increasing rationalism made him slightly ashamed of his boyish prayer.

[2] Christie is mistaken in suggesting that he died in 1634; the records show that he appeared before the Court of Wards on 16 Nov. 1635.

[3] For Noy and Herbert, see articles in D.N.B.; for Ashley's death, 28 Nov. 1635, Sir R. Baker, Chronicle (1684), p. 417; copies of orders of the Court of Wards in Shaftesbury Papers, XXXII, 7 and references to fees in ibid. XXXIII, 8.

Anthony Ashley Cooper when the boy came of age. With regard to the Cooper family home at Rockbourne which Mr. Tregonwell bought, the result was rather more fortunate, though not through the Court of Wards; for it turned out that Rockbourne was entailed, and not available for sale to pay the Cooper debts. Anthony Ashley Cooper generously agreed with Tregonwell's grandson that the latter should lease the manor, after which it should revert to himself. Other issues, however, remained outstanding almost until the Court of Wards itself was overtaken by civil war. Its last order on the Cooper estates is dated 22 November 1641.

Shaftesbury's own estimate of his losses from what he called 'the injustice and oppression of that court' was a round £20,000,[1] which when added to the estimate of over £35,000 for his father's debts must have made a considerable hole in the fortune he inherited. So great had been the Ashley and Cooper estates, however, that he was very far from being ruined or even reduced to poverty. Early in 1638 a survey was made of the lands remaining to him, and it was calculated that a yearly revenue of £2,349. 15s. 9d. was improvable to a 'total of the present and contingent estate' of £7,007. 15s. 9d.[2] Though this latter figure was over-optimistic, it is sufficiently clear that young Sir Anthony Ashley Cooper was wealthier than the average country squire. His income may be compared with the £2,800 which Gregory King estimated as the average income of the peerage in 1688, and the £880 estimated income of the baronets.[3] The silver spoon in his mouth at birth had not had to be completely melted down to satisfy his creditors. It may be added here that, although precise accounts are never available, his estates were always competently administered throughout his life, and he never needed ministerial office to establish his fortunes, like Arlington, or to repair the ravages produced in his fortune by gambling, like Sunderland. It was always financially possible for him to pursue an independent political line.

This meant that, in spite of his losses, as he grew to manhood he had no particular need to economize, and could keep up a standard of living appropriate to his station in life as a young baronet. He was allowed his own hawks and hounds from the age of twelve. In these circumstances it is not surprising that when Sir Daniel Norton, with whom he had lived for nearly five years, died early in 1636, there were several claimants to the position of his guardian. Lady Norton, whom he certainly respected, hoped that he would remain in the Norton household, and that a promising friendship between him and her youngest daughter Elizabeth would ripen into marriage; 'and truly', said Shaftesbury recollecting this in the tran-

[1] Christie, i, App. I, p. viii.
[2] Shaftesbury Papers, II, 33.
[3] A. Browning, *English Historical Documents*, vol. viii, *1660–1714* (1953), p. 516. According to Professor Stone's calculations (*The Crisis of the Aristocracy, 1558–1641*, 1965, p. 761) the mean gross rental of the peers was higher in 1641, but nevertheless a third of them had a gross rental of less than £2,200.

quillity of old age, 'if the condition of my litigious fortune had not neces-
sitated me to other thoughts for support and protection, the sweetness of
the disposition of that young lady had made me look no further for a wife'.
Another possible guardian was Sir Walter Earle, whose son Thomas was
the same age as Anthony and his closest friend. Sir Walter was an old
soldier who kept green the memory of his campaigns against the Catholics
and Spaniards in the Low Countries by hanging his house at Charborough
with maps and planning his garden in the shape of the redoubts and fortifications where he had served. More important, he was one of the famous
Five Knights who had been imprisoned for refusing to pay Charles I's
forced loan in 1627, and as a member for Dorset had joined in the demand
for a Petition of Right; so that here in his friend's home at Charborough as
in the Norton household, Anthony would certainly hear politics talked from
the point of view of the parliamentary opposition. However, neither sentiment nor friendship with Thomas Earle decided his choice of guardian.
Apparently since he was fourteen he was now free to select his own
guardian, and he chose his uncle, and Sir Daniel Norton's co-trustee,
Edward Tooker, as being 'most versed in the affairs of his estate, and a man
of honest, prudent reputation'. It was a prudent and mature judgement for
a boy of his age when no doubt it would have been easier to stay where he
was in Southwick, and he never had cause to regret it, to judge from the
tribute which he paid to his uncle's memory.[1]

Anthony, his brother George and sister Philippa accordingly moved to
Tooker's house at Salisbury, and in the next year spent the greater part
of their time either in that cathedral town, or in a country house not far
away at Madington. No doubt this was a further addition to an experience
already more varied than that of most boys of a similar background; but
the nature of Edward Tooker's influence upon his nephew cannot be
ascertained, for he seems to have been content to live his own life in the
country with no political views strong enough to leave any record.[2]

The next normal stage in the development of a young man of Sir
Anthony Ashley Cooper's social class was undoubtedly a period at one or
other university. Since his grandfather's youth the well-known invasion of
the universities by the gentry had taken place, and Oxford and Cambridge
now provided some humanistic education and served as a finishing school
for the sons of such families as the Ashleys and Coopers after they had
received their preliminary education at the hands of private tutors. Anthony
had had three tutors, the first, Aaron Guerdon, chosen, as previously
described, by his grandfather, the second, in the Norton household, named
Fletcher, of whom we are told only that he was 'a very excellent teacher of

---

[1] Christie, i, App. I, p. x. For Sir Walter Earle, cf. S. R. Gardiner, *History of England
1603–42* (1894), v. 364; vi. 213, 253, 268. Tooker's accounts survive in the Muniment
Room at Wimborne St. Giles, numbered vols. 16 and 17. Tooker had married a sister of
Sir John Cooper.

[2] He did, however, accept office as sheriff, after the Civil War. See p. 60 below.

grammar', and the third, in the Tooker household, who left so little mark that Shaftesbury could not recall his name, but only that he was an M.A. of Oriel College. The time had now come for him to remove to Oxford, and in March 1637 when he was nearly sixteen he was entered at Exeter College.

Then as in other centuries Exeter College was a very natural choice for a young man from the south-west, and was full of undergraduates from Cornwall, Devon and Dorset. There may therefore be no special significance in Anthony Ashley Cooper's appearance in that particular college, not so very far from Sir Thomas Bodley's newly extended library. Exeter College had, however, a very considerable reputation at this time, thanks to its Rector, Dr. John Prideaux, and the 'industrious and careful tutors' whom he appointed, so that 'in short time many were fitted to do service in the Church and State'. Dr. Prideaux, whose personal pupil Anthony became, was generally respected for his sincere piety, honesty, 'plain and downright behaviour', and his scholarship. A previous biographer has contrasted the fervent Puritanism in Sir Daniel Norton's household with the 'Anglicanism in its best form' which young Anthony would find in Exeter College chapel under the Rector, but there is more to be said than this. Though he was later a bishop, Dr. Prideaux's Anglicanism was emphatically not of the Laudian type; indeed, he was a strong upholder of the Calvinist doctrine of predestination, and, as Regius Professor of Divinity as well as Rector of Exeter, a vehement opponent of the newly fashionable Arminian doctrines. In 1627 his description of the Arminian, Peter Heylyn, as 'Bellarminian' (alluding to the Cardinal) indicated clearly his view that the new doctrines were a dangerous half-way house to Popery, and in 1633 he was in trouble with the authorities again for his anti-Arminian views on the authority of the Church. Indeed, a recent historian of the universities has listed him among 'the university Puritans'; this may be going too far of a man who later became a bishop and a Royalist, but his nomination to the see of Worcester in November 1641 was obviously intended as a 'moderate' appointment to mollify some of the opposition at the time of the Grand Remonstrance. Whether by accident or design, therefore, Anthony Ashley Cooper had fallen on that Oxford college which was most likely to encourage an independent, critical attitude on religious questions rather than a conforming orthodoxy. Anthony à Wood later commented on the number of Exeter men who, as a result of the principles they sucked in there, proved to be 'no great friends either to the Church or State'.[1]

How much his formal education was continued during his stay at Oxford

[1] C. W. Boase, *Registrum Collegii Exoniensis* (1894), pp. c–civ; Wood, *Athenae Oxonienses* (1691–2), ii. 68–71, 181–3; C. E. Mallet, *A History of the University of Oxford* (1924), ii. 305–6; John Selden, *Table Talk*, ed. Sir F. Pollock (1927), p. 110; Mark H. Curtis, *Oxford and Cambridge in Transition, 1558–1642* (1959), p. 189; H. R. Trevor-Roper, *Archbishop Laud* (1939), pp. 113–14; Brown, p. 22.

must remain doubtful. He stayed there a little less than a year, and in that limited period he had to pay visits to London during the legal terms to be present at the interminable litigation in the Court of Wards; so that early in 1638 he was entered at Lincoln's Inn. From his own account it appears that he took part in the disputations which encouraged undergraduates to argue a case before an audience; he no doubt became familiar with more classical authors and to some extent with Dr. Prideaux's divinity, and became a reader in the Bodleian, *per dispensationem*. But as sometimes happens with undergraduates who are not primarily concerned with academic scholarship and a successful university career, Oxford's educative value lay in teaching him how to use the advantages which birth had given him, so as to manage and lead men. Forty years on, growing older and older, Shaftesbury's memories of his undergraduate days were of successes of this sort, and not of more intellectual excitements.

He came to Oxford well provided with servants (his servitor, Mr. Hussey, later becoming 'minister' of the parish of Hinton Martin in his gift), with horses, and with money as much as he wanted; he boasted proudly 'that my name in the buttery book willingly owned twice the expense of any in the University'. This has been shown to be an exaggeration,[1] like much else in Shaftesbury's account of his youth. Old men are rarely modest about their doings in undergraduate days, and he was certainly no exception to this rule. However, he did run up a heavy buttery bill, and the striking thing is that (according to his own account) the money was spent not on self-indulgence and personal luxury, but on 'obliging by entertainments the better sort and supporting divers of the activest of the lower rank with giving them leave to eat when in distress upon my expense'—all good training in the art of using wealth to make friends and clients, which was essential to a successful man of quality in the seventeenth century. He would also rescue from prison impecunious scholars who had been caught in the act of stealing poultry, buying the farmers off at considerable cost, and winning popularity in return. Altogether his wealth, his birth, and his 'proficiency in learning, and natural affability' (as he himself complacently said, when looking back) made him a natural leader. On three occasions he used his power against authority. When the senior fellows of the college made an attempt to reduce the strength of the beer, a matter on which undergraduates might be expected to be sensitive, it was to Sir Anthony Ashley Cooper that they resorted for advice; with characteristic prudence he advised those who depended on their studies for a livelihood to keep out, and led the rest to strike their names out of the buttery book, thus bringing the authorities to terms. He also led the freshmen's opposition to the barbaric initiation custom of 'tucking', whereby freshmen had the skin scratched from their chins by their seniors (including the Earl of Pembroke's son) and were then forced

[1] Boase, op. cit. p. cx, n.

to drink a glass of water and salt. If his own account is to be believed, he not only gave the signal for the free fight which followed, but controlled his forces, employing 'my authority' to use prisoners as hostages 'to make terms for us'. He also describes how he often led the college forces against Christ Church when the inter-college disputations on some logical proposition turned from arguments to blows and each side tried to drive the other downstairs: 'I was often one of the disputants, and gave up the sign and order for their beginning, but being not strong of body was always guarded from violence by two or three of the sturdiest youths.' As a result of these unacademic methods of argument, Laud had to impose an absolute ban on all inter-college disputations between Christ Church and Exeter. No doubt all this was exaggerated in the telling; but the realization that in spite of his own insignificant physique he could manipulate men taller and stronger than himself must have encouraged his self-esteem.[1]

Attendance at an inn of court to acquire some legal knowledge was as much part of the country gentleman's equipment as attendance at a university; and as a prospective J.P., as well as one who had already enough personal experience to realize how indispensable a knowledge of the law could be, Sir Anthony Ashley Cooper was entered at Lincoln's Inn on 18 February 1638. Aggravatingly, however, he tells us nothing of his stay there. A note of 'Queries' includes '8. When Dr. Reynolds and Mr. Carroll [Joseph Caryl] were preachers at Lincoln's Inn', and this may be a hint that these two Puritan preachers influenced him more than any legal luminaries; for Lincoln's Inn was in many ways a Puritan one—it was, after all, Prynne's Inn. In later life, he was to have political dealings with Lord Wharton, James Harrington and (more sinisterly) Edmund Warcup, all of whom were entered at Lincoln's Inn within a few days of Ashley Cooper, but we know nothing of any conversations they may have had at that time; nor do we know much of his acquaintance with Falkland, who by a curious coincidence was entered on the same day.[2] That his attendance during the Easter Term of 1638 was regular we know from an itemized account, still preserved in the Muniment Room at Wimborne St. Giles, of his expenses for dinner and supper: they amounted to £33, plus 13s. 3d. for drink (mostly sack at 1s. 2d. a quart, with a little white wine at 7d. a quart, and claret at 3½d. a pint). It may be that here he began to lay the foundations of the legal knowledge that later encouraged him to assume the responsibilities of Lord Chancellor, but it is more likely that this was the result of his marriage.

Marriage may perhaps be said to complete a young man's education, and it is therefore fitting that we should describe Ashley Cooper's first marriage

[1] Christie, i, App. I, pp. xi-xiii; Laud, *History of his Chancellorship, etc.* in *Works* (1853), vol. 5, pt. 1, p. 191.
[2] Christie, i, App. I, p. iv. n.: *Records of . . . Lincoln's Inn. Vol. I. Admissions, 1420–1799* (1896), p. 234. Cf. p. 42 below for Falkland.

before taking stock of him on the threshold of manhood. He was only seventeen when he began to look for a wife, perhaps because he also wanted a father-in-law who could help him on in the world and aid him in any further law-suits with unfriendly neighbours. Certainly this dominated the actual choice which he made, for, in spite of the 'dotage on astrology' of which Burnet later accused him, he rejected the advice of his old astrologer friend, Dr. Olivian, to marry the sister of a neighbour named Rogers, and instead paid court to Margaret, one of several daughters of Lord Keeper Coventry himself. One would have expected that a young man like Ashley Cooper would have his marriage arranged for him by his guardian Tooker; but as Shaftesbury describes it, although his uncle suggested the match, the decision was his own. Nor was the marriage entirely one of convenience, inasmuch as he was definitely attracted to Margaret rather than to either of her unmarried sisters. In his old age he remembered how he had been so bashful and tongue-tied before Margaret, while he was 'very talkative and good company' to her sisters, that their mother mistakenly thought he preferred one of them. But this romantic misunderstanding was satisfactorily cleared up, and on 25 February 1639 the marriage took place. What we know of their ten years of married life suggests that they were happy ones. Margaret seems to have been reasonably intelligent for her age and class, sweet-natured, and devoted to her husband, while he was certainly fond of her, if we may judge from the private tribute in his diary when she died.[1]

Like his father, Ashley Cooper found it natural enough to settle down in his father-in-law's household; and during 1639 apart from visits to Wimborne St. Giles they lived in the Lord Keeper's houses at Durham House in the Strand, and at Canonbury, in Islington. Here therefore he came under the influence of Lord Coventry, at an impressionable time of life, and precisely when the political situation was becoming threatening: the first Bishops' War broke out in the spring of 1639. In an age when scarcely any royal minister was free from attack, either on grounds of policy or on charges of corruption, Lord Coventry, who had held the office of Lord Keeper since 1625, enjoyed a remarkably large measure of respect. He was upright and honest, not elaborately eloquent, but, according to Clarendon, possessing 'a strange power of making himself believed'. Other judges, like Finch, might be suspected of giving political verdicts to suit the King's needs; Coventry had maintained his independence, refusing to be subservient to Buckingham at the beginning of the reign, in the 1630s joining in accusing Portland of corruption and opposing Portland's scheme for a Spanish alliance. It is true that he was not called upon to play any part in the most controversial cases, like those of Hampden and Prynne; true also that he died in a fortunate hour, in January 1640, before he was called upon to take a stand in the political crisis which was looming up;

[1] Christie, i. App. I, pp. xiii–xiv; App. II, p. lii. Margaret's dowry was £4,000.

and finally that, in Clarendon's phrase, he was 'rather exceedingly liked than passionately beloved'. None the less, it was no small achievement that he was able to maintain a reputation for integrity and devotion to the law and Protestantism in a Court which was suspected of financial dishonesty and of favouring arbitrary government and Roman Catholicism. Moreover, he was able to pass on this rather prickly, independent, Protestant and patriotic attitude to his two best-known sons, Henry and William. Henry, who at this time was twenty-one, lived to be Secretary of State under Charles II yet was never impugned, like his fellow-ministers of the 1670s, for favouring either France or Popery; William, who was about eleven in 1639, was alternately in office and in opposition under the Restoration, but in neither did he compromise with principle or allow himself to become one of a factious, selfish clique. The atmosphere of the Coventry household (like that of Dr. Prideaux) was calculated to foster independent thought, rather than unquestioning adherence to any 'party line'. In June 1639 the Lord Keeper would not support the King's desire to enforce payment of a loan by the City of London (where his younger brother Walter was a merchant) and it was reported that his dying advice to the King was to be patient with Parliament when it met.[1]

We know also that, quite apart from any influence on his political outlook, Anthony Ashley Cooper was deeply impressed by his father-in-law's administration of the law. Having no professional legal experience, even an ambitious young man like him could hardly have dreamed that one day he too would carry the Great Seal and preside in the Court of Chancery, with the still more august title of Lord Chancellor; but when in 1672 that unlikely event came about, he based the organization of his household and the reforms of his Court on what he could remember of Durham House over thirty years earlier.

One other service the Lord Keeper may have performed for his son-in-law, although there is no positive evidence to support it. It would be the most natural thing in the world for him to take his son-in-law along to Whitehall. There, some day in 1639, he very probably stood for the first time in the presence of his King; and somewhere along the corridors of that rabbit-warren of a palace he may even have seen a boy of nine, the Prince of Wales whom Van Dyck painted in silks and satins and lace collar, who would one day be his master and later still his antagonist, King Charles II. If there was such a meeting, neither the young man of eighteen nor the boy of nine, nor any other Englishman in that year, could possibly have foreseen what strange revolutions they and England would see in the next fifty years. But it was already clear that events were beinning to move to a crisis which would compel Anthony Ashley Cooper to make up his mind where he stood and where his ambitions lay. Before

---

[1] Clarendon, *Rebellion*, i. 56–59, 172; S. R. Gardiner, *History of England 1603–42* (1894), vii. 355, 357, ix. 39, 84 *et al.*

attempting to define his attitude at the beginning of the critical decade of the 1640s, it may be as well to conclude this chapter by taking stock of the character which birth, natural abilities, and environment had produced.

If we take first his physical endowment, he inherited the short stature of his grandfather. He was not only below the average height, but markedly so; so that letter-writers of the Restoration period could speak of 'the little man' or 'the little peer' without any possibility of being misunderstood. The 'pygmy body' as Dryden called it was already plagued by ill-health. The internal condition for which John Locke later operated caused him as a younger man to suffer almost daily a violent pain in his left side, which lasted for about an hour until it subsided into a dull ache. Allowing for the exaggeration which men commonly employ when speaking of their ailments and operations, we must nevertheless imagine that this was a considerable handicap which would have broken the spirit of some men and driven others to deaden the pain in alcohol. Ashley Cooper, however, always kept himself well under control, and never allowed the weakness of his body to dictate the sort of life he should lead. In youth he remained cheerful and rejected all pity, while having the acumen to notice that his endurance under almost daily pain made him 'interesting' to the ladies and young people whose company he kept.[1] In age a strong will prevented his body from interfering with anything he wanted to do, and it is surprising how little, except in 1668, ill-health kept him away from work.

Portraits show him looking unflinchingly, and sometimes a little quizzically, directly at the painter from a three-quarter face position. The features are clearly marked, particularly the long nose; the lips are often compressed, but often a suggestion of humour is present. With increasing age the lines become harder, but never show the grim, unscrupulous, villainous features which one might perhaps conjure up from Dryden's lines. In comparison with many of the faces to be seen in the portraits which appeared almost mass-produced from the studios of Lely and others, it is (particularly in Greenhill's painting in the National Portrait Gallery) a face showing character, composure, calm resolution and intelligence, and by no means unattractive.

In intelligence he was clearly above the average, and wide-ranging in his interests. His education had been in some ways scrappy and unsystematic, with three successive private tutors and short spells at Oxford and Lincoln's Inn; but he derived from it at least the educated gentleman's usual knowledge of the classics (enabling him to make apposite allusions to *Carthago delenda est*, Sempronia, and the like in his speeches) and enough of the law and of history on which to build at a later date. Further than this it is difficult to go on the subject of his intellectual attainments at the age of eighteen; we know something of the books he possessed and bought later in life and the varied interests they represented. Burnet was to

---

[1] Christie, i, App. I, p. xxi; cf. p. 33 below.

complain that although he was very ready to express his opinion on any
subject, his knowledge rarely went very deep, but like other statements
made by Burnet about people he disagreed with, this deserves to be taken
with a good deal of salt, and in some ways might be taken as a tribute to
Ashley Cooper's versatility.[1] One deficiency may be detected in the intellectual equipment with which his education provided him. In a period when
many Englishmen of his age and class travelled abroad—and still more were
to do so, whether voluntarily or involuntarily, after the collapse of the
Royalist cause in 1646—Ashley Cooper did not. He never lived abroad,
except for a few days in Holland in May 1660, and the last two months of
his life. It is not fanciful to detect in him a certain insularity of outlook as
compared with the cosmopolitan experience of Charles II. He could read
French, but did not speak it well; it is unlikely that he could converse easily
in any foreign language, and this may have been one reason why he was
never on very familiar terms with French, Dutch or Spanish ambassadors.

What effect did his upbringing have upon his religious ideas and experience? Here we have already noted the number of Puritan influences to
which he was subjected from time to time. Even Dr. Prideaux was uncompromisingly predestinarian. To the various influences of Aaron Guerdon, Sir Daniel Norton, his friends the Earles, Dr. Prideaux, Reynolds and
Caryl must also be added another, not previously noticed by Shaftesbury's
biographers. This was his friendship with, and patronage of, the noted
Puritan preacher William Strong, who in 1640 was presented to the living
of Moor Crichel, only three miles from Wimborne St. Giles. Later after
the Civil War Strong gathered an Independent congregation, including
many parliament men and persons of quality, which met in Westminster
Abbey; and at the Restoration in 1660 his remains had the distinction of
being dug up from the Abbey and thrown into a pit in St. Margaret's
churchyard. He had the reputation of a learned, laborious and profound
preacher. A letter survives,[2] written during the Civil War, and acknowledging with sincere gratitude the help given him by Sir Anthony Ashley
Cooper: the implication certainly is that the two men were not so far apart
in religious outlook and 'I know no friend but yourself to whom I can
commit them [my children] or anything else'. The difficulty is that we
possess no contemporary letters of Ashley Cooper's own. From his later
speeches biblical references can be detected, sometimes however to the less
obviously devotional books like the Song of Solomon and Esther. What can
be most easily found in all the later stages of his career is a constant dislike
of all forms of clerical authority, whether in politics or in enforcing any
kind of religious conformity, and it is probable that throughout he belonged

[1] Burnet, i. 173.
[2] Shaftesbury Papers, VI B, 397. For Strong, see article in D.N.B.; B. Brook, Lives
of the Puritans (1813), iii. 196–200.

to that section of Puritan opinion in which dislike of clerical pretensions was, consciously or unconsciously, the main factor rather than to any section with strong dogmatic views. He was capable of taking an extremely detached view of his first Puritan tutor, Aaron Guerdon, who 'had neither piety proportionable to the great profession he made nor judgement and parts to support the good opinion he had of himself', so that any Puritan feeling on his part was not sufficient to blind him to the defects of individual Puritans.[1] To this we may add the obvious fact that not only the Puritan but the Anglican influences in his early life, such as that of his father-in-law Lord Coventry, were always unequivocally Protestant and opposed to the fashionable Roman Catholicism at Court or to anything which seemed to lean in the direction of Popery. The opposition to Popery with which Shaftesbury's name was later identified can undoubtedly be traced back to these early influences; but further than that the evidence does not allow us to be specific on matters of doctrine.

The over-riding impression of his education is above all that it was not purely bookish and theoretical, but that, in his own words, 'my business called me early to the thoughts and considerations of a man'.[2] His experience in the Court of Wards taught him some of the realities of political power. Both in London and in Oxford he realized what could be done by the skilful handling of men; and he early became conscious that by birth, wealth, intelligence and skill in personal relationships he was qualified to play an important part in whatever field of activity he chose. Otherwise he would not have gone down to Dorsetshire in the summer of 1639, when still barely eighteen, and chosen to take part in the weekly gatherings of the gentry of the eastern half of the county, when they met at the bowling-green at Handley, only three or four miles along the lanes from Wimborne St. Giles. Nor was he content to be merely an observer and a listener as his seniors played bowls, drank and talked politics. He amused himself by making insinuations about Richard Rogers, whose sister he had declined to marry and who had afterwards been his rival for the hand of Margaret Coventry. Rogers was in his estimation 'a very worthy able gentleman, and one that thought so well of himself as gave him a value with others'; he made the mistake of parading his coach and six horses and giving himself airs of pretended superiority over his fellow gentry. Ashley Cooper was able to exploit this—'besides', he complacently remarked in his memoirs, 'my affable, easy temper, now with care improved, rendered the stiffness of his demeanour more visible'—and to suggest to Rogers's neighbours that Rogers 'expected to command us all, and valued himself to the Court as already doing so'. This last remark suggests that there may have been political overtones to the personal rivalry; but the real significance of the episode lies in the young man's realization that he could diagnose the weaknesses of his neighbours and turn them to his own advantage. It was

[1] Christie, i. App. I, p. vi.   [2] Ibid. p. xi.

a realization that flattered his self-esteem and encouraged him to weigh up other people ever more keenly and critically.[1]

It is striking that when, forty years later, he looked back on these gatherings of the Dorset gentry in those distant days before the great dividing line of the Civil War, he could remember vividly the personalities of his neighbours and describe them sharply, and without any suggestion of doubt or uncertainty, in vignettes of one or two sentences. The criticisms are pointed, but detached and without real animosity; these are long dead people recollected in tranquillity. Some of these character-sketches include the observation that the person was 'a favourer of the Puritans', or 'inclined to the Puritan', like Sir Walter Earle, or 'a great enemy to the Puritans', like Sir John Strangeways, and, apart from the geographical division into the east and west of the county, this is the only suggestion of classification. But the real interest is in the delineation of character, good points and bad, suggesting that the failure to continue the autobiography was a serious loss to literature as well as history. One extended sketch has indeed been often reprinted in anthologies. This is the description of Henry Hastings, his godfather, who lived only two miles away at Woodlands, and whose full-length portrait still hangs at St. Giles. It is, however, important to point out, since some have looked on Hastings as 'the typical squire', that Shaftesbury himself portrays him as 'an original in our age, or rather the copy of our nobility in ancient days in hunting and not warlike times'. Part of his attraction to Shaftesbury was as a survival from an earlier and simpler age, a man who lived to be a hundred, but could always read and write without spectacles, and mounted his horse without help, and until past eighty rode to the death of a stag as well as any. He is portrayed affectionately and with relish as a man of simple tastes for country pleasures, hunting and eating, with the Bible and the Book of Martyrs representing his religion and no indication of any other intellectual interests; and affectionate as it is, it suggests that the writer did not share the limited horizons which it implies.[2] Not that Ashley Cooper did not enjoy country life; for, although he was no great hunter, he took a considerable interest in his stock and his fruit-trees all through life, and was quite capable of passing on a homely recipe for the making of beer, or a tip for curing the sore eye of a horse by blowing powdered roast beef into it.[3]

As a young man he had some other accomplishments equally difficult to reconcile with the grim picture of Achitophel; he was in demand for his gifts in palmistry and fortune-telling, but even here it was characteristic of him to make use of a young man in his service to wheedle the necessary

[1] Christie, i, App. I, pp. xiii–xv, xx–xxi. For a contrasting tribute to Rogers's 'rare temper and excellent understanding', and 'zeal to the public' [i.e. to the Royalist cause], see Clarendon, *Rebellion*, iii. 76–77.

[2] Christie, i, App. I, pp. xv–xvii.

[3] MSS. Locke c 42, fo. 166; MSS. Locke f 4, fo. 143.

background information out of the maids in the nursery.[1] But such pastimes as this, pleasant as they were, were never able to absorb his full attention.

Amongst the Dorset men of quality whom he knew, there was one even more precocious young man, who was equally anxious to play his part in the political scene, and whose path was to cross Ashley Cooper's on more than one occasion. This was George, Lord Digby, who at the age of twelve had made a strong impression when he had appeared at the bar of the House of Lords to plead for his father, the Earl of Bristol. With his good looks, audacity and quick wit, great things were expected of him; Ashley Cooper only noted that he 'gave himself disadvantages with a pedantic stiffness of affectation'.[2] Nine years older than Ashley Cooper, he was obviously someone to emulate. Digby and Ashley Cooper were two of the most prominent Dorset men of the century; and it was important that the former was twenty-seven and the latter still only eighteen, when at the end of 1639 the signs were clear that Charles I's personal government was collapsing and parliamentary life would shortly be resumed. It is a pity that we do not know what was said about politics in those gatherings at Handley bowling green.

[1] Christie, i. App. I, pp. xxii–xxiii.
[2] Christie, i. App. I, pp. xviii–xix.

CHAPTER III

THE YOUNG MAN IN CIVIL WAR (1640-45)

> A martial hero first, with early care
> Blown, like a pygmy by the winds, to war;
> A beardless chief, a rebel ere a man,
> So young his hatred to his Prince began.
>
> DRYDEN, *The Medal*

THE county of Dorset is not one of the largest or most populous of English counties. Lying some hundred miles from London, and with no large towns within its boundaries, it has not played a particularly prominent part in English history. Nevertheless its inhabitants could not fairly be written off in 1640 as backwoodsmen, interested only in their crops and in local affairs. Not only did the wool from the backs of the many sheep grazing on the Downs (possibly two thousand on the Cooper estates)[1] make them concerned in the prosperity of the clothing industry of Wiltshire and the success of its exports; but fishing vessels from Poole especially, and a few from Weymouth and Lyme, tossed on the stormy waves of the Atlantic to bring back fish from the waters round Newfoundland. From the county town of Dorchester, where the famous Puritan John White had been rector of Holy Trinity since 1606, a colony of Dorset men had gone out to found a new Dorchester in Massachusetts—it is significant that Shaftesbury described the inspirer of the Massachusetts Company as 'one of the wisest and subtlest of that sort of men [i.e. Puritans]',[2] and the suggestion may be put forward that it was here as a young man that Ashley Cooper's attention was first directed towards colonization.

In addition to these incentives to take an interest in a wider world, there was a special reason why Dorset gentry and merchants should be interested in what went on at Westminster, and in the prospects for a new election in 1640. The county was generously provided with parliamentary seats. Twenty members sat for Dorset and its boroughs; and if we include the two neighbouring counties of Wiltshire and Hampshire (whose boundaries ran within seven or eight miles of Wimborne St. Giles) the total rose to eighty, or one sixth of the full membership of the House of Commons within a radius of fifty miles of Ashley Cooper's home. Nothing could be better calculated than this over-representation to arouse an interest in

---

[1] In 1668 he had 1,650 sheep and in 1670 2,759 at Wimborne alone; Shaftesbury Papers, IV, 166, 187.

[2] Christie, i, App. I, p. xx.

politics. It is true that at many general elections the interest would lie almost entirely in the rivalries of families exercising their social influence to secure the election of a relative or protégé for reasons of prestige; but in 1640 it was also a question of who should ventilate the gentry's grievances in the House. In the past fifteen years Dorset men had had many complaints. Loud had been the outcry in 1626–9 over the forced billeting in Dorset towns and villages of the troops raised for Buckingham's misguided expeditions to France. Ship-money had been at least as difficult to collect there as anywhere else, and many later Royalists shared the general dislike of it, so that in Dorset as elsewhere, if the Civil War had been fought between those for and those against ship-money the King would have had few supporters. Indeed in the ports along the Dorset coast the discontent was aggravated because the tax did not even seem to be achieving its pretended object: Barbary pirates continued to intercept ships from the ports of Poole and Weymouth.[1] Nor was the High Church religious policy of Archbishop Laud more popular. Puritan influence was especially strong in Dorchester, which had been the home of the Rev. John White for over thirty years, and which was from Clarendon's point of view 'the most malignant town in England'; but Poole had also a long tradition of extreme Protestantism, and Laud once complained that there were Puritans in nearly every parish in Dorset.[2] Here as elsewhere it is possible that the presence of some well-known recusant families contributed to foster a more zealous and more consciously Protestant religious feeling.

For these reasons it is not surprising that out of the twenty Dorset members who in March 1640 were elected to the Short Parliament some three-quarters were local men who went up to Westminster in a decidedly critical frame of mind (though, as will be seen, not all of them later fought against the King). Ashley Cooper was not one of this group. Though it was not unknown for boys of eighteen to appear in the House of Commons, it would not have been easy to win a seat in the circumstances of 1640 when there were many older aspirants. However a combination of good fortune, tact and useful connexions unexpectedly gave him a seat at Tewkesbury, in Gloucestershire. On a recent visit to the seat of the Coventry family at Croome D'Abitôt in Worcestershire, he and all the neighbouring gentry were invited by the corporation of Tewkesbury to a hunt followed by a dinner. According to his own story (told with no pretence at modesty) he ingratiated himself with the town bailiffs and chief burgesses, first of all by his fortitude and cheerfulness during his daily visitation of pain, and later at the dinner by defending the corporation and the fare provided against the sarcasms of Sir Henry Spiller, 'a crafty perverse rich man' who was important as a member of the Queen's

[1] Mrs. E. Fripp in the *Victoria County History for Dorset*, ii (1908), 146–9; A. R. Bayley, *The Civil War in Dorset* (1910), ch. i.

[2] Miss M. M. C. Calthrop in *V.C.H. Dorset*, ii. 30–35; Clarendon, *Rebellion*, iii. 127, 158.

C

Council, but strongly disliked as 'a bitter enemy of the town and Puritans as rather inclined the Popish way'. It is intriguing to read of this first attempt to ally with the Puritan susceptibilities of the townspeople against a 'popishly affected' courtier—the forerunner of attempts on a larger scale in the reign of Charles II. A dispute entered into partly to oblige his hosts and partly for the satisfaction of the personal contest yielded unexpected dividends, for, in his own words, 'this gained the townsmen's hearts, and their wives to boot; I was made free of the town, and the next parliament, though absent, without a penny charge, was chosen Burgess by an unanimous vote'. So at least runs his own account. It must be remembered, however, that he was not a completely unconnected outsider. Not far over the Worcestershire border lay the estates of his late father-in-law, the Lord Keeper; and his stepmother also had had estates locally. She had married as her third husband Sir Edward Alford, who now appeared on the scene to take the second seat for Tewkesbury. These connexions cannot have been a disadvantage, to say the least. No young man of eighteen could have succeeded without them. Yet the part played in his success by his handling of men must have further stimulated his consciousness of his own abilities, the more so as his brother-in-law John Coventry mismanaged his canvassing in Somerset and was rejected there. His achievement may even have served to console him for the fact that in spite of his insinuations his local rival Richard Rogers was elected one of the knights of the shire for Dorset.[1]

Ashley Cooper thus began his long parliamentary career as one of the youngest members of the Short Parliament, which met on 13 April 1640, called by the King to vote money so that he could expel the Scots and reverse the decision of the first Bishops' War. In the proceedings of this parliament, however, there is no sign of his future greatness; so far from his bursting upon the scene as a youthful prodigy, anything that he may have said or done is veiled in complete obscurity. It was perhaps prudent for one so inexperienced to keep silence, and to observe; and in any case the session lasted barely three weeks, before on 5 May Charles dissolved Parliament. The theme of this short session had been the persistent refusal of the House of Commons to vote subsidies until ship-money and other grievances had been settled in the way they wanted; and Ashley Cooper was obviously intelligent enough to absorb the first axiom of all parliamentary politics in the seventeenth century, namely that a strict control of the purse-strings was the most obvious and the most effective weapon in the House's armoury when it sought to change royal policy; and the second axiom, that the King's most obvious and most effective counter-weapon lay in his unrestricted power of prorogation or dissolution. It has been

---

[1] Christie, i. App. I, pp. xxi–xxii; for Alford, cf. M. F. Keeler, *The Long Parliament 1640–1* (Philadelphia, 1954), pp. 83–84; J. G. Alford, *Alford Family Notes* (1908), pp. 38–42; and for John Coventry, see his letter to Cooper, 29 Feb. 1640, in Christie, i. 33–34.

further suggested that the young man 'learned lessons in technique that he never forgot' by watching the master hand of Pym at work in these three short weeks[1]; but he left no written impressions from which this can be substantiated. Similarly, his early upbringing and known later views make it probable that he resented Convocation's remaining in being after the dissolution of Parliament and voting High Church canons to regulate religion; but no contemporary corroborative evidence survives.

It was thirteen long years before he could again establish himself in Parliament. Charles's dissolution of the Short Parliament gained a few months' respite, at the price of making matters worse for himself when, after the fiasco of the second Bishops' War, he had to call Parliament again. This time the electors of Tewkesbury were no longer willing to offer Ashley Cooper a seat. The competition was greater, and relationship to a dead Lord Keeper no longer an advantage, more especially as the young Coventrys (with whom he still lived at Durham House in the Strand) were showing themselves to be supporters of the Court. Consequently Ashley Cooper does not seem even to have taken part in the disputed election at Tewkesbury, though Sir Edward Alford again participated in it.[2] Nor was a seat any easier to win in his own county of Dorset, where in that summer of 1640 opinion had hardened still further against Charles; scarcely any ship-money had been raised except by distress,[3] and the 600 men who were unwillingly assembled as the county's contribution against the Scots battered one officer to death on their way north, and dwindled to a mere 340 before one of them was shot in front of the rest in order to instil some discipline.[4] When the elections for the Long Parliament were held in October 1640, therefore, Ashley Cooper saw his neighbours elect a predominance of members who would support the opposition. Of the twenty-two Dorset members, twelve were definitely Parliamentarians in the Civil War, and a further five or six, though later Royalists, were probably considered to be opponents of the Court when elected. In neighbouring Wiltshire only thirteen out of thirty-seven members were later Royalists, and in Hampshire only eight out of twenty-eight members.[5] Ashley Cooper must have been aware of the overwhelmingly critical attitude of those classes which elected members to the House of Commons, and it is likely enough that he was present at the county meeting at Dorchester in October, when the Dorset gentry drew up a list of their grievances for their member, Lord Digby, to present to the Long Parliament: '(1) ship money; (2) pressing soldiers, and raising moneys concerning the same; (3) monopolies; (4) the new canons, and the oath to be taken by lawyers and divines, etc.; (5) the oath required to be taken by church officers to

---

[1] Brown, pp. 34, 36–37.   [2] Keeler, op. cit. pp. 47–48.
[3] C.S.P.D. 1640, pp. 57, 241, 551, 598–9.
[4] Ibid. pp. 55, 204, 291, 316, 334–5, 491, 558–9.
[5] Keeler, op. cit. pp. 44, 70, 48.

present according to articles new and unusual.'[1] This is an interesting foreshadowing of the famous electoral instructions to members of the Oxford Parliament of 1681; but there is no sign that in 1640 Ashley Cooper was anything more than a mere observer of his neighbours' discontent.

He had not, however, abandoned his parliamentary ambitions, and in December 1640, when the Long Parliament had been sitting for a month, an opportunity suddenly presented itself to enter the House as it were by a back door. William Herbert, second son of the Earl of Pembroke, had been elected both for Monmouthshire and for the Pembroke pocket borough of Downton. He now chose to sit for the Welsh county, leaving a vacancy at Downton, which lay only a few miles across the Wiltshire border from Wimborne St. Giles, and where Ashley Cooper's father had owned a burgage.[2] There followed the unusual occurrence of a disputed election in what was normally a Pembroke private preserve, for the Earls of Pembroke were lords of the manor and the electors few. The candidates were Ashley Cooper, and another young man only a few months older, Richard, the son of Lord Gorges, whose seat was not far away. Unfortunately we know next to nothing about this election, and it is impossible even to be sure which was the Pembroke candidate. Relations between the Ashleys and the Herberts were usually good, and William Herbert had actually been at Exeter College when Ashley Cooper entered it; on the other hand, it had been William Herbert's ear that he had boxed to start the famous 'tucking' riot. All that we know is that the deputy bailiff and about thirty-three burgesses voted for Gorges, and the bailiff and about the same number for Cooper. Even supposing that the bailiff's vote suggests Pembroke support for Cooper, it would not be easy to deduce from this what Cooper's political attitude was at this time. The Earl, an outspoken, hot-tempered man, of bad morals but allegedly Puritan tendencies, was Lord Chamberlain and had put in one member, Sir Edward Griffin, who was a Gentleman of the Privy Chamber and later a Royalist; on the other hand the Earl was never on good terms with Queen Henrietta Maria, and about this time began the change in political course which was to take him into the Parliamentarian camp.[3]

Ashley Cooper was never able to define his own attitude to the problems facing the country in 1640–1 in any speech to the House, for it was not until 1660 that he was able to establish his claim to the Downton seat. According to his own account, 'at the Committee for Privileges it was clearly decided for Sir Anthony, yet no report yet made of it' to the House. In point of fact, the matter was nevertheless discussed by the House on 18 March 1641, when a petition from Denzil Holles was read, referring to

---

[1] W. A. Shaw, *A History of the English Church during the Civil Wars . . .* (1900), i. 9.

[2] M. J. Hawkins, *Sales of Wards in Somerset* (1965), p. 100. The Raleigh family into which Philippa Ashley had married also owned property at Downton: G. Matcham in *The History of Modern Wiltshire: the Hundred of Downton*, ed. R. C. Hoare (1834), pp. 35–37.

[3] Keeler, op. cit. pp. 69–71; *D.N.B.* for Philip, Earl of Pembroke.

his long litigation with Sir Anthony Ashley Cooper in the Court of Wards
over the disputed manors of Damerham and Martin, and asking that
Cooper should not be admitted to take his seat since he was under age.
Other members argued that there were others in the House besides Cooper
who were under twenty-one, and eventually the House took no action on
Holles's petition. The practical effect was, however, that, thanks to Holles's
obstructive influence in the Commons, the Downton election dispute
never came before the House, and was not decided either for or against
Cooper for nineteen years.[1]

Thus, although at one point a favourable ruling seemed possible,
Ashley Cooper's hopes of a seat were baulked, and he was unable to take
any part in the critical sessions of 1641–2. His political career was delayed,
and also he was enabled to remain uncommitted until after the beginning
of the Civil War. In the Commons, under the pressure of attending,
speaking and voting, the likelihood is that he would have had to declare
himself much earlier, and at a time when the Coventry relatives with
whom he was still living were strongly Royalist and opposed to Strafford's
attainder. Apart from other considerations, Anne Coventry had married
Strafford's nephew, Sir William Savile. His relatives and friends (in all
parts of the House, for his Puritan friend, Thomas Earle, was a member[2])
could keep him well informed of what was going on, and he could join
the fashionable company which thronged Westminster Hall to witness the
trial of Black Tom Tyrant. From Strafford's impeachment he could
absorb the third great axiom of the seventeenth-century parliamentarian,
that impeachment by the House of Commons before the House of Lords
as judges was (in spite of the difficulties involved) the greatest threat that
a royal minister had to face, and an indirect means of securing ministers
of whom the House approved. Loss of the royal favour was a disaster, but
impeachment on charges of treason could, if proved, mean the loss of
one's head. And even when Strafford's impeachment had to be abandoned
in favour of the method of passing a bill of attainder, there was another
lesson to be learned from the crowds which shouted for 'Justice' at
Westminster and Whitehall to secure the assent of the Lords and the
King: in addition to those classes which filled Parliament, those people
who in the time of Shaftesbury's dominance in 1678–81 acquired the new
name of 'the mob' had a part to play in politics.

Kept out from the House of Commons while these exciting events were
taking place, Ashley Cooper did at this time make his first appearance before
the House of Lords where he was later to shine. One John Bishop came
forward to claim either the benefit of the lease of a house or farm which
Ashley Cooper's father had granted him, or the bond of £1,000 into which

---

[1] Christie, i, App. II, p. xxvii; Locke, *Works* (1823), ix. 271; *The Journal of Sir
Simonds D'Ewes from the beginning of the Long Parliament to the opening of the Trial of the
Earl of Strafford*, ed. W. Notestein (Yale University Press, 1923), pp. 344, 366, 504–5.

[2] And his father was one of the managers of Strafford's impeachment.

Sir John Cooper had entered. Taking advantage of the inquiries which were going on into the activities of the prerogative courts, Bishop was able to get the matter taken up by a committee of the House of Lords instead of by the Court of Wards. On 12 March Ashley Cooper and his guardian and trustee, Mr. Tooker, appeared before this committee in the famous Painted Chamber; and finally, on 31 May, the case was decided at the bar of the House itself. It was not a very successful first appearance in that august chamber. Like so much of the litigation arising from Sir John's encumbered estate, this case, after further delays, obstruction and expense, ended in defeat for Tooker and his ward, and they had to pay the thousand pounds.[1] It was twenty years to the month before Ashley Cooper appeared again in the House of Lords—this time, in the changed world of the Restoration, to take his seat among the peers.

In the period between Strafford's death and the outbreak of civil war scarcely anything is known about Ashley Cooper's doings or thoughts; indeed, for two years the only source of information about him which we possess is the bare record of his movements, which he compiled a few years later. After his father-in-law's death in January 1640, Sir Anthony and Lady Cooper had continued to live with the dowager Lady Coventry at Durham House and Canonbury for another year, until Lady Coventry 'left off housekeeping'. Then had followed a period in which Ashley Cooper had kept house with his brother-in-law, the second Lord Coventry, at Dorchester House in Covent Garden until he began a series of visits to Lady Cooper's married sisters, in different parts of the country. The first of these, to Lady Hare at Stow Bardolph in Norfolk, took place 'in 1641', but this could refer to any period up to 25 March 1642, under our calendar. It looks as though Ashley Cooper may have been one of the many who left London after the King's departure from Whitehall in January 1642, but if so it is significant that he did not join the Court. Instead, at the end of March he and Lady Cooper moved further to Rufford in Nottinghamshire, the home of another of his sisters-in-law who had married Sir William Savile; and there he may have met his little nephew, George Savile, then a boy of nine, who later as Lord Halifax was to be first collaborator and then bitter opponent of Shaftesbury and the Whigs. From Rufford he paid a flying visit to London, to Dorset, and to Lord Coventry's country seat at Croome d'Abitôt in Worcestershire, before returning to his wife in Nottinghamshire. He was thus back in Rufford when the King appeared in the county, and when the famous occasion of the raising of the royal standard at Nottingham on 22 August confirmed to all men that the issue between King and Parliament would have to be settled by force of arms.[2]

[1] Shaftesbury Papers, XXXII, 7; L.J. iv. 154, 246, 261, 271, 284; H.M.C. Fourth Report (House of Lords MSS.), pp. 47, 56, 69, 73, 77.
[2] Christie, i, App. II, p. xxvii. This record (written in 1646) must not be confused with the autobiographical fragment of his later years in Appendix I.

Along with everyone else in his class, therefore, Ashley Cooper was confronted with a difficult choice. For those who regard the Civil War as a clear-cut issue of principle it is disconcerting to find that large numbers of people did not instinctively rush to arms as convinced Roundheads or Cavaliers. Clarendon commented disgustedly at the time on the slowness and reluctance with which many people took up arms, and as modern research examines the local scene county by county this impression is abundantly confirmed. Cowardice, indifference, a prudent, inglorious desire to choose the winning side, a conflict between interest and political or religious principle, a feeling that neither side was wholly in the right— all these different motives combined to strengthen the country gentleman's natural disinclination to fight his friends and neighbours, with whom he sat on Quarter Sessions, rode to hunt, drank and bowled on the bowling-green. Many who had no doubt which side they hoped would win nevertheless hoped that the issue would be decided by someone else fighting a short campaign somewhere else in the country; even so convinced a partisan as Sir Thomas Fairfax was willing to sign a local truce in Yorkshire until Parliament countermanded it from Westminster.[1]

It is clear that Ashley Cooper belonged somewhere in this body of opinion. From Rufford he rode over to Nottingham to see King Charles with his two sons, Charles Prince of Wales aged twelve, and James Duke of York, aged nine. It is not certain that he was actually present at the ceremony when the royal standard was raised, as earlier writers have stated, but when Charles left Nottingham for Derby on 13 September, he went with him. Yet he is careful to insist that this was 'only as a spectator, having not as yet adhered against the Parliament', and this is borne out by the fact that he did not accompany the King beyond Derby, or return to Dorset where fighting had just broken out, but instead retired northwards away from the scene of military operations.[2]

He left no explanation of his own conduct at this point, but his career as a whole does not suggest that either cowardice or indifference can account for his neutrality. Nor do caution and self-preservation seem to fit the case. Whatever view is taken of his later changes of side, they were often accompanied by considerable risks, and were not the result of hedging; and an ambitious young man of twenty-one would be more, not less, ready to run risks. It is easier to explain his hesitation by considering the opposing influences in his life. He had lived in the household of Sir Daniel Norton, found a friend in another leading opposition family—that of the Earles—had listened to Puritan preachers and had himself come into conflict with 'the Establishment'. On the other hand, since early in 1639 he

---

[1] A. Woolrych, 'Yorkshire's Treaty of Neutrality', *History Today* (1956), pp. 696–704. Cf. D. H. Pennington and I. A. Roots, *The Committee at Stafford, 1643–5* (1957), p. xx, and A. C. Wood, *Nottinghamshire in the Civil War* (1937), pp. 23–25; also Clarendon, *Rebellion*, ii. 460–1.

[2] Christie, i, App. II, p. xxvii.

had attached himself to the Coventry household, and although his in-laws might not approve wholeheartedly of everything that the King had done, there was no doubt of their Royalism in 1642. His wife's brother-in-law at Rufford, Sir William Savile, with whom he was staying, had attacked ship-money in the Short Parliament and continued critical until his uncle Strafford's attainder, but now became Royalist leader in those areas of South Yorkshire and Nottinghamshire where his interests lay; and if Ashley Cooper's politics had been determined by those ideas of 'connexion' to which some historians have accustomed us, he would have joined the Royalist cause without delay. It is yet another sign of his maturity of judgement and independence of mind that he did not follow the immediately easy and obvious course.

Instead, although he was made a deputy-lieutenant for his native county, he refrained from making his way there, and the only sign that he inclined towards the Royalist rather than the Parliamentarian side was that he and his wife took care to remain in Royalist-occupied country. From Rufford they withdrew northwards to another of Sir William Savile's houses at Thornhill near Wakefield, and then, when that area became 'unquiet' through the activities of the Roundheads in the West Riding clothing area, they went with Lady Savile and another sister-in-law to Bishop Auckland, Durham and Newcastle, where the Marquis of Newcastle was making his preparations for a Royalist advance southwards in the spring. At the beginning of February 1643, even county Durham was so unquiet that Sir Anthony and the ladies journeyed in the depths of winter across the Pennines, and down through Lancashire and Cheshire to Shropshire, where they stayed in the country houses of yet another sister-in-law, Lady Thynne. There he left the ladies when, in the spring of 1643, he decided that he must return to Dorset, make his choice and take his part in the approaching campaign.[1] Contrary to expectation, the issue had not been quickly decided in 1642, or by any compromise settlement in the winter, and, however reluctantly, any man of spirit, political interest and ambition must decide which side he wanted to win and work for it.

Dorset lay to the west of that famous and entirely imaginary line from Hull to Portsmouth, and yet it included many critics of the King's government and had returned predominantly opposition members to the Commons in 1640. By 1642, however, the county was much more evenly divided, for Lord Digby, volatile, restless and not naturally a revolutionary, 'a singular person, whose life was one contradiction', had abandoned his earlier attitude of opposition to become one of the King's more reckless and disastrous advisers; and he had been followed by others in the local gentry whose conservative instincts had been offended by Arminianism and ship-money in the 1630s, but were now still more alarmed by the radical demands of Pym and his colleagues. Amongst these were the Strangeways

---

[1] Christie, i, App. II, pp. xxvii–xxviii.

family (two of them M.P.s) whose estates were considerable, especially in the western half of the county round their house at Abbotsbury. On the other hand, Denzil Holles, the Earles, the Trenchards, and other Puritan gentry had the support of the Puritan and clothing town of Dorchester, and of the seaports of Poole, Weymouth and Lyme. In so far as the fighting in Dorset had any strategic importance, it lay in the denial of these ports to the Royalists, so that they could not bring in foreign supplies through them, and were hindered in their plans to advance eastwards along the South coast. In the campaign of 1642, the only events of significance had been the fortification of these towns, and the Parliamentarian capture of Digby's stronghold of Sherborne Castle, after an earlier failure.[1] In view of what follows it is also interesting to note that early in March 1643, Sir Thomas Trenchard and Mr. John Browne, on behalf of Parliament, and Sir John Strangeways, Mr. Rogers, Mr. Phillips and others on the Royalist side, 'agreed upon an accommodation to assist one another and to oppose any force whatsoever that should attempt to enter the county of Dorset'. There was even talk of extending this to cover the four counties of Somerset, Dorset, Devon and Cornwall. Nothing came of it, probably because within a few days Sir William Waller advanced into Dorset with larger Parliamentarian forces than anyone could cope with, and accordingly this local agreement was swept into limbo along with similar ones in Yorkshire and elsewhere; but this disinclination of neighbours who were strong partisans to fight one another explains Ashley Cooper's course of action in the summer of 1643.[2]

During that summer he certainly threw in his lot with the Royalists, and raised at his own expense a regiment of foot, of which he became colonel, and a troop of horse, of which he became captain.[3] He also continued to ingratiate himself with the Royalist commander in the West, the Marquis of Hertford. Hertford was a man who, in Clarendon's view, possessed many good qualities, but 'though he was a man of very good parts, and conversant in books both in Latin and Greek languages, and of a clear courage . . . yet he was so wholly given up to a country life, where he lived in splendour, that he had an aversion, and even an unaptness, for business'.[4] In fact his qualifications for his position lay rather in his aristocratic birth and loyalty than in any military experience, and since he had never been at all prominent at Court, and was married to a sister of the Earl of Essex, his moderate opinions did not win him much support at the King's headquarters in Oxford. On the other hand, Prince Rupert and Prince Maurice, who had a modicum of German military training, were much younger, and inexperienced in personal relationships; and from this a cleavage was to develop, in which Ashley Cooper was to be concerned.

---

[1] A. R. Bayley, *The Great Civil War in Dorset* (1910), ch. ii.
[2] Ibid. pp. 63–65.   [3] Christie, i, App. II, pp. xxviii–xxix.
[4] Clarendon, *Rebellion*, ii. 529. Cf. also iii. 128–9.

According to Cooper's own account, he was also able to win some in-fluence over his neighbours in Dorset (where his old rival, Richard Rogers, died this same spring, leaving a vacancy to be filled among the Royalist leaders). He tells us that at some unspecified date he 'was by the gentlemen of the county desired to attend the King with their desires and the state of the county'.[1] He gives us no details of what happened at this interview, but fifty years later his friend John Locke wrote an account of a conversation between Ashley Cooper and Charles, and it is likely that he derived his knowledge of it from Shaftesbury himself: Locke's diaries contain references showing that he and Shaftesbury discussed past histori-cal events. Needless to say, a memoir written so long afterwards (and a decade after Shaftesbury could have given him the necessary information) might be expected to contain inaccuracies, and yet cannot be dismissed as a complete fabrication. As will be seen, the essence of it fits in with what we know from other sources.

According to John Locke, Ashley Cooper 'was brought one day to King Charles I by the lord Falkland, his friend'. This in itself is an interesting corroborative detail. Not only had Falkland been entered at Lincoln's Inn on the same day as Cooper, so that they would be expected to know one another; but also it is well known that by the summer of 1643 Falkland was relapsing into that mood of disillusion and despair which led him eventually to seek death at the battle of Newbury in September. He certainly belonged to those who could see no hope for the future in the complete victory of either side, and could be expected to sympathize with any attempt to reach an honourable compromise. This was in effect what Ashley Cooper now proposed, beginning with the bold declaration 'that he thought he could put an end to the war if his majesty pleased'. He argued that 'the gentlemen and men of estates, who first engaged in this war' were now weary of it and would be glad to be 'at quiet at home again, if they could be assured of a redress of their grievances, and have their rights and liberties secured to them.' Accordingly he asked the King for authority to treat with the parliamentary garrisons, beginning in his own county of Dorset, assuring them of a personal amnesty which would 'reinstate all things in the same posture they were before the war, and then a free parliament should do what more remained to be done for the settle-ment of the nation'. It was based on an accurate knowledge of the state of mind of many of his fellow Dorset property-owners, but none the less it was an exceedingly naïve proposal. Over the whole country too violent passions had been raised to be appeased by a reference to the vague recipe of a 'free parliament', and an unknown settlement; Charles himself was not in a mood to deal with parliaments; and it would have been impossible to arrange any form of disarmament or control over the executive while such a new parliament was summoned and worked out its solution. In short,

---

[1] Christie, i. App. II, p. xxviii.

the barrier of distrust between King and Parliament had become in-surmountable, and the struggle would have to be fought to a finish. It is not surprising that, according to Locke, Charles remarked that Ashley Cooper 'was a very young man for such an undertaking'. However, anything which led parliamentary garrisons to lay down their arms without committing the King to very much would be useful, and Cooper was a sufficiently wealthy and influential local landlord to be worth conciliating, and so he was sent with some vague powers.[1]

The most likely date for this interview (if we are right in believing that Locke's story is based on fact) is July 1643,[2] and there is evidence that in that month Ashley Cooper was engaged in some private negotiations for the surrender of Dorchester to the Royalists. However, on this occasion his boundless self-confidence proved to be unjustified. Nothing had been achieved, when the military balance was suddenly changed in the Royalists' favour by the battle of Roundway Down and the fall of the great city of Bristol. Influenced by 'some correspondence with the chief gentlemen of Dorsetshire, who were ready to join with any considerable party for the King, and had some probable hopes that the small garrisons upon the coast would not make a tedious resistance' (according to Clarendon), the King ordered Lord Carnarvon and Prince Maurice to advance into Dorset.[3] On 3 August, three of the chief gentlemen of Dorset wrote as royal commissioners calling upon the Mayor and Corporation of Dor-chester to surrender. The first of these three was Sir Anthony Ashley Cooper, and the second Sir Gerard Napier, his neighbour at Moor Crichel, who was far from being an extreme Royalist partisan; in May he had contributed money to the Parliamentarians and assured Sir Walter Earle of his intention to resume his seat in the House of Commons, and after a brief spell of Royalism he, like Cooper, went back to the side of Parliament. The tone of their 'ultimatum' to Dorchester is astonishingly gentle, considering that it represented overwhelming force.

> Gentlemen,
> Lately as private friends we moved you to return to your allegiance in laying down those arms which you have raised: but now as commissioners from his Majesty we have power to accept of your submission if you will be so happy to yourselves as to tender it. If therefore you can yet submit yourselves and render your town to His Majesty's service, send us some reasonable conditions upon which you will yield and we will give you our speedy resolution. . . .[4]

[1] Locke, *Works* (1823), ix. 266–7; Christie, i. 40 n.
[2] Miss Brown (p. 42) suggests that it took place during Cooper's journey home from Shropshire in March 1643; but at that point, after a lengthy absence from Dorset, he could hardly claim any up-to-date knowledge of the state of opinion there.
[3] Clarendon, *Rebellion*, iii. 127.
[4] Printed in Bayley, op. cit. pp. 100–1. Miss M. F. Keeler's account of Sir Gerard Napier in *The Long Parliament* (Philadelphia, 1954), pp. 283–4, is incomplete; cf. the report of Sir Walter Earle and John Browne, 17 May 1643, printed by Bayley, p. 73, and see also ibid. pp. 31, 107. His wife was a sister-in-law of John Coventry.

Whether induced by the remarkably conciliatory tone of this letter, or knowing that if the much stronger walls of Bristol had been unable to resist the Royalist storm, the much flimsier ones of Dorchester had no chance of holding out, the Mayor and Corporation surrendered their city without offering any resistance. Within a few days the inhabitants of Weymouth and Portland did the same.[1] Yet Ashley Cooper's hopes that their surrender might be the basis for conciliation were immediately baffled by the behaviour of Prince Maurice's troops, who paid no attention to the niceties of the political situation and were simply concerned with enjoying the fruits of victory. They ignored their leaders' agreement not to plunder Dorchester and Weymouth. At the former place they did not restrict themselves to plundering the house of the Puritan patriarch, John White, and at Weymouth their behaviour was no better. The Earl of Carnarvon was so disgusted at this breach of agreement that he threw up his command and returned to the King. Poole and Lyme both refused to surrender, and indeed John Locke relates that Ashley Cooper warned 'the other garrisons, he was in treaty with, to stand upon their guard, for that he could not secure his articles to them'. According to Locke, Cooper 'could not forbear to express his resentments to the prince; so that there passed some pretty hot words between them'. The Royalist indiscipline meant indeed the complete breakdown of any schemes of reconciliation.[2]

It is probable that some of the 'pretty hot words' which were exchanged with Prince Maurice involved a more personal issue. Ashley Cooper claimed to have a promise from the Marquis of Hertford (as commander of the royal forces in the west) that he should be made governor of Weymouth, with a deputy in Portland. Prince Maurice on the other hand had an officer on whom he wished to bestow them. Cooper clearly set great store on getting this governorship for himself, whether because he still had some political schemes concerning it, or because he prized it as an honour. No sooner had Weymouth been taken than he hastened away to Bristol to find the Marquis of Hertford and remind him of his promise; and the marquis was persuaded by his arguments. What followed was partly an argument between the politicians and the soldiers, with the Marquis of Hertford anxious to conciliate a young gentleman 'of a fair and plentiful fortune' and some useful local influence, and Prince Maurice wanting to see Weymouth and Portland in the hands of experienced soldiers, not a rich young amateur. In addition there was a considerable

---

[1] Cf. also the letter written by William Constantine, Recorder and M.P. for Poole, urging the Mayor and Corporation of Poole to surrender on suitable terms (Bayley, pp. 108–11). This letter, written significantly from Wimborne, appears to have been written later than the date of 15 July with which it is endorsed. Miss Wedgwood, *The King's War*, p. 236, is wrong in saying that Poole surrendered.

[2] Clarendon, *Rebellion*, iii. 157–9; Bayley, pp. 100–2; Locke, *Works* (1823), ix. 267. Cf. also Burnet, i. 172. Burnet, like Locke, probably derived his information from Shaftesbury himself.

personal antipathy between the marquis and the prince, and each con-ceived that his personal honour was involved. For some days a furious controversy raged; the curious thing is that eventually Cooper's successor surrendered Weymouth back to Parliament without striking a blow, and to defend himself for this produced a certificate from Prince Maurice that the town was untenable. Many people were however involved in the argument, and among them Edward Hyde, whose political career now for the first time crossed that of Anthony Ashley Cooper. At this time in the prime of life at thirty-five, and a good deal more genial and flexible in his ideas than he later became in his more formal and sententious days as Earl of Clarendon, Hyde too had striven as long as it seemed practicable to build a bridge between King and Parliament; and up to this point their political outlooks had not been markedly different, except for Hyde's greater age and experience and consequent need to commit himself earlier and further to the King's service. The two men had known one another for some time, probably as fellow-members of the Short Parliament, and now Ashley Cooper sought to enlist Hyde's influence as Chancellor of the Exchequer and an important adviser to the King. He asked Hyde's assis-tance 'that, after so much charge he had been put to in the expectation of it and to prepare for it [i.e. in the enlisting of men in his regiment] he might not be exposed to the mirth and contempt of the country'.

Hyde both agreed to write 'very earnestly' to the King, and also wrote to his friends Falkland and Culpeper to lend their support; and then finally when he himself had rejoined the King, he pressed the case himself and overcame Charles's reluctance to disoblige his nephew Maurice. In going to these lengths Hyde was partly influenced by a desire to prevent the Marquis of Hertford from going home in a sulk, but he also seems to have set some store by Ashley Cooper's support, and genuinely thought it worth winning. His whole account of these events in Dorset in the *History of the Rebellion* seems based on the idea that it was a pity that the Marquis of Hertford, with his greater political experience, had not been in charge of the expedition instead of Prince Maurice, and thus been in a position to take better advantage of the co-operation offered by the 'chief gentlemen of Dorsetshire'.[1] All therefore brings us back to the belief that Locke's story of the interview between Ashley Cooper and Charles I has a kernel of truth, and that Cooper was disappointed at the outcome of his grand scheme.

So far as the governorship of Weymouth was concerned, on 10 August 1643, the same day as he summoned Gloucester to surrender, Charles wrote to Hertford, putting forward a characteristic solution.[2] Ashley Cooper and his nominee in Portland were to be allowed to retain their posts for the time being, but in view of 'the youth of the one and the want in

---

[1] Clarendon, *Rebellion*, iii. 127–9, 157–9, 163–5, 362–3.
[2] Printed by Christie, i. 45–46.

both of experience in martial affairs' Hertford was recommended to persuade them to resign as soon as they could do so without it looking like disgrace; he was then to consult with Maurice to find abler soldiers, if possible also with sufficient local interest to be acceptable to the Dorsetshire gentry. This meant in practice that Ashley Cooper retained his post until the end of the year, and in the meantime he was given other honours too. He was made sheriff of Dorset and 'president of the council of war for those parts'.[1]

This last was a very high-sounding title, but no evidence survives to show Ashley Cooper playing any part in any Royalist operations in this autumn to cope with the enemy garrison at Poole. Indeed, when Lord Hopton met the leading county Royalists at Blandford and tried to arrange for a contribution of £1,000 a week to be paid, Cooper went without Hopton's knowledge to Oxford to obstruct it.[2] For any other reference to his activities in these last months before he went over to Parliament, we must go again to Locke's memoir, which describes a supposed second attempt to bring the Civil War to an end. This time it originated not with an interview with the King, but from a casual interview with a lawyer, John Fountain, in an inn at Hungerford, not far from Newbury (was this at the time of the battle in September 1643?). Fountain was a strange person, a lawyer, who, when called upon by Parliament in 1642 to contribute to a loan, had had the temerity to argue that forced loans were illegal by the terms of the Petition of Right, and had received the reply that though the King might not levy them, Parliament could. He had indeed been imprisoned, and in consequence became a Royalist. Later, in 1645, he was certainly concerned in the formation of the famous Clubmen in the west country, who embarrassed Parliament particularly by threatening action against incursions by the troops of either side.[3] According to Locke, Ashley Cooper and Fountain agreed in deploring the ruin which war was bringing to the country, and in thinking 'that the countries all through England should arm and endeavour to suppress the armies on both sides', once again on the basis of a general amnesty and elections for a new parliament 'for redressing the grievances, and settling the nation'. Cooper is said to have worked a good deal on this scheme, which however failed because all those who promised to join did not act at the time appointed. Clearly there is much exaggeration in Locke's story, and the use of the term 'Clubmen' to describe this 'third force' in 1643 is anachronistic; but this does not dispose of the whole story, which could include the beginnings of something which later became one factor in the movement of the Clubmen. Locke finally suggests that Ashley Cooper's activities aroused the King's distrust, and that, rather

---

[1] Christie, i. App. II, p. xxix.

[2] Bayley, p. 125; C. E. H. C. Healey, *Bellum Civile* (Somerset Record Soc. 1902), pp. 63–64.

[3] For Fountain, see Gardiner, *History of the Great Civil War* (1897), i. 35; Clarendon, *Rebellion*, iii. 505.

than accept a suspicious invitation from the King to go to Oxford, or meet Lord Goring, 'who lay with an army in those parts', Cooper, to avoid arrest, 'went whither he was driven, into the parliament quarters, and took shelter in Portsmouth'. The details here present some difficulty, since there is some doubt where precisely Lord Goring was at the time; the question remains whether or not this was the motive for Ashley Cooper's action in taking refuge in the parliamentary lines on 24 February 1644.[1]

Clarendon, with his customary propensity for putting down other people's actions to personal motives rather than considerations of principle, thought that Ashley Cooper's change of sides was the result of pique on having to give up his governorship of Weymouth.[2] Quite apart from Clarendon's limited insight in general into the motives of those who differed from him, this notion is thoroughly unconvincing in Cooper's own case. In a letter to Hyde from Weymouth on 29 December,[3] there is no hint of any ill-feeling towards his successor, Colonel Ashburnham, whom he complimented on doing all he could. But in any case, the governorship of the small port of Weymouth was a petty honour in comparison with others, such as the shrievalty, and still more the peerage which he was offered shortly before he went over. This offer rests only on Ashley Cooper's own account, written two years later, but there is nothing implausible about it. Others with no greater claims gained such honours at Oxford, if they played their cards properly; and Cooper claimed that only two days before leaving 'he received a letter from the King's own hand of large promises and thanks for his service'[4] (and the invitation to Oxford to which Locke referred?). Moreover, even if there had been adequate grounds for discontent at the treatment he was receiving, they would surely have been likely to lead to a withdrawal into neutrality rather than a change of sides. Going over to Parliament from motives of hurt pride would have been cutting off his nose to spite his face; it meant leaving the greater part of his estates in Somerset, Wiltshire and Dorset in Royalist hands to be plundered.

A second possible explanation, equally to Ashley Cooper's discredit, is that he went over to Parliament because he foresaw that that was the winning side; a precocious Machiavellian political sense made him give up his estates to be plundered now in the belief that all would turn out to his advantage in the end when Parliament won. This idea is based on hindsight, at once with Ashley Cooper's later career in mind, and with our

---

[1] Locke, *Works* (1823), ix. 268–9. The author of *Rawleigh Redivivus* (1683), pp. 16–18, says that Cooper as sheriff had called 'the whole county from sixteen years old' to a meeting at Dorchester, but went over to Parliament before this meeting took place. There are so many errors in the story, however, that it is difficult to tell whether there is any residuum of historical fact in it. [2] *Rebellion*, iii. 362.

[3] Printed by Miss Brown, p. 44 n. When before a parliamentary committee, he said that he gave up his governorship in the first week of January (Christie, i. 49).

[4] Christie, i, App. II, p. xxix.

knowledge that in 1644 and 1645 the King was in fact overborne by superior resources. But no contemporary at the end of 1643 could feel sure that Parliament would win; if the House of Commons had been so confident of victory, they would not have made the alliance with the Scots, and the King's forces did not exactly feel doomed to defeat. Ashley Cooper, in his letter of 29 December 1643, had been pessimistic about the situation in money and manpower in Dorset for the Royalists, but no more so than many a local commander on either side writing to his government for assistance. To ask us to believe that, when still only twenty-two, he made a cold calculation to give up his estates for the present in order to get them back (all being well) at some uncertain future date is too much. Nor did he carry with him any useful information to enable him to ingratiate himself with Parliament, which imposed a £500 composition fine upon him.

It is better to remember that Ashley Cooper had never been a wholehearted, unquestioning Royalist partisan. He had raised his regiment of foot and troop of horse at his own expense, but not until nearly a year after the fighting began. So far as we know, he had engaged in no fighting himself. Whether we accept Locke's memoir in full or not, the signs are that he had always been a moderate. To such a man the developments at the King's Court in the second half of 1643 would be disturbing. The return of Queen Henrietta Maria strengthened the hand of the more reckless, absolutist, Catholic faction as against the constitutionalists, and, in Locke's words, 'it was the soldiers of fortune who were best looked upon at Court, and had the commands and power put into their hands'; their only idea was complete conquest of the enemy. Such views could be amply supported from Clarendon's own account of the Royalist scene, and his own difficulties there. In September 1643 Falkland had ridden to his death in the gap in the hedge at Newbury, and then news began to arrive from Ireland of the so-called Cessation or truce with the Irish Catholic rebels, and of Charles's endeavours to bring over Irish troops in time for the campaign of 1644. In these circumstances it is not surprising that others besides Ashley Cooper began to consider a parliamentary victory as at any rate the lesser of two evils. Sir Edward Dering preceded him, complaining when he reached Westminster of the number of Catholic officers in the King's army, of the general view at Oxford that a settlement must be imposed 'by conquest', and of the difficulty of reconciling the Cessation with the King's professed policy in England.[1] There were others too, stimulated to make up their minds by Parliament's offer, dated 30 January, of pardon to those who came in before 1 March 1644.

Ashley Cooper himself wrote, in an autobiographical sketch prefixed to a diary of 1646 which no other eye could be expected to see, that he took this

---

[1] Gardiner, *History of the Great Civil War* (1897), i. 301; C. V. Wedgwood, *The King's War* (1958), pp. 259–63, 292–3; J. Rushworth, *Historical Collections* (1692), pt. iii, ii. 383–4.

step because he saw that the King's aim was 'destructive to religion and the state'; and, further on, that he left his estates to the mercy of the enemy 'resolving to cast himself on God and to follow the dictates of a good conscience'.[1] This description of his own motives may seem repellently sanctimonious; but it may rest on truth, whether or not we accept Locke's additional statement that he was afraid of being arrested by the King's side if he remained. It certainly seems to the present writer the most likely of the three possible theories.

At all events, Ashley Cooper claimed to have given up his commissions to Colonel Ashburnham early in January 1644, and to have resolved to go over to Parliament before he heard of Parliament's proclamation. He made his way to the commander at Hurst Castle—the same shingly promontory jutting out into the waters of the Solent that the King was himself to know a few years later—on 24 February, and thence by way of the Isle of Wight and Portsmouth he travelled up to London. There on 6 March he made a statement before a parliamentary committee, to the effect that he had come because he was fully satisfied that the Royalists had 'no intention . . . for the promoting or preserving of the Protestant religion and the liberties of the kingdom'. He made a virtue of having left estates worth £3,400 per annum behind the King's lines, and, while producing a certificate that he had appeared before the key date of 1 March, said that he had come without attempting to take advantage of any conditions, solely because he now believed that Parliament's cause was just. Further, he was prepared to take the Covenant which was now the general test of loyalty to the Presbyterian cause.[2]

By the terms of Parliament's offer he was guaranteed his life and personal liberty, but his estates were nominally at Parliament's disposal—when they were won from the enemy, that is.[3] But he was not by any means a penniless fugitive. His flight had not been undertaken on a sudden, momentary impulse, and no doubt he had been able to make suitable financial preparations. He was even able to establish himself at Dorchester House, in Covent Garden, where he lived with his brother-in-law, the second Lord Coventry, in 1641. There, before the end of March, he was reunited with his wife, whom he had not seen since leaving her behind in Shropshire twelve months previously. The fact that in the extremely meagre record of his movements which he himself made he made mention of this reunion is a reminder of his affectionate relationship with his wife.[4] Neither then nor at any other time was Achitophel the cold, calculating politician who sacrificed all personal relationships on the altar of political intrigue.

[1] Christie, i, App. II, p. xxix.
[2] Notes printed from the Royalist Composition Papers by Christie, i. 49–51.
[3] Rushworth, pt. iii, ii. 500–1.
[4] Christie, i, App. II, p. xxix.

In the spring of 1644 Ashley Cooper remained in London with his wife, awaiting news from the battle fronts as events moved to a crisis in the North, while in his own county the little port of Lyme held out with great gallantry for Parliament against Prince Maurice. Before the Royalist fortunes in the North collapsed for ever as the July darkness fell on Marston Moor, there had been a reversal on a lesser scale in Dorset. In mid-June the Earl of Essex advanced into the county, and the Royalists abandoned the siege of Lyme. On 17 June Weymouth surrendered to the Parliamentarians without putting up any resistance; Ashley Cooper's successor as governor there, Colonel Ashburnham, thought it better to concentrate on holding Portland Castle. After installing his own nominee, Colonel William Sydenham, as the new governor of Weymouth, Essex ordered him to deliver such goods there as belonged to Sir Anthony Cooper to his brother, Captain George Cooper, for conveyance to Hurst Castle; an order which suggests that within four months of changing sides Sir Anthony was able somehow to wield a surprising amount of influence with the commander-in-chief.[1]

This was soon to be even more strikingly demonstrated. After Essex had passed on on his ill-fated march further into the south-west, the usual Parliamentary County Committee was left behind in Dorset to continue the fighting against the remaining Royalist garrisons (particularly at Wareham), and to contribute what they could to the main Parliamentary war effort. At the beginning of July this committee, perhaps influenced by Ashley Cooper's friend Thomas Earle who was a member of it, wrote asking for Cooper to come and join them; and on 10 July the House of Commons gave the necessary permission.[2] Hastening down to Dorset, he immediately entered the ranks of the leading supporters of Parliament in the county. In spite of youth, military inexperience and Royalist past, he was nevertheless able, by a combination of his local position, wealth, personality and efficiency, rapidly to win a position of trust. In the next four months he played a leading part in the military operations without a breath of distrust about his loyalty to his new cause.

On 3 August he was asked by the Dorset committee to serve as 'field marshall' to a brigade of horse and foot,[3] and within a week he had played his part in an attack on the town of Wareham. The Royalist garrison here had made a special nuisance of itself by its raids on the surrounding country, and its surrender was extremely welcome. Some accounts suggest that under the more experienced command of Lieutenant-General Middleton Ashley Cooper performed great deeds of valour in this attack, which was probably his baptism of fire; but it is well known that accounts extolling the prowess of local commanders cannot always be trusted, since some of

[1] Bayley, pp. 194–7; Egerton MSS. 2126, fo. 12.
[2] Christie, loc. cit.; C.J. iii. 556.
[3] Copy in Shaftesbury Papers, II, 43.

THE YOUNG MAN IN CIVIL WAR

them were aware of the importance of 'public relations' in order to bring
their names to official notice. Cooper was not one of those who signed the
terms on which the Royalist garrison surrendered. On the other hand, it is
significant that he was the man selected to ride post-haste to London to
carry the news to the House of Commons. On 14 August he appeared at
the bar of the House to present letters from Colonel Jephson and the Dorset
committee. How far he was allowed to supplement these letters verbally
is uncertain, but he certainly gained personally from his conduct during
this episode. Accepting the county committee's recommendation, the
House voted to add him to their numbers, and also referred his case to the
Committee for Sequestrations at Goldsmiths' Hall, for consideration of
the terms on which his estates should be restored to him. The committee
reported with speed and leniency, and eight days later on 22 August the
House agreed that he should be allowed to compound for £500. This was
even more lenient than it sounded since Ashley Cooper was never in fact
called upon to pay.[1]

Back in Dorset, Ashley Cooper rapidly began to make his presence felt
on the county committee, many of whose letters carry his signature first,
along with that of his friend Thomas Earle.[2] September 1644 was indeed
a busy month. Not only was the county now divided fairly equally between
the two parties, with the garrisons of each able to raid the estates of the
other, but Dorset also felt the consequences of events elsewhere. After
Essex's surrender to King Charles at Lostwithiel in Cornwall, there were
returning foot-soldiers to be taken care of and refitted; and General
Waller advanced on behalf of Parliament to examine the military situation,
only to fall back before the King's return eastwards. Charles spent the
first fortnight of October in the county, and the last night of his stay was at
Cranborne, very close to Wimborne St. Giles. All this meant much feverish
activity for the County Committee, and plenty of scope for Ashley Cooper's
organizing ability, powers of leadership and rapid decision. The result was
that when Charles had passed through and Dorset was once again contested
by the local forces of the two parties, Cooper emerged the commander-in-
chief of some 1,500 men against the Royalist commander Sir Lewis Dyve.
Longer-serving soldiers like Colonel Sydenham were apparently willing to
serve under him.

With this force Ashley Cooper claimed one highly successful skirmish
over the enemy, and then early in November advanced to attack the home
of Sir John Strangeways at Abbotsbury in west Dorset. The passage of
arms which followed has attained some notoriety. The essential facts are
not in doubt; they can be derived from Ashley Cooper's own report to the

---

[1] Christie, i, App. II, p. xxx; Bayley, pp. 208–10; *C.J.* iii. 589, 603; J. Vicars, *Parliamentary Chronicle* (1646), iv. 5; *Wareham taken by Parliament* (1644); MSS. Tanner 61, fos. 43,
45, 48.
[2] Add. MSS. 29319.

Dorset committee (which claimed no credit for personal gallantry) and from the account of one of his officers (which gave him some).[1]

After the first summons to the garrison to surrender had been refused in the growing November darkness, Ashley Cooper's men evicted some of them from the nearby church, and then Cooper sent a second summons, with a warning that if this was refused and he was forced to storm the house, no quarter would be given. The garrison paid no attention to this warning, and Cooper was left to drive them from the windows of the house by concentrated fire, and then to get his men in close in the darkness to prise open the ground-floor windows with iron bars and throw in lighted faggots. It took some six hours to do this, and about fifteen casualties were lost in killed and wounded, but eventually Sir John and Colonel James Strangeways found themselves with a fire which they could not control, and they then called out for quarter. Ashley Cooper reported (without any shamefacedness) that he refused to give quarter, as he was 'entitled' to do by the commonly accepted 'rules of war' of the period.

This would not have been by any means the only or the first 'atrocity' of the war; apart from other stormed garrisons, there were some ugly scenes, as when in July Dorset Royalists had hanged twelve prisoners in retaliation for seven hanged by Parliament previously.[2] Nor would this have been the result of any feelings of vindictiveness or personal enmity for the Strangeways family. By the cold light of reason a case could be made out for showing no mercy. As Ashley Cooper himself explained, he wanted to deter other Royalist garrisons from prolonging their resistance and inflicting casualties in confidence that they would be spared in the end; and in the next two years many lives were certainly lost in the futile defence of country-houses and castles dotted up and down the country. Nevertheless the idea of shooting down men who were cornered in a burning house and ready to surrender is repellently cold-blooded, and (whatever the merits of the calculation about the total loss of life in country-houses) most people will rejoice that cold logic was overborne by the warmer humanity of Colonel and Major Sydenham, who rode round to the other side of the house and granted quarter from there. But the episode reveals a defect not only in Ashley Cooper's humanity but also in his broader political sense. There could be no guarantee that such an atrocity as he contemplated would have the deterrent effect intended; but one atrocity would certainly lead to another, and the long-term result would be to perpetuate bitterness between the two factions and to make worse and far more numerous vendettas. There is a sense in which (in spite of Machiavelli) magnanimity is in the long run the greatest political wisdom.

As it was, the Strangeways family did not feel well disposed to Ashley

---

[1] Both printed by Christie, i. 62–67, the latter from Vicars's *Parliamentary Chronicle* (1646), iv. 67–68.   [2] Bayley, pp. 204–5.

Cooper after this episode, all the more so because while the Parliament-arians were plundering the house, the fire reached a magazine and blew it up. Perhaps they derived some satisfaction from the fact that a few soldiers were killed and thirty or forty injured by the explosion; but the combined effects of fire and explosion led to Abbotsbury being burned to the ground. Not unnaturally they were left with a score to pay off in the distant future.

Some recommendations of Ashley Cooper's about the military situation in the county at this time show a similar cold and calculating spirit.[1] Wareham was difficult both to provision and to defend; the Royalists in Corfe Castle could be contained more effectively from Lulworth than from Wareham; the inhabitants of Wareham were 'almost all dreadful malignants, besides the keeping it will certainly starve more honest men than the destroying it will undo knaves'. So why not destroy the town of Wareham altogether? These and other suggestions made a complete change from his attitude in 1643; no thought of a compromise settlement now, but a determination to achieve complete victory by the speediest and most effective means, regardless of other considerations. These opinions on military matters also show once again a remarkable self-confidence in one whose experience was so limited; and although his suggestions about Wareham were not accepted by the Dorset committee, it is clear that he was coming to be regarded as the leading Parliamentarian taking part in the fighting. Not only was he active, energetic, zealous for the cause and competent, but he was probably able to make a substantial and much-needed contribution to the committee's financial resources. When in December 1644 the commander of the garrison at Wareham was in desper-ate straits to pay his men, it was to Ashley Cooper that he wrote for 'money, money'; and although it may be that he only wanted Cooper to use his influence with the committee for this purpose, it is likely that he had Cooper's extensive estates in mind as well.[2]

In this same month of December he saw his last piece of active service, when he received orders to leave the county and go to the relief of Colonel Robert Blake in Taunton. This was successfully accomplished without incident, the Royalist besiegers retiring as Ashley Cooper's force ap-proached, and the only point of interest is whether in describing himself in his diary as commander-in-chief for this military operation he was accurate or boastfully exaggerating his own exploits. Contemporaries seem to have regarded Major-General Holborn as the true commander. The truth may be that Ashley Cooper commanded the Dorset contingent, which joined the main force under the experienced Holborn, along with two hundred more under Colonel Ludlow, and that the relief was accom-plished by their co-operation. But neither Ashley Cooper's diary reference,

---

[1] Cooper to the governor of Poole, n.d., printed by Christie, i. 68–70.
[2] R. Butler to Ashley Cooper, 18 Dec. 1644, printed in Christie, i. 71.

nor the letter in which he reported the expedition's success to the Earl of Essex, can justly be the basis for any conclusions about his alleged vanity. His report to Essex was very impersonal and matter-of-fact, and the really significant point about it is that Essex passed it on, to be read to the House of Commons on 24 December; and his account of the situation at Taunton was persuasive enough to lead the House to resolve on sending reinforcements. Whatever his prowess with the sword, his ability to persuade was to have more lasting significance.[1]

This Taunton expedition marked the end of his military career. On 17 May 1645, it is true, the 'committee of Lords and Commons for the safety of the Associated Western Counties' (including his enemy Denzil Holles, and his bosom friend Thomas Earle) sent him instructions to raise forces for the reduction of the Royalists at Corfe Castle; but nothing ever came of this, apparently because the troops on which Ashley Cooper principally depended were occupied elsewhere.[2] Why no other task was assigned to him is something of a mystery, for in 1645 much remained to be done to clear Dorset and the West of Royalists, and also to cope with the famous movement of Clubmen who congregated in that summer not so very far from Wimborne St. Giles. One possibility is that his lack of employment was connected with the Self-Denying Ordinance which on 3 April barred all members of Parliament from any military command. As will be seen, Ashley Cooper still regarded himself as the rightful member for Downton, and naturally would not wish to imply that he was not by retaining his commissions. However this would not explain why nothing is heard of his activities earlier in 1645, for instance when a Royalist force surprised Parliament's garrison at Weymouth. It may be that the explanation is to be found not in any subtle political manoeuvring, but in ordinary ill-health. In June and July he spent six weeks with his wife at Tonbridge, drinking the waters.

It was while he and Lady Cooper were at Tonbridge that the battles were fought at Naseby and Langport which put Parliament's victory beyond all doubt. In six years of married life they had lived through crisis and civil war, and now it was certain that there was no possibility of putting the clock back to those days of early 1639, when King Charles I had wielded untrammelled authority over an ordered and peaceful, if discontented, England. Like everyone else in that summer of 1645 the Coopers had to adjust themselves to a changed world. How should a man of birth, wealth, a precocious political intelligence and ambition chart his course? What should he do in the reconstruction of the country's political and religious life which must now follow? If he pondered these things as he

---

[1] Christie, i. 72–74 and xxx; Gardiner, *History of the Great Civil War* (1898), ii. 97–98; *C.S.P.D. 1644–5*, pp. 113–14, 124, 196; J. Vicars, *Parliamentary Chronicle* (1646), iv. 77–78; Ludlow, *Memoirs*, ed. C. H. Firth (1894), i. 107–8; *C.J.* iii. 734.

[2] Bayley, pp. 295–6.

sipped the Tonbridge spa waters, we may be sure that he did not do so in any spirit of anxiety about what the future might bring, but in a mood of complete self-confidence as at all times of his career. After all, in the years now past he had faced some tricky problems with success, when other promising young men, like that Lord Digby with whom he had talked on the bowling-greens of Dorset, had gone to disaster. Many Royalists indeed would say in years to come that he had saved himself by treason while other and better men had found death or ruin for their loyalty; Cavalier memories were long-lived and in simple terms. To others, however, and to the present writer, it seems inadequate to think of his career thus far merely in terms of successful survival by means of a timely desertion; rather this was a man who, after initial uncertainty, had decided that Parliament's cause was the nearer to his own outlook, had assisted it and seen it triumph.

CHAPTER IV

OFF STAGE (1645–52)

If you can look into the seeds of time,
And say which grain will grow, and which will not,
Speak then to me . . .

DURING the Civil War Sir Anthony Ashley Cooper had made no decisive mark on English history. If he had died at this point his career would have been of interest only to the local historian of Dorset. None the less he had become personally acquainted with many of the great men on both sides; his local position, wealth and precociousness had made his support worth seeking, and finally, in the service of Parliament he had shown at least a measure of competence and won the confidence of his colleagues. In the normal course of events a young man of twenty-four with such assets, such a record, and such ambition would be expected to go on quickly to greater things.

Yet for the next seven years he made no progress towards political power and influence, and in 1652 he was no better known than he had been in 1645. This was largely because of his failure at the outset to secure election to the House of Commons. In 1645 his hopes of at last establishing his claim to the Downton seat must have been high. He could rely on the influence of his Dorset neighbours, the Earles. Young Thomas Earle was his closest friend and Thomas's father, Sir Walter, was a veteran Parliamentarian whose opinion would carry weight. He made some declaration of 'his great affection to the Parliament, and his enmity to the King's party from whom he had revolted', and seemed to be 'in great favour and trust'. On 1 September the journals of the House of Commons record an order that Sir Walter Earle should report to the House on the Downton election dispute on the following Saturday, and there can be no doubt that this report would have been favourable. But the cup was dashed from his lips. The very next entry in the Journals records a resolution 'that no person that hath been in actual war against this Parliament, shall be admitted to sit as a member in this Parliament'. Ashley Cooper was automatically debarred from sitting. Nothing was heard of Sir Walter's report on Downton, and the same resolution equally prevented Cooper from standing as a candidate at any of the local by-elections for 'Recruiters' to take the place of expelled Royalist members. The proximity of the two orders in the proceedings of the House makes it plain that the Downton order led to the general resolution, and it is probable that we must again see here the influence of enemies who were determined to keep him out.[1]

Thus he remained outside the Long Parliament, which seemed in September 1645 to be the place where the great political decisions were made. Rather curiously, there is no trace of his renewing his attempts to get the Downton dispute settled at any later date; did he come round to the view that it was actually better for him to remain outside the House? Like his absence from the opening sessions of the Long Parliament in 1640–1, so now his absence in 1645–52 prevented him from becoming too closely identified with any political group. If he had been in the House in 1648, for instance, he might well have been purged by Colonel Pride, as happened to both the Earles and Denzil Holles. But the real difficulty for the biographer is that Ashley Cooper's unimportance at the time means that there are few references to him in the contemporary sources, and consequently there is very little evidence from which his attitude to the great events of these years can be deduced. We are largely reduced to the most meagre of diaries which Ashley Cooper kept of his own movements.

One exception to this lies in two episodes which are recounted by John Locke in the memoirs to which reference has previously been made.[2] The first relates to the period in July 1645 when Holles was under attack in the House for his behaviour when, as a parliamentary commissioner, he had negotiated with the King, and (Locke says) Ashley Cooper, who was known to be on bad terms with him, was called upon at the bar of the House to say whether he had heard anything about it when at Oxford. This Cooper obstinately refused to say, on the ingenious grounds that 'whatever answer he made, it would be a confession that, if he had known anything to the disadvantage of Mr. Holles, he would have taken that dishonourable way' of wreaking his revenge. He held to this position in the face alike of threats and of inducements from his friends; and according to Locke, the outcome was the exchange of compliments by Holles and Cooper, and the formation of a firm friendship between the two men instead of their previous enmity. Scorn has been poured on this romantic story, because Ashley Cooper had changed sides twelve months before Holles's conversations with the King (which were at Oxford, not Uxbridge, as Locke alleged), and therefore could have had no knowledge of them. Clearly the story cannot be accepted as it stands. The details at least have been seriously confused, and there is obvious exaggeration in Locke's dramatic picture of Ashley Cooper waiting in the lobby of the House and 'unmoved expecting his doom' while the House debated whether or not to send him to the Tower. Nevertheless one hesitates to dismiss the story as a complete fabrication, because somewhere about this time there was undoubtedly a reconciliation between Holles and Ashley Cooper, and by 30 March 1646 Cooper was holding his manorial court at Damerham, one of the two manors which

---

[1] *C.J.* iv. 260.
[2] *Works* (1823), ix. 270–2, 278–9.

had been the bones of contention between them. Holles, ever 'haughtily stiff' was not naturally ready to forget and forgive, and it is likely that there was some obligation to induce him to give up what he conceived to be his rights. By some means Ashley Cooper had won over a dangerous enemy. It is worth noting that Holles was also accused of maintaining secret communications with Digby at Oxford throughout the war, and it is possible that Ashley Cooper, who knew Digby, might have had evidence to give on this charge, and not the main one.[1]

Locke goes on to say that Cooper formed the habit of calling on Holles, and that one morning (which must have been at the end of May 1647) he found Holles planning an attack on Oliver Cromwell for his approval of the seizure of the King by Cornet Joyce and the army leaders. Cooper argued that Holles could accomplish his desire to get rid of a dangerous commander more effectively by sending him out of the way to campaign in Ireland; Holles however regarded this as an evasion, persisted with his head-on collision with Cromwell and the Army, and paid the penalty for his inflexibility. On 3 June Cromwell left to join the Army, and not long afterwards the Army, ignoring the constitutional forms and the traditional respect for Parliament on which Holles had relied, turned out Holles and ten other leading Presbyterians from the House. Here again Locke has not got the details right, and telescopes the expulsion of the eleven M.P.s in 1647 with Pride's Purge in December 1648. But it would not be in the least surprising to find Ashley Cooper taking a more realistic view of the political situation than Holles, and talking of it to Locke twenty or thirty years later.

This is the only hint which we possess that Ashley Cooper preferred the cause of the 'Presbyterian' politicians to that of the Army officers, though this is what we might expect from a general view of his career as a whole. For the rest, nothing is known of his reactions to the great events which he witnessed in these years. Though he had friends who could keep him well informed of what was going on, his diary is bare of political comment. There is nothing to indicate any interest in the immense ferment of Leveller ideas in 1647, and the more democratic concepts which were put forward in pamphlets and at the Putney debates; nothing on the Second Civil War, except that in July 1648 he was made one of the commissioners for the militia in Dorset; no reference to the exclusion of his friends from the House in Pride's Purge; no mention of the most sensational event of the whole century, the execution of a king on a public scaffold in Whitehall; indeed in the critical months of December 1648 and January 1649 he was uncharacteristically away from the centre of political activity in London, whither he returned from Dorset only on the day after the King's execution. All is wrapped in silence.

---

[1] Christie, i. 40, n., xxxiv. There is however no reference to Cooper in Holles's own account of the charges against him (*Memoirs*, 1699, pp. 38–41).

Though the diary says nothing about all these great national events, it is possible to glean from it information about his public activities locally in Dorset. Though the Long Parliament was not willing to accept him as a member at Westminster, it was prepared to thrust local tasks upon him, and Ashley Cooper was ready to perform them, to do his duty and acquire greater experience and reputation. In October 1645, after his failure over the Downton election, he resumed his place on the Dorset county committee, 'most commonly as chairman', as he records to his own satisfaction. On 1 October he joined in writing to the Speaker, painting a melancholy picture of plague and famine at Poole, and pleading that the burden of the garrisons which the county had to support was too heavy. Having represented the interests of his neighbours in this way, two months later he and Colonel Bingham were deputed to travel to Fairfax's camp before Exeter to ask for assistance to rid themselves of the nuisance of Corfe Castle, which was still holding out for the King. He did not however return to Dorset to be present at the final submission of the Royalists in Corfe and Portland or at every routine committee meeting; instead his record of his movements from 1646 onwards shows him making periodical visits to his native county, in the course of which he occasionally attended the county committee (although the Minutes record his presence only four times after September 1646) or served in other local capacities. On 1 October he 'went to Shaftesbury to the council of war for Massey's brigade, and got them removed out of Dorset'. In the next two years he was frequently a commissioner for the levying of tax assessments in Dorset and Wiltshire, and in 1648 one of the commissioners for the militia.[1]

The most exalted position to which Parliament appointed him (in December 1646) was that of High Sheriff for Wiltshire. He had served for a short period in 1643 as sheriff of Dorset for the King, so that his case was rather unusual. A sheriff's duties were already becoming more honorific than practical, and even the honour was dearly bought, for the expenditure involved was considerable: sheriffs were expected to be open-handed and generous in their hospitality on the great occasions. Ashley Cooper had to rent a house next to the Deanery in the cathedral close at Salisbury, and when the time came for the assizes to be held, he had sixty men in livery and kept an 'ordinary' at the Angel inn where all visiting gentlemen could be entertained at his expense—4s. for the gentlemen, 2s. for their men, 'and a cellar'. This lavishness was not simply, in the jargon of the twentieth century, a 'status symbol', or a desire to keep up with others who had held the same position; it will be seen that when much later he was Lord Chancellor he had a strong sense of the majesty of the law and the need for

---

[1] Christie, i, App. II, pp. xxx sqq. Cf. also Bayley, p. 292; *H.M.C. Portland MSS.*, i. 279; *Acts and Ordinances of the Interregnum*, ed. C. H. Firth and R. S. Rait (1911), i. 964, 977, 1081, 1095, 1236, 1241, 1244; *Minute Books of the Dorset Standing Committee, 1646–50*, ed. C. H. Mayo (1902), pp. 318–28, 421–7, 492–3.

those in political authority to put up an impressive front for the benefit of people at large. For the most part the sheriff was an impressive figure-head; the only important action recorded is in March 1647, when he 'raised the country twice, and beat out the soldiers designed for Ireland, who quartered on the county without order, and committed many robberies'. He was not the man to tolerate such disorders. In February 1648 he received his writ of discharge from Mr. Tooker, who curiously enough succeeded his nephew in the office.

At the Assizes he saw his hapless fellow-men facing capital charges, and on the commission of oyer and terminer and at Quarter Sessions he helped to sit in judgement on them. He chalked up the score in his diary: 'Nine hanged, only three burnt in the hand'; 'seven condemned to die, four for horse-stealing, two for robbery, one for killing his wife'; 'five condemned to die, two women for murdering their children, one of them a married woman'. It was a pitiless age, in which human life was of little account, and Cooper's attitude was not greatly different from that of his contemporaries, though it must be said in his favour that he joined in several successful petitions for reprieve, two of them on the excuse that the criminal had fought on the right, or Parliamentary, side in the Civil War. On one point it is surprising to find him sharing the common outlook: it is rather disconcerting to find a man apparently so cool and rational recording without comment that, in the case of one man who had broken his wife's neck, 'it was proved that, he touching her body the day after, her nose bled fresh'.[1] The common currency of such superstitions as this, even among intelligent people, and the sort of 'proof' of guilt which they were ready to accept, must be borne in mind when one considers the atmosphere in which the notorious Popish Plot trials were conducted.

It is natural to ask whether the proclamation of a Republic made any difference to Ashley Cooper's willingness to undertake local duties. The answer is that in February 1649 the new régime again made him a justice of the quorum for Wiltshire and Dorset, and of oyer and terminer for the Western circuit, but that he was not actually sworn until 16 August. There may therefore have been some slight hesitation here about serving the Commonwealth, but in April he had been appointed a commissioner to regulate the 'contribution' or tax paid by his two counties, so that any hesitation cannot be pressed too far, and it would be quite profitless to speculate on motives. In January and February 1650 we find him not only subscribing the Engagement of loyalty to the Republic, but agreeing to serve on a commission tendering the Engagement to others.[2]

For the rest, the diary contains a record of all his movements from 1646 to 1650.[3] These are the movements of a man who is neither content to

---

[1] Christie, i, App. II, pp. xxxiv, xxxvii.
[2] Christie, i, App. II, pp. li–liv; *Acts and Ordinances of the Interregnum*, ed. C. H. Firth and R. S. Rait (1911), ii. 33, 45, 296, 311, 464, 480.   [3] Christie, i, App. II, pp. xxxii–lv.

live the ordinary life of a country squire living on his estates through every season, nor prepared to settle permanently in the capital. In four and a half years he spent a total of approximately two and a half in the West, whether at Wimborne St. Giles or (while sheriff of Wiltshire) at Salisbury, holding his manorial courts or attending the county committee, or paying social visits to his neighbours or being present at Quarter Sessions. In the same period he spent a total of nearly two years in or around London. He lodged with various people, and at other times refers to 'our own house' next to the Hatton house in Holborn. There were also frequent visits to Oxted in Surrey, the home of yet another of his wife's relatives, her aunt, Lady Capel. His wife indeed stayed for long spells at Oxted while he pursued his business in London or elsewhere.

There are other signs besides this that his ties with the Coventry 'connexion' remained strong for some years, even though most of the Coventrys were Royalist. From the brief notes of financial transactions it appears that on several occasions he sealed bonds for his brother-in-law, John Coventry, to enable the latter to borrow money.

However, from 1649 onwards Ashley Cooper's connexion with the Coventrys began to weaken, for in that year his wife died. They had been very happy, except that there were no children. In July 1646 his wife had one miscarriage, when her brother threw her against a bed-post in the course of some horse-play; in March 1647, there was a second miscarriage, and in December of the same year there was a stillborn girl.[1] All these are recorded without comment, for such hazards had to be accepted in the seventeenth century. In 1649 Lady Cooper became pregnant for the fourth time, and by July she was within six weeks of giving birth to the long-awaited child. But on 10 July, 'just as she was sitting down to supper', she 'fell suddenly into an apoplectical convulsive fit'. After a time she recovered 'and spake and kissed me', but a quarter of an hour later she had a second fit. This time she did not recover, and did not speak again before she died at noon next day.

There follows in Ashley Cooper's diary his tribute to his wife.

'She was a lovely beautiful fair woman, a religious devout Christian, of admirable wit and wisdom, beyond any I ever knew, yet the most sweet, affectionate, and observant wife in the world. Chaste without a suspicion of the most envious to the highest assurance of her husband, of a most noble and bountiful mind, yet very provident in the least things, exceeding all in anything she undertook, housewifery, preserving, works with the needle, cookery, so that her wit and judgment were expressed in all things, free from any pride or forwardness. She was in discourse and counsel far beyond any woman.'[2]

Now it is well known that no man is on oath in his tributes to the dead, but this tribute occurs in a private diary, most of the entries in which are

---

[1] Christie, i, App. II, pp. xxxvi–xxxvii, xlii, xlvi.   [2] Ibid. p. lii.

arid and matter-of-fact in the extreme, and it is clearly intended to be an accurate description. It is unemotional, or rather the emotions are kept firmly under control—no wild outpourings of passionate feeling for Ashley Cooper, but every word chosen with care. Yet it is not fanciful to see underlying the calm phrases a real affection. He was not a cold, solely political animal. It is obvious that he shared some of the customary ideas of the seventeenth century on what a wife should be to her husband: she was expected to be 'observant' of his wishes, and a good mistress of his household. But the reference to discourse and counsel suggests an intellectual companionship, and the over-riding impression is of a happy relationship brought to an untimely end.

No childless man of property was expected to remain a widower, and within less than a year, on 15 April 1650, Ashley Cooper married for a second time. His bride again came from a noble family: indeed Lady Frances Cecil had more distinguished forebears than Lady Margaret Coventry had had. The current Leveller ideas and the abolition of the House of Lords under the Commonwealth evidently did not affect Ashley Cooper's desire to have a wife from a family in the hereditary peerage. However, the seventeenth-century Cecils were by no means the unbending conservatives that they later became. Lady Frances's brother, the Earl of Exeter, was too young to have taken any part in the fighting, but the leading member of the house of Cecil at this time, the Earl of Salisbury, had thrown in his lot with Parliament. After the abolition of the House of Lords in 1649, this aristocrat went so far as to gain election to the Commons, and at the time of the marriage he was a member of the Republican Council of State. Clarendon paints a singularly unflattering, but not impartial picture of his character and motives.[1] He was Ashley Cooper's neighbour in Cranborne Chase, and in the eyes of the world Cooper's match with Lady Frances Cecil was a most suitable one, in which one man of property took a wife from another propertied and titled family of not very dissimilar political outlook.

Virtually nothing is known of Lady Frances herself. She was seventeen when she married, and nineteen when she died in 1652. At St. Giles there is an unremarkable portrait of her, anachronistically alleged to be by Van Dyck. She was, however, the mother of Ashley Cooper's heir. The first son, born in 1651, must have been one of the first babies to be christened by the name of Cecil: Cooper, who bore the name of his mother's family, followed this precedent and paid a similar compliment on this occasion. Cecil, however, died in childhood, and it was the second son (to whom Cooper gave his own names of Anthony Ashley), who lived to be the butt of Dryden's malice and eventually became the second Earl of Shaftesbury.

Sir Anthony and Lady Cooper took new London lodgings, which by a

---

[1] *Rebellion*, ii. 542–3.

curious coincidence were in the Strand next to Exeter House, later to be his residence under the Restoration.[1] But in 1649 and 1650 his diary refers more and more to Wimborne St. Giles as 'home'. Before 1645 it is doubtful how much of his youth he had actually spent there—he had lived in many different places; but he was obviously settling down there and on 19 March 1650 (a month before his second marriage) his diary contains the entry 'I laid the first stone of my house at St. Giles.'[2] This was not a period when very many country gentlemen chose to build; the times were very unsettled and, with Charles II proclaimed in Scotland and few people able to be confident that the Commonwealth would last, it could well be argued that it would be prudent to wait. It was once again typical of Ashley Cooper's self-assurance and belief in his own abilities to cope with any political situation, that he should choose 1650 as the year in which to begin. Unfortunately no documents survive from this year to tell us how and by whom the new house, which replaced the older one he had known in his youth, was planned. One authority, who has described the house as 'one of the very first buildings to have been erected in the English classic style, apart from those derived directly from Palladio by Inigo Jones', suggests that Ashley Cooper 'may well have designed it himself with the help of men who had worked under Inigo Jones'. Twenty years later he is found writing a memorandum to his steward containing orders for its decoration, alteration and completion.[3] So many alterations have since been made both to the inside and to the outside of the house, that it is not easy to imagine it as it was when first it was built. Two further wings were added in the eighteenth century; the red bricks with stone facings of which the house was built were treated with stucco a little later; originally the house had a low roof and battlements all round it; the seventeenth-century entrance, though it still survives, is an entrance no longer; and the east façade may have been remodelled in the eighteenth century. The fourth and fifth Earls of Shaftesbury were responsible for much internal embellishment and redecoration, knocking four rooms into one to make a state dining-room, and roofing over an open courtyard to make the present panelled hall. Apart from one or two chimney-pieces, a plaster ceiling and some family portraits the interior has more of the eighteenth century than the seventeenth.[4] Nevertheless it is possible to form certain impressions of what the original must have been like. It must have been big enough to entertain a king on occasion (in 1665), but it was not in the least grandiose or ostentatious. In size and cost it fell far short of the great houses of Jacobean or Georgian times, and it never became a great political centre for the region in the way that they did. Though Shaftesbury did occasionally

---

[1] Christie, i, App. II, p. lv.   [2] Ibid.
[3] Shaftesbury Papers, IV, 183.
[4] Christopher Hussey, in *Country Life*, 10–24 Sept. 1943, and see the booklet on St. Giles's House by R. W. Symonds, F.S.A. (1960).

entertain political associates there, he does not seem to have done this extensively; when in later life he retired to St. Giles in the summer he seems to have done so rather to recuperate, to supervise his estate and to enjoy his beloved fruit-trees. It was a nicely-proportioned building, well within the means of its builder, and well suited to his position in society in the 1650s.

One other development in Ashley Cooper's personal life in these years after the Civil War may be mentioned. It was now that he began to add to his income from his landed estates, investments in commerce and in plantations overseas. These interests of his are not well-documented; no accounts or legal records survive in the Shaftesbury Papers other than a few brief references in his diary, and we possess hardly any information on the interesting question who his commercial associates were, except that his brother George Cooper married a daughter of one Mr. Oldfield of London, a 'sugar baker'.[1] He was much interested in the profits to be obtained from the import of sugar from the West Indies, and on 23 March 1646, there is the first recorded reference to 'my plantation in the Barbadoes'. On 1 April of the same year there is a note of two boys from Wimborne St. Giles and the neighbouring village of Gussage, both of them aged fifteen, who 'bound themselves to me for seven years for the Barbadoes, to give them 5l. a piece at the term's end'. He made arrangements for his Barbados agent's bills of exchange to be paid by the famous financier and merchant, Martin Noell.[2]

Investment in sugar plantations led by an insensible but natural progression to the slave trade, and towards the end of 1646 he had a quarter share in a little ship called the *Rose*, bound for the Guinea coast. After a year on the usual triangular trade the *Rose* returned in November 1647 ('blessed be God!' he piously noted in his diary). At first he hoped to double his money, but in the end had to be content with breaking even.[3] It is natural to suppose that this was not his only commercial venture at this time, and that he now began to acquire that interest in trade and colonial enterprise which bore fruit under the Restoration.

When, in September 1651, Charles II paid a fleeting visit to Dorset as a hunted fugitive after the battle of Worcester, Sir Anthony Ashley Cooper was a man of thirty. He was one of the leading landowners in his county; his new house was rising at Wimborne St. Giles and no doubt claiming a good deal of attention; his wife was carrying the child who was to be his heir; he had his estates and other interests to superintend.

But so far as public affairs were concerned, he had only the local duties of a magistrate and of a commissioner for the raising of taxation. There seemed no outlet for his unbounded energies and versatile abilities on the

[1] Christie, i, App. II, p. xliv.
[2] Ibid. pp. xxxiv, xxxvi, xli.
[3] Ibid. p. xlvi; cf. Brown, p. 151.

national stage, which was occupied by the Republicans in the Rump and the Council of State and by Cromwell and his officers. The time had now come, however, when he was to advance further into the limelight. On 17 January 1652, he was named a member of a commission for legal reform. The train of events had begun which was to lead him to service under Oliver Cromwell and to his first political opportunities.

CHAPTER V

THE APPRENTICE POLITICIAN (1652–4)

Next this, (how wildly will ambition steer!)
A vermin wriggling in the usurper's ear,
Bartering his venal wit for sums of gold,
He cast himself into the saint-like mould;
Groaned, sighed and prayed, while godliness was gain,
The loudest bag-pipe of the squeaking train.

ON the surface Ashley Cooper's association with Oliver Cromwell is one of the most difficult episodes in his career to explain. 'Can two walk together except they be agreed?' The stereotyped picture of Cromwell is of a rough, homespun, plainly dressed country squire turned soldier, animated by an intense religious experience and a burning faith in 'the glorious cause of the people of God'; a man carried by circumstance and the support of his devoted Ironsides into a military dictatorship, wielding supreme power and yet at the same time remaining defiantly proud of his warts. Ashley Cooper on the other hand is commonly thought of as a man of the world, cultivated, intelligent, adaptable, able to move without incongruity in Restoration society where Cromwell would have been completely out of place; a man whose religion was at best deistic, and who in politics was temperamentally a rebel against authority. What was it that brought two such different personalities temporarily together, so that rumour even mentioned the possibility of Ashley Cooper marrying Cromwell's daughter?

Dryden gives one possible answer to this question. Whether because of 'ambition' or 'for sums of gold'—he is not altogether consistent here—Ashley Cooper ingratiated himself with the Protector by assuming a hypocritical pretence of 'godliness', as 'the loudest bag-pipe of the squeaking train'. Of course Shaftesbury could have retaliated by pointing out that King Charles II also had 'squeaked' a Presbyterian tune for political advantage in Scotland in 1650, and by reminding Dryden's readers that the poet's own views about 'the usurper' had changed over the years. But such counter-attacks, however valid, would leave the main question unanswered. Is there any other possible explanation of Ashley Cooper's relationship with Cromwell?

The first part of the answer must be that undoubtedly they had more in common than might appear at first sight. In religion, for instance, they shared a belief in religious toleration, at least for all Protestants who did not threaten to disturb public order. Ashley Cooper had at all times a dislike for compulsion in religious matters and a marked distaste for ecclesiastical authority; though the term 'Presbyterian' has sometimes been mistakenly applied to him in the period before 1660, there is no sign that at any time he favoured a policy of rigid conformity, whether Presbyterian or any other. He wanted an established church, maintained from tithes or some other public source, but with other dissenting congregations existing freely by its side. His services could therefore be easily and naturally used by Cromwell to further what the Protector always maintained was his primary aim. It is quite unnecessary to suppose that Ashley Cooper had to put on any hypocritical act in order to impress Cromwell, and there is no evidence to suggest that he did in fact pretend to be one of the 'Saints'. Dryden's lines refer to nothing more than the common Tory view that the Barebones Parliament was composed entirely of extreme religious enthusiasts, and that any member of it must have been either a religious maniac or a hypocrite. It is superfluous now to disprove this outmoded view, and in any case we shall find later that in the debates of the Barebones Parliament Ashley Cooper belonged to the conservative group which opposed the extremists. The pages of the Royalist news-sheet *Mercurius Academicus*, under 2 March 1646, contain a long story alleging that Ashley Cooper and his brother George attempted to force a fanatical preacher on the congregation at Wimborne (Minster); but it is difficult to attach much credence to this tale, since Ashley Cooper had not in fact been in Dorset for the previous two months. His private diary contains a couple of expressions of thanks to God for the safe return of his ship and for recovery from a tertian ague,[1] but that is all. All that can properly be inferred from the available evidence of his youth and upbringing is that he was a convinced Protestant, with friends like the Rev. William Strong among the Independents but no trace of any desire to impose any settlement on others. As for the undoubted deistic tendencies of his later years, it is more likely that (as with other intelligent people) they were the result of growing dissatisfaction with a religion based on revelation, and disillusionment after living through some of the religious excesses of the Commonwealth period, than that they were present from youth upwards.

In religion, then, there was no incongruity in Ashley Cooper's co-operating for a time with Cromwell. In politics, too, they were both opportunists, so far as constitutional means were concerned, believing that no form of government was sacred, but that political arrangements should be adapted to suit the needs of the time. In each case contemporary enemies would have said that the motive for political change was personal ambition; both men would have defended themselves by saying that they were genuine believers in a parliamentary system, seeking to put the government of the country back on to a workable constitutional basis, neither Royalist nor doctrinaire Republican.

---

[1] Christie, i, App. II, pp. xlvi–xlvii. For a discussion of Dryden's charge of lewdness, see pp. [211–15] below.

Finally, the two men shared a common interest in legal reform. It was in all probability this that drew Ashley Cooper to Cromwell's notice. On 17 January 1652 his name was the last of twenty-one on a commission appointed to aid the Rump's committee for the reform of the laws.[1] Acceptance of membership of this commission drew him into service under the Republic for the first time, except for minor local duties. There is no direct evidence to tell us why he decided to commit himself in this way; but it is fair to emphasize that an interest in the law persisted through-out his career, from the time when he lived in Lord Keeper Coventry's household to the time when he himself became Lord Chancellor and beyond—suggesting that it was not a temporary means of political advance-ment. He believed that law was too important a matter to be left only to lawyers.

At this point the Rump of the Long Parliament and the Council of State which it had nominated had governed England for three years, but they had done little to satisfy the aspirations of the Levellers and many of the rank and file in Cromwell's army pressed for reforms to help the small man who was entangled in the expensive complexities of the law. One ordinance, it is true, declared that all legal proceedings should henceforth be in English,[2] but nothing further had been accomplished. To appease the restive, therefore, the Rump had decided to call in outside assistance, 'to take into consideration what inconveniencies there are in the law, and how the mischiefs that grow from the delays, the chargeableness, and the irregularities in the proceedings of the law, may be prevented . . .'. A committee of members of the Rump had been appointed to consider the names of suitable outsiders, and later 'to receive from them, such things as shall be prepared by them'; and it is evidence of the subject's importance that this committee was headed by Cromwell himself, and included both generals like Fleetwood and Harrison, and civilian Republicans like Algernon Sidney, Bulstrode Whitelocke and Haslerig. Cromwell was one of three who were directed 'to take special care of it'. The committee also included Carew Raleigh (husband of Ashley Cooper's stepgrandmother) and Colonel Richard Norton (his old playmate at Southwick), and it may have been they who put forward his name for appointment to the body of outsiders, which for the sake of clarity we shall call the commission. Its other twenty members were a strange assortment, including as they did moderate legal experts like the great Matthew Hale, army officers such as Desborough, Tomlinson and Packer, and enthusiasts like 'the strenuous Puritan' Hugh Peters—the outspoken army chaplain who was rumoured to have been present on Charles I's scaffold, and who was to be sentenced to death in 1660 by a group of judges including Ashley Cooper. In short,

---

[1] *C.J.* vii. 58, 67, 73, 74.
[2] *Acts and Ordinances of the Interregnum*, ed. C. H. Firth and R. S. Rait (1911), ii. 455–6, 510–11.

membership of this body would bring Ashley Cooper into contact with many of the most important people of the day—on the one hand generals, from Cromwell to 'Saints' like Harrison, and on the other the Republican politicians such as Haslerig and Sidney, who upheld the cause of parliamentary government based on a narrow, property-owning oligarchy.[1]

The commission sat at intervals for over twelve months, and had not completed its task when the Rump came to its untimely end in April 1653.[2] During this period it discussed a wide range of subjects, from the registration of marriages and the provision of civil ceremonies performed by justices of the peace, to the question of allowing prisoners counsel on matters of fact as well as law and permitting the witnesses for the defence to give evidence under oath. None of these ideas, however, was passed into law by the Rump. Different groups put the blame for delay on to one another; the lawyers complained of the impracticability of the suggestions of the ignorant laymen, more especially Peters, while the laymen, and petitioners from outside, complained even more vociferously of the obstructive tactics of legal vested interests. No doubt there were, then as always, people who favoured referring problems to a committee, or, better still, two committees, as a means of shelving them. For instance, the Rump, urged on by petitioners who included Commissary-General Whalley and others close to Cromwell, referred to the commission the question of legislation for a general registry of land, which it was thought would prevent future disputes about land ownership. In January 1653, after lengthy technical discussion, the commission sent back the draft of a bill for county registries, accompanied by other bills on equally thorny subjects: one to reform Chancery, speed up its proceedings and regulate its fees; another setting up 'county judicatures' with powers to hear and determine all matters which justices of the peace, justices of oyer and terminer, and justices of gaol delivery had heard in the past; and another relating to criminal procedure. This last measure was a characteristic mixture of enlightenment and moral vindictiveness. It abolished the pressing to death between sheets of lead of prisoners who refused to plead and allowed prisoners counsel at all times, but provided that the right hand of murderers should be cut off before execution; ordered that women should never be burnt but hanged like other criminals; and laid it down that perjurers should have their ears cut off and their nostrils slit and seared with a hot iron, but supplied preachers to instruct and pray with prisoners. Taken together, these four bills would have supplied almost infinite material for argument even if the Rump had had no other preoccupations. On 11 January 1653, the Rump ordered that every Wednesday be set aside for

---

[1] Another member of the commission was that same lawyer John Fountain with whom Ashley Cooper was said to have schemed in his Royalist days in 1643. See p. 46 above.

[2] Its proceedings for the first six months are to be found in Add. MSS. 35,863, and copies of bills drafted are in the Shaftesbury Papers, XXXIII, 13.

considering bills of legal reform 'and that nothing do intervene'; on the 26th the registry bill was actually given first and second readings, but on 2 February it was referred back to a further select committee with powers to confer with the commission on which Ashley Cooper sat. This select committee was led by Cromwell, but there the bill stuck, to the mounting discontent of Cromwell and many of his soldiers who had a particular interest in it.[1]

What was Ashley Cooper's part in the activities of the commission, as it met three days a week 'in the House heretofore called the Lords' House', drafting and discussing these bills? Notes survive for their proceedings in the first six months, for four of which he attended regularly.[2] Occasionally pointed remarks which attracted the secretary's attention are recorded, and some of these are Ashley Cooper's. 'Our laws not like Medes and Persians—inconv[eniences] can be removed afterwards. Future reason is not excluded.' 'Nothing in the world hath a mathematical perfection.' Such dicta as these suggest that Ashley Cooper wanted to press on quickly with legislation, even though it might require later improvement, rather than delay to cope with minor legal objections. On 2 April 1652, he was a member of a delegation which discussed with the commissioners of the Great Seal the best way to approach the prickly question of the reform of Chancery—a permanent interest of his. From 17 May until the notes end on 23 July 1652, he was absent, probably in the country, and thereafter the commission's proceedings are entirely anonymous. It is impossible to tell whether all the bills put forward had his approval. What may be legitimately deduced, however, is that his abilities quickly attracted attention. The last man to be appointed to the commission in January 1652, he was the first to be named when, with his colleagues, he was made a judge for the probate of wills in March 1653.[3] Whether he ever officiated in this capacity is uncertain—according to the ordinance the appointment was to last until 1 October; but within a few months he was to become a member of the Council of State itself, and this must have been because his share in the work of legal reform had won favourable notice from Cromwell and other influential officers. He had sufficient knowledge of the law to believe that the existing system was not sacrosanct, without necessarily agreeing with the wilder suggestions.

On 20 April 1653, finally exasperated by the Rump, Cromwell made his famous decision to 'take away the bauble', and dissolve what was left of the Long Parliament of 1640; the law reform commission naturally ended with it. In the next few weeks Cromwell went on to adopt Major-General Harrison's suggestion that, in preparation for the coming of the Fifth

[1] *Somers Tracts* (1811), vi. 177–245; F. A. Inderwick, *The Interregnum* (1891), pp. 205–12; *C.J.* vii. 213, 218, 221–2, 246, 249–51, 253.

[2] Miss Brown (p. 53) is mistaken in saying that he was not present until 15 Mar. 1652; he missed only the opening meeting on 30 Jan., Add. MSS. 35,863.

[3] *Acts and Ordinances of the Interregnum*, ed. C. H. Firth and R. S. Rait (1911), ii. 702.

Monarchy, that of Jesus Christ, the godliest people should take command, and on this principle a new, nominated assembly was called, known forever to history by its derisive nickname of the Barebones Parliament. When this assembly met on 4 July it included Ashley Cooper among its members. Precisely how he secured nomination is another of the irritating blanks in his career at this time. Gardiner conjectured that he owed his seat rather to the Army Council than to the recommendation of the Congregational churches of Wiltshire, the county for which he sat in preference to Dorset, where two former colleagues of the Civil War, Colonels William Sydenham and John Bingham, were favoured. But the great historian was only guessing, and there is no means of telling whether he was right.[1] All that we know for certain is that he met with the rest, and like others was allocated lodgings in Whitehall Palace,[2] so that he could observe the changes which had taken place there since he had walked its corridors with Lord Keeper Coventry fourteen years earlier.

The prominence into which Ashley Cooper sprang from the very beginning of the Barebones Parliament is striking. Though it is true that many of his fellow-members were without parliamentary experience, so too was he; yet he early became a leader. On the day after Oliver Cromwell had made his opening speech to the members assembled in the Council Chamber at Whitehall, Ashley Cooper's name was the first in a delegation of eight which besought the Lord General to join in their deliberations. Within the next fortnight he was appointed to some of the most important committees: to the committee to consider the propriety of incumbents in tithes, evidently to be one of the principal bones of contention; to the committee on the advancement of learning, a cherished ideal of the members; to the committee on law reform, to carry forward the work which the previous committee had begun; and to the small committee on foreign affairs.[3] Most important of all, on 14 July the assembly elected him to serve on the Council of State which constituted the executive government of the country. He was the last but one of the thirty-one people elected, but none the less it was a testimony to the impression his abilities had made in the previous sixteen months.[4]

Simultaneous membership of the Council of State and the so-called parliament gave Ashley Cooper a great opportunity. Obviously it gave him a different type of experience, and greater insight into politics, corresponding to junior ministerial office for a rising modern politician. It enabled him on the one hand to act as an intermediary between the government and the assembly, reporting the wishes of the former to the members in something like the fashion of front-bench spokesmen in more modern times; and on the other hand he had the knowledge, authority and

---

[1] *History of the Commonwealth and Protectorate 1649–56* (1903), ii. 282.
[2] Dutch deputies, 8/18 July, in *Thurloe State Papers*, ed. T. Birch (1742), i. 338; *C.S.P.D. 1653–4*, pp. 12, 23, 71, 95. [3] *C.J.* vii. 281–7. [4] Ibid. p. 285.

ability to become a party leader. From the earliest days of the new régime in July 1653, it was clear that there was a split in both the Council of State and the Assembly. On 15 July the House discussed a motion that no minister should be maintained from the proceeds of tithes after 3 November. The previous question was defeated by 68 votes to 43; and when later the problem whether incumbents had a property in tithes or not was discussed, this was referred to a committee by the narrower margin of 56 votes to 49. In both votes Ashley Cooper was one of the tellers for the majority, and Major-General Harrison one of those for the minority, and this corresponded to a division in the ranks of the Parliament which persisted throughout its five months of existence.[1] On one side stood the Fifth Monarchy men and other 'Saints' and radicals like Harrison who believed that what they conceived to be God's will should be done, and done quickly, though the heavens fell. On the other side stood more moderate men like Ashley Cooper, not by any means rigidly conservative since in some measures of reform they joined; even the abolition of tithes they were prepared to accept provided that lay-impropriators received compensation, and provided that some other form of ministers' maintenance was arranged first.[2] In fact they had at once a greater respect for existing property rights, a greater practicality and a greater sense of what was politically possible. Between the two groups Cromwell vacillated, convinced that it was his duty not to interfere, and, in the first weeks at least, with divided sympathies.[3] At the beginning of September he is reported as remarking, 'I am more troubled now with the fool than with the knave',[4] and as time went on the conservative element in his make-up asserted itself against the visionary radicalism of Harrison. In the Parliament's early days, however, he was still on good terms with Harrison, whose suggestion he had adopted in nominating the assembly in the first place. It was not for some weeks that he became convinced that the Parliament was not likely to achieve the hopes which he had cherished; and the decided line which Ashley Cooper took from the very outset cannot have been due to any calculation to play the game of the Lord General who in the last resort possessed the power which counted.

Ashley Cooper's part in the struggle cannot be described in detail, since no reports of debates have survived. Even the information in the *Commons Journals* is more meagre than it might have been, since many of the controversies were fought out in committee. Yet though we possess no knowledge of the arguments which he used in his speeches, it is noticeable that

---

[1] *C.J.* vii. 285–6.

[2] See the account (by a radical) in *An Exact Relation of the Proceedings and Transactions of the Late Parliament . . .* , in *Somers Tracts* (1811), vi. 270.

[3] H. R. Trevor-Roper, 'Oliver Cromwell and his Parliaments', in *Essays presented to Sir Lewis Namier* (1956), pp. 19–27. Professor Trevor-Roper is wrong in stating (ibid. p. 34) that Ashley Cooper was excluded in Pride's Purge.

[4] Newsletter cited by Gardiner, *History of the Commonwealth and Protectorate, 1649–56* (1903), ii. 302.

his name is to be found as one of the tellers in several of the most important divisions. In the early divisions, like those on tithes already mentioned, his side was usually narrowly victorious; but as time went on there were more and more occasions on which they were defeated. Tithes having been successfully shelved for some months, the most important differences were over matters of law. On some of the measures foreshadowed by the law reform commission of 1652–3 there was substantial agreement, and Ashley Cooper is found redrafting one clause in the bill authorizing civil marriages and requiring registration of births, marriages and deaths, in accordance with the sense of the debate.[1] Other useful and non-contentious measures were also passed. But many members of the Parliament, while demanding a complete overhaul of the legal system, began to manifest a distressing contempt for those 'caterpillars of the land', the lawyers, whose professional advice was dismissed as the outcome of prejudice and self-interest. Ashley Cooper had enough legal experience and enough legal friends to distrust the enthusiasms of ill-informed laymen who wanted the laws to be 'easy, plain, and short', and 'reduced into the bigness of a pocket-book'. Whether he judged this laudable endeavour to be impracticable, or feared the nature of the law which the pocket-book would contain, on 19 August he opposed the motion that there should be a committee appointed 'to consider of a new body of laws'. He was beaten, and a committee largely of extremists was named, but the task of compression defeated even their eagerness.[2]

More urgent was the problem of what to do with the Court of Chancery. The criticisms of its 'dilatoriness, chargeableness, and a faculty of letting blood the people in the purse veins' were so universal—one 'knowing gentleman' maintained that there were 23,000 cases pending, some of them for many years—that on 5 August a motion that Chancery 'be forthwith taken away' was carried without a division. This was easily agreed, but the awkward problem what arrangements to make to deal with those 23,000 cases and other future ones took much more time to solve. On 15 October, in order to compel some action, the extremists carried a motion that all proceedings in Chancery should be suspended for a month; and when two days later a bill embodying this motion was debated, Ashley Cooper was one of the tellers against it, together with Cromwell's physician, Dr. Goddard. The votes were equal, and the bill was thrown out by the casting vote of the Speaker. Two further bills were rejected alternately by moderates and extremists, each of whom was able to baulk the others, and a third bill, whose aim was to see that 'any ordinary cause might be determined and ended for twenty or forty shillings' unfortunately suffered the same fate as so many Chancery proceedings, and was still pending when the Parliament came to an end.[3]

[1] C.J. vii. 300–1.
[2] An Exact Relation . . . , Somers Tracts, vi. 276–8; C.J. vii. 304.
[3] Somers Tracts, vi. 275–6; C.J. vii. 296, 335, 338, 340, 346.

This was satisfactory from the government's point of view, but the margin was perilously narrow. Equally disturbing for Cromwell was the attempt of some members to change the basis on which the monthly assessment was levied, so as to remove the inequalities between county and county. Though some redistribution of the tax would have been equitable, it would have delayed the voting of the money on which the army depended for its pay; and Ashley Cooper must have been representing the official view when on 8 November he was teller for a successful motion that the assessment be divided among the counties in the same way as previously.[1]

In another key motion, however, Ashley Cooper was beaten, when on 17 November it was carried that a bill be brought in to take away the power of patrons to present to benefices. On this basic question of the manner of appointment of clergy Ashley Cooper clearly preferred to maintain the traditional privileges of his class rather than adopt any congregationalist scheme; and for the same reasons he would naturally approve the report of the committee on tithes when at last it was presented on 2 December. This report maintained the principle of payment of the clergy by tithes, and gave rise to five days of debate, 'many arguments and scriptures being alleged'. Eventually, when the arguments and the supply of texts had been exhausted, on 10 December the House reached a division on the first clause of the report. This provided for the appointment of commissioners to tour the country and eject 'ignorant, profane, and scandalous ministers' and settle 'godly and able persons' in the vacant places; it thus went some way to meet the general desire for reform but implied the maintenance of the essentials of an established church rather than the adoption of any voluntary system. The result of this vote would presage that of the vote on the main question of tithes, and it went in favour of the radicals by the narrow margin of 56 votes to 54.[2]

Ashley Cooper was not one of the tellers for the conservatives in this last division, but it may safely be deduced from his part in the dissolution of Parliament two days later that he shared their dislike of the radicals' religious proposals. The story of the dissolution is well enough known. To talk of the radicals having 'control over the whole assembly' and to describe the Cromwellian conservatives as 'panic stricken at their revolutionary designs' is to go too far; rather a deadlock had arisen, with both sides so equally balanced that neither had been able to pass its wishes into law; but certainly on 11 December the conservatives decided that the Barebones Parliament had nothing further to offer them, and after consultation with some of Cromwell's officers and the Speaker decided on their famous course of going to the House early on the 12th and passing a hasty vote dissolving themselves before the radicals arrived in sufficient

---

[1] *Somers Tracts*, vi. 273–4; *C.J.* vii. 347.
[2] Ibid. vi. 278–81; *C.J.* vii. 352, 361, 363.

numbers to prevent them. In that last scene of self-dissolution the lead was taken by two other Councillors of State, Sir Charles Wolseley and Colonel Sydenham, but the former was relatively younger and less experienced and the latter was an old Dorset colleague of Ashley Cooper's, and it is not surprising to find Ashley Cooper's name mentioned. He may have played more than a mere supporting part behind the scenes. The radical author of *An Exact Relation of the Proceedings and Transactions of the late Parliament* reserved a special thrust for him, replying to complaints that the army's pay had been endangered by saying that at any rate the radicals 'can say, they never were in arms against the parliament and army, nor were ever in Oxford, or any other garrisons that stood in opposition to them'.[1] Ashley Cooper had not succeeded in living down his Royalist past.

This did not, however, harm his relationship with Oliver Cromwell, who was, as ever, prepared to use the services of anyone who seemed willing to work with him in the public interest. The Lord General's earlier friendship with Major-General Harrison had by now evaporated, and his genuine desire for some law reform shrank before the prospect of the upheaval in the legal and religious systems which the radicals clearly wanted. By December 1653, he and Cooper shared an equally low opinion of the Parliament. They might not be so demonstrative about it as the Chancery lawyers, who having 'feared for the loss of their great Diana' celebrated their escape from the reformers with bonfires and large quantities of sack; but they shared the feeling that it was time to make a fresh start. By this time, also, Cromwell had seen a good deal of Ashley Cooper over the table in the Council of State, and had been able to form an impression of his assiduity and ability. Except for a period at the beginning of September, when he had been given a fortnight's leave to go into the country, he had been one of the most regular attenders at the Council Board; and it was a striking testimony to his qualities of mind and personality that only a month after his appointment he was nominated to act as President of the Council for the next fortnight. When the time came to renew the Council of State on 2 November, the moderates in Parliament voted him in tenth, though in July he had only squeezed in thirtieth.[2] Plainly he had recommended himself by showing a considerable grasp of the business.

What was this business, in the second half of 1653? From the mass of routine three main issues stand out. The first of these related to foreign affairs, and particularly to the war with the Dutch which was in progress.

---

[1] *Somers Tracts*, vi. 274 (where the anonymous gentleman referred to is much more likely to be Ashley Cooper than Wolseley, who had only been a boy in the Civil War) and pp. 282–4; pamphlet quoted by H. A. Glass, *The Barbone Parliament* (1899), p. 113 (where 'Sidney' should read 'Sydenham'); *Clarke Papers*, ed. C. H. Firth (Camden Society, 1899), iii. 9.

[2] *C.S.P.D. 1652–3*, pp. xxxvii–xl, and *C.S.P.D. 1653–4*, pp. xxxvi–xxxvii (tables of attendances); *C.S.P.D. 1653–4*, p. 92; *C.J.* vii. 344.

July 1653, when Ashley Cooper entered the Council, was also the month of Admiral Tromp's defeat and death off Scheveningen at the hands of Monk. On the day of his election he was made one of the councillors who were to meet the Dutch deputies then in England; and a fortnight later he was made a member of the Council's special committee on foreign affairs, which eventually met as often as three mornings a week. He thus had to discuss negotiations to bring to an end the first of those struggles which he afterwards compared with the Punic wars—wars between two eternal rivals whose interests were utterly irreconcilable. There is no means of telling what opinions he expressed. The Council of State and its committees were very heterogeneous bodies; at one extreme there were those who wanted to fight on until the Dutch were completely crushed and even incorporated into a political union of the two countries; at the other extreme there were those like Cromwell himself who viewed with distaste a war with another Protestant Republic. Since Ashley Cooper was later a member of the Protestant Council of State which made peace with the Dutch in April 1654, it may be surmised that he was not one of the uncompromising wing in 1653, but there is no supporting evidence. Nor is it possible to tell what his position was in relation to Cromwell's diplomacy towards France and Spain, from whom the Protector would in the end have to choose one as ally and the other as enemy. All that can certainly be said is that he was initiated into the world of international politics and into the technique of conferences with foreign envoys.[1]

Secondly, during the fortnight when he was President of the Council he was involved in the *cause célèbre* of John Lilburne. The decision to prosecute this awkwardly individualistic Leveller had been taken before Ashley Cooper joined the Council, and the trial actually began on the previous day; but when on 20 August the jury brought in a verdict of 'Not Guilty of any crime worthy of death', the aggrieved members of the Barebones Parliament directed the Council of State to supply a report. After the judges and jury had been summoned before the Council, sitting under Ashley Cooper's presidency, it fell to him to present the report to Parliament on 27 August. It is noticeable that he made no recommendation on behalf of the Council of State; the onus was carefully thrust on Parliament to direct the Council 'to take some course for the further securing Lt. Col. John Lilburne for the peace of the nation'. Nevertheless it is ironical to find the future sponsor of the Habeas Corpus Act one of an executive responsible for arbitrary imprisonment; and in 1654 this irony was to become even more pointed. Meanwhile, on 19 September 1653 the inspirer of the Whig journalism of the Exclusion crisis was the first member of a committee 'to consider what measures are fit for suppressing scandalous

---

[1] *C.S.P.D. 1653–4*, pp. 26, 53, 87, 90, 223; cf. S. R. Gardiner, *History of the Commonwealth and Protectorate* (1903), vol. iii, chs. xxx, xxxi; and W. C. Abbott, *The Writings and Speeches of Oliver Cromwell* (Harvard, 1937–47), iii. 78–80, 84–86, 121–5.

pamphlets'.[1] As always, a politician's attitude to criticism depends on whether he is in office or out.

Thirdly, as a member of the Council of State he was necessarily concerned with guarding against Royalist conspiracies, the more so as one of these took place in his native county of Dorset; and we catch a glimpse of him as one of those who interrogated Colonel Robert Phelips for his part in it. Phelips's own account of the episode to Hyde may perhaps present himself in too heroic a light; but as he describes it Ashley Cooper's interrogatory technique was the familiar one of the iron hand in the velvet glove. He began with flattery of Phelips's qualities and local influence, recalled that Phelips was an old aquaintance of his, and, when Phelips refused to answer his 'friendly' questions, concluded with: 'Truly, I pity you; you will cast yourself away by standing upon these punctilios of honour.' The method may be compared with the mixture of blandishments and threats (veiled or otherwise) which he used on the Popish Plot Examinations committee. On this occasion it had no effect, and it is possible that Ashley Cooper regretted the necessity of questioning an old friend; at all events Phelips did not suffer for his refusal to 'co-operate'.[2]

On none of these matters is there any evidence of differences of outlook between Ashley Cooper and Cromwell and the officers who thought as he did; and no contemporary expressed any surprise when Ashley Cooper's name was amongst the fifteen selected to form the new Council of State in the provisions of the Instrument of Government, which in December 1653 established Cromwell as Lord Protector. One curious rumour even suggested that Ashley Cooper was to become Lord Chancellor.[3] This was the sort of wildly exaggerated rumour which invariably circulates in unsettled times and does not mean that such an appointment was ever seriously considered; but it does suggest that Ashley Cooper was regarded as being very close to the men who mattered, and interested primarily in the law, even though it was to be nineteen years before he attained the heights of the Chancellorship under a very different régime from that of Cromwell.

There is certainly no sign that Ashley Cooper was in any way reluctant to accept the new Instrument of Government, even though this paper constitution rested basically on no more authority than that of Lambert and the other army officers who drew it up. It has been tentatively suggested that his advice may have been in some measure taken in the new arrangements, and even Cromwell may have consulted him before accepting it himself; but this is pure conjecture.[4] Ashley Cooper never found it necessary to give his own account of his reasons for agreeing to serve in 'the

---

[1] Gardiner, op. cit. ii. 292–300; C.J. vii. 309; Pauline Gregg, Free-born John (1961), ch. 28; C.S.P.D. 1653–4, p. 200.

[2] MSS. Clar., 46, fos. 182–3; Brown, pp. 56–57; Thurloe State Papers, ed. T. Birch (1742), i. 409.   [3] Thurloe State Papers, i. 645.

[4] Gardiner, op. cit. iii. 3. The statement by Burnet which Gardiner quotes is however much more applicable to the circumstances of December 1654 than those of December

usurper's' Council of State; but it is not difficult to discern the political merits which the Instrument would have had from his point of view. It established the executive authority of a single person in the Lord Protector, and yet imposed constitutional checks upon him; he was to govern 'in all things by the advice' of his Council, and there was to be a resumption of parliamentary life on at any rate a better basis than that of the purely nominated Barebones Parliament. In religion there was to be the non-persecuting established church, surrounded by voluntary congregations, which the moderates in the Barebones Parliament had wanted; it was to continue to be maintained by tithes until better provision could be made, 'less subject to scruple and contention, and more certain than the present'. The document as a whole was realistic in that it rested on the armed force which dominated everything in England in December, 1653, and yet it seemed capable of development into a more constitutional régime. Some serious drawbacks implicit in it were to become apparent in 1654, but at the time a case could easily be made out for Ashley Cooper's acceptance of service under it, quite apart from any question of personal ambition. It was an entirely natural development from Ashley Cooper's course of political action in 1653.[1]

Between December 1653, and June 1654, he was an assiduous attender at the Protector's Council of State, except for a fortnight at the end of February when he probably went into the country.[2] It must have been an extremely busy life, for in the first two months alone the Council's records show that he was assigned some fifty special tasks, usually in conjunction with three or four other councillors. He presented to the Council various ordinances regulating the new régime, continuing the powers of courts and commissioners; he and another member drew up the Protector's treason act; he was on a committee to regulate the justices of the peace and present names to Council; he presented to Council an ordinance for the great level of the Fens, strengthening the powers of the Earl of Bedford and other Adventurers to levy dues and punish local saboteurs.[3] From the great variety of committees on which he served we may also select one appointed on 13 June to consider the number of writs of *habeas corpus* being issued to free prisoners committed by the Lord Protector and Council. The *habeas corpus* procedure was evidently as much of a nuisance to Cromwell as it had been to Charles I, and three months earlier the Council, including Ashley Cooper, had approved the removal of John

---

1653. (See pp. 86–7 below.) It is interesting to note that Gardiner credited Ashley Cooper with certain consistent principles, such as a dislike of clerical domination and support of religious toleration, rather than with personal ambition.

[1] For the text of the Instrument see S. R. Gardiner, *Constitutional Documents of the Puritan Revolution, 1625–1660* (1906), pp. 405–17.

[2] *C.S.P.D. 1653–4*, pp. xxxv–xl; *C.S.P.D. 1654*, pp. xxxvi–xliv.

[3] *C.S.P.D. 1653–4*, pp. 301, 308–10, 318, 344; *C.S.P.D. 1654*, p. 146; *Acts and Ordinances . . .*, ii. 824–35, 899–902.

Lilburne to Jersey, where the writ would not run. Thus, ironically, began the evasion of the *habeas corpus* system which was to be stopped by the so-called 'Shaftesbury Act' of 1679.[1]

For the rest, in view of Ashley Cooper's later career it is important to note that in 1654 he was appointed to more committees on financial and trade matters than in the previous year; his interests were widening to include every department of government. He was thus one of those commissioned to draw up an ordinance touching the excise; 'to consider the setting forth a settled revenue for the Lord Protector's household'; and to consider the best ways of rating taxes. When the Muscovy Company sent in a petition, and it was agreed that an official agent of the Lord Protector should be sent to Russia to revive and extend the old trade between the two countries, it was Ashley Cooper who put before the Council a draft of the letter from Cromwell to the Tsar which the agent was to carry.[2]

In all this there is ample evidence of activity, but little to differentiate Ashley Cooper's contribution from that of other members of the Council. This is equally true of foreign affairs, on which we know that there was considerable difference of opinion among the councillors without certainly knowing where Ashley Cooper himself stood. On bringing the Dutch war to an end, it is true, there is no evidence of disagreement; after the zealots of the Barebones Parliament had disappeared from the scene, all the signs are that Cromwell went ahead to the treaty of 5 April 1654, without opposition from any of his council. Though the treaty did not finally settle any problem arising out of the intense commercial rivalry between the two countries, there was little prospect of gaining more by continuing an expensive war.[3] What was much more difficult to decide, however, was England's policy as between France and Spain. Should she adopt a policy of hostility towards France, as advocated by Lambert and other officers? or a policy of alliance with France against Spain, and a war against the traditional enemy in the Caribbean, as advocated by Sir Gilbert Pickering, Walter Strickland, and other councillors? On 4 April the Council appointed commissioners to negotiate with the two foreign ambassadors: Ashley Cooper, Strickland and Viscount Lisle to treat with the French ambassador, and Lambert, Pickering and Edward Montagu with the Spanish. Too much cannot, however, be read into these appointments, which might indeed imply that there were representatives of each school of thought in each group. Moreover, although Ashley Cooper had addressed the French ambassador at his official reception, the latter reported when

---

[1] *C.S.P.D. 1654*, pp. 208, 33–34; cf. pp. 108–9 below.
[2] *C.S.P.D. 1653–4*, pp. 345, 362–4, 381, 397, 401; *C.S.P.D. 1654*, pp. 73, 108, 187, 202–3, 219.
[3] Ashley Cooper was not one of the six commissioners who signed the treaty (see W. C. Abbott, *The Writings and Speeches of Oliver Cromwell* (1937–47), iii. 905).

serious negotiations began that the English commissioners had been changed, and thereafter referred in his dispatches to 'my commissioners' without naming them.

It is thus impossible to define Ashley Cooper's part (if any) in the negotiations, and the same is true of the foreign policy debates in the Council; for instance, notes of the arguments used in Council on 20 April do not indicate who spoke on each side. On this occasion the opinion of the majority seems to have favoured war with Spain, but there were opponents who argued that this would ruin the important trade in cloth to Spain, and also the Newfoundland fishing trade, 'whereby only we import yearly from Spain £150,000'. It has been supposed that this view was put forward by Lambert, who came from Yorkshire with its important clothing interests, but Wiltshire and Dorset, where Ashley Cooper had his estates, were also deeply concerned in the cloth trade, and the mention of fish is a reminder that vessels from the port of Poole fished in the waters off Newfoundland and exported some of their catch to the Roman Catholic countries of the Mediterranean. There is just a suggestion here, therefore, that Ashley Cooper, aware both of the national importance of the export trade in cloth to Spain and the local interests of his county, may have preferred to maintain peaceful relations with Spain.[1]

If this was the case, Ashley Cooper was eventually on the losing side, for the majority of the Council took the view that economic relations with Spain in Europe need not be affected in any case by a naval campaign in the West Indies. The old Elizabethan prejudices against Spain were still strong, and moreover France seemed likely to prove a more satisfactory ally. In another debate in Council on 20 July (when Ashley Cooper was away in the country electioneering) Lambert maintained against Cromwell his opposition to war with Spain; but within a few weeks of this preparations for the "Western design' were under way.[2] English imperialism was to take its course at the expense of the hated Spanish Papists.

Whilst all these matters were under discussion, Ashley Cooper was not much in the public eye, as compared, for instance, with Major-General Lambert. Yet he was certainly welcome in the Cromwell household, which in the spring of 1654 moved from the Cockpit to take over the whole of Whitehall and began to look more and more like a Court—not, it is true, a Court with the aesthetic tastes of Charles I, nor with the more dissipated ones of Charles II, but equally not the narrowly 'puritanical' society of popular legend. Ashley Cooper was a man of considerable personal charm, able to get on good terms with people of very different character and background at all times in his life; Cromwell was by no means so narrow in his

---

[1] Gardiner, *History of the Commonwealth and Protectorate, 1649-56* (1903), vol. iii, ch. xxxiii, esp. pp. 119-21, 127-8; *C.S.P.D. 1654*, pp. 53-54, 73, 82; de Baas, 28 Mar./ 2 Apr.; Bordeaux, 20-30 Apr.; *Clarke Papers*, ed. C. H. Firth (Camden Society, 1899), iii. 203-6. [2] *Clarke Papers*, iii. 207; Gardiner, iii. 162, n. 2.

outlook and interests as Royalist writers would have us believe, and was also willing to take into his circle many different people. A hostile witness quotes Cromwell as saying that he could not fathom 'that Marcus Tullius Cicero, the little man with three names'[1]; and the two men could never be called intimate friends. But Cromwell's son Henry, the ablest and most interesting of his children, can certainly be called a friend of Ashley Cooper's; we possess a letter to Henry, written three years after Ashley Cooper had broken with the Protector, in terms which suggested that a genuine affection and respect persisted.[2] Cromwell also had an unmarried daughter, Mary, a girl of seventeen. Ashley Cooper was now a widower for the second time, Lady Frances Cooper having died on 31 December 1652, and although he was a man of thirty-three, such a difference in age was no obstacle in the seventeenth century. One or two contemporaries connected their names, and we shall find Ludlow attributing his breach with Cromwell in December 1654 to the Protector's refusal to give him Mary's hand in marriage. It has even been suggested that when, in later life, Shaftesbury told Burnet that Cromwell had offered to make him king, he was alluding, probably in jest, to this possible marriage into the Protector's family.[3] It would however be safer to regard this gossip merely as evidence that for a time Ashley Cooper was a welcome visitor in Cromwell's household.

From midsummer 1654, another factor entered the political situation. By the terms of the Instrument of Government a parliament was to meet on 3 September, and an attempt would have to be made to achieve harmony between it and the Lord Protector's government. Trouble could be expected both from those Republicans who disliked all idea of government by 'a single person', whether he had the title of King or Protector, and from those who regarded Cromwell's position as founded not on right but on military force, and saw no reason why they should accept as the country's constitution an Instrument drawn up by a small group of army officers. One possible way of forestalling such criticism was by securing the election of the right sort of people from the government's point of view, and it so happens that the election about which most is known is the very Wiltshire election in which Ashley Cooper, even though he was offered safe seats by the boroughs of Poole and Tewkesbury, chose to engage. Although Cromwell himself had doubts about the propriety of interfering in elections, Ashley Cooper engaged in a thoroughgoing electioneering campaign.

By the terms of the Instrument there were to be ten members for the county of Wiltshire, all of them to be elected by one body of constituents, those who possessed property valued at £200. Two opposing lists of candidates were therefore drawn up. One of these, headed by Ashley

---

[1] J. Warner, History of the English Persecution of Catholics and the Presbyterian Plot, ed. J. A. Birrell for the Catholic Record Society, 1953, i. 27, 183; cf. also Martyn, i. 168.
[2] Christie, i. 135–6.
[3] Memoirs of Edmund Ludlow, ed. C. H. Firth (1894), vol. i, p. lxxi; Wood, Athenae Oxonienses (1820), iv. 71; Burnet, i. 173; Brown, pp. 62–63. Cf. p. 88 below.

F

Cooper, was markedly the more conservative, but contained people from very different backgrounds; there were four men who had been secluded from the Long Parliament by the Army in 1648, and two lawyers who had actually fought for the King in the Civil War, besides two ex-members of the Rump. On these grounds Ludlow sneered at Ashley Cooper as 'a man of a healing and reconciling spirit, of all interests that agree in the greatening of himself'. The other list was headed by the name of Edmund Ludlow, and no doubt consisted of conscientious and determined Republicans like himself. It is to be noted, however, that Ludlow was absent in Dublin; his account of the election is not based on first-hand evidence, and is infused by the bitterest prejudice. Like many conscientious people, he was very ready to impute the worst of motives to others who disagreed with him, and he wrote his memoirs as a soured exile in Switzerland, mindful of his Republican friends who had lost lives or estates by sticking to the 'honest cause' while Ashley Cooper had risen to the peerage and to office under Charles II by deserting at the right time. In these circumstances it would be too much to expect an impartial account, even though the two men had co-operated in the relief of Taunton in 1644.

Before the election meeting was held, Ashley Cooper's party made every effort to whip up support, with the assistance of a strong association of clergy who wished at all costs to maintain an established church, based on tithes, against the pure voluntaryism wanted by the radicals of the Barebones Parliament in 1653. According to a hostile pamphleteer, they branded Ludlow's group as Anabaptists and Levellers, arranged to distribute 'a list of the ten to be chosen . . . to every one that appeareth for the best interest' and exhorted one another 'to remember the last men that met at Westminster what they were voting for'. From Ludlow's statement that they cited 'the parishes and every particular person therein to appear', it looks as though there was something like canvassing to get voters to turn out on election day. In addition to this 'packing of the cards' which Ludlow regarded as unfair, he accused them of winning over the vital support of the under-sheriff, who was to conduct the election meeting in the absence of the high sheriff.

So many voters (and others) put in an appearance on election day that the meeting was adjourned from Wilton to Stonehenge. There the prehistoric stones witnessed a unique scene. Ashley Cooper made an electioneering speech, 'labouring to convince them that it was desirable to choose such as were of healing spirits, and not such as were for the putting of all things into confusion and disorder'. It was apparently one of those speeches by front-bench government spokesmen which are commonly described as 'statesmanlike'. It might be regarded as the usual defence by a conservative of the *status quo*, but a case could also be made out for the view that in the long run it was only by adopting such a combination of 'healing spirits' that they could consolidate some of the gains they had made; it was this failure of the opponents of the Royalists to heal their differences that eventually led to the Restoration. At all events, Ashley Cooper's speech was supported by the Rev. Mr. Adoniram Byfield, 'a busy clergyman', and by other 'politique state parsons' who bawled 'No Ludlow, No Ludlow', and other slogans until they were hoarse. Eventually Ashley Cooper and his colleagues were declared elected, with Ludlow's supporters claiming that they had a true majority of those who were properly qualified to vote. The merits of their contention it is naturally impossible to determine, and the interest of the election lies in the more modern political techniques employed in it rather than in the accuracy of the final poll.[1]

The Wiltshire contest thus ended satisfactorily from the Protector's point of view, and with a view to the approaching Parliament two ordinances were directed to the two vexed questions which brought down the Barebones Parliament. On 21 August a long ordinance attempted to cut down the complications and expense of suits in Chancery, and on 28 August a second ordinance set up commissioners, on the lines suggested by the Barebones Parliament's committee, to eject 'scandalous, ignorant and insufficient ministers and schoolmasters'. Ashley Cooper was one of the members of the Council of State appointed to consider this ordinance, and was one of the commissioners nominated for Dorset and Wiltshire to remove ministers guilty of holding blasphemous and atheistic opinions; or of 'profane cursing or swearing', 'adultery, fornication, drunkenness, common haunting of taverns or ale-houses, frequent quarrelling or fighting, frequent playing at cards or dice . . .'; of using the Book of Common Prayer, or encouraging 'morris-dances, may-poles, stage-plays, or such like licentious practices, by which men are encouraged in a loose and profane conversation'; or of declaring their disaffection to the present government. There is no evidence, however, that Ashley Cooper actually sat in judgement on any minister accused of any of these lurid offences; indeed, the need to be present in Parliament must have detained him in London. In a different way, he was able to intervene in the religious affairs of his neighbourhood without leaving the capital, for at about the same time he procured from the Council an ordinance sensibly uniting the two local rectories of Wimborne St. Giles and All Saints to form one parish.[2]

Before Parliament met, someone in the Council of State proposed, as an additional safeguard, to call upon all members to take a personal engagement to do nothing to alter the government as settled by the Instrument in a single person and Parliament, under penalty of exclusion from the House. The elections had already confirmed that this would be the basic

---

[1] *The Memoirs of Edmund Ludlow*, ed. C. H. Firth (1894), i. 388–90; *The Copy of a Letter sent out of Wiltshire . . .*, printed, ibid. i. 545–8; *An Apology for the Ministers of the County of Wilts* (1654); S. T. Bindoff in *Victoria County History of Wiltshire* (1957), v. 150–1.

[2] *Acts and Ordinances of the Interregnum*, ed. C. H. Firth and R. S. Rait (1911), ii. 949–90; *C.S.P.D. 1654*, pp. 308, 330; Shaftesbury Papers II, 64.

issue to be fought out in the first weeks of the session. The radical reformers of the Barebones Parliament had been almost entirely eliminated, and with them the danger from the extreme Left, but instead determined Republicans like Bradshaw, Haslerig and Scot had been returned who would be certain to challenge a constitution giving political power to the Army's commander-in-chief. Against these, both the soldiers who had intended the Instrument to maintain their own political position, and the constitutionalists who saw in the Instrument the best chance of developing a constitutional monarchy, must combine to uphold at least the Instrument's essential features; and the latter, probably including Ashley Cooper, induced Cromwell to decline the proposed engagement, which would certainly have appeared to many members an unwarranted interference with Parliament's freedom of debate.[1]

Instead, Cromwell's opening speech struck many of the same notes as Ashley Cooper and his Wiltshire supporters had done. He posed as the saviour of society against Levellers and Fifth Monarchists, stressed the need for 'healing and settling', maintained his support of freedom of conscience but sought to conciliate conservatives by declaring that religion should not be admitted as a cloak for licentiousness, appealed in reviewing foreign affairs to the old hatred of Spain, and, on the basis of this declaration of policy, called upon Parliament immediately to consider the Instrument. All this apparently made good political sense; the hope was that an acceptably conservative policy would induce members to consider the constitutional system as a whole to be satisfactory, and vote their immediate approval. The attempt failed, however, before the parliamentary experience of the Republicans who insisted on the supremacy of Parliament and, by implication, Parliament's power to alter, or even abolish, the Instrument as the House alone thought fit. In the discussions which followed in committee of the whole House, the situation was uncertain; and, not daring to wait for a vote, Cromwell decided to use compulsion. On 12 September, after a long self-justificatory speech, he required all members to sign a Recognition in the form discussed before the opening of the session, namely, to be faithful to the Lord Protector and Commonwealth, and not to 'propose or give my consent to alter the Government, as it is settled in a single person and a Parliament'. Rather than sign this Recognition, Bradshaw, Haslerig and the irreconcilables stayed away.[2]

There followed then a significant episode which it has been suggested must be placed to the credit of Ashley Cooper. On 14 September the House voted that the Recognition applied only to the central principle of the Instrument—government by a single person and a Parliament—and did

---

[1] Gardiner, op. cit. iii. 176–8.
[2] W. C. Abbott, *Writings and Speeches of Oliver Cromwell* (Harvard, 1937–47), vol. iii. ch. x; Gardiner, op. cit. iii. 178–96; *Diary of Thomas Burton*, ed. J. T. Rutt (1828), vol. i. pp. xix–xxxviii.

not imply approval of its detailed provisions; and a week later another vote declared that the terms of the Instrument were alterable by Parliament, with the consent of the Protector. This was a compromise which once again made possible agreement on a parliamentary basis for the government, and it must have been the work of a shrewd tactician with a good grasp of the political situation, to act as an intermediary between Cromwell and the Council of State and the House. It has been very plausibly suggested that Ashley Cooper could have been the man.[1] Such an action would be consistent with everything else that is known of Ashley Cooper's political actions in the years 1653–5; but once again it has to be said that no positive evidence exists to prove or disprove it. The important debates took place in committee of the whole House, so that we do not possess even the names of the tellers in the vital divisions to enable us to draw conclusions as in the case of the Barebones Parliament. This is equally true of the debates which followed over the next four months on the detailed terms of the Instrument. No extensive notes of the speeches survive,[2] and it is impossible to glean very much from the purposes and composition of the committees on which Ashley Cooper served.

It is therefore unnecessary to recount in full the inexorable process by which Parliament in effect asserted its right to control fundamental decisions which Cromwell and the officers thought had been settled in their own way by the Instrument. We may note in passing that on 27 November Ashley Cooper was one of the two unsuccessful tellers against a motion restoring the old forty-shilling freehold county franchise, which the Instrument had replaced by a voting qualification of £200 worth of property of any kind, real or personal. The fact that the other teller against the motion was Cromwell's ineffectual eldest son Richard suggests that Ashley Cooper joined with the 'Court party' (as contemporaries called it) in favouring the extension of the vote in the counties to other types of property besides freehold land: such a point was not fundamental, and the vote was in fact followed by a compromise.[3] But by December earlier hopes of reaching a satisfactory agreement on essentials had almost evaporated. An example of the way in which the majority sought to impose its wishes by adding evasive provisos to the Instrument is to be found in the members' discussions on religion. They accepted the principle of freedom of conscience which had been laid down, and agreed that no bill to restrain it should pass without the consent of both Parliament and Protector, but added a proviso that bills to restrain atheism, blasphemy, 'damnable heresies', etc., should be subject only to the Protector's suspensory veto for twenty days, thus driving a coach and horses through the clause. The

[1] Gardiner, op. cit. iii. 196–7; H. R. Trevor-Roper, 'Oliver Cromwell and his Parliaments', in *Essays presented to Sir Lewis Namier* (1956), pp. 34–35, 37.

[2] The notes of Guibon Goddard printed in the introduction to volume one of Thomas Burton's diary mention very few names.

[3] *C.J.* vii. 391.

Cromwellians replied by calling for a committee to consider the enumeration and specification of these vaguely damnable heresies, and Ashley Cooper was one of the many members nominated to this committee. The enthralling task of listing and defining heresies might have occupied them for some time, but it so happened that it was incarnated (if that metaphor is permissible in reference to a Socinian) in the person of John Biddle, whose books against the Holy Spirit and other aspects of Trinitarian theology were condemned by the committee and the House.[1]

There is no evidence to tell us whether Ashley Cooper agreed or not with the majority view here: the rest of his career would suggest that he was unlikely to support an intolerant attitude towards a harmless unorthodox thinker. But this episode and others showed Cromwell that control over things that he valued was in danger of passing out of his hands, and that these issues might be decided by Parliament in ways that he did not like.

The voting of taxes for the upkeep of the army was urgent, and some members showed a disposition to use control of revenue as a political weapon in the traditional manner. By the middle of December it was clear to an intelligent observer that a breach between Protector and Parliament was likely, and that the attempt to turn a military state into a civil one was collapsing. A dissolution could be expected when the five months' minimum session under the terms of the Instrument had been completed; and that would mean a military dictatorship. The rule of the Major-Generals was already foreshadowed. It is in this context that we should consider the suggestion, supported by Ashley Cooper in a constitutional debate in committee of the whole House, that the problem of Cromwell's powers should be solved by making him King.

This was not the first time that hints of this kind had been made, for it appears that when Lambert and his fellow-officers had first put the Instrument of Government before Cromwell a year earlier, they had urged him to take the title of King.[2] If there was to be a Single Person at the head of the executive, why not give him the familiar title? Again in October 1654, when Parliament had been debating the Protector's place in the constitution, Lambert had vainly wanted the Protectorship to be made hereditary instead of elective[3]: if successful this would have given Cromwell one of the most obvious attributes of monarchy, and made the title a natural next step. Now in December 1654, the suggestion to make Cromwell king was a last desperate throw in an attempt to 'civilize' the government of the country and make possible a return to constitutional life instead of the rule of the sword. As king Cromwell need not necessarily have all the powers which Charles I had still enjoyed in 1642, but he would be able to

---

[1] *C.J.* vii. 398–401.
[2] Cf. his speech of 27 Feb. 1657 in Abbott, op. cit. iv. 417; Burton, i. 382.
[3] Burton, vol. i, p. li.

veto bills with which he disagreed (for instance, on religious matters), while Parliament on the other hand would retain its control of finance. The parliamentary game would be played on the old lines, the succession would be provided for, and a return to something like normality would be possible. Accordingly on 23 December a member named Augustine Garland, himself a regicide but not a particularly prominent one, proposed that the title of King should be offered to Cromwell. He was supported by Ashley Cooper and Henry Cromwell.[1]

At the Restoration when the memory of a proposal to make the usurper king must have been decidedly awkward, Ashley Cooper defended it to Burnet by asserting that his real motive in putting it forward was to ruin Cromwell,[2] presumably by arousing Republican prejudice against him. The mention of Ashley Cooper's name in conjunction with that of Henry Cromwell makes this highly unlikely. But though the move was sincerely meant, it had little prospect of success at this point. Later in 1657 more people realized the advantages to be gained from it, and Cromwell could have taken the title if he had wished; but in December 1654 it is significant that the proposal was not even pressed to a division. Nor did it excite as much popular discussion as might have been expected. This suggests that even if all the Cromwellians had been mobilized in full support, opinion in the House and Army was not yet ready for it.

At all events, the failure of this attempt meant that Ashley Cooper had come to the parting of the ways. With a dissolution imminent, he must either choose Cromwellian military rule and continued office in the Council of State, or join the parliamentary opposition as a private gentleman again. On 28 December he attended the Council for the last time. On the day of the next meeting, 5 January 1655, he was missing. On this same day, news-sheets under the influence of the government began to hint that the five months minimum parliamentary session might be calculated as lunar, and not calendar months; and the House granted an entirely inadequate sum for the Army.[3] Some days later Ashley Cooper marked his new position by moving a resolution making illegal the collection or payment of revenue not authorized by parliamentary grant,[4] and on 22 January Cromwell dissolved Parliament, with a speech in which he declared that he was opposed to making the government hereditary in his family.

Ashley Cooper's period of co-operation with the Lord Protector thus came to an end. Nowhere did he explain his reasons for leaving the Protector's service at this particular time, but this was a logical step for him to take on purely political grounds. It is difficult to reconcile his decision with an alleged resolve 'to ruin or to rule the state': if he had

---

[1] *Clarke Papers*, ed. C. H. Firth (Camden Society, 1899), iii. 16; *C.S.P. Ven. 1655–6*, p. 4.   [2] Burnet, i. 173.
[3] Gardiner, op. cit. iii. 236–40; *C.S.P.D. 1654*, p. xliii.
[4] MSS Rawl., A. 31, fo. 364.

been solely concerned with the exercise of power, regardless of principle, he could have remained in office under the all-powerful military dictator instead of retiring into private life and obscurity. It is true that Edmund Ludlow attributed his going into opposition to Cromwell's refusal to give him Mary Cromwell's hand in marriage. But it would be wrong to accept Ludlow's word about this without good contemporary corroboration. He was animated by bitter hostility when he wrote; he was in Dublin all through 1654; and his account contains two demonstrable errors, in that Ashley Cooper was not 'dismissed the Council' but ceased to attend, and was not replaced by Colonel Mackworth, who had been a member of the Council for some time already.[1] No strictly contemporary corroboration of Ludlow exists. There is no good reason why we should not accept that Ashley Cooper's motives, first for accepting office and then for leaving it, were legitimate political ones. In spite of Dryden he did not gain financially either from having a place on the Council of State (for which he himself later declared that he had received no salary)[2] or from relinquishing it. He changed his political affiliations, as many do in times of revolution, but it is quite possible that there was a real consistency underlying the change.

[1] *Memoirs of Edmund Ludlow*, ed. C. H. Firth (1894), vol. i. p. lxxi. Miss Brown, p. 63, suspects that Cooper's defection was partly due to the success of Lambert in a rivalry for Cromwell's favour; but there is no evidence to support this.

[2] *Parliamentary History of England* (1808), iv. 78.

CHAPTER VI

THE APPRENTICE OPPOSITION LEADER
(1655-9)

> Besides, their pace was formal, grave, and slack;
> His nimble wit outran the heavy pack.
> Yet still he found his fortune at a stay,
> Whole droves of blockheads choking up his way;
> They took, but not rewarded, his advice;
> Villain and wit exact a double price.
>
> *The Medal*

HAVING decided to stay away from the Council of State, Ashley Cooper found himself suffering the common fate of opposition leaders in the seventeenth century. From 22 January 1655 until the opening of the next parliamentary session on 17 September 1656, he was reduced to silence. With no public platform on which to express his views, he could only look on while Cromwell levied taxes on his own authority and ruled as a military dictator through his major-generals.

There was one possible alternative to biding his time in this way; and that was through participation in Royalist conspiracy. There were those at Charles II's exiled court who remembered that Ashley Cooper had once been a Royalist and the son-in-law of Lord Keeper Coventry, and who jumped to the conclusion that, having left Cromwell's service, he had returned to the path of righteousness and Royalism. On 26 February 1655 the King wrote personally offering forgiveness and reward to Ashley Cooper if he would do his part towards a restoration. The grounds on which Charles based his appeal are interesting: 'your experience tells you how unsettled all things must be, till I am restored to that which belongs to me, which would restore peace to the nation, and you are master of too good a fortune not to desire that security.'[1] All gentlemen of fortune, in fact, should have the good sense to support a restoration as the best means towards orderly government and the peaceful enjoyment of their property. But Ashley Cooper rejected this opportunity of re-insuring himself with the Royalist cause; he chose not to enter into any relations with the Court. Any reply would certainly have been preserved and used by Clarendon, but none exists. While, therefore, some of his Wiltshire and Dorset neighbours took part in the ill-fated rising of Colonel Penruddock in March 1655, Ashley Cooper remained aloof. When, after the inevitable failure at Salisbury, the equally inevitable commission of oyer and terminer

[1] Printed by Miss Brown, p. 64.

was appointed to try the prisoners, Ashley Cooper's own name was not among the judges, but his brother George's was.[1]

One step which Ashley Cooper took in 1655 did, however, bring him closer to two important Cavalier families. On 30 August he married for the third time. The wife he chose was Margaret Spencer, sister of the first Earl of Sunderland, who had been killed fighting for the King at Newbury. Her nephew, the second Earl of Sunderland, was still a boy of fourteen in 1655, but (like Ashley Cooper's other nephew by his first marriage, Sir George Savile) he was to play an important part in English politics and in Ashley Cooper's personal fortunes. The marriage also brought him closer to another Royalist family which in 1655 seemed to be of greater potential importance than either Spencers or Saviles. His new wife was the niece of Thomas Wriothesley, Earl of Southampton,[2] the most respected of those Cavaliers who had chosen to remain in retirement on their estates in England rather than follow King Charles into exile. In the pages of Clarendon (whose close friend he was) he appears to us as a well-meaning, upright, respectable, cautious peer, of unimpeachable loyalty to the Stuart cause and to the Anglican Church, and yet without much energy and without any disposition to take risks on impossible escapades like Penruddock's. He attempted to resist the taxation imposed on Royalists by Cromwell's major-generals in 1655, but entered into no conspiracies, and in spite of his birth and background was not even a member of the Sealed Knot, the group of five on whom Hyde principally relied in England. He was one of those well-born Cavaliers who, having great possessions, preferred waiting for a restoration to working actively to bring one about. None the less, Ashley Cooper's connexion with Southampton (who had estates near to his own in the New Forest) was to prove advantageous to him when the Restoration did take place in 1660.

How far the marriage was the outcome of deliberate political calculation, and how far it was simply a matter of finding a well-born and well-endowed wife (for she brought a dowry of £4,000) it is impossible to tell. But whatever the motives behind it, the marriage, though childless, proved to be as happy as Ashley Cooper's first one had been, until it was broken by Shaftesbury's death twenty-eight years later. After ten years of married life, we find him writing to his wife as 'my dearest', and ending with a reference to 'that treasure God has given me in so faithful and affectionate a wife, to whom I ever vow myself, a most sincere and truly affectionate husband'.[3] Though epistolary forms of address were often flowery in that age, this was not the language of convention. Margaret repaid him with even greater devotion, sharing in his imprisonment in the Tower, pathetically alarmed by rumours of danger to him at Oxford

---

[1] C.S.P.D. 1655, p. 114.   [2] Her mother Penelope was Southampton's sister.
[3] Printed by Christie, i. 286–8.

in 1681, and eventually becoming a deeply mourning widow. When she was married, she was a woman of twenty-eight, self-effacing, and sincerely religious; she would rise at five for her lengthy devotions. That she was also by no means unintelligent may be inferred from her relationship with John Locke after the latter had joined her husband's household. When Locke was in France in 1675–9 he translated three religious essays by the Jansenist Nicole and dedicated them to Lady Shaftesbury in terms which again go beyond the usual empty flatteries of such prefaces. She does not appear to have been particularly interested in politics, and still less to have become a 'political hostess'; but she supplied her husband with a happy and well-run home in a period under the Restoration which (apart from the Russells) is not normally associated with happy and well-matched family life.[1]

The marriage did not mean that Ashley Cooper abandoned the family ties which he had formed through his first wife. His nephew Sir George Savile had narrowly escaped being involved in the plans for a Royalist rising in February and March 1655, and thereafter, like other Royalists, was subject to the punitive taxation imposed by Cromwell and his major-generals. To help his nephew, Ashley Cooper in October 1656 was, with William Coventry and others, a party to a complicated collusive arrangement whereby Sir George Savile conveyed away some of his estates in Derbyshire, Yorkshire and Shropshire, and received them back in 1659 when the coast was clear.[2] Such transactions were not uncommon in a period of revolution, when one naturally lent one's relatives a helping hand across the political barriers. Equally it was natural for Ashley Cooper to be a party when the marriage settlement was made on the occasion of his nephew's marriage on 30 December 1656 to Lady Dorothy Spencer (thus adding another link to the Coventry-Savile-Cooper-Spencer chain).[3] But such obligations as these may not have helped relations between the two men in the long run. Relations between uncle and nephew in politics are never easy, particularly when both are intelligent and ambitious, and a sense of past obligation may sometimes breed resentment rather than gratitude. As will be seen in a later chapter, Viscount Halifax's separation from the Whigs in 1679 was partly a reaction against political sub-ordination to his uncle.

In June 1656, the long lull in the parliamentary life of the country came to an end when the Lord Protector consented to the summoning of his second Parliament under the terms of the Instrument of Government. Once again Ashley Cooper was elected as one of the members for Wiltshire, but this time without any of the furore which had accompanied his election in 1654. His career in this session was however of the shortest. He may

<hr>

[1] *Rawleigh Redivivus* (1683), p. 13; *Discourses translated from Nicole's essays by John Locke* (1828), pp. xxiii–xxvii.

[2] From deeds in papers at present being sorted at Chatsworth.   [3] Ibid.

have been present in Westminster Abbey on 17 September to hear the Rev. John Owen preach the opening sermon, and he may afterwards have joined the other members in the Painted Chamber for the Protector's speech, in which Cromwell this time added to his condemnation of Levellers and Fifth Monarchy men an attack on those who called themselves 'Commonwealthsmen', some of whom were 'men of fortune and great estates'. If Ashley Cooper felt himself to be among those aimed at under this description, his fears were soon confirmed. When the members went from the Painted Chamber to the House they found the door guarded by three colonels with a troop of soldiers. Only those members who could produce a ticket certifying the Council of State's approval were permitted to enter, and Ashley Cooper, with three other Wiltshire members, was among those excluded.

In adopting this course the Council of State claimed to be acting by virtue of clause 17 in the Instrument, which provided that members should be 'persons of known integrity, fearing God, and of good conversation'. The aspersion on Ashley Cooper was no more justified than on Haslerig, Scot, Colonel Birch and others who were excluded; it was a pretext to keep out those who, it was feared, would make trouble for the government. Ashley Cooper was one of seventy-nine who wrote to the Speaker, complaining that they were kept back from doing their duty by soldiers at the lobby door. When Sir George Booth, a member for Cheshire, presented this letter on 18 September, some of the members took up the cause of the secluded members as a breach of parliamentary privilege, but after four days of debate they were defeated by the government's supporters, and Ashley Cooper had to resign himself to his fate. Some of the excluded members, said a newsletter, 'are gone into the country discontented, and will not apply themselves to the Council; others are guilty and dare not'. A printed protest was prepared on their behalf, pointing out that no King had ever dared to treat his Parliament thus, attacking the Protector for assuming 'an absolute sovereignty as if he came down from the throne of God' and claiming that the consent of 'the body of the people in Parliament' was needed to make his authority legitimate. Boxes containing a thousand copies of this were sent to various people for distribution. Among the ninety-eight names of excluded members which were appended to it was Ashley Cooper's; but no firm conclusion can be based on this, for it is known that some of the members concerned denied all knowledge of it, and names may have been printed without permission by the anonymous propagandist author.[1]

---

[1] C. H. Firth, *The Last Years of the Protectorate, 1656–8* (1909), i. 1–23, n. 1; W. C. Abbott, *The Writings and Speeches of Oliver Cromwell* (Harvard, 1937–47), iv. 257–85; *C.J.* vii. 424–6; B. Whitelocke, *Memorials* (1682), pp. 639–43; *Clarke Papers*, ed. C. H. Firth (Camden Society, 1899), iii. 72–75; *Thurloe State Papers*, ed. T. Birch (1742), v. 456, 490; R. C. H. Catterall, 'A Suspicious Document in Whitelocke's *Memorials*', *E.H.R.* (1901), pp. 737–9.

Thereupon Ashley Cooper disappears into obscurity for over a year. Except for one letter addressed to Henry Cromwell in Ireland on private business[1] nothing whatever is known of him until this same Parliament met again, after a long adjournment, in January 1658.

This time Ashley Cooper was able to take his seat. In the meantime the constitution had once again been changed, in the persistent endeavour to cloak military government with parliamentary forms and to make the result more like the traditional one. Cromwell had refused the offer of the title of king, but had accepted an amended version of the Humble Petition and Advice which had been put forward by the Parliament from which Ashley Cooper and others had been excluded. He was to be allowed to nominate his successor, and to appoint whoever he wished to constitute a new, second chamber. Since this 'other house' would obviously be subservient to himself, Cromwell felt that he could afford to yield to the demand that as part of the settlement the excluded members should be allowed to return; and Ashley Cooper came back with the rest. It is probable that, had he wished, he could have been one of those nominated by the Protector to the 'other house'; he had the necessary qualifications of birth, fortune and ability which were badly needed to make this new assembly respectable in that age. Cromwell would probably have been willing to let bygones be bygones, for he included among the nominees his stiffly doctrinaire Republican opponent, Sir Arthur Haslerig, who however refused the honour. It is likely, therefore, that the omission of Ashley Cooper's name from the list means that he was known now to be an irreconcilable opponent. On 19 January, the day before the opening of the new session, Cromwell issued a warrant releasing him from the fine of £500 imposed upon him as a delinquent in 1644,[2] but if this was an attempt to disarm him, it failed completely.

The new parliamentary session lasted only a fortnight. Cromwell found this as disappointing as all his previous attempts to find a representative body which would co-operate harmoniously with him, and Ashley Cooper was among those who frustrated him. He entered the House on 25 January,[3] in time to hear the Protector's long speech urging Puritans, in the interests of international Protestantism, national trade and defence, to stop tearing and rending one another. Let members heed the danger from the Cavalier party, Cromwell urged, and attend to the urgent needs of the poor unpaid army; let them count their blessings of 'peace and the gospel', and have 'one heart and soul'. But the text which the Protector quoted, that the Lord 'will speak peace to his people and to his saints, that they turn not again to folly', fell on stony ground. From Cromwell's point of view, the

[1] Christie, i. 135–6.
[2] Shaftesbury Papers, I, 13. Ashley Cooper's petition, in response to which this warrant was said to be issued, is not extant and it is not known when it was made.
[3] *Clarke Papers*, ed. C. H. Firth (Camden Society, 1899), iii. 133 n.

strictly Republican members of the House turned to folly from the beginning.[1]

The issue over which battle was joined was that of the 'other house' which the Humble Petition and Advice had brought into existence. The problem of its title, and therefore its powers, had been raised already on 22 January, when the House had received a message from 'the Lords', and was called upon to decide whether to reply to them under this title. After a 'day of humiliation' on the 27th with sermons and devotions lasting from ten until five-thirty, the struggle began in earnest next day. The opposition were unable to obtain that the House should go into grand committee, but thanks to their parliamentary experience the practical effect was the same. After a week they were still talking. Some Republicans, like Haslerig and the regicide Thomas Scot, were clearly opposed to any second chamber: glorifying 'that victorious Parliament' which had abolished both monarchy and Lords in 1649, attacking the Lords' record in the year before their abolition, and claiming to speak for posterity, they objected to anything which 'puts a negative upon the people' or might become 'a co-ordinate power' with the House. Others were not necessarily opposed to all second chambers, but did object to one consisting of the Protector's nominees and able to block the wishes of the Commons in his interests. Neither group was willing to acknowledge a 'House of Lords' which might aspire to the powers of the traditional body of that name.[2]

Ashley Cooper does not appear to have belonged to the more extreme group of critics. The notes which survive of speeches made in these debates are scrappy and often not easy to follow: when Ashley Cooper is recorded as remarking that 'Some are neither for another House, nor for the title', it is impossible for us to know certainly whether he was merely stating a fact, or including himself amongst those opposed to 'another House' whatever its title. But his interventions in debate were concerned less with abstract principles of political theory than with the immediate, tactical parliamentary situation. He insisted vainly that the subject is of such vital importance that a grand committee was appropriate, 'and cannot be denied'. He argued against the idea that the House could send a reply to 'the Lords' without implying anything about the other House's title. 'Admit Lords, and admit all', he declared. 'There is nothing but a compliment to call a man Lord', he said in his longest speech on 3 February; 'but if one calls himself Lord of my manor, I shall be loth to give him the title, lest he claim the manor'. Lawyers would confirm the importance of names like 'King', or 'Lords': 'Words are the keys of the cabinets of things. Let us first take the people's jewels out, before you part with that cabinet.' 'Consider, let us not lay

---

[1] Abbott, op. cit. p. iv.

[2] *C.J.* vii. 588–92: *Diary of Thomas Burton*, ed. J. T. Rutt (1828), ii. 372–470; C. H. Firth, *The Last Years of the Protectorate, 1656–8* (1909), ii. 16–41.

foundations that we may repent.'[1] By such arguments as these, he helped to make his fellow-members face the issue of 'the other house' instead of turning to government business. It may be reasonably suspected that his real intention was to obstruct Cromwell's attempt to give military rule constitutional trappings, rather than to indulge a constitutional objection to second chambers. Thus, at all events, the later upholder of the privileges of the House of Lords in *Shirley* v. *Fagg* fought against Cromwell's upper house.

These obstructionist tactics were successful to the extent that they led Cromwell to abandon his last constitutional experiment. In dissolving Parliament after a session lasting only a fortnight he was influenced partly by the futility of the debates, and partly by the news that a monster Republican petition signed by thousands of people was being prepared in London to threaten his position. In the Exclusion crisis of 1679–80 Ashley Cooper was to be concerned in the large-scale organization of petitions, and it is tempting to wonder whether he had anything to do with this earlier example of a means to use outdoor pressure in support of a parliamentary struggle; but such evidence as is available refers only to former members of the Rump such as Haslerig and Scot, and suggests that when the petition was presented to the House on 4 February they intended to propose the recall of the Rump, in which Ashley Cooper had no seat. He was given no chance to express his views on it,[2] for Cromwell forestalled his opponents by hastily journeying to the House in a hired hackney coach. Summoning the members to the Lords' House, he made another speech in his own justification, calling upon God to 'be judge between you and me', and dissolved this, his last Parliament. In the hasty manner in which the dissolution was carried out, it is comparable with the famous end of the Oxford Parliament of 1681.[3]

As so often in the seventeenth century, the opposition's success in provoking a dissolution carried with it its own penalty—that of silent impotence until the government was forced to summon a new session. Once more Ashley Cooper falls into obscurity. No mention of his name is to be found either in the state papers of Cromwell's secretary of state, Thurloe, nor in those of the exiled King Charles's principal minister, Edward Hyde. He was not engaging in underhand conspiracy, but biding his time until he had a further opportunity in Parliament. Finally he reappeared when there was again an assembly in St. Stephen's, in February 1659.

[1] Burton, ii. 378, 392, 401, 419, 433–5.
[2] When the petition was presented in the next session on 15 Feb. 1659, Ashley Cooper was not recorded as taking part in the debate: Burton, iii. 288–96. Burton, however, was not present during the whole of the proceedings in the House.
[3] Firth, op. cit. ii. 30–41; Firth, 'Letters concerning the dissolution of Cromwell's last Parliament, 1658', in *E.H.R.* 1892, pp. 102–10; Bordeaux, 4/14 Feb. 1658, in *Thurloe State Papers*, ed. T. Birch (1742), vi. 778; Payne to Nieuport, 5/15 Feb., ibid. vi. 781–2; Thurloe to Henry Cromwell, 13 July 1658, ibid. vii. 269.

In the intervening twelve months, however, there had been a fundamental change in the situation. Contemporaries saw something momentous
and symbolic in the great storm which raged on the eve of the anniversary
of the Lord Protector's victories at Dunbar and Worcester, 3 September
1658. When the tempest had blown itself out, the leader who had over-
shadowed the entire political scene lay dead, and in his place there stood
the most insignificant of men, Richard Cromwell. The striking fact about
Richard is that, although he was thus thrust into a position of responsibility
in a period of revolution, his many political opponents all regarded him
without any malice. When later deposed, he was left unmolested, even by
the returning Royalists. 'Without guile or gall', he had not the strength of
will or character necessary to make enemies—or to rule. His only positive
qualification for his position was the mere fact that he was his father's
eldest son; and he never found anyone capable of acting as the power
behind the throne. When he first succeeded as Lord Protector there was a
lull, in which his father's officers promised their devotion and loyal
addresses came in large numbers from all over the country, but this soon
proved to be a mockery. After men had had time to observe and to think,
it seemed to them less and less likely that the Protectorate would last, and
more and more tempting to devise something in its place. Army officers
could not long respect their new leader who was without military experience; and if Oliver had not been able to dominate Parliament, it was
improbable that Richard could. Moreover, one of his decisions gave an
obvious opening to his experienced Republican opponents. The Humble
Petition and Advice had talked of reforming the system of representation,
but the last Parliament had not sat for long enough to do this; accordingly
Richard decided that the English members should be elected on the old,
pre-war basis, but that Scotland and Ireland should send members as under
the terms of the Instrument, and that his father's 'other house', appointed
under the provisions of the Humble Petition and Advice, should sit once
more. Such a mixture of constitutions could have no authority except
Richard's personal edict, and it should have been obvious that as soon as
Haslerig, Scot, Ashley Cooper and others met together, they would
challenge it. Nothing was secure.

The return to the old constituencies made no difference to Ashley
Cooper. As in 1654 he was elected first by the borough of Poole, but
waived his right to this seat when he was chosen for the more exalted
county seat of Wiltshire.[1] For some unknown reason he missed the opening
days of the new session, and it is significant that when he appeared on 5
February, the diarist Thomas Burton noted his arrival.[2] He was expected
to be one of the government's leading opponents once more. On his first
day in the House he intervened briefly in two debates, and although

---

[1] *C.J.* vii. 616, 622.
[2] Burton, iii. 80.

neither of these was very important his contributions are revealing. One concerned a simple-minded man, who having been jokingly told by a friend that he had been elected to Parliament, was discovered sitting on the benches of the House without any right to be there. Many members took this as an affront and talked of sending him to the Tower; others suspected him of distributing pamphlets and wanted him to be thoroughly examined about this. Amid the excited speeches Ashley Cooper took a cool, detached view: the man was 'inconsiderable', and though he should be sent to the common Newgate prison as punishment for his intrusion, he should not be made to incriminate himself under examination. This common-sense and relatively liberal view eventually prevailed. Ashley Cooper's second speech was on a motion for a committee on the mainten-ance of ministers in Wales—always one of 'the darker corners of the land' for Puritans.[1] He agreed about the urgency of supplying clergy for Welsh livings, commenting 'I have passed through Wales, and found churches all unsupplied, except a few grocers, or such persons, that have formerly served for two years'. Though personally more tolerant than the average, he had evidently not much sympathy for the 'grocers or such persons' of less education who filled some of the pulpits during the Protectorate. His own preferences were always for the more learned type of preacher— Reynolds or Caryll, Strong, or later Stillingfleet. He was duly placed on the committee which was appointed.[2]

Such minor issues were soon lost from view in the smoke of battle joined over the whole of the constitution. This battle raged for three months, during which no legislation at all was passed and the Republican opposition made a determined effort to convert a Protectorate which they regarded as merely an expression of military force into a truly parliamentary régime, though not a democratic one. The tough, unyielding Haslerig, who had been one of the Five Members of 1642, and Scot, whose character and opinions alike were summed up in the exultant justification of the execution of Charles I, 'not done in a hole or corner, but in the face of God and of all men', wanted to get back to the political and social policies of the Rump in 1649–53, however unrepresentative it had been. The much subtler mind of Sir Henry Vane did not share all their views and prejudices, but found them preferable to the rule of swordsmen, with Richard Cromwell as their figurehead; and Ashley Cooper too joined in refusing to accept the Humble Petition and Advice.

They had been given their chance by Secretary of State Thurloe, who had brought in a bill to recognize Richard Cromwell as Protector. Haslerig, Scot, and Henry Neville had already indicated their intention to broaden the debate on this bill to include the whole constitution of the Protectorate —even the Protector's 'negative voice' and control over the armed forces.

---

[1] Cf. Christopher Hill, 'Puritans and "the dark corners of the land"', in *Trans. Roy. Hist. Soc.*, 1963, pp. 77–102. [2] Burton, iii. 80, 83; *C.J.* vii. 600.

When the time came for the bill's second reading two days after Ashley Cooper's arrival, that is, on 7 February, Haslerig began with an immense historical lecture lasting three hours for the benefit of those members who were too young to remember all the events of the previous twenty years. Glorifying the achievements of the Commonwealth between 1649 and 1653, he complained bitterly of everything which had happened since under the Protectorate. He claimed that the Parliament which had presented the Humble Petition and Advice in 1657 'was a forced Parliament, because some of us were forced out', whereas the present assembly was 'the freest, clearest and most undoubted representative' since 1653: they were 'the supreme power' and had the right and duty to settle everything as they liked. Other members talked of the Humble Petition being 'but a sandy foundation', having been carried by only three votes in a House from which a hundred members had been excluded and in which Scots and Irish members nominated by the government had carried the day.[1] Everything, in fact, was to be thrown back into the melting-pot, and Parliament was to do the remoulding.

The 'Court party' (as the Republicans called the supporters of the Protectorate) was by no means without supporters in the House, for there were many who thought the mild rule of a man like Richard would be the best guarantee against both a Royalist restoration and the naked rule of the sword of the major-generals. But they were no match for their experienced opponents, especially as the Speaker failed to supply the customary guidance from the Chair and allowed protracted and unnecessary arguments about procedure. The Republicans were able 'to spin out the debate with long speeches', educating some of the young new members in the process. In the first few days Ashley Cooper did not speak, except on one occasion to support an adjournment and so allow further speeches, when the 'Court party' wanted the question put without further delay. He reserved his main effort until the debate had reached a critical moment on its fifth consecutive day (11 February). By that time it had been proposed to add to the main motion recognizing Richard Cromwell further words reserving the House's right to discuss the two points of the control over the militia and the Protector's 'negative voice' or veto. The Speaker was about to put these additional words to the vote, when Ashley Cooper intervened at the last moment to urge that the motion should be put as a whole. His aim was, he said, 'to assert his [Richard Cromwell's] authority together with the liberty of the people. This will be security and indemnity to all'. He compared the situation with that in 1654, when, after recognizing

---

[1] Burton, iii. 86 sqq. For all these debates, cf. Godfrey Davies, *The Restoration of Charles II, 1658–1660* (1955), chapters IV and V; and Slingsby Bethel, *A true and Impartial Narrative . . .* in *Somers Tracts* (1811), vi. 477–86, for a Republican account. MSS. Lansdowne 823 contains letters sent to Henry Cromwell in Ireland with accounts of the debates. Ludlow, who was a member, also has an account (*Memoirs*, ed. C. H. Firth, 1894, ii. 51–71).

the authority of a 'single person', the House had been permitted by the Cromwellians themselves to discuss 'the interest of the people' and the detailed provisions of the Instrument of Government. In the same way they should now pass a resolution which would allow discussion of the Humble Petition and Advice. This last he attacked in extreme, and even extravagant terms. 'If the Florentine and he that sat in the great chair of the world [i.e. Machiavelli and Pope Alexander VI[1]], had all met together, they could not have made any thing so absolute.' Having the aid of the other House, the government would be short only of money. If any resolution implying acceptance of the Humble Petition were carried, the results would be disastrous for posterity. In all this there was no direct personal attack on Richard Cromwell, and no explicit refusal to allow him the title of Protector; the purpose stated was to preserve both the interests of Protector and 'the people'. This last noun he used several times without ever attempting to define it, and the same vagueness may be observed in the high-sounding statement that 'Englishmen's minds are free, and better taught in their liberties now than ever'. As in so many Republican and later Whig statements, the general sentiments are unexceptionable, but the question who is included as 'the people' and 'Englishmen' is left un-answered.[2]

After a further day's debate, in the course of which Ashley Cooper and others contended that the very use of the word 'recognize' would imply acceptance of all the powers claimed by the Protector under the Humble Petition and Advice,[3] the House finally voted on 14 February. The result was superficially a victory for the Cromwellians, but in practice a gain for the opposition. It was resolved that there should be no additional clauses to the motion that Richard Cromwell be recognized as Lord Protector; and thus the specific references to the militia and the 'negative voice' which Ashley Cooper and others had advocated were lost by a majority of 89 votes. It was then agreed without a division, however, that before the bill of recognition was committed, 'this House do declare such additional clauses to be part of the bill, as may bound the power of the Chief Magistrate; and fully secure the rights and privileges of Parliament, and the liberties and rights of the people', and that the previous vote should not be binding until the whole bill was passed. Thus the opposition were enabled to fight again another day; and the pattern for the session was set, with the numerical majority on the government's side, but with the debating skill and parliamentary experience on that of the opposition, redressing the balance.[4]

[1] Cf. Christie, i. 150 n.
[2] Burton, iii. 150, 227–9, 286, for Ashley Cooper's speeches.
[3] Ibid. pp. 276–7.
[4] C.J. vii. 603; J. Barwick to Hyde, 16 Feb., Thurloe State Papers, vii. 615; Annesley to H. Cromwell, 15 Feb., in MSS. Lansdowne 823, fo. 216; F. Aungier to same, ibid. fos. 218–19.

On 17 February the House proceeded to carry out its intention to debate the bounds of Richard Cromwell's power, with Haslerig, Vane and other Republicans desiring to uphold the supremacy of Parliament, and Henry Neville, ever the constitutional theorist, wanting in effect to turn the House into a constituent assembly. The Cromwellians sought to evade discussion of the 'negative voice' of the Protector by urging that the position of the 'other house' should be settled first, the Attorney-General stating explicitly that 'if there be a negative voice elsewhere, perhaps I shall agree the Chief Magistrate shall have none'. In arguing thus he admitted what was patent to all, that the 'other house' consisted entirely of officers and other nominees of the government, and, that if its position was acknowledged by all, it could be relied on to block any unpalatable measures proposed by the House of Commons. If the 'other house' were accepted, therefore, the government would win a considerable success; and therefore the opposition fought against discussing it and favoured first establishing the constitutional limits of the Protector's powers. Here Ashley Cooper emphatically joined with them. In answer to the Attorney-General's argument, he suggested that the reverse of it was also true: 'unless you know what power your single person shall have, how will you declare the power of the other House . . .?' Proceeding to the heart of the matter, he said: 'I have not heard that debated yet, whether we are upon the footing of the Petition and Advice, or on a new foundation, or on the old constitution. I think we are yet to be supposed to be upon the foot of the old constitution, unless something appears to the contrary.' By 'the old constitution' he presumably meant that in operation before the Rump had been illegally turned out by Cromwell's use of naked force in 1653: like Haslerig, Scot and Vane, he conveniently overlooked that the Rump itself owed its position to an earlier use of force by the army in Pride's Purge in 1648, and he also passed over the fact that by accepting membership of Cromwell's Council of State in 1653 he had in some sense condoned the eviction of the Rump. He was now turning his back on his Cromwellian past, and coming close to the position of the Republicans. On this occasion he shared in their defeat, for the government supporters carried the motion that the other house should be considered first by the large majority of 217 votes to 86.[1]

This, however, turned out for the government to be the sort of victory which was worse than defeat. Once more, as in 1658, the House began to flounder in the morass of endless inconclusive debates about the 'other House'. It is true that this time they began by resolving without a division that it should be part of the Bill of Recognition to declare the Parliament to consist of two houses. But there remained infinite scope for debate on the powers and composition of the other house. Should it be the other

---

[1] Burton, iii. 335; *C.J.* vii. 605.

house nominated by Oliver Cromwell, consisting of his officers and supporters, and apparently prepared to carry out the wishes of the Protector or whoever advised him? or should the House recognize the rights of the 'old peers', that is, those members of the House of Lords who had fought faithfully for the parliamentary cause? Should the other House's constitutional powers or its composition be determined first? Such questions made possible endless, confused debates before it was even possible to agree on what motion the House should vote. Ashley Cooper criticized what he considered to be the illogical course of the debate. 'One while it is argued for right', he complained, '. . . and then they fly off to conveniency.' His argument was that 'the first question ought to be, whether there be a right or no; for, where there is a right . . . there is a duty; and then matters of convenience or inconvenience is out of doors'. He therefore advocated considering first whether the 'old lords' or the new (Cromwellian) lords had a right to sit, and then discussing what the limits of their authority should be; and, as might be expected from his speeches in the session of 1658, he made it clear that his own sympathies were emphatically opposed to the new lords, 'who have already a vast power in their hands, and dangerous to the people'.[1]

Not all of the opposition speakers accepted this line of argument, that the composition of the other House should be decided first: it is interesting to find one Republican member, Knightley, saying that trying to impose bounds on the other House, once constituted, would be like the men of Gotham who tried to hedge in the cuckoo—an illustration which was to become a commonplace twenty years later, when the Whigs argued that no legal limitations would be adequate to restrain a Popish successor.[2] In the end, however, after the debate had raged intermittently for about a fortnight, the House began to show a disposition to put 'persons' before 'bounds'; but then the opposition began to find (to their alarm) that the vote was not likely to take place in the way they wanted. A motion was proposed, that the House would transact with the persons now sitting in the other House as a house of Parliament, with an additional vague proviso to the effect that this should not 'exclude the rights of the old peers that have been faithful'. This was an ingenious move by the government supporters to get their main point—an 'other house' of officers and nominees—carried at the possible cost of including the old peers, who were fewer in number. The Cromwellians would remain entrenched in the other House, whatever the effects produced on the Commons by elections. Ashley Cooper therefore found that the question of right which he had advocated was likely to be decided in a way that he did not want; and on 7 March he spoke again at length against such a formulation of the question before the House. He attacked the additional clause which

[1] Burton, iii. 418–19.
[2] Ibid. iii. 511.

claimed to preserve the rights of the old peers, describing it accurately as 'but a shoeing-horn' to assist in the settling of the main issue to the Cromwellians' satisfaction. While pretending to safeguard the rights of the old peers, the clause would in reality destroy their claim to constitute the upper house. 'Let us consider what we can say to posterity. . . . Your laws and liberties are all gone. Two negatives are in one hand. An army is in your legislature, and 1,300,000l per annum for ever. To say that a law made under force shall be a good law, and binding in reason, is against all reason.' His argument here was that if the motion was carried, the Army officers would be able to perpetuate themselves in power, thanks to their control of the other House and of the Protector, 'two negatives' which could block anything that the elected representatives of the people wanted; the terms of the Humble Petition and Advice would guarantee them an income, even though that 'law' had been passed after the forcible expulsion of himself and many other members. There would be in effect a military dictatorship. 'You might have had as good a government three hundred years ago.' In his peroration he declared that he could not transact with the other House 'because it is against the rights of others, the rights of this House, and the rights of the nation', and appealed for the motion to be put without its misleading addendum, so that there could be a straight vote for or against it.[1]

Among those who expressed a similar view in this debate, two or three names are of interest and significance. Sir George Booth, a rich Cheshire Presbyterian who had fought in the Civil War, was later to lead a premature rebellion against the Commonwealth in August 1659; Colonel Morley early in 1660 occupied the key position of Lieutenant of the Tower and was eventually brought to acquiesce in the plans which led to the Restoration. More important than either was William Morrice, a Devonian who, like Ashley Cooper, had been at Exeter College, a man of integrity and some pretensions to scholarship who larded his speeches with a frequent use of Latin tags, suitable for every occasion. A worthy, learned and respectable man, who was later to be a friend, and not merely a political associate, of Ashley Cooper's, his importance lay not so much in any supreme ability or oratorical skill as in his wife's relationship to General Monk, the commander-in-chief in Scotland. He too was to have his part to play in the Restoration. Though their spoken opinions coincided, their secret desires did not. Booth was in advance of the others in his decision that a Restoration of the monarchy would be most likely to bring with it the sort of parliamentary régime which they all wanted.

The debate of 7 March proved to be unusually protracted, for the Cromwellians were more and more determined to carry their point against the obstructive, filibustering tactics of the opposition. A motion for

---

[1] Burton, iv. 50–52.

adjournment to Wednesday the 9th was defeated by one vote, and midnight drew near; one member who kept notes recorded ruefully that one Mr. Sadler 'would have spoken, if he had not been taken down by Sir Ashley Cooper and others, who prayed to shorten the debate, or else to adjourn'. At 1 a.m. the House did adjourn, but only until the same afternoon, and now the opposition could not hold off the vote much longer. Ashley Cooper made one further speech,[1] reiterating his former arguments, and saying that much as he respected the old peers and wanted them restored, he objected to bringing them back as a minor part of the other House nominated under the Humble Petition and Advice. He urged again that the motion should be put without its additional clause; but by 195 votes to 188 this clause was added. The main motion thus amended was on the point of being put to the House, and the opposition was certain to be beaten. Haslerig complained that some members had withdrawn, and then another member dragged in a further red herring, by questioning the right of the members for Scotland and Ireland to sit and vote. This successfully diverted the House on to another trail, and at 9 p.m. the House once again adjourned without taking a vote on the motion, the Speaker by this time 'ready to die in the chair'.

For the next fortnight the House followed this new track. There were sixty members sitting for Scottish and Irish seats, almost all of them owing their election to government influence—some, it was said, had been no nearer to Scotland than Gray's Inn[2]—and in a divided House they were able to sway the balance in the government's favour. This became, therefore, the keenest-fought of party issues, with the opposition giving ground inch by inch and raising every possible obstruction to delay the victory of the Cromwellians. Haslerig, taking a full part as usual, remarked on one occasion that 'if an angel should come from Heaven, there would not one man's vote be altered in this debate,'[3] but neither he nor anyone else would curtail their speeches on that account; and on another day the general exasperation after ten hours' debate was so great that there was 'a great noise and horrid confusion' lasting for an hour, and 'Mr. Young compared it to a cockpit'.[4] Though not as frequent a speaker as Haslerig and Vane, and some others, Ashley Cooper had his contribution to make. He supported the motion that the Scots should withdraw while their case was being considered, and backed Vane's proposal that the writs of summons to Scottish members in this and earlier parliaments should be read and compared. In a longer oration he went to the heart of the matter, and attacked the Petition and Advice itself as a constitution imposed by Oliver Cromwell after some members had been prevented from taking their seats

---

[1] Burton, iv. 83–84. The debates for 7 and 8 Mar. are ibid. pp. 46–90; cf. *C.J.* vii. 611–12, and MSS. Lansdowne 823, fos. 239–47.

[2] Bethel, *Brief Narrative*, in *Somers Tracts* (1811), vi. 484.

[3] Burton, iv. 205.   [4] Ibid. iv. 138.

in 1656. 'It was under force. If a law under force must bind, *actum est de lege*.' He made it clear that his objection was not to union with Scotland itself; under the Restoration he was to be one of the commissioners appointed to consider a union. 'They [the Scots] are persons very fit to be united to us; of the same religion; the same continent. They have been faithful and assisting to you. I am as much for the freedom of that nation as any man; but he that wishes his son well, does not give him his land till he come out of his guardian's house.' The present members, he added, 'either come now on the account of their own interest, or upon the interest of the Chief Magistrate', and were not truly independent. His basic complaint, like that of Morrice, who spoke next, and Sir Henry Vane, was against the way in which the terms of Scottish representation had been virtually dictated by the Protector, and were not the outcome of a legal settlement. When the Cromwellians formulated a motion stating simply that the Scottish members should continue to sit, he tried to insist that the motion should rather deal explicitly with their legal right. 'In order of nature', he maintained, 'legal right must be considered before any prudential.' In this, however, as in everything else, he and the opposition were defeated when they were at last brought to a vote, and the majority succeeded in establishing that first Scottish and then Irish members should be allowed to continue to sit.[1]

On 28 March, therefore, the House at last returned to its motion that it should transact with the other House. Once again Ashley Cooper voiced his opposition, maintaining correctly that the proviso purporting to conserve the rights of the old peers was worthless, for the motion was 'clearly putting others in their place, and is setting up a thing that is quite contrary. The [alleged] saving of their rights is the clear proscription of their rights. You are upon the greatest piece of prerogative that ever was.' In the other House, he said, the Protector would possess 'a whole negative', a way of blocking all proceedings that Richard Cromwell, or whoever controlled him, did not like.[2] On this day, however, the debate on the other House petered out remarkably quickly; many members had clearly had more than enough of it, and perhaps the opposition was caught napping, for when the House began to vote at midday Haslerig and Vane were both absent. Ashley Cooper fought a delaying action, making a long speech until the House was 'fuller of those of his party',[3] and seconding Scot's proposal that if the other House was to be recognized, it should be only for the duration of the existing Parliament: the other House would be limited in

---

[1] Burton, iv. 106, 108, 110, 170, 189, 212–13, 226, for Ashley Cooper's speeches.

[2] Ibid. iv. 284.

[3] Ibid. iv. 286–7. Christie, i. 160–4 and App. IV, considered that this long speech was to be identified with the pamphlet, *A Seasonable Speech, made by a Worthy Member of Parliament in the House of Commons, March, 1659*, but there is no evidence for this. See C. H. Firth in *Clarke Papers* (Camden Society, 1889), iii. 189, n., and *The House of Lords during the Civil War* (1910), p. 259, n.; also Brown, p. 73.

time, if not in any other way. Among those who spoke in support were Morrice, once again, and Carew Raleigh, the second husband of Lady Philippa Ashley. Anxious to establish their main point, the 'Court party' accepted this amendment, and the opposition then proposed to add the further words, 'and no longer unless confirmed by Act of Parliament'. In answer to the argument that such an addition would cast doubt on everything done since 1649 which had not been confirmed by Act of Parliament, Ashley Cooper could see no such danger: 'It shakes not yourselves, unless you distrust your senses. I could as ill venture as any man, without an indemnity.' But the addition was rejected, and in the end the motion to transact with the other House was carried by the surprisingly large majority of 198 votes to 125.[1]

After two months of debate, the essential features of the constitution of the Protectorate had been confirmed, and it might seem that the protracted efforts of the Republicans had been in vain. Nevertheless Richard Cromwell's government had been crippled by the delay. No legislation had been enacted, and no new supply bill had been passed to cope with the government's ever-increasing debts, which a committee estimated on 7 April to be over two millions.[2] Most serious of all, many in the Army were coming to feel that their views and interests were being attacked in Parliament and insufficiently defended by the Protector. The debates in Parliament were full of uncomplimentary remarks about soldiers and their influence on government, and officers with seats reported these outside the House, increasing the distrust between civilian politicians and the Army. Some officers feared that their past activities might be questioned. Major-General Butler was attacked in the House for his illegal actions in Northamptonshire, and his bold defence that his actions were done under Oliver Cromwell's orders only added fuel to the flames. Though some members 'laboured to wash him', Scot answered them that 'The arguments for him are as much as to say, "we must be ruled by the army"; and I am against that'. Butler was impeached, and Ashley Cooper, though his remarks about the Army in general had been less tactless than many, was a member of the committee appointed to draw up the articles of impeachment.[3] Many officers must have been conscious that they had not always adhered to the letter of the law; and if major-generals were not safe, and a plea of superior orders was not accepted, who could be sure of escaping?

Further, the Army had to look on while nothing was done to cope with the mounting arrears in their pay. On one occasion Ashley Cooper had supported a motion to fix a day to consider this problem,[4] for it was clearly dangerous to drive the Army beyond endurance; but as parliamentarians he and the rest of the opposition were naturally conscious that control of supply was their most obvious weapon, and they were reluctant to free

---

[1] Burton, iv. 277–94; *C.J.* vii. 621. [2] *C.J.* vii. 627–31.
[3] Burton, iv. 403–12; *C.J.* vii. 636–7. [4] Burton, iv. 139–40.

the government from its difficulties. On 29 March a government supporter introduced a bill purporting to end the excise some years, and the customs duties some months, after the Protector's death: apparently a measure likely to satisfy the constitutionalists, but in reality an ingenious method of confirming the Protector's right to levy these duties for life. Haslerig proposed that the bill should be 'laid by' while members considered it; Ashley Cooper went further. 'There is nought can destroy us like that which we like. I am apt to suspect this bill.' He argued that, as a money bill, it should not have been introduced without a formal order of the House, and moved that it should be rejected and another bill brought in granting tonnage and poundage for a limited period. Nevertheless the bill was read a second time two days later, by which time all the Republicans had joined in opposing what was effectively the grant of taxes for life. 'A matter of twelve or thirteen lines is to settle the greatest revenue that ever was', said Haslerig; and Scot complained that the money was not for the Protector, but 'for your army', forty of whom were in the other House. Neville argued that Parliament would not be sitting at all but for the financial necessity, and appealed to members to 'consider your own constitution before you settle your revenue'. Ashley Cooper shared Neville's fears that the bill might be followed by a dissolution. 'Once declare money, they may go on without you.' Very sensibly he declared that he did not want any vote passed discountenancing the levying of customs and excise at the moment, and instead his remedy was to propose a vote that the duties should not be levied after the end of this Parliament unless Parliament had first agreed; this would be the best possible guarantee that the session would continue. He read out his motion, declaring that Neville had drafted it. Debate on it was later adjourned, and never resumed; but neither was the bill passed. The soldiers who heard of it were not encouraged to hope for new revenue to satisfy their arrears, when there was some uncertainty even about the government's right to continue to levy the existing duties. When the government's debts were debated, Haslerig and others talked of retrench-ment, and complained of the number of officers.[1]

Finally, many in the Army were disturbed by signs that Parliament was threatening to interfere with the religious liberty which they valued. The Declaration which was drawn up to give the reasons for a proposed fast complained in strong terms about blasphemies and damnable heresies against Jesus, the Holy Spirit, and 'the word of God, the only rule of faith and life, by denying the authority thereof, and crying up the light in the hearts of sinful men, as the rule and guide of all their actions'. Since the Declaration went on to complain about the remissness of the civil magis-trates 'in permitting the growth of these abominations', Quakers and all holders of unorthodox opinions could fear repression in the future.

---

[1] Burton, iv. 294–9, 309–12, 319–27, 362–7; Ashley Cooper's speeches are on pp. 296–7, 324. See also *C.J.* vii. 621, 627–31.

Ashley Cooper was one of the seventeen members selected to draft this Declaration; but so was Sir Henry Vane, who afterwards attacked it vehemently as 'a coercing the conscience'. The only recorded sentence of any speech by Ashley Cooper in the debate refers only to the importance of the subject without giving any decided opinion; so that all we can say about his attitude is that his support of toleration at other times and his general agreement with Vane in this present session suggest that he probably disliked it too.[1]

It is not surprising that all these events aroused much dissatisfaction in the Army, which saw some of its ideals and interests endangered by the Parliament. There was an alarming growth in the number of councils and meetings held by officers, who themselves began to split into factions. Some followed Lambert and some Fleetwood; some sought salvation by approaches to the 'Commonwealthsmen' who had, after all, governed with reasonable success between 1649 and 1653, while others remained loyal to Oliver's son; and some of the other ranks showed signs of wanting to hold meetings of their own and to advocate more radical solutions.[2] The outcome of three weeks caballing behind the scenes was that Major-General Fleetwood finally decided to take action. When Oliver had dissolved the Parliament of 1658, Fleetwood had expressed doubts and been called 'a milksop' for his pains; now, his tearfully morbid piety strengthened by much 'waiting on the Lord', he too decided to take forcible action against a Parliament of which he disapproved. He and other officers who met at Wallingford House compelled Richard Cromwell to dissolve Parliament on 22 April. It is impossible to say what part Ashley Cooper had in the conversations and manoeuvrings which preceded this further cutting of the Gordian knot; other Republicans like Vane and Haslerig had certainly had their share, but no speech of Ashley Cooper's in the House is recorded in the last three weeks of the session, and no newsletter mentions his name in any intrigue. Perhaps he was merely waiting and seeing.

Thus came to an end the fifth Parliament in which he had been a member. It is noteworthy that all five, the Short Parliament, the Barebones Parliament and the three Protectorate Parliaments in 1654, 1658 and 1659, had been assemblies in which a group of determined men, fluent speakers and skilful parliamentary tacticians, had been able to baulk the wishes of the government, even when they had been in a minority. The lesson learned cannot have been lost on the future leader of the 'Country Party', who had watched the politicians of an older generation than himself at work. In this last session the stubborn pertinacity of Haslerig, as awkward an opponent for the Protectors as he had been for Charles I, the impulsive outspokenness of Scot, the compound of idealism and cold realism in Sir Henry Vane, the

---

[1] *C.J.* vii. 622–6; Burton, iv. 300–1, 328–49.

[2] For the state of opinion in the Army, cf. A. H. Woolrych, 'The Good Old Cause and the fall of the Protectorate', *Cambridge Historical Journal* (1957), pp. 133–61.

aristocratic but unorthodox theorizing of Henry Neville, had taught him a great deal; and at the same time he himself had not been content to be a mere onlooker.

The question arises, how intimate was the co-operation between him and these other men? One debate has already been noticed in which he made a long time-consuming speech until the House was 'fuller of those of his party',[1] and although one needs to be wary of the use of the word 'party' in the seventeenth century, the implication here is surely of more than casual agreement. A contemporary writing to Henry Cromwell in Ireland referred in the same spirit to 'Sir Arthur Haslerig, Sir Hen. Vane, Ludlow, Lambert, Scot, Sir Ant. Ashley Cooper, Neville, and all that gang',[2] and they are almost invariably to be found on the same side. We have seen Ashley Cooper putting forward to the House a resolution drafted by Neville,[3] and on an earlier occasion when Neville had been accused vaguely of atheism and blasphemy, Ashley Cooper had joined with Haslerig, Vane and Scot in calling for the matter to be 'clearly made out' so that a precise charge could be given a precise answer.[4] It looks as though there was more than a loose agreement in their common opposition to the constitution of the Humble Petition and Advice and in their constant upholding of an oligarchic, but liberally interpreted, rule of law against military rule; though it does not follow that they were agreed on the form of government which they wanted to put in place of the Protectorate.

There remain two postscripts to be added to this account of Ashley Cooper's activities in this session. The first of these concerns his attitude to some of the prisoners who appeared at the bar of the House. One who appeared, his petition for release sponsored by his father-in-law Fairfax, was the second Duke of Buckingham. Thus Achitophel for the first time met Zimri, and supported his application. Declaring that he had 'not so much as a correspondence with this person', he urged the House not to leave arbitrary precedents even where Royalists like Buckingham were concerned. Another prisoner who appeared at the bar, after three years in prison in Jersey, was Major-General Overton, and here again, although Overton's radicalism was disliked, Ashley Cooper joined the opposition in pressing for the release of a man against whom no charge had been brought. In his speech he pointed out an additional reason for declaring the warrant illegal, namely that he was sent to a place where the *habeas corpus* writ would not reach, for 'I am clearly of opinion, and all the Long Robe at the committee of grievances were of that opinion, that a *habeas corpus* lies not to Jersey'. As a result he was put on a committee ordered to bring in a bill 'concerning persons committed to prison in any of the islands

---

[1] p. 104 above.
[2] F. Aungier to H. Cromwell, 14 Feb., in Lansdowne MSS. 823, fo. 219; and cf. H. Sankey to the same, 8 Mar., ibid. fo. 247.
[3] p. 106 above.   [4] Burton, iii. 300.

belonging to this commonwealth, out of the reach of an *Habeas Corpus*'. Thus, although he had been a member of the Councils of State which had taken arbitrary action against Lilburne in 1653–4, he began to press for a Habeas Corpus Amendment Act, though it was to be twenty years before, under vastly different circumstances, such an act reached the statute-book.[1]

One further speech is worthy of remark, dealing this time with foreign policy. In the Baltic, from which England drew vital naval supplies in addition to her other trade, the Danes and the Swedes were resuming their perennial struggle for control of the Sound at its entrance, and Richard Cromwell's government wished to send a fleet to watch over England's interests. Many English sympathies were with the Swedes, partly because Charles X was misguidedly regarded as a Protestant hero, and partly because the Danes were supported by the Dutch, whom Scot described in a famous phrase as England's 'rivals for the fairest mistress in all Christendom, trade'. In a long speech containing historical references to Henry V and Renaissance Italy, Ashley Cooper took a different view.[2] He was against referring the matter to the Protector and his Council to decide, because that might imply war, 'and doth it not signify that you will have no regard to treaties and amities, but merely to interest of state? If you will begin a war, it must be upon clear grounds . . . the justness of the quarrel stated. . . .' In his view the Swedes and not the Danes were the aggressors, and the Dutch would be perfectly justified in coming to the aid of their allies. Moreover Swedish control over the Sound would be much more dangerous than Danish or even Dutch, because the Swede was more warlike. 'He may overrun Spain, Denmark, Pomerania, Italy, and make himself master of this part of the world.' This last preposterous statement he defended by saying that the Swede's Viking predecessors 'overran the whole world'. Finally he linked the issue of foreign policy with the struggle over the constitution, arguing that the House should retain control over the power of war and peace in a way which suggested that the domestic issue was probably his real concern.[3]

It is surprising to find this attack on 'interest of state' and this support of international morality on the lips of the statesman who co-operated in the attack on the Dutch in 1672, and equally to find the author of the famous *Delenda est Carthago* speech of 1673 so tolerant of the Dutch in 1659. But the speech is interesting in other ways too, for it is typical of all his speeches recorded in this session. Its arguments are coolly rational, not buoyed up by attempts to arouse emotional or religious prejudice; its illustrations are drawn not from the Bible nor the classics but from history; its aim was to cut through tangled irrelevancies in order to reach the

---

[1] Burton, iii. 370, iv. 158; *C.J.* viii. 614.

[2] Though his view of the situation in the Baltic was not basically very far removed from the official policy of the Protectorate. See M. Roberts's article, 'Cromwell and the Baltic', in *E.H.R.* (1961), pp. 402–46.

[3] Burton, iii. 465–71.

essential principles involved. Less prepossessing was the tendency to spoil a good argument by pressing it to absurd extremes, for, ignorant as many Englishmen were of Sweden, it is difficult to take seriously his picture of the results of helping Sweden. In this session much of his mental make-up is laid bare; it remains to be seen which of the characteristics there revealed were to be modified and which confirmed by the added experience which the years would bring.

CHAPTER VII

THE APPRENTICE CONSPIRATOR (1659–60)

> Power was his aim: but thrown from that pretence
> The wretch turned loyal in his own defence,
> And malice reconciled him to his Prince.
> *The Medal*

I had rather live under a regulated and well-bounded King ... than under any government with Tyrannie.—*John Lilburne*

THE twelve months which followed the dissolution of the last Protectorate Parliament on 22 April 1659, saw one of the most complete reversals of fortune in English history. At their beginning all parties had their hopes and their fears; but not the most naïvely optimistic Royalist nor the most gloomily pessimistic Republican could have foreseen that Charles II would return unopposed at their end. It was natural that conscientious supporters of the Commonwealth like Ludlow and Hutchinson who saw the abrupt collapse of the Good Old Cause and the ruin of their personal fortunes should have extremely hostile opinions of former colleagues like Ashley Cooper, who not only survived this cataclysm but emerged from it with a title and office. Ludlow, looking back on Ashley Cooper's record, concluded that he was already a secret Royalist in the spring of 1659, that his activities were treacherous throughout, and that he aimed at reducing everything to confusion so that the King would benefit.[1] On the other hand, Tory writers in or after the Exclusion crisis claimed that his true sympathies were always Republican, and that his conversion to the Restoration was late and insincere and aimed only at self-preservation.[2] Which was right? or is there some more creditable explanation? At what point, and from what motives, did he decide that the King's return would be preferable to a continuation of the Commonwealth?

There can be no doubt that in the spring of 1659 the Royalists already entertained hopes of winning Ashley Cooper back, and the Republicans suspicions of his treachery. This seems, however, to have been the natural outcome of Ashley Cooper's relationship to his former Royalist father-in-law, Coventry, and his present Royalist uncle-in-law, Southampton, combined with his vehement opposition to the Protectorate; and if he had been a Royalist once, might he not become one again? There is, however, no evidence of any positive action on Ashley Cooper's part at

---

[1] E.g. *Memoirs*, ed. C. H. Firth (1894), ii. 83, 85, 116, 155.
[2] E.g. Roger North, *Examen* (1740), p. 41.

this point which would justify these ideas; and what he actually did is a more reliable guide than the opinions he was merely reputed to hold.

The dissolution of Parliament which the army officers had compelled was followed within a fortnight by their decision to recall the Rump which Cromwell had expelled in 1653. This was a surprising solution, because it should have been obvious that the Republicans who had suffered at the hands of the Army in 1653 and had spoken out against military influence in the recent session would inevitably seek to subject the Army to their control; and this the army grandees would in the last resort be unwilling to accept. But there was no satisfactory alternative. It was impossible to risk a free Parliament under the old franchise, for that would have brought in a Royalist or Presbyterian majority; none of the grandees now sympathized with Leveller solutions; and none of the theoretical constitutions which were being bandied about had any hope of commanding agreement. The Rump had, after all, been reasonably successful in the way it had conducted the Good Old Cause; it had at least a dubious air of legality about it; and secret conversations had led Lambert and some of his colleagues to believe that Vane and others might look sympathetically on their claims for more pay, might provide the sort of political and religious solutions that they wanted, and would in time be prepared to give way to a more representative body. The Rump might provide settled government, and it might at least vote some taxes. Accordingly, on 7 May, Speaker Lenthall led his band of former colleagues back into St. Stephen's, in smaller numbers than they had been before, but even more conscious of their right to be there and to govern the country. It was not long before Richard Cromwell quietly disappeared from the scene.[1]

There is no evidence that Ashley Cooper took part in any of the conversations which preceded the recall of the Rump; but afterwards he took immediate action in order to take part in the new régime. Two days later, on 9 May, he attempted to enter the Rump, by reviving yet again his old claim to sit for the borough of Downton. Nineteen years after the election had taken place, there were still those who contested it; the matter was shelved once more by referring it to a committee which never reported. Ludlow states frankly that 'we could find no better way to put him off (so far had he insinuated into the members)' than this, and those who distrusted his loyalty revealed their suspicions in this way.[2] Four days later, however, Ashley Cooper's supporters were more successful in another attempt. The House decided to appoint a Council of State consisting of thirty-one members to form an Executive. Ten of these were to be non-members of the House, and at the end of the afternoon of 19 May seven of these were chosen. Fairfax was complimented by being selected first (he never took his seat); Lambert, Desborough and Berry were rewarded

---

[1] Cf. Godfrey Davies, *The Restoration of Charles II, 1658–1660* (1955), ch. vi.
[2] *C.J.* vii. 646; Ludlow, *Memoirs*, ii. 85.

for their part in bringing back the Rump, and Bradshaw, who had presided over the Court of Justice in 1649, was an equally obvious fifth. Then a London merchant named Love suddenly proposed Ashley Cooper, in consideration (says Ludlow) of his activities in the last Parliament, 'though his affections were well known to be to another interest', and Neville proposed Sir Horatio Townshend, 'which two motions being upon the rising of the House made on a sudden before any could recollect themselves to speak against them . . . were consented to'.[1]

Townshend, whose father had been a Cavalier, was already so much of a Royalist that he went into the country to avoid sitting on the Council, and attempts were made to induce Ashley Cooper to follow the same course in order to avoid making the Army suspicious of the new régime. To this, however, Ashley Cooper would not consent; he appeared in the Council and boldly asked for the oath of loyalty to the Commonwealth 'without a single person, kingship or house of peers' to be administered to him. His colleague in the opposition in the previous Parliament, Thomas Scot, attempted to remove him by declaring that one of his spies had sent him word of a correspondence between Ashley Cooper and Charles II's principal minister, Hyde. Ashley Cooper vigorously denied this, 'and his expressions were so high, that they bred in some the more suspicion of him: but at this time he was believed', the more so because Scot made the mistake of attacking Bulstrode Whitelocke at the same time, and because it turned out that the source of his information against both was only 'a beggarly Irish friar'. Ashley Cooper was therefore allowed to take his seat on the Council of State, even though some of its other members were distrustful of him.[2]

Nevertheless, his protestations were sincere, for in this same month he rejected Royalist approaches to him. Charles wrote a second personal letter, which made no more impression than his earlier letter of 1655. Ashley Cooper courteously remarked to the agent who carried it, that he knew he had gone too far to expect the King's forgiveness, and had heard that his estates were forfeited and given away to Hyde. Hyde, when he received Mordaunt's report, recognized this for the evasion it was; it simply meant that Ashley Cooper was giving a polite refusal, not a rude rebuff. If he had been a mere time-server, he ought to have taken this obvious opportunity to reinsure his political future, but instead he neglected it. Another Royalist agent in England, Brodrick, a man of far more reckless optimism than Mordaunt, wrote enthusiastically that Ashley Cooper had engaged to provide three or four hundred horse in Dorset for the projected rebellion; but since the same letter refers to an entirely imaginary correspondence between Lambert and Charles, this letter can

---

[1] *C.J.* vii. 652; Ludlow, op. cit. ii. 83. It was perhaps because Ashley Cooper was elected to the Council as a non-Parliamentarian that the committee never reported on the Downton case.
[2] Ludlow, op. cit. ii. 85; Whitelocke, *Memorials* (1682), p. 680.

H

be taken only as an example of the delusions which kept up the flagging spirits of the Royalists. The last word here belongs to Mordaunt, who noted with disgust that 'Sir A. A. Cooper is rotten and sits' on the Council.[1]

He did indeed sit on the Council during the month of June 1659, and the natural explanation is that at this time he still regarded the Rump and its Council of State as the best possible, or perhaps the least objectionable, political solution. The suggestion that he took part in the work of the Council merely in order to foment trouble between the Rump and the Army[2] is impossible to credit, in view of what follows. He did his share of the committee work, helping to meet foreign ambassadors and, using his growing circle of acquaintances in the City, persuading the East India Company to lend £15,000 in the government's dire need of ready money.[3] Nevertheless, his position must have been an awkward one; he was distrusted by some of his colleagues, and he was not, like most of them, a member of the Rump, where the really important issues were debated. This was a serious disadvantage.

At the same time it became steadily clearer that the Rump had no more prospect of commanding wide support in the country than Richard Cromwell's Protectorate had had. Fewer than a hundred members commonly took part in debates, and some of those who had been forcibly secluded by Pride's Purge in 1648 were again refused permission to enter when they tried to do so. A promise not to sit beyond May 1660 did not make the Rump seem any less unrepresentative in the meantime. Failing to win over outsiders, the members quarrelled among themselves and with their natural supporters in the Army, who discovered to their dismay that the Rump which they had reinstalled to protect them was inevitably trying to bring them under its control. The Act of Indemnity which was passed did not satisfy their expectations, and the decision that all officers should hold their commissions from the Speaker had as an inevitable corollary that officers of whom the Rump disapproved could be dismissed. Nor could the Rump do anything to cope with the Army's arrears of pay, which mounted steadily every month. While dissatisfaction grew in all ranks of the Army, the members of the Council began to differ in their attitude towards it: Haslerig, stiff and uncompromising as ever, sought to maintain civilian control over the Army at all costs, and even though the more acutely observant Vane saw that something must be done to avoid losing the military support on which they depended, 'jealous and hot words' passed between Fleetwood and him.[4] Cracks were appearing in the front presented

---

[1] Hyde to Mordaunt, 3/13 June and 23 June/3 July; Brodrick to Hyde, 23 May, and Mordaunt to Hyde, 16 June, in *Clarendon State Papers* (1786), iii. 488, 512, 477–8, 490.

[2] Ludlow, op. cit. ii. 85.

[3] The Council's Minutes at this time are in the Bodleian Library, MSS. Rawlinson. C 179.

[4] *Diary of Sir Archibald Johnston of Wariston*, vol. iii (Scottish History Society, 1940), ed. J. D. Ogilvie, p. 123.

by the Commonwealthsmen, and a further military *coup d'état* became more and more probable.

If Ashley Cooper had been the deliberate trouble-maker depicted by Ludlow, he would have revelled in this situation; but instead he left the Council and retired to his home at Wimborne. The date of his last appearance on the Council was July 11 at a season when a politician could naturally withdraw for a spell to become the country gentleman on his estates; but the fact that he remained there for six weeks and did not return until he was arrested and compelled to do so, even though a rebellion had broken out in the meantime, suggests that his retirement was the result of some dissatisfaction or disillusionment. The possibility that this had already gone so far that he sympathized with the Royalist rebellion may be ruled out, because there is no hint of it in any Royalist correspondence at the time. It was natural, however, that he should be under suspicion, for, apart from his Royalist relatives, he had been friendly with Sir George Booth, who on 31 July appeared in the field in Cheshire, demanding explicitly a free Parliament, and implicitly a Royalist restoration. One Major James Dewey, who had sat in the previous Parliament for Wareham, picked up one or two hints which might serve as a justification for questioning Ashley Cooper. A boy named Nicholas testified that he had carried a letter from Booth to Ashley Cooper, and been civilly received, though nothing was known of what the letter contained; and a neighbour reported a dinner-table conversation at Wimborne St. Giles, in which, discussing the latest news of Booth's rising, Ashley Cooper had remarked that 'he knew Booth when they were Parliament men together, and was sorry he had undertaken the present business; also that he was a Presbyterian, and accounted an honest man, and reported 5,000 strong'. To the discerning the terms of this remark should have indicated that Ashley Cooper was not conspiring with Booth; but on this, the scantiest of evidence, Major Dewey had him arrested. The Council itself evidently thought the evidence thin, for they ordered his release and merely wrote inviting him to come to London and submit to questioning. A committee consisting of more than half the Council's members investigated and reported on 12 September completely acquitting him. Two days later Neville, on behalf of the Council, passed on this resolution to Parliament, which accepted it without a division. If anyone had any reservations, these were kept silent, and were indeed unjustified. It is significant that the arrest and release attracted no comment on the Royalist side.[1]

Thus exonerated, Ashley Cooper resumed his seat on the Council, but the Council's own days were now numbered. The inevitable conflict between Haslerig and the civilian politicians who formed a majority in

[1] Bayley, op. cit. pp. 383–5; *Calendar of Clarendon State Papers*, iv, ed. F. J. Routledge (1932), pp. 315–48; *C.S.P.D. 1659–60*, pp. 140, 143, 155, 184, 189; Ludlow, op. cit. ii. 116; *C.J.* vii. 768, 778.

Council and Rump on the one hand, and the Wallingford House group of army grandees on the other, had been postponed by the need for common action against Booth; but when the danger of rebellion had receded, they were free to quarrel again. Lambert and other officers who had been concerned in putting down the rising returned self-confident and at the same time resentful that their efforts were not better rewarded. Their petitions to Parliament were interpreted as being threatening, and finally on 12 October, the members, perhaps hoping for help from Monk and the Army in Scotland, brought their own doom upon them by depriving Lambert, Desborough and other officers of their commissions, dismissing Fleetwood from his position as commander-in-chief, and resting the command instead in seven commissioners, of whom Fleetwood was one but Haslerig was another. Lambert had already been threatened with the Tower by Haslerig, recklessly uncompromising to the last; and the predictable result was that next morning Lambert's men stopped the Speaker from entering Palace Yard and brought the Rump's session to an abrupt and arbitrary end. At one time there appeared to be a possibility that Colonel Morley's regiment would obey Haslerig's orders and defend their occupation of Westminster Hall, but in the end they dispersed without bloodshed, refusing to fire on their colleagues in the Good Old Cause.

Unable to meet as a Parliament, the Republicans remained a majority on the Council of State and could still pose as the rightful executive of the country. Ashley Cooper was one of the councillors who met on 14 October and sought to order the Army officers to withdraw from Westminster and to permit the Rump to meet again; and on the following day he and others rejected a proposal that the Council should adjourn until the end of November. These were only empty gestures of defiance, and Ashley Cooper, Haslerig, Neville and others recognized this by not returning to any other Council meeting. Other members continued to sit until the 25th, after which the council of officers nominated a Committee of Safety of twenty-three members to replace it.[1]

Thus once more Ashley Cooper rejected the possibility of clinging to power (for he could have joined the Committee of Safety, as did Sir Henry Vane, seeing here the best chance for the Good Old Cause) in favour of taking part in a determined opposition to the all-powerful military régime. He threw in his lot with Scot, Haslerig, Neville, Morley and four others who continued to meet in secret, claiming to be the rightful Council of State still. It does not necessarily follow that he desired the recall of the Rump for its own sake, as did Haslerig; but in the circumstances of October 1659 the Rump's return represented the overthrow of military rule, and the return of at least a form of constitutional government. It was the most

---

[1] For these events, cf. Godfrey Davies, op. cit. pp. 144–58; *C.S.P.D. 1659–60*, pp. 251, 253; *Diary of Sir Archibald Johnston of Wariston*, vol. iii (Scottish History Society, 1940), ed. J. D. Ogilvie, pp. 143–6.

practical basis on which to rally opposition to the new Committee of Safety, because many who were not convinced supporters of the Rump might yet accept it as a stepping-stone towards further changes. It is impossible to say precisely what eventual solution Ashley Cooper contemplated at this moment, and likely enough that he was concentrating on the immediate objective of breaking the power of the army grandees. At all events, he now betook himself to conspiracy, with all its risks and excitements.

There were several directions in which the opposition could look for the support they needed to overthrow the new military government. They could look to Scotland, and investigate the possibility of calling in Monk and his army against Lambert and Fleetwood; they could seek to tamper with key garrisons, such as those in Portsmouth and the Tower of London; they could seek to mobilize the growing discontent of all classes in the City of London; they could look to the fleet in the mouth of the Thames under its commander, John Lawson. Of these, Monk was obviously the most important for he was the popular and uncontested leader of a substantial number of troops. A professional soldier, competent but unimaginative, completely unsubtle, tossed about by no wind of doctrine, he was able to maintain a sphinx-like pose all the better because he did not yet know the answer to the riddle himself. So far as his personal aims were concerned, he had no ambitions to wield political power, wanting only a position which would give enough honour and wealth to satisfy the covetousness of his wife; and though he was animated by a certain bluff, soldierly patriotism, and was anxious to see a settled government established, he had no clear idea how this was to be done except for the general belief, by no means universal among soldiers of that or any other period, that soldiers ought to obey a civilian authority. His reaction to the news of the expulsion of the Rump was therefore one of disapproval, manifested immediately in letters to Fleetwood, Lambert and Lenthall. However, in answer to Fleetwood's appeal, he agreed to send three commissioners, Colonel Timothy Wilkes, Lieutenant-Colonel John Clobery and Colonel Ralph Knight, to discuss matters in London.

These three commissioners reached London and by 15 November had made an agreement in which they went considerably beyond their instructions. Instead of insisting on the return of the Rump they accepted the summons of a Parliament under new arrangements to be fixed with the approval of a general council of officers representing the whole Army and Navy. The qualifications of members of this new Parliament would be fixed by a committee on which members of the Army's Committee of Safety were a majority, and it was plain that what was contemplated was a Parliament arranged by the officers and willing to fit in with their requirements, not one which would provide effective control over them. Having unwisely agreed to this, on the following day the commissioners nevertheless agreed to meet Ashley Cooper and Haslerig, on behalf of the secret council of nine. In a private room at the Fleece Tavern, in Covent Garden, Ashley Cooper and Haslerig put their case in the way they thought most likely to appeal to Monk. First they suggested that the best which Monk could hope for from co-operation with Fleetwood and the rest was 'to be gently laid aside, and then ruined with some more artifice and caution than other men', whereas if he declared for the recall of the Rump he was certain to be made commander-in-chief. To this they added a practical argument of a different kind. They claimed to have a wide measure of secret support from 'a great correspondence and interest with the inferior officers and common soldiers of every troop and company' stationed near London, thus exploiting the difference of interest between the grandees and the rank and file; and in addition they had the important garrison of Portsmouth 'at our devotion', and secret promises of assistance from Vice-Admiral Lawson and from Fairfax. Their party, they insisted, was stronger than it might appear. To judge from Ashley Cooper's later account of these conversations no time was spent on defending the abstract justice of their cause; but the practical considerations were sufficient to convince Clobery and Knight, though not Wilkes (the most extreme of the commissioners) that the secret council's plans promised better than the agreement just signed with the Army's Committee of Safety. Whether Clobery and Knight's accounts of these conversations persuaded Monk to find reasons for evading this agreement it is impossible to say; it is likely enough that he would in any case have persisted with his declared intention to secure the return of the Rump. Yet at the very least such information must have helped him to pursue his course, and equally the letter which all nine members of the secret council wrote to him, followed by their commission appointing him commander-in-chief of all forces in England and Scotland, supplied him with any constitutional trappings which he needed for his intervention. Authorized to march into any part of England and destroy any forces hostile to Parliament, he proceeded with his preparations to cross the Tweed.[1]

While they were waiting for Monk, Ashley Cooper and the other members of the secret council of nine sought to win over others to their cause. The important garrison of Portsmouth was one of the government's vulnerable points, since its commander, Colonel Whetham, was not loyal to the new military régime. He was Ashley Cooper's 'friend and very long acquaintance', and John Locke tells a story, probably derived from his patron, that one day when the two men met by chance in Westminster Hall Ashley Cooper asked Whetham whether he would put Portsmouth into his hands if he should happen to have an occasion for it? Whetham promised that he would, and on 3 December he welcomed into Portsmouth

---

[1] Godfrey Davies, op cit., ch. x; Sir R. Baker, *Chronicle* (1684), pp. 670–3; *Clarke Papers*, ed. C. H. Firth, (1901), iv. 63–141; Ashley Cooper's account in Christie, i. 195–6. It should be noted that Ashley Cooper's account was a description of his own activities in these events, not a historical narrative of the period; hence the frequent use of the first person is not so egotistical as it might appear.

Haslerig, Morley and another member of the council of nine. Ashley Cooper was not with them, however, perhaps because he had important business in the capital, where an attempt on the Tower itself was being planned.[1]

In London Ashley Cooper had received a commission to command all the forces there which were expected to revolt against the Army's Committee of Safety. In after-life the memory of this commission evidently gave him some amusement, for as general he had not one soldier, and his concern was to hide the commission where no hostile eye could see it. He was under such suspicion that he was arrested and taken to Wallingford House to appear before General Fleetwood. The meeting between the two men gave Ashley Cooper a further pleasant recollection of the way in which he outwitted his interrogator. The examination was not a particularly terrifying one, for Fleetwood was not by temperament an inquisitor, but 'naturally an obliging man' in Ashley Cooper's own phrase; indeed the interview is one more example of his pathetic inadequacy for the situation in which he found himself. He suspected Ashley Cooper of planning to raise the standard of revolt in the western counties of Dorset and Wiltshire where his estates lay. Since Ashley Cooper's plots concerned not the West but London, he was able to assure Fleetwood upon his word and honour that this was not so, thus continuing to be deceitful without telling a direct lie. He went further, and offered to give Fleetwood his parole not to leave London without the general's permission, and left a free man, smiling up his sleeve with characteristic self-satisfaction. He was not, however, out of danger, for other officers realized what a mistake Fleetwood had made. Returning home to his house in Covent Garden at ten o'clock the following night, he found a man knocking at his door. After they had discussed some trivial piece of business, the stranger said good-night and turned back from the entry in which they stood into the street, while Ashley Cooper made as if to go into his house. No sooner was the stranger out of sight, however, than Ashley Cooper also turned back into the street and went to his barber's home near by. This proved to be a shrewd move, for the stranger was an officer who had a file of soldiers waiting nearby at the corner of the Half Moon Tavern, and the conversation had been his way of making sure that Ashley Cooper was at home. The soldiers broke into the house, and, unable to understand how their man had escaped, ran their swords into the hangings and broke open boxes and trunks in their search for papers. Lady Cooper was badly frightened, the more because her little seven-year-old stepson was lying ill of small-pox at the time; but the searchers did not find her husband's incriminating commission, nor Ashley Cooper himself. He slipped away into the City, and remained there in hiding and disguise for some days. In all probability his life had not been

[1] Christie, i. 196; Locke, *Works* (1823), ix. 275. The name Metham printed in Locke's *Works* is evidently the result of a misreading of Locke's capital letter.

at stake, for the Wallingford House officers were not a bloodthirsty set of men; but such incidents test a man's nerve, and the man who surmounts such a test naturally has his self-esteem enhanced.[1]

He was not idle in his new hiding-place in the City. He and some of his colleagues had arranged with the Lieutenant of the Tower, Colonel Fitch, that early on the morning of Monday, 12 December, he should open the gate of the Tower, to allow him to leave in his coach. Colonel Okey and his men, waiting in readiness nearby, would seize this opportunity, rush the gate, and seize the Tower in the interests of the secret Council of State. The scheme does not sound very convincing, and the attempt was never actually made because, warned by the Lord Mayor, Desborough went to the Tower, and arrested and replaced Fitch. But even this failure could be turned to some account, for it could be made the occasion for a propagandist appeal seeking to exploit the mounting discontent of Londoners and the growing demoralization of the troops.

The council of army grandees at Wallingford House had never been popular in London. More and more it seemed that their arbitrary intervention in politics had been only in their own interests. It was difficult to find any kind of theoretical or practical justification for the régime of the Committee of Safety, and in the winter of 1659–60 unsettled political conditions went hand-in-hand with a serious trade depression. Amongst the more well-to-do classes hatred of a revolutionary situation in which it was difficult to plan for the future was restrained by fear of provoking the 'swordsmen' to intervene in the City. On 9 November an attempt by Scot and Ashley Cooper to induce the Common Council to petition for a restoration of the Long Parliament had failed.[2] But the apprentices and 'young men that were newly out of their times', living nearer the poverty line, were more immediately affected by the slump, more scornful of 'the Committee of Shifty' and, perhaps encouraged by some of their employers, less patient. Many petty insults culminated in the riot of 5 December, when they vented their feelings on the troops of one-eyed Colonel Hewson, whom they despised as an 'old blind cobbler' whose low birth gave him no better right to command than themselves. The troops were pelted with old shoes and turnip-tops, brickbats and tiles and lumps of ice, and inevitably in the end they retaliated by firing. Yet the troops themselves cannot have been unaffected by all this. It is never pleasant to be jeered at and pelted by the ordinary people for whom one claims to be fighting, more especially when one's pay is months in arrears and only the officers seem to be prospering.

---

[1] Christie, i. 197–8; Locke, op. cit. ix. 275–7. Locke is mistaken in writing that Lambert was in London at this time, but this does not invalidate the essentials of his story, which accord well enough with Shaftesbury's own account and were obviously derived from him.

[2] *Diary of Sir Archibald Johnston of Wariston*, vol. iii (Scottish History Society, 1940), ed. J. D. Ogilvie, p. 152.

This was an ideal situation for the propagandist, and already on 16 November *The Remonstrance and Protestation of the Well-Affected People of the Cities of London and Westminster, and Other the Cities and Places within the Commonwealth of England* had appeared, protesting against the 'interruption' of Parliament by the swordsmen, and complaining that Englishmen suffered from the greatest oppression that ever poor freeborn people lay under. The authorship of this is uncertain, and Ashley Cooper was only one of some four hundred and fifty people 'men of quality' whose names were appended, along with Fairfax, Wildman, Monk, Lawson and a great variety of others. The remonstrance is however interesting because of the representative character which it claimed; the names included the Lord Mayor and Common Council of London, 'and out of every city and town that was in any account four or five person[s] of quality. . . . This did look as if it [had] been the truest thing in the world.' Whether Ashley Cooper had any hand in drawing it up or not, the tract invites comparison with the addresses which were sent up in the Exclusion crisis in 1679–80.

The failure of the attempt on the Tower gave occasion for another pamphlet, in the composition of which Ashley Cooper was certainly directly concerned. This took the form of an 'open letter' to Fleetwood from Ashley Cooper, Scot, Josias Berners and John Weaver, in which they admitted and defended their attempt to seize the Tower, since true legal authority over all garrisons belonged to the Council of State of which they were members, and not to any 'single person, junto, or pack of men at Whitehall or Wallingford House'. To appeal to the common prejudice against soldiers, they used the episode of Ashley Cooper's own attempted arrest—the 'sending for one of our number by a party of soldiers, as if red coats and muskets were a *non obstante* to all laws and public privilege'. They taunted Fleetwood with 'the shame you have brought upon God's people', 'the breach of faith to the Parliament from whom you have received your commission', and 'the misery you have led the poor soldiers into, who, instead of being the instruments of renewing and settling the peace and liberty of these nations, enjoying the honour and quiet thereof, their arrears fully paid, future pay and advancement settled and established in order and with the blessing of their countrymen, are now become the instruments of nine men's[1] ambition, have made the whole nation their enemies, and are exposed again to the hardship and hazard of a new unnatural war'. This skilful playing on the doubts and distrusts of the common soldier was followed by an appeal to them to regard Monk as a divinely sent deliverer, in spite of all aspersions upon him, 'being warranted in his present actings by especial commission and authority from the

---

[1] Probably, as Christie suggests, the nine officers, led by Lambert and Desborough, who had promoted an address hostile to the Rump, and been cashiered for it just before its dissolution. Cf. Godfrey Davies, op. cit. p. 151.

Council of State, whereas yours [Fleetwood's] is that only of the sword'. Finally, they dismissed the new Parliament which the Committee of Safety had promised to call as a puppet body 'whose liberty and safety either of meeting or debating must be at your pleasure', and whose members would be nothing but 'your assessors and tax-gatherers'. Rather 'the present interrupted Parliament' (the Rump) was the sole lawful authority, and the one 'which can only be hoped to make the sword subservient to the civil interest, and settle the government in the hands of the people by successive and free parliaments unlawfully denied to them'.[1]

Ashley Cooper was the first of the four to sign the document, ahead even of Scot, who was nominally President of the secret Council of State. The reference to his own escape, and perhaps that to 'successive and free parliaments', suggests his hand rather than that of Scot, for whom free parliaments were not urgent; and the document has the sharp thrust at the enemy's vulnerable points which was characteristic at all times of Ashley Cooper. It is impossible to assess how considerable was its effect upon its readers; no doubt it did not produce a sharp change in public opinion, but only contributed to intensify a mood which was already present. But it can safely be said that all this was part of the store of varied experience on which he could draw when another critical and confused situation arose in the days of Exclusion.

All these events taken together helped to demoralize the officers at Wallingford House. With their forces under Lambert in the North disintegrating and plainly reluctant to fight against Monk, they had the news that the troops sent to recapture Portsmouth had gone over to Haslerig, and that other places too had declared for 'a free Parliament', among them Lyme and Poole in Ashley Cooper's own county of Dorset.[2] In the capital they were violently unpopular, and most of them can have had little real conviction of the justice of their cause. Another blow came when Vice-Admiral Lawson brought his fleet into the Thames, declared with his captains for the return of the Rump, and rejected all Vane's efforts to persuade him that the best way of preserving the 'good old cause' was by co-operating with the army grandees.[3] Fleetwood's nerve, never very strong, completely failed him, and the power of the grandees, apparently so overwhelming only a month or two earlier, collapsed with remarkable

---

[1] Ludlow, op. cit. ii. 169; J. V[ernon] to Col. John Jones, 12 Dec., in *Calendar of Clarendon State Papers*, iv. ed. F. J. Routledge (1932), p. 481; *The Diurnal of Thomas Rugg, 1659–1661*, ed. W. L. Sachse (Royal Historical Society, 1961), pp. 9–15. For the letter to Fleetwood, see Christie, i, App. V, pp. lxxiv–lxxvii, or *Somers Tracts* (1811), vi. 542–4.

[2] J. S[haw] to Hyde, 15/25 Dec., in *Calendar of Clarendon State Papers*, iv. 483.

[3] Vane was forestalled by three opposition spokesmen who boarded Lawson's ship first. Clarendon (*Rebellion*, vi. 159) states that these three were 'Sir Anthony Ashley Cooper and two others, members of Parliament', but since Ashley Cooper makes no mention of this in his own account, it is more probable that they were Scot, Okey, and Streater, as stated in Granville Penn's *Memorials of Sir William Penn* (1833), ii. 186–91.

suddenness and completeness. On 23 December the troops themselves assembled in Lincoln's Inn Fields—one wonders how the rendezvous was arranged—and declared their resolve to live and die with the Parliament and to accept the orders of the Council of State. Then they marched into Chancery Lane and stopped before the house of the Speaker of the Long Parliament, William Lenthall; they submitted to him and departed obediently but noisily, loosing off volleys of shot. That evening Lenthall, Ashley Cooper and three others visited the Lord Mayor and informed him that the Rump of the Parliament would soon meet again. Their next step was to proceed to the Tower and accept the submission of Major Miller, who had taken Fitch's place in command there. Lenthall formally nominated Ashley Cooper, Berners and Weaver, three of the four who had planned the attack a fortnight earlier, to serve as commissioners, and then departed, leaving £20 for the guards to have a drink. Thus another revolution was accomplished, remarkably without bloodshed.[1]

Ashley Cooper had taken his full share in the risks of the previous two months, and this was reflected in some of the orders which the Rump made after resuming its sessions on 26 December. He was one of the seven commissioners given temporary control over the armed forces until the return to London of Haslerig and two others, the survivors of a previous commission of seven appointed in October. Acting with urgency, Ashley Cooper and his colleagues sent orders the same night, informing Lambert's officers in the north of the change and carefully instructing them to march to new quarters in suitably dispersed directions. On the 28th his new-found authority disappeared with the arrival of Haslerig post-haste, and his temporary authority over the Tower lasted only until 7 January, when his friend Colonel Morley was made Lieutenant there. But there were ample compensations. On 2 January Parliament voted for a new Council of State, and of the ten non-members for whom the House voted, Ashley Cooper received the largest number of votes, ahead even of Monk and Fairfax, instead of sneaking in just before the adjournment as he had done previously in May. Three days later his friends in the House secured the appointment of a committee to examine the rights and wrongs of the Downton election, and this time the committee reported with exemplary speed. On 7 January, 1660, he took his seat. It was just over nineteen years since, as a young man of nineteen, he had stood for election in the little Wiltshire borough, in those long-distant days before the flood of civil war and revolution had begun to submerge the traditional landmarks. Now, as a middle-aged man of 38, he was to watch the waters recede.[2]

The Rump had no sooner returned to St. Stephen's than its sixty members found themselves as unpopular as Fleetwood and his fellow-officers had been. Most of those who had clamoured for its return had done

<hr />

[1] *The Diurnal of Thomas Rugg, 1659–1661*, ed. W. L. Sachse (1961), p. 22; *Public Intelligencer*, 19–26 Dec. 1659.   [2] *C.J.* vii. 797, 801, 804–5; Christie, i. 198–9.

so only as a means of getting rid of the Army's Committee of Safety, and not because of any passionate devotion to the Rump itself. There was a loud demand that the Rump, instead of restricting its membership to those who had taken the Republican Engagement of 1649, should readmit those members who had been secluded in that and the previous year. To some this was mere justice, to convert an oligarchy into a representative Parliament; but to many the readmission of the secluded members would be a means to get the Rump to dissolve itself, so that a new and free Parliament could be elected which would vote for the return of the King. Not all those who were beginning to contemplate a Restoration wanted an unconditional one, for there were 'Presbyterians' who thought of imposing on Charles II terms such as those put forward to Charles I in the so-called Treaty of Newport in 1648; but the demands for a free Parliament which began to roll in from the provinces were naturally supported whenever possible by Royalists who rightly thought it the best way to secure their aims. The Rump, however, made no concessions to these feelings. Vane was expelled as a punishment for his co-operation with the grandees, but the majority under Haslerig, Scot, Neville and their colleagues were unwavering. On 27 December some of the secluded members who tried to take their seats were prevented from doing so, and on 3 January the House voted to fill itself up, not by readmitting them, but by ordering new elections on some unspecified date and with qualifications to be decided for the new members. A Bill was introduced, disabling those of different political views from voting or being elected. The Rump plainly meant to perpetuate itself. By the middle of January pamphlet attacks upon it had begun to appear in large numbers. In the succinct words of a diarist, 'There was those that made very jeering things against the Parliament's Rump and had them printed and gave them away for nothing to poor girls for to sell, the more because they was forbid'.[1]

For some time contemporaries were unsure of Ashley Cooper's attitude to this situation. In November he had professed his devotion to the Commonwealth 'so to the life' that even his enemy Ludlow was temporarily convinced. Those members of the Rump who elected him to the Council of State presumably did so because they thought he would support their cause, and when he took his seat for Downton he once more subscribed to the Engagement to be faithful to the Commonwealth. When an additional clause renouncing Charles Stuart was put to the members of the Council of State, he was one of the majority who declined to take it[2]; but this does not necessarily mean more than that, like so impeccable a Republican as

---

[1] Godfrey Davies, op. cit. pp. 256–9; *Diurnal of Thomas Rugg*, p. 28; *C.J.* vii. 803, 806–7.

[2] Sir R. Baker, *Chronicle* (1684), p. 678. It is possible that he never attended the Council of State; certainly the table of attendances in *C.S.P.D. 1659–60*, p. xxv shows him always as missing, though this table is compiled only from the names of those who signed letters and warrants (ibid. xxi–xxii). But cf. p. 127 below.

Colonel Hutchinson, he would not commit himself to unequivocal resistance in all circumstances. He still made no attempt to secure his future by entering into any correspondence with the exiled Court. His Royalist relatives sought to find plausible excuses for his behaviour, but 'Will Sir Anthony Ashley Cooper ever serve the King?' wrote Hyde plaintively in mid-January. Hyde was frankly baffled by Ashley Cooper; he could not understand why he should be so 'mad' when he was related through his wife to 'one of the most worthy persons of the nation' (Southampton); in spite of his past record he had done nothing which he could not forgive himself or from which he could not retreat. Why did he not take the sensible course in good time? In the meantime, Royalists in England were very wary of him.[1]

Nevertheless in this same month of January there were signs that Ashley Cooper had parted company with Haslerig, Scot, Neville and their brand of Republicanism. The Royalist agent Mordaunt reported the growth of two diametrically opposite parties in the Rump: one party of twenty-three with Ashley Cooper, 'who acts Cicero', and some sixteen with Neville, 'who represents Anthony'. Neville, we are told, 'argues for liberty in so general a sense, that he is *de nouveau* concluded an atheist'. Morley and Weaver are reported as combining with Ashley Cooper in these debates, but unfortunately no parliamentary diaries exist to enable us to penetrate further into them: a member who jotted down notes of speeches made at this time would have made himself rather unpopular. Unsympathetic observers paid left-handed compliments to Ashley Cooper's skill as a debater at this time: Mordaunt's comment was that he 'hath his tongue well hung, and words at will', and Ludlow referred more savagely to his 'smooth tongue and insinuating carriage', while Haslerig 'began to lose ground, and all that he said in the House or elsewhere to go for nothing'. Ludlow suffered once again from Ashley Cooper's parliamentary skill, for when the Council of State recommended that he and three colleagues should be given power over Ireland, Ashley Cooper, Weaver and others procured the adjournment of the debate for three days, thus giving time for a charge of high treason against Ludlow to be introduced. The upshot was that the House appointed commissioners for Ireland, led by Sir Charles Coote, who were more palatable to Monk and prepared to follow his lead in the days to come.[2] On other measures of the Rump there was more agreement, especially on the remodelling of the regiments to get rid of the officers who had supported the régime of the Committee of Safety. Contemporaries put the number of cashiered officers at 'near one

---

[1] Ludlow, op. cit. ii. 155; *C.J.* vii. 801, 805; *Memoirs of Colonel Hutchinson*, by Lucy Hutchinson (Everyman ed. 1908), p. 313; Brodrick to Hyde, 30 Dec., *Clarendon State Papers* (1786), iii. 637; Hyde to Brodrick, 13/23 Jan., *Calendar of Clarendon State Papers*, iv, ed. F. J. Routledge (1932), p. 517; Hyde to [Willoughby], 11/21 Feb., ibid. p. 557–8; [Major Wood] to John Shaw for [Hyde], 20 Jan., ibid. p. 525.

[2] Mordaunt to the King, 16 Jan., *Clarendon State Papers* (1786), iii. 650; Ludlow, op. cit. ii. 205–6, 209–11; *C.J.* vii. 815–16.

thousand' or even fifteen hundred, though this may have been an exaggeration. Thus Haslerig and his faction wreaked their revenge on their former enemies, while Ashley Cooper and others saw the Army being so drastically remodelled that it would not be able to organize any effective united opposition to the decisions which Monk would take. It is not without significance that Ashley Cooper himself was given Fleetwood's own former regiment, 'modelled it with officers for his turn', and when he sent a troop away on special service obtained pay for it in advance.[1]

In the meantime it became steadily clearer that the real issues must await the arrival of the *deus ex machina*, General Monk, slowly and deliberately descending on to the stage from the far North. Though the recall of the Rump had satisfied his main aim, he nevertheless marched southwards, greeted on his way by a succession of addresses from town and county appealing for a free Parliament: the suggestion has been made that these addresses had a common origin, possibly in William Prynne,[2] and whether this is so or not, they must have been in Shaftesbury's mind later at the time of the petitioning movement of 1679–80. None could tell what Monk would do when he arrived, but the Republicans feared the worst. In a last attempt to secure Ashley Cooper's co-operation, Haslerig and Scot offered him the command of the Army if he would march it against Monk. It is difficult to take this offer quite as seriously as he himself did when he related it in a fragment of autobiography, in view of Lambert's later failure; but his story is that he rejected the invitation, not as impractical (for Monk's army was small and the London regiments jealous of the 'Coldstreamers'), but because 'I had given General Monk my word to be his friend, and therefore could not break it; besides, I assured myself he was doing that that I and all good men prayed for, and therefore was not to be disturbed, but rather assisted by all that sincerely wished the public good'. This, he went on, underlining the lesson of a life-time of politics in a way which will surprise those who regard him as a selfish time-server, made him as unpopular with the Commonwealthsmen as Monk, 'or rather worse, inasmuch as principles are less reconcilable than interests'.[3]

The statement that Ashley Cooper had given his word to be Monk's friend indicates that the two men had been in touch before Monk arrived in London, but no correspondence survives except for one letter of the previous June when Monk was writing to many members of the Council of State.[4] It is unlikely, however, that they had reached any close understanding. In order to follow the course of events in the three weeks after

---

[1] *Diurnal of Thomas Rugg*, p. 30; Ludlow, op. cit. ii. 204–6; *C.J.* vii. 808, 815, 817; *C.S.P.D. 1659–60*, pp. 322, 591; Shaftesbury Papers I, 14. Wariston (*Diary*, ed. J. D. Ogilvie, iii. 174) has a curious statement that Ashley Cooper discovered two priests in Fleetwood's regiment. [2] D. Ogg, *England in the Reign of Charles II* (1934), i. 20, 26.
[3] Christie, i. 204–5.
[4] Ibid. i. 183–4. Monk sent Ashley Cooper his 'service' from Nottingham on 21 January (*Clarke Papers*, ed. C. H. Firth, Camden Society, 1901, iv. 251).

Monk's entry into London on 3 February, it is necessary to bear in mind that no-one could fathom what Monk was planning, and perhaps until the eleventh hour he did not know himself. A pamphlet *Pedigree and Descent of His Excellency General Monk* traced his ancestors back to King Edward III, and even earlier to that Richard, brother of Henry III, who had been King of the Romans. Such a pedigree existed to cater for those who anticipated that Monk would set up for himself; and those who thought on these lines suspected that he was being secretly encouraged by the French ambassador, as a counterpoise to the alliance between Charles II and Spain. There was no foundation for this, but it was a natural error. Shaftesbury, recollecting these critical days in old age, wrote that Monk 'treated at the same time with all sorts of men, and appointed a select number of several sorts to confer together . . . intermixing them as he thought fit, sometimes two, sometimes three parties together, keeping the world in a great uncertainty, and (if myself and others that were nearest him were not mistaken) himself too'.[1] Clarendon's view of Monk was not dissimilar: 'it is glory enough to his memory that he was instrumental in bringing those mighty things to pass, which he had neither wisdom to foresee, nor courage to attempt, nor understanding to continue.'[2]

The Rumpers themselves brought matters to a head. On 8 February the Common Council of the City of London received a petition which seemed to foreshadow a strike of taxpayers in the City until there was a representative Parliament. Later in the day, Ashley Cooper and his colleague Weaver were travelling in a coach along Fleet Street when they were stopped by an officer, who told them that an important meeting was evidently in progress in the Council Chamber, because the doors had been locked and guards posted to prevent anyone entering. Haslerig and his supporters had decided to take drastic action against the City; they wanted to quarter troops there, to unhinge the gates, wedge the portcullises and arrest eleven prominent citizens, and at the same time to embroil Monk with the City. They had therefore summoned a special meeting of the Council to press Monk to carry out these orders, and they had taken care to leave Ashley Cooper and other possible opponents uninvited. Hastening in their coach to Whitehall, Ashley Cooper and Weaver knocked at each of the doors of the Council Chamber in turn, but without effect; and they were no more successful when they enlisted the help of Mrs. Monk, for they could get no door opened and not even a word of answer to Mrs. Monk's knocks and calls for her husband. Baffled, they withdrew to Mrs. Monk's lodgings— no doubt Ashley Cooper used his opportunity to get on better terms with that redoubtable lady, who had considerable influence over her husband— and remained there until two o'clock in the morning, when the Council broke up and Monk reappeared. Confronted with a unanimous body of councillors who had called upon him to keep his promises to obey the

---

[1] Christie, i. 210.   [2] Clarendon, *Rebellion*, vi. 164.

lawful orders of the lawful authorities, and without Ashley Cooper or any-one else present to suggest an evasion, he had reluctantly agreed to take the action required against the City, and, having given his word, he would not go back on it in spite of all the appeals of Mrs. Monk, Ashley Cooper and Weaver. Next morning his troops appeared in the City and began their work of destruction, while Haslerig appeared in the House, triumphantly congratulating himself that Monk would after all obey the Rump's orders, and remarking: 'All is our own, he will be honest.' When a letter arrived from Monk suggesting that it was not necessary to carry out the destruction in full, the Rump replied that he must not only unhinge the gates and portcullis but destroy them, and this Monk reluctantly did. At the same time the Rump ordered that the Common Council of London should be declared null and void, and a new one elected under suitable qualifications. In essence they were imposing their will by armed force in the same way as they had deplored when it had been done by Cromwell and Lambert. The Journals record no opposition in the Rump to this course of action; perhaps Ashley Cooper and others who thought like him stayed away.

On the evening of 10 February Monk returned to Whitehall, having completed his work, and knowing how unpopular it was and how grudgingly many of his soldiers had undertaken it. At the same time he learned that the Rump, instead of confirming him as commander-in-chief, had decided that there should be five commissioners to control the Army. In Whitehall he was subjected to pressure from all sides. According to Ashley Cooper 'his lady, Sir Thomas Clarges, myself, and some other of this friends' represented to him how awkwardly he was now placed between a thoroughly disliked Rump and the City. There were other consultations as well, particularly with some of his officers, and it is impossible to be certain whose advice was most influential; yet it must be remembered that in May Monk specially recommended Ashley Cooper for appointment to Charles II's Privy Council when he did not so strongly press the claims of Clarges and others who also claimed the honour of giving the decisive advice. At all events, Monk returned to the City, having signed, together with his officers, a letter to the Parliament. This recalled that the Scots army had undertaken not only to restore the Parliament but to vindicate the liberties of the people; urged the grievance of the unrepresentative character of Parliament, and demanded that writs should be issued within a week for the filling of all vacant seats, so that the people might be assured of their undoubted right to a succession of parliaments. It was not so much the actual demands as the implications which mattered: Monk was not content with remaining a passive instrument of the Rump, but was adopting some of the popular demands. This was immediately realized. Pepys, walking in Westminster Hall, noted how 'the countenance of men in the Hall was all changed with joy' within half an hour, while Ludlow from the opposite point of view remarked on the dejection of his fellow-Republicans in the

House. Haslerig went out in anger, and a Quaker at the door took him by the arm and exclaimed: 'Thou man, will thy beast carry thee no longer? Thou must fall!' He remained as inflexible as ever: he was not the man to seek to make terms for himself. The same afternoon the House debated the appointment of the five new army commissioners. The first four elected were evenly balanced, with Haslerig and Walton acting as a counterpoise to Monk and Morley. For the decisive fifth place Monk's friends proposed Ashley Cooper, but the other side carried it for Alured by 30 votes to 15, and further declined to make Monk a member of the quorum. The news naturally served only to confirm Monk in his new policy, and in an address to the Lord Mayor and Common Council he told them publicly both how distasteful he had found his task of pulling down the gates, and what were the contents of his letter to the Parliament. The result was the famous outburst of popular rejoicing that evening (11 February), with bells ringing, bonfires burning and rumps roasting for hours. Though Pepys and others saw people helping on the festive spirit by giving away money to buy drink, there is no reason to doubt that this was a genuine outburst of feeling, comparable with Mafeking night and VE day. In the Shaftesbury household it was long remembered how Ashley Cooper returned home with Col. Alexander Popham from the Guildhall, where he had been helping to reconcile Monk with the City authorities, and found his coach surrounded by people shouting 'Down with the Rumps!' He leaned out of the coach, and with his usual quickness of wit turned jeers into cheers by retorting 'What, gentlemen, not one good piece in a rump?'[1]

If any evidence were needed of the unpopularity of the Rump, these incidents should have supplied it, but Monk delayed nine days before taking further action to compel the Rump to readmit the secluded members. In the past two or three months he had made many professions of his readiness to obey the orders of the Rump, and he made more remarks of his devotion to a Commonwealth in these very days. Even supposing that he had definitely made up his mind about the secluded members, he was reluctant to use force if the leaders of the Rump could be brought to accept them in any other way. He therefore encouraged meetings between Haslerig and others on the one side and some of the secluded members and their supporters on the other. On the 14th Haslerig attended with Scot and two others, while Chief Justice Oliver St. John brought Ashley Cooper,

---

[1] Shaftesbury's own account of the events of 8–11 Feb. is in Christie, i. 206–9. His memory was at fault in thinking that the vote on the five army commissioners preceded Monk's letter of the 11th, but otherwise there is no reason to doubt that his narrative is correct in essentials. See also *C.J.* vii. 837–8, 840–1; Ludlow, op. cit. ii. 218–24, 231; Pepys, 9–11 Feb. 1660; Sir R. Baker, op. cit. pp. 684–7; J. Collins in *H.M.C. Leybourne-Popham MSS.*, pp. 215–20; T. Gumble, *The Life of General Monk* (1671), pp. 235–54; Martyn, i. 226; *Old Parliamentary History* (1760), xxii. 92–93, 98–103, and cf. Godfrey Davies, op. cit. pp. 277–83.

together with the latter's relative by marriage, Carew Raleigh, and
Reynolds. A second and larger meeting included Ashley Cooper's friend
Weaver, Colonel Hutchinson (with whom he was also on good terms at
this period), and, amongst the secluded members themselves, Arthur
Annesley, Colonel Popham and Colonel Richard Norton, Ashley Cooper's
former playmate at Southwick. These meetings, however, produced only
a quarrel between Annesley and Haslerig and broke up in confusion, and
although pressed by Fairfax in a declaration from Yorkshire, Monk had
done nothing when yet another crisis was reached on 20 February. By
this time the Rump had completed an act providing for new elections to
fill all vacant seats, with appropriate restrictions to ensure that only men
who thought as they did should be elected. If the members secluded in
1648 were to be admitted, it was now or never. They met, and decided to
make a renewed attempt to claim their seats next morning. The news of
this leaked to the Council of State, who sent to tell Monk and received
assurances from him that he would prevent it.[1]

In this crisis Ashley Cooper took a hand. That afternoon he was waiting
on Mrs. Monk, when an army officer, Colonel Markham, the brother-in-
law of his friend Weaver, came and told him that he had just met Haslerig
and Scot leaving the General, and had overheard them promising one
another the satisfaction of 'securing' Sir Anthony Cooper before noon
next day. Thus warned, Ashley Cooper went immediately to Monk to find
out what was going on. Eventually he got Monk to admit that in return
for the sole command of all the forces he had promised Haslerig and Scot
to return from his present lodgings in the City to Whitehall, 'and to support
their interest and obey their commands'. Monk undertook that Ashley
Cooper should not be molested, but the latter was not satisfied. Promising
to return at supper-time, he went off to Mrs. Monk (with whom he was
obviously on good terms) and persuaded her to send for her brother
Thomas Clarges, another relative, Colonel Clobery, and Colonel Knight.
With these three, those on whom Monk most relied, Ashley Cooper and
Mrs. Monk set to work to persuade Monk to change his mind. From
supper-time until three in the morning they argued, while the candles
burned low and the fires were replenished on that February night. Finally,
in the early hours, they were successful. Monk promised to restore the
secluded members to their places that very morning, and commissioned
Clarges and Ashley Cooper to summon them to attend him at Whitehall
at nine o'clock. There was no time for sleep as they went from place to
place with their news. By eight a considerable number had been assembled
in the Drury Lane house of their most prominent leader, Arthur Annesley;

[1] Ludlow, op. cit. ii. 228, 233–5; *Mercurius Politicus*, 16–23 Feb. 1660; Monk to
Haslerig, 15 Feb., in *Clarke Papers*, ed. C. H. Firth (Camden Society, 1901), iv. 264; Sir
R. Baker, op. cit. p. 687; J. Collins in *H.M.C. Leybourne-Popham MSS.*, pp. 221–2;
T. Gumble, *The Life of General Monk* (1671), pp. 260–1.

thence they travelled west to that part of Whitehall called the Prince's lodgings. Here there also came Sir Arthur Haslerig to wait upon Monk, knowing nothing of what had happened during the night. Coming into the room, and seeing those present, he realized that in effect the game was up. His face went pale with fury, and he went up to Ashley Cooper and passionately said that all this was his doing, but it should cost blood; to which Ashley Cooper suavely replied, his own if he pleased, but Sir Anthony Cooper would not be secured that morning. And in the next hour seventy-three of the members secluded in 1648 returned to the House, before a guard led, according to one account, by Ashley Cooper.[1]

So runs Shaftesbury's own account of these events, when he looked back upon them in later life. Modern writers commenting upon his story have been disposed to comment upon his alleged lack of modesty, and to suspect him of exaggeration; but there is no good reason to doubt his accuracy. There is ample evidence from other sources that Monk did change his tactics overnight[2]; and in some respects the narrative, so far from being egotistical, is restrained. Shaftesbury in his recollections makes no attempt to assert or even hint that his own arguments were more effective upon Monk than those of Clarges and the others: it is left for the reader to remember, from a view of his whole career, that his ability and persuasiveness were likely to have been far greater than theirs. On one point only is some caution warranted. According to Shaftesbury, Monk admitted that he had reached 'a full agreement' with Haslerig and Scot, and had promised 'to support their interest and obey their commands'. It may well be that if Monk had really made such a full agreement with the Commonwealthsmen, he was not sincere in it, but hoped in time to achieve by the by-elections which they had promised the same results as Ashley Cooper and others wanted to bring about by immediately admitting the secluded members. On the surface both methods might produce a full, representative Parliament instead of a Rump; but Ashley Cooper with his greater political experience saw that the Rump would hedge the by-election candidates round with 'the strictest qualifications imaginable, that none but such as were zealous men of the party might get amongst them'. In his view the Commonwealthsmen's design 'was to have continued a legislative power in themselves, their friends, and their posterity, and never settle a government that might be equal and just to the people; whose security could lie in nothing so much as that their representatives should, in a short time, annual or biennial, be accountable to them, and now eligible by them'.[3] In these words he linked his advocacy of a full,

---

[1] Christie, i. 211–12; R. Coke, *Detection of the Court and State of England* (1719), ii. 95.

[2] Cf. Ludlow, op. cit. ii. 235; and Monk's own letter to Fairfax, 18 Feb., in *H.M.C. Leybourne-Popham MSS.*, pp. 154–5.

[3] Christie, i. 209–10. For the qualifications which the Rump desired to impose upon new members, see *Old Parliamentary History* (1760), xxii. 131–2.

free Parliament in 1660 with the Whig demand for annual parliaments twenty years later.

The returning secluded members swamped the Rumpers and rapidly made it plain that the Republican cause was doomed. They immediately appointed a new Council of State consisting entirely of 'Presbyterians' and others who had had no part in the trial of Charles I and were not committed either by principle or self-interest to a Republic: naturally Ashley Cooper was among them.[1] It is true that, while most people concluded that a Restoration was on the way, Monk's own attitude was still equivocal. In his speech to the secluded members before their restoration he had still talked of establishing a commonwealth without a King or House of Lords,[2] and it was a month before he would see the Royalist Sir John Grenville and give him a message for the King. It appears that in the meantime Haslerig may have made one final effort to win over Monk by offering him either the crown or the Protectorship for himself; and in later years a story was current in the Shaftesbury household that the French ambassador, Bordeaux, had promised French assistance for such a move, but had been foiled by the co-operation of Mrs. Monk, Thomas Clarges, and Ashley Cooper, whose skilful oblique hints in Council forced Monk to declare that he had no such ambitions. In fact Bordeaux engaged in no intrigues to persuade Monk to set up on his own account; but Ashley Cooper may genuinely have suspected French policy at this point and sought to guard against it. Such stories are further evidence that no-one could be absolutely sure of Monk until the eleventh hour; but even these doubts rapidly faded as February passed into March 1660.[3]

It was at this time, and at this time only, that Ashley Cooper at last drew closer to the Royalists. On 24 February Lady Willoughby, one of Hyde's correspondents in London, wrote that Sir Anthony was 'his Majesty's fast friend', but added her fears that his Presbyterianism might show itself when the terms of a restoration were being discussed. Hyde in his reply stated specifically that Lady Willoughby's letter was 'the first that gives us the least assurance of Sir Anthony . . . nor do I take him to be a person at all concerned in Presbytery, except in the ambition of it, and when once he intends well, I suppose he will be advised by those who will give him good counsel, and particularly by my Lord Southampton, whose niece he hath married'. Hyde was still inclined to be sceptical whether Ashley Cooper really did 'intend well', until Lady Willoughby replied that her authority was William Coventry. Then he welcomed the news. As he wrote to another of his correspondents, Brodrick, 'I am heartily

---

[1] *C.J.* vii. 849.

[2] *Old Parliamentary History* (1760), xxii. 140–3.

[3] Sir R. Baker, op. cit. pp. 693, 695; Locke, op. cit. ix. 279–81. In his despatch of 31 May/10 June Bordeaux explicitly denied rumours that he had encouraged Monk to become Protector: Guizot, *Monk* (1851), pp. 375–6; cf. also 7/17 June, ibid. p. 382.

glad you seem confident of Sir An. Ashley Cooper, of whose good inclinations we have heard little, and for whom I have always had a particular
esteem, and do heartily wish he would propose to himself frankly to serve
the King, in which I will undertake he shall receive his own account and I
know he can merit it very well'. The news seemed to be sufficiently promising for Hyde to make an effort to get into touch with Ashley Cooper; and a
natural agent to choose for this purpose was the latter's brother-in-law
Henry Coventry, who could carry over a personal letter from the King
and join his persuasions to those of William Coventry.[1]

Hyde's first draft of this letter on 15/25 March differed significantly
from the one which the King had signed in February 1655.[2] That letter
had appealed to Ashley Cooper's self-interest, as a man of property;
but this time Charles was to send his assurance that 'I value myself upon
being a good Englishman, and do as much, if not more, than any man,
desire the peace, happiness, and security of the nation, and why you, who
have so fair a share in it, should not be willing to assist me in the right way
of procuring it, I cannot imagine: I am sure you have some very near
friends, who will encourage you to it, and who will pass their words to
you and for me, if you could have any doubt of my kindness . . .'.[3] Thus
the appeal to self-interest was combined now with one to patriotism, and
the letter was not without its ironies for the future, as Henry Coventry
carried it from Brussels to London.

There are two significant points to be made about the reconciliation
between Ashley Cooper and the King which Henry was now to mediate.
One was the importance which the King and Hyde clearly placed upon
winning Ashley Cooper: there are signs that Henry Coventry was authorized to hold out hopes of a title for him, if he thought it necessary.[4] And
secondly, the invitation to a reconciliation came late and from the King's
side. If Ashley Cooper had been the cynical time-server sometimes
portrayed, one would have expected him to make an earlier attempt to
make terms for himself with the King, and sell his support. Instead, no
bargain had been arranged when his brother-in-law arrived in London
early in April.

It is natural to wonder whether there was not a reason for Ashley
Cooper's marked lack of eagerness to ingratiate himself. By the middle of
March it was reasonably certain that the King would be invited to return:
the House had voted that the Engagement to be true to the Commonwealth
as now established should be taken off the file, and made arrangements
for a general election for a new Parliament to meet on April 25; and a
painter had prudently obliterated the famous inscription 'Exit tyrannus,

---

[1] Lady Willoughby to Hyde, 24 Feb., MSS. Clar. 70, fo. 27; Hyde to Lady Willoughby,
3/13 Mar., ibid. fo. 83; Lady Willoughby to Hyde, 9 Mar., ibid. fo. 120; Hyde to Lady
Willoughby, 17/27 Mar., ibid. fo. 190, and to Brodrick, 14/24 Mar., fo. 157.
[2] p. 89 above.   [3] Printed by Brown, p. 94.   [4] See p. 135 below.

Regum ultimus' on the statue of Charles I on the Exchange. It did not take a soothsayer to foretell that England would shortly have a King again. There remained, however, the important problem of the terms on which Charles should be permitted to come back. Former Parliamentarians and so-called 'Presbyterians' wanted assurances both of their personal safety and about the political and religious policy which the King would pursue; rather than admit him on his own terms they talked of sending him proposals similar to those of the so-called Treaty of Newport in 1648. There were meetings attended by Parliamentarian peers like Bedford, Manchester, Northumberland and Wharton, and sympathizers from the ranks of the Council of State such as Pierrepont, Waller, Denzil Holles, and Sir Gilbert Gerard. One Royalist correspondent mentions Ashley Cooper's attendance at one such meeting at Suffolk House.[1] It is thus possible that he took part in these discussions, though he can hardly have been prominent in them. It is conceivable that this could have had something to do with his delay in submitting himself unconditionally to the King.

The attempt to put forward terms for a restoration was in any case a forlorn hope. It ran across the plain trend of public opinion, and anyone who obstinately held out for terms merely risked forfeiting the King's favour in the future; and in the end the Declaration of Breda seemed to promise the same result without a formal negotiation. It was Monk who had suggested, by way of Sir John Grenville, that the King should issue such a manifesto, promising in general terms an amnesty and liberty for 'tender consciences' and undertaking to consult with Parliament on these ticklish points, as also on the problems of land ownership and army pay. The Declaration of Breda was such a striking success in sweeping away all talk of a 'treaty' that one wonders whether Monk himself was subtle enough to suggest it of his own accord. Did one of his advisers put forward the idea? Monk's trusted relative William Morrice, who was now with him in London, could have done so; so too could Ashley Cooper, always a skilful tactician and possibly realizing that such promises were all they were likely to get before the Royalist restoration had proceeded too far. But there is no evidence available to support or to rule out such speculation.

What is certain is that in these months of April and May Ashley Cooper was close to Monk, and working hard in the Council of State for him. He was becoming the indispensable man on any committee, the man who has all the facts and figures at his finger-tips. The most important administrative problem was the control over the armed forces and the collection of all the information about their numbers and the extent of their arrears of pay. An order of 19 March ordered that the committees of Council for

---

[1] Mordaunt to Hyde, 19 Apr., *Clarendon State Papers* (1786), iii. 729–30; cf. Slingsby to Hyde, 23 Mar., ibid. p. 705, and 11 Apr., ibid. p. 726, and Mordaunt to the King, 24–26 Apr., *Calendar of Clarendon State Papers*, iv, ed. F. J. Routledge (1932), p. 674; J. Collins in *H.M.C. Leybourne-Popham MSS.*, p. 230.

the public revenue and for the establishment of the Army and Navy should meet every morning an hour before the Council's own meeting, and 'confer together as they shall see occasion for the better understanding of the public incomes and issues, and consider how the public expenses may be borne by the receipts with some overplus towards answering the public debts of the Commonwealth'. Further, 'when either of the said committees shall have any matters to report to the Council the same shall from time to time be in the first place heard . . . and Sir Anthony Ashley Cooper is desired to take care hereof'. When the committees reported to Council they commonly did so through Ashley Cooper; it was also to him that Admiral Montagu wrote, promising the necessary information about the Fleet. Ashley Cooper could not bring forward any magical solution to the problem of the Commonwealth's heavy debts; but when the Restoration took place he was the man with the facts which the new government would require.[1] At the same time he was also collaborating in persuading army officers to subscribe an Engagement to accept the decisions of the forth-coming new Parliament.[2]

His brother-in-law Henry Coventry, arriving with Charles II's letter at the beginning of April, found him immersed in these activities. Henry's reception was wholly satisfactory: he wrote back to Hyde that Cooper had 'promised as much both in relation to your friend [the King] and yourself as I could ask him and there was no need of the motive, which I still keep in my own breast'. The 'motive' was probably the promise of a title which Henry was empowered to make if necessary to gain a valuable supporter, but which he found to be needless. 'I am not better disposed to serve your friend [the King] thoroughly, and without merchandising than he pretends [claims] to be . . . '. Others still regarded Ashley Cooper as 'too full of tricks', not knowing quite what to expect of him even when the Convention Parliament met on 25 April; but there can be no doubt that by this time his mind was fully made up. He rejoiced in tones still charac-teristically Puritan at the failure of Lambert's final attempt at revolt: 'Thus God has blasted the wicked in their reputations and bloody designs, and I hope will bless us with a happy settlement. . . .' On 4 May Henry Coventry wrote again to Hyde, repeating his certainty of Ashley Cooper's loyalty and even adding that Cooper claimed to have frustrated an attempt by Clarges to turn General Monk against Hyde; and again he went on, 'I have made no mention concerning making him ought and that for many reasons too large to write in this cipher; I conceive his inclination to be more for business than title'. This opinion that Ashley Cooper set more store by opportunities for work than by empty honours is significant;

[1] See the Shaftesbury Papers, especially III, 75 and 79; II, 56; VI B, 444; VII, 554, and XXXIII, 14, for documents illustrating these activities; cf. also *C.S.P.D. 1659–60*, p. 405.

[2] Sir R. Baker, op. cit. p. 697.

and it marked him off from most of the others who now began to clamour for favours from the King.[1]

On the following day, 5 May, Henry Coventry had an opportunity to write more fully and without the hindrance of cipher, by way of a reliable messenger. He thought the winning over of Ashley Cooper sufficiently important to warrant a lengthy account of their conversation. He began by describing how he had conveyed the King's message, and told Ashley Cooper that Charles 'desired not an acquisition of Sir A[nthony] barely as an expedient for this present conjuncture, but as one from whose abilities and insight in the affairs of the nation, he hoped in all occasions services of advantage'. On Hyde's behalf he denied that the latter had ever begged for the grant of Ashley Cooper's estates from the King, and stressed 'the respect you [Hyde] profess to his person and the desire you had of making a friendship with him'. In reply Ashley Cooper had promised to serve the King 'with all the powers he had', and then launched out on a lengthy apologia for his conduct under the interregnum. 'He acknowledged to me', Coventry wrote, 'that Cromwell had for some time abused, and dec[ei]ved him, but that it had lasted not long, and that from his first parting with him[he n]ever had other opinion, but that the King would come in, nor other desire than that he should. That he had ever since made use of all occasions that conducted to it, the hindering any other government to settle being a point as he thought most material, he had been as far as he could instrumental in it.' His explanation for not getting in touch with the King for whose restoration he thus claimed to have worked for the past five years was that 'the business, being to be done by appearing other than what he was, secrecy was the most necessary part of it, and the less he was thought to be the King's friend, the more he had the power of being it'. As far as his attitude towards Hyde was concerned, he had never believed the rumours of Hyde's designs on his estates, and hoped that Hyde would remain the King's chief minister, 'as one that have contributed what you could for the preservation both of our religion and the right church government' and as one who could be relied on to oppose French plots to the contrary.[2]

To this last passage we shall return later when discussing Ashley Cooper's relationship with Clarendon, and also his attitude towards France and French influence at Charles II's Court. For the present it is important to consider the claim which Henry Coventry made on his behalf—the claim that his repentance and return to Royalism was not the last-minute affair which it appeared to be, but a matter of several years' standing, and that

---

[1] H. Coventry to Hyde, 20 Apr., MSS. Clar. 71, fo. 339; Mordaunt to the King, 24–26 Apr., *Calendar of Clarendon State Papers*, iv, ed. F. J. Routledge (1932), p. 674; Ashley Cooper to Montagu, 23 Apr., printed by Christie, i. 219; H. Coventry to Hyde, 4 May, MSS. Clar. 72, fo. 180.

[2] Printed in Brown, pp. 97–98. Unfortunately Miss Brown's only comment on Ashley Cooper's apologia was that 'the reader may accept it or not as he chooses'.

all his political activities were devoted to that end. This was the line taken by all Shaftesbury's later apologists in reply to the insistence of the Tories that his Royalism had never been sincere, but only expedient. John Locke, for instance, wrote that 'Sir A. had laid the plan [of the Restoration] in his head a long time before, and carried it on', and others also asserted that, so far from being a traitor, Shaftesbury was the man to whom King Charles really owed his return.[1] Equally the Republican Ludlow on his side believed that Ashley Cooper had been a concealed Royalist since his break with Oliver Cromwell.[2] What evidence is there in support of this? The answer must surely be that there is none. It was natural in May 1660 that Ashley Cooper (or Henry Coventry on his behalf) should want to put the best possible face on his past actions for the benefit of the King whose return to power was imminent; but Hyde, or Charles if he read the letter, may well have reflected that there was nothing at all to corroborate this unlikely claim to have been for years a Royalist without revealing himself to any other Royalist. Nothing but Shaftesbury's later reputation for Machiavellian cunning could ever have induced anyone to believe that his conversion was more than a few months old. When, in February 1660, he helped to turn Monk against the Rump and to persuade him to recall the secluded members, he must have foreseen the trend of events which then led to the Restoration; but it does not follow from this that he had anticipated it in the period in 1659 when he had been co-operating with Haslerig and the other Republican politicians.

Was he then the ambitious time-server the Tories alleged, who at a late hour joined a winning cause, in which he did not really believe, to suit his own personal interests? At this point it is relevant to compare this apologia of 1660 with a later one, also written for the King's eyes. In the winter of 1677–8 he lay imprisoned in the Tower for his opposition to the King: he had been unable to secure freedom through the law-courts, and must consider some sort of appeal for leniency from Charles.[3] In these circumstances he drafted a letter which would describe his past services to the King. After a reference to the book of Job—'my integrity will I hold fast, and will not let it go; my heart shall not reproach me so long as I live'[4]— he went on:

I had the honour to have a principal hand in your restoration; neither did I act in it, but on a principle of piety and honour: I never betrayed (as your majesty knows) the party or councils I was of. I kept no correspondence with, nor I made no secret addresses to your majesty; neither did I endeavour to obtain any private terms or articles for myself, or reward for what I had or should do. In whatever I did toward the service of your majesty, I was solely acted by the sense of that

---

[1] Locke, op. cit. ix. 281. Cf. also *Rawleigh Redivivus* (1683), pp. 36–39, and other anonymous panegyrics after Shaftesbury's death.

[2] *Memoirs*, ed. C. H. Firth (1894), ii. 83, 85, 116, 155.

[3] See p. 435 below. [4] Job xxvii. 5, 6 (not quite accurately quoted).

duty I owed to God, the English nation, and your majesty's just right and title. I saw the hand of Providence, that has led us through various forms of government, and had given power into the hands of several sorts of men, but he had given none of them a heart to use it as they should; they all fell to the prey, sought not the good or settlement of the nation, endeavoured only the enlargement and continuance of their own authority, and grasped at those very powers they had complained of so much, and for which so bloody and so fatal a war had been raised and continued in the bowels of the nation. I observed the leaders of the great parties of religion, both laity and clergy, ready and forward to deliver up the rights and liberties of the people, and to introduce an absolute dominion; so that tyranny might be established in the hands of those that favoured their way, and with whom they might have hopes to divide the present spoil, having no eye to posterity, or thought of future things.

He then refers immediately to Lambert's eviction of the Rump in October 1659, and begins a narrative at that point.[1]

This dignified defence claims far less than Henry Coventry had claimed for him in his letter. Although it was in his interest to put his services, and thus Charles's obligation to him, as high as possible, there is no suggestion here that he had been converted back to Royalism as soon as he left Oliver Cromwell's service at the end of 1654. Rather the implication is that he began to contemplate a return of the monarchy some time towards the end of 1659, when 'several sorts of men' had in turn disillusioned him, and convinced him that they 'endeavoured only the enlargement and continuance of their own authority'. This was his main grievance against the Commonwealthsmen with whom he had originally co-operated: by the end of 1659 it was certain that Haslerig and his colleagues in the Rump had no intention of allowing anything like a free election, and it was natural that Ashley Cooper—and many others—should be forced to the conclusion that the best way to bring about a return to truly parliamentary government was by bringing back the King and the old constitution: there is no evidence that he ever considered the Leveller alternative. The cynic, or the reader of Dryden, may perhaps be dubious about Shaftesbury's talk of 'integrity', of his duties to God and the English nation, and of the rights and liberties of the people: were these high-sounding phrases possibly hypocritical, or the mere rationalization of self-interest? Such a solution has a superficial simplicity about it which may appeal to readers inclined to distrust these abstractions, and believe that all politicians' motives are selfish, but it will scarcely fit the facts. A selfish man concerned only with personal advancement would have sought to communicate with Charles II

---

[1] The letter is printed in Locke's *Works* (1823), ix. 282–3, and Christie, ii. 251–3. The narrative part of it lasts for only two sentences, and then breaks off at the same point in time and with the same words ('in Scotland') as the beginning of the autobiographical fragment previously used (pp. 118–20, 123, 126–9, 131 above) (printed by Christie, i. 195–9, 204–12). It may be that Shaftesbury at first intended his story as an apologia to the King and then changed it into a narrative for his own satisfaction—or that of posterity. There is no proof that the letter was actually delivered to the King.

and bargain for himself: Shaftesbury was able to boast truthfully that he had not done so. Alternatively, a cynic who was unsure of the outcome and anxious only to preserve himself could have followed passively in Monk's wake until the issue was certain: Shaftesbury had not done this either, but had endeavoured to push Monk on in the way he preferred. Putting aside for the time being all knowledge of Shaftesbury's later career, and judging solely from his actions in 1659–60, one is forced to the conclusion that his conversion to a monarchical restoration was the result of a genuine political conviction. This was, as we have seen, Hyde's interpretation at the time.

There is certainly one phrase in Shaftesbury's justification of which one may be sceptical. This is his reference to 'your majesty's just right and title'. After 1660 such an acknowledgement was obviously *de rigueur*, and a man appealing for royal clemency would have to make it; but in the 1650s he had certainly not thought of the problem in these terms. In the spring of 1660 signatures were canvassed for an address of thanksgiving from the nobility and gentry of Dorset. It was presented to the King at Whitehall on 12 June by a deputation which included, besides Ashley Cooper, two members of the Strangeways family.[1] As they knelt together in homage, the Strangeways may well have thought back to the day in 1644 when Ashley Cooper had burnt down their house at Abbotsbury, and reflected with bitterness on the way in which those who had borne the heat and burden of the day were being made equal (or less than equal, for Ashley Cooper was a Privy Councillor) to those who had come in at the eleventh hour. Where the Cavaliers could boast of their consistent loyalty to a divinely appointed monarch, Ashley Cooper's reasons for joining Charles II were entirely utilitarian. In his eyes, Republicanism had been tried, and found wanting, and in the circumstances it was politically expedient in the interests of 'the people' to return to the old trinity of King, Lords and Commons. Between the attitudes of the Cavaliers and Ashley Cooper there lay a whole world of difference; and though the two motives might seem to be working towards the same end in the 1660s, the Exclusion crisis was to show that the reconciliation was not final.

[1] Bayley, op. cit. p. 387.

CHAPTER VIII

THE KING'S SERVANT (1660-1)

Him in the anguish of his soul he served,
Rewarded faster still than he deserved.

The Medal

WHEN the Convention Parliament met on 25 April 1660, Ashley
Cooper sat, as a matter of course, as one of its members for the
county of Wiltshire. No one was likely to oppose a man who had
his Royalist connexions and local influence, and who was known to be close
to Monk. It was equally natural that he should be chosen when, having
decided to acknowledge Charles II unconditionally as King, the House of
Commons voted on 8 May for twelve commissioners to carry across its
expressions of loyalty and a present of £50,000. Indeed, he had an additional claim in that he was one of the three members sent to borrow the
money from the financiers of the City of London.[1]

The end of the week therefore found him on board ship, crossing to the
continent for the first time. Amongst his companions there were his friend
Sir George Booth, Fairfax, whom he had always respected, and his former
enemy Denzil Holles, reappearing after a decade of political obscurity.
Each of them had a chequered past; each of them must have been wonder-
ing what the future would bring. The political situation was entirely
changed, and quite unlike anything that any of them had known before;
and the all-important personality of the new King was an unknown
quantity. Ashley Cooper had last seen Charles, then a boy of thirteen, at
Oxford in 1643. Since then, there had been rumours, but no accurate
knowledge had been possible. What little he could do to smooth his
reception, he did; along with many others, he took with him a gift of
money to supplement Parliament's grant, for he knew that Charles was so
poor that everything would be welcome.[2]

The meeting took place on 16 May at The Hague, whither Charles
had just moved from Breda. When Ashley Cooper was ushered in to the
royal presence, along with his colleagues, to kiss the royal hand, he found
first of all that its owner towered over him, at least a foot taller: we may
leave it to the psychologists to speculate on the way this difference in
height affected their relationship. Of stronger physique and better health,
a more sensual disposition and quite different tastes, Charles yet had one

---

[1] *C.J.* viii. 15; Dering's Parliamentary Diary, 2 May (cit. Godfrey Davies, *The Restoration of Charles II*, 1955, p. 345 n.)   [2] Burnet, *Supplement*, p. 59.

thing in common with Ashley Cooper: he too could say that he had been forced to learn the world faster than his book, and that his business had called him early to the thoughts and considerations of a man. But whereas Ashley Cooper had had to contend with the corruption and oppression of the Court of Wards, Charles's royal birth had forced him to play for higher stakes. For the rest of his life he bored his helpless courtiers by repeating, at the slightest provocation, the story of his escape after the battle of Worcester; and between 1651 and 1660 he had had to play the difficult part of the royal pretender, begging for help from foreign rulers, patronized and used or scorned as their turn was served, and surrounded by poverty-stricken, quarrelsome and intriguing courtiers. In one way this experience had the same effect upon him as Ashley Cooper's: emerging successfully, he too had complete self-confidence in his ability to use and manipulate men, whatever their prejudices and interests. He based this confidence less rationally upon his power 'to read physiognomies', but still he was prepared to use other people for his own purposes irrespective of their past careers and backgrounds. He might not altogether trust Ashley Cooper, but he was prepared to employ him as long as there was profit to be derived from his services, more especially since he liked good conversation and Ashley Cooper knew how to pay his court. Superficially, also, their attitudes to religion were similar, in that both had come to dislike religious 'enthusiasm' and equally persecution, at least for strictly religious purposes: but they approached this problem from different standpoints. Ashley Cooper favoured toleration for Dissent because he inclined to a rationalist, latitudinarian freedom of thought and because he retained a Puritan dislike for clerical authority; Charles favoured indulgence for Catholics, not because his own views were any more mystical, but because he inclined to Catholicism as a support for legitimate authority. Politically, their experience had equipped them in different ways. Charles's years on the continent had given him a greater knowledge of European politics and personalities and a greater skill in diplomacy; on the other hand, though he prided himself on being a true Englishman, having been out of England between the ages of fourteen and thirty he had no first-hand knowledge of England and Englishmen such as Ashley Cooper had gained from close contact with his neighbours in the Dorset and Wiltshire squirearchy and his colleagues in Parliament and the City of London. Equally he knew nothing of the precedents, routines and red tape with which Englishmen still governed their country, in spite of an apparently revolutionary upheaval; and having had little to administer, he had little experience in, or taste for, detailed administration. For this he preferred to rely on people like Ashley Cooper, who in 1660 had a more accurate and detailed knowledge of conditions in England than anyone at Charles II's Court. In the short run, therefore, Ashley Cooper might serve, and the King reward; ultimately, their co-operation might break up.

The short run was a good deal shorter in the relations of Ashley Cooper
with James, Duke of York. There is no hint that the two men ever got on
well with one another. Duller of intellect, less opportunistic and adaptable,
and more authoritarian than his brother, James had fallen more under
French influences. Charles had for the most part been surrounded by good
Englishmen like Hyde; James had served with the French armies and never
lost the habits of mind which he had formed from contact with French
nobles. He had definite ideas about the position of a King or his heir
presumptive and the place of a subject, and Ashley Cooper never fitted
into this pattern. Perhaps the interview on 16 May did not give Ashley
Cooper much insight into James's mind, any more than he was able to
predict the future greatness of the nine-year-old Prince of Orange who
was also present; but it was not long before the antipathy was evident.
Ashley Cooper and James differed *toto caelo* on every political and religious
subject.

If it was important for Ashley Cooper to meet his new royal master and
the heir to the throne, it mattered almost as much to meet and weigh up
the people in whom the King placed his trust. Foremost among these was
a man whom Ashley Cooper had known long before, Edward Hyde. They
had been fellow-members of the Short Parliament, and it is possible that
their acquaintance dated even further back, for Wimborne St. Giles was
not so far from the Hyde property in Wiltshire. They had been on good
terms at Oxford in 1643, when Hyde had at first sympathized with young
Ashley Cooper's plans in Dorset.[1] Reading between the lines of Hyde's
remarks in his histories and his correspondence in 1659–60, it is possible
to detect that he respected the promising talents of his junior, but was at a
loss to understand him.[2] He found Ashley Cooper of a 'slippery humour',[3]
and was perplexed to know why he did not attach himself firmly to one
political group or one patron. Ashley Cooper on his side may have been
sincere when he told Henry Coventry, in this month of 1660, that he
respected Hyde's Protestantism and his refusal to submit to foreign
influences; for he could remember how Hyde had stood for moderate
Protestant constitutionalism in opposition to Queen Henrietta Maria and
her clique at Oxford. When some people in Monk's entourage had tried
to persuade the General that Hyde ought not to be allowed to return with
his master, Ashley Cooper had helped to frustrate them by saying that if
Hyde did not come back 'the foreign interest' would triumph.[4] Hyde was
a man of good sense, who could be relied on not to pursue an extreme or
vindictive policy in the delicate situation of 1660. Yet Ashley Cooper
found that in the intervening sixteen years since they had last met Hyde
had changed in one respect; he was a martyr to 'gout' or arthritis. Even

[1] p. 45 above.
[2] E.g. Hyde to [Lady Willoughby], 11/21 Feb., MSS. Clar. 69, fo. 131.
[3] Clarendon, *Continuation*, i. 278.   [4] Mordaunt to Hyde, 5 May, MSS. Clar. 72, fo. 234*.

today the twisted handwriting which survives tells its tale of gnarled fingers. He was more elderly in manner than his fifty-two years would suggest, and he was both old enough to be Charles's father and ready to read paternal moral lectures to him. When Hyde and Charles had left Oxford in 1644 Hyde had been thirty-six to the Prince's fourteen, and the disparity in age had never been fully overcome. They belonged to different generations. Indeed Ashley Cooper found that Charles was surrounded by counsellors older than himself: Nicholas was sixty-seven, Culpeper sixty, Ormond fifty. Himself nearly thirty-nine, Ashley Cooper was closer in age to the King. He was one of the set of men who in the early 1660s could be companions to the King as well as ministers. This was to be a matter of political importance in due course; but in 1660 Hyde's influence with his master seemed to be invincible.

The few days which Ashley Cooper and his fellow-commissioners spent in Holland were full of meetings, banqueting, and assessments of new acquaintances. Amongst the festivities there was one unpleasant incident, a coach-spill which was later blamed for his internal abscess.[1] This accident probably occurred just before the royal embarkation on 23 May, but it did not prevent him from going on board and joining in the King's triumphant progress by way of Dover, Canterbury and Blackheath to London. Thus he was able to witness the crowds of Cavaliers who flocked to greet Charles because they recognized him not only as King but as All-Provider, the giver of places and pensions and titles. The King's function as the fountain of honour was one of the new facts of life to be reckoned with, though unfortunately a second fact was that there were never enough favours to go round. The climax of importunity came at Canterbury, with an element of comedy in it. Monk presented the King with a long list of persons whom he recommended, including no less than seventy privy councillors. Charles, in no position to oppose anything on which Monk insisted, was in some confusion, but he had the good sense to pocket the paper and show it privately to Hyde, who in turn discovered by way of Morrice that Monk had promised to put forward all these names, but cared little what happened to most of them. There were however one or two people to whom Monk gave a special recommendation. Amongst these were Morrice, who became a privy councillor and second Secretary of State, and Ashley Cooper himself, who became a privy councillor. If Monk's recommendation needed any further support, this came from Ashley Cooper's relationship to the Earl of Southampton, the most respected of the Cavaliers who had remained in England: it was thought that Southampton would be able to keep his nephew by marriage on the strait and narrow path of loyalty.[2]

And so, on 29 May, the royal cavalcade reached Blackheath, where the

---

[1] *Rawleigh Redivivus* (1683), p. 48.
[2] Clarendon, *Continuation*, i. 278.

troops were drawn up to await it. Ashley Cooper had left it some time before, to appear at the head of his regiment: if any of his men harboured unworthy thoughts of their colonel as a turncoat, they were wise enough to leave no evidence for history. He was probably as realistic about their feelings as Charles, when the latter remarked that it 'could be nobody's fault but his own that he had stayed so long abroad, when all mankind wished him so heartily at home'.[1]

For the next six months the possibility hung over the new government that the Army would rebel against the defeat of its hopes. In this period Ashley Cooper's duties were twofold. He was a privy councillor—not one of the inner ring commonly known as the 'committee of foreign affairs', which discussed in advance all major issues of policy, but one who could be assigned to special committees whenever the need arose. In the second place, he was a member of parliament as well as a privy councillor, and could therefore act as a front-bench government spokesman, guiding the House of Commons in the direction which the government required. This function was also performed by Morrice, Holles and Arthur Annesley. Annesley, who had been one of the 'Presbyterian' secluded members returning to politics in February 1660, was recorded as intervening rather more frequently, but Ashley Cooper was certainly one of those on whom the government relied, in a House which was divided between Royalists and ex-Parliamentarians. The situation was a particularly delicate one, for a House which the government could not be certain of controlling had to be persuaded to settle some urgent and controversial problems. It was vital to secure from the Commons money with which to pay off the Army, and until this was raised and the former Ironsides disbanded it was necessary to prevent any revival of discontent. This meant that an act of indemnity had to be passed and vindictive attacks by the Royalists on their former opponents prevented, while it was safest to postpone a religious settlement to a more opportune time.

Ashley Cooper did his share in helping to moderate dangerous animosities in the debates on the Indemnity Act. On at least one occasion he had a personal interest in the subduing of faction, for he was attacked by Prynne and another member 'for putting his hand to the Instrument to settle the Protector', but nothing is known of the way in which he evaded this charge. But he was not solely concerned with self-preservation. He supported Annesley's endeavour to secure an additional fourteen days' grace for those regicides who had not surrendered by the time limit laid down in the proclamation. A few days later, when there was a further attack on the former supporters of the Protectorate in a proposal that all who had held office in those years should be made to refund their salaries, 'Sir Anth. Ashley Cooper closed the debate, with saying, He might freely

---

[1] A. Browning, *English Historical Documents 1660–1714* (1953), p. 60; Clarendon, *Continuation*, i. 268.

speak, because he never received any salary: but he looked upon the proviso as dangerous to the peace of the nation; adding That it reached gen. Monk, and admiral Montagu, after the house had given them thanks, and thousands besides'. This skilful argument (for only the boldest opponent would care to be identified with a proposal hostile to the all-powerful General) contributed to the rejection of the proviso by 181 votes to 151. Another proviso which would have affected a whole category of people was aimed at excluding from the general pardon those who would not take the oaths of allegiance and supremacy. This proviso Ashley Cooper at first supported, but later he yielded to the arguments of members like Holles 'and said though he were no friend to Papists yet wished not to press it but to lay it aside at present'. The fact was that the imposition of such tests as qualifications for indemnity at such a moment would have excluded not only Roman Catholics (who had not been conspicuous followers of Cromwell!) but also many Republicans and sectaries in the Army; so that here too Ashley Cooper's view was the more moderate one.[1]

He also helped to save some individuals from attempts by their enemies to exclude them from the general amnesty. Haslerig, who within the previous eighteen months had been first a parliamentary colleague and then an opponent, was obviously a marked man for many Royalists, as a consistent and unrepentant Republican. After the events of February 1660, when Ashley Cooper and Haslerig had taken up diametrically opposed positions, it might have been expected that Ashley Cooper would leave him to his fate; but instead he argued that only those who had been guilty of shedding Charles I's blood should be punished, 'and said, He thought this man not considerable enough'. This was not a very warm or complimentary reference, but it was the only type of argument likely to save Haslerig's life. Colonel Birch, speaking on behalf of Monk, threw his weight into the same scale, and Haslerig escaped by 141 votes to 116. Ashley Cooper also signed a certificate in favour of another former Republican colleague, Colonel Hutchinson, and spoke in favour of the regicide Col. George Fleetwood, and Col. Croxton, who had sat in judgement on some Royalist peers. He did his share to enable all these to escape at least with their lives. Thus he was not unmindful of some former acquaintances whom, if he had been completely self-regarding, he might have abandoned to their enemies.[2]

Others whom he had known he was unable to save, and indeed he was called upon to take part in putting them to death. The Act of Indemnity which received the royal assent on 29 August 1660 gave an amnesty to the

---

[1] S. Charlton to Sir R. Leveson, 3 June 1660, in *H.M.C. Report V*, p. 205; Bodleian Library, MS. Dep. f. 9 (Spencer Bowman's Parliamentary Diary), fos. 38, 52; *Old Parliamentary History*, xxii (1760), p. 370.

[2] Ibid. xxii. 444–5; *H.M.C. Seventh Report, House of Lords MSS.*, pp. 120–1, 159–60; Spencer Bowman's Diary (above), fo. 152.

K

great majority of the King's opponents, but several victims were selected as scapegoats from amongst those who had contributed directly to the death of Charles I. Along with Monk, Montagu and Denzil Holles, Ashley Cooper was placed on the special commission which was set up to try these regicides. Before him in court there appeared the chaplain Hugh Peters, who had served with him on the law reform commission of 1652–3; Major-General Harrison, who had sat with him on the Council of State in 1653; and Thomas Scot, who less than a year previously had joined with him in planning to seize the Tower of London and in signing the propaganda letter to Fleetwood. The result of the trials was a foregone conclusion, and these three were among the ten who met their deaths with all the barbarities attendant upon cases of treason. Naturally there were those who looked upon Ashley Cooper's participation in sentencing former colleagues wtih special abhorrence. Colonel Hutchinson (although Ashley Cooper had sought to help him personally) recalled that when they had been discussing the possibility of a Restoration in the spring of 1660, Ashley Cooper had vehemently protested that not a hair of any man's head nor a penny of any man's estate should be touched for what had passed; and yet here he now was, sitting in judgement upon them.[1]

The treachery was not as black as it seemed; it is necessary to keep the facts in proportion. If anyone at the beginning of 1660 had been told that a Restoration would take place at the cost of only ten deaths,[2] he would have considered it a miracle: the promise to Hutchinson had been substantially kept. Again, the ex-Parliamentarians and ex-supporters of the Commonwealth on the bench drew a sharp distinction between themselves and those who had actually helped to bring the King to the scaffold. But perhaps most important in Ashley Cooper's case is that he had no real choice in the matter. Having once thrown in his lot with the Restoration, he could not refuse to show his loyalty by serving on the commission; and when he had agreed to serve, there was nothing he could conceivably have done which could have saved men like Peters and Scot who had gloried in the King's execution. They were past all human aid, and Ashley Cooper was not the man to throw himself away in a totally lost cause on behalf of people whose outlook he did not share. He seems to have kept silence during the trial, unlike some of his fellow-judges; and in the next few days the men he had known were hanged, disembowelled and quartered at Charing Cross. Not long afterwards he took part in the committee stage of a bill attainting Oliver Cromwell,[3] as a result of which his former master (and almost his father-in-law) with whom he had many times conversed, was dug up, and the head was stuck, green and grinning, on one of the pinnacles of Westminster Hall for all to see. These were reminders to any politician of the penalty of opposing his king and finishing on the losing

---

[1] *State Trials*, vi. 986 sqq; Lucy Hutchinson, *Memoirs of Colonel Hutchinson* (Everyman ed. 1908), pp. 314–15.   [2] Plus that of Sir Henry Vane in 1662.   [3] *C.J.* viii. 177–8.

side; and they must have been in Shaftesbury's mind at the end of his life when the Exclusionist cause began to slide into defeat.

Co-operating in this way with the government's plan to pass the Act of Indemnity for the people at large and to execute a few regicides as examples, Ashley Cooper also joined in the government's desire to put off discussion of the religious problem. In the important debate of 16 July he declared that 'our religion was too much inter-mixed with interest; neither was it ripe enough now to handle religion; but moved the whole committee might be adjourned for three months and this debate laid aside'.[1] After a debate lasting seven hours, this motion was carried, and the House was able to turn from matters of religion to matters which were, from the government's point of view, more urgent. Apart from the indemnity bill, we find Cooper and Annesley together acting as tellers for a motion to resume the debate on tunnage and poundage, and carrying it by 153 votes to 112.[2] By such efforts the government was enabled to raise some money, to adjourn Parliament (13 September), and to begin disbanding the Army,[3] before it had to take any action to implement Charles's promise about religion in the Declaration of Breda.

On 22 October 1660, discussions between Anglicans and Presbyterians which had been fostered by Charles and Clarendon culminated in a meeting at the latter's lodgings at Worcester House, and this was followed by the publication three days later of the so-called Worcester House Declaration. While professing his own preference for episcopacy and for the Prayer Book service, Charles promised temporarily to meet Presbyterian objections by modifying the powers of the bishops and by allowing some latitude in the ceremonial to be used. When Parliament again met and the Presbyterian members of the House of Commons sought to convert the Declaration into an Act, however, the government turned against this move and successfully defeated it. The consequence was that neither contemporaries nor historians could be sure whether the Declaration represented a genuine attempt to comprehend some at least of the Puritans within a broader national church by making suitable concessions, or whether it was only a tactical move to keep the Presbyterians in play for a little longer.[4] For an assessment of Charles's and Clarendon's religious policy this is a crucial episode which is wrapped in impenetrable darkness; and the darkness covers also Ashley Cooper's attitude at this point. According to Baxter the laymen present at the decisive meeting at Worcester House

---

[1] Bodl. Libr. MS. Dep. f. 9, fo. 83ᵛ; cf. *C.S.P. Ven.*, *1659–61*, p. 176.

[2] *C.J.* viii. 91.

[3] At Ashley Cooper's suggestion the order in which regiments were to be paid off and disbanded was determined by the drawing of lots. *Old Parliamentary History*, xxii (1760), 473.

[4] See R. F. Bosher, *The Restoration Settlement of the Church* (1951), pp. 184 sqq., and Anne Whiteman, 'The Restoration of the Church of England', in *From Uniformity to Unity*, ed. G. F. Nuttall and O. Chadwick (1962), pp. 60–72, for conflicting views.

included (besides the King and Clarendon) Albemarle, Ormond, Manchester, Holles, Annesley, 'etc.', and it is impossible to know whether this 'etc.' included Ashley Cooper or not. Equally the surviving notes of the parliamentary debates on the Declaration make no reference to him: he was not concerned in the committee stage of the bill, nor does he seem to have spoken in the debate on 28 November when the bill was finally defeated, though his friend Morrice joined other government spokesmen in arguing against it.[1] It looks as though he remained in the background at this time, in spite of his interest in religious affairs at other times, but the reason one can only guess at. It does not appear that he was ever on close terms with the Presbyterian ministers who took part in the Worcester House discussions—when he wanted to consult Baxter in 1665 he had to do so through Sir John Trevor[2]—and it might be that, like some Independents who voted against the bill, he feared that the broader church contemplated would be one intolerant to those Puritan sectaries who remained outside it. Or he might have concluded that whatever its merits the Declaration was not intended to be a permanent settlement, and seen no point in involving himself in it. Between these and other conjectural explanations it is impossible to choose: one can only state the fact that he did not make any contribution to the discussion which attracted the notice of contemporaries, and thus at least did not embarrass the government which he was serving, before it was securely established.

By the beginning of December 1660, however, Charles and Clarendon were able to feel much safer. The disbandment of the Army was well advanced, and Ashley Cooper's regiment, which he had taken over from Fleetwood in the previous January, was one of those which had been paid off[3] after its colonel had made 'a pertinent speech'. Besides the immense financial efforts required for this, the House of Commons had been induced to do something at least for the King's permanent revenue, though time was soon to reveal its inadequacy. Ashley Cooper had been a member of some of the House's committees on the disbandment of the Army, and on the Poll Bill which was the rough and ready means of raising some of the money necessary for this.[4] His work on these committees went unreported, but in one full-dress financial debate he expressed decided views about the form which the King's regular revenue should take. Speaking from the bitter experience of his own youth, he joined in the general outcry against the Court of Wards, the abolition of which by the Long

[1] C.J. viii. 182; Old Parliamentary History, xxvii (1761), 27–31.

[2] Reliquiae Baxterianae (1696), p. 445. This is the only reference Baxter makes to Ashley Cooper. Indeed, though the latter was on friendly terms with many Dissenting laymen after 1660, the only Dissenting minister with whom he seems to have had any connexion (so far as I can recall) was the famous Baptist merchant-pastor William Kiffin.

[3] Sir Charles Firth and Godfrey Davies, The Regimental History of Cromwell's Army (1940), i. 100–1; Shaftesbury Papers, VII, 469.   [4] C.J. viii. 109, 160, 177.

Parliament was the one ordinance that no Cavalier squire desired to reverse. The difficulty lay in the form of compensation which should be given to the King for not reviving his former rights of wardship. Some Presbyterian members, including Annesley, Prynne and Clarges, wanted a land tax to be paid by the same gentry classes who had been in the Court's clutches; but others preferred a continuation of the Long Parliament's excise duties, which would fall on all consumers. Amongst this group was Ashley Cooper, and on 21 November 1660, they carried the day by 151 votes to 149.[1] In this he showed the attitude of a wealthy landed proprietor; but it is also possible that the excise suited the government better, in that money could more easily be raised in advance on its security.

The journals of the House of Commons contain many further entries which illustrate his new-found status as a privy-councillor member, even when we catch no echoes of the opinions he expressed. He was frequently one of the small group of members appointed to manage conferences with the Lords over disputed amendments to bills; this was the case with the Indemnity Bill, the Poll Bill, and the Militia Bill.[2] On other occasions it was he who reported the King's wishes to the House. On 23 July he reported to the House the King's readiness to withdraw a temporary ban on the export of cloth pending the enactment of a customs duty, in answer to the House's petition; and on 13 September he reported the King's acceptance of the House's desires about the Court of Wards, the settling of ministers, leases of crown land, and timber in the Forest of Dean.[3] Finally on 14 December there is even the piquant spectacle of Ashley Cooper helping to damp down the excited protests of his old friend Sir Walter Earle and others against the disorderly behaviour of Royalist militia.[4] He was one of a small group who supplied the indispensable link between executive and legislature. On the whole they were remarkably successful, in comparison with the government spokesmen in later Parliaments, especially when one considers the shakiness of the new government's position and the fact that so many of the members had previously been on opposite sides in a civil war. All in all, when the Convention was dissolved on 29 December Charles had no reason to be dissatisfied with his new servants' parliamentary work for him.

Ashley Cooper, however, had many other tasks thrust upon him in addition to his services in the House and its committees. There were meetings of the Privy Council, and this body too had its committees on a great variety of topics. He was not a member of the most important of them, the 'committee of foreign affairs'; but he was very early placed on a committee to deal with the plantations, which was intended to meet on two afternoons every week (4 July). Other committees in which he was

---

[1] *Old Parliamentary History*, xxiii (1761), 21; cf. ibid. xxii. 415.
[2] *C.J.* viii. 124, 128, 130, 157, 163, 165, 168, 188.
[3] Ibid. pp. 99, 171.   [4] *Old Parliamentary History*, xxiii (1761), 53.

included were authorized to receive proposals from the Swedish envoy, to discuss relations with the United Provinces, to deal with the Navy, to examine the magazines and buildings of the Tower of London; the list could be extended to illustrate the range of his interests.[1] He was in demand because he had acquired so much knowledge of current problems in the three months before the Restoration, but also because he was the sort of person who could usefully be placed on any committee, who could be relied on to grasp a problem quickly and give a decisive opinion upon it. Between 1660 and November 1664, he was placed on forty-one of fifty-four Council committees, and this fact speaks for itself.[2] He was one of the hard workers of whom, in a particularly chaotic situation, the new government stood sorely in need.

His reward came in the spring of 1661. The elections which were taking place were the first for over twenty years in which he had no direct personal interest. He was no longer concerned with winning a seat in the House of Commons, for, having by now worked his passage, he received a peerage. On 20 April he became Lord Ashley, taking his title not from a place or from his father's name, but from his grandfather. His patent of creation referred to his part in helping Monk to bring about the Restoration, and described him as *fide erga nos summa, affectuque erga patriam integerrimo praestans*, in the effusive way of such documents. The horoscope which was cast on his nativity at this time did not indicate that these two qualities of loyalty to his king and love of his country were ever to conflict.[3] On 11 May he took his seat on the peers' bench in the House of Lords, having been introduced by Lords Windsor and Hatton. Precisely why these two sponsored him is not clear, for neither was a close friend, though both had some colonial interests.[4]

Thus he exchanged the status of knight of the shire for that of a peer of the realm. Though he had attained only the most junior rank in the peerage (unlike his collaborator Annesley, who received the earldom of Anglesey), he had moved up the social and political scale. No politician in the reign of Charles II ever regretted being 'kicked upstairs', and few expressed any scorn for titles: certainly Ashley never did, and no doubt he was suitably gratified by his promotion. Perhaps, however, he was equally pleased by the second reward which came his way. Two days after his introduction into the House of Lords, he was appointed Chancellor of the Exchequer and Under-Treasurer, so that for the first time he gained administrative office in addition to his membership of the Privy Council.

Clarendon ascribed the appointment to the influence of Ashley's uncle

[1] S.P. Charles II, 204, fos. 139 sqq.
[2] E. R. Turner, *The Privy Council of England in the Seventeenth and Eighteenth Centuries, 1603–1784* (1927–8), ii. 369.
[3] MSS. Ashmole 838, fo. 36; MSS. Ashmole 243 (unnumbered).
[4] *L.J.* xi. 249–50. Windsor became governor of Jamaica in July 1661.

by marriage, the Earl of Southampton, who was now Lord Treasurer, and commented grudgingly that '[Ashley's] parts well enough qualified him for the discharge [of this office]; though some other qualifications of his, as well known, brought no advantage to His Majesty by that promotion'.[1] There can indeed be no doubt of his business ability, his diligence and mastery of detail. Not only devoted servants like Locke and Stringer, but hard-working administrators like Pepys, and observers like the French ambassador Comminges all paid tribute to him. Yet these qualities had to be exercised largely on routine matters; they could not easily be brought to bear upon the intractable financial problem as a whole. The main responsibility here must inevitably fall upon Southampton, and Southampton, though honest and well-meaning enough, was inadequate for the extremely difficult financial situation in which he found himself. He did not possess the drive, initiative and authority which were necessary. He abdicated from the responsibility of advising the King on the numerous petitions for grants and favours which came in, and was incapable of fighting for the necessary Treasury control over the departments; he had not the personality either to influence the members of the House of Commons to vote more money, or to insist that the King should attempt to cut his coat according to his cloth. Faced by a crippling debt and inadequate revenue, he could do little but drift helplessly along, retaining his office at the insistence of his friend Clarendon until he died.[2]

This may be part of the explanation for the deteriorating relations between Ashley and Southampton. At the beginning of the reign they collaborated in other matters besides financial ones: the bishops laid the blame for Southampton's desire to moderate the Church settlement and conciliate the Presbyterians 'on the great ascendant that Ashley was observed to have over him'.[3] On the other hand, Clarendon, writing of the period at the end of 1664 just before the outbreak of the Dutch war, asserted that 'the treasurer . . . exceedingly disdained the behaviour of his nephew . . . who he well knew had by new friendships cancelled all the obligations to him'.[4] A year later it seems that Southampton was relying more upon his secretary, Sir Philip Warwick. Charles II then told Clarendon, after commending the 'good old man's' integrity, that 'he was not fit for the office he held: that he did not understand the mystery of that place, nor could in his nature [go through] with the necessary obligations of it. That his bodily infirmities were such, that many times he could not be spoken with for two or three days, so that there could be no despatch: of which everybody complained, and by which his business suffered very much. That all men knew that all the business was done by Sir Philip Warwick, whom, though a very honest man, he did not think fit to be

---

[1] Clarendon, *Continuation*, i. 315.
[2] S. B. Baxter, *The Development of the Treasury, 1660–1702* (1957), pp. 9–11, 259–61.
[3] Burnet, *Supplement*, p. 57.   [4] Clarendon, *Continuation*, ii. 91.

treasurer; which he was to all effects, the treasurer himself doing nothing but signing the papers which the other prepared for him. . . .'[1] This is one of the most remarkable descriptions ever made by a king of his lord treasurer in time of war; yet Southampton was permitted to retain his position until his death eighteen months later. It must have been an extremely frustrating experience to serve as Chancellor of the Exchequer under such a superior, when the administration was suffering from an impossible burden of debt and the House of Commons would not vote sufficient money to satisfy all the greedy claimants.

Ashley's papers therefore include estimates of the King's revenue, expenditure and debts,[2] but estimates, however accurate, could not alter a situation over the main features of which he had no control. Some of his routine duties were discussed in a surviving paper on the office and duties of the Chancellor of the Exchequer which described him as 'an officer empowered and entrusted to put in execution the laws and customs which are of force for the timely answering bringing in and taking the accompts and revenue thereof'.[3] The Exchequer did not directly collect most of the revenue, but it controlled the tax agents, commissioners or farmers who did, and those who claimed to have spent the proceeds: at least all accomptants had to produce their accounts for approval.[4] Accordingly the Chancellor of the Exchequer had to concern himself with a wide range of subjects, and this is reflected in the surviving Shaftesbury Papers,[5] which include documents submitted to him on many minor topics, from the sheriffs' accounts and the product of the office of first-fruits to the farming of the right to mine tin, the production of alum, and the administration of the King's lands in the Duchy of Cornwall and his rights in the New Forest and the Forest of Dean. Papers relating to the more important branches of the royal revenue are few and of doubtful significance. All are in miscellaneous handwritings, unsigned, rarely with any indication of Ashley's own views, and it is difficult to know how much importance to attach to the mere fact that a document has been preserved. A man's papers may be kept for a variety of reasons—or chances, and certainly there is no indication of any system to account for Ashley's. They are more impressive for their bulk and variety than for the light they throw on his ideas, although occasionally there are some hints. One anonymous writer advocated the collection of the taxes by the traditional officer, the sheriff, and not by a specially appointed receiver, 'commonly a person of no visible estate in the country or elsewhere', whose bailiffs are 'very extortive and grievous to the people'. Elsewhere there is a draft of an Act

---

[1] Clarendon, *Continuation*, ii. 234.
[2] E.g. Shaftesbury Papers, III, 90, 98, 105; VII, 479.
[3] Ibid. VII, 577.
[4] S. B. Baxter, op. cit. has no section directly on the duties of the Chancellor of the Exchequer; but cf. pp. 1–2, 33–35, 109–12.
[5] *Passim* in bundles III to VII, XXXII, etc.

for this purpose. It would be dangerous to conclude from this that Ashley seriously contemplated a return to the medieval practice of relying on the sheriffs; but it is interesting to compare a circular letter written by South-ampton and Ashley to all justices of the peace in 1662 about the farming of the excise. This quoted with approval Parliament's desire that the farm 'might be in the hands of such as were best known in the country and so likeliest to govern it to their content', and called upon the justices to make recommendations. This might represent a desire on Ashley's part to rely on local people of some wealth and position, rather than people 'of no visible estate in the country or elsewhere'; and as such it could be argued that this fitted in with what is known of Ashley's general political outlook.[1] But such hints cannot be pressed too far, and on the important subject of his relations with the bankers from whom the government borrowed there is no light whatsoever.

The years between Ashley's appointment in 1661 and the beginning of the Dutch war nearly four years later were a period of continuous hand-to-mouth struggle to satisfy petitioners and creditors from inadequate resources. Amongst the Cavaliers who clamoured for payment of pensions promised by the King there was even Elizabeth, daughter of the Queen of Bohemia and Rupert's sister, who wrote to Ashley from abroad to ask for favoured treatment.[2] All kinds of influence were employed at Charles's Court to secure priority of payment, as it became realized that the House of Commons had provided neither enough money to pay off the debts which the government had inherited, nor sufficient taxes to raise the £1,200,000 which they had recognized as appropriate for the King's normal annual revenue. Such expedients as a voluntary present to the King, to which Ashley himself contributed £300,[3] were of little avail; Queen Catherine of Braganza's dowry was being offered as security for loans in September 1661, eight months before she landed, and negotiations to get the money from the Portuguese at the most advantageous rate of exchange were a preoccupation for many months.[4] Creditors strove to get their debts secured upon a reliable branch of the royal revenue; and in February 1662, Southampton and Ashley tried to regulate the system of payment of debts assigned upon the customs, by directing that they should be repaid 'in course', that is, in the order in which they had been incurred. Compared with Downing's later scheme for repayment of loans 'in course', this was less rigid, for Southampton retained the power to give 'particular directions to the contrary', and this may have been one reason why the measure proved to be inadequate. In November 1662, a warrant had to be issued to the Lord Treasurer to permit no more assignations upon Customs, Excise and Hearth money until existing charges totalling £745,000 had been met, and in August 1663, the King

[1] Shaftesbury Papers, VII, 472, 533; C.T.B. 1660–7, pp. 401–3.
[2] Christie, i. 275.   [3] Shaftesbury Papers, XXXIV, 21.   [4] Cf. ibid. VII, 478.

had to issue a stoppage on all pensions, and to cut down household expenditure by suspending wages and food allowances to courtiers with places in the household.[1]

The Chancellor of the Exchequer was thus at the centre of a throng of competing claims and complaints. Some of those who were dissatisfied, together with those who had to vote and pay the taxes, were not slow to criticize the administration for alleged incompetence and corruption, which certainly existed although they were not the root cause of the financial difficulties. Ashley can undoubtedly be acquitted of incompetence, of which indeed no enemy ever accused him. One of Pepys's informants portrayed Ashley as almost the only capable and industrious man amongst the ministers: 'Sir John Hebden, the Russia Resident, did tell me how he is vexed to see things at Court ordered as they are by nobody that attends to business, but every man himself or his own pleasures. He cries up my Lord Ashley to be almost the only man that he sees to look after business, and with the ease and mastery that he wonders at him.'[2] Was his ability also used to his own financial advantage at the expense of the King and the taxpayer?

The official salary of the Chancellor of the Exchequer was a mere £200 per annum, which was made up to £1,000 to equal the salary of the Barons of the Exchequer with whom he sat to judge revenue cases.[3] But as in almost all offices in the seventeenth century, the salary was less important than the fees and perquisites which went with it. It has been estimated that before the Civil War fees paid to the Chancellor of the Exchequer had amounted to between £2,000 and £3,000 per year.[4] Accounts which survive among the Shaftesbury Papers give a total of only £3,381. 16s. 10d. for the period between 1662 and 1672,[5] but this cannot refer to the total profits of the place; these were as it were 'official' fees payable on writs, leases, patents, commissions, etc. It was within his power to supplement his income in other, less authorized ways, and there were some who thought that he did. Captain Cock, a commissioner for the sick and wounded in the Dutch war of 1665, told Pepys disgustedly that 'My Lord Treasurer, he minds his ease, and lets things go how they will; if he can have his £8,000 per annum, and a game at l'ombre, he is well. My Lord Chancellor, he minds getting of money, and nothing else; and my Lord Ashley will rob the Devil and the Altar, but he will get money if it be to be got.'[6] But there is no reason to suppose that this is a fairer estimate of Ashley than it is of Southampton and Clarendon; these were the cynical remarks of a man with a little inside knowledge trying to impress credulous gossip-seekers like Pepys. Again, Ashley was not left unscathed by the anonymous

[1] C.T.B. 1660–7, p. 358; C.S.P.D. 1661–2, p. 577; C.S.P.D. 1663–4, pp. 250, 255.
[2] Pepys, 6 June 1663; cf. also 27 May 1663.   [3] Shaftesbury Papers, VII, 508(1).
[4] G. E. Aylmer, The King's Servants (1961), p. 243. Unfortunately, however, no evidence is cited for this estimate.   [5] XXXVI, 26.   [6] Pepys, 9 Sept. 1665.

pamphleteers: a libel scattered in Westminster Hall at the meeting of Parliament in October 1669, flaying the Cabal and others, described Ashley as 'knavery bound up in little, the very abridgement of villainy. The world calleth him an ingenious man; I suppose it is because he is not hanged. . . . He is said to understand the King's revenue. No wonder, for he hath a share in every farm.'[1] There is only one piece of evidence related to this last statement that he went into partnership with some of the tax-farmers. Shortly after the Restoration the King had paid a debt to Sir Nicholas Crisp by giving him the right to a customs duty on foreign spice until £20,000 had been paid off; and when in the 1670s Danby had a covetous eye on the reversion to this tax, which he said was not authorized by law, he remarked that his plans would 'be opposed by my Lord Shaftesbury, he having a present share with Sir Nicholas Crisp'.[2] But no further details of this transaction are known. Those personal accounts of Ashley's which survive give no hint of his being involved with Crisp or any other tax-farmer, and one can fairly say only that no definite evidence exists to prove or disprove dishonest financial dealings with tax-farmers.

Another possible means of making corrupt gains was through the Chancellor of the Exchequer's powers of patronage, for there can be no doubt that he was in a position at least to influence the appointment of officials and tax-farmers. Here too, however, evidence is lacking. But it is relevant to mention the case of one man who made Shaftesbury a gift of money during his period as Lord Chancellor. When, towards the end of 1681, Shaftesbury was in the Tower awaiting trial for high treason, and consequently it was both safe and meritorious to join in hunting him down, one Adderley, Clerk of the Peace for Middlesex, brought a case against him. He alleged that he had paid Shaftesbury a bribe of 500 guineas without getting any valuable consideration in return, and claimed them back. He proved satisfactorily that he had paid the money; but the defence proved in reply that Shaftesbury had decided a dispute over a place in Adderley's favour, and that it was only two months afterwards that the plaintiff 'voluntarily made a present' of the money, 'which the Court looked upon as consideration enough'. The Court not only directed the jury to find for the defendant, but censured Adderley; and the most striking fact of all is that both friend and foe regarded Shaftesbury as amply justified by this evidence.[3] The acceptance of money under such

---

[1] The Alarum, printed in A. Browning, English Historical Documents 1660–1714 (1953), p. 235.

[2] Undated memorandum by Danby, Add. MSS. 28042, fo. 76; for the original warrant for Crisp's benefit, see Court Minutes of the East India Company 1660–3, ed. E. B. Sainsbury (1907–29), pp. 271, 284.

[3] See, for instance, the newsletter in C.S.P.D. 1680–1, p. 562; The Loyal Protestant and True Domestick Intelligence (Nath. Thompson), 12 Nov. 1681; The Impartial Protestant Mercury (Richard Janeway), 11–15 Nov. 1681. Cf. also Shaftesbury Papers, IV, 232, for a grant of the Clerkship of the Peace in Middlesex to W. Adderley by the Earl of Craven as Custos Rotulorum, 5 Nov. 1672.

circumstances was within the ordinary code of morality of the day, and not regarded as corrupt. Shaftesbury was no worse, and no better, than his contemporaries in this respect.

There remains the most serious accusation against Ashley's honesty. This arose from a claim for what were called defalcations. Financiers who had undertaken to farm a tax or contracted to supply the government could ask for allowances to be made in their favour if their profits were reduced unreasonably by war, plague, fire, or other extraordinary circumstance, and the question how much allowance should be made was then debated by the Council or by a specially appointed committee. The Chancellor of the Exchequer's support would be extremely valuable, if not decisive, if it could be secured by money or some other inducement. In the summer of 1666 Yeabsley, Lanyon, and Alsopp, the contractors for the supply of victuals to Tangier, presented a claim of this kind, basing it on the loss of some of their ships during the Dutch war. They had always believed in making friends of the mammon of unrighteousness, for when their contract had been made Samuel Pepys had benefited to the extent of £300 per annum in return for using his influence in their favour; and now Yeabsley himself told Pepys that Ashley had accepted a bribe of £100.

This would appear to be conclusive; but a judge would have to warn a jury of the dangers of accepting the uncorroborated evidence of an accomplice, such as Yeabsley was, and there are some curious features in this case which may raise doubts. On four separate occasions when Pepys was present at the Tangier committee he marvelled at the closeness with which Ashley inquired into the accounts, 'and yet with all the discretion imaginable.' Pepys would clearly have suspected nothing if he had not had secret information from Yeabsley. Again, it is surprising to find that the bribe allegedly offered to Ashley, a rich and powerful man, was only half the gains of the far humbler Pepys from the transaction; for Pepys, while criticizing the mote in his superior's eye, was prepared to overlook the beam in his own, and to call his money by the genteel name of profit, and not the nasty one of a bribe. Could it be that Yeabsley was seeking to convince Pepys that he could continue his support of the contractors in safety?[1]

In general it is fair to conclude that Ashley, like other members of the administration, may have accepted money from some of those with whom he had business dealings, but that if so he did not do it on a scale or in a manner which invited attack. His freedom from attack on this point is remarkable when one considers the vulnerability of his position as Chancellor of the Exchequer in a government accused of waste, peculation and embezzlement on a large scale, and also the number of his enemies both in the 1660s and at a later date. Neither the anonymous *Advices to a Painter*

[1] Pepys, 16 July 1664; 11, 20, 21 and 30 May 1666; 9, 14 and 15 June 1666; 23 Sept. 1667.

of this period, nor Dryden and other Tory writers in the reaction after the Popish Plot, made the vehement references to corruption which one would expect if his reputation was black. Contemporaries plainly did not think that his conduct was particularly bad, and although they criticized him on many other grounds they did not do so because he was thought to have rendered the King inefficient or dishonest service.

During the 1660s, therefore, Ashley was engaged in hard, administrative work. When Parliament was sitting he must have been especially busy, attending the House of Lords, the Privy Council and their committees, and performing a wide variety of duties connected with the Exchequer. There is an obvious contrast here between Ashley and his later colleague in the 'Country Party', the Duke of Buckingham, who never did any regular administrative work of any consequence. Shaftesbury is often thought of as parliamentary leader, political intriguer and demagogue; but in the background, at least, there are to be seen the years of unspectacular, unremitting and useful service in office under Charles II.

CHAPTER IX

THE SURVIVAL OF THE FITTEST—I (1661-5)

> Behold him now exalted into trust,
> His counsels oft convenient, seldom just;
> Even in the most sincere advice he gave
> He had a grudging still to be a knave . . .
> At best, as little honest as he could,
> And, like white witches, mischievously good.
>
> *The Medal*

ON 23 April 1661, Charles II was at last crowned king over an apparently contented people; and among the barons who advanced two by two in procession to Westminster Abbey, 'carrying their caps of crimson velvet, turn'd up with miniver, in their hands', was the newly created Lord Ashley of Wimborne St. Giles. We are told that 'towards the end of dinner-time . . . it began to thunder and lighten very smartly', and that some naturally interpreted this as ominous[1]; but most people regarded the coronation and its festivities as another symbol of the national reconciliation.

Yet amongst those who walked in pairs on this occasion there were many different species of politician—men with widely varying ideas and habits and backgrounds, both Royalist and Parliamentarian, who would inevitably vie for power to pursue their own policies or serve their own interests. All politics is in some sense a matter of the survival of the fittest, but this was more than usually true at the Court of Charles II. They were all ambitious and therefore all rivals. And amongst them Ashley occupied a special position. There were other ex-Parliamentarians amongst Charles's privy councillors, but (apart from Monk, who had a unique claim on the royal gratitude) he was the only one who had been a Republican and a servant of Cromwell. In a Court filled with Cavaliers, and a Court in which Butler's *Hudibras* appealed to the dominant mood, he was likely to find himself exposed and isolated unless he showed himself to be particularly adaptable.

He was able to commend himself partly through his Royalist uncle, the Lord Treasurer, and partly by making himself useful in a minor role in the administration. But in addition he was also able to win friends by means of his personal charm. Within a year or two ex-Royalists like Prince Rupert and the Earl of Craven were both friends and business partners. He was on good terms with the Duke of Richmond, who was his

---

[1] Sir R. Baker, *Chronicle* (1684), pp. 739, 748.

Lord-Lieutenant in Dorset, and with Seth Ward, Bishop of Salisbury.[1] 'A man of great business and yet of pleasure, and drolling too',[2] his company was acceptable in the supper-time gatherings below stairs in the rooms of Lady Castlemaine, where the King and his cronies entertained themselves. He made himself agreeable on the one hand to Sir Henry Bennet, later Earl of Arlington, and on the other to the Duke of Buckingham. The former bore proudly across his nose a black sticking-plaster concealing or emphasizing the honourable scar which he had won in a Civil War cavalry skirmish; and since then he had acquired from a stay as the King's representative in Spain a kind of Spanish gravity, the deferential good manners of a courtier, the art of anticipating the King's wishes and sharing his tastes. The mercurial, irrepressible Buckingham, however, relied for his favour with the King on a familiarity which derived from the days when they had been first playmates, and then young men sowing their wild oats, together; and he maintained this intimacy with witty convivial conversation and extravagant ideas, in turn 'chymist, fiddler, statesman, and buffoon'. Temperamentally Arlington and Buckingham were poles apart; but Ashley got on well enough with both. So, too, he did at first with the Earl of Lauderdale, who gradually asserted himself as the King's representative in Scotland, and who at this date still combined some intellectual interests with his coarse, brutal behaviour.

These were all new acquaintances, but there was also one who reappeared at the Restoration after Ashley had last seen him at Oxford in 1643. This was the Earl of Bristol, once the admired youthful prodigy on the Dorset bowling-greens of Ashley's youth. Since he had abandoned his original discontent and joined the Court in 1641, Digby had been the rash, and unsuccessful, adviser of the arrest of the Five Members, and had given equally unwise counsel, both political and military, at Oxford; and in exile in 1657 he had startlingly been converted to Roman Catholicism, though to his dismay he found that he lost his Secretaryship of State as a result. Neither his religious nor his political extremism was likely to commend itself to the moderate, cautious Hyde, and from 1657 onwards their relationship went from bad to worse. When, at the Restoration, Bristol found himself without office, and without as much reward as he thought himself entitled to expect, he put this down to the machinations of his former colleague, who was now the all-powerful Lord Chancellor; and it was not long before his resentment became public and political. In the years 1661–3 Ashley, like others, had to decide whether to remain supporting Clarendon, or whether to throw in his lot with Bristol in the latter's reckless attempts to undermine the Chancellor.

There were two major fields of policy in which disagreement was possible. The first of these was the finding of a bride for Charles, whose

[1] Cf. Walter Pope, The Life of . . . Seth [Ward], Lord Bishop of Salisbury (1697), pp. 88–89.   [2] Pepys, 15 May 1663.

marriage to Catherine of Braganza was decided on in May 1661, and finally accomplished a year later. And secondly there were the measures taken to re-establish the Church of England, pressed on strongly by the overwhelmingly Anglican majority in the House of Commons. In both cases Bristol and Clarendon differed in their ideas, and in both Ashley inclined more to the position taken up by Bristol.

The Portuguese marriage, which has been described as 'intrinsically a victory for Clarendon over his rivals',[1] was not accomplished without opposition. It was strongly encouraged by Louis XIV, for it implied English support for the Portuguese in their struggle for independence from France's rival, Spain; and there were those in London who were more jealous of French power than they were tempted by the commercial concessions which the marriage treaty promised. The Spanish ambassador in London, Watteville, with the aid of the so-called 'Spanish' faction at Court, therefore sought to hinder the marriage, putting forward alternative candidates for the honour of being Charles II's queen. There was no Spanish Infanta available, but Bristol went to Italy to inspect the Princesses of Parma: in vain, however, for on 9 May 1661 the Privy Council accepted Catherine as Charles's prospective bride. But it was many months before she landed in England, and in the meantime Watteville tried to work up opposition to the Portuguese alliance among the King's ministers. Little is known of the details of his intrigues, which eventually led to his recall at Charles's request in February 1662,[2] but there is an interesting letter from Louis XIV to his London ambassador, D'Estrades, referring to a plot against Clarendon and the marriage which he favoured. According to Louis, a cabal was agitating against the treaty with Portugal on the pretext that its commercial clauses had already been infringed by a further treaty between Portugal and the Dutch, and alleging also that the alliance would inevitably bring with it a rupture with Spain, with the consequent loss of the valuable English trade with that country.[3] Hostility to the Dutch, dislike of Portuguese sugar competition, fear of France and a disinclination to break with Spain are motifs which reappear constantly in the political views of the merchant classes in this period, and from time to time also in the career of Ashley, who is mentioned by name as one of the cabal. As has been seen,[4] one of Clarendon's merits in Ashley's eyes in 1660 had been his resistance to French influences at the court of the Stuarts. Now that Clarendon and the French both favoured a Portuguese marriage, Ashley along with Bristol was opposed to it.

Thus informed by his master, the French ambassador hastened to pass on his fears to Charles II, and reported to Louis the results of his conversation. Charles had explained that he wanted to ruin Anglesey,

---

[1] Sir Keith Feiling, *British Foreign Policy 1660–72* (1930), p. 52. (Chapter ii of this work contains the authoritative account of the complicated foreign policy of 1660–2.)
[2] Ibid. p. 42.   [3] Louis XIV to D'Estrades, 6/16 Sept. 1661.   [4] p. 136 above.

Dorchester and 'Cooper' amongst the pro-Spanish faction; as far as Monk, Ormond and Bristol (whom D'Estrades had also named) were concerned, he was sure of them, and their opposition did not matter.[1] Plainly Charles still cared little for the ways of the recent converts to the Royalist cause, and desired to get rid of them at the earliest opportunity. As yet Ashley had not succeeded in ingratiating himself in the King's favour.

The marriage to Catherine of Braganza duly took place in May 1662, and thereafter ceased to be of any great political importance until it became clear that the Queen could not provide the heir who was needed. In the same month the Act of Uniformity received the royal assent, and the resettlement of the Church was complete. On the main principle of Anglican predominance there was no dispute among Charles's advisers; but the question remained whether, if only from motives of expediency, any concessions should be made to the Puritans in order to avoid driving them to desperation. The first two acts of the so-called Clarendon Code substantially represented the victory of the extremists, with the aid of the triumphant Anglican majority in the Cavalier House of Commons: the Corporation Act of 1661 was designed to restrict municipal office to Anglicans, and the Act of Uniformity of 1662 to restrict the possession of benefices to episcopally ordained clergy who were prepared to give their assent and consent to a largely unaltered Book of Common Prayer. It is now known that the latter Act was more rigorous than Clarendon himself intended,[2] and to that extent it is unlikely that there was a sharp cleavage of opinion between Ashley and the Lord Chancellor. Ashley's uncle Southampton was reputed to favour concessions to the Puritans in order to 'heal the Church', and the bishops blamed Ashley's influence for this,[3] but Ashley did not attract attention to himself by any intervention in the debates. He was not present at the decisive conference between Lords and Commons on the Corporation Act on 19 December 1661, and was not even included in the committee of the House of Lords on the Act of Uniformity.[4] On 8 May, when the House finally debated amendments from the Commons which made the Act more stringent, he was not

[1] D'Estrades, 19/29 Sept. 1661.

[2] Cf. K. Feiling, 'Clarendon and the Act of Uniformity', in *E.H.R.* (1929), pp. 289–91, and *History of the Tory Party, 1640–1714* (1924), pp. 104 sqq. I am, however, unable fully to accept the extreme conclusions of G. R. Abernathy, 'Clarendon and the Declaration of Indulgence', in the *Journal of Ecclesiastical History* (1960), pp. 55–73.

[3] Burnet, *Supplement*, p. 57.

[4] *L.J.* xi. 356, 366, 450. Martyn in his eighteenth-century biography of Shaftesbury maintained that Ashley vehemently opposed the Corporation Act (i. 255–6, cf. 260). This could represent a tradition in the Shaftesbury household, but it is inconceivable that Ashley in 1661 used the arguments which Martyn puts into his mouth, to the effect that the Act 'was the most effectual method which could be contrived for lodging the executive power of the government in the hands of such persons as would make no difficulty of subjecting the whole nation to an absolute tyranny both of church and state'. Probably Martyn was here ascribing to him opinions derived from his later career and principles in opposition.

L

recorded as being present. Neither he nor any other peer recorded any protest against the Bill. Protest would have availed nothing. The natural conclusion is that Ashley, considering his past career, found it best to lie low in the debates, and he certainly did not propose to attend any Puritan conventicle. John Highmore, who had been Rector of Wimborne St. Giles since 1655, made no difficulty in conforming; and Ashley, like many other ex-Puritans of his class, joined a Latitudinarian, anti-clerical party within the re-established Church of England, ready to lend a helping hand to the Dissenters when the opportunity arose. Such an opportunity might present itself in conjunction with an attempt to provide indulgence for the King's Roman Catholic friends, and this brought him once more into contact with the Earl of Bristol and a small group of influential courtiers.

It had soon become common knowledge in political circles that Charles was well disposed towards Catholics. Catholics had helped him in his flight after the battle of Worcester, had been loyal to him in exile, and now continued in his household. Charles was known to have expressed his disgust of the sanguinary penal laws, and several politicians sought to avail themselves of Charles's inclinations. Bristol had become converted to Catholicism in 1657; Bennet, who to Clarendon's chagrin replaced Nicholas as Secretary of State in October 1662, was rumoured to be 'popishly affected', and eventually, like his master, was admitted on his death-bed into the Roman Catholic Church. Among other allies at Court this group enjoyed the powerful aid of Lady Castlemaine, the royal mistress, of whom Clarendon had made an inveterate enemy. She was spiteful, hot-tempered, volatile, and greedy, but she knew how to entertain the King. Quite apart from her physical attractions, she knew how to provide convivial company for him in her famous supper-parties, and the conversation had a way of turning to politics of which Clarendon did not approve. Amongst this group Bristol in particular staked his political future on providing the toleration for Catholics which he knew Charles wanted, and which he knew Clarendon was reluctant to give.

The first attempt to ease the position of the Catholics had been made in July 1661, when a bill had been introduced into the House of Lords to repeal various clauses in the penal laws, and also the Act of 1593 against Dissenters—thus early it was realized that the best method of helping the Catholics was in conjunction with the relief of Dissenters. Bristol spoke warmly for the bill, whereupon Clarendon opposed it, 'rather to be contrary to the Earl of Bristol than on purpose to harm the Catholics',[1] and perhaps also because he did not wish to run the risk of antagonizing Protestant feeling in the House of Commons. Ashley was not prominent in the debate, but he was put on the large committee, headed by the Duke

[1] D'Estrades, 15/25 July 1661; cf. also 19/29 Aug. 1661, and Clarendon, *Continuation*, i. 536–9.

of York, to which the bill was referred.[1] The bill, however, perished with the prorogation ten days later, and the attempt to secure an indulgence for Catholics was not renewed until December 1662, when the situation had been modified in two ways.

In the first place, there were rumours that Clarendon's influence with the King had declined considerably in comparison with that of Bristol and the opposing cabal. The Dutch ambassador had noticed the existence of 'envious enemies' of the Chancellor in May 1662, and in October they were successful in procuring the replacement of Secretary Nicholas by Sir Henry Bennet. Though Nicholas was elderly and no longer equal to his duties, while Bennet had considerable knowledge of foreign affairs, the change was regarded by many as the work of Bristol and others to eject a client of Clarendon's and substitute a friend of the rising cabal.[2]

Secondly, in August 1662 there had taken place the Great Ejection of Puritan ministers as a result of the Act of Uniformity. Over a thousand clergy left their benefices rather than take the tests which the Act prescribed. Another attempt to ease the lot of the Catholics might now depend upon the support of those who wanted to indulge Protestants, and observers noted with surprise that Lady Castlemaine was 'the fiercest solicitor these ejected Presbyterian ministers have'.[3] Amongst the King's ministers the ex-Presbyterian Lord Privy Seal, Robartes, could be expected to help them. So too could Ashley, whose importance people were now beginning to note: rumour even reached Ormond in Dublin that in a general ministerial reshuffle Ashley was to replace Morrice as the second Secretary of State and Bennet's colleague.[4] Moreover, Clarendon himself had always been uneasy about the rigour of the Act of Uniformity, and, if only because of fears of the dangers to public order which might result, had taken part in efforts to modify it; so that he could hardly now come out in opposition to a measure of indulgence.[5]

This was the background to the issue of a Declaration on 26 December 1662, in which Charles defended himself against the charge that he had broken his pledge at Breda to give 'a liberty to tender consciences'. He said that it had been necessary to give the re-establishment of the Church of England priority over the grant of indulgence to dissenters from it; but now that the former objective had been achieved by the Act of Uniformity, he would try to help those with tender and peaceable consciences by inclining Parliament in its next session to concur in a bill, which would permit him to exercise his inherent power of dispensing people from the penal laws. As a reward for their loyal services to the Royalist cause, Roman

[1] L.J. xi. 310–11.
[2] De Wiquefort in C.S.P.D. 1661–2, pp. 371–2 (cf. also C.S.P. Ven. 1661–4, p. 164); Ormond to Clarendon, 19 Oct. 1662, in MSS. Carte 143, fo. 18.
[3] O'Neill to Ormond, 2 Sept. 1662, MSS. Carte 32, fo. 3.
[4] Ormond to Clarendon, 20 Oct., MSS. Carte 143, fo. 23.
[5] See the articles of Feiling and Abernathy, quoted above, p. 161, n. 2.

Catholics would be allowed to share in the benefits of such an act, though they were not to be given an official toleration or to be permitted to proselytize. Clarendon, writing in old age and exile and portraying himself as a consistent and uncompromising Anglican throughout, ascribed the responsibility for the Declaration to Ashley, 'out of his in-differency to religion', Bennet, 'out of his good will to the Roman Catholics', and Robartes, 'whose interest was most in the Presbyterians', and to these Bristol must undoubtedly be added. But (though this could not be inferred from the terms of his own narrative) the Declaration was also shown to the Lord Chancellor, bed-ridden with gout in Worcester House, and Clarendon had not objected to it in principle, though he had complained about 'several parts' of it, and doubted its 'seasonableness' because he feared that it might raise suspicions that the King was too favourable to Roman Catholics. The indulgence was a policy in which friends of the Catholics, friends of the Dissenters, and those Anglicans who yet feared or disliked making Dissenters desperate, might tempor-arily combine. Only later were the differences in outlook to result in division.[1]

In form this was a declaration of policy which would not be operative until Parliament could be persuaded to pass a bill to the same effect. When Parliament met on 18 February 1663, however, the House of Com-mons, in spite of its overwhelmingly Royalist composition, proceeded in the next few days to draw up an address calling for the withdrawal of the indulgence and denying the King's claim to a dispensing power on which the Declaration had been based. Charles, in need of money, was not in a position to resist this; but Ashley and Robartes were not prepared to admit defeat without a struggle. On 23 February Robartes introduced his Dispensing Bill into the House of Lords. This is often regarded merely as an attempt to put the Declaration into the form of a bill, but in fact there is an important difference between the two. The bill was explicitly di-rected to help Protestants and afforded no sort of relief to Roman Catholics. It authorized the King to dispense with the Act of Uniformity and any other laws enjoining conformity to the established church, and to grant licences to subjects of the Protestant religion, of whose inoffensive and peaceable disposition he was persuaded, to enjoy the use and exercise of their religion and worship, though these differed from the public rule; provided that no such indulgence or dispensation should extend to tolerating the use or exercise of the Popish or Roman Catholic religion, or to enable anyone disabled from holding public office to do so.[2] Such a bill might perhaps be supported by Catholics as a prelude to a possible relaxation of

---

[1] A. Browning, *English Historical Documents 1660–1714* (1953), pp. 371–4; Clarendon, *Continuation*, ii. 93; Ormond to Bennet, 14 Jan. 1663, MSS. Carte 143, fo. 63; Bennet to Ormond, 13 Jan. 1663, and Clarendon to Ormond, 31 Jan., in T. H. Lister, *Life of Edward, Earl of Clarendon* (1837), iii. 231–3; loc. cit. in previous note.

[2] Christie, vol. i, pp. lxxix–lxxxi.

the penal laws in their own favour, and opposed by Anglicans on the same ground; but in itself it was designed explicitly to aid Protestant dissenters alone. As such it was fully consistent with Ashley's policy at all other times of tolerating Nonconformists but not necessarily Papists.

The bill received its first and second readings and then passed into committee. The critical stage was reached on 12 March, when Clarendon, who had previously been kept away by his gout, attended for the first time and declared his opposition to it. The Lord Chancellor had been far from an uncompromising opponent of the Declaration of Indulgence when it had been first issued, and had indeed drafted a message to the House of Commons in support of it. However, when the draft bill had been read to the committee of foreign affairs, Clarendon and Southampton had both opposed it, not because it was too indulgent to Puritans, but because it was 'a thing that could never find the concurrence of either or both houses, and which would raise a jealousy in both, and in the people generally, of his affection to the papists, which would not be good for either'. These doubts about the 'seasonableness' rather than the merits of the measure had naturally been strengthened by the opening debates in both houses. When Clarendon was fit enough to attend the House of Lords, he naturally felt that it was his task to protect the government from any suspicion of unsoundness in religion, and to preserve his own reputation from the rumour that he personally had drawn up the bill. At first, however, according to his own account he left it to the bishops and to Southampton to lead the attack on the bill.[1]

At this point the Lord Privy Seal, Robartes, who had originally sponsored the bill, abandoned it. He could see the way the wind was blowing, and the political risks involved, and he remained silent. It was left to Ashley to defend the bill and the royal dispensing power on which it was based. Declining to follow the lead of his relative Southampton, he 'adhered firmly to his point, spake often and with great sharpness of wit, and had a cadence in his words and pronunciation that drew attention' in the grand committee of the House. He, the former member of the Cromwellian Council of State, posed as the loyal supporter of the royal prerogative while the great officers of the crown opposed it; and he professed to be the more surprised at this, 'because nobody knew more than they the King's unshakeable firmness in his religion, that had resisted and vanquished so many great temptations', and therefore they above all should have been willing to trust the King with the powers claimed for him. This taunt about his alleged unwillingness to trust Charles stung Clarendon, as Ashley

---

[1] *L.J.* xi. 482–92; G. R. Abernathy, op. cit. pp. 68–73; Clarendon, *Continuation*, ii. 93–100. It does not seem to me that Clarendon's own account of the bill can be written off as completely as Professor Abernathy suggests, though it is plainly distorted and chronologically confused, and incorrectly states that the decisive debate took place on the second reading. Comminges, 9/19 Apr. 1663, asserts that at one point Clarendon directly opposed the Declaration in a speech in the House of Lords.

had known it would. Pulling himself with difficulty to his feet, the Lord Chancellor agreed that Charles was 'more worthy to be trusted than any man alive', but contended that this was not the point: the bill 'confounded all notions of religion and erected a chaos of policy to overthrow all religion and government' and Charles would find the trust placed in him extremely embarrassing. Clarendon was in some pain as he spoke—it was the first time he had even dragged himself to the House after some months of confinement to his room—and in the heat of the debate he was led on by Ashley to commit himself much further than he had intended, and further than he later felt to have been wise. Complaining of the 'wildness and illimitedness' of the bill, he described it as 'ship-money in religion, that nobody could know the end of, or where it would rest'; and if it were passed, 'Dr. Goffe or any other apostate from the church of England' might be made a bishop.

Clarendon's general contention was justified, in that the bill would have handed over dangerously sweeping powers to the royal discretion. Ashley, the future Whig leader, was in the wrong in striving to enhance the royal prerogative in religion in this way; and some have interpreted this episode as one example of his readiness to adopt whatever extreme view suited his political ambition at any particular time. There is however an alternative explanation. In debate Ashley was always prone to use whatever argument seemed tactically best suited to outmanoeuvre his opponents in order to reach his policy objective—the famous *Delenda est Carthago* speech was another instance of this.[1] Given that his objective was to secure toleration for the Puritans, and that the most zealous Royalists would inevitably be the fiercest opponents of this, it was tactically skilful to suggest that loyal Anglicans ought to be able to trust their King, and this line of argument obviously embarrassed Clarendon. In the circumstances of 1663 it was the way most likely to overcome the Anglicanism of the Cavalier Parliament. That this interpretation of Ashley's actions is the more probable (as against the view that he was merely currying favour with Charles by supporting a policy of indulgence) is further suggested by the fact that the bill contained no provision for Catholics, and by Clarendon's statement that 'the lord Ashley got no ground' with the King as a result of his efforts. On the whole it appears that his honesty and consistency of aim in religion may be recognized here, but not his political wisdom in the long run; though even here it must be said that James's use of the dispensing power could not have been foreseen in 1663, and that at that precise moment there was no reason to believe that Roman Catholicism was a serious political danger.

The obnoxious bill was dropped, and Clarendon's opposition to it won him some temporary popularity in the Commons[2], but this was at the cost of

[1] See pp. 316–17 below.
[2] For this session, cf. D. T. Witcombe, "The Cavalier House of Commons: the session of 1663", *Bull. Inst. Hist. Res.* (1959), pp. 181–91.

his favour with Charles. Previously he had not been an uncompromising opponent of indulgence; now, however, he had expressed views from which it would be impossible to turn back, in terms which were not palatable to the King, who had originally backed the bill. Charles expostulated with him, and though a reconciliation was achieved, Clarendon later wrote that 'from that time he never had the same credit with him [the King] as he had before'. His personal enemies were correspondingly encouraged, and in the spring of 1663 there were frequent rumours that a cabal was threatening his position. At the end of March the French ambassador reported that Bristol, Ashley, Robartes, Morrice and Bennet were co-operating; and ten days later he elaborated on this. Describing Ashley as the only man who could be set against Clarendon for intelligence and firmness, he declared that Ashley did not restrain himself from speaking freely about the Lord Chancellor and directly contradicting him. Ashley had even gone so far as to suggest to the King that Clarendon's family connexion with the Duke of York was harmful to the royal interests; he was shrewd and a very good courtier, and people suspected that Bristol, Bennet, Morrice and the rest of them might stir up *quelque mauvaise affaire* for the Lord Chancellor. This is the first recorded mention of Ashley's long hostility to the Duke of York.[1]

This line of gossip in due course reached Samuel Pepys, who noted in his diary on 15 May that Bristol, Buckingham, Bennet, Ashley and Sir Charles Berkeley between them had 'cast my Lord Chancellor upon his back, past ever getting up again'. He followed up this intriguing comparison between the old man and an overturned sheep helplessly waving its legs in the air, with an interesting comment on Ashley in particular. 'But stranger to hear, how my Lord Ashley, by my Lord Bristol's means . . . is got into favour, so much that, being a man of great business and yet of pleasure, and drolling too, he, it is thought, will be made Lord Treasurer upon the death or removal of the good old man [Southampton].' He added, as an explanation of the co-operation between Ashley and the Catholic Earl of Bristol, that Ashley had been brought over to the Catholic party against the bishops, 'whom he hates to the death, and publicly rails against them, not that he is become a Catholic, but merely opposes the bishops'. There was thus a clear distinction maintained between the standpoints of the two men: Ashley, unlike Bristol and Bennet, gave no good grounds for any belief that he was ready to buy the royal favour by favouring Catholicism himself. However, they were able to act together temporarily against established authority in religion; and in June the French ambassador reported home that Bristol was trying to get Ashley, *le plus agréable parleur d'Angleterre*, admitted to the foreign committee. At the same time Ashley was acting as intermediary in negotiations for the marriage of Bristol's daughter to Lord Sunderland; and he was assisting

[1] Comminges, 30 Mar./9 Apr. and 9/19 Apr. 1663.

Bennet in the interests of the proprietors of recently drained lands in the Fens, in which Bristol may also have been concerned.[1]

It is abundantly clear, therefore, that in the spring of 1663 Ashley was on friendly terms with his Dorset neighbour, the Earl of Bristol, and with others who were commonly regarded as Clarendon's rivals at Court. Yet it has to be remembered that he still maintained some connexions at least with the Chancellor, since on 24 March they and seven others had become joint proprietors of the projected colony of Carolina. Collaboration in this cherished scheme does not suggest uncompromising hostility between the two men; and this is noteworthy when one considers whether Ashley was involved in Bristol's rash attempt to impeach Clarendon in July 1663. No doubt Bristol presumed upon his friendships with Ashley, Bennet, and others; but it does not follow that the men were joined together in con-spiracy. A contemporary describing the crisis went so far as to say that Bristol had among his friends 'the Queen mother . . . all the nobility dis-obliged (not to say abused) by the Chancellor . . . Lord Ashley Cooper, on many old and new scores . . . and indeed almost all the rest of that House [the Lords], and the whole body of the Commons unless a lawyer or two preferred by the Chancellor, nay shall I say, all the people in England that have been sound in their religion and constant in their loyalty . . .'.[2] No doubt some such over-optimistic calculation was in Bristol's mind, but when it came to the point not one of the friends for whose support he hoped proved to be committed to him. Everyone commented on the absurdity and inconsistency of the charges of high treason which he brought—he, a Catholic, accusing Clarendon of favouring Popery—and the whole episode reads much more like the reckless bid of one desperate man (as Clarendon himself portrays it) than the result of a political combination. The only sign of preparation on Bristol's part was that he 'endeavouring to interest the people in his quarrel . . . quitted his ordinary way of going to the Lords' House, and came through the Great Hall and Exchequer Chamber, with his hat in his hand, saluting with a sad and humble countenance all the crowd that followed, wishing him all success. He showed himself several days upon the Exchange and told many considerable merchants his story . . .'.[3] This was an interesting foreshadowing of the later Whig appeals from the Court to the City, but in the circumstances of 1663 it had little relevance.

Bristol's bid failed as dismally and disastrously as the gamble which he had advised twenty years earlier in the impeachment of the Five Members.

[1] Pepys, 15 May 1663; Ruvigny, 15/25 June; O'Neill to Ormond, 27 June, MSS. Carte 32, fo. 625; Bennet to Ashley, 11 May, in Shaftesbury Papers, IV, 121; Wm. Garret to Bennet, 1 June, in C.S.P.D. 1663–4, p. 160.

[2] Salusbury to E. of Huntingdon, 13 July 1663, in MSS. Carte 77, fo. 524. Compare with this account of Bristol's fall that of O'Neill to Ormond, 11 July, MSS. Carte 32, fo. 708; and Clarendon's own story, ii. 22–28.

[3] O'Neill to Ormond, 7 Aug., MSS. Carte 33, fo. 34.

When he presented his charges of high treason, no one in the House of Lords supported him. In the course of his reply Clarendon questioned whether, even if the articles could be substantiated, they would amount to treason, and asked that the judges should be called upon to deliver their opinion on this. On this point Ashley did intervene to urge that the House itself was competent to pronounce, as the highest court: 'the judgment of the judges was nothing in the presence of their lordships, but only as they were the properest men to bring precedents; but nothing to interpret the law to their lordships, but only the inducements of their persuasions.'[1] On this technical point that the judges' opinion was only advisory and not binding, Ashley won agreement, but nevertheless the House proceeded to accept the judges' finding against Bristol in this particular case, and there is no evidence that Ashley disputed it. At the same time the House received a message from the King in which Charles gave his firm backing to his Chancellor, and Bristol was helpless to proceed any further. Before long he had to go into hiding to avoid a royal warrant for his apprehension; it was four years before he was able to return to the Court or to the Lords, and he never again recovered any political importance.

Ashley was in no way involved in Bristol's ruin: he continued with his position in the Privy Council and as Chancellor of the Exchequer unaffected. Nevertheless he must have pondered the implications of the affair. For all Bristol's faults, which were many, he had behind him many years of service in times of difficulty and misfortune. Now, in a matter of a week or two, he sank from a position of some influence to one of complete impotence. In the political rivalry of the period the stakes were high and ruin was apt to be complete, particularly if a man had relied on the royal favour rather than on some more permanent asset.

He did not, however, draw the moral that he must play for safety. In the interval between the prorogation of Parliament on 27 July 1663 and its reassembly on 16 March 1664 the gossip-mongers continued to associate his name with those who were reputed to be trying to undermine Clarendon's position. It is in this period that he is coupled for the first time with Lauderdale, the Scottish nobleman on whom Charles came more and more to rely for the government of his turbulent northern kingdom. Lauderdale's historical reputation is one of the blackest, and those who suffered the grim torture of the boot under his rule of Scotland have had ample revenge in the pages of Burnet and those who have written about the period. In the ensuing period Shaftesbury himself was to be one of the most vehement critics of his authoritarian grip on Scottish political and religious life. Yet his most unpleasant characteristics were perhaps not obvious to Englishmen in 1663. His character was to deteriorate progressively with advancing years. Even Burnet speaks respectfully of his earlier intellectual interests and knowledge of Greek, Latin, Hebrew,

[1] Pepys, 23 Sept. 1667.

divinity and history, but as time went on it is clear that he became increasingly coarsened and brutalized. His development from a relatively ingenuous young man into one of the most repellent politicians of his day is reflected in the portraits which were painted of him in different periods: contemporaries ascribed it to his association with the selfish, greedy Countess of Dysart, his mistress and later second wife, and to some extent it may also have been the familiar result of the exercise of power, corrupting him and enabling him to indulge his native violence and bad temper. In the early years of the Restoration, however, though his manner was rather more frank and boisterous than was usual at Charles's Court, the deterioration had not progressed very far and had not attracted the notice of English observers; and there was not the obvious gap between his political outlook and general tastes and those of Ashley which later developed.

In the first six months of 1664 the association of the two men attracted the notice of those who were eagerly on the look-out for signs that Clarendon's influence was weakening. The French ambassador named them amongst those who in January were alleged to be aiming at Clarendon's 'total ruin' by 'all sorts of means, both open and concealed'. Pepys too mentions them as 'opening high against the Chancellor' in readiness for the meeting of Parliament. Four months later Comminges again referred to 'Lauderdale's cabal', in which he was alleged to have united with Ashley, Robartes and others striving to destroy Clarendon in the course of 'the debauches which go on daily here'. The story was that in the course of their drinking with the King they were in the habit of making scornful remarks about the Chancellor, and that Charles made his own contribution to the fun.[1] Too much, however, should not be read into this kind of tittle-tattle. It is evidence that there were people who enjoyed a joke with the King at Clarendon's expense, and, so far as Ashley is concerned, that he did not unquestioningly follow the Chancellor's lead; but this falls a long way short of the definite political combination which the French ambassador expected. The surviving evidence of the parliamentary session of 1664 betrays no hint of disagreement on any political issue.

It had been thought that some of Bristol's friends might take up his cause, but when he sent a letter to the Lords in order to get his case debated there, Ashley was amongst those in favour of sending it on unopened to the King. The interpretation of one of the peers was that 'Lauderdale and Ashley Cooper are now quite silent, and as I suppose, taken into the Chancellor's friendship'.[2] On religious policy the King's ministers seem also to have preserved a reasonably united front. It is possible that neither Clarendon nor Ashley was altogether happy about

---

[1] Comminges, 25 Jan./4 Feb. and 26 May/5 June 1664; Pepys, 1 Feb. 1664.

[2] MSS. Rawl. A. 130, fo. 5; Lord Salisbury to Lord Huntingdon, 22 Mar. 1664, MSS. Carte 76, fo. 7; Bristol's petition to the Lords, c. 19 Mar., MSS. Clar. 80, fos. 153–4; and to the King, 20 Mar., ibid. 81, fos. 151–2.

the severe penalties which the Conventicle Act of 1664 imposed upon lay Dissenters,[1] but it was politically necessary to accept the view of the Anglicans in the House of Commons on this if the government was to achieve its more urgent objectives. One of these was the replacement of the Triennial Act of 1641 by a more innocuous measure, which, while accepting the principle that there should be no longer interval than three years before parliamentary sessions, abolished the machinery for elections which the earlier Act had provided. The effect was to restore the King's power to summon Parliament only as and when he thought fit; this was to be demonstrated at the end of the reign when there was in fact a period of four years in which no Parliament was summoned. Undoubtedly the King's ministers in 1664 went to some trouble to procure the repeal of the Act of 1641 which they regarded as an unreasonable restriction on the royal prerogative.[2] It has been suggested that Ashley contributed to achieve the desired result. There survives a list of members of the House of Commons, in his writing and from internal evidence compiled at this time, and there is a special mark (the letter 'S') against the names of office-holders and 'King's servants', whose votes the King might normally expect.[3] This could well represent a calculation of the voting strength likely to be available on the Triennial Bill, but the evidence is not conclusive; it is possible that the list had a financial objective in mind, or even that it is not connected with any specific measure. Nothing is known of any part which Ashley took in managing the House of Commons at this time.

At the same time there were growing signs of a demand for war with the Dutch.[4] There was already a long history of commercial rivalry between English and Dutch merchants, both in European waters and across the seas, and from one point of view the surprising thing is, not that there were three Anglo-Dutch wars in the middle of the century, but that there were only three. However those commercial interests whose competition with the Dutch had been bitterest had not always been able to make their views felt in the circles where state policy was made; and also domestic matters had taken precedence over foreign. Once before, in the days of the Rump, those interests in the City which were hostile to the Dutch had been successful in getting their rulers to adopt their policy, and war had followed. Now in 1664 there was again a situation in which merchants and governing classes tended to come together. To the old anti-Dutch feelings of the East India Company, excluded from the Spice Islands, and of the

---

[1] Ashley was one of the Lords' 'managers' at a conference with the Commons, 13 May 1664 (L.J. xi. 616).

[2] Caroline Robbins, 'The Repeal of the Triennial Act in 1664', in *Huntington Library Quarterly* (1948–9), pp. 121–40.

[3] J. R. Jones, 'Court Dependants in 1664', in *Bull. Inst. Hist. Res.* (1961), pp. 81–91.

[4] Cf. K. Feiling, op. cit. and C. H. Wilson, *Profit and Power* (1957), esp. chs. viii and ix; N. Japikse, *De Verwikkelingen tusschen de Republiek en Engeland 1660–5* (The Hague, 1900).

supporters of the Navigation Act policy who saw in the New Netherlands a loophole in their control over trade to the American plantations, were added those of the newer interests which invested in the Company of the Royal Fisheries and the Royal Africa Company. These included members of the House of Commons and influential people at Court from the Duke of York downwards. In addition to those investors who were brought sharply up against the competition of the Dutch in the fisheries and the slave trade from West Africa to the New World, there were others at Court who saw in a naval war prospects of both laurels and prize money. Both at Court and in Parliament pressure for war began to mount. Against the general current of opinion the King, Clarendon and Southampton held out as long as they could, knowing only too well how difficult their financial situation was, and how unprepared they were to fight a war.

Ashley was in a position to appreciate both sides of the argument. His interest in trade was well known, and he had many commercial connexions in the City who would retail to him their grievances against the Dutch.[1] On the other hand none knew better than the Chancellor of the Exchequer what the financial difficulties were likely to be. It is tempting to assume that, because he had been a member of the Council of State in the Commonwealth's Dutch war, and was to be a party to the third attack on the Dutch in 1672, he was one of the instigators of the second Dutch war too; but in fact there is no satisfactory evidence of his taking a very decided attitude in 1664. On 22 April he was one of seven peers appointed to manage a conference with the Commons, at which a young man named Clifford, now coming to the fore for the first time, represented all the complaints which the trading companies had to make against their Dutch competitors; and the upshot was that Lords and Commons joined in an address asking the King to protect trade from Dutch depredations. But since the reluctant Clarendon was also one of the managers of this conference, it is impossible to infer very much from it.[2]

On this occasion the King was able to divert the general desire for hostilities by means of a general promise to demand redress from the States-General, but events during the summer months, particularly hostilities on the coast of Guinea, made it impossible for him to hold back any longer. When he met Parliament again on 24 November he made it plain that his intentions were warlike; and Ashley was on the deputation of five from the House of Lords which had the dual task of thanking the King for his speech and thanking the City of London for supplying money to assist the government in its preparations.[3]

Those like Clarendon and Southampton who had been cautious and reluctant now had to combine with the war party in a common effort to make the best of the naval conflict which broke out in European waters in

---

[1] For his trading interests, see ch. XII below.
[2] *L.J.* xi. 599–600.   [3] *L.J.* xi. 627.

1665. For Ashley the war meant additional duties, both of a national and a local kind. He was responsible for the impressment of seamen from his native county of Dorset, and set about the task with characteristic thoroughness by calling for lists of names, occupations and ages of all the seamen available in Poole and the other local ports—an instance of his methodical procedure.[1] More important, however, was his appointment as Treasurer of Prize Money, responsible to the King alone for receiving and paying out the money.

Clarendon gives a long account of Ashley's appointment to this office,[2] saying that he himself knew nothing of it until 'one evening a servant of the Lord Ashley came to the chancellor with a bill signed, and desired in his master's name "that it might be sealed that night" '. The bill provided that Ashley should account for and pay out all proceeds from the sale of captured Dutch ships as directed by the King alone, without reference to the normal Exchequer routine. Any departure from the traditional procedure was bound to send the conservative Chancellor up in arms, and he went to the King and objected that 'his majesty might be abominably cozened', and also that the grant was derogatory to Lord Treasurer Southampton. Charles's reply was to get Ashley to pay Clarendon a visit and talk matters over. Ashley (so Clarendon wrote) told him 'with some sullenness "that the king had given him the office and knew best what is good for his own service, and that except his majesty retracted his grant, he would look to enjoy the benefit of it" '. He was willing that the terms of his commission should be amended in order to avoid any suspicion of putting an affront upon Southampton, but 'in all other respects he was resolved to run the hazard'. Southampton himself, 'though he knew that he was not well used, and exceedingly disdained the behaviour of his nephew', refused to intervene; and in the end Charles sent 'a positive order' to Clarendon to seal the commission. Faced by this, Clarendon gave way, though very unwillingly, 'because he very well knew, that few men knew the Lord Ashley better than the king himself did, or had a worse opinion of his integrity'. He attributed Ashley's success to the new friendships he had made, 'which could remove or reconcile all prejudices' on Charles's part: he alleged that Ashley had 'a league offensive and defensive' with Sir Henry Bennet and William Coventry, and above all 'had got an entire trust with the lady [Castlemaine] who very well understood the benefit such an officer would be to her'.

This account thus alleges that Ashley used the help of other intriguers in order to prevail over the King's better judgement and to gain for himself a lucrative office and for Charles new money for his pleasures. If it could be accepted as objective history it would be a heavy indictment of Ashley's

---

[1] Shaftesbury Papers, IV, 132–6; VII, 550–66.
[2] Clarendon, *Continuation*, ii. 82–92; cf. the despatches of the French ambassadors, 12/22 Dec., 29 Dec./5 Jan., 2/12 and 9/19 Jan. 1665.

conduct and motives; but when considered in its context it plainly derives from Clarendon's constant refusal to admit that any of his opponents could possibly have other than personal and selfish motives for their actions, particularly when these were innovations. Clarendon's obsession with an alleged 'league offensive and defensive' of his enemies must be discounted. The whole career of that prickly but honest individualist, William Coventry, suggests that he was not the man to engage in a close political combination; his real offence was that he was prepared to express forthright opinions of his own in contradiction to Clarendon.[1] Clarendon's imputations of unworthy motives to his opponents[2] must not blind us to the fact that there were some good reasons for the extraordinary appointment of a special treasurer of the prize money instead of relying on the usual but slow and cumbersome practice of the Exchequer. The experience of the first Dutch war had shown that prizes were particularly subject to embezzlement, and that unless reliable commissioners were appointed the normal Exchequer machinery was powerless to exercise effective control. John Sparrow, Richard Blackwall, Humphrey Blake, and other commissioners of prize goods under the Commonwealth had been accused in 1661 of being no less than £110,000 in arrears,[3] and as late as 1670 the Blackwall affair was still not closed.[4] In all probability there were many prize goods sold or embezzled of which the Exchequer had no knowledge, in addition to the arrears which were claimed. In 1664 Dutch prizes were expected to yield as much as they had done before, and for many at Court they were one of the main attractions of the war. There was a fierce scramble for commissionerships and other advantages. Among others, Samuel Pepys after dinner one night 'had much discourse tending to profit with Sir W. Batten, how to get ourselves into the prize office or some other fair way of obliging the King to consider us in our extraordinary pains'. Pepys was unable to get into the prize office, but he was able to profit from some skilful bargains in prize goods, in partnership with Captain Cock, one of the commissioners for the care of sick and wounded; whether his activities in this direction constituted 'a fair way' may be debated. The Duke of York himself wanted something to be done to prevent both the seamen and the public from being defrauded of their shares in the prizes.[5]

There was therefore a strong case for appointing a Prize Commission of leading Privy Councillors, and as their Treasurer an energetic minister,

[1] The contrast between Clarendon's picture of Coventry and that which may be gained from the pages of Pepys's *Diary* is very instructive.

[2] And the imputations of the French ambassadors, who explained their diplomatic failure in terms of the supposedly interested motives of Charles's ministers; see below pp. 177–9.

[3] *C.S.P.D. 1663–4*, p. 36. The Duchess of Albemarle alleged that Blackwell owed £321,000. Ibid. p. 42.　　　　[4] *C.S.P.D. 1670*, p. 297.

[5] Pepys, 16 Nov. 1664; Duke of York to Bennet, 24 Nov., *C.S.P.D. 1664–5*, p. 89.

already fully conversant with the critical financial situation and practised in extorting arrears from reluctant tax collectors, who would be directly responsible for all money derived from prize sales and would see that it was used for ends approved by the King. The appointment of a special Treasurer also had other advantages. Money paid into the Exchequer might be claimed by importunate creditors for services rendered in the past; money in a separate prize account could be devoted to the immediate needs of the war.

Ashley's accounts were not questioned by contemporaries, either by so keen and knowledgeable a critic as Pepys, when he was given (probably deliberately) an opportunity to look over them, or by the parliamentary commission of accounts which did its best to unearth evidence of scandals after the war was over. Ashley's responsibility was only to receive the money and pay it out in obedience to the King's instructions, but in any case there is little in the use made of the money which could be called seriously discreditable. Pepys thought that there were 'many sums to the Privy Purse, but not so many . . . as I thought there had been'[1]; in fact, they amounted to only £7,000 out of over £400,000. 'Secret service' payments—a term which might cover many different uses—amounted to £26,387, including £3,252 for the notorious Chiffinch and £586 for T. Lloyd, against one of whose payments is written 'for Madam Palmer'. Payments for royal buildings and to Mr. Gomeldon for jewels[2] amount to a further £31,404. But by far the largest proportion of the prize money, amounting to £147,551, went to the Navy Treasurer, Sir George Carteret, for the use of the fleet; and rewards to sea-commanders and others, criticized by Pepys but not altogether unjustifiable, accounted for £23,924. Pepys himself received £20,000 for the garrison at Tangier. The payments with which a modern auditor might find most fault are those connected with the running costs of the Prize Office. 'Incidental charges' amounted to £43,372, salaries to subordinate officers were £21,570 and salaries to the thirty Prize Sub-commissioners at the various ports were £23,200, so that expenses amounted to nearly twenty per cent of the gross proceeds of prize sales, for a period of about two and a half years.[3] It is not surprising that in January 1666 complaint was made of the expense of the numerous sub-commissioners, considering that they were frequently absent on parliamentary duty, and as a consequence severe reductions of staff were made.[4] The thirty posts as sub-commissioners were systematically given as

[1] Pepys, 23 Sept. 1667.

[2] In the seventeenth century jewels were not suitable presents only for women; they might, for instance, be given as parting gifts to foreign ambassadors.

[3] The remainder of the proceeds was spent in miscellaneous ways, e.g. payment of guards and regiments, upkeep of fortifications, allowances to Customs and Excise, etc. I have taken these figures from an analysis of accounts in the Shaftesbury Papers, esp. XL, 39, 41; they are not identical with those given by Dr. W. A. Shaw in C.T.B. 1667–8, pp. xxii–xxiv, but the differences are only minor ones.

[4] MS. book in Shaftesbury Papers, XXXVIII, 32.

rewards for services rendered to the Royalist cause. Twenty-two out of thirty were knights or baronets; no less than twenty-six were members of the House of Commons, and all were associated with the 'Court Party'.[1] It is therefore likely that the appointments had a political motive, that of strengthening the loyalists in the Commons for the future, as well as rewarding past loyalty. Not all these ex-Cavaliers, however, were loyal to Clarendon, who was hated for the 'ingratitude' which the Restoration government had shown to them, and was finally impeached in 1667 by a pack of Cavaliers, amongst them at least two of these sub-commissioners, Seymour and Clifford.

Apart from this political motive it seems that organization was planned in order to cope with much more numerous captures than were actually made, but it was not merely to provide money for Charles's personal extravagances nor to provide perquisites for Ashley. The Dutch ambassador reported to his masters that Ashley as Treasurer for Prizes was to be paid £1,500 per annum and Arlington as Comptroller £1,000, with £500 for the Principal Commissioners,[2] but no mention of any of these payments is made in the prize accounts, nor has it been possible to trace them elsewhere.[3] Perhaps only the sub-commissioners were paid in view of the dire financial distress piling up at the end of the war.

In the early months of 1665 the prospects of a rich haul of enemy shipping, the proceeds of which would pass through Ashley's hands, made him a more important person than he had previously been under the Restoration. One letter-writer commented that 'Lauderdale and Ashley, the only persons that stuck to him [Bristol] are most in favour of all the counsellors of state' and seemed to be eclipsing the Chancellor, who was not being so frequently visited by the King as formerly.[4] Ashley's name also began to occur more frequently in the despatches of the French ambassador, who on 9 January reported with astonishment that Bennet and Ashley seemed now to be confidants of Clarendon—something which he had thought out of the question a year previously; but, he asked with

---

[1] Their names are: *London*: Mr. (later Sir) E. Seymour, Sir T. Clifford, Sir T. Strickland, Mr. J. Ashburnham, Mr. E Windham, Sir E. Pooley, Sir H. North, Sir J. Talbot. *Portsmouth*: Sir H. Bennet, Sir P. Honeywood, A. Newport, P. Prideaux. *Bristol*: Sir J. Ernle, Sir J. Knight, Sir F. Dodington. *Plymouth*: Sir J. Skelton, Sir J. Trelawny, Sir J. Coryton, Sir E. Fortescue. *Hull*: Col. Kirkby, Col. Gilby, Sir J. Crosland. *Newcastle*: Sir J. Morley or Marley, Sir F. Anderson, Sir T. Higgins, Col. Villiers. *Dover*: Sir T. Peyton, Sir E. Massey, Sir F. Clerke, Col. Strode. Their political affiliations may be checked from the lists printed in the third volume of Browning, *Danby*.

[2] Despatch dated 3/13 Feb. 1665, Add. MSS. 17677, OOO; cf. also Comminges, Verneuil and Courtin to Louis XIV, 24 Apr./4 May and 11/21 May 1665.

[3] But on 8 May 1669 £1,500 from the prize money was paid to Sir Stephen Fox, the Army Paymaster. On 23 July Fox was ordered to pay £500 each to Lauderdale, Arlington and Ashley from this money. (*C.S.P.D. 1668–9*, pp. 317, 422). This may have been a roundabout method of paying a salary—or on the other hand there may be some explanation of which we can know nothing.

[4] T. Salusbury to E. of Huntingdon, 9 Jan. 1665, in *H.M.C. Hastings MSS*, ii. 148.

rhetorical cynicism, what could ambition and self-interest, supported by their master's goodwill, not achieve?[1] This despatch, however, is out of line with the rest of Comminges's reports at this time, which generally insist that the war was being carried on against Clarendon's will, by his rivals, Lauderdale, Ashley, Bennet and Coventry.

This was not a matter of mere academic interest to the French, for Louis XIV could not be indifferent to the struggle between the English and the Dutch. By a treaty signed in 1662 Louis was an ally of the Dutch and under an obligation to come to their assistance when attacked; and moreover he was afraid that the war might result in an English victory and English domination of the seas if he did nothing. On the other hand he did not wish to make an enemy of a king who had always seemed well-disposed to him, and least of all to drive Charles into the arms of his real enemies, the Hapsburgs. It would suit him best to mediate between the English and the Dutch and induce them to make up their differences. For this purpose he decided to add to his ambassador in London, Comminges, a second diplomat in Courtin and an illegitimate son of Henry IV, the duc de Verneuil, who would (by the standards ruling in the seventeenth century) add special lustre to the embassy. These three—the so-called *célèbre ambassade*[2]—found to their surprise that their master was not generally liked in England, and that there were even many Englishmen who welcomed the prospect of fighting against French as well as Dutch. Knowing that Clarendon's former hostility to French influence had largely evaporated, they put down this unaccountable anti-French feeling in the spring of 1665 to the interested motives of an anti-Clarendonian cabal, and to the Prize Commissioners in particular. These, they reported, all belonged to the same cabal and wanted war: either they did not like France because they were devoted to the interest of Spain, or (they added, with complacent flattery) 'they are not afraid of Your Majesty's power because they are not aware of it'. Into the first of these two categories they put Bennet (who had previously been the King's representative in Madrid); in the second they placed Monk, Ashley and Lauderdale. Monk and Ashley were only informed of the affairs of England, where they were *en grande considération*, Monk because of his popularity and Ashley because of his ability; both thought that under the protection of the Channel and the English fleet, they had nothing to fear from any foreigners. The ambassadors went on to allege that Ashley had been made Prize Treasurer so that this cabal could profit from seizures of enemy shipping, and since these had been below expectations, a further declaration of war must be sought to

---

[1] Comminges, 9/19 Jan. 1665. Note however that this letter is of the same date as that quoted in the previous note, which puts the opposite point of view. This is a good illustration of the unreliability of some of this gossip.

[2] See their instructions, printed by J. Jusserand, *Recueil des Instructions Données aux Ambassadeurs de la France*, vol. xxiv. *Angleterre* (1929), i. 345–74.

provide them with the gains they wanted—war 'with all nations' if necessary.[1]

It was typical of a general weakness in French diplomacy that they should
ascribe the growing anti-French hostility in London to a small, self-
interested cabal aiming at personal profit. Elsewhere in their despatches
there are hints that the ambassadors themselves were not altogether satisfied with this as an explanation of the fact that 'almost all the English
want war with France as much as they wanted it with Holland'.[2] So far as
Ashley's motives are concerned, the ambassadors had no special means of
divining them: they were merely guessing. It may be that the matter of
prizes did enter into the reasons why Ashley advocated an extension of
the war, but in a quite different way. Arlington told the Frenchmen that
the aim of the Prize Commissioners was to win the war by destroying
Dutch trade. The Dutch were at a disadvantage geographically, in that
much of their shipping had to run the gauntlet of English privateers as
they sailed up the Channel; and the lesson of the Commonwealth's war
against the United Provinces had been that the Dutch suffered far more
from an interruption of their commerce than they did from naval battles.
Ashley strove to apply the lesson in 1665, as he later did in 1672–3. But
he knew that the Dutch were evading English privateers by putting their
ships under French flags and then buying them back by means of bogus
contracts as soon as they reached Flushing or some other Dutch port.
Moreover trade with France, in wine, salt, and other products, was vital to
the Dutch economy, and if England could interrupt it by a declaration of
war on France as well as the United Provinces, it might be possible to
strike a decisive blow at Dutch commercial strength. The French ambassadors reported this line of argument to Louis XIV but declared it to
be merely an excuse to cover up a greed for booty; however it may well
have been the real reason for Ashley's undoubted advocacy of war with
France.[3]

In the summer of 1665 also the Frenchmen continued to interpret the
anti-French opinions of Lord Arlington (as Bennet had now become),
Ashley and Lauderdale as part of a general campaign waged against
Clarendon, with the aid of the famous convivial suppers at Lady Castlemaine's. In June they even brought the Duke of York over to their view.
The French ambassadors vainly tried to stem the tide by means of a talk
with the King. They represented to Charles their fears that people close
to him might for their own private interests endeavour to spoil his friendly
disposition towards France. Charles's reply was that he knew those people
and understood their designs; for the present he had to pay attention to
the wishes of Parliament and people, but when the time came he would

---

[1] Despatch of 11/21 May 1665.
[2] 22 May/1 June. Cf. K. Feiling, op. cit. pp. 139–50.
[3] Despatch of 11/21 May.

know how to take the line which suited his own interests best. At another time he talked of his esteem for Louis XIV and his natural inclination towards France, where he had been given sustenance in his time of need. This talk of his own friendliness for France in the midst of self-interested ministers and ignorant Parliament and people was to be one of Charles's main diplomatic tactics in conversations with French ambassadors for the rest of his life. One can never be sure how far Charles meant anything that he said at any time, and this could be merely an insincere excuse for doing nothing to meet the wishes of the Frenchmen; but there is a plain difference in tone between his own attitude towards France and that of Ashley.[1]

Charles's reference to 'those people' and understanding 'their designs' suggests that his relations with Ashley may not have been so close as some contemporaries thought at this time. On the surface, however, Ashley seemed to be genuinely in the royal favour. On 10 August Charles did him the honour of a surprise visit to his house at Wimborne St. Giles, and later in the month the King and Queen were 'very handsomely entertained' there. In September Charles stayed there for some days 'with some select persons', but this time he left the Queen at Salisbury. Visitors to St. Giles may still see a leather case in the form of a book, bearing the Royal arms and containing a pair of scales for weighing drugs. Charles, who had been complaining at Salisbury 'of the great pain of the colic', left them behind at St. Giles.[2]

While the King and Ashley were dining and drinking together at St. Giles and hunting across the Dorset countryside, the plague-carts were out in the streets of London, carrying the dead bodies of the poor to some hastily dug grave. A visitation of the plague was no novelty in seventeenth-century London, but the scale of the 1665 epidemic was altogether exceptional and quite terrifying. No convincing cure was known (although the quacks had a variety of suggestions) and the only precaution against contracting the dread disease was that of staying away from the capital. The number who could evade the danger was limited, but they included all those who owed attendance to the King. For them to stay in the country was not cowardice but common sense; and it was considered equally natural that the parliamentary session of the autumn of 1665 should be held, not in London but in Oxford. There the members assembled on 9 October (though the attendance was markedly thinner than usual) and the Court established itself in some of the Oxford colleges and led a life which scandalized the College dons.

Sixteen years later there was to be another Parliament at Oxford, in vastly different circumstances. The session of 1665 was almost as brief—

<hr>

[1] Despatches of 11/21 May, 27 May/6 June, 1/11 June, 12/22 June, 22 June/2 July.
[2] Letters of Sir Robert Moray to H. Slingsby of 10 Aug., 1 and 9 Sept., in the papers of Sir R. Graham, *H.M.C. Sixth Report*, p. 336; MSS. Clar. 88, fo. 5.

it lasted just over three weeks—but it was far less dramatic, and though the House of Commons needed careful handling, the members were not yet in a Whiggish mood. They duly voted a further £1,250,000 to supplement the two and a half millions which they had granted less than a year previously, and their loyalty to the established order in church and state was such as to be almost embarrassing to the government. In the Five Mile Act they forbade Nonconformist ministers ejected in 1662 even to approach within five miles of any town or of their former parish, unless they would take a non-resistance oath; to which was appended a promise that they would not endeavour 'any alteration of government, either in church or state'. At the same time another bill sought to impose a similar oath on the whole nation. If this had been taken literally it would have made permanent the Restoration settlement and ruled out all political change or religious indulgence. Ashley's uncle Southampton felt that this went much too far: supported by the ex-Puritans Manchester and Wharton, and by Ashley, he opposed the Five Mile Act as inhumane, and the oath as 'unlawful and unnecessary', but was overborne by the Duke of York and by the solid vote of the bench of bishops. The second bill however was successfully blocked; it would have been altogether too impolitic, and it was narrowly defeated even in the House of Commons. When Danby later tried to introduce a similar test in 1675, opposition pamphleteers noted the irony that the bill of 1665 had been beaten by his own vote and those of two of his relatives.[1]

In these debates at least there were no signs of latent Whiggery in the House of Commons which an opposition leader could exploit. Two other subjects of debate were more ominous from the government's point of view. The House sent a deputation to request the King that the accounts of the Navy and of the Ordnance should be presented to them in the next session[2]; and many gentry members expressed themselves forcibly about the competition they were facing from the importation of Irish cattle. One observer said that the House was more heated about this than on any subject since the 1641 bill to exclude the bishops from the House of Lords. An Irish Cattle Bill passed through the lower House, only to be terminated in the Lords by the prorogation. Charles foresaw that in the next session he would have to accept such a bill if he was to get any money, but for the

---

[1] The text of the Five Mile Act is in Browning, *Documents*, pp. 382–4. The account of the Lords' proceedings in MSS. Rawl. A. 130, fo. 56, does not mention Ashley among the Bill's opponents, nor do the notes printed by Caroline Robbins, in 'The Oxford Session of the Long Parliament of Charles II, 9–31 October 1665', *Bull. Inst. Hist. Res.*, 1946–8, pp. 220–4; the *Letter from a Person of Quality to a Friend in the Country*, written in the Shaftesbury entourage in 1675, does (*Parliamentary History*, iv. p. xl). Perhaps Ashley played only a supporting role behind his Anglican uncle; alternatively he may have spoken up only in the committee to which he was appointed, and not with Southampton on the third reading on 30 Oct. (*L.J.* xi. 697 does not record him as present on the latter occasion, though this is not conclusive).

[2] A. Marvell, *Works*, ed. H. S. Margoliouth (1927), ii (*Letters*), 41.

time being the Duke of Ormond in Ireland could breathe more freely. Ashley was to have much to say about Irish cattle in the next session, but at this time he seems to have remained silent.[1]

Evidently the country gentlemen who sat in the Commons had strong views and were far from easy to manage, but for the present they did vote the money required for a further campaign against the Dutch in 1666. The fact that the supply bill contained restrictions on the King's use of the money was not the House's doing, but that of some of the King's own advisers; and the controversy about it was largely fought out behind the scenes. In this controversy Ashley played an important part, but once again the only account of it is that of the embittered Clarendon, who as before refuses to give him credit for any motives of genuine policy.

It is clear from Clarendon's own account[2] that he had little appreciation of what Sir George Downing was trying to do by his financial proposals. That tough, hard-headed businessman had served both the Commonwealth and Charles II as ambassador at The Hague, and he had there witnessed the relatively easy supply of credit at the disposal of the Dutch. The States-General found many lenders at a comparatively low interest, while Charles II was dependent on a few big bankers, who for their loans demanded interest at six per cent, plus a further 'consideration' of four per cent, and priority of repayment when the parliamentary supply reached the Exchequer. Downing's aim was essentially that other private persons should be encouraged to make small loans at lower interest on the security of the Act which the Commons was just passing to give the King £1,250,000. Accordingly he proposed first of all that the proceeds of the Act should be appropriated entirely for the purposes of the war, and not to the repayment of past creditors; and secondly that it should be laid down in the Act that people who would lend money or supply goods on the Act's security should be guaranteed repayment strictly 'in course' by means of a system of registering loans in order as they were made. Whereas formerly the big bankers and other importunate and influential creditors had been able to demand priority of repayment, everyone would now get his fair turn. It seemed a good idea; with the aid of Arlington and William Coventry, Charles was persuaded to agree; and accordingly Downing introduced his proviso into the House of Commons with a suitable rabble-rousing attack on the bankers as 'bloodsuckers and extortioners' which he knew would go down well with the country gentlemen.[3]

Clarendon interpreted this as part of a plot by Arlington and Coventry to undermine his own position by removing his friend, Lord Treasurer Southampton. The gout and the stone from which the old man suffered were naturally an embarrassment to the efficient conduct of business in

---

[1] MSS. Carte 34, fos. 442–464, contain accounts of the fortunes of this Bill from several correspondents of Ormond.   [2] Clarendon, *Continuation*, ii. 213 sqq.

[3] See the relevant portion of the Act in Browning, *Documents*, pp. 174–5.

wartime, and the complaint was made that he had to leave much of the Treasury work to his secretary, Sir Philip Warwick. 'And towards fastening this reproach they had the contribution of the Lord Ashley, who was good at looking into other men's offices, and was not pleased to see Sir Philip Warwick's credit greater than his with the Treasurer, and his advice more followed. And the other two [Arlington and Coventry] had craftily insinuated to him, that he would make a much better Treasurer, which, whilst he thought they were in earnest, prevailed with him not only to suggest materials to them for that reproach, but to inculcate the same to the King upon several occasions; but when he discovered that they intended nothing of advantage to his particular, he withdrew from that intrigue, though in all other particulars he sided with them.' The sneer is obvious: Ashley first joined with Arlington and Coventry in the hope of being made treasurer himself, and then abandoned them when he found he was being duped. The same explanation is given for Ashley's change of mind over the Downing proviso. According to Clarendon he at first supported it, but later, 'whether he found himself left out in the most secret part of it, or not enough considered it it, [Ashley] passionately inveighed against it, both publicly and privately, and according to the fertility of his wit and invention, found more objections against it than anybody else had done'. The King was sufficiently impressed to decide that the matter should be debated by all those concerned, and since Clarendon was once again crippled with gout, the meeting took place in his bedroom. Though Clarendon disliked this and any other innovation, he had not seen the offending proviso beforehand, and Southampton himself had read it only an hour or two before. Accordingly it was left to Ashley to attack the plan and describe its probable ill effects, and this he did 'with great clearness and evidence of reason, and would have enlarged with some sharpness upon the advisers of it'. In this personal attack, Ashley for once over-reached himself, for the King stopped him by taking the responsibility upon himself; but the objections to the scheme were substantial ones. In the first place, if once such a clause were admitted into a supply bill, it would inevitably be put into later ones, and the result would be that the king's advisers would be deprived of all flexibility of action in the use of the money they received, which would have to be allocated automatically to creditors in their turn, whatever more urgent demands there were. Secondly, it was pointed out that the bankers had been approached for loans as soon as the House of Commons had passed its vote for supply, and before the Downing proviso had been introduced; since the proviso laid it down expressly that the proceeds of the supply should not be applied to debts contracted previously, the bankers were left without security for the money they had just advanced. The government's credit with them would inevitably be seriously prejudiced for the future. Charles was so much impressed by the force of these arguments that he wanted the proviso to be amended to take them into account, but it proved to be too late for this to be arranged, and the bill with the Downing proviso passed into law.

There is no means of corroborating this story, but it contains nothing implausible, provided that the facts narrated are carefully distinguished from the motives imputed by Clarendon. Clarendon was unable to take a detached view. He could not regard the episode as anything but a dishonourable attempt by his enemies, directed against his friend Southampton; and so far as Ashley was concerned, he could not imagine how Ashley could have changed his mind for honest reasons. Yet it seems perfectly possible that Ashley could have been attracted by Downing's scheme at first, and then turned against it, not from personal pique but because he realized what the consequences were likely to be. For some time the goldsmiths refused to lend money under the new system,[1] and the small loans to the Exchequer which it had been hoped to encourage did not materialize in sufficient numbers. The middle of a war and a critical financial situation were scarcely the right circumstances for a revision of the credit system, whatever its long-term merits. It was not difficult for Ashley, with his connexions and knowledge of the City, to foresee the results of the Act, and it is unnecessary to accept the accusations of personal motives made by a political opponent in order to account for his opposition to the scheme.

In the same way it is easy to see now that, even if Ashley did toy with the idea of bringing about Southampton's retirement, this was advisable from a national and not merely a personal point of view. The Lord Treasurer was honest but not the financial genius that was required, and was not even in good health. Charles recognized this when he asked Clarendon to persuade Southampton to resign,[2] and it is clear that the Chancellor did a disservice when he and the Duke of York dissuaded the King from his plan of putting the Treasury into commission. If the Treasury Commissioners of 1667 had been appointed eighteen months earlier, many difficulties might have been avoided,[3] but Southampton was retained because Clarendon thought he needed him to bolster up his own position. Clarendon's own view was not so purely patriotic as he thought, and equally the actions of his enemies were not so purely selfish as he maintained. Ashley was probably not on bad terms with his uncle; they had recently acted together over the Five Mile Act, and also in a vain attempt to get the post of Master of the Horse to the Queen for Mr. Robert Spencer.[4]

---

[1] Pepys, 27 Nov. and 8 Dec. 1665. For a contrary view, see George Walsh to H. Slingsby, 20 Feb. 1666, in *H.M.C. Sixth Report*, p. 337; but Pepys's opinion is not lightly to be discarded.

[2] Clarendon, *Continuation*, ii. 234. Cf. pp. 151–2 above, for Charles's description of Southampton at this time.

[3] This was Sir W. Coventry's opinion. See Pepys, 27 Dec. 1667.

[4] Southwell to Ormond, 12 Oct. 1665. MSS. Carte 34, fo. 431.

An attempt to induce his uncle to accept an honourable retirement need not have been discreditable to either, if the successor was in better health and of greater financial knowledge. However, by the end of the year it was clear that Southampton was to remain Treasurer until the stone from which he suffered proved fatal[1]; and the financial position became steadily worse.

Looking back at this point on the years 1661–5 covered by this chapter, it may be recognized that they take much of their political character from the fact that the obvious passport to political advancement was the favour of the King. Observers were naturally preoccupied with trying to determine which courtier was rising or falling in the King's estimation; and those correspondents of Ormond who scribbled off their gossip to Dublin often tended to report in these terms on what was happening in the corridors of Whitehall or in Lady Castlemaine's private rooms. Clarendon, conscious of the steadily deteriorating personal relationship between himself and his master and unable to ascribe his downfall to any political inadequacies of his own, also tended to look back upon the period in the same way, in terms of personal manoeuvres. Consequently the period takes on the appearance of a cynical struggle for the survival of the fittest, in which Bristol went under in 1663, and Clarendon in 1667. Yet there were after all important decisions of policy reached in these years, and it would be rash to assume that the arguments used counted for nothing to those who put them forward. So far as Ashley was concerned, it would be foolish to suppose that he was without the politician's usual instinct for self-preservation or his common hopes for advancement; but it would be equally unjustifiable to ignore the fact that at every turn there was a genuine political case to be made out for the course which he took.

If, however, the ambitious politician had, before 1666, been pre-occupied with the need to win and keep the royal favour, from that year onwards a new element entered into the situation. Politicians had also to concern themselves with the possibility of attack by the House of Commons, and the struggle for the survival of the fittest took on a new form.

---

[1] Southwell to Ormond, 30 Dec. 1665. Ibid. fo. 537.

CHAPTER X

THE SURVIVAL OF THE FITTEST—II (1666–8)

BEFORE the parliamentary session which began on 21 September 1666 it had scarcely been possible to accuse the Cavalier House of Commons of reviving the habits of mind which had led to the Civil War. Sometimes, indeed, its loyalty to King and Church of England had been so great as to be embarrassing, particularly because in 1661–3 its Anglicanism had been more zealous than the King's. Certainly the House had required the most careful management, and even so it had failed to provide the King with as much money as he had hoped; but it could not be said to have contemplated anything in the nature of an attack on the King's ministers.

All this was changed by the failures of the Dutch War. The successful pursuit of the previous (Cromwellian) war against the Dutch had encouraged extravagant hopes of rapid victory and seizures of enemy ships, but these early hopes had been disappointed. The battle of Lowestoft had been hailed as a great triumph, but there was a widespread feeling that it had not been properly followed up, and the Four Days Battle of 1666 had ended in defeat because faulty intelligence had led Monk and Prince Rupert to divide their forces. When the members came up to Westminster in the autumn of 1666 victory seemed no nearer than eighteen months previously, and though utterly unprecedented sums had been voted for the war, they had all been spent, and still creditors were unpaid and starving seamen thronged the streets. It would be a ticklish business to induce the House to vote for more, and neither the King's ministers nor his Chancellor of the Exchequer could be very hopeful.

Since the end of the previous session letter-writers with a keen eye for political intrigues had had little to report about Ashley except his ill-health. In the early months of 1666 he suffered frequently from the illness for which an operation was later necessary,[1] and spent considerable time resting at St. Giles or taking the waters at Astrop, near Oxford. For this reason he was unable to intervene, even had he so desired, in the interests of Samuel Farmer, who had come to England to complain against Governor Willoughby of Barbados, Ashley's enemy and Clarendon's friend.[2] The

---

[1] Sir Paul Neile to H. Slingsby, 15 Feb. 1666, in *H.M.C. Sixth Report*, p. 337; P. Vares to the same, 2 and 22 Mar., ibid. p. 338; Sir R. Moray to the same, 14 Apr., ibid. p. 338; H. Savile to Lady Dorothy Savile, 31 May, in *Savile Correspondence*, ed. W. D. Cooper (Camden Soc. 1857), p. 6.

[2] Capt. John Grant to R. Harley, 16 Feb. and 10 Mar. 1666, in *H.M.C. Portland Papers*, pt. iii, pp. 295–6; cf. the articles of impeachment against Clarendon in 1667.

attempt to interest Ashley in this case seems to imply that he was still thought of as a potential opponent of the Chancellor; but this is the only indication of their relations in 1666. It is definitely known, however, that in this period he remained on intimate terms with Lauderdale,[1] and as will be seen this attracted some comment in the session which began on 21 September.

As Charles's ministers were contemplating without enthusiasm the prospect of appealing to the House of Commons for more money, another blow of Fate or human carelessness increased their plight. This was the disaster of the Great Fire of London. As the flames swept across the capital destroying all the timbered buildings in their path, Ashley was one of those who attempted to cope with the situation. He helped to organize the work of men brought from the neighbouring countryside with tools to assist in putting down the fire,[2] and he and Holles were responsible for very sensibly committing to protective custody a servant of the Portuguese ambassador who was accused of throwing 'a fireball' into a house.[3] The idea that the Fire was a Papist conspiracy, which was later to become part of the Whig mythology, was widespread at the time—as many as eighteen months later the Lord Mayor, Aldermen and Common Council of the City were offering 'new matter' to the House of Commons 'to prove it a design'[4]—but in 1666 these hysterical fears were not important because neither Ashley nor anyone else sought to turn them to political account. The Fire affected the situation in quite a different way, by crippling the yield of the King's taxes. The dislocation of trade reduced the proceeds of both customs and excise duties, and people who had lost their chimneys were naturally not inclined to pay their chimney tax. The King and his ministers were even more dependent on the House of Commons than they otherwise would have been.

At the same time they had grounds for apprehension about the House's probable activities. It was easy to anticipate that there would be a demand for an inquiry into the expenditure of money granted for the war, into the reasons why it had proved insufficient to pay seamen and contractors, and into allegations of waste and peculation, before any more money was voted. The two people most likely to bear the brunt of such an inquiry were Ashley as Prize Treasurer and Sir George Carteret as Treasurer of the Navy. Clarendon thought that Carteret (who was a 'Clarendonian') 'was a punctual officer and a good accountant', but Ashley 'had more reason to be troubled . . . he well knew that there were great sums issued, which could not be put into any public account, so that his perplexity in

---

[1] Various correspondents of Slingsby, in H.M.C. Sixth Report, pp. 136–40, 338; Lauderdale to Ashley, 30 May 1666, in Shaftesbury Papers, IV, 146.

[2] Order of Council of 7 Sept. 1666, to be found in Shaftesbury Papers, IV, 151.

[3] Clarendon, Continuation, ii. 283–4.

[4] Newsletter to Sir Willoughby Aston, 31 Mar. 1668, in Add. MSS. 36916, fo. 87; cf. also fos. 105, 116.

several respects was not small'.[1] In the event the attack was to be concentrated on Carteret, and the prize accounts show that no such 'great sums' had been issued as Clarendon suspected; but the possibility remains that a desire to divert the House's attention elsewhere may have influenced Ashley's attitude to the House's other preoccupation at this time.

This was the bill to prohibit the importation of Irish fat cattle, which was introduced by Sir R. Temple on the very first day of the new session. Ashley was to second Buckingham in vehement support of this bill, but it must first be noticed that the agitation for the bill was by no means their creation. A similar bill had been introduced in the Lords as far back as 1663, and in the Oxford session of October 1665, a second bill was 'carried on with as much popular heat as was seen when the bishops were in 1641 pulled out of the House of Lords'.[2] In the interval between the two sessions the agitation did not abate, and more than a month before Parliament again met, the reports reaching Arlington from the country made him anxious.[3] The Irish Cattle Bill, then, was something more than a mere intrigue concocted as a parliamentary tactical move or in the interests of a few opponents of Ormond—for whatever purposes certain politicians tried to use it. The country gentry who sat in the Commons, and particularly those from the South-West, believed that the disastrous decline in rents, probably due in fact to a combination of slump, war and plague, was the result of the competition between English cattle and fat cattle imported from Ireland; and they took it as axiomatic that the interests of the King's English subjects should be preferred to those of the Irish. Ashley was in touch with his neighbours on their estates in Dorset, and knew the violence of the prejudices aroused; and it is conceivable that he genuinely shared them, unenlightened as they were. Certainly he shared the common English view that the welfare of Ireland was as nothing compared with English interests.

It was therefore clear from the beginning of the session that the Irish Cattle Bill would be strongly pressed. On October 13 it was carried in the Commons by a majority of 57,[4] and was brought into the Lords by Edward Seymour and others on 19 October. There it became the subject of violent debates in which Ashley and Buckingham strongly supported it, and the 'elder statesmen' such as Clarendon sought to throw it out. Once again the question arises of Ashley's motives for his course of action.

Various discreditable reasons have been given, the most common being that he and Buckingham were animated by hatred of the Duke of Ormond, the Lord Lieutenant of Ireland. Clarendon wrote that Ashley 'could not

---

[1] Clarendon, *Continuation*, ii. 319–20.

[2] T. Carte, *Life of Ormond* (1736), iv. 245, probably based on Conway's letter to Ormond, MSS. Carte 34, fo. 464.

[3] Arlington to Ormond, 14 Aug. 1666, ibid. 46, fo. 353.

[4] Brodrick to Ormond, 13 Oct. 1666, ibid. 35, fo. 101. Arlington gives the voting as 165 to 104, ibid. 46, fo. 385.

forbear to urge it as an argument for the prosecuting it, "that if this bill did not pass, all the rents in Ireland would rise in a vast proportion, and those in England fall as much, so that in a year or two the Duke of Ormond would have a greater revenue than the Earl of Northumberland"; which made a visible impression in many, as a thing not to be endured'.[1] There is no reason to suppose that Clarendon invented Ashley's use of this argument (if such it can be called); the problem is whether it accurately represents an unreasoning jealousy of Ormond, or whether it was a means of playing upon the envy of others as a means to some political end. It is true that Ashley and Ormond were never on good terms with one another. From the mass of correspondence with his friends which survives, Ormond comes down to us as a man of integrity and unusually blameless personal life, dignified, patriotic, a sincere Anglican; a man whose sympathies were limited by his social class but within those limits were genuine; a man whose loyal service to the Royalist cause in times of danger and exile had been rewarded in the nature of things with power and wealth in Ireland after the Restoration. Some of his contemporaries, however, looked on him rather differently. They saw a man who professed to be a Protestant but whose parents, brothers, sisters and almost all of his Irish relatives were Catholic. Many, amongst them Ashley, remembered how in the course of his duty to the King he had gone to the length of signing a truce in 1643, and treaties in 1646 and 1649, with those Irish rebels whose Popish atrocities had become part of the Puritan legend. They disliked the excessive rewards (estimated at £72,000) which he had received, distrusted the almost vice-regal authority which he wielded, and feared that it was being used against the interests of the Protestant minority in Ireland with whom they sympathized; and they missed no opportunity of striking at him.[2]

After the allegation that Ashley was motivated by envy, Clarendon added for good measure that he was suffering from a drop in his own rents, and also that he wanted to divert the critics in the Commons from paying too much attention to his prize accounts. Conway, one of Ormond's correspondents, talked of 'an implacable hatred to your person from the Duke of Buckingham, my Lord Ashley, Lord Lauderdale, and others of their party', and accused Ashley and Lauderdale of an intrigue to engross the trade in cattle from Scotland after Irish cattle had been excluded. This last impracticable scheme sounds like the wild invention of a partisan imputing dishonesty to an opponent; and it would be a mistake to think more highly of Conway's further suspicion that the affair might 'conceal

---

[1] Clarendon, *Continuation*, ii. 332.

[2] It is also possible that Buckingham had some personal animus against Ormond after the breakdown of a proposed marriage alliance between the two families in 1664 (cf. Ormond to Buckingham, 30 July 1664, MSS. Carte 49, fo. 267, and an unknown correspondent of Ormond, 10 Aug. 1667, ibid. 35, fo. 650). But temperamentally Buckingham and Ormond were at opposite poles, and dislike was natural.

a secret design to make the Duke of Monmouth' Lord Lieutenant of Ireland, something which neither Ormond nor Clarendon would swallow.[1]

What emerges from all this is that Ormond's friends believed that, whatever Ashley's motives were, they must be bad ones; after all, he had once supported the Republic, and therefore was bound to be dishonest. But there is also a possible political motive to be considered. Clarendon, as we have said, alleged that Ashley hoped to divert the Commons from their demand for accounts in order to save himself from their criticism; but such an enquiry would be quite as unwelcome to the King as to Ashley. If the House's grievances about Irish cattle were satisfied, the embarrassing demand for an audit might be evaded, whereas to oppose the popular current might lead to disaster and a refusal to vote the money which was essential. If the session is regarded in this way, it is found that as a result of the heat engendered by the Irish cattle issue Charles was able to avoid the demands for a commission of inquiry for three months, and then instead of acceding to the House's bill he nominated his own commission, and on much more favourable terms than might have been expected earlier. Conway suspected that the cattle bill's supporters would not have dared to speak as they had done without some indulgence by the King, and in the end it was 'by the King's particular command' that the House of Lords accepted the crucial clause in the Commons' bill. Sir William Coventry openly argued that in the King's difficult position his only sensible course was to accept the Commons' demand; and even Arlington, although he had acquired extensive estates of his own in Ireland, defended the King's decision to consent to the bill by saying that 'the truth is the nation as well as both Houses of Parliament have so possessed themselves with the opinion of advantages they shall have by the stop of Irish cattle that without the hazard almost of a rebellion His Majesty could not deny it'.[2] If this is so, may Ashley's advocacy of the bill not have been in part a matter of political tactics?

It is possible that all or some of these motives concurred. What is certain is that Ashley had no hesitation about his course of action, and that he pursued it with considerable violence of language. At the same time he attempted to play on the Lords' jealousies of the Irish peers by proposing in the committee of privileges that the Irish nobility should be 'degraded from taking any place in England', that is that they should lose any right of precedence over English commoners; and he was rumoured to be planning to alter the Book of Rates so as to force Ireland to import foreign commodities only through England. On the Irish Cattle Bill itself, when

[1] Conway to Ormond, 13 Nov. 1666, MSS. Carte 35, fo. 126, and 27 Nov., ibid. fo. 148; Ormond to Conway, 8 Dec., MSS. Carte 49, fo. 367. An amendment to the Bill, permitting the import of Scottish cattle but not Irish, was finally lost.

[2] Conway to Ormond, 13 Nov. 1666, MSS. Carte 35, fo. 126; and 14 Jan. 1667, ibid. fo. 30; Arlington to Ormond, 19 Jan. 1667, MSS. Carte 46, fo. 440.

the Irish party tried to insert a proviso exempting from its provisions a supply of fat cattle to relieve distress in London after the Great Fire, Ashley vehemently attacked the clause as a wrecking amendment, and proposed that the meat for the charity should be brought in, not on the hoof, but as barrelled beef, although others who knew Ireland urged that this was impracticable. On 19 November he went on in this strain, attacking the proviso 'as a thing politically contrived to frustrate the end of the Bill', until Ormond's eldest son Ossory, who sat in the House of Lords by virtue of an English peerage, could stand it no longer. Losing his temper, he exclaimed that such language could only come from one who had belonged to Oliver Cromwell's Council. Ashley found it politic to consider himself insulted by this reminder of his past, which should have been obliterated by the Act of Indemnity; he sprang up and said that Ossory 'must give him reparation, or he would take it his own way'. This was fighting talk. Ashley would have fared ill in a duel, for Ossory was younger, physically stronger, an officer and skilled swordsman; but he knew well that the House would intervene in his favour. Ossory was reprimanded and compelled to apologize for his words. The incident was a triumph for Ashley, but it was also a reminder that, even though he had now been in the King's service for six years, his past had not been buried; for many Royalists, he would always remain a man who had deserted to the enemy, and served Cromwell.[1]

On 23 November the bill passed the House of Lords by 63 votes to 47, 'all the bishops included against' it.[2] But this did not end the disputes, as the Lords had replaced the word 'nuisance' in the bill, which in common law would have prevented the King from granting dispensations from its provisions, by the innocuous words 'detriment and mischief'. The Commons refused to give way, insisting that all possibility of dispensations must be prevented, and they were supported by a minority of the Lords, including Ashley, Buckingham, and Lucas, who risked losing the royal favour by saying 'that it was no diminution of the royal prerogative to make laws indispensable; most laws made for the King's benefit were so, as treason, praemunire, etc. and all laws of highest penalty; the bill would be frustrate without it—no other word so proper'. This was a decidedly Whiggish argument, more appropriate to the mood of the Exclusion period than to that of the Restoration, and it can scarcely have pleased Charles. Ashley suggested as a 'compromise' that the word 'nuisance' might be changed into 'felony' or 'praemunire', which would have the same practical effect. In reply Clarendon 'drolled very well' and thought that the import of

---

[1] Conway to Ormond, 13 Nov. 1666, loc. cit.; Pepys, 19 Nov. 1666; Proceedings of the House of Lords, 19 Nov., in MSS. Rawl. A. 130, fo. 67. T. Carte, op. cit. iv. 273, says that during the debate Ashley also fell out with the ex-Presbyterian Anglesey, who had worked with him in 1660 but had extensive Irish interests.

[2] Conway to Ormond, 27 Nov., MSS. Carte 35, fo. 148.

THE SURVIVAL OF THE FITTEST—II   191

Irish cattle 'might as reasonably be called Adultery'; but sarcasm was all in vain. In the end, on 14 January 1667, the Lords accepted the Commons' point of view, after the King had induced the Duke of York, most of the bishops and many other peers to absent themselves from the decisive vote.[1] As a result the money bill was passed almost immediately afterwards, and Charles was able to prorogue Parliament on 8 February, by which time the royal commission of inquiry into the war accounts had still not commenced operations.

To that extent, yielding to the Commons' demands over Irish cattle paid dividends, and there was therefore a political case to be made for the course taken by Ashley, Sir William Coventry and others in supporting the bill. What is less easy to condone is the intemperate vehemence with which he advocated it—a disagreeable feature not to be found earlier in his career. In these years his health was deteriorating and he may have been in pain from his cyst: this may be a partial explanation. But anything to do with Ireland always seems to have brought out the worst in him. In this connexion two conversations with Conway early in 1667 illuminated his attitude to Irish problems. In the first, Ashley attacked 'those lords that have driven the English out of the seaports and corporate towns, and filled them up with Irish'. Ill-informed as this criticism may have been, it illustrates a definite view that there should be a Protestant and English ascendancy; and in the second conversation he declared that the best means of achieving this would be by means of a parliamentary union between England and Ireland. Conway began this conversation with a piece of outrageous flattery, suggesting that no man was so likely to become Lord Lieutenant of Ireland in the near future as Ashley, but that Ashley had made his position impossible by his recent attacks on the Irish interest, which would alienate everyone there. 'He answered me,' wrote Conway, "twas true they had done an unnatural act [in prohibiting the import of Irish cattle], but the fault was in the present government, which by the settlement of Ireland [at the Restoration], the Book of Rates, and other principles of government did endeavour to divide the interest of the two kingdoms, whereas he desired they should be united, and sit in one Parliament, and then all these Acts would fall to the ground.' Claiming that he really had Irish interests at heart, he promised 'to befriend all proposals for the relief of Ireland', particularly in the matter of liberty of conscience, though according to Conway he had 'exclaimed against' this during the Oxford session: it is not known whether liberty of conscience to Catholics or to Presbyterian and ex-Cromwellian settlers is referred to here. Conway thought all this to be 'matter for raillery'; in his own estimation he had been deluding a dangerous enemy of Ireland by holding out the prospect of command there. But in spite of the admission that the Irish Cattle Bill had

[1] Proceedings of the House of Lords, 17 Dec. 1666, MSS. Rawl. A. 130, fo. 71; Conway to Ormond, 29 Dec. 1666 and 14 Jan. 1667, MSS. Carte 35, fos. 197 and 30.

been 'an unnatural act', made necessary by temporary tactical considerations, the basic ideas outlined here were considered ones, consistently held.[1] The type of parliamentary union advocated came naturally to one who had once been a member of the Council of State under the Instrument of Government, and it may be compared with the union with Scotland which he supported in 1669.[2]

In this episode of the Irish Cattle Bill Ashley for the first time stood on the same side as a discontented majority of the House of Commons, in opposition to the King's principal minister; for Clarendon with characteristic honesty and inflexibility refused to fall in with the general demand for a measure which he believed to be unjust, whatever the tactical considerations in favour of it. There had been rumours that the bill would be followed by an impeachment of Clarendon, either in the next session or even in this,[3] for by now Clarendon's unpopularity was growing faster than his new palace in Piccadilly, and the royal favour was evaporating equally quickly. Within a year the old man was dismissed, in August 1667, and forced into exile four months later. In the normal course of events one could expect that Ashley, whose name had been consistently among those of Clarendon's opponents from at least 1663 until the Irish Cattle Bill, would be one of the politicians who hounded Clarendon to his downfall. Yet certainly he took no part in it, and by the end of 1667 he was even being described as a Clarendonian and out of favour. What happened to produce this change, precisely when, if Ashley were concerned with his own advancement, one would have expected him to run with the pack?

All the signs are that in 1667 Ashley was in a position of political isolation and that he cared little about it. He quarrelled even with his brother-in-law, Sir William Coventry, though the latter agreed that it was advisable to give way over Irish cattle. The two men took different views about the sale of prize goods. A year previously Pepys had recorded 'very high words' between them, in the course of which Ashley 'did snuff and talk as high to him, as he used to do to any ordinary seaman'.[4] In January 1667 there was a further dispute about some prize goods which were suitable for use by the Navy. After Pepys had procured an order from the King that the goods should be made available for the Navy, Ashley first yielded, but then insisted on selling them according to the normal procedure to anyone who would buy them.[5] Such a decision cannot have been welcome to

---

[1] Conway to Ormond, 5 and 19 Jan. 1677, MSS. Carte 35, fos. 240, 259. In the Shaftesbury Papers, L, 16 and 48, there is a document, with corrections in Ashley's own hand, favouring the Protestant English at the expense of the class of 'innocent' Irish papists constituted by the Act of Settlement.   [2] See below, pp. 271–2.

[3] Conway to Ormond, 27 Nov. and 29 Dec. 1666, MSS. Carte 35, fos. 148, 197.

[4] Pepys, 21 Mar. 1666 (quoting Sir W. Warren).

[5] Pepys, 16 and 19 Jan. 1667. Sir Arthur Bryant, *Pepys, the Man in the Making* (1934), p. 321, deduces from this that Ashley wanted to secure a rake-off for himself, but it seems equally reasonable to suppose a departmental difference in policy, the Navy needing goods for the war and Ashley being more concerned about ready money to satisfy the many

Coventry, who on a similar occasion later 'did plainly desire that it might be declared whether the proceeds were to go to the helping of the war or no'.[1] There was apparently friction between the Lord High Admiral's secretary, clamouring for stores for the fleet, and the Prize Treasurer and Chancellor of the Exchequer, at his wits' end to procure cash to satisfy creditors; and when once the decision had been taken to seek for peace and to lay up the battle fleet in 1667, the latter felt that his need was the more urgent. The result was that Ashley was estranged from Sir William Coventry, who in August 1667 was the man most insistent on bringing down the Chancellor. At the same time, Buckingham, with whom he had co-operated in the recent session, was exiled from court; on 25 February 1667 the Duke was put out of the Privy Council, his post in the royal bedchamber, and all his commissions, and he absconded. Another friend, Lauderdale, was in Scotland. Finally, if Clarendon is to be believed,[2] he was not at this time on good terms with the King himself.

Ashley was thus in some isolation when his superior, Lord Treasurer Southampton, died in May 1667, and Charles, impressed by the success of the Ordnance in commission, determined to put the Treasury into commission also. Albemarle was to be the figurehead, with Ashley, Sir Thomas Clifford (at this time Arlington's protégé), Sir W. Coventry (coming from the department with the greatest expenditure) and Sir John Duncombe (previously on the Ordnance commission) as colleagues. According to Clarendon, the King had not originally intended to appoint Ashley as one of the commissioners, on the ground that 'the lord Ashley gave him some trouble, and he [Charles] said enough to make it manifest that he thought him not fit to be amongst them: yet he knew not how to put him out of his place . . .'. Clarendon had to remind the King that if Ashley retained his position as Chancellor of the Exchequer, it would not be seemly to omit him from the Treasury Commission; and Charles gave way, though he would not specify that Ashley must be one of the quorum. 'And Ashley rather chose to be degraded than to dispute it'.[3]

Thus Ashley squeezed on to the Treasury Commission only because he could not conveniently be left off it. However Clarendon's expectation that Ashley would be elbowed out in favour of 'those three who were designed for it' was soon falsified, for after the Commission had decided to meet twice a week at 3 p.m., and twice more at 8 a.m., he attended regularly,[4] and must have played a prominent part, since, after all, his

---

demands upon him. Otherwise it is scarcely probable that he would have dared to challenge a direct order from the King.

[1] Pepys, 3 Apr. 1667. On this occasion Pepys agreed with Coventry; but the transaction the latter advocated would have been to the advantage of the contractor, Lanyon, from whose Tangier contract Pepys benefited.

[2] Clarendon, *Continuation*, ii. 413–14.   [3] Ibid.

[4] The statement in S. B. Baxter, *The Development of the Treasury, 1660–1702* (1957), p. 11 n., is misleading, for it takes no account of Ashley's prolonged illness in 1668.

experience of financial affairs was by far the greatest. Indeed, he is said to have made the disgruntled comment that the other commissioners understood nothing,[1] and his hand may be seen in the Commission's early proceedings. Its first action under his presidency was to issue orders for the systematic collection of information, 'to know how far all the branches of the revenue or the extraordinaries given by Parliament are anticipated', to know the expenditure of the great departments 'and to compute what the debt is which remains unpaid of that expense'.[2] Such attempts to collect all the facts on which policy could be based were characteristic of all the commissions and committees on which Ashley served, such as the Councils of Trade. The results are to be found in the Shaftesbury Papers, which include details of 'the ordinary charge of H.M. Navy as it stood the 1 January 1667', showing the wages payable to each class of sailor and workman in the yards. At midsummer 1667 £384,368 was owing to ships in service, and £113,407 was owing to the yards on 25 March 1667; but a later estimate of the debt of the Navy alone on 1 September reached £1,331,768, equivalent to nearly eighteen months of ordinary peace-time revenue. Of this £74,322 dated back at least to 1664, and no less than £477,178 was pay owing to seamen.[3]

By collecting this information, the Commission was enabled for the first time to exercise adequate Treasury control over the activities of the spending departments. It is no wonder that the Treasurer of the Navy, Sir George Carteret, was 'mightily displeased'; 'he hath reason', said Pepys, 'for it will eclipse him'.[4] Others at Court were displeased by the Commission's second step, which was to apply to the King 'that before any warrant be signed by His Majesty for issuing money or charging the revenue or making any grant of any part thereof my Lords be acquainted with the address made to His Majesty concerning it, and make their report of their opinion to him as to the matter of fact and as to the condition and present state of the revenue'.[5] This surely stemmed from the Chancellor of the Exchequer's experience of the haphazard way in which many grants had been made in the past to courtiers, without the financial officers of the Crown being able to express a preliminary opinion. Pepys applauded these first steps of the Treasury Commissioners, thinking that 'the King will find such benefit by them as he will desire to have them continue'.[6]

Unfortunately these activities were far too late to have any influence on the course of the war. Within a fortnight of the Commission's appointment the humiliating disaster of the Medway occurred, when the Dutch captured Sheerness, broke the chain across the river which was supposed

---

[1] Pepys, 31 May 1667.
[2] C.T.B. 1667–8, p. 2 (27 May 1667).
[3] All these details are to be found in a MS. book labelled 'memo about Prize Office', Shaftesbury Papers, XXXVIII, 36.   [4] Pepys, 31 May 1667.
[5] C.T.B. 1667–8, pp. 2–3; cf. Baxter, op. cit. pp. 12–13, for the significance of this step.
[6] Pepys, 31 May 1667; cf. also 3 June.

to protect the British capital ships at their moorings, towed away the flag-ship, the *Royal Charles*, and burnt others. For a day or two the panic in London was great, because none knew what further attack the Dutch had in mind. Samuel Pepys was among those who thought it prudent to collect together all the ready cash that he could lay his hands on; his father and wife took it into the country and there buried it in the garden, to his dismay, 'in open daylight' one Sunday morning.[1] But when the alarm subsided, it was succeeded by an outcry for the punishment of those whose neglect had led to the disaster. When, Clarendon's opposition having been overruled, the House of Commons met at the end of July 1667, the loudest opposition came, not from ex-Parliamentarian members, but from old and loyal Cavaliers. Protests against the army which the King had raised were voiced by Sir Thomas Tomkins, 'an old Cavalier and sequestered in Cromwell's time', and 'seconded by five other old Cavaliers',[2] and the temper of the House was so ominous that Charles was relieved to be able to prorogue Parliament on 29 July, having heard that the peace negotiations with the Dutch at Breda had been successfully completed.

Yet this did not avoid a parliamentary crisis; it merely postponed it for two months. Money was no longer needed to fight the Dutch, but when Parliament met again on 10 October it would still be necessary to appeal to it for financial assistance to avert a complete breakdown. As the Treasury Commissioners examined the situation, they estimated that the Crown's debts were over £2,000,000, and that 'we are in a regular established way of spending £600,000 above the income of His Majesty's revenue', and though severe attacks were made on perquisites such as the Navy Treasurer's poundage from victualling contracts and the new commissioners were 'a terror to all bankers, accomptants, patentees, etc.', yet all these retrench-ments could not solve the problem.[3] At the same time alarming reports were coming from the country. At Yarmouth one observer 'could take this for the year 1641. . . . The people are as insolent in their speeches against those that govern and mutter and murmur as if there were as great a difference between the King and Parliament; nay, they are come to taking parts to justify and condemn.' At Minehead it was said that Parliament had been prorogued because the King 'would not have any person called to account that had the management of the public treasury'.[4]

In these circumstances one obvious line of escape for the government was by making the unpopular Clarendon the scapegoat for all. The Lord Chancellor had clearly outlived his usefulness; perhaps the prorogation of

---

[1] Pepys, 13, 19 June.

[2] See the interesting account given by one of Ormond's correspondents, in MSS. Carte 35, fos. 649–50.

[3] Arlington to Ormond, 3 Aug., MSS. Carte 46, fo. 520; Sir A. Brodrick to Ormond, 3 and 13 Aug., ibid. 35, fos. 595–6, 632.

[4] R. Bower to Williamson, 5 Aug., *C.S.P.D. 1667*, p. 360; J. Maurice to Williamson, 27 Aug., ibid. p. 420.

29 July had saved him even then from an impeachment planned for that very morning, and an impeachment could certainly be expected in the next session.[1] A series of interviews with members of Parliament such as Clifford, Osborne, Carr, Littleton and Seymour served to convince the King that Clarendon must go, both in order to make possible harmonious relations with the House and in Clarendon's own interest, to protect him from attack.[2] Clarendon's opponents within the Privy Council, whether from motives of ambition or because (like Sir William Coventry) they saw in him an obstacle to necessary reforms, also applied pressure on the King. Even Clarendon's son-in-law, the Duke of York, at first accepted the view that it would be wise for him to retire, and mentioned it to him some days before 27 August.[3] The old man foolishly would not co-operate with the inevitable; there was one last pathetic interview with the King after which his enemy Lady Castlemaine ran out in her smock 'and stood joying herself at the old man's going away', and on 30 August he was dismissed.

At this juncture one would expect to find Ashley among those urging this course on the King; after all, observers had consistently ranked him among Clarendon's opponents for the last four years, and from the point of view of political tactics, and indeed of self-preservation, the obvious policy was at least to swim with the tide. Yet Ashley did nothing. At this crisis he retired to Wimborne St. Giles. He attended the meetings of the Treasury Commission on 31 July, and did not reappear until the 26th of August when Charles's decision had certainly been reached. August then as now was a time when country gentlemen expected to be on their estates and not in London; nevertheless others did not leave the capital at this crisis. One observer attributed his retirement to disapproval of the Commission's policy, 'not well understanding how to break contracts solemnly made by His Majesty in the presence of all his great ministers after long deliberation, for valuable considerations, and passed the Great Seal with all formalities of ratification . . .'. But even if this was so, absence from the scene of intrigue was remarkable in one with such a reputation for political manoeuvring as Ashley.[4]

In November, when Clarendon was impeached by the House of Commons, Ashley's conduct was even more striking. He did not merely remain ostentatiously aloof from the attack on the old man, but on one important issue he took a positive stand on the side of Clarendon's friends. Though his actions did not earn Clarendon's gratitude when the latter wrote his life, the ex-Chancellor's son Rochester later acknowledged to Ashley's grandson that Ashley had opposed the motion in the Lords to

---

[1] Loc. cit. p. 195, n. 2.   [2] Burnet, i. 451.

[3] Arlington to Ormond, 27 Aug. 1667, MSS. Carte 46, fo. 540. His previous letter, dated the 24th, makes no mention of the Chancellor's retirement.

[4] C.T.B. 1667–8, pp. 49–70 (for Ashley's attendances); Sir A. Brodrick to Ormond, 13 Aug. 1667, MSS. Carte 35, fo. 632.

commit Clarendon to the Tower on a general charge of treason by the Commons. He argued, along with the majority in the Lords, that Clarendon should not be committed to custody unless detailed charges were brought, and this view prevailed against all that Buckingham, Bristol, Arlington and others could do. He was then present at a series of conferences between Lords and Commons in which each House held out against the other on this question of commitment, and at the last of these conferences, on 29 November, he got in a shrewd blow at the Cavaliers in the Commons, and Waller in particular, by maintaining that if specific charges had been demanded when Strafford had been committed in 1640, a great blow to the Royalist cause would have been avoided. The Lords maintained their view by a majority of 60 votes to 12, and the issue was still in the balance when Clarendon at last responded to the King's hints and fled the country. Clarendon had been alarmed by attempts to 'incense the people' against him; and Ashley had not lessened his alarm by reporting a remark of Edward Seymour's, 'that the people would pull down the Chancellor's house first, and then those of all the lords who adhered to him'.[1]

This last remark is a reminder that Ashley's actions risked involving him in the unpopularity of Clarendon amongst the Londoners. At the same time his course was generally thought to be directly opposed to the King's own wishes. Charles had instructed the Solicitor-General, Heneage Finch, at the beginning of the session 'to promote the business' against Clarendon,[2] and it was widely suspected that the activities of the ex-Chancellor's enemies were not unwelcome to him. By the end of the year there was talk of dismissing from the Council Ashley, other ex-Puritans such as Anglesey, Holles and Morrice, and the Archbishop of Canterbury: 'these men do suffer only for their constancy to the Chancellor, or at least from the King's illwill against him.'[3]

Ashley had thus imperilled his political prospects by refusing to abandon the fallen Chancellor whom he had frequently opposed in past years. This remarkable change is mysterious. It is true that Ashley's original motives for opposition to Clarendon had partly disappeared with the decline of the Chancellor's influence and the greater freedom given to Ashley and others in their attempts to cope with the financial and administrative chaos; and

[1] Martyn, *Life of Shaftesbury*, i. 329, n.; *L.J.* xii. 141–2, 144, 147, 149; J. Milward, *Diary* (ed. 1938), p. 147; Grey, i. 51 (dated 25 Nov.); Sir A. Brodrick to Ormond, 30 Nov., MSS. Carte 35, fo. 871; Clarendon, *Continuation*, ii. 484. This last is the only reference to Ashley in Clarendon's own account of his fall. Clayton Roberts is able to describe 'The Impeachment of the Earl of Clarendon' in *Camb. Hist. Jour.* (1957), pp. 1–18, without alluding to Ashley in any way.

[2] Conway to Ormond, 15 Oct., MSS. Carte 35, fo. 764.

[3] Pepys, 30 Dec. 1667 (based on a conversation with Sir G. Carteret). On 5 Jan. 1668 he was told that the design to replace them by members of the House of Commons had been abandoned, as it might merely make more enemies for the King. Cf. Ossory to Ormond, 4 Jan., MSS. Carte 220, fo. 326: '. . . for the others [Anglesey and Ashley] I believe fear more than love will preserve them from any disgrace . . .'.

after Clarendon's dismissal at the end of August Charles had made it clear that he was no longer to be reckoned with in the formulation of policy. But this in itself does not explain why Ashley not only failed to join in an overwhelming movement which was thought to have the backing of the King himself, but actually exposed himself by speaking against the proposal to commit Clarendon to the Tower. The suggestion has been made that he was 'actuated by a sense of fair play',[1] and though this cannot be accepted in quite so naïve a form, it does perhaps hint at the truth. In Clarendon a trusted minister who had served the monarchy faithfully in good times and in bad for twenty-five years had been jettisoned by the King to appease the wrath of the Commons; he had not simply been dismissed from office (for which a good case could be made out) but might lose his life as the result of a charge of treason, the injustice of which was patent to any cool and unprejudiced observer. If this could happen to a statesman with Clarendon's record, what was Ashley's own position? Whether or not he suspected that Charles had little real liking for him, the whole episode glaringly showed up the insecurity of royal favour; if Clarendon were not protected by the King from the wild charges of the Commons, Ashley could hardly expect to be, and he had every reason to try to prevent the setting up of a disastrous precedent for the impeachment of fallen ministers. It was a matter of common prudence for a minister under the Restoration to oppose the committal of a peer to the Tower on general, unsubstantiated charges of treason by a hostile House of Commons.

As Ashley heard the news of the indignities which the old man had to suffer before he found a refuge for his last years in the South of France, he must have digested the obvious political lesson that other unsuccessful statesmen might become (in Ashley's own phrase) 'travellers to Montpellier'.[2] In his speech as Lord Chancellor on Sir Thomas Osborne's appointment as Lord Treasurer six years later, his theme was that 'however happy you have been in arriving to this high station, yet *Parti tueri non minor est virtus*'.[3] In 1667–8, however, such cynical reflections did not incline him to seek safety by hitching his fortunes to those of anyone else. The French ambassador indeed reported that Ashley and Anglesey were trying to form a 'third party' in Parliament, a party of moderates under the nominal leadership of the Earl of Northumberland; and that possibly Arlington belonged to them because of his dislike of Buckingham's brusque and arrogant manner. As Ruvigny was Southampton's brother-in-law and through his connexions was better placed than other Frenchmen to penetrate English political alliances, his opinion is not to be ignored. But the truth seems to be that Ashley was to be found in different political company as the issues changed. In some respects he was to be found on the same side as his former ally over the Irish Cattle Bill, the Duke of

---

[1] Brown, p. 183.   [2] Cf. p. 268 below.
[3] Shaftesbury Papers, V, 251; Christie, vol. ii. pp. lxxi–lxxii.

Buckingham; in others they were opposed. In November 1667 they had taken different views of Clarendon's impeachment, and in January 1668 Buckingham used his considerable powers of sarcasm against Ashley's speech on the Act of Accounts. Of their attitude to a rumoured scheme for a bill to divorce the Queen, or 'a bill to affirm that the King was married to the Duke of Monmouth's mother', nothing is known at this time, though as will be seen they both advocated similar schemes later.[1] On Irish affairs, on the other hand, they continued to have much in common.

As the most important of Clarendon's friends, the Duke of Ormond was an obvious target for attack, and here Ashley was generally thought to be in league with the erratic Buckingham. In the autumn of 1667, even before the meeting of Parliament which was to attack Clarendon, rumours had reached Dublin that inquiries were being made into Ormond's administration of Ireland and that men with complaints were being received by Ashley. Within a week of the opening of the session it was discovered that an impeachment of Ormond was being prepared, and a copy of the articles was actually procured for Ormond's benefit. In the following month this news was corroborated from a different quarter, with the additional information that both Buckingham and Ashley were concerned, and that the attack was to be begun in the House of Commons by Sir Thomas Littleton. There were three main points on which Ormond might be vulnerable. One was a petition by a Dublin alderman named Barker against a verdict by Ormond and his Irish Privy Council. This was discussed in the English Privy Council on 11 October, and Barker's appeal was then rejected after a long debate in which both Buckingham and Ashley had supported his case. The matter was then taken up in the Commons by Seymour, who declared that the affair 'began in bribery and ended in corruption'. The affair dragged on there until March 1668, as did a second petition, that of the Adventurers against the terms of the Act of Explanation, but both were eventually crowded out by more important business. A third possible line of attack was on the financial administration of Ireland. Ever since the Restoration Ireland had had to be subsidized from the English Exchequer, and it was natural for the Treasury Commissioners to extend their attempts at retrenchment to this field. A special committee was formed to cut down Irish expenditure, from the numerous pensions to the wages of the Lord Lieutenant's trumpeters, and also to make big reductions in the Irish army. At the same time inquiries were also made into wasteful administration in the past, and even Conway was instrumental in providing Ashley with ammunition for this purpose. Anxiety about these machinations against him led to Ormond's arrival in London on 6 May 1668, in order to defend himself against possible attacks; but in the end nothing came of all this sniping. It may well be that Ormond's

---

[1] Ruvigny, 22 Nov./2 Dec. 1667; Pepys, 4 Jan. 1668; Conway to Ormond, 5 Nov. 1667, MSS. Carte 36, fo. 25. Cf. also his letter of 30 Nov., ibid. 873, and Pepys, 30 Dec.

correspondents exaggerated these causes of alarm, since no direct attack on him was ever mounted; but there is enough evidence to show that he was strongly disliked, and that Buckingham and Ashley were among those who disliked him most.[1] Whatever one thinks of Ashley's consistency in other respects, there can be no doubt of his consistent attitude towards Ormond.

The session of 1668 closed with the deadlock between the two Houses over the case of *Skinner* v. *East India Company*, which put a stop to all other business. This case had been pending in the Privy Council since 1663 and Ashley had then been a member of a committee appointed to consider it; Skinner's cause had been strongly taken up on this committee by Lord Robartes, but no agreement was reached, and the matter was referred to the Lords in March 1668. The principle of the Lords' claim to original jurisdiction in the case was not accepted by the Commons, especially as one of their members, the East India merchant Sir Samuel Barnardiston, was involved in the defence and called upon to appear at the bar of the other House. In the dispute which followed Ashley was twice a manager for the Lords at conferences of the two Houses, but there is no record of what he said.[2]

It was later suspected that this quarrel between the two Houses was deliberately brought on by politicians who wanted a dissolution, and that among these was Ashley, since Skinner was alleged to be one of his dependants, and Barnardiston was later on a prominent Whig.[3] This is plausible, but it may be only hindsight, the result of later experience of *Shirley* v. *Fagg* and other cases; there is no contemporary corroboration of these suspicions, and it is not easy to see how a dissolution at this point could have benefited Ashley. It is not necessary to see deep-laid intrigues behind the origin of this dispute.[4] After its eclipse under the Commonwealth, the House of Lords was naturally very anxious to assert its importance by maintaining every possible privilege. This jealous defence of its rights was at the bottom of the numerous disputes between the two Houses during the reign, and Ashley shared the attitude to the full. In 1663 he had maintained that the Lords need not accept the judges' opinion

---

[1] Ossory to Ormond, 24 Sept. 1667, MSS. Carte 220, fo. 288; Conway to Ormond, 15 and 22 Oct., ibid. 35, fos. 764, 778; Orrery to Ormond, 19 Nov., in T. Morrice, *Orrery State Papers* (1743), ii. 323; Ossory to Ormond, 12 Oct., MSS. Carte 220, fo. 296; P. Forster to Ormond, 28 Jan. 1668, ibid. 36, fo. 123, where Ashley may be the Treasury Commissioner whom 'I need not name'; Conway to Ashley, 28 Feb., Shaftesbury Papers, L, 12 (the figures which Conway forwarded were actually provided by an unnamed 'noble author'); and cf. Carte, op. cit. iv. 311–47.

[2] *Court Minutes of the East India Company*, ed. E. B. Sainsbury (1907–29), *1660–3*, pp. 309–35, 344; *1664–7*, pp. 210, 252–3; *1668–70*, pp. xvii and 18; *H.M.C. Eighth Report*, pp. 107, 167–74; cf. also A. Marvell, *Letters*, ed. H. M. Margoliouth (1927), p. 74.

[3] J. Ralph, *History of England* . . . (1744), i. 172.

[4] In a later session Buckingham seems to have desired to use the deadlock to advise a dissolution, but there is no evidence that even then Ashley had any part in it. See below, pp. 273–5.

on what constituted treason; in 1667 he had opposed the committal of Clarendon to the Tower when the Commons had demanded it as a right; in 1671 he was to maintain the right of the Lords to amend money bills, to the natural annoyance of the Commons. On other occasions he sought to protect peers' personal privileges, for instance the freedom of their houses from search. In October 1665 he and some colleagues ruined a bill 'for regulating all people in time of the plague' by adding a proviso 'that nothing therein contained . . . should extend to any peer of the realm, nor should his house be shut up by any officer though infected'; the Commons refused to accept this selfish and short-sighted proviso, and in the end a useful bill failed to pass, not for any serious political reason, but because he and his class preferred to stand on their dignity.[1] It is true that in 1671 he and Halifax vainly attempted to pass a bill reforming some of the worst abuses of privilege, and for instance enabling peers and their servants to be sued in the law courts[2]; but this did not progress far enough to become an issue between the two Houses. Once a matter of privilege was in dispute between Lords and Commons, Ashley always sided with the majority of his own House, as jealous as anyone to maintain its independent place in the constitution. In 1658 and 1659 he had attacked the Cromwellian 'other house' because its members were entirely dependent on the Protector and simply a hindrance to the development of any true parliamentary life.[3] Now that he was himself one of the upper House under the Restoration, not unnaturally he was disinclined to take such a radical view. Even in his later opposition period, when he was repeatedly outnumbered by the Court peers, his concern was to make use of the political facilities for obstruction offered by the Lords (in contrast to the 'other House') and not to abolish them. In the society and the political system which he envisaged, the lay peerage always had a place, where Cromwell's army officer 'peers' had not.

---

[1] Brodrick to Ormond, 2 Nov. 1665, MSS. Carte 34, fo. 468. Cf. A. Marvell, op. cit. p. 40.

[2] *L.J.* xii. 448; *H.M.C. Eighth Report, House of Lords MSS.*, p. 153.

[3] See pp. 94–95, 101–5 above.

CHAPTER XI

JOHN LOCKE AND THE SHAFTESBURY HOUSEHOLD

A<small>T</small> the end of May 1668 the ill-health from which Lord Ashley had suffered for years approached a crisis. During a particularly bad night he was suddenly seized with excessive vomiting, and next day the physicians administered their customary cure-all, a purgative, but all that this did was to turn the patient's face a rusty red. In the next few days his doctors vainly prescribed a course of 'anti-icterics and chaly-beates',[1] and purging pills, until after a bout of acute pain a soft tumour the size of an ostrich-egg suddenly sprang up below the ensiform cartilage. Several days of treatment failed to reduce this tumour, and the drastic decision had to be taken, to kill or cure by means of a surgical operation.

If Ashley had died under the surgeon's knife at this point, the footsteps which he would have left on the sands of time would have been of the faintest. He would have been remembered, if at all, only as a minor figure who had played some part in helping on the Restoration and earned sub-ordinate office as a result. He would have been of approximately the same political stature as Anglesey or Morrice. When in February 1668 the permanent committees of the Privy Council had been reorganized, he had (after nearly eight years' service) still not been placed on the most important of them, the king's 'cabinet council' or 'committee of foreign affairs'.[2] His death at the age of forty-seven would have left no obvious void in English political life.

He did not die, and the development of English Whiggism and liberalism was modified, because two years previously he had met John Locke, divined his genius, and admitted him into his household. Locke's greatness also lay in the future. Eleven years younger than Ashley, he was no longer a young man, but he had not found his true métier in life; he had been Lecturer in Greek and later in Rhetoric at Christ Church, dabbled in experimental science with Boyle, studied medicine and been on a minor diplomatic mission to the Elector of Brandenburg at Cleves. He had written nothing of note, and what we know of his views in the years just after the Restoration suggests that they were not yet particularly liberal. The accidental meeting of Ashley and Locke in 1666 was of crucial im-portance to both.

---

[1] According to *O.E.D.* an anti-icteric is a medicine used against jaundice; a chalybeate is one impregnated with iron.
[2] S.P. Charles II, vol. 276, fo. 251.

There are two accounts of the way in which the meeting took place, both, however, written some forty years later and therefore possibly unreliable in detail. Ashley's grandson, the third Earl of Shaftesbury, thought that the introduction was performed by one Mr. Bennet, a friend of Locke's, 'steward' of Ashley's and later M.P. for Shaftesbury.[1] Locke's closest friend in later life, Lady Masham, said that a medical friend and Fellow of New College, Doctor Thomas, asked Locke to go to Ashley, and apologize for a messenger's failure to deliver some spa water from Astrop, in north Oxfordshire, which Ashley had come to Oxford to drink.[2] Both incidents may have taken place, but at this distance of time it is impossible to determine which of them came first. But whether Bennet or Thomas had the credit, the important fact was that Ashley and Locke were immediately attracted to one another and took pleasure in conversing, not merely on Ashley's health, but on a wide variety of questions. When Ashley left Oxford, he did not forget his new acquaintance. It was probably through his influence that Clarendon wrote as Chancellor of the University to his Vice-Chancellor, recommending that Mr. John Locke be awarded the degree of Doctor of Medicine without having first gone to the lectures required for the degree of Bachelor; and when this attempt proved unsuccessful, it was Ashley's friend, the Secretary of State Sir William Morrice, who signed a royal warrant which gave Locke a royal dispensation from taking holy orders, as he would normally have had to do in order to retain his Studentship at Christ Church.[3] Finally, in the spring of 1667 Ashley invited Locke to come and live in his household in London—and Locke accepted the invitation. He did not give up his Christ Church Studentship, and from time to time he returned to Oxford, but he had now turned his back on the life of a college tutor, and from 1667 to 1675 he was rather to be thought of as a member of Ashley's household than of an Oxford college.

So it came about that Locke was at hand when the crisis came in Ashley's ill-health, and to him Ashley turned for advice. The great philosopher had long been interested in medicine; he had never practised it, but since 1652 he had kept notebooks with jottings about remedies, and he had been friendly with people like Richard Lower and David Thomas who were interested in medical research.[4] Sometime in 1667 he had also met Thomas Sydenham, the greatest physician of the day—the introduction may have been performed by Ashley, since the Sydenhams were a Dorset family who had served with him on the Parliamentary side in the Civil War, and

---

[1] The Earl's story is in a letter to J. Le Clerc, 8 Feb. 1705, the original of which is in the Amsterdam University Library, Remonstrants' MSS. J. 20.

[2] Damaris Masham to Le Clerc, 12 Jan. 1705, ibid. J. 57a. Both accounts of the meeting are printed by Maurice Cranston, *John Locke* (1957), pp. 93–95; but the letter of David Thomas's which he also prints does not in fact prove that Thomas was the first to bring the two men together.   [3] Shaftesbury Papers, XLVII, 8 and 22.

[4] Cf. M. Cranston, op. cit. esp. pp. 40 and n., 90–93.

Thomas Sydenham lived close to Ashley's London house and prescribed for the household.[1] Locke and Sydenham both stressed the need to base medical practice on keen observation of cases rather than on theoretical speculation; and in accordance with this principle Locke kept careful notes of Ashley's case and its history, and these notes still survive.[2] They are so full that modern doctors can diagnose that the patient was suffering from a hydatid cyst of the liver, and that the tradition that Ashley's internal abscess or 'tumour' had been caused by a coach-spill in Holland in 1660[3] was incorrect.

A hydatid cyst is caused by a parasite transmitted through dogs and sheep, and is therefore uncommon now except in such countries as Australia and New Zealand. The severe pains in his left side of which he had complained in youth may or may not mean that such a cyst had already developed, but certainly there were symptoms directly attributable to this in 1656. It was then that Ashley himself first noticed the existence of a painless internal tumour, 'about the anterior region of the liver' which caused just sufficient swelling to be visible when a hand was applied to it. At the same time over-exercise produced a deep redness in the skin, and a burning fever; but the doctors took the view that this was simply an unusual malformation in the liver and was no cause for alarm. Since 1656 the tumour had been accompanied by recurring bouts of that most depressing of ailments, jaundice; and Ashley had had to struggle with the languor, loss of appetite, weakness and irritation which jaundice produces, by frequently drinking *acidulae*, that is, cold spa waters with a sharp and pungent taste. From 1666 attacks of ill-health had been more and more frequent; and what happened at the end of May 1668 was the rupture of the cyst. Ashley's condition was now acute, and some more drastic remedy than spa waters must be found.

In the seventeenth century a surgical operation was a terrifying experience. Brandy might deaden some of the pain, but could not be a complete anaesthetic or reduce greatly the shock; and even if the surgeon's knowledge of anatomy was adequate, his ignorance of antisepsis was total, and the proportion of patients who died under his knife was high. An operation was something to be undertaken only in a desperate emergency, and many brave men (for instance, Southampton) preferred to undergo agonies of pain and a slow death, rather than risk it. It took immense

---

[1] Shaftesbury Papers, IV, 216; and cf. K. Dewhurst's article on 'Sydenham's *Original Treatise on Smallpox*, with a preface, and dedication to the Earl of Shaftesbury, by John Locke', in *Medical History*, Oct. 1959, pp. 278–302.

[2] Shaftesbury Papers, XLVII, 2. They were studied by Sir W. Osler in an article on 'John Locke as a Physician', reprinted from the *Lancet* in *An Alabama Student and other biographical essays* (1908), pp. 80–96. I am indebted to my former colleague Professor A. W. Kay for medical advice on Shaftesbury's illness and operation. See also K. Dewhurst, *John Locke, Physician and Philosopher* (1963), pp. 36–37.

[3] p. 143 above.

courage and will-power both to submit to an operation and to advise and
superintend one. It was to Locke that the Shaftesburys were permanently
grateful for the success of this one, though it is unlikely that he wielded
the knife himself. One account has it that Locke's friend, the well-known
Doctor Thomas Willis, gave his advice, and that the actual operation was
performed by a surgeon named Knollys,[1] but the Shaftesbury household
was in no doubt whose was the responsibility and the honour of saving his
life.

The cautery, or hot knife, was applied on 12 June, and for six weeks
thereafter Locke made daily observations of his patient's condition. For a
long time Ashley's friends had no hope of his recovery, but on the 23rd
he was able to get up, and by the middle of July, though far from recovered,
he was transacting business.[2] There was a short period when he had a chill,
and the famous 'sympathetic powder' was prescribed for him, but by
25 July his recovery was so assured that Locke abandoned his note-taking.
One difficult decision had to be taken. In the course of the operation a
tube was inserted to drain matter from the abscess, and the question was
whether this tube should be removed or whether it should remain permanently there. Characteristically Ashley solved this problem by systematically putting a list of questions to Sydenham and other doctors;
they were his questions and not Locke's, for he asked in the first person
'Whether I may travel in a coach, ride on horseback, boat, or use any such
exercise safely with a pipe in of this length?'[3] After comparing the
answers, it was decided to keep the pipe open to allow for possible further
drainage. Present-day medical opinion would not be in favour of this
solution because healing would be more difficult and there would be a
serious risk of infection; but though the tube would be something of a
nuisance, it would not necessarily cause much discomfort. At all events,
for the rest of his life he was unique amongst men in possessing the famous
tube which led later Tory pamphleteers to christen him 'Tapski' as though
he were a barrel of beer with a tap—perhaps in combination with other
jokes about a Cooper. Whether the knowledge that he was unique in his
way had any psychological effect upon him is a mystery into which it is
impossible to penetrate.

Ashley's debt to John Locke could never be repaid, in the nature of
things, though Ashley at a later stage allowed him to buy for only £800

---

[1] *Rawleigh Redivivus* (1683), p. 48. The author of this anonymous life of Shaftesbury
probably had access to his household, but gets the date of the operation and other details
wrong. He omits all reference to Locke's part in the operation, but Locke's dislike of
publicity was always intense, and no doubt was particularly great in the circumstances of
1683. For Willis, see the article in the *D.N.B.*, and also that by Sir Charles Symonds in
The Royal Society, its Origins and Founders (1960), pp. 91–97.

[2] Pepys, 19 June 1668; newsletter of 23 June in *H.M.C. Fleming MSS.*, p. 7; newsletter of 4 July in Add. MSS. 36916, fo. 107; John Nicholas to Sir E. Nicholas, 16 July,
in MSS. Eger. 2539, fo. 232.   [3] Osler, loc. cit.

an annuity of £100 per year, secured on a farm at Kingston in Dorset.[1] It is significant that the annuity was not a gift but a sale on favourable terms. Locke was not an employee of Ashley's, to be rewarded for services rendered; he was a friend, with other sources of income, who had been invited to live in Ashley's household.

In 1667 this household was settled at Exeter House, on the northern and less fashionable side of the Strand. Earlier Ashley had rented a house in Queen Street, Lincoln's Inn Fields, but this was not grand enough for a peer nor near enough to the centre of government for a Chancellor of the Exchequer. Accordingly he had decided to rent Exeter House, rather nearer to Whitehall than to the City, and where his second wife's Cecil relatives had lived. The house stood on the site of the modern Exeter Street, almost opposite the old Savoy Palace, while behind it there was still a garden which the Dutch ambassadors found attractive. The building had been begun by Sir Thomas Palmer in the reign of Edward VI, had been completed by Lord Burleigh and passed on to his eldest son the Earl of Exeter. It had been described at the beginning of the seventeenth century as 'a very fair house raised with bricks, proportionably adorned with four turrets placed at the four quarters of the house; within it is curiously beautified with rare devices, and especially the oratory, placed in an angle of the great chamber'. In the chapel attached to it Evelyn had attended Anglican communion during the difficult days of the Protectorate, and had been arrested there by Cromwell's troopers on Christmas Day, 1657. At different times the house had been occupied by Spanish and Dutch ambassadors, for after the first Earl of Exeter's death the Cecils had not lived there themselves, preferring to let it until, when Ashley's lease expired in 1676, they pulled it down to make way for building. This was probably because it was too large, inconvenient and expensive to run. When Burleigh had lived there he had had 'fourscore persons in family', that is in his household, but not many could afford to live on the scale of Queen Elizabeth's Lord Treasurer. Ashley thus had an impressive London house suitable for a greater officer than the Chancellor of the Exchequer, though he did not rent the whole of it until he became Lord Chancellor, when the rent was increased from £200 to £250 per annum.[2]

Ashley's household fell far short of Lord Burleigh's eighty; even after he had become Lord Chancellor in 1672 only thirty-six names were listed in his 'family'. One has the impression that many of these were men who originated from the neighbourhood of his estate in Dorset. Of the origins

---

[1] Cf. Locke to Edward Clarke, 16 May 1692, printed in M. Cranston, op. cit. pp. 355–6.

[2] *Survey of London*, vol. xviii, *The Strand*, ed. Sir G. Gater and W. H. Godfrey (1937), p. 125, and cf. Plate 1b; Norden's *Middlesex*, cit. H. B. Wheatley, *London Past and Present* (1891), i. 343 (note that Wheatley does not sufficiently distinguish between Burleigh/Exeter House and Cecil House); Evelyn, iii. 203–4 and n.; Hoboken, 5/15 and 12/22 Oct. 1660, in Add. MSS. 17677, X; the rent from accounts in Shaftesbury Papers, XL, 44 and XLI, 54.

of Thomas Stringer, the blindly devoted servant who kept his household accounts, unfortunately little is known, but the fact that he lies buried at Ivychurch, just across the Wiltshire border, is probably not without significance. Peter Percival, who acted as Ashley's banker at least in later life, married Stringer's sister, and was probably related to one James Percival who had given evidence before the Court of Wards on Sir Anthony Ashley Cooper's behalf; a document of 1663 refers to three acres called Heath Close, at Wimborne St. Giles, 'lately in the possession of James Percival, gent'. Ned Stillingfleet, a page, may have been related to the famous divine of that name, whose birthplace was at Cranborne, only a mile or two from St. Giles. When Shaftesbury became Lord Chancellor and wanted his portrait painted, it was to a native of Salisbury, Greenhill, that he turned; and it was to Greenhill that he paid £100 to take the son of his bailiff at St. Giles, Hughes, as an apprentice. Doctor Sydenham, to whom reference has already been made, prescribed medicines for the household's ailments. The local ties were very strong, and may have helped to give Ashley devoted service; for it is significant that in his hour of need in 1681, when anyone turning King's evidence could have earned ample reward, none of his servants did so.[1]

Some of Stringer's accounts for the Ashley household in these years survive. Between Lady Day 1668 and Lady Day 1671, Stringer received £17,871 and paid out £17,231; the corresponding figures for 1671–2 were £22,973[2] and £23,984, and for 1672–3 they were £16,519 and £16,569.[3] However, these totals are not to be identified with income and expenditure[4]; for the receipts included money received from bankers and others— repayment of loans or other financial transactions—and from the maturing of government 'orders in course' in which Ashley had dealt, while the disbursements included both investments and payments for the purchase of land.

Thus the impressive figure of £23,984 spent in 1671–2 includes £12,040 paid for the purchase of land and fee-farm rents and between £3,000 and £4,000 in investments, mainly in the Whalebone Company; the exact figure cannot be determined because only the names of some men receiving payment are given, without any indication of the nature of the transaction. A further difficulty is that these accounts are not comprehensive. They refer only to the money passing through Stringer's own hands, and he was not Ashley's only accountant. His figures of receipt for 1671–2, to which

[1] Shaftesbury Papers, IV, 236; II, 16; IV, 122, 205, 216.
[2] From the total of £23,613 a balance in hand in 1671 of £640 must be deducted; Professor Rich (see below) has omitted to do this.
[3] Shaftesbury Papers, XL, 44; XLI, 54; IV, 216.
[4] As was done by E. E. Rich, in 'The First Earl of Shaftesbury's Colonial Policy', *Trans. Roy. Hist. Soc.* (1957), p. 56. Professor Rich noticed that the 'expenditure' included many investment payments but none the less suggested that 'the scale of living at the Restoration Court' might be deduced from these totals.

reference has been made, include only £315 in income from rents (this from the 'Ely rents' in Holborn) plus the sum of £1,608 received from Charles Cheswell or Chiswell, who was probably Ashley's principal account-ant on his country estates. But his total income from land must have been considerably in excess of this. A set of rentals, preserved in the Muniment Room at St. Giles House, shows an income from land in Dorset and Wilt-shire of £25,295 over a period of seven and a half years from 1668 to 1675, or an average of £3,373 *per annum*; the corresponding rentals for 1675–9 are lost, but those for 1679–81 show an income from land (excluding the 'Ely rents') of £5,977 or £2,988 *per annum*.

Even these figures do not include receipts from the sale of produce, stock, timber, etc., on the home farm in these years. That these may have been substantial appears from the probably incomplete sum of £2,348 received from the sale of stock and surplus milk between Michaelmas 1675 and Lady Day 1678, and from the sum of £2,204 received from the sale of the timber from 1,415 trees in 1679 and 1680. Equally Stringer's accounts contain entries of some disbursements relating to the estates and not others. There are references to £464 'abated unto several tenants in consideration of hard times' and allowances of £642 to tenants for improvements on their holdings; on the other hand, we do not know the cost of the 908 sheep added to the stock at Wimborne in or shortly before 1670,[1] or how much was spent on improvements to St. Giles House.

In short, the absence of a proper comprehensive account of all Ashley's financial affairs makes it impossible to arrive at a firm figure for his income and expenditure in a given year; but it is possible to form some impressions of the scale of his operations. Firstly, the money which passed through the hands of Stringer alone in one year, 1671–2, ran well into five figures. Of this, £2,666. 13s. 4d. was Ashley's salary as one of three Treasury Commissioners,[2] and a further £200 came from his office as Chancellor of the Exchequer. The amount derived from fees, official and unofficial, cannot be fixed, but Ashley received a further £2,000 'upon an order of £2,000 charged unto the fee-farm rents in Edw. Rogers's name for secret service dated 3 Oct 1671'. Of this £1,781 was paid out to Rogers in small amounts before the end of the financial year.[3] Secondly, £15,268 passed through Stringer's hands as the proceeds of various short-term private financial transactions; this includes £1,247 from the banker Horneby, £3,558 upon four bonds from the East India Company dated 26 July 1671, and £8,560 from Treasury orders which had previously been assigned to him by two great financiers, Sir John Banks and Sir Robert Viner. Of this £693 represents interest on the capital sums repaid (at annual rates ranging from 5 per cent in the case of the East India Company,

---

[1] Shaftesbury Papers, IV, 187.
[2] Albemarle had died, and Coventry had been dismissed.
[3] Cf. *C.T.B., 1669–72*, pp. 753, 938.

to 10 per cent). The amount involved in these transactions is considerably greater than the sums which Ashley invested in Carolina, the Royal Africa Company or the Hudson's Bay Company.[1] It is possible, however, that the receipts may have been inflated by the realization of assets, either to buy land or because the Stop of the Exchequer was impending.[2] In 1671 he consolidated his estates by buying Cranborne Chase from Lord Arundel for £2,200; and in addition he spent some £4,500 on purchasing fee-farm rents in reversion of the Queen. Thus he seized opportunities to add to his estates, and in the long run this third source of income, from land, at over £3,000 per annum would remain the most important. Loss of office, when it came, would naturally mean a serious reduction in income, but not a catastrophic one.

As has been seen, the figure of £23,984 spent in twelve months in 1671–2 needs considerable reduction to reach the amount which can really be termed expenditure. In addition to purchase of land, investments, and payments to people who were probably other accomptants, there was an allowance of £700 each half-year for Ashley's son, and a personal allowance of £75 each quarter for Lady Ashley, plus £342 per annum which seems to have been the rent of a farm settled upon her. (In 1672–3 Lady Ashley had two additional gifts of £100, plus a further item of £100 paid for '5 pearls for my Lady's necklace'.) In this year £2,178 of Stringer's disbursements can be definitely assigned to household and personal expenditure for his master. Servants' wages amounted to £193, all in small quarterly payments additional to their board down to 'Alice in the scolary', who received the princely sum of £1. 2s. 6d. each quarter; bills paid to various tradesmen came to £269, plus £5. 15s. 'given to tradesmen's boxes' at Christmas 1671; the stables cost £152, plus £45 for a new coach; a total of £159 was spent on hangings and £64 on damask. Hangings were expensive: there is a bill of 1671 'For four pieces of hangings of the history of Hero and Leander £132. 10s.', and in 1674 '24⅜ ells flem. of tapestry of the design of the Apostles at 45s. per ell' cost £54. 16s. 10d. Some of the bills for hangings may have been for the embellishment of St. Giles with which Ashley was also concerned at the time. The payments relate to every aspect of a nobleman's life at this time. The 'charges of Mr. John Cooper's[3] sickness and funeral' in January 1672 amounted to £54. 15s., including ten shillings for 'the minister of the Savoy praying with him'. Elsewhere preserved among the Shaftesbury Papers there is a bill of £31 for medicines supplied at Dr. Sydenham's prescription in a period of some ten weeks in the autumn of 1673; during this short period scarcely a day went by without a clyster, cordial, julep or purging pill being prescribed for somebody in the household, which suggests that it must have been full of hypochondriacs. There are scattered references to Lord Ashley's charity:

[1] See below, ch. xii.   [2] See below, p. 296.
[3] I have not been able to discover John Cooper's relationship to the family.

o

five shillings 'to the poor people at the gate when my Lord was going into the country' in 1669, sixpence 'to a poor man at Marrowbone' [Marylebone], another sixpence 'to a poor man in Lincoln's Inn Fields', five shillings for a scholar at Charterhouse, and £9. 11s. 8d. each quarter to alms-people at St. Giles, in the almshouses which his grandfather had built there.[1]

The general impression derived from all this is that Ashley was thoroughly businesslike, but not mean; willing to spend to keep up his position in society, but not extravagantly so; and above all in complete control of his financial affairs, unlike Buckingham or Sunderland, to quote only two contemporary examples. It is significant that there is no hint of any gambling losses. Certainly there was never any danger of his falling into the hands of creditors, or having a stop of his own private exchequer.

The Exeter House in which John Locke took up his residence was therefore the house of a nobleman who was able to indulge himself as he thought fit. Obviously Ashley's main interest for most of his life lay in politics, but there was another less serious side. He once remarked to Locke, 'that there were in every one, two men, the wise and the foolish, and that each of them must be allowed his turn. If you would have the wise, the grave, and the serious, always to rule and have the sway, the fool would grow so peevish and troublesome, that he would put the wise man out of order, and make him fit for nothing: he must have his times of being let loose to follow his fancies, and play his gambols, if you would have your business go on smoothly'.[2] Some of his relaxations were those of the normal country gentleman: he liked to retire to Dorset whenever he was free to do so, or, when business kept him in London, he diverted himself by making plans for St. Giles, or by changing those which he had previously drawn up. He instructed his bailiff to prepare a model of a chapel, 'with a little vault under it for burying'; directed 'that the stair be made out of the designed dining-room into the terrace in the garden', and that 'a bathing-room [be] made under that which was intended for the cabanett and a door opened out of the hall into it, and that door into the long green walk be made up'; arranged that if Hughes would supply him with the necessary measurements he would send 'chimney pieces for the new dressing room and drawing room of Plymouth or Chichester marble'. Out of doors he planned a winter greenhouse '60 foot long and 16 foot broad in the clear'; talked of two pigeon-houses, 'one in my new designed warren in Allhallows fields', and of cutting 'a new river from the hatches in the hopgarden unto Philipston ford'. Above all he was interested in the progress of his fruit-trees, and was always on the look-out for new grafts. When Locke returned from France in 1679 he brought to please his patron some *Observations*

[1] These examples are taken from various bills in IV, 216, in addition to the more formal accounts for 1668–70 and 1671–3 in XL, 44 and XLI, 54.

[2] Locke, *Works* (1823), ix. 272.

upon the growth and culture of vines and olives: the production of silk and the preservation of fruits with a short dedicatory letter.[1] Ashley was not particularly addicted to hunting or other energetic sports, perhaps because his health would not permit it, but he noted in his diary the dates of all the horse-fairs.[2]

There is no evidence that Ashley had any intention of filling his house with an expensive collection of paintings and *objets d'art*. Such pictures as survive at Wimborne St. Giles from this period are almost all portraits of members of the family, and those are not numerous.[3] Ashley had not the aesthetic tastes of collectors like Sunderland or Walpole. Again, there is nothing to suggest that he included among his relaxations any special interest either in contemporary poetry or in the Restoration theatre. No doubt he went to the play from time to time, as did everyone else; but not with the same interest as the King or the Duke of Buckingham. In his lighter moments he liked a game of cards, and he enjoyed the pleasures of conversation, and was by Burnet's admission very entertaining company.[4] Certainly when he was at Exeter House he did not live the life of a recluse; he was not interested only in politics, business and his family. His circle of acquaintances was extremely wide. They were drawn from all ranks of society and from every type of political background, and unlike Clarendon (who could never bring himself to mention Lady Castlemaine by name, but only under the highly inappropriate title of 'the lady') he was not inhibited by any moral censoriousness from consorting with the King's mistresses. Indeed the question arises whether Ashley did not sink even lower and include in 'his times of being let loose to follow his fancies, and play his gambols' an addiction to the pleasures of the brothel, as his enemies later alleged.

'His open lewdness he could ne'er disguise', wrote Dryden in *The Medal*—having, be it noted, omitted any reference to this in his earlier and more famous character-sketch of Achitophel. Burnet—writing from a very different political point of view, but not one favourable to Shaftesbury —also described him as lewd, and remarked that 'his morals were of a piece with his religion', that is, that he had very little of either morality or Christianity.[5] The nearest we get to a specific charge against him is Roger North's famous description:

---

[1] Printed ibid. x. 323 sqq., from a first edition published in 1766.

[2] Shaftesbury Papers, IV, 183, 196–8, 206, 208; Christie, ii. 49–51.

[3] An inventory of the pictures at Thanet House in 1682 lists thirty-two, all but two of them portraits, but comparatively few of these are now to be seen at St. Giles House.

[4] Third Earl of Shaftesbury to J. Le Clerc, 8 Feb. 1705, Amsterdam University Library, Remonstrants' MSS., J. 20; Burnet, *Supplement*, p. 58.

[5] Burnet, i. 173; *Supplement*, p. 59. For a Catholic statement, cf. J. Warner, *History of the English Persecution of Catholics and the Presbyterian Plot*, ed. J. A. Birrell for the Catholic Record Society (1953), i. 27, 183. The remark here that Charles II called Shaftesbury 'the Chief Lecher' may be a curious reflection of the famous anecdote, see pp. 214–15 below.

'And, whether out of inclination, custom, or policy, I will not determine, it is certain he was not behindhand, with the Court, in the modish pleasures of the time; and to what excess of libertinism they were commonly grown, is no secret. There was a deformed old gentleman called Sir P. Neal, who, they say, sat for the picture of Sydrophel[1] in *Hudibras*, and, about town, was called the Lord Shaftesbury's groom, because he watered his mares (I forbear the vulgar word) in Hyde Park with Rhenish wine and sugar, and not seldom a bait of cheese cakes.' This lurid account has some peculiar features: no-one would suspect from it that the 'deformed old gentleman', Sir Paul Neile, who is alleged to have performed this function for the Whig leader, was the son of a former Archbishop of Canterbury, a considerable mathematician and a founder Fellow of the Royal Society. However, no doubt it is within the bounds of possibility that a son of an archbishop, and F.R.S., might have acted as North says; certainly he was a business partner of Ashley's in mining projects. For the present it is sufficient to note that this story of North's was not a strictly contemporary account; it was the recollection at least twenty-five years later of a fierce Tory partisan, anxious to reply to Whig historians by painting as black a picture as possible of the Exclusion crisis and all who were concerned in it.[2]

There are also to be considered numerous alleged references to Shaftesbury's lewdness in plays performed in the years of reaction from 1679 onwards. Montagu Summers printed a long list of supposed identifications of characters in these plays who represented Shaftesbury: Sir Timothy Treat-All in *The City Heiress* by Aphra Behn; the Chancellor in *The siege of Constantinople* by Nevil Payne; Marius Senior in *The History and Fall of Caius Marius* by Otway; Ismael in *The Loyal Brother* by Southerne; Wolsey in *Virtue Betrayed, or, Anna Bullen*, by John Banks; the Podesta in *The City Politiques* by Crowne; Arius in *Constantine the Great* by Lee; Benducar in *Don Sebastian* by Dryden.[3] The very length and variety of this list from Marius to Wolsey is enough to show the absurdity of the identification. A reading of the plays confirms that no man could be so Protean as to appear in all these shapes, and that no collection of dramatists could be so incompetent as to portray him in so many different ways. The two city plays, *The City Heiress* and *The City Politiques*, have obviously topical overtones, but in the former Sir Timothy Treat-All (whom Mr. Summers alleges to be 'a full length portrait' of Shaftesbury), if this is a

---

[1] Sydrophel was an astrologer on whom Butler poured ridicule in Part II, Canto III of his poem; but he was not there accused of being a pander.

[2] *Examen* (1740), p. 60; article on Neile by C. A. Ronan and Sir H. Hartley in *The Royal Society, its Origins and Founders* (1960), pp. 159–65; R. Surtees, *History and Antiquities of the County Palatine of Durham* (1816), vol. i, p. lxxxix. For Neile's business relationship with Ashley, see below, p. 229.

[3] Ed. M. Summers, *Complete Works of Thomas Otway* (1926), iii. 274–6, 278; cf. also vol. i, p. lxxxviii n.

portrait at all, is much closer to the Whig alderman Sir Thomas Player, and in the latter (in which the political parallels are evident) the Podesta must represent a Whig sheriff or Lord Mayor of London.[1] Elsewhere it is plain that these dramatists had a repertoire of anti-Whig allusions on which they could draw to make Tory courtiers laugh and cheer, but the use made of these does not add up to a portrait of any one Whig.

This is relevant when we consider the most famous of the alleged representations of Shaftesbury on the stage, as Antonio in *Venice Preserved*. In this play, which was first performed in February 1682, Thomas Otway based his plot on a story by the Abbé Saint Réal of a plot against the Republic of Venice, and as such it could be turned by the government to refer to Whig plots: Charles II attended on the poet's benefit day, and the Duke of York made his first public appearance at it after his return from exile. The part of Antonio, one of the Venetian senators, provides comic relief. He is shown in crudely farcical scenes with a courtesan, Aquilina, his 'Nicky-Nacky', whom he urges to erotic flagellation. The name Antonio is obviously the same as Shaftesbury's, and their ages were similar but not exactly so (Antonio is 61 in the play,[2] while Shaftesbury was 60 when it was first performed); but in other respects they are unlike—for instance, Antonio is on the side of established authority, whereas in 1682 Shaftesbury was regarded as a revolutionary. From the political point of view Shaftesbury is much closer to another character in the same play, Renault, who is a professional conspirator against the state. Where Antonio is merely a fool, Renault is the dangerous villain that the Tories deemed Shaftesbury to be. It is true that Renault makes an attempt on the chastity of the heroine, but this is necessary for the mechanics of the plot. In his Prologue Otway describes Renault and Antonio. After talking generally of plots in Venice and England, he goes on:

> Here is a Traitour too, that's very old,
> Turbulent, subtle, mischievous and bold,
> Bloudy, revengefull, and to crown his part,
> Loves fumbling with a Wench, with all his heart;
> Till after having many changes pass'd,
> In spight of Age (thanks Heaven) is hang'd at last:
> Next is a Senatour that keeps a Whore,
> In Venice none a higher office bore;
> To lewdness every night the Letcher ran,
> Shew me, all London, such another man,
> Match him at Mother Creswold's if you can.

From the description of Antonio in the last five lines, the sentence 'To lewdness every might the Letcher ran', has often been quoted to Shaftesbury's discredit.[3] On the other hand the characterization of Renault—

---

[1] Possibly Slingsby Bethel (cf. *Dramatic Works of John Crowne* (1873–4), ii. 138–9, 161–3, and the reference to 'a person of quality' [not in the play] on p. 132).

[2] Act III, scene 1, line 40.   [3] E.g. M. Cranston, op. cit. p. 108.

'very old, turbulent, subtle, mischievous and bold'—sounds exactly like a Tory view of Shaftesbury. There is plainly a difficulty here, from which come authorities try to escape by saying that Otway portrays him 'clearly and unmistakably' both as Antonio, the fool, and Renault, the knave, and trying to provide explanations for his presence on both sides at once in the play.[1] But this is surely a *reductio ad absurdum*, and there must be a better solution. One possibility is that the character of Antonio was originally intended to allude not to Shaftesbury, but to Sir Thomas Player. 'In Venice none a higher office bore' than Player, who was permanent Chamberlain of the City of London; and though well past middle age he was notorious for his whoring: he was the 'railing Rabsheka' of the second part of *Absalom and Achitophel*, 'a saint that can both flesh and spirit use, Alike haunt conventicles and the stews'. One of the stews that he frequented was Mother Creswell's notorious bawdy-house in Moorfields.[2] He was a frequent target for government satirists, and but for the simple matter of the name Antonio he would be a much more likely subject for the caricature. Was the name Antonio chosen for the character as an afterthought, to transfer the ridicule from a lesser man to the government's principal enemy? Or was it simply that, after all, Antonio was a not uncommon name for a merchant of Venice?

Be that as it may, this theatrical tradition would be very unsafe ground on which to base a charge of lechery against Shaftesbury. This is equally true of the scurrilous references which appear in the anonymous poems of Tory satirists in the years 1681–3 of reaction. The significant point is that all these charges are made either in the period after 1680 when Shaftesbury's name was dragged through the mud, or in 'reminiscences' after his death. With one solitary exception, all contemporary records known to the present writer are silent about any alleged unchastity of Shaftesbury's before he was sixty; Pepys, whose prurient imagination missed little, and who knew Ashley, has nothing to say about any escapades in Hyde Park, and contemporary letters which refer to the adulteries of Buckingham, Monmouth and others are equally silent. The one exception can scarcely be dignified by the name of evidence. It is the famous anecdote which relates how one day when Shaftesbury was Lord Chancellor in 1672 or 1673, he was walking with full solemnity to the royal presence chamber, accompanied by a sergeant carrying the mace and his purse-bearer carrying the great seal. Charles, watching him approach and wishing to deflate his pomposity, remarked to the courtiers standing by, 'Here comes the greatest whoremaster in England'; only for Shaftesbury to get the better

---

[1] Z. S. Fink, *The Classical Republicans* (Evanston, 1945), pp. 144–8. Cf. also T. Thornton's edition of Otway's *Works* (1813), vol. i, p. xxxviii n., and iii. 7; *The Dramatic Censor* (1770), i. 313; R. G. Ham, *Otway and Lee* (New Haven, 1931), p. 190; Summers, op. cit. iii. 274.

[2] Cf. *London's Loyalty*, quoted by Summers, op. cit. iii. 275; *The Last Will and Testament of the Charter of London*, cit. J. Kinsley, *The Poems of John Dryden* (1958), iv. 1924.

of him with the quick repartee, 'Of a subject, Sire'.[1] This retort was so telling that the story was widely remembered; but it is impossible to be sure how literally Charles's remark was intended. This apart, in the period when Shaftesbury was in office there is nothing at all to set against the fact that his wife was devoted to him; and though happily married men do sometimes go off the rails, they are at least less likely than others to do so.

Finally, if it is true that all these scurrilities relate to the period when he was an elderly opponent to be discredited, this means also that they all relate to the period after his operation and the installation of the tap in his side to drain off matter from his abscess. The anonymous satirists of 1681–3 often refer to this tap and his alleged lewdness together,[2] and they believed, or affected to believe, that his internal abscess had a venereal origin. It is at least possible that the scurrilous rumours of unchastity derived from such a crude and ignorant view about the reasons for the operation performed under John Locke's supervision.

Thus, having described the household at Exeter House, we return to the subject of the friendship between its head and John Locke. Recent Lockian scholarship has fully confirmed the vital importance of this friendship in the development of the greatest of English philosophers,[3] and it is time now to consider the influence which they had upon one another.

John Locke's place in the household was quite unlike that of anyone else at Exeter House. In the first place, it may be said that it was not in any way that of a paid employee. Locke was invited to enjoy Ashley's hospitality freely, he was permitted to buy an annuity on favourable terms and was for a time promoted to two minor posts[4]; but he was not Ashley's servant. He worked and wrote entirely as he thought fit, and when he chose left London for his rooms at Christ Church or on two longer trips into France. If Locke was left free in this way, it was equally true that he did not make vast material gains from his association with Ashley; no doubt he lived a more comfortable life unrestricted by any financial anxiety, but on the other hand he did not become a rich man, and at the same time he had always other sources of income. Sometimes his place was more like that of the intellectual 'brains trusts' which some twentieth-century politicians have cultivated to provide them with ideas, but this comparison cannot be pressed too far—Ashley had plenty of ideas of his own without relying on other people to provide them, and Locke on his

---

[1] Cf. p. 211, n.5 above. For a distortion of it, see *Memoirs of the Life of Anthony late Earl of Shaftesbury, with a Speech of the English Consul at Amsterdam concerning him* . . . (1683), p. 9.

[2] E.g. *The Last Will and Testament of Anthony, King of Poland* (1683), lines 27–30:
> To thee [Armstrong] I do bequeath my brace of whores,
> Long kept to draw the humours from my sores;
> For you they'll serve as well as Silver Tap,
> For women give, and sometimes cure a Clap.

[3] M. Cranston, op. cit. esp. chs. ix–xii, xiv–xvi; *Two Treaties of Civil Government*, ed. P. Laslett (1960), pp. 25–37.   [4] See pp. 260, 311 below.

side always had his own pursuits and was never fully occupied with Ashley's business. In the last analysis the simple fact is that the two men found one another's company congenial. Even the consideration that Locke's medical skill had saved Ashley's life was not allowed to embarrass them.

Like Ashley, John Locke came from the West Country—indeed although his birthplace was in Somerset his grandfather had originally come from Dorset. Like Ashley, he had been subjected in youth to Puritan and Parliamentarian influences: he had been too young to fight himself, but his father had been a captain, and his father's colonel, Alexander Popham, had secured his entry into Westminster School. (Popham was known to Ashley—he too had been suspected of complicity in Sir George Booth's rising in 1659,[1] and, after being a member of the Rump, was elected to the Cavalier Parliament.) Like Ashley, Locke had disliked the worst excesses of the extremist enthusiasts during the Commonwealth, had reacted against them and welcomed the Restoration when it came. Like Ashley, Locke had emerged into the new world of the Restoration with a coolly rational attitude towards religion and politics. And Locke was extremely versatile— no narrow specialist, his interests ranged over a wide field—medical, scientific, educational, religious, philosophical, political. So far as politics was concerned, Locke had no ambitions of his own—or no doubt Ashley could have provided him with a seat for a Dorset constituency; and how far he entered into Ashley's political secrets must remain for ever a mystery. But equally he was far from being the kind of abstract thinker who remains in his study remote from the world of affairs, erecting academic theories (if indeed such thinkers really exist). He was interested in the urgent political questions of the day, and thanks to Ashley he had now been brought much nearer to the places where decisions were actually taken than Hobbes or Filmer had ever been.

On his side Ashley was capable of meeting Locke at most of these points of interest, and perhaps even of suggesting new ones. As we have seen, his formal education had probably been incomplete; but he had by no means allowed his intellectual abilities to stop developing when he left the university, and he too ranged widely even when he was active in politics. Charles II's remark that Ashley knew more law than all his judges and more divinity than all his bishops may have been sarcastic; and Burnet (who disapproved of his dubious religious orthodoxy) remarked grudgingly that 'he had a general knowledge of the slighter parts of learning, but understood little to the bottom; so he triumphed in a rambling way of talking, but argued slightly when he was held close to any point'.[2] But

---

[1] Godfrey Davies, *The Restoration of Charles II* (1955), pp. 128–9. But the letter quoted by Cranston, op. cit. p. 106, does not refer to this rising at all, but to the overthrow of the Army's régime in December of the same year. Mr. Cranston also states wrongly that Sir Anthony Ashley Cooper was tried and acquitted.   [2] Burnet, i. 173.

Locke, who probably conversed more with him than did either Charles or Burnet, thought differently, admiring his penetration. As a friend wrote after Locke's death:

> I wish I could . . . give you a full notion of the idea which Mr. Locke had of that nobleman's merit. He lost no opportunity of speaking to it, and that in a manner which sufficiently showed he spoke from his heart. Though my Lord Shaftesbury had not spent much time in reading, nothing, in Mr. Locke's opinion, could be more just than the judgement he passed upon the books which fell into his hands. He presently saw through the design of a work, and without much heeding the words, which he ran over with vast rapidity, he immediately found whether the author was master of his subject, and whether his reasonings were exact.[1]

Another reference to this priceless faculty of being able to pick out the gist of a book and assess it quickly occurs in the recollections of Lady Masham, Locke's patroness in the years after the Revolution, of what Locke had told her about Shaftesbury:

> . . . But if my Lord was pleased with the company of Mr. Locke, Mr. Locke was yet more so with that of my Lord Ashley, and he has often said, that it perfectly charmed him.
>
> The conversation of men of good parts, bred with all the advantages which people of quality have, is not ordinarily more different from that of mere scholars, than my Lord Ashley's was distinguished from that of other men's of his own rank, and position, by peculiar agreements.
>
> This great man, esteemed by all parties in his country to be the ablest and most consummate statesman in it, if not of the age he lived in; who had a compass of thought, soundness of judgment, and sharpness of penetration that (in some extraordinary instances of his sagacity) has been fancied almost more than merely human, was no less admirable in the qualities and accomplishments that fit men for society.
>
> He was very communicative in his nature: he had conversed with books a good deal; but with men much more; and having been deeply engaged in the public affairs of his time at an age when others were scarce thought fit to begin to meddle with them, he had, whilst young, acquired that experience of things, and knowledge of men, which few have till they are old; and though this permitted him not the leisure to be any great reader, yet being able (as he was) presently to discern the strength of any argument, and where the weight of it turned; having besides the advantage of an excellent memory, he always understood more of the books he read from a cursory reading of them than most other men did who dwelt longer upon them.
>
> As he had every qualification of an excellent speaker (in which great endowment he was esteemed to surpass all who were his contemporaries in either House of Parliament) there was in his wit as much vivacity as there was strength and profoundness in his judgment: to which being added a temper naturally

---

[1] *The Character of Mr. Locke*, by Mr. *Peter Coste*, translated in Locke's *Works* (1823), x. 167–8. The passage goes on to pay tribute to Shaftesbury's political acumen, for which cf. Locke's own memoir, ibid. ix. 272–3.

gay (unalloyed with melancholy even in age, and under his greatest troubles) this happy conjuncture gave ever to his most ordinary conversation a very peculiar and agreeable mixture of mirth with instruction; which was still so much the more pleasing, in that as he himself was always easy, he loved that others should be so in his company, being a great enemy to constraint and formality, having, above all men, the art of living familiarly without lessening anything at all of his dignity. Everything in him was natural, and had a noble air of freedom, expressive of the character of a mind that abhorred slavery, not because he could not be the master, but because he could not suffer such an indignity to human nature, and these qualities (so far as they were capable of it) he inspired into all that were about him. In short, Mr. Locke, so long as he lived, remembered with much delight the time he had spent in my Lord Shaftesbury's conversation; and never spoke of his known abilities with esteem only, but even with admiration.

If those to whom the character of Mr. Locke is best known, may from hence conceive a very high idea of my Lord Shaftesbury, it is certain that those who knew my Lord Shaftesbury do never represent Mr. Locke to themselves as a man more extraordinary, than when they recall to their remembrance that singular esteem my Lord Shaftesbury had of him.

That two such persons should find an uncommon delight in the company of each other, is not to be wondered at; though perhaps it has rarely been known that so firm and lasting a friendship (for so I must call it) has been so suddenly contracted.[1]

This is a striking description of the friendship between the two, and of the nature of the attraction which Ashley had for the younger man. In one respect perhaps it does Ashley less than justice, when it is said that his other preoccupations 'permitted him not the leisure to be any great reader'. Possibly he was no great reader by Locke's standards, but these were academic and high. Certainly the books which Ashley bought were both numerous and extremely varied. Histories, law reports, fugitive pamphlets, Evelyn's *Calendarium Hortense*, Bishop Wilkinson's book on the nature of religion are all to be found in two casual bookseller's bills.[2] 'A list of books which my Lord Shaftesbury carried into the country' compiled by Locke in May 1674 is particularly remarkable.[3] Some of the books represent the obvious interests of the country gentleman: The Duke of Newcastle's *New Method . . . to dress horses* (1667); J. Parkinson's *Paradisi in sole, paradisus terrestris, or a garden of flowers, with a kitchen garden and an orchard* (1629); Gervase Markham's *English husbandman* and his *Country Farmer* (1616); Thomas de Gray's *Complete Horseman* (1639) and the older book by T. Blundeville, *The fower chiefyst offices belongyng to Horseman-shippe* (1565–6); W. Blith's *English Improver, or a New survey of husbandry* (first published 1649). All these were books which ran through several editions in the seventeenth century, for obvious reasons; Cato's and

---

[1] Damaris Masham to Le Clerc, 12 Jan. 1705, Amsterdam University Library, Remonstrants' MSS., J. 57a.   [2] Shaftesbury Papers, IV. 216.
[3] Ibid. V. 278.

Columella's *De Re Rustica* were probably less common. F. Fulton's collection of statutes and M. Dalton's *Country Justice* were probably owned by many J.P.s. J. Collins's *Introduction to merchants' accounts* (3rd ed. 1674) is an addition which needs no comment. But more intellectual interests of different kinds were represented by an edition of Terence, and eight volumes of the *Philosophical Transactions* of the Royal Society; and there were various historical works, including three volumes of de Thou, John Fowler's *History of the troubles of Suethland and Poland* (1656), two volumes of the memoirs of Jeannin and an edition of Baker's *Chronicle*. There were Jeremy Taylor's *Discourses* and something vaguely listed as 'Latitudinarians', and finally there were works of political theory such as Harrington's *Oceana* and *Art of Lawgiving*, and the *De Jure Ecclesiasticorum* of 'Lucius Antistius Constans', sometimes thought to be Spinoza, or, more probably, de la Court.

Some of these books which Shaftesbury took with him to St. Giles may have been bought for him by Locke, for there are numerous entries in the latter's diaries of purchases made for his patron.[1] At other times the two men lent one another books: one particularly intriguing case of this was the loan of 'Lawson's book of the English government' in 1679 when Locke may have been beginning his own work on that subject.[2] Political theory was obviously one of their common interests. When in 1672 John Aubrey recommended Locke to read Hobbes's *Dialogue between a Philosopher and a Student of the Common Laws of England*, he found it natural to add: 'I have a conceit that if your Lord saw it he would like it.' Four years later Shaftesbury sent Stringer special instructions to procure 'the Earl of Clarendon's book against Mr. Hobbes, well bound and gilt and titled on the back', but unfortunately we do not know who he thought had the better of the controversy.[3] One must imagine that there were many informal conversations about such books as these, and that they had their share in influencing the development of the ideas later formulated in Locke's *Two Treatises of Civil Government*.

The decade during which Locke entered Exeter House was also the period of the first efflorescence of the Royal Society. Experimental science was fashionable, and Ashley, like everyone else, took some interest in the Society's activities. His first recorded appearance at the meetings in Gresham's College was on 30 December 1663. On that occasion one of the topics discussed was the effect upon eels of the kind of water in which they

---

[1] See some examples of books on political subjects mentioned in Mr. P. Laslett's list of books available to Locke, in his edition of *Two Treatises of Government* (1960), pp. 133–45, Notes column.

[2] Ibid., p. 59 n. Cf. A. H. Maclean, 'George Lawson and John Locke', in *Cambridge Historical Journal*, 1947, pp. 69–77. Unfortunately it is impossible to be certain whether the book lent was *Politica sacra et civilis* (1660) or the *Examination of the Political Part of Leviathan* (1657); nor is it clear who lent it to whom.

[3] Brown, p. 206; Shaftesbury Papers, VIA, 300.

lived, and Ashley intervened to say that he had observed that eels from muddy water tasted rank, but in spring water the taste became sweet. It was perhaps this remark about the eels of his native county which led someone to christen him 'the Dorsetshire eel', *anguilla Dorsettensis*, 'because he could wriggle out of anyone's grasp'[1]: Clarendon too applied the adjective 'slippery' to him, and this may have been one of the smart witticisms at Whitehall. Later in the same evening when the great chemist Boyle was talking about his experiments with 'spirits of wine' (alcohol), Ashley recommended the redstreak apple 'for yielding a very rich liquor of a long duration, and for being a constant bearer' and offered to have a bottle of cider sent from Wimborne St. Giles so that Boyle might distil it and compare it with the alcohol which he had produced from wine. Ashley seems to have been mainly interested in such everyday observations as this and also in the inventions of Prince Rupert, and on this basis the Society welcomed him, elected him a Fellow, and later to the Society's Council, its committee 'to consider and improve all mechanical inventions' and its 'georgical [i.e. agricultural] committee'.[2] His attendance was very infrequent and his interest not sustained—he probably had too many other irons in the fire—but his circle of acquaintances included several people who were much more closely involved than himself, such as Sir Robert Moray, Sir Edward Harley, Sir Paul Neile, and John Evelyn; and when Locke began to live at Exeter House it seems that some scientific experiments were performed there, and that equipment for them was ordered in Ashley's name as well as Locke's. A later writer included Ashley among a number of 'worthy peers and gentlemen' who followed the King's example, 'erected laboratories in their own houses, and laid their hands to the crucibles and melting-pots'.[3]

In short, Exeter House was a place where almost any intellectual interest could be cultivated, and where all sorts and conditions of men, princes, politicians, merchants, medical men, scientists, might be met from time to time. It could be expected that anyone living there would come into much more varied and more stimulating company than could be found at the Oxford University of that day. And it was very far from being a place where Locke could sit in seclusion, peacefully reading and writing abstract philosophical works without the concerns of the world pressing in upon him; rather was it a hive of activity which grew ever busier as the years passed by. It is true that at Exeter House in 1671 Locke began to write drafts of what later became the *Essay Concerning Human Understanding*, but it is significant that this was never completed while he

---

[1] J. Warner, op. cit. i. 27, 183. There may, however, be a punning contrast between the name Shaftesbury and the word *shaftling*, meaning a variety of eel.

[2] T. Birch, *History of the Royal Society* (1756–7), i. 332, 335, 350, 365–6, 406–7, 498; iii. 112.

[3] M. Cranston, op. cit. p. 109 (based on a notebook of Locke's now privately owned in the United States); M[oses] S[tringer], *Opera Mineralia Explicata* (1713), p. 276.

was in Ashley's household.[1] This does not mean that Ashley was un-interested in problems of the theory of knowledge—indeed he possessed an incomplete copy of parts of Locke's original draft—but that Locke's attention was to some extent diverted by his patron's other concerns, in which he became involved.

How far Ashley confided in Locke the details of his political plans it is impossible to tell with any certainty; but Locke undoubtedly was close to him in his plans for his family. The dangerous operation of 1668 drew attention to the fact that his hopes of founding a noble family depended upon his son, Anthony Ashley Cooper, then a boy of sixteen and still un-married.

This was the 'unfeathered two-legged thing, a son . . . born a shapeless lump, like anarchy', of Dryden's satire. The description, if it can be called such, is obviously exaggerated, but none the less the boy must have been a serious disappointment to his father. When he grew to manhood he was quite unable to give effective support to his father's political schemes; he was found a seat in the House of Commons for Weymouth and Melcombe Regis when he was only eighteen (a few months younger than his father had been when elected for Downton), and his name is occasionally to be found in the *Commons Journals* as Teller in a division, but he is never found as a speaker, and in the last two of the Exclusion Parliaments he did not even stand for re-election. Perhaps the best commentary on his political nullity is to be found in the knowledge that he was left entirely unmolested at the time of the Rye House Plot and the Tory reaction at the end of the reign, and during the Monmouth rebellion at the beginning of the next. Both in 1685 and in 1688 he was left completely out of the calculations of all parties. The few letters of his which survive are laboriously written in a large, shaky hand, and do not suggest that he found writing a pleasurable occupation or engaged in it frequently. The anonymous pamphleteer who in 1683 wrote *The Last Will and Testament of Anthony, King of Poland* put into Shaftesbury's mouth the lines:

> Therefore I leave my soul unto my son,
> For he, as wise men think, as yet has none.

Although it is impossible to place reliance on this sort of scurrility, it seems probable that the intellectual equipment of Ashley's son was at best only ordinary, and it is certain that he was handicapped by chronic ill-health. According to a note written by the fourth Earl of Shaftesbury

[1] M. Cranston, op. cit. pp. 140–1. When Shaftesbury's papers were seized at the time of his arrest in 1681, they included '4 sheets beginning: The Light of Nature is reason set up in the soul at 1st by God, in man's creation; 2nd by Christ'. It has been suggested that this may have been the opening of an epistemological essay by Shaftesbury himself, which has since been lost (P. Laslett: 'Locke and the First Earl of Shaftesbury', in *Mind*, 1952, p. 92 n.). This is not impossible, but since very few of Shaftesbury's surviving papers were written by him, it cannot be taken as certain that this was. It might just as easily have been a paper sent to him by some other author.

in the eighteenth century, the family tradition was that 'by an unhappy mistake committed in misapplying a mercurial medicine for a disorder he had fallen into when but fifteen years old' he was 'so debilitated that he was confined almost altogether within doors and disabled from stirring much in public affairs'.[1] Mercury treatment was commonly given in the seventeenth century for the disease of syphilis, and it is natural to think that this must have been the 'disorder' vaguely described here. Having written this down, the fourth earl crossed out most of the sentence, and substituted a statement that he was 'so afflicted with the gout that he was confined . . .', etc. Whether this was the result of more accurate knowledge or only of a greater sense of delicacy one cannot be sure. What is certain is that young Anthony Ashley Cooper was already in poor health before he attained to manhood, and that it was an urgent matter to find him a wife who could give him an heir to carry on the family line.

In choosing a bride for his son Ashley was not primarily concerned with making a useful political alliance. In later years he gave some advice to his grandson on this point: 'Remember that thou choose a wife out of a worthy honest family that are beloved in their country, that have gained and maintained their estates by honest means; and that have brought up their family accordingly healthy and well bred. Honours and riches may be obtained many ways, but good blood, good relations, healthy families and good society is what gives the truest satisfaction.'[2] But there were other considerations too: when he could finally report to his old friend Morrice that his search had been successful, he wrote of his satisfaction that his son had married 'a virtuous, discreet well-humoured lady, great and necessary additions to her birth and fortune'.[3] Such a paragon had not been easy to find. He turned first to the niece of the fourth Earl of Warwick, a peer of definitely Parliamentarian past[4] but (being crippled by gout) no obvious political importance under the Restoration. These negotiations broke down in September 1668, because the two men could not agree on the terms of the marriage settlement. Two months later John Evelyn, dining with Ashley, was asked for his assistance to obtain the hand of his niece, but nothing came of this proposal either, though it shows that Ashley was not exclusively preoccupied with the idea of marrying into the aristocracy.[5] Finally the choice fell on Dorothy Manners, a daughter of the Earl of Rutland, who had also been a moderate Parliamentarian during the Civil War; he had remained at Westminster and had been offered some official tasks but had usually asked to be excused from them on grounds of

---

[1] Shaftesbury Papers, XXI, 225.   [2] Shaftesbury Papers, XX, 128.   [3] Christie, ii. 44.
[4] He was the son of the Parliamentarian Lord High Admiral; his nephew had married Frances Cromwell, and he had himself sat in Parliament during the Commonwealth, but like Ashley had been one of the commissioners deputed to go over to meet Charles II in 1660. His wife was the Puritan Countess of Warwick whose *Autobiography* was ed. by Croker for the Percy Society in 1848.
[5] Shaftesbury Papers, IV, 169; Evelyn, 27 Nov. 1668.

ill-health. Williamson's description of him as 'a harmless soft man' is sufficient indication of his political weight, and although the matrimonial affairs of his son Lord Roos were to be of some political consequence a year later, he too shrank from being committed to any political grouping. Socially, therefore, the match was a good one, but there was no very obvious political advantage to be derived from it.

According to the third Earl of Shaftesbury (who was the offspring of this marriage), Lady Dorothy was chosen as a possible bride by Locke, 'who being already so good a judge of men, my grandfather doubted not of his equal judgment in women'.[1] However this may be, Locke helped a great deal with the wedding arrangements. He travelled with young Anthony Ashley Cooper to the Rutland house at Belvoir, and it was to him that Ashley sent 'another jewel' with instructions that the young man should 'present his lady with both together' a day or two before leaving. In a further letter Ashley told Locke of his intention to reach Belvoir on 24 September 1669 for the wedding, and he concluded with what was for him an unusual epistolary flourish: 'Sir, you have in the greatest concerns of my life been so successively and prudently kind to me that it renders me eternally, Your affectionate and faithful friend, Ashley.'[2]

After the wedding young Ashley Cooper and Lady Dorothy lived at Exeter House and at Wimborne St. Giles, with an allowance of £1,400 from Lord Ashley. So far from finding Ashley a grim, villainous ogre, she seems to have taken to him immediately; this at least is the impression to be derived from the references to her father-in-law in Lady Dorothy's letters to Locke, with whom she was also on good terms. It was Locke, the family friend and physician, who supervised Lady Dorothy's pregnancies. After one miscarriage the joking hopes which Ashley and Locke had exchanged when the wedding was celebrated were fulfilled, when on 26 February 1671 a third Anthony Ashley Cooper was born.[3] Other grandchildren were born in the following years, but all Ashley's hopes for his family were concentrated in this first grandson, who eventually attained eminence in a very different field as the author of the *Characteristics*. On 19 March 1674, shortly after the boy's third birthday, his father was persuaded to sign a deed constituting the grandfather guardian of Anthony and his younger brother John, with the right to appoint whom he thought fit to become guardians after his death until the boys reached the age of twenty-one.[4] The grandfather in fact hoped to keep the boy under his own

---

[1] Third Earl of Shaftesbury to Jean Le Clerc, 8 Feb. 1705, Amsterdam University Library, Remonstrants' MSS. J. 20. According to Cranston, op. cit. p. 121, 'it was certainly he [Locke] who negotiated the terms of the marriage', but he gives no evidence for this, and it seems improbable.

[2] Letters of 29 Aug. and 16 Sept. 1669, printed by Christie, ii. 35–37.

[3] Lady Dorothy Ashley to Locke, 1 and 15 July 1671, ibid. pp. 38–39; Ashley to Locke, 5 Oct. 1669, ibid. p. 37.

[4] Shaftesbury Papers, XX, 2. It does not appear that Shaftesbury in fact made any provision for this before his death in 1683.

supervision, and he relied upon John Locke, first to provide the medical care essential in an age of such high infant mortality, and later to assist him in planning the boy's education.

Locke was thus a friend of the family, helpful to Ashley in some of his most intimate personal affairs. There remains the much more important question how far this intimacy extended on matters of public concern, and how far it affected the development of Locke's ideas on the nature and extent of political authority.

It is now generally recognized that Locke's early political writings (first published in 1954) were distinctly authoritarian in emphasis. ' "The voice of the people is the voice of God." Surely, we have been taught by a most unhappy lesson how doubtful, how fallacious this maxim is, how productive of evils, and with how much party spirit and with what cruel intent this ill-omened proverb has been flung wide [lately] among the common people [*vulgus*].'[1] This was the inference which he had drawn from the experience of the Civil War and Commonwealth, when shortly after the Restoration he had argued that the 'law of nature' could not be known from the general consent of men. He had not gone to the opposite extreme of adopting a theory of Divine Right, but in an unpublished tract on the *Civil Magistrate* he had argued the need for 'the largeness of the governor's power' to restrain the impatient multitude; and in answer to one Edward Bagshawe's defence of religious toleration he had maintained explicitly that 'the magistrate of every nation, what way so ever created, must necessarily have an absolute and arbitrary power over all the indifferent actions of his people', that is in all matters where the commands of God were not specific.[2] The need for obedience to lawfully constituted authority had been uppermost in his mind, not the freedom of the individual; it was a far cry from this to the *Letters on Toleration*.

In these early writings he had been preoccupied not with 'the way magistrates were created' but with the extent of their authority, particularly in religion. How far were 'magistrates' entitled to enforce their own kind of conformity in 'things indifferent'? When Locke came to Exeter House in 1667 this was still the main preoccupation of Locke's political thought. The basis of royal power was not at that time in question; the possibility of James Duke of York's succession was still remote, and Charles II was not in open conflict with his Parliament. Religious toleration, however, was very much a live issue. The House of Commons had recently insisted on enacting the so-called 'Clarendon Code', but there were those who hoped for greater religious freedom, and amongst these was Ashley. It was at this time that Locke made at least four drafts of a more substantial essay on toleration[3]; but now there was a marked change of emphasis. This time,

[1] Ed. W. von Leyden (1954), p. 161.

[2] P. Laslett, op. cit. pp. 19–22; M. Cranston, op. cit. pp. 59–63; MSS. Locke e. 7 and c. 28.

[3] One of these drafts, now in the Shaftesbury Papers, was printed by H. R. Fox Bourne, *Life of John Locke* (1876), i. 174–94. For the others, see M. Cranston, op. cit. p. 111 n.

in steering between absolute obedience and universal liberty in matters of conscience, he began by 'lay[ing] this down for a foundation, which I think will not be questioned or denied, viz. That the whole trust, power, and authority of the magistrate is vested in him for no other purpose but to be made use of for the good, preservation and peace of men in that society over which he is set'. Without examining the arguments for and against Divine Right, he pointed out that it was contradictory to Magna Carta. Then, 'this being premised, that the magistrate ought to do or meddle with nothing but barely in order to securing the civil peace and property of his subjects', he went on to divide men's opinions and actions into three kinds. First, there were 'purely speculative opinions, as the belief of the Trinity', and 'the place, time, and manner of worshipping my God': these should have unlimited freedom because they did not concern government and society, but were 'a thing wholly between God and me', while 'the magistrate is but umpire between man and man'. As examples of actions in which the magistrate had no business to interfere, because they injured no one and created no disturbance, he chose 'kneeling or sitting in the sacrament', 'wearing a cope or surplice', adult baptism, 'whether I pray with or without a form'—precisely the points which the Act of Uniformity and Conventicle Act claimed to settle. In such matters, Locke maintained, 'every man hath a perfect uncontrollable liberty'. In his second category, of opinions and actions 'such as, in their own nature, are neither good nor bad, but yet concern society and men's conversations one with another', the magistrate was allowed more powers: he might in extreme cases prohibit the publishing of dangerous opinions, but he must be absolutely convinced that 'the peace, safety, or security of his people' were at stake, and he must not try to compel a man to renounce opinions merely held in private. Thirdly, in regard to actions which were good or bad in themselves, the magistrate must leave it to God to reward virtue and to punish vice; the magistrate's business was to interfere only when a man's actions affected other people.

Thus there was a marked change in Locke's views: in 1667 he still did not advocate complete toleration, but he was prepared to concede far more freedom than he had been only a few years earlier, and implicitly attacked the Clarendon Code. This change has been attributed to the influence of his new patron, Ashley: one authority has gone so far as to state that Locke's 'association with the acknowledged champion of religious freedom swiftly transformed the traditionalist and authoritarian views' which he had expressed earlier.[1] This may be claiming a little too much. Locke may well have begun to modify his views before his meeting with Ashley,[2] and the change simply reflected the different political background: previously

---

[1] P. Laslett, op. cit. p. 29.
[2] He had been favourably impressed by his experience of the religious toleration which he had found at Cleves.

P

he had been preoccupied with the need for stability after a period of confusion, but in 1667 this worry had receded and he was more concerned with
the contemporary situation in which a rigid and exclusive Anglican Church
had enlisted the aid of the secular authorities to force its opinions upon a
persecuted and no longer dangerous minority. Nevertheless Locke's
friendship with Ashley must at least have reinforced his changed views and
stimulated him to set them down. From 1667 onwards the two men
thought alike on this subject. And in the concluding portion of his essay
Locke used arguments through which Ashley's influence does seem to
shine. At some length he argues to exclude Papists from the toleration
which he was prepared to give to Dissenters. He did this partly because
'where they have power, they think themselves bound to deny it [toleration]
to others', partly because they were subject to an infallible pope who could
dispense them from their oaths of allegiance to their prince, and partly
on the rather unconvincing ground that force was likely to be more effective
with Papists than with Dissenters, against whom it would be both wrong
and futile. Catholics were 'less apt to be pitied than others, because they
receive no other usage than what the cruelty of their own principles and
practices are known to deserve'; and restraint of them would encourage
the formation of a Protestant front against them such as was later to be one
plank in the platform of Shaftesbury and the Whigs. Finally Locke concluded his paper with a series of points of which he proposed to write
when he had more leisure, such as a defence of latitudinarianism in doctrine
and forms of worship. The first of these seven points was 'to show what
influence toleration is like to have upon the number and industry of your
people, on which depends the power and riches of the kingdom'. This
practical argument would have been unlikely to appeal to a philosopher in
an Oxford study; but the idea that religious toleration was good for trade
and the national prosperity was characteristic of his new patron.

At this point, therefore, the relatively liberal ideas of Locke and Ashley
on freedom of conscience for Protestants link with their interest in matters
of trade and colonization—an interest which was greatest in the years
between 1667 and 1673, and which deserves a chapter to itself.

CHAPTER XII

TRADE AND PLANTATIONS

SHAFTESBURY'S interest in matters of trade and overseas expansion was so obvious that some have regarded him as a representative of the rising new capitalistic forces in society. There is evidently some justification for this, although it should be emphasized that the profits of land and office provided a larger proportion of his personal income than those from trade, and further, that the success of the No Popery slogans of his opposition period was precisely that they appealed to discontented elements in all classes, not merely commercial ones. When these two considerable reservations have been made, and when the conclusion has been drawn that one must be wary of trying to fit Shaftesbury tightly into a theory of social development, the fact remains that he was more keenly interested in matters of trade and overseas expansion than any other important politician of his day.

In the period following the Restoration trade and colonization were indissolubly linked. When, in 1672, a single Council of Trade and Plantations was set up under Shaftesbury's presidency instead of separate bodies for each, this was a logical step recognizing the course of economic development, which was making trade in colonial produce far more important in the national economy. Shaftesbury was interested in such matters both in his capacity as a minister of the King and as a private person. As Chancellor of the Exchequer and from 1667 one of the Treasury Commissioners, he was recognized to have an obvious interest in anything which could increase the royal revenue from customs duties. Accordingly many petitions were referred in the earlier years of the Restoration to Southampton and himself for report, and some people wrote directly to him, basing their appeal on this assumption. This revenue interest was no doubt one reason why he was appointed to almost every committee of the privy council on any commercial or colonial subject. But he was not merely a Treasury representative on those committees. His interest dated back to the days before he became Chancellor of the Exchequer in 1661. He had indeed been a member of various colonial committees of the Commonwealth Councils of State in 1653 and 1654.[1] In 1660 he was promptly appointed to the privy council's committee for trade and plantations, and later in the same year to the select council of trade and to the select council for plantations, on which both merchants and ministers sat. Both these latter two bodies

---

[1] C.S.P. Col. Amer. and W. Indies 1574–1660, pp. 412, 414, 416. He was not a member of the Council for Trade and Navigation appointed in Nov. 1655 (C.S.P.D. 1655–6, pp. 1–2) or of any committee in the years 1655–9, as wrongly stated by Brown, pp. 130–1.

became rapidly moribund, but, as will be seen, he had much to do with their resuscitation in a different form in 1668 and 1670 respectively, and in September 1672 he became president of a combined body with the title of Council of Trade and Plantations.[1] As such he was the nearest to a minister for colonial affairs that England had yet seen, but naturally this official interest ceased after his dismissal from the Lord Chancellorship at the end of 1673.

As a private person, he had his commercial investments. We shall never know how extensive these were: as usual in the seventeenth century, such investments left far fewer records than dealings in land, since there was no need to keep the relevant papers once the transaction had been completed. Occasionally one lights upon a casual reference; for instance, in the accounts which his servant Stringer kept in 1671–2 there is a reference to £2,800 paid in three instalments to Mr. Kiffin 'upon the accompt of whalebone', and in the following year Kiffin repaid £2,505. This looks like a short-term investment in the Whalebone Company which was one of the interests of the famous Baptist merchant-pastor, with whom it is interesting to find that Ashley had business dealings; but the complete transaction cannot be reconstructed.[2] A surviving indenture dated 4 February 1674 provided that Shaftesbury should contribute £2,500, Kiffin £1,500, Locke £500 and one Maurice Hunt £500 as joint stock for trade in the buying and selling of raw silk,[3] but nothing more is known of this. It is only the investments over longer periods that have left substantial traces. Of these only two relate to enterprises within England, and in both he was in association with Prince Rupert. In 1668, as the respective governors of the two societies, they completed the union of the Mines Royal and the Mineral and Battery Works into one company. The question how this company was to exploit its rights under the charter was solved in 1671 by the signing of a contract for the working of the Mines Royal in the counties of Cardigan and Merioneth by a subsidiary company of undertakers who had shares of £100, to which their liability was limited. With the total capital of £4,000 the undertakers were to lease the mines for 41 years and to buy for £870 the lease of the smelting and refining mills, last held by one William Dickinson of the Middle Temple. Ashley himself had two shares of £100, as did Rupert, and all orders for appointments and dismissals and for any expenditure of over £20 were subject to confirmation by one of them. Amongst the shareholders were prominent financiers like Edward Backwell

---

[1] For all these bodies see C. M. Andrews, *British Committees, Commissions, and Councils of Trade and Plantations*, Johns Hopkins University Studies, XXVI (1908).

[2] Shaftesbury Papers, XL, 44, XLI, 54; *Remarkable passages in the Life of William Kiffin*, ed. W. Orme (1823); *D.N.B.* This seems to have been a time when the whaling activities of the Greenland Adventurers had ceased, and others were anticipating the Act of 1673 which threw the trade open. (W. R. Scott, *The Constitution and Finance of English, Scottish and Irish Joint-Stock Companies to 1720* (1910), ii. 74–75.)

[3] Indenture preserved in the Muniment Room at St. Giles House.

(who was to be Treasurer), Bucknall, Sir Robert Viner, and Sir John Shaw. Sir Paul Neile was to be one of the standing committee, as was Edmund Warcup, who was later to be first Shaftesbury's instrument and then an opponent during the Popish Plot. An even more sinister figure associated with the enterprise was an ex-Cromwellian soldier, Colonel John Rumsey, who was to be Chief Steward of the Mines with a salary of £100 and a free share in the company: Rumsey was to lose his life for his share in the Rye House Plot. In addition to these mining interests in Cardigan and Merioneth, Ashley investigated with Sir Edward Harley (another ex-Puritan and father of the statesman of Anne's reign) the possibility of mining in Herefordshire, and did actually mine at Dulverton in Somerset and in Derbyshire. How profitable these enterprises were one cannot tell. Fifty years earlier it was rumoured that Sir Hugh Middleton had paid £400 per annum in rent for the Welsh mines, and had profited at the rate of £2,000 per month; but it is most unlikely that the Mines Royal were still as lucrative as that in the reign of Charles II. The significant point is the small size of Ashley's investment—£200 out of a total of £4,000—suggesting that it was highly speculative.[1]

The same may also be said of the partnership with Rupert to exploit the Prince's invention. This was a new metallurgical process, the most obvious practical application of which was in the manufacture of cannon. Rupert was granted a patent by the King for fourteen years, and it was then agreed that Ashley and Sir Thomas Chicheley, Master of the Ordnance, who had married a sister of Ashley's first wife, should supply the necessary funds. They were to be first repaid from the profits; half of the remainder of the profits was to go to Rupert, and a quarter each to Ashley and Chicheley. Inevitably they looked to the Navy to buy their guns, and Tory writers later pointed out what a 'jolly triumvirate' this was for the purpose: consisting of Rupert, the King's cousin, courtier, and naval commander, Ashley, Chancellor of the Exchequer and Treasury Commissioner, who could expedite payment for the guns, and Chicheley 'to make bargains and to order fit quantities'. As a business partnership it seemed ideal, but matters did not turn out very well. In 1676 they decided that it was best to sub-contract their rights to one John Browne of Horsmonden, Kent, in return for a royalty of £20 per ton, but unfortunately he soon died, and within three years his widow and one William Dyke owed £11,450 to Rupert, Ashley, and Chicheley. In order to make sales in sufficient quantities Browne at some point offered the guns at £30 per ton (or less than

---

[1] M[oses] S[tringer], *Opera Mineralia Explicata* (1713), p. ix; Sir John Pettus, *Fodinae Regales* (1670), pp. 25–26, 33; *Articles of Agreement between His Highness Prince Rupert and divers Noble and Honourable Persons and others, Undertakers for working of Mines Royal in the Counties of Cardigan and Merioneth . . .* (1670[/1]); Sir E. Harley to Ashley, 17 Dec. 1663, Shaftesbury Papers, VII, 548; minutes in ibid. V, 246; Shaftesbury to Stringer, 15 July, 15 Aug., 23 Oct. 1676, ibid. VIA, 298, 299, 301; and to Sir Thomas Price, 5 Sept. 1677, ibid. VIA, 310.

£20, according to Roger North's usual exaggeration) instead of the £60 which the King had previously paid, and at the end of the reign this made Tories suspect that the whole affair was nothing but a racket, especially when Colonel George Legge, Lieutenant-General of the Ordnance, gave it as his opinion that the new guns were no better than the old. But one has to be wary of all statements made, like this one, in 1683. It may be that if the enterprise was unsound, this was the result of a not uncommon over-optimism on the part of the inventor and his partners, and not of crooked dealings on their part. How much Ashley benefited from the partnership it is impossible to say, but in the end he was left with a substantial bad debt on his hands.[1]

The investments were evidently pioneering enterprises which left little mark on the economic life of the country. Ashley's overseas investments show the same pioneering element but they had much more important consequences.

Ashley had been interested in lands across the seas ever since he had been a young man. His grandfather had been one of the Virginia Company; his neighbours in Dorset, under the influence of John White of Dorchester, had subscribed to the Massachusetts Bay Company; the fishermen of Poole sailed to Newfoundland. Philippa Ashley's second marriage to the son of Sir Walter Raleigh may have diverted his attention further south, and it was originally in the Caribbean that he was interested. There from about 1640 onwards the cultivation of sugar began to spread rapidly, until it was by far the most valuable of all colonial products. The English island of Barbados was well suited to the cultivation of sugar, and, like others, young Anthony Ashley Cooper spotted the opportunity, and in the year 1646 he was joint owner of a plantation there of some 205 acres, employing twenty-one white servants and nine adult black slaves. Two local boys from the neighbourhood of Wimborne St. Giles bound themselves to him for seven years' service, in return for £5 at the end of that period. The curiously small number of slaves did not mean, however, that he was not alive to the economic advantages of negro labour; and in the year 1646 he had a fourth share in a ship, the *Rose*, which had been away for a year in the 'Guinea Trade'. This might refer to the trade in the gums, wood, ivory and other products of the West African coast, but it is more likely to refer to the usual triangular trade.[2]

In 1655 he sold his share of the Barbados plantation (105 acres) for the sum of £1,020, either because it was difficult to find a reliable local agent and thus profits were uncertain, or because he foresaw a decline in the

---

[1] Shaftesbury Papers, XLVI B, 94–100, VIA, 297, 313; R. North, *Examen* (1740), p. 52; notes dictated by Pepys in 1683, in *Samuel Pepys's Naval Minutes*, ed. J. R. Tanner (Navy Records Society, vol. lx, 1926), pp. 225, 372. According to Defoe, the secret of the metallurgical process died with Rupert in 1682: *Essay upon Projects* (1697), pp. 25–26, cit. W. R. Scott, ii. 428 n.

[2] Shaftesbury Papers, XLIX, 1, 2a; Christie, vol. i, pp. xxxiv, xxxvi, xli, xlvi.

prosperity of Barbados through competition with other producers of sugar. Thereafter he had no financial interest of his own in any colony until on 24 March 1663 he became one of the proprietors to whom Carolina was granted by royal charter.

Carolina had originally been granted to Sir Robert Heath as far back as 1629, but at the Restoration it was still empty of settlers. We do not know precisely when or how Ashley's interest was first directed to the area, but the initiative for petitioning the King for a charter probably came from those two of the eight new proprietors who had actually crossed the Atlantic. One of these, Sir John Colleton, had been a planter in Barbados, whence some Barbadians had visited Carolina; and Sir William Berkeley had governed Virginia for the Stuarts and knew in that way of the large, unexploited territory to the south of that colony. It is likely enough that they approached Ashley, and others too: Berkeley's brother Lord Berkeley of Stratton, who had married a City heiress and had money to invest; Monk, now the Duke of Albemarle but by no means a titled figurehead, perhaps because Colleton was a relative; the Earl of Craven, a rich courtier who had inherited a City fortune; Sir George Carteret, Treasurer of the Navy, who also had money at his disposal[1]; and finally Clarendon, whose political support would be valuable. These eight formed a powerful consortium, but in order to appreciate their action one has to remember that in 1663 they agreed to contribute an original capital of only £25 each. Investment was by no means large, or aimed at producing quick profits; and, as will be seen, the policy pursued in developing the colony was essentially a political one, based on long-term considerations of the general good of the plantation and not simply on the immediate financial gain of the proprietors. It is significant that Ashley's interest in the scheme was more sustained than that of any of the other proprietors.

Two years later, in 1665, Ashley became interested in another area across the Atlantic. While the Court was at Oxford there came to it two Frenchmen, Groseilliers and Radisson, to urge the merits of a new route to the lucrative furs of North America by sea to Hudson's Bay. Charles II listened attentively, awarded them a pension of forty shillings per week, and then put them into the hands of Sir John Colleton's son, Sir Peter, and thus with the Carolina group, who knew from experience the value of beaver and other furs. The Dutch war prevented any immediate action from being taken, but by 1667 an informal group was already in existence, preparing for a voyage to Hudson's Bay. In 1668 Ashley contributed £200 when 'Founder's shares' were subscribed for, and others who contributed either now or later were Prince Rupert, the Earl of Craven, and Sir Paul Neile, his partners in his other business enterprises. Some years later he

---

[1] After the conquest of New Netherlands from the Dutch in 1664 Carteret and Lord Berkeley received a grant of the area which came to be known as New Jersey. Carteret had previously been governor of Jersey in the Channel Islands.

held £1,100 out of the Hudson's Bay Company's stock of £10,500; and on 24 November 1673, that is, after his dismissal from power by the King, he was chosen Deputy-Governor of the Company. Nor was he content to occupy this position nominally. He was a very regular attender at General Courts and committees, and the Hudson's Bay Company's historians have paid generous tributes to the order and decision which marked the Company's activities under his influence in these critical early years. This was certainly not a case of a nobleman merely lending his name to the Company's prospectus, but of a man as deeply immersed in the company's affairs as anyone. Nevertheless the difficulties of beginning a new trade in an area such as the Bay were obviously considerable, and the Company paid no dividend until 1684. Whether from discouragement, or more probably because of the awkwardness of being concerned with a company in which the Duke of York was then also concerned, Shaftesbury sold the last of his stock in 1679, having contributed some of his energy and of his capital to help open up this new English trade, but probably without having drawn much personal profit from it.[1]

Further south, in the same year (1670) as the Hudson's Bay Company received its charter, Ashley's attention was drawn by two merchants, John Darrell and Hugh Wentworth, to the existence of a settlement at New Providence in the Bahama Islands. They suggested that Ashley and the other Carolina proprietors should take steps to secure a charter for the development of this group of islands, and this Ashley did. One of the reasons which Darrell and Wentworth had given for securing the islands was strategic, for they argued that Spain would be prevented from securing a possible base from which Carolina could be attacked; but Ashley's interest was characteristically positive. He sought to develop the islands in the same way as he did Carolina, and in the autumn of 1672 he and his co-proprietors entered into an agreement to set up a company which would trade with the mainland. The company included Darrell, William Kiffin (with whom Ashley had invested money in the Whalebone Company) and other members, and also members of Ashley's household, including both Thomas Stringer and John Locke. Once again, however, the hopes placed in the Company, in which Ashley had a tenth share, proved to have been over-optimistic. Ashley's ideas of building up a trade in European commodities with the Spaniards in Florida and Cuba came to very little, at least in part because people in the Bahamas were disinclined to accept direction from thousands of miles away; there were the usual difficulties

---

[1] E. E. Rich, *The Hudson's Bay Company, 1670–1870* (Hudson's Bay Record Society, XXI, 1958), i. 13, 23–31, 38–39, 78, 82, 84–86; *Minutes of the Hudson's Bay Company, 1671–4*, ed. Rich with intro. by Sir John Clapham (1942), pp. xxvi, lvii–lix, 71, 86, 222; ibid. *1679–84*, intro. by G. N. Clark (1945), vol. i, p. xxi. From accounts preserved in the Muniment Room at Wimborne St. Giles it appears that for six shares Shaftesbury received back exactly the purchase price of £600, but that for the last three shares he had to be content with £285.

with interlopers, and the agents on whom Ashley depended were unreliable. Nevertheless when John Locke sold out his stock in the Bahama Adventurers in 1676, he found that it had appreciated usefully in value.[1] Another idea was of 'throwing away some money' on some experimental planting of Ashley's own in the Bahamas, but Sir Peter Colleton with his experience of local conditions advised against it; and there remained only an interest in 'the rarities and other observable things in the Bahama Islands . . . the strange plants, birds, or beasts you have there. And if there be any pretty ones amongst them that will endure the sea to send them to me.'[2] The proposal for a plantation in the Bahamas was probably given up; but in 1671 Ashley acquired two lots of twenty-five acres each in a different group of islands, that of the Bermudas. For some years he was Governor of the Somers Islands Company which ruled Bermuda, but little is known of his activities here except for two letters which he signed—one of them demanding peremptorily the enforcement of the Navigation laws on tobacco, and the other, to judge from its tone, not drafted by himself.[3]

Finally, Ashley also invested in the Royal Africa Company, which was re-formed in November 1671 to monopolize the supply of slaves to Britain's transatlantic possessions.[4] The amount of stock which he held in the early months was £2,000—only the Duke of York and Sir Robert Viner contributed more—and no doubt it was on his advice that John Locke risked £400. Other familiar names among the investors are those of some of his partners in Carolina, the Hudson's Bay and the Bahamas: the Earl of Craven, Sir George Carteret and Sir Peter Colleton.[5] It seems a little unjust of the Royal Africa Company's historian to dismiss the 'ephemeral enthusiasms' of Ashley so lightly.[6] As with the Hudson's Bay Company, Ashley's interest was not confined to investment. Two months after the Company's re-formation, on 10 January 1672, he was elected its Sub-Governor, serving under the Duke of York as Governor, and probably doing more of the work than James. He was re-elected in the following year, and though he was succeeded in January 1674 by his friend Sir John Banks, he was elected to the Court of Assistants. While it is true that the Company made a slow start on account of the Dutch war of 1672, and that he sold the last of his stock in 1677 (possibly because of his bad relations

---

[1] M. Cranston, *John Locke*, p. 115 n., says that Locke obtained £127. 10s. for £100 stock.
[2] *Collections*, v. 160–1, 422–4.
[3] Shaftesbury Papers, XLIX, 15, 16; J. H. Lefroy, *Memorials of the Discovery and Early Settlement of the Bermudas or Somers Islands, 1511–1587* (1879), ii. 361–3, 370–3, 385; *C.S.P. Col. 1669–74*, p. 513; [P. Trott], *A True Relation of the just and unjust Proceedings of the Somers-Islands-Company* (1676). He must have been Governor at least from 1671 to 1674, but the exact dates are unknown.
[4] He had not originally been a member of the first Company of Royal Adventurers trading to Africa, but had joined it between 1663 and 1667 (*Documents illustrative of the History of the Slave Trade to America*, ed. Elizabeth Donnan, Washington, 1930, i. 169 n., 170). [5] K. G. Davies, *The Royal Africa Company* (1957), p. 65.
[6] Ibid. p. 68.

with James), the fact remains that he had presided over the beginnings of another important overseas enterprise, the unsoundness of which did not develop until later.[1]

Viewed as a whole, Ashley's commercial undertakings were spread over a wide area of thousands of miles. There are however some interesting omissions from them. He had some financial dealings with the greatest trading company of all, the East India Company, but no concern with its management. There are one or two amongst his surviving papers which refer to the Company, but these are only of the type which any politician might possess at a time when the spice trade was being disputed with the Dutch. The absence of any closer connexion with the Company was certainly not attributable to any objection in principle to monopoly grants to chartered trading companies, such as many of the Company's critics put forward. His own concerns in Carolina and the Bahamas, in the Hudson's Bay and Royal Africa Companies, were all based on royal charters or grants to small groups of proprietors. Moreover, from time to time he had political associates amongst the leading merchants in the East India Company, such as Papillon and Dubois, the two Whig sheriffs during the Exclusion Crisis, and Sir Samuel Barnardiston, and on occasion he was even prepared to use his influence to obtain posts with the Company for dependents.[2] His failure to take part in the highest counsels of the East India Company is rather symptomatic of a lack of any special interest in long-established concerns. Similarly he was not active in the Levant Company, and in the new American colonies he shows no sign of any particular interest in the older colonies of New England. He was attracted to the new, pioneering enterprises, to new companies, new trades, and new plantations further south. His capitalistic instincts took him not to the older and safer trades, but to new ones which were just beginning to develop. And, reviewing all these overseas enterprises, we may reasonably conclude that he was attracted by the challenge of planning the course of development at least as much as by greed of gain. Moreover, neither the amounts invested nor the profits made were very great. The amounts invested in Carolina and the Hudson's Bay and Royal Africa Companies together were far less than the amount invested in the purchase of English land in the year 1671–2. We have no means of knowing exactly what profit

---

[1] In August 1676 he instructed Stringer to sell 'as much of my Guinea stocks as will sell for thirty per cent profit or better' (Christie, ii. 225), but evidently did not find a ready purchaser. In April 1677 he received £1,936 for his remaining sixteen shares—considerably less than 30 per cent; but in 1676 he had drawn the first two dividends of the Company, amounting to £275, so that he had made a reasonable gain for five years of investment. For Ashley's stock transactions, see P.R.O., T 70/100, fos. 8, 27, 106–8, 120, 128, 131, 152, 167, and cf. Davies, op. cit. pp. 72 n., 73 n. The figure of £1,936 is taken from accounts preserved in the Muniment Room at St. Giles House.

[2] Shaftesbury Papers, L, pt. 1, 1–4; *Court Minutes of the East India Company, 1668–70* ed. Sainsbury, p. 310; and cf. p. 208 above. The amount of money involved is large (£3,558), but was only placed with the Company for a few months.

they yielded, but all the indications are that this profit was of decidedly minor importance when compared with his income from other sources.

One further general observation may be made about Ashley's activities in these trading and colonizing enterprises. The reader may have noticed how many of the dates quoted belong to the period between 1667 and 1674. The Carolina charter dated from 1663, but the fortunes of the colony flagged when the first impulse was spent, and after the Treaty of Breda there was almost a fresh start, with Ashley more prominent among the proprietors than he had been earlier. The years in which Ashley was most active in Carolina and elsewhere were precisely those middle years of the reign—incidentally the years when Ashley and Locke were closely associated. In the last years of his life he restricted himself more and more to his cherished projects for Carolina: this was a period when his income from office had disappeared and when his activities in opposition left him with much less leisure.

With all these different irons in the fire, as politician, investor and colonizer Ashley was as well-informed about England's transatlantic trade and possessions as any man in England who had not actually crossed the ocean himself; and this at a vital time in English overseas expansion. The nature of his own personal contribution to this growth and the extent to which it depended on consistent principles remain to be defined.

Before Locke entered his household in 1667 it is difficult to distinguish Ashley's views from those of his many colleagues on the various bodies on which he served. There was the Privy Council's standing committee on trade and plantations, appointed on 4 July 1660, and consisting of ten members who were instructed to meet on two afternoons each week; and there were smaller *ad hoc* committees of the Privy Council dealing with specific problems which came up. There was the Council of Trade, whose commission was dated 7 November 1660, which consisted of sixty-two members, some of them politicians and some traders, and which was given comprehensive authority to inquire into any problem connected with foreign trade. There was the Council for Foreign Plantations, also a mixed body of forty-eight politicians and merchants, which received its commission on 1 December 1660 to obtain information about every English colony and those of foreign states and to report on them.[1] When the Council held its first meeting on 7 January 1661 Ashley was the only privy councillor present. Both these bodies had their subcommittees. Finally there were the different committees of Parliament which considered bills on matters of trade at the committee stage in the legislative process. On all these Ashley sat, and from his record it may safely be inferred that he was

---

[1] C. M. Andrews, *British Committees, Commissions, and Councils of Trade and Plantations, 1622–75* (Baltimore, 1908), pp. 61–85; *C.S.P.D. 1660–1*, pp. 319, 353–4; A. P. Thornton, *West-India Policy under the Restoration* (1956), pp. 5–14; P.R.O., C O 1/14, no. 59, 1–27.

not a silent or an uninfluential member, but in such large and unwieldy bodies there is no means of establishing the extent of his influence or the nature of the advice which he gave. The many memoranda submitted to him and surviving in his papers bear no evidence of his opinion about them.[1] The nearest one can get is in connexion with matters on which his uncle Southampton and he were jointly asked to report as Lord Treasurer and Chancellor of the Exchequer: one would expect that the report would reflect the views of Ashley as the man with the greater experience of the issues. Such a matter was the proposal to make Dover once again a free port for composition trade, that is, permitting re-export of goods imported, without the payment of customs dues at the full rate. Such a trade had existed under the personal rule of Charles I, but an attempt to revive it under the Protectorate had failed. Southampton and Ashley were in favour of allowing this for a trial period of three years, as being 'to the advantage of your Majesty's Customs and the good of that town. But how far it will be beneficial to either in respect of those ties and observances that are put upon trade by the late Act of Navigation, without some trial and experience we cannot determine, the farmers of your Majesty's Customs certifying that for the advance of trade there will be a necessity of some dispensation to be made of the said Act; and the Council of Trade being of opinion that that Act be inviolably kept'. There was a conflict of opinion here over the Navigation Act's stipulation that foreign goods must be imported only direct from their country of origin; the Council of Trade wishing to adhere rigidly to this in the interests of English shipping, and the Customs Farmers wishing to relax this in the interests of encouraging the Dover composition trade. Southampton and Ashley accepted the farmers' point of view, and their report was adopted in an Order of Council of 28 June 1661. This was an eminently sensible and non-doctrinaire attitude.[2] At the same time, however, neither Southampton nor Ashley, neither customs farmers nor Council of Trade, would hear of any relaxation in the Navigation Act's provisions dealing with goods from the plantations, which were not to be included in the composition trade at all. On this basic point all were in agreement. Ashley fully shared the view that the profits of all trade with the colonies should be reserved for Englishmen. Scots were to be excluded from the colonial trade along with all other foreigners. Southampton and Ashley reported that they had conferred about this with the Customs Commissioners, 'some principal merchants and some Parliament men principally employed for framing' the Navigation Act;

---

[1] Occasionally there are jottings which are of little use, e.g. a paper in his handwriting headed 'ironwork', with reasons for and against, in parallel columns, but no full explanation or conclusion: Shaftesbury Papers, VII, 484.

[2] C.T.B. 1660–7, pp. 117, 247, 250; C.S.P.D. 1661–2, p. 19; Andrews, op. cit. p. 82; D. Ogg, England in the Reign of Charles II (1955), i. 234 sqq.; M. P. Ashley, Financial and Commercial Policy under the Cromwellian Protectorate (1962), pp. 29, 150–1; R. W. K. Hinton, The Eastland Trade and the Common Weal (1959), pp. 93–94, 165, 213–18.

and had come down heavily in favour of the view that to admit the Scots would be 'contrary to the main end of the Act of Parliament which aimed at the increase of English shipping and employment of English mariners'. The more Scots were admitted into the trade, the fewer English ships and sailors would be employed, especially as the Scots could 'undersail' them; and the Customs would lose. Ashley firmly set the interests of the King's English subjects above those of his Scottish ones, just as he set the interests of English over those of Irish landowners at the time of the Irish Cattle Bill.[1]

Such glimpses suggest that Ashley's attitude was not greatly different from that of most people of his day. Another matter on which he was called to pronounce was the subject of a petition by Francis Cradock. Cradock was one of a number of people who had made proposals during the Interregnum for the setting up of a first English bank. Recognizing that these ideas 'though approved by many are not as yet countenanced by any', he now suggested that they should be tried out elsewhere, and that he should be empowered to set up such a bank in Barbados where he had a grant of the office of Provost-Marshal. In 1654 Ashley had been concerned in putting before Cromwell a different set of proposals by Henry Robinson[2]; but in 1661 he was cautious. He had 'no confidence in the success of the first experiment of new inventions, especially in matters of this nature'; in England such novelties 'will hardly gain credit with a people apt to make more difficulties than God and nature hath made them', but nevertheless he could see no reason why an experiment should not be authorized in Barbados, at the risk of the undertakers, especially if a quarter of the profits were to go to the Governor as part of the island's public revenue. Accordingly a warrant was issued on 9 December 1661 in favour of Cradock, Thomas Elliott, and Sir John Colleton. At the same time steps were taken to protect the interests of the planters by restricting the rate of interest to 6 per cent, while on the other hand no creditor was to be compelled to accept payment in sugar, so that an attempt would have been made simultaneously to solve these two critical plantation problems; but characteristically Clarendon held up the passing of the grant, and the Cradock bank in fact never came into existence. Ashley's willingness to experiment was thwarted.[3]

At the time of this incident Colleton and Ashley were not yet partners in the proprietorship of Carolina, but they were acquainted. Possibly indeed they had known one another since the time when Ashley, like Colleton, had owned a sugar plantation in Barbados. Certainly in the decade which

[1] C.T.B. 1660–7, pp. 305–6; Acts of the Privy Council, Colonial Series, 1613–80, p. 318.
[2] Ashley, op. cit. pp. 11, 33–34; C.S.P.D. 1653–4, pp. 364, 366.
[3] C.S.P. Col. 1661–8, pp. 59–60, 62; Acts of the Privy Council, Colonial Series, 1613–80, p. 325; F. Cradock, Expedient for taking away all impositions and for raising a revenue without taxes (1660).

followed their association meant (so far as Barbados was concerned) that Ashley was on the side of those planters in the island who disliked their Governor, Lord Willoughby of Parham. Ashley indeed thought that Willoughby should not be permitted to be Governor of Barbados as well as owner of the colony of Surinam, in Guiana. In a joint report Southampton and he urged that Willoughby might attract planters and labourers from Barbados to Surinam, in his own interests, instead of allowing those who wished to emigrate to go to Jamaica, where they were needed. Their opposition, however, was in vain. Willoughby was both made Governor of Barbados and allowed to retain Surinam in partnership with Clarendon's son, Lawrence Hyde.[1] Thus Ashley was brought into opposition to Clarendon and his clients in the colonies as well as in home politics, and when in 1666 Samuel Farmer, Speaker of the Barbados Assembly, was shipped back to London to answer charges made by Willoughby, it was to Ashley that he looked for help. Farmer, who had induced the Assembly to refuse supplies and had been described by the indignant Governor as 'a great Magna Carta man and Petition of Right maker', was a Whig before his time; but unfortunately Ashley was convalescing at St. Giles and unable to take his part.[2]

It was partly dissatisfaction with economic and political conditions in Barbados that led planters like the Colletons to investigate the possibility of colonizing the remaining vacant section of the eastern American seaboard between Virginia and the Spaniards in Florida. The charter which was issued on 24 March 1663 granted to eight proprietors including Ashley the land between the thirty-sixth and thirty-first parallels: an immense area some three hundred and fifty miles from north to south and extending across America 'as far as the South Seas', known to possess flowing, navigable rivers and thought to have fertile soil which could be better exploited than by the Indian tribes who inhabited it. The new proprietors of this land were given the most comprehensive powers. Not only were they to possess it in free and common socage in return for a nominal rent of twenty marks a year, but they were empowered to appoint all governors, magistrates and other officers, civil and military; to erect manors with courts baron and courts leet; to grant any titles they chose, as long as these were not the same as English titles; to exercise martial law in case of rebellion. They could import into England certain specified commodities, such as silks, wines, currants, oil and olives, free of duty for the seven years after the first shipment; on the other hand they could impose what customs duties they thought fit in Carolina. In religion the

---

[1] *C.S.P. Col. 1661–8*, p. 92; Thornton, op. cit. pp. 27–39.
[2] Ibid. pp. 65, 133–4; Captain John Grant to Sir R. Harley, 16 Feb. and 10 Mar. 1667, *H.M.C. Portland MSS.*, iii. 295–6; *Acts of the Privy Council, Colonial Series, 1613–80*, pp. 404–5, 409, 422; V. T. Harlow, *A History of Barbados, 1625–85* (1926), pp. 145, 157, 159.

proprietors were granted the patronage of all churches which might be erected: the Church of England was to be established. There were two possible restrictions: they were authorized to make any law 'according to their best discretion of and with the advice assent and approbation of the Freemen of the said Province or of the greater part of them or of their delegates or deputies'; and there was to be liberty of conscience for those who could not conform to the liturgies and ceremonies of the Church of England. One can easily imagine that these provisions for an elected assembly and for toleration were particularly welcome to Ashley, though it would be a mistake to assume that they were specially inserted by his influence: they were obvious political measures which probably occurred to others of the proprietors as essential in order to attract colonists in the circumstances of the time.[1] Nevertheless it is worth stressing that in the precise month when Ashley was being defeated over the attempt to implement Charles II's Declaration of Indulgence of 1662 by means of the Robartes bill, the Carolina charter was embodying the same principles of toleration in a distant land where Parliament's intolerance was of no account: the ideas of the future were to be applied to the colonies even though Anglican persecution was being revived in the mother-country. However, the colonists' political and religious rights were not to be complete and unconditional; the authority of the proprietors was safeguarded, for the freemen were to assemble only 'from time to time . . . in such manner and form as to them [the Proprietors] shall think meet', and the toleration too was to be a prerogative toleration—'such indulgencies and dispensations as in their discretion they might see fit and reasonable'. All in all, the eight Lords Proprietors were to have more absolute powers in their colony than King Charles II ever enjoyed in England, and Ashley, the future leader of the Whigs, was inevitably in a very different political position of authority.[2]

There is no evidence that Ashley had a greater share than his colleagues in drafting this charter; and equally there is no evidence that he had a greater share than they in organizing the plantation of the colony in the next four years. It is true that Clarendon could give little more effective

---

[1] The Privy Council's Plantations Committee had previously agreed unanimously that liberty of conscience should be granted to all settlers in Surinam: C.S.P. Col. 1661–8, p. 92.

[2] For the general history of Carolina under the Proprietors, cf. C. M. Andrews, The Colonial Period of American History (New Haven, 1937), vol. iii, chs. v–vi; W. F. Craven, The Southern Colonies in the Seventeenth Century (1949) (vol. i. of A History of the South), chs. ix, xi; J. A. Doyle, The English in America: Virginia, Maryland, and the Carolinas (1882); E. McCrady, The History of South Carolina under the Proprietary Government (New York, 1897); D. D. Wallace, History of South Carolina (New York 1934), chs. vi–x; Brown, ch. x. Shaftesbury Papers relating to Carolina were published in the Collections of the South Carolina Historical Society, N.S. vol. v. (Charleston, 1897) (cited hereafter as Collections); and cf. also North Carolina Colonial Records (Raleigh, 1886), vol. i. The most important are summarized in C.S.P. Col., and since these volumes are more easily accessible I have referred to them where the summaries are adequate.

help after the first few months of its existence, when as Lord Chancellor he assisted in beating off rivals who pretended to have prior claims to ownership of the colony[1] inherited from the Heath patent of 1629, and Sir William Berkeley was once again across the ocean governing Virginia; but the other six met on 23 May 1663 and took their first decisions. They agreed each to pay £25 to Sir John Colleton to cover immediate expenses, and then proceeded to share out the bear's skin. Twenty thousand acres in each settlement were to be reserved for the proprietors, and the court-houses and other official buildings were to be erected on these sites; and maps were to be printed 'and some declaration drawn to invite planters'.[2] This Declaration duly appeared on 21 August. As inducements the 'under-takers' of any group willing to embark were to be permitted to present to the proprietors a short list of thirteen names, out of which the proprietors were to choose one as Governor and six to be his Council. Two deputies elected from each Carolina parish by the freeholders were to make their own laws, provided that they were not repugnant to the laws of England and that they must be submitted to the proprietors for ratification. The attention of prospective settlers was drawn to the customs concessions set out in the charter; and each 'undertaker' in the first five years of the colony was to receive a hundred acres of land with additions if he carried servants with him, in return for which the proprietors would expect one halfpenny per acre.[3]

These promises of self-government, freedom from customs duties on exotic commodities, and cheap land were intended to be impressive on paper, but they attracted very few English settlers. Barbados and New England seemed more promising fields of recruitment. There had been a previous settlement of New Englanders in the neighbourhood of Cape Fear, but they had found it far from the Utopia they had hoped for, and had abandoned it; and the promises of liberty of conscience were presumably intended primarily to appeal to others to renew the attempt. In Bar-bados, however, the Lords Proprietors had ready agents in the persons of Peter Colleton, a son of Sir John, and Colonel Thomas Modyford, a relative of the Duke of Albemarle; evidently the governor, Lord Willoughby, was unwilling to see some of his subjects depart, but his reluctance could be overcome by a letter from Albemarle, or, if that failed, a missive from the King. Accordingly in 1663 one Captain William Hilton sailed from Barbados on two voyages of exploration, from which he re-turned with some Indians, a map which he had constructed, and en-couraging reports that he had found 'as good land and as well timbered as any we have seen in any part of the world, sufficient to accommodate thousands of our English nation'; and in October 1665 Sir John Yeamans, a friend of the Colletons, left Barbados with a number of colonists, who

---

[1] Order of the Privy Council, 12 Aug. 1663, C.S.P. Col. 1661–8, p. 152.
[2] Minutes of the meeting, ibid. p. 133.   [3] Ibid. pp. 154–5.

after a stormy voyage landed at the mouth of the Cape Fear river and, having been promised 500 acres for every 1,000 pounds of sugar contributed, founded the first settlement of 'Charles Town'. In the meantime the Lords Proprietors also tried to bring under their control an independent settlement of Virginians, who had moved southward before 1663 into the districts along the northern shore of Albemarle Sound; through Sir William Berkeley, who ruled in Virginia, they appointed one William Drummond as governor there, and in June 1665 they obtained a second charter which extended their territory north of the thirty-sixth parallel and thus made sure of including the Albemarle settlement within it. In this charter and in other documents various attempts had been made to develop the principles put forward in the original charter. The 'Concessions and Agreements' put before the Cape Fear settlers went so far as to lay it down that the governor should not be allowed to levy taxes without the consent of the elected assembly, and promised liberty of conscience to all, 'they behaving themselves peaceably and quietly and not using this liberty to licentiousness nor to the civil injury or outward disturbance of others, any law statute or clause . . . of this realm of England to the contrary hereof in any wise notwithstanding'.[1]

These inducements, and the more materialistic ones of cheap land, were impressive on paper, but they cut no ice with colonists who had to struggle for survival. The Cape Fear settlement was dogged with bad luck; the settlers' first voyage had been extremely stormy, two of the ships were damaged and all the equipment, arms and ammunition lost; the captain of a relieving vessel was made so desperate by contrary winds that he went mad and jumped overboard; it turned out that Cape Fear was not a good choice for the site, and that other areas further south were healthier and more fertile; and the quit-rents which had seemed light beforehand turned out to be very irksome to struggling farmers. By the summer of 1667 all these discontents had reached such a pitch that the colonists had had enough, and they abandoned the farms into which they had put so much effort. The only Europeans left in the whole extent of Carolina five years after the charter had been granted were those on the shores of Albemarle Sound, and their presence was not due in any way to the efforts of the proprietors. The names of some of the proprietors had been given to counties and to geographical features, but apart from that the eight partners had as yet left no mark on the territory that they owned.

So far, it is true, they had spent little money on it either. A balance sheet of April 1666 showed that they had contributed only £75 each; over half of the total of £600 had been spent on fees for the two charters, and the rest on the purchase of arms and ammunition.[2] At this point they could easily have cut their losses and abandoned the project, as earlier grantees

---

[1] *C.S.P. Col. 1661–8*, pp. 154–5, 157, 159, 160, 166, 267–9; *North Carolina Colonial Records*, i. 75–92.　　　　[2] *C.S.P. Col. 1661–8*, p. 379.

had done. But now Ashley, hitherto practically indistinguishable from his colleagues, began to come to the fore and to supply the necessary driving-power. Clarendon was in exile from 1667; Albemarle, less active than before, was to die in 1670; Sir John Colleton had died and been succeeded by his son Peter; Carteret was over seventy and the Berkeleys and Craven all more than sixty. It was largely for Ashley to accept the challenge of making something more of Carolina than had yet been done. Fortunately the situation in England was improving; the country was beginning to recover from the depression which had been brought by the Dutch war, the Plague and the Fire, and there was an opportunity to revive interest in colonization.

As before when colonists had had to be attracted, the first step was to paint a picture of the conditions which would prevail in the new world to which they would go. But this time there was available to do this John Locke himself, a thinker interested in the origins of societies; and in 1669, the prologue to another effort was the famous *Fundamental Constitutions of Carolina.*

The *Fundamental Constitutions* have been printed in many editions of Locke's works since 1720, and students of Locke have long known of a corrected copy in Locke's own hand, preserved among the Shaftesbury Papers. Accordingly many have assumed that Locke was entirely respons-ible for producing them; on the other hand the opposite opinion had been expressed that they 'may be supposed to represent Shaftesbury's ideas written down by that philosopher'. But it is inconceivable either that Locke was given *carte blanche* to make his own theoretical construction without consulting the ideas, interests and practical experience of Ashley and the other proprietors, or that he acted merely as an amanuensis copying down without comment what Ashley dictated. A letter from Sir Peter Colleton to Locke refers to 'that excellent form of government in the composure of which you had so great a hand'. The *Constitutions* must be the outcome of many informal exchanges of ideas between the two men. One must presume that if the two men ever disagreed about any of the provisions, the decision would necessarily be taken by the proprietor, and not by his secretary, and to that extent it is safer to regard the finished version as representing Ashley's ideas rather than Locke's; but it is unlikely that they differed in essentials. On at least one clause, as we shall see, there is a suggestion that others of the proprietors intervened.[1]

At the same time it would be a mistake to exaggerate the originality of the *Fundamental Constitutions*, the main principles of which had already

[1] Cf. H. R. Fox Bourne, *Life of John Locke* (1876), i. 239 n.; Brown, p. 156 (cf. ibid. 323 for the author's discovery of a copy in the Bodleian endorsed in a contemporary hand: 'made by Anth: Earl of Shaftesbury'); MSS. Locke, c. 6, fo. 215; *Thirty-Third Report of the Deputy Keeper of the Public Records* (1872), pp. 258–69; Locke, *Works* (1823), x. 175–99; [Des Maizeaux], *A Collection of Several Pieces of Mr. John Locke* (1720), Dedication (not paginated).

been foreshadowed in some of the earlier inducements which had been offered to prospective colonists. What the *Fundamental Constitutions* essentially did was to set down these ideas in much more elaborate detail to form a coherent whole. The preamble began by recalling the King's grant of Carolina, with privileges 'as large and ample as the County Palatine of Durham'; by virtue of those privileges the *Constitutions* had been prepared 'for the better settlement of the government of the said place, and establishing the interest of the Lords Proprietors with equality, and without confusion; and that the government of the Province may be made most agreeable to the monarchy under which we live and of which this province is a part, and that we may avoid erecting a numerous democracy'. Thus the key-note was struck at the outset: it was to be liberal, but not by any means levelling; and though it made provision for 'the people', *demos* was not to rule.

In pursuance of these ideals, the first clauses dealt with the position of the proprietors. The eldest Lord Proprietor was always to be the Palatine, succeeded on his death by the oldest survivor; and there were to be seven other chief officers, an admiral, chamberlain, chancellor, constable, chief justice, high steward, and treasurer, to be filled by the other seven proprietors at first by lot. Ashley's choice was that of Chief Justice. Later when there was a vacancy in any of these seven offices the oldest of the survivors was to succeed to it if he wished; thus any disputes over precedence amongst the proprietors would be decided by seniority. Until 1701 a proprietor was permitted either to sell or to bequeath his proprietorship, but after that date he was to be prevented from doing so; a proprietorship was then to descend to heirs male, and there were elaborate provisions for the succession should these be lacking. There would forever be eight proprietors in Carolina.

The land of Carolina was to be divided into units called counties, each consisting of exactly 480,000 acres, or 750 square miles (about three-quarters of the area of Dorset). One-fifth of each county was to be divided into eight signories, one for each proprietor. One fifth of each county was to be divided into eight baronies for a local hereditary nobility; four for a Landgrave, and two each for two Caciques. The remaining three-fifths of each county was for 'the people', a term which evidently might include either a lord of the manor (a unit consisting of not less than 3,000 and not more than 12,000 acres) or someone with very much less. The *Constitutions* themselves make no mention of the exact area to be offered to immigrants, probably so that the proprietors could vary it as they thought fit, but in fact every freeman entering the colony before 25 March 1670 was offered 150 acres, with a similar amount for every manservant (white or black) that he brought with him and 100 acres for women servants and boys; these figures were reduced until 70 and 60 acres respectively were offered to those who settled between March 1671 and March 1672. Servants at the expiration of their time would receive 100 acres for themselves.[1] The *Constitutions* did specify the quit-rent payable for this, namely a penny per acre, payable annually after 1689 only. In every signory, barony and manor there was provision for the lord to hold a court leet on the English model from which there was to be no appeal, and there was a curious provision for a class of leetmen who voluntarily bound themselves to the soil in return for ten acres of land rented to them by their lord on marriage.

There were to be eight supreme courts corresponding to the eight offices held by the eight proprietors. Their respective jurisdictions were carefully defined—for instance, the Chancellor's Court dealt with all matters of state and treaties with Indians, all invasions of the law of liberty of conscience, all invasions of the public peace upon pretence of religion, and the control of printing, while the Chamberlain's Court had the seemingly less practical task, in a colony of pioneers, of dealing with all ceremonies and heraldry, and with the more useful work of the registration of births, deaths and marriages. Together the eight proprietors (or their deputies) and the forty-two counsellors who sat with them on these Courts were to constitute a Grand Council which would meet on the first Tuesday in each month. Amongst other duties the Grand Council would prepare all matters which were to be put before Parliament: here the historian is irresistibly reminded of that device of Stuart absolutism in Scotland, the Lords of the Articles, though it has also been suggested that the Council was derived from Harrington's idea that the laws should be 'initiated by the best and resolved by the most'.[2]

Parliament was to meet automatically every two years, as was the case in most of the experimental constitutions put forward by the Levellers and others after the Civil War; but it was to be different from them in that it included in the same chamber a hereditary element consisting of the eight proprietors (or their deputies), and the hereditary nobility of the landgraves and caciques (of whom it will be remembered that there were three to each county) and an elective element of four freemen from each county: thus there would be a nice balance. In 1672 Ashley stated his aim here explicitly: 'Having been so careful to balance one another's power to prevent the engrossing it into any one hand that the Palatine himself and so his Deputy the Governor hath but his limited proportion of it suited to the dispatch of affairs.'[3] Voters for the elected members must be freemen possessing at least fifty acres. Since this was less than the amount offered to each settler before 1672, this franchise was not so restrictive as it might sound; but servants were excluded as a matter of course, just as they were in the Leveller schemes. More significant was the decision that in order to

---

[1] *C.S.P. Col. 1669–74*, p. 33.   [2] Andrews, op. cit. iii. 216.

[3] Since the number of counties was not defined, it was unclear which element would eventually be in a slight majority, but at first the nobility was lacking and therefore inferior in numbers. Ashley to West and the rest of the Council, 20 June 1672, *Collections*, v. 401.

qualify for election members must possess at least five hundred acres. This was not especially reactionary in the circumstances of 1669; what it meant essentially was that the political superiority of the landed interests which existed in the English House of Commons in practice would be enshrined in the Carolina constitution. As an additional safeguard for the interests of the proprietors, laws were to remain in force only for two years unless ratified by the Palatine and at least three of his colleagues.

Some clauses relating to the law in the new colony recall issues in debate when Ashley had been a member of the law reform committee and of the Barebones Parliament in 1652–3. There was much insistence on the registration of all births, marriages and deaths. All land transfers were also to be registered, as English radicals had demanded under the Commonwealth. Assize juries need not agree, but could reach majority verdicts. Laws were automatically to come to an end one hundred years after their enactment, thus preventing the continuation of anachronisms because problems were too thorny to touch. And finally there was a provision that in Carolina's courts no lawyers should be permitted to plead for gain. This was a direct imitation of Virginian laws of 1647 and 1658, but it also recalls the disrespect which Ashley had on occasion expressed for the legal profession.

Towards the end of the document is to be found a group of clauses amplifying the promises made in earlier years about liberty of conscience. No man could be a freeman who did not 'acknowledge a God, and that God is publicly and solemnly to be worshipped', but within this broadest of categories 'any seven or more persons agreeing in any religion' could be officially recognized, provided that they did not abuse people who thought differently. Thus Jews could be admitted, and the susceptibilities of Quakers and others who scrupled the taking of oaths were catered for, twenty years before the English Toleration Act, by means of an affirmation. On the other hand, a later clause inserted in 1670 declared that 'as the country comes to be sufficiently planted . . . it shall belong to the Parliament to take care for the building of churches and the public maintenance of divines, to be employed in the exercise of religion, according to the Church of England; which being the only true and orthodox, and the national religion of the King's dominions is so also of Carolina, and therefore it alone shall be allowed to receive public maintenance by grant of Parliament'. Some of Locke's friends later maintained that Locke had told them that this clause providing for the establishment of the Church of England as the state church was inserted contrary to his wishes by 'some of the chief of the proprietors'.[1] If this statement was correct, it might refer to some of Ashley's colleagues, anxious not to seem too unorthodox at a time when the House of Commons was rejecting comprehensive schemes and reaffirming its Anglicanism; but it might also apply to Ashley himself.

---

[1] Locke, *Works* (1823), x. 194 and n. (derived from [Des Maizeaux], *A Collection of Several Pieces of Mr. John Locke* (1720), p. 42 and n.)

It will be recalled that during the Commonwealth he had maintained that there should be an established church, publicly maintained but without coercive powers, and accompanied by free conventicles of such people as could not conform to it. The Carolina constitution would have brought into existence precisely this state of affairs, without any inconsistency on Ashley's part. However, it would be futile to press this speculation too far. Dissenters settling in Carolina would obviously be reluctant to contribute money to support a Church in which they had no part; and it was probably for this reason that no effort was made to implement this clause during Ashley's lifetime. It seems to have been only in 1698 that the first Act was passed 'to settle a maintenance on a minister of the Church of England in Charles Town'.[1]

One reason given for the liberty of conscience contained in the *Fundamental Constitutions* was the need to consider the Indian tribes and to convince them, by peaceful persuasion and good example rather than by force, of the reasonableness of Christianity. This was an excellent principle, to which too many European colonizers had failed to adhere in the past. It was however the only reference in the *Constitutions* to the existence of a native population which was for many years to be more numerous than the white immigrants. It will be seen that Ashley's Indian policy was not unenlightened, but there was no question of giving them any legal status or land rights under the constitution. Again, it was laid down that negro slaves might belong to any church (whether it was that of their master or not) but it was stated without any ambiguity in terms which would satisfy any prospective planter that 'every freeman of Carolina shall have absolute power and authority over his negro slave of what opinion or religion soever'. Slavery was to be an essential part of the new colony from the beginning.

Looking back from the vantage-point gained by three hundred years of subsequent American history, it is easy to see that many of the detailed provisions of the *Constitutions* could never have become permanent. They were too cut-and-dried to be successfully imposed without amendment upon a new, pioneering community thousands of miles from the study in Exeter House. Inevitably they seem hopelessly artificial, with their attempt at mathematical subdivision of the land into exactly proportioned units irrespective of the hills and swamps they might contain. The very names 'landgrave' and 'cacique' (or 'Cassock' as the colonists mispronounced it[2]) smack of the doctrinaire inventions of the abstract political thinker. Too much should not be made of the outlandishness of these names: by the terms of their charter the proprietors were empowered to create titles but forbidden to use those in existence in England, and therefore Locke

---

[1] E. McCrady, *The History of South Carolina under the Proprietary Government 1670–1719* (New York, 1897), p. 332.
[2] W. F. Craven, *The Southern Colonies in the Seventeenth Century* (1949), p. 339.

adopted the 'landgrave' from Germany[1] and the 'cacique' from the Spanish name for an Indian chief. It is also true that the attempt to transplant manors and courts leet across the Atlantic was not so anachronistically medieval as it sounds, nor was it confined to Carolina; nevertheless it is unlikely that any were successfully brought into existence there.[2] Landgraves and caciques there were, but there was no great rivalry to obtain these titles, and almost always they expired with the original holder. But whatever the merits and demerits of separate proposals such as these, there was the overall objection that the proprietors were powerless to keep the colonists strictly to them if the colonists chose to ignore them. The *Fundamental Constitutions* suffered from the same defect as the Agreement of the People, and all the paper constitutions of the Commonwealth period, that they assumed a general acceptance of them which did not in fact exist. Locke and Ashley tried to guard against this by laying down that all freemen must subscribe to them before becoming qualified to own an estate, and by declaring that no-one should be able to interpret or comment upon them; but experience of the Instrument of Government and the Humble Petition and Advice should have suggested that sooner or later people were bound to question whether the *Fundamental Constitutions* were like the stone tablets of the law, immune to criticism, and eventually (though not until after Shaftesbury's death) this came to pass.

The likelihood that the eventual reality would correspond exactly with the blueprint was therefore remote; but the *Constitutions* cannot on that account be dismissed as impractical and worthless. The proprietors themselves did not regard them during Shaftesbury's lifetime as being so 'sacred and unalterable' in practice as they sometimes declared. Instead of being rigidly doctrinaire, they stated from the beginning that their aim was only to 'come as nigh the aforesaid model as is practicable',[3] and in 1670 and 1682 amended versions were published. The *Constitutions* were in fact a kind of prospectus, setting out (in rather more than the generalities of the original charter) the kind of society it was hoped to bring into existence in Carolina, in such a way as to appeal to potential immigrants while at the same time forming a base for the exercise of the authority of the proprietors. It has been pointed out, for instance, that when stripped of its curious verbiage the plan to establish a nobility based on large-scale land ownership was 'a very practical promotional device',[4] to encourage men of means or enterprise, and this description may well be applied to the whole of the document. While the *Constitutions* certainly reflect Ashley's and Locke's preference for a landed aristocracy ruling its inferiors

[1] Hardly from 'the usages of northern England' (ibid. p. 339 and Andrews, op. cit. iii. 215).

[2] Andrews, op. cit. iii. 219 and n. Shaftesbury again made provision for a class of voluntary leetmen in the instructions given to Andrew Percival for setting up a plantation of his own on the Edisto River in 1674: *C.S.P. Col. 1669–74*, p. 586.

[3] *Collections*, v. 120.   [4] Craven, op. cit. p. 341.

in the countryside, with political institutions embodying a balance between this propertied class, the smaller landowners and the demands of 'prerogative', and with toleration in religion, this was not simply empty theorizing; it had to attract colonists and encourage unidealistic fellow-proprietors to invest. In these circumstances it would be unwise to examine too closely the similarities and the differences between the plans for Carolina and Harrington's *Oceana*.[1] It is likely enough that Ashley had read *Oceana* but he may simply have been drawing, to suit his practical purposes, on ideas which were in the air.

The *Fundamental Constitutions* were approved by the proprietors in July 1669. At the same time Ashley and his partners decided on a new departure in policy. Instead of relying entirely on colonists who could be enticed from Barbados, New England, and other settlements already existing across the Atlantic, they determined to fit out an expedition of their own from England. Having contributed only £75 each before 1666, they now undertook to give £500 each for the purchase of ships, arms and tools, and a further £200 in each of the next four years. The minutest inventory was drawn up of all the stores purchased. There were new sails and rigging for the ships; biscuits and beef, beer and brandy, candles and 'garden seeds'; shirts and drawers, needles and thread; 'a flag for the fort at Carolina' and a drum; swords and powder; hammers and saws, nails and 'skrues', spades and shovels, kettles and frying pans; bricks and grindstones and cartwheels; fishing-lines; glass beads and hatchets to trade with the Indians; knives and 'sizzards'; a surgeon's chest and instruments. It is astonishing to see the variety of goods thought essential to found a new civilized community in 1669.[2]

Three ships, the *Carolina*, the *Port Royal* and the *Albemarle*, with about one hundred and forty persons on board (the majority of them belonging to the 'servant' class) sailed from the Downs in August 1669 under the command of one Joseph West. Two of the ships were cast away before reaching their destination, but the largest of them, the *Carolina*, after touching at Kinsale, Barbados, and Bermuda, finally appeared on the coasts of the promised land in March of the following year. Port Royal, where the expedition had been instructed by the proprietors to land, was not much liked; St. Helena Sound, in spite of its peach trees, was rejected as being 'in the very chaps of the Spaniards'; and finally, influenced by reports of friendly Indians, they settled further north, at a point twenty-five miles up the Ashley River where a marsh, cutting off all but a neck of fifty yards of access to the mainland, made the site easily defensible. There the colonists established their headquarters, though Ashley immediately

[1] Russell Smith, *Harrington and his Oceana*, pp. 157–61; cf. Andrews, op. cit. iii. 213 and n.

[2] The total cost was £3,200 and the amount actually given by the proprietors in 1669 was £2,645. *Collections*, v. 91–93, 134–52.

realized that the site was marshy and unhealthy and urged a move to
higher ground. In 1680 the colonists acted on this advice, and moved
downstream to the junction of the Ashley with the Cooper river. On this
spot, which was a better port, more healthy and easy to defend, they built
Charles Town—an ironical conjuncture of Ashley, Cooper and Charles II
at a time when they were at loggerheads in England. When Shaftesbury
died in 1683 it was still a smaller settlement than that further north on
Albemarle Sound; but it was the nucleus of what became in the eighteenth
century the largest town south of Philadelphia. This was not the result of
accident; for the instructions which went with the expedition of 1669
stressed the importance of settling in towns in marked contrast to the
state of affairs in Virginia. At a later date, indeed, Ashley insisted that one
reason why New England had developed so much faster than Virginia was
the practice of 'planting in towns'; and in 1672 he carried his insistence
to the point of a kind of town planning. He wanted the port to be built on
higher ground than the first low-lying unhealthy site, with a main street a
hundred feet wide, other streets at least sixty feet wide, and alleys between
the houses at least eight feet wide; each householder was to be limited to
a square of 300 feet for his house, but was allocated other land outside the
town for his main holding. 'Be the buildings never so mean and thin at
first yet as the town increases in riches and people the void spaces will be
filled up and the buildings will grow more beautiful.' The aim was clearly
to bring into existence a spacious, open town far different from cramped,
haphazardly-developed seventeenth-century London. Though the details
of the plan were not fully adhered to by the settlers (as might be expected),
Charles Town after 1680 became the first American town to have the
straight, broad streets with intersections at a right angle which later
became common.[1] Joseph West had been supplied with other instructions
before leaving. He had orders to obtain at Barbados supplies of cotton
seed, indigo seed, ginger roots, sugar canes, vines and olives, all of which
were to be planted experimentally in different kinds of soil and at different
seasons in Carolina. This epitomizes the constant policy of trying to find
which tropical or 'Mediterranean' crops would grow in the colony—and
not relying on any one of them to the extent that the Barbados sugar
planters had mistakenly done. This was not a new policy in 1669: the
proprietors had intended it from the beginning. Albemarle in 1663–4 had
written to the Governor of Barbados of the advantages of growing crops
not yet produced in other plantations, and conversely of preventing
competition in 'commodities which your plantation abounds in', and
amongst his suggestions had been that of rice; and with reference to the
Albemarle Sound settlement instructions had been given that where
possible the proprietors' own lands should be chosen looking to the south,

[1] C.S.P. Col. 1669–74, pp. 32–33, 195 (but 'some' in line 42 should be 'none'), 197,
209–10, 260–1, 294.

so that vines could be grown.[1] Nevertheless there is evidence that this experimental planting was a special interest of Ashley's; he talked of 'throwing away some money' on it in the Bahamas too,[2] and it may be compared with his interest in the growing of different stocks of fruit trees on his home estate at Wimborne St. Giles, at once the work of a practical, businesslike landowner and a kind of hobby. When Locke returned from his visit to France in 1679, he helped to satisfy this taste by presenting his friend with his *Observations upon the growth and culture of vines and olives*.[3] Ashley did not live to see his policy fully justified. The first crops of ginger and indigo were destroyed by drought. Though a barrel of rice was shipped out to Joseph West in January 1672, it was ten to twenty years later before rice fully established itself as a crop specially suited to the swamps of Carolina and to negro slave labour,[4] and cotton was not successful until later. Nevertheless it is not fanciful to trace these eventual successes to the far-seeing original policy encouraged by the proprietors, and Ashley especially among them.

Along with their seeds and cuttings the immigrants carried arms and ammunition. This, however, was intended solely for purposes of self-defence. The instructions which went with the expedition directed that in order to avoid offending the Indians, no-one was to be allowed to take up land within two and a half miles of any Indian village: this was a form of self-denial which other European settlers had not always practised in the past. It was also laid down that no Indian was on any pretext to be made a slave or taken out of the country without his own consent. But these good resolutions were more easily made on the eastern shores of the Atlantic than they were kept on the western. Some Indian tribes, particularly the Westoes, were fiercer and less friendly than those who had given the first colonists a welcome, and were reported to be cannibals; and conversely as the colonists occupied more and more land they could only do so at the expense of the Indians. Ashley preferred to forcible conquest the method of 'purchasing' the land from them: it was at once more humane, cheaper and less troublesome, and accordingly in March 1675 we find Andrew Percival acquiring a large area for the proprietors 'for and in consideration of a valuable piece of cloth, hatchets, beads and other goods and manufactures'. But others were less patient; relations with the Westoes in particular were apt to be bad. There was one short punitive expedition against a tribe in the autumn of 1671, and in spite of temporary treaties of friendship there had eventually to be a large-scale war against the Westoes early in the 1680s. In all such matters, as was to be expected, Ashley was more moderate than those who actually lived amongst the Indians; for instance, he and the other proprietors repeated their ban on the Indian

---

[1] *C.S.P. Col. 1669-74*, pp. 33-34; ibid. *1661-8*, p. 157; *North Carolina Colonial Records*, i. 51.   [2] p. 233 above.
[3] Locke, op. cit. (1823), x. 323 sqq.   [4] Craven, op. cit. p. 356.

slave trade, but in vain. But Ashley's policy towards the Indian tribes did not arise from pure motives of humanity. He would have liked to prevent the settlers from peaceful trading with the Indians as well. He conceived that the prosperous development of the colonists should rest on agriculture. As he wrote on one occasion, 'we aim not at the profit of merchants, but the encouragement of landlords'. He was not entirely consistent in this, because in 1677, when reports reached him of the profits to be obtained from trade with the Indians, he adopted a different policy, and sought to reserve for the proprietors trade with the more distant tribes like the Westoes and the Cussatoes, while permitting the colonists to deal with tribes nearer to their settlements on the coast. But in this he was merely trying to win for the proprietors some compensation for the money which they had put into the colony, while restricting the settlers to the trade which he could not in any case prevent, and his main aim of establishing a community based on the cultivation of land remained unaffected.[1]

For similar reasons Ashley strove always to maintain friendly relations with the Spaniards in Florida. There was no question of returning to the kind of Puritan, anti-Spanish raids which had been favoured by many in the days before the Civil War. There would have been some justification for hostility, because the Spaniards not unnaturally disapproved of English settlements being established in areas which they themselves claimed. When the 1669–70 expedition first appeared on the coast of Carolina, the Spaniards seized a few of the English who went ashore, including one John Rivers who was Ashley's agent and a relative,[2] and took them captive to their own station at St. Augustine. For some years the colonists had to be on their guard against a possible hostile expedition from St. Augustine, and Spanish fomenting of Indian tribes against them was frequently a nuisance. Yet Ashley did not seize any opportunity to retaliate, nor did he attempt to enlist the power of the English state or to influence English policy in Europe against Spain. Rather did he abstain from anything which might give offence to the Spanish. When reports reached him that precious metals had been discovered, he wrote back that these rumours should be suppressed, 'for fear our people being tempted by the hopes of present gain should forsake their plantation and so run themselves into certain ruin which has followed all those who formerly (though in greater numbers than we have there now) marched into this country in search of gold and silver', because the region concerned was claimed by the Spaniards and could not be occupied without fighting. 'Planting and trade is both our design and your interest and if you will but therein follow our directions we shall lay a way open to you to get all the Spaniards' riches in that

---

[1] McCrady, op. cit. pp. 118, 141, 146–7, 177–80, 189–90; V. Crane, *The Southern Frontier, 1670–1732* (Durham, N. Carolina, 1928), pp. 1–21, 118; C.S.P. Col. 1669–74, p. 579; C.S.P. Col. 1677–80, pp. 60–61.

[2] I have not been able to discover the precise relationship.

country with their consent, and without any hazard to yourselves.' In the same way he tried to build up a trade between the Bahamas and Florida.[1]

It will be seen that Ashley had very definite ideas about the lines on which his colony should be developed. He took a proprietorial interest in it, in every sense of the term. But the trouble was that the colonists in the swamps of Carolina, planting and clearing and struggling with hostile Indians and uncertain whether they would be able to make a living or not, saw no reason to respect leadership from thousands of miles away by a man who had never even seen the coasts of Carolina. They felt no debt of gratitude to him; they regarded such success as they enjoyed as the result of their own pioneering efforts, and while they had no choice but to acknowledge that by the royal charter the proprietors had some legal claims, they disregarded them whenever they could. As soon as they were sufficiently established to have no need of any assistance from the proprietors, they resented their authority. And in these circumstances the proprietors always found it difficult to assert their authority. Ashley in particular could send a continuous stream of instructions to the Governors and proprietorial agents across the ocean, but inevitably many of them could safely be disregarded. To do them justice, the Governors were in a difficult position between the complaints of the colonists on their doorstep and the instructions of Ashley and his colleagues on the other side of the Atlantic; but the first Governor, an old Puritan named Colonel Sayle, was nearly eighty and not equal to his task, and Sir John Yeamans, the Barbadian who had been governor of the Cape Fear colony and, recommended by Sir P. Colleton, succeeded when Sayle died, seems to have been liked by no-one. Ashley came to think that 'in this which is my Darling' Yeamans's self-seeking was a positive danger.[2] The efforts to establish a colonial aristocracy which would be a support for authority also took a long time to produce any result; at the end of 1671 we find Ashley writing that colonists needed to be in a condition to stock and furnish themselves, and that he was 'not very fond of more company unless they be substantial men'.[3] However it must not be thought that he paid no attention to what the colonists themselves wanted; he maintained the spirit of the *Fundamental Constitutions* to the extent of insisting that a Parliament 'must upon no terms be refused the people; the proprietors have no design but to maintain them in their perfect liberty'.[4] Bodies bearing the solemn title of 'Parliament' in fact met in 1671 and 1672 (though the 'electorate' of freemen must have been

---

[1] McCrady, op. cit. pp. 127, 129–30, 169–71; Ashley to Henry Woodward, 10 Apr. 1671, in *Collections*, v. 316, and also to Sayle, 13 May 1671, ibid. p. 327.

[2] Cf. his warning letter to Yeamans, 20 June 1672, *C.S.P. Col. 1669–74*, pp. 374–5, his letter to West and the rest of the Council of the same date, ibid. pp. 376–7; to Sir Peter Colleton, 27 Nov. 1672, pp. 436–7; to Yeamans and Council, 18 May 1674, pp. 578–9.

[3] *C.S.P. Col. 1669–74*, p. 295.

[4] Brown, p. 162; *C.S.P. Col. 1669–74*, p. 209.

exceedingly small) and elected five of their number to serve on the Governor's Grand Council as members for the people.[1]

In the years following the landing of 1670 Ashley had to occupy himself with all these problems. He had to listen to the complaints of different parties in the colony (and answer them all as 'your very affectionate friend'); he had to see that the trading interests of the proprietors were not sacrificed to those of the colonists on the spot; he had to employ alternate exhortation and rebuke to persuade people that the interests of proprietors and colonists alike lay in the joint pursuing of the policies which he advocated. Though the proprietors such as Craven, Carteret and Colleton were by no means ciphers, we know that the main burden fell upon Ashley (who became Palatine of the colony in 1670[2]) because many of the documents have been preserved for us by John Locke, who acted as his secretary on Carolina matters until 1675. He kept 'minutes of meetings of the Lords Proprietors of Carolina'[3] at Exeter House, with jottings of decisions reached and expenditure approved, and 'extracts' or summaries of letters received: on a rare occasion in 1674 when Shaftesbury was absent from such a meeting the three proprietors who attended suspended a decision until they had written to ask for 'his advice what they should do therein and in the rest of the affairs of Carolina, wherein they desired his assistance to put that business in the right course, he having as they think a perfect scheme of it in his head . . .'.[4] But most useful of all are Ashley's replies to letters from Carolina. These are preserved for us in a letter-book among the Shaftesbury Papers.[5]

In all the bulk of the surviving Shaftesbury Papers there are singularly few of Shaftesbury's own letters. Those on Carolina (which there was no need to destroy with those on English politics in the last desperate days of Shaftesbury's life) easily outnumber all those on other subjects, and they are the more interesting on that account. They are always written directly to the point, crystal-clear in meaning and with scarcely a word wasted—the letters of a methodical businessman sizing up the situation without ambiguity, doubt or hesitation. And though there was certainly an element of idealism implicit in the enterprise which he called 'my Darling', he never appealed to altruism or sentiment in others; his letters always referred to the long-term prosperity of the colonists and the profits of the proprietors as the two aims to which all steps were to be directed. He himself was confident that these two aims were not at all contradictory, though the colonists must often have thought that he drove a hard bargain

[1] McCrady, op. cit. pp. 156, 161.
[2] When Lord Berkeley of Stratton went to Ireland he appointed Ashley his Deputy as Palatine: C.S.P. Col. 1669–74, p. 60.
[3] MSS. Locke c. 30, fos. 1–11; cf. Shaftesbury Papers, XLVIII, 39, 53, 77, 84, 95, printed in Collections, v. 222–5, 245–53, 256–64, 346–56, 386–9.
[4] MSS. Locke c. 30, fo. 4.
[5] Shaftesbury Papers XLVIII, 55.

with them. The proprietors' original instructions to the agent and store-keeper Joseph West provided for repayment with ten per cent interest for stores issued to them, and Ashley insisted on strict accounts being kept 'that so we may be repaid in work, timber or goods, as may best consist with the ease of the planters. . . . For if we be not satisfied that we have fair dealings we shall stop our supplying.' In the same letter he warned West to be on his guard that Sir Peter Colleton with his trading connexions in Barbados did not gain an unfair advantage over the other proprietors. Ashley was not the man to overlook anything. Later he relaxed his prices to colonists to some extent: 'we intend from time to time to furnish our stores that industrious people who will pay ready truck may be supplied with things they want at reasonable and moderate rates, but do not intend that the lazy or debauched who will never be good for themselves or the plantation shall run further in our debts to the increase of our charge and disparagement of our settlement.'[1] This was not so much the voice of the moneylender anxious to extract every possible penny from debtors, as that of a master warning that the settlers cannot expect to live for ever on the proprietors' charity: Carolina was a business proposition. His mind was not in the least rigid and he could usually resist the temptation to take short cuts to quick profits at the expense of future developments: equally he could use encouragement or rebuke where he thought it would be more likely to produce results from his correspondent.

By the beginning of 1672, as a result of all this effort, the settlement on Ashley River still consisted of only 278 men, 69 women and 59 children,[2] struggling to maintain themselves alive rather than to earn a rapid fortune; but there was no thought of evacuating it like the earlier settlement at Cape Fear. To that extent the proprietors' investment had earned a dividend; but no more tangible profits had come to them. No accounts survive of income derived either from land or from trade on the proprietors' account to counterbalance all the bills paid; but everything suggests that profits remained something to be anticipated in the distant future, not a present reality. In 1674 the proprietors expressed their dissatisfaction with Yeamans's governorship, complaining that he had no thought 'how we might be repaid either our past debts which already amounts to several thousand pounds or be better answered for the future'. All the arrangements for repayment by the colonists for the stores which had been doled out to them had broken down. Yeamans was replaced by Joseph West, and Shaftesbury persuaded his colleagues to inaugurate the new régime by contributing £100 per annum each for the next seven years to provide further urgently needed stores. But when these arrived in the colony they only added more to the mountain of bad debts, and a letter of Shaftesbury's dated 10 June 1675 (at the height of his struggle with Danby) breathes exasperation in every line: it spoke of apprehensions 'that by the expense

---

[1] *Collections*, v. 128–9, 317, 366.   [2] *C.S.P. Col. 1669–74*, p. 321.

of 9 or £10,000 we have purchased nothing but the charge of maintaining 5 or 600 people who expect to live upon us', and made proposals for cutting the proprietors' losses and wiping clean the slate. So far as profits from his new colony were concerned, he proposed in future to set his hopes on a private plantation to be set up under Andrew Percival (a relative of his banker) on the Edisto River, and he insisted that this should not be under the control of the Governor and Council at Charles Town. 'For it is as bad as a state of war for men that are in want to have the making laws over men that have estates.'[1]

In these same years 1667–74 when Ashley as a private person, with John Locke as his secretary, was struggling to solve the problems of colonial policy in one area, he was also involved in the consideration of government policy in matters of trade and the plantations; and here too he interested Locke in the same matters. In January 1668 when the standing committees of the Privy Council were reorganized, Ashley was inevitably placed on the committee for trade and plantations.[2] But he was also in favour of returning to the device employed in 1660, of setting up a Council of Trade consisting partly of ministers and partly of merchant experts who would be able to collect accurate information about the colonies, act as a link between the City and the Privy Council and supply advice when asked to do so. The Council of 1660 was moribund, but it appears that in October 1667 Ashley advocated reviving it.[3] In August 1668 when he was convalescing from his operation, he was in touch with Benjamin Worsley, a man whose interest in colonial trade dated back at least twenty years: he had been secretary of the Commonwealth's Council of Trade in 1650, and claimed to have been the first advocate of the Navigation Act.[4] In a ten-page memorandum addressed to Ashley he drew attention to 'the peculiar advantages which this nation hath by the trade of our plantations', which unlike other trades was free from restrictions imposed by other nations, and the profits of which were exclusively British; went on to argue that previous policy had been defective, permitting the over-production of some commodities and the neglect of others, while no statistical information was gathered to facilitate action; and advocated the establishment of a Council to study all these connected problems systematically. It is fair to connect the influence of Worsley and Ashley with the setting up of the Council of Trade which received its commission in October.[5]

The Council of Trade of 1668 consisted of 42 members (later increased

---

[1] *C.S.P. Col. 1669–74*, pp. 578, 584–7; *1675–6*, pp. 240–1 (but the figures £90,000 and £100,000 should read £9,000 and £10,000). In 1728 when the charter was surrendered to the Crown seven proprietors shared £22,500 compensation. (McCrady, op. cit. p. 679). For Carolina after 1674, see below, pp. 364–6, 433, 705–7.

[2] Andrews, *British Committees*, pp. 88–91.   [3] *C.S.P. Col. 1661–8*, p. 511.

[4] See his letter of 8 Nov. 1661, MSS. Clar. 75, fos. 300–1.

[5] Worsley to Ashley, 14 Aug. 1668, Shaftesbury Papers, XLIX, 26; cf. also ibid. 8. The Council's Instructions are summarized in *C.S.P.D. 1667–8*, pp. 607–8.

to 48). They were a motley collection of people, including as they did ministers, courtiers, merchants like Josiah Child and Thomas Papillon, men like Worsley and Sir George Downing who were experienced in the ways of the Dutch; its secretary was Pierre Du Moulin, who later deserted to the Dutch in 1672.[1] Like the Council of 1660, it suffered from unwieldy membership and from the fact that it was only an advisory and not a decision-taking body, and it was probably for that reason that after about two years it began to languish once again. Little is known about the nature of the discussions which went on; but two of the Council's reports to the King, both of them signed by Ashley among others, require a mention. In November 1668 they complained about the permission which had been granted to the Dutch to continue their trade with New York for seven years, and talked about the Navigation Act as the principle by which everything should be governed; and a second report on 4 December made various proposals to stop the connivance of colonial governors in breaches of the Act. There is no support here for the view which has been put forward that Ashley did not incline to enforce the old colonial system.[2]

The most important economic issues of 1669 were however debated elsewhere than in the Council of Trade. When Parliament met in October of that year the House of Lords proceeded to appoint a large committee to consider 'the fall of rents and decay of trade within the kingdom': Ashley was for some reason not an original member, but was added to it on 25 October. The most contentious proposal before this committee was that made by Josiah Child, the great East India Company merchant, who knew from observation of the Dutch the advantages to be obtained from low interest rates and sought to obtain them by reducing the legal maximum rate from 6 per cent to 4. Others who gave evidence disagreed, either because they thought that 4 per cent would be unfair or unattractive to lenders, and money would become scarce, or because they argued that low rates would favour the great moneyed men and drive smaller men out of business. The committee adopted Child's view by thirteen votes to one, but when its report was debated by the House, the peers were not satisfied; and the matter was referred back to the committee, with a request that the Earl of Anglesey, Viscount Halifax, Lord Lucas and Lord Ashley should choose 'three or four of a side of the ablest persons they know, to speak for it and against it, before the said committee'. After the experts had had their say, the committee adhered to its former view, significantly deciding that the lowering of interest rates would drive up the value of land; but

[1] See K. H. D. Haley, *William of Orange and the English Opposition 1672–4* (1953), *passim*.

[2] Andrews, op. cit. pp. 91–95; *C.S.P. Col. 1661–8*, pp. 624–5, 629–30; cf. below, p. 262. When the members of the Council attended upon the King on 9 Nov. Ashley was their 'spokesman': *Bulstrode Papers* of Alfred Morrison (1897), i. 72.

the House of Lords refused to accept even this appeal to the pockets of landowners, and rejected the proposal. Where did Ashley stand in this debate of the economists? There is no direct evidence, but we do possess the ideas of John Locke on the subject. Locke had had no previous occasion to study economic matters, and it is probable that his attention was drawn to them, as also to Carolina, by his patron at Exeter House. Locke's treatise, which was later fetched out from its pigeon-hole and became the basis of *Some Considerations on the Lowering of Interest and Raising the Value of Money* (published in 1692), was directly opposed to Child. His basic conception was that 'the price of the hire of money' could not be regulated by law. The forces of supply and demand must inevitably operate, and legal restrictions would only make borrowing more difficult, encourage perjury and hinder trade. Interest rates should be left to the free play of the market. Sir William Coventry endorsed his contemporary copy of the treatise, 'By Mr. Locke directed by Lord Ashley', and this suggests that Ashley shared Locke's *laissez-faire* views on the subject. It is observable that Benjamin Worsley, on whom Ashley relied for advice on colonial questions, was also opposed to Child on this matter.[1]

The committee of the House of Lords made other recommendations to deal with the fall of rents and decay of trade. They revived the old idea of a register of titles to land, urged a bill of naturalization to remedy 'the want of people in England', and finally declared 'that some ease and relaxation in ecclesiastical matters will be a means of improving the trade of this kingdom'.[2] These ideas are connected with a document which has often been regarded as describing Ashley's views on the relationship between religious toleration and commercial prosperity. It takes the form of a letter following up a previous conversation with the King at Windsor on the subject of the economic depression, and puts forward all these three remedies.[3] Thirty years ago it was pointed out that the only surviving copy of this letter (preserved in the Shaftesbury Papers) was unsigned, that the endorsement 'Ld. Sh. Advice to his Majesty about trade' was not a contemporary one, and that therefore the authorship was uncertain; but this has not prevented historians from continuing to regard the paper

---

[1] *L.J.* xii. 254, 273–4, 277, 280; *H.M.C. Eighth Report*, pp. 133–4; Add. MSS. 32094, fo. 289; F. R. Harris, *The Life of Edward Montagu, First Earl of Sandwich* (1912), ii. 309–10; W. Letwin, *The Origins of Scientific Economics* (1963), pp. 155–62.

[2] *L.J.* xii. 273–4, 284.

[3] Shaftesbury Papers, XLIX, 8, printed by Martyn, i. 369–76, and Christie, ii, App. I, pp. v–ix. Copying from Martyn and not from the original, Christie makes some serious errors, e.g. in the first paragraph on page viii he omits the important concluding words 'or shall have a special dispensation from your Majesty'; and the fifth paragraph on the same page should read: '. . . that all and every other sort of Nonconformists may have liberty to assemble, for the exercise of their own manner of worship but that only, as your Majesty shall prescribe, and in such public places as your Majesty shall approve, and the Nonconformists can procure, and the doors of the meeting-places do stand open. . . .'

R

as setting out his ideas.[1] And superficially they do, for all his life he was concerned with toleration and trade. Nevertheless internal evidence shows that Ashley cannot have written the letter. The central argument is that trade is suffering from a decline in population, which is partly the result of the loss of 'above two hundred and fifty thousand (*sic*) persons' in the Plague and Dutch War, and partly the result of people transporting themselves to the American plantations 'to enjoy the liberty of their mistaken consciences'; therefore freedom of worship must be permitted (and bills for a land register and naturalization introduced) in order to encourage foreigners to immigrate and to discourage Englishmen from emigrating. The wild estimate of losses from plague and war, and the uncharacteristic phrase 'liberty of their mistaken consciences' might give us pause; but much more than that, it is impossible to believe that Ashley could have used arguments against emigration to the colonies. As recently as August 1669, he and his co-proprietors had spent £3,000 in fitting out ships to carry English settlers to Carolina. No colonizer such as he would conceivably have written of 'the drain that carries away the natives from us'. Once this glaring inconsistency has been noticed, it follows that the paper was not his, but was passed on to him by the King. It may be that Ashley then adopted the practical proposals without accepting the arguments which the unknown author used to advance them; certainly the committee adopted them, but nothing came of them before the prorogation of Parliament.

Once the discussions in Parliament had lapsed, it remained for the standing committee of Privy Council and for the Council of Trade to debate matters of commercial policy. On 30 July 1670, however, a third body was set up, with the title of Council for Foreign Plantations. This new departure was not simply the result of a feeling that the colonies deserved special treatment from other, purely English, economic problems; the new Council was to be organized more effectively. Instead of being a large, amorphous body of more than forty members, giving a little of their spare time when they were so disposed, it was to contain a nucleus of ten salaried members, one of whom, the Earl of Sandwich, was to act as President. John Evelyn became an additional paid member in 1671. Ashley, Arlington and a few other ministers were also allowed to attend *ex officio*; and Benjamin Worsley was to receive an allowance of £300 for giving assistance and advice. The result was to set up a much more professional and businesslike body, which met more regularly and worked more consistently than previous ones. Its instructions began by imposing upon it all kinds of fact-finding duties. They were to inquire into the present condition of all the colonies; into the powers given to the governors and into any 'neglect or miscarrriage' committed by them; into the population of planters, servants and slaves. They were given authority to correspond

[1] Cf. Brown, p. 143; M. Cranston, op. cit. p. 130.

directly with governors on such problems as these, and to advise with them about the production of timber and naval stores—an urgently needed contribution to naval defence. We catch an echo of the problems of Carolina in a clause directing the councillors to inquire into the possibility of better species of cotton, ginger, cocoa and other crops and to encourage their planting; and as in Carolina the governors were to be specifically enjoined to give no provocation either to the Indians or to their French, Spanish and Dutch neighbours. Indians who placed themselves under English protection were to be protected both from other Indians and from violence and injustice at the hands of English colonists. In such respects these instructions are consistent with the policies being pursued by Ashley and the Carolina proprietors; and a clause directing the Council to inquire into the provision of slaves and the disputes between the 'Guinea Company' (i.e. the Royal Adventurers trading to Africa) and the American plantations reminds us that a year later Ashley was one of those who took part in that company's reorganization as the Royal Africa Company. Thus the aims of the private colonizer and the politician coincided; and the general object was to be so to 'regulate the trade of our whole plantations, that they may be most serviceable one unto another, and as the whole unto these our Kingdoms so these our Kingdoms unto them'. For this purpose the Council was to take care that the Navigation Acts were duly executed, and it was also empowered to send for copies of all colonial laws, so that any which were 'inconvenient or contrary to the laws of this land, or to the honour and justice of our government' might be disallowed. Such were the principles of the colonial system which was envisaged.[1]

The Council for Plantations which was thus established met once a week or oftener for the next two years. An entry in Evelyn's diary describes his first attendance at a meeting on 26 May 1671; this was held in the Earl of Bristol's house in Queen's Street, which was rented to provide a headquarters for the Council between that month and February 1672. There was even talk of the erection of a building in Whitehall to be used as a colonial office. This never came to pass, but clearly the Council was regarded as something more than a mere committee amongst many which met periodically; it had its paid members and its regular office staff including a secretary, three clerks, a messenger, a doorkeeper, a porter, a maid, and a chamberkeeper, with an allowance of £1,000 per annum for contingent expenses. It promised in fact to be the nucleus of a new department. Its energy was so highly regarded, in comparison with that of the Council of Trade, that in September 1672 a further reorganization took place. The two councils were now combined into one Council of Trade and Foreign Plantations. The membership of this was largely identical with that of the successful Council of Foreign Plantations; but

[1] C. M. Andrews, op. cit. pp. 117–26; R. P. Bieber, 'The British Plantation Councils of 1670–4', *E.H.R.* (1925), pp. 93–106.

the latter's head, the Earl of Sandwich, had been killed in the battle of Sole Bay, and Ashley (who in the meantime had become Earl of Shaftesbury) became President, with an increased salary of £800 per annum to add to his other emoluments. Benjamin Worsley, whom he had previously consulted on colonial matters, became the Council's secretary until, a year later, he declined to comply with the provisions of the Test Act and was succeeded by none other than John Locke.

From this it is plain that Shaftesbury was the driving force behind the Council, even though his many other commitments prevented him from being its most regular attender. It is not surprising to find a draft of the Council's instructions in the Shaftesbury Papers, nor to discover that the first meeting to consider the instructions was held at Exeter House. The draft differs from previous instructions principally in being more specific about the subjects on which the Council was to collect information. It does not repeat the instruction given to the previous Council in 1670 to see to the strict execution of the Navigation Acts; on the contrary, clauses directing the Council to consider the opening of free ports for the landing and re-export of foreign commodities, and the advantages to be obtained from 'giving way (according to the example of other nations [i.e. the Dutch]) to a more open and free trade than that of companies and corporations'[1] suggest an open-minded outlook on commercial problems. On the other hand, one of the subjects to be investigated was the revenues due to the Crown from the plantations and the way in which they were collected. In general, the instructions strike the reader as being less concerned with the enunciation of principles of policy to be enforced than with the collection of facts on which policy decisions could be taken, without tying anyone's hands in any way.

The combined Council met for the first time on 13 October 1672, and during the next year continued to meet at least once a week at Villiers House in King Street near Whitehall, which was rented from the Duchess of Cleveland. It was as active as the previous Council of Plantations of 1670 had been; and the question which has to be faced is whether from the comparatively scanty record of the activities of these two councils between 1670 and 1674 any consistent outlook can be discerned.

In practice the taking of policy decisions could not be so easily postponed until after the collection of the information which the councils' instructions envisaged. There were, for instance, petitioners who clamoured for redress of their grievances, and whose cases had wide general implications. The most awkward case of this type came before the Council of Plantations in the spring of 1671, when Ferdinando Gorges and Robert Mason laid claim to Maine and New Hampshire respectively. Settlers from Massachusetts had moved into these areas during the Interregnum, and after the Restoration the colony of Massachusetts had ignored an

---

[1] Evelyn, 1 Sept. 1672; Andrews, op. cit. pp. 127-32.

unfavourable decision by a royal commission of 1664, so that the petitions of Gorges and Mason raised the whole problem of the exercise of the royal authority in New England. At the first meeting of the Council which John Evelyn attended 'great were the debates, in what style to write to them; for the condition of that colony was such as they were able to contest with all our plantations about them, and fear there was, of their altogether breaking from all dependence on this nation ... some of our Council were for sending them a menacing letter, which those who better understood the touchy and peevish humour of that colony were utterly against'. The party of caution prevailed, deciding that 'only a conciliatory paper' should be sent at first. Later someone made the ingenious proposal that commissioners should be sent to New England with open instructions to settle the boundary dispute, and secret orders to report back on 'the condition of those colonies; and whether they were of such power, as to be able to resist his Majesty and declare for themselves as independent of the Crown, as we were told and which of late years made them refractory'. This might seem like an investigation of the practicability of taking firm action, but even if commissioners had actually been sent, the effect would have been to postpone the need to take a decision for many months; but in fact, though the matter was talked about at intervals for months, no one ever went, and the matter was quietly dropped. The members of the Plantation Council had spent much time and energy in inquiry and discussion, but to positively no effect. The people of Massachusetts were left to their own devices until after Shaftesbury's fall from power, when in 1676 Edward Randolph was sent over in pursuance of a different policy.[1]

The issue of the way in which the colonies were to be controlled was also raised by the requirement that the Plantations Council should study all colonial laws and recommend their approval or annulment to the King and Privy Council. It might be expected that the Council would devote particular attention to this duty, but this the Council emphatically did not do. It has been calculated that, of thirty-four acts signed by the governor of Jamaica on 14 May 1672, three were approved and four disallowed by the Council by June 1673. 'No further record of these laws is found until March 1674, and then when the council desired to act upon the remainder, they could not be found.'[2] A possible means of control was thus neglected, and colonies were left to adopt the expedient of re-enacting their laws after the initial period of two years for which they were valid had expired.

The only important act of policy in these years was the passing of a new Navigation law in 1673, which in order to stop up a loophole put duties on the enumerated commodities when shipped from one plantation to another, and even provided for the appointment of a staff of officials to

---

[1] Evelyn, 26 May, 6, 20, 21 June, 4 July, 3 Aug. 1671, 12 Feb. 1672; Bieber, op. cit. pp. 104–5 (citing the Journal of the Council for Plantations, which is now in the Library of Congress). [2] Bieber, op. cit. p. 104.

enforce the laws. But this Act does not seem to have been passed at the prompting of the Council of Trade and Plantations; it arose rather from a motion in the House of Commons, the officials were to be appointed not by the Council but by the Customs Commissioners, and nothing was done to implement it before Shaftesbury's fall from office later in the same year.[1]

There is therefore a striking contrast between the energy displayed by the councils in inquiring into many minor matters,[2] and their failure to take any major initiative. In spite of Shaftesbury's undoubted knowledge and keen interest, the councils which he inspired and over which he presided left little permanent mark on English colonial development. One authority has sought to explain this strange feature by suggesting that Shaftesbury's abstention from any drastic action was deliberate; he contrasts 'the negligent tolerance over which Shaftesbury had presided' with the attempts made in the decade after 1676, particularly by James, to assert the royal authority and take up a tougher attitude towards the colonists.[3] But while Shaftesbury's attitude was certainly different from James's in this as in all other subjects, it would be too much of a paradox to suppose that he promoted the setting-up of a Plantations Council in order *not* to take any positive action. A policy of 'negligent tolerance' could presumably have been pursued without the aid of any special council. Rather do the Instructions of 1670 and 1672 suggest that the Council was intended to prepare the way for a proper, coherent colonial policy; there was no hint that the colonists were to be left to themselves. The explanation for the failure to work out such a policy must be sought elsewhere, in the circumstances in which the Council had to deliberate. Between 1670 and 1673 the principal preoccupations of Shaftesbury and his fellow-ministers were the preparation for, and the waging of, a new war with the Dutch, together with the domestic problems raised by the Declaration of Indulgence and the parliamentary difficulties to which this gave rise. Not only did these problems represent the first call on Shaftesbury's own time, but they meant that it was not a propitious period to tackle colonial problems while a war was either impending or actually being fought. Before a peaceful and relatively settled political situation was restored, he had fallen from the royal favour in the autumn of 1673.

It may be that in this way a great opportunity was missed, for it was to be many years before a statesman of Shaftesbury's qualifications, influence

---

[1] L. A. Harper, *The English Navigation Laws* (New York, 1939), p. 160; G. L. Beer, *The Old Colonial System, 1660–1754* (New York, 1912), i. 80–83; *C.J.* ix. 252.

[2] See the list of heads of business compiled by Andrews, op. cit. pp. 133–51.

[3] E. E. Rich, 'The First Earl of Shaftesbury's Colonial Policy', in *Trans. Roy. Hist. Soc.* (1957), pp. 47–70. Apart from some inaccuracies which it is unnecessary to list, this article seems to me to read more into the available evidence than it will bear (cf. the remarks on Shaftesbury's attitude towards the Dutch). It is fair to recall, however, Professor Rich's own cautious remark, p. 70: 'This may be placing Shaftesbury's purpose in too clear a light and it must be admitted that such an interpretation would be pure surmise based upon his general character and opinions'.

and ability to get things done was able to appraise the problems of colonial government. What kind of policy he would have pursued had he been able to give it his undivided attention it is naturally difficult to say, but the signs are that it would have been a thoroughly empirical one. He was not committed to any policy of rigid enforcement of the Navigation laws, but was prepared to consider modification of these where it was sensible to do so. He was not interested, like James, in the enforcement of royal authority as an end in itself. As in Carolina, he acted on the assumption that the interests of the English authorities and of the colonists could be reconciled, and was prepared to concede a definite place to the assemblies of the colonists themselves and to take account of their representations; on the other hand, he was not the man to abdicate from all power and leave the colonists to go their own way. In these respects he was better equipped to tackle the problem than, for instance, James. Whether he could have solved it must be forever doubtful; it may well be that the difficulties of distance and divergence of interest were insuperable, and that in any case succeeding English statesmen would have been preoccupied with problems on their own doorstep. That he would not have left the colonies to drift is certain.

It is significant that when in November 1673 he was deprived of the Lord Chancellorship he was not immediately removed from his position as President of the Council of Trade and Plantations as well. Precisely when he was coming to the parting of the ways with the King, he secured the appointment of John Locke as the Council's secretary (15 October), and in the same month when a report reached London of the capture of New York by the Dutch, he was active in making plans to retake it. On 13 November, four days after he had lost the seals, he spoke to the Council on a proposal to prohibit the importation of wool; he opposed this, on the ground that a ban was impracticable, and that in any case it would not achieve its object of helping English woollen manufacture. The real causes of the current decline in this, he argued, were the lack of labour and 'some difficulties that lay upon our trade by reason of the Act of Navigation'. Accordingly the Council decided to consider 'a better way for the mainten-ance of the poor, the present law by encouraging them in their idleness very much hindering the manufacturers of England', and also the Navigation Act and interest rates: the social attitude implicit in this reference to the poor law needs no comment. On 17 February 1674, when the Council was considering the best way of reviewing colonial laws, discussion was adjourned to a later meeting until the Earl of Shaftesbury could be present; and it was not until the following month that the Earl ceased altogether to attend. By that time it would have been futile to do so, for his recommenda-tion would have been the best means of securing rejection of a proposal by Danby and the Privy Council. The Council itself was left to languish, with the salaries of its members unpaid, until in December 1674 the King dissolved it. Later in 1679 Shaftesbury was for a time head of the Privy Council's committee on trade and foreign plantations, but in effect his ambitions to take charge of colonial policy came to an end at the beginning of 1674. Thereafter his interest in colonial affairs was confined to his 'darling' project in Carolina, and elsewhere he was left without direct influence.[1]

But not quite without indirect influence. For, over a decade after his death, and over twenty years after the dissolution of the Council of which John Locke was secretary, Locke was instrumental in the creation of the Board of Trade. In this, as in other respects, Locke carried on the interests to which his patron had introduced him.[2]

Reviewing Ashley's economic and colonizing activities as a whole, it is impossible to say that he was truly original in any of them, but only that he was abreast of the latest ideas and did what he could to foster them. Like most Englishmen of his day, he accepted the general principles of the Navigation Act policy which was the main development of his lifetime, but took a less rigid view of them than, for instance, Sir George Downing, and was prepared at least to examine the case for modifications. In other respects it is possible to detect some paradoxes in what he did. He was interested in a variety of commercial enterprises, yet as far as we can tell these were not the basis of his own income. He had many friends among the merchants who looked to him for help and leadership, yet the society which he had planned to found in Carolina would be based on a landed aristocracy in which merchants were offered no place. He was a private proprietor in Carolina at a time when the trend was towards bringing the colonies under the supervision of the English state, and when the Councils of which he was a member were intended as instruments in this process. He was an efficient, hard-headed businessman who was however prepared to forgo immediate returns on his investments in exchange for some highly speculative good in the future, in which all concerned would participate. Yet, looked at in another way, these paradoxes are more apparent than real. Behind his actions there lay the confident assumption that the enlightened self-interest of individuals such as himself, acting in accordance with rational principles, would operate to the general good of all Englishmen and colonists. The basis of society should be the landed interest, but (once the foundations had been securely laid) not an exclusively landed interest. Commerce and investment had a valuable and respectable contribution to make to the general prosperity, and a sensible landlord might engage in both. Merchants, moneyed men and landed interest were not in conflict: they could all be harmonized, and even the

[1] *Documents Relative to the Colonial History of the State of New York*, ed. E. B. O'Callaghan and J. R. Brodhead (Albany, 1853), iii. 209–13; Brown, p. 148 (citing the Journal in the Library of Congress); Andrews, pp. 149–50.

[2] P. Laslett, 'John Locke, The Great Recoinage, and the Origins of the Board of Trade, 1695–8', in the *William and Mary Quarterly* (1957), pp. 370–402.

class of voluntary leetmen whom he invited to come under his protection would benefit. All could enjoy the benefits of liberty of conscience (except Catholics and others who might wish to disturb it); all, except those who were too poor to be trusted, could have political rights and make their opinions felt. A wise, beneficent government would listen to their representations and would rule, not simply to preserve its own position and rivet its authority more firmly upon its subjects, but for the general good. The question remained how far the government of the Stuarts measured up to this test.

CHAPTER XIII

THE BREAKING OF THE TRIPLE BOND
(1668–70)

> . . . Resolved to ruin or to rule the state;
> To compass this the triple bond he broke,
> The pillars of the public safety shook,
> And fitted Israel for a foreign yoke.
>
> *Absalom and Achitophel*

SHLEY'S critical illness in the summer of 1668 meant perforce that for some months he was out of the main stream of English politics. Being the man he was, it is unlikely that his restless mind was inactive during this period, but it was not until 4 September that he returned to his place on the Treasury Commission, and in October he had the King's permission to retire to the country for a fortnight.[1] His return, reinvigorated and freed from the jaundice which had harassed him for some years past, is an appropriate point at which to take stock of his political position.

Since the Restoration which he had helped to bring about he had tended always to take up a more independent line of action. At first he had co-operated fully in establishing the new régime, managing the Convention and supplying administrative assistance in all manner of ways; but as time went on some dissatisfaction had made itself felt. Especially in 1663 contemporaries had ranged him among those younger politicians who disliked the dominance of Clarendon. It might be claimed that in his support of religious indulgence he was nevertheless in accord with the real inclinations of his master King Charles; but in 1666 and 1667 he had gone further and taken up attitudes which he must have known would be distasteful to the King. Both at the time of the Irish Cattle Act and at the time of Clarendon's fall, he had followed a line of his own, instead of adhering simply to Charles's wishes. This was not simply a matter of the growing self-confidence of a politician who, having a doubtful past, had had to work his passage. As time went on, it became apparent that the Restoration met some of his needs better than others. It had got rid of the Army and supplied much more settled political conditions; on the other hand Anglican intolerance had triumphed in religion, the government's foreign policy (at least until the Triple Alliance of 1668) had been a singularly inglorious one, and neither the financial position of the government nor the economic

---

[1] Downing to Duncombe, 4 Sept., *C.T.B., 1667–8*, p. 615; Arlington to Williamson, 8 Oct., *C.S.P.D. 1668–9*, p. 8.

life of the country was in 1668 in a very healthy condition. The new régime therefore had a decidedly mixed record. At the same time, a man who holds ministerial office does not readily give up hope that he and his colleagues will be able to effect an improvement.

These colleagues too were an unusually disparate set of people. The unlucky coincidence that the initials of five of them (Clifford, Arlington, Buckingham, Ashley and Lauderdale) combined to spell the word CABAL has misled many people into thinking of them as a group who together formed a 'ministry' to replace that of Clarendon,[1] when in fact they disagreed on many points of policy and when their personal relations were far from harmonious. Not until the end of 1670 did they agree on any act of policy, and then, as will be seen, two of the five were tricking the other three. Moreover, until then there was nothing to mark off these five from others in the Privy Council such as Sir William Coventry.[2] And finally, the five were not by any means of equal weight in the King's counsels. Arlington and Buckingham dominated the scene which Clarendon had left, and contemporaries thought of these two as rivals for the royal favour. The more formal Arlington was a complete contrast to the splendidly erratic Buckingham in temperament and political outlook, and in addition the latter had a grudge against the Secretary of State for signing a warrant for his arrest in the spring of 1667. Though Charles arranged one or two temporary 'reconciliations' the rivalry between these two men was one of the basic political facts between the years 1668 and 1673.

In comparison with these two Ashley was still, in 1668, a figure of lesser importance. Having stood aloof from the hue and cry against Clarendon, he had been left in a position of isolation, and so far from being a member of any 'cabal', he was not a member of the so-called committee of foreign affairs which consisted of the King's innermost advisers. He had some affinities, it is true, with both Arlington and Buckingham: he had co-operated with Arlington over the Declaration of Indulgence of 1662 and was never thereafter on really hostile terms with him: even in 1681, when the two were definitely in opposed political camps, it was Arlington whom he asked to present to the King his petition for release from the Tower. With Buckingham he had in common a desire to do something for the Dissenters, a readiness to talk to ex-Commonwealthmen, and a hostility to Ormond and his Irish policy, while no doubt they found one another good company. Yet while he had no personal hostility to either, he had no admiration for either as a politician, and there are signs that his attitude to their intrigues was one of detachment and even cynicism. In the autumn of 1669 he had occasion to write to his old friend Sir William Morrice, who had retired from his Secretaryship of State to his books in the West Country, and had not appeared in London for the meeting of Parliament.

[1] E.g. M. Cranston, *John Locke* (1957), p. 110.
[2] Coventry was dismissed by the King early in 1669.

After talking of his son's marriage, he went on: 'I am sorry for my own sake not to enjoy you here this session, but you are in a better place. The Lapland knots are untied, and we are in horrid storms.[1] Those that hunted together [*sc.* Arlington and Buckingham, who had "hunted" Clarendon] now hunt one another, and at horse play the Master of the Horse [Buckingham] must have the better. The division about Skinner's business of the two Houses is by the state chemists like to be improved into a new Parliament. No man of our age has seen a time of more expectation, which is the next step to confusion.' In the following summer Morrice wrote back in terms of warm friendship, concluding with the hope 'that, before you need it for old age, you may have a staff to support you and the nation', that is, the official staff of the Lord Treasurer. Ashley's reply was to say: 'Since I knew you we have had a constant and uninterrupted friendship, I daresay not in thought, which is a miracle in the place we lived. You are the only happy man that have got off the stage with the love and esteem of all. We are in the storm, and in dispute what shall be our event, whether Knights of the Garter or travellers to Montpellier'—Montpellier being the place where Clarendon had settled in his final exile in the South of France. These letters breathe a certain rueful disillusionment with what the twentieth century would call the 'rat-race' of politics at Whitehall and Westminster. They suggest a sense of the insecurity of political life (which Clarendon's fall had emphasized) without any hint that any worth-while objective was being achieved.[2]

This mood would not have been improved if Ashley had been aware of what was taking place behind the scenes at this time. Having thrown off the tutelage of Clarendon, King Charles was left with ministers who were little older than himself and had less experience of international affairs. He was encouraged to pursue, by devious methods, his own foreign policy. Ever since his return to England in 1660 he had hankered after a closer alliance with Louis XIV. Louis was well endowed with money and even with men who might be useful to Charles in his precarious control over his kingdom; and abroad he cared little whether Louis won control over Western Europe on land if with French asssistance he could rule the waves. For some years, however, he had little success in his efforts to achieve intimacy with Louis: Louis had many fair words, but in 1666 he kept his treaty obligations to his Dutch allies, and the mere existence of a hostile French fleet made difficulties for the English. But the events of 1667 and 1668 produced a sudden transformation in the international situation. While the war at sea was brought to an end by the Treaty of

---

[1] Lapland was supposed to be inhabited by witches who had the power to raise storms. Ashley appears to combine a reference to this superstition with one to the older story of Aeolus, who tied up the winds in a bag for Odysseus, only for Odysseus' crew to untie the bag, release the winds and be caught in the resulting tempest.

[2] Ashley to Morrice, 30 Oct. 1669 and 5 July 1670; Morrice to Ashley, 21 June 1670, in Christie, ii. 44–47.

Breda, Louis XIV laid claim to the Spanish Netherlands by the right of 'devolution' and began to pour troops into Flanders, to the alarm of the Dutch Pensionary, De Witt. In January 1668, Sir William Temple hastened over to The Hague to negotiate with De Witt the famous alliance which, with the later adhesion of Sweden, became known as the Triple Alliance. Its declared aim was to restrict Louis's conquests, and by the Treaty of Aix-la-Chapelle Louis did indeed content himself with less than he might otherwise have gained. Yet while Charles had adopted this apparently anti-French policy, he continued to let his fellow-monarch and cousin know that he had done this with the greatest reluctance: his real desire was, as he had always said, an alliance with Louis. Though English public opinion had taken the Triple Alliance at its face value as a popular means of restraining the over-powerful, absolutist, Roman Catholic monarch of France, Charles had never intended it as a permanent policy: it was for him only a temporary device to break the alliance between French and Dutch which had previously existed, and to drive up the value of his own friendship in the eyes of Louis. In this it amply succeeded. Louis's indignation was reserved for the 'ingratitude' of the Republican, Protestant, Dutch merchants, and in 1668 he resolved to destroy them, and clear away the principal obstacle to his expansionist designs. For this purpose he wanted the English alliance to which he had previously shown himself lukewarm. Charles's chance had come.

The Anglo-French alliance against the Dutch which both kings now wanted was not, however, to be negotiated by the ordinary diplomatic methods. Instead, on 20 January 1669 Charles sent to his sister, the Duchess of Orleans, a cipher which she could use in her correspondence with him. Poor 'Minette', a pathetic figure beloved of all who knew her except her jealous, morose husband, devoted the last years of her life to bringing together her admired brother Charles and her brother-in-law, Louis XIV, in the interests, as she believed, of both kings and of the Catholic Church. Five days after Charles had sent her the cipher, with a letter to pass to Louis, he held a private meeting with his brother James, Arlington, the latter's protégé Sir Thomas Clifford, and Lord Arundel, a leading member of the Catholic nobility. He told them that he had called them together to consider the best means of 'settling the Catholic religion in his kingdoms, and . . . the time most proper to declare himself'. He spoke, we are told, 'even with tears in his eyes, and added, That they were to go about it as wise men and good Catholics ought to do',[1] that is, by enlisting Louis's help. The effect of this edifying scene was heightened by the fact that it was staged on 25 January 1669, the day on which the Church traditionally celebrated the conversion of Saint Paul. Whether his conversion was as sincere as Paul's, and still more whether he was prepared in the last resort to take the same risks for his faith, may well be doubted; but the fact

[1] Ed. J. S. Clarke, *Life of James II* (1816), pp. 441–2.

remains that by using Henrietta as an intermediary and by asking Louis to help him to declare himself a Catholic, he deliberately introduced a new element into the negotiations. No doubt it was partly a device to extract a little more money (two million livres, or about £150,000) from Louis, but much more, it was a means of achieving a special relationship with him, much more confidential than in a normal treaty. He was so convinced that it was in his own interest, and England's, to be attached to the fortunes of the most powerful monarch in Europe that he was willing to give a valuable hostage; for the 'Catholic secret' would have ruined Charles if Louis had allowed it to leak out, and for the rest of the reign it prevented him from pursuing a truly independent foreign policy.

From this time onwards, then, the 'triple bond' which England had formed with the United Provinces and Sweden at the beginning of 1668 was being steadily gnawed away by Charles, with the complicity of Arlington and Clifford, until the Secret Treaty of Dover was signed in May 1670. Neither Arlington nor Clifford was at this time a completely convinced Catholic, and Arlington, who had not previously been accounted a friend of France, was much less certain of the merits of the new policy than his all-or-nothing protégé, but both like good courtiers were willing to follow the lead of their King, and the promise of advancement. No other of the King's accredited ministers was aware of this revolution in English foreign policy which was going on in secret in 1669 and early 1670; yet this was the really important intrigue which was taking place, and Charles must have been much amused by some of the schemes and activities on which others spent their energy. In public, for instance, Buckingham often seemed to be the one who enjoyed most of the King's favour; in private it was Arlington and Clifford who had his confidence, and there was much play-acting for the benefit of observers at Court whose occupation it was to divine whose star was in the ascendant and whose was falling.

Ashley was one of the many who were deluded. In the winter of 1668-9 he was generally thought to be veering towards Buckingham's side in the factious dispute. The French ambassador reported that he was Buckingham's candidate for the office of Lord Treasurer (in opposition to Arlington, who wanted it for himself) and even that he was prepared to offer money for it. Ambassador Colbert de Croissy (brother of the great Colbert) later heard that Holles, Coventry, Ashley and Anglesey could be depended on with Buckingham to support an alliance with France; and that Buckingham, seeking to win over all Clarendon's former 'friends and creatures', was already sure of Ashley.[1] He heard this from Sir Ellis Leighton, not the most reliable of informants, who for his own purposes was trying to give an inflated idea of his patron Buckingham's importance, and it would be unwise to rely on him for evidence that either Ashley or Sir William

---

[1] Colbert de Croissy, 5/15 and 19/29 Oct., 5/15 Nov. 1668. The mention of Sir William Coventry's name as a supporter of France does not inspire confidence.

Coventry was a friend of France; but as regards the relationship between Ashley and Buckingham others had the same impression as he did. Pepys heard that Ashley 'is turning about as fast as he can to the Duke of Buckingham's side, being in danger, it seems, of being otherwise out of play, which would not be convenient for him'.[1] Pepys's cynical interpretation was suggested by the fact that 'the Duke of Buckingham's side' certainly appeared to be the winning one. In February 1669 the Duke at last achieved his aim of getting the Duke of Ormond replaced by the ex-Presbyterian Robartes as Lord Lieutenant of Ireland, and in the same month Sir William Coventry, cut to the quick by being put on the stage in one of Buckingham's plays, challenged the Duke to a duel, only to find himself turned out of the Council and sent to the Tower at the King's command. In both cases Charles had other reasons for dismissing these men, as he hinted to his sister Henrietta,[2] but observers naturally thought that Buckingham's influence was the real cause. A few days later Buckingham was one of the select party who left with the King for Newmarket, so that ostensibly his favour with the King both in pleasure and business was high. On the other hand, while he was with Charles at Newmarket Ashley and Lauderdale were reported to be caballing with Arlington and Ormond against him at Hampton Court; this is a reminder, if one were needed, that much of the gossip about supposed political alliances has not necessarily a firm basis in fact.[3]

One scheme in which Buckingham, Arlington and Ashley were all concerned in the summer of 1669 was a proposal for a union with Scotland. In the previous year there had been abortive negotiations for a commercial union, and now a Scottish peer, the Earl of Tweeddale, pressed for a more far-reaching scheme of legislative union. On 25 June 1669, Ashley was admitted to a meeting of the committee of foreign affairs, at which the principal subject for discussion was a list of nineteen articles drawn up by a number of ministers, including Buckingham, Arlington, Ashley, Lauderdale and Tweeddale. As befitted a former member of the Council of State under the Instrument of Government, Ashley favoured the idea of union, and he strongly backed up Tweeddale when the latter urged that the King should nominate commissioners on his own authority to represent the two kingdoms in discussions, instead of leaving the nomination to be authorized by Act of Parliament as in 1604. At the time he was certainly prepared to make full use of royal powers to avoid delay, provided the cause was good enough. But he and Tweeddale were overruled, and the expected delay followed. After the necessary Acts had eventually been passed in 1670, English and Scottish commissioners gathered in September 1670, but

---

[1] Pepys, 12 Feb. 1669.

[2] Charles to Henrietta, 7 Mar. 1669, translated in C. H. Hartmann, *The King My Brother* (1954), p. 245.

[3] Newsletter in *H.M.C. Fleming MSS.*, p. 62; Colbert, 18/28 Mar.

when the Scots proved unwilling to consider a reduction of their existing parliamentary representation in any future combined Parliament, the meeting was adjourned and never reconvened. Since the scheme had first been mooted, both Lauderdale's own position and the King's authority in Scotland had been strengthened by the Act of Supremacy and the Militia Act which the Scottish Parliament had passed. With Scotland apparently firmly in control, there was no incentive to press on to union, especially as foreign affairs were claiming priority; and Ashley and others acquiesced in this situation, with how much reluctance is unknown.[1]

Some of the preoccupations which took precedence were inevitably parliamentary. There had been a long recess since May 1668, but all recesses come to an end. In August 1669 most politicians were diverting themselves in the ways traditional at that season: the King, on a hunting expedition in the New Forest, was inevitably invited to 'the little great Lord Ashley's house' at Wimborne St. Giles, though a slight shadow was cast on the proceedings by the news of the death of the Queen-Mother, Henrietta Maria, in France, and Ashley attended a meeting of those who were on the spot at Southampton to consider what this involved.[2] But behind all the diversions there lay the problem of the policy which the King should be advised to pursue towards Parliament when it met in October. There were those who thought that the Cavalier Parliament should not be allowed to reassemble at all: they favoured a dissolution in the hope that new elections might produce a House of Commons which would do the King's business better. At one point the French ambassador thought that both Buckingham and Arlington, though rivals in other respects, favoured this course of action because they were afraid of being impeached by the present lower House. There were still many followers of Clarendon in it, looking for an opportunity to revenge the fate of their fallen leader, and elections might get rid of them. It was also thought that Buckingham hoped to gain influence with his Dissenting friends by procuring the dissolution of the Parliament which had enacted the 'Clarendon Code'. However Charles was reluctant to dispense with the services of members who had been elected at the Cavalier high-water period in 1661, and who included many of his own office-holders, household servants, and dependants: there was a real danger that a new House of Commons might be more difficult to manage, not less. But there was a possibility that Charles's reluctance might be overcome if it was demonstrated that the existing House was impossible to work with; and it was rumoured that,

---

[1] Foreign Entry Book 176, 25 June 1669; Burnet, i. 505, 511; *Lauderdale Papers*, ed. O. Airy, vol. ii (Camden Society, 1885) esp. pp. 147–50, 159–63; *The Cromwellian Union*, ed. C. S. Terry (Scottish History Society, Edinburgh, 1902), Appendix, pp. 187–224; Sir George Mackenzie, *Memoirs of the Affairs of Scotland* (Edinburgh, 1821), pp. 193–212; Maurice Lee, Jr., *The Cabal* (Urbana, 1965), pp. 42–69.

[2] Capt. E. Fox to Sir R. Harley, 26 Aug. 1669, in *H.M.C. Portland MSS.*, iii. 311; Foreign Entry Book 176, 4 Sept. 1669.

with this in mind, Buckingham, Sir Thomas Osborne and others were planning to revive the dispute between Commons and Lords over the case of *Skinner* v. *East India Company* which had bedevilled the end of the previous session. It was to this that Ashley was alluding in the letter to Morrice previously quoted, when he said that 'Skinner's business . . . is by the state chemists like to be improved into a new parliament', shortly after the new session began.[1]

The second day of the new session (20 October 1669) was enlivened by the scattering of an anonymous libel, *The Alarum*, in Westminster Hall. The author, evidently an ex-Republican, gave a rather highly coloured warning against attempts to suppress popular liberties by the manipulation, bribery or intimidation of the House of Commons. It was the sort of argument about the growth of arbitrary government which was common Whig propaganda in the next decade; but on this occasion the future Whig leader was among those who were mercilessly attacked by name as tools of the obnoxious policy. 'Shall I forget my Lord Ashley? Good God! what a knave is here? This is knavery bound up in little, the very abridge ment of villainy. The world calls him an ingenious man; I suppose it is because he is not hanged, a thing he deserveth at least once a day. . . . His business at this time is to go of errands to Parliament men to convince them by his own experience how wise a thing it is to be a knave.' Arlington, Clifford, and Sir Thomas Littleton ('an angry man against the Court' who had recently been silenced by being made joint Treasurer of the Navy) were also abused by name; Buckingham, still the favourite of the radicals for joining with the government's critics in the years 1666 to 1668, was not. However the writer of this pamphlet, though he possessed a nice turn in invective, was a few years in advance of his time, and his work made no impact on the parliamentary debates.[2]

Instead the House turned once more to worry the bone of Skinner's case. In fairness to Buckingham, however, it must be said that (at least publicly) he tried to reconcile the two Houses; he warned the Lords not to reject outright the Commons' bill abolishing their claim to an original jurisdiction in certain cases because, he said, a dissolution might follow and a new House might be more violent than the present one, and because the privilege to which the Lords were clinging was an unnecessary one anyway. It seems that in order to justify his claim to the King to be able to manage the unruly Commons, he was at this time trying to ally his supporters with those of the Duke of York. Nothing is known of Ashley's activities in this connexion; but his reference to 'Skinner's business' in his

---

[1] Colbert, 18/28 Mar., 1/11, 15/25, 19/29 Apr. 1669; Ormond to Arran, 31 July 1669, MSS. Carte 50, fo. 58; Colbert, 21/31 Oct.; Lindenov (Danish ambassador), 5, 9, 12 Oct., in *The First Triple Alliance*, ed. W. Westergaard (New Haven, 1947), pp. 165–6, 168, 169–70.

[2] The most telling extracts from the paper are printed by Andrew Browning, *English Historical Documents*, vol. viii, *1660–1714* (1953), pp. 233–6.

S

letter to Morrice rather suggests indifference.[1] He was more interested in
the committee which the House of Lords set up to consider the causes of
the decay in trade, and the debates on the rate of interest which were
described in the previous chapter.[2] Another matter which claimed some
of his attention was the report which the commissioners for accounts at
long last made on the financial administration of the Dutch war of 1665
to 1667. After struggling for two years with the complexities of the government's accounting, they found it impossible to bring anything home to
anybody. So far as Ashley's prize accounts were concerned, they had no
serious allegations to make against him. There was vague talk of embezzlements at the ports in accordance with popular rumour, and the commissioners 'have used their best means to find out embezzlements, but
cannot encourage expectations of their making discoveries answerable to
the embezzlements'. After such a confession of defeat it is not surprising
to find that attendance at the Lords' committee on the report was very
slack, and nothing came of its debates. In the Commons' committee on
the same subject Ashley also escaped attack. The main weight of the
critics there fell on the former Treasurer of the Navy, Sir George Carteret,
in whose favour Ashley had written a letter to say that he and Carteret had
both on occasion pledged their own personal credits on behalf of the
government's urgent needs for the war. He would not try to make Carteret
a general scapegoat for the collective sins of the government,[3] nor on the
other hand try to divert anger on to the heads of the unpopular bankers.
'Neither can we complain of the bankers for it, since I believe we have
owed some of them near a million at a time, so frankly did they venture in
the King's affairs when they could command money. . . .' Since the government still needed loans from the bankers, he discreetly refrained from
saying that their profits were proportionate, although in the next year or
two at least he came to feel that they were excessive.[4]

In December 1669 Skinner's case produced the inevitable deadlock
between the two Houses, and the equally inevitable prorogation. An attempt
at a fresh start was made with a new parliamentary session on 14 February
1670, for the King was now desperately in need of financial assistance.
The problem was how to prevent Skinner's case from wrecking this session
as it had wrecked the two previous ones. It was Ashley who found the
solution. He suggested that the King should propose that each House should
erase from its journals all the previous resolutions relating to the matter;
neither House would then have given way, and the legal point would be
left conveniently unsettled. Skinner's mouth was apparently closed by
vague promises from Ashley of some compensation for the damages he

---

[1] Sandwich MS. Journal, 11 Nov. 1669, printed in F. R. Harris, *Life of the First Earl
of Sandwich* (1912), ii. 308; Colbert, 25 Nov./5 Dec.; Browning, *Danby* i. 73–75, iii.
33–42; p. 268 above.   [2] pp. 256–7 above.
[3] Carteret was, it must be remembered, a fellow-proprietor of Carolina.
[4] *H.M.C. Eighth Report*, i. 129, 131; *L.J.* xii. 261–2.

was claiming from the East India Company. These were not fulfilled, for the matter came up before the committee of foreign affairs again in 1671, when Ashley was instructed 'to endeavour to bring the East India Company to pay him £5,000. If he then refuse to accept it, the King has done what is fit in it.' Ashley's connexions with East India directors such as Sir John Banks could be used to the government's advantage.[1]

The Commons adopted Ashley's solution with some relief. The French ambassador thought that the friends of the Dissenters were disappointed that the dispute had not led Charles to dissolve his Anglican House of Commons, but that others were tired of the tedious squabble, and afraid that it might drive Charles to unparliamentary measures—even to alliance with France! Little did they know! Eventually an additional supply of £100,000 per annum was agreed on. From the King's point of view, any money was better than none, but £100,000 was little enough in comparison with the mountain of debt which was crushing his government; and on 18 March Ashley had to present to the House of Lords a bill to enable the King to sell some fee-farm rents, and so obtain some ready money by disposing of some of his permanent resources.[2]

Even the £100,000 of parliamentary supply was obtained from the Commons only as the price of the King's consent to a second and stiffer Conventicle Act, which was intended to stop some of the loopholes in the previous Act of 1664: for instance, it imposed penalties on Justices of the Peace and constables who turned a blind eye to the illegal meetings of their Nonconformist friends. When the bill went through the House of Lords some peers, ex-Presbyterians and others, opposed it and signed a formal Protest against it, but neither Ashley nor Buckingham did so, probably because it would have been futile to set the King's ministers against the House of Commons, and start a new dispute between the Houses. It may reasonably be surmised, however, that Ashley joined in the amendments by which the upper House reduced the penalties which the Commons wished to impose for attendance at conventicles. All reference to imprisonment was eliminated, and fines cut down by more than half. The Lords also made another amendment which attracted some attention, and of which Ashley disapproved. To the Commons' proviso 'that neither this Act, nor anything therein contained, shall extend to invalidate or avoid His Majesty's supremacy in ecclesiastical affairs . . .', the Lords added 'or to destroy any of His Majesty's rights, powers, or prerogatives, belonging to the imperial Crown of this realm, or at any time exercised or enjoyed by himself, or any of His Majesty's royal predecessors'. In spite of the fact that most of them were ex-Cavaliers, the Commons regarded

---

[1] J. Macpherson, *Original Papers* (1775), i. 53; Skinner's petition (undated), *Court Minutes of the East India Company, 1668–70*, ed. E. P. Sainsbury (1929), p. 397 (wrongly assigned to the year 1668 in *C.S.P.D. 1668–9*, p. 131); Foreign Entry Book 176, 2 July 1671.   [2] Colbert, 23 Feb./5 Mar. 1670; *L.J.* xii. 313; *H.M.C. Eighth Report*, p. 142.

this clause with grave suspicion, because it might be taken to imply the loss of everything which Kings had conceded to Parliaments in the past. Not all of them would have gone so far as Andrew Marvell, who wrote 'There was never so compendious a piece of absolute universal tyranny', but the House threw it out. The Lords widely accepted this, and at the conference at which they informed the Commons, it was noted that Ashley said of this proviso that 'the Commons had done very well in their amendments of it'. He was carefully dissociating himself from any suspicion of excessively exalting the royal prerogative.[1]

Overlapping with the debates on the Conventicle Bill there were other debates on a much more sensational bill, even though it was in appearance only a private one. Lord Roos, eldest son of the Earl of Rutland and brother-in-law of Ashley's son, had a wife who was a notorious and promiscuous adulteress. An Act had previously declared her children to be illegitimate, and in a church court Roos had obtained a 'divorce', but this only amounted to a legal separation from bed and board: it did not authorize him to re-marry. Accordingly he now moved for a second bill, dissolving his marriage and enabling him to marry again, and the question of principle was raised, whether Parliament was competent to pass such an Act and authorize a divorce. It was a delicate domestic problem; but it was more than that. On all sides the bill was regarded as a *ballon d'essai* to see if the King could be enabled to divorce the Queen and remarry.

By 1670 it was clear to everyone that Queen Catherine of Braganza was not going to bear Charles any children. From very soon after their marriage it had been rumoured that she was incapable of bearing children, and even that Clarendon had deliberately arranged the marriage in the interests of his son-in-law, the Duke of York, and thus of his own grandchildren. Once or twice there had been hopes of a child, but each time they had been disappointed, until on the last occasion, on 7 June 1669, a pet fox, jumping on to the Queen's bed, brought about a miscarriage. Thus a pet fox may have produced one of those dynastic accidents which modify the course of history. For the rest of Charles's life one of the central facts of English politics was that he happened to have no legitimate children. And a second basic fact was that his brother James was not universally beloved, and that there were those who did not welcome the prospect of his succeeding to the throne; this was the case even before James was known to be a Roman Catholic. To the end of his life James retained a pathetic memory of the days when he had been 'the darling of the nation' after his part in the sea-fight with the Dutch off Lowestoft in 1665, and he could not grasp why he lost this temporary popularity; but when in the summer of 1667 some people were thinking dark thoughts about the way in which the troops raised by the government might be used, it was James who was suspected

---

[1] *L.J.* xii. 325–6; *H.M.C. Eighth Report*, p. 142; *C.J.* ix. 148; A. Grey, *Debates* (1769), i. 246–50, 265; Marvell, *Works*, vol. ii, *Letters*, ed. H. M. Margoliouth (1927), p. 303.

of advising Charles to solve his difficulties by the use of force, rather than recall Parliament.[1] James was known to be much more authoritarian in temperament than his brother, and though his religion might be uncertain, his political views were not. In addition, those who had overthrown his father-in-law Clarendon had reason to fear that he would neither forget nor forgive.

In 1670 the King was in robust health and might reasonably be expected to live for many years. Nevertheless he would not live for ever, and the heir to the throne was necessarily a powerful political figure. There were already those who would breathe more freely if James did not occupy that position.

One way of evicting James from his position as heir would be to induce Charles to declare that he had been married to the mother of his son, the Duke of Monmouth. The exceptional honour of the dukedom which Charles bestowed upon him was not the only way in which Monmouth was indulged; it was easily observable that Charles was far more fond of him than of any other of his brood of illegitimate children. Almost from the Restoration, therefore, there had seemed a possibility that Charles might announce that Monmouth was legitimate[2]; perhaps he had after all been married to Lucy Walter, however unlikely that worthless creature may have seemed as a queen. In the autumn of 1667, when Charles turned against Clarendon but James obstinately defended his father-in-law, there was a fresh wave of rumours. This was not simply the kind of half-informed gossip which Pepys habitually picked up; Lord Conway wrote to Ormond in Dublin of his fears 'that either a bill of divorce is to follow, or a bill to affirm that the King was married to the Duke of Monmouth's mother, as Clarendon told me'. If no less a person than Clarendon thought that these were political possibilities, then they deserved serious consideration. Long afterwards, at the time of the Rye House Plot, the King himself confided to James that Ashley and the Earl of Carlisle had proposed that he should 'own' the Duke of Monmouth. Buckingham made the same proposal, but 'the King would not consent to this: yet he put it by in such a manner as made them all conclude, he wished it might be done, but did not know how to bring it about . . .'. Eventually, this refusal became more definite, but not before Buckingham had convinced himself that Charles was not irrevocably committed to the succession of James. Since this means was not feasible, he fell back on the alternative policy of procuring a divorce from the Queen on the grounds of her barrenness, so that Charles could remarry and raise a new heir. The Roos remarriage bill, if carried, would supply an admirable precedent for the principle of a divorce.[3]

---

[1] Pepys, 27, 29 July, 16 Nov. 1667.
[2] For such rumours, cf. Pepys, 27 Oct. 1662, 4, 14, 15 May, 9 Nov. 1663, 20 Jan., 8, 22 Feb. 1664, 16 Dec. 1666.
[3] Pepys, 11, 14 Sept., 4 Nov. 1667; Conway to Ormond, 5 Nov. 1667, MSS. Carte 36,

The bill therefore became a subject of bitter dispute. The Duke of York and all his supporters fought it: on the other hand Ashley was instrumental in bringing Lauderdale and Buckingham to combine to push the bill. The Earl of Anglesey also supported the bill, though it was commented that both his son and Ashley's might have a claim on the inheritance if Lord Roos died childless. The debates were long—that on 17 March lasted until almost ten at night, an unprecedented time for the House of Lords—and the majorities were small. Men noted with surprise that 'my Lord Buckingham sat it out to the last' with unusual conscientiousness. It was soon suspected that behind the scenes the King was in favour of the bill, particularly after 21 March, when to the astonishment of all Charles appeared in the House and calmly announced that he intended to revive a practice of his long-dead predecessors and attend the House's debates informally himself. Thereafter it became his practice to stand there comfortably with his back to the fire, listening to the debates (which he described as better than going to a play) and able to have a private word with individual peers when this might be useful. His first appearance in the House came during a debate on the Conventicle Bill, but it was widely supposed that his real aim was to influence the debates on the Roos private bill.[1]

At the House of Lords' debate on the third reading, which took place in the King's presence on 28 March, Ashley spoke strongly in favour of granting Roos permission to remarry. In so doing he made clear his own general attitude to the subject of marriage and divorce. Before the time of the Council of Trent, he argued, marriage was a civil contract and managed by the civil magistrate; this was as it should be, since nothing in Scripture could be produced to the contrary—it was not necessary to find a positive text permitting a certain course of action, or this would disqualify many laws. So far as such cases as Roos's was concerned, the Council of Antioch in A.D. 436 had allowed remarriage—'in this case and divers others'. Till marriage was made a sacrament by the Council of Trent, he repeated, it was never taken wholly out of the hands of the civil magistrate; 'and even the church of Rome never left this case desperate, but found place to relieve many great and able families as there was occasion'. He went on to quote the medieval canon lawyer, Lyndwood, as saying that if either party to a marriage entered a monastery the marriage was entirely dissolved; implying that if the principle of dissolution and therefore remarriage was admitted in

---

fo. 25; J. Macpherson, op. cit. i. 44; Burnet, i. 469–70; Colbert, 10/20 June 1669. Cf. also Marvell's opinion that 'Lauderdale at one ear talks to the King of Monmouth and Buckingham at the other of a new Queen'. (Letter to Popple, 21 Mar. 1670, in *Works*, ed. H. M. Margoliouth, 1927, ii. 302.)

[1] Conway to Sir G. Rawdon, 15 Mar., in *Rawdon Papers*, ed. E. Berwick (1819), pp. 239–40; Marvell to Popple, 21 Mar. and 14 Apr., op. cit. pp. 301–3; Orrery to Conway, 12 and 19 Mar. in *C.S.P. Ireland, 1669–70*, pp. 85, 88–89; *L.J.* xii. 300, 311, 316, 318; Burnet, i. 471–2, 492–3; Colbert, 24 Mar./3 Apr.

such cases, it must be possible in others too.[1] The significant feature of all this is not the questionable interpretation of medieval thinking on marriage, or the knowledge of early church history, or the inconsistency of declaring it a matter for the state and then appealing to a Church Council, but the strongly secular outlook implicit in the whole argument. Marriage was not a sacrament but a civil contract, and matrimonial cases should be decided by the 'civil magistrate' and not by any church court or in deference to the views of the bishops (who were almost unanimously opposed to the bill). An appeal to Scripture should only be decisive where it contained a specific command. This was consistent with his thinking at other times. He had once been a member of the Barebones Parliament which had legislated for the solemnization and registration of marriages by Justices of the Peace; and frequently during his lifetime he was opposed to the authority of the Church, particularly of the bishops, intervening in the affairs of laymen. He was abreast of a growing, secularizing movement of thought, and his arguments were not simply concocted for temporary political purposes, though these certainly existed, for by backing the bill Ashley was unmistakably throwing in his lot with the opponents of James, Duke of York, although he had not to fear (like Buckingham and others) that James would revenge the fall of Clarendon. The fact was that in ideas (political and religious) and in temperament he and James were becoming more and more antipathetic to one another.

The bill passed the House of Lords in spite of the protests of James and his friends and the bishops, and it then went through the Commons more easily, though here too there was a highly vocal minority.[2] Lord Roos was successful; the question remained whether the precedent of a divorce would be used to benefit the King. For some days possible new brides for him were a fascinating topic of conversation. Marvell wrote that 'the King disavows it, yet he has said in public, he knew not why a woman might not be divorced for barrenness, as a man for impotency'. Baptist May, the notorious Keeper of the Privy Purse, who was in the intrigue, later claimed that matters had gone so far that a day was fixed for a motion to be made in the House of Commons; but three days beforehand, he said, the King sent for him and told him 'that matter must be let alone, for it would not do'. Wilder schemes of getting rid of the Queen were also talked of: it was said that Buckingham proposed kidnapping her and sending her to a plantation (was Carolina intended?), 'when she would be well and carefully looked to, but never heard of any more', and Parliament could grant a divorce on grounds of desertion. Charles rejected this idea with horror, saying that 'it was a wicked thing to make a poor lady miserable, only

[1] Sandwich MSS. Journal, quoted in F. R. Harris, *Life of the First Earl of Sandwich* (1912), ii. 328–9.
[2] *L.J.* xii. 328–9; *C.J.* ix. 150; Grey, i. 251–63; Orrery to Conway, 3 Apr., *C.S.P. Ireland 1669–70*, p. 103.

because she was his wife, and had no children by him, which was no fault of hers'; but he was said to have contemplated an alternative proposal that the Queen should be persuaded to become a nun, until it became clear that she was not attracted to the idea. Lady Castlemaine, now the Duchess of Cleveland, also disliked the idea of a new Queen who would be a rival to herself.[1]

The point in all this is that the King was prepared to countenance talk of all sorts of schemes for a divorce, but that when he was called on to take action, he drew back. It may be that he did seriously consider a divorce, but it is more likely that he was playing an elaborate game to divert attention from his negotiations with Louis XIV. Behind this smokescreen the preparations for the Secret Treaty of Dover were being completed—it was signed within six weeks of the royal assent being given to the Roos bill—and it suited him admirably to have all but one or two of his ministers preoccupied with debates and intrigues of this kind. It was on gaining the long-desired French alliance that he was concentrating his efforts, and at this time anything else must be subordinated to it. One such scheme at a time was enough. If this is the correct interpretation of Charles's conduct, then like much of his dissimulation it was successful in the short run, for no one suspected what was to happen at Dover; but in the long run, as usual, it had serious disadvantages. Ashley and others remembered that once the King had been prepared at least to consider the possibility of ridding himself of the Queen and depriving James of the succession. If he had considered it once, he might do so again, particularly if a suitable amount of pressure was exercised to overcome his show of reluctance. The result was to be evident in the turbulent days of the Exclusion crisis.

Nothing is known of Ashley's relationship with his prospective victim, Catherine of Braganza, at any time in the reign. She had as little wit or beauty to commend herself to him as to Charles. On the other hand, it is known that he was on friendly terms with two or three of the King's mistresses. Possibly in 1670 he was supposed to have 'managed' one of them, the daughter of a clergyman named Robarts. She must have been unique amongst Charles's loves, for in spite of 'many scandalous disorders' she retained a lively sense of sin and eventually died a most edifying death.[2] She sounds a most unlikely companion for Charles, whose loves were said to 'be the effects of health and a good constitution, with as little mixture of the seraphic part as ever man had',[3] and we are not told in what the 'management' consisted. At an earlier date Ashley had attended Lady Castlemaine's famous supper parties, and yet he also contrived to win the friendship of Frances Stuart, the original Britannia whose figure graced English coins. That this was not merely a matter of ingratiating himself

---

[1] Marvell, op. cit. ii. 303; Burnet, i. 472–4 (derived from May and Sir Robert Moray).
[2] Burnet, i. 475.
[3] Halifax's 'Character of Charles II', in the *Life* by H. C. Foxcroft (1898), ii. 348.

with a powerful favourite is shown by the fact that the friendship continued after Frances Stuart, rejecting Charles's advances, had eloped with the Duke of Richmond. Richmond was Lord Lieutenant of Dorsetshire and a friend of Ashley's, and in 1669 Ashley did what he could to recover for him the royal favour which the elopement had cost him: he prompted the Duke on the best way to approach Charles in order to obtain an embassy to Poland. These relations with royal favourites are a reminder that Ashley moved easily and without constraint at Charles's Court, as he did in all other circles: he was catholic in his friendships, if in nothing else.[1]

In May 1670, however, came the hour of a different royal favourite, the King's sister Henrietta, Duchess of Orleans. For three weeks Ashley and Sir John Duncombe sat alone at the Treasury Board in London, while their colleague was with the King, the Court and the French ambassador at Dover, welcoming 'Minette'. There amidst all the festivities the secret treaty was signed which, if it had been successful, would have secured for Louis XIV dominance over Western Europe, and would have tied Charles II's fortune to his. The treaty provided first of all that Charles should declare himself a Catholic: he was to choose his own time for this, but was to receive immediately two million livres (£150,000), and should Charles's declaration make his subjects rebellious, Louis was to assist him with 6,000 troops. The second half of the treaty provided that Louis and Charles jointly should attack the Dutch Republic. Charles was to provide the larger share of the naval forces (fifty ships as against thirty), while Louis provided the bulk of the land forces and an annual subsidy of three million livres (£225,000). The gains which Charles was to make from the war were defined and limited to Sluis, Cadzand and Walcheren at the mouth of the River Scheldt. Louis's prospective gains were undefined and unlimited.

This momentous treaty was signed without immediately arousing the suspicions of anyone. Henrietta's visit was so brief, and dancing and feasting took up so much of it that it seemed impossible that any serious negotiation could have been carried on. Even later, when men suspected the existence of a secret and sinister understanding with Louis, it was commonly supposed that this had first been suggested, not completed, by Henrietta at Dover. Charles's success in hoodwinking his people, and all his ministers save Arlington and Clifford, was complete. Nevertheless the preparation needed for a renewed war against the Dutch would be considerable. A week after the Court had returned to London, the King himself, with James and some of the naval officials, attended the meeting of the Treasury Commissioners to examine the extent of the Navy's debts and the cost of repairs to the ships. It was 'ordered that the preparations of the

---

[1] Ashley to Duke of Richmond, 9 Aug. 1669, Add. MSS. 21947, fo. 247. The reference to a rumour of Ashley's death in the Duchess's letter to her husband, 6 Sept., ibid. pp. 259–60, seems more likely to refer to a later illness in 1670. Cf. C. H. Hartmann, *La Belle Stuart* (1924), pp. 168 sqq., 181.

Navy be gone in hand with all speed', and shortly afterwards Pepys and the Navy Victualler attended to provide further information about the financial needs of the Navy.[1] In these circumstances Charles decided that he must associate three more of his ministers, Buckingham, Lauderdale and Ashley, with his plans for a Dutch war, though not with the so-called Catholic clauses of the Treaty. Buckingham was the most dangerous to his scheme, for in so far as it was ever possible to predict anything about him, he was likely to oppose any policy which Arlington advocated, and his connexions with members of the Commons might be very awkward for the King, as they had been for Clarendon in 1667. Ashley was probably taken into the scheme because in his position on the Treasury Commission he was likely to guess the purpose for which money was being spent on the Navy, and possibly also because he was thought likely to want a war against England's chief commercial competitor. Lauderdale was selected partly as a friend of the other two, and partly because his recent successes in Scotland had shown what a useful servant of the King he might be.

The method which Charles chose to enlist their support was a charac-teristic one. Weighing up Buckingham's character to a nicety, he deter-mined to play on his vanity and encourage him to suggest a French alliance against the Dutch as though it was his own idea. This was the more easily done because Buckingham had actually suggested a French alliance three years earlier, and with the aid of his client Sir Ellis Leighton kept up friendly relations with the French ambassador; and the bait of being the commander of the English contingent which accompanied Louis's army was dangled before him. Thus tempted, Buckingham came out with a brilliant new plan for a French alliance. At a 'cabal conference' at the beginning of July, he proposed it to his colleagues. The French ambassador later heard that Buckingham was enthusiastic; that Lauderdale, 'who always, and rightly, puts himself on the side to which he sees his master leaning', was of the same opinion, and that Ashley was not opposed to it, but said that in a matter of such importance he wanted some time to consider it.[2]

Thus Ashley was the last of the 'Cabal' to fall in with the idea of a French alliance against the Dutch. Yet by a curious fate he more than any of the others became associated with the policy involved. Others besides Dryden saddled him with the responsibility for 'breaking the triple bond', and going over from the Dutch side to the French, not realizing that the responsibility was essentially Charles's own. This was primarily because of the vehemence of the famous *Delenda est Carthago* speech to Parliament in February 1673. Even Ashley's grandson and his apologists felt un-comfortable about this and sought to apologize for it; the speech was said to have been prepared by the foreign committee for him reluctantly to deliver, and he was supposed to have been so disturbed that he had to have

[1] 14 June and 1 July 1670, in *C.T.B. 1669–72*, pp. 450, 469.   [2] Colbert, 4/14 July 1670.

Locke standing at his elbow with a written copy, ready to prompt him.[1] Such explanations do not carry much conviction, and on the basis of this speech almost entirely he has commonly been portrayed as the most impassioned of all the enemies of the Dutch—one who believed that English and Dutch were as irreconcilable as Romans and Carthaginians had been. With his well-known interest in trade and colonization, this hatred of the Dutch seemed consistent. Yet this interpretation of the speech, in spite of its sensational use of the phrase *Delenda est Carthago*, is a mistaken one. More will be said of it in its proper chronological place[2]; it is sufficient here to say that the apparent vehemence was purely tactical, designed to carry away the House of Commons on a wave of wartime emotion and secure money for a policy which the House had not begun. His real opinions were not necessarily so extreme, and certainly the policy he defended in the speech was not one which he had first devised. He was not so zealous an enemy of the Dutch as Clifford, who had wanted a third Dutch war almost from the end of the second. But he did adopt the idea of a third Dutch war, and for two years he took part in preparations for it without any sign of reluctance. The simple fact was that for two decades Ashley had listened to the complaints of English merchants about Dutch competition, and war was only too obvious a course. Not having been on the committee of foreign affairs, he had had nothing to do with the policy of the Triple Alliance in January 1668. And precisely in the critical month of July 1670, when he was called upon to decide, Ashley was made one of the royal commissioners appointed to discuss with the Dutch ambassador a projected treaty on overseas trade which had hung fire for the past two years. In the conversations which followed Van Beuningen was full of professions of good-will and the need for co-operation between the two peoples in Europe, but he also made it plain that the Dutch would make no concessions in the East Indies or elsewhere overseas. These could only be obtained by force.[3]

If there was to be a war, it made good military sense to seek a French alliance. In the previous war, when the French had been on the side of the Dutch, the French fleet had been large enough to be of a considerable nuisance value, and it was plainly better to have it under English control next time. Still more, Louis XIV's armies could invade the United Provinces from the land side and force the Dutch to concentrate their war effort on defending themselves there. The question remained whether other aspects of the problem were of more importance than the military one. Could England view with equanimity the possibility of Louis XIV winning land victories and power even greater than he already possessed?

[1] Third Earl of Shaftesbury to Jean Le Clerc, 8 Feb. 1705, Amsterdam University Library, Remonstrants MSS., J. 20.   [2] See pp. 316–17 below.
[3] Foreign Entry Book 176, 10 July 1670; Van Beuningen, 23 July/2 Aug., 13/23 Aug., Add. MSS. 17677, BB.

Ashley had never liked France or the political and religious system over which the Bourbons ruled. Back in 1643 at Oxford he had disliked the influence which Henrietta Maria, a daughter of France, had exercised over the counsels of Charles I. When he had been a member of Cromwell's Council of State, discussing the possibilities of choosing either France or Spain as an ally against the other, it seems that he may have preferred Spain. In 1660 one of the reasons why he had favoured the return of Hyde when others wished to exclude him was the belief that Hyde would oppose foreign, i.e. French, influence over the King. In 1665 he had welcomed the extension of the war to include France. He had never, like Buckingham, been dazzled by the magnificence of Louis XIV's Court, nor was he at any time on familiar terms with any French ambassador, as were Buckingham, Arlington, Clifford, Holles, and others. This may safely be inferred from the very scanty references to conversations with him in the ambassadors' despatches, and the tone of those few which are to be found. Furthermore, the opinion of the merchant classes in the City of London, with which Ashley was well familiar, was steadily hardening against France. It was axiomatic that the balance of trade with France was as unfavourable as that with Spain was favourable, and nothing ever came of proposals for an Anglo-French commercial treaty.[1] Again, the statement which is often made that the Anglo-French colonial rivalry of the following century could not have been foreseen in 1670 is completely erroneous. There were those at the time who did foresee it. Amongst them was Benjamin Worsley, whom we have seen advising Ashley in the Councils of Trade and Plantations. In a memorandum addressed to Ashley on 14 August 1668 Worsley complained about Colbert's protective tariffs; in a later one of 24 February 1669, dealing with Jamaica, he talked at length of the danger of French ambitions in the Caribbean, and recommended that England should co-operate with Spain against them.[2] Indeed in 1666 the French had seized several of the Leeward Islands from the English, and the long negotiations which dragged on about the restoration of the English portion of St. Kitts, although it was of no great importance in itself, were symptomatic of a growing incompatibility of interest in the area. Ashley was well aware of all this, and in so far as he wanted friendly relations between his Carolina and Bahamas colonies and the Spaniards in Florida, it may be thought that he inclined to Worsley's view.

For all these reasons it is unlikely that Ashley was particularly enthusiastic about the prospect of a French alliance, even though he was entirely unaware of the 'Catholic design' and Charles's desire to reach a special relationship with Louis XIV. For him (in contrast to Charles) the French alliance was essentially a short-term expedient to achieve victory over the Dutch, not a permanent feature of English diplomacy. As such an expedient

[1] Cf. Margaret Priestley, 'London Merchants and Opposition Politics in Charles II's Reign', *Bull. Inst. Hist. Res.* (1956), pp. 205–19.   [2] Shaftesbury Papers, XLIX, 26, 4.

it came very near achieving its objective, for in 1672 the Dutch survived the invasion of Turenne's army by the narrowest possible margin. But Ashley, like Charles, may be criticized for failing to appreciate what the consequences of victory would have been. Inroads into the commercial supremacy of the Dutch would have been bought at the expense of leaving Louis XIV the master of north-western Europe. With the Dutch defeated, Spain and the Emperor helpless, he would have been able to pursue freely his expansionist aims in Flanders and on the Rhine; he could have acquired the domination over the Low Countries which it has always been a cardinal point of English foreign policy to prevent. It is true that Louis promised to maintain his Treaty of Aix-la-Chapelle of 1668 with Spain, but had he been victorious in 1672 he could have ignored this promise with impunity; and had Carlos II of Spain died in the 1670s (as appeared likely) Louis could have fought a Spanish succession war under much more advantageous conditions than he did thirty years later. The implicit price of the French alliance was the prospect of having to accept such a situation. Ashley was too insular in outlook to appreciate the danger properly. With his interests mainly in England or overseas, he cared comparatively little what went on across the Channel. Neither in 1668 nor in 1677–8 when other Englishmen were concerned about the fate of Flanders is there much evidence of his interest in it: at all events it was low in his list of priorities, as it was for Charles. It was fortunate for England and for Europe that William of Orange inspired resistance to the danger of a Bourbon supremacy on land.

So Ashley allowed himself to become the accomplice of Charles II in his foreign policy, and all through the autumn of 1670 he was associated in negotiations with the French ambassador, until on 21 December he signed a treaty, together with Clifford, Arlington, Buckingham and Lauderdale. It was this treaty alone, therefore, which permits historians to speak of a CABAL; it is commonly called the *traité simulé* or bogus treaty, because it was designed to delude Ashley, Buckingham and Lauderdale to accept a line of action which had already been agreed on in the previous Secret Treaty. As was only to be expected, the treaty confined itself to speaking of the proposed war on the Dutch and made no mention of the 'Catholic clauses'; by arrangement between Louis and Charles, the subsidy promised to enable the King to declare himself a Catholic was concealed in a total of £375,000 promised for the war. In one respect Ashley, Buckingham and Lauderdale had proved hard bargainers; they insisted on adding to the English share of the spoils the islands of Goeree and Woorne. The French anbassador complained privately to Charles that this was more than had been promised in the Treaty of Dover, but he received no satisfaction, and Goeree and Woorne were added to Sluis, Cadzand and Walcheren to make doubly sure of future English control of the mouths of the Scheldt and Rhine.[1]

---

[1] Cf. Sir K. Feiling, *British Foreign Policy 1660–72* (1930), p. 313; Colbert, 6/16 and 13/23 Oct.

Interrupted by another serious illness in September 1670, which even led to 'a very strong report that my Lord Ashley should be dead',[1] Ashley threw himself into these negotiations and identified himself completely with the new policy. Sir William Temple, the great advocate of friendship between English and Dutch, returning from Holland and calling on Arlington, was surprised and hurt to be kept waiting for an hour and a half while the Secretary conferred with Ashley. Buckingham, Ashley and Lauderdale were so eager for war that they urged that the attack should be brought forward to the spring of 1671 instead of being left until 1672. Ashley was also reported to be endeavouring 'par l'adresse de son esprit' to break off the agreement which the second Secretary of State, Sir John Trevor, had reached with the Dutch over the colony of Surinam in Guiana; alleged ill-treatment of English proprietors was needed as a possible pretext for war. Having made up his mind on war, he was as unscrupulous as any of his colleagues about the way in which war was to be brought on.[2]

All this meant that Ashley was now a much more important figure than he had previously been. Still not so prominent in the King's counsels as Arlington or Buckingham, he was nevertheless one of the five signatories of the *traité simulé* and thus one of the five on whom the King depended for the carrying out of his new policy. It was natural that in the course of these same months in the autumn of 1670 he became a regular member of the 'cabinet council', or committee of foreign affairs, which was competent to discuss all confidential matters. Ashley was a useful man for Charles to have on it in a number of different ways; for instance, when the committee discussed 'a factious endeavour in the City to put by Sir Richard Ford for being chosen mayor', Ashley was asked to 'speak with such of the City in this matter, as he can influence'.[3] In the City, in Parliament, in the Councils of Trade and Plantations, at the Treasury Board, at the committee of foreign affairs and in the King's innermost counsels, Ashley was a man who had to be considered when the year 1670 gave way to 1671, and it is not surprising that as the months passed by there were more and more rumours of political promotion for him. What Ashley did not realize was the way in which he had been made a cat's-paw of the King's foreign policy. Charles, watching him engaged in the long mock negotiations with Colbert de Croissy, must have laughed up his sleeve and congratulated himself on his powers of manipulation; he still regarded Ashley as a former member of Cromwell's Council of State who could not, like Arlington, be trusted with his real secrets, but of whom he could make good use. It was not a promising basis for a cordial, or a permanent, relationship.

[1] Downing to Duncombe, 8 Sept. 1670, *C.T.B. 1669–72*, p. 661.
[2] Temple to Sir J. Temple, 12/22 Nov. 1670, *Works* (1754), iii. 495–6; Colbert, 23 Oct./ 2 Nov. and 22 Sept./2 Oct. (quoting Lauderdale).
[3] Foreign Entry Book 176, 23 Sept. 1670.

CHAPTER XIV

MONEY, RELIGION, AND WAR (1670-2)

> How can the nation ever thrive
> Whilst 'tis governed by these five,
> The Formal Ass, the Mastiff Dog,
> The Mole, the Devil and the Hog.[1]

ONE of the many fallacious statements commonly made about the Secret Treaty of Dover is that Charles was driven into the arms of Louis XIV by the niggardliness of his House of Commons. From the financial point of view, the proposal to wage another war made a bad situation worse. So far from postponing bankruptcy, the treaty accelerated it; for the £150,000 which Charles had squeezed out of Louis by means of the 'Catholic clause' was miserably inadequate for the preparations which were required, and the annual subsidy of £225,000 would not be due until 1672. These sums must be compared with the two and a half millions which Parliament had voted at the end of 1664, shortly before the beginning of the previous war; and there was the added consideration that the burden of debt was far greater in 1670 than in 1664, and the government's credit correspondingly weaker. The French money would undeniably be useful, but far more would have to be found somehow from some other sources. This preoccupation was central to all the deliberations of the King's ministers between the signing of the *traité simulé* in December 1670 and the outbreak of war in March 1672.

Inevitably much of the task fell upon Ashley. He was Chancellor of the Exchequer and had been concerned with the royal revenues ever since 1661, so that he had far longer experience than his two colleagues on the Treasury Commission, Sir Thomas Clifford and Sir John Duncombe. He had invaluable acquaintances in the City whom he could press to lend money[2]; and he had the right businesslike approach. He saw that the King's forts and castles were not exempted from excise duty, cut down the claims of the King's ambassadors for extravagant allowances and those of the excise farmers for excessive defalcations, complained bitterly of the lack of method in the Navy Office, and insisted that every assistance should be given to the Chimney money farmers to levy their unpopular tax.[3] Sir Thomas Clifford, eager, impulsive, hot-headed and ready for extreme

---

[1] Add. MSS. 23722, fo. 4ᵛ. A marginal note identifies the five as Arlington, Treasurer Clifford, Chancellor 'Cooper', Buckingham and Lauderdale.
[2] Cf. Downing to Ashley, 29 Oct. 1669, in *C.T.B. 1669-72*, p. 293.
[3] Ibid. pp. 10, 188, 285, 147, 151, 352; Pepys, 12 Feb. 1669.

courses, was rapidly growing in the royal favour, but at the beginning of
1671 he could not compete in experience, and men naturally speculated
that Ashley would be promoted to be Lord Treasurer.[1]

Yet Ashley and his colleagues were powerless to arrest the steady
deterioration of the financial position. Economies in expenditure could
hardly have saved enough, but in any case they would have needed stiffer
royal backing than they received at the court of Charles II. Some capital
assets could be sold; Ashley had introduced into the previous parliamentary session a bill for the sale of the King's fee-farm rents. There
remained the possibility of an appeal to the House of Commons for assistance in fitting out the Navy. Ironically such an appeal had been made at
the opening of a new session on 24 October 1670, that is, after the signing
of the Treaty of Dover and while Ashley and the other members of the
Cabal were engaged in negotiating the *traité simulé*. Yet Sir Orlando
Bridgeman, who had been Lord Keeper since the fall of Clarendon but
was not in the secret, was permitted by his colleagues to appeal for money
to enable the King to meet his obligations under the Triple Alliance which
was secretly being discarded; this was the theme of the Lord Keeper's
speech in support of the King's address to both Houses.[2] Ashley must
have read it (for he was not present) with rather mixed feelings, and in fact
Charles's government eventually had to pay the inevitable price of such
deception, by forfeiting the trust of the House of Commons. But the
future could take care of itself; the immediate question was whether the
House would vote the money. On 27 October Clifford and Downing
outlined the financial position to the Commons, estimating 'the debt at
interest' at £1,300,000, and the 'charge of setting out the Navy' at £800,000,
and appealing for additional subsidies to meet these needs.[3]

For some time the outcome did not look very hopeful. A proposal for
the obvious Land Tax was rejected,[4] and various inadequate expedients
were discussed. One of these, a proposal for a tax on playhouses, led to a
sensational incident involving Ashley's nephew by his first marriage, Sir
John Coventry. When courtier members complained that this would be a
tax on the King's pleasures, Coventry inquired whether the King's pleasures
lay among the men or the women that acted—a reference to Nell Gwyn
and others—and was rewarded by having his nose slit by some Court
bravos one dark night on his way home from the tavern. The incident
draws attention to the rooted disinclination of country gentlemen like
Coventry to supply money for the extravagances of Charles and his
Court—a disinclination which was to be one motive for the growth of the
'Country party' which Shaftesbury was later to lead. When the incident

[1] Add. MSS. 36916, fo. 222.

[2] *L.J.* xii. 352–3. The speech had previously been approved by the committee of foreign
affairs (including Ashley and all the so-called Cabal) on 16 Oct. (Foreign Entry Book 176).

[3] Grey, i. 270–1.   [4] Debate of 1 Dec. ibid., i. 314–17.

occurred it seemed to bode ill for Charles's hopes of supply; while the House of Commons was passing an avenging bill, the new Customs farmers were behindhand with their advances of ready money, and at the end of January 1671 the Navy Victualler was proclaiming desperately that without money he could not go on.[1] One possibility of saving money which Ashley considered at this point was the evacuation of the expensive garrison of Tangier, which Catherine of Braganza had brought in her dowry[2]; but for the moment Tangier was reprieved.

Yet from this point matters took a turn for the better from the government's point of view. After Ashley had helped to smooth over a difference between the two Houses over the clauses of the Coventry Act,[3] the House of Commons proved to be, if not as generous as Charles would have liked, then at least more generous than he might have expected. In addition to a subsidy bill, they passed a bill imposing duties on legal proceedings and an additional excise bill; and a fourth bill would have increased the duties on imports of sugar and tobacco. On this bill, however, the members of the Cabal were at odds with one another, with the result that another dispute arose between the two Houses, Parliament was finally prorogued, and a bill which would have produced at least £160,000 per annum[4] was lost. The occasion for the dispute was the different rates to be imposed on imported refined and unrefined sugar, a matter in which the interests of the London merchants and refiners and those of the colonial planters conflicted. In the House of Commons the London sugar refiners secured the adoption of their view. Whereas previously the duty on white sugar had been three and a third times that on brown, unrefined sugar, the House was persuaded to fix the rates at $1d.$ per lb., and $\frac{1}{4}d.$ per lb., respectively. But those Barbados planters who wished to profit from refining their own sugar on the spot now protested, and, including one of Ashley's partners in the colonization of Carolina, set to work to organize the presentation of their case to the House of Lords. In their fight to reduce the rate on white sugar they were supported by papers written by Benjamin Worsley, and they succeeded in convincing Buckingham, Halifax, Ashley, the Earl of Sandwich, and others. In his manuscript journal Sandwich himself assumed full responsibility for the reduction in the duty on unrefined sugar in committee in the House of Lords, 'that being principally carried out by me (though my Lord Ashley also was fully of the same mind and did a good part therein)'.[5] Ashley was suspected of being influenced by personal interest here, but he had sold his Barbados plantation twenty years earlier, and was not in fact a partner with Colleton in the Barbados trade as some

---

[1] Foreign Entry Book 176, 29 Jan., 5, 12 Feb. 1671.
[2] Luke's Journal, 4 Feb., Add. MSS. 36528, quoted by E. M. G. Routh, *Tangier* (1912), p. 236.   [3] *L.J.* xii. 419; Grey, op. cit. i. 377–83, 387.
[4] Sandwich's estimate; see his MS. Journal, quoted in F. R. Harris, *Life of the First Earl of Sandwich* (1912), ii. 335. Others put the figure higher.
[5] Ibid.

T

said.[1] Though they did share an interest in Carolina, and Ashley may have been influenced to some extent by that, it is better to point to the conjunction of the opinions of the three 'colonial experts', Sandwich, the President of the newly formed Council of Plantations, Ashley, its inspirer, and Worsley, its adviser. From the point of view of the development of the colonies there was a good case for favouring the interests of the sugar planters, whose prosperity had been much affected of late by overproduction and competition from other sources. It is significant that when a committee of the House of Lords prepared a reasoned statement for a conference with the Commons on 12 April, they referred not only to the rightful proportion of the duties on brown and white sugar, but to the desirability of defeating French, Dutch and Brazilian competition by underselling; 'and if once we could become the sole or principal vendor of sugar in Europe, the advantages to this kingdom thereby would be more than is needful to enumerate upon this occasion'. The document is generally concerned with long-term colonial policy rather than considerations of immediate self-interest.[2]

It was a complex problem on which the committee of the House of Lords accepted the opinion of its colonial pundits, and resolved without a division to reduce the duty on imported white sugar from $1d.$ to $\frac{5}{8}d.$ per lb.; the duty on brown sugar was to remain at $\frac{1}{4}d.$ Ashley reported this amendment to the House, which accepted it, and the bill was returned to the Commons. Sandwich was convinced that the Commons would have accepted the changes but for the opposition of what he called 'the Court party' under the influence of Arlington, who he said wanted to impute to his rival Buckingham (who favoured the amendment) the obstruction of a money bill, and so to destroy his favour with the King. It is certain that a prominent part was played in the Commons discussions by Sir Robert Carr, Clifford, Sir Richard Temple, and other followers of Arlington, who could stand forth to the Commons as champions of their rights in money bills, and to the King as the opponents of a reduction of duty and consequent loss of revenue. Under their influence the issue of colonial policy disappeared from sight before the constitutional issue of whether the Lords had a right to amend money bills, and a deadlock rapidly developed. At a conference between the two Houses Ashley defended the rights of the peers and pointed to what the logical result of the Commons' denial of them might be: 'This will invert the course of Parliaments; by the same nature, freedom of debate, and all parliamentary things, fall; and by the same reason, anything of any foreign nature whatsoever' might be tacked to a money

[1] C.S.P.D. 1671, p. 497.

[2] L.J. xii. 486–7. For literature on both sides of the question see Shaftesbury Papers, XLIV, 75; C.S.P.D. 1671, pp. 117–120; C.S.P. Col. 1669–74, pp. 214–16; H.M.C. Ninth Report, pt. ii, House of Lords MSS. pp. 8–9, 10–13. The best account is in G. L. Beer, The Old Colonial System (1912), pt. i, i. 149–59.

bill without the Lords being able to discuss it. Ashley was maintaining his characteristic view of the independent position of the House of Lords in the constitution, though it would be wrong to blame him for the outcome; it was a view which the peers as a whole not unnaturally shared without any need for instigation by anyone. The Commons however did not shrink back before the revolutionary prospect which Ashley described, and, led by courtiers, obstinately defended the principle which eventually triumphed under the Liberal heirs of the Whigs and the 'Country Party'.[1]

The King promptly prorogued Parliament on 22 April 1671, and the bill for additional impositions was therefore lost, and Charles deprived of much-needed supplies. Buckingham later told Colbert that it was not his fault but Arlington's; Arlington had persuaded the King to prorogue, without Buckingham having any part in it, and contrary to the promise Buckingham and Ashley had given the House from the King only the previous day; a million pounds sterling had been lost for the sake of a week or ten days' patience. He went on to argue that Parliament would have to be recalled anyway to provide the money needed for the war.[2] But in this he was wrong. Charles now decided that it was futile to look to the House of Commons for assistance, and, as a result of repeated prorogations, Parliament was not allowed to meet again until February 1673. If Buckingham and Ashley urged that Parliament should be called, they could be reminded of the futility of the debates on this bill and the 'millions' which had been lost,[3] and they found themselves willy-nilly embarked on a non-parliamentary course of policy which only success could excuse.

The episode is also significant in another way: it marks a definite decline in Buckingham's importance. Much of this had come from the way in which, in the sessions of 1667 and 1668, he had claimed to influence the attitudes of the House of Commons through his followers there; the events of 1671 had shown how limited this influence was, and in any case it was not now proposed to allow the House to meet. Though Buckingham had exalted ideas of his own abilities as a diplomat and a general, no-one else shared them, and he was incapable of any administrative duties more onerous than those of Master of the Horse; he could contribute nothing to the war effort. On the other hand Ashley's importance was increasing with the King's need for able servants to prepare for and run the war. He became regarded less as a supporter of Buckingham and more as a power in his own right. He was still on good terms with Buckingham—in February he had shared with the King the dishonourable duty of being godparents to the son of the Countess of Shrewsbury, who was impudently

---

[1] Sandwich's Journal, in F. R. Harris, ii. 334–5; *L.J.* xii. 482, 483, 486–7, 494–8, 502–4, 506; Grey, i. 433–42.

[2] Colbert, 4/14 July 1671.

[3] Ibid. 30 Oct./9 Nov. 1671.

christened George after the man everyone knew to be his father[1]; and in August the connexion took on a new form. The prorogation had exposed the Duke to the clamours of his numerous creditors. His debts were calculated at £133,587—almost a kingly sum—and a scheme was prepared by which Ashley, Sir John Trevor, Sir Thomas Osborne, Sir Robert Moray, and Dr. John Tillotson were to act as his trustees, paying him a yearly income of £5,000 and selling or leasing the rest of his estates for the creditors' benefit.[2]

There were many controversial topics on which the 'Cabal' could disagree, apart from the sugar duty. In February 1671, Ashley, Buckingham, Anglesey, Holles and Trevor had been appointed to examine 'all the papers, orders, and writings concerning the settlement of Ireland from first to last', and such a magnificently vague commission to venture into the morass of Irish affairs frequently suggested trouble.[3] There were arguments on the question who should further be admitted into the secret of the forthcoming Dutch war. Buckingham and Ashley vainly opposed the inclusion of Ormond and Prince Rupert—for no other reason than personal animosity, the French ambassador thought; but as far as Ashley and Rupert were concerned, this was quite wrong, for they were business partners. If Ashley did wish to keep him ignorant, it must have been to keep down the numbers in the secret. Yet one of the few recorded instances of Ashley's paying a visit to the French ambassador was on the occasion of the admission to the secret of his brother-in-law, Henry Coventry, newly appointed minister to Stockholm.[4] At the same time Buckingham and Ashley were trying to bind Anglesey closely to their party. The latter had laboured under a sense of grievance ever since he had been relieved of the Treasurership of the Navy in 1668, and in spite of his disclaimers in his diary he was flattered by hints that he might return to public office. They dined together on several occasions during June and July, and Buckingham talked of making Anglesey Lord Chancellor. Ashley too talked of giving Anglesey the Great Seal at present weakly held by Sir Orlando Bridgeman: he 'complimented me about the Lord Keeper's place, being pleased to tell me none would fill it better, and that if he had any power he would endeavour it'. In October, however, Anglesey was disgusted to learn that Ashley's professions of friendship were accompanied by inquiries behind his back into his gains in Ireland. 'God forgive this false man and pretended friend!' he scrawled in his diary, and his temper cannot have

---

[1] Newsletter, 21 Feb. 1671, Add. MSS. 36916, fo. 211.

[2] Shaftesbury Papers, XLI, 46. Abstracts of his rent-rolls in the years 1668–71 showed an income varying from £8,357 to £9,085 per half year. Marvell's information was remarkably accurate: letter to a frlend in Persia, 9 Aug. 1671, in *Poems and Letters*, ed. Margoliouth (1927), ii. 310. How long the arrangement lasted is not known.

[3] Shaftesbury Papers, L, 17, 18; B. M. Lauderdale Papers, Add. MSS. 23135, fos. 61–3; *C.S.P.D. 1671*, pp. 358, 410.

[4] Colbert, 18/28 May, 31 July/10 Aug. 1671.

been improved by the feeling that, since as Annesley and Ashley Cooper they had sat in the Convention, he had been passed by the latter in the race for political power.[1]

These faction fights of course aroused the disgust of the French ambassador, who still described Ashley as depending entirely upon Buckingham, an intelligent and eloquent man, but very self-seeking and capable of thoroughly spoiling and confusing matters, particularly in Parliament. Colbert de Croissy learned with some satisfaction that Buckingham, Lauderdale and Ashley had all received a solemn warning from the King: if any quarrels amongst his ministers harmed the great design, the person responsible would suffer. Lauderdale and Ashley were said to be 'somewhat mortified' by it: Buckingham was probably too graceless to bother.[2] It is plain that Ashley's reputation with the French was bad: he was regarded as being neither a friend of France nor a consistently loyal servant of Charles II. In these circumstances it was not unnatural that Louis XIV and Louvois should be alarmed at rumours that Ashley was to be made Lord Treasurer, because (wrote the English ambassador in Paris) 'they are afraid your affairs would be in people's hands they cannot think at bottom well affected either to monarchy or the great design you are now upon . . .'.[3] Time was to show that in this suspicion they were quite right.

In the autumn of 1671 rumours were prevalent that Ashley's promotion to the Treasurership was imminent, though one observer shrewdly suggested that 'money matters were so out of order, that he was too wise to accept it'[4]; the office might be more burdensome than rewarding. The rumours were intensified after the great change which took place in customs administration in September. This came about as a result of the misbehaviour of the new farmers, whose farm was due to begin at Michaelmas, and who thought they were so indispensable that they could improve on their terms. But when they offered to renounce their contract, Charles, having already had the advantage of an advance payment of £60,000, boldly called their bluff and agreed. It was too near to Michaelmas to find another syndicate, and so Ashley and Clifford proposed that the customs revenue should instead be collected directly by the King's own commissioners. The commissioners appointed included two merchants put forward by Ashley, namely Upton and Millington (the latter a fellow-member of Ashley's in the Hudson's Bay Company), and Clifford's nominee, Garroway; their secretary, John Man, was a merchant from

---

[1] Anglesey's diary, 4, 24 June, 19 July, 26 Aug., 8 Oct., in *H.M.C. Thirteenth Report*, pt. vi, pp. 263–9.

[2] Colbert, 18/28 Sept., 30 Oct./9 Nov. 1671.

[3] R. Montagu to Charles II, 13/23 Sept. 1671, in *H.M.C. Buccleuch MSS.*, i. 502–3.

[4] R. Brockenden to Sir R. Paston, 2 Sept. 1671, *H.M.C. Sixth Report*, p. 369 (giving as his authority 'the gentleman I writ you it was said should be his [Ashley's] secretary)'. Cf. Anglesey's diary, 26 Aug. 1671, *H.M.C. Thirteenth Report*, pt. vi, p. 267.

Dorset, later to be put forward by Ashley for the parliamentary constituency of Melcombe Regis. Thus Ashley was partly responsible for a momentous change in the taxation system, which had a good reception from the London merchants and eventually redounded to the profit of the King.[1] Incidentally it also added a great source of patronage to the Treasury Commissioners, who agreed to take turns in recommending men for the positions of tidesmen, landwaiters and other small posts at the ports, though this did not immediately reach the proportions characteristic of the eighteenth century.[2] There were many people who supposed that the next step after setting up Customs Commissioners was to appoint a Lord Treasurer to supervise them, and that Ashley was the obvious choice, and once rumour even reached the point of saying that he was to be given the Staff 'tomorrow', but nothing came of it.[3] Thereafter Ashley was prominent in beating down a demand for defalcations from the old customs farmers from £139,000 to £40,000,[4] but he was never formally offered the most lucrative post in the King's service. Whether this was because Charles fought shy of entrusting it to him, or whether Ashley made it clear that he did not want such a difficult task as would be involved is not known; the fact was that he did not become Lord Treasurer, and from December 1671 his influence on the Treasury Board began to decline before that of Clifford.

It was Clifford who was responsible for the act commonly known to history as the Stop of the Exchequer. In this case, as in that of the 'breaking of the triple bond', there were those who were ready to believe the worst of Ashley and load the blame upon him[5]; he was after all the man thought to have most influence in financial matters. But in addition to the evidence of well-informed contemporaries like Evelyn and Temple, notes have now been discovered in Clifford's papers suggesting that he had considered the possibility of a 'stop' as early as 1667, and had studied precedents in the reigns of Edward III and Elizabeth.[6] For this reason it would also be wrong to pay any attention to the silly story that Ashley dropped hints of

---

[1] The best account is in Martyn Ryder to George Treby, 9 Sept. 1671, *H.M.C. Fitzherbert MSS.*, p. 7; cf. also Sir Thomas Osborne's letter of 3 Oct., in *H.M.C. Lonsdale MSS.*, p. 95. According to various correspondents the Duchess of Cleveland and others had been heavily bribed by the defeated farmers: see Marvell's letter to a friend in Persia, 9 Aug., op. cit. ii. 310, and Colbert, 11/21 Sept. The Danish ambassador Lindenov has a curious account in *The First Triple Alliance*, ed. W. Westergaard (New Haven, 1947), but his despatch of 22 Sept. is unintelligible as it stands: either Lindenov misunderstood his informant, or the translator misunderstood Lindenov.

[2] *C.T.B. 1669–72*, pp. 955, 972, 980, 1039; Shaftesbury Papers, XLI, 47.

[3] Ryder to Treby, loc. cit.; newsletter, 23 Sept., Add. MSS. 36916, fo. 230.

[4] *C.T.B. 1669–72*, p. 961 (13 Nov. 1671).

[5] E.g. Burnet, i. 550; R. North, *Examen* (1740), p. 37; and the authors of *Plain Dealing is a Jewel, and Honesty the Best Policy, Somers Tracts* (1812), viii. 244.

[6] Evelyn, 12 Mar. 1672; Sir W. Temple to Sir J. Temple, 23 Mar. 1672, in *Works* (1754), iii. 506; A. Browning, 'The Stop of the Exchequer', in *History*, vol. xiv. (1930); W. A. Shaw, *C.T.B. 1669–72*, Introduction, pp. lix–lxiii; C. H. Hartmann, *Clifford of the Cabal* (1937), pp. 214–15.

this solution to Charles's financial troubles to Clifford in the course of a drinking bout.[1] In any case the policy was an obvious one; it did not need a financial genius to devise it. By the end of 1671 the government's debts and at the same time its needs for money to fit out the fleet had at last reached a completely impossible level. These years have been described by one authority as 'a financiers' paradise',[2] in which bankers could virtually fix their own terms for loans. The problem which had so exercised the House of Lords in 1669, of whether the legal rate of interest should be reduced from six per cent to four, was entirely beside the point where the government's own borrowing was concerned. And finally a time was reached when Lombard Street refused to advance any more money at all.[3] When this happened the government was left with one method of raising money at the bankers' expense, by stopping the repayment of the 'orders in course' under the system inaugurated by the 'Downing proviso' in 1665. Some of these represented loans made by the bankers from the beginning; others had been bought up by them from the governments' creditors at a high rate of discount; and under the terms of the various subsidy acts they should have been repaid in order as the proceeds of the taxes reached the Exchequer. If repayment was stopped, then the proceeds of the taxes would become available for current expenditure; and all that was needed was for a man of Clifford's boldness and unscrupulousness to propose it.

There was a tradition in the Shaftesbury household that the Stop was first proposed by Clifford in the summer of 1671, when Ashley opposed it and it was put aside. When the idea was revived at the New Year Ashley drew up his reasons against it, and went to Whitehall for a two hours' discussion with the King, Clifford, and Lauderdale. These reasons survive in the handwriting of his secretary Stringer, who went with him to Whitehall. The measure was contrary to common justice, the law, and the King's own promises; it would 'ruin thousands', including 'a multitude of poor widows and orphans' who had deposited their money with the bankers; it would cause 'the greatest damp on trade' ever known, and thus affect the revenue; and the example of Spain had shown that such measures were disastrous.[4] It was not that he had any love for the bankers: in a letter written to John Locke on the subject two years later he conceded that there was some weight in the case against them, 'that the bankers were grown destructive to the nation' by the extortionate rate of interest they charged to private borrowers, while in the King's affairs they were not content with twelve per cent interest, but bought up all the King's

---

[1] L. Echard, *History of England* (1720), p. 879.

[2] D. C. Coleman, *Sir John Banks* (1963), p. 41.

[3] R. Langhorne to L. Hatton, 6 Jan. 1672, printed in A. Browning, *English Historical Documents 1660–1714* (1953), p. 353.

[4] Martyn, i. 415–16, no doubt derived from Stringer. In this case there are no good reasons for doubting Stringer's and Martyn's story. The reasons are also printed by Christie, ii. 59–60.

assignations at twenty or thirty per cent profit. He had no illusions about the bankers; his objection was to the effect which the measure might have on the general prosperity and on the King's own finances through the blow which it gave to the whole credit system. The trouble was, as Temple noted, that the opponents of the Stop could produce no alternative when challenged by Clifford to do so. Once the Dover policy had been embarked upon, the money had to be obtained for it by hook or by crook. All that Ashley could do was to dissociate himself from it as best he could; he claimed that afterwards he and Duncombe left 'all paying and borrowing of money' to Clifford. This did not save him from being blamed, and his enemies even said that he had taken advantage of his advance knowledge by withdrawing his own deposits from the bankers' hands in time. There is no evidence of this in the accounts kept by Stringer in the days immediately preceding the Stop. What they do show is that between the end of October and the beginning of December Ashley had been calling in short term loans, cashing assignments in his own possession, and buying land in Cranborne Chase with the proceeds. But there was nothing improper about this; it was at most the action of a prudent businessman in a financial situation which he knew to be uncertain.[1]

The Stop of the Exchequer, in January 1672, was the most sensational event of that winter, even though it did not in fact ruin as many poor widows and orphans as Ashley and other pessimists had forecast, but at the same time momentous negotiations were being undertaken in secret with the Nonconformists which were a prelude to the issue of the Declaration of Indulgence in March. Little is known of the government's relations with the 'fanatics' through the notorious Colonel Blood and other intermediaries, except for a series of minute, scarcely legible and scarcely intelligible jottings made by Arlington's under-secretary, Joseph Williamson. From these it appears that Ashley, Arlington, Buckingham and Lauderdale all had their rival connexions with groups of Dissenters, but it is impossible to tell precisely what was going on. In October 1671 the committee of foreign affairs decided to pardon some of the 'Phanaticks', 'they declaring and promising to live peaceably hereafter'.[2] There is no reference to any further discussion of the matter 'as to a liberty in matters ecclesiastical' in this committee until 6 March 1672, within a few days of the treacherous attack on the Dutch Smyrna fleet which began the war. The Declaration of Indulgence and the draft declaration of war passed the committee on consecutive days (14 and 15 March), and they were clearly intended to be complementary. For some members of the committee it was necessary to

---

[1] Shaftesbury to Locke, 23 Nov. 1674, Christie, ii. 61–64; Temple, loc. cit. p. 294, n. 6; Burnet, i. 550; Shaftesbury Papers, XL, 44.

[2] *C.S.P.D. 1671*, pp. 496–7, 533–4, 560–1, 562–3, 568–70, 581; *1671–2*, pp. 8–9, 14, 27–28, 28–29, 35, 44–46; *Add. 1660–85*, pp. 341–2 (notes extending from Sept. to Dec. 1671); Foreign Entry Book 176, 22 Oct. 1671.

conciliate the Dissenters in order to induce them not to sympathize too much with their Dutch co-religionaries; for the 'Catholic' members both steps were intended to launch Charles II's great design; and for Ashley and Buckingham it was the achievement of a religious toleration which they had always wanted. Thus there was no opposition in principle in the committee of foreign affairs, and discussion ran solely on the King's legal powers to issue a Declaration, and on its terms.

Ashley, who had supported the Declaration of 1662, had never had any doubts about the King's ecclesiastical supremacy, and consequently the legality of what was proposed. On 6 March he supported Clifford's view that the King could appoint a Vicar-General and so 'may declare heresies, excommunicate, burn, etc.' He, Clifford and Lauderdale were commissioned 'to consider how the law stands as to this, and what the King has in his power', and John Locke duly provided Ashley with the necessary information, upholding the royal supremacy in ecclesiastical affairs in documents still extant. Whether the same three drafted the declaration itself, or if not, who did, is uncertain; but after some discussion of the terms, in which Ashley's views were not recorded, the Declaration was read and approved in the committee of foreign affairs on 14 March 1672. From its starting-point that the forcible measures of the previous decade had proved unable to solve the religious problem, and that some indulgence would be beneficial to the national unity and trading prosperity, it proceeded to reassure Anglicans that tithes and benefices would continue to be restricted to orthodox clergy, and then to suspend all penal laws in matters of religion. Dissenting congregations were to be allowed to worship publicly in meeting-places and under preachers licensed by the government. Catholic recusants were not to be allowed the same freedom of public worship, but were simply to be conceded freedom from all statutory fines and penalties, and some play was made with this to argue that Papists gained less from the Declaration of Indulgence than did Dissenters; but everyone realized that this argument was unreal, because in practice Catholics could always attend mass either in the household of a Catholic peer, or in the Queen's chapel, or in the chapels kept by the ambassadors of Catholic foreign powers specially for the purpose.[1]

As will be seen, Ashley stubbornly maintained the justice and legality of the Declaration for a year, even when the Commons strongly attacked it, until Charles himself decided to abandon it; and even after he had joined in a common opposition to Charles with many politicians who had attacked the Declaration he still maintained that it had been the right policy. In 1675, the pamphlet *Letter to a Person of Quality*, which was clearly an authorized statement of Shaftesbury's views, contained a full defence of the King's religious supremacy, and of his powers to dispense

---

[1] Foreign Entry Book 177, 6, 9, 11, 14 Mar. 1672; Shaftesbury Papers, VI B, 427, 430; Browning, *Documents* pp. 387–8.

from Acts of Parliament when Parliament was not sitting. In a supposed conversation between Shaftesbury and the author of the pamphlet, the former maintained that 'without a power always in being of dispensing upon occasion, was to suppose a constitution extremely imperfect and impracticable', and to provide for this need by keeping Parliament permanently in session would be 'no other than a perfect tyranny'. This was his bold answer to the argument that if by a declaration the King could suspend penal laws in religion, he could dispense with any act: he was prepared to see this done where the occasion was good enough, subject to Parliament's right to annul such an indulgence when it met. As to the alleged threat to the Church of England, on the contrary (he maintained) 'the Declaration was extremely their interest, for the narrow bottom they had placed themselves upon, and the measures they had proceeded by, so contrary to the properties and liberties of the nation, must needs in a short time prove fatal to them, whereas this led them into another way to live peaceably with the dissenting and differing Protestants, both at home and abroad, and so by necessity and unavoidable consequences, to become the head of them all'. 'As to the Protestant religion', the author of the pamphlet wrote, 'he told me plainly, it was for the preserving of that and that only, that he heartily joined in the Declaration.' If the Church of England insisted on 'a rigid, blind, and undisputed conformity', this would play into the hands of a possible Popish successor. The argument that the Declaration really favoured the Papists he answered by correctly pointing out that in practice they gained no more by it than they had enjoyed before with the tacit consent of the bishops—the Dissenters were 'the only men disturbed before' by the Conventicle Acts; and in any case 'Papists ought to have no other pressure laid upon them, but to be made incapable of office, court, or arms'. In conclusion, Shaftesbury 'desired me seriously to weigh, whether liberty and property were likely to be maintained long, in a country like ours, where trade is so absolutely necessary to the very being as well as the prosperity of it . . . if articles and matters of religion should become the only accessible ways to civil rights'.[1]

Although this pamphlet was written with the definite purpose of putting the most favourable construction upon Shaftesbury's career for the benefit of the public in the political circumstances of 1675, when due allowance has been made for this it does represent his considered and consistent view on religious toleration. He has sometimes been represented as being ready for his own purposes to make concessions to Papists in 1672 only to become a passionate, extreme enemy later; his real attitude was more moderate, more reasonable and more consistent. His main concern in 1672 was with the Dissenters, in the interests of national liberty, 'property', and trade. Some surprise has been expressed that after the Declaration was

---

[1] Locke's *Works* (1823), x. 204–8. For some discussion whether Locke was the author of the pamphlet, see pp. 391–3 below.

issued he took no part in procuring licenses for particular congregations, but the natural channel for this was by way of the offices of the Secretaries of State, and there was no need for him to intervene.[1] Having helped to secure the principle, he could stand by and leave the routine work to others.

There was plenty of other work for him to do, for by this time hostilities had broken out. Ashley shares with his colleagues and his King the responsibility for the discreditable manner in which the war began. Twelve months previously he had been one of the commissioners appointed to negotiate an alliance with the Dutch ambassador Boreel, the intention being never to bring these negotiations to a serious conclusion but only to delude, and to keep every dispute open as a pretext for the war on which they were determined.[2] In January he had joined with Clifford, Buckingham and Lauderdale in pressing for the war to be opened by a sudden attack on Cadzand,[3] but a decision was deferred until the spring. It had been planned to begin operations in May, but at the beginning of March the news arrived that a large Dutch fleet of merchantmen from Smyrna in the Levant was sailing up the Channel. The temptation to make prizes of them was too great to resist. Ashley was not present in the foreign committee on 4 March when the order to bring in all Dutch ships was first made, but he was there next day when the order was repeated and more detailed arrangements made. There is no record of any protest by Ashley, and no evidence that at any later date he had any compunction about it, as had the Earl of Ossory who took part in the attack. His view of international affairs was the Machiavellian one that ordinary standards of morality did not apply, and that all things were permissible to gain an advantage over an enemy. He was not, like Buckingham, Lauderdale and Arlington, commissioned to avoid the King having any embarrassing contact with the extraordinary Dutch ambassador Meerman at this time, but when Arlington defined the task as 'to break with them, and yet lay the breach at their door' he was silent. It was after all the logical continuation of the policy which had been decided on in 1670.[4]

The attack on the Smyrna fleet proved to be an ignominious failure, but it committed England to war, and an official declaration soon followed. Two years later when defending himself to the House of Commons, Buckingham maintained that 'I and my Lord Shaftesbury were of the opinion not to begin a war, without advice of the Parliament, and the affections of the people, that the Parliament might join it',[5] but if this remark had any truth in it it cannot have applied to this month of March

[1] G. L. Turner, *Original Records of Early Nonconformity* (1914), iii. 252. Some licences were applied for through Robert Blayney, who had been Ashley's secretary; ibid. iii. 476–8.

[2] Boreel's despatches, 7/17 Mar. 1671 and following, Add. MSS. 17677, PPP; Foreign Entry Book 176, 12 Mar.   [3] Colbert, 11/21 Jan. 1672.

[4] Foreign Entry Book 176, 4 Mar.; 177, 5, 6, 8 Mar. 1672.

[5] 14 Jan. 1674; Grey, op. cit. ii. 261.

1672. The very fact of the issue of a Declaration of Indulgence at the same time as hostilities began meant that a meeting of Parliament could not be contemplated for some time. The new policy in finance, in religion, and in war was essentially the King's policy, in which the co-operation of Parliament could not be sought.

This made it essential that the members of the 'Cabal' should be kept together and induced to sink their personal disagreements in the common effort. With this in mind, the declaration of war was followed by a distribution of honours. Buckingham, who was already a duke, could be promoted no higher; but Ashley and Arlington were given earldoms, Clifford a barony and Lauderdale a dukedom. The choice of a title for his earldom presented Ashley with a difficulty; Dorset and Southampton, Dorchester and Salisbury, all belonged to different peers. He solved the problem characteristically, not by attempting to revive some old titles in his favour, but by choosing a new one from the market town of Shaftesbury some twelve miles from his house at Wimborne St. Giles. He became Earl of Shaftesbury and Baron Cooper of Paulet (a Somerset manor of his), and the title by which his grandfather had set so much store, that of Lord Ashley, became the courtesy title of his eldest son. His motto too was not in Latin, but in English: a very simple one, 'Love, Serve'—though the cynics might have noted that the object of his love and service was left discreetly vague.

Fortified by this honour, Shaftesbury immediately threw himself into the plans for the naval campaign. Through March, April and May the 'foreign committee' met with great frequency—sometimes even twice a day—to settle a great variety of problems. Some were diplomatic, involving relations with Spain and Hamburg, in which Shaftesbury concerned himself with the interests of the merchants that the war should not lead to a dislocation of trade. Others were more immediately practical: there were arrangements to be made for pressing seamen, for exempting colliers bringing coal to London, and for sending spies to Holland. He became, too, one of the Commissioners of Appeal in all cases relating to prizes, drawing a salary of £800 per annum, though the post of Prize Treasurer was not revived for his benefit. In comparison with the last war he took a much more direct interest in the equipping of the fleet and in its strategy. At the beginning of April he went down to Sheerness with the Duke of York, Clifford, 'and others of the great men'. A month later he was to be found at a meeting discussing the relative merits of Dungeness and the Downs as a station for the fleet; and then when the King, Duke of York, Arlington and others went down to Portsmouth it was decided that in their absence Prince Rupert, Lauderdale and Shaftesbury should 'meet about the matters of the war'. It is typical of all the committees which Shaftesbury dominated that, at the very first meeting of this triumvirate on 4 May, they called for several lists of information: lists of ships, stores required, the victualling situation, stores held of cordage, pitch, hemp, tar, etc., the condition of fireships, what hulks there were and where. Pepys and his colleagues at the Admiralty had to scurry around to provide the facts, and soon disturbing deficiencies were revealed, particularly in pitch and tar. When the King returned to London, the 'Navy officers' were asked why they now said they were short of £100,000 worth of stores when they had previously said they had enough for all summer, and Clifford as usual was vehement in his criticisms. 'Writing I understand not', remarked Shaftesbury; 'doing the business, I do', and in accordance with these sentiments he, Clifford and Sir Thomas Osborne were empowered to visit the dockyards at Deptford, Woolwich and Chatham, to see the state of affairs for themselves. On 30 May the 'officers of the Navy' were ordered to sit every morning at Shaftesbury's rooms in Whitehall. All this activity required money, and Shaftesbury was needed to assist in the negotiation of an agreement between Osborne, the Treasurer of the Navy, and Sir John Banks, a prominent financier and Governor of the East India Company. Finally Banks was induced to advance more money urgently in return for favoured treatment of the King's previous debts to him, repayment of which had been involved in the Stop of the Exchequer.[1]

In spite of all this effort, the battle of Sole Bay, in which Shaftesbury's old colleague Sandwich was killed, was no better than a draw. It was followed by a dispute over strategy in which Shaftesbury and the Duke of York were to be found on opposite sides. At a meeting of the foreign committee held unusually at sea, on board the *Prince* at the Nore, James proposed to sail straight for De Ruyter and force him either to a second battle or to retreat into port. Shaftesbury opposed this. Apart from the consideration that there would not be sufficient money to refit the fleet again that year, the experience of three Dutch wars dating back to 1652 had convinced him that naval battles were not decisive, but that a dislocation of Dutch trade could be. He proposed an attempt to intercept the returning Dutch East India fleet, which might in any case yield valuable prizes. This view was adopted by Charles and the committee, but the plan failed because the merchantmen were able to slip through the English fleet in a storm and reach port safely.[2]

In other ways too Shaftesbury recognized the importance of trade in wartime. When sailors from British East Indiamen were pressed into the service of the Navy, he and Clifford wrote to Portsmouth to order them to be replaced. When a valuable East Indiaman was captured by Dutch privateers and taken into the port of Bergen, it was to Shaftesbury that the

---

[1] Foreign Entry Book 177, esp. 6 Mar., 1, 8, 9, 13, 22 Apr., 2, 4, 5, 6, 8, 9, 13, 15, 30 May; *C.S.P.D. 1671–2*, pp. 419, 438, 450–1, 470–1; W. Coventry to H. Coventry, 5 Apr., Coventry Papers at Longleat, vol. 104, fo. 86; D. C. Coleman, *Sir John Banks* (1963), p. 60.

[2] J. S. Clarke, *Life of James II* (1816), p. 478; Foreign Entry Book 176, 22 June 1672.

Company wrote to ask for help to retake it. Some months later Shaftesbury asserted his conviction that 'he that can trade best, will carry on the war longest'.[1] This argument was sound enough up to a point; but it did not take sufficient account of the difficulties which Charles and his ministers would inevitably face in getting enough money to fight a second campaign in 1673. Accordingly, in September Shaftesbury changed the opinion he had expressed in June, and urged that everything should be staked on a battle, followed by a landing on the Dutch coast, in order to end the war in 1672. This made better sense in September than in June, as at that late season it would not be so urgent to fit the fleet out again immediately after a battle, and thus the money for it would not have to be so urgently found. Shaftesbury and Rupert were noticed taking some of the flag officers aside to win support for their plan. But James also reversed his previous view, arguing that now it was too late; it was too dangerous to expose the ships to possible westerly autumn gales off the coast of Holland. Charles's own technical knowledge convinced him that James was right; he overruled Rupert and Shaftesbury, and ordered that the fleet should not go to sea again in 1672.[2]

The campaign at sea had therefore achieved nothing. On land, on the other hand, the armies of Louis XIV had won some sensational successes. Turenne's famous march had carried the French into the heart of the United Provinces; and early in June Louis arrived in Utrecht, convinced that he had the Dutch at his mercy. This had created some difficulties for the English government. On the one hand it was disagreeable to have English failure contrasted with French success; there were sure to be some Englishmen who were jealous of Louis XIV and alarmed at the prospect of seeing him master of the Low Countries. On the other hand, there was the possibility that Louis might seize his opportunity to make gains for himself without doing anything to secure the agreed share of the loot for Charles. To meet this danger, Shaftesbury's nephew Halifax had been sent on a special embassy to the camp of Louis XIV; and then, in case he was not an ambassador of sufficient weight, Arlington and Buckingham crossed the Channel. If only one of the two rivals had been sent, the one who stayed at home would inevitably have been critical; the only safe course was to send both. To such straits Charles's policy was reduced. After some typical vacillations on Buckingham's part, he and Arlington secured a new treaty which bound both the allies not to make a separate peace without the other; but Charles was still afraid that Louis might leave him in the lurch.[3] A development which promised better for him was the overthrow of the Dutch Pensionary Jan de Witt. The wave of

---

[1] *C.S.P.D. 1672*, pp. 270–1 (23 June); Sir John Banks to Shaftesbury, 10 Aug., ibid. pp. 468–9 (cf. Foreign Entry Book 177, 8 Aug.); Foreign Entry Book 177, 8 Nov.

[2] Clarke, op. cit. pp. 480–1; cf. R. North, *Examen* (1740), p. 51.

[3] Foreign Entry Book 177, 31 July 1672.

pro-Orange sentiment whose strength was demonstrated by the terrible lynching of de Witt and his brother carried into power William of Orange, a young man not yet twenty-two. William had paid a visit to England in the winter of 1670, had seemed dull and unenterprising and had not then impressed either Charles or anyone else with any glimpse of his future greatness. Someone of his youth and inexperience, in a desperate situation, might reasonably be expected to accept the patronage of his uncle Charles II; it could even be in his interest to do so, for with Charles's help he might be able to attain sovereignty over the Dutch and found a dynasty. It was some time before Charles realized that his stubborn nephew would not play the part of protégé for which he wanted to cast him; for William did offer to make concessions, through a series of agents who crossed the North Sea, and he was tempted by the chance of sovereignty. But he insisted that the concessions which he offered—the flag, payment for the right to fish off the English coast, a war indemnity, and Sluis as a 'cautionary town'—should be part of a separate Anglo-Dutch peace treaty which would leave him free to fight against Louis XIV. A separate treaty was something which Charles dared not contemplate—he was irrevocably tied to France by the Treaty of Dover—but in the autumn of 1672 there still seemed a chance that William would be 'sensible', drop his demand for a separate peace and agree to a general one. In that event the risks which Charles had taken would be triumphantly vindicated.[1]

This was the situation which Charles and his ministers had to consider in the autumn of 1672. Any bellicosity which they might once have had, had by this time evaporated. When the news of the 'accident' to de Witt arrived, Shaftesbury joined with others in seeking to take advantage of it to 'send underhand' to William and try to set a peace treaty on foot; he did not rant about *Delenda est Carthago* on this occasion. While the correspondence was being carried on, however, the important decision had to be taken whether Parliament should meet at its appointed time in October, or be further prorogued. Among those who favoured prorogation until February 1673 were Shaftesbury and his relative Henry Coventry, who had now become the second Secretary of State. Shaftesbury considered that an early meeting of Parliament might spoil the prospects of peace negotiations, because it would encourage the Dutch to wait and see what the House of Commons's mood would be; whereas on the other hand if a successful peace could be settled before the Houses assembled, 'it will be a powerful argument to the Parliament to give money'. This was the general view of the foreign committee; as under-secretary Williamson had noted earlier, 'Seemed concluded on all hands no treaty of peace could be depending while the Parliament sits, for the infinite danger there may be in

---

[1] N. Japikse, *Correspondentie van Willem III en van Hans Willem Bentinck* (The Hague, 1927–35), II. i. 80, 96, 103, 114–16; cf. P. Geyl, *Oranje en Stuart* (Utrecht, 1939), pp. 480 sqq.

having all the circumstances of it misrepresented by secret whispers to leading men of the House, by which the King's business in the House would be obstructed and his reputation abroad lost . . .'.[1]

All through the summer of 1672, therefore, Shaftesbury's energies were fully occupied in support of the Dutch war; in the autumn he favoured a postponement of the recall of Parliament; and although he looked forward to a treaty there was no question of it being peace at any price. The story of his clerk, Stringer, that in these months he learned of Charles's Catholic designs, and worked with Prince Rupert and Henry Coventry to oppose them, may therefore be disregarded. There was no sign yet of any rift between him and the King. Something of a mystery attaches, however, to Stringer's next sentences, for he tells a circumstantial story to the effect that Shaftesbury, hearing that the Treasurer's Staff was to be thrust upon him, and being reluctant to take it, evaded it by going into the country for two months. Details of the houses visited are given, and these are corroborated by Stringer's surviving accounts of the expenses incurred (though the journey lasted one month, not two). But it does not follow that the alleged motive for the absence from London was the correct one. Whereas there had been prolific rumours of impending promotion in the autumn of 1671, there are none recorded in September 1672. The journey may have had a more innocent explanation; it may have been mere recreation, and this is the more likely because it coincided with the King's absence at Newmarket.[2]

Shaftesbury returned to London at the end of October, and on the thirtieth of that month, when Parliament met to be formally reprorogued until February, he was introduced into the House of Lords under his new title, between the Earls of Bridgewater and Dover. Paying the usual fees, which amounted to £15.10s., he took his seat on the earls' bench.[3] Not long afterwards he achieved a still greater honour, when the Great Seal was withdrawn from Lord Keeper Bridgeman, who had held it since Clarendon's fall in 1667, and given to Shaftesbury with the title of Lord Chancellor—the highest position which a subject could attain. The post of Lord Treasurer, which had earlier been associated with his name, and was probably more lucrative to its holder, was given instead to Clifford.

Several reasons have been suggested for the dismissal of Bridgeman, and in all of them there may be some measure of truth. Bridgeman had declined to affix the Great Seal to the Declaration of Indulgence. It is also probable that he had refused to agree to a proclamation of 'martial law', to keep the troops collected for the proposed expedition to Holland under military discipline. He had objected to this as being contrary to the Petition of Right, and Shaftesbury had been instructed to confer with Solicitor-

---

[1] Foreign Entry Book 177, 18, 20 Aug., 15, 16 Sept.; Colbert, 16/26 Sept.
[2] Christie, ii, pp. xxiv–xxvi; Shaftesbury Papers, IV, 231.
[3] *L.J.* xii. 519; account in Shaftesbury Papers, IV, 216.

General North about this.[1] Apparently Bridgeman was never persuaded, because no commissions of martial law had been signed by November. Thirdly, there may have been a difference over the 'suits of the bankers'. The bankers who had been hard hit by the Stop of the Exchequer, amongst them Horneby with whom Shaftesbury had had dealings, were now hampered by threats of law-suits from the people who had deposited money with them; they claimed that their plight was due entirely to the government's action, and that in all fairness they were entitled to a proclamation to stop their creditors from suing. This matter was discussed in the foreign committee and in Council on 8 November, a week before Bridgeman's dismissal. There is no record of what views the Lord Keeper expressed, but contemporaries suspected that this problem was relevant to his fall.[2]

As all these legal questions certainly cropped up towards the end of 1672, it has often been implied that Shaftesbury, a layman and a courtier, was appointed to succeed 'that good old man' Bridgeman, the trained lawyer, in order to sanction uses of the royal prerogative which were not in strict accordance with the law.[3] But this view is not very strongly supported by the measures which Shaftesbury actually took with regard to each of these problems. The Declaration of Indulgence had already been in operation for eight months without serious inconvenience from Bridgeman's refusal to affix the Great Seal, and it was not until 9 December, three weeks after Shaftesbury's appointment, that, in a meeting of the foreign committee, 'His Majesty now directs that it be passed the Great Seal accordingly'.[4] It is true that this slightly strengthened the government's position with a view to the meeting of Parliament in February, but the Declaration certainly would not stand or fall according to whether or not it had passed the Great Seal. With regard to 'martial law', legal advisers were not lacking to maintain that the government's view was correct, amongst them Attorney-General Finch, who was himself to be Lord Keeper a year later, and Solicitor-General North.[5] Thus there were lawyers available to succeed Bridgeman without calling upon a layman like Shaftesbury to take the responsibility, but in any event it had been possible to do without martial law throughout the campaigning season, it cannot have

---

[1] Foreign Entry Book 177, 16 June 1672. By 'martial law' was meant solely the power to try soldiers by military courts; it was not intended to apply to the civil population.

[2] Foreign Entry Book 177; W. A. Shaw, *C.T.B. 1672–5*, pp. li–liii; Charles Hatton to Lord Hatton, 19 Nov. 1672, *Hatton Correspondence*, ed. E. M. Thompson (Camden Society, 1878), pp. 101–2 ('But this is but guess and that by the most ignorant'); R. North, *Examen* (1740), pp. 38–39; J. Copleston to the Duke of Richmond, 25 Nov., Add. MSS. 21948, fo. 427.

[3] Cf. *C.S.P. Ven. 1671–2*, p. 318. Miss Brown, p. 200, suggests that Bridgeman 'may have been sounded and refused' to issue writs for bye-elections to be held during the prorogation, but there is no evidence that this was considered before 17 November, and in any case, according to Clifford, Bridgeman was not opposed to the issue of writs during a prorogation: Foreign Entry Book 177, 30 Jan. 1673.

[4] Foreign Entry Book 177.   [5] Ibid. 1 Oct. 1672.

been a particularly urgent problem in November, and no commission for martial law was issued. Finally, in the matter of the suits against Backwell and other bankers, Shaftesbury granted only a temporary injunction to hold up their creditors.[1]

This all suggests that these legal problems were only incidental to the dismissal of Bridgeman and the appointment of Shaftesbury. They may have contributed to Charles's irritation with the former; they cannot by themselves account for Charles's choice of the latter. The really important facts were that Bridgeman had been appointed solely as an innocuous successor to Clarendon, was not closely linked with any faction among the King's ministers, was never admitted to the King's secret designs, was of no great political significance, and could therefore be dispensed with as soon as it was convenient. His 'frequent sicknesses and not attending business was become a great grievance to the people'.[2] Shaftesbury, on the other hand, had shown both zeal and ability since the war had first been planned; and by the middle of November hopes that the Dutch would sue for peace were fast evaporating. Ahead lay another campaign in 1673, and before that an appeal to Parliament for money, with disputes about the Declaration of Indulgence and about foreign policy probable. It was natural for Charles to try to bind the ablest of the Cabal to his service, and by raising him to high office to hope that he could win Shaftesbury's support and use his great gifts for all his schemes. This is probably the true significance of the experiment of making Shaftesbury Chancellor. Yet at the same time Charles had some misgivings. Evidently feeling some need of reassurance, he approached the old, faithful Cavalier elder statesman, the Duke of Ormond, and taking him aside into a window alcove, asked him what he thought of his giving the Seals to Shaftesbury. Had he done prudently or not? Ormond's reply was: 'Your Majesty has doubtless acted very prudently in so doing, if you know how to get them from him again.' In his opinion Shaftesbury was not a man merely to follow where the King led.[3]

And so Shaftesbury paid his fees and gave his presents on becoming Lord Chancellor: £16 'at the Council for swearing'; £6. 9s. to the Grooms of His Majesty's Bedchamber; £10 to the serjeant trumpeter; £2. 3s. to the Kettle Drums; £1 to the parish waits; and finally £2 to the porters at the Great Gate of the palace of Whitehall.[4] He had come further in the world than even his doting grandfather could have hoped; but in one week under a year he was to lose his new-found honour.

[1] R. North, op cit. p. 47.
[2] J. Copleston to the Duke of Richmond, 25 Nov., Add. MSS. 21948, fo. 427.
[3] J. Carte, Life of Ormond (1736), iv. 484.
[4] Accounts in Shaftesbury Papers, IV, 216.

CHAPTER XV

ABBETHDIN AND CATO (1672–3)

A little bobtailed Lord, urchin of state,
A praysfull Barebones Peer whom all men hate,
Amphibious animal, half fool, half knave,
Begged silence and this grave blind counsel gave.

The Gambol, A Dream of the Grand Cabal[1]

SHAFTESBURY entered upon his duties as Lord Chancellor as though he expected to be there carrying them out for a long time. There was no suggestion that he thought of his position as precarious. Work had already been in progress for some time (under the supervision of His Majesty's Surveyor of Works, 'Doctor' Christopher Wren) on improvements to his lodgings in the Privy Garden at Whitehall; now he proceeded in addition to extend his lease of Exeter House to the whole of the building, and to spend about £730 on alterations to that, between January and April 1673.[2] It was to be made into a dwelling fit for a Chancellor, for Shaftesbury strongly believed in the importance of external magnificence as a support to those in authority. Addressing a newly appointed judge, he recommended to him 'the port and way of living suitable to the dignity of your place, and what the King allows you. There is not anything that gains more reputation and respect to the Government than that doth; and let me tell you, magistrates as well as merchants are supported by their reputation'. In his own household, he acted according to the same principles.[3]

For a model he took, not Clarendon but his father-in-law, Lord Keeper Coventry, whom he had admired in those long-distant days before the Civil War, when conditions had been very different. Perhaps a desire to emulate his father-in-law had helped to make him prefer the Chancellorship to the Treasurership. Now he had lists drawn up of 'the Lord Keeper's servants in Lord Coventry's time', and a descriptive account of the way in which he spent his day during term-time.[4] Coventry evidently lived a very regular, formalized life, and this was reflected in Shaftesbury's own

---

[1] *Poems on Affairs of State* (1697), p. 148.

[2] Accounts in Shaftesbury Papers, IV, 216, and XLI, 54.

[3] Speech to Baron Thurland, 24 Jan. 1673, Christie, ii. lxi. The stress on 'reputation' recurs elsewhere, e.g. in the *Delenda est Carthago* speech: 'Reputation is the great support of war or peace', *L.J.* xii. 526. Cf. also Stringer: 'Our Earl also knowing that all governments do subsist more by reputation and credit than power or force . . . '. (Christie, ii, p. xxvii). In this emphasis Shaftesbury puts his finger on the central weakness of Charles II's government.

[4] Shaftesbury Papers, XXX, 20, 77; XLI, 52. Christie mistakenly thought that the second of these applied to Shaftesbury's own household: ii. 169–72.

plans, when he 'settled his family' at Christmas 1672. The account which we possess mentions the names of thirty-six men, from Mr. Hodges, the chaplain, Mr. Stringer, steward of the house, Mr. Bennett, one of his secretaries, and Mr. Locke, 'Secretary for the clergy', down to the cooks, porters, and footmen. There were careful regulations laying down who should sit at which table, what were to be the mealtimes and who was entitled to what meat. The four men just named were to sit at the Steward's table and have wine; they were also authorized to keep servants of their own in Shaftesbury's livery. Everything was worked out in detail; for instance, 'The yeoman of the wine-cellar and butler are to provide cards and dice and are to have the benefit of play in the dining rooms and drawing rooms. In the rooms below the under-butler is to have the benefit. The yeoman of the great room, groom of the great room, usher of the hall and groom of the hall are to put all the money that is given them and all manner of profits or advantages whatsoever into a common stock which is to be divided according unto these proportions . . .' and the document goes on to fix the share of the tips and perquisites which each of these four were to have, in a manner of which the twentieth century would approve. The profits of the Lord Keeper's place from which all this establishment would have to be maintained, including fees, 23s. per day for diet, and about £600 in New Year's gifts from 'lawyers and officers of the court', were estimated at £2,440 per annum.[1]

It was in keeping with all this that Shaftesbury decided to revive the old practice of riding to Westminster Hall on horseback, accompanied by all the judges and law officers, on the first day of the new term. On the morning of 23 January 1673, they were 'entertained at a splendid and magnificent treat' at Exeter House; and then the procession began. Beadles, constables, and the court crier led the way; then followed all the minor Chancery officials, the students of the Inns of Court invited for the occasion, the registrars, the barristers at law, the Sealer to the Great Seal, the Chase Wax to the Great Seal and others, the Seal-bearer, carrying the purse containing the Great Seal, the Serjeant at Arms attending the Great Seal, carrying the mace, 'after whom came the Lord High Chancellor himself on horseback, being richly arrayed; the Gentleman of his Horse, attended by a page, a groom, and six footmen walking along by his stirrup'. There followed the judges, in order of seniority, and finally the Attorney-General, Solicitor-General, King's Counsel, Masters of Chancery and others. Amid crowds of bystanders they passed along the Strand and King Street to Westminster Hall. The result was not quite as dignified as Shaftesbury would have liked; there was some 'curveting' among the horses, and one leading luminary of the law, Judge Twisden, found that his horsemanship was unequal to the occasion, and bit the dust. For this

---

[1] Shaftesbury Papers, IV, 236; XXX, 21.

reason there were some who ridiculed the idea as a silly freak, revived
from the days when there were fewer coaches to feed the vanity of a
pompous ass. But this would be unfair. Although Clarendon, who suffered
from gout, had not ridden in such a procession, the judges as a body had
ridden to Westminster Hall until the death of Lord Chief Justice Sir
Robert Hyde in 1665.[1] The procession was not a long-disused one, and the
motive behind it was basically that behind all state processions and
ceremonial.

Shaftesbury's readiness to accept the position of Lord Chancellor and
therefore to preside over Chancery was one of the most striking instances
of his self-confidence, for his formal legal training was scanty. It is true
that he had, like many country gentlemen, spent some of his youth at an
Inn of Court, that as Chancellor of the Exchequer he had on occasion sat
in the Exchequer Court,[2] and possibly that the equitable jurisdiction of
Chancery required less technical legal knowledge than some other courts;
but nevertheless it was many years since a layman had been appointed. The
fact was that Shaftesbury considered that his own common sense was the
equal of all the lawyers' experience; and curiously no astonishment was
expressed either at his appointment or because he filled the position at
least adequately. Stringer said that there were some of his enemies who
hoped that his new duties 'would have gravelled and confounded him',
and the existence of some jealousy of him amongst the lawyers and officials
of Chancery may be deduced from Roger North's sarcasms[3]—no 'outsider'
could easily be accepted amongst them—but his chancellorship was soon
accepted as a matter of course. Within a month, indeed, a contemporary
noted that 'the new Lord Chancellor is very active in his office, and has
gained great reputation in the administration of the Court, so that he
bears his authority high'.[4] The most striking tribute of all is the famous one
from an enemy:

> In Israel's courts ne'er sat an Abbethdin,
> With more discerning eyes or hands more clean,
> Unbrib'd, unsought, the wretched to redress,
> Swift to despatch and easy of access . . .

Various explanations have been offered for the insertion of such an unexpected panegyric in the middle of a bitter partisan attack, but the
simplest and the best is that the lines were true, and were known to be
true. It is impossible now to tell from the records of the cases how discerning his eyes really were, but they certainly suggest that he was 'swift
of despatch'; he wasted no words and no time in deciding a case himself

---

[1] *Rawleigh Redivivus* (1683), pp. 73–76; R. North, *Examen* (1740), p. 57; J. Aubrey,
Brief Lives, ed. A. Clark (1898), i. 302–3. SP Car. II 332, no. 186.
[2] S. B. Baxter, *The Development of the Treasury, 1660–1702* (1957), p. 33.
[3] Christie, ii, p. xxvii; R. North, op. cit., pp. 46, 58–59.
[4] 'J. T.' to William Arton, 17 Dec., in the Rijksarchief at The Hague, Fagel papers 244.

or in referring it to commissioners. He tried to cut through the technicalities and circumlocutions of Chancery, unpalatable as this was to all the conservative lawyers of the Court. One simple and obvious reform which he introduced from the very first day in court was an order that the 'registers' should begin by reading aloud the decrees they had set down the day before, so that any errors could be corrected. This was no doubt one reason why there were so few appeals from his judgments.[1]

Shaftesbury had also more far-reaching ideas for the reform of Chancery. His interest in this dated back at least to the days when he had sat on the committee appointed to advise the Rump in 1652. Then and in the Barebones Parliament he had listened to exasperated complaints against the court's slowness, and the consequent accumulation of cases, delay and expense. In 1661 Clarendon and the Master of the Rolls, Sir Harbottle Grimston, had issued some orders to cope with all this, but they had not been sufficiently comprehensive to effect the vast improvement which was necessary. Shaftesbury projected a far more complete reorganization, and he asked for the opinions of the law officers and others upon his draft. Unfortunately his plans were dropped when he fell from power. A great legal historian's opinion of Shaftesbury's orders was that they constituted 'a complete code of procedure: and they show that Shaftesbury was quite able to appreciate the principles which should underline the procedure of the court, and the main evils against which it was necessary to guard'; and elsewhere, that 'if Shaftesbury had held office longer, his talents and experience as an administrator might have effected some valuable reforms in the organization of the court, and the litigant would have rejoiced in his clear intellect and impatience of unnecessary delay'. In the field of legal reform as in that of colonial policy, his fall meant the loss of an opportunity.[2]

The duties of the Lord Chancellor also extended into many by-ways, from the custody of idiots and lunatics to the issue to shipwrecked sailors of licences to beg.[3] He also had under his control considerable ecclesiastical patronage, and characteristically he had lists made of the value of the livings at the King's disposal. He was particularly concerned with the number of livings in the King's gift which were filled by clergy whom the King had not presented; such unauthorized people, having no legal title or responsibility, would be likely to be both negligent and wasteful of the property of the benefice, and there was a danger that in the long run the King's right of presentation would be totally lost. He therefore called on some of the bishops to provide him with lists of the livings in the King's gift, with the names of their holders and whether they officiated as incumbents duly presented, 'or otherwise put in'; and in future if the

---

[1] P.R.O., C 37/191; Locke to Clarke, 4 May 1693, in *Correspondence of John Locke and Edward Clarke*, ed. B. Rand (1927), p. 374.
[2] Shaftesbury Papers, XLII, 58; Sir William Holdsworth, *History of English Law* (1922-7), vi. 614-15, 526-7. 					[3] *C.S.P.D. 1672-3*, p. 181.

bishops found it necessary to put in a curate, they were to notify him of the curate's name and stipend.[1]

John Locke became his Secretary of Presentations and opened a book recording the petitions of clergy for vacant benefices, with Shaftesbury's fiat appended. The second entry is the humble petition of John Highmore, Clerk, Master of Arts (the Rector of Wimborne St. Giles) for a prebend in the cathedral church of Bath and Wells: but this attempt to cash in on his patron's favour was foiled, because Locke noted that the former incumbent was not dead, and so the grant was void. Another of Shaftesbury's chaplains, Nathaniel Hodges, was also unlucky at first, for a prebend at Ely was recalled and given to someone else; but Hodges had not long to wait, for by May 1673 he was in possession of prebends both at Norwich and at Gloucester, and exempted from the twenty-one days residence which he was legally required to keep there. Shaftesbury made no bones about using his patronage in the customary manner of the period, for the benefit of his own dependants.[2]

Another duty was to make formal speeches on suitable occasions, particularly when high officers of state and judges took their oaths on appointment. Such speeches are not generally remarkable for profundity, sincerity or systematic exposition of political ideas; but Shaftesbury's speeches bear all the signs of being very carefully composed, and he had them all printed, however brief, for the benefit of the public. Two of them, in the winter of 1672-3, are especially interesting: the first of them was made on 5 December 1672, when his colleague Clifford, newly appointed Lord Treasurer, took his oath in the Exchequer.[3] Addressing him, Shaftesbury said that he was greatly honoured to be chosen by a King,

who, without flattery I may say, is as great a master in the knowledge of men and things, as this, or any other age hath produced; and let me say farther, it is not only your honour, that you are chosen by him, but it is your safety too, that you have him to serve with whom no subtle insinuations of any near him, nor the aspiring interest of a favourite, shall ever prevail against those that serve him well. Nor can his servants fear to be sacrificed to the malice, fury or mistake of a more swelling popular greatness. A Prince under whom the unfortunate fall gently. A prince, in a word, that best of all mankind, deserves the title of *deliciae humani generis*.

To a casual reader this might simply seem unpleasingly fulsome flattery of Charles, to be contrasted with the speaker's later disloyalty. But Clifford and the others who listened to it must have thought very differently of it. They could easily recall that the subtle insinuations of Clarendon's enemies had undermined him, that Clarendon had been sacrificed to the anger of Parliament, that Clarendon had not fallen at all gently, for at that

[1] Shaftesbury Papers, XLII, 59; V, 257.
[2] MSS. Locke c. 44, fos. 1, 3; *C.S.P.D. 1673*, pp. 508-9.
[3] Christie, ii, pp. lviii-lix.

moment he was spending his last years in distant exile. The speech was in fact an outspoken indication that Charles's ministers would expect stronger support from the King in the parliamentary session which was approaching, than Clarendon had received in 1667.

Allusion has already been made to the speech to Baron Thurland on his appointment as one of the Barons of the Exchequer Court, on 24 January 1673.[1] It contains some interesting remarks on a judge's duties to King and to subject.

. . . In the first place, you are to maintain the King's prerogative; and let not the King's prerogative, and the Law, be two things with you. For the King's prerogative is law, and the principal part of the law; and therefore, in maintaining that, you maintain the law. The government of England is so excellently inter-woven, that every part of the prerogative hath a broad mixture of the interest of the subject; the ease and safety of the people being inseparable from the greatness and security of the Crown.

. . . let me recommend to you, so to manage the King's justice and revenue, as the King may have most profit, and the subject least vexation.

As an example of this, he put Thurland on his guard against being too ready to allow the courts to send out processes for small sums:

. . . when you consider, how much the officers of this Court and the under-sheriffs get by process upon small sums, more than the King's duty comes to, and upon what sort of people this falls, to wit, the farmer, husbandman, and clothier in the country, that is generally the collector, constable, and tithingman; and so disturbs the industrious part of the nation, you will think it fit to make that the last way, when no other will serve.[2]

Thus he endeavours to reconcile the interests of government and of the governed. It is not a very profound piece of argument—it states an ideal but is very vague about the means by which the ideal is to be realized. Nonetheless the insistence on the needs of 'the industrious part of the nation' is of some significance. In 1673 he still identified them with those of an enlightened monarchical régime. Here again, as in the previous speech, too much stress must not be laid on an apparent contrast between the words of 1673 and the deeds of a decade later. Even under the pressure of the Exclusion crisis he did not contemplate Republicanism and rejected the wholesale 'limitations' which Halifax wished to impose on the royal authority; his aim was rather to see a suitable successor on the throne, exercising the royal prerogative, than to abolish it. His belief remained in an 'excellently interwoven' constitution, perhaps not so very far removed from that of the eighteenth-century Whigs, in which the powers of the Crown were used for the benefit of 'the industrious part of the nation'. The difficulty was that the Stuarts never quite filled the bill.

---

[1] Christie, ii, pp. lix–lxi.
[2] Cf. however his remarks on the chimney money, C.T.B. 1669–72, p. 352, though it may reasonably be argued that the nature of chimney money made it something of a special case.

Both these speeches in different ways reflected the political situation at the time they were delivered. Public opinion (using that phrase to indicate the opinion of those classes with parliamentary influence) was becoming all-important with the approach of the new session on 4 February 1673. From the House of Commons would be required approval both for Charles's foreign policy and for the religious policy of the Declaration of Indulgence; and the necessity of meeting the House could not be evaded, since it alone could supply the money which was necessary for a further naval campaign. The realization of this influenced almost every decision taken by the committee of foreign affairs. For instance, the committee had to face the prospect that Spain, realizing that a Dutch defeat would destroy the biggest obstacle to a French annexation of Flanders, would join the Dutch and declare war on Louis XIV. This might mean that England would have to break with Spain too, destroying a trade which was recognized as being peculiarly profitable to England and endangering the considerable assets which English merchants had in Spain. On this problem Charles and Shaftesbury took different views: whereas the King wanted tactful warning to be given to the merchants, the earl thought it less likely that Spain, whatever her inclination, would risk declaring war, and was opposed at all costs to alarming the merchants. For once James agreed with Shaftesbury, and their opinion prevailed and was vindicated. The possibility of a thoroughly unpopular war with Spain was minimized, and to that extent it would be easier to defend the King's foreign policy to Parliament.[1]

Another unpleasant possibility, however, remained—the possibility that Dutch agents might seek to exploit the discontent of members of Parliament and turn it against the French alliance. Fears of this were stimulated when on 14 January two Dutchmen landed at Harwich from the packet-boat. One of them, Zas, had been in England previously in December, seeking to open unofficial peace negotiations on behalf of William of Orange, and Shaftesbury had then agreed with Clifford that Zas should be sent away 'only do it with kindness. . . . Show him what the King has done towards a Peace, only convince him the King will expect Towns'—a view with which James agreed. Shaftesbury had not then feared any ill effects in Parliament from Zas's arrival, but several other members of the foreign committee had suspected that his negotiations were merely a cloak for attempts to stir up trouble. Zas's reappearance three weeks before the meeting of Parliament without proper credentials seemed to confirm this suspicion: it was altogether too much of a coincidence.[2] Moreover his companion, a notary named Arton, carried with him a letter, addressed to Shaftesbury, from Pierre Du Moulin.

Du Moulin was an embittered Huguenot with a life-long hatred of

---

[1] Foreign Entry Book 177, 24, 25, 26 Nov.

[2] Ibid. 11 Dec. 1672; Mayor of Harwich to Arlington, 14 Jan. 1673, *C.S.P.D. 1672–3*, p. 428.

Popery and of Louis XIV, who had first become a naturalized Englishman and had sought a career for himself in the English service, but had inevitably fallen out of favour when the Triple Alliance policy had been replaced by a French alliance. He had now fled the country and was devoting all his ideological fervour to the service of William of Orange as the best remaining bulwark against French aggression; and having convinced William of his ability and knowledge of English conditions, he was now trying to re-form connexions with influential Englishmen whom he had previously known, so that they might be turned against Charles's pro-French policy.[1] He had been secretary to the Council of Trade, and so was acquainted with Shaftesbury and knew that he was far from being a devoted friend of France. It was a natural step to write from The Hague to Shaftesbury, appealing for a private interview in which 'I have things to propose to you, which would fully satisfy you how far I am an Englishman'. He asked that this interview should take place in absolute secrecy—he said that Lauderdale might be informed but preferred that the matter should be strictly between himself and Shaftesbury.[2] When a letter in this strain was found in Arton's possession, it was inevitably, and rightly, interpreted as having a sinister purpose—that of dividing the members of the Cabal. This was explicitly confirmed when on 24 January the Foreign Committee read a long report from William Howard, their spy in Holland (who was, however, really a 'double agent'). The letter may have revived Charles's suspicions of a Lord Chancellor in whom he had never had complete confidence: he announced his intention of examining Arton himself. It was rumoured that Zas and Arton had admitted to having instructions to communicate with two other peers of notoriously anti-French sentiments, Holles and Halifax, but in fact they held out against all questioning. To this the members of the Cabal showed their own characteristic reactions. Lauderdale, brutal and entirely unscrupulous, briefly recommended that Zas should be first racked and then hanged. Clifford, equally extreme but not so much of a sadist, favoured hanging only. Buckingham favoured 'getting to the bottom of the design rather than taking away his life'. Arlington said nothing. Shaftesbury, more subtle than Lauderdale or Clifford, was prepared to use the threat of torture but not to carry it out: 'Go as far to torment him as you can. Show him the rack, tell him of it, but not execute it.' He was prepared to go far along the road of mental cruelty in order to exercise pressure on the prisoners, but not to inflict senseless physical cruelty. This more moderate policy was adopted, and Lauderdale and Secretary Coventry were commissioned to show Zas and Arton the rack on the following morning.[3]

---

[1] Cf. my *William of Orange and the English Opposition, 1672–4* (1953), *passim*; and see ch. v. for a fuller treatment of the Zas and Arton episode.

[2] 30 Dec. 1672, *C.S.P.D. 1672–3*, pp. 325–6.

[3] Foreign Entry Book 177, 19, 24, 25, 26, 28 Jan. 1673; B. Woodroffe (chaplain to the

The two Dutchmen held out against this terrible threat, even when it was wielded by Lauderdale. Perhaps, indeed, they had nothing more to tell than Charles and his ministers already knew. They were then sent back to their respective cells in the Tower. There was talk of a commission to try them, and even of applying torture 'yet not so as to lame or disable them', but in the end they were left to languish there, until one escaped and peace released the other.[1] Yet the episode was not without its consequences. It may have helped to revive the distrust of Shaftesbury to which Charles was always prone. And equally it may have made Shaftesbury feel that in order to dissipate any doubts on the part of the King, he must show himself a particularly emphatic supporter of the King's foreign policy. It was precisely in these days when Zas and Arton were being examined that he was preparing the *Delenda est Carthago* speech.

By this time the parliamentary session was only a week away. The 'foreign committee' had long been making its preparations for it; in few sessions can the government have planned so carefully to try to secure a favourable majority. As far back as 24 November, the problem of the choice of a suitable Speaker had been discussed. Shaftesbury, after mentioning Sir Robert Howard (who was present) 'but that he is seen in the Treasury', and Robert Milward (who was also present), had misgivings about Sir Job Charlton, fearing 'his zeal to run with his own opinion against the King's measures . . .'. It is not surprising that Charlton was an unwelcome choice for Shaftesbury, for in the Convention Charlton 'was very violent' against him as a Cromwellian; but there seemed no satisfactory alternative, and the Speakership was therefore offered to Charlton, with a suitable pension to act as an incentive.[2] Other measures were a meeting of those Privy Councillors who had seats in the Commons,[3] a further meeting at Arlington's house of 'such as the Lord Chancellor, Lord Treasurer, and Earl of Arlington shall think fit', and the reading of Shaftesbury's official speech as Lord Chancellor in the foreign committee, where it was 'allowed with one or two alterations'.[4] Most important, however, was the issue by Shaftesbury of writs to fill the thirty-six seats which had fallen vacant during the long prorogation. Shaftesbury, with Locke's aid, was well prepared with precedents for this, but the normal practice was for writs to be issued by the Speaker; and as the writs were issued suddenly after the middle of January, 1673, the move was rightly

---

Duke of York) to the Earl of Huntingdon, 30 Jan. 1673, *H.M.C. Hastings Papers*, ii. 161–2; note of Arton's examination, 27 Jan., S.P. Charles II, 332, fo. 217; Howard's letter of 17/27 Jan., S.P. 84/183, fos. 69–72.

[1] Foreign Entry Book 177, 1 Feb., 13 Apr.; *C.S.P.D. 1673*, pp. 53–54, 95, 144.

[2] Foreign Entry Book 177; S. Charlton to Sir R. Leveson, 3 June 1660, *H.M.C. Fifth Report*, p. 205.

[3] *C.S.P.D. 1672–3*, p. 630; Foreign Entry Book 177, 19, 30 Jan., 2 Feb. 1673.

[4] Ibid. 28 Jan.

interpreted as an attempt to increase the number of members with an interest in voting supplies and supporting the King's policy. There were some who thought it a still more sinister plan of Shaftesbury's to fill the vacancies with 'creatures of his own'; and he did back both his brother, George Cooper, at Poole, and John Man, secretary to the Customs Commissioners, for another Dorset seat at Melcombe Regis. But an analysis of the members returned shows clearly that the great majority later belonged to the 'Court Party', and almost all of them could be expected to vote for supplies for the King. Even Thomas Papillon, later a Whig, who was elected at Dover, was bound to vote for money, since in 1673 he was Victualler to the Navy. At Chester Shaftesbury used his influence to try to get the later Whig, William Williams, to withdraw in favour of Robert Werden, a client of the Duke of York. The issue of the writs was not an attempt to build up a party of Shaftesbury's own, but to strengthen the government's support in the Commons. It was proof that in January 1673, he was still prepared to throw his whole weight into the struggle to win financial assistance for the King and the war against the Dutch.[1]

The famous *Delenda est Carthago* speech at the opening of Parliament on 5 February 1673 was directed to the same end. After Charles had begun by announcing his uncompromising intention of standing by the Declaration of Indulgence and raising more armed forces to continue the war in the summer, Shaftesbury proceeded to a much longer exposition of the King's policy. He began by saying that 'His Majesty had called you sooner, and his affairs required it, but that he was resolved to give you all the ease and vacancy to your own private concerns, and the people as much respite from payments and taxes, as the necessity of his business, or their preservation, would permit'. As an excuse for not consulting Parliament earlier about the war, this can have deceived no-one. He then went on to the main matter of his speech, a justification of the attack on the Dutch, and the need of money to pursue it. Recapitulating the usual grievances against the Dutch, he skilfully reminded the Commons that they had seen the danger as far back as 1664, 'but it could not then be so well-timed, or our alliances so well made. But you judged aright, that at any rate *Delenda est Carthago*, that government was to be brought down, and therefore the King may well say to you, This is your war. He took his measures from you, and they were just and right ones. . . .' He further appealed to the patriotism of members to show the world how futile it was to send over agents like the two now in the Tower, by voting large supplies to complete the defeat of the Dutch. After supplies had been voted for the war, the Commons might consider what could be done for the bankers who had been affected by the Stop of the Exchequer. His references to the Declaration of Indulgence consisted mainly of vague praise of His Majesty's

---

[1] Foreign Entry Book 177, 30 Jan. 1673; Shaftesbury Papers, XLVII, 8; R. North, op. cit. p. 56; Shaftesbury to Williams, 16 Jan. 1673, Christie, ii. 127.

devotion to the Church of England; and in a fulsome peroration he concluded with the hope that 'this Triple Alliance of King, Parliament, and
people, may never be dissolved'. This was a curiously impertinent attempt
to use the emotions of approval associated with the phrase 'the Triple
Alliance' to support the reversal of the policy of the original alliance
of 1668.[1]

Viewed in its context, the phrase *Delenda est Carthago*[2] was not a reckless,
impassioned outburst of a vehement hater of the Dutch, but part of the
calculated argument of a politician putting the government's case in the
best tactical way. His contention was that the war of 1672 had not been
the result of a merely personal policy of the King's, but was only the logical
continuation of a policy for which Parliament itself had pressed in 1664.
Parliament, he was saying, had foreseen then that the rivalry between
English and Dutch was as fundamental as that between Romans and
Carthaginians had been, 'and therefore the King may well say to you,
This is *your* war', and the House of Commons could not avoid voting
money to support it. This was such an obviously sensible line to take in the
circumstances, that it is unnecessary to suppose (with some of Shaftesbury's
friends who later tried to explain the speech away)[3] that it had been
written by other members of the Cabal for him reluctantly to deliver.
The speech had certainly been submitted to the foreign committee and
'allowed with one or two alterations',[4] but there is no reason to suppose
that these alterations were fundamental, and no strictly contemporary
hint that it did not represent his views. Given that Shaftesbury had
signed the *traité simulé* and joined in the attack on the Dutch, the
speech was only a continuation of the same policy.

The speech was both skilful and successful. It had been planned that
after the formal opening was over, the House of Commons should be
sent to its own hall 'to make some brisk resolution' upon the King's
speech before opposition could be properly organized.[5] There followed a
long debate lasting four hours in the February evening by the flickering
light of one solitary candle on the clerk's table. When that had almost
burnt down in its socket the Court supporters reluctantly agreed to an
adjournment of the debate until Friday. But the debate on Friday, 7
February, went much better from the government's point of view. The
foreign policy set out in Shaftesbury's speech and upheld also by Secretary

---

[1] *L.J.* xii. 524–7; Christie, ii, pp. lxiii–lxix.
[2] Cato's words had occurred to others besides Shaftesbury. Cf. my *William of Orange
and the English Opposition 1672–4* (1953), p. 68, for an extract from an unsigned letter in
Du Moulin's papers, dated 10 Oct./31 Sept. (*sic*), 1672.
[3] Cf. Stringer, who claimed that he had transcribed Shaftesbury's first version of the
speech and then seen the speech much altered by 'the Council' (Christie, ii, pp. xxxiv–vi),
and the statement of Shaftesbury's grandson that Locke had to stand near, ready to prompt
his master if he fumbled words which were not his own: Shaftesbury to Le Clerc, 8 Feb.
1705, Amsterdam University Library, Remonstrants' MSS., J 20.
[4] Foreign Entry Book 177, 28 Jan.   [5] Ibid. 2 Feb.

Henry Coventry, was not seriously challenged; and in the end the House voted *nemine contradicente* that £1,260,000 should be raised over a period of eighteen months. So far, so good. The reason why the vote had been delayed a couple of days was not any explicit opposition to the war, but a feeling that redress of grievances should be given priority. One minor grievance had already been settled.

At the Commons' preliminary meeting on 4 February the legality of Shaftesbury's issue of writs for bye-elections during the recess was disputed. No sooner had a Speaker been elected than Colonel Sir Giles Strangeways raised the matter. It was nearly thirty years since young Sir Anthony Ashley Cooper had burnt down the Strangeways' house at Abbotsbury during the Civil War, but no doubt the memory still rankled. But Strangeways had a much more direct interest in the matter too: his son Thomas had opposed Shaftesbury's brother George at Poole, and his protégé John Man at Melcombe Regis, and had been beaten at both places —a severe blow to his prestige amongst the Dorset gentry. It is not surprising that he was to be found in the van of the attack on 4 February. After the official speeches on the following day, the King added a postscript inviting the House to examine the precedents for the issue of writs by his order during a recess, in the confidence that precedents would justify what had been done; but on 6 February the House by 169 votes to 103 refused to appoint a committee to inspect the precedents, and declared the elections void without more ado. As one supporter of the Court sadly noted, the majority of members cared little about the precedents and much more about the constitutional point of the 'inconveniences which might arise upon this power in the Chancellor'. The thirty-six members therefore had to file out of the House. Many of them were re-elected at the bye-elections which followed, but they came back too late to influence the most important decisions which the House had to take; and George Cooper was not among them, for it seems that a bargain was struck by which he withdrew in favour of Thomas Strangeways at Poole, and John Man was chosen again at Melcombe Regis. Shaftesbury was mortified by the declaration that his writs had been illegal; but it is doubtful whether he had grounds for complaint of lack of adequate support from the King, as some have suggested. The subject had been raised *before* the King alluded to it in his speech on 5 February; and the point was one on which the plainly expressed wishes of the majority of the House of Commons had to be accepted.[1]

The matter of the writs was in any case only a minor one. Much more serious was that of the Declaration of Indulgence. On 8 February some

---

[1] For the debates of 4–7 Feb. 1673, see *The Parliamentary Journal of Sir Edward Dering, 1670–3*, ed. B. D. Henning (1940), pp. 103–12; Grey, ii. 2–11; *L.J.* xii. 526–7; *C.J.* ix. 248. For the elections at Poole and Melcombe Regis, cf. *C.S.P.D. 1672–3*, pp. 300, 304, 322–3, 510–11, 572–3.

of the leaders who had joined in the vote of the previous day for supply, such as Sir Thomas Meres and Strangeways, made plain the price which they expected the government to pay in return. Though the Declaration was not without its defenders, they were overborne by weight of numbers and of argument. The critics' main concern was not with the toleration of Dissenters, but with the encouragement given to Popery, and they argued also that the King's power to suspend laws, if once admitted, might be extended to other statutes as well as penal laws in matters of religion. Henry Powle declared that 'The consequence of this is direful; the King by this may change religion as he pleases; we are confident of him, but knows not what succession may be'. Fears of James, Duke of York, were probably in the minds of many, though even Powle did not state them explicitly. Strangeways, as might have been expected, tried to turn the debate against his enemy Shaftesbury: he thought that the House might enquire whether Lord Keeper Bridgeman had not refused to affix the Great Seal to the Declaration because he thought it illegal, and sneeringly observed that he 'would not have those that are not lawyers, or divines, prescribe out of their profession. . . . In point of law, would have the King advised by those that profess the law.' But this oblique attack on the Lord Chancellor was not taken up by anyone else.[1] For once, the House was less interested in personalities than in establishing the illegality of the Declaration. Rejecting the more respectful method of a petition to the King, the House resolved by 168 votes to 116 that penal statutes in matters ecclesiastical could not be suspended except by Act of Parliament, and appointed a committee to draw up an address communicating their vote to the King. And while awaiting a reply to this address they declined to make progress with the money bill, for, as Buckingham observed in the committee of foreign affairs, 'they know every man there, that as soon as the bill is passed, their time is over'.[2]

The foreign committee was thus confronted with an awkward problem. Would it be possible both to cling to the Declaration and to obtain the money bill? If not, which should they choose? At first the ministers were united in trying to cope with the difficulty by diversions. Shaftesbury and James, Duke of York, for once were in agreement that they should 'keep the House sweet', and gain time by getting the government's supporters to suggest, firstly, that the House should seek the concurrence of the Lords to

[1] Grey, ii. 25. J. Oldmixon, *History of England during the reigns of the Royal House of Stuart* (1730), pp. 571–2, gives a melodramatic account of an impending impeachment of Shaftesbury which was diverted by the latter's offer to Sir Robert Howard of the reversion to the Auditorship of the Exchequer. This Howard did receive on 6 March 1673 (*C.S.P.D. 1673*, p. 18). But it was not in Shaftesbury's gift, Sir Robert Howard was a supporter of the Declaration and usually on the same political side as the Chancellor, and there is no corroboration of any attempt at impeachment, which in any case could hardly have been evaded by bribery of one man.

[2] Dering, op. cit. pp. 114–16; Grey, ii. 13–26; *C.J.* ix. 251; For. Entry Book 177, 16 Feb.

their address, and secondly, that a bill be introduced to give ease to Dissenters, and the address be re-drafted to take account of this. Such a bill would meet the professions of many critics in the Commons that their objections to the Declaration were constitutional and not directed against its purpose of relieving Dissenters; and it might divide many Anglicans from them. But these tactics failed. On 14 February the Commons did agree that a bill should be brought in for the ease of Protestant Dissenters, but they refused to hold up their address to the King or to spend time in seeking the concurrence of the Lords. The ministers were left with the same problem as before, thrust back upon them.[1]

On the same day cracks began to develop in the unity of the foreign committee. Arlington and Clifford urged that the King should 'be kind in the handling of this address', but Shaftesbury insisted: 'Yet so as not to quit the point of right, but answer cross to the point. Rather lose money than lose rights. And at last state the point to the House of Lords and engage them in it, who will certainly determine otherwise.' Two days later there was a longer debate on whether or not it was desirable to encourage the Lords to take up the matter. Arlington, temperamentally the most timid of the Cabal, hoped that the Lords would not do so 'till the King sees whether he shall have anything or not', and Secretary Henry Coventry, fearful of a second Medway disaster, was also anxious to have the money bill first; but Shaftesbury said that he 'would be glad the House of Lords would vote the King's Declaration good etc. whenever they are disposed to it'. The King's matter-of-fact view was that 'upon the whole matter let the Money Bill be first got. What is the discretion for a man to be angry to his own hurt? And have a care not to be left without a fleet this spring.' Buckingham found points to be made on both sides. As the dilemma became sharper this divergence of opinion steadily grew. Shaftesbury set greatest store by maintaining the principle of the Declaration; Charles cared little for it in comparison with the need to fit out a fleet in support of his French alliance.[2]

On 22 February Sir Thomas Meres bluntly stated in the Commons 'that a gracious answer from the King to this address would very much smooth the passage of the money bill'; and two days later the King's answer came pat. It reflected Shaftesbury's advice, maintaining the King's ecclesiastical supremacy but denying any claim to be able to suspend laws in which the properties, rights and liberties of his subjects were affected. His only intention, he asserted, was 'to take off the penalties inflicted upon the Dissenters', and while he would not give up the prerogative which he claimed he offered to concur in any bill which was presented to him for the same purpose. But the House was not to be diverted from the constitutional principle at stake. Even those who favoured a bill for the ease of

[1] Foreign Entry Book 177, 12 Feb. 1673; Grey, ii. 26–37.
[2] Foreign Entry Book 177, 14, 16 Feb. 1673.

Dissenters refused to accept it as a reason for abandoning the issue of the Declaration; and any dissensions over the bill were more than offset by the united hostility which all the members of the opposition showed towards Popery. 'Let us take care,' said Meres, 'that, whilst we dispute the indulging the Protestant subjects, the third dog does not take the bone from us both.' On 26 February 'the Court side' was outvoted and a new address sent to the King which included the ominous phrase, reminiscent of the days of James I and Charles I, that he had been 'misinformed' about his powers, and asked for 'a full and satisfactory answer'.[1]

Faced by this stubborn attitude of the Commons, Shaftesbury, Clifford, Lauderdale and Buckingham were even prepared to advocate dissolving Parliament and calling a new one. So at least the French ambassador was told by Arlington, who did not think the Declaration was worth such a drastic step. Nor did the King, who decided instead to adopt Shaftesbury's original advice and see whether support from the House of Lords could redress the balance. In a short speech on 1 March he asked for their advice, and called upon the Lord Chancellor to read the Commons' addresses and his reply. Shaftesbury drew attention to a phrase in the address of 26 February which talked of the legislative power residing in 'your Majesty and your two Houses of Parliament'. From this he inferred 'a co-ordination of the three estates' of Parliament, in which the King was reduced to being merely one of three. 'I am commanded', he said, 'to open to you what foundation this co-ordination laid for the late [civil] war; it produced the ordinances [e.g. the Militia Ordinance of 1642] which were the cause of it. Co-ordination makes the two Houses equal with His Majesty in the legislature, whereas the sanction of laws is in the King alone.' If the argument was Shaftesbury's own, it was a feeble one, which in a few years time he would have repudiated; it was at best a debating attempt to appeal to the monarchist sentiments of the Royalist peers. In this it was only partially successful, for the Lords, not explicitly approving the Declaration, voted simply that 'the King's answer to the House of Commons, in referring the points now controverted to a Parliamentary way by Bill, is good and gracious', and appointed a committee under Shaftesbury's chairmanship to prepare a bill of their own. Clifford and Anglesey each put forward proposals to this committee. The Lord Treasurer's bill would have removed the 'jealousy' given by the Declaration by giving the King 'power (if it be not in him already) to suspend penal statutes in matters ecclesiastical out of time of Parliament'; but 'except it be in great exigences and emergencies' the King would not suspend such statutes wholesale without naming them. Anglesey's bill, on the other hand, would have denied the King any such power, but gone on to enact the suspension of certain statutes for five years. It has been

---

[1] Dering, op. cit. p. 128; C.J. ix. 256, 257; Grey, ii. 62–69.

suggested that Clifford's proposal was made by arrangement with Shaftesbury, and that the latter was 'counselling moderation'. The former may
well be true, for Clifford's bill fitted in well enough with the ideas Shaftesbury expressed on other occasions; but there was no question of moderation, for though the bill would have provided certain minor restrictions,
the central principle of the Declaration of Indulgence would have been
confirmed by it. There was no real compromise in it.[1]

At this point, however, the essential intransigence of Shaftesbury and
Clifford was rendered fruitless. By now Charles had had enough. On the
same day as Clifford's proposals were discussed, he determined to abandon
Shaftesbury's policy, and to cancel the Declaration. According to the
French ambassador, on the previous day (Thursday, 6 March) the King
had seemed determined to go to the length of dissolving Parliament in
order to preserve his prerogative; but on Friday morning, after hearing a
message from Louis XIV in which the French King urged him to give
way and hinted at further financial assistance, he changed his mind.
Possibly Charles had made up his mind earlier, and kept up a pretence for
Colbert's benefit until he had a prospect of suitable promises from Louis.
At all events the game was up. The Venetian ambassador was told that the
debate in the foreign committee lasted six hours before the decision was
accepted by all; but next day the cancellation of the Declaration was
announced to both Houses, Shaftesbury himself performing this unpalatable task in the Lords. Thanks to the King were voted, and the
Commons promptly went into committee on supply. It was as simple as
that.[2]

Yet there was still another hurdle to surmount before the money bill
was passed for which the King had given up the Declaration. Not content
with that, and an address to the King against Popery more vehement than
any previous one, the House of Commons had carried its hatred of Popery
still further. On the motion of William Sacheverell they had turned their
attention to the numbers of Catholics who were known to hold commissions
in the armed forces and places at Court, and from their alarm had come
a Test Act incapacitating all persons who did not take the Anglican
sacrament and make a declaration against transubstantiation from holding
either civil or military office. The bill had been generally approved by the
Commons, but inevitably there was the fear that it might not get through
the Lords before the end of the session. Once again Sir Thomas Meres's
advice was the traditional parliamentary tactic: as he expressed it, he
'would not have this [money] Bill sent up to hinder them, to make a
parenthesis in business there to interrupt them', and the weight of opinion

---

[1] Colbert, 27 Feb./9 Mar. (J. Dalrymple, *Memoirs*, 1773, ii. 89); *L.J.* xii. 539, 543;
Shaftesbury Papers, VI B, 431 (a paper giving reasons for referring the dispute to the
Lords); *H.M.C. Tenth Report*, pt. vi, Braye MSS., pp. 181–2; *H.M.C. Ninth Report*,
pt. ii, *House of Lords MSS.* p. 25; Brown, pp. 207–10.

[2] Colbert, 10/20 Mar.; *C.S.P. Ven. 1673–5*, p. 27; *L.J.* xii. 549; *C.J.* ix. 265–6.

was on his side. It was ordered that the engrossed money bill should not be considered until 21 March, when the attitude of the Lords to the Test bill would be clear.[1]

When Shaftesbury, sitting on the woolsack, received the Test Act from a deputation of members from the Commons, he asked whether they had not brought the money bill as well, and to his surprise was told that they had not. The Lords responded to this stimulus by rushing the Test bill through all its stages. The first reading took place on 13 March, the second reading on the 14th, and the House went into committee on the 15th. After a sub-committee under Shaftesbury's chairmanship had prepared some amendments on minor points, the bill passed on 20 March with provisos exempting the household servants of the Duke of York and the Queen from its provisions. After conferences between the Houses it was agreed that the Duke of York's servants should be subject to the requirements of the Act, like those of any other Catholics, but that exemptions should be given to present members of the Queen's household.[2]

On these terms the Test Act passed, followed by the long-awaited money bill, but not before the last debates in the Lords brought to light some deep divergences between the King's ministers. In the course of the debate on 20 March Clifford made an impulsive, violent attack on the Test Act. As he later told James, when he went to the House he did not intend to speak, but when the time came 'he could not resist the inspiration of God'. In vehement terms he said that it 'ought to be spurred out of the House as a dirty bill', described it as *monstrum horrendum ingens*, and objected to the Lords' tame acquiescence in the Commons' decision on what were purely church matters—for that was what the declaration against transubstantiation amounted to in the bill. James and some of the bishops were inclined to approve; but Shaftesbury saved the situation by making an equally strongly-worded reply to Clifford.

The sight of the Lord Chancellor and Lord Treasurer publicly at odds with one another over a major matter of policy would have been remarkable at any time. As it was the episode firmly established the reputation of Clifford as a zealot for the Catholic cause, and of Shaftesbury as a Protestant hero. Both then and since Clifford's action has seemed perfectly consistent with his actions at other times, but Shaftesbury's action has appeared to be a reversal of the policy of religious indulgence in which he had previously co-operated with Clifford; for support of the Test Act confining office to Anglicans seems irreconcilable with support for a Declaration of Indulgence. It looks almost like a desertion of the government for the opposition; and modern historians have tried to explain it, either by supposing (with Colbert de Croissy) that Arlington had betrayed the

---

[1] Grey, ii. 108–15; Dering, p. 139. (Debate of 15 Mar.)

[2] *L.J.* xii. 554, 557, 567–9; *H.M.C. Ninth Report*, pt. ii, p. 29; Grey, ii. 137–54, 157–9; Colbert, 17/27 Mar.

secret of the Treaty of Dover to Shaftesbury in order to revenge himself on the man who had deprived him of the Treasurership; or by supposing that Shaftesbury had guessed the secret of the Treaty from Clifford's actions; or even by supposing that Clifford told Shaftesbury himself, thinking that the latter had no real religious convictions anyway and was not averse to Popery. Shaftesbury's resentment at learning that he had been a victim of such gross deception might well lead him to mutiny, it has been argued. Alternatively, there is the more cynical suspicion to be considered, that Shaftesbury was simply saving himself by going over to the popular side. But all these guesses are wide of the mark, for three reasons. Firstly, there is no satisfactory evidence that Shaftesbury did suspect what happened at Dover. If he had done so, he or his pamphleteers would surely have alluded to it; but Whig propaganda, when it referred to the Dover meeting at all, suggested that it was the *beginning* of a negotiation, and not the end of it.[1] In the second place, Shaftesbury's reply to Clifford made good political sense from the King's own point of view. As Charles and Arlington both told the French ambassador, Clifford's act had revived the violence of the opposition in the Commons and endangered the money bill at the last; there was dark talk of 'evil counsellors' and rumours of impending impeachments of Clifford and Lauderdale which were only narrowly averted. As Colbert de Croissy reported back to Louis XIV, it was extremely silly of Clifford to speak up for the Catholics after Charles had given up the Declaration of Indulgence, accepted an address against Popery and promised to take action against it: Clifford was risking again the loss of the money for which the King had already given up one of his cherished prerogatives. Colbert's report contains no disapproving mention of Shaftesbury's speech, which can easily be interpreted as an attempt to repair the harm which Clifford's speech had done.[2]

In the third place, support of the Declaration of Indulgence and support of the Test Act are not so inconsistent as they might appear to be at first sight in an advocate of toleration for Dissenters. Nowadays freedom of worship and religious equality go hand in hand; but in the seventeenth century it was possible to believe that Dissenters should be tolerated but nevertheless excluded from public office. Moreover, Dissenters themselves were prepared to be content with this in 1673. In an earlier period they

---

[1] Cf. the short reference in A. Marvell, *Growth of Popery*; *Works*, ed. Grosart (1875), iv. 266. Stringer, in his account of these years, refers to the 'Dover articles' as though they provided for the assistance of French troops to restore Roman Catholicism (Christie, ii, pp. xxxvii, xl, xliii); but he wrote about 1700 and it may only be a guess. In other respects Stringer's account of his master's actions in 1672–3 can be shown to be inconsistent with better sources such as the Foreign Entry Books which are strictly contemporary. I know of no strictly contemporary references to 'the Dover articles'.

[2] Colbert, 17/27 Mar., 22 Mar./1 Apr., 24 Mar./3 Apr., 10/20 Nov. 1673; Grey ii. 152; Burnet, ii. 9–13 (confusing the debates on the Test Act with those on the Declaration of Indulgence); V. Barbour, *Arlington* (American Historical Association, 1914), pp. 209–10; Brown, p. 209.

would have demanded much more; but now Alderman Love, one of the members for the City of London who presented their views to the House of Commons, asked simply that 'you will permit those that are preachers to preach'. In any case many prominent Puritans had taken the Anglican sacrament in the past,[1] and in the years to come many found it possible to do so to qualify for office. It is significant that the passing of the Test Act was not received with loud howls of Nonconformist protest.[2] Nor was there any attempt later in the reign to repeal it. Dissenters accepted it (as the Commons had intended it) as a measure designed not against themselves, but against Popery; and as good Protestants they supported it. For his own part, Shaftesbury's support of religious toleration had at all times been intended to help Protestant Dissenters; he had never at any time expressed any sympathy with Roman Catholics; and it is scarcely likely that Shaftesbury felt any regret at seeing Catholics excluded from office in the administration and from commissions in the Army and Navy, or regarded himself as going back on his previous ideas.

There is one more positive piece of evidence that Shaftesbury's support of the Test Act did not represent an abandonment of his previous religious policy. In the concluding days of the session, the Bill for the Ease of Dissenters passed through the House of Commons. Many Anglican members had been very lukewarm to it; they had reluctantly accepted the necessity for such a bill, either to demonstrate that their opposition to the Declaration of Indulgence was based on a hatred of Popery and not of Protestant Dissent, or, in some cases, in response to the government's own pressure. Its provisions were very limited, and the requirements of the oath of allegiance and subscription to the Thirty-Nine Articles would have excluded many sectaries from any benefit. Passed without much enthusiasm, and much diluted in the process, the bill was sent up to the Lords, and three amendments to it were debated on 25, 26 and 27 March. One of the clauses inserted at this stage would have given the King power to issue proclamations on religious matters, 'if he saw cause either of liberty or restraint'. When the bill reappeared in the Commons with this clause in it, Sir Thomas Meres immediately pointed out that 'the Proclamation is the same in effect as the Declaration', and though not all the former critics of the Declaration took this view, the majority asked for a conference with the Lords over it. At this conference on 29 March Shaftesbury defended the Lords' view that the King should be recognized to have power to regulate the operation of the bill by proclamation; and incidentally he opposed the Commons' endeavour to restrict the 'ease' which they proposed to give, to men who were willing to subscribe to the Thirty-Nine

---

[1] N. Sykes, *From Sheldon to Secker* (1958), pp. 96–97.

[2] Grey, ii. 40. Cf. the anonymous author of the paper on trade and religion printed by Christie, ii. v–ix, and discussed above, pp. 257–8; he too wanted religious freedom for Dissenters at the price of exclusion from office, and without benefit to Roman Catholics.

Articles, for, he said, 'the Anabaptists are men of good lives, and are good traders'. Returning to their own House, on what they already knew to be the last day of the session, the Commons debated the principle of proclamations in religious matters. Some were in favour, some against; but it was Shaftesbury's old antagonist, Strangeways, who had the last word. He suspected 'that some that made these arguments in the Lords' House had a hand in the Declaration', an obvious innuendo against the Chancellor. Before any question could be put to the vote, Black Rod knocked at the door to summon the members to the adjournment ceremony. The House was adjourned until the end of October. Since it was an adjournment and not a prorogation, the bill was not killed; but by October the political situation had entirely changed. When the House reassembled nothing more was heard of the bill, or of the King's right to pursue a policy towards Dissent by means of proclamations.[1]

The interest of this episode lies in the tenacity of purpose which is revealed in Shaftesbury. To the bitter end he stood by his policy of securing indulgence for Nonconformists by means of an exercise of a form of the royal dispensing power in ecclesiastical matters; he saw more hope of an enlightened, liberal religious policy in that than in the House of Commons which ever since 1661 had shown itself to be exclusively Anglican. But now that the session was over, his hopes lay in ruins; and more than that, the suspicion was growing that the royal family's inclinations towards indulgence sprang from a positive plan to favour the Roman Catholicism which Shaftesbury abominated. The day after the adjournment (30 March) was Easter Sunday, and it was noticed that for the second year in succession James, Duke of York, abstained from taking the Easter communion according to the rites of the Church of England.

[1] *L.J.* xii. 571–5, 579–80; *C.J.* ix. 279–81; Grey, ii. 163–73, 177–80; Roger Thomas in *From Uniformity to Unity*, ed. G. F. Nuttall and O. Chadwick (1962), pp. 212–14.

CHAPTER XVI

THE PARTING OF THE WAYS (1673)

On Monday the 27th of [blank] are to be sold at Public Sale by inch of candle at the Royal Coffee house near Charing Cross these following goods in several parcels.

1 Lot. One whole piece of the Duchess of Cleveland's honesty . . .

2 Lot. Two ells of Nell Gwyn's virginity in 3 pieces . . .

4 Lot. Two rich royal camlet cloaks faced with the Protestant religion and very little the worse for wearing . . .

5 Lot. Two whole pieces of the Duke of Buckingham's religion, 7 yards wide . . .

6 Lot. 14 yds ¾ of a Chancellor's loyalty in 5 remnants, the first of his late Majesty's colour, the 2ᵈ orange tawny, the 3d of Praise God Bare-bones, the 4th of the Protector, the 5th of his present Majesty's colour, prized at a noble p. yard, to advance 2d p. yard each bidding.

7 L. Some remnants more ready mixed, and fit for the loom if the Chancellor live and have good luck to exercise his talent.

8 L. A box of curious legerdemaines of Haver-du-pois, among whom is an Act for stealing away a Chancellor's head from the block and laying a Treasurer's head instead of it,[1] a new invention of the Lord Chancellor's and Lord St. John's . . .

17 L. A very fine Cabal cage with 5 or 6 Canary birds all of differing notes to make the better consort . . .

19 L. Two accurate maps, the one of a new Queen and the other of making the Duke of Monmouth legitimate, both *secundum artem* and of the Chancellor's own drawing, to be presented to Parliament next sessions, valued at his neck and to be advanced at discretion . . .

29 L. Two whole pieces of new fashioned paradoxes, the one to suppress Popery by the suppression of the Protestant interest abroad, the other to maintain liberty by the raising of a standing army at home . . .

34 L. Contains the old Solemn League and Covenant, His Majesty's declaration from Breda with that of the 15th of March 1671 [/2], his royal proclamations against Catholics, and that of paying the bankers, with the present sacrament, valued altogether at 5 groats.

35 L. Two dozen of French wenches the one half paid by his Majesty to keep him right to the Protestant religion, the other to incline him to the Catholics, managed by the two factions in the Cabal . . .

41 L. The art of making brick without straw, written by Stephen Primate the Lord Craven's secretary of the burnt buildings, wherein is showed

[1] A reference to the Lords' debate on the Test Act.

a cheap and expeditious way for building any part of the City, whenever it shall be burned again, intended for the Queen Mother, but
since dedicated to His Highness the Duke of York . . .[1]

THE satirist who expressed his scorn of the Court in this manner in
the spring of 1673 did not make any significant distinction between
Shaftesbury and the rest of his colleagues. Shaftesbury too was one
of 'them', to be assailed like all the others. There was no indication here
of the transformation from a royal servant to an opposition hero which was
to take place in the next few months. Yet the reasons for the change were
already inherent in the situation when he wrote.

Apart from the usual spice of sexual references, and the caricatured
personalities, the most striking feature of the satire is the persistent
implication that the religion of the two royal brothers was unsound. Some
of Charles's opinions when discussing religion had given rise to considerable dissatisfaction; in December 1672 he had argued to Sir Robert Moray
'that our Saviour would certainly leave some body or power to whom the
Church might have recourse for solution of difficulties, and then he very
well knew where that power must be lodged',[2] a remark so close to a
typically Roman Catholic line of reasoning that it had caused some alarm.
But it was more generally thought that Charles had no strong religious
convictions of any kind, whereas James was suspected to have positive
Catholic beliefs. This had been implicit in all the debates of the House of
Commons on the Declaration of Indulgence: Powle's way of expressing
a widespread feeling had been to say that 'we are confident of him [the
King], but knows not what succession may be'. Events occurred which
reinforced this feeling. There was the open opposition of Lord Treasurer
Clifford (known to be close to James) to the Test Act; and James's
deliberate refusal to dispel doubts by taking the Easter communion with
his brother. One day as the Lord Treasurer's coach, with its blinds drawn,
turned into the Strand, it overturned and spilled out, along with Clifford,
a priest in full robes on his way to mass at Somerset House; and so it was
not surprising that, rather than take the transubstantiation test and the
Anglican sacrament as the Test Act had just prescribed, Clifford preferred
to give up his high office and retire to his Devon home, to die there in
mysterious circumstances a few months later. As if this was not enough,
James proceeded to give up his own office as Lord High Admiral, which he
had held since the Restoration and was known to love. From now on, it

---

[1] The full text is printed by Lady Newton, *Lyme Letters 1660–1760* (1925), pp. 85–92.
[2] T. Thynne to William Coventry, 2 Jan. 1673, Thynne Papers at Longleat, xvi. fos. 54–
5. According to Stringer (Christie, ii, pp. xxii–xxiii, Martyn, i. 402–4) Buckingham and
Lauderdale both found Charles at his devotions in the Queen's oratory, and told Ashley
of this, c. 1672; but if this were so one would expect to find more echoes of it before
Stringer wrote at the end of the century.

was an open secret that the heir to the throne was a Catholic, and for the next sixteen years this was the central fact of English politics.

It would be easy to imagine that the widespread hatred of Popery, and of James as its personification, during these years was something fabricated by politicians for their own purposes; it would be easy, but it would be quite wrong. There is plenty of evidence for the existence of these anti-Popish sentiments in the previous decade when there was no very obvious political benefit to be gained from them: one has only to remember the wild rumours which had gained credence about the origins of the Fire of London.[1] They may be partly explained as an irrational phobia deriving from popular memories of the previous century, of Gunpowder Plot, the Armada, and Smithfield; but the cry of 'No Popery' also had a more rational basis. Anyone reviewing the history of Europe since the Reformation might very reasonably conclude that Protestantism and Catholicism could not easily co-exist within one state; that in determining which should triumph the influence of the ruler could be decisive; and that a Protestant people with a Catholic ruler might be in a parlous plight. Many intelligent people feared the encroachments of Popery—not that they were all religious zealots, but because they dreaded the political, economic and social, as well as religious, consequences which they feared Popery would bring. The cry of 'No Popery' was raised not only by fools and knaves. It is impossible to read the notes of speeches in the Commons between 1673 and 1681 without realizing that, when due allowance has been made for the inevitable exaggerations, propaganda and tactical manoeuvring of politicians, they meant much of what they said, and felt it deeply.

Nothing in James's character, in his views or his political activities, helped to dissipate such fears. It has recently been suggested that James sincerely believed in religious toleration, not in a Catholic conformity to which all would have to submit[2]; but whether or not this was true, it was certainly not obvious to contemporaries. Not only Protestants, but indiscreet Catholics like Coleman who was at one time James's secretary, expected James's accession to mean the triumph of Catholicism. Of course optimists could believe that Charles might well outlive his younger brother; Charles was easy-going enough, and no crusader for religious principle, and everything might be safe as long as he was King. The trouble about this line of thought was that events seemed to show that Catholic influences were already becoming strong. Irish priests were to be seen at the Queen's palace at Somerset House and at Court; the King's old mistress, the Duchess of Cleveland, and his newer one, Mlle de la Quérouaille, were both Catholics; many officers in the forces raised for the war were Catholics, until they were evicted by the operation of the Test Act; the

[1] Cf. p. 186 above.
[2] Cf. M. P. Ashley, in *Historical Essays 1600–1750 presented to David Ogg*, ed. H. E. Bell and R. L. Ollard (1963), pp. 185–202.

Declaration of Indulgence was not generally thought to have been motivated by a love of the Stuarts' former Puritan enemies. On top of all this, from the spring of 1673 onwards, Dutch pamphlet propaganda hawked on the streets of London began to insinuate that the French alliance was not in England's true interests, and that there was more in the friendship between the English Court and Louis XIV than met the eye. In the parliamentary session of February to March 1673 Charles's foreign policy had not been seriously questioned; but about the beginning of March Pierre Du Moulin's great pamphlet, *England's Appeal from the Private Cabal at Whitehall to the Great Council of the nation, the Lords and Commons in Parliament assembled*, began to foster doubts.[1] The pamphlet professed not to desire 'to raise a jealousy between His Majesty and his people', and therefore concentrated on the dangers of allowing Louis XIV to continue with his aggressive policy; but it drew attention, for instance, to the French ambassador's statement at Vienna that the war against the Dutch was a war of religion, and to Louis XIV's demands for public Catholic worship in the Netherlands, paid for out of the public revenue. It was easy to believe that an alliance with the most powerful Roman Catholic monarch in Europe concealed some secret understanding about English domestic politics; as in fact it did, in the Catholic clauses of the Treaty of Dover.

As people began to worry about these possibilities, the 'five or six Canary birds in the Cabal Cage' all sang different notes, but did not make better harmony. Shaftesbury was certain to take a different view from Clifford: he had never been cordially disposed to James, and at the time of the Roos divorce case he had already canvassed methods of preventing the succession falling to him. When the news of James's failure to take the Anglican sacrament at Easter (30 March) reverberated through London, therefore, his immediate reaction was to join a group of members of Parliament who were pressing the King to divorce Catherine of Braganza; and James told Colbert de Croissy that Shaftesbury and his adherents wanted to get the King to marry a Protestant princess, and to detach him at all costs from his friendship with Louis XIV. The Venetian ambassador in London, who also had much of his information from James, reported that the King had 'become aware of the unfaithfulness of the Chancellor', and this probably reflects Shaftesbury's readiness to co-operate with James's enemies at this point. By June the knowledge of the enmity between the two men had become public, for a pamphlet purporting to be a letter from Shaftesbury to James to win him back from Popery was current in London.[2] Another complication was that James was a widower, anxious to marry again and

---

[1] Cf. my *William of Orange and the English Opposition 1672–4* (1953), pp. 97–111.

[2] Colbert, 7/17 Apr.; Alberti, 11/21 Apr., *C.S.P. Ven. 1673–5*, p. 37; H. Ball to Williamson, 26 June 1673, in *Letters addressed from London to Sir Joseph Williamson*, ed. W. D. Christie (Camden Society, 1874), i. 67. I have not been able to trace a copy of the pamphlet referred to.

produce a son; and his choice fell on a Roman Catholic princess. After negotiations for a marriage to an Austrian archduchess had broken down, he took a bride who was a French protégée, Mary of Modena. In planning this marriage for the autumn of 1673, James was nailing his colours to the mast and revealing them as a combination of the Roman purple and the white of the Bourbons.

By midsummer, therefore, Charles was well aware that his brother and his Lord Chancellor were at loggerheads: an unfortunate development from his own point of view. He talked to the French ambassador at this time of the possibility that when Parliament met bills might be introduced to send James into exile and to exclude Roman Catholic princes from the throne, so that the first known mention of exclusion came from the lips of the King himself.[1] In such a situation it would be difficult to tolerate a Chancellor whom Charles could not trust on such a vital matter as his brother's right to the succession. And at the same time Charles began to suspect that Shaftesbury was intriguing with the enemy in an attempt to overturn his foreign policy; the problem is whether these suspicions were justified.

Until the Easter of 1673 there had been no sign of any disloyalty on Shaftesbury's part to his master's policy of allying with Louis XIV against the Dutch. Though Shaftesbury had made it plain that he disliked the prospect of an extension of the war to include Spain, he was by no means alone in this. It is true that when Arlington was persuading Colbert de Croissy that it would be inadvisable for France to press for common action against Spain, he used the argument that other members of Charles's Council were reluctant; but in doing so he was being insincere, for in secret he joined with Shaftesbury and the other members of the foreign committee in opposing a breach with Spain, which all knew to be violently unpopular. On this the committee was unanimous.[2] Nor was there any marked divergence of opinion between the ministers over the peace congress which was to meet in the spring. At first Charles and Shaftesbury had agreed to insist on Dunkirk as a suitable place for negotiations, rather than Aix, which was Louis XIV's suggestion. Later, when they gave way and consented to a still more distant conference at Cologne, there was little divergence of opinion on the terms on which the English negotiators were to insist. Charles and Shaftesbury agreed on the necessity at all costs of securing 'cautionary towns' from the Dutch in preference to a merely monetary indemnity; and it was the Duke of York who would 'rather part with any [of] the towns, rather towns and all, than lose the peace'.[3] In fact the instructions given to the English ambassadors, Sir Joseph Williamson and Sir Leoline Jenkins, at all times to co-operate with their French colleagues, made all negotiation fruitless since the Dutch were prepared only to

[1] Colbert, 30 June/10 July.
[2] Colbert, 17/27 Dec. 1672, 10/20 Feb. 1673; Foreign Entry Book 177, 11 Feb. 1673.
[3] Ibid. 26 Jan., 31 Mar., 28 Apr.

consider a separate peace with England; but there is no evidence available that Shaftesbury objected to those instructions, and at the same time he was busily engaged in pressing on the preparations of the fleet.[1]

At the beginning of June, however—precisely the time when James was giving up his post as Lord High Admiral—Shaftesbury was reported to be having doubts. Arlington told the French ambassador that the Chancellor had been one of those who had been having talks with 'the principal members of Parliament' who were planning to break the French alliance when the next session came in October; but, Arlington continued, he had argued to Shaftesbury that after giving way over religion it was all the more necessary to maintain that the French alliance was a matter only for the King and his Council, in which 'the people' had no right to interfere; and, he said, Shaftesbury had agreed. He advised Colbert de Croissy to pay Shaftesbury a visit and say that he expected that the Chancellor, as one of the principal promoters of the French alliance, would continue to do all he could to make it permanent. This the Frenchman did; and after one of the few recorded talks between him and Shaftesbury, he returned satisfied with some vague protestations of good-will which the latter had made. But within a few weeks, Charles II himself told Colbert de Croissy that all Shaftesbury's protestations were dishonest (*fourbes*), 'like all the actions of that minister', whom he described as the weakest and worst-intentioned of men. The King now suspected that from weakness (a singular mis-reading of Shaftesbury's character) the Chancellor had yielded to popular clamour and was now working against the French alliance while professing to work for it. And there can be no doubt that Charles came to believe that Shaftesbury went to the length of co-operating with the Dutch agents inspired by Du Moulin, who were working underground in England. There were one or two circumstances which fed this suspicion: for instance, when the Spanish diplomat Don Bernardo de Salinas brought over to London a letter from William of Orange to the King, it was remarked that Shaftesbury had an interview with him which lasted for three hours. Charles promptly asked his Chancellor how much money the Spaniards had offered him; and when Shaftesbury protested against this imputation, commented that the Spaniards were not treating him properly, for they had offered Arlington £40,000. It was a joke which concealed a sneer.[2]

Sir William Temple was one contemporary who was ready to believe anything of Shaftesbury and suspected him of treasonable relations with the Dutch. After William of Orange and Pierre Du Moulin had achieved their object of forcing England out of the war by means of their propaganda, and Temple had gone over to The Hague as ambassador, he presumed upon his friendship with the Prince to ask him which Englishmen had been involved in plots for a rebellion against Charles in alliance

---

[1] Shaftesbury to [Rupert], 14 May, in Coventry Papers at Longleat, vol. 2, fo. 34.
[2] Colbert, 12/22 June, 30 June/10 July, 31 July/10 Aug.

with the Dutch. William made the only possible reply, and declined to betray friends, thus maintaining distrust at no cost to himself; and neither Temple nor Charles ever knew precisely who intrigued with the Dutch in 1673.[1] It is impossible for the historian to be certain either, but the evidence which survives, though admittedly incomplete, suggests when dispassionately surveyed that it is highly unlikely that Shaftesbury was implicated. There is one concrete fact showing that by May 1673 he would have liked to negotiate peace directly with the Dutch, aside from the formal proceedings at Cologne: in that month he and some other Englishmen (said to include the very respectable Duke of Ormond) sent to Holland one 'Colonel Alexander', an alias which concealed the identity of Augustus Coronel, a financier who had handled the dowry brought by Catherine of Braganza in 1662. Coronel crossed the Channel, with what instructions is not known, and died there before he could bring back William of Orange's peace proposals. But Coronel claimed to have Charles's permission for his errand, and there is corroboration for this. At the most the episode showed that Shaftesbury was disposed to seek an end to the war if one could be obtained. It did not even mean that thereafter he was complimented by the Dutch: when Du Moulin wrote to his English friends at the end of October he referred in extremely scathing terms to 'grand speakers' who might be 'forced to *delere* some of their new *delendas*', and observed sarcastically that if Shaftesbury's speech at the beginning of the approaching session 'doth this country [the Dutch Republic] as much good as the *delenda Carthago* hath done, my Lord Chancellor will be the best friend they have ever had'. This was not the language of a man who regarded Shaftesbury as an actual or potential ally.[2] Moreover, we shall see that one of the basic facts of the period when Shaftesbury was an opposition leader is the striking absence of any known correspondence between him and William of Orange. There is no sign that they were ever in touch with one another, and if this is true of the years 1674 to 1683, it is likely to be true of 1673 also.[3]

Shaftesbury must therefore be acquitted of underhand intrigues with the Dutch; but the fact remains that, justly or unjustly, he was under suspicion, and, in view of his known attitude to James, Duke of York, regarded as disaffected. His words were carefully noted; and there was some surprised comment on his official speech on the occasion when the new Lord Treasurer, Sir Thomas Osborne (better known to history under his later title of Earl of Danby) took his oath in the Exchequer on 26 June 1673. Like all his speeches, this one was printed—Shaftesbury was no

[1] Temple, *Works*, i. 206-7.

[2] Rijksarchief, Fagel 253; and for other uncomplimentary references to Shaftesbury in Du Moulin's correspondence, suggesting that the two were not allies, cf. ibid. 252, no. 150, and ibid. 251.

[3] For fuller discussion of this, see my *William of Orange and the English Opposition 1672-4* (1953), pp. 116-19 and sources there quoted.

believer in hiding his light under a bushel; and the public observed with interest his remarks on the art of keeping hold of the position one has reached. 'And let me say to your Lordship, that however happy you have been in arriving to this high station, yet *Parta tueri non minor est virtus*. Many great men have proved unfortunate in not observing that the address and means to attain great things, are oftentimes very different from those that are necessary to maintain a sure and long possession of them.' The new Lord Treasurer did not conceal that he found this homily on the insecurity of high office not altogether to his liking[1]; and in the following weeks there was a spate of rumours about impending ministerial changes.[2] None of these materialized, however, and Shaftesbury remained in office in spite of his suspected disloyalty, possibly because Charles considered him less dangerous in office than he would be out of it.

In August the naval battle off the Texel ended, like the others, in-decisively, and any surviving hopes of beating the Dutch to their knees disappeared. The battle had other consequences, too, because the failure of the French fleet to render satisfactory assistance to the English admiral, Prince Rupert, when reported and magnified in English newsletters, nourished a popular fear that Louis XIV was allowing the Dutch and British fleets to destroy one another, to the advantage of France and of Roman Catholicism. And the same incident led to a strengthening of the ties between Rupert and Shaftesbury. For some years they had been business partners; now in September 1673 Rupert and Shaftesbury 'are observed to converse very much together and are very great, and indeed I see his Highness's coach often at his door. They are looked upon to be great Parliament men, and for the interest of Old England. . . .' It is not far-fetched to see in this a deliberate attempt on Shaftesbury's part to set up Rupert as a 'Protestant admiral' in opposition to James.[3]

As the meeting of Parliament which had been fixed for 20 October drew nearer, the government's difficulties became greater and the Lord Chancellor's attitude more doubtful. On 6 October the Spanish governor at Brussels, Count Monterey, began hostile operations against the French, and three days later Louis XIV declared war on Spain. There seemed a serious possibility that England would have to fall in behind Louis, and the calamity which Shaftesbury and others had long feared, of a break in the vital English trade with Spain, seemed imminent. The effect on the City was immediate. 'The fears of a war with Spain are so great in the City that it's their common cry, We shall be ruined if we do; the merchants thinking it as bad a mischief as can possibly come to them.' It was a golden

---

[1] Christie, ii, pp. lxxi–lxxii; Sir W. Coventry to T. Thynne, 7 July, Thynne Papers at Longleat, xvi, fos. 142–3.

[2] *Letters to Sir Joseph Williamson*, ed. W. D. Christie (Camden Society, 1874), i. 99, 102–3, 108, 117, 119, 121, 151.

[3] H. Ball to Williamson, 19 Sept., ibid. ii. 21–22; Colbert, 1/11 Sept.

opportunity for the renewal of the Dutch propaganda offensive against English foreign policy, which took place in this critical month of October.[1] But it was an equally unfortunate moment for the first approach to this country of James's bride, Mary of Modena, who, having been married to him by proxy, was now about to cross the Channel. It is significant that at this time there was also a rumour that the King had 'had lately three sad fits of an apoplexy'; the rumour was probably false (since it was reported by only one observer), but it implied an awareness of what hung on the King's life, and a dislike of the prospect of James's succession. Charles himself complained bitterly that the behaviour of his brother was the cause of the principal difficulties that he would have to surmount; while Arlington forecast that there would be proposals for James's banishment and that the fear of his succession would lead to measures to enable the King to remarry.[2]

No great genius was needed to foresee that the House of Commons would combine an attack on the French alliance with an attempt to prevent the completion of James's marriage to Mary of Modena. Unfortunately Shaftesbury's activities at this time have to be viewed entirely through the eyes of hostile observers, and the only certain fact about them is that the Lord Chancellor was now under such great suspicion that it was possible to believe almost anything of him. At the end of September, it is true, the French ambassador had reported home that the King thought he had brought back the Chancellor to his duty, 'but he is a poor man of whom it is impossible to be sure'. In October, Colbert de Croissy thought that Shaftesbury was co-operating with Arlington, who had long had mis-givings about the war, to halt it; he believed, incorrectly, that the pair of them were behind a secret trip which William Howard paid to his friend Pierre Du Moulin in Holland.[3] What this proves is simply that Shaftesbury was now believed to be closer to the viewpoint of the opposition than to that of the King. Yet he did not attempt to resign his office. In the seven-teenth century few politicians ever voluntarily resigned office and gave up its profits and its power; the idea of deliberately 'going into opposition' was thoroughly unnatural to them from every point of view. As experience since the Restoration had shown, they normally preferred to retain office and to press their opinions within the government circle against their opponents there—and to seek the favour of a King who was generally believed to be unusually susceptible to persuasion and to pressure. In such a way Bristol, from within the Court, had attempted to undermine Clarendon in 1663; in such a way, with the assistance of parliamentary

---

[1] Ball to Williamson, 17 Oct., op. cit. ii. 45; Haley, *William of Orange* . . ., pp. 127–30.
[2] Ball to Williamson, 10 Oct., op. cit. ii. 35; Colbert, 20/30 Oct.
[3] Colbert, 25 Sept./5 Oct., 20/30 Oct., 27 Oct./6 Nov. For evidence that Shaftesbury and Arlington were on good terms with one another at this time, cf. T. Ross to Williamson, 3 Oct., in *Letters to Williamson*, ii. 29–30.

pressure, Clarendon's enemies had finally succeeded in overthrowing him in 1667; in such a way Arlington and Buckingham had intrigued against one another ever since. If Shaftesbury wanted to work against James, Duke of York, the natural way to do this was from his powerful position as Lord Chancellor, not by 'going into opposition'; and this was what he did until James persuaded his brother that it was best to be rid of him.

It had been arranged that when Parliament met on 20 October (having been adjourned since March) it should be prorogued for a few days and a new session begun on the 27th. This would forestall possible objections that it was wrong to pass two money bills in one session; and it might enable Mary of Modena to arrive in the country, so that James could consummate his marriage with her before the House of Commons could protest against it. So the intention was that the proceedings should be entirely formal in character. The Speaker was instructed not to take the chair in the Commons until Black Rod was ready, and so he did not make his appearance until half-past ten. But as soon as he had arrived the House insisted that he should take the chair, and then Henry Powle argued that 'we had been very careful to prevent Popery, but it was in vain to suppress it elsewhere if it got footing so near the throne', that the Duke was going to marry an Italian lady who was 'kin to two cardinals', and that the House should send an address to the King asking that the match should not be consummated. The ex-Cromwellian colonel John Birch with his usual bluntness of speech seconded this motion, with a reference to earlier Popish alliances from the time of the Spanish match; and the courtiers were powerless to prevent the address from being carried. It amounted to a slap in James's face; and it was only possible because Black Rod arrived late on the scene. The preliminaries in the House of Lords had taken a long time; there were several new peers who had to be introduced for the first time, and Shaftesbury, who as Lord Chancellor presided over the House, insisted that all the formalities should be meticulously observed while James bit his nails in impatience. James believed that the delay was deliberate, and he was probably right. If he had not previously pressed Charles to dismiss Shaftesbury, he began to do so now.[1]

The week which followed gave an opportunity for many political talks and combinations; and in the course of it one observer, Sir William Temple, wrote a letter describing the parliamentary situation and distinguishing between different groups in the House. One, including Garroway, Sir Robert Thomas, Sacheverell, Cavendish, and William Russell, supported by Shaftesbury's nephew Halifax in the Lords, 'would run up to the height and fall upon the ministers, especially Buckingham, Arlington, Lauderdale, and their carriage, particularly in the business of the war', to force themselves into office and bring about a complete reversal of policy;

[1] *Parliamentary Journal of Sir E. Dering, 1670–3*, pp. 149–51; J. S. Clarke, *Life of James II* (1816), p. 485; Burnet, ii. 36; *C.S.P. Ven. 1673–5*, p. 161.

a second group, including Powle and Strangeways, was more moderate, wanting to 'secure the business of religion [and] break the war with Holland' but not to attack the ministers personally; and a third, led by Sir John Holland, was prepared to vote money for the King 'with pretence of not perfecting it unless peace be made', as a means of 'securing the business of money under a show of moderation and popular aims'. Fourthly, there was a group (the size of which Temple leaves entirely vague), led by Shaftesbury in the Lords, and by Sir Robert Howard, Secretary to the Treasury, in the Commons. In their case, in contrast to the other three groups, Temple says nothing of their attitude to the war; instead he says simply that the party 'is made chiefly to carry on the business of the divorce'. Evidently Shaftesbury was trying to revive the plan suggested in 1670, of persuading Charles to divorce Catherine of Braganza, marry again and beget some Protestant heirs who would exclude James from the succession. Once again Charles did not immediately reject the idea: according to Temple, 'The King seems sometimes very earnest in it, and sometimes cold, and in all these matters is either so uncertain or disgusted that those who are nearest him know not yet what will be the issue'. Charles's indecision may have been genuine, for he was indeed in a very perplexing situation between his obligations to Louis (on which it would be dangerous to default) and the disaffection of a Parliament which was hostile both to his foreign policy and to his Roman Catholic brother. At about this time Shaftesbury, along with Arlington, the Duke of Ormond, and Secretary Henry Coventry, joined in advising him to send James away from the Court for a while, for the King's good and his own; and again Charles did not immediately reject the idea. Instead he sent the four of them to make the suggestion to James in person. Not unnaturally James was indignant: he said that he would obey any orders that the King gave, but would look on those who gave that advice as his enemies. He redoubled his efforts to get Charles to dismiss Shaftesbury.[1]

Charles, however, still thought that Shaftesbury could render him some service at the beginning of the new session, as he had done with his *Delenda est Carthago* speech at the beginning of the last. In his own speech on 27 October Charles's line was that he would have liked to welcome the members of Parliament with the news of peace with the Dutch, but that the Dutch negotiators at the peace congress in Cologne had shown themselves intransigent, and therefore he must ask for more war supplies. At the same time he offered a general assurance that he would keep his promises about 'religion and property', and said that he would be 'very ready to give you fresh instances of my zeal for preserving the established religion and laws,

---

[1] Temple to Essex, 25 Oct., in *Essex Papers*, ed. O. Airy and C. E. Pike (Camden Society, 1890–1913), i. 130–3; Burnet, ii. 42; *C.S.P. Ven. 1673–5*, p. 177; York to Lauderdale, 4 Dec., in *Lauderdale Papers*, ed. Airy (Camden Society, 1884–5), iii. 5–6. It is not certain whether the attempt to get James to withdraw took place before or after 20 October.

as often as any occasion shall require'. As usual, it then fell to the Lord
Chancellor to develop these points at greater length, in a speech which had
been approved by the Council as a whole. Inevitably it made a nice
contrast with the *Delenda est Carthago* speech. In asking for war supplies
and enumerating the peace terms on which the government was insisting,
he spoke only of the Dutch being made to salute the English flag, to pay
'a small rent' for fishing off the British coasts, and to accept 'a fair adjust-
ment of commerce' in the East Indies. All demands to occupy any Dutch
towns were abandoned, and the term Carthaginian was applied only to
the 'Lovesteine party' of De Witt: now that William of Orange was in
power, it would no longer be necessary to fight to the death. As for 'religion
and property', he remarked simply that the King 'hath not yet learned to
deny you anything; and he believes your wisdom and moderation is such,
he never shall . . .', and concluded the official portion of his speech with
an appeal for money to repay the debt owing to the bankers, and thus
rescue the 'widows and orphans' who were the bankers' own creditors.
Then, pointedly remarking 'I have no more in command', he proceeded
to add a postcript of his own: 'I have no more in command; and therefore
shall conclude, with my own hearty prayers, that this session may equal,
nay exceed, the honour of the last; that it may perfect what the last begun
for the safety of the King and kingdom; that it may be ever famous for
having established upon a durable foundation our religion, laws, and
properties; that we may not be tossed with boisterous winds, nor overtaken
by a sudden dead calm; but that a fair gale may carry you, in a steady,
even, and resolved way, into the ports of wisdom and security.'

This may have been only a fulsome peroration; but there were those who
saw in it implicit encouragement to the House of Commons to continue
the anti-Catholic policy of the Test Act in the previous session and take
further steps to secure the nation from a Catholic successor. And certainly
the deliberate distinction drawn between the official part of the speech
and the personal postscript is odd. It can only have strengthened the
suspicions which some people had of him.[1]

As it proved, the House of Commons needed little encouragement.
Three days later, on 30 October, by 186 votes to 88 they persisted in a
further address to the King against the Duke of York's marriage; and
on the following day, in grand committee, there was a wholesale attack on
the French alliance, begun by William Russell, who talked of being
'betrayed by those about the King' and proposed a flat refusal of all money.
Others were more moderate than Russell, Cavendish and Sacheverell;
and the final vote was less extreme. It was agreed that no money should
be given until the end of the eighteen months which the previous money
bill in March had been supposed to cover, 'unless it shall appear that the
obstinacy of the Dutch shall make a supply necessary'—this last clause

[1] *L.J.* xii. 589.

being added at the motion of Sir William Coventry, who by this time was one of the most responsible and respected members of the Country Party. But even in this modified form the resolution was a disaster for the King. He had no money left to continue the war, and the debate had shown, in the words of the French ambassador, that there were not four people in the entire House who did not think that the sole means of maintaining the Protestant religion was to make peace with the Dutch, and in every way possible to oppose the plans of Louis XIV. Moreover several speakers attacked not only the King's foreign policy but the 'villainous counsellors' who had advised it. It was only a matter of time before these villains were named, and once the process had begun no-one could tell where it would stop. Obviously from the point of view of the King and his ministers the Commons had to be forestalled, and after some discussion in Council whether there should be a prorogation or dissolution, the King appeared in the House of Lords on the morning of 4 November to prorogue Parliament until 7 January. Before Black Rod could knock at the door of the House of Commons to summon the members to listen to the royal speech, Sir Robert Thomas just had to time mention the name of one 'evil counsellor', the Duke of Lauderdale. The King's speech was short and to the point: there was to be a short recess, 'that all good men may recollect themselves against the meeting', and during this recess Charles undertook 'to let all my subjects see, that no care can be greater than my own, in the effectual suppressing of Popery'. That Charles had here put his finger on the real issue was shown by what happened next day, when the anniversary of Gunpowder Plot was celebrated by more than ordinary zeal. At six o'clock 'in the Poultry the burning of the whore of Babylon' was acted, 'with great applause'; and later there were more bonfires than at any time in the previous thirty years—more than two hundred of them between Temple Bar and Aldgate, and 'the young fry made the effigies of popes, carried them in procession, and there burnt them'.[1]

What was Shaftesbury doing backstage while all these events were being played out in view of the public? 'His house', wrote one observer, 'is the best place without comparison to know where the wind stands.'[2] He certainly knew many of the M.P.s who were actors; did he prompt them in any way? Had he anything to do with the preliminary meeting of Parliament men on the evening of Wednesday the 29th 'about uniting'?[3] We have no certain knowledge; all that we can do is to examine the

---

[1] For this session see Grey, ii. 182–223; *Parliamentary Journal of Sir Edward Dering, 1670–3*, pp. 151–61; *C.J.* ix. 285; *L.J.* xii. 593; Colbert, 3/13, 17/27 Nov.; T. Derham to Williamson, 5 Nov., in *Letters to Williamson*, ii. 61–62; Arlington to Jenkins and Williamson, 4 Nov., S.P. 105/221, fo. 387; Sir T. Player to Williamson, 10 Nov., *Letters to Williamson*, ii. 67; Charles Hatton to L. Hatton, 6 Nov., in *Hatton Correspondence*, ed. E. M. Thompson (Camden Society 1878), i. 119; *C.S.P.D. 1673–5*, p. 8; and cf. my *William of Orange and the English Opposition 1672–4* (1953), pp. 133–43.   [2] Derham, as in previous note.
[3] Sir T. Player to Williamson, 3 Nov., in *Letters to Williamson*, ii. 55–56.

speeches of Sir Robert Howard, M.P. for Stockbridge, whom Temple had coupled with Shaftesbury in the previous week. Howard had spoken on 20 October in favour of the address against James's marriage to Mary of Modena, 'with expressions that the danger of Popery was now greater than ever' and suggestions that 'none of that profession might ever be married to any of the royal family'—which could be interpreted as an oblique reference to the Queen. On 30 October he supported a motion that all members of both Houses (presumably including James) should have to take the Test against transubstantiation; a bill was ordered to be prepared for this purpose. And on 31 October in the foreign policy debate, although as befitted his position as Secretary to the Treasury he opposed Russell's motion against any grant of money, he did so in an odd way by seeking to divert the House's attention to religious grievances. 'Seek ye first the kingdom of God', he proclaimed; 'settle religion, and all things will be added.' He was in fact beating the No Popery drum with vigour, in a way fully consistent with Shaftesbury's enmity to James at this time; and it might reasonably be suspected that the two men were co-operating.[1]

The King also suspected his Lord Chancellor of making trouble in another way, by stirring up hatred of Lauderdale. Shaftesbury and Lauderdale had formerly been friends, particularly about the year 1665; but by 1673 they were equally bitter enemies. Lauderdale had lost a great many of his friends in recent years; his character had coarsened considerably—whether or not the influence of the Countess of Dysart was responsible for this—and also he was revealed as an ever more uncompromising upholder of the King's authority in Scotland. In the Scottish Parliament he carried all before him: in 1669 the Scottish Militia Act gave the King power to use his Scottish forces in any part of his dominions and not merely in Scotland, and it appears that in February 1673 at the height of the dispute over the Declaration of Indulgence he let fall a suggestion that they should be used in England against the parliamentary opposition. As a result he became violently unpopular; and about the same time Shaftesbury ceased to be a visitor to Ham House. Amongst the Exeter House circle was a Scot, Sir Robert Moray, the well-known Fellow of the Royal Society, a man who shared some of Shaftesbury's intellectual interests and in politics was connected with the growing Scottish opposition to Lauderdale. Moray too accused Lauderdale of having 'betrayed his country', and it was noticed that he dined several times with Shaftesbury in the summer of 1673. Moray died suddenly on 4 July, but to these meetings between Moray and Shaftesbury Lauderdale later attributed the rise of opposition to him in the Scottish Parliament. Some time in the following months Shaftesbury began to press the Duke

---

[1] Temple, loc. cit. p. 337 n.; Dering, op. cit. p. 151; Grey, ii. 196, 201.

of Monmouth to aspire to replace Lauderdale as the King's Commissioner in Scotland; for Monmouth, who was now in his mid-twenties, was old enough to be used as a political tool. By October 1673 the enmity between Shaftesbury and Lauderdale was a matter of common knowledge. A political observer, talking of a possible attack on Lauderdale in the English Parliament, commented that 'among the Lords his principal antagonist is the little one once his great confidant [Shaftesbury] who (though his Grace said he would crush the little worm with his great toe) most believe will wriggle from under him and trip up his heels . . .'.[1]

When, therefore, Lauderdale's name was mentioned in the Commons on 4 November, it was natural to suppose that the 'little worm' was at work tripping up his enemy's heels. Lauderdale was preparing to meet the Scottish Parliament on 12 November; and both he and the King expected trouble beforehand, and were prepared to ascribe it to the correspondence which Shaftesbury kept up with some Scottish peers.[2] Foremost among Lauderdale's enemies north of the Border were the Duke of Hamilton and Lord Tweeddale, the latter of whom sent his son, Lord Yester, to London on the day before the Scottish Parliament was due to meet for the purpose, as Lauderdale supposed, of plotting to replace him by Monmouth. The events of 12 November seemed to confirm Lauderdale's suspicions, for in the usually docile Scottish Parliament there was a strong attack led by Hamilton on the committee which controlled its business, the Lords of the Articles—'that excellent constitution of the Articles which is the security of monarchical government here', in Lauderdale's own words. He had to circumvent it by adjourning Parliament and asking for the King's authority to redress grievances about salt, brandy and tobacco; and so when in a few days the news of Shaftesbury's dismissal reached Edinburgh, Lauderdale welcomed it—'I bore it with great moderation'. Shaftesbury certainly took a keen interest in Scottish affairs, and it may well be that Lauderdale and Charles were right in suspecting that he had been trying to 'make a flame' in Scotland too—and this would not be discreditable, for Lauderdale's heavy-handed rule had little to commend it. Yet it must be emphasized that there is no proof available; and Lauderdale had every incentive to put down the opposition to the intrigues of an unscrupulous enemy rather than to genuine and justifiable discontent with his government. Though Lauderdale would not admit it, there was enough real discontent to evoke the attacks on him in both Parliaments without the necessity for any outside instigator. If Shaftesbury is to be held responsible,

---

[1] A. Robertson, *Life of Sir Robert Moray* (1922), pp. 146–7; H. Ball to Williamson, 7 July, *Letters to Williamson*, i. 94; Burnet, ii. 39; Kincardine to Lauderdale, 18 Dec., *Lauderdale Papers*, ed. O. Airy (Camden Society, 1884–5), iii. 11–12; T. Ross to Williamson, 3 Oct., *Letters to Williamson*, ii. 29.

[2] This is clear from Lauderdale's letter to Charles Maitland, 18 Nov., in *Lauderdale Papers*, ii. 245.

it can only be on the basis of that most misleading of all proverbs, that there is no smoke without fire.[1]

The fact remains that, whether rightly or not, Charles believed that Shaftesbury was engaging in that sort of activity at the beginning of November 1673. He believed that Shaftesbury was capable of intriguing with Scottish malcontents and with the agents of the Dutch, and knew him to be at daggers drawn with James. It was indeed becoming impossible for Shaftesbury and James to sit at the same Council Board: on one occasion James sent for the Lord Chancellor, abused him and called him a madman,[2] and he was constantly urging Charles to 'make an example' of him. In such a situation Shaftesbury seemed to Charles more dangerous than useful; Charles privately called him *fourbe* and *fripon* to the French ambassador, and after the parliamentary debate on 31 October decided that he must go. The tradition in the Shaftesbury household was that the decision was taken on 3 November at a supper-party in the lodgings of the Duchess of Portsmouth, when Colbert de Croissy, Lord Treasurer Danby and others 'drank his Majesty to a great height' and persuaded him to dissolve Parliament, turn out Shaftesbury, and 'set up for himself'; but in fact the King had some days earlier made a reasoned decision to dispense with the services of his Chancellor and rely for the future on Danby and his friends. But Charles waited until Parliament had been prorogued before he took action. On 7 November Shaftesbury sought a talk with him when the Council meeting was over, and in a room at the end of the Privy Gallery 'talked with that briskness unto the King as made him tremble'— or so Shaftesbury's familiars believed. This interview evidently led Shaftesbury to believe that his days as Chancellor were over, for on the morning of Sunday, 9 November, he took another opportunity to ask the King whether, if he was to be dismissed, it could be done without contempt. To this Charles readily agreed; and it was arranged that the King should send formally to Exeter House for the seals at four o'clock that afternoon. In the meantime Charles and Shaftesbury left for chapel smiling and talking together, to the chagrin of some of the courtiers who had been looking forward to Shaftesbury's fall; but their discomfiture did not last for long. At 4 p.m. Shaftesbury's brother-in-law, Secretary of State Henry Coventry, arrived to request formally that he should give up the seals; at the same time he brought with him a royal pardon for 'all treasons, rebellions, murders, negligences, concealments, or other crimes committed before 5 November 1673', which Shaftesbury had had the forethought to arrange for himself. Thus provided, he gave up the seals with

---

[1] Loc. cit. in previous note; and cf. Lauderdale to Maitland, 13 Nov., ibid. ii. 241; Charles II to Lauderdale, 29 Nov., ibid. iii. 2; Lauderdale to Charles, 20 Nov., ibid. iii. 16–17, and 1 Dec., ibid. iii. 2–4; York to Lauderdale, 4 Dec., ibid. iii. 5–6; Kincardine to Lauderdale, 18, 29 Dec., ibid. iii. 11–12, 18.

[2] Alberti, 7/17, 14/24 Nov. in *C.S.P. Ven. 1673–5*, pp. 175, 176.

an air of cheerfulness, and a remark that 'It is only laying down my gown, and putting on my sword'.[1]

The news was received with general rejoicing by the Queen, who was threatened by Shaftesbury's revival of the project to procure a divorce for the King, and by the Duke of York, who was generally supposed to have had the greatest share in bringing about his fall. They congratulated the French ambassador on the disgrace of a man who was the greatest enemy of France and 'the most knavish, unjust, and dishonest man in England'. Others took a melancholy view of the event: they were said to include Prince Rupert (who visited him on the day of his dismissal) and, more strangely, the Duke of Ormond—possibly because Ormond too regarded it as a triumph for French influence and disliked it. Many, however, did not immediately regard Shaftesbury's dismissal as final; after all, he had held office continuously since the Restoration, and had been considered the best administrator in the government. Within a week there were rumours that he would be taken back into the royal favour. Nor did Shaftesbury himself make it plain that he was to be regarded in future as hostile to the royal government: on 15 November he was present at the Council of Trade and Plantations, of which he remained President, and led its members in urging and planning an expedition for the recapture of New York from the Dutch. It is probable, too, that for some weeks he continued to appear at Court, hiding his resentment under a smile and continuing to press his political views. The King and his ministers, more-over, were far from united in their attitude to him. One well-informed observer reported that Shaftesbury had been twice commanded to leave town, and had refused to stir; but the Earl of Arlington plainly disliked the prospect of driving him into opposition and worked to reconcile him to the King. Optimistically he told Colbert de Croissy that he was con-vinced that he had 'brought back the Chancellor to his duty' and that Shaftesbury on his side was determined to recover the King's favour by working to satisfy him. He suggested that the French ambassador should help to win Shaftesbury, who was 'not insensitive to offers of money'; through Shaftesbury it would be possible to secure the most extreme members of parliament, 'over whom he has great power'.[2]

Colbert de Croissy had no liking at all for Shaftesbury, but he recog-nized that he was a dangerous enemy whom it would be valuable to win over. Accordingly he sent his colleague Ruvigny to Shaftesbury to assure

---

[1] Colbert, 30 Oct./9 Nov., 3/13 Nov.; Stringer's Memoir in Christie, ii, pp. xl–xlii and n.; C.S.P.D. 1673-5, p. 11; notes by Finch in Finch Papers, H.M.C. Seventh Report, pp. 514–15. Stringer's account is evidence of what Shaftesbury's servants saw and believed; what it purports to say about events behind the scenes is demonstrably unreliable.

[2] Colbert, 10/20 Nov.; Rawleigh Redivivus (1683), pp. 86–87; Major T. Fairfax to Williamson, 17 Nov., Letters to Williamson, ii. 79; C.S.P. Col. 1669-74, pp. 532-3; Conway to Essex, 22 Nov., Essex Papers, ed. O. Airy (Camden Society, 1890), i. 142; Colbert, 17/27 Nov., 27 Nov./7 Dec.

him of Louis XIV's favour and to promise him £10,000 'to reward whoever he wished'. Shaftesbury received him at Exeter House, and had a
long talk in private, in the presence only of an interpreter, 'because', as his
steward Stringer later wrote, 'our Earl was not very exact in speaking
French, though he understood it perfectly well'. According to Stringer,
Ruvigny came on behalf of both the kings of England and of France, and
Shaftesbury was offered, not only 10,000 guineas, but a dukedom and
whatever office he chose; he would 'not only be First Minister of state
here, but have what command he pleased in France'. This is obviously an
exaggeration: even though Stringer was one of those who waited on Ruvigny
to his coach afterwards, and claimed to have heard what had passed from
the lips of his master, it is safer to accept Ruvigny's own account to Colbert
de Croissy of the terms he offered and of Shaftesbury's reaction to them.
Shaftesbury did not reject the proposal with a display of indignation; he
gave the Frenchman a polite reception, and, though he did not accept the
money, he left Ruvigny under the impression that eventually he would
find a pretext to do so. King Charles knew of the offer and thought that
the money would do useful service in at least neutralizing his former minister; indeed on the evening of the day of Ruvigny's visit the King confirmed
the offer himself, in a private talk with Shaftesbury at eight o'clock in that
most useful of private places in Whitehall, the lodgings of Mr. Chiffinch.[1]

In the end, however, nothing came of all this. Shaftesbury did not take
the bribe: evidently Ruvigny had mistaken a courteous refusal for a coy
willingness to be pressed. The courtesy of the refusal and the talk with the
King that followed it suggest that he was prepared to negotiate, but not
crudely in terms of money; there were issues of policy which would also
have to be settled in the way that he wanted. The policy with which he was
generally identified now was one of friendship with Spain rather than
France, and peace with Holland in foreign affairs; and at home he was said
to be offering the King a reconciliation with Parliament and the money
Charles needed, if Charles would repudiate his Queen and make a second
marriage, the offspring of which would exclude James and his children from
the succession. For a little while the issue hung in the balance; as late as
11 December, over a month after Shaftesbury's dismissal, it was possible
for an observer to write that Shaftesbury's 'interest they report is as good
as ever; and the side whereof he is they report to be much stronger than
the other and more prevalent'. In his view there were two parties at Court,
one including the Duke of Ormond, Arlington, Shaftesbury and Secretary
Coventry, and the other including Buckingham, Lord Treasurer Danby, the
Speaker Edward Seymour, and Lauderdale 'if he were there'. The first
party seemed to be the stronger.[2]

[1] Colbert, 27 Nov./7 Dec.; Christie, ii, pp. xliv–xlv.
[2] Alberti, 28 Nov./8 Dec., 12/22 Dec. in *C.S.P. Ven. 1673–5*, pp. 183, 189; R. Jones
(?James) to Conway, 11 Dec. 1673, in *Letters to Williamson*, ii. 92.

Either Charles had definite misgivings about driving Shaftesbury into opposition, or it suited him to let it appear so. But as the date of the next parliamentary session (7 January) drew near it became necessary for him to make a final choice; and that choice was not for Shaftesbury, but for the new Lord Treasurer Danby and his idea of trying to appeal to the loyalist sentiments of the Anglican and Cavalier squires in the House by a return to an Anglican and Cavalier policy. Shaftesbury still attended some meetings of the Council of Trade and Plantations as late as March 1674,[1] but to all intents and purposes his chances of recovering the King's favour had evaporated by the end of 1673. The parting of the ways had come.

Thus ended a period of thirteen years in Shaftesbury's life, in the course of which he had served the Restoration government. It is a curious fact that the man who is generally notorious as the leader of a violent and extreme Opposition actually spent longer as a minister of Charles II. As Chancellor of the Exchequer, Treasury Commissioner, President of the Council of Trade and Lord Chancellor he had taken as full a share as anyone of the burden of administrative work; and one must not lose sight of this fact when one considers the opposition period which followed. He was not the kind of factious politician who is adept at purely destructive criticism without having anything constructive to offer; he knew the problems of government from the inside as well as any man alive. One might say that past experience fitted him to be a minister of the crown, taking advantage of all the power and perquisites attached to office, rather than a hostile critic, spending his own money to fight a difficult political battle against all the resources at the disposal of the King. It was not a change which most seventeenth-century politicians would naturally relish.

Yet Shaftesbury's position amongst the King's ministers had always been anomalous; it differed from that of most of his colleagues. For Charles and for James, for Louis XIV and the French ambassadors, for Clarendon and Ormond, Arlington and Clifford, Bristol and Buckingham, the ultimate political virtue of a minister was his zeal to anticipate and execute the desires of his King. Clarendon especially might seek to guide the King in the paths he thought best; Arlington and Danby might have misgivings about the wisdom of Charles's alliance; but as soon as they realized the King's firm purpose, they fell in with it. Even Bristol and Buckingham, though they sought by intrigues in Parliament to enhance their political value to the King and to embarrass their rivals for power, nevertheless sought to win the royal favour by anticipating what they conceived Charles's real wishes to be. In no case was this obedience complete and uncritical, but in the last resort, these men had all been Royalists whose careers had been based on personal loyalty to the King as their principal

[1] *C.S.P. Col. 1669–74*, p. 551; MSS. Rawlinson A, fos. 86, 89; Shaftesbury Papers, XLIX, 8.

political guide.[1] For Shaftesbury, however, this was not the case. He was the only non-Royalist who attained the front rank among Charles's advisers. Others who had served the Commonwealth and Protectorate entered the Privy Council at the Restoration, but he was unique in achieving real eminence. Monk's influence on policy was negligible, Anglesey, Holles, Downing and others filled second-rank posts, but only to Shaftesbury came a real share in political power. In this respect he was marked off from the rest of Charles's 'inner circle'; however the differences between Shaftesbury and the rest might be obscured, in the long run he was separated from them because for him loyalty to the King was not an end in itself. He had supported the Restoration not from any conviction of Charles's inherent right, but because, after he had tried other expedients, a monarchical régime seemed most likely to provide the government and the society he wanted. Times might change, and ultimately he might find it necessary to oppose the policy of Charles II. In a sense, he was always a Whig.

It may have been an appreciation of this that led Charles repeatedly to distrust him. This distrust was not produced for the first time by the events of 1673; it is not the case that he enjoyed the King's favour until that date and forfeited it by his behaviour in that year. He had been admitted to the Privy Council in 1660 because 'it was believed that his slippery humour would be easily restrained and fixed by his uncle Southampton'; and to this remark in a later passage Clarendon added scornfully that 'few men knew the Lord Ashley better than the King himself did, or had a worse opinion of his integrity'. Charles did not trust him with the secret of the negotiations leading up to the Treaty of Dover, and when he appointed him to the Chancellorship he evidently had misgivings, to judge from his remarks at the time to Ormond. For all Shaftesbury's skill as a courtier, he was never really close to the King, and he kept his position mainly because Charles, confident of his power to manage other men however 'slippery' their 'humour' might be, counted on utilizing his abilities.

On his side Shaftesbury was probably not unaware of Charles's opinion of him. He had, too, been warned by Clarendon's fall and exile of the insecurity of royal favour, and he knew that the struggle for it might lead politicians to become Knights of the Garter or travellers to Montpellier, in his own expressive phrase. For him too, his relationship with the King was merely one of convenience; he would not lightly abandon the responsibilities and profits of office, but he would not cling to them at all costs, until death did them part. This was the situation when in 1673 events drew attention to the person of the heir to the throne, James, Duke of York, a man whose religion and politics and connexion with France were

---

[1] Buckingham had returned to England and married Mary Fairfax in 1657, and this was perhaps one reason why Charles did not put so much trust in him as in others.

disliked by Shaftesbury as by many others in the kingdom. At first he tried to work against James from his position as Lord Chancellor; but this was an impossible situation which Charles could not tolerate for long. He could allow factions amongst his own ministers, but not one aimed so directly at his own brother. The exclusion of Shaftesbury from office was the result; and for the rest of his life Shaftesbury's central aim was the exclusion of James from the throne.

CHAPTER XVII

THE 'COUNTRY PARTY' (1674–5)

> Now, manifest of crimes contrived long since,
> He stood at bold defiance with his Prince,
> Held up the buckler of the people's cause
> Against the crown, and skulked behind the laws.
>
> *Absalom and Achitophel*

'A KIND of Job's second edition' was the description given to
Shaftesbury's fall by one of his later panegyrists.[1] His ruin was
in reality far from being as complete as Job's. Dismissal meant a
substantial loss of income, but he remained a rich man. Still, loss of office
did mean something of a revolution in his manner of life. For the past
thirteen years his life had been centred on Whitehall; he must have known
every inch of the way his coach jolted along the Strand, past the Savoy
and Charing Cross to the royal palace. Apart from the usual interruptions,
particularly in August, when he retired to St. Giles or visited friends in
the country, much of his time had been spent in the royal palace, attending
the meetings of the Privy Council, the committee of foreign affairs, or other
committees, or the Treasury Commissioners. Not that the life of a seventeenth-century minister was as consistently arduous as that of a twentieth-
century one; but for a man who liked business there was usually something calling for attention, and even when there was not, a man could mix
business and pleasure by attending on the King, either formally in the
King's own apartments or informally in those of his mistresses in the
evening.

Sometimes before 1673 Shaftesbury's coach would carry him past the
royal palace at Whitehall and on to that earlier royal palace of Westminster.
There in term-time the law courts sat in Westminster Hall; and there,
rather less frequently, sat Parliament in the Parliament House. Presiding
from the woolsack over the debates of the House of Lords had been one of
his most august responsibilities; but when Parliament had not been sitting
there had been many other political activities for him. From 1674 this
was not so; for the future politics would consist very largely of the parliamentary sessions, punctuated by long recesses in which it was possible
only to make preparations for future parliamentary sessions. When Parliament met, Shaftesbury was a figure of importance. When it was not sitting
there was little he could do and he might even be ignored. It was the

[1] *Memoirs and essay for the just vindication of the Earl of Shaftesbury*, printed by Samuel
Lee, 1681.

inevitable fate of an opposition peer in the conditions of the seventeenth century; he could only look on, talk to his friends and make plans in private. He could make no speeches and get nothing done; and he was powerless to accelerate the time when the King chose to allow Parliament to sit. Until then, he was politically helpless.

In three years and three months after Shaftesbury's fall from power Parliament was allowed to sit for a total of less than five months, in three separate sessions. While these lasted he could indeed be feverishly active. But it would be a mistake to assume even then that he had stepped from the Chancellorship of which he had been deprived into the acknowledged leadership of an opposition party. Even if such a party could be said to exist in 1674, he could hardly claim to lead it. Even in the Whig heyday of the Exclusion crisis it is foolish to talk as though all the Whigs were Shaftesbury's obedient 'henchmen', ready to do his bidding without question; and in 1674, though Shaftesbury had acquired some reputation as a Protestant hero by his opposition to James, men could also remember that he had been a zealous supporter of the unpopular Declaration of Indulgence and the (by now) equally unpopular war with the Dutch. Many would be wary of him.

In the House of Lords certainly there was as yet nothing which could be described as an opposition 'party'. There were one or two individual critics of the general trend of government policy or particular aspects of it. There were a few peers of Puritan and Parliamentarian antecedents, like Lord Wharton or Shaftesbury's old Dorset neighbour, Denzil, Lord Holles; but experience had taught them to be cautious and they were a far less compact group than the Roman Catholic peers who would follow the lead of the Duke of York, or than the twenty-six bishops who with only one or two exceptions could normally be relied on to vote solidly in the way the King and Danby wanted them to do. There were other individual peers like Arlington who were envious and resentful of Danby's rise to power and might welcome an opportunity to undermine him if they could; but they would do so from within the Court and within the Council. They had neither interest nor inclination to cut themselves off from the royal favour for the doubtful pleasures of becoming part of what the eighteenth century was to know and dislike as a 'formed' opposition. It is true that one distinguished authority claims to have identified what he calls 'the Sidney-Capel-Howard connexion—an extraordinarily extensive family alliance which included many of the titled houses which at one time or another sided with Parliament during the Civil War and which in the 1670s numbered at least a dozen in the House of Lords and probably twice that number in the Commons'; but when this alleged 'connexion' is examined in detail, it scarcely shows the 'remarkable correlation between family relationship and common political action' which is claimed for it.[1]

[1] R. Walcott, *English Politics in the early Eighteenth Century* (1956), pp. 78–79 and n.

Politicians might on occasion avail themselves of their relationships by marriage to other politicians; social contacts could easily merge into political co-operation; but the sad truth is that a politician could normally count among his relatives by marriage some of his opponents as well as some of his friends. Shaftesbury had among his own relatives in the House of Lords two nephews by marriage who were to become front-rank politicians; in both cases the fact of the relationship had a certain importance, but in the end neither of them became Whigs under his leadership. One of them, Halifax, had as sharp a tongue, as critical an outlook and as coolly rational a cast of mind as Shaftesbury had; and he had also that consciousness of frustrated ability which frequently goes to make an opposition leader; but in the end he 'trimmed' and turned against Exclusion. The other, Sunderland, was also able and ambitious, and at one time in 1680 expediency did lead him to support Exclusion; but normally he pursued his taste for power and his greed for wealth by seeking office from the King—he was certainly no Whig. Both nephews might temporarily work with their uncle Shaftesbury, but neither was ever willing to accept him as an unquestioned leader.

In the House of Lords, then, the prospects for Shaftesbury did not appear to be very bright; and should they ever become brighter the King could always dim them again by creating a batch of new peers. In the House of Commons, however, there was already in existence by the end of 1673 something which may be described as a 'Country party', as long as we understand by the term 'party' a relatively loose and informal political grouping, which might change its composition to some extent with changing circumstances. Sir Thomas Meres had pointed to the existence of such a grouping in February 1673 when in a speech he referred to 'this side of the House', and 'that side'. Secretary Henry Coventry had protested that these terms were 'not parliamentary', and that Meres was trying to make a distinction between 'country gentlemen' and 'courtiers' which did not exist[1]; but he was trying to lock the stable-door long after the horse had bolted. For it was a natural instinct for members of parliament who were conscious of possessing a similar political outlook to wish to sit together in the House, to talk over parliamentary business and to plan their tactics, and this instinct had only been strengthened by the repeated sessions of the Cavalier Parliament which had enabled members to form friendships—and enmities. The instinct was developed by the steadily growing political sophistication of the period, and naturally it was most developed among those who were conscious of themselves as 'country gentlemen' struggling to cope with a flashy, extravagant, corrupt and untrustworthy Court which monopolized the royal favour. The names 'Court' and 'Country' were not first applied to political groupings in the reign of Charles II; they had been

---

[1] Grey, ii. 52; *Parliamentary Diary of Sir Edward Dering*, ed. B. D. Henning (1940), pp. 128–9.

used, for instance, in a not dissimilar situation in the 1620s, when there had also been members who thought of themselves as representing their 'country'[1] against a selfish, corrupt, unpatriotic Court clique dominated by Charles I's favourite Buckingham. In the atmosphere of the Restoration there had seemed at first no reason for reviving such a distinction: the accepted view was that the return of Charles II and the government he set up were desired by all sections of the community, and the sixty members of the Cavalier Parliament who had fought against the King in the Civil War lay low, conscious no doubt that they were only a small minority in an overwhelmingly Royalist House. With the years they had become more assertive and had been reinforced by others who entered the House at some of the numerous by-elections—such as William Sacheverell, who in 1670 became a member for Derbyshire; but of more importance had been the disillusionment which many ex-Cavalier members felt with the government. Some were frustrated by their exclusion from the favours which the fortunate few at Court enjoyed. Many disliked voting taxes which would be squandered (it seemed) on a Court which was even more dissolute and wasteful than most Courts; not many ventured to express themselves as forcibly about this as did Sir John Coventry, but others certainly felt the same in private, for the few who dared to speak their mind were not immediately overwhelmed by the reprobation of all the rest. Amongst such men the disastrous outcome of the war of 1665–7 had produced a large volume of criticism of the waste and mismanagement of the government's resources, so much so that in 1667–8 the Commons had already been dangerously out of hand from the King's point of view. But by the end of 1673 the situation was very much worse, because criticisms of waste and mismanagement had been reinforced by suspicions of the whole trend of government policy both at home and abroad. In its connexion with Louis XIV the government seemed to be allying itself with the forces of reaction against those of sweetness and light in politics and religion; and in the person of James the same unpleasant tendencies were dangerously entrenched close to the centre of power in England.

This did not mean that by the end of 1673 all the members had chosen the 'side' of the House to which they belonged: many still thought of themselves as being independent of any 'faction', and hard as Danby and Williamson tried to classify them they could never produce more than very approximate lists of the groupings in the House as a whole. Nevertheless, uncertain and variable as might be the affiliations of some members, there were others about whom no-one had any doubt—members whom Charles II and the French ambassador could describe as *les malintentionnés* because they could be relied upon to oppose the government on almost any issue that came up. They included such men as Sir William Coventry,

---

[1] The word 'country' was commonly used in the seventeenth century for 'county'.

Lord Cavendish, William Russell, Meres, Sacheverell, Lee, Thomas, Powle, Littleton, Garroway, and Sir Robert Howard. Such men were plainly in the habit of meeting together and talking politics. They were a very loose grouping, acknowledging no leader and indeed consisting largely of individualists: Coventry, for instance, was very widely respected and his interventions in debate carried great weight with many members, but he did not aspire to the position of a party leader, nor would the others have accepted him if he had. It was simply that they naturally compared notes and, when appropriate, decided what course they wished the House's proceedings should follow and sought to direct it. Like all opposition groups they contained some who were temperamentally 'agin the government' and others who had either been disappointed of office in the past or hoped to force themselves into it in the future, as well as others who were genuinely concerned about the issues involved; and no doubt, political psychology being what it is, many found it possible to combine all these motives without any thought of inconsistency.

Their secret consultations are naturally wrapped in mystery; one catches glimpses, for instance of a meeting on 29 October 1673 'about uniting',[1] but one possesses no details of what took place there. The biographer of Shaftesbury is equally in the dark, and likely to remain so, about the nature of his relations with them before 1673. It may safely be inferred that since 1661 he had become personally acquainted with many members, but it is impossible to tell with which of them he was at all intimate. Amongst his papers there survives a list of all the members, dating from 1664, in which all the King's servants and dependants in the House are listed.[2] In 1669 a hostile pamphleteer refers to Ashley's business at that time as being 'to go of errands to Parliament men to convince them by his own experience how wise a thing it is to be a knave',[3] but no specific information is available about any such 'errands'. What one may say in general terms is that in the judgment of contemporary observers his influence over members was very much less than that of either Arlington or Buckingham in the years 1667–71; but that in the summer of 1673 the French ambassador began to be very preoccupied with the possible effects of his parliamentary connexions. It was primarily for this reason that Ruvigny offered his bribe to Shaftesbury at the end of the year.

There is one other scrap of evidence, of dubious value in itself; it derives from the account of these years written by Shaftesbury's steward Stringer about 1700. In the course of a generally unreliable account he refers to a visit paid to 'our Earl' at Exeter House early in February 1673 by 'Lord St. John, the Lord Russell, Sir Thomas Littleton, Mr. Powle, and others of the leading members of the other side'; they warned him of an impending attack on his action in issuing by-election writs without

---

[1] p. 339 above.   [2] p. 171 above.
[3] *The Alarum;* A. Browning, *English Historical Documents, 1660–1714* (1953), p. 235.

the Speaker's authority, and 'our Earl, to divert them from what was intended against him, turned them upon those matters of Popery which were of great moment and consequence unto the kingdom'.[1] This last may be no more than a guess inspired by hindsight (like the allegation that Clifford had bribed members to make the attack over the writs), but the meeting may have taken place, and may be the earliest indication of consultations between Shaftesbury and Russell. They had long known one another, for Russell had married a daughter of the Earl of Southampton, who was thus cousin to Lady Shaftesbury; but in the course of the following decade Russell became the member of the House of Commons on whom Shaftesbury could most rely. The friendship was an important one, not only because Russell was heir to one of the richest of all the English noble families, but because he was a man of good reputation—'an honest, worthy gentleman, without tricks or private ambition, and . . . known to venture as great a stake perhaps as any subject of England'. He was generally liked, respected and trusted; and after his execution in 1683 it was all the easier to build him up into a Whig martyr because it seemed entirely consistent with the whole of his life that he should give it up for the cause. He was not a profound thinker or a politician of first-rate ability, but a man of simple, clear-cut ideas to which he clung—in the words of a Whig admirer, Burnet, 'a slow man, and of little discourse'; a man, in fact, who would be ready to follow a more powerful mind than his own in pursuit of the ideals of parliamentary and Protestant government, and toleration for Dissenters. As time went on Shaftesbury acquired a greater ascendancy over him.[2]

He could, however, claim no such ascendancy over the Country Party's other leaders in 1673, for at no time were they prepared unconditionally to follow his lead—not even at the time of the Exclusion crisis. Of those just listed as prominent in the session of 1673 Sir William Coventry, Lord Cavendish, Henry Powle and Sir Thomas Littleton voted against the first Exclusion Bill in 1679, and William Garroway and Sir Robert Howard absented themselves from the division. This should be a warning to us not to ascribe too great a coherence to the 'Country Party' or too great an influence over it to Shaftesbury. The view of one experienced observer, Sir William Coventry, was that the House would not submit to leadership of any sort: 'he shall no longer believe himself to lead the House of Commons than he follows it.'[3] In so far as the House could be manipulated at all, it would have to be done by a combination of rational argument and appeals to no-Popery prejudices powerful enough to overcome the individualism of the members.

There was another consideration which weakened Shaftesbury when

[1] Christie, ii, p. xxix.
[2] Temple, *Works*, i. 532; Burnet, ii. 91.
[3] Coventry to T. Thynne, 31 Mar. 1673, Thynne MSS. at Longleat, vol. xvi, fo. 104.

the time came for the new parliamentary session in January 1674. Though in the previous year he had won some popular reputation as an opponent of the Duke of York, he was effectively debarred from taking a prominent part in the two main issues which the opposition would inevitably raise. Firstly, this month marked the climax of the Dutch propaganda offensive against Charles II's French alliance; as a result of a particularly successful combination of rational argument and appeals to prejudice, organized from The Hague by Pierre Du Moulin, it could be forecast that the opposition would attempt to refuse further war supplies and force the King to make peace with the Dutch.[1] Shaftesbury too had by this time come round to the view that peace was necessary, but the man who had talked of *Delenda est Carthago* and of the Dutch as England's eternal enemy was in a poor position to lead a peace offensive. Secondly, the opposition in the House of Commons would attack the ministers responsible for the past policies which they detested; Lauderdale, Arlington and Buckingham all had reason to feel themselves threatened. Shaftesbury would have welcomed the downfall of the first of these three, but he had no reason to wish for the downfall of the other two: in the previous autumn his name had often been mentioned in conjunction with Arlington's, and he and Buckingham had much in common. And in any case it would be difficult to dissociate Arlington's and Buckingham's responsibility for acts of policy (such as the French alliance and the Declaration of Indulgence) from Shaftesbury's own. On both these issues he would have to lie low. His main concern was with measures to restrict the position of a Popish successor or to exclude him; but in the excitement over foreign policy and over impeachments he would find difficulty in getting priority for it.

On Wednesday, 7 January 1674, Charles again met his Parliament, having no choice but to do so. By now he had no stomach left for the war against the Dutch, but he dared not default on his obligations to Louis XIV under the Secret Treaty of Dover until it was obvious even to the French that he could get no money with which to fight; and in any case he did not want to lose his friendship with Louis if he could possibly avoid it. He therefore determined on one final attempt to persuade the Commons to vote supplies to continue the fight. With at least 400 members packed in at the bar of the Lords—an unusually large attendance for the first day of a new session—Charles combined assertions that the Dutch had made no serious peace proposals with general reassurances about religion and property; and then concluded with an offer to show a committee of the two Houses his treaty with France, in order to prove that it contained no secret articles of dangerous consequence as rumour alleged. By this he meant not the Secret Treaty of Dover itself, nor the *traité simulé* which Shaftesbury and his four Cabal colleagues had signed in

---

[1] Cf. my *William of Orange and the English Opposition*, chs. viii-ix.

December 1670, but a third innocuous treaty signed in February 1672 and known to all the members of the Privy Council. Even Charles, accustomed as he was to dissimulation (or lying), 'fumbled' as he asserted that 'there is no other treaty with France . . . which shall not be made known'. However he was able to end by saying that 'having thus freely trusted you, I do not doubt but you will have a care of my honour, and the good of the kingdom'; and his speech and that of Lord Keeper Finch with its long account of the negotiations with the Dutch were received with unusual applause by the packed crowd of listeners. When the Commons returned to their own chamber, Sir Thomas Meres had to avert a vote of thanks to the King by moving an adjournment until the 12th to give time for consideration.[1]

In the intervening five days a further instalment of Dutch propaganda arrived which blew great holes in Finch's account of the negotiations and demonstrated the unreasonableness of Charles II's diplomatic position, while a *Relation of the most material matters handled in Parliament, relating to religion, property, and the liberty of the subject* . . . appeared, printing the Commons' votes in the sessions of 1673 with a commentary stressing the danger of Popery and the French alliance.[2] It was these propagandist pamphlets which largely made the King's speech fruitless and meant that the Commons reassembled on 12 January as discontented with the war as ever; but in the meantime Shaftesbury had also shown his hand in the House of Lords, which had not adjourned. He had affronted the Duke of York by insisting that he must sit on the dukes' bench and not in the chair on the King's left which was habitually reserved for the Prince of Wales.[3] On 8 January the House debated religion, and Shaftesbury began to beat the anti-Popery drum as loud as he could. He said he had been told that in the neighbourhood of London there were more than 16,000 Catholics ready for desperate measures; no one could be safe as long as they were at liberty at the gates of the City, and the House must think seriously about ways to prevent a massacre which might take place any day. This quite unscrupulous speech carried the House with it; Bristol, himself a Catholic, took the lead in proposing to address the King to remove all Papists from the neighbourhood of London, and only York and two others dared to oppose it. Thus James had already been placed in a position of isolation. On 12 January there was another ominous episode; the Lords interrogated a boy of thirteen 'who surprised my lords by his answers and by a resolution not usual in one of his age'. The boy said that he had found in the street a paper (which he handed in) saying that King and Parliament were in danger from gunpowder or massacre, and that the writer who gave this

---

[1] *C.J.* ix. 291; Grey, ii. 225; Ruvigny, 8/18 Jan.; Conway to Essex, 10 Jan., *Essex Papers*, ed. O. Airy and C. E. Pike (Camden Society, 1890–1913), i. 161.

[2] Haley, *William of Orange and the English Opposition, 1672–4* (1953), pp. 160–7.

[3] Alberti, 23 Jan./2 Feb., *C.S.P. Ven. 1673–5*, p. 206.

warning was a Catholic in the service of a Catholic. It is impossible to say whether Shaftesbury or any one else had prompted the boy to present this reminder of Gunpowder Plot, or whether he merely noted for future use the effect which such a 'warning' of a Catholic plot could have. As the King watched from his habitual position in front of the fire, the peers took it all with the utmost seriousness. In the Commons they were more vehement. There were motions to ask the King to order the Lords-Lieutenant to put the militia in a state of readiness, and to command the Lord Mayor to see that the trained bands could be put under arms if necessary for the defence of King and Parliament. One man who suggested that the King's guards were enough was shouted down.[1]

On the same day the two Houses agreed to join in an address to the King for a general fast-day—referring in their petition to differences and divisions 'chiefly occasioned by the undermining contrivances of Popish recusants'. Having thus set the tone for their labours, the Commons resolved to proceed first to redress grievances, 'the Protestant religion, our liberties and properties, effectually secured; and to suppress Popery, and remove all persons and counsellors Popishly affected, or otherwise obnoxious or dangerous to the government'. By the time the four hundred members returned to their lodgings from Westminster, 'late and weary', the Commons had made their attitude unmistakable. The fact that the House did vote thanks to the King for 'the gracious promises and assurances' in his speech meant little; what was far more important was that during the debate members had vented their feelings against the war and against 'ill ministers'. One of the most outspoken was Sir Thomas Clarges, who had collaborated with Monk and Sir Anthony Ashley Cooper back in 1660. Now he wanted a new Test Act, and 'Religion, after the King's death, secured', and complained about the Catholic priests still to be seen in Whitehall in defiance of royal proclamations. His contention that the House should give priority to its attacks on counsellors was generally accepted, and in the next few days Lauderdale, Buckingham and Arlington in turn had the limelight shining disagreeably upon them. Lauderdale's fate was a foregone conclusion; a motion that the King should be addressed to remove him from his counsels as a person proved dangerous and obnoxious to the government was easily carried. Buckingham tried to avert a similar fate by offering to waive his privilege as a peer and come to the bar of the Commons to answer questions. When the House finally agreed to this, Buckingham unconvincingly tried to escape responsibility for the policies of recent years by putting the blame upon Arlington, and by declaring, for instance, that he and Shaftesbury had wanted to meet Parliament before beginning the war against the Dutch. It was all in vain; a

---

[1] Ruvigny, 11/21 Jan. (but probably written early on the 12th. Shaftesbury's name is wrongly written Shrewsbury); *L.J.* xii. 601, 604–5; Alberti, 16/26 Jan., *C.S.P. Ven. 1673–5*, p. 201; 'J. Nicholas', 9/19 Jan. in Rijksarchief, Fagel 244.

similar address to that against Lauderdale was duly carried, and the episode served only to show how the large amount of support which Buckingham had enjoyed in the Commons in 1667–8 had evaporated. Arlington was more successful: not usually accounted a good speaker, he surprised even his friends by the defence he put up when he in turn appeared at the bar of the Commons, giving replies which seemed frank and yet put responsibility for unpopular policies upon the whole of the Privy Council. His friends in the House rallied round him, and eventually a paradoxical position was reached in which they wanted an impeachment (counting on a triumphant acquittal) and his enemies wanted only an address for his removal similar to the two previous ones.[1]

During these debates people's attention was naturally fixed on the House of Commons—and Shaftesbury's attention with the rest. Yet the Duke of York at least thought that he was not merely an idle spectator; he told Ruvigny, who was now Louis XIV's official ambassador in London, of meetings at Lord Holles's house attended by Lords Carlisle, Shaftesbury, Salisbury, Fauconberg, and others 'where they concerted together the matters which were to be proposed in the lower house, where those lords had great influence'.[2] The names are all those of ex-Parliamentarian peers. Holles was one of the Five Members; Carlisle had fought against the King at Worcester, sat in the Barebones Parliament and the Council of State with Sir Anthony Ashley Cooper, had been a major-general in 1655 and a member of Cromwell's Upper House in 1658. Like Cooper, he had been suspected of complicity in Sir George Booth's rebellion in 1659, and had been rewarded for his conversion to royalism by a privy councillorship and a peerage. Fauconberg had married Oliver Cromwell's daughter Mary—the same with whom Sir Anthony Ashley Cooper's name had once been coupled; Salisbury was a younger man whose grandfather had taken Parliament's side in the Civil War and sat in the Commons under the Commonwealth, and whose wife, a daughter of the Earl of Rutland, was the sister of Shaftesbury's daughter-in-law. It is noteworthy that their meetings were not held at Exeter House, but at the home of the veteran Lord Holles whose nominal leadership would be more easily accepted. James was so alarmed by their activities that he wanted an early dissolution of Parliament, but he may have exaggerated their influence over the House of Commons. Certainly it is easy to discover their plans for the House of Lords, into which it was intended to introduce some motions on 24 January.

They were forestalled in this, for on that day Charles appeared in the House himself to produce to Parliament some peace proposals which he

---

[1] For these debates, see *C.J.* ix. 291–6; Grey, ii. 225–328; *Letters to Williamson*, vol. ii, *passim* for the month of January; Ruvigny, 15/25 Jan.; 'J.T.'s letters of 20, 23, 27 Jan. in the Rijksarchief at The Hague, Fagel 244; Haley, op. cit. pp. 167–72.

[2] Ruvigny, 22 Jan./1 Feb.

had received from the Dutch by way of the Spanish ambassador in London. On these proposals he desired the advice of the two Houses. This was an unusual abdication from the normal Stuart position that peace and war were matters for the King alone, but, as usual with Charles, it had a clever tactical purpose. If the House of Commons rejected them as inadequate— and certainly they brought England no concrete gain whatever for two years of warfare—then the House would have to supply money to secure better terms; if on the other hand the House voted them to be acceptable, then the French would be convinced that he had no choice left but to make a separate peace with the Dutch. Accordingly he asked the two Houses to give him their advice and assistance, appealing to them at the same time to 'have a care of my honour, and the honour and safety of the nation', to which he was, as always, sensitive.[1]

The instinctive reaction of the opposition was to play for time to allow them to consider the situation. In the Lords it was decided to debate foreign affairs on Monday, the 26th, and Shaftesbury's colleagues pressed on in the meantime with the motions they had planned. Salisbury led the way with a motion for a bill to provide for the education of the Duke of York's children as Protestants. Carlisle seconded this, and moved a further bill laying down that in future neither the King nor any prince of the blood should marry a Catholic without the consent of Parliament; Halifax then moved for the disarming of all Catholics and reputed Catholics, and Lord Mordaunt for the removal of all English Catholic priests from the Queen, leaving her only with Portuguese ones. A committee was appointed to prepare a bill for these purposes. In the course of the debate the King himself had received an affront. Noticing two Catholic peers whispering to him, Lord Clare protested that 'he knew not why the King should whisper to any unless it were to direct them how to give their votes, and moved that the King might be desired to withdraw out of the House, and leave them to a free debate'. Shaftesbury had said little for the present; his turn would come when the bill had been drawn up and its clauses were debated.[2]

The House of Commons also adjourned its foreign policy debate until the 26th. Those members who were in touch with the Dutch agents in London had received no advance notice of the peace proposals and feared a trick on Charles's part. Others were torn between a desire to see an end to a war they detested and the fear that peace would release Charles from his difficulties and his dependence on Parliament for money. Over the weekend there were frantic consultations with the Dutch agents, Trenchard and Medley—consultations in which, to judge from their correspondence with Du Moulin, Shaftesbury was not himself involved—and the outcome

[1] *L.J.* xii. 616–18; Haley, op. cit. pp. 174–8.
[2] *L.J.* xii. 618; J. Macpherson, *Original Papers* (1776), i. 71; unsigned letter dated 29 Jan., in Rijksarchief, Fagel 244.

was, after two days' debate, that the King was advised to treat with the States-General 'in order to a speedy peace', but the House would express no opinion on whether the articles before it were satisfactory or not. The House of Lords reached a similar decision on 28 January, having taken advantage of the King's offer to show them the French alliance of 2/12 February 1672 known to all the Council. Shaftesbury's face as he heard the treaty read would have repaid study; for he, as a signatory of the earlier *traité simulé*, knew that the affair was a trick but was not in a position to say so. In both Houses the debates were rather confused, and Arlington noted: 'One thing was very remarkable in the debates of each House, that no man opposed the coming to a speedy peace, but those that had most professedly railed at the war before, and now saw His Majesty in a fair way, by this expedient, of breaking through those snares they had laid for him.' Lord Conway's opinion was similar: 'Those who thought the French alliance a grievance, do now think a peace . . . to be the greater grievance, so that one may see they designed only to fetter the King and take their advantages. . . .'[1]

Much as the opposition wanted peace, it carried with it the awkward disadvantage that it would prevent any implicit bargain such as that by which the King's revocation of the Declaration of Indulgence and consent to the Test Act had been extorted. What they could not foresee was the speed with which Charles would make the peace now that he and the French had been convinced that it was quite impracticable for England to stay in the war. Negotiations which, conducted at the normal diplomatic speed, might have taken months were completed in ten days, and the Treaty of Westminster, by which England gave up her attempt to destroy the Dutch, was signed on 9 February. The ratifications, however, still had to be exchanged, and in the meantime the opposition pressed on with its bills in both Houses.

In the Commons the first Habeas Corpus bill to tighten up the subject's protection against arbitrary imprisonment was given three readings; a Test Bill would have eliminated Roman Catholics from the House of Lords; an address to the King asserted that any standing army was a grievance and petitioned him to dismiss all troops raised since January 1663; another bill foreshadowed the provision of the Act of Settlement that judges should hold office during good behaviour and no longer at the royal pleasure. As Conway commented, 'fear of the Duke [of York] makes them every day fetter the Crown'. One member, Birch, with typical bluntness declared that 'though we have no reason to misdoubt the King, yet we tremble to think what we may come under', and Clarges thought that this was the time to take care against coming under a bad prince, and talked of the

---

[1] Haley, op. cit. pp. 178–82; Grey, ii. 338–57; C.J. ix. 299; L.J. xii. 622; 'J.T.', letter of 29 Jan. in the Rijksarchief, Fagel 244; Arlington to Jenkins and Williamson, 30 Jan., S.P. 81/71, fo. 169; Conway to Essex, 27 Jan., *Essex Papers*, i. 168.

persecution under Queen Mary. In the House of Lords James was present
to listen to arguments which were just as offensive to him. These arose
from the bill for securing the Protestant religion, which the Lords had
ordered to be drawn up on 24 January. On 10 February, when the House
was discussing the clause to prevent a prince of the blood from marrying
a Roman Catholic without the consent of Parliament, Carlisle proposed,
and Halifax seconded, that the penalty for a breach of this clause should be
exclusion from the succession. When Peterborough described this as a
'horrid notion', Shaftesbury interposed to defend it and to say that there
were precedents for it (presumably he was thinking of Tudor acts of
succession). It is true that he said that the clause should not be retrospective (in which case it would not apply to James's marriage to Mary of
Modena), but contemporaries saw the hidden trap. If once exclusion were
declared to be legally possible in any set of circumstances, then it would be
possible to bring in a more explicit Exclusion Bill later; the whole principle
of exclusion was being debated already. Two contemporaries actually
wrote that the debate took place on a motion to declare Papists to be incapable of succeeding, but it seems improbable that the matter was as
explicit as that. Certainly Shaftesbury found that he had called down a
host of opponents upon his head. The Archbishop of York, supported by
the Bishop of Winchester and 'cheered by the rest of the bishops', put
forward the pure divine right theory that obedience was due, not only to a
Popish King, but to a tyrant and even a pagan, and described the proposal
as 'diabolical'; and Lord Keeper Finch pointed out that no less a person
than Queen Elizabeth had once been declared ineligible by Act of Parliament but fortunately had succeeded none the less. Before this weight of
opinion Shaftesbury and his allies found it advisable to drop their proposal,
and it was decided that there should be no penalty for a breach of this
clause in the bill.[1]

All this was thought to be the result of 'a combination betwixt the dis-
contented and turbulent Commons in the south-east corner of our house
and some hotspurs in the Upper (the Earl of Shaftesbury, the Lord
Halifax, the Earl of Salisbury and Earl of Clare being the most forward)'.
Halifax had now joined the 'cabal' at Lord Holles's house, and so too had
Buckingham, whom Shaftesbury was helping to evade the charges brought
against him by the relatives of his mistress the Countess of Shrewsbury.
By 21 February the Habeas Corpus Bill had passed through all its stages
in the Commons and was in committee in the Lords (Shaftesbury being a
member of the committee); and the bill for the better securing the Protestant
religion had received its first reading (Shaftesbury having reported from
the sub-committee at work on it). Other measures were reported to be in

---

[1] Grey, ii. 389–99, 415–17; Macpherson, op. cit. i. 72; Alberti, 13/23 Feb., *C.S.P. Ven.*
1673–5, pp. 220–1; Kincardine to Lauderdale, 10 Feb., *Lauderdale Papers*, ed. O. Airy
(Camden Society, 1885), iii. 32–33.

contemplation. It was said that Shaftesbury and Carlisle were to propose the disbanding of the Duke of York's regiment of guards. The French ambassador heard that Shaftesbury had accepted the responsibility for presenting a petition about the danger to Ireland; France was said to have 'intelligences and cabals' there, and it was alleged that her admiral the Comte d'Estrées had planned to land there if the last sea-battle against the Dutch had been a victory. Though these were only 'facts in the air', commented the French ambassador, Shaftesbury would not have failed to make a great show of them if he had had the opportunity. There were said to be 'Republican drifts' in the City of London designed to bring it under the rule of the Common Council. And finally it was rumoured that on 25 February there would be a direct attack on the Duke of York, and perhaps even a charge of treason.[1]

By this time Charles had had enough. It was not worth waiting any longer to see if the House of Commons could be persuaded to vote any money. 'The King says, he had rather be a poor King than no King'.[2] It was too risky even to wait until the arrival of the ratification of the Treaty of Westminster. By now he knew that Louis XIV had not taken offence at the treaty, and he was safe on that side. On 24 February he went down to the Parliament House and announced a prorogation until 10 November. All the bills which Commons and Lords had prepared therefore lapsed.

The prorogation came as a great shock to the leaders of the Country Party, who had evidently thought that Charles would have to allow Parliament to sit until a money bill had been passed to relieve him of his financial difficulties. Some feared that the prorogation was a prelude to a *coup d'état*. Lord St. John, Sir Thomas Lee, Sir Robert Thomas, Sir Nicholas Carew, Sir Eliab Harvey, Sacheverell, 'and many others' abandoned a dinner which they had ordered at the Swan Tavern in King Street on the familiar Whig principle that convivial entertainments lubricated political transactions, and hurried into the City. One member who was found burning his papers remarked, *liberavi animam meam*. These fears were groundless, but nevertheless the prorogation was a severe blow. 'I never saw such a consternation as was among the members of both Houses; every man amazed and reproaching one another that they had sat so long upon eggs and could hatch nothing.' This was an underestimate, for it was no small success to have forced the King to make a separate peace with the Dutch; but certainly all the other eggs were addled. Shaftesbury had gone far along the road which he and the Whigs were to travel in the Exclusion crisis, but all the measures he had planned to cope with the problem of a

---

[1] Sir Gilbert Talbot to Williamson, 28 Feb., in *Letters to Williamson*, ii. 156–7; Aungier to Essex, 27 Jan. and Conway to Essex, 27 Jan., in *Essex Papers*, i. 167–8; *L.J.* xii. 640, 647; *H.M.C. Ninth Report*, pt. ii. p. 45; Macpherson, op. cit. i. 72; Ruvigny, 26 Feb./ 8 Mar., 2/12 Mar.; Alberti, 27 Feb./9 Mar., in *C.S.P. Ven. 1673–5*, p. 232.

[2] Conway to Essex, 28 Feb., *Essex Papers*, i. 181.

Popish successor had achieved nothing.[1] And the Country Party was not again to be in such a powerful position until the end of 1678.

From Shaftesbury's conduct in this session certain points can be securely established. In the first place, he had gone much further than he would have needed to do if he had been a mere time-server, concerned to save his own skin. He had gone far to extremes; even exclusion was in his mind as a political possibility to be considered, though he was not yet committed to it. In the second place, if the political objective of the Exclusion crisis had been foreshadowed, so too had the main method to be employed to achieve it; Shaftesbury had already shown himself prepared to exaggerate to the limits of credibility to establish the point which he wished to make about the dangers to be expected from Popery. Thirdly, there is no evidence in the Dutch archives that, having been dismissed by Charles and having declared his hostility to James, he entered into any relations with the agents of William of Orange. Had he done so it is likely that some hint of it would have survived. William was in the habit of keeping letters from prominent Englishmen—they might be useful to him some day—but he kept none from Shaftesbury and no drafts of any letters to him. William was not Shaftesbury's hope for the future; after all he was a Stuart, like his uncles. Shaftesbury would have to work out other plans for the situation after Charles's death.

It may be doubted whether Shaftesbury was deterred from entering into relations with William by any scruples about dealing with a hostile power. He would adopt any means to reach an end which he thought desirable. The question remains whether an incident involving Samuel Pepys at this time is or is not an unpleasant illustration of this.

Samuel Pepys's work as Clerk of the Acts had long ago brought him into contact with the Duke of York in his position as Lord High Admiral. His work for the Navy had earned him James's patronage, and whatever he thought of James's religion he always saw in him a prince who was devoted to the interests of English sea-power. By 1674 he was generally considered to be James's man; and this meant that members of the House of Commons who were hostile to James were hostile to him too, and disliked his election as member for Castle Rising. On 10 February, when a dispute over this election was being considered, Sir Robert Thomas led the way in accusing Pepys of being a concealed Roman Catholic himself. He was credibly informed, he said, that Pepys had said that 'our religion came out of Henry the eighth's codpiece'; and to this heinous accusation he added a more serious one, that some persons had told him that they had seen an 'altar, and a crucifix upon it' in Pepys's house. Finally Thomas, James Herbert and Lord St. John all said that they had heard this from Shaftesbury; Littleton, who had also been present at the time, asked to be excused,

---

[1] Talbot to Williamson, as in p. 361, n. 1; 'Nic. Smyth', 25 Feb., Rijksarchief, Fagel 244; Conway to Essex, 24 Feb., Essex Papers, i, 179–80.

possibly because in his time as Navy Treasurer he had been friendly with Pepys. Thomas also claimed that Sir John Banks (a friend alike to Pepys and Shaftesbury) had seen the dreadful altar and crucifix.

The House deputed Sir William Coventry, Meres and Garroway to wait upon Shaftesbury and hear what he had to say. On the result hung Pepys's election to the House of Commons; if proved to be a Catholic he would be expelled. In the period covered by the *Diary* the Chancellor of the Exchequer and the Clerk of the Acts had frequently met, and though there is no sign of cordiality between them, there is no hint of hostility either; Pepys several times expressed his admiration for the other's business abilities though he had no high opinion of his honesty. When the deputation called to see Shaftesbury, the latter categorically denied that he ever saw an altar in Pepys's house. 'As to the crucifix . . . he had some imperfect memory, before the Navy Office was burnt [in the Fire of 1666] of seeing somewhat, which he conceived to be a crucifix, but does not remember whether it was painted or carved,[1] and that his memory is so very imperfect in it, that if he were upon his oath, he could give no farther testimony.' Next day Shaftesbury's 'gentleman' brought a letter to Sir Thomas Meres to the same effect. Shaftesbury pointed out that it was some years since he had been at Pepys's lodging, and that when he had been there he had not been concerned with taking note of things so that he could testify on oath; but he was sure he would have remembered an altar had he seen one. About Pepys's general religious orthodoxy he refrained from saying anything, one way or the other. Since Banks positively declared that he had no ground for believing Pepys a Catholic, it was on Shaftesbury's uncertain testimony that Pepys's reputation depended. Back in the House, however, Thomas, Herbert and St. John all said that originally Shaftesbury had been much more definite: St. John said that he had heard him refer to the altar and crucifix six or seven times. The House had taken no decision when the prorogation took place.

Pepys's view of the matter was clear: he thought that Shaftesbury had refrained from substantiating or denying the charge of Catholicism in order that the mud might stick. He went to seek Shaftesbury and remonstrate with him, but Shaftesbury refused to see him; and Pepys vented his righteous indignation in a letter and a speech in the House, in the course of which he claimed that Shaftesbury had wished him success in the by-election at Castle Rising, and then written underhand to promote the interests of his rival. Plainly he was prepared to believe anything about so bad a man.

What are we to think of this matter? Was it a piece of Machiavellianism on Shaftesbury's part? Pepys's admirers would have us think so. It is difficult to be sure, but on the evidence available it seems best to acquit

---

[1] By a 'crucifix' was meant any kind of representation of the Crucifixion. Pepys had in fact possessed what was probably a print (Pepys, 20 July, 3 Nov. 1666).

Shaftesbury of planning to ruin Pepys. Had he really wished to ruin Pepys he could easily have done so. In all probability he had made the statement attributed to him about the altar and crucifix, though perhaps only as a dinner-table exaggeration. Had he chosen to repeat it for the benefit of the House of Commons, Pepys would have found it impossible to disprove; and the fact that he did not do so, but said that his memory was uncertain, suggests not that he was devoid of scruples, but that he had some, and that on this occasion at least he would not repeat gossip which would 'smear' a political opponent.[1]

In a sense Pepys had the last laugh on this occasion, for after the pro-rogation he could continue with his work at the Admiralty, whereas Shaftesbury was left without office and without any political platform from which to express his opinions. While the session had lasted, he had made some impression on the critics of the government; he had gone some way to demonstrate that he was no longer one of the ministers against whom they were protesting; but the prorogation cut all this short. On 23 March 1674, he was to be found still acting in his capacity as President of the Council of Trade and Plantations and signing a draft commission and instructions for Colonel Morgan, the new Deputy Governor of Jamaica; and in mid-April there was a rumour that he had again been received in audience by the King. But in May, perhaps to demonstrate that there was nothing in this rumour, or in answer to the protestations of James and Danby, the last faint connexion between Shaftesbury and the King was cut. On 19 May he was expelled from the Privy Council, and this was followed by his replacement as Lord Lieutenant of Dorset by Lord Paulet. Charles went further and ordered Shaftesbury to leave town; he was afraid of Shaftesbury's relationship with the new Dutch ambassadors who had rented part of Exeter House as their London residence, though nothing in their secret despatches suggests that his suspicions were justified. Shaftesbury waited for a meeting of the Hudson's Bay Company's com-mittee on 3 June—long enough to show that when he left London it would be to suit his own convenience—and then left for St. Giles House, carrying with him a large number of books.[2]

Shaftesbury was now unemployed and silent. This did not mean that he was altogether without something to occupy his mind. A stay at St. Giles was not uncongenial to him; he was far from conceiving it as a

---

[1] Grey, ii. 407–12, 420–1, 426–33; C.J. ix. 306, 309; Coventry Papers at Longleat, ii. fo. 40; Shaftesbury to Meres, 10 Feb., Christie, ii. 195–6; A. Bryant, Samuel Pepys: The Years of Peril (1948 ed.), pp. 110–16.

[2] MSS. Rawl. A. 256, fos. 86, 89; Alberti, 24 Apr./4 May, C.S.P. Ven. 1673–5, p. 253; Ruvigny, 27 Apr./7 May and 25 May/4 June; Minutes of the Hudson's Bay Company, 1671–4, ed. E. E. Rich (1942), pp. 102–4, 110–12, 115; Shaftesbury Papers, V, 278. Cf. also J. Macpherson, Original Papers (1776), i. 72–73; but some of the events described here as taking place in March 1674 might more appropriately be assigned to 1676, e.g. the attempt to promote a petition for the calling of Parliament, and Shaftesbury's plan to buy a house in the City.

disagreeable exile from London; he was full of plans for developing his estates, planting and stocking them. He also had his grandchildren to plan for. Evidently doubting the capacity of his son Ashley to look after them, in March 1674 he persuaded Ashley to sign a document giving him the guardianship of them until they came of age, and the right to nominate another guardian to take over the responsibility after his death.[1] The eldest grandchild, the future philosopher Earl of Shaftesbury, now three, was a precocious boy in an age when people believed in starting education early, and his education had to be planned in conjunction with John Locke. In 1674 also he had his colonial interests to pursue. Particularly in the first six months of the year he was active in the Hudson's Bay Company, where he enjoyed almost the position of managing director. In June 1674 when he paid a hasty visit to London, rumour talked of his appointment as Lord High Steward for the trial of a peer; but what he did in London was to take out a further £300 worth of stock in the Hudson's Bay Company, and attend its General Court, which was held at Exeter House on 29 June.[2] In the previous month his enforced leisure had enabled him to make new plans for his 'darling' Carolina. On 6 May the Lords Proprietors agreed to provide an additional £100 each for seven years for the purchase of stores, clothing, etc., for the settlement on the Ashley River; and this was followed by a scorching letter (surely inspired by Shaftesbury though Craven and Carteret also signed it) dismissing Sir John Yeamans and making Shaftesbury's servant, the faithful Joseph West, Governor of the colony. But apart from the fortunes of the colony as a whole, Shaftesbury was now concerned with developing a new plantation which would bring in at least some compensation for the money he had spent in America. On 23 May he signed instructions to Andrew Percival, evidently a relative of the Dorset Peter Percival who was his banker. Percival was commissioned to found a new plantation on Locke Island on the Edisto River, including a signiory of Shaftesbury's own. It was intended to be a fresh start, south of the struggling colony on the Ashley River—a fresh start geographically, that is, but on similar principles. Percival's instructions contain all the familiar themes. There was to be experimental planting of crops: Indian corn, Irish potatoes, English wheat, and perhaps cassava from Bermuda. Planters must be prepared to settle in townships. Provision was made for a similar class of voluntary leetmen to that adumbrated in the *Fundamental Constitutions*: those willing to enter his service would receive after two years a house, sixty acres of copyhold land, common for three or four cows, and two cows, two sows, and fifteen bushels of corn; and their descendants were to settle on the land and receive ten acres for themselves on marriage. There were to be friendly relations with the Spaniards in

---

[1] Shaftesbury Papers, XX, 2.
[2] *Minutes of the Hudson's Bay Company*, op. cit. *passim*, and pp. 115, 117, 120; Sir W. Coventry to Thomas Thynne, 27 June, in Thynne Papers at Longleat, xvi. fo. 184.

Florida: a letter was to be sent from Shaftesbury's agent Henry Woodward to the Spanish governor, telling him that of all the English nobility Shaftesbury was the best-disposed to Spain, and prepared for a commerce with them 'in some convenient place about or beyond Port Royal so as to give jealousy to neither side and with as much secrecy and by as few persons as he pleases...'. Finally, there were to be friendly relations brought about with the Indians through the efforts of Woodward. As a matter of fact it was Woodward who won the most striking success: he returned from a trip into the interior with promises of skins and Indian slaves, and since it was not to Edisto that he returned, but to Shaftesbury's signiory of St. Giles Cussoe on the Ashley River, it was there that his own plantation was developed. Like all the signiories planned in the *Fundamental Constitutions*, it was intended to be 12,000 acres in extent.[1]

During 1674 and early 1675 he was preoccupied with all this. From time to time the other proprietors, the Earl of Craven, Lord Berkeley and Sir George Carteret, meeting in London, directed their secretary, John Locke, to write to Shaftesbury for advice; and on other occasions Locke sent summaries of letters arriving from Carolina down to his patron in Dorset.[2] But it is difficult to imagine that all this fully occupied the restless energies of a man like Shaftesbury. Surely his eyes were fixed on the date of 10 November to which Parliament was prorogued; then Charles would have to meet his discontented Commons to appeal for money. If this was his expectation, it was to be disappointed, for in September it was announced that Parliament would be prorogued further until April 1675. Since the end of the last session, the improvement in the King's position had been sufficient to allow him to dispense with Parliament for a further five months.

This improvement was mainly the work of the former Sir Thomas Osborne and Lord Latimer, who already in June 1674 had received the earldom of Danby as a recognition of his services. That tough ex-Yorkshire squire, a man of considerable business ability though no great ideals or intellectual range, had risen to the challenge which the situation presented to him. His energy equalled his ambition, and already he had accomplished a great deal. When he had first taken the oath before Shaftesbury in June 1673 he had not been generally regarded as a figure in the front rank; he had been thought of as a protégé of the Duke of Buckingham and the Duke of York, who had supported his promotion to the Treasurership in succession to Clifford. But Charles had chosen well for his purposes; and within twelve months Danby had emerged as a statesman in his own right, patronized by no-one. Buckingham and Arlington had both been discredited with the King by their behaviour in the parliamentary crisis; and Danby seized his opportunity with both hands. His first success came in

---

[1] *C.S.P. Col. 1669–74*, pp. 576–7, 578–9, 584–7.
[2] MSS. Locke, c. 30, fos. 4–8.

his handling of the financial situation, which for a time turned unexpectedly in the King's favour. Danby insisted on retrenchments in expenditure, and, taught by the experience of his dependence on an unruly Parliament in the previous year, Charles for once was prepared to give his Treasurer the backing that mattered. To meet the immediate needs, a temporary stop was put on all salaries and pensions, in spite of the complaints of the courtiers. At the same time income was increased: Danby was able to exact better terms from the syndicates which farmed the Excise and the Hearth money, and the yield of the Customs duties also increased sharply. Not all of this was the result of Danby's own efforts; the trend had begun in the time of his predecessor and was strengthened by the commercial profits of English neutrality during the war which still raged on the Continent; but as always the credit for a startling improvement in the economic situation went to the minister in office at the time, and certainly Danby was businesslike enough to make the most of it. Charles's problems were not completely cured, but his financial state of health had improved out of all recognition.[1]

Yet Danby was not only a financier. He had his ideas about general policy too. On foreign affairs he was not well-informed, but he had no liking for France, and when he turned for advice to Sir William Temple (who became ambassador at The Hague again in 1674) his antipathy to France was strengthened. Sensitive to the opinion of the class from which he came, he eventually began to favour co-operation with William of Orange against Louis XIV. But he could not hope to convert Charles to this reversal of his former policy until he had strengthened his claims on the King. To his initial financial success he strove to add something which no-one had previously achieved, control on the King's behalf of the House of Commons.

His recipe for this was an appeal to the Cavalier and Anglican sentiments of the county squires in the Commons. As Sir Thomas Osborne he had sat in the House himself, and he had realized that most of the members were not naturally radical either in politics or in religion. Like himself, they had Cavalier backgrounds and prided themselves on their loyalty to the King and to the established Church of England; and that they had been tempted into opposition was the result of their doubts of the soundness of the religion and the patriotism of the King's ministers. If this soundness could be rediscovered and stressed, a Court Party might be built up on this basis. In the course of time he was to develop other, more 'corrupt' methods of doing this; but in the winter of 1674–5 he seems to have been more concerned with reviving their loyalties to Church and King. This was not merely the device of a parliamentary tactician; it fitted in with his own principles, even if these cannot be rated very highly.

---

[1] Browning, *Danby*, i. 128–32.

At the end of 1674 he encouraged conferences amongst the bishops, and the eventual outcome of these was an Order of Council, dated 3 February 1675. On the one side it provided for the enforcement of the penal laws against Catholics; the suppression of Catholic worship except in the chapels of the Queen and foreign ambassadors and the prevention of Englishmen attending even there; the banishment of priests from England and of Catholic laymen from Court; and the recall of Englishmen from foreign seminaries. On the other side it struck at the Puritans by ordering the enforcement of the Conventicle Act and the suppression of worship not in accordance with the Book of Common Prayer.[1] This assertion of Anglican orthodoxy was symbolized by proposals to erect a brass statue of Charles I at Charing Cross and to reinter the Martyr King with appropriate magnificence. Loyal Cavaliers and Anglicans would, it was hoped, rally to 'God's own cause', though they would scarcely have used that phrase.

This result was not gained by Danby without some opposition from within the Court circle itself. It may be surmised that the King was not too pleased with this reversal of the policy of indulgence which he had formerly countenanced; but probably the failure of Arlington's bid at this time to arrange a marriage between Princess Mary and William of Orange[2] made it essential to find some other means to conciliate Protestant sentiment in the Commons. James, however, had a stronger dislike of a policy of Anglican orthodoxy which seemed to threaten Catholics as much as Puritans. Little as he cared for Presbyterianism or sectarianism, he was tempted on this as on other occasions in his life to make use of Protestant Dissent for the sake of his Catholic friends. At the beginning of January, therefore, while Danby, Lauderdale, Lord Keeper Finch and others were conferring with the bishops, James made overtures to Bedford, Holles, Halifax, Carlisle, Fauconberg, Salisbury and Newport.[3] All but the first and last of these had certainly taken part in the attacks on him in the previous parliamentary session, but all of them had some sympathy with the Puritans who were again being threatened with persecution, and they did not reject James's proposals out of hand.

Shaftesbury was not in London at the time, for he had been spending his first Christmas for some years in Dorset. There, some time before the middle of January, he received a visit from Lord Mordaunt which attracted a great deal of attention. Mordaunt too had been a vehement opponent of Popery in the last session, but since then he had been reconciled to the extent that he had been promised the succession to Lord Hawley's place as Gentleman of the Bedchamber to the Duke. His mission was attended

---

[1] *C.S.P.D. 1673–5*, pp. 548–51, 568; MSS. Carte 72, fos. 61–62.

[2] For Arlington's fruitless journey to The Hague, cf. Browning, *Danby*, i. 142–5, and Haley, op. cit. pp. 209–14.

[3] W. Harbord to Essex, 9 Jan. 1675, *Essex Papers*, ed. O. Airy and C. E. Pike (1890–1913), i. 285.

with just sufficient secrecy to attract attention, and it led to much speculation. Some said that he went to Dorset on behalf of the King, or the Duke,
or both, and that the journey was a prelude to Shaftesbury's return to
Court and to favour; it was still difficult for people to realize that a man of
his ability and experience might be permanently disgraced. It was suggested, too, that it was expedient to have an understanding with him before
Parliament met, and that he was being offered either the post of Lord
Lieutenant of Ireland, or the more startling position of Vicar-General in
ecclesiastical affairs which had been held previously only by Thomas
Cromwell. There had been talk of reviving it at the time of the proclamation
of the Declaration of Indulgence in 1672.[1] There survives in the Shaftesbury
Papers a paper of uncertain date and authorship, but endorsed by John
Locke, advocating the appointment of a vicar-general to reform abuses
which the bishops had failed to correct.[2] Plainly some one in authority
was toying with the idea of such an appointment, for it would have been
a most unlikely rumour for anyone to invent. On the other hand, there was
an alternative theory about Mordaunt's mission. Some said that he went,
not from the King or Duke, but 'from some other lords, with whom his
lordship did use here to consult', that is, the group of peers who had
joined in the anti-Popery motions of the last session and whom James had
now approached; the motive here might be to invite Shaftesbury to allow
himself to be reconciled to the Court, but more probably simply to inform
him of developments in London, ask his advice, and 'know upon what
measures, and with what temper he would appear if the Parliament should
meet'.[3]

Shaftesbury's own words and actions make this last theory the most
probable.[4] He cannot have been displeased to be the centre of attention,
or to have Holles and Bedford anxiously writing to him not to make a
sudden agreement with the Court. And for some time he took care to
keep both friends and enemies guessing. He sent back via Mordaunt 'a
dexterous insignificant answer', and a hint that he might come up to town
the following week (when the law term began) and bring his daughter-in-
law to lie in at London. But he did not appear as he had promised.[5]

Instead, on 3 February he wrote a letter which received a large amount

---

[1] p. 297 above.

[2] VI B, 430. It cannot however be proved that the paper was carried to Shaftesbury by
Mordaunt, as Miss Brown considers 'very probable' (p. 226).

[3] For the conflicting speculations about Mordaunt's journey, cf. Harbord to Essex, 16
and 23 Jan., *Essex Papers*, i. 286, 289; Alberti, 15/25 Jan., 22 Jan./1 Feb., *C.S.P.D. 1673–5*,
pp. 346–349; Southwell to Ormond, 16 Jan., MSS. Carte 72, fo. 255; Col. Fitzpatrick to
[Ormond?], 29 Jan., MSS. Carte 243, fo. 189.

[4] In this I disagree with Miss Brown (loc. cit.), on the ground that she has attached
insufficient weight to the references to Mordaunt in Shaftesbury's letter of 3 Feb., and to
the concluding sentences of Southwell's letter of 16 Jan. (see note below).

[5] Marvell to Sir H. Thompson [end Jan.]. *Poems and Letters*, ed. H. M. Margoliouth
(1927), ii. 317; Southwell to Ormond, 16, 23, 26 Jan., MSS. Carte 72, fos. 255, 257, 259.

of publicity. It was addressed to 'my dear Lord Carlisle' who had co-operated with him previously. It began: 'I very much approve of what my Lord Mordaunt told me you were about, and should if I had been in Town readily have joined with you, or upon the first notice have come up; for 'tis certainly all our duties and particularly mine (that have borne such offices under the Crown) to improve any opportunity of a good correspondence or understanding between the Royal Family and the People, and not to leave it possible for the King to apprehend that we stand on any terms not as good to him as necessary to us.' Thus he agreed that it was right for Carlisle and his colleagues to listen to what the King and his brother had to say, and to proffer advice; indeed, he went on to justify the lords against possible attacks by Parliament on them as 'undertakers', using the historical argument that 'through all the Northern kingdoms' kings had always been in the habit of taking the advice of 'the most considerable and active of the nobility' when Parliament was not sitting. 'Besides,' he went on, 'there are none so likely as we, nor time so proper as now, to give the only advice I know truly serviceable to the King, affectionate to the Duke, or sincere unto the country, which is, a new Parliament, which I dare undertake at any time to convince your lordship, is the clear interest of all three.' Combining in this way a profession of loyalty to King and Duke and a declaration of policy, he continued his manifesto—for it was that—by apologizing for not coming up to London as he had intended, and had told Mordaunt. This was the result of all the rumours that 'a great office with a strange name is preparing for me'. 'I am ashamed I was thought so easy a fool by them should know me better. But I will assure your lordship, there is no place or condition will invite me to Court during this Parliament nor until I see the King thinks frequent new Parliaments as much his interest as they are the people's right; for until then, I can neither serve the King as well as I would, or think a great place safe enough for a second adventure.' As if this stinging rebuke to those who had conjured up the idea of making him Vicar-General was not enough, he added that 'I think it would not be unwise for the men in great office that are at ease, and where they would be, to be ordinary civil to a man in my condition; since they may be assured that all their places put together, shall not buy me from my principles'. He asked Carlisle to show the letter to Salisbury, Fauconberg and Holles, promised to 'obey' when they summoned him to London, and concluded with a sarcastic reference to Lord Halifax and Sir William Coventry, who, he implied, had, unlike himself, been prepared last summer to abandon their principles and accept office, but had been unsuccessful in getting it. The sarcasm was probably unjustified, to judge from Coventry's own account of his visit to Windsor.[1] Copies of this letter were made and passed from hand to hand in

---

[1] To Tho. Thynne, 11 Aug. 1674, in the Thynne Papers at Longleat, vol. xvi, fo. 192. Shaftesbury's letter was printed by Miss Brown, pp. 226–7.

London; to judge from the number of copies which survive in collections of manuscripts of the period, not merely Carlisle and his three friends, but anyone interested in politics must have seen it. Evidently there was much discussion about its meaning. Some naïvely accepted the assurances of loyalty to the King and Duke at their face value. Carlisle showed it to the King, 'because it sets forth the great pacification of that lord's [Shaftesbury's] mind', and Sir Robert Southwell, reporting to Ormond in Dublin, referred to 'my lord Shaftesbury's late pacific letter'. Others were intrigued by the sarcasm of the references to Halifax and Coventry, on which Charles's characteristic remark was that 'these great wits cannot agree who should be uppermost' (for he disliked all three equally).[1] But the real significance of the letter was quite different. It lay in the assertion, for all the world to see, that he would not be 'bought from his principles' and that the only cure to the political ills of the time was the dissolution of the Cavalier Parliament and the summoning 'of frequent new ones'. The terms in which this was stated to be 'the people's right' made compromise on the point impossible, in spite of the vague assurances of willingness to serve the King; for Charles was unlikely to exchange the Royalists elected in 1661 for a set of new members who might include more ex-Parliamentarians. By the time he saw the letter, he had already committed himself to Danby's policy of dealing with the existing Parliament and appealing to its Anglicanism; but he would hardly have negotiated with Shaftesbury in any case. The letter was not really designed for the King at all; it was meant for 'the angry party within and without' Parliament.

It may, however, have been carefully calculated not to alienate the Duke of York. Considering the relationship between the two men in the previous two years, it is remarkable that the letter contains no attack, open or hidden, on James. Instead it suggested that a new Parliament was as much in the interest of James as anyone. On frequent occasions in the past James had already urged a dissolution upon his brother. This had been his reaction, for instance, to the clamours of the Commons in the debates on the Declaration of Indulgence; if the members were obstreperous, the King should either rule without them or try what a new election could do. And since Catholics were affected by Danby's Anglican policy as much as Puritans, James's dislike for the present House of Commons might be reinforced.

The tactics to be pursued in the next three parliamentary sessions were already foreshadowed. Instead of pressing on with the direct attacks on James which had begun in 1674, it was necessary first, with James's own support if it was available, to bring about a dissolution—and a new Parliament which, in Shaftesbury's judgment, would be even more critical and hostile to Popery. It took four years and the Popish Plot to achieve the new Parliament that he now demanded.

[1] Southwell to Ormond, 20, 27 Feb., MSS. Carte 38, fos. 276, 277–8.

CHAPTER XVIII

DANBY'S TEST (1675)

Straining above our Nature does no Good;
We must sink back to our old Flesh and Blood.
As by our little MATCHIAVEL we find,
That nimblest Creature of the busy Kind:
His legs are crippled, and his Body shakes,
Yet his bold Mind, that all this Bustle makes,
No Pity of its poor Companion takes;
What Gravity can hold from laughing out,
To see that lug his feeble Limbs about?
Like Hounds ill-coupled, Jowler is so strong.
He jades poor Trip, and drags him all-along.
'Tis such a cruelty as ne'er was known,
To use a Body thus, tho' 'tis one's own.
Yet this vain Comfort in his Mind he keeps;
His Soul is soaring, while his Body creeps.
Alas! that Soaring, to those few who know,
Is but a busy Flutt'ring here below.
So visionary Brains ascend the Sky,
While on the Ground entranc'd the Wretches lie;
And so late Fops have fancy'd they can fly.

An Essay on Satire written in the year 1675,
by John Sheffield, Earl of Mulgrave[1]

BEFORE the opening of the new parliamentary session on 13 April
1675, members of the opposition had been able to make some
preparations; indeed there was talk of meetings held in some counties,
and the legality of these was questioned.[2] William Sacheverell came up
primed with precedents from the reigns of Edward III, Richard II, and
Henry IV, from which on 14 April he and others agreed that sessions
ought not to be terminated until all business was completed; if established,
this would have removed the King's prerogative to prorogue Parliament
as it suited him, and would have been the equivalent of the Act of 1641
protecting the Long Parliament against being dissolved without its own
consent.[3] Members of the 'Country Party' in the Commons also came up
provided with a programme of legislation which they desired to see enacted
—probably all bills which had been introduced in the previous session and

---

[1] *Works* (1740), i. 116–17.
[2] 'J.A.', in *C.S.P.D. 1673–5*, p. 604.
[3] *C.J.* ix. 316, 317, 321; *C.S.P.D. 1675–6*, p. 65; Alberti, 16/26 Apr., *C.S.P. Ven.
1673–5*, p. 393; Van Beuningen, 16/26 Apr., Add. MSS. 17677, QQQ; Grey, iii. 19–22.

killed by the prorogation. Within the first week a Test Act to prevent Papists from sitting in either House of Parliament was proposed, and a Habeas Corpus bill and a bill for the prevention of illegal exaction of money from the subject were given a first reading. There was talk of other anti-Popery bills, including one preventing princes of the blood from marrying Roman Catholics.[1] Finally, it was planned to pass another address for the removal of the hated Lauderdale, and, still more drastically, articles had been drawn up for the impeachment of Lord Treasurer Danby.

All this constituted a direct attack on the King's ministers and pre-rogatives, to be carried out in the lower House; it indicated clearly the presence there of a group of irreconcilables. No doubt Shaftesbury knew beforehand what was afoot; what share he had in planning it is unknown. We do not even know how long before the session he arrived in London. The circumstance that the attack on Danby was begun on 26 April by William Russell may appear suspicious, but Danby himself blamed Arlington, who had never liked him and disliked his promotion to the coveted Treasurership.[2] The only hint about Shaftesbury's activities consists of renewed rumours that he had sought to return to the good graces of the Duke of York; the Venetian ambassador even reported that he had 'humbled himself' to James, and reported that Bedford and Holles 'and the rest of the confederates' in the Lords had offered a reconciliation on the basis of joint resistance to Danby's policy of Anglican conformity, and James's resumption of the office of Lord High Admiral.[3] It would be dangerous, however, to read into this anything more than a tactical attempt to drive a wedge between James and Danby, and improve the opposition's prospects against the phalanx of Royalist peers and bishops. Certainly the 'heads for a bill for securing the Protestant religion' which had been discussed in the previous session were promptly taken up again in the first week of the session in the Lords.[4]

But Shaftesbury was never given time to develop his plans for action in the Lords, whatever they may have been. Instead Danby seized the initiative. The note was struck by the King's opening speech on 13 April, when he appealed to the Anglican and Cavalier sentiments of his hearers. Referring to 'the pernicious designs of ill men' (presumably including Shaftesbury) who wanted to compel him to dissolve Parliament and call

[1] C.J. ix. 317–19; Van Beuningen, loc. cit.

[2] Browning, Danby, i. 155–9; Ruvigny, 8 Apr., cit. ibid. 155, n.

[3] Alberti, 9/19 Apr., C.S.P. Ven. 1673–5, p. 391. I am inclined to believe that the story in the Life of James II, ed. J. S. Clarke (1816), i. 513, about an approach by 'Lord Russell and other considerable men of the party' to James, relates to April 1675 and not April 1678, when it would have been hardly appropriate to describe the offers as being made 'a little before the meeting of Parliament'. This phrase would hardly apply to the short recess from 15 to 29 Apr. 1678.

[4] L.J. xii. 659–61; H.M.C. Ninth Report, Part II, House of Lords MSS. p. 43.

a new one, 'when I consider, how much the greatest part of this Parliament have either themselves, or their fathers, given me testimony of their affections and loyalty, I should be extreme loth to oblige those enemies, by parting with such friends. . . . I have done as much as on my part was possible, to extinguish the fears and jealousies of Popery; and will leave nothing undone, that may shew my zeal to the Protestant religion, as it is established in the Church of England, from which I will never depart. . . .' The precise meaning of this manifesto became clearer two days later, when Danby's brother-in-law, the Earl of Lindsey, brought in a 'bill to prevent the dangers which may arise from persons disaffected to the government', that is, rebellious Puritans. All members of both Houses of Parliament and all office-holders were to be required to make a declaration that taking up arms against the King was not lawful upon any pretence whatsoever, and to swear not at any time to endeavour the alteration of the government in Church or State. Such a non-resistance declaration had previously been imposed on members of corporations, militia officers, and clergy, and a similar bill extending it had been narrowly defeated in the Oxford session of 1665 by the votes of Danby and Lindsey themselves. It was now revived in an attempt to return to the old party lines between Royalist and Parliamentarian, Anglican and Puritan, in the expectation that the government's position in Parliament would be strengthened. Straying Cavaliers might be brought back to the fold.[1]

The 'country lords' put out a kind of manifesto of their own in reply to the King on 13 April. Objecting to a motion that thanks be presented to the King for his gracious speech, they had been outvoted, but ten of them (including Shaftesbury) had entered a Protest in the Journals on the ground that this was not consistent with the House's usual freedom of debate. Protests of this kind were unusual, and the adoption of this method, with the publicity which it gave to the outvoted minority and the reasons which they gave for their opposition, amounted to an acceptance of Danby's challenge.[2]

On the first reading the country lords put up no great opposition as they waited to see more of the use to which the government intended to put the bill. When the second reading took place on 20 April, the battle began in earnest. The Lord Keeper, Finch, and others painted a lurid picture of the large number of 'fanatics' still in the country and the dangerous and rebellious principles which were still current. It was a picture which bore little relation to the peaceful state of the country, and as a crude attempt to revive antagonisms which the Act of Oblivion of 1660 had been intended to put to sleep, the opposition attacked it; and before the government could carry its motion for the bill's committal, it had to face unusually

---

[1] *C.J.* ix. 314–15; *L.J.* xii. 659; Alberti, 16/26 Apr., *C.S.P. Ven. 1673–5*, pp. 393–4.
[2] *L.J.* xii. 655.

long debates, lasting until nine or ten at night on four different days—
something quite uncommon for the period. The opposition delayed the
bill as long as they could. First they moved that the bill entrenched upon
peers' privileges and should be thrown out; when the motion was heavily
defeated twenty-three lords, including Shaftesbury, Buckingham, Salisbury, Halifax, and the (second) Earl of Clarendon had a protest entered
in the Journals, on the ground that a bill imposing an oath on peers with
the penalty of exclusion from the House was 'the highest invasion of the
liberties and privileges of the peerage that possibly may be'. Then they
moved that the problem of how far peers' privileges were affected should
be referred to a committee of the whole House for argument; and after
this was beaten off, it was late on the 26th before the bill was sent for its
committee stage by 53 votes to 37. This time Shaftesbury was one of
twelve peers who signed a protest against the subversion of peers' privilege,
the attack on freedom of speech ('it being necessary to all government to
have freedom of voice and debates') and the rigidity of a bill which ruled
out any alteration in Church or State however much political prudence
'or Christian compassion to Protestant Dissenters' might require it. The
terms of the Protest aroused considerable resentment among the government supporters, some of whom even suggested that the twelve should be
sent to the Tower for their insolence. In the end they carried a motion that
the reasons given by the opposition peers reflected upon the honour of
the House. To this the opposition replied defiantly with a new Protest,
signed by Shaftesbury, Buckingham, Salisbury, Clarendon, Holles, Halifax,
Wharton, and fifteen others, against the majority's 'discountenancing of
the very liberty of protesting'.[1]

Many peers obviously had misgivings about the possibility of exclusion
of themselves or their colleagues from the House for refusing the oath
required by the bill, and the motion that this matter of peers' privilege
should be referred to a committee of the whole House was lost only by
39 votes to 38. 'If some had not been at dinner', wrote one observer, 'it
[the Bill] had been cast out with indignation'.[2] But this vote was exceptional. The government might have the worst of the argument, but it
could count on the best of the voting. Many of the lay peers had ties of
one sort or another with the King, who attended the debates regularly.
Above all, there was what the opposition described as 'the dead weight',
meaning the bishops, who voted consistently for the bill. Against them
Shaftesbury was supported by Buckingham (who had now finally separated
from his former protégé Danby) and Halifax. Two on whom he had

---

[1] *Letter from a Person of Quality to his Friend in the Country*, in Locke's *Works* (1823),
x. 211–17; *L.J.* xii. 664–71; *H.M.C. Ninth Report*, ii 51; Van Beuningen, 23 Apr./3 May
in Add. MSS. 17677, QQQ; Alberti, 23 Apr./3 May, 30 Apr./10 May, *C.S.P. Ven.
1673–5*, pp. 397–9, 401; W. Denton to Sir R. Verney, 24 Apr., *H.M.C. Seventh Report*, p.
492; notes in Wharton Papers, MSS. Carte 79, fo. 17.   [2] Denton, loc. cit.

counted, Carlisle and Fauconberg, had abandoned the struggle: Carlisle had accepted the governorship of Jamaica, and Fauconberg, the opposition remarked with disgust, had an office at Court to keep. But others played valuable supporting parts: Holles, Wharton, Salisbury and Bedford were all to the fore. They were joined by some moderate Anglicans, like Clarendon, who disliked Danby's policy or had personal reasons for opposing him. All in all, they were not a group of extremists, for of the thirty-two peers who signed one or more of the six Protests of the session, only nine were later to vote for the Exclusion Bill of 1680, and eight were actually to vote against it.[1] Nor did the thirty-two form a coherent, disciplined 'party', for none of the six Protests was signed by more than twenty-three of them. By themselves they could only delay the inevitable; if they were to have any chance of achieving numerical equality, they had only one hope, namely to enlist the support of the Catholic peers, including James, who were as much affected by the bill as the Puritans. Accordingly Shaftesbury 'dinned this in their ears, . . . that, if this Act passed, the next would be to test them out of the House'. This was indeed the obvious truth, for there was already a bill for the exclusion of Catholics from Parliament under study in the Commons. The possibility that the Catholic peers might join the opposition to the bill was real enough for Danby himself to take action to forestall it, by moving that peers might not be incapacitated from sitting by the oath required in the bill. The Duke of York moved that there should be a standing order to this effect applying to all bills, and this was agreed to. Shaftesbury joined in the agreement with the rest, for tactical reasons. Three years later, when the Test Act of 1678 was being debated, and reference was made to this standing order of 1675, Shaftesbury only smiled, remarked that the House was master of its own orders, and quoted the maxim that *leges posteriores priores abrogant*; a course that did not improve the Catholics' already low opinion of his sincerity, though, as will be seen later, he was only repeating an argument of Lord Keeper Finch.[2]

Danby's acceptance of the standing order effectively defeated Shaftesbury's hopes of enlisting the support of the Catholic peers against the bill. James sometimes vacillated—plainly he did not like a bill which aimed at strengthening Anglican conformity—but he liked the possibility of being accused of disloyalty to the King still less, and he would not vote with the 'enemies of monarchy' against the ministers and the policy that Charles approved.[3] Shaftesbury and the rest were left in a hopeless minority.

They were not discouraged by this. They were determined to fight the

---

[1] E. S. Turberville, 'The House of Lords under Charles II', *E.H.R.* (1930), p. 58; cf. Browning, *Danby*, iii. 122–5.

[2] *L.J.* xii. 673; J. Macpherson, *Original Papers* (1775), i. 80–81; Roger North, *Examen* (1740), pp. 63–64.

[3] Cf. Alberti, 30 Apr./10 May, *C.S.P. Ven. 1673–5*, pp. 401–2; Burnet, ii. 82.

committee stage of the bill, clause by clause. At the least they hoped to
obtain some propagandist advantage out of their opposition to Danby's
policy of Anglican intolerance. When the committee reported progress to
the House on 4 May, Shaftesbury was one of fifteen peers who signed yet
another Protest for entry in the Journals; and it was evident from the
length of this Protest that it was not intended merely for purposes of record,
but to appeal to the public 'out of doors'. Thereafter, in order to avoid
more such Protests, Danby decided that the committee should report
back no more until it had completed its deliberations on the bill; but the
debates had by now attracted so much attention that they could hardly be
kept secret.[1]

The committee (which was a committee of the whole House) began
with a debate on the principle of imposing oaths on anyone. Here Halifax
made a characteristic mordant speech about the futility of oaths in general,
saying with biting scorn that even if all the town was sworn not to rob,
no man would sleep with open doors or without locking up his plate.
Oaths, he said, made difficulties not for the wicked, but for 'some honest,
conscientious men, who would never have prejudiced the government'.
But he was voted down: oaths were still too much in accord with the
mentality of established authorities in that day. Next it had to be decided
who was to take the oath; at first it was to be applicable only to office-
holders, until after some hours Lord Keeper Finch proposed to add all
privy councillors, justices of the peace, and members of both Houses.
When the recent standing order was quoted against this, Finch argued
(three years before Shaftesbury) that the peers were masters of their own
orders, and the interpretation of them; and when the majority upheld him,
it was against this that the minority Protest of 4 May was directed. There
then followed some long debates on the declaration which all these categories of people were first to be called upon to subscribe: 'I, A.B., do
declare, that it is not lawful, upon any pretence whatsoever, to take up
arms against the King, and that I do abhor that traitorous position, of
taking arms by his authority, against his person, or against those that are
commissioned by him.' Against this extreme statement of the doctrine of
non-resistance the opposition argued that there might be at least some
extreme positions in which resistance was justifiable: 'it necessarily brings
in the debate in every man's mind, how there can be a distinction then left
between absolute and bounded monarchies, if monarchs have only the
fear of God, and no fear of human resistance to restrain them.' Suppose
the King of France acquired a title to the throne of England, and avowed
a design to change the English religion, and make his government here as
absolute as in France; would resistance not be justifiable then? What
about historical examples, as when Henry VI of England had been a

---

[1] *L.J.* xii. 677, 681–2; *H.M.C. Ninth Report*, ii. 51; *Letter from a Person of Quality*,
op. cit. x. 217–19.

prisoner doing what the Yorkists told him to do? or when Charles VI of France disinherited the Dauphin in favour of Katherine and Henry V? or when King James 'of blessed memory' was kidnapped as a child? Were their supporters not justified in 'taking arms by his authority against his person, or against those that are commissioned by him'? And would not this last clause in the declaration justify the oppressions of a standing army, or the illegal raising of taxation?—'and however happy we are now, either in the present prince, or those we have in prospect, yet the suppositions are not extravagant, when we consider kings are but men, and compassed with more temptations than others.'[1]

Nevertheless all these arguments were voted down by the 'dead weight', and the committee passed on to discuss the central oath, which, after some minor amendments had been accepted by the government, read: 'I do swear that I will not endeavour to alter the Protestant religion, or the government of either Church or State.' Against the first half of this oath Shaftesbury argued at length on 12 May. He urged, first of all, 'that it is a far different thing to believe, or to be fully persuaded of the truth of the doctrine of our Church, and to swear never to endeavour to alter; which last must be utterly unlawful, unless you place infallibility either in the Church or yourself; you being otherwise obliged to alter, whenever a clearer or better light comes to you'. Following up this idea that religious truth was not something fixed or static, but something which needed to be looked at again in 'a clearer or better light', he boldly asked where, in any case, it was possible to find what was meant by 'the Protestant religion'. His opponents thought that this provided them with an opportunity for a crushing retort: Lord Keeper Finch mockingly asked that it might not be told in Gath, nor published in the streets of Askalon, that a lord of such eminence and ability, and a professed Protestant, should not know what was meant by 'the Protestant religion'; and Seth Ward, the bishop of Winchester, presented the elementary information, for Shaftesbury's benefit, that the Protestant religion was comprehended in the Thirty-Nine Articles, the Liturgy, the Catechism, the Homilies, and the Canons. In so doing they fell into the trap which Shaftesbury had laid for them. He pointed out that some of the Thirty-Nine Articles were contrary to the doctrines preached from the pulpits under the Restoration: for instance, in the seventeenth and eighteenth Articles he detected the doctrine of pre-destination which few Anglicans retained; the nineteenth, he said, defined the Church 'directly as the Independents do'; and the twentieth was confused and contradictory. The Liturgy could not be regarded as sacred,

---

[1] *L.J.* xii. 674–7, 681–2, 685; *H.M.C. Ninth Report*, ii. 51–52; *Letter from a Person of Quality*, op. cit., x. 219–26. The author of this propagandist pamphlet probably does less than justice to the arguments of Danby, Finch, and the bishops; but there is no reason to suppose that he misrepresents those of the opposition, and it is for these that he is quoted.

being man-made and dating only from 1662; and Shaftesbury took the opportunity to attack the Act of Uniformity. So far from uniting Protestants, it had served to divide them: for instance, the insistence on episcopal ordination meant that Puritans were excluded while converted Papists could take a benefice without re-ordination, and in any case the clause was an innovation, for it ran counter to the practice of the Church of England from the Reformation to 1662, and it benefited only the Pope and Louis XIV, since it hampered English relations with Continental Protestants. It might therefore be a positive duty to try 'to restore the liturgy to what it was in Queen Elizabeth's days'. The Catechism and the Book of Homilies could both be improved; and as for the Canons, they were still 'the old Popish canons', unrevised. It would be hard to impose an oath preventing people from advocating alterations to any of the bishop's five criteria of Protestantism.

These weighty arguments made a deep impression on moderate opinion in the House—so much so, that Danby was in serious difficulties when one of Shaftesbury's supporters, Lord Grey of Rolleston, moved that the words 'by force or fraud' be inserted into the oath, thus legitimizing attempts to alter the religious settlement by other and constitutional methods. The Duke of York and the Bishop of Rochester both supported this amendment; the opposition joyfully closed with it, seeing that it would stultify the whole of Danby's test bill; but in the nick of time Danby saw his danger, rallied his party, and voted down the amendment. When the sitting was drawing to a close, after darkness had fallen, there were heated scenes. The government tried to insist that the vote should apply to the whole of the oath: the opposition argued that it should apply only to the first half of it, ending with the words 'the Protestant religion'. 'Standing up in a lump together' they shouted at the top of their voices, 'Adjourn', and silence was only obtained when Danby and Finch accepted their point.[1]

The struggle was continued on other days and at equal length. The opposition argued that the oath against altering Church or State would remove Parliament's legislative functions and reduce it to a money-giving body, for every new Act of Parliament amounted to an alteration in the state; and no state could be regarded as perfect, as though it had been handed down on sacred tablets from Mount Sinai. It was also contended that the oath would prevent even private converse on politics. But always 'the major vote answered all objections'. Finally, on 31 May, the committee debated the penalties to be imposed for refusing to take the oath. By this time the Court peers had had so much argument, and had had so much the worst of it, that many preferred to remain silent until the time came for the division. Late at night Buckingham mocked them in a speech of

[1] *Letter from a Person of Quality*, op. cit. x. 226–31; *L.J.* xii. 690; *H.M.C. Ninth Report*, ii. 52.

'eloquent and well-placed nonsense', until at midnight the last vote was taken, and the peers streamed out, relieved or frustrated.[1]

Thus in fact the whole struggle ended, for the bill proceeded no further before the prorogation. It had been a parliamentary battle of unprecedented length, extending over days of parliamentary time, and some of those days' debates lasting until after dark or even until midnight. It was 'the greatest and longest debate in the House of Lords' that Burnet could remember; and he also commented that in it Shaftesbury distinguished himself more than ever before, opposing the doctrine of non-resistance and the permanent preservation of the *status quo* in Church and State. Once he spoke for a whole hour—in those days an extremely long speech; and always he had to watch his words, for an incautious word about resistance to authority, or one which could be interpreted as reflecting on the King, might have led to the Court majority sending him to the Tower, as they did later in 1677.[2] The debate defined Shaftesbury's political position in a way from which it would be impossible for him to recede. Though Buckingham and others had taken part in it, he now stood out as the uncompromising opponent of the Court, committed to the principles that he had put forward. It can be said that he had taken one side in a debate between conflicting political philosophies. Yet it would be a mistake to conclude from its terms and from the nature of Danby's Test Bill that the debate was simply about abstractions, adopted by each side for propagandist purposes. There were concrete issues at stake. If Danby's test had been applied to all office-holders, justices of the peace and members of Parliament, it would have made difficulties for many conscientious people; it could have been the basis for a government purge; and it could have seriously embarrassed any later attempts at 'alterations' in the existing order.

That this was ruled out was due primarily to the success of Shaftesbury and his allies in obstructing and protracting the debate. If twenty or thirty peers could hold the bill up for so long, then it was clear that the much larger opposition in the House of Commons could hold it up for much longer, even if the lower House could be diverted from its other preoccupations. It was not practical politics for the bill to be sent down to the tender mercies of the 'Country Party' in the Commons: it was not simply that parliamentary business was blocked by the famous case of *Shirley* v. *Fagg*, which must be kept in its proper perspective.

In the meantime the opposition in the Commons had been finding it unexpectedly difficult to make headway. In the session of January 1674 they had carried all before them; now they found themselves committed to a much more even and hard-fought battle. The endeavour to use alleged medieval precedents to see that a parliamentary session lasted as long as

---

[1] *Letter from a Person of Quality*, op. cit. x. 231–40; *H.M.C.*, loc. cit.; Francis Godolphin to Essex, 1 June, in *Essex Papers*, ed. O. Airy and C. E. Pike (Camden Society, 1890–1913), ii. 23. [2] Burnet, ii. 81–84.

there was still unfinished business, and thus deprive the King of his right
of prorogation, had petered out for lack of support. The attempt to impeach Danby, begun on 26 April by Russell, had ended in ignominious
failure.[1] The Habeas Corpus Bill passed the House, but a Place Bill aimed
at the court dependants in the House was rejected on the second reading.[2]
Against this, Danby's efforts to induce the members to vote money for the
fleet were thwarted by the opposition, and a bill was even drawn up appropriating the existing Customs duties for the Navy's use—where taxation
was concerned the government's critics could always count on the reluctance of members to return home and break the news of new taxes to their
neighbours.[3] But the ease of this success in the matter of money was
counterbalanced by the difficulty which the 'Country Party' had in imposing its view on foreign policy. In 1674 they had effectively forced the
King to give up his French alliance and leave the war by the Treaty of
Westminster; but now they found it much harder to force Charles to recall
the British troops which had taken service in the French army. Their
presence with Louis XIV's troops (which were now making important
captures from Spain in Flanders and Franche-Comté) excited a good deal
of resentment which was fanned by the ambassadors of the Confederate
powers in London; and, led by Sir Thomas Littleton, on 19 April the
Commons did resolve without difficulty on an address to the King asking
him to recall his subjects in the service of France. After delaying as long
as he could Charles replied on 8 May agreeing to forbid further French
recruiting, but saying that he could not in honour recall the troops who had
been fighting with Louis XIV before the Treaty of Westminster was signed.
Then followed two unusually heated debates. The first of these, in grand
committee on 10 May, ended in disorder. When the members voted on a
motion that a further address should be sent to the King, the two sides
were almost exactly equal with about 135 votes each, but the tellers could
not agree on the figures. A heated argument ensued, in which 'hot and
provoking discourses and gestures passed on both sides, especially betwixt
Lord Cavendish and Sir John Hanmer' (the teller for the 'Court Party').
Russell had to prevent Cavendish from drawing his sword; Cavendish was
also accused of spitting in Hanmer's face, though his friends excused this
as the accidental result of a natural 'eagerness of speech'. Some of the
'young gallants' of the Country Party jumped over the seats to join
Cavendish; other members, more neutral, more cautious or more intent
on seeing what was happening, stood on the upper benches to watch the
fun, expecting bloodshed at any moment. After half an hour an ugly scene
was brought to an end by the Speaker's action in recovering the mace and
turning the Grand Committee into a sitting of the House. This brought
members to their senses, but another hard-fought debate took place next

---

[1] Browning, i. 155–60.   [2] C.J. ix. 331; ibid. 326–7; Grey, iii. 69–74.
[3] C.J. ix. 330; Grey, iii. 34–40, 96–102.

day. Secretary Henry Coventry brought a message from the King agreeing now to recall those who had gone over into the French service since the Treaty of Westminster. The opposition were still not satisfied and moved that the King should be asked to recall *all* of his subjects (that is, including those who had crossed before the peace treaty). Once again, in an unusually crowded House, the result of the vote was uncertain until the tellers jointly reported a victory for the government by the narrowest possible margin, 173 votes to 172.[1]

The closeness of these debates meant that tempers in the Commons were as inflamed as in the Lords, and it was this which made the case of *Shirley* v. *Fagg* so explosive. The dispute between Dr. Thomas Shirley and Sir John Fagg, M.P., had dragged its way through Chancery until on 30 April the doctor appealed to the House of Lords; and, having heard his petition, the Lords gave Fagg a week in which to reply. In the Chancery court Fagg had waived his privilege as a member of the House of Commons, but now he could not appear before the bar of the Lords without asking the leave of his own House. After referring the matter to a small committee (which did not consist of extremists)[2] the Commons sent up a message to the Lords asking the peers to have regard to the privileges of their House. The Lords replied asserting their 'undoubted right . . . to receive and determine . . . appeals from inferior courts, though a member of either House be concerned', and Shaftesbury, who had evidently taken part in the debate, signed a Protest complaining that the terms of this answer were too conciliatory. Eight other peers signed the Protest, and most of them were allied with Shaftesbury in fighting Danby's Test Bill. There can be no doubt that Shaftesbury had decided to use this case as a means of wrecking the session, by setting the two Houses at loggerheads. How soon he conceived the idea of using it to compel not merely a prorogation but a dissolution and new elections, is not so clear, but certainly he strove to make the discord even worse. Shaftesbury later told Burnet that the whole matter was 'laid by himself', and some have supposed that the case was brought to the Lords at his instigation in the first place; Fagg was later to be an Exclusionist. This however seems to be going further than the evidence will permit. Fagg did not himself seek to insist on his privilege as a member of the Commons. He had waived it at earlier stages in the case; he appeared at the bar of the Lords on 7 May to ask for five more days in which to present his answer; and seems to have been genuinely concerned that if he did not appear before the Lords, his case might go by default. Others took a far more rigorous view of his privileges than he

[1] *C.J.* ix. 319, 321, 333–5; Grey, iii. 3–9, 115–39; Ruvigny, 19/29 Apr., 22 Apr./2 May, 13/23 May, in F. Mignet, *Négotiations Relatives à la succession d'Espagne* (1835–42), iv. 345, 350–1; Van Beuningen, 20/30 Apr., 7/17, 11/21 May, in Add. MSS. 17677, QQQ. (Van Beuningen's despatches contribute additional details on all the proceedings of this session.)

[2] Its members were Sir Trevor Williams, Mr. Hales, Sir R. Carr, and Sir A. Irby.

did himself. It seems best to assume that the case was not a collusive one, and that when Shaftesbury said that it was 'laid by himself' he meant that he saw its possibilities early, and worked systematically to exploit them.[1]

The small cloud which on the horizon had seemed no bigger than a man's hand approached with great rapidity and became a storm-cloud of large proportions. On 12 May (the day following the two heated debates on foreign policy) Fagg put in his answer to Shirley's petition to the Lords, but the Commons promptly ordered him to proceed no further without their special leave, and sent for Shirley to account for what they conceived to be a breach of privilege.[2] Two days later the officer of the Serjeant-at-arms found Shirley in the lobby of the House of Lords and unwisely tried to serve the Speaker's warrant on him there. Shirley called for assistance to Lord Mohun, a young rakehell peer whose political affiliations were with the opposition, and Mohun snatched the warrant from the officer's hand and took it into the House of Lords, where the peers were indignant at the intrusion into their lobby which he reported to them. Shaftesbury was one of three peers deputed to draft an offensive message to the Commons inquiring whether the 'paper signed Edward Seymour' was authentic. In the meantime the Commons had heard of the incident and sent one of their members, Lord Ancram, to deliver a complaint about Mohun's action. Ancram was kept waiting some hours for an unsatisfactory answer, and in the Painted Chamber he had an unpleasant encounter with Mohun, who took care to tell him that the Lord Keeper had received the Commons' message 'fleering and laughing'. All this lost nothing in the telling when Ancram returned to his own House, and the reaction of the members was what might have been expected. What was not so predictable was the encouragement which the Speaker gave to them, perhaps on the instructions of the Earl of Danby, who saw the dispute as a means of obtaining popularity for the government in the Commons by its identification with the cause of their privileges.[3]

In the days that followed, the duel between Shaftesbury and Danby over the Test Bill in the Lords was paralleled by a second duel, in which Danby and his supporters espoused the cause of Commons' privileges while Shaftesbury and his colleagues defended the right of the Lords to act as a court of appeal in all cases. The fact that two other cases involving members of the Commons, Onslow and Dalmahoy, came before the Lords

---

[1] *L.J.* xii. 673–4, 679–81; *C.J.* ix. 329–30, 333; Grey, iii. 112–15, 269–75; Burnet, ii. 85; Marvell, *Growth of Popery* in *Works*, ed. Grosart (1872), iv. 310.

[2] Unfortunately this debate was not reported by Grey and we do not know who inspired this motion; though on 5 June Vaughan claimed the 'credit' for 'opening the matter' in the Commons (ibid. iii. 263).

[3] In this I follow Browning, *Danby*, i. 162. It should be noted, however, that Danby later blamed Speaker Seymour for 'promoting the difference betwixt the Houses' (ibid. ii. 71), and it may be that Danby acquiesced with some reluctance in a policy which Seymour had begun. *C.J.* ix. 335–9; *L.J.* xii. 689–92; Grey, iii. 140–56; *H.M.C. Ninth Report*, ii. 57.

on appeal within a few days of *Shirley* v. *Fagg* did not help to cool tempers. The Commons resolved that anyone appearing at the bar of the Lords in a suit against any M.P. was acting in breach of their privileges; the Lords insisted on their right, and positive duty in the interests of justice, to hear all appeals. Conferences between the two Houses (at which Shaftesbury was one of the peers present) had no result, and the usual adjournment over Whitsuntide had no effect either, for on 28 May no member of the Commons even put in an appearance at a conference with the Lords, and later the House went further and passed a resolution denying that any appeal lay to the Lords from any court of equity. To enforce their view, they sent for the counsel who had appeared against Dalmahoy, and ordered them into custody. The Lords replied by deputing Anglesey, Bridgewater, Shaftesbury and Holles to draw up an order for their release—an order which was couched in very extreme language—and entrusted it to Black Rod for enforcement. The climax came on 4 June, when Speaker Seymour, passing through Westminster Hall on his way to the House, found one of the offending counsel, Sir Francis Pemberton, there and arrested him; and the Serjeant, accompanied by thirty or forty members, took three other counsel from the bars at which they were pleading.[1]

By this time the King had given orders for his apartments at Windsor to be prepared, and it was obvious that the session would speedily be at an end. There were not wanting those who sought to persuade Charles that it was hopeless to expect anything from the present House of Commons, and that he should dissolve it and call a new one. This would have suited Shaftesbury's aim (as expressed in his letter to Lord Carlisle) perfectly; but Danby and Charles were wiser than to adopt it, foreseeing as they did that a new House of Commons was likely to be less, not more amenable. Instead, on 5 June, the King assembled both Houses in the Banqueting Hall, and the Lord Keeper read a prepared statement attributing the present state of affairs to the designs of 'ill men' who wanted to procure a dissolution. Having scored this propaganda point, which was probably not lost on those members of the Commons who did not wish to risk losing their seats, Charles waited four more days while the Houses continued to wrangle over the four luckless counsel (who were now in the Tower), and then prorogued them until October with a speech which again complained of 'the ill designs of our enemies'.[2]

Amongst those enemies was certainly to be included Shaftesbury, for whom the prorogation represented a triumph in his efforts to obstruct the policy of Danby. Yet on Sunday, 13 June, observers noted with surprise that Shaftesbury and the Marquis of Winchester, neither of whom had

---

[1] *C.J.* ix. 339–54; *L.J.* xii. 694–723; Grey, iii. 156–260; *H.M.C. Ninth Report*, ii. 53–54.
[2] *C.J.* ix. 354–7; *L.J.* xii. 724–9; Grey, iii. 260–89; Alberti and Sarotti, 28 May/7 June, 4/14 June, *C.S.P. Ven. 1675–6*, pp. 412–13, 416; Ruvigny, 27 May/6 June; Van Beuningen, 4/14, 8/18 June, Add. MSS. 17677, QQQ.

been seen at Court for twelve months, were admitted to kiss the King's hand. Even more surprisingly, it was supposed that this was the work of the Duke of York, who was known to dislike Danby's Anglican policy. For months rumours had reached the Venetian ambassadors of negotiations between James and the opposition for common action against Danby: there had been talk of a declaration of indulgence and of permitting James to resume his position as Lord High Admiral. Now it seemed that a dissolution and new elections might suit both James and the Country Party. An undated document surviving in the Shaftesbury Papers refers to proposals brought by Sir Thomas Littleton and Sir John Baber (a Presbyterian doctor at Court who was often a party to schemes for an indulgence) on behalf of James; they offered that James would procure the calling of a new Parliament and the removal of Danby, and asked what the King might expect in return. The reply was in the most general terms: Shaftesbury was sure that a new Parliament would at its first meeting 'be most forward to express their readiness to do them [Charles and James] all good service, and to settle a thorough and lasting confidence between the Crown and the subject'.[1] The vagueness of this clearly reveals the purely tactical nature of Shaftesbury's purpose in listening to such proposals: if only he could secure a new Parliament, by whatever means, he expected it would be more favourable to the 'Country Party' than to the Court, and he would then be in a position to 'settle a thorough and lasting confidence between the Crown and the subject' in the way he thought best. Accordingly he did not reject James's offers out of hand. He was always prepared to represent himself as a loyal subject of Charles, and ready to kiss his hand; while Charles for his part disliked committing himself to one minister, whether Danby or anyone else, and was always prepared to keep open relations with others whatever their record. There followed a tussle in which Danby sought to point out the disastrous consequences of such behaviour. For a few days it seemed touch and go; on 18 June James refused to confer with Danby, and had a private talk lasting two hours with Shaftesbury. But in the end Danby won: on 24 June Shaftesbury received orders from the King to stay away from Court in future.[2]

Shaftesbury was left to pay his usual summer visit to his country estates in Dorset. By now, in his mid-fifties, he was feebler and his contemporaries were beginning to remark on his weakness,[3] and a visit to his well-loved

---

[1] Shaftesbury Papers, XXX, 64. It should be stressed that this document is undated, and Christie (ii. 283–4) places it in April 1678, combining it with the story in J. S. Clarke, *Life of James II* (1816), i. 513; but see p. 373, n. 3 above for the view that the story is wrongly dated in Clarke. A date in 1675 seems much more probable.

[2] George Scott to James Scott, 17 and 26 June, *H.M.C. Laing MSS.*, i. 403, 404; Van Beuningen, 18/28 June, Add. MSS. 17677, QQQ; W. Harbord to Essex, 19 June, *Essex Papers*, ed. O. Airy and C. E. Pike (Camden Society, 1890–1913), ii. 32–33; von Schwerin, 25 June/5 July, *Briefe aus England*, ed. L. von Orlich (Berlin, 1837), p. 31.

[3] See the extract from *An Essay on Satire written in the year 1675* by John Sheffield, Earl of Mulgrave, quoted above in the epigraph to this chapter.

country house must have done something to refresh his weary body. But even at Wimborne St. Giles his restless mind found work to do. He busied himself drawing up careful regulations for his household at mealtimes. Besides his own table, there was to be a Steward's Table for the eight most important members of the household, 'to be set with fresh victuals a little after my Lord's'. Fifteen more were to sit at the Gentlemen Waiters' table and seven at the Grooms' Table, together with the servants of the visitors; these had to wait until the Earl's dinner was over and to dine from the warmed-up victuals left over from his table. Eleven women sat at the Maids' Table, to dine from the food left over from the Steward's Table, supplemented from the kitchen; and last of all eleven of the boys, their digestive juices no doubt stimulated by this time, ate up what was left over from all the tables, except for the scraps which 'William Bryant and the Dairy-Boy' were to carry out, under the supervision of the porter, to the poor people at the gate. Further orders laid down who was to bring in and who to clear away the plates of food. It was a carefully regulated hierarchy, organized evidently in the most businesslike and economical fashion. It was also a large household; at dinner-time at Wimborne St. Giles, Shaftesbury, his family, his visitors and his servants must have been seventy or more in number. Even an ex-Lord Chancellor must have a position to maintain.[1]

Life at Wimborne St. Giles, in spite of the distance from London, did not mean a holiday from political preoccupations. During that month of July 1675 his old Dorset rival, Colonel Strangeways, died, consoled in his last days by his admission into the Privy Council. It would not be possible to hold a by-election for a new Knight of the Shire until Parliament met in October and the Speaker authorized the sending of a writ; and this meant that the gathering in of the harvest was accompanied by prolonged eager discussion who the new member should be. One candidate was Lord Digby, the son of Shaftesbury's one-time political ally, the Earl of Bristol. According to the long account written by Shaftesbury himself of what followed, he did not at first oppose Digby; he would have preferred the later Whig Mr. Freke of Shroughton to stand, but Freke would not do so. Accordingly when the gentlemen of the eastern half of the county assembled 'at the usual meeting' one Saturday at Blandford, the general talk was that no-one would stand against him 'but that we were all for him, as indeed I was at that time'. Accordingly Shaftesbury proposed, 'at the hunting and to the company at Mr. Freke's afterwards, that we might send to my Lord Digby and the gentlemen of the west [of Dorset] to give us a meeting at Blandford, and there unanimously and friendly agree on the election'. The others did not agree—Shaftesbury was by no means in a position to carry his neighbours with him; but these seemed to be the normal preliminaries to a county election.

---

[1] Christie, ii. 211–14.

On the following day, however, Shaftesbury learned (so he said) that Digby was corresponding with the Court ('some of our great men above'), and decided that he was not a suitable candidate. He bestirred himself to find another. Mr. Browne of Frampton refused to stand; but another possibility was Mr. Moore of Haychurch, whom a government correspondent described as 'the greatest upholder of illegal meetings of any in this county'—a Dissenter or at least a protector of Dissenters. Shaftesbury was canvassing support for him when the news reached Digby, a hot-headed young man who concluded that Shaftesbury, while promising support for him in the open, was working in an underhand fashion against him, as befitted a man of Shaftesbury's dubious political past. While Digby was in this heated mood, the two men chanced to meet on 27 August at Fernditch Lodge, the home of Mr. John Tregonwell. Digby took Shaftesbury aside to expostulate with him; he almost threw the older man to the ground, and even drew his sword. He was restrained from using it, but vented his ill-temper in abuse: 'You are against the King, and for seditions and factions, and for a Commonwealth, and I will prove it, and by God we will have your head next Parliament.'[1]

These words were carefully noted down by Shaftesbury's son, his chaplain, and three of his servants,[2] and Shaftesbury used them as the basis for legal action against Digby, from whom he eventually recovered £1,000 in damages.[3] More immediately the incident did not harm Digby's electoral prospects, for the Cavaliers rallied round him against a man of notorious 'dissenting principles' like Moore, and the Bishop of Bristol sent his secretary into Dorset to distribute letters to the local clergy. They were urged to vote for Digby themselves and to engage as many of the forty-shilling freeholders as possible to do the same, 'for at this time it's both our interest and duty so to do, as we honour the King and love the peace of Church and State'. Moore on the other hand was supported by the Nonconformists and by 'the commonalty', who were less numerous than Digby's followers among the gentry, in spite of Shaftesbury's journeys with his candidate to whip up votes. In the end, after Shaftesbury had spent £640 on the election, Digby won an overwhelming victory by over 1,700 votes to 520: Shaftesbury's influence in his own county was comparatively weak.[4] The real significance of the whole episode is as an

---

[1] Shaftesbury to Mr. Bennett, 28 Aug., Christie, ii. 216–18; N. Osborne to Williamson, 28 July, 16 Aug., *C.S.P.D. 1675–6*, pp. 232, 263; A. Thorold to Williamson, 4 Aug., ibid. 245; R. Ingram to W. Ernle, [29 Aug.], Coventry Papers ii. fo. 40; W. Fanshaw to Locke, 14 Sept., Shaftesbury Papers, V, 289.

[2] Ibid. V, 287.

[3] Cf. p. 407–8, below.

[4] Copy of the Bishop's letter in Christie, ii. 218 n.; N. Osborne to Williamson, 2 Oct., *C.S.P.D. 1675–6*, p. 331; R. Biles to Williamson, 18 Oct., ibid. p. 353; A. Thorold to Williamson, 20 Oct., ibid. p. 355. The total of £640 is taken from Stringer's accounts at St. Giles, but no details are given.

illustration of the revival of old animosities between Anglican and Puritan, and between Royalist and Parliamentarian. Fifteen years after the Act of Oblivion the old enmities remained obstinately alive, and indeed Danby's objective had been precisely to revive them at the expense of the common Protestant hostility to Popery which had been so dangerous to the government in 1673 and 1674.

Shaftesbury remained in Dorset until the week before Parliament was due to reassemble. No doubt he kept in touch with other politicians in London in these months, but if so none of the letters survives. During the 'close season' between the parliamentary sessions, however, some important developments had been taking place in his rival Danby's activities. Some of the voting in the House of Commons in May had been so close as to demonstrate that even ten votes could sway the balance: and Danby occupied himself with measures to see that the 'Court Party' polled its full strength in the House. The summer of 1675 was the period when the real organization of the system of Excise pensioners took place. By the autumn between twenty-three and thirty-four members of Parliament had pensions on the Excise totalling £10,000 a year, and other members already held Commissionerships of Customs and other minor offices. It was expected that these office-holders would attend and vote in the House; and with the same end in view the Secretaries of State wrote to members who were thought to be well-disposed to the Court a special letter summoning them to appear promptly for the October session. These measures to build up a 'Court Party' were probably neither so sinister nor so effective as the opposition feared. It is improbable that the pensions induced their holders to do violence to their true convictions: an examination would show that for the most part they acted as one would expect from their past political record, and the purpose of the pensions was less as a crude bribe than to ensure that members were in their places in the House when they were needed. Pensions and letters of summons were to some extent the counterpart of the modern Party whips, without being so successful: Danby could never in fact be sure of the block of dependable voters that he wanted. But the opposition naturally disliked these developments intensely; they supposed that the grants of pensions and offices were even more numerous than was actually the case; they resented the expenditure of the proceeds of taxes for such dubious purposes; they regarded it as an attempt to pervert by bribery the normal course of voting, which they liked naïvely to think was the result of a consideration of the arguments used in the course of the preceding debate, and the merits of the case under discussion; they interpreted it as an entirely corrupt attempt to build up a 'Court Party' which would avoid the risk of a dissolution and new elections. In the previous session they had vainly attempted to deal with the problem of the office-holders in the House by means of a Place Bill, but this had been thrown out. For Shaftesbury all this cannot but have reinforced his desire for a dissolution and a new Parliament. More frequent elections would certainly reduce the effectiveness of Danby's method.[1]

Others besides Danby saw the importance of winning support, by whatever method, within the House of Commons. The ambassadors of the Dutch, the Spaniards and the other powers which were fighting against France hoped to follow up their success in forcing Charles to make the Treaty of Westminster in 1674. That success had been won very largely by means of the arguments of the pamphlet propaganda organized by Du Moulin; the Confederate ambassadors knew that Englishmen had no need of bribes to convert members to a sense of the dangers of French aggression, and confined themselves mainly to giving dinners and to supplying Sir Thomas Littleton, Lord Cavendish and other members with information about the progress of the French armies and the British troops which were serving with them.[2] The French ambassador, Ruvigny, on the other hand, had less confidence in his ability to defend Louis XIV's expansionist policies by means of argument than in the efficacy of the money with which Louis XIV supplied him. In the last session he had spent over £3,000; now he asked for more than £20,000. With its aid, and by fostering a common distrust of Danby's policy, he strove to encourage a union of the opposition and the followers of the Duke of York against Danby; in this way Charles might be compelled to dissolve Parliament, and the possibility of Parliament forcing Charles into an anti-French foreign policy might be avoided. Ruvigny had an entrée into opposition circles by his relationship with Russell; and in the Duke of York's former secretary, Coleman, he had an agent who was prepared to distribute French money amongst members to procure the dissolution which he believed to be in the interests of his master and his Roman Catholic religion. Some of the opposition toyed with Ruvigny's overtures, and a few accepted his money; but they did not temper the Country Party's hostility to France in the next session, and the effect of all this was minimal. Louis XIV himself had no confidence in it, and preferred at the end of August to reach an agreement with Charles, who on his side disliked committing himself to Danby's plan to manage the House of Commons. Accordingly Louis and Charles privately agreed that if the October session proved to be as unmanageable as the last, Parliament should be prorogued for a long period, and the money which Charles needed should come to him instead from France. Charles thus entered the October session with a valuable insurance.[3]

There is no evidence that Shaftesbury, absent in Dorset, had any part

[1] Cf. Browning, *Danby*, i. 167–73.

[2] The evidence for this must await publication in an article by the present writer in the near future.

[3] Ruvigny, 12/22 July, 29 July/9 Aug., 9/19 Aug; F. Mignet, op. cit. iv. 364–70. Browning, i. 165, seems to me to overrate Ruvigny's success in persuading the opposition 'to moderate their anti-French zeal'. It would be difficult to demonstrate this from the events of the next session.

in the opposition's conversations with Ruvigny, whose despatches make
no mention of him. Rather was he concerned with convincing a wider
circle of opinion. While Danby and Ruvigny preoccupied themselves with
the members of the House, Shaftesbury, who hoped for new elections in
any case, was embarking on an appeal to the public in the pamphlet
Letter from a Person of Quality to his Friend in the Country.

This massive pamphlet, some 15,000 words in length, was obviously
propagandist in purpose. When it appeared on the streets at the beginning
of November it sold at first for 1s., 'and now valued at 20s.', as one letter-
writer reported.[1] It set out to portray Danby's recent Test Bill as the
culmination of a project which had existed since the Restoration 'to make
a distinct Party from the rest of the nation of the high Episcopal Man,
and of the old Cavaliers, who are to swallow the hopes of enjoying all the
power and office of the kingdom. . . . Next, they design to have the government of the Church sworn to as unalterable, and so tacitly owned to be
of Divine Right. . . . Then, in requital to the crown, they declare the government absolute and arbitrary, and allow monarchy, as well as episcopacy,
to be *Jure Divino*, and not to be bounded by any human laws. And to
secure all this, they resolve to take away the power and opportunity of
Parliament to alter any thing in the Church or State, only leaving them as
an instrument to raise money, and to pass such laws as the Church shall
have a mind to. . . .' This alleged plot, which was coupled with a plan to
keep up a standing army, was then traced from the Corporation Act, the Militia Act, the Act of Uniformity and the Five Mile Act to the Declaration of
Indulgence of 1672, with an account of a conversation with Clifford in which
the latter maintained that the King 'might settle what religion he pleased,
and carry the government to what height he would', with the aid of an
imperceptible increase in the armed forces. Following this lengthy introduction to set the scene, the main section of the pamphlet described the
debates on Danby's Test Bill in considerable detail, with the names of the
opposition speakers and the arguments which they used—and not only
Shaftesbury's. Each peer received his word of praise for his part in obstructing the non-resistance Test and even the Catholic lords who had disliked
Danby's Anglicanism received a faint compliment. 'If they were safe in their
estates, and yet kept out of office, their votes in that House would not be
most unsafe to England of any sort of men in it.' The tactical purpose of
this is obvious—without abandoning the Test Act of 1673 to keep open
the possibility of enlisting Catholic support for the immediate aim of
procuring a dissolution. The opposition peers were further praised for
upholding the privileges of their class (against the test, and implicitly
against the Commons in *Shirley* v. *Fagg*): 'it must be a great mistake

---

[1] W. Fall to Sir R. Verney, 11 Nov., *H.M.C. Seventh Report*, pp. 466–7. The *Letter
from a Person of Quality* is conveniently available in the *Parliamentary History*, iv, pp.
xxxviii–lxvii, and in Locke's *Works* (1823), x. 200–46.

in councils, or worse, that there should be so much pains taken by the Court, to debase and bring low the House of peers, if a military government be not intended by some. For the power of a peerage and a Standing Army are like two buckets, the proportion that one goes down, the other exactly goes up.'

The concluding pages of the pamphlet referred once again to the alleged aim of persons unnamed to introduce absolute and arbitrary government in Church and State with the help of military force. Charles himself was exonerated from the plot: 'I cannot believe that the King himself will ever design any such thing; for he is not of a temper robust and laborious enough to deal with such a sort of men. . . .' But that there was a plot, dating back to Archbishop Laud and the notorious Canons of 1640, to set up a monarchy of Divine Right, and abolish Magna Carta and 'the rights and liberties of the people', the author had no doubt. In his peroration he defined the objective of the unnamed plotters as being so to order matters 'that priest and prince may, like Castor and Pollux, be worshipped together as divine, in the same temple, by us poor lay-subjects'.

The 'conspiracy theory' of politics always has its attractions: it is always convenient to say that 'they' are responsible for the ills of the present, with no references more precise than those to 'the Court' and to Castor and Pollux. In the circumstances of 1675 the pamphlet appealed at once to ex-Parliamentarians with long memories going back to the Canons of 1640, to those who were puzzled by, and suspicious of, Charles's religious and foreign policy, and to those who could not understand why Danby had unreasonably attempted to revive old animosities by his deliberate policy. The existence of such a dark, sinister conspiracy would explain much. It is easy now to see that no such conscious and consistent plot, dating back to the Restoration, existed; and in any case Shaftesbury had been a member of the ministry alleged to have prosecuted the plot. At the same time, however, it must be realized that if Danby's policy had succeeded—if he had managed to manipulate Parliament, to make the King financially independent, to obtain the support of an exclusive established Church, and to raise some armed forces—in the long run the constitutional consequences might not have been so very different from those which the author feared. There would always have been the temptation to extend the royal authority further when confronted by difficulties. For an illustration of this one has only to read the memorandum which Danby submitted to the King in 1677, justifying a policy of opposition to France (among other reasons) because of the advantages which the King would have from 'being put into a condition of arms'.[1]

There were those who maintained that the pamphlet was written by John Locke. In *A Collection of Several Pieces of Mr. John Locke, published*

---

[1] Browning, *Danby*, ii. 68–69; p. 434 below.

by Mr. Des Maizeaux under the direction of Anthony Collins, esquire (1720), Des Maizeaux's dedication[1] had something to say about the composition both of the *Fundamental Constitution of Carolina* and of the *Letter from a Person of Quality*. In regard to the latter, he wrote that 'my Lord Shaftesbury, who was at the head of the country party, thought it necessary to publish an exact relation of everything that had passed upon that occasion. . . . But though this lord had all the faculties of an orator; yet, not having time to exercise himself in the art of writing, he desired Mr. Locke to draw up this relation; which he did under his lordship's inspection, and only committed to writing what my Lord Shaftesbury did in a manner dictate to him. Accordingly you will find in it a great many strokes, which could proceed from nobody but my Lord Shaftesbury himself; and, among others, the characters and eulogiums of such lords as had signalized themselves in the cause of public liberty.'[2]

It will be noticed that this account of a kind of collaboration is much more circumstantial than a mere casual attribution of authorship to Locke alone. Moreover, there is no question of Des Maizeaux being indiscriminate in ascribing political pamphlets to Locke; the *Letter from a Person of Quality* was the only one to appear in the *Collection*. Des Maizeaux had it from Collins, who had it from Locke's cousin and executor, Peter King. Finally, there is other evidence of a tradition in the Shaftesbury household that Locke was concerned in writing the pamphlet; for the third earl, talking in 1705 of Locke's literary services to his patron, wrote that 'it was for something of this kind that got air' that Locke went abroad. 'His health served as a very just excuse.' This plainly refers to Locke's departure for the Continent at the beginning of November 1675, just a day or two after the House of Lords solemnly ordered that the pamphlet should be burnt by the common hangman at the Royal Exchange and also in the Old Palace Yard at Westminster, and set up a committee to find the pamphlet's author, publisher and printer.[3] Locke's decision to leave was not in fact a sudden one, and his state of health was more than a mere excuse, but it was an odd coincidence that it should be particularly bad at this time. Against this we have to set Locke's solemn protestation, in a letter to the Earl of Pembroke, 'in the presence of God that I am not the author, not only of any libel, but not of any pamphlet or treatise whatever in part good, bad, or indifferent'. This might seem conclusive; but if Des Maizeaux was right about the way in which the pamphlet was 'in a manner dictated' by Shaftesbury, there was room for equivocation about authorship. Nor could a man be blamed for equivocation in the circumstances of 1684, when the theory of non-resistance held sway. Within the

---

[1] Printed in Locke's *Works* (1823), x. 149–59.
[2] Ibid. x. 151–2.
[3] The Lords took action on 8 Nov. and Locke landed at Calais on the 14th (Cranston, op. cit. p. 161).

previous twelve months Algernon Sidney's writings had been used as evidence to put him to death; and the author of the *Letter from a Person of Quality*, which argued that in some situations resistance to the King might be justifiable, might have been exposed to the same fate if he could have been identified and apprehended.[1]

The possibility that Locke had a hand in the pamphlet, therefore, cannot be so easily ruled out as some would have us believe.[2] There is plenty of internal evidence to show that the author, whoever he was, moved freely in circles which one would have expected to be closed to the ordinary scribbler; he quotes conversations, not only with Shaftesbury but with Clifford. All this falls short of proof positive; but whether the author was in fact Locke or not, it is clear that he wrote with Shaftesbury's authorization and under his guidance.[3] He presented at length Shaftesbury's defence of his share in promoting the Declaration of Indulgence; he had intimate knowledge of the debates in the Lords such as no ordinary commoner could have possessed; he bestowed praise on the opposition peers in a way which could only have been planned to encourage them to act together in the next session. Finally, the very length and expense of the pamphlet, and the need to organize its printing and its distribution without risking seizure of the copies by the government, all pointed to the existence of a man like Shaftesbury behind it. It can be taken as certain that the *Letter* was very much in Shaftesbury's mind as he journeyed up to London for the opening of Parliament on 13 October.

Shaftesbury was in no hurry to leave Dorset, for on 2 October he was still at Weymouth putting his name and influence behind the candidature of Mr. Moore.[4] Members of the 'Country Party' in the Commons were holding meetings to concert action, and some of the 'Presbyterian party' were offering, through Ruvigny, to vote the King £1,000,000 in return for the King's abandonment of Danby's Anglicanism and support for a bill giving liberty of conscience: this broke down because Charles very naturally insisted on having the money first.[5] Shaftesbury's plans were quite different: he proposed deliberately to revive the dispute over *Shirley*

---

[1] Third Earl of Shaftesbury to Jean Le Clerc, 8 Feb. 1705, in Remonstrants MSS. J 20, Amsterdam University Library; *L.J.* xiii. 13; Locke to Pembroke, 3 Dec. 1684, in Christie, i. 261 n. It should be added that Locke did not include the *Letter* in the list of 'all the books whereof I am the author, which have been published without my name to them' which he included in the codicil to his will. (Cf. Lady Masham to Leibniz, 24 Nov. 1704, in Leibniz, *Philosophischen Schriften*, ed. Gerhardt (1875–90), iii. 366, a reference for which I am indebted to Mr. E. S. de Beer).

[2] Christie, loc. cit.; H. R. Fox Bourne, *Life of John Locke* (1876), i. 336.

[3] Cf. the statement in *A Pacquet of Advices and Animadversions sent from London to the Men of Shaftesbury*, pp. 1–2, quoted p. 415 below, and J. Basnage, *Annales des Provinces-Unies* (1726), ii. 585–93. Basnage says that his account of these events is based on 'what milord Shaftesbury told us'.

[4] N. Osborne to Williamson, 2 Oct., *C.S.P.D. 1675–6*, p. 331.

[5] Cavendish to Sir Robert Thomas, 8 Oct., B.M. Egerton MSS. 3330 (at present unfoliated); F. Mignet, op. cit. iv. 371, citing Ruvigny, 14/24, 21/31 Oct.

v. *Fagg* and produce a new deadlock between the two Houses. If a second session were ruined in this way the King would surely have to fall back on a dissolution and new elections, to try to secure a Parliament which would vote him the money he needed. In such a new Parliament Shaftesbury believed that the opposition would be stronger than the 'Court Party', and in a position to force through its legislative programme.

In his opening speech on 13 October King Charles expressed the hope 'that no disputes like those of the last session would arise, or at any rate that the discussion of them might be deferred until urgent business had been completed. On 19 October Dr. Thomas Shirley again presented his petition, and Lord Mohun moved that it be taken into consideration. Long debates ensued on six different days. On the second of these (20 October) Danby tried to divert the petition by showing that it was intended for factious motives. Some days before, he said, the King had personally asked Shirley to delay his petition, 'to which he answered he could not, for that he was obliged by some persons of honour to bring it in'. When Shirley had been asked who these 'persons of honour' were, he had desired to be excused; and Danby wanted the House to examine him. But there were too many peers who felt that they must uphold the principle of the Lords' judicial powers, and on their pride and resentment against the Commons' actions in the previous session Shaftesbury sought to play, in a long speech of which a version later appeared in print. This printed version was probably more dogmatically expressed than the actual utterance, because there was no possibility of being interrupted and called to account by his fellow-peers; but there is no reason to doubt that it represents Shaftesbury's true views.[1]

'My Lords, Our all is at stake', he began dramatically, 'and therefore you must give me leave to speak freely before we part with it.' His argument was that the Lords' right to judge appeals from Chancery was an essential part of their privileges, of the constitution and consequently of 'the people's' rights. He made mincemeat of Lord Keeper Finch's unfortunate attempts to persuade the House that Shirley's was 'a doubtful case', and that it had best be postponed to avoid causing a breach with the Commons. Such an argument, he urged, would 'overthrow the law of nature, and all the laws of property and right in the world . . .'. 'If the obstinacy of the party in the wrong shall be made an unanswerable argument for the other party to recede, and give up his just rights, how long shall the people keep their liberties or the princes . . . their prerogatives? How long shall the husband maintain his dominion, or any man his property?' Having thus applied the principle at stake to both public and private life, he

---

[1] *L.J.* xiii. 4, 8, 9; O. von Schwerin, *Briefe aus England* (Berlin, 1837), p. 37; *H.M.C. Ninth Report*, ii. 57; *Memoirs of Sir John Reresby*, ed. A. Browning (1936), p. 102; Browning, *Danby*, i. 180. Shaftesbury's speech was printed as one of *Two Speeches* (?Amsterdam, 1675); in *Somers Tracts* (1812), viii. 42–48 (misdated 20 Nov.); in *Parliamentary History of England* (1808), iv. 791–9; and in Christie, ii, pp. lxxxiv–xciv.

inquired why in any case, if to avoid a breach was all-important, had the Court Party in the Commons allowed the resolutions against the Lords' judicial powers to pass without opposition? Referring to the fact that in Scotland the King had declared against appeals in Parliament, not without complaint, he agreed that 'during this king's time' Charles could be relied upon to make proper use of his power to appoint and dismiss judges; 'yet who can see how future princes may use this power, and how judges may be made not of men of ability and integrity, but men of relation and dependence, and who will do what they are commanded; and all men's causes come to be judged, and estates disposed on, as great men at court please?' The appeal powers of the House of Lords were a necessary safeguard.

Turning to examine the Bishop of Salisbury's contention that the hearing of causes and appeals was not so important that it ought not to give way to 'the reason of state', he elaborated his defence of the Lords' judicial powers. 'This matter is no less than your whole judicature; and your judicature is the life and soul of the dignity of the peerage in England; you will quickly grow burthensome, if you grow useless; you have now the greatest and most useful end of Parliaments principally in you, which is not to make new laws, but to redress grievances, and to maintain the old land marks.' The equitable jurisdiction which the Lords claimed was better than reliance on 'intricate, long, perplexed statutes' which only made work for the lawyers. And even if the bishop had been right in claiming that what was at issue was not the judicial powers of the Lords, but only the Lords' right to summon members of the Commons, 'if you part with this undoubted right merely for asking, where will the asking stop?' From pointing thus to the danger of allowing the Commons to have their own way, he naturally went on to defend the position of the Lords in the English constitution: '. . . it is not only your concern that you maintain yourselves in it, but it is the concern of the poorest man in England, that you keep your station. . . . What are empty titles? What is present power, or riches, and a great estate, wherein I have no firm or fixed property? It is the constitution of the government, and maintaining it, that secures your lordships and every man else in what he hath . . . it is not only your interest, but the interest of the nation, that you maintain your rights . . . for . . . there is no prince that ever governed without nobility or an army; if you will not have one, you must have the other, or the monarchy cannot long support, or keep itself from tumbling into a democratical republic. . . . And I therefore declare, that I will serve my prince as a peer, but will not destroy the peerage to serve him. . . .' The concluding passages of the speech incorporated a warning of the danger from France (perhaps even of a French invasion of Ireland), and another attack on the divine right theories of the bishops, with references to Laud, the Canons of 1640, and the preachings of the Arminian clergy before the Civil War, similar to the concluding section of the *Letter from a Person of Quality*.

Obviously this speech had the immediate tactical objective of reviving the dispute over *Shirley* v. *Fagg* and forcing a deadlock between the two Houses. Yet it was more than just a skilful debating speech. It enunciated a clearly defined general theory of the place of Shaftesbury's own class in the constitution of the country: the peers were, he claimed, endowed with certain powers to protect the 'property' of every man, even the poorest, against the dangers on the one hand of an absolute monarchy based on armed force, and on the other hand of 'tumbling into a democratical republic'. That was the function of the aristocracy in the House of Lords. It was a theory from which neither Shaftesbury nor the later Whigs would depart.

Whereas Danby wanted to postpone the hearing of Shirley's case for six weeks (to about 1 December), Shaftesbury wanted it to be delayed for only three weeks (to 10 November). Finally, on 4 November, the Lords decided by 43 votes to 23 on a compromise, fixing the case for 20 November.[1] This meant that anything which either the government or the opposition wished to achieve in the House of Commons would have to be completed before that date, when there was certain to be a deadlock which would make further progress impossible.

While the Lords had been preoccupied with Shirley's petition, the battle in the Commons had been just as even as in the last session. By dint of his pensions and the 'whips' which the Secretaries of State had sent out Danby had hoped to increase the Court Party's vote; on the other hand some members of the opposition, while apprehensive of Danby's activities, encouraged the Spanish ambassador to believe that they might muster as many as 238 votes.[2] Neither side had calculated correctly. In the first three weeks no important issue was decided by a majority of more than eleven, while one division had to be settled by the casting vote of the chairman of the committee.

The most important subject to be debated was, as so often, that of money. The King's Speech had asked for supplies to enable him to take off the heavy 'anticipations' which clogged his income for at least a year ahead and provide for his creditors, and secondly to enable him to strengthen the Navy by building some new ships. The opposition was entirely opposed to helping the King out of his difficulties by dealing with the anticipations. Even a moderate member like Sir John Holland could criticize the expense of the Court and look back nostalgically but most unrealistically to the time of Edward III, 'who reigned above fifty years [but] never had near

---

[1] *L.J.* xiii. 11–12; *H.M.C. Ninth Report*, ii. 57–58. 'By naming so distant a date the Lords had clearly shown their inclination towards moderate courses', says Professor Browning (*Danby*, i. 181); but when the date was finally fixed 20 Nov. was not very far ahead, and the delay was due less to the Lords' 'moderation' than to Danby's success in prolonging the original debate. He had taken a leaf out of Shaftesbury's book, pursuing the filibustering policy which the opposition had employed against the Test.

[2] Ronquillo [n.d. but ? 11/21 Oct.], A[mbassade de l'] E[spagne à La] H[aye], vol. 488.

this King's supply'; and the 'Country Party' could also make play with the idea that the anticipations were only the result of the generally execrated war of 1672 and the French alliance, and therefore did not merit any action to clear them away. On 19 October, therefore, after the previous vote had ended in a tie broken by the chairman of the committee, the committee decided by 172 votes to 165 to do nothing about the anticipations. On the matter of the building of ships, however, the government for some time had opinion on its side. Moderate members sympathized with the desire to build some ships; and even the opposition recognized the danger of the increase in French naval strength, to which Shaftesbury himself had pointed in his speech in the Lords on 20 October. Accordingly they did not try to oppose a direct negative to the Court on this issue; instead they strove to restrict the sum granted, so that it could not be used to relieve the government's other financial embarrassments, and also they brought in a bill to appropriate the proceeds of the Customs duties to the needs of the Navy in the traditional medieval manner. If this had been successful it would have made intolerable difficulties for the government. So too would a motion that the money for the ships should be paid, not into the Exchequer but into the Chamber of the City of London. This was proposed by Sir Nicholas Carew but was voted down by the Court by 171 votes to 160, with Russell and Cavendish acting as the tellers for the minority. On 4 November the House, in grand committee, voted the sum of £300,000 for the ships—a disappointing amount from Danby's point of view; but the voting (163 votes to 157) was sufficiently close for him to direct his supporters in the House of Commons to make an effort to increase it.[1]

From this time, however (the same day as the Lords took their decision about the date of Shirley's hearing), everything went wrong from the government's point of view. On 6 November the attempt to persuade the House to increase the committee's vote to £380,000 failed by 176 votes to 150, with Russell and Cavendish being tellers for the opposition. This was a sign that in spite of Danby's efforts the Court Party's voting strength was slipping away. Its members were evidently unable or disinclined to face long sittings. Two days later, when they went out into the December darkness to obtain some food, the opposition carried a motion for candles by 143 to 118, and followed this up by seizing the opportunity to tack to the motion for a land tax to raise the £300,000 a clause 'that no other charge be laid upon the subject this session of Parliament'. Worse, from the government's point of view, was to follow, for on 11 November Sir Thomas Meres moved that the bill for appropriating the proceeds of the Customs to the use of the Navy should be annexed to the bill for money to build the new ships; and in spite of the Court Party's efforts to secure

[1] For these debates see *C.J.* ix. 357–68; Grey, iii. 290–411; *Poems and Letters of Andrew Marvell*, ed. H. M. Margoliouth (1927), vol. ii, *Letters*, pp. 159–65.

an adjournment, late at night the motion was carried by 151 votes to 124. Danby's pensions had not, after all, been sufficient to sway the 'Pensionary Parliament'. Since the appropriation of the Customs duties would undermine the whole of the government's financial arrangements, the money for the ships would have to be abandoned. Moreover, in these weeks the 'Country Party' had made progress with several bills which would have restricted the King's prerogatives or his foreign policy: a habeas corpus bill; a bill against unparliamentary taxation; a second Test bill to exclude Catholics from Parliament; a bill to provide that unless a treaty of commerce was signed in the next six months all French trade should be banned; and a bill to prevent the King's subjects from entering the French armed forces—for in spite of the money employed by Ruvigny, the House would no longer be satisfied with royal proclamations against this. All these bills would be extremely embarrassing to the government. In short, by 11 November there was little point in the government going on with the session, and, so far from a dispute between the two Houses being unwelcome, it might supply a much-needed excuse to bring the session to an end.[1]

It would be tempting, but unjustifiable, to ascribe this result to the machinations of outsiders influencing the members of the Commons, as they certainly sought to do. Ronquillo, the Spanish ambassador, took great credit to himself, thinking that the House was obstructing the King's pro-French foreign policy as a result of his conversations with some (unnamed) M.P.s, but it is doubtful whether these talks did more than encourage members along a path which they would have followed in any case.[2] So far as Shaftesbury is concerned, the outcome cannot have been altogether unwelcome to him; it suited him admirably to keep the King in financial difficulties, and no doubt he kept in touch with some of the leaders in the Commons, and even gave them the benefit of his advice on the tactics to be pursued. But it would be wrong to think of men like Meres, Powle, Sacheverell and Sir William Coventry being manipulated by him. So far from their carrying out his instructions, in this session their objective was quite different from his. They set a value on the legislative programme which they had begun, and they were plainly reluctant to see it brought to a premature end as a result of *Shirley* v. *Fagg*. Shaftesbury, on the other hand, had no confidence that the present Parliament would do what he wanted it to do; his aim was to bring it to an end by manufacturing a deadlock which would induce the King to dissolve it and hold new elections. If Shaftesbury's hand is to be seen anywhere in these debates, it is in the speech of Sir Harbottle Grimston on 25 October. This curiously-named member was an old acquaintance of Shaftesbury's—a former

---

[1] *C.J.* ix. 368–74; Grey, iii. 411–59; Marvell, op. cit. ii. 167.

[2] Ronquillo, 19/29 Oct., 22 Oct./1 Nov., A.E.H. 488. There is no hint of any conversations between Ronquillo and Shaftesbury; nor, incidentally, is there any evidence that Ronquillo spent large sums of money.

Roundhead member of the Long Parliament who in 1660 had made his peace (like Ashley Cooper) and become Master of the Rolls and Speaker of the Convention Parliament. Now an old man of over seventy and resting on the wealth which he had acquired over the years, he did not often trouble to attend the Commons; but now he came forward with a motion for an address to the King 'to set a period to this Parliament', on the ground that frequent Parliaments were a right of the subject. He did not find a seconder. Sir Thomas Lee, a prominent member of the Country Party, was 'one of those that think this Parliament may have good effect'. On the other side Sir Edward Seymour was able to get in some telling blows at the 'strict conjunction between the Fanatic and the Papist, to dissolve this Parliament'; and another Country member, Sir Thomas Meres, passed Grimston's motion off as the desire of 'an ancient man' who, like Saint Paul, 'had a desire to depart'. He complained that five or six times bills had been cut to pieces by prorogations, and that he was tired of hearing them read.[1]

This was no great disappointment to Shaftesbury, who had only to wait, as he thought, until Shirley's case did the work for him. In the meantime, there were one or two minor excitements. On 8 November he absented himself for once from the Lords, while the peers condemned his *Letter from a Person of Quality* and set up a committee to find out who had printed it. He was in no danger of discovery, for he had covered his tracks too well. Widow Knight, when interrogated, said that the books had been left in her shop while she was out, and no-one had ever called for payment; and there the trail ended.[2] There was a moment of greater physical danger when a pistol shot aimed at him (or so it was said) passed between the coach and the coachman.[3] This alarm over, the time came on 13 November when the Commons could no longer avoid taking cognizance of the fact that Shirley's hearing had been fixed for only a week later. It was Sir Eliab Harvey, one of the Country Party, who asked for instructions on behalf of his friend Fagg. This put the opposition into a dilemma, torn between the desire 'not to lose the fruits of this session' and that to 'preserve the rights of the House', in the words of Garroway. After an adjournment over the weekend to consider their position, they contented themselves on the 15th with a simple resolution declaring Shirley's appeal to be a breach of privilege, and ordering Fagg not to appear before the Lords. Two days later Sir John Holland proposed that the House should ask for a conference with the Lords 'to represent to them the good bills pending on religion, liberties and properties', and to ask them to postpone the case until these bills were completed. It is significant that the reaction of Secretary of State Henry Coventry, no doubt on

---

[1] Grey, iii. 341–6.
[2] *L.J.* xiii. 13–16; *H.M.C. Ninth Report*, ii. 66; *C.S.P.D. 1675–6*, pp. 395–6.
[3] W. Denton to Sir R. Verney, 13, 25 Nov., *H.M.C. Seventh Report*, p. 493.

instructions, was to agree that it was 'not for your honour' to postpone
the issue in this way: the government no longer cared what happened. As
for the opposition, they were split: some, like Sir William Coventry and
Lord Cavendish, supported Holland; others, such as Sacheverell, Lee,
Meres, Garroway and Littleton, wanted a vote asserting the House's
rights. But the House resolved by 158 votes to 102 not to put the question
'that there lies no appeal to the judicature of the Lords in Parliament from
courts of equity', and decided instead to ask for a conference. By 130
votes to 84 they decided to omit some possibly inflammatory words
from their request. In this division the amount of cross-voting among the
parties was remarked on; but it is to be noted that one of the tellers for the
minority of extremists was one of Shaftesbury's associates, Sir Samuel
Barnardiston.[1]

This relative moderation was ill requited. On 19 November ten peers,
including Shaftesbury, duly attended the conference with the Commons;
but after they had reported back to their own House, the Lords sent no
answer to the request for a postponement of Shirley's hearing, and merely
reaffirmed their decision to hear it next day. When Sir William Coventry
interrupted a debate to give this news, the reaction of the Commons was
unanimous: realizing that a compromise was out of the question, members
vied with one another to pass a motion declaring that anyone prosecuting
an appeal from a court of equity before the Lords should be deemed a
betrayer of the rights and privileges of the Commons of England, and
proceeded against accordingly. They ordered that copies of this resolution
should be posted up on Westminster Hall gate, and elsewhere.[2]

Next morning Lord Grey of Rolleston, a peer who had co-operated
with Shaftesbury over Danby's Test Bill, told the Lords that he had seen
this on Westminster Hall gate, and had been prevented by two members of
the Commons from taking it down. The peers reacted by unanimously
voting the paper to be 'illegal, unparliamentary, and tending to the dissolution of the government': there was no sign here, any more than there
was in the Commons, of the government trying to restrain the general
feeling. Then, however, Lord Mohun, the hot-headed young peer who
had been to the fore in the disputes in June, got up and made a motion
that, as a means of bringing the dispute to an end, the King should be
addressed to dissolve the Parliament and call a new one. Shaftesbury
seconded this proposal in a longer and more elaborate speech which made
it evident that a plan had been prepared beforehand. A long and heated
debate occurred, in which the Earl of Bristol made almost his last appearance after a career of forty years: it was not, however, a very dignified
one, for he vented his spite for the slander action which had been brought

---

[1] *C.J.* ix. 376–9; Grey, iv. 9–15, 27–39, 42–49; Marvell, op. cit. ii. 169–70; Sarotti,
19/29 Nov., *C.S.P. Ven. 1673–5*, p. 490.
[2] *C.J.* ix. 380–1; *L.J.* xiii. 29; Grey, iv. 50–53.

against his son on Mohun (who was a witness) and on Shaftesbury. He boldly accused Shaftesbury of being the author of the *Letter from a Person of Quality* which the House had condemned. Like everything else which Bristol had attempted, this was a failure: the House entered in its journal a resolution that nothing Bristol had said had made any impression upon them to Shaftesbury's prejudice, and ordered Bristol to ask for pardon. Later in the debate there was a further altercation between Shaftesbury and Danby's ally Lord Arundel of Trerice, both of whom had to be formally enjoined 'that there be no further proceedings to any resentment' outside the House.

The hungry, ill-tempered peers continued their debate until nine o'clock at night, for Danby had been caught napping: it became evident that the motion to spite the Commons by dissolving them would win the support of some moderates and of the Duke of York and the Catholic lords, and Danby had to send out to muster every possible vote for a close division. Finally when Lords Lauderdale and Maynard appeared, he felt safe enough to allow the vote to proceed. Of the peers present 41 voted for the address and 33 (including all the bishops present) against it, but when proxies had been counted the two sides were equal with 48 votes each. In the nick of time the Earl of Ailesbury came in, and although he had not heard any of the debate, he was allowed to settle the matter. Casting his vote and a proxy which he held against the address, he brought about its defeat by 50 votes to 48. Shaftesbury and twenty-one others duly entered a protest in the journals of the House, on the grounds that there should be 'frequent and new' Parliaments; that members should not be allowed to 'engross so great a trust . . . the mutual correspondence and interest of those who choose and are chosen admitting great variations in length of time'; that 'the long continuance . . . must . . . naturally endanger the producing of factions and parties, and the carrying on of particular interests and designs, rather than the public good'; and that the actions of the Commons had made any work impracticable.[1]

Although the address had been formally defeated, the narrowness of the defeat amounted to a moral victory for the opposition. A House of Lords which six months earlier could have been expected to provide an automatic majority for the government was now almost equally divided. At the same time all Danby's hopes of achieving control of Parliament and financial assistance had been defeated; the only question which remained was whether the session should be terminated by a prorogation or a dissolution. Shaftesbury sought to exploit the division which the debate had revealed between the Duke of York and Danby by sending a complimentary message to James by way of the Catholic Lord Stafford; James's voting as he did (he said) had gained much on many who were formerly

---

[1] *L.J.* xiii. 32–33; Schwerin, 23 Nov./3 Dec. in *Briefe aus England*, pp. 41–42; newsletter in *C.S.P.D. 1675–6*, pp. 413–14; cf. Browning, *Danby*, i. 182–4, iii. 125–6.

his enemies, and if James would only use his influence with the King to bring about a dissolution, a new Parliament would be readier to grant the Papists 'a toleration' than the present one.[1]

But whether James was deluded by this or not, Charles was determined against a dissolution. And he had a secret asset which Shaftesbury had not been able to take into his calculations. Although he had received no grant from the Commons, he could fall back on the secret agreement which he had made with Louis XIV in August. He had been promised £100,000 a year if he would dissolve a Parliament which was so obviously hostile to France; he could now say that while he was not prepared to yield to pressure from his enemies for a dissolution, he would certainly agree to an unusually long prorogation. Louis XIV himself would be content with an arrangement which made him sure of English neutrality in the year to come. And the French subsidy might be supplemented by some economies and reorganization. Danby would be extremely reluctant to accept this dependence on France, but as his alternative policy had failed he was not in a position to resist. Accordingly at the meeting of the Council on the evening of Sunday, 21 November, it was decided to prorogue Parliament for fifteen months, until 15 February 1677.

Thus Shaftesbury was baulked. He had helped to thwart Danby's attempt to gain control over Parliament; but he had achieved nothing positive, and not only had he failed to force a dissolution, but he had to wait fifteen months before even the present Parliament was permitted to meet again. Probably some contemporaries felt disposed to criticize his tactics during the last session, and to regret the loss of the 'good bills' which lapsed at the end of it. Yet it may well be that Shaftesbury was right in thinking that the habeas corpus bill and other restrictive legislation would only be permitted by the government to pass when they were backed by an overwhelming majority of the Commons and of articulate public opinion outside it. Little reliance could be placed on a House so evenly matched as the present one, and Danby's dubious methods of building up a 'Court Party' might easily bear fruit. All in all, it still seemed best to Shaftesbury to stake everything on compelling a dissolution, and this remained in his mind during the long recess which followed.

[1] Burnet, ii. 102.

CHAPTER XIX

TO THANET HOUSE—AND THE TOWER (1676-7)

SHAFTESBURY did not choose to retire to Dorset as soon as the session was over. He was not unmindful of his estate—for which he hoped to obtain some trees from France through the good offices of John Locke[1]—but there were some things which he could do in London and not in Dorset. One was to arrange[2] for the publication of a version of his speech of 20 October on *Shirley* v. *Fagg*, in conjunction with a speech made by the Duke of Buckingham on 16 November when seeking leave to bring in a bill for the ease of Dissenters. These *Two Speeches* duly appeared, with Amsterdam on the title-page as the place where they were printed; but the probability is that the press was not a hundred miles from Exeter House. It is uncertain whether Shaftesbury was also concerned in the publication of *Two Seasonable Discourses*, the first of which purported to consist of arguments used in the debate of 20 November: it repeated the same doctrine of the importance of the hereditary nobility 'to keep the balance of the government steady', affirmed that King, Lords and a frequently renewed Commons were each a necessary part of the legislature, and argued the necessity for a new parliament in the interests alike of the King (who would be supported with money), the Church (which would be secured), the Dissenters (who would be protected), and the Catholics (who would be relieved from the penal laws if they stayed away from Court and government office).[3] This was the programme of Shaftesbury and those who thought with him; and these pamphlets, following the *Letter from a Person of Quality*, may be interpreted as the beginning of a deliberate propaganda campaign aimed especially at the people of London.

The reaction of Danby and the government was first of all to try to suppress the coffee-houses where these pamphlets were passed from hand to hand and discussed over the new, fashionable drinks of coffee, chocolate, tea and sherbet. Shaftesbury had his own favourite resort—'John's coffee-house', where he was said to 'vent out all his thoughts and designs'.[4] Taverns could not easily be controlled, but there seemed to be a possibility that coffee-houses could. On 29 December 1675, a proclamation ordered their suppression. Before the storm of disapproval which arose the government had to withdraw, contenting itself with a compromise by which the

---

[1] Stringer to Locke, 25 Nov. 1675, MS Locke, c. 19, fo. 116.

[2] Direct evidence of this is lacking; but it is impossible to believe that the speech appeared without his authorization.

[3] Reprinted in *Parliamentary History*, iv, pp. lxxi–lxxx; *State Tracts* (1689), pp. 65–71.

[4] Williamson's notes, 18 Feb. 1676, *C.S.P.D. 1675–6*, p. 563.

coffee-sellers entered into recognizances not to permit scandalous papers to be brought into their houses or false and scandalous reports against the government to be uttered there.[1] With these attempts to suppress hostile opinion in London may be linked action to persuade the City authorities to enforce the Conventicle Act against Dissenters.[2]

These measures naturally excited much resentment, and it is against this background that we must consider an attempt by the King to bluff Shaftesbury into leaving London. On 15 February 1676, Charles sent for Sir Joseph Williamson (who had taken Arlington's place as Secretary of State in 1674), and in the Privy Garden instructed him to take a message to Shaftesbury: 'that he had information that he was very busy here in town in matters that he ought not, and that His Majesty thought it were much better he were at home in the country . . . that the King knows more than it may be he thinks he does, and that this is the King's advice. . . .' Next day Williamson paid a call on Shaftesbury at Exeter House, and after a visitor, Sir Edward Harley, had withdrawn, he passed on the King's advice. Shaftesbury's reply cloaked a plain refusal to be bluffed in the appropriate courtly language. He asked Williamson to 'return his humble duty' to the King, saying with a sneer that 'His Majesty's desire, advice, inclination, fancy, or call it what I would, should be in all things observed of him with all dutifulness'; but the King was misinformed about his activities. 'He did not use to see any company, two or three it may be so, but nothing in the least relating to public business; at no time had he in any company meddled with anything relating to the King or the public, possibly a word now and then in jest he might come out with, but nothing serious or in earnest, nor had he ever said anything of that kind as to the King himself, of others possibly he might.' The business which kept him in London was private business: he was considering whether to let or sell Exeter House, or to pull it down and 'let it into tenements'; he was thinking of disposing of his Royal Africa Company stock and his own plantation in Carolina.[3] 'These were the businesses that kept him in town, and he had rather be made a prisoner here in town, where his business was, than make himself a prisoner in the country separated from his business. . . . He meddled with none but his own private business, which was enough for him. In Parliament he declares his opinion to the King, as matters call for it, but otherwise he meddles not, a word in jest or so he may possibly let fall but never of the King; of others maybe he may.' Recent appearances on the Exchange had no ulterior motive. 'He filled his head with his own little business. A man's head must be full of something; some statesmen

---

[1] Browning, *Danby*, i. 194–5.

[2] This may be followed in the despatches of van Beuningen, Add. MSS. 17677, RRR, *passim*, and cf. Schwerin, 29 Feb./10 Mar., *Briefe aus England*, p. 53.

[3] To this he might have added the sub-contracting of the manufacture of guns in accordance with Rupert's invention; Shaftesbury Papers, VI A, 297, above, p. 229.

suffered themselves to die for fear of troubling their heads with business, but that he loved to fill his head with business.' He seems also to have mentioned the possibility that, if things went well, in three or four years' time he might be in a position to form a syndicate to farm the King's customs.

This was the reply which Williamson carefully noted down and took back to the King. It is an illuminating reply in relation to Shaftesbury's evident psychological compulsion to 'fill his head with business'; his restless mind could not bear to be unoccupied. But his references to his activities are rather disingenuous; whether or not he was engaged in anything which could be called an 'intrigue', it is impossible to believe that his friendships and his conversation were as unpolitical as he made them out to be. On the following day Williamson's friend Lord O'Brien called at Exeter House and found there the young Earl of Salisbury, Sir Thomas Littleton, Sir Samuel Barnardiston, and Thomas Papillon: the first three of these had all been active in the parliamentary opposition in 1675, and the Huguenot merchant and contractor Papillon had made himself so obnoxious that Charles personally exercised his influence to prevent his election to the Sub-governorship of the East India Company.[1] The following day O'Brien found there Sir Robert Clayton, 'extorting Ishban', the Whig goldsmith and financier who was later to be Lord Mayor in 1679–80, and Sir Robert Peyton, another City magnate who was also to be a strong Exclusionist in the first twelve months of the Popish Plot crisis. It would have been a remarkable act of self-denial if such company had refrained from discussing politics. Danby certainly did not believe it. He urged Charles to send Shaftesbury to the Tower, and Charles was willing; the only thing that saved Shaftesbury at this point was the reluctance of Williamson, as Secretary of State, to sign the necessary warrant. He did not want to accept the responsibility of sending Shaftesbury to the Tower without a well-grounded charge against him. Parliament was still twelve months away, but he feared the complaints which it might make. In the end Charles accepted his point of view, and Shaftesbury went scot-free.

The episode had no direct consequences, but it shows that Danby was prepared to be quite as unscrupulous in his dealings with his opponents as any opposition leader: he could contemplate imprisoning Shaftesbury without any definite charge against him. Each man was prepared to raise the stakes, but there was a certain justice in the fact that ultimately Danby had a longer spell in the Tower than his enemy. For the time being Shaftesbury had the satisfaction of having bluffed it out successfully. The story of his interview with Williamson lost nothing in the telling: it was reported that he had boldly told the Secretary 'that he would be glad to see the six Privy Councillors that would sign the warrant'. Such a tale of

---

[1] *C.S.P.D. 1676–7*, pp. 75–81 (17–21 Apr. 1676).

defiance would not lessen his appeal to the discontented elements in the City.[1]

During the spring of 1676, therefore, Shaftesbury remained in London, and rumour coupled his name with that of Buckingham in 'populaires menées' appealing to the Londoners.[2] In March there was a rumour that some interested parties had also tried to bring about a reconciliation between him and Lauderdale. Before the opening of the last session the two men had actually been brought to meet for the first time for two years at the house of Mr. Edmund Warcup, 'but when they met the question between them was, who sent for each other, and both denying they had ever sent such a message, and understanding it only to be an invitation by Mr. Warcup to them both, they parted as strange as they met, and both blamed Mr. Warcup'. After that both were reluctant to risk a second affront: the gap between the one-time friends was now very wide. Yet needs must if the devil drives, and anything which might undermine Danby's position might be considered: there seems to have been a new negotiation between Lauderdale and his secretary and Shaftesbury, in which the latter made it plain that his terms for a reconciliation would be that Lauderdale should desert Danby, 'whose counsel he knew would destroy King and kingdom'. Lauderdale had little liking for Danby, but when it came to the point he would not turn against the powerful Lord Treasurer, and the 'reconciliation' therefore lapsed.[3]

In Holy Week this year James, Duke of York, declined even to accompany the King to the royal chapel, and his apostasy from the Church of England was plain for all to see. This was followed by a spate of rumours of impending conversions of peers to Roman Catholicism, and there were even stories current in London that James's elder daughter Mary was to be married to the Dauphin of France.[4] There was no basis for these stories, which are evidence only of people's readiness to believe in the possibility of a Roman Catholic dynasty inheriting the succession to Protestant England. In view of the censorship there was the unhealthy situation in which such fears could not be openly expressed and discussed; they were pent up, only to break out with increased violence in the years to follow. In the same way Londoners were dismayed by the successes which Louis XIV was winning on the Continent. His armies were early in the field this year, and by 1 May they had already captured two important fortresses, those

---

[1] Notes by Williamson, 15–18, 22 Feb., in *C.S.P.D. 1675–6*, pp. 559–61, 562, 562–3; unsigned letter, 17 Feb., MSS. Carte 228, fo. 101; Schwerin, as in note 2, p. 404; van Beuningen, 22 Feb./3 Mar., Add. MSS. 17677, RRR.

[2] Van Beuningen, 10/20 Mar., 31 Mar./10 Apr.

[3] Add. MSS. 28045, fos. 39–40 ('Received from Mr. Browne, 20th Feb. 1676/7); 'The Journals of Edmund Warcup, 1676–84', ed. K. Feiling and F. R. D. Needham, *E.H.R.* (1925), p. 241. For Warcup, see below p. 421.

[4] Van Beuningen, 28 Mar./7 Apr., 31 Mar./10 Apr., 7/17, 14/24 Apr.; Schwerin, 30 May/9 June, *Briefe aus England*, p. 57.

of Condé and Bouchain. It was known that in spite of the Commons' protests and the royal proclamation of 1675, French recruiting of British troops to serve in Louis's armies was still continuing without Charles's government doing anything effective to suppress it[1]; so that British subjects were contributing to the extension of Bourbon power, and might eventually, on their return to England, be available as trained soldiers for the increase of Stuart authority as well. Yet this too could not be discussed; the next meeting of Parliament lay nine months ahead, and in the meantime there was nothing but frustration. There were some within the King's Council (including Shaftesbury's business partner, Prince Rupert, as well as James, Arlington, Williamson and the Duke of Ormond) who wanted to have the old Parliament dissolved and a new one called; but Danby's influence was proof against them. He was able to convince the King that in view of James's recent conduct new elections were too dangerous— members might demand concrete assurances to protect Protestantism; and in addition he claimed to have won over more than 150 additional members of the present Parliament by his blandishments and his cruder offers of 'gratifications' to suitable people.[2]

For Charles and Danby, therefore, the summer of 1676 was pleasant and unusually peaceful; for Shaftesbury it was uncommonly frustrating. He did, however, derive some solace from the successful outcome of his case against Digby. Recalling from his days at Lincoln's Inn the stories of Sir Edward Coke's first case,[3] he had brought the words that Digby had uttered within the provisions of the statute of *scandalum magnatum* of the reign of Richard II, protecting peers from abuse by commoners. The case came up for trial before a jury of Wiltshire gentlemen on 28 April, when both sides attended with numerous friends and partisans. 'There were many brisk things said and reflections made', amongst others by the later Lord Chief Justice, Sir William Scroggs, whom we meet here as one of Digby's counsel. The evidence that Digby had uttered the words complained of was too strong to be denied—Lord Mohun was one of Shaftesbury's witnesses—and the scandalous nature of the words was equally undeniable. When Scroggs saw that his side was likely to lose, 'in a very rallying tone and gesture [Scroggs] give [sic] his Lordship a Mark . . .' which cannot have endeared him to the Earl for the future. Shaftesbury was awarded £1,000 damages, plus costs. There were those who said that he was disappointed not to get more; but he gave his gains to the fund for the rebuilding of the city of Northampton (which had suffered severely

[1] Cf. Louis's instructions to his new ambassador in London, Courtin, 5/15 Apr.; *Recueil des Instructions . . . XXIV, Angleterre 1666–90*, ed. J. Jusserand (1929), p. 196.

[2] Charles Hatton to Lord Hatton, 25 May, *Hatton Correspondence*, ed. E. M. Thompson (Camden Society, 1878), i. 128–9; Courtin, 12/22 June; Van Beuningen, 16/26 June; Browning, *Danby*, i. 191–3, 198–9.

[3] C. D. Bowen, *The Lion and the Throne* (1957), pp. 60–61.

from fire)[1] and celebrated his victory by giving a dinner to the jurors at
10s. a head. It must have been a very convivial occasion, for the thirty-two
men present shared 103 bottles of wine, including twenty-four bottles of
Canary at 2s. 6d. each and '12 botteles of shampane' at 2s. each. Defeat
rankled with Digby, even though his friends in Dorset raised a subscription
to enable him to pay the damages. Imitating Coke, he asked for arrest of
judgement on the technical ground that the old statute of *scandalum
magnatum* had not been correctly recited in Shaftesbury's declaration,
and Scroggs solemnly got up in court and argued that the Latin word
contrafacere did not literally mean 'devise'. This and another quibble
equally characteristic of the law-courts of the time—no wonder Shaftesbury
was impatient with professional lawyers!—were finally swept away at the
beginning of June, much to the satisfaction of the Earl's faithful servant
Thomas Stringer, who described it all in a letter to John Locke in France.[2]

Stringer's letters to Locke,[3] besides acknowledging presents of a box of
orange trees for Lady Shaftesbury and vine cuttings for the Earl, also
refer to the household's plans to leave Exeter House after some fifteen
years there. Exeter House had been a suitable dwelling for an aspiring
royal minister, but for an opposition politician with a reduced income it
was inconvenient and expensive. Some months earlier, after renting the
house for many years, Shaftesbury had apparently bought it as a speculation[4]; after some debate on how best to exploit his purchase, he disposed
of it in March 1676 to builders who would pull it down and rebuild new,
smaller dwellings on the site. By the terms of the sale he had to leave
Exeter House by midsummer. Until he could find another suitable
London house he took a temporary place in St. Martin's Lane, where his
goods were to be stored. A bill for some of the removal costs survives.
Besides small sums for 'tax', cords, and wire staples, it includes twelve
shillings 'for 3 women's work 3 days to clean the house', £8. 6s. 2d. to
five porters for ten days' work, £5. 5s. 'for carrying of 70 loads of goods
from Exeter House to St. Martin's Lane', and 11s. 9d. 'for drink given to
the porters'.[5] Removal was evidently thirsty work. At the same time the
Shaftesbury family arrangements were altered; Lord and Lady Ashley
with two of their children were to leave Wimborne St. Giles and, after
staying for the rest of the summer and the winter at Haddon Hall at the
expense of Lady Ashley's relatives, were to set up house on their own not
far away from Wimborne at Martin. Young 'Mr. Anthony', the apple of

---

[1] In Nov. 1675 Shaftesbury had been on a committee of the House of Lords for the
rebuilding of Northampton, *L.J.* xiii. 31.
[2] *Modern Reports*, ii. 98; W. Ellis to J. Ellis, 28 Apr., Add. MSS. 28930, fos. 87–88;
bill in Shaftesbury Papers, IV, 216; Charles Hatton to Lord Hatton, 11, 18 May, *Hatton
Correspondence*, i. 123–4, 126; Stringer to Locke, 5 June, Christie, ii. 222–3.
[3] As above, and 6/16 Apr., ibid. pp. 221–2.
[4] Williamson's notes in *C.S.P.D. 1675–6*, p. 560.
[5] Shaftesbury Papers, IV, 216.

his grandfather's eye, was to remain at St. Giles under the Earl's personal care. There Shaftesbury and his wife intended to stay from June until at least Michaelmas, while enquiries were made at leisure for a new house in London.

The intention had been that they should leave for Dorset about the middle of June, but an event took place which detained them in London a little longer. On 24 June, at the usual meeting at the Guildhall for the election of sheriffs, one Francis Jenks, a linen draper in Cornhill, got up and made a sensational speech. After referring to some recent fires which were popularly supposed to be the result of arson by persons unknown[1]; to the trade depression, which he attributed to the combined effects of French tariffs, French competition in silks, and French privateers; and to 'the just apprehension that is upon the minds of good men, of danger to His Majesty's person, and the Protestant religion', he propounded as his solution to these problems a deputation to the Lord Mayor and Aldermen, to desire a Common Council to be called to petition the King to call a new Parliament, in accordance with the statutes of 4 and 36 Edward III. These two ancient statutes, which declared that Parliament should be held every year, were the basis of the contention that the present Parliament, having been prorogued for more than twelve months, stood *ipso facto* dissolved, and should be replaced by another.

The mention of a new Parliament was greeted with numerous shouts of 'Well moved, well moved'; but this was all the satisfaction that Jenks received. The City authorities so handled the matter that his request was evaded, and he was summoned before the Privy Council to account for his action. There he justified his right to debate 'whatever he thinks for the service of the King and the good of the City' in such a 'presumptuous and arrogant manner' that he was committed to the Gatehouse. The King's concern was to find out who had prompted Jenks to make the speech: Jenks naturally declined to say, but there can be no doubt that Charles was right in blaming 'Alderman George', his jocular nickname for his old companion Buckingham, who had recently taken a house in the City and was supposed to be seeking election as an alderman. As for Shaftesbury, much as he wanted a new parliament, he opposed Buckingham and Jenks in this: he argued that the step was premature and had no chance of success. He may well have known about it in advance and stayed in London to await events, but he had no confidence in the outcome. His assessment was more realistic than Buckingham's; and yet, although Jenks had not achieved his aim of a petition to the King, he had successfully ventilated the issue, and he became something of a popular martyr for his cause. Refusing to petition the King for release, he sought a writ of *habeas corpus* instead. An anonymous *Account of the Proceedings at Guildhall* gave what

---

[1] Cf. *C.S.P.D. 1676–7*, pp. 173–4, 183–4, 186–7, 192.

purported to be his speech, with the addition of a later speech of a strongly anti-Papist character. Repeating Jenks's arguments, it enquired also: 'if the presumptive heir of the Crown be a Roman Catholique, what security can be given that the King shall live eight or nine months?[1] And what safety is there provided for the Protestant religion, if a Catholick shall possess the Crown?' A Lincolnshire gentleman, Sir Philip Monckton, was also in trouble with the Privy Council for making similar remarks about the danger from Popery. Some people were already in the right frame of mind for belief in a Popish Plot.[2]

The incident made plain that the relationship between Shaftesbury and Buckingham was not altogether smooth. Buckingham was not prepared to accept Shaftesbury's leadership; Shaftesbury had no confidence in Buckingham's judgement, and he did not wait in London to take part in the efforts made to secure the release of the latter's protégé, Jenks. On 2 July spectators noticed him at Lord Cornwallis's trial for murder, sitting 'just in the King's sight' and whispering all the time to Lords Wharton and Mohun[3]; and then he was not seen again in London for four months or more. We know little of his activities in the course of this extended holiday, except for a few letters of instructions which he sent from St. Giles House to his steward Stringer in London, mainly on business matters. He asked for prompt statements of account, and entrusted Stringer with the sale of some of his Royal Africa stock and one of his shares in the Bahamas, so that the proceeds could be used to make a purchase of some more land adjacent to his estate. His more intellectual interests were represented in the letters by a request for a copy of 'the Earl of Clarendon's book against Mr. Hobbes, well bound and gilt and titled on the back', which had just been posthumously published; but nothing is known of his opinion of the work.[4]

There was also the matter of finding a London house for the winter. In July there had been talk of Shaftesbury buying Russell House in Southampton Square, but the Earl rejected this on the ground that he was not rich enough; he could only afford to rent a house. In October he received an offer of Thanet House from Lord Thanet. There was some difficulty about the amount of rent, because Shaftesbury insisted that he

---

[1] I.e. until Parliament was due to meet in Feb. 1677.

[2] For Jenks's case see State Trials, vi. 1189–1208, including An Account of the Proceedings at Guildhall (which is also fairly fully printed in C.S.P.D. 1676–7, pp. 253–6); van Beuningen, 27 June/7 July; Courtin, 29 June/9 July, 10/20, 13/23 July; Charles Hatton to Lord Hatton, 29 June, Hatton Correspondence, ed. E. M. Thompson (Camden Society 1878), i. 132–3; Marvell to Sir Edward Harley, 1 July, Works, ed. H. M. Margoliouth (1927), ii. 322 and to Popple, 17 July, ibid. 325; Southwell to Essex, 4 July, Essex Papers, ii. 63–64; Anglesey to Essex, 25 July, ibid. 69–70; C.S.P.D. 1676–7, pp. 184, 193–5, 215 (which should be dated 9 July), 285, 296, 313. For Monckton, see also ibid. pp. 145–6 (which should be dated 5 July), 174–8, 194–5, 207, 293.

[3] Charles Hatton to Lord Hatton, 2 July, Hatton Correspondence, i. 136.

[4] Shaftesbury to Stringer, 15 and 20 Aug., Christie, ii. 225–6.

could not afford to pay more than £160 a year; but some time in the following weeks the two men agreed on terms, and Thanet House was the Earl's London home for the rest of his life.[1]

Thanet House stood in Aldersgate Street, so that the move to it from Exeter House was a move from the West End back into the City of London, in the reverse of what was now the fashionable direction. We have seen that Buckingham had made a similar move earlier in the year,[2] and it had been attributed to a desire to take part in City politics and perhaps even become an alderman himself. Too much should not, however, be read into Shaftesbury's own decision to take up residence in the City, which may have been less of a deliberate act of policy than it has sometimes been represented. Certainly his initial reason for leaving Exeter House had been financial, not political; and when he decided on Thanet House he had been looking round for several months and presumably had to take any suitable opportunity which presented itself. Nor must it be imagined that in Thanet House Shaftesbury would be the only aristocrat in a commercial neighbourhood. Thanet House itself was not an ancient house, having been built for the Earls of Thanet by Inigo Jones. A little higher up the street, on the same side, stood Lauderdale House, the London residence of the Duke of Lauderdale, who has never been accused of having Whig or radical affiliations. Another house in Aldersgate was the residence of the Marquis of Dorchester, until it was sold after his death in 1680 to the bishops of London and Henry Compton lived there. The neighbourhood had other associations, it is true: Milton had had a 'pretty garden-house' near by; there was a Quaker meeting-place called the Mouth to which the body of 'Free-born John' Lilburne had been conveyed on his death on 29 August 1657, and where the Society of Friends met for over a century.[3] At some other informal religious society—possibly Anglican, possibly Moravian— meeting in Aldersgate, on 24 May 1738, John Wesley's heart was to be 'strangely warmed' during the reading of Luther's Preface to Romans.[4] But it was not by any means an inappropriate area for a nobleman to settle in, and no-one made any special comment on it at the time. Yet ultimately, in the Exclusion Crisis, there can be no doubt that residence at Thanet House presented advantages for him; it was undoubtedly handier for his supporters in the City, and it was much easier for people to slip in to see him unobtrusively than it would have been if he had still been living in the Strand.

It was not until 27 November that Shaftesbury returned to London to

---

[1] Stringer to Locke, 8 July; Shaftesbury to Stringer, 15 July, 23 Oct., Christie, ii. 224–5. The precise date of the contract is not known.

[2] Buckingham's house was in Dowgate.

[3] See the references to the 'Bull and Mouth' in Wesley's Journal, 10 Oct. 1756, 17 Feb. 1758, 21 Dec. 1763.

[4] H. B. Wheatley, *London Past and Present* (1891), i. 22–25; W. Wilson, *History and Antiquities of Dissenting Churches and Meeting Houses in London, Westminster and Southwark* (1810), iii. 357–8, 363–5.

make his preparations for the session which, as confirmed by royal proclamation on 20 December, was to begin on 15 February 1677. Already before his return people had been seen in the streets wearing a green ribbon, and the rumour ran that these were Shaftesbury's 'party'.[1] But this is misleading, and it is quite wrong to believe that at this point Shaftesbury 'was well established as the head of a definite political party, the Country Party, in distinction from the Court Party'.[2] From previous sessions he now enjoyed a powerful reputation as an able and determined opponent of the Court, but this did not mean that other opponents of the Court were prepared to obey his lead. On the contrary, the events of February 1677 were to show precisely that he could not command their support; when it came to the point only three other peers and not many more of the Commons were prepared to adopt the tactics which he planned.

This was because Shaftesbury was determined to stake everything upon an attempt to establish what Jenks had earlier suggested. By the terms of the statutes of 4 and 36 Edward III, he argued, a prorogation for more than twelve months was illegal, and therefore the Cavalier Parliament had lapsed and must be replaced by another. This was by no means the only possible avenue of attack on the government. On 27 October the Common Council of the City of London drew up an address to the King complaining about the depredations of French privateers on English merchant shipping and more generally about the heavily unfavourable balance of trade with France; and someone was at work promoting similar addresses from Bristol and other ports and instructions to their members in Parliament.[3] Feeling against Louis XIV's military and economic policy was mounting so high that it could have been the basis for a sincere concerted attack on Charles's attitude of benevolent neutrality towards France; and this was what the ambassadors of France's Confederate enemies wanted. But Shaftesbury remained firmly of the opinion that a more radical House of Commons was the essential prerequisite for the forcing of the policies he wanted upon the King; and he believed that he could obtain this.

This was a serious misjudgement. In the House of Commons itself it was only to be expected that many members would not relish the prospect of loss of their seats and perhaps exposure to their creditors. Dissolutions are never popular with the members of elected bodies; and even Country members who wanted one disliked having it imposed upon them by the Upper House.[4] For that was Shaftesbury's intention: his address to the King for a dissolution at the end of the last session had been rejected by

---

[1] Courtin, 23 Oct./2 Nov. Green had been the colour of the Levellers.

[2] Brown, p. 237.

[3] 'T.B.' to Williamson, 28 Oct., *C.S.P.D. 1676–7*, pp. 388–9; Sir Alan Broderick to Laurence Hyde, 27 Oct., *Correspondence of Clarendon and Rochester*, ed. S. W. Singer (1828), i. 1–2; Courtin, 16/26 Nov. Cf. Margaret Priestley, 'London Merchants and Opposition Politics in Charles II's Reign', *Bull. Inst. Hist. Res.* (1956), pp. 205–19.

[4] W. Harbord to Essex, 17 Dec., *Essex Papers*, ii. 86.

only two votes. If that narrow defeat could be changed into a narrow victory, then the Lords would refuse to deal with the Commons, and the King's financial difficulties would compel him to try what a new Parliament would do. But the trouble about this line of action was that the vote of 20 November 1675 was quite abnormal, in the heat of *Shirley* v. *Fagg*, and Shaftesbury could not count on keeping together those who had voted together then. Buckingham certainly had identified himself with the same policy, but the trouble was that he expected the leadership for himself, and there was a misunderstanding between them which caused much embarrassment.[1] Halifax and Winchester both disliked the plan and refused to co-operate in it.[2] Mohun's hot-headedness had led him into one duel too many, and in January 1677 he lay incapacitated by a wound from which he never fully recovered.[3] Lord Townshend, when appealed to for his attendance, excused himself on the ground that he was 'fit for nothing' because of gout, though he sent Shaftesbury his proxy.[4] Anglesey, usually a stickler for the nicer points of the law, listened to Shaftesbury's arguments,[5] but in the end rejected them. Only the aged Puritan peer Lord Wharton (won over partly by an intermediary named Murray[6]), and the younger Earl of Salisbury were firmly committed to speak in support of Shaftesbury and Buckingham; and some others such as Holles dithered uncertainly, to remain silent when the test came.

Most serious of all was Shaftesbury's failure to win the support of the Duke of York and the Catholic peers for a new Parliament. With their aid he had come within two votes of passing the address of 20 November 1675; without it he would fall well short. There were not wanting those who sought to persuade James that his interest lay in co-operating with Shaftesbury. Notably the French ambassador, Courtin, urged that if Danby would not agree to prorogue or dissolve Parliament, James should declare openly against him, and inform Shaftesbury of this.[7] This must not be taken to imply that Courtin was in touch with Shaftesbury at this time— on the contrary, the Earl was maintaining publicly that the only means for Charles and James to win back popularity was to join Louis XIV's enemies[8]—but it would suit Louis XIV admirably if the new session could be put into the same kind of disorder as the last one, leaving the Sun King to press on in Europe without the fear of public opinion ranging England with his enemies. James was at first uncertain. Wharton was sent to him (while Shaftesbury and Holles approached Lords Bellasis, Arundel

---

[1] Information of Thomas Garway, 4 Oct., *C.S.P.D. 1676–7*, p. 352; 'T.B.', 30 Dec., 13 Jan., 28 Jan., ibid. pp. 476, 506, 523.

[2] Burnet, ii. 117; J. Macpherson, *Original Papers* (1775), i. 84.

[3] Lady Chaworth to Lord Roos, *H.M.C. Rutland MSS.*, ii. 35, 37; Prideaux to Ellis, 2 Feb., in *Letters of Humphrey Prideaux to John Ellis*, ed. E. M. Thompson (Camden Society, 1875), p. 57.   [4] 2 Feb. 1677, Add. MSS. 41654, fo. 30.

[5] Lady Chaworth to Lord Roos, 30 Dec. 1676, op. cit. ii. 35.

[6] Sir Philip Musgrave to Williamson, 9 Oct. 1676, *C.S.P.D. 1676–7*, pp. 358–9.

[7] Courtin, 2/12 Nov.   [8] Courtin, 25 Jan./4 Feb. 1677.

of Wardour and other Catholic peers) and James did not reject out of hand Wharton's argument that Parliament was now legally dissolved; instead he reserved his opinion until he had heard the forthcoming debate in the House of Lords. But James was temperamentally disinclined to take part in any formed opposition to the King's ministers, which he regarded as disloyal and factious; and, much as he disliked Danby and his policy, it was obvious that Shaftesbury's approaches did not arise from any feelings of friendship towards him—they were purely tactical. James's natural suspicion was fortified by the circumstance that one of the pamphlets published by Shaftesbury's party, *Some Considerations upon the Question whether the Parliament is dissolved*, on its last page answered the argument that prorogation was a matter solely for the royal prerogative by arguing that Acts of Parliament might not only restrict that, but 'can bind, limit, restrain and govern the descent and inheritance of the Crown itself, and all rights and titles thereto', as in Tudor times. Shaftesbury and Wharton sent word to James that this had been inserted without their knowledge; but Buckingham, exculpating himself, said on the contrary that Shaftesbury had drafted it and caused it to be put in. Whether this was a foretaste of the Exclusion Bill, or only a threat to frighten James into co-operation, James's reaction was the same: he would vote against Shaftesbury, and all the latter's assurances that there would be no attack on him had no effect.[1]

Finally, Shaftesbury laboured under the disadvantage that all this activity necessarily made his plan evident, and Danby was enabled to be ready with his counter-attack. Indeed, Danby could employ the government's resources to hinder his opponent. One way of dealing with the arguments of pamphlets backed by Shaftesbury, such as *The Grand Question concerning the prorogation of this Parliament*, was to suppress them and order the arrest of the man who had caused it to be printed, Dr. Nicholas Cary.[2] At the same time the man whom Danby had entrusted with the task of suppressing anonymous unlicensed pamphlets, Sir Roger L'Estrange, saw to it that *A Pacquet of Advices and Animadversions sent from London to the Men of Shaftesbury* was left unmolested, for this was the government's reply to the *Letter from a Person of Quality*, saved up in order to produce the maximum effect by allowing it to appear on the streets just before the new session began.[3]

[1] J. Macpherson, op. cit. i. 79–80; J. S. Clarke, *Life of James II* (1816), i. 504–5; memoranda by Lord O'Brien, 7, 10 Feb., *C.S.P.D. 1676–7*, pp. 541–2.

[2] Ibid. p. 543; cf. 'T.B.', 11 Feb., ibid. p. 550. The House of Lords was later told that the proofs of the pamphlet had been corrected by Cary, who received the manuscript in Chancery Lane from the servant of a gentleman, but that all attempts to entrap Cary into admitting that the gentleman was Lord Holles had failed: *L.J.* xiii. 54–56; *H.M.C. Ninth Report*, ii. 70–73; Marvell, *Poems and Letters*, ed. H. M. Margoliouth (1927), ii. 178.

[3] L'Estrange to Samuel Mearn, 4 Feb., *H.M.C. Fourth Report*, p. 231. Scroggs's letter to Danby, n.d., Add. MSS. 28053, fo. 114, may refer to the planning of this attack on 'that little lord', Shaftesbury.

The author of this *Pacquet of Advices*, which was some 40,000 words in length, was reputed to be Marchamont Needham, who had once been in the 1640s the most notorious journalist of his day, first for Parliament and then for the King; he had then passed into the service of the Common-wealth and the Protector, but was now available (rather ironically, in view of the line his argument took) for the journalistic defence of the Church of England against its enemies—or rather its enemy.[1] For the whole pamphlet was a caustic attack on Shaftesbury—'Mephistopheles, the Faery Fiend that haunts both Houses; of whom I have been told, the witty Duke of Buckingham likened him to Will-with-a-Wisp, that uses to lead men out of the way; then leaves them at last in a ditch and darkness, and nimbly retreats for self-security'. This telling quotation of a remark which had presumably been made by Buckingham at the end of 1673 is characteristic: the writer had both an eye to the weak points in his enemy's armour and the literary skill to draw the attention of the public to them. In form his work was a reply to the *Letter from a Person of Quality*, 'which I will not call his; though those that have ask'd him do say he but faintly denies it; and in such phrases as signified plain enough that he would not for all the world be thought the author, or at least the intelligencer'. But it was less a reply than a counter-attack, in which references to the *Letter*'s theory of a conspiracy dating back to the Restoration were accompanied by a commentary based less on argument than on satirical references to Shaftesbury's own career over the same years. 'Once upon a time (as I remember) the Old King [Charles I] had a Dorsetshire-eel by the tail; which then slipt into the hands of [the Presbyterian] party: And when we thought ourselves sure of him, whip, he was gone, and, in a trice, com-menced a Brother-Independent . . .' and so on; until, like the unjust steward making preparations for being turned out of his stewardship, he made his last turn in 1673. 'Now (I suppose) he hath lived to see the utmost of his old trade of juggling, having juggled himself out of all at Court; and being past hope of juggling himself in again (all his feats being well understood, there—) he sets up at t'other end o' th' Town, to juggle up a mutiny in the City; in hope to find combustible matter there to set fire to in the country. . . .' It was a powerful indictment; it was set out in pithy, quotable, colloquial language; it was all good fun; it rested on the fact that Shaftesbury had for thirteen years been a member of the government which he was now opposing; and it appealed to the perpetual readiness of the man in the street to believe that a politician who changes his affiliations must do so for dishonest or ambitious reasons and cannot possess any inner consistency.

---

[1] Needham (for whom see C. H. Firth's article in *D.N.B.*) was believed to be the author by Shaftesbury and his supporters; cf. *C.S.P.D. 1677–8*, pp. 226–7; *Rawleigh Redivivus* (1683), pt. ii, pp. 8–9; *No Protestant Plot*, pt. iii, p. 58, where he is said to have been introduced to Danby by Justice Warcup. But it is not impossible that L'Estrange's hand was to be found in it.

The strategic purpose of all this was to argue that all the recent discontents were attributable to the machinations of 'that small boutefeu', and had no independent foundations. Let all moderate men be on their guard lest they be tempted to make trouble merely to subserve the ambitions of a Mephistopheles. For this objective it was necessary to exaggerate and put down everything which had occurred to his diabolical instigation: Jenks and his proposal at the Guildhall; the addresses from the counties in November 1676. Shaftesbury's agents were portrayed as here, there and everywhere, ready to revive the Old Faction of Forty One, and even to use the dreadful arguments of John Lilburne against a Long Parliament which 'ingrossed a trust of the people'. All in all, the pamphlet must have exasperated the many members of the Country Party (some of whom had Cavalier antecedents) who did not accept Shaftesbury's leadership and now saw themselves identified with him or portrayed as his puppets; and some of those for whose assistance he had hoped fell away from him. Shaftesbury's followers regarded the failure of their bid in this month of February 1677 as mainly the result of this pamphlet. Out of twenty peers who had been in a firm league (so Shaftesbury was reported to have said) sixteen 'dropped off upon perusal and well-digestion of that book'.[1]

Before Parliament even met, therefore, it was already clear that Shaftesbury's bid to declare that it was dissolved was likely to fail. The King was confident that it would,[2] and Shaftesbury's own doubts were increasing. This must be the explanation of the remarks he made to one of Danby's associates. Making a pretext to send for the Deputy-Paymaster of the Forces, Lemuel Kingdon, two days before the opening of the session, Shaftesbury professed that he bore no ill-will towards Danby, and had no desire to replace him as Lord Treasurer, 'for my Lord Shaftesbury said he aimed not at particular things but public good; but for my Lord of Ormond, there was my Lord Treasurer's danger, and he wondered he did not see it, for Sir William Coventry and my Lord of Ormond were in counsels together against my Lord Treasurer to bring in Sir William Coventry and their party', which included Halifax and the Marquis of Winchester, Danby's avowed enemies.[3] This obvious attempt at troublemaking between Danby and Ormond, which at the same time illustrated the poor relations between Shaftesbury and his nephew Halifax and brother-in-law Coventry, met with no response from the Treasurer and can only have encouraged him in the counter-attack he was planning to make while his opponents were few and divided.

On 15 February the King opened the new session with a speech which blamed his opponents for the misfortunes of the previous sessions and

---

[1] Anonymous notes, Add. MSS. 28047, fo. 199, printed by Browning, *Danby*, i. 218, n. 3.

[2] Lady Chaworth to Lord Roos, 7 Feb., *H.M.C. Rutland MSS.*, ii. 37.

[3] Kingdon's letter printed by Browning, *Danby*, i. 213 n.

called upon the Houses to avoid all occasions of difference between them for the future; 'and let all men judge who is most for arbitrary government, they that foment such differences as tend to dissolve all Parliaments; or I, that would preserve this and all Parliaments from being made useless by such dissensions'. Having got in this telling blow, he made more specific requests for money to build ships in the interests of national defence, and for the renewal of the additional excise granted in 1671. The Lord Keeper Finch followed this up with a longer speech, full of platitudinous references to the ship of state and appealing to conservatives to rally round to the defence of the peace of State and Church against innovations. He stressed the need 'not to remove the ancient landmarks',[1] and complained of 'the strange diffidence and distrust, which, like a general infection, begins to spread itself into almost all the corners of the land'. This was simply the result of 'the artifice of ill men', and was of the same type as the jealousies which had produced the Civil War. He made one oblique reference to the nature of this distrust, when he inquired: 'Would any man, that doth but give himself to think, refuse to enjoy and take comfort in the blessings that are present, only for future changes and alterations?' This appeal to Cavaliers to remember the lessons of the past and to forget the problems which a Popish successor might raise, he followed up with a peroration urging them: 'Away with those ill-meant distinctions between the Court and the Country! . . . for the first men that ever began to distinguish of their duty never left off, till they had quite distinguished themselves out of all their allegiance. . . .'

With this appeal ringing in their ears, the members of the Commons went to their own chamber. As soon as the Lords were left on their own, the Duke of Buckingham rose, 'in great bravery in liveries of blue', and argued that by the statutes of Edward III no Parliament was legally in existence. He bolstered the legal arguments with incitements to prejudice against the Commons, who 'look upon themselves as a standing senate, and as a number of men picked out to be legislators for the rest of their lives. And if that be the case, my lords, they have reason to believe themselves our equals'; the balance of the constitution was being destroyed, and a dissolution was desirable as well as legal. As soon as he had finished, Danby's cousin, Lord Frecheville, got up and, without attempting to controvert his arguments, 'moved that he might be called to the bar, and then be proceeded with as should be thought fit'. This motion, seconded by Lord Arundel of Trerice, and supported later by Danby, was a warning to the less determined members of the opposition, and only Shaftesbury, Salisbury and Wharton gave their backing to Buckingham. Halifax, Berkshire and Winchester all maintained that these lords were (in spite of Frecheville's motion) in order in giving their opinion, but they did not

---

[1] Proverbs, xxii. 28 and xxiii. 10.

DD

agree that Parliament stood dissolved; Holles, speaking late, seems to have argued that a dissolution was desirable, but not that the prorogation amounted to one. All Shaftesbury's eloquence and his citations of 50 Edward III and 9 Henry IV were in vain, and even the suggestion that the judges should be consulted found no favour.

Danby could probably have forced a vote quite quickly, but he chose to wait until his 'couriers' had brought him word that Shaftesbury's supporters had failed in a parallel endeavour in the House of Commons. There Sir John Mallet, Sir Philip Monckton, Lord Cavendish and William Russell, had raised the issue of the legality of the session, only to find that even colleagues in the 'Country Party' such as Grimston, Sacheverell, Garroway, Powle and Meres did not accept their point of view and were willing to mark their independence of any leadership by Shaftesbury. About three o'clock the debate petered out without Shaftesbury's few supporters even daring to force a vote.[1] As soon as the news reached Danby, he brought matters to a head in the Upper House, and it was easily agreed that Buckingham's motion should be laid aside.

The poverty of the support for Shaftesbury's 'party' had been amply demonstrated, but Danby was not satisfied with this: he wanted at least to humiliate Shaftesbury and perhaps to exclude him from the House's debates, with the aid of the substantial majority he knew he possessed. He had his excuse and he wished to make the most of it. Accordingly he moved that the House should now consider what to do with the lords who had, he said, conspired to maintain that Parliament had been dissolved; and the man who Shaftesbury had insinuated was Danby's secret enemy, Ormond, led the way by naming the man he hated far more, the Duke of Buckingham. Danby moved that Shaftesbury, Salisbury and Wharton might also be called to account. He could not achieve this object that same evening, for there were those who regarded it as an abuse of the power of the majority, and a danger to freedom of speech, to punish a defeated opposition, the more so as the debate had been allowed to continue for four or five hours without being ruled out of order. About eight o'clock in the evening he had to agree to an adjournment,[2] but next day he easily carried his point. By 53 votes (including those of the bishops) to 30 the four lords were ordered to withdraw. Salisbury was then called in

---

[1] On 17 Feb., while agreeing that there was no question of Parliament being dissolved, the opposition did try to question whether the King's action in 1675 should not be considered an adjournment instead of a prorogation, but were defeated on the previous question by 193 votes to 142. (Grey, iv. 81–95; Sir Cyril Wyche to Essex, 17 Feb., *Essex Papers*, ii. 101–2).

[2] For the events of 15 Feb., see *L.J.* xiii. 36–41; three sets of notes of the Lords' debates in MSS. Carte 79, fos. 31–43; J. S. Clarke, op. cit. i. 505–6; Marvell, *Growth of Popery* (*Works*, ed. Grosart), iv. 319–22; Buckingham's speech printed in *Parliamentary History*, iv. 814–24; Lady Chaworth to Lord Roos, 17 Feb., *H.M.C. Rutland MSS.*, ii. 38; Burnet, ii. 117–18; and for the debate in the Commons, *C.J.* ix. 382–3; Grey, iv. 63–77; Marvell, *Letters* (ed. Margoliouth), ii. 172–3.

first to his place; evidently the government wished to make things easier for him than the others and to separate him from them if possible, for he was told that if he would go to the bar and on his knees ask pardon of the King and the House he would be forgiven, and even when he had peremptorily refused, he was given time to consider it while some of his friends persuaded him to give way, but under Shaftesbury's advice he held firm. He was therefore ordered to the bar and sentenced to the Tower. Wharton was offered the same loophole for escape as Salisbury, and, shrinking from Salisbury's fate, he did try to maintain that he had already agreed that he had been mistaken, and that this amounted to an apology; but when called upon to make a more explicit submission he had sufficient Puritan stiffness to refuse, and he too was sentenced to the Tower. Buckingham had slipped away on some pretext; he had to be summoned back next day by Black Rod to share the same punishment as the other three, and his temporary evasion only served still further to reduce his already diminished popularity. Shaftesbury was the real enemy of the government; unlike Salisbury and Wharton he was called immediately to the bar and not to his place, and required to acknowledge that he had been guilty of 'an ill-advised action' for which he humbly begged pardon of the King and the House. In reply he made 'a long and humble speech' but said that he could not retract his opinion. To the undoubted satisfaction of Danby and the King, he was packed off to the Tower as well. As a final insulting gesture of defiance, he first persuaded Salisbury to ask for permission to have his own cook in the Tower, and then made the same request himself. It was greeted with a mixture of laughter, contempt and anger—Charles resented the implication that poison might be used, as Shaftesbury had known he would—but the House agreed.[1]

For Shaftesbury this was not only defeat but disaster. The Tower would not be so uncomfortable a prison for him as Newgate might be for criminals or Quakers, for a nobleman expected to be treated as befitted a 'person of quality'; but worse than the discomforts of imprisonment was the fact that it meant political impotence. The only possible consolation of martyrdom was that it might excite some popular sympathy with victims whose only crime, after all, was that they had maintained a different legal view from the government. With this in mind, Shaftesbury asked that instead of being taken from Westminster to the Tower by water, which he pleaded might be dangerous to his health, he should be transported by coach— through the streets of the City of London. But there were no demonstrations in his favour. That night, indeed, some of the more well-to-do citizens lit bonfires in front of the Exchange and elsewhere to celebrate the lords'

---

[1] *State Trials*, vi. 1298–1301 (for proceedings in the Lords, which were erased from the Journals by order of the House in 1680); MSS. Carte 79, fo. 38; Courtin, 19 Feb./1 Mar.; Lady Chaworth to L. Roos, 17, 20 Feb., *H.M.C. Rutland MSS.*, ii. 38–39; Van Beuningen, 20 Feb./2 Mar., Add. MSS. 17677, DD.

imprisonment, and although it was said that 'the common people' did not approve, the cause of freedom of speech against governmental suppression did not find any defenders in public. Buckingham was no more successful in arousing public sympathy when he made the same request next day[1]; and the four lords could only fall back on the thought that they were suffering for their principles, and that their suffering might be expected to come to an end with the parliamentary session, probably at Easter. In the meantime they might perhaps be able to receive visitors and so keep in touch with what was happening in Parliament, and they might be permitted to talk and plan amongst themselves in the Tower.

Even these last hopes were largely disappointed. The Lieutenant of the Tower put his prisoners into separate apartments 'with two trusty warders apiece' to permit no-one to have access to them but approved servants. The Guard was doubled for their benefit. When the prisoners' wives appeared, the Lieutenant found them 'very troublesome', but resisted all their importunities and told them that they needed permission either from the Lords or the King. Amongst other visitors who were turned away were Shaftesbury's son, Lord Cavendish, William Russell and Thomas Wharton. On 17 February the majority in the Lords, no doubt exasperated by the prisoners' request for their own cooks, laid down rigorous regulations for their imprisonment. They were to be allowed to meet only at Church—and even this freedom was taken away after the first Sunday, when they were seen to be whispering together throughout the divine service—and none was to be permitted to visit them without the leave of the House, other than their necessary attendants and servants. In spite of the attempts of Lord Cavendish and Sir Scrope Howe to make trouble over this in the Commons, the lower House tacitly agreed that its members would have to seek the permission of the Lords like anyone else.[2]

The upshot was that the prisoners' ladies were allowed to visit without restriction, or even to stay in the Tower if they wished: the seventeenth century was too civilized, at least where 'persons of quality' were concerned, to separate husband and wife without the most serious of reasons. Permission was given for others to visit fairly freely,[3] but Danby was able to keep a watch on the names of all visitors, and in the circumstances no one person could apply too often for leave. Though Halifax paid a weekly

[1] Van Beuningen, loc. cit.; Sarotti, 23 Feb./5 Mar.; [Sir John Robinson to the King] 20 Feb., *C.S.P.D. 1676–7*, p. 564.

[2] Sir John Robinson, loc. cit.; Add. MSS. 28091, fo. 29 (probably notes of Thomas Neale, member for Petersfield); MSS. Carte 79, fo. 39; Courtin, 19 Feb./1 Mar., 22 Feb./ 4 Mar.; Lady Chaworth to Lord Roos, 20 Feb., as in previous note; Grey, iv. 101–2.

[3] The names of those authorized were erased from the Lords' Journals by the House's order in 1680, but are to be found in MSS. Rawl. A.76, without however any indication which of the prisoners any person was to visit. It may, for instance, be safely inferred that Sir Peter Colleton was visiting Shaftesbury on Carolina business; other cases are more doubtful until Shaftesbury was alone in the Tower.

visit, it would not be possible for anyone sitting in the Tower to control the tactics of his followers in Parliament at all closely.

In this situation an approach was made to Shaftesbury by agents who acted, or purported to act, on behalf of Danby. The main intermediary employed (rather reluctantly, according to his own account) was Edmund Warcup, one-time captain in Anthony Ashley Cooper's regiment in January 1660, and since 1667 at least a farmer of the excise for Wiltshire and Dorset, so that he was known to both Shaftesbury and to Lord Treasurer Danby. Acting on the prompting of some of the people in the political underworld of the time, who claimed to be able to interpret Danby's wishes and even talked of the chancellorship for Shaftesbury if he would co-operate, Warcup went to Lady Shaftesbury. He told her that if Shaftesbury would 'well assure for his faithful loyalty and true service to the King and an inviolable friendship to the Lord Treasurer', the latter would mediate for his liberation and restoration to favour. Lady Shaftesbury greeted him with friendliness and a characteristic domestic reminiscence: she recalled that the first time Warcup had visited her was when her stepson (now Lord Ashley) had smallpox, and now, she said, her grandson had it. But, knowing her husband, she anticipated that he would not separate from his 'partners', but would stand on his honour; and so it proved when she took Warcup's message to him. She reported to Warcup that her husband had said he 'had been much injured,—he said against all rules: that he had been always faithful, that he stood upon his honour, and would not treat, but if the Treasurer, or any other who had injured him, would labour his enlargement, etc., he should gratefully accept, and then 'twas time to treat'. This amounted to a rejection of Danby's offer— if indeed it was his. It could have been a genuine offer, following up Shaftesbury's conversation with Kingdon not many days before; but acceptance of it would have discredited Shaftesbury permanently in all opposition circles and would have meant the abandonment of the friendships and the policies which he had pursued since 1674. He rejected it, as usual, civilly but firmly; and settled down to wait in the Tower for better days. It was only two months to Easter, when the end of the session would probably mean release in any case, and perhaps after that there might be better days, with himself as a martyr-hero of the opposition.[1]

---

[1] K. Feiling and F. R. D. Needham, 'The Journals of Edmund Warcup', in *E.H.R.* (1925), pp. 240–1; 'received from Mr. Browne 20th Feb. 1676/7', Add. MSS. 28045, fos. 39–40. Browning makes no mention of this episode in his life of Danby.

CHAPTER XX

IMPRISONMENT AND RELEASE (1677-8)

... seeing the Tower agreed not with his constitution ... it was his best way to return to the bar, there to submit and beg mercy of His Majesty, and the right honourable House, and from that most noble theatre preach repentance to all that had been perverted by his doctrine and example. Which he having done, what remains, but that he may spend the rest of his days with the blessing of a convert, the comfort of a good conscience. ...

Honesty's Best Policy

THE news which reached Shaftesbury in the Tower cannot have been very palatable to him, for the government was more successful in this session than it had been for many years. The House of Commons was induced to vote £600,000 for the building of thirty new ships, whereas in 1675 the most that they would have been willing to concede was £300,000; and this time the opposition's attempt to tack on a clause appropriating the Customs for the use of the Navy was defeated by the large majority of 51. A week later the House renewed the additional excise for a further period of three years. Notwithstanding opposition fears that the money might enable the ministers to rule without calling Parliament, the King's financial position had been considerably eased; and it looked as though Danby's attempts by pensions and other inducements to build up a 'Court Party' on which he could depend were proving successful. The 'Country' members introduced a Habeas Corpus Bill and a bill for the recall of British troops in the French service, but there seemed no more likelihood that these would pass in this session than in earlier ones, though the French ambassador was told that the latter bill would be allowed to go through the Commons, to be obstructed later in the Lords.[1]

The government's two weakest points, precisely because they were the two on which there was the greatest public concern, were the Roman Catholicism of the heir to the throne and a foreign policy which seemed to favour France. Danby attempted to cover up the first of these two weaknesses by himself putting forward a bill against Popery, the most important provision of which laid down for the protection of the Church of England that a Roman Catholic king would no longer have the unrestricted right to appoint its bishops. He would be permitted only to select from a short list of three names drawn up by the other bishops of the province. It was also provided that the education of his children should be supervised by the archbishops and three other bishops. The fact that

[1] Courtin, 26 Feb./8 Mar. 1677.

James's agreement to these clauses had been obtained in advance secured an easy passage for the bill through the Lords; but it also confirmed the view of the Commons that the bill was inadequate to bind a Catholic king. 'No wonder the Lords send you down such a Bill as this', said the outspoken Sir John Mallet, 'while they keep such wise and understanding Lords in the Tower.' Many members were reluctant to trust themselves to the Protestantism of bishops, who had since Laud's day devoted themselves to supporting the monarch and upholding his divine right, whether he were Protestant or Catholic. "'Tis a pretty experiment', sneered Andrew Marvell. 'Just a trial, whether the Loadstone will attract the Iron, or the Iron the Loadstone.' Who could think that a body of men so dependent on the King as the bishops must naturally be would dare to defy him? There might be bishops, as well as a vicar, of Bray. In the reigns of Henry VIII, Edward VI, Mary and Elizabeth the bishops had been powerless to restrain the monarch from making the changes which he or she wanted. Another member pointed out that the monarch also selected the judges, 'and, no doubt, upon any dispute hereafter upon this Bill, the judges will give it for the King'. Implicit in many of the arguments against the effectiveness and the desirability of limitations on the royal prerogative was already the idea that a monarch of the wrong religion should be excluded, though no-one specifically said this and one cannot tell how many members realized where the argument was leading. As often, the most reckless was Mallet, who moved that 'if there were any great man, though ever so great about the King, who might be suspected not to be a friend to our religion, he might have the tests offered to him . . . and he might be removed from Court, if he refuses them'. This motion was greeted with silence, until another member changed the subject. It was not yet time to come out into the open, however preoccupied members might be with the problem of the succession, which cropped up in many different ways— for instance in the debate on the validity of the royal charter making Newark a parliamentary borough, when Henry Powle argued against conceding such an indefinite power in the King. 'We may put the case, that the King has a mind to alter religion, without altering the constitution of this House. Whether boroughs sending fifty Papists, might not be predominant. . . .'[1]

The Lords' bill against Popery, which one member, Hale, dismissed as being 'like empty casks for whales to play with, and rattles for children to keep them quiet', was sent into committee and buried while the House busied itself with a bill of its own which would have imposed stiffer

---

[1] *L.J.* xiii. 48–51, 56, 57; *H.M.C. Ninth Report*, ii. 81–82; Marvell, *Growth of Popery*, in *Works*, ed. Grosart (1872), iv. 340–52; Courtin, 26 Feb./8 Mar.; *C.J.* ix. 402–3, 406–7; Grey, iv. 204, 284–96, 318–26; Add. MSS. 28091, fos. 39, 59–60. It was rather ironical that although in the end Newark was permitted to send members, Shaftesbury's friend Sir Paul Neile was declared not validly elected: *C.J.* ix. 403; Grey, iv. 297–304.

penalties upon recusants, but which did not succeed in reaching the statute-book either. All this was ominous, indicating as it did the serious attitude which people had to the succession problem well before the hysteria of the Popish Plot, and in circumstances when the concern could not be attributed to the machinations of Shaftesbury, since he was in the Tower. But at the time, in the spring of 1677, problems of foreign policy looked very much more urgent, for Louis XIV's successes were arousing general concern. Once again the French armies were ready to begin their campaign before the Confederates were prepared to oppose them. Valenciennes, Cambrai and St. Omer all fell, and early in April the French won a battle at Cassel. It became a question whether the whole of Flanders would not fall, city by city, into Louis's hands, if England did not intervene.

At the beginning of the session opposition members of the Commons had again taken up the issue of the British troops which were still in French service, and were still, with the connivance of Lauderdale, receiving recruits from Scotland. To many this state of affairs was a continuing proof of the untrustworthiness of the government's attitude to foreign problems, and of its subservience to France, and accordingly a bill was introduced to recall the obnoxious soldiers. This time no reliance was placed on addresses to the King or on royal proclamations. But the news of the loss of Valenciennes led the Commons to adopt a more urgent and positive approach, and on the same day, 6 March, they voted without a division for an address asking the King to make alliances for the preserva-tion of the Spanish Netherlands. Charles found such an address unwelcome —he valued his understanding with Louis, and disliked the risks of war and dependence on the financial grants of the Commons which such a foreign policy would entail; Danby on the other hand was not well-disposed to French influence and wished to secure the popularity which an anti-French policy might bring.[1]

In this explosive situation it so happened that the last batch of Scots troops for the French armies to be shipped from Leith was captured by a Spanish privateer and taken into the port of Ostend. Two of the Scots, William Herriot and John Dewar, then were given their liberty on con-dition that they would go to London and report to the Spanish embassy at Wild House, in Lincoln's Inn Fields; and there the Spanish consul, Fonseca, a man of long experience and many commercial and political connexions in the capital, passed them on to John Harrington and Robert Murray.[2]

---

[1] For foreign policy problems in 1677, cf. Browning, *Danby*, chs. xi. and xii, *passim*, and my article on 'The Anglo-Dutch Rapprochement of 1677', in *E.H.R.* (1958), pp. 614–48.
[2] For the general history of this case, see *C.S.P.D. 1677–8*, pp. 12–13, 14–17, 21, 22, 24, 27–28, 318–19, 329; Schwerin, 20/30 Mar., *Briefe*, pp. 104–5; Marvell, *Growth of Popery*, in *Works*, ed. Grosart (1872), iv. 334; Coventry Papers at Longleat, xiii. fo. 82; Grey, iv. 255–83; Add. MSS. 28091, fos. 46–51; Courtin, 19/29 Mar.

John Harrington was a native of Weymouth and a 'cousin' of Shaftesbury's,[1] and Murray had been the intermediary between the Earl and Lord Wharton in the previous autumn.[2] Both (but especially Harrington) had been frequent guests at Shaftesbury's dinner-table in the last months at Exeter House.[3] Both were in a position to interpret Shaftesbury's wishes: Harrington in 1676 had strongly supported Jenks's arguments, and had been heard by shocked Royalists to make the appalling statement 'that the King was bound to a law as well as others, and that the Government was in the three estates, and that taking up arms unless against all three was no rebellion'. He and Murray now set to work to persuade Herriot and Dewar to describe how the Scottish government had facilitated the French recruiting, promising on Shaftesbury's behalf that 'they should not want', and even (so Herriot later declared) that Herriot should be made Shaftesbury's tailor.[4] Eventually Herriot and Dewar were taken to a Master of Chancery, and signed a deposition alleging not only that recruiting in Scotland had gone on with the government's connivance, but that unwilling recruits had been kept in the public prisons, tried in twos like malefactors, and had even had their ears cut off: later they excused these lurid details to the Secretary of State by alleging that they had not read the document that they had signed. They were then told to wait in the neighbourhood of Westminster until a suitable opportunity was found to get them to repeat their story at the bar of the House of Commons. This would have been extremely awkward for the government, but before the opportunity occurred Secretary of State Williamson's agents discovered what was afoot. Herriot was interrogated and Harrington and Murray were arrested. Before the Privy Council Harrington behaved rather indiscreetly; in answer to the King's questions, he said 'It may be so—I'll answer you no more'. 'I'll ask you no more', Charles replied, and committed him to the Tower, where he was kept in close confinement, without pen, ink and paper. On his way to the Tower he had had the presence of mind to sign his name at the bottom of a blank sheet of paper and slip this to a bystander, so that his friends could write in a petition to the House of Commons; but when Sacheverell presented this, and Harrington, Herriot and Murray were heard in turn at the bar, the House refused to take the case up. Herriot's

---

[1] C.S.P.D. 1677–8, p. 22. I have not been able to discover his precise relationship to Shaftesbury.

[2] p. 413 above; and cf. Lauderdale to Danby, 28 Aug. 1677, Lauderdale Papers, iii. 86–87.

[3] Catering accounts now at St. Giles House show, with other details, the names of guests between Oct. 1675 and July 1676, but this information is not so illuminating as might have been expected. Guests were few in number, and not very varied. Apart from Harrington, the most frequent visitors were, in order, Lords Mohun and Wharton and Mr. [Thomas] Wharton.

[4] H. Coventry to Sir Wm. Godolphin, 19/29 Mar., S.P. 94/64, fo. 33; C.S.P.D. 1677–8, p. 15; Grey, iv. 278. Murray, however, said that Herriot 'was offered 20l. and to be in the King's Tailor's service if he would not make affidavit', ibid. pp. 279–80.

repudiation of the affidavit, his story of how it had been procured, and Harrington's contempt of the Privy Council and his obvious intrigues with the representatives of a foreign power made members fight shy of adopting him. Harrington went back to the Tower, for his case eventually to add to the arguments of those who wanted to fortify the *habeas corpus* procedure against such arbitrary action by the Executive. The government had had a narrow escape from what could have been a very dangerous story.

The whole episode rebounded very heavily on Shaftesbury. There was no evidence that he had prompted the actions of Harrington and Murray,[1] but it was well known that they were close to him, and it was plain that if Shaftesbury were released other similar machinations might follow. Charles and Danby were determined that he must be kept out of harm's way in the Tower. Charles was extremely irritated by the Spaniards' intrigues with his discontented subjects; Danby, on the other hand, could not afford to have to contend with Shaftesbury at a time when he was trying to press on the King an anti-French policy to suit the wishes of the Commons. It was the worst possible moment for an attempt to secure the release of the four lords, and the manner of it was as bad. On 20 March, a month after their imprisonment, but only a week after Harrington's arrest, Lord Delamere moved in the House of Lords that since four of their members were imprisoned 'upon a punctilio only', they might now be set free. No doubt he meant that their offence was not serious enough to justify confinement for more than a month (as indeed was true, by any ordinary standards of justice); but Danby was able to argue that at least the prisoners should present a petition for release before the House considered it. Only Halifax, the second Earl of Clarendon and the Earl of Berkshire supported Delamere, who narrowly escaped being sent to join the other four for his temerity in describing their offence as a mere punctilio.[2]

Still, as Shaftesbury's steward Stringer wrote on 9 April to his friend John Locke, absent in France, it seemed that Easter would bring a prorogation and with it release for his hero. 'There have been great endeavours against our little friend but the air is now grown very clear, and the season towards the end of a stormy winter, puts us in expectation of fair weather at hand. We hear of no other discourses concerning your 2 other friends Mr. H. and S. but that this fine month of April that gives life and freshness to all other things, will send them out of a dirty stinking air from ill-meaning, base and despicable company, into a sweet and pleasant country

---

[1] Their names are not among the authorized visitors to the Tower listed in MSS. Rawl. A. 76, but it is possible that they had visited their patron in the guise of servants. Murray indeed admitted on 17 Mar., that he had accompanied Lord Ashley on a visit to Shaftesbury, but 'above a fortnight ago' (i.e. before the two Scots arrived in London), Grey, iv. 279. Little is heard of Harrington and Murray in the Popish Plot period.

[2] W. Fall to Sir R. Verney, 23 Mar., *H.M.C. Seventh Report*, p. 469; Courtin, 22 Mar./1 Apr.

to receive the delightful embraces of their wives and mistresses. . . .'[1] The rude awakening came two days later, when Sir Joseph Williamson told the Commons that the King meant 'by short adjournments, to October, to have the Parliament within call, upon emergencies'. Neither the session nor the lords' imprisonment would come to an end. The decision to have an adjournment instead of a prorogation was partly the result of considerations of foreign policy, for Danby still hoped to persuade the Commons to give the money and the King to give the orders for preparations against France; but the French ambassador privately knew that, come what may, dangerous opponents must be kept in prison.[2]

The immediate result was to make some of the four lords consider whether they might not seek to escape from the 'dirty, stinking air' of the Tower by means now of some token submission to the King. On the last day of the session, the oldest and weakest of the Lords, Wharton, petitioned for release, at least for a time, on the grounds of age, colic in his stomach, and urgent family concerns. The House referred this plea for compassion to the King, who gave him permission to retire to Woburn until Parliament met again on 21 May.[3] A few days later, the other three sent a joint petition to the King, asking civilly for the favour of liberation but without any apology or acknowledgement that they had been in error. Shaftesbury's gentleman, Shepherd, carried this petition to Charles at Newmarket, but the atmosphere of Newmarket had not softened him at all. He told Shepherd that 'he came post, but his answer would not be so hasty', and having turned the matter over at his leisure, sent word that the very fact of a joint petition suggested the 'confederacy' for which they had been imprisoned; if however they had petitioned separately, this suspicion would have been removed, 'and in his apprehension some deserved more favour than others'. Responding to this hint, each peer drew up a separate petition and persuaded a friend to present it: Shaftesbury's was handed in by his brother-in-law, Secretary Henry Coventry, Salisbury's by the Earl of Suffolk, and Buckingham's by the Earl of Middlesex. But they were no more apologetic than before, and no more successful than before. At the committee of foreign affairs Charles observed with some satisfaction that the petitions were 'very short of what they themselves must know to be necessary to precede their enlargement'.[4]

The meeting of Parliament on 21 May produced no relief for the

---

[1] MSS. Locke, c. 19, fo. 129.

[2] Grey, iv. 343 (cf. the Chancellor's statement to the Lords, 13 Apr., *C.S.P.D. 1677–8*, p. 87); Courtin, 29 Mar./8 Apr.

[3] *H.M.C. Ninth Report*, ii. 95; *C.S.P.D. 1677–8*, p. 92; Coventry Papers at Longleat, ii, fo. 90.

[4] Coventry Papers, ii, fos. 92, 96, 97; Lady Russell to William Russell [? April], *Life and Letters of Lady Russell* (1819), pp. 186–7; Charles Hatton to L. Hatton [May], *Hatton Correspondence*, i. 146–7; Courtin, 3/13 May; Henry Savile to Halifax, *Savile Correspondence*, ed. W. D. Cooper (Camden Society, 1857), p. 50; Charles Bertie to John Cooke, 12 May, Coventry Papers, v, fo. 158.

prisoners, for in only a week there was another adjournment. The Commons addressed the King 'to enter into a league, offensive and defensive, with the States General of the United Provinces' and to make alliances with other Confederate powers after that. Only after these alliances had been concluded would they grant supplies; and Charles, who had never liked the prospect of turning against France as Danby advocated, seized the opportunity to adjourn Parliament with an unusually sharp rebuke to the Commons for invading his 'fundamental power of making peace and war'. It was certain that the rebuke would be much resented, and that agreement over foreign policy was out of the question for some time to come; and when the King personally declared that although the adjournment was formally only until 16 July 'I do not intend you shall sit till winter, unless there should happen any urgent occasions', everyone realized that he meant what he said. The peers had to face a long imprisonment, and the French ambassador was quite clear in his mind that that was precisely the purpose of having an adjournment and not a prorogation.[1]

The peers' reaction was to imitate Wharton and seek some excuse to appeal to Charles's good nature for temporary release. Salisbury asked for permission to go to Hatfield on the ground that his own health was impaired, and that his wife, who was near her confinement, was endangering her life by staying with him in the Tower. Charles, partly from good nature but partly to achieve his aim of dividing his opponents, gave Salisbury freedom to go to Hatfield until the end of the month. Buckingham also petitioned on health grounds, referring to the 'growing distemper prevailing every day more and more upon me, from which I cannot hope to be released, without the change of air'. This and two other petitions had no direct result, but on 21 June the influence of Nell Gwyn procured for the Duke a warrant to leave the Tower for two days to inspect his new buildings at Cliveden, and it is probable that a private meeting laid the foundations for a reconciliation between the King and the old companion of his pleasures. Shaftesbury, however, had no success. His petition, delivered to the King on 1 June by his brother-in-law Henry Coventry, asked briefly for leave to go to his house in Dorset 'in consideration of his health and private affairs', but in vain. He had no Nell Gwyn to plead for him, and he was too dangerous an opponent to receive mercy. He determined on a different course of action.[2]

Convinced that he was entitled to bail, Shaftesbury instructed that on 23 June an application should be made for a writ of *habeas corpus* at the King's Bench bar. There were those who foresaw that he was unlikely to be able to induce the Court of King's Bench to go counter to an order of

---

[1] *C.J.* ix. 426; Courtin, 28 May/7 June; Browning, *Danby*, i. 230–2; Haley, 'Anglo-Dutch Rapprochement of 1677', in *E.H.R.* (1958), pp. 630–1.

[2] *C.S.P.D. 1677–8*, pp. 166, 205; Coventry Papers, fos. 99–100, 102, 103, 106; Lady Burghclere, *Duke of Buckingham* (1903), pp. 324–30; Shaftesbury to Coventry, 1 June, printed by Brown, p. 244.

the House of Lords, and that he would only exasperate King and peers still further by appealing over their heads to the judges. But Shaftesbury was convinced that he had suffered four months' imprisonment while innocent of any crime, simply because he had exercised his right as a peer to speak his mind in the House. He had been the victim of an abuse of the power of the majority to get rid of a dangerous enemy, and in a sense he could claim to represent liberty against oppression. At all events his case aroused great excitement when it was heard on 29 June. At midnight people were banging on the door of Westminster Hall to get in. By four in the morning there were no places left, and some were paying four silver crowns to get within easy hearing. In the course of the morning several were carried fainting out of the throng.

Williams and Wallop, Shaftesbury's counsel, argued that the warrant for his commitment was too vague and general, and that the fact that commitment was by the House of Peers made no difference, for the court was obliged to declare the law in all cases brought before it; otherwise 'the party would be without remedy for his liberty, if he could not find it here'. The Attorney-General, Solicitor-General, and the veteran lawyer Maynard all argued that there could be no interference with a commitment by the Lords. At this point Shaftesbury himself took up the argument; he began by saying that he had not intended to speak—but he was after all a former Chancellor and well capable of presenting his own case. He denied that his case was, as the Crown lawyers maintained, that King's Bench was 'greater than' the House of Lords, but maintained that there was a jurisdiction that the Lords did not meddle with, namely applications for writs of *habeas corpus*, which were proper to be argued here—'and I do not think it a kindness to the Lords to make them absolute and above the law, for so I humbly conceive this must do, if it be adjudged that they by a general warrant, or without any particular cause assigned, do commit me, or any other man, to a perpetual and indefinite imprisonment; and, my lords, I am not so inconsiderable a person, but what you do in my case, must be law for every man in England'. After flourishing Magna Carta, he took up an admission which the Attorney-General had made, that the King's pleasure could release him without reference to the Lords. At the bar of King's Bench, he said, he was *coram rege*, and since the King was deemed to be present the Court could and should release him. A minister in similar case might be released by a pardon or a prorogation; there was no such possibility for anyone else, and if his own commitment was legal, why should not forty members of parliament, or even more, suffer the same fate? 'If in this case there can be no relief, no man can foresee what will be hereafter.' And, stressing again that 'it will be a precedent that in future ages may concern every man in England', he concluded by saying that he would not insist on complete release, but was very willing to tender whatever bail the Court laid down.

Rather surprisingly some of the judges did agree that 'such a commitment by an ordinary Court of Justice would have been ill and uncertain', but they declined to interfere with an order of Parliament while the session was still technically in progress. Shaftesbury was remanded back to the Tower. There was 'much murmuring' about it and much argument whether his course of action had been wise—argument which no doubt was given added sharpness by the appearance about this time of a second *Pacquet of Animadversions to the Men of Shaftesbury*. But the truth is that nothing but the very humblest of submissions could have procured his release, and he preferred to make his stand for a principle in which he believed.[1]

As a retaliation for his impertinence in applying for a writ of *habeas corpus*, the King determined to make his imprisonment in the Tower stiffer than before. 'Our old friend is still in limbo and now closer confined than ever', Stringer reported to Locke on 13 July. Charles personally called for a list of the persons Shaftesbury deemed necessary to have regular access to him. From the list Charles struck out the names of Shaftesbury's steward Stringer, his solicitor Hoskins, his gentleman of the horse, Shepherd, his 'factor for all merchant affairs', Saxby, his Dorset steward Cheswell, his secretary Wilson, his kinsman and trustee Sir William Cooper, and the master of the ship plying to Carolina; he gave permission to visit only to Lord Ashley, five men servants, some women-servants, a physician, surgeon and apothecary. All others would have to seek permission through the Secretary of State. It would appear that since Easter no restrictions had been placed on visiting, but that they were now revived.[2] At the same time Shaftesbury also lost the solace that he was not the only one in trouble, for Wharton, Salisbury and Buckingham all finally made their peace. When Parliament met briefly on 16 July there were petitions ready for presentation to the Lords, but there was no chance to present them before the House obeyed the King's command to adjourn again immediately; and the trio then made up their minds to seek freedom from the King. Salisbury, who had received permission to stay at Hatfield for a further month, decided before the end of it to make his submission for having offended the King and the House of Lords, and Charles accepted this. Wharton, too, was jestingly told to 'go, and sin no more'. Buckingham,

---

[1] Henry Savile to Halifax, 24 June, *Savile Correspondence*, p. 62; Marvell to Sir E. Harley, 30 June, in *Works*, ed. H. M. Margoliouth (1927), ii. 327; Sarotti, 6/16 July; Shaftesbury Papers, VI A, no. 306; MSS. Locke, f 2, pp. 282–6; Christie, ii, pp. xciv–xcvi; *State Trials*, vi. 1269–1310; 'T.B.', 3 and 8 July, *C.S.P.D. 1677–8*, pp. 226, 233, 378.

[2] Christie, ii. 239; *C.S.P.D. 1677–8*, pp. 224, 235, 236, 257–8. A list of Shaftesbury's visitors between 25 July and 18 Feb. 1678 may be compiled from ibid. 267–9, 272, 274, 296, 687–8. Permission seems to have been granted fairly freely after about 20 Aug. to the people struck off Shaftesbury's list (above) and other servants and business visitors like Sir Paul Neile, Sir Peter Colleton and Henry Kemp. The number of 'political' visitors was markedly smaller than in the spring of 1677, either because permission was refused or because they were away in the country; e.g. in seven months Halifax visited only three times, and Russell visited only once before the end of the year.

solemnly pleading that he had contracted 'a very dangerous distemper' by his confinement, through the offices of 'Nelly, Middlesex, Rochester and the merry gang' at Court received temporary leave for a month, and soon he too made the formal submission necessary to make his leave permanent. There were reports that before he left the Tower there were recriminations between him and Shaftesbury. The latter was said to have described the Duke as 'giddy' and 'inconstant' (which was true enough). When the Duke's coach came into the courtyard to take him away, Shaftesbury looked out of the window, and remarked with a sneer, 'What, my lord, are you leaving us so soon?' To which the Duke replied that someone as 'giddy pated' as he could not bear to remain too long in one place, and went his way to freedom, leaving Shaftesbury steadfast, but in jail.[1]

Shaftesbury's steadfastness did not prevent him from sending another petition to the King, but once again this was not apologetic but based solely on grounds of health; he asked for leave to go to Wimborne St. Giles until Michaelmas, for both he and his wife had been ill and were likely to become worse if they remained in the Tower during the hot weather. When Lady Shaftesbury presented the petition on 2 August, Charles received her courteously, but his usual good nature (from which the other three had profited) did not extend to her husband. As he told the foreign committee, 'If my Lord thinks this an ill air, the King will think of some other prison in a better air', and there the matter rested. Naturally Shaftesbury did not press to be removed to a different prison; he remained where he was in the grim old fortress, determined not even to try whether an abject submission would be more effectual.[2]

The most important result of this continued imprisonment was to help to make Shaftesbury the hope of the hardened core of malcontents who could never be reconciled to the regime of the King and Danby. Whereas Buckingham by his submission and return to Court had demonstrated his fickleness, Shaftesbury preferred to remain a prisoner. *The Animadversions to the Men of Shaftesbury* had pointed to his political record and suggested that it was that of a time-server; the months spent in the Tower did not fit in with this assessment, and pamphlets on the *Case of the Lords in the Tower concerning the illegality of their commitment* argued that he was unjustly imprisoned. Another story which went the rounds strengthened the view that he was a martyr. It was said that on 16 July the Roman Catholic peer Lord Stafford had paid him a visit to the Tower, and hinted that there was one way of escape for him. 'I suppose I comprehend your

---

[1] Courtin, 16/26 July; *C.S.P.D. 1677–8*, pp. 260–2, 290; Marvell to Sir E. Harley, 7 Aug., in *Poems and Letters*, ed. H. M. Margoliouth (1927), ii. 328–9; Lady Burghclere, op. cit. p. 330. Buckingham's friends apparently spread rumours that Shaftesbury would have deserted him earlier if Salisbury had not interposed to reconcile them: Martin Clifford to Shaftesbury, 7 Aug., Shaftesbury Papers, VI A, 309.

[2] *C.S.P.D. 1677–8*, p. 282; Foreign Entry Book, 3 Aug., S.P. 104/180; newsletter, 8 Aug., in MSS. Carte 79, fo. 114.

Lordship', said Shaftesbury. 'You would have the Duke [of York] to write a new creed for me and I to subscribe it. But I shall never do it. He has done his worst to me, yet would do worse if it were in his power. He would have my head, but I shall yet wear it in despite of him and live perhaps to come betwixt him and his great hopes.' If indeed he uttered these words, he believed, or affected to believe, that James rather than Danby was responsible for the punishment which had been inflicted on him. In any case, the propagandist use to which the words could be put is sufficiently obvious. Over a year before the idea of excluding James was explicitly put forward, there were those who looked to Shaftesbury as the Protestant leader who would come between James and 'his great hopes', though there were still those who had doubts.[1]

No-one would have chosen the Tower as a residence, but it was not a desperately uncomfortable dungeon for a man who was able to adapt himself to the life. This Shaftesbury was able to do, with the aid of his wife (who lived with him) and a number of servants who waited upon him. Though his petition had complained of ill-health, in fact apart from one 'fit of the gout' his physical condition improved. In October his steward Stringer wrote to John Locke, who was still in France, that his master was 'better in his health, fresher in his complexion and fatter in his body' than he had ever known him. His mental alertness he maintained principally with the aid of books, maps and papers which were sent in to him. Locke was commissioned to send him over some maps on which he could follow the course of the campaigns which were being fought by Louis XIV and his opponents; and Locke also lent some books which the Earl promised to keep separately and return. These, Stringer said, proved 'a very good entertainment'; and while Shaftesbury had more time than usual to read books himself, he remembered also to provide for the education of his small grandson, and sent to Locke to enquire from what books the Dauphin had learned Latin.[2]

Shaftesbury also whiled away the time in congenial fashion by collecting political information. There survives in the Muniments Room at Wimborne St. Giles a manuscript book which contains some of the results of his labours. At one end of the book there are different lists of the 'ministers and great men' and army officers of the different European countries, usually in a clerk's hand, but with brief annotations in Shaftesbury's own: thus the Dutchman van Beuningen was noted as 'Emb: [ambassador] in Eng: ill man—'. It was a kind of *Who's Who* of continental nobilities. The earliest list was dated Christmas 1676; others were dated 1677 and other years after his release down to the year 1682, suggesting that he found it helpful to keep his information up to date to the very end. At the other

---

[1] *C.S.P.D. 1677–8*, pp. 691–2; Marvell to Harley, as in note 1, p. 431; 'T.B.' to Williamson, 12 Aug., *C.S.P.D. 1677–8*, p. 302.

[2] Stringer to Locke, 16 Aug., 5 Oct., printed in Christie, ii. 248–9, 250.

end of the book there are local lists of the gentlemen of his native Dorset-shire, by divisions and hundreds, many of them prefixed by the letters *v* or *w* in Shaftesbury's hand. Then, after another Namierization of the cardinals of the Catholic Church, there follow the two lists most valuable for the historian. These contain the names of all the peers and members of the Commons in May 1677 (but kept up to date with notes of deaths and replacements at by-elections). Again, the names are prefixed with the letter *v* (for vile) or *w* (for worthy); indeed, degrees of vileness and worthiness are measured by doubling or trebling the letter. It was a working list of the members of Parliament on whom he and his enemies respectively could depend.

He also had his estates and his business interests to look after, with the aid of the servants and partners who visited him. Some of the news they brought was unwelcome, as when the Earl learned that he had been the principal victim of 'a great gang of deer stealers' who had seized the opportunity of his absence to kill as many as a thousand of the deer in his park.[1] Other news was rather better, for in 1677 there seemed at last some prospect of reward for the hundreds of pounds which he had poured into Carolina. From his own plantation on Ashley River his agent Andrew Percival began to send back deer-skins and beaver furs, which were a profitable commodity; and about this time Shaftesbury also began to exploit other possibilities afforded by the friendly relations opened up by his Indian trader, Henry Woodward, with the tribe of the Westoes. These included a trade in Indian slaves, which Shaftesbury had originally for-bidden to the Carolina settlers. Now Shaftesbury, Sir Peter Colleton and three of their colleagues formed a company to carry it on jointly, while a proclamation declared that this inland trade was a monopoly of the colony's proprietors and the settlers were left only that within a hundred miles of the coast. From now on the returns from Carolina began at least to keep pace with Shaftesbury's expenditure.[2] There were also decisions to be taken about his silver mining and about the sub-contracting of the manufacture of guns using Prince Rupert's metallurgical discoveries; on the other hand he sold sixteen shares in the Royal Africa Company for £121 each at the end of April. The lighter side of life is reflected too in surviving accounts of his personal expenditure: there are small amounts (£3. 15s. and £10) entered as 'lost at play', and a guinea paid for the luxury of a pound of tea.[3]

---

[1] Newsletter of 14 Aug., MSS. Carte 79, fo. 117. Cf. Sir W. Portman to Shaftesbury, 1 Aug., Shaftesbury Papers, VI A, 308, on unspecified business connected with estates in Dorset and Somerset; and cf. also Shaftesbury to Mr. Uvedale, 4 Nov. 1678, ibid. VI A, 329.

[2] Andrew Percival's accounts in the Muniment Room at St. Giles House show £2,468.17s. 2d. on the credit side and £2,140. 17s. 11d. on the debit side, including allow-ances for interest, for the years 1678-June 1680. See also *C.S.P. Col. 1677-80*, pp. 59-61.

[3] Shaftesbury to Sir Thomas Price, 5 Sept., to Thos. Bennet, 9 Nov., and to Sir Thos. Chichley, 5 Dec., Shaftesbury Papers, VI A, 310, 313-15; accounts for 1677 at St. Giles House. For these business interests see pp. 228-30, 233-4 above.

But books, maps, profits and losses, cards and tea could not compensate for the enforced isolation from political activity. It was not that he was ignorant of what was going on in the outside world: he paid his shilling or 1s. 4d. for copies of the Haarlem and Brussels gazettes which brought news of the campaigns in the Low Countries, and no doubt the visitors who came supplied him with other information. But he was powerless to influence the course of events, and the course of events seemed to be disastrous. At home the King and Danby seemed comfortably placed, and beyond the reach of criticism; James could expect the succession; and abroad Louis XIV, with whom Charles and James had always sought to associate their fortunes, was going from success to success. The coalition against him was creaking more and more ominously. His great enemy William of Orange, harassed by the rise of a peace party within the cities of Holland and by the inefficiencies, jealousies and suspicions of his Spanish allies, could make no headway. In August 1677 he had to give up an attempt to besiege Charleroi in rather ignominious circumstances: there were those who said that he had betrayed the allied cause at the instigation of his uncle, Charles II, and was seeking his own advantage with his uncle's aid.[1]

In September the prisoner in the Tower heard the news that William was to come over to England to visit his uncle, and (as rumour had it) to marry James's daughter Mary; and on 21 October the engagement was duly announced. Danby had been pressing the idea of an anti-French policy upon Charles for some time: the experience of the last session had shown that the government's weakest point was its benevolent neutrality to Louis XIV, and Danby had privately urged on the King the advantages of adopting a different foreign policy in order to secure more harmonious relations with his Parliament and people—or to adopt the more authoritarian line which would be possible if the King was once 'in a condition of arms'.[2] Charles had no intention of going as far as Danby wanted him to do in the direction of making Louis XIV an enemy—the memory of the Catholic clauses in the Treaty of Dover left him scarcely free to pursue a fully independent foreign policy; but William's military failures in 1677 and his request for Mary's hand seemed to suggest that his nephew might at last accept his guidance and might enable him to mediate an end to an embarrassing war. And so he commanded his reluctant brother to agree to the marriage of William and Mary.

To the opposition the marriage seemed to mean that William, himself a Stuart on his mother's side, had accepted the leadership of his uncles in some political conspiracy. Some of those who had looked to him in 1673–4 now distrusted him; there were even those who regarded the marriage as a

---

[1] Haley, 'Anglo-Dutch Rapprochement of 1677', in *E.H.R.* (1958), pp. 635 sqq.
[2] Danby's memoranda of 4 Apr. and June 1677 in Browning, *Danby*, ii. 66–71.

contrivance of Louis XIV.[1] To us, looking back with our knowledge of William's later career, this seems absurd; but it was not so in the circumstances of 1677. William was then already the determined opponent of Louis, but he had not the gift of explaining his position and disarming the suspicions which clustered round him; nor did the behaviour of his Orangist supporters in the United Provinces suggest that he would be any more tender to the political rights of his opponents than any other Stuart. Nor were many of the opposition able to meet the Prince, to talk with him and see for themselves. It was not without significance for the history of the Exclusion years that Shaftesbury himself was debarred from seeing him. The only time when the two men actually met was during William's previous visit to England at the end of 1670, when as a young man only just twenty he had given no sign of his true qualities. Shaftesbury had no opportunity to revise his opinion by personal contact.

Five days after the announcement of the marriage all the suspicions about it seemed to be confirmed, for a proclamation declared that Parliament would meet on its appointed day, 3 December, only to be adjourned further until 4 April. This was a bitter blow for Shaftesbury personally: he could look forward to almost indefinite detention. After eight months stone walls were coming to look very like a prison. His enemies sneered at him in a play, *Sir Popular Wisdom or the Politician*, which was supposed to have royal patronage.[2] Disconsolately he began to wonder whether there was any means of escape without admitting that he had been in the wrong. He drafted a personal letter to the King, pleading 'not only my innocence towards your majesty; for "my integrity will I hold fast, and will not let it go; my heart shall not reproach me so long as I live".'[3] He then embarked upon an account of his services at the Restoration.[4] At the same time he drafted a letter to James: 'Sir, I humbly confess I never thought my person or my principles acceptable to your Royal Highness; but at that juncture of time and occasion when I was committed, I had no reason to expect you should be my severe enemy. Reputation is the greatest concern of great dealers in the world; great princes are the greatest dealers; no reputation more their interest than to be thought merciful, relievers of the distressed, and maintainers of the ancient laws and rights of their country. This I ever wish may attend your Royal Highness, and that I may be one instance of it.' Another letter to an unnamed peer took a different line: it appealed for compassion, on the ground that the adjournment to April seemed like 'an age to an old infirm man, especially shut up in a winter's prison', but it also argued that his imprisonment was a bad constitutional precedent, and went on: 'Your intercession to His Majesty, if it be general,

---

[1] Add. MSS. 28091, fo. 61; Southwell to Ormond, 18, 22, 25 Sept., *H.M.C. Ormond MSS.*, iv. 376–7; and references in my article (see above, p. 434, n. 1), p. 648.
[2] Marvell to Sir E. Harley, 17 Nov., in *Poems and Letters*, ii. 330.
[3] Job xxvii. 6.   [4] pp. 137–8 above.

is not like to be refused; if you are single, yet you have done honourably; and what I should have done for you.' This would have been an appeal for members of the peerage to take up his cause with the King.[1]

These letters were never sent, probably because of the transformation in the political scene at the beginning of December. The Earl of Feversham had been sent over to Louis XIV with proposals which it had been thought could have been the basis of a peace settlement; they would have involved the surrender by Louis of some of the cities which his forces had captured in Flanders, but he would have retained others, and Franche-Comté. On 2 December Feversham reported back with the news that Louis had rejected the proposals out of hand, and had not even made any counter-proposals. This left Charles in an awkward predicament: either he must give up his hopes of mediating between William and Louis, watch the war continue, and meet further pressure for action against France when Parliament met; or he must at least threaten action in support of William to make Louis see reason. Under Danby's urging Charles rather uneasily chose the latter alternative. On 3 December Parliament was adjourned, not until April, but only until 15 January; and the government began to make diplomatic and military preparations to threaten war against France.[2]

In this new situation Shaftesbury made one further petition to the King, again pleading not repentance but ill-health, 'and your petitioner well knowing your Majesty's innate goodness and leniency cannot think him the only person of all your subjects that is exempted from the benefit of it; especially since there is no man more devoted and faithful to your Majesty's government, person and interest'. In spite of its fulsome language, this was a declaration of defiance; and the failure of the petition must have been expected. Shaftesbury settled down to wait for a few weeks longer.[3]

During the months of December and January the sound reached him of the drums beating through the streets as recruits were raised for the armed forces. His visitors brought him news of the excited discussion which was going on about all this. Some who had long advocated action against France welcomed Charles's belated conversion to the idea. Others could not believe in it. In all opposition groups there is a natural tendency to oppose whatever policy is pursued by the government. Not only personal ambition but the very heat engendered by political conflict makes the primary objective of an opposition that of beating the other side, the wickedness of whose policy and motives can be taken for granted. Charles was indignant about one member of Parliament who, when told that it was

---

[1] The letters are printed in Locke's *Works* (1823), ix. 282–4. They are undated, but the last clearly, and the others in all probability, belong to the period between 26 Oct. and 3 Dec.

[2] Haley, op. cit. pp. 644–6.

[3] Coventry Papers at Longleat, ii. fo. 113. Miss Brown, p. 248, attributes another undated petition (ibid. fo. 110) to this period, but it appears more likely to be one of February 1678; see p. 439 below.

still uncertain whether war or peace would follow, said that it was all the same to him what the King chose, for he would every time maintain the opposite of the Court's choice.[1] In 1678 this powerful political instinct was supported by strong rational arguments. Charles had watched the French conquests of the past six years with apparent equanimity, and resisted all pressure to take action against them; was he really sincere in wanting to hold them up now? Observers noted that Charles, James, and the French ambassador Barrillon were frequently seen together, and 'separated laughing'.[2] The King's principal mistress had the English title of Duchess of Portsmouth, but she remained a Frenchwoman, on good confidential terms with Barrillon, whom she was privately informing that Charles did not really want the war that he was threatening.[3] If Charles was serious, why had he not called Parliament before January, and why did he then adjourn it further from 15 to 28 January? In any case, from their contacts with the Confederate ambassadors in London, Sir Thomas Littleton and others knew something of the diplomatic negotiations which were going on; they knew that Charles was prepared to see Louis make some substantial conquests, and that the reason why no settlement had been reached was disagreement over one or two towns in Flanders, principally Tournai. Was the government perhaps really aiming at securing a Parliamentary grant of money, and then using it not for war but to secure financial independence? Was it really aiming at raising troops, which could then be used for some nefarious purpose against parliamentary liberties? The times through which men had lived did not suggest that it was impossible, or even unlikely. The Spanish ambassador, Borgomanero, would not trust English troops into Ostend.[4] Some members were beginning to visit Barrillon and try to find out what they could from him.[5]

There were even some members who talked of safeguarding themselves against the newly raised troops by demanding the right to nominate their officers,[6] but in the end they decided to impose upon the King their own conception of the war. Instead of a limited war to restrict Louis's conquests, they called upon Charles for a total war, including a prohibition of all French trade, until Louis had been pushed back to the boundaries of the

---

[1] Schwerin, 8/18 Jan., 1678, *Briefe aus England*, p. 183.

[2] Sarotti, 4/14 Jan., in MS. continuation of *C.S.P. Ven.*

[3] Barrillon, 24 Jan./3 Feb.

[4] For all this, cf. C. L. Grose, 'The Anglo-Dutch Alliance of 1678' (1924), pp. 349–72, 526–51, Browning, *Danby*, ch. xii, and see Borgomanero's despatches, esp. that of 29 Jan./8 Feb. with its reference to the distrust of 'Lords Halifax, Holles, Cavendish and Winchester and all Littleton's party'. I propose to write in more detail elsewhere about the relations between members of Parliament and foreign ambassadors in the years 1677–8.

[5] Cf. Barrillon 14/24 Jan., 30 Jan./9 Feb. The first of these despatches refers to a visit from Buckingham's confidant, Sir Ellis Leighton, who one letter-writer says was sent by Buckingham and Shaftesbury into France (Daniel Finch to Sir J. Finch, 14 Jan., *H.M.C. Finch MSS.*, ii. 36); but Barrillon makes no mention of Shaftesbury.

[6] Barrillon, 14/24 Jan.

Treaty of the Pyrenees, and promised assistance when treaties for this purpose were produced. It was not until 18 February that the government secured, by a majority of only twenty, a promise of £1,000,000, 'for enabling His Majesty to enter into an actual war', and even then the details of how it should be raised would still have to be worked out. Three days earlier the Commons had, much to James's chagrin, rejected the Lords' Bill for 'explaining' the Test Act of 1673, suspecting that it would be used to give commissions to people who were 'popishly affected', and perhaps even to excuse 'a great person' from the Test; and refused to read the Secretary of State's list of the army officers and proposals for their 'entertainment'.[1] And about the same time there appeared on the scene Marvell's famous pamphlet, *The Growth of Popery and Arbitrary Government in England*. 'There has now for divers years a design been carried on to change the lawful government of England into an absolute tyranny, and to convert the established Protestant religion into downright Popery', it began. After laying down that, unlike other countries, England had only a limited monarchy, and delivering a slashing attack on the idolatries, corruptions and past inhumanities of Roman Catholicism, the pamphlet embarked on a narrative of an alleged conspiracy by persons unnamed 'to introduce a French slavery and . . . to establish the Roman idolatry'. This conspiracy was traced through from 1665 to 1678, with full weight given to the failure of the government to do anything to meet the French danger, and to the number of members of Parliament who 'are received into pensions, and know their pay-day, which they never fail of: insomuch that a great officer was pleased to say, "That they came about him like so many jack-daws for cheese at the end of every session" '. Like all influential pamphlets, it put into epigrammatic expression what many were already obscurely feeling; and if the names of the alleged conspirators were not given, the reader could supply them for himself.[2]

It was in this situation that Shaftesbury (to whom the pamphlet referred in laudatory terms[3]) decided that he must humiliate himself to the King and Lords for his release, to take part in all these activities. On 13 February he wrote to his brother-in-law, Secretary Henry Coventry, to ask him to tell the King that he was resolved to submit to the House's order, and to 'beg to be restored to (the King's) favour' like the other three lords. Unfortunately this preliminary step, though necessary, gave the King and Danby time to prepare their counter-measures; they were determined not to let Shaftesbury out if they could possibly avoid it. Next day in the Lords Halifax presented his uncle's petition, which said that he was ready

---

[1] *C.J.*, ix. 439–40; Grey, v. 153–5; Southwell to Ormond, 16 Feb., in *H.M.C. Ormond MSS.*, N.S. iv. 403–4; Barrillon, 18/28 Feb.; Sarotti, 15/25 Feb. (typescript continuation).

[2] Printed in Grosart's edition of Marvell's *Works* (1824), iv. 248–424. For the date of the pamphlet's appearance, cf. *C.S.P.D. 1677–8*, p. 659 (19 Feb.), and *C.S.P.D. 1678*, p. 110 (21 Feb.).

[3] Op. cit. iv. 291–2, 309, 316–17, 409.

to make his submission according to the House's directions, and he was supported by Clarendon and Essex 'and faintly by the Duke of Buckingham and some others'; but James and Danby were ready with arguments to oppose it. Danby argued that Shaftesbury had not made due application to the King, and that his action in appealing by *habeas corpus* in the previous June amounted to an additional contempt; so the petition was thrown out.[1]

In the following week the Earl tried again. He sent a further petition to the King, this time formally acknowledging that in maintaining that Parliament was dissolved he had been guilty of an 'ill-advised action' for which he asked pardon. The Marquis of Winchester presented a similar petition to the Lords for him on 20 February. It should have been abject enough for any neutral, for the word *humble* was used by Shaftesbury seven times in two short paragraphs—and another petition to the King raised the score to ten—but even this degree of humility was not sufficient. The Lord Chancellor, Finch, told the House on the King's behalf that the King had not thought fit to declare his opinion until the peers had taken into consideration the Earl's attempt to free himself by appealing to the King's Bench. Acting on this hint, the House resolved by some four votes to order the records of that appeal to be brought for inspection. Next day Shaftesbury tried to forestall this new attempt to keep him in the Tower by 'casting himself at your lordships' feet' and acknowledging, in another petition presented by Holles, that he might have erred in this too; but the Lords resolved that it was a breach of privilege for any peer committed by the House to bring a suit of *habeas corpus*. All that the Earl was granted, was permission to defend himself at the bar of the House against this further charge, and James did not seem to regret the late dinners which these debates made necessary, for his enemy was still far from free.[2]

On 25 February, when Shaftesbury was due to appear at the bar, Charles had his dinner taken to Westminster for him: it was a wise precaution, for the debate lasted all day until five o'clock. Shaftesbury made a full apology for all his actions, saying that he would never have brought his *habeas corpus* if he had realized that it involved a breach of privilege. His eloquence, his show of repentance, the danger to his health to which he referred, and perhaps the feeling that he had been more than adequately punished for what he had said a year earlier—if indeed that was a crime— had their effect, notwithstanding the opposition of the King's ministers

[1] Shaftesbury to H. Coventry, 13 Feb., Coventry MSS., ii. fo. 132; to the King, [n.d.], ibid. fo. 112; *H.M.C. Ninth Report*, ii. 102; Lady Chaworth to L. Roos, 16 Feb., *H.M.C. Rutland MSS.*, ii. 46; Southwell to Ormond, 16 Feb., *H.M.C. Ormond*, N.S. iv. 404.
[2] Petitions to the King, n.d., Coventry MSS. ii, fos. 94, 110; to the House, Add. MSS. 15892, fo. 57; *C.S.P.D. 1677–8*, pp. 660, 662–3; Van Beuningen, 22 Feb./4 Mar., Add. MSS. 17677, DD; *H.M.C. Ninth Report*, ii. 102; *State Letters of Henry Earl of Clarendon*, ed. S. W. Singer (1828), i. 7, 8.

and the bishops, and Danby had to fall back on his last line of defence. His supporter, Lord Arundel of Trerice, reported that on that famous occasion in the King's Bench the Earl had spoken some words 'of a dangerous nature'. Danby and James both seconded this vigorously, but in the end unsuccessfully, because they could not prove that the Earl had uttered the words complained of. The two shorthand writers who were called in, Rushworth and Blayney, said that after the trial in Westminster Hall their versions of the proceedings had not agreed, they had concocted a joint account and consequently could not swear to Shaftesbury's words. (Blayney had earlier served in his household, and Rushworth later voted for Exclusion.) In these circumstances Danby's arguments seemed vindictive and unreasonable. Shaftesbury was called on to recite a prescribed form of words to the House, and remanded to the Tower only until the King had been formally addressed for his release.[1]

To Danby's mortification, therefore, on 27 February, 1678, Shaftesbury again took his place in the House of Lords, at a very inconvenient moment for the government. Apparently there was one last attempt to bluff him into staying away, for Charles let it be known that he wished him to go off to Dorset until the session was over; but Shaftesbury's reply was that he had grown so used to the Tower that he would rather go back there than leave London.[2] Yet some propaganda advantage could be obtained for the government from Shaftesbury's humble acknowledgement of error, and a pamphlet duly appeared, called *Honesty's Best Policy, or, Penitence the sum of Prudence*. Quoting Scripture, 'He that turns many to righteousness, shall shine as the stars for ever and ever',[3] the anonymous author considered it 'a charitable public-good work' to publicize Shaftesbury's repentance so that others might be encouraged to follow his example. All his humble petitions, and the speech he had made on 25 February, were printed *verbatim*. Much of the rest of the pamphlet described recent events in a way similar to that of the *Pacquet of Advices to the Men of Shaftesbury*; the Earl was again accused of stirring up the discontent of the previous years, by seeking popularity on the Exchange, inciting Jenks, holding 'many a costly dinner, and deep potations, for the putting as many members as they could out of their senses', and instituting 'offices of intelligence, to coin news for the coffee-houses; and an academy for inventing seditious and treasonable pamphlets, with directions how to print and spread them, to edify both City and kingdom into an oblivion of their allegiance . . . and for the quickening of a diligent correspondence of their country-agents, with the supreme Council of the Directors at London'. As in the previous pamphlet, readers were warned against a terrible Machiavellian figure who

---

[1] Barrillon, 25 Feb./7 Mar.; Christie, ii. 258–9; *C.S.P.D. 1677–8*, pp. 672–3; Lady Chaworth to Lord Roos, 26 Feb., *H.M.C. Rutland MSS.*, ii. 47; Southwell to Ormond, 28 Feb., *H.M.C. Ormond MSS.*, N.S. iv. 408.

[2] Schwerin, 1/11 Mar., *Briefe aus England*, p. 223.   [3] Daniel xii. 3.

was alleged to be manipulating everything. But the writer also took the opportunity to score a few points against Andrew Marvell's *Growth of Popery*, which had appeared in the meantime, and had praised Shaftesbury. At the time when Popery was alleged to be growing before 1673, Shaftesbury had been in power, and a passage was quoted from his speech to Parliament on 5 February 1673, to the effect that the Church of England was the King's constant care, and that religion was safe. The writer went on to contend that Shaftesbury was unlucky to have as his defender a man like the writer of the *Growth of Popery* who attacked Parliament, Duke of York, ministers and Court, and even the King. 'It looks ugly; but far be it from us, to think that there is any understanding betwixt him and the author. 'Tis only his lordship's ill luck, that in divers other pamphlets the knaves have been so bold as to commend him: and who can help it?'

The writer thus scored some polemical points and made some skilful insinuations about Shaftesbury's secret machinations, at the expense of eventually contributing to make him the opposition leader and hero which he scarcely was as yet. There is no satisfactory evidence that he had yet a very great following either inside or outside Parliament. No doubt the 'martyrdom' of his imprisonment helped to raise his standing with many inveterate opponents of the government; but his release was not greeted with bonfires or any show of popular enthusiasm. The Lords who had released him had not done so from any devotion to his person. Even Salisbury had given his support only by proxy; and, curiously enough, the Earl owed something to the help afforded by a few of the Catholic peers who did not follow James's lead, perhaps because as a minority group themselves they too feared the possibility of future victimization in the same way as Shaftesbury. One new supporter for the Earl was, however, Arthur Capel, Earl of Essex. Essex's grandmother had been Shaftesbury's stepmother, and the house at Cassiobury in Hertfordshire was well known to Anthony Ashley Cooper in his boyhood; but more than this is needed to account for his gravitation into the opposition. He was an upright, serious, conscientious and independent-minded man, widely respected by all except the friends of his rival in Ireland, Ormond: 'a sober, wise, judicious, and pondering person, not illiterate beyond the rate of most noblemen in this age, very well versed in English history and affairs, industrious, frugal and every way accomplished', according to Evelyn, who was just the man to appreciate these virtues when they were unfashionable at Charles's Court. His background was far from being one of rebellion; indeed, his father's Royalism had cost his head in 1649, and it was this, and his obvious honesty, which earned him the Lord-Lieutenancy of Ireland in 1672. During Essex's period of office he had corresponded with Shaftesbury in terms of respect and had acquired a dislike of almost everyone at the English Court. Now, his complaints of corruption and Catholic influence aggravated by his replacement as Lord

Lieutenant by Ormond, he took the first step on the road which led eventually to suicide after the Rye House Plot.[1]

No sooner was Shaftesbury back in the Lords than he complained that his menial servant Cowper had been arrested at the suit of Mrs. Anne Hustwhatt and other creditors. The committee of privileges, to which this incident was referred, never reported, and the matter was probably Shaftesbury's way of announcing that he was once more in his place and a person who could not be ignored with impunity.[2] But the main battle was not now being fought in the Lords, where the government's position was for the moment unchallengeable.

Shaftesbury's release coincided with the sensational news of the surrender of the great city of Ghent to the forces of Louis XIV. The news was a few days premature, but what was certain was that the French armies had begun their campaign long before the Dutch and such forces as the Spaniards could muster would be able to make headway. Charles II professed to share the desire of many Englishmen to rescue Flanders from the grasp of France; the question in the minds of the men of the 'Country Party' was whether he could be trusted with the money and the armed forces necessary to save it. No sooner was the question asked than they answered 'No'. This was partly the result of their interpretation of the active help or benevolent neutrality which Charles had afforded to Louis between 1672 and 1677; it was partly a result of prejudice; and it was partly their conclusion from the evidence of their eyes, which showed them that the French ambassador, Barrillon, and the King's French mistress, the Duchess of Portsmouth, were no less intimate with Charles than they had been before. Precisely at this time, too, the younger Ruvigny returned after conveying a message to Louis XIV; and this mission was looked upon with great disfavour even though no one outside the King's circle knew that the peace terms which he had conveyed included a provision for a large French subsidy for the King. On his return Ruvigny was known to have paid an immediate visit to the Duke of York, and to have stayed with him for two hours.[3]

The opposition leaders were positive, therefore, that they must oppose the King's foreign policy, or what was officially declared to be the King's foreign policy, of threatening to join the Confederates against France; and what mattered was whether they could prevent the House of Commons

---

[1] Salisbury to Shaftesbury, 23 Feb., Shaftesbury Papers, VI A, 323; Barrillon, 25 Feb./7 Mar., 27 Feb./9 Mar.; Southwell to Ormond, 2 Mar., *H.M.C. Ormond MSS.*, N.S. iv. 411; Christie, ii. 101–2, xlvii–liv; Evelyn, ed. E. S. De Beer (1955), iv. 201. Evelyn was unduly disparaging about Essex's 'illiteracy'.

[2] *H.M.C. Ninth Report*, ii. 107.

[3] Southwell to Ormond, 2 Mar., *H.M.C. Ormond MSS.*, N.S. iv. 410; Waldstein, 1/11, 18/28 Mar., Klopp, ii. 98, 91, n. 1; cf. speeches of Clarges and William Harbord in the debate of 14 Mar., Grey, v. 234, 241; and the account of the debate in MSS. Carte 72, fo. 359. See Browning, *Danby*, i. 271, for the context of Ruvigny's mission in Danby's policy.

from supporting that policy. There were three different tactics which they might adopt. One was to put pressure to bear on the King to bring to an end the existing state of uncertainty by declaring war on France; in this way Charles might either be induced to commit himself at last, or have his insincerity revealed. On 14 March, therefore, Sir Gilbert Gerrard moved that the House should address the King for an immediate declaration of war, and the opposition had so much the better of the argument in grand committee, that proposals for the dismissal of Barrillon and the recall of the English ambassadors from Paris and Nijmegen were added without a division.[1] Embarrassed by such an address at a time when he had completed neither his military preparations nor his alliances, Danby gained time by persuading the House to ask for the concurrence of the Lords, and foreign policy was debated there on the 16th and 18th. Along with Essex, Halifax, Buckingham, Holles, Clarendon and Wharton Shaftesbury pressed for an immediate declaration of war. Shaftesbury was able to score one good debating point against Danby, who claimed to have a paper in his pocket in which the Spanish ambassador, Borgomanero, declared himself against an immediate declaration of war. Shaftesbury lured him on to repeat this statement and then called upon him to produce the paper in question, thus reducing Danby to confusion because, as Shaftesbury had known or guessed, the context of Borgomanero's statement had been an urgent demand for Danby to press on with the still incomplete alliances with the Confederate powers. But though the Earl enjoyed this little triumph, the vote was strongly in the government's favour. The address was sent back to the Commons with the word 'immediately' replaced by 'with all the expedition that can possibly consist with the safety of your Majesty's affairs', and all reference to ambassadors omitted.[2] Since the Commons would not agree to this, the address never reached the King: but Danby's evasion of it did not lessen the suspicion of the government's policy.

The opposition had, however, a second and quite contrary tactical move at their disposal at this same period. If they could not find out in any other way whether the newly raised troops were to be used against France or not, they might make a secret approach to Barrillon on the basis that it was not in the interests either of the opposition or of Louis XIV for Charles to become too powerful, and see what could be discovered.

There had been contacts with the French ambassador well before Shaftesbury's release from the Tower. They had been made easier by the relationship between Russell and Barrillon's colleague Ruvigny, who also had the advantage of being a Protestant and was thus acceptable to many Englishmen. By the beginning of February Holles, Buckingham and Russell were talking to Ruvigny and predicting that the Commons would

---

[1] *C.J.* ix. 454–5; Grey, v. 223–50; MSS. Carte 72, fos. 359–62.

[2] *L.J.* xiii. 185–6; Borgomanero, 23 Mar./2 Apr.; Southwell to Ormond, 19 Mar., *H.M.C. Ormond MSS.*, N.S. iv. 416–17; Schwerin, 19/29 Mar., *Briefe*, pp. 233–4.

not vote supplies. At the beginning of March, when Ruvigny returned from his brief errand to France, there were more important talks. He brought assurances to Holles and Russell that Louis was convinced that it was not in his interest to make Charles absolute master of his kingdom, and would help to bring about the dissolution of Parliament which they wanted. In reply Russell promised to work underhand to prevent further votes of money for Charles and to attach unacceptable conditions to the money already voted; and he promised to bring Shaftesbury into this line of action as 'the only man to whom he would speak frankly about it'. But he was uneasy, suspecting that Louis was really willing that Charles should declare war on him in order to get money and then make peace. To dispel this suspicion, Ruvigny offered money to assist in persuading the Commons not to vote the money which Charles needed, and asked for the names of members who could be bribed. This offer Russell rejected (on this occasion at least); what he wanted at this time was simply the assurance that there was no secret understanding between Charles and Louis, and this he had now received to his satisfaction. They agreed to aim at bringing about a dissolution, and it was arranged that Ruvigny should meet Shaftesbury 'one of these days' at Russell's house.[1]

Whether this meeting actually took place is very doubtful: it is certainly not described in Barrillon's despatches. But at the beginning of April Barrillon did report that Buckingham, Shaftesbury, Russell and Holles had given him to understand (*m'ont fait entendre*) that they were afraid of the uses to which the new levies might be put. There was the possibility that they might be used to strengthen the royal authority, and then (they insinuated) Charles would be able to turn all England's resources against Louis; so would it not be best for Louis, as well as for themselves, if he were now to call upon Charles to say clearly whether he was meditating peace or war? In parrying this request Barrillon saw clearly that its purpose was once more to make sure that there was no secret engagement between the two kings, and he noted that none of the politicians named, with the possible exception of Buckingham, would enter into any formal engagement with France.[2] These were exploratory talks, and nothing more. At some unknown date later on, Russell among others accepted French money, though it would be impossible to prove that this induced them to take any political action which they would not have taken without it. So far as Shaftesbury is concerned, it is uncertain whether the phrase quoted above implies his presence at an actual meeting, but in any case no later meetings are even hinted at. In the Popish Plot period there is no sign that he and Barrillon were personally acquainted; and it can be taken as certain that he did not receive any French money at any time. Barrillon did think it

---

[1] Barrillon, 4/14 Feb., 14/24 Feb., 4/14 Mar. (J. Dalrymple, *Memoirs of Great Britain and Ireland*, 1771–3, ii, App. 131–2), 14/24 Mar., (ibid. 134–5).
[2] 1/11 Apr., ibid. pp. 136–8.

policy to pay money to Thomas Bennet, who was close to the Earl; but if he had thought he had any kind of pecuniary link with the Earl himself he would certainly have mentioned it, and he did not do so. Indeed at one point Ralph Montagu urged Barrillon to offer Shaftesbury a bribe in terms which plainly implied that no such connexion already existed.[1] Whatever the guilt of Russell and others in accepting money secretly from a foreign power which they denounced in public, all that Shaftesbury derived from his contact with the French through Russell was some useful information about the state of the relations between Louis XIV and Charles II.

In all probability Shaftesbury was most active in pursuing a third tactical plan to attack the government's position. Some members of the 'Country Party' might still wish to push the King into a patriotic war with France, but he had little faith in that. He preferred to bring out into the open the hatred of Popery and the suspicions of the government's 'soundness' on religion which had long existed, and which were now fostered by the sight of James, Duke of York's obvious eagerness to be in command of troops. Whatever foreign policy might be best to halt the advance of Bourbon absolutism and Catholicism on the Continent, the basic fact of English domestic politics remained what it had been since 1673, the Catholicism of the heir to the throne. Until this had been dealt with, agreement on anything else was impossible.

It is significant that on 14 March, when other members of the Country Party were more concerned with foreign affairs and pressing the King to declare war, Shaftesbury's ally Russell was anxious for the grand committee to consider 'the apprehensions we are under of Popery, and a standing army', and there was support for the idea that Catholics must be rigorously excluded from the armed forces.[2] Two days later Russell returned to the attack and successfully moved for a day on which to debate the growth and progress of Popery, and rumours reached James that it was intended to move that all recusants should be forbidden to possess arms. Danby sent for some of his friends in the Commons to warn them to oppose motions which were designed only 'to give jealousy of the government', and he was successful in deferring the debate until the day fixed for Parliament's adjournment, 27 March. But when that day came, some one in the opposition (possibly Shaftesbury), had laid his plans with particular care. One Arnold, who was later to attain some notoriety by a faked attack on him during the Popish Plot,[3] was brought to the bar of the House to describe the activities of Catholic priests in Monmouthshire. It seems that he and others had been turned out of the commission of peace after

---

[1] Barrillon, 4/14 Dec. 1679, and cf. pp. 567–8 below.

[2] The Test Act of 1673 excluded Catholics only from commands and places of trust within the realm of England and in the navy. It might therefore have been possible for James to command forces in Flanders. Grey, v. 224, 241–2; Barrillon, 16/26 Mar.

[3] J. Pollock, *The Popish Plot* (1903), pp. 273–4, 394–9.

helping in the defeat of the Marquis of Worcester's candidate at a by-election, and had been replaced by others who 'were kind to their Popish neighbours'; and having lamented his hardships to 'some of the members' they persuaded him to tell his story to the House. At the bar he talked of Mass being celebrated both in public and in private; of a Jesuit college in the county; and of Worcester's steward, 'an undoubted Papist', being made a justice of the peace. The House, roused by this appalling news, voted Arnold their thanks, and when some of Worcester's friends foolishly hissed the motion, they were told for their pains that Arnold's was 'a cause, for which every of them that deserved to sit there, ought to fry in the fire if the occasion required'. Fortunately the members did not have to go to those melodramatic lengths; instead, spurred on by Russell, they adopted the more prosaic course of planning a conference with the Lords on the suppression of Popery when they next met, and then dispersed for Easter. But the incident was one more reminder, if it were needed, of the amount of inflammable material which might easily burst into flame, either by spontaneous combustion, or by arson. Four days later Charles spoke at length to Barrillon about the distrust caused by his brother's religion, and about the failure of all attempts to reassure people.[1]

Except for two short meetings which were mainly taken up with the election of a new Speaker during the real or supposed illness of Sir Edward Seymour, the House did not meet again until 29 April. In the meantime the likelihood of England being involved in war had diminished. The Dutch peace party, in spite of all William of Orange's efforts, were suggesting that the political situation in England made it vain to hope for effective English help and persuaded the States-General to negotiate with Louis XIV; the Spaniards, whatever their public protestations, secretly recognized the necessity of peace and were concerned only with using the possibility of English assistance to extract better terms from Louis. Danby was reluctant to abandon hope of winning popularity for himself and Charles by a policy of hostility to France; but Charles had never had much stomach for war, and was concerned only with escaping from it by doing sufficient to satisfy public opinion and William of Orange, and not enough to lose the friendship of Louis XIV, from whom he hoped for a large new subsidy as part of a general settlement. On his instructions Danby reluctantly despatched the letter of 25 March which asked Louis (vainly) for 6 million livres a year for three years, and which later figured in his impeachment.[2] Of all this the opposition leaders knew nothing. Those who were in contact with Barrillon continued anxiously to seek for assurances that there was no secret understanding between his master and Charles II, and for the

---

[1] Grey, v. 253; C.J. ix. 459, 462–3; Barrillon, 18/28 Mar., 28 Mar./7 Apr., 1/11 Apr.; Reresby, pp. 136–7; MSS. Carte 72, fos. 382–3. Sir Thomas Clarges claimed acquaintance with Arnold (Grey, v. 275–6).

[2] Browning, *Danby*, i. 271–3, 305–9.

moment Barrillon was able honestly to give them.[1] The decreasing likelihood of war, however, made it increasingly urgent to secure the disbanding of Charles's new forces, and this became the immediate objective of many of the opposition.

While Danby strove to keep together his disintegrating Court Party, probably by an increase in the amount of 'secret service money' paid to members,[2] some one in opposition was financing the publication of the pamphlet *A Seasonable Argument to Persuade all the Grand Juries in England to Petition for a new Parliament, or A List of the Principal Labourers in the Great Design of Popery and Arbitrary Power, who have Betrayed their Country to the Conspirators and Bargained with them to maintain a Standing Army in England under the Command of the Bigoted Popish Duke, who by the Assistance of the Lord Lauderdale's Scotch Army, the Forces in Ireland, and those in France, hopes to bring all back to Rome*. This listed and exaggerated the number of members who had Court offices and pensions.[3] And from 15 April a committee of the Commons sat to review Arnold's evidence and prepare for the planned conference with the Lords on Popery.[4]

Their chance came on the opening day of the new session. After Lord Chancellor Finch had made a long speech justifying the King's foreign policy in the last twelve months, putting the blame for an unsatisfactory situation on others, and with apparent frankness asking the Houses for their advice, the House turned to the report of its committee on Popery. The Reasons which the committee proposed to offer to the Lords for the enactment of new penal laws detailed the information of Arnold and others about Catholic priests, J.P.s, and sympathizers in the 'black spot' of Monmouthshire, and then, after arguing the inefficacy of the existing penal laws, concluded by asking for a speedy remedy, 'because the Commons cannot think it suitable to their trust to lay any further charge upon the people, how urgent soever the occasion be that require it, till their minds be satisfied' on this matter of Popery. In spite of the courtiers' protests that the committee had no authority to include this refusal of taxation, the majority insisted on retaining this clause. 'You cannot save the Protestant religion', declared Sir Thomas Meres dramatically, 'but by this paper. Farewell Parliaments and all laws and government, and the Protestant religion, for they are all one'. To the King, who was 'in a rage', to the Confederates and the French it was proof that the Commons could not be relied on to support any active foreign policy which Charles might pursue, and it was now a foregone conclusion that the war would come to a speedy end to the advantage of France. Three days later Ruvigny carried

---

[1] Barrillon, 15/25, 18/28 Apr., 25 Apr./5 May, 29 Apr./9 May.
[2] Browning, *Danby*, i. 274–5.
[3] *C.S.P.D. 1678*, p. 98; *English Historical Documents, 1660–1714* (1953), pp. 237–49.
[4] Grey, v. 269–76; Southwell to Ormond, *H.M.C. Ormond MSS.*, N.S. iv. 422.

over to Louis Charles's acceptance of the terms which the French had put forward at the peace conference in Nijmegen.[1]

On 4 May the Lords discussed the Commons' Reasons about Popery, and at last after many months ordered their Growth of Popery Bill to be read for a second time two days later. The Lords were less excitable on the subject, and less inclined to hurry on something which they knew would be unpalatable to the King and to the heir to the throne. The only peer whose speech attracted attention was Shaftesbury, who maintained that the chief danger did not come from priests or Jesuits or other Catholics living quietly in the counties, 'but from those who live in this city and apply themselves to an arbitrary government and to introduce the Catholic religion entirely, and there are great personages . . .'. As he spoke these words a look and gesture indicated the Duke of York, who was present. Shaftesbury was identifying himself with that section of the Commons which was preoccupied with James.[2]

It is possible that Shaftesbury had something to do with the Commons' outburst on 7 May, when, taking advantage of the absence of some of the courtiers at dinner, the Country Party forced through a resolution that the King be asked to remove his councillors, and specifically Shaftesbury's enemy Lauderdale. It is significant that Danby's supporter, Sir Edmund Jennings, tried to counter-attack by suggesting that the present misfortunes dated from the Stop of the Exchequer, the Declaration of Indulgence, and the breaking of the Triple Alliance, with which Court propaganda had tried to associate Shaftesbury's name; and it was the Earl's friend, Russell, who seconded the proposal that Lauderdale be named in the address. Lauderdale, of course, did not suffer in any way, for Charles had no intention of removing the man who controlled Scotland; but the King was unusually bad-tempered about it, losing his normal self-control 'which never transported him beyond an innocent puffing and spitting'.[3] For this vote on top of the preceding ones indicated that the House was, in spite of all Danby's efforts, out of control; and James, giving up his ambitions of military glory, told his nephew William that peace was necessary, 'for now the ill men in the House strike directly at the King's authority' and aimed at leaving him the powers only of a Doge of Venice.[4]

The session continued for two more months, and no peace was actually signed at Nijmegen until 31 July. Almost nothing is known of Shaftesbury's activities during this period, and so it is not necessary to describe the course

---

[1] C.J. ix. 464–71; Grey, v. 276–87; Temple, Works, i. 354–5; Mignet, Négotiations Relatives à la succession d'Espagne, iv. 572–4.

[2] L.J. xiii. 212; Sarotti, 10/20 May (unpublished section of C.S.P. Ven. in P.R.O.); Barrillon, 5/15 May.

[3] Grey, v. 321*–61, esp. pp. 335*, 358; Fountainhall, Historical Observations, p. 148, cit. by Airy, in Burnet, ii. 149, n. 2. Henry Savile, who had voted for the Address, was ordered out of the King's sight and presence 'for ever'.

[4] James to William, 21 May, C.S.P.D. 1678, pp. 182–3.

of events in detail. The essential facts are that the King and Danby wished to retain the Army in being until the peace was signed; they needed it as a diplomatic counter to influence peace terms and to induce Louis to pay a subsidy in return for England's benevolent neutrality. Many of the opposition, on the other hand, feared a possible *coup d'autorité* by the government to extricate itself from its difficulties with the aid of the troops in and around London. The sound of their drums beating as they marched to take the Test Act oaths led Sir John Coventry to exclaim in the House that 'These redcoats may fight against Magna Charta', and these alarmist sentiments were widely shared.[1] There were still some opposition leaders, like Littleton, who clung as long as they could to an unrealistic hope of fighting the French in alliance with the Holy Roman Emperor; but most wanted to see the troops disbanded as soon as possible, and were prepared to vote taxes to pay them off with much more alacrity than they had shown to pay for a possible war.

The bill which was prepared laid down that the troops should be disbanded by 30 June, and one little fact which attracted some attention was that the King's illegitimate son, the Duke of Monmouth, who had not previously been beloved by the opposition, was winning some popularity by talking publicly about the need for such a prompt disbandment, even though the Duke of York disliked it.[2] But while the bill was still in committee in the Lords the meandering course of the diplomatic negotiations at the peace congress at Nijmegen took one last temporary turn, which did not ultimately affect the terms of the Treaty but did affect Anglo-French relations. Louis XIV's ambassadors announced that his forces would not evacuate those Flanders towns which he had promised to return to Spain until the lost possessions of his Swedish ally had been returned. This was greeted everywhere as a trick to enable him to continue the war against a coalition which was by now in complete disarray; and Charles himself resented it as a breach of faith. He knew that he could not justify either to his subjects or to his nephew William a situation in which Louis remained in possession of everything that he had conquered since 1672; and he determined that he and the Dutch must act together against it. Accordingly on 19 June he relayed to the Lords a Dutch appeal to hold up the disbandment of the Army, and two days later the Lords amended the date of disbandment in the bill from 30 June to 27 July in the case of the forces in England, and 24 August for the forces which were already in Flanders or were to be sent there.

Some of the Commons were frankly bewildered by all this. Was there to be war after all? The feeling of frustration was expressed by Littleton, who had once clamoured for war, but now (said Secretary Williamson) 'told me, we had so foiled them, they would never be more for war'. But

---

[1] Barrillon, 23 May/2 June, 6/16 June; Grey, v. 287.
[2] Barrillon, 3/13 June.

FF

the general feeling was that this was no more serious than Charles's previous professions of readiness to resist France. Even some of Danby's followers, like Reresby, saw Charles, James and Barrillon 'very merry and intimate' at the Duchess of Portsmouth's lodgings, and concluded that the new talk of a war was not in earnest. Members of the Country Party were alarmed; they felt that the crisis had been manufactured as an excuse to keep the Army in being, and that some plot between the Court and William lay beneath it. It was odd that the King's message came on the day after the rejection of a request by him for an additional increase of £300,000 a year in his ordinary peace-time revenue. At the same time James's very keenness to win popularity by a policy of hostility to France only made him more distrusted and more unpopular.[1]

The opposition in the Commons, therefore, although depleted in numbers because many had gone into the country thinking that the session was dead, seized on the constitutional issue of the Lords' inability to amend a money bill, and threw out the peers' amendment. The Lords, on the other side, maintained their view and rejected a proviso which the lower House put forward as a compromise: Shaftesbury, Wharton, Essex and two others signed a protest. The peers' action was, as the Brandenburg ambassador noted, only a sham-fight (*ein Spiegelfechten*), encouraged by the King to enable him to keep his troops together in the meantime. In the end the Commons preserved their constitutional rights by combining the Disbanding Bill with another covering the cost of the military preparations made in the previous twelve months; this new comprehensive measure went through, and on 15 July Parliament was prorogued, first until 1 August, and eventually until October.[2] The international situation remained uncertain for another fortnight. Sir William Temple on the King's behalf negotiated a treaty in which England and the United Provinces declared that, if before 1/11 August Louis XIV had not agreed to evacuate the Flanders towns in question, they would declare war on him. But, as might have been expected, on the very day on which a Dutch ultimatum expired, Louis's ambassadors found an excuse to recede from their position and to agree to the evacuation. The French and Dutch signed the Treaty of Nijmegen, and in spite of William of Orange's attempt to defeat the French army a few days later before the news of the peace had officially reached him, the long foreign crisis was over.

By the Treaty of Nijmegen Charles of England was freed from the embarrassments which Louis XIV's successes had caused him in the last two years. He was no longer perpetually faced with the agonizing choice

---

[1] *L.J.* xiii. 255, 257; *C.J.* ix. 501–2; Grey, vi. 108; Longford to Ormond, 22 June, *H.M.C. Ormond MSS.*, N.S. iv. 152; *C.S.P.D. 1678*, p. 225; Van Beuningen and van Leeuwen, 21 June/1 July, Add. MSS. 17677, SSS; Reresby, p. 149; Barrillon, 24 June/4 July, 25 June/5 July, 1/11, 15/25 July; Schwerin, 28 June/8 July, *Briefe*, p. 288.

[2] *C.J.* ix. 503–11; Longford to Ormond, as in previous note, 152–3; *L.J.* xiii. 259–60, 289; Schwerin, 5/15 July, p. 292.

between yielding to the pressure of public opinion and his minister Danby to declare war, and the friendship with Louis which be valued. To outward appearance he was stronger because of that, and stronger too because he had not in fact disbanded his forces, and had used the money which the Supply Bill had appropriated for that purpose to maintain them. The drawback was that sooner or later the forces would have to be paid off, and that in the autumn the House of Commons would meet in a mood of exasperation at the way in which the government's policy had oscillated, and declarations of hostility to France had ended in a peace which consolidated most of Louis's gains. Moreover, Charles's general financial needs remained unsolved; Danby had failed to induce the Commons to add to the King's ordinary revenue; and at the same time the hope of obtaining a French subsidy had been lost. On 17/27 May it had been agreed that there should be one as the price of England's peace settlement, but the one consequence of the Anglo-Dutch co-operation in June and July had been to wreck this agreement. One of the basic facts of the next two and a half years is that Charles had to contend with his Parliaments without French money to help him out of his difficulties.

However, these disadvantages were all hidden from the Country Party. From their point of view all their efforts in the last eighteen months had achieved nothing. On the Continent Louis XIV's power had increased and the coalition against him, not having received English help, had broken up. At home none of the legislation which they wanted had been passed, as members pointed out when for the fourth time they vainly sent up to the Lords a bill to exclude Papists from the House. In the Commons they were just strong enough to baulk the Court, but not strong enough, in face of all Danby's pensions, to take command of the House; and in the Lords, after Shaftesbury's failure in 1677, they were helpless. The hated Army was still in existence; and the problem of an heir to the throne who was addicted to Catholicism and of an authoritarian cast of mind grew steadily more urgent as the King grew older.

Shaftesbury must have been reflecting on these lines when, correctly deciding that there would be no war, he set out on 25 July for his Dorset estates.[1] He had just celebrated his fifty-seventh birthday: he was not an old man by twentieth-century standards, but his health had never been good, and now he was bent and walked with the aid of a stick. As events turned out, he had only four and a half years to live; and at the end of July 1678, his political prospects seemed to be dim. He had burnt his boats and was the Court's most inveterate and dangerous enemy,[2] but he

---

[1] The date is discoverable from an account book, now at Wimborne St. Giles, which details the expenses of the journey.

[2] Cf. the Speaker's letter to Williamson, 28 July, C.S.P.D. 1678, pp. 321-2, for the latter's desire to guard against any action by Shaftesbury at the brief meeting of Parliament on 1 August.

was far from being the acknowledged leader of all the forces hostile to the Court. His positive successes since his dismissal in 1673 had been few. When he journeyed to the house at Wimborne St. Giles to refresh himself on the estates which he had not seen since the end of 1676, only an unquestionable optimist could have hoped to make his mark on English politics.

Yet by the time he returned in October his own political prospects and those of the Court and the Country Parties had completely changed. For Titus Oates had made his 'revelations' about the Popish Plot.

CHAPTER XXI

THE POPISH PLOT (1678)

O N 13 August 1678, as King Charles II was about to go for his
daily stroll in St. James's Park, he was stopped by one Christopher
Kirkby, a gentleman at his Court who sometimes helped him when
the fancy took him to pursue some dilettante experiments in chemistry
in the royal laboratory. Presuming on this acquaintance, Kirkby waylaid
his master on his way out of the Palace and told him of a Jesuit plot to kill
him, either by shooting or, if that failed, by poison. Charles was very cool
about the matter: he continued his usual walk regardless of any armed
Catholics who might be waiting to assassinate him. This was probably less
an act of deliberate personal courage than a correct reading of Kirkby's
character, which Charles knew to be extremely unbalanced where Catholics
were concerned; and anyway since 1660 there had been frequent idle talk
of plots against him, both Puritan and Catholic, and nothing had come of
any of it. At that very moment Cromwell's son-in-law, John Claypole,
was in the Tower accused of discussing the possibility of ambushing the
King and the Duke of York on their way to Newmarket.[1] Such tales had to
be investigated as a matter of routine, but by 1678 they were not taken very
seriously.

Yet this plot was to be blown up into something much greater than
anything which had preceded it; for behind Kirkby was the half-crazed
preacher Dr. Israel Tonge, 'hardly ever without a plot in his head, and a
pen in his hand', and behind Tonge loomed the monstrous figure of the
loathsome Titus Oates, whose considerable gifts for successful lying
happened to coincide with the political needs of the hour. 'The one bred
the maggots, and the other vented them.'[2] And the Plot stories which they
propagated were the centre of British politics for the next four years.

The whole Popish Plot episode deserves the revulsion which most
people have felt about it ever since: no-one could pretend that the atmosphere of hysteria and lying was anything but discreditable. Yet at the outset
a warning against exaggeration is necessary. Many of our ideas about the
crisis are clouded by the writing of nineteenth-century British historians
who lived in a time of settled constitutional development and did not find
it easy to project themselves into the situation of 1678; and the more Whig
they were in sympathy, the more zealous their defence of the Glorious
Revolution of 1688, the more anxious they were to dissociate themselves
from the violence and hysteria of 1678 and to regard them as an aberration.

[1] C.S.P.D. 1678, pp. 295, 299, 301, 359; State Trials, viii. 428.
[2] R. L'Estrange, Brief History of the Times (1687–8), iii. 3.

Yet to a historian of the twentieth century the curious feature of the crisis is how little violence there actually was. With our knowledge of the passions which can be roused by different ideologies and man's propensity for rioting in support of them, it is striking to see how few lives were lost in these years. Some thirty-five people lost their lives by judicial process[1]; there was not one death as a result of rioting. Elections were rowdy, but then they were commonly so before the nineteenth-century Reform Bills. Much has been made of the Pope-burning processions celebrating the anniversaries of Gunpowder Plot and the accession of Queen Elizabeth; but the really significant point to be made about these demonstrations is that when they were over people went home quietly—or if not quietly, without loss of life or notable destruction of property. Tory propaganda insisted that ''41 is come again', but there was less mob action than in 1641, not more. No mob demonstrated outside Whitehall and Westminster as they had done at the time of Strafford's trial. It is true that Charles II possessed more guards than his father had, but they were not very numerous, and, as the Catholic Father Warner noted,[2] they and two small guns, 'mere terrors for children', would have been a pitifully thin defence against an organized and determined *journée*. To someone familiar with European history since 1789, the Popish Plot crisis is remarkably orderly.

Our ideas of the Popish Plot are also warped by the notion that any honest, sensible person ought to have seen through the farrago of nonsense which Titus Oates put forward—with his talk of plans for poisoning or stabbing the King or shooting him with a silver bullet, and for risings in Scotland and Ireland, all based on letters which Oates claimed to have seen but of which he could not produce even a copy in corroboration. The only supporting evidence he could offer were the letters sent to the Duke of York's confessor, Father Bedingfield, and these were forged. Moreover, when Oates appeared before the Council on 28 and 29 September, the King had no difficulty in tripping him up; how then could anyone but a complete knave or a complete fool believe him?

To answer this question it is necessary to remember that the King probably had a piece of knowledge which was not available to the general public. The centre of Oates's revelations was a Jesuit 'consult', which he said had been held in London at the White Horse Tavern on 24 April 1678: there, he said (with much circumstantial detail), the Jesuits had laid their plans to kill the King. Now Oates, who had been in the Jesuit seminary at St. Omer, was right in his contention that a 'consult' had been held on that date; but it had been held, not at the White Horse Tavern but in the Duke of York's own quarters at St. James's Palace. On this central detail, therefore, James certainly and Charles probably were aware

---

[1] The calculation of Sir George Clark, *The Later Stuarts* (ed. 1955), p. 94.
[2] *History of the English Persecution of Catholics and the Presbyterian Plot*, ed. T. A. Birrell (1953), ii. 320, 416.

that Oates was perjured, but they dared not say so. All that Charles could do was to ask Oates questions about the colour of the hair of Don John of Spain, and the site of the Jesuits' house in Paris, and elicit false answers. But Charles's own ministers round the Council Board were less impressed by this than by the assurance with which Oates 'identified' the handwriting of the letters which had been sent to Father Bedingfield. These were folded so that only a line or two could be read, but Oates named their supposed writers instantly, and when asked why the handwriting was not in the writers' normal hand, confidently replied that they were in the habit of disguising their hands in case letters were intercepted. The Council, encouraged by Danby for his own purposes, unanimously decided that the matter must be further investigated, and ordered the immediate arrest of the people whom Oates named. Among these was one Edward Coleman, whom Oates mentioned as something of an afterthought. It was Danby himself who insisted that the warrant for his arrest should provide for the seizure of his papers.[1]

Edward Coleman had been secretary, first to the Duke and later to the Duchess of York. Converted and educated by Jesuits, his devotion to his new religion was equalled only by his indiscretion, for he looked only to the day when the Duke would succeed to the throne and Catholicism would triumph, and he worked to prepare for that day. He was dogmatic of opinion, ambitious, and not above bribing members of Parliament with money supplied by the French ambassador, and not prepared tamely to wait for a lead from others higher placed than himself. When Danby had found Coleman's name not present in Oates's original revelations, he had asked about it, 'my Lord intimating that Coleman must needs be busy in the plot if any were on foot'. He had kept up a correspondence with Louis XIV's confessors—a correspondence the vagueness of which was sometimes almost more disastrous than the most precise details could have been, for the letters talked in general terms of the glorious prospects which lay ahead for the Catholic religion. One letter, when translated, was found to indulge in extravagant hopes for the 'conversion of three kingdoms' and 'the utter subduing of a pestilent heresy'. Another, dated 29 September 1675, described how Coleman had tried to arrange a French offer of a subsidy in return for a dissolution of Parliament by the King. Worse, he hinted that such intrigues were approved by the Duke of York.[2] But his crowning folly was that, when warned by James that there was a warrant out for his arrest, he neither escaped nor destroyed all his papers. In a drawer under a table were found letters relating to 1674, 1675, and part of

[1] For the Privy Council meetings of 28 and 29 Sept., see Privy Council Register, P.R.O. 2/66, fos. 392–7; Southwell to Ormond, 1 Oct. 1678, H.M.C. Ormond MSS., N.S. iv. 455–6, and 22 Nov. 1682, Add. MSS. 38015, fo. 278; J. S. Clarke, Life of James II (1816), i. 518–21, 534; Burnet, ii. 160; Barrillon, 30 Sept./10 Oct.; S.P. Car. II 409.

[2] J. Pollock, The Popish Plot (1903), pp. 31–44; C.J. ix. 525–9; Sir George Treby, A Collection of Letters (1681).

1676; and the fact that the letters for the last two years were missing only led people to suppose that they must have been even more incriminating than those which had been permitted to survive. When the letters were read to a committee of the Privy Council on 4 October the lords were 'all amazed'.[1] Even though Oates, when confronted with Coleman, had failed to recognize him, there appeared now to be corroboration of the existence of a Popish Plot. Charles himself was not unshaken: although he obstinately refused to believe in a plot to murder him, he was prepared to believe that there were too many Jesuits in the country, that they were not 'quiet men', and that they were prepared to engage in indiscreet and even treasonable intrigues to establish their religion. At Newmarket it was observed that he spoke with unusual bitterness of Catholics, and said that Coleman could not escape the death sentence if justice was done; and when back in London he made it plain how incensed he was with Coleman. He told those who waited on him that Coleman's letters 'contained plainly a design to introduce Popery', but that he 'did not believe there was any design upon his life'.[2] But this was a distinction which could not easily be appreciated by people who (unlike Charles) had grown up with the idea that Catholics were people who were capable of anything in the service of their Church. It was only too easy for people to jump to the conclusion that, since Catholics hoped that the succession of James would bring about the triumph of their religion, they would be prepared to hasten the day by assassinating Charles, and to seek French assistance for their purposes. It was difficult to believe in the obvious guilt of Coleman, and not in the veracity of the man who had informed against him. Charles's own councillors, who were in by far the best position to distinguish truth from falsehood, were unable to do so. 'If he be a liar', wrote honest Henry Coventry of Oates, 'he is the greatest and adroitest I ever saw', and that was before Coleman's letters, the genuineness of which no-one could contest, had been read. As for Lord Treasurer Danby, he was positively eager to accept the 'revelations' of Catholic plots and exploit them to rally the Court Party in the Commons: he hoped, misguidedly, that all Protestants would unite in defence of the monarchy and of Protestantism, and that the maintenance of the armed forces could be justified by the need to protect the King. He was the keenest advocate of prosecuting the Plot, and the action against Coleman had been his doing.[3]

---

[1] Southwell to Ormond, 5 Oct., *H.M.C. Ormond MSS.*, N.S. iv. 457-8.

[2] The King's attitude can be traced in Southwell to Ormond, 1 Oct., ibid., iv. 457; Barrillon, 30 Sept./10 Oct., 7/17, 10/20, 21/31 Oct.; Southwell to Ormond 15 and 19 Oct., op. cit. iv. 459-60; Reresby, 23 and 25 Oct., pp. 153-4. Cf. also the Catholic Lord Stafford's opinion of Coleman, as given to Archbishop Sancroft in the Tower, 21 Jan. 1679: 'he seemed to acknowledge Coleman's plot; and added, that he never could like, or brook that fellow, when he was in the hottest of his career' (MSS. Tanner 39, fo. 159).

[3] Coventry to Ormond, 1 Oct., *H.M.C. Ormond MSS.*, N.S. iv. 207; Browning, *Danby*, i. 290-7; J. S. Clarke, op. cit. i. 522-3.

At first, therefore, news of the Plot leaked out to the public from government sources; and at first, therefore, many of the opposition who were in London disbelieved it. In their view it was a trick designed to free the Lord Treasurer from his difficulties, to induce the Commons to vote money, and to permit the retention of the armed forces. So Burnet was told by Littleton and Powle: so too the French ambassador was told by his informants.[1] It must be remembered that no-one outside the government was yet familiar with Oates's prowess as a convincing liar; and it was some time before the text of Coleman's letters became public. After the way in which they had been deceived (as they thought) by Danby's foreign policy over the last twelve months, the major concern of such as Littleton and Powle was to ruin Danby and to secure the disbandment of the dangerous troops. For that purpose they were even prepared to approach James during the month of September, seeking once again to divide him from Danby; but James, with whom the reference to the succession in the pamphlet of January 1677[2] still rankled, refused these overtures.[3] Some were ready to sound the French in the belief that Louis XIV too wanted the English troops disbanded and Danby dismissed, and in the hope that French money could be obtained to meet their own needs. In August the Duke of Buckingham had paid a mysterious visit to France whence he had returned with vague assurances which he hoped to convert into money from the funds at the disposal of the French ambassador in London.[4] Barrillon was also visited by M. Falaiseau, who had been a member of the household of the former English ambassador to Versailles, Ralph Montagu; by Montagu himself, an unscrupulous rogue who, having failed to satisfy his greed and ambition in office, and having been dismissed from his embassy for paying court to the King's illegitimate daughter, sought to put his knowledge of the secrets of Danby's foreign policy at the disposal of the opposition; by William Harbord, who like Montagu was a personal enemy of Danby's; and by the well-known doctrinaire aristocratic Republican, Algernon Sidney, who had just returned from exile for the first time since 1660.[5] For all these the primary objective was the ruin of Danby, and at first the Plot stories seemed to them a trick which was more likely to strengthen than to weaken his position. One opposition leader who foresaw that the Plot might spell more danger to the Court and particularly to the Duke of York was Lord Halifax[6]; and at the beginning of October there was an ominous revival of talk of the possibility of divorcing the

---

[1] Burnet, ii. 156; Barrillon, 30 Sept./10 Oct., 3/13 Oct.
[2] p. 414 above.
[3] Barrillon, 16/26 Sept. Browning, op. cit. i. 297, assumes that Shaftesbury was concerned in this, but the Earl was absent and I know of no evidence to justify the assumption.
[4] Sunderland to Henry Coventry, 27 Aug./6 Sept., H.M.C. Fourth Report, p. 245; Barrillon, 16/26 Sept., 10/20 Oct.
[5] Barrillon, 26 Sept./6 Oct., 30 Sept./10 Oct., 10/20, 14/24, 17/27 Oct., 24 Oct./3 Nov.
[6] Burnet, ii. 156.

King and remarrying him to a Protestant[1]; but the no-Popery panic had not spread much further amongst the public than in the previous winter, until the news burst upon London, first of the disappearance and then of the death of Sir Edmund Berry Godfrey—the most famous of unsolved historical murder mysteries.

Sir Edmund Berry Godfrey was the magistrate before whom Titus Oates had sworn to the truth of his information, and with whom he had left a copy of his depositions before attending the Council on 28 September—probably for use if the Council refused to bother with his story. Godfrey had been chosen for the purpose because he was popularly believed to be a zealous Protestant unlikely to be deterred by any threats from authority. In reality his character was not so straightforward: amongst his friends was Coleman, whom he met and with whom he talked privately after he had read Oates's depositions; and he suffered from a morbid melancholy such as had already led some of his relatives to commit suicide. But the tall, stooping figure of this middle-aged, bachelor magistrate was well known in London and Westminster, and when, five days after his disappearance, his dead body was found on Primrose Hill with the neck broken, marks of strangulation, and his own sword sticking through it, the immediate conclusion was that he had been murdered by Jesuits because he knew too much about the Plot. What he could have known that Oates was not still in a position to divulge, was not really clear: it has been left to a modern historian to suggest that Coleman might have told him that the Jesuit 'consult' of 24 April 1678 had been held in St. James's and not in the White Horse Tavern, but there is no evidence that Coleman passed on that secret. Contrariwise, it has been suggested that Coleman might have told him of the way in which he had bribed opposition members of Parliament with French money, but there is no confirmation either of this possible motive for murder by the opposition. Oates himself had the obvious possible motive of murder to secure credence for his story, but although his career contained almost every crime in the calendar, it did not include crimes of violence. A modern generation reared on detective stories has found another possible murderer in the homicidal maniac, the Earl of Pembroke, who had been presented for murder six months previously by a grand jury of which Godfrey had been the foreman: the trouble about this ingenious theory is that there is no evidence that Pembroke was in London at this time.[2] The contemporary Tory apologist Roger L'Estrange, writing in a time of reaction, did not try to throw the blame on the defeated Whigs, but contented himself with trying to show that Godfrey's hereditary suicidal tendencies had led him to take his own

---

[1] Barrillon, 7/17, 17/27 Oct., 24 Oct./3 Nov. In the last of these despatches it is stated that James's friends believed that Danby was behind this talk.

[2] He did not attend the House of Lords until 5 Dec. He was at no time a regular attender, and may or may not have been in London.

life; if that were true the implication would be that his death was dressed up to look like murder, either for political motives, or by the dead man's brothers to prevent the suicide's property from falling to the Crown—for in spite of L'Estrange, it is impossible to believe that Godfrey found his own way to the spot on Primrose Hill and inflicted all the wounds upon himself. Between all these possibilities the historian has insufficient evidence to decide,[1] and the biographer of Shaftesbury may be absolved from examining them further, since the Earl, being in Dorset at the time, can hardly have been directly concerned. What mattered from his point of view was that Godfrey was almost universally believed to have been killed by Papists; that the precise details of criminals, time, and place were mysterious; and that whatever the true motive, political, ideological or financial, it continued to operate, both under Whig domination and under Tory reaction, so that the real accomplices never betrayed one another for reward.

The immediate effect of the discovery of Godfrey's body was to convince most people that a Popish Plot really existed. In L'Estrange's words, the murder 'proved' the plot, and the plot 'proved' the murder. The murder 'stopped all mouths, and answered all objections'.[2] People naturally believed at once in the general truth of Oates's revelations, in the guilt of Coleman and in Godfrey's murder by Catholic assassins; in the general excitement it would have been very difficult for people to exercise their critical faculties and to believe in one, but not in the others, of these three articles of faith.[3] And once having committed oneself on these points, it was psychologically difficult to change one's mind, and politically difficult to admit in public any doubts which did arise, lest they break the common Protestant unity against the Catholic enemy, and foil the general desire to provide in some way for the situation which would arise when Charles died and his Catholic brother claimed the throne.

It was to this situation that Shaftesbury came when he returned to London on the eve of the opening of the new parliamentary session on 21 October. It was not a situation of his own making. Oates's 'revelations' redounded so much to the Earl's political advantage that it is natural to suspect that the Earl instigated them[4]—the more so as Shaftesbury

---

[1] Of the many works on this subject, we may cite J. Pollock, *The Popish Plot* (1903); A. Marks, *Who Killed Sir Edmund Berry Godfrey?* (1905); J. D. Carr, *The Murder of Sir Edmund Berry Godfrey* (1936); Roger L'Estrange, *Brief History of the Times* (1687–8); J. G. Muddiman, 'The Mystery of Sir Edmund Berry Godfrey', in *National Review*, September 1924.   [2] L'Estrange, op. cit. iii. 10.

[3] Cf. Maynard's speech on 28 Nov. in Grey, vi. 295.

[4] This was Charles's view, or so he told Burnet (ii. 179). The argument that they were instigated by the opposition was also later put forward by Lord Keeper North (MS. memorandum printed by J. Dalrymple, *Memoirs of Great Britain and Ireland* (1773), ii. 320–1; cf. Roger North, *Examen* (1740) p. 216), but his suppositions seem to me over-subtle, and on at least one point (number four) in error. It is significant that this private memorandum by a Tory makes no attack on Shaftesbury personally: the implication is that the Plot was planned by persons unknown.

certainly patronized the arch-informer later on—but a dispassionate examination of the available evidence makes this most unlikely. It is true that Shaftesbury's political correspondence for these months in Dorset (as for the rest of his life) has not survived to show how far he was in touch with events in London; but it is intrinsically improbable that he could have controlled them from ninety miles' distance, and inconceivable that he should have remained in the country as long as he did if he had any advance knowledge of what was to take place.[1] Moreover neither the timing nor the contents of Oates's original revelations suggest the hand of a master-plotter. Mid-August, when the Plot was first brought to the government's notice, was, then as now, a dead political season, and scarcely the moment which a calculating politician would have chosen to launch a scheme to influence the course of events in a Parliament which would not meet for some time. Most important of all, Oates's statements not only contained much that was implausible; they contained much that was extremely inconvenient later on from Shaftesbury's point of view. It is striking to see how Oates violently attacked the Jesuits, but at the same time took great care not to involve the Duke of York, but to make out that the Jesuits were ready to murder him as well as the King if necessary. 'If they saw that His Royal Highness did not answer their expectations, they would dispose of him, as they did intend to dispose of his brother'; and some London fathers were described as saying that they dared not trust the Duke of York with the secret because, although he 'was a good Catholic, yet he had a tender affection to the King'. And as late as 30 October, after some of Coleman's letters had seemed to throw suspicion upon the Duke, Oates went out of his way to volunteer to give the House of Lords his reasons why he thought the Duke of York was wholly innocent—inventing 'evidence' for the purpose with his usual facility. It would have suited the Exclusionists much better if James's innocence had been left more ambiguous: but it was not until the beginning of November that Oates definitely decided that his advantage lay in throwing in his lot with the opposition, who lionized him, while Charles and James plainly disliked him.[2] It will not do to imagine that Oates's care to exculpate James was the result of specially subtle tactics on the opposition's part to ensure that Oates received a hearing; it is much more natural to suppose that at the

[1] The evidence for Shaftesbury's movements is derived from his personal accounts at Wimborne St. Giles. These show travelling expenses for his journey down into Dorset on 25–27 July; payments for beagles on 22 Aug., 23 Sept. and 12 Oct.; 10s. 'given the decoy man that came from Lyndhurst' (in the New Forest) on 26 Sept.; and £2. 2s. 6d. 'paid Haskall the helper in the stables for 17 weeks to this day' on 21 Oct. The next entry, with no date added, is £4. 6s. 6d. for 'the house bill' at Andover on the road to London. Since Shaftesbury is recorded as being present in the Lords on 21 Oct. (L.J. xiii. 293), it is possible that there may be an error of one day.

[2] Articles 4, 23, 24, 29, 60 of Oates's narrative to the Lords on 31 Oct., L.J. xiii. 313–330 (article 60 being one of those added to the forty-three of his original information); H.M.C. House of Lords MSS., 1678–88, pp. 5–6; L.J. xiii. 309–10.

outset Oates and Tonge were adventurers seeking their own advantage by
such crude forgeries as the Bedingfield letters, and looking in the first
place to the government, to the Lord Treasurer and to the established
Church[1] as the obvious source of patronage. And for some weeks Danby
proved willing to take them up. It is significant that the Catholics themselves,
bad as their opinion of Shaftesbury was, blamed Danby for launching the
Plot in the first place.[2]

But if the situation had not been made by Shaftesbury, it could certainly
be exploited by him. After the frustrations of the last three years, he was
presented with a No-Popery slogan which could appeal to all classes: to
rich landowners like 'Tom of Ten Thousand' and discontented, but
loyally Protestant country squires; to City magnates like Sir Robert
Clayton, to merchants like Barnardiston and Papillon, to artisans like
Stephen College, and to the poor seamen of Wapping. It appealed to
zealous Anglicans, to Dissenters, and to secular-minded people who disliked all clerical pretensions. It appealed to ex-Cromwellians, to many ex-
Cavaliers, and to all who for many years had doubted the Protestant
soundness of the government's religious policy. To all such people the
prospect of the succession of a Catholic king with strongly authoritarian
temperament had long been distasteful, and talk of the King's assassination
and the publication of Coleman's letters suddenly made it much nearer.
And of all the opposition leaders Shaftesbury was in the best position to
take advantage of this. Until now he had not been the unquestioned leader
of all the forces hostile to the government: in the Lords neither Buckingham
nor Halifax was prone to regard himself as a subordinate, and in the
Commons there were many whose record of opposition went back further
than Shaftesbury's, and some who did not view his changing record with
favour. Sir William Coventry had never liked him, and there were others
like Littleton and Powle who shared some of his opinions but not others,
and were indeed later to vote against Exclusion. In any case his imprisonment in 1677 had prevented him from acting as an effective leader for
twelve months, and even for the session of January to July 1678 the main
lines of opposition policy had been formulated before he left the Tower.
But now Shaftesbury stood out as the man who had been right all the
time, the man who had paid for his rightness by loss of office in 1673 and
imprisonment in 1677-8 when others had been unscathed; the man whose
public hostility to James went back to 1673 and whose semi-public
hostility went back to the time of the Roos divorce case. The very publicity
which government propaganda attacks had given to him, however telling

---

[1] For Oates's original appeal to Anglicanism rather than Dissent, cf. articles 35, 43,
and 51 of his narrative, which accused the Jesuits of sending messengers to Scotland to
stir up people [i.e. Covenanters] to fight for liberty of conscience. Shaftesbury could hardly
have inspired this complaint.

[2] Father Warner, *History of the English Persecution and the Presbyterian Plot*, ed. T. A.
Birrell (Catholic Record Society, 1953), i. 33, 189–90; J. S. Clarke, op. cit. i. 546.

when they were first made, now worked to his advantage; and in the months to come this man who had at least made clear his uncompromising hostility to the government would be listened to with increased respect.

'Let the Treasurer cry as loud as he pleases against Popery, and think to put himself at the head of the Plot, I will cry a note louder and soon take his place', Shaftesbury was quoted as saying.[1] Whether or not he actually uttered these words, they certainly represented his policy. How much of Oates's story he believed may well be doubted, but he certainly was prepared to make use of it in order to destroy the Catholic plans for the next reign. Never did he make any remark hinting at the slightest doubt of the complete accuracy of everything that Oates said. Once having embarked upon a policy of patronizing Oates, it was impossible to turn back; and the policy led to more and more unpleasant consequences which could not be predicted at the outset. At the beginning, Oates's evidence by itself, however dreadful, could not hang anyone except Coleman, whose letters supplied additional evidence of activities which could in law be deemed treasonable; the main evidence would supply political ammunition only. But a succession of new informers, encouraged by Oates's gains, came forward with new discoveries and new lies; and, patronizing Oates, Shaftesbury had little choice but to patronize them too. It may be doubted whether Shaftesbury actually put the words into their mouths; this would have been too dangerous, for he might have been 'trepanned', betrayed to the Court, and accused of subornation of witnesses; and no convincing evidence of this was supplied when he was in the Tower in 1681. In any case it was unnecessary for Shaftesbury to put the words into their mouths; for the informers were well aware, from their conversations with one another, of what would be plausible and of what information the Whigs would be prepared to take up. Shaftesbury's function was not that of author but of impresario. Whenever it was within his power, he would produce them on stage at the moment and in the manner in which they would have the greatest political effect.[2] And a disreputable lot they were. We do not know whether Shaftesbury used their services with reluctance. He can scarcely have derived any pleasure from it, and it may well be that he simply decided that he would give a hearing to anyone who came forward, extract any political advantage that he could, and leave the law courts to take care of the criminal accusations. The end, perhaps, would justify the means, and, once having started, 'returning were as tedious as go o'er'. But no historian could extenuate everything which was done in his name; and it was poetic justice that in the end the lies of the Popish Plot brought defeat.

For what purposes, then, did Shaftesbury propose to make use of the

---

[1] Clarke, loc. cit.

[2] This does not imply that they were *all* produced by him: some were completely independent.

no-Popery panic? From the outset his objective was to attack the Duke of York. Others of the opposition, as we have seen, were more intent on bringing down the Lord Treasurer—sometimes, as in Montagu's case, for personal reasons—and in September 1678 had been prepared to seek James's assistance for this; Shaftesbury would have none of it, and made clear his antipathy from the very beginning of the new session. In 1675 approaches had been made to James for temporary tactical reasons in the debates on Danby's Test; in 1678 there was no reason to renew them. Equally Shaftesbury did not, like some other leaders of the Country Party (for example, Buckingham), put any great reliance on French assistance to get rid of Charles's troops. It is likely that he listened to what Buckingham and Holles, Littleton and others had to tell him of their conversations with the French ambassador—it was useful to have information about French policy, but it is very noticeable that he refrained from entering into any direct relationship with Barrillon, even to bring about the common aim of the disbandment of the Army. The fall of Danby, the disbandment of the Army, and the replacement of the Cavalier Parliament might well come in the course of events; but the vital concern was with the problem of the succession.

There were two possible policies open to him here—policies of Exclusion and of 'limitations'. One might seek to debar James from succeeding at all, or one might permit him to succeed, but hope to make him harmless by imposing in advance restrictions on his powers both in Church and State. The latter was a more straightforward, legal, and constitutional method, which would not deprive James of his natural right to succeed his brother. Restrictions on royal powers might seem more in line with the course of English constitutional development than the drastic course of excluding the man who was entitled to succeed by the normal hereditary principle which applied to the transmission of estates. But for both strategic and tactical reasons Shaftesbury rejected the idea of limitations which would tie James's hands. In the long run, how effective would these restrictions be? To use illustrations of which contemporaries were very fond, would not a Parliament which enacted such legislation be like the men of the village of Gotham who built a hedge round the cuckoo in order to keep him in? Or like those who sought to bind Samson with withes? Those who knew James believed that he would not rest content with any restrictions on his prerogative, and that with the immense prestige attaching to monarchy he would have little difficulty in escaping from them; and events in the next reign were to prove them right, for James's use of the dispensing and suspending powers enabled him to free himself from a host of statutes enacted by past Parliaments, and to pursue political and religious policies which were disliked both by Whigs and by Tories. In the end, the Bill of Rights was only made possible by the exclusion of James. The short-term, tactical arguments against a policy of limitations were also very strong.

Although Charles professed himself willing to consent to restrictions on the power of a Catholic successor, was he sincere in this? Since January 1674 the Country Party had repeatedly tried to pass legislation, including a Habeas Corpus Act, and a Test Act to exclude Catholics from Parliament, but the bills had been repeatedly terminated by prorogations. Effective limitations would be complicated, and at least involve lengthy discussion; the possibilities for obstruction would be considerable, particularly with a House of Lords which was largely dependent on the Court, and it might be simply a matter of the King waiting until the temporary agitation had subsided, and then seizing a suitable opportunity to employ his power of prorogation. An Exclusion Bill on the other hand presented a simple, clear-cut issue which would force people to take sides, and which might be quickly settled. There was, it was true, a danger that James might not accept the deprivation of his divine rights by human agency, and that Charles's death might be followed by civil war; but it was arguable that this danger existed whichever policy was pursued, and that an Act of Exclusion laid the best foundation for action to prevent it.

So at least Shaftesbury and the Exclusionists reasoned; and, having reasoned, had to provide an alternative successor. Here it is to be noticed that Shaftesbury never explicitly committed himself to the claims of the Duke of Monmouth, and there are signs that he would have preferred a different solution if it could be arranged. His support of the Roos Divorce Bill in 1670 had been explained in terms of a scheme to divorce the King from Queen Catherine of Braganza and re-marry him to a Protestant. No-one doubted that if this happened the King would beget a Protestant heir. The scheme was again being canvassed in London in October 1678, and it promised many political advantages. It would be the solution which James was least in a position to resist, and a solution which believers in the divine right of hereditary succession might accept without much difficulty: it would be easier to defend than the fiction of the Black Box in which some said the marriage papers of Monmouth's mother had been kept. Although some might regret it on Catherine's behalf, she could be assured of a comfortable retirement. But the difficulty about this solution was that it depended on the King's willingness to co-operate; one simply cannot arrange for the divorce of a man who does not ask to be divorced; and Charles, cynical as he was on other occasions, and unfaithful though he was repeatedly to the Queen, felt that he could not in honour repudiate her. Perhaps, too, he shrank from the scenes which would take place with his aggrieved brother; at all events he would not accept this way of escape from his difficulties. There remained, however, the possibility that he might be compelled to accept it, or that he might be induced to accept it for Catherine's own sake, to preserve her from attack; and at more than one point it is likely that this possibility was in people's minds. It was certainly a long time before Shaftesbury ruled it out.

A second possibility was that James might be excluded in the interests of the next heir, namely his elder daughter Mary, who was married to William of Orange. There could be no doubt of their Protestantism, and there were already those, like Halifax, who hoped that they would succeed, guarantee Protestantism in England and bring England into the scales against Louis XIV. But there were difficulties in this solution too, from Shaftesbury's own point of view. William was a Stuart, and by his present marriage he had aligned himself with his uncles. So at least it seemed; and Shaftesbury, unlike Halifax, had no personal knowledge of William from which to appreciate that the Prince had preserved a very independent outlook. Reports of the way in which William's influence was exercised in the Netherlands suggested that he was somewhat authoritarian in outlook, and that, at best, English political liberties would be subordinate to the needs of his foreign policy on the Continent. It was indeed possible that he might be tempted away from the side of his uncle James by the promise of the English throne; but it was certain that if he were, and if he would take part in an attempt to exclude James, he would be far from a tool in the Exclusionists' hands—he would expect to guide events, and the Exclusionists did not sufficiently trust him. Moreover, apart from these guesses and prejudices, there was one solid fact which made it undesirable for the Exclusionists to stake their fate on William and Mary. Mary's claim to the succession might be superseded by the birth of a brother. James's second wife, Mary of Modena, was still only twenty; only a year previously she had borne a son, the Duke of Cambridge, who lived for a few weeks, and there might be more sons to follow. To hope for the succession of Mary and William meant a gamble, and the possibility that another settlement might be needed later on; as indeed was found when the Old Pretender was born on 10 June, 1688.

There remained the claims of the King's illegitimate son, the Duke of Monmouth. The possibility of his legitimization had been rumoured since at least 1662,[1] the more so because of all the King's natural children Monmouth was always very much his father's favourite, and because there was much gossip that the King had indeed been married to Monmouth's mother but could not afford to acknowledge it publicly on account of her low birth. Certainly he had been indulged with everything that he could wish for at Court. Public opinion varied considerably about him. At times he had been regarded as being as much of a waster as anyone at Charles's Court; his bravos had been involved in the notorious assault on Sir John Coventry in 1670, and the fact that he had commanded the English auxiliary forces with Louis XIV in 1672 and 1673 had won him no friends. But he was handsome and open-handed, and his dissolute behaviour could be forgiven as a temporary excess of youth; and one conclusion which can

---

[1] Pepys, 27 Oct., 31 Dec. 1662; 4, 14, 15 May, 9 Nov. 1663; 20 Jan., 8, 22 Feb. 1664; 16 Dec. 1666; 11, 16 Sept., 4 Nov. 1667; 23 Nov. 1668.

clearly be derived from his short career is that he had it in him to appeal as a heroic figure to the lower classes in the capital and provinces alike. Above all, he was the natural counterpoise to James. To Monmouth gravitated all who disliked the King's brother and whose wishful thinking led them to hope that somehow, somewhere, evidence of Lucy Walter's marriage might relegate James to the background—and also those dissolute adventurers who saw attachment to him as a means of personal advancement. As for Shaftesbury, he had had every opportunity to weigh up Monmouth's qualities and weaknesses, ever since the time when the latter, as a boy of 16, had accompanied his father to Wimborne St. Giles in 1665. He was not impressed by any qualities of mind or character that he could detect, and it is significant that when he drew up his lists of the peers to while away his stay in the Tower, he prefixed Monmouth's name with three 'v's'—the maximum amount of 'vileness'. In 1677 he evidently regarded Monmouth as part of the established system that he was combating, and as one who would vote with the Court. But in the Exclusion crisis he could see Monmouth's willingness to be tempted by the mirage of a crown, his willingness to seek popularity, and his willingness to accept guidance without taking any initiatives of his own. It is a striking commentary on Monmouth's weakness that he was prepared to co-operate with Shaftesbury without getting from the Earl any explicit, public commitment to his claims in return. 'The Protestant Duke' was tempted to that path which was eventually to lead to the ditch not five miles from Shaftesbury's house at Wimborne St. Giles where he was found cowering after the battle of Sedgemoor.

Such was Shaftesbury's secretiveness that it is impossible to say whether he ever finally made up his mind about the successor to Charles whom he would like to see, but he was at any rate willing to use Monmouth for his purposes. What must be emphasized, however, is that in his attempts to regulate the succession he was not governed by the expectation that he would live to see it, and to be himself the power behind a puppet king. No one in 1678 would have expected Shaftesbury to live longer than Charles— unless indeed Charles was assassinated. The King was nine years younger than the Earl, and in incomparably better health—active and vigorous, he had never had a serious illness, while Shaftesbury was weakened by persistent ill-health and walked with the aid of a stick. Even though men are often over-optimistic about their own longevity, it is likely that Shaftesbury was trying to provide for a future which he would not himself see.

It is likely, too, that he was something of an 'old man in a hurry'. Both his age and the political situation meant that if he was to be successful he must strike quickly and make the most of the turn that public opinion was taking. For, in conclusion, the last of the common fallacies about the Exclusion crisis is that, in resisting Exclusion, it was Charles who was facing overwhelming odds; in reality the odds were much more even, and perhaps actually against the success of Shaftesbury and the Whigs. Certainly Shaftesbury was in a weaker position than Pym was in 1641. Charles II's financial position was far from good, but it was immeasurably better than Charles I's had been, and this, combined with the fact that there was no Act on this occasion preventing the dissolution of Parliament without its own consent, meant that he could dispense with Parliament for nearly eighteen months in 1679-80. When Parliament was not sitting the Whigs could do nothing to press their case; they were almost helpless until the next session. When without means of constitutional agitation, they were unable to employ force. Not only were the magazines and the Navy, Scotland and Ireland firmly under the King's thumb, as they were not in 1642, but the very memory of the Civil War and its aftermath worked against them; the Tories' strongest propaganda slogan was that ' '41 had come again'. Shaftesbury could rely on constitutional methods only; or, in other words, he must keep the 'No-Popery' feeling at such a fever-heat that it would be more potent than the immense assets of sentiment, patronage, and power at the disposal of the King. Only an overwhelming pressure of public and parliamentary opinion could coerce the King into a policy of Exclusion: hence the constant temptation to employ ever more disreputable methods to maintain the agitation. Charles, on the other hand, once he had made up his mind to stand by his brother's rights, had the simpler task of keeping his nerve, biding his time and choosing the right moment to assert the powers at his disposal—a task which suited his opportunistic talents. For neither he, nor for that matter Shaftesbury, was in a position in October 1678 to forecast the course which events would take. Fortunately it is not given to politicians to divine the future more than a short time ahead; and though both Shaftesbury and Charles knew where they wanted ultimately to be, there were many surprises awaiting them on the road there.

CHAPTER XXII

THE END OF THE CAVALIER PARLIAMENT
(1678–9)

OBSERVERS commented that in comparison with previous sessions the attendance at the opening day on 21 October was thin.[1] Evidently neither side had thought it necessary to organize supporters in the expectation of urgent decisions being taken. Stories of the Plot took time to penetrate into distant counties, and it was only four days since Sir Edmund Berry Godfrey's dead body had been discovered in the ditch on Primrose Hill. Like Shaftesbury, the country gentry were in no hurry to arrive in the capital; but when they did arrive they found more excitement than at any time for years. Enterprising booksellers were already cashing in on the situation by publishing anti-Catholic pamphlets[2]; there was silly talk of a plan for massacring all Anglicans in London in one day, and Buckingham and Halifax, who had been there for some time, were telling the French ambassador of their plans to urge Parliament on against the Catholics in order to drive a wedge between Danby and the Duke of York.[3] The previous session had been dominated by issues of foreign policy, but the situation had now been transformed and it was widely realized that the Duke of York might be in danger.

Standing at the bar of the House of Lords, the members of the Commons listened to the King's opening speech, and found to their surprise only the briefest reference to the topic which was on everyone's lips. 'I shall forbear any opinion, lest I may seem to say too much, or too little: but I will leave the matter to the law' and in the meantime take every possible care to prevent people from contriving to introduce Popery; and the rest of his speech related to the 'well-securing what was left of Flanders', and the familiar theme of the need for money. This was less the result of deliberate policy than of the conflict of opinion between the King's brother and his principal minister, the former of whom was endangered by the Plot while the latter still wished to exploit it and demonstrate his Protestantism. This meant that the initiative passed straight into the hands of the opposition. In the Commons, although some of Danby's friends played their part, the Privy Councillors with seats refrained from taking any lead, and one government man noted that 'many of the country gentlemen were much scandalized to see none of the other side speak a word, but all the agitation of the matter

---

[1] Southwell to Ormond, 22 Oct., *H.M.C. Ormond MSS.*, N.S. iv. 460; Barrillon, 24 Oct./ 3 Nov. Anchitel Grey's notes on debates in the Commons begin a week later on 28 Oct.
[2] Van Beuningen, 18/28 Oct., Add. MSS. 17677, SSS; Sarotti, 25 Oct./4 Nov.
[3] Barrillon, 17/27 Oct.

left to them, though it concerned the King's security'. Quickly the opposition took charge of the investigations into the Plot, both in the House and in the special committee which was appointed, while at their request the Secretaries of State saw that members were provided with all the relevant documents.[1] Meanwhile in the House of Lords Shaftesbury threw down the gauntlet at the outset by moving that the regiment of Lord Dumbarton, which had fought in Louis XIV's service for several years and was thought to contain many Catholics, Irish and others, should be sent a hundred miles off; the peers agreed that there should be no formal Address for sending the troops further afield, 'but it was presumed the thing would be done'. Shaftesbury's intention had been simply to be offensive to the Duke of York, and for that purpose he had carefully included in his speech a reference to the number of Catholics in the company of Lord Roscommon who was Master of the Horse to the Duchess of York.[2]

Oates appeared first before the Lower House, on three consecutive days, and on these, his first public appearances, he made an enormous impression even on those who were not predisposed to believe him. One of Ormond's London correspondents, marvelling at the scope of Oates's unconfirmed statements about people who had always been loyal, yet remarked that 'The accuser is so positive in his charge, so exact in all circumstances, so agreeing with himself in the whole, and each particular, and swears it with such assurance, that it seems impossible to be a fiction'; and another writer, Sir Robert Southwell, Clerk to the Council and member of Parliament, though intelligent enough to see the weaknesses in Oates's 'loose and tottering fabric which would easily tumble if it stood alone', observed that the past indulgence given to Papists, the phraseology of Coleman's letters and the 'impudent murder' of Sir Edmund Berry Godfrey 'bring credit to what Mr. Oates has pronounced, and would do so, were it ten times wilder and more extravagant than it is'. Certainly the overwhelming majority had no doubts, and after sitting until ten o'clock at night behind locked doors on 24 October, they asked the Lord Chief Justice to issue warrants for the arrest of five Catholic peers, Lords Arundel, Bellasis, Petre, Powis, and Stafford, who, Oates now swore, had received commissions to act in the overthrow of the government. Oates did not embroider other important parts of his narrative, and in particular he still insisted that the Duke of York knew nothing about the plot. Yet James's position was bound to be affected: the Test Bill which was rushed through the House unopposed within a week in order to exclude all Catholic peers would have excluded James by implication. Some members were still suspicious about the whole thing, as though it were a government

---

[1] *L.J.* xiii. 293; *C.J.* ix. 516–18; Southwell to Ormond, op. cit. 461.

[2] *H.M.C. House of Lords MSS., 1678–88*, p. 54; W. Denton to Sir R. Verney, 24 Oct., *H.M.C. Seventh Report*, p. 494; Barrillon, 24 Oct./3 Nov.; report in Modena archives by Ronchi, 24 Oct./3 Nov., in Campana de Cavelli, *Les Derniers Stuarts* (1871), i. 235.

trick, and a significant attempt to get the Votes of the House printed for public consumption failed; but by the end of the month the hunt of the Papists was well in progress and it was not being controlled by the government, which was criticized for its inaction between the middle of August and Oates's appearance at the Council on 28 September.[1]

The Lords were not a whit backward, and Shaftesbury found himself accepted from the start as one of the House's leaders, and a member of almost all the important committees—though not on the committee which drew up an address to advise the King on the precautions to be taken for his personal safety: it was Monmouth who reported the committee's opinion that all Papists excepting servants of the Queen and the Duchess of York should be hindered from coming to court, that no Papist should have any part in preparing the King's meals, that the 'great concourse of mean and unwarranted people' frequenting the palace and following the King in St. James's Park should be restricted, and that all the palace locks should be changed. Shaftesbury, however, joined Winchester, Halifax and Essex and Bridgewater in preparing an address asking the King for a proclamation to remove all Papists from London, and he was on another committee with instructions to inspect the constables of London and Middlesex to see if any were open or concealed Papists. On 26 October, too, he, along with Danby, Essex, Clarendon, and the Bishop of London, was instructed to examine Coleman and other prisoners in Newgate, and 'to use all encouragement to them for further discovery'.[2]

This committee reported on 29 October that it had detected some lies and elicited some interesting admissions. One Jesuit had agreed that, as Oates had said, a Jesuit congregation had been held on 24 April. But Coleman had been as indiscreet as ever. First he had asked to speak to the King and the Duke of York, and when asked why, he said 'that it was to know how to govern himself, as to naming the Duke'. He had admitted delivering one letter from Louis XIV's confessor, Father Ferrier, to James; said that James was acquainted with his own correspondence with Ferrier, 'not perhaps with every letter, but in general'; denied that he had corresponded with Louis's later confessor, Père La Chaise, until the committee produced an actual letter to him; and agreed that a visit which he had paid to the Papal inter-nuncio at Brussels had been paid with James's knowledge. Shaftesbury and others promptly moved that these interesting facts should be communicated to the Commons with a view to joint action by the two Houses. James had to rise and defend himself, saying that any letters which he had written to foreign ecclesiastics had only been to recommend individuals to them, and that Coleman was 'a shameless liar' revenging

---

[1] *C.J.* ix. 518–22; Van Beuningen, 25 Oct./4 Nov., Add. MSS. 17677, DD; Barrillon, 28 Oct./7 Nov.; *C.S.P.D. 1678*, p. 480; MSS. Rawl. D 720, fo. 157; Sir Cyril Wyche to Ormond, 26 Oct., *H.M.C. Ormond MSS.*, N.S. iv. 221; Southwell to Ormond, 26 Oct., ibid. pp. 461–4; Grey, vi. 118–20.   [2] *L.J.* xiii. 298–300, 303–5.

himself for his dismissal from the Duke's service. Not all the peers found this answer altogether convincing. Shaftesbury's motion was defeated, but by less than twenty votes, and it was remarked that five bishops had voted against the Duke's party: even the 'dead weight' was not so inert as formerly. Only Shaftesbury and Essex signed a formal Protest for entry in the Journals of the House, but it was at this time that there was the first talk of an Association on similar lines to that formed to defend Elizabeth against Mary Queen of Scots, 'with other hints that relate to the succession'.[1]

Ironically, it was left to Titus Oates himself to come to James's defence, volunteering to appear at the bar of the House to give his reasons why he believed James to be wholly innocent; and his 'authoritative' statement had some effect.[2] But it did not save James from direct attack. On 2 November Shaftesbury first proposed that the Lords should agree with a unanimous resolution which the Commons had communicated to them, 'that this House is of opinion, that there hath been, and still is, a damnable and hellish plot contrived and carried on by the Popish Recusants, for the assassinating and murdering the King, and for subverting the government, and rooting out and destroying the Protestant religion'. Having established this, he went on to open a new debate. In the presence of the King and the Duke of York, he declared that the House must deal with this plot and without regard for personal considerations. Though one must not lose sight of the respect due to a royal brother, and though one must recognize the Duke's experience, bravery, constancy, and resolution, the fact that the Duke had chosen a different religion from that laid down by law made these qualities more dangerous than praiseworthy, so it was necessary to remove the Duke from the King's Council and even from his presence. This drastic motion was supported by Lords Essex, Halifax, Gerrard of Brandon, and Winchester, and also by five bishops including the strongly 'Protestant bishop', Henry Compton of London, who was usually to be found working with Danby. The tone of the speeches was moderate, except for that of Gerrard who said that for a long time people had not known who was King, and whether there was one king or two. James's friends restrained him from what would have been a vehement defence; instead his cause was defended principally by his brother-in-law, the second Earl of Clarendon. Danby also spoke for him, but there were some who found his speech ambiguous. In the end Shaftesbury did not press his motion to a division, when it would probably have been defeated; his supporters proposed that the debate should be adjourned until another day, but readily accepted the Court's argument that it would be disrespectful to have a

---

[1] L.J. xiii. 307–8; Southwell to Ormond, 29 Oct., op. cit. iv. 465; James to William of Orange, 29 Oct., H.M.C. Foljambe MSS., p. 123; MSS. Carte 81, fo. 361; Sarotti, 1/11 Nov. (unpublished C.S.P. Ven.); Schwerin, 29 Oct./8 Nov., 1/11 Nov., Briefe, pp. 342, 345.

[2] H.M.C. House of Lords MSS., 1678–88, p. 6; L.J. xiii. 309–10; W. Denton to Sir R. Verney, 30 Oct., H.M.C. Seventh Report, pp. 494–5.

formal entry in the Journals. The tactical purpose of the debate had been achieved, namely that of encouraging the Commons to make a more violent attack.[1]

That this was realized by the King was shown at the committee of foreign affairs next day. The King gave positive orders that his ministers and their friends should oppose any similar motion in the House of Commons; but after the committee had risen, he took James on one side and asked him to forbear coming to the committee and meddling in public business for the present. James reluctantly obeyed, and made a declaration to that effect in the House of Lords on 4 November; Shaftesbury and Buckingham rather impudently wanted this published in a proclamation, so that it should be made clear that James's decision was taken to satisfy the general desire of the nation, not the suspicion of a few individuals, but the general feeling of the Lords was against this.[2] But this declaration did not prevent the Country Party from pressing on with the plans which had been laid for the House of Commons on that same day. After the Speaker had reported on the visit which he and five other members had made on the previous day to Coleman in Newgate, and the House had consequently been heated by hearing again how Coleman had begun his correspondence with the Duke's knowledge, Russell moved for an address to the King, asking that the Duke be removed from his presence and councils. It was noted that Russell's words were 'in a style beyond his way of speaking', and certainly they were in precisely the same tone as Shaftesbury's speech two days earlier; the speech had plainly been prepared in consultation. The motion was seconded by Henry Booth, son of the Booth who had rebelled against the Commonwealth in 1659. The opposition's arguments were notably less extreme than they became later in the Exclusion crisis. Only Sacheverell boldly asked 'whether the King and the Parliament may not dispose of the succession of the Crown? and whether it be not *Praemunire* to say the contrary?' Others who later voted for Exclusion, like Birch, Meres, and Capel, whether sincerely or for tactical reasons simply argued for the present that Tudor experience had shown 'the variable temper of the nation' and its willingness to accept different religious settlements in different reigns; that even in the Civil War only the twentieth part of the nation were in action while the other nineteen stood still; and so legislation was necessary to secure the Church. This legislation the Duke would hinder if he were present at Court; in spite of his own innocence 'this Plot had not been, if the Duke were not what he is', and his very

---

[1] *L.J.* xiii. 333; Borgomanero, 4/14 Nov.; Schwerin, 5/15 Nov., *Briefe*, pp. 346–7; van Beuningen, 5/15 Nov., Add. MSS. 17677, SSS; Barrillon, 4/14 Nov. (In Baschet's transcript 'Baret' should read 'Jaret', i.e. Gerrard); Southwell to Ormond, 2 Nov., *H.M.C. Ormond MSS.*, N.S. iv. 466; [Southwell?] to Ormond, 5 Nov., MSS. Carte 72, fo. 403.

[2] J. S. Clarke, *Life of James II* (1816), i. 524; Henry Thynne to Ormond, 5 Nov., *H.M.C. Ormond MSS.*, N.S. iv. 227; Schwerin, 5/15 Nov., *Briefe*, pp. 347–8; Barrillon, 4/14 Nov.; Reresby, p. 156.

virtues had helped to produce the present situation. It was also hinted that the Duke's influence was responsible for the attack on the Dutch in 1672—to which courtiers retaliated by recommending an inquiry into those who put the Great Seal to the Declaration of Indulgence, consented to receive French money for that same war, and later printed arguments for the dissolution of Parliament, i.e. Shaftesbury. Finally the opposition's moderation led them to agree to an adjournment of the debate without pressing for a vote. It was suggested that this was to avoid breaking the unanimity of the House in all its previous actions in this session, and to see whether the Test Act now in the House of Lords would pass without hindrance; perhaps even James would 'voluntarily' withdraw from the Court as he had already withdrawn from Council. At all events the opposition were willing to wait a little while to see; the debate was adjourned to the 8th, and then to a later date, because by that time other developments were expected.[1]

Shaftesbury was busier than he had ever been. He had to attend the sittings of the Lords for much of the day and consult with members of the Commons about tactics there for much of the evening. He was deputed to interrogate Coleman in Newgate and the five arrested Catholic peers in the Tower; he was appointed to almost every committee connected with the Plot. Some of these were on trivial matters which yet had to be taken seriously while they lasted; there was a committee to investigate a mysterious knocking heard at night in Old Palace Yard, and another to investigate the stocks of fireworks, or explosives, kept by a French Papist named Choqueux.[2] These inquiries were soon completed, but there was no end to the activities of the main Plot Committee which the Lords had set up at the beginning of the session. Consisting of all the fifty-five peers present in the House on the day when it was constituted, it met commonly both before and after the formal sittings of the House, at 9 a.m. and 4 p.m., with the broadest of mandates to inquire into the Plot and to read the papers communicated to it by the King, including Coleman's letters.[3] It soon became apparent that there was more material than the Committee could easily cope with, and accordingly it gave a welcome to Buckingham's proposal on 28 October to set up a special sub-committee 'to enquire into the business of Sir E. Godfrey'. Buckingham's first request was for Winchester and Halifax to be joined with him; but two days later Shaftesbury was added, and next day Essex and the Bishop of London made the number up to six, with powers to examine and if necessary commit into custody. At first Buckingham's crony, the old Leveller plotter Major Wildman, was its secretary, but this function was later handed over to

---

[1] C.J. ix. 532–3, 536; Grey, vi. 132–49, 165–9; [Southwell to Ormond], 5 Nov., MSS. Carte 72, fos. 403–6 and 9 Nov., H.M.C. Ormond MSS., N.S. iv. 467; C.S.P.D. 1678, p. 503.

[2] H.M.C. House of Lords MSS., 1678–88, pp. 18–19.

[3] Its proceedings are calendared in H.M.C. House of Lords MSS. 1678–88, pp. 1 sqq.

Shaftesbury's own steward, his loyal servant Thomas Stringer, and for this reason notes of their meetings are now preserved amongst the Shaftesbury Papers.[1]

For all its eagerness this sub-committee never discovered anything of value about Godfrey's death, but its members interrogated anyone who was reported to it as being a suspect. Their methods were not pretty. They relied entirely on the extraction of confessions by means of a mixture of inducements and threats. But this was normal in the seventeenth century, when the government had virtually no means of detection and often could convict only by the confession of accomplices, by whatever means these were obtained.[2] What was peculiar about the interrogations of 1678 was that the possible rewards for a timely confession were unusually large; a man might not only escape a bullying interrogation and possible conviction himself, but he might also hope for the positive advantages which were beginning to fall the way of Titus Oates, and, as in Oates's case, these rewards might go not only to those who confessed the truth but to those who invented a plausible and convenient falsehood. And the question which has to be examined is whether Shaftesbury as an interrogator tried not merely to extract the truth but to encourage the swearing of untruths for his political purposes.

There is some evidence to suggest that he did, but most of it dates from the period of reaction after Shaftesbury's death and is therefore suspect. Just as after 1940 every man had his story of the blitz, so after 1678 every man had his story of the Plot, and it lost nothing in the telling. It is not necessary to postulate deliberate distortion in order to detect exaggeration in the statements made to Secretary of State Jenkins and the Tory propagandist L'Estrange, who were not likely to disbelieve anything against Shaftesbury. For instance, Mrs. Mary Gibbon of St. Martin's-in-the-Fields, an old friend of Godfrey's, complained that she had been sorely abused for hinting inconveniently that Godfrey might not have been murdered by the Papists, but might have committed suicide. Before the committee, 'her first salutation was from Lord Shaftesbury, who said, you damned woman, what devilish paper is this you have given in? and questioned her on oath who writ it, and gave her most opprobious language, and often threatened her that, if she would not confess that Sir John Banks, Mr. Pepys and M. du Puy[3] contrived the matter in it, she would be thrown into prison for her life or torn to pieces by the rabble or worried as the dogs worry the cats. The Duke of Buckingham said, if you were a

---

[1] *H.M.C. House of Lords MSS. 1678–88*, pp. 46, 49; *L.J.* xiii. 310; *State Trials*, vii. 1196 (for Wildman); Shaftesbury Papers, XLIII, 63.

[2] The House of Commons, for instance, was prepared to hold out an assurance of a pardon to induce Coleman to confess: Grey, vi. 131–2.

[3] Banks was actually a friend of Shaftesbury's, and the reference to du Puy is anachronistic, for it was not until 1681 that he (a servant of James's) was accused of participation in the murder.

man, I would sheath my sword in your heart's blood . . .'. At least these lurid threats, if they were uttered, brought no actual harm to Mrs. Gibbon. William Bromwell and John Walters, a baker and a blacksmith, two of the three people who had found Godfrey's body in the ditch, were imprisoned some weeks on suspicion (for which there was some slight justification[1]) that they were expecting to find it there and might have been hired 'by some great Roman Catholics' to find it there. Bromwell said (years later) that he was threatened by Shaftesbury with hanging and offered £500 reward by Wildman; Walters said that, after threats, Shaftesbury took him 'aside into a by-closet, speaking to him to this effect, "Honest Smug the Smith, thou look'st like an honest fellow, thou shalt shoe my horses, and I'll make a man of thee": saying further, "tell me who murdered this man, and who set thee to find him out? What Papists dost thou work for?" ' but Walters claimed to have been unaffected by this sinister offer, if such it was. More sensational was the story of Francis Corrall, a hackney coachman with an unfortunate propensity for telling tall stories to attract attention. Having impressed his friends one day at the tavern with a tale that he had been stopped by four mysterious armed men and asked to convey what he thought must have been Godfrey's body in his coach, he found that his remarks had been conveyed to the Lords' sub-committee and to his dismay he was summoned before them at Wallingford House. There (he later said) he was first offered the official reward for the discovery of Godfrey's murderers, and then, when he could supply no information, his sufferings began. First Shaftesbury threatened him, rather improbably, with 'a barrel of nails . . . to put thee in, and roll thee down a hill'; then, more simply, 'thou shalt *Die*'. After a spell in a very nasty dungeon, he was examined a second time, threatened this time with being starved to death, and returned to the condemned hole, where he would have killed himself in despair 'if his knife had not dropped out of his hand'. At a third interview, when Shaftesbury had threatened him with a dreadful trial and hanging if he would not confess and Corrall had dramatically replied (so he said) by saying that the Day of Judgement would be still worse if he swore falsely, Shaftesbury sent him back to Newgate to 'lie and rot', and when he pleaded that he had a wife and children, 'the Lord Shaftesbury answered, Let his wife and children starve'. Back in the condemned hole and reading the twentieth chapter of Revelations, he was terrified by 'a rattling of chains' and told that 'the Devil will have you'; had 'two great holes worn in his right leg [and] one in his left' by the irons, and was reduced to drinking his own water. It is an impressive story, which must have earned him many drinks in the tavern, but it is rather spoiled by the fact that on one occasion, after the Popish midwife, Mrs. Cellier, had got herself into trouble by publishing it, Corrall signed a deposition before the Lord Mayor categorically denying everything that

[1] Shaftesbury Papers, loc. cit.

Mrs. Cellier had said about him, and Mrs. Corrall contradicted the charges of torture and brutality in open court.[1]

It would be rash to build any view of Shaftesbury's character on such evidence as that. One may assume that he would be a formidable inquisitor, but nothing more; and the crude threats attributed to him here contrast sharply with the much subtler tactics employed in the much more serious case of Samuel Atkins.

Samuel Atkins was the clerk of a much greater Samuel, Samuel Pepys, and he was certainly the victim of a deliberate attempt to entrap him by his namesake Charles Atkins, a naval captain with a bad record and a thoroughly unpleasant character, but, as the son of Sir Jonathan Atkins and nephew of Sir Philip Howard, M.P., a man who could claim credence. On 30 October Charles Atkins appeared before the Council to say that, according to Samuel Atkins, his master and Godfrey were on bad terms; that Samuel Atkins had enquired whether one Child was reliable; and that Child had later tried to induce him to join in murdering some person unknown. It is quite clear that the aim of these lies was to induce Samuel Atkins to swear against his master, whose Protestantism had been questioned in the Commons in 1674 and whose work at the Admiralty was patronized by the Duke of York. If any suspicion of being involved in Godfrey's murder fell on Pepys, this could only further weaken the position of James as Pepys's patron. What is doubtful is whether the scheme was Charles Atkins's own, in the expectation of reward, or that of some greater person— his uncle, Sir Philip Howard, who took the deposition (though he voted later against exclusion) or someone higher in the opposition's counsels. One would have thought that Shaftesbury or Buckingham would have been aware that Pepys could not in fact have been involved in the murder, since he was at Newmarket at the time; but perhaps this is not conclusive.

At all events, having appeared before the Council, Samuel Atkins, a young man just twenty-one, was passed on to the Lords' sub-committee, sitting at Winchester House in Lincoln's Inn Fields. It was Shaftesbury who led the questioning, and he treated the young man's denials very gently, did not bully him, addressed him civilly as 'Mr. Atkins', got him to agree that there was no reason to suppose that Charles had any grudge against him ('and to tell you truly', said the Earl, 'I do not think he has wit enough to invent such a lie'), and showed him what a predicament he was in. At the end, beginning with Buckingham, the lords all pitied him and urged him not to be obstinate; and with the greatest of reluctance Shaftesbury said that since there was such a positive oath against him, they had no option but to commit him to Newgate. In Newgate there was none of the horrendous treatment of which Corrall complained (or boasted);

---

[1] C.S.P.D. January–June 1683, p. 127; R. L'Estrange, Brief History of The Times (1687–8), iii. 97–106; Matthias Fowler's deposition, 1 Nov. in Shaftesbury Papers, XLIII, 63; Mrs. Cellier, Malice Defeated (1680); State Trials, viii. 1183–1218.

he enjoyed the relative comfort of being confined in the house of the Keeper of the prison, Captain Richardson. There he was left for a few days to meditate on his plight and the advantages of making a confession.[1]

On 6 November, at his own request, he appeared again before the sub-committee; but to try to confute Charles Atkins, not to confess. Even supposing that he had said to Capt. Atkins what the latter swore he did, Samuel declared, he would have to say now that it was baseless, 'and that it must arise purely from my own invention . . . and pray, my lords, what will come on't?' Then, according to the narrative which Samuel later prepared for Pepys, 'Nay, nay', says my Lord Shaftesbury, 'Leave us to make the use of it; do you but confess it, you shall be safe, and we'll apply it'.[2] The young man obstinately refused to 'tell a lie to any man's prejudice'; whereupon Shaftesbury called upon Samuel and Charles to look one another in the face, and asked the latter whether he had belied Samuel. 'May be you have been mistaken; pray consider it, and remember the injury you'll do this man, if this be not true. You won't have more to answer for before God, if you should waste and destroy an emperor and his country, than you'll have if you wrongfully ruin him, who is in himself (as every man is) a little emperor.' The two men gazed at one another, until Charles, a little unnerved, threw down his pipe on to the table, and asked 'Why should I say so, my lords, if he had not told me?' An impasse had been reached, and after Shaftesbury had tried to find out if any of the books which Samuel was in the habit of reading aloud to his master Pepys were Popish ones, he recommitted him to Newgate. Charles Atkins asked for and obtained permission to see him there; and perhaps this was the most objectionable feature of the proceedings, for, if Samuel was willing, it made it possible for the two Atkins to concoct a joint story against Pepys. Into this story, moreover, a third person might be invited.

This was William Bedloe, the second of the Popish Plot informers, who now appeared on the scene to volunteer evidence about the death of Godfrey. His mother and sister both lived in Chepstow, Monmouthshire, in that same area where Catholic activities had been brought to the attention of an indignant House of Commons six months earlier. He had a long record of dishonesty, robbery, and confidence trickery. He was inferior to Oates, not in wickedness but in inventive powers and assurance; as a witness he was apt to be almost inaudible in Court and reluctant to swear positively. This however was the result of caution, not compunction. At the outset his aim was not to indulge in too many risks, but to invent

---

[1] *C.S.P.D. 1678*, p. 494; *L.J.* xiii. 353; Henry Coventry to Shaftesbury, 1 Nov., Shaftesbury Papers, VI A, 328; MSS. Rawlinson A 173, fos. 114–32; *State Trials*, vi. 1473–89 for Samuel Atkins's story; MSS. Rawlinson A. 181, fos. 11–24, for an earlier manuscript version of it. See also Sir Arthur Bryant, *Samuel Pepys: The Years of Peril* (1935), ch. ix.

[2] It should be noted, however, that these important words do not occur in the earlier version of Samuel's story in MSS. Rawl. A 181.

sufficient to earn the sum of £500 which had been offered by royal proclamation to anyone who could give information about Godfrey's death,
and for this purpose he proposed to incriminate people not in custody and
whose whereabouts were unknown. Leaving London after the proclamation
had appeared, he wrote from Bristol to offer his story to the government,
and finally told it to Secretary Henry Coventry in the King's presence on
7 November. He inculpated three Jesuits (especially one Lefebvre or Le
Fere), a gentleman of Lord Bellasis, and an under-writer in the Queen's
chapel, and declared that Godfrey had been murdered in one of the rooms
in the Queen's palace at Somerset House. It is not necessary to see any
political motive in this last invention: it was well known that Somerset
House was a large, sprawling place with many rooms to which many
Catholics and others resorted, and in which many things occurred which
were quite unknown to the mistress of the household. To this story
Bedloe appended one or two tales about the Plot for good measure: there
were 30,000 Spaniards to meet at Santiago disguised as pilgrims, who
were to land at Milford Haven, while others from Flanders landed in
Bridlington Bay. The wild implausibility of this indicates clearly that no
master politician's hand was behind Bedloe; and the lack of direct corroboration of Oates's story suggests that Oates was not responsible either,
though the two men had met. But in the evening of the same day Bedloe
paid a visit to another of his acquaintances, Charles Atkins,[1] and this
helped him to 'remember' some further details. When he was examined
by the Lords' Plot committee next day, Bedloe declared that one of the men
he had seen with Godfrey's dead body at Somerset House had
owned himself to be Pepys's clerk, Mr. Atkins.[2] That morning Samuel
Atkins, in his bed at Newgate, was awakened by Charles, who, with tears
in his eyes, told him what Bedloe was prepared to swear against him.
Samuel's only chance, it appeared, was to confess before it was too late[3];
and it was further suggested that he should admit to having asked Charles
to accuse Pepys of the murder to 'keep it off from the Duke of York'.
Here Charles Atkins's political objective was nakedly revealed; but Samuel
would have none of it. That afternoon he was confronted with Bedloe
before the lords of the Godfrey sub-committee. Fortunately the most that
Bedloe would say was that Samuel was very like the man he had seen with
Godfrey's body; he would not positively swear the identification. Fortified

---

[1] There is, however, no evidence that Oates and Charles Atkins knew one another.

[2] For Bedloe's appearance on the scene, see R. L'Estrange, op. cit. iii. 5–6, 24–25;
Bedloe, 31 Oct., *C.S.P.D. 1678*, p. 495; J. Pollock, *The Popish Plot* (1903), pp. 384–7
(slight verbal corrections in *C.S.P.D. 1678*, p. 507); Burnet, ii. 168–9; *L.J.* xiii. 343, 350–3;
MSS. Carte 81, fos. 424–5; MSS. Rawlinson A 181, fo. 26. The account of Bedloe in
M. Petherick, *Restoration Rogues* (1951), pp. 40–102, is enjoyable but not altogether
reliable.

[3] 'There is nothing can hurt you, but your fortune may be made by it; and what need
you care for your master?' These words are attributed to Charles in the version printed in
the *State Trials*, vi. 1483, but not in the MS. in Rawlinson A 181, fo. 19.

by this circumstance, Samuel was able to hold out against Shaftesbury's last urgings to him to 'confess all you know' and save his life, and went back to Newgate to wait patiently to be put on trial for complicity in the murder. Before the trial took place some weeks later the pressure had been taken off him by the appearance of much stronger 'evidence' from the third informer, Prance, against three other wretches; and by the tireless activities of Pepys to establish an unbreakable alibi for his clerk, which the latter himself had forgotten; and the result was an easy acquittal.

This story is based on Samuel Atkins's own narrative, but this rings true in its essentials, when some allowance has been made for rhetorical exaggeration of his protestations that he could not tell a lie, even to save his life. The question is, what interpretation is the biographer to place on Shaftesbury's conduct of the interrogations. There was less direct bullying than one might expect; for the most part Shaftesbury's attitude was that of one reasonable man speaking to another; but was all this a subtle attempt to persuade Atkins to invent charges against his master? Atkins himself plainly thought that it was, and so too did Pepys, who by now was willing to believe almost anything about Shaftesbury. There can be no doubt that the young man was under considerable temptation to betray a master with whom he was not on particularly good terms, and that he deserved the utmost credit for holding out against it. But there seems insufficient evidence to convict Shaftesbury positively of attempted subornation in this case, rather than the normal investigator's pressure to secure a confession; it is safer to leave it an open question, and to add that our knowledge of Shaftesbury's handling of other informers strongly suggests that he would have exploited anything that Atkins had said, whether the methods employed to elicit it may be deemed legitimate or not.

Bedloe's own story could easily be turned to political use. However incredible some of the details, it seemed to supply general confirmation of the existence of a plot. Winchester, reporting from the sub-committee to the House of Lords, made a virtue of Bedloe's reluctance to swear positively against Atkins; he had been 'very careful and exact in his testimony'. So good a courtier as Sir John Ernle, Chancellor of the Exchequer, thought that Bedloe had confirmed Oates's testimony. Members of the opposition privately agreed that his story of a Spanish invasion was ridiculous, but thought that the leaders of the plot might have spread such rumours to encourage the rank and file; and in any case, they said, there could be no doubt of the existence of a plot against English liberties which made it necessary to take precautions against the succession of a Catholic to the throne. Even courtiers agreed on this, carried away by the general torrent of feeling in the capital.[1]

Charles therefore found it necessary to make some concessions to this current of opinion, the more so as his principal minister, Danby, was also

[1] *L.J.* xiii. 350; Grey, vi. 212; Barrillon, 14/24 Nov.

anxious to win favour by passing legislation to 'pare the nails of a Popish successor'. His action was not so much a particularly cunning scheme to throw the opposition into disarray, as something almost forced upon him. On 9 November, two days after the appearance of Bedloe, Charles appeared before his houses of Parliament, and made a speech. Thanking the assembled peers and M.P.s for their care for his personal safety, he went on to assert his readiness to do his part to establish 'a firm security of the Protestant religion' 'not only during my time . . . but in all future Ages'. These words were greeted with loud applause, some members even thinking that they presaged the King's agreement to a measure which would ensure a Protestant succession. But the King went on to qualify his opening statement. 'And therefore I am come to assure you, that whatsoever reasonable Bills you shall present, to be passed into laws, to make you safe in the reign of any successor (so as they tend not to impeach the right of succession, nor the descent of the Crown in the true line, and so as they restrain not my power, nor the just rights of any Protestant successor) shall find from me a ready concurrence'. When the Commons were back in their own chamber, Sacheverell immediately complained that this tied their hands from ensuring that the successor was a Protestant; and he pertinently inquired of the Cavaliers whether, if a Catholic successor did not keep to the conditions of any 'reasonable bills', subjects would have a right to resist him? This was an obvious weakness of the policy of limitations, but the House declined to proceed with the debate, or to take up their adjourned debate on the motion to ask the King to exclude James from his presence and counsels. Instead they preferred to wait and see what happened to the Test Bill which they had sent up to the Lords. This would be a test in another sense—a test of the possibility of enacting effective anti-Catholic legislation. Public opinion was less inhibited, interpreting the speech as more far-reaching than it was. There were bells and bonfires and wine flowing as people reported it as a sign that there would be a Protestant successor and even that he would be Monmouth. Toasts were drunk to the King, Monmouth, and Shaftesbury as 'the only three pillars of all safety', and next day a rumour that Shaftesbury was to be sent to the Tower caused considerable restlessness. Shaftesbury's prominence was by this time exciting the distrust and jealousy of the former popular hero, Buckingham.[1]

The Commons therefore waited impatiently for news of the fate of the Test Act to exclude Catholics from Parliament. As Thomas Bennet, the young protégé of Shaftesbury's who had recently succeeded his father as M.P. for the borough of Shaftesbury, with an impulsive disregard for syntax, expressed it, 'If the Popish Lords be in the House, and the Duke

---

[1] L.J. xiii. 345; Grey, vi. 172–4; Reresby, 7 Nov., p. 157; Southwell to Ormond, 9, 12, and 16 Nov., H.M.C. Ormond MSS., N.S. iv. 467–8, 470, 473–4; Schwerin, 12/22 Nov., Briefe, p. 352; van Beuningen, 12/22 Nov., Add. MSS. 17677, DD; Barrillon, 14/24 Nov.

be a Papist, we can do nothing without this Bill', and it was useless to think of enacting limitations. A succession of reminders was sent to the upper House, and even the possibility of sending the Speaker with one was canvassed.[1] The Lords spent several days on the bill between 28 October, when they had received it, and 20 November. In committee on 7 November the Catholic peers sought to remind the House, and Shaftesbury in particular, of the order adopted by the House during the struggle over Danby's test three years earlier, to the effect that no oath should be permitted to take away any peer's place in Parliament.[2] Shaftesbury smiled blandly and quoted the Lord Keeper's remark during those debates, that the House was master of its own orders, and *leges posteriores priores abrogant*; and the House easily agreed on the principle that peers must take the oaths of allegiance and supremacy to retain their places. On 15 November, by a majority of five, the Catholics, with the aid of some of the bishops, passed an amendment, the effect of which was that peers should not lose their places if they refused the offensive Declaration against transubstantiation and the invocation of saints which the Commons had inserted in the Bill; but this was reversed at the report stage (20 November). So far all had gone well, but slowly, for the opposition, but at this point James got up and asked the favour of a special proviso to exempt him from the terms of the bill. His conscience was too tender for him to take the oath. He swore that he had no intention of subverting the government, and ended with 'an angry aspect' and ominous words that if they refused him this they would throw him into despair, and he did not know what this might eventually induce him to do: let them think of what they were doing, because the mischief would indeed be great for him, but many others also might have to suffer, if he was not considered in the manner due to him. Moved or alarmed by this, the House accepted the proviso, and the bill passed by a majority variously reported at 6, 12, and 20. It was noticed that Danby was not present, and that Monmouth went out before the debate ended to avoid voting: James complained bitterly to the King of this, of Monmouth's 'affecting of popularity' and of his friendship with Essex and Wharton, and alleged that Monmouth permitted his health to be drunk as Prince of Wales.[3]

The bill was therefore returned to the Commons for their approval of this new proviso. Danby, abandoning his somewhat equivocal attitude to James, rallied all his forces in support, and for once the Court speakers were numerous while most of the opposition sat silent or shouted 'Coleman's

---

[1] Grey, vi. 186–9, 204–9; Schwerin, 15/25 Nov., op. cit. p. 354.

[2] Cf. p. 376 above.

[3] *L.J.* xiii. 308, 335, 341, 344, 347, 349, 354–5, 358, 359, 360, 362, 363–4, 365–6; *H.M.C. House of Lords MSS. 1678–88*, pp. 61; R. North, *Examen* (1740), p. 64; Southwell to Ormond, 16 Nov., *H.M.C. Ormond MSS.*, N.S. iv. 473; MSS. Carte 81, fo. 380; Sarotti, 22 Nov./2 Dec. and 29 Nov./9 Dec.; Waldstein, 22 Nov./2 Dec., in Klopp, ii. 178–9; Barrillon, 21 Nov./1 Dec.; Clarke, *Life of James II* (1816), i. 525–6.

letters' and 'To the question'. When the House did come to the question, the proviso was accepted by 158 votes to 156, to the intense chagrin of opposition members like Sacheverell and Bennet who foreshadowed Shaftesbury's view that the bill was now worthless. Tempers were so heated that there was even an ugly scene in the lobby.[1] But the opposition's defeat was less important in itself than because it threw into relief the inherent weakness of the idea of solving the problem of the succession by restrictive legislation. After three weeks in the Lords the Court majority there had successfully inserted a destructive proviso into the bill, and as a result of Danby's efforts (including, it was rumoured, extensive bribery) the Commons had been brought to accept it. Could not a similar process be expected for every measure introduced to limit the powers of a Popish successor? Other events also suggested this. The Lords, again, after a speech from James, declined to concur with the Commons' proposal that three of Coleman's letters should be printed,[2] and the proposal fell to the ground. Catholics were still to be seen in the royal palaces, which were described as 'harbours for Papists', and even in the Court of Requests adjacent to where the Commons were sitting. The failure to recall immediately the British ambassador in Madrid (the Catholic Sir William Godolphin), the King's reported remarks disparaging the 'Plot' and even the prayers devised by the bishops for the official fast day all seemed to suggest that the government was not sufficiently serious about the plot. Sir Joseph Williamson, the Secretary of State, had to admit in the House that he had recently countersigned orders granting army commissions to Papists and dispensing them from the oaths required by the Test Act of 1673. In a wave of indignation the House swept aside Williamson's feeble explanation that he had to sign many documents put before him without reading them, and sent him to the Tower; and the speech in which the King informed them next day that he had released his minister was not calculated to soothe. Bennet, Shaftesbury's dependant, seized his chance to emphasize that 'it is not the ministers do this, but he that made them [the Duke of York]; from thence they have their succour and assistance'.[3]

All this seemed to some people to show that not much reliance could be placed on the promises which the King had made on 9 November to facilitate measures for the security of the Protestant religion; and on the day after the opposition's defeat over the Test Act proviso William Sacheverell, whose views almost invariably coincided with Shaftesbury's, talked in the Commons of debating the condition which the King had laid down

---

[1] C.J. ix. 543; Grey, vi. 240–60; Southwell to Ormond, 21 Nov., MSS. Carte 38, fos. 664–9; Barrillon, 25 Nov./5 Dec.

[2] L.J. xiii. 349; Southwell to Ormond, 12 Nov., H.M.C. Ormond MSS., N.S. iv. 470; Barrillon, 14/24 Nov. Nevertheless unofficial and unlicensed copies of the letters most damaging to the Duke of York were on the streets early in December (Van Beuningen, 10/20 Dec., Add. MSS. 17677, DD).

[3] Grey, vi. 165–72, 189–99, 216–38; Southwell to Ormond, 19 Nov., op. cit. iv. 475–8.

that the succession should not be disturbed. Unless they 'leaped over' that condition, how would it be possible to make any Association similar to that in Queen Elizabeth's time, to protect the monarch from being assassinated in the Catholic interest? But the majority of the members were not yet disposed openly to debate Exclusion; they preferred to follow the advice of Speaker Seymour, who in Grand Committee made a long speech warning against causing a civil war by 'making the heir of the Crown desperate', and advocating various proposals for the easier conviction of Papists and for limitations on the power of a future Popish prince. Some members thought this evidence that the King really meant what he had said in his speech.[1]

At this point, however, the informers again took a hand. On 13 November Oates had already had an interview with the King in which he had talked of the Queen's correspondence with the Jesuits, and gifts to them; and next day Bedloe at the bar of the Commons had declared that he had 'something to say against a great person near the King', but dared not do so until he had a general pardon, which would cover him against misprision of treason.[2] Now on Sunday, 24 November, through the agency of Dr. Tonge, Lady Gerard of Bromley,[3] and the wife of a gentleman of the bed-chamber, Mrs. Elliott, Oates obtained a second interview with Charles. Claiming most implausibly that on the previous occasion he had been inhibited by the presence of Secretary Williamson, this time he made no bones about accusing Queen Catherine of conspiring the death of her husband. He had, he said, seen a letter from her physician, Sir George Wakeman, to a Jesuit named Ashby, in which Wakeman accepted the idea of poisoning the King and said that the Queen had engaged him to do it; and in an ante-chamber he had even heard the Queen vow to 'revenge the violation of her bed'. Within a few days Bedloe followed with some similar inventions, including a story of a consultation attended by the Queen, Lords Bellasis and Powis (two of the five Catholic peers now in the Tower), two 'persons of quality', and others, to agree to 'taking off the King'. When asked at the bar of the Commons if the two unnamed persons were not the Duke of York and the Duke of Norfolk, Bedloe ambiguously answered that 'for any thing he knew, they might be they, he did not know but they might be they'.

These accusations so obviously fitted in with the known desire of Shaftesbury and others to divorce the Queen from the King that Charles immediately jumped to the conclusion that Oates had been prompted by

---

[1] Grey, vi. 262–8; Southwell to Ormond, 23 Nov., op. cit. iv. 478–9.
[2] *C.S.P.D. 1678*, p. 519; Grey, vi. 199, 209–10, 274–8.
[3] Pollock (*Popish Plot*, p. 230) says that Lady Gerard was 'in close connection with the Whig leaders', but this seems to be the result of confusing the Gerards of Bromley with those of Brandon. The dowager Lady Gerard of Bromley was the widow of a former Royalist exile; and there was a younger Lady Gerard who had just married their son, a boy of sixteen.

the villainous Earl. So sure was he, that within an hour of hearing Oates's statement he sent guards to keep a close watch upon the informer and to carry off all his papers. Great must have been Charles's delight when a letter from Shaftesbury was found among them, but it contained only a general exhortation to Oates to discover boldly and sincerely the whole conspiracy, without any exaggeration! James, as usual misreading the situation, promised himself that Oates was now so secured that he could not get away, and all his villainies would be found out at last; but instead the close watch kept by the guards on Oates only infuriated a House of Commons which by now had made him a hero. Whether Oates had in fact been prompted is far from certain. The suspicion is natural; yet not only is positive evidence lacking, but the 'discoveries', in spite of their apparent advantages to the opposition, were at once crude and premature. No one who knew the mild, inoffensive Queen Catherine and her pathetic devotion to her faithless husband could believe her capable of poisoning him, and the attempt to make capital out of the stories petered out. It is not unlikely that Oates and Bedloe, aware of the fact that a royal divorce was being talked of as a solution to the succession problem,[1] put their heads together and, in the hope of reward, concocted stories to facilitate it. In the process their haste spoiled the whole idea; Buckingham's comment when he heard the news was said to have been that it was not yet time to bring the Queen forward.[2]

'I do not believe a story, because Mr. Oates and Mr. Bedloe say it is true; but because it is probable to be true, therefore I believe it', declared one member of the Commons, Silas Titus. 'That which pushed the Commons on with rounder heat in this great matter', wrote a Court observer, Sir Robert Southwell, 'was, first, the assurance and vigour of the witnesses, as if they would live and die on the truth of what they said; next the opinion (doubted of by none) that the doctrine of Rome authorises all evil to come by their ends, and makes most bold with those that are most resigned to it; and lastly that the slender thread of the King's single life is, under God, the only bulwark of their present safety'. Nevertheless, warned by the Solicitor General, Sir Francis Winnington, that the evidence might not justify an immediate charge against the Queen, the House contented itself with an apparently unanimous address to the King for the removal of the Queen and all Papists from Court: this would restrict her to her palace at Somerset House, and incidentally restrict the Duke of York to

---

[1] Cf. p. 464 above.

[2] *C.S.P.D. 1678*, pp. 538–9; Barrillon, 25 Nov./5 Dec.; *L.J.* xiii. 385–92; Southwell to Ormond, 26 Nov., *H.M.C. Ormond MSS.*, N.S. iv. 480–1; Salvetti, 29 Nov./9 Dec., in Anna M. Crinò, *Il Popish Plot* (Rome, 1954), p. 52; Marquis to Marchioness of Worcester, 26 Nov., *H.M.C. Beaufort MSS.*, pp. 73–74; Duke of York to Prince of Orange, 26 Nov., *H.M.C. Foljambe MSS.*, p. 125; *C.J.* ix. 549–50; Grey, vi. 287–300; *C.S.P.D. 1678*, p. 550; *Lettre éscrite de Mons à un Amy à Paris* (1679), a translated summary of which is in *H.M.C. House of Lords MSS., 1678–88*, p. 99.

St. James's.[1] But the Lords, on 29 November, would not hear of concurring in this address. Unlike many of the Commons, most of the peers were personally acquainted with the Queen and could not credit the accusation. Though the debate was long, only eleven peers at the most (some sources said five, six or eight) voted for the address. Among them, needless to say, was Shaftesbury; but, since Halifax is often said to have been more scrupulous than his uncle, it is necessary to add that Halifax voted in the same way. Only two peers would join Shaftesbury in signing a Protest.[2]

One result of this failure to shake the position of the Queen was increased interest in that of Monmouth. Stories reached James[3] of cabals which united Monmouth 'with my Lord Russell, Mr. Montagu, Sir Henry Capel, and others of that gang'; Monmouth's crony Sir Thomas Armstrong was reported to have said that even if the King did not make his son Prince of Wales, he had witnesses ready to swear that Charles had been married to Mrs. Barlow, Monmouth's mother. Charles privately insisted that, well as he loved his son, 'he had rather see him hanged' than declared legitimate; but he was not sorry that some of his opponents were flattering themselves that he might consent. Monmouth could be kept under control, unlike some others (possibly the Prince of Orange?), and in any case the opposition would not be able to agree about his claims. Only a fortnight earlier Cavendish and Littleton had found fault with the wording of commissions directed without qualifications 'to our dear and entirely beloved son'. Many peers would certainly resent the elevation of a bastard. It is noticeable that Shaftesbury's own name was not among those of Monmouth's supporters quoted above, and possible that he was still pondering which course he ought to take.[4]

Encouraged by the failure of the attempt against the Queen, on the next day, 30 November, Charles announced his reluctant consent to the Test Act (which 'might hereafter be of ill consequence') and his decision to veto a Militia Bill which had been presented to him at the same time. This bill had arisen from a motion by Sir Gilbert Gerrard in the Commons on 18 November, that the King should be asked to order part of the militia to be in readiness to defend the country against Papist rebellion; Shaftesbury's dependant Bennet, in seconding, stressed the advantages of relying on the militia so that the King might have no further need for the army

[1] Grey, loc. cit.; Southwell to Ormond, 30 Nov., *H.M.C. Ormond MSS.*, N.S. iv. 484.

[2] Grey, *C.J.* and Southwell, loc. cit.; *L.J.* xiii. 392; Ossory to Duchess of Ormond, 30 Nov., *H.M.C. Ormond MSS.*, N.S. iv. 255; M. of Worcester to [the Marchioness, not Bedloe (*sic*) as stated by the editor], n.d., *H.M.C. Beaufort MSS.*, p. 82; Van Beuningen, 29 Nov./9 Dec., Add. MSS. 17677, DD; Barrillon, 2/12 Dec.; 'Lords who voted for the Address . . .' in MSS. Carte 81, fo. 387 (Wharton Papers).

[3] Possibly through Baptist May, who was said to have been the only one present at the cabals who disagreed with the others (J. S. Clarke, op. cit. i. 530–2). See also James to the Prince of Orange, 9 Dec., *H.M.C. Foljambe MSS.*, p. 125, and Barrillon, 12/22 Dec.

[4] Burnet, ii. 179; Grey, vi. 225.

which he had raised, and perhaps not even for his paid guards. When the Lords were asked to concur in the address a committee (which did not include Shaftesbury) reported that there was no legal power to keep the militia together for more than a fortnight without payment; and so a bill was rushed through both Houses empowering the Deputy Lieutenants to keep the militia in being for forty-two days. No Privy Councillor objected to the bill, and when Charles, warned at the last minute by Burnet of the danger of allowing the militia to escape from his control and become a tool of the opposition, imposed his veto, this came as a shock to the members of the Commons. The mood of frustration which had long been simmering was now approaching the boil. All the important measures attempted since the beginning of the session had been blocked, presumably by the influence of the Duke of York or the Earl of Danby, who stood out head and shoulders above all the ministers. In the early days of December, therefore, the opposition declined the government's offer to accept an amended militia bill and preferred to work up this feeling against 'the ministers' without immediately attacking the hated Lord Treasurer. Sacheverell, a man of extreme views coldly and rationally expressed, led the way; Bennet, excitable and vehement, made a violent defence of the militia and a violent attack on crypto-Papists, ending 'till we remove wife, friend, brother, and sister—till then, you'll never do good'; Clarges answered the old Royalist Birkenhead's fear that the situation was more and more like that of 1641 by arguing that 'now Popery is plainly coming in, more than in 1641, since we have a person so near the Crown, that has been perverted'; and finally some even of 'the Court's friends' were in favour of an address to the King, representing the dangerous situation, complaining of misrepresentation of their proceedings to the King and his adhering to 'private counsel' rather than that of Parliament.[1]

All this suited Shaftesbury's book admirably. Though so far he had few concrete successes, matters were progressing the way he wanted them to. He could afford to be jocular at the expense of Lord Wharton, his former ally who had abandoned him in the Tower, as they took the oaths prescribed by the Test Act. When the Puritan Wharton's turn came, he expressed some hypersensitive scruples that it was 'idolatry' to kiss the Bible on which the oath was taken. With deadly accuracy Shaftesbury said 'he hoped kissing was no idolatry, for if 't were then they must forbear kissing their wives'.[2] Wharton kissed the Book next day. For the rest, Shaftesbury attracted comparatively little attention in the Lords, except when he reported on a dangerous situation in that same county of Monmouthshire which had earlier become notorious. Captain Spalding, the

---

[1] *C.J.* ix. 541, 544–7; Grey, vi. 212–16, 270–1, 300–20; *L.J.* xiii. 372, 394; Burnet, ii. 178; Southwell to Ormond, 3 Dec., *H.M.C. Ormond MSS.*, N.S. iv. 486–7; Reresby, 2 Dec., p. 161.

[2] John Verney to Sir R. Verney, 15 Dec., *H.M.C. Seventh Report*, p. 471; *L.J.* xiii, 396, 398; MSS. Carte 81, fos. 390, 396.

governor of Chepstow Castle, was far less scrupulous than Lord Wharton
about oaths: in an age which set such store by them he was accused of
making the reckless statement that 'he could and would be ready to take
any oath that could be devised'. Shaftesbury used this horrifying remark
as an example of the unreliability of the King's armed forces,[1] and a few
days later declared threateningly in the House that involved in the Popish
Plot there were a number of 'considerable people' who had not yet been
named.[2] But the additional restrictions on rank-and-file Catholics which
the Lords debated were only incidental to his main purpose of excluding
their head from the succession; and Shaftesbury was more active in the
House's plot committee which still sat every morning before the House's
own sitting began. He was 'the great giant that speaks to all, and they say
with strange freedom, and admirable eloquence. My Lord Halifax is his
second, and so is my Lord Winchester; but none so close, so constant, and
so relied on by him as the Earl of Essex'. These four kept up close relations
with the committee which the Commons had set up to prosecute the five
Catholic peers whom Oates and Bedloe had accused—having taken that
prosecution out of the hands of ministers whom they could not trust.[3]

In private, however, Shaftesbury was more concerned with the mine
which was now ready to blow up Danby, and with it the Court's whole
position, already shaky, in the Commons. This was not something invented
by Shaftesbury; the mine would certainly have been dug and exploded
in any case, though Shaftesbury was probably consulted about its timing
and was certainly prepared to exploit it when the moment came. Ralph
Montagu, the former English ambassador in Paris who had been disgraced in the previous summer, wanted both revenge and financial gain.
He resented Danby's refusal to see him made Secretary of State, and,
having lost not only his hopes of that office but his embassy, sought to turn
to account the assets which remained to him, namely the letters which
Danby had written to him in the previous winter about negotiations for a
French subsidy. The deadliest of these was a letter of 25 March 1678,
five days after the King had assented to a Poll Bill providing money for
'an actual war' against Louis XIV; Danby, reluctantly accepting Charles's
view that the chance of a successful war had gone, had instructed Montagu
to ask Louis for 6 million livres a year for three years as part of a general
peace settlement. Actually, while Danby had always been reluctant to ask
for French money (and was bitterly disliked by France), Montagu had been
eager to ask for more; but this did not stop him from using the letter to
ruin Danby, or from himself accepting money from the French ambassador

---

[1] *L.J.* xiii. 401, 404; *H.M.C. House of Lords MSS., 1678–88*, p. 75; Marquis to Marchioness of Worcester, 5 Dec., *H.M.C. Beaufort MSS.*, p. 75.

[2] Barrillon, 9/19 Dec.

[3] Southwell to Ormond, 10 Dec., MSS. Carte 38, fo. 678; *H.M.C. House of Lords MSS.,
1678–88*, pp. 14–15; Grey, vi. 320–5; Southwell to Ormond, 7 Dec., *H.M.C. Ormond
MSS.*, N.S. iv. 487–9.

to do so. He was quite unprincipled in the matter. He knew that as soon as he published this and other correspondence, there would be a tremendous outcry from the Commons; the opposition had argued that the government's warlike professions had been intended to deceive, and this would prove it. The revelations would fit perfectly with the long-standing suspicions, strengthened by Coleman's papers, that there was a serious conspiracy against English liberties and English Protestantism, based on a secret understanding with Louis XIV. The only puzzling feature is Montagu's delay in producing the incriminating letters. Shortly after the beginning of the session he had entered the House in a by-election at Northampton, defeating Danby's candidate, Sir William Temple, with the aid of William Harbord and other influential opposition members in whom he had confided. The sheriff delayed matters by sending in a return in Temple's favour, and it was only on 11 November that the House unanimously approved Montagu's petition against this return.[1] By this time he had his plans laid with Barrillon, who was eager to promise money to drive Danby from power; and it was widely rumoured that he would accuse Danby,[2] but five weeks later he had not risen in his seat. The reason seems to have been in the first place that the opposition hoped to drive a wedge between Danby and the Duke of York. Originally, as we have seen, Danby had sought to use the Plot to demonstrate his own Protestantism by anti-Catholic measures, and James himself had distrusted him and feared that he would join in the demand that James should leave the Court.[3] By the beginning of December the opposition's hopes of this had evaporated[4]; but then it was thought best to wait until a bill had been passed for the disbandment of the armed forces raised in the past twelve months, so that it should not be in Danby's power to use them in a coup d'état. 'Until this be perfected, they cannot speak plain English.' Barrillon was willing enough to wait until he had seen the last of the Army; it was his aim to deprive Charles II of all means of pursuing any independent line in foreign policy; and indeed he was willing to spend money for the purpose. It was at this time, when the bill voting money for the paying-off of the soldiers was being debated, that Barrillon gave out the largest of the money presents to opposition leaders which, when they came to light a century later, drew the odium of historians upon them; yet it is as certain as that night follows day that the members concerned would have acted in the same way without any French money, so eager were they to see the last of these forces. It is highly improbable that these notorious bribes changed a single vote.[5]

---

[1] Browning, Danby, i. 301 and n.
[2] Cf. Reresby's warning to Danby, 18 Nov., Reresby, p. 159.
[3] Barrillon, 14/24 Nov.; Reresby, pp. 157–8.
[4] Southwell to Ormond, 10 Dec., MSS. Carte 38, fo. 678.
[5] Newsletter, MSS. Carte 72, fo. 429; Duke of York to Prince of Orange, 17 Dec., H.M.C. Foljambe MSS., p. 126; Barrillon, 12/22 Nov. The only contentious feature

Unlike Montagu, Littleton, Powle, Harbord, and others, Shaftesbury received no money, and did not see the French ambassador, but he probably knew well enough what was going on, through Russell and Bennet who were in the secret. It was in any case a very 'open' secret. As the days went by, there were more and more references in public to people who 'diverted the public counsels from any good issue', and even had 'stifled the Plot' by doing nothing for six weeks between 13 August and Oates's appearance before the Council on 28 September; in private some talked of the letters in Montagu's possession. The government expected the attack to come on 17 December.[1] When that day passed quietly, Danby determined to wait no longer, but to seize the initiative with a counter-attack accusing Montagu of holding secret conferences with the Papal nuncio in Paris. To obtain material for this accusation, and possibly incidentally to secure the letters which Montagu intended to produce, the Privy Council ordered the seizure of all Montagu's papers. But as in the attempt a month previously to seize Oates's papers, the result was to make matters worse for the government. The material hoped for was not found; the most important of the letters were elsewhere; and the effect on the Commons was to make members sympathetic to the victims of this seizure, the more so as in this case the victim was one of themselves, and privilege and precedents might be involved. Sir John Ernle, the Chancellor of the Exchequer, officially informed the House of the steps taken against their member, taking care not to do so until the House was about to adjourn at one o'clock. At first Montagu's friends concentrated on asking whether the information on which the Council's order was grounded was on oath in the proper legal form—and after some discussion the House resolved on an address to the King to inquire about this, and about the precise charge made against Montagu. The King sent word that, since he was busy in the Lords, he would receive this Address later at Whitehall; and at this point the day's proceedings might have come to an end. But in the meantime the opposition members had had time for hasty consultations amongst themselves, and perhaps with their friends in the Lords, including Shaftesbury; and now Montagu rose for the first time and announced his belief that the reason for the seizure of his papers was that he had 'letters of great consequence . . . to produce, of the designs of a great minister of state'. William Harbord, Bennet, Cavendish, Russell, and others made it plain that they had seen the letters, and when it was revealed that the box containing them had escaped seizure Russell, Harbord, and two others were sent to bring it to the House immediately. Montagu then, at the

---

about the disbanding bill was the question whether the money should be paid into the Exchequer or into the Chamber of London; the principle of providing money for the disbandment was accepted by all.

[1] Southwell to Ormond, 7, 17 Dec., *H.M.C. Ormond MSS.*, N.S. iv. 488, 490; Grey, vi. 322–3 (Sjt. Stringer), 326–7 (Clarges and Powle); Duke of York, as in previous note.

command of the House, took out two letters, the second of which was that of 25 March 1678, with hypocritical remarks of his sorrow that so great a minister had brought this guilt upon himself; it had been his intention, he said, to have acquainted Secretary Coventry with the papers, and 'out of duty and respect to the King' he would not have revealed them but for the House's command.

The House received them in a stunned silence. Characteristically it was Bennet, Shaftesbury's man, who broke it. 'I wonder the House sits so silent when they see themselves sold for six millions of livres to the French. . . . Now we see who has played all this game; who has repeated all the sharp answers to our addresses, and raised an army for no war. . . . I would impeach the Treasurer of High Treason.' This set the tone for the debate which followed; until at ten o'clock at night the motion that the question for the impeachment should be put was carried by 179 votes to 116. This was an unusually large majority in a House in which single figure majorities had not been uncommon; and it meant that Danby's laboriously constructed Court Party now lay in ruins. In the next two days his counterattacks failed. When he sent to the House letters mentioning Ruvigny's intrigues with 'Lord Russell and other malcontents' in the previous winter, the House easily accepted Russell's lying denial ('I defy any man alive to charge me with any dealing with the French'); and the proposed articles of impeachment were carried one by one, in spite of the efforts of Danby's supporters, by what were fairly comfortable majorities (varying from 50 to 24) in this Parliament. Not only that, but the majorities included royal servants like Sir Francis Winnington, the Solicitor-General, Sir Stephen Fox, Paymaster to the Forces, Sir Robert Howard, the Auditor, and the sailor Sir Robert Holmes (all of whom lost their offices as a consequence) and there were strong rumours that Speaker Seymour had quarrelled with the Lord Treasurer. Danby's control over the House of Commons had gone for ever; and Bennet was allowed to remark, without contradiction, that 'this is only the difference between Coleman and the Treasurer, that Coleman dealt with the King of France's confessor about money to bring in Popery, and the Treasurer dealt with the French King's ministers for money'.[1]

Danby still retained a strong position in the Lords, which, when it received the Commons' impeachment on 23 December, declined by a majority of twenty even to order him to withdraw from the House while the matter was debated. On 27 December a roughly similar majority decided that Danby should not be committed to custody. Eighteen peers protested

---

[1] For the debates of 19–21 Dec., see *C.J.* ix. 559–62; Grey, vi. 337–87; [Southwell to Ormond, 21 Dec., MSS. Carte 38, fos. 682–3; Sir Cyril Wyche to Ormond, 21 Dec., *H.M.C. Ormond MSS.*, N.S. iv. 285–6; Fox to Ormond, 28 Dec., ibid. 290–1; L. Herbert to M. of Worcester, 24 Dec., *H.M.C. Beaufort MSS.*, pp. 79–80; W. Paston to Lord Yarmouth, 18 Dec. (*sic*), *H.M.C., Sixth Report*, p. 389; Barrillon, 19/29 Dec., 23 Dec./ 2 Jan., 26 Dec./5 Jan.; Browning, *Danby*, i. 301–8.

against the first decision and fifteen against the second; Shaftesbury, Buckingham, Winchester, Halifax, and Wharton (but not Monmouth, who voted with the Court) signing on each occasion.[1] There were all the makings of a deadlock between the majority in the Commons and Danby's friends in the Lords, including the 'dead weight' of the bishops; but it is to be doubted whether the opposition was disappointed by this prospect. The King could not afford such a deadlock: it would not give him the money which he needed, it would dangerously inflame an already over-heated public opinion, and there was no knowing what further secrets might be revealed in the course of a prolonged dispute between Danby and Montagu. Charles was in a very difficult position, and in the continued refusal of the French to aid him, he would have to make some concession.

At the same time other problems were pressing on Charles. The Plot had begun to levy its toll of blood. Coleman had met his death earlier in the month, and Charles neither regretted his passing nor thought the terrible sentence unjust. But he felt differently about the three Jesuits, Ireland, Pickering, and Grove, who had been convicted on 17 December on the perjured evidence of Oates and Bedloe. 'He well remembered what his father suffered for consenting to the Earl of Strafford's death' and was determined not to shed innocent blood if he could avoid it; but his councillors would not accept responsibility for a reprieve, while Parliament was in session. Danby joined the others in arguing that the Jesuits had had a fair trial and that their blood was on the heads of witnesses and jury, and Lord Chancellor Finch made it clear that he would rather give up the Great Seal than affix it to a pardon. Only a prorogation could enable Charles to prolong the lives of the condemned men.[2]

Moreover, Charles had a third reason for a prorogation, in that the vigour with which Shaftesbury and his colleagues on the Lords' Plot committee and Godfrey sub-committee had pressed their investigations had attracted other informers to come forward with new 'evidence'. In contrast with Charles's creditable reluctance to shed innocent blood, Shaftesbury betrayed no sign of unease. He had, it is true, nothing to do with the prosecutions in the trials, and where he could do a good turn without giving up any political advantage he would do so: having visited the Catholic barrister Richard Langhorn in Newgate he obtained from the Lords permission for the prisoner's friends to have access to him.[3] But for political advantage he did patronize the witnesses and in one case he discouraged

---

[1] *L.J.* xiii. 432–4, 441; *H.M.C. House of Lords MSS., 1678–88*, p. 85; Reresby, p. 166; Barrillon, 26 Dec./5 Jan., 30 Dec./9 Jan.; Van Beuningen, 27 Dec./6 Jan., Add. MSS. 17677, EE; Browning, *Danby*, i. 309–10, iii. 129–33.

[2] Barrillon, 26 Dec./5 Jan.; Southwell to Ormond, 28 and 31 Dec., *H.M.C. Ormond MSS.*, N.S. iv. 492, 495; Grey, vi. 394–9; Williamson's notes, 31 Dec., *C.S.P.D. 1678*, p. 595.

[3] *State Trials*, vii. 510–11; Southwell to Ormond, 17 Dec., op. cit. iv. 489; *L.J.* xiii. 418, 421. It does not appear to have been Shaftesbury's fault that Langhorn did not receive longer notice of his trial.

criticism of them. One William Stayley, the son of a Catholic goldsmith, had been sentenced to death for an alleged remark in a tavern that 'he would kill the King himself'; and Gilbert Burnet, distrusting the character of his Scots compatriots who had given evidence, went about letting people know what 'profligate wretches' they were, and hoping that men's lives would not be taken upon such testimony. Shaftesbury had no direct interest in the case, but he 'could not bear the discourse. He said we must support the evidence, and that all those who undermined the credit of the witnesses were to be looked upon as public enemies.'[1] This was his consistent attitude, and in the short run it brought him political gain. Others were encouraged to come forward with supplementary information about the Plot, and thus keep up the anti-Catholic panic which he could use to force through Exclusion.

The first of these witnesses, however, was an involuntary one, betrayed to the authorities by an aggrieved lodger, who had been dunned for arrears of rent and suspected of purloining a silver tankard belonging to his landlord. This landlord was Miles Prance, a Roman Catholic silversmith in Holborn, who in the course of his trade had naturally accepted many commissions from Catholics, including Grove, Pickering, and Ireland. As ill-luck would have it, the only three nights when Prance had slept away from home in the last two years were the three of Sir Edmund Berry Godfrey's disappearance, and he was never able to supply convincing evidence of where he had been. Moreover, when an opportunity was provided for Bedloe to see him, in an eating-house inappropriately called Heaven, Bedloe immediately claimed to recognize him as one of the men he had seen, by the light of a dark lanthorn, round Godfrey's corpse in a room in Somerset House. Prance was promptly brought before the House of Lords' investigating committee, including Shaftesbury, and closely questioned. At first Prance denied hotly that he was privy to Godfrey's murder, but when left to cool his heels in Newgate he realized the desperate position he was in. He was a rather ordinary married tradesman, who liked his drink and had little interest in politics, but now found himself plunged by circumstances into a world of which he had no experience. He was petrified by fear, and he took the obvious way out. As it was put later by the Tory L'Estrange, he had the choice 'whether being innocent he would confess himself to be a murderer, and so escape; or deny it, and hang: but charity began at home, and he chose the perjury'.[2] When examined at the Council Board on Christmas Eve, and when promised his pardon by the King if he confessed, he gave a long circumstantial account of Godfrey's murder, incriminating three entirely innocent acquaintances named Green, Berry, and Hill who had connexions with Somerset House. Five

---

[1] *State Trials*, vi. 1501–12; Burnet, ii. 171–2. It is fair to say that the evidence suggests that the words complained of were indeed spoken. Cf. Pollock, op. cit. pp. 323–6.

[2] L'Estrange, op. cit. iii. 14.

days later, however, whether tormented by conscience or by fears that he would lose his Catholic customers, he asked for a private interview with the King, and recanted all that he had said. Years later he tried to extenuate his perjury by telling a rather melodramatic story: on his first morning in the prison 'up comes a person to himself wholly unknown, lays down a paper upon a form just by him, and so goes his way. Soon after this, comes another, with a candle; sets it down, and leaves him.' By the light of this obliging candle, Prance said, he read details of the Plot and Bedloe's evidence about Godfrey—'hints of what he was to swear to'; and when examined at Thanet House by Shaftesbury and three other peers, he was threatened with hanging if he did not confess; told that 'there must be *great persons* in it' and bid not to spare the King himself. Thus Prance excused himself in later years. When he recanted on 29 December, however, he said nothing of all this; his story was in almost total disagreement with Bedloe's; and there were none of the reflections upon the Queen and the Duke which could have been expected if Shaftesbury had prompted him. The Privy Councillors suspected that he had been tampered with to make a false recantation, not suborned to make a false confession, and the Lord Chancellor questioned him narrowly and suggested showing him the rack. Prance was no sooner back in Newgate than he recanted his recantation. It was a peculiar business, and time was needed to unravel it. It was also necessary to prevent Shaftesbury and the opposition from making political capital out of the fact (as Charles himself now considered it) that Godfrey had been murdered in the Queen's palace.[1]

In the meantime Stephen Dugdale had voluntarily come forward with further information against Lord Stafford. When the Earl of Essex reported this to the Lords they heard a kind of corroboration of Oates's story of the Jesuit plot to assassinate the King, with the interesting embellishment that the Duke of Monmouth was to be killed as well; and observers noticed that now Monmouth was at work giving the King 'the same impressions which the bulk of his subjects have', was at odds with Danby, 'and appears of late to be more a man of business than was expected he would prove'. He was making a bid for popularity. But the value of Dugdale's evidence could not quickly be assessed; his deposition had been sent to the Earl of Essex from Staffordshire, and nothing was known about him in London.[2]

---

[1] *H.M.C. House of Lords MSS., 1678–88*, pp. 51–52; *L.J.* xiii. 431, 436–9; Williamson's notes in *C.S.P.D. 1678*, pp. 586–7, 592–3; Southwell to Ormond, 24, 28, 31 Dec., *H.M.C. Ormond MSS.*, N.S. iv. 490–1, 492, 494; MSS. Rawlinson A 136, fos. 417–19; Capt. Richardson's evidence at the trial of Green, Berry, and Hill, *State Trials*, vii. 177–8; J. S. Clarke, op. cit. i. 535; L'Estrange, op. cit. iii. 26–27, 51–53, 62–63, 80. See J. Pollock, op. cit., pp. 120–48, for the interesting but to me unconvincing theory that Prance's story of the manner and place of Godfrey's murder was true in essentials, though not in involving Green, Berry, and Hill. Prance pleaded guilty to a charge of perjury in 1686.

[2] *L.J.* xiii. 442–3; Southwell to Ormond, 28 Dec., op. cit. iv. 492; *H.M.C. Fitzherbert MSS.*, p. 118.

All these factors together, Danby, the Jesuits, Prance, and Dugdale, combined to make some breathing-space urgently necessary for the King. Late on the 27th he sent out orders that the next day the Lords were to meet in their robes, presumably for a prorogation. Within a few hours he countermanded these orders, it was rumoured at the instigation of Prince Rupert. But on 30 December he did take the decision: he prorogued Parliament until 4 February, promising in the meantime to disband the Army and to 'prosecute the Plot'.[1] It was a desperate decision, involving the loss of the Disbanding Bill and the supplies which it promised for the purpose, and it was widely interpreted and criticized as a move to save Danby, though Danby, to escape the odium, insisted that he had nothing to do with it.[2]

James, writing to his nephew in Holland, was full of optimism about the good effect which the prorogation might have,[3] but as usual he misread the situation. Only five weeks were gained, at the cost of increasing the Commons' venom against Danby and the almost complete distrust of the government which Montagu's revelations, on top of the events of the past years, had produced. When Charles appealed to the French ambassador, Barrillon smiled and gave fair words, but made it plain that Charles had not yet expiated his alliance with William of Orange and his semi-independent line in foreign affairs a year earlier.[4] As it turned out, neither Prance nor Dugdale produced any deadly information against the Queen or James, but in general their evidence did a great deal to reinforce the conviction that there had indeed been a Catholic Plot. After his first recantation, the withdrawal of that, and a second recantation, the wretched Prance had spent ten days of mental agony (or, his jailers said, feigned madness) until the committee of Privy Councillors whom Charles had appointed to conduct examinations had decided 'that he spoke plainest when he was in irons'; and the combination of irons and a cold dank dungeon (it was freezing, and he had neither bed nor blanket for some days) led him eventually to make up his mind. After the 'raving talk' and the outbursts of tears had subsided, he returned to his first story; he made no effort to harmonize it with Bedloe's story, but none of the Privy Councillors was disposed to inquire into the many contradictions, and the doomed three, Green, Berry, and Hill, had no facilities for doing so.[5] As for Stephen Dugdale, when he arrived in London from Staffordshire, he made a big

---

[1] Southwell to Ormond, 28, 31 Dec., op. cit. 492, 494; Van Beuningen, 31 Dec./10 Jan., Add. MSS. 17677, EE; Barrillon, 30 Dec./9 Jan.; L.J. xiii. 447.

[2] Southwell to Ormond, 4 Jan., MSS. Carte 39, fo. 1. But cf. the letter to Col. Fitzpatrick, 4 Jan., MSS. Carte 38, fo. 617, which dismisses this as pretence.

[3] Archives de la Maison d'Orange-Nassau, ed. G. Groen van Prinsterer (The Hague and Utrecht, 1858–62), II. v. 367.

[4] Barrillon, 26 Dec./5 Jan., 30 Dec./9 Jan., 2/12 Jan.

[5] MSS. Rawlinson A 136, fos. 28–29, 32, 35–36, 38–39, 45–47, 50–52, 60, 67–69; Coventry Papers, vol. xi. fos. 357–9; C.S.P.D. 1679–80, pp. 27–28, 33–34.

impression, not only on the opposition but on courtiers like Secretary Coventry and Sir Robert Southwell, as a 'plain and honest' witness. He had been for fourteen years the steward of the Catholic peer Lord Aston at Tixall in Staffordshire, and, coming as he did from a rather higher social class than other Plot informers, seemed by the standards of the seventeenth century to be a more credible witness: it was not until later that he stood revealed as a dishonest steward, since Lord Aston did not dare to press any charges at this point. Southwell was 'as convinced as of my creed' that there was 'a most hellish design' against the King's life, and Charles too, though still certain that Oates and Bedloe were perjurers and impostors, after hearing Dugdale, could no longer help believing that there was a conspiracy against his person, and that there might be some factual foundation for Oates's and Bedloe's inventions. The Speaker paid Dugdale's debts, and the King ordered that he should be lodged in Monmouth's house.[1]

This was the period in which belief in the existence of a Plot was most general. Even Catholics, it was said, were beginning to suspect that there might be some truth in the stories, and to put the blame on the abominable practices of the Jesuits.[2] For Protestants enterprising cutlers manufactured some thousands of daggers, bearing on one side the words *pro religione Protestantium*, and on the other, under a death's head, *Memento Godfrey, 12 October 78*. Women carried them to defend themselves from a possible Popish massacre, and the French ambassador claimed to have seen them in the hands of persons of quality, until they were officially banned.[3] The City was full of wild rumours of impending French invasion, which were not diminished by the Lord Mayor's action in chaining the streets and increasing the guards. Two of Danby's letters to Montagu were printed. The 'rabble' congregated outside Newgate and the Recorder's House clamouring to know when the three convicted Jesuits would be executed. And the general feeling against the prorogation was so great that 'the Green Ribbon men' talked in their club that the nation was sold to the French,

---

[1] *H.M.C. Fitzherbert MSS.*, pp. 118–39; Coventry to Ormond, 14 Jan., *H.M.C. Ormond MSS.*, N.S. iv. 303; Southwell to Ormond, 14 Jan., op. cit. iv. 497; Committee of Council for Examinations, MSS. Rawlinson A 136, fos. 29, 49, 104–6; Barrillon, 16/26 Jan.; Van Beuningen, 10/20 Jan., Add. MSS. 17677, EE. At Stafford's trial in Dec. 1680 Dugdale swore that he had been told by the Jesuit Evers that the Duke of York had sent orders for Godfrey's murder, and, to explain why he had not said so before, the Earl of Essex told Burnet that he had in fact said so at his first examination (8 Jan. 1679), but the King told him to keep this quiet since it was only hearsay, and therefore valueless in law, and would add to the fury against James (Burnet, ii. 190–1). But it is impossible to believe that such a statement could have been kept quiet even if Essex (who examined him) and Dugdale had wished to do so. Pollock (*Popish Plot*, p. 341) says that Dugdale told the story in his information of 21 March 1679, but the source he cites (*H.M.C. Fitzherbert MSS.*, p. 135) makes no mention of it.

[2] Salvetti, 10/20 Jan., in Anna M. Crinò, *Il Popish Plot* (Rome, 1954), p. 58. Cf. Sancroft's conversation with Stafford in the Tower, 21 Jan., MSS. Tanner 39, fo. 159.

[3] Barrillon, 16/26 Jan.; P.C. Reg. 2/67, fo. 21.

that Parliament would not meet again if Whitehall could do without it, and that everything was governed by the King's French mistress, the Duchess of Portsmouth, the Duke of York, Danby, and the French ambassador.[1]

It is not surprising that Charles was reading the history of 1641 and fearing a similar course of events in 1679.[2] Clearly he had to make some concessions. Before the pressure of his councillors and the opinion of his judges he had to abandon his idea of leaving the three Jesuits alive until the falsity of Oates's and Bedloe's evidence was revealed: having heard Dugdale's additional evidence, he gave the order for the execution of Ireland and Grove, while leaving Pickering whom Dugdale had not mentioned. His efforts to dispose of the case of the five Catholic lords in the Tower during the prorogation were blocked by the judges' opinion that an impeachment could not be tried out of Parliament.[3] Inevitably the question had to be faced whether to meet again a Commons which would have been angered even more by the prorogation. On 20 January the King declared in Council for a further prorogation from 4 to 25 February, only to change his mind the same evening. He was contemplating the alternative of a dissolution, and new elections. The Duke of York had for years been convinced that from the Catholic point of view no House of Commons could be worse than the present one; and since Montagu's revelations the same was true of Danby, who sought therefore to reach a bargain with some of the Country Party. He offered them the new parliament which they wanted, and undertook to get the Duke sent out of the way before it met; he was the more willing to do this when he was told that Shaftesbury and his party, using George Pitt, the member for the Dorset constituency of Wareham, as an intermediary, were trying to turn James against him. In return Danby was promised safety from impeachment in the new parliament, provided that he gave up the Treasury and retired from politics; and supply would be provided for the King. The trouble about this bargain was that the parliamentarians who made it could not speak for their colleagues. The aged Presbyterian Lord Holles was no longer an influential figure, and even if Littleton, Boscawen, and Hampden were sincere, they could not commit Shaftesbury, who was not directly involved. But in a desperate situation this seemed to offer the best chance, and on 24 January the King announced his decision to dissolve Parliament and call a new one for 6 March. He did not ask his Council's advice because, he said, he found everybody more afraid to displease the Parliament than him.[4]

[1] Letter to Col. Fitzpatrick, 4 Jan., MSS. Carte 38, fos. 617–18; C.S.P.D. 1679–80, pp. 19–25.   [2] Southwell to Ormond, 4 Jan., MSS. Carte 39, fo. 1.
[3] Ibid.; C.S.P.D. 1679–80, p. 44.
[4] Secretary Coventry to Ormond, 21 Jan., H.M.C. Ormond MSS., N.S. iv. 306; Sir Charles Lyttleton to Lord Hatton, 21 Jan., Hatton Correspondence, ed. E. M. Thompson (Camden Society, 1878), i. 170; Burnet, ii. 187–8; Reresby, p. 168; Barrillon, 30 Jan./ 9 Feb.; Robert Brent to Danby, 21 Jan., Add. MSS. 28053, fo. 133; C.S.P.D. 1679–80, pp. 50, 52.

So ended the Cavalier Parliament after eighteen years, unlamented by anyone. Indeed the rejoicing in London was so great as to indicate quite clearly that Charles's decision had been a mistake.[1] Not least among those who rejoiced were the four lords who had been imprisoned in 1677 for maintaining that Parliament then stood dissolved, and especially Shaftesbury, who had been released from the Tower less than twelve months before. Shaftesbury boasted that the dissolution was his doing.[2] This was untrue, in the sense that he had not been a party to the negotiation of Lord Holles and his group which had influenced Danby. But in the sense that for the past four years he had striven to compel a dissolution, and that he had done more than any other single man to obstruct Danby's efforts to build up a permanent Court majority, his triumph was justified. Danby and the King had at last been brought to admit that they could not control the old Parliament; it remained to be seen what could be done with the new.

[1] Barrillon, 27 Jan./6 Feb., 30 Jan./9 Feb.; Van Beuningen, 28 Jan./7 Feb., Add. MSS. 17677, EE.
[2] Southwell to Thomas Henshaw, 22 Nov. 1682, Add. MSS. 38015, fo. 278.

CHAPTER XXIII

THE FIRST EXCLUSION BILL
(JANUARY–MAY 1679)

Suppose there were a lion in the lobby, one cries shut the door and keep him out. No, says another, open the door and let us chain him when he comes in.

(Silas Titus, 7 Jan. 1681)

A T the beginning of 1679 Shaftesbury had built up a greater influence in Parliament than any other opposition leader. But outside Parliament he stood out even more as the great hero of the opposition to the Court. He had a strong hold on the affections of a large section of the City. Rumours of a plot against his life had led some of the citizens to pay for a special guard,[1] and when Miles Prance finally decided to be an informer rather than a victim of the Plot, he thought it worth while to include in his inventions a story of four fellow-tradesmen who had said that Shaftesbury as the great persecutor of the Catholics must be 'taken off'. Fortunately there was no corroboration, and one of the four, Adamson, actually went to Thanet House to protest his innocence, only for Shaftesbury to refuse to see him 'unless he would make some discovery'; and since Adamson insisted that he had no discovery to make, the men eventually escaped after some weeks of uneasiness.[2]

All politicians were well aware of London's importance in their calculations. It included perhaps one-tenth of the total population of the country, and considerably more than that of its easily realizable wealth. Amongst its citizens were virtually all those from whom governments could hope to borrow money, and as a body they formed the public opinion which could most easily be influenced, organized and mobilized by oppositions. Others besides Shaftesbury could remember the vital part played by the City in the events of the 1640s,[3] and the pamphlets which circulated there did so because their authors expected not only to gain financial reward, but to influence events. Members of Parliament might be predominantly gentry, but they were very much open to the atmosphere of the capital in or near which they resided during sessions, and from which they derived their news at other times. Again, the technique of exploiting citizens' petitions, which Pym had used in 1641, could be employed once more.

---

[1] P. Legh to his wife, 31 Dec., in Lady Newton, *Lyme Letters, 1660–1760* (1925), p. 74; Van Beuningen, 7/17 Jan., Add. MSS. 17677 EE. Cf. p. 480 above.

[2] MSS. Rawlinson, A 136, fos. 46, 144; W. Lloyd in Coventry Papers, xi. fo. 357; *C.S.P.D. 1679–80*, pp. 28, 185; *L.J.* xiii. 467–8, 474, 486, 492–3.

[3] Cf. Valerie Pearl, *The City of London and the Outbreak of the Puritan Revolution* (1961).

When the fate of the Test Act was in doubt, an observer wrote: 'And so tuned and so united is this great engine at the present that I do more than fear, if addresses from the Commons will not move the Lords to the expediting of the Bill, they will hear of addresses from another place'; and after the prorogation there was talk of asking the Lord Mayor to present a petition to the King.[1]

From this point of view Shaftesbury's house in Aldersgate now proved to be a very convenient party headquarters. Danby's spies, indeed, thought that he had a printing-press there, but this was probably a misinterpretation of a remark by one of the Earl's servants 'that my Lord Shaftesbury could have what he pleased printed, and that in a night's time'. Certainly printing-presses were easily accessible, and the government's control over them was not very effective. In principle it is highly likely that some of the many Whig pamphlets published in the next three years were commissioned by Shaftesbury; but (with one or two exceptions) there is insufficient evidence to enable us to distinguish them from the mass of libels written to cash in on a ready market.[2] A second significant activity in which Danby's spies plausibly thought that the Earl was engaged was in giving instructions to his supporters in the City, notably Sir Robert Peyton, Sir Thomas Player, and Francis Jenks; there was talk of calling a Common Hall, of its 'keeping a correspondency' with the opposition in Parliament, of addresses and petitions already prepared, and of similar efforts at Bristol, Chester, 'and all the considerable corporations in England'. As yet these activities were subterranean; it was only later that they had a direct influence on the course of events. And the same may be said of a third form of activity reported by Danby's informers, namely the messages said to be passing between the Duke of Monmouth's creatures, Shaftesbury and Buckingham—messages carried by Stringer, and also by Shepherd and the one-legged Francis Charlton, who were to acquire a notoriety in the Rye House Plot. Certainly Ralph Montagu had been sounding out the possibilities of French support for declaring Monmouth Prince of Wales; but there are indications that Shaftesbury was very doubtful about the Duke. When he classified the members of the new Parliament, he included the Duke's boon companion, Sir Thomas Armstrong, and his secretary, James Vernon, amongst the courtiers.[3]

Shaftesbury was preoccupied with such matters as these as he waited in London. He was not tempted to go down into Dorset, for it was bitter

---

[1] Southwell to Ormond, 16 Nov., *H.M.C. Ormond MSS.*, N.S. iv. 474; 'T.B.', 13 Jan., *C.S.P.D. 1679–80*, pp. 19–20; Ellis to [?Ormond], 18 Jan., MSS. Carte 243, fo. 429.

[2] Cf. O. W. Furley, "The Whig Exclusionists: Pamphlet Literature in the Exclusion Campaign, 1679–81', in *Cambridge Historical Journal* (1957), pp. 20–21. Mr. Furley's conclusion is that 'the precise relationship between Shaftesbury and his "hackney scribblers" remains a matter for speculation'.

[3] Letters to Danby in Add. MSS. 28049, fos. 30–35, 28047, fos. 47–48; Barrillon, 13/23, 16/26, 20/30 Jan.; for list of members, cf. p. 500, n. 4 below.

winter weather and the Thames was frozen hard: when one of the fires which so alarmed the Whigs broke out in Southwark, the engines had to use the contents of many barrels of beer to stop it.[1] Evidently he was so confident of success in the elections that he felt it unnecessary to go to Dorset in person. From Thanet House he helped to arrange the candidature of Thomas Wharton and Richard Hampden for Buckinghamshire,[2] and, along with the Marquis of Winchester, sent letters warning their friends not to choose Puritan 'fanatics' and so alienate moderate opinion: when some of these were intercepted 'the King was much pleased, and said he had not heard so much good of them a great while'. But no elaborate central organization was necessary or was used in order to achieve the electoral triumph which followed. Though in many places local factors and personal rivalries played their usual part, there is also evidence, in many of the counties and larger boroughs, that a general political feeling secured the elimination of Court candidates and the election of opposition men. Certainly it was not a victory which was achieved by any Whig manipulation of rotten boroughs, and there is no good reason for doubting that the result reflected the opinions of the politically conscious classes. Dining one day at Lord Shaftesbury's, Lady Russell found her host in a jocular mood. The Earl told Sacheverell, who was one of the guests, that 'my Lord Russell was a greater man than he, for he was but one knight, and Lord Russell would be two'—that is, would be returned knight of the shire by two different counties.[3]

When all the results were in Shaftesbury proceeded to draw up a list classifying the members in four categories. 153 members were marked 'ow', that is, 'old' (members of the previous parliament) and 'worthy', and 149 were 'nH', 'new' and 'honest'. 98 were 'ov', 'old' and 'vile', and 60 were 'nB', 'new' and 'bad' and 36, all newly elected members, were marked as doubtful. The total of 302 opposition members against 158 Courtiers was over-optimistic, but not very much so. The list brings out very clearly the two main features of the results, namely the large opposition majority of nearly two to one, which had replaced the almost evenly divided House of a year earlier, and the large influx of new men. 245 members, or nearly half the House, would be sitting for the first time, and they would need careful leading in the way their guides wanted them to go.[4]

At first Charles persuaded himself that, since so many 'men of estates' had been chosen, the new Parliament would be 'more moderated'; 'having

---

[1] Luttrell, i. 7. It is noteworthy that the fire was reported both by Barrillon, 27 Jan./ 6 Feb., and by Van Beuningen, 27 Jan./6 Feb.

[2] Lord Wharton to his son, 27 Jan., MSS. Carte 79, fo. 168; cf. J. R. Jones, *The First Whigs* (1961), pp. 45–47.

[3] Jones, op. cit. pp. 34–48; Lady Russell to Lord Russell, [?13] and 15 Feb., in [Mary Berry], *Life of Lady Russell* (1819), pp. 204–6.

[4] The list is printed by Jones, 'Shaftesbury's "Worthy Men" ', in *Bull. Inst. Hist. Res.* xxx (1957), 232–41.

such good stakes to lose, [they] would be very unwilling to throw cross and pile again, for all they had in the world'.[1] But it was plain that some concessions would have to be made before he met Parliament. On 7 February he dismissed Sir Joseph Williamson, his loyal, but uninspired and unpopular, Secretary of State, and replaced him two days later by the Earl of Sunderland. This was the first important political office (other than that of ambassador) to be held by Sunderland, who was a very different man from the second-rank figure that he had succeeded. Greedy for office both on account of the power it might give and on account of the money he needed to gratify his expensive tastes, he was not a man tamely to follow the initiatives of others—he was a heavy gambler in public as well as in private life. But the notoriety which he was later to attain in James II's reign could not easily have been predicted in 1679, when he was relatively little known. What was realized was that he was Shaftesbury's nephew by marriage, so that it might be hoped that he would be free from some of the attacks and insinuations made against Charles's ministers in the past; and also that he had an understanding with the King's French mistress, the Duchess of Portsmouth, which might be advantageous to both. Contemporaries were wont to exaggerate the influence which Charles's 'dearest Fubbs' had over policy, but nevertheless her friendship was a useful asset. Quite soon after Sunderland was in office, it was rumoured that he and the Duchess had joined Monmouth, Essex, and Shaftesbury to ruin Danby.[2]

Williamson's dismissal, however, would by itself fall far short of what was necessary to conciliate the new Parliament. Danby's solution was that of sending the Duke of York out of the country, at least until the storm had blown over. Though since the beginning of November James had refrained from attending the Privy Council, his continued presence at Court where he could influence the King was an obvious irritant to public opinion (as well as to Danby), and it was easy to argue that it would be wise for him to go away. James was unwilling, and (precisely as Shaftesbury suspected) would have preferred the King to attempt to rule by armed force; but Charles wisely rejected this idea, and after the failure of an attempt by the Archbishop of Canterbury and the Bishop of Winchester to convert James back to Anglicanism, Charles decided that his brother must go. In some ways Charles was not sorry to see him leave, for he disliked James's importunities and was well aware what a political liability he was. And so, after Danby had drafted a letter in which the King ordered James to go beyond the sea, and after James had reluctantly agreed, provided that Charles signed a declaration that he had never married or contracted to

---

[1] J. S. Clarke, *Life of James II* (1816), i. 543.

[2] Temple, *Works*, i. 398, 413 (speaking of the period shortly after his return to England on 2 Mar.). It is doubtful whether Browning is right in implying that Sunderland was Danby's choice (Browning, *Danby*, i. 313).

marry any woman but Queen Catherine, the time came for the two brothers to separate. At nine o'clock on the morning of 3 March, three days before Parliament was due to meet, the Duke and Duchess of York left for exile in Brussels.[1]

Preserved in the Shaftesbury Papers there is a document headed 'The Present State of the Kingdom at the opening of the Parliament'.[2] It is not in Shaftesbury's own handwriting, but its tone suggests strongly his authorship. It may even have been intended for publication as a pamphlet, and countermanded because after James's departure some of it was no longer applicable. At all events it may safely be taken as representing his views. Beginning the review by an analysis of the European situation, the paper represented the Treaty of Nijmegen as a great French triumph, won with the assistance of English policy. William of Orange's marriage to James's elder daughter had aroused the suspicion of the States party in Holland that there was a plot against their liberties; they had therefore forsaken the coalition against France and had been followed separately by Spain, the Emperor, and the minor princes. Thus Louis had broken up his enemies more effectively by his diplomacy than by the efforts of his armies; and 'all the wise Protestants' talked of 'a secret universal Catholic league carried on by the clergy for the utter extirpation of the Protestant religion out of the world. And this they all say cannot be carried on without the full concurrence of the English Court'. (This was an extremely crude view of the situation, but not an entirely unreasonable one in the light of the very limited knowledge at the disposal of people outside the official circle, and one which was sincerely held by many honest people.) The review of home affairs began with a somewhat contemptuous description of the King. 'The King, who if he had been so happy as to have been born a private gentleman, had certainly passed for a man of good parts, excellent breeding and well natured, hath now, being a Prince, brought his affairs to that pass, that there is not a person in the world, man or woman, at home or abroad, that does rely upon him, or put any confidence in his word or friendship'. 'His brother, his minister and his mistress' governed everything, while people 'hardly slept this winter, for fear of fire and massacring by the Papists, whilst they suspect the Government itself to be in the Plot, and that their best security for the King's religion is the Act of Parliament [of 1661] which forbids on a grievous penalty to say he is of any other'. This last sneer about the unsoundness of Charles's Protestantism was followed by a bitter attack on the triumvirate. There was, first, the Duchess of Portsmouth, 'a very indifferent beauty: and of

---

[1] Danby's memorandum about the Duke of York, in Browning, *Danby*, ii. 90–91; Clarke, op. cit. i. 537–41; Barrillon, 24 Feb./6 Mar.; Southwell to Ormond, 22 Feb., MSS. Carte 39, fo. 21; *H.M.C. Lindsey MSS.*, p. 401; Charles Hatton to Lord Hatton, 4 Mar., *Hatton Correspondence*, i. 177; Coventry Papers at Longleat, ii. fo. 167; *H.M.C. Le Fleming MSS.*, p. 157.

[2] Printed by Christie, ii. 281–3, 309–14.

wit hardly enough for a woman' who had become the royal mistress through Buckingham at Dover, 'it being absolutely necessary . . . that our King should have a mistress of the King of France's choosing, that the secrets of our counsels may be known and discovered to him, and the severest of his commands may be more softly conveyed to us'. There was Danby, 'a plausible well-spoken man, of good address, and cut out naturally for a courtier; but one of no depth of judgement at all in any matter' who owed his position as Treasurer to James's favour and Clifford's recommendation, though now it was doubtful whether he might not sacrifice the Queen and the Duke to the Protestant interest. To this last insinuation was added another, that Danby's enmity to Monmouth was the result of his daughter's marriage to another of the King's illegitimate sons, the Earl of Plymouth. And finally there was James, 'in every way a perfect Stuart, and hath the advantage of his brother only that he hath ambition and thoughts of attaining something he hath not, which gives him industry and address, even beyond his natural parts; yet his conduct, courage, judgement or honour are not much to be confided in'. It was suggested that James's Catholicism was political, aimed at securing a party for himself and deterring the Pope from agreeing to the Queen's divorce, and yet suited his temper, 'heady, violent and bloody'. 'His elder brother is much the abler man, and hates him perfectly, and he knows it: yet he hath the ascendant over him, and by little arts and importunity doth much with him and seems to govern all'; and his aim was the introduction of a military and arbitrary government in his brother's lifetime, in order to secure quiet possession of the Crown for himself later on.

The exaggeration, prejudice, and partisanship of these character-sketches needs no comment; nor does the fact that they nevertheless contained a substantial element of truth. What requires more emphasis is the underestimation, not of the King's abilities, but of his will-power to resist pressure upon him. Implicit in the memorandum is the idea that if the King could be separated from the influence of his brother, his ministers, and his mistress, he could be brought to comply with the wishes of the nation. By March 1679 James had been exiled and Danby's period of office was almost over; but the next six months were to show that the expectation that Charles would then yield was a mistaken one, and to make the political duel one between Shaftesbury and the King, instead of between him and James or Danby.

Charles for his part opened his new Parliament with a typically disingenuous speech, in which he tried to make a virtue of his consent to the Test Act, the execution of the convicted Jesuits, his disbandment of part of the Army, and finally the exile of his brother. Since those assembled knew that all these steps had been taken reluctantly, they were not particularly impressed; and the demand for money to pay for his expenses and debts and the needs of national defence was not likely to have much success.

Finally, the King's peroration that he hoped this would prove to be 'an healing Parliament' in which he would be defended from the calumny 'of those worst of men, who endeavour to render me and my government odious to my people', was quite without effect, as the opening proceedings in the Commons showed.[1]

The relationship between Danby and the Speaker of the Commons, Edward Seymour, had always alternated between a close political alliance and moods of distrust, and now the latter predominated. Seymour may, like other office-holders, have resented the revelation that Danby had been negotiating for French subsidies at a time when they had been defending in the Commons the idea that the government was sincerely opposed to France; and in any case he did not wish to be involved in Danby's probable ruin. Danby, who still lay under an impeachment, felt that he could not rely on his co-operation, and it was arranged to propose Sir Thomas Meres as the new Speaker instead; but for precisely the same reason, and in order to maintain the principle that the Speaker was the House's servant, the majority insisted on Seymour rather than Meres, who had formerly been a prominent Country Party leader but was now suspected to have formed friendships with Danby's brother-in-law, the Earl of Lindsey.[2] Under Danby's persuasion, the King then proceeded to insist on his prerogative right to disapprove of a Speaker, and through the Lord Chancellor refused to accept Seymour and ordered them to make another choice. This produced a heated dispute between the government and the Commons, and the King could only resolve the deadlock by proroguing Parliament from 13 to 15 March. When the new session opened Seymour wisely stayed away, and the dispute was settled by the election of a third member, a nonentity named Gregory, whom the King approved.

On the surface this represented a victory for the King and Danby, in that the distrusted Seymour was kept out of the chair, and the royal right to approve a Speaker was not lost.[3] But in reality the episode played into the hands of Shaftesbury and the opposition. The passions roused annihilated any goodwill which the government might have gained from James's exile, and heated opinion against Danby, from whose advice and in whose interest the quarrel had arisen. Bennet talked of 'the designs of ill men, who have thrown this bone amongst us', and others too used this metaphor to illustrate their view that the incident was a device to obstruct the House's work by fostering divisions. It is noticeable that when the dispute was settled Gregory's name was proposed, not by the Privy Councillors as had been customary, but by Russell and Cavendish, and it can be taken for

---

[1] *L.J.* xiii. 449–50.

[2] 'They thus in great haste cried out, No, no, away with him, no upstarts' (MSS. Rawlinson A 137, unfoliated).

[3] But it was not asserted at the beginning of the next Parliament in October 1680 (see p. 593 below).

granted that this was the result of consultations with their friend Shaftesbury. In many ways Gregory suited the opposition better than the slippery Seymour would have done. When he presented himself for royal approval in the Lords, the luckless Lord Chancellor, Finch, permitted Shaftesbury to score one final debating point. In answer to the Speaker's customary request for the House's privileges, Finch said 'that what His Majesty had created by his power, he would protect by his kindness'. Shaftesbury dealt roughly with this remark on the ground that it might revive the dispute, and the government was so much on the defensive that it agreed that the Chancellor's speech should not be entered, as normally, in the Journals.[1]

It was precisely when the Commons were in this mood that the news began to leak out that the hated Danby, who lay under an impeachment for high treason, was to be allowed to retire with a marquisate and a pension of £5,000 a year for life. It was not even certain that his retirement from the Treasury would be permanent, for the five commissioners whom it was intended to nominate in his place included at least two of his creatures who might keep his place warm until he wanted it back. This was an incredibly indiscreet and provocative proposal. In the Lords Shaftesbury moved that the House should petition the King not to do an act which might alienate the affections of his subjects; Halifax ironically opposed this, saying that his lordship must have been 'imposed upon by a flamm report, for it was impossible to imagine that the King could ever be prevailed upon to do an act so ungrateful to his people'. In the end the pension was stopped at the Great Seal, and Danby found it wiser not to use the warrant for the marquisate which he had received; but by now the damage had been done, and the Commons were in full cry after him.[2]

Shaftesbury for his part was bound to co-operate with the leaders of the Lower House in their attempt to call Danby to account. If he could be removed from the King's side the Court Party would be left leaderless, for there was no obvious successor as the head of the ministry. Lord Chancellor Finch, timid, irresolute, and with little influence, was likely to prove a broken reed; Sunderland, even if he proved reliable, was inexperienced; and Charles would be left open to direct pressure upon him. In addition Shaftesbury had a personal score to settle with the man who had been responsible for his own impeachment. Yet it would be a mistake to suppose that he was dominated by a feeling of vindictiveness, for in comparison with some of Danby's enemies in the Commons who were literally out for

[1] Grey, vi. 403–39, vii. 1–4; Charles Hatton to L. Hatton, 8 Mar., and 18 Mar., *Hatton Correspondence*, i. 179–81, 183–4; E. Cooke to Ormond, 8 Mar., *H.M.C. Ormond MSS.*, N.S. iv. 345–7; Southwell to Ormond, 8 Mar., ibid. iv. 498–9; Daniel Finch to Sir J. Finch, 2 June, *H.M.C. Finch MSS.*, ii. 47; Danby's memorandum, Browning, *Danby*, ii. 71–72; Ranelagh to Conway, 8 Mar., *C.S.P.D. 1679–80*, p. 98; Van Beuningen, 14/24 Mar., Add. MSS. 17677, EE; Browning, *Danby*, i. 317–20; Jones, op. cit. pp. 49–50.

[2] Ranelagh to Conway, 18 Mar., *C.S.P.D. 1679–80*, p. 103; Charles Hatton to Lord Hatton, 18 Mar., *Hatton Correspondence*, i. 183–4; E. Cooke to Ormond, 18 Mar., *H.M.C. Ormond MSS.*, N.S. iv. 360.

his blood, he would have been satisfied with the effective removal of Danby from the political scene by a banishment similar to Clarendon's. This would serve his purpose; it would avoid any dangerous raising of the stakes; and it would avoid spending the energies of a favourable House of Commons on revenge, when they were needed to attain the more basic objective of Exclusion. Unfortunately for him, Shaftesbury could not foresee the legal tangle which was to follow in the proceedings against Danby, and in which his control over the Country Party in the Commons was shown to be far from complete. So far from his being the unquestioned leader over a docile body of 'henchmen', he had to follow their wishes when their passions were roused. Reluctant as the evidence suggests he was, he dared not allow himself to lag behind opinion in the lower House.

On 18 and 19 March, therefore, Shaftesbury began by maintaining in the Lords that all impeachment proceedings were unaffected by the dissolution of the last Parliament. Otherwise, he said, 'it would destroy the judicature' and stultify the whole process of impeachment. Since any other decision would have not only aided Danby, but released the five generally hated Catholic lords who lay under Oates's accusation, Shaftesbury was able to carry this point against the Lord Chancellor, Lauderdale, and all the bishops save one.[1] Next day, the Lords gave Danby a week to put in a written answer to the charges against him[2]; but in the next few days his position collapsed. First of all, Oates and Bedloe appeared before the Commons (whether at Shaftesbury's instigation one cannot tell) and complained of alleged discouragements offered them by the Court; and after much feigned reluctance Bedloe swore that Danby had offered him 'a great sum of money' and a yacht to take him out of the country, if he would desist from his evidence against the Queen and the Catholic lords in the Tower. The effect on the Commons can easily be imagined, and there seemed a real possibility that the Lords might accept their request that Danby be committed to custody.[3] Charles's sense of obligation to his minister, and his fear of what Danby might say under pressure, alike led him to intervene at this point, and on 22 March he appeared before the two Houses to announce that he had given Danby a full pardon; that the letters which were the basis of the charges against the Earl had been written by his order; that he had dismissed him from Court and Council; and that the Houses should proceed with 'public business' instead of the impeachment. This the King did in the belief that the pardon would bring the impeachment to a halt, the more so as he reminded the Houses that Shaftesbury and Buckingham had been awarded similar pardons when dismissed from office in 1673. But this was a serious mistake on the King's part; the

---

[1] *L.J.* xiii. 464, 466; Van Beuningen, 21/31 Mar., Add. MSS. 17677, EE; notes on debate in MSS. Carte 228, fos. 229–30; *H.M.C. Hastings MSS.*, iv. 301.

[2] *L.J.* xiii. 469.

[3] Grey, vii. 9–19; *C.J.* ix. 573; MSS. Rawlinson A 137, unfoliated (Bedloe's testimony); *L.J.* xiii. 470.

opposition in the Commons were able to point out that there had been no charges against Shaftesbury and Buckingham, and, led once again by the impulsive Bennet, refused to accept that an impeachment could be stultified in this way. Instead they once again asked the Lords to commit Danby, and the general feeling was such that the Solicitor-General, Finch, found it advisable to exculpate his father, the Lord Chancellor, by revealing that the latter had declined to affix the Great Seal to the pardon, and Charles had personally ordered an officer to do it instead.

In this situation Shaftesbury's solution was to propose[1] to the Lords that a bill should be immediately brought in to banish Danby from the King's presence, declare him incapable of holding any office or pension, and deprive him of his seat in the House. The committee which was ordered to prepare such a bill included among its thirteen members Shaftesbury, Monmouth, Winchester, Essex, Halifax, Wharton, Grey of Wark, and Holles, and it is plain from this that the opposition in the Lords would have been satisfied by it. The penalties for Danby would have been drastic, but less than those which would follow a sentence for high treason; and Shaftesbury would have been content with making him politically ineffective in this way. There were signs that Charles on his side would have been prepared to agree, but he was faced by remonstrances from Danby which he could not ignore, and instead, during the weekend he sent an order to his former minister to avoid committal to the Tower by going into hiding.[2]

If either now or at any time within the next three weeks Danby had followed the example of Clarendon in 1667 and fled the country, the matter would have ended there, and Parliament could have proceeded to other business (including Exclusion). That this did not happen was not the result of any extraordinarily far-sighted cunning on the King's part, but of Danby's superior toughness in comparison with the heartbroken, worn out old man who had fled twelve years earlier. Reluctantly he did agree to go into hiding on 24 March when he heard from Charles that the Lords were on the point of arresting him, but it was well known that he was still in the country, and not a thousand miles from Whitehall.[3]

The Commons now refused to follow Shaftesbury's lead, and even when the Lords stiffened their bill against Danby at the committee stage by introducing a clause to banish him from the country they refused to accept it—rejected the bill, indeed, on the second reading. Instead they proceeded with a bill of their own, a bill for attainting Danby if he did not quickly

---

[1] That this was Shaftesbury's proposal is clear from Van Beuningen, 25 Mar./4 Apr., Add. MSS. 17677, EE.

[2] For the events of 22 Mar. see *C.J.* ix. 573–4; Grey, vii. 19–54; Ranelagh to Conway, 22 Mar., *C.S.P.D. 1679–80*; p. 106; Winnington's speech in MSS. Rawlinson A 137; *L.J.* xiii. 471–2; *H.M.C. House of Lords MSS. 1678–88*, pp. 86–87; Browning, *Danby*, ii. 76–77; Add. MSS. 28043, fo. 7. For the manner in which Danby's pardon passed the Great Seal on 1 Mar., cf. *H.M.C. Finch MSS.* ii. 50; Grey, vii. 53–54, 55–56.

[3] Danby to Hatton, 28 Mar., *Hatton Correspondence*, i. 185; Reresby, p. 173; *L.J.* xiii. 474–6.

surrender himself and submit to trial. This in turn was too drastic for the Lords who amended this bill of attainder into a bill for banishment similar to that passed against Clarendon in 1667; only if Danby did not surrender, and was found in England after 1 May, would he suffer the penalties of attainder. This produced a fortnight of deadlock in which the Lords advocated exile and the Commons insisted that attainder was the only appropriate penalty for a man who had fled to avoid charges of high treason. Shaftesbury's position in the interchanges was clear. He fully sympathized with the Commons' hatred of Danby. Indeed, he said, using a metaphor of the countryside, 'we have now shot one rook, but there are a whole flock that will still endanger devouring our corn; therefore I am for hanging them up to affright others'; to which the Earl of Northampton replied that once he had destroyed a rookery of which his neighbourhood complained, 'but after[wards] the corn was devoured worse than before, for there was a little grub at the root that devoured more than the rooks had done'—a sneer at Shaftesbury's small stature. But Shaftesbury's vehemence against Danby was kept in restraint by his cool political head. There seemed little chance of quickly getting the consent of Lords or King to attainder, and in any case Danby's exile would serve him equally well. Accordingly he did not even organize protests by the minority of opposition peers against the majority's modification of the Commons' Bill; instead he adopted the majority view and identified himself with their efforts to persuade the Commons at a series of conferences. On 10 April, at a free conference, he appealed to his allies, Powle, Sacheverell and others. 'We do not say the Bill [as sent up by the Commons] is not just, or that it is hard: nor doth what we offer arise from any compassion to the gentleman, but from reason of state. Consider this man's art, power, and interest. I wish (and so we have all reason) that we were rid of him . . . it is time we should deliver ourselves from this meteor that hangs over us. . . . If this Parliament recover not England, we may despair of it, there being such an assembly of persons of that estate, worth and integrity. . . .' As an inducement to these worthy persons to dispose of Danby by the quickest possible method and to proceed to more basic matters (i.e. Exclusion, though he did not name it), he made a virtue of the Lords' admission that they ought to have committed Danby in the first place, and hinted that the Commons might increase Danby's punishment to anything short of actual attainder.[1]

---

[1] *C.J.* ix. 574-7, 579, 581, 584-5, 588-94; Grey, vii. 54-63, 55*, 60*-62*, 89, 91-97, 102-3; *L.J.* xiii. 479, 481, 493-7, 504-6, 508-10; *H.M.C. House of Lords MSS. 1678-88*, pp. 95-97, 110-12; Edward Cooke to Ormond, 29 Mar., *H.M.C. Ormond MSS.*, N.S. v. 9-10 and 2 Apr., ibid. v. 30-31; Barrillon, 3/13 Apr.; notes on conference of 10 Apr. in MSS. Carte 81, fos. 585-6. According to Algernon Sidney (*Letters of the Hon. Algernon Sydney to the Hon. Henry Savile*, 1742, p. 21) Shaftesbury, Essex and Halifax themselves amended the Commons' bill to one of attainder 'in compliance unto the King's desires', but Sidney and Shaftesbury disliked one another and the former's statement must be treated with caution.

Yet Shaftesbury's authority over his so-called 'party' in the Commons was insufficient to obtain what he wanted. Long-serving members of the Commons who were jealous of the House's rights were determined to prevent any constitutional precedent which might possibly weaken their ability to bring ministers to book by means of an impeachment in the future. Personal enemies of Danby, like Ralph Montagu, were determined to exact their full pound of flesh; and they now included one dangerous new speaker in Sir Francis Winnington, the former Solicitor-General whom Danby had dismissed in December and whose speech setting out the legal arguments against the validity of the King's pardon had attracted much attention.[1] And the many new members were anxious to show that they were not backward in defending the rights of the House which they had just entered; observers noticed that they were even worse disposed to Danby than the old hands.[2] Moreover there was an excellent logical case for saying that a man accused of high treason should either face a trial or be dealt with as a traitor. One or two of the Country Party, such as 'my Lord Shaftesbury's Mr. Bennet',[3] dared to suggest a different view; but others of Shaftesbury's associates, such as Russell, preferred to remain silent. The irony of it was that, like Shaftesbury, the King would have preferred Danby to go into either voluntary or compulsory exile—he could not afford to have his recent foreign policy raked over at a public trial, and of course could not decently consent to an act of attainder. Paradoxically Danby, fearing the King was only too ready to dispose of him by banishment, preferred the issue to be fought over the more extreme measure of attainder, and even on one occasion suggested that his friends should vote for it, in the belief that Charles would have to veto it.[4]

Finally on 14 April the Lords bowed to the superior logic of the Commons' case, and passed the Commons' bill of attainder by the narrow majority of 39 votes to 36. Shaftesbury and his friends now voted for the bill; and the Earl moved that since a man's life was at issue the bishops, who normally supported Danby, should withdraw. Six did so, and seven remained to vote against the bill, while the issue of the bishops' right to vote in capital cases was left formally undecided, to complicate matters in the future.[5] Thereupon, as Danby had probably foreseen, in order to avoid having to accept or reject the bill, Charles reluctantly gave his minister permission to surrender to Black Rod. This was not a piece of Machiavellian

---

[1] Grey, vii. 25–9; MSS. Rawlinson A 137, unfoliated; Burnet, ii. 207–8; *C.J.* ix. 579.

[2] Barrillon, 27 Mar./6 Apr.; Van Beuningen, 8/18 Apr., Add. MSS. 17677, EE.

[3] E. Cooke to Ormond, 8 Apr., *H.M.C. Ormond MSS.*, N.S. v. 38.

[4] Danby to Lauderdale, 2 Apr., Browning, *Life of Danby*, ii. 77–78; and to Latimer, 12 Apr., ibid. ii. 80. Cf. the note on the last page; and see Barrillon's despatch above for the belief that the Duchess of Portsmouth's influence over the King was being exercised against Danby.

[5] *L.J.* xiii. 514–16; Charles Hatton to L. Hatton, 15 Apr., *Hatton Correspondence*, i. 186; E. Cooke to Ormond, 15 Apr., *H.M.C. Ormond MSS.*, N.S. v. 48; Browning, *Danby*, i. 326–9, and division list, ibid. iii. 148–51.

cunning designed to produce the disputes which followed over Danby's trial; the fact was that the King had no possible alternative. On April 16, fourteen months after Shaftesbury's release from the Tower, Danby passed within its walls, facing much more serious charges and destined to stay there for much longer than his rival had done.

Yet, as members were beginning to notice, Parliament was now six weeks old and had achieved nothing constructive. The Commons had passed once again a Habeas Corpus amendment act similar to those which had failed to reach the final stage of royal assent in the previous Parliament; Russell, on their behalf, had carried up to the Lords the articles of impeachment against the five accused Catholic peers; and the House had disciplined and expelled one member, Edward Sackville, who had dared to make the accurate but inopportune statement that Oates was 'a lying rogue', so that other doubters would keep silent in future.[1] But attention had been so concentrated on the 'malevolent comet' (Danby) that it had been impossible to raise the fundamental issue of the succession, and since in Shaftesbury's plans this must first be raised in the Commons, there was little he could do in the Lords but wait.

What he did try to do was to draw attention to alleged Popish influences in many different quarters and thus keep the pot boiling. On 25 March, on a motion for an inquiry into 'the state of the nation' he was outspoken. 'I do not know well how what I have to say may be received, for I never study either to make my court well, or to be popular; I always speak what I am commanded by the dictates of the Spirit within me'. (The Spirit also dictated that his remarks should be available for printing and distribution in London and Norwich).[2] 'We have a little Sister, and she hath no breasts; what shall we do for our sister in the day when she shall be spoken for? if she be a wall, we will build on her a palace of silver; if she be a door, we will enclose her with bonds of cedar'. This text from one of the less commonly studied books of the Bible[3] was admirably calculated to make his hearers sit up. He proceeded to identify the 'little sisters without breasts' as the French Protestant churches, which were a 'wall and defence' to England, and the kingdoms of Scotland and Ireland, which were 'two doors, either to let in good or mischief upon us'. There followed a violent attack on Lauderdale's regime in Scotland. 'Popery and slavery, like two little sisters, go hand in hand, and sometimes one goes first, sometimes the other; but wheresoever the one enters, the other is always following close at hand. In England, popery was to have brought in slavery; in Scotland, slavery went

---

[1] In addition Jones, op. cit. pp. 53–54, has drawn attention to an interesting parliamentary reform bill which received a first and second reading before fading out. But the bill attracted so little contemporary comment and was followed up so inadequately that it is difficult to attach much importance to it.

[2] See the endorsement on the copy in Add. MSS. 38847, fo. 76b. The speech is most conveniently accessible in the *Parliamentary History*, iv. 1116–18, and Christie, ii. pp. xcix–cii.   [3] Song of Songs, viii. 8, 9.

before, and popery was to follow'. The 'ancient nobility and gentry' of Scotland had been deprived of their ancestral authority, subjected to arbitrary imprisonment, and plundered by the 'Highland host', and until this was put right it was impossible to believe that the intentions of the King's government in England were genuine. The King should be asked to see that the Act of 1669 which made the Scottish militia available 'to invade us upon all occasions' was repealed. As for Ireland, Shaftesbury remarked sarcastically that Douglas's regiment, which had served with Louis XIV for several years, had been sent there 'to secure us against the French'. The seaports and inland towns alike were full of Papists whose arms had been restored to them, and Ireland could not long continue in English hands unless better care were taken of it.

These last remarks were interpreted by the impulsive Earl of Ossory as an attack on his father, the Duke of Ormond, Lord-Lieutenant of Ireland, and after defending his father's administration he retaliated against Shaftesbury. 'Having spoke of what he [Ormond] had done, I presume with the same truth to tell your Lordships what he has not done. He never advised the breaking of the Triple League. He never advised the shutting up of the Exchequer. He never advised the declaration for toleration. . . . He was not author of that most excellent position of *Delenda est Carthago*. . . .' Shaftesbury said afterwards that his own attack had been aimed not at Ormond but at such people as the Irish Colonel Fitzpatrick, and Ossory and Ormond found it expedient to pretend to accept this explanation; but they did not trust him and the son's letters at this time were full of rumours that Shaftesbury was intriguing to undermine the Lord-Lieutenant's position in Essex's favour.[1]

While attacking Popish and absolutist influences in Scotland and Ireland, Shaftesbury did not neglect matters nearer home. He complained of Papists among the garrison of the Tower, and with supporting 'evidence' from Titus Oates tried to get its lieutenant, Sir John Robinson, replaced; he complained of unsound elements in the fleet and other garrisons such as Portsmouth, 'urging it was well known who had put all officers in'— the Duke of York. He even introduced to the bar of the House of Lords a man, Sidway, who claimed to know that the episcopal bench was not thoroughly sound in its Protestantism. The Bishop of Ely, Sidway said, had discouraged him from leaving the Roman church, saying that it 'was a better religion than it was generally believed to be'. Unfortunately for

---

[1] MSS. Carte 47, fo. 247; Ossory to Ormond, 22 Mar., 25 Mar., 12 Apr., 15 Apr., *H.M.C. Ormond MSS.*, N.S. iv. 366, v. 1, 40, 45–46; Longford to Ormond, 29 Mar., ibid. v. 4; Sir Cyril Wyche to Ormond, 1 Apr., ibid. v. 21; Ormond to Ossory, 31 Mar., ibid. v. 22; Capt. J. St. Leger to H. Gascoigne, 31 Mar., ibid. v. 22; Cooke to Ormond, 15 Apr., ibid. v. 49; Southwell to Ormond, 19 Apr., ibid. iv, pp. xx–xxiv, and 22 Apr., ibid. iv. 505; Ossory to the Duchess of Ormond, 19 Apr., ibid. v. 54; *L.J.* xiii. 478, 488–91, 493, 532. The Prince of Orange's congratulatory letter to Ossory on his speech is confirmation that he was not in touch with Shaftesbury; T. Carte, *Life of Ormond* (1851), v. 136.

Shaftesbury, when he pointed out one of the bishops and asked Sidway whether this was not the Bishop of Ely, Sidway was unable to recognize him; and it was also obvious that Sidway had never been to Rome as he claimed. Even so, when the courtiers and bishops wished to vindicate the honour of their colleague and commit Sidway to prison for an untrue and frivolous information, this was carried only by 32 votes to 28, and Shaftesbury, Halifax and seven others signed a protest against this treatment of 'the King's evidence'. This was a good example of the Earl's readiness to bring forward any informer who presented himself.[1]

There was one way only by which the King could clear his ministers of such vague aspersions as these of being 'Popishly affected', and that was to bring some of the critics themselves into the ministry. Charles could hope that (in the words of the axiom later formulated by Mirabeau) *un Jacobin ministre ne serait pas un ministre jacobin*. Some of the opposition might be convinced by entering the King's councils that there were really no sinister influences at work there; others might be converted by the satisfaction of their self-interest. Accordingly one of the most upright of the Country Party, the Earl of Essex, was made one of the Commissioners of the Treasury in succession to Danby, and seemed to be 'in very good grace' with the King.[2] Lord Cavendish was brought to Court at the King's own request, and Shaftesbury too dined with his nephew Sunderland at Whitehall, with the King's approval. It was the first time that they had been permitted to go to Court since 1675, and Sunderland and the royal mistress, the Duchess of Portsmouth, were thought to be the instigators.[3]

Sir William Temple it was, however, who claimed to originate the precise form of the reform of the Privy Council which now took place. That diplomat had recently returned from his embassy in the Netherlands, where he had been enthusiastic in his sympathy for William of Orange's efforts to restrain French aggression; and it was still his hope to bring England into an anti-French coalition in Europe, and for this purpose he wanted an all-party coalition in England to take power. His idea, in which Lord Chancellor Finch, Essex, and Sunderland concurred, was that the Privy Council should be reduced to thirty in number. Half of these were to be office-holders and half Lords and Commoners of 'credit and sway' in Parliament without being thought 'either principled or interested against the government'. Other artificial features of the new construction were the pairs of dukes, marquises, earls, viscounts, barons, and bishops that it

[1] E. Cooke to Ormond, 29 Mar., 5 Apr., 8 Apr., *H.M.C. Ormond MSS.*, N.S. v. 8–9, 33, 36; *L.J.* xiii. 499, 502; *H.M.C. House of Lords MSS. 1678–88*, p. 121; Roger Morrice, Entry Book P (in Dr. Williams's Library), fos. 158–9.

[2] Henry Coventry to Ormond, 8 Apr., op. cit. v. 39.

[3] Ossory to Ormond, 29 Mar., op. cit. v. 5; Van Beuningen, 1/11 Apr., Add. MSS. 17677, EE; Barrillon, 10/20, 17/27 Apr.; Southwell's memorandum, 19 Apr., *H.M.C. Ormond MSS.*, N.S. iv. xxi; James to Prince of Orange, 28 Apr./8 May, *H.M.C. Foljambe MSS.*, p. 129; Sidney's *Diary of the Times of Charles the Second*, ed. R. W. Blencowe (1843), i. 15.

contained, so that satirical observers said 'they went into the Council as Beasts into the Ark'. The detested Lauderdale sat side by side with some of his fiercest enemies, like Russell and Cavendish. Monmouth was there, and Ormond, Arlington, Winchester, Salisbury, Sunderland, Essex, Bath (representing the Danby interest), Holles, and Temple. Of the front-rank politicians of the previous decade (apart from Danby) only the Duke of Buckingham was missing: he was now only a shadow of his former self, and could safely be ignored. Two names particularly aroused discussion between the King, Temple, and the others who wanted the reform. One was that of Halifax, whom Temple wanted to include as an opponent of France but whom Charles strongly disliked for his sharpness of tongue and independence of mind. In the end Charles reluctantly allowed himself to be persuaded, and then went on to say that there was another, who, if he were left out, might do as much mischief as any. This was Lord Shaftesbury. Temple was horrified; the last person whom he wished to include was the perpetrator of the *Delenda est Carthago* speech against the Dutch, with whom Temple wanted to ally. But Finch, Essex, and Sunderland overbore him. They argued further that an ex-Chancellor would not be satisfied with an ordinary councillor's place, and resurrected for him the formal position of Lord President of the Council, which had not been filled since 1631, unless the presidency of the Council of State in the Interregnum be counted. This would, they hoped, be suitably honorific without carrying with it much executive authority outside the Council.[1]

In proposing Shaftesbury's inclusion Charles had no cunning idea of fostering the split between the Earl and Halifax which soon occurred; this is clear from his evident reluctance to include Halifax at all, regarding him as an inveterate enemy of monarchy. Charles did not take Temple's idea very seriously; he had no intention of trusting his new councillors and intended only to use them as a means of gaining time. 'God's fish! they have put a set of men about me, but they shall know nothing'. In this situation he might just as well take in Shaftesbury as anyone else. According to Sunderland, Charles thought Shaftesbury 'was only angry in revenge, because he was not employed', and this might be a sop to make him harmless.[2] The attitude of Sunderland himself and the Duchess of Portsmouth was probably not very different: it was a matter of conciliating a potentially dangerous enemy.

Shaftesbury made no bones about accepting his new office, though he had no illusions about the feelings with which the King regarded him.

[1] Temple, *Works*, i. 413–18, 473–7; Burnet, ii. 208–9; R. North (1740), *Examen*, pp. 75–6. For the reformed Privy Council, cf. E. R. Turner, 'The Privy Council of 1679', in *E.H.R.* (1915), pp. 251–70, and G. Davies, 'Council and Cabinet, 1679–88', ibid. (1922), pp. 47–66.

[2] According to Barrillon (21 Apr./1 May), Charles was reminded that both Strafford and Danby had begun as opponents of the Crown, only to become its most zealous servants.

Few politicians in the seventeenth century refused office, and one who had been so loud in criticisms of the ministers' Protestantism would have found it particularly difficult logically to turn down a superficially genuine offer to reform the ministry so that it would include more popular ministers. Nor was he the man to refuse an opportunity to draw nearer to the secrets of government and the levers of power. He had always claimed to be a loyal servant of his King and until the offer was proved to be not genuine he had to accept it. And his inclusion in the Privy Council served to impress waverers that the King was allowing himself to be won over to the opposition's views. Many courtiers were greatly discouraged. It was not overlooked that Shaftesbury and Monmouth were in the Council, while James was in exile in Brussels; and there were those who took their measures accordingly.

The principal disadvantage for the opposition in entering the Privy Council was that others might interpret it as 'selling out' to the Court. Some members of the Commons thought it 'a new court-juggle'; some were jealous of those who had gained office, more especially those like Montagu who were themselves disappointed. On Easter Monday (21 April), when the King announced the creation of his new Privy Council, the reception given to the announcement was less than enthusiastic; and in the City even the bonfires ordered by the Lord Mayor evoked less response than had been hoped.[1] Within ten days a bill was introduced into the Commons which would have provided that any member accepting office would have to submit himself for re-election; and the efforts of Henry Powle and others of the new councillors to persuade their former colleagues in the opposition to vote money for the Navy were treated almost with contempt. Shaftesbury's own past record, with its many twists and turns, made him especially vulnerable to suspicions that he had once more changed sides, and to exculpate himself he made a point of demonstrating his continued independence of outlook in the Lords. When the Lord Chancellor happened to express his dissatisfaction with the implication in the royal declaration that Prince Rupert was entitled to sit on the new Council by virtue of being a prince of the blood, Shaftesbury prefaced his defence of his business partner with the remark that his judgement would not alter with his place, and his conscience would always guide his tongue. And an even better opportunity came when the Lords were debating whether the oaths designed to drive Catholics from London should also be applicable to Quakers and other Dissenting sects. The bishops and other courtiers carried their view that there should be no distinction between Protestant and Catholic Dissenters from the established church, triumphing over Shaftesbury, who spoke with great vehemence and said loudly that if he

---

[1] So Barrillon in his despatch of the same day. It is fair, however, to say that Van Beuningen had a quite contrary impression (22 Apr./2 May, Add. MSS. 17677, EE), as had Temple, *Works*, i. 417.

had thought he would be unable to get his own way in a matter of such consequence he would not have returned to office: he wanted his place in the Council only to serve his country and strive for the safety and advantage of the whole nation. Though defeated in the vote Shaftesbury achieved his object of demonstrating that his outlook had not changed. To remove any doubt he remarked on another occasion that he 'neither could live *with* or *under a Papist*'. His opposition to James was as extreme as ever.[1] At the same time in the Commons his zealous supporter Bennet was declaring that though the Council had been reformed, no good could reasonably be expected from it as long as it still included one man (Lauderdale) who was advancing arbitrary power in Scotland, and another (Anglesey or Ormond?) who had thirty masses a day said for him in Ireland. For good measure he followed this up with an attack on James's protégé, Samuel Pepys.[2]

In these circumstances it was naïve of James's friends to suggest that now Shaftesbury was in office he might be more amenable, and that therefore James should write an encouraging letter to the Earl. James was quite prepared to believe that Shaftesbury's former principles meant nothing, but could not bring himself to write directly. Instead he authorized his friend Col. George Legge to sound Shaftesbury through Lord Townshend, and tell the Earl that it was in his power to recover James's favour; Legge was to say that James's opposition to the Earl was only on the King's account, and now that Shaftesbury was on good terms with the King, James too was prepared to forgive the past, but not to conform to the Church of England.[3] This offer to let bygones be bygones was fully as insincere as anything of which James suspected 'Little Sincerity' (the nickname which he and Charles gave to the Earl). No reports of Shaftesbury's reaction to it survive, but the old adage that actions speak louder than words applies in this case too, and Shaftesbury's actions were of unqualified hostility to the Duke of York.

It is likely that Shaftesbury was kept fully informed of the activities of the Commons' Committee of Secrecy which was meeting regularly to plan a course of action in the house of a lawyer-member, Serjeant Ellis, 'every room being divided into sub-committees'.[4] To say that he directed those activities would be considerably more hazardous, but he certainly influenced them. At the appropriate moment Lady Shaftesbury's butler came forward with a tale that a French army of 60,000 men was ready to cross the Channel

[1] *C.J.* ix. 599, 609; Barrillon, 24 Apr./4 May; Cooke to Ormond, 26 Apr., 2 May, *H.M.C. Ormond MSS.*, N.S. v. 67, 75–76; A. Sidney to H. Savile, 28 Apr., 15 May, *Letters of the hon. Algernon Sydney to the hon. Henry Savile* (1742), pp. 42–43, 55; *L.J.* xiii. 549.

[2] Sidney to Savile, 28 Apr., op. cit. p. 45; Southwell to Ormond, 26 and 29 Apr., op. cit. iv. 506, 507.

[3] James to Legge, 28 Apr./8 May, *H.M.C. Dartmouth MSS.*, pp. 32–33.

[4] Charles Bertie to Danby, 26 Apr., *H.M.C. Lindsey MSS.*, p. 407.

and assist the English Catholics, bringing James with them.[1] There also survives in the Shaftesbury Papers what appears to be an advance copy of the report made by Serjeant Rigby on behalf of a committee appointed to investigate some recent fires in London.[2] A maidservant named Elizabeth Oxley and a man named Nicholas Stubbs 'confessed' that they had been set on to commit arson by a priest named Gifford. Both these interesting reports were presented to the Commons together on 26 April, and the House resolved, *nemine contradicente*, to sit next day to consider ways of protecting the Protestant religion against Papists, 'both in the reign of His Majesty and his successors'. Next day would be Sunday, a day when the House sat only in the most exceptional circumstances; but the better the day, the better the deed.

In a highly charged atmosphere one of the first speakers was Bennet, who traced the Plot back to Clifford's ministry and declared that all Coleman's letters had been sent by the Duke of York's command. 'The Duke of York', he went on, 'has as much right to succeed his brother, if he die without heirs, (which God forbid!) as my son has to inherit my estate after me. Therefore I desire that by some law we may have power to arm ourselves against him, if he would bring in Popery amongst us. If the King have a son, then we are out of fear; but if a way cannot be found out that the King may have a son [i.e. by divorcing the Queen?] then we are to go another way to work. I do believe that this Plot had not been carried on without the Duke of York's approbation. . . .' As to what the 'other way' was to be, he made no explicit suggestion except that the lawyers be asked to report whether an attainder would be wiped out if the person attainted secured possession of the Crown; but what mattered was that the attack on the Duke was more outspoken than on any previous occasion, and the Duke was accused of lending his approval to the Plot. Later on Bennet made an interjection describing the debate as being 'about a Protestant successor', but the time was not yet ripe for an Exclusion Bill to be mentioned. Even Russell spoke only for a bill 'to secure our religion and properties in case of a Popish successor'. Others talked of an Association Bill similar to that passed in 1585 to protect Queen Elizabeth from plots in the interest of a Catholic heir. In the end the House agreed, again without dissent, 'that the Duke of York being a Papist, and the hopes of his coming such to the Crown, have given the greatest countenance and encouragement to the present conspiracies and designs of the Papists against the King and the Protestant religion'. The first stage had been accomplished; shortly it would sink into members' minds that the logical consequence

---

[1] It should be stated, however, that this is derived only from the *Life of James II*, i. 546–7, and that the details given there do not include even the butler's name.

[2] Shaftesbury Papers, VI A, 337. The nature of the slight differences from the report printed in *C.J.* ix. 603–4, for instance in the first sentence, suggests that this was an advance copy, and not one taken afterwards from the Journals. Unfortunately the debate of 26 Apr. is not recorded by Grey.

was Exclusion. Three days later the debate would be resumed, with the Committee of Secrecy producing all the references to the Duke in Coleman's letters.[1]

It was necessary for Charles to make some attempt to forestall this, and before the debate of 30 April could begin the Commons were summoned up to the bar of the House of Lords. There the King tried to divert attention from Exclusion by reminding the Houses of the urgent need to proceed with the Plot prosecutions, complete the disbandment of the Army and provide for the fleet; after which the Lord Chancellor reiterated the King's readiness to consent to any laws for the future of Protestantism, 'so as the same extend not to alter the descent of the Crown in the right line, nor to defeat the succession'. He made the King's promise more concrete than it had been in the previous November; Charles would agree to legislation preventing a Popish successor from making any ecclesiastical appointments at all or from putting in or removing Privy Councillors, Lords Lieutenant or naval officers without the approval of Parliament. In addition he reminded the Houses that the King's successor would be dependent on Parliament for money. Superficially at least, these appeared to be satisfactory safeguards.[2]

These offers had been debated at an extraordinary meeting of the Privy Council lasting for three hours on the previous evening. It is not clear whether they were designed by Charles or whether he accepted suggestions made by a group which was emerging amongst the councillors, consisting of Sunderland, Essex, and Halifax. Certainly Shaftesbury was the only councillor of note who opposed them. In all probability he had already decided in private that he preferred a policy of exclusion to one of limitations; now he had to bring his preference further into the light of day, and he did this by maintaining to his fellow-councillors that the proposals were 'too like a Republic', and that in any case there could be no effective security against James if once he gained possession of the Crown. In this, however, he seems to have been alone at the Council Board; and whether or not this was Charles's design, this marks a definite stage in Shaftesbury's separation from some of his former opposition colleagues, notably his nephew Halifax, who preferred 'limitations'. Of their rapidly growing enmity more will be said later.[3]

The Council's extraordinary meeting had been resumed at eight o'clock in the morning, before these offers were made to Parliament; but the register shows that this time Shaftesbury did not attend, no doubt because he was hastily getting in touch with some of his followers. Even so the King's and Chancellor's speeches were received with loud hums of

---

[1] C.J. ix. 605; Grey, vii. 137–52.   [2] L.J. xiii. 547.

[3] Southwell to Ormond, 29 Apr., H.M.C. Ormond MSS., N.S. iv. 507; Daniel Finch to Sir J. Finch, 2 June, H.M.C. Finch MSS., ii. 52; Temple, Works, iv. 419–22; Burnet, ii. 213. Burnet follows this with a reasonable summary of the arguments for and against exclusion.

approval. Many felt that they conceded all that was needed; and even Bennet's impetuosity took the form this time of moving for extraordinary thanks to the King. Other members competed for the honour of seconding the motion. It was left to Sacheverell, in a long and carefully prepared speech, to argue that the proposals were 'merely to delude the people with security, when there is none'. Supposing a Popish successor refused to accept these restrictions and used the armed forces, what then? Other experienced members, without going so far as to talk of 'deluding the people', were cautious about voting thanks: as one of them, Titus, said, 'I would use the King, as we use God Almighty; we give thanks for fair weather and rain, but we give no thanks for clouds. Rain must fall first, clouds may blow over; the rain may be prorogued, and perhaps we may give thanks for nothing'. It was best to wait until the promised bills had been passed.[1]

This caution prevailed, and the debate was adjourned for five days. In the meantime the suspicion rapidly asserted itself that, in accordance with the past history of the reign, this was a characteristic trick of the King's, to induce Parliament implicitly to confirm James's right to the succession— 'a little gilding to cover a poisonous pill'. Perhaps only Exclusion would really be safe? The possibility was now being seriously canvassed, though its advocates could not agree whether the Prince of Orange or the Duke of Monmouth should become the heir. 'I do not know three of a mind', wrote Algernon Sidney, 'and . . . a spirit of giddiness reigns amongst us, far beyond any I have ever observed in my life'.[2]

By the time the Commons resumed their debate on 11 May the Exclusionists' hold over the House had been restored. Various circumstances suggested that the King's proffer of co-operation was not sincerely intended. The impeachment of Danby and of the five Catholic peers was apparently being obstructed by the Court peers and bishops in the Upper House, which voted, over Shaftesbury's protests, against the appointment of a joint committee of the two Houses to discuss the impeachment procedure, and declined to rule that the bishops had no vote in capital cases. Outside Parliament a mysterious fire burned down the new prison in Clerkenwell which included some Catholic priests among its prisoners; and the rumours which spread like the fire said that Papists were responsible, that the Duke of York's return would take place any day, and that the despatch of sixteen small guns from London to Portsmouth was connected with this.[3] The prevalent excitement was heightened by the tactics

---

[1] Grey, vii. 159–64; Van Beuningen, 2/12 May, Add. MSS. 17677, EE; E. Cooke to Ormond, 30 Apr., *H.M.C. Ormond MSS.*, N.S. v. 74–75.

[2] 5/15 May, in *Letters . . . to the hon. Henry Savile*, pp. 51–54. Cf. Southwell to Ormond, 3 May, *H.M.C. Ormond MSS.*, N.S. iv. 508.

[3] J. Verney to Sir R. Verney, 12 May, *H.M.C. Seventh Report*, p. 471; Southwell to Ormond, 10 May, *H.M.C. Ormond MSS.*, N.S. iv. 510; E. of Burlington to Ormond, 13 May, ibid. v. 93; Algernon Sidney to H. Savile, 12 May, op. cit. pp. 66–67; Grey, vii. 261–4.

of the opposition in the Commons. There was talk there of 'Samson's being betrayed by his Delilah, and Solomon outwitted by strange women, and that no good could be expected whilst the French interest and the Popish both were centred in one person . . . and she admitted a place in the King's bosom'; for in spite of the English-sounding nick-name which Charles had given to his 'dearest Fubbs', it was easy to arouse prejudice against the Duchess of Portsmouth as a Papist and a foreigner.[1] And on the day before the critical debate was to take place, the opposition tried to force Charles Bertie to produce the accounts of the secret service money which he had paid out to Court M.P.s during Danby's period at the Treasury. The fact that Bertie could not or rather would not do so was almost as useful to the opposition as the production of the accounts would have been.[2] It contributed to build the conviction that there was something irretrievably rotten in Charles's government.

It was in this mood that the House met on 11 May—once again a Sunday—and one or two minor matters which delayed the opening of the debate seemed to suspicious minds like deliberate obstruction. At about three o'clock in the afternoon Sir George Treby, chairman of the Committee of Secrecy, began by reading some of the references to the Duke of York in the correspondence which had been seized from Coleman. Russell added another letter 'of a more desperate style and matter than any of the rest', and then Bennet moved for an address to the King to ask that the Duke of York should not be permitted to return to England without the consent of Parliament. This set the ball rolling: others gave it added impetus, suggesting a bill of banishment, until it fell to Sir Thomas Player to move for an Exclusion Bill. In the debate which followed the most notable feature was the number of formerly prominent leaders of the Country Party who opposed such a bill, including Henry Powle, Cavendish, Littleton, and Sir Henry Capel of those who had entered the Council, and also Sir William Coventry and Sir William Hickman, who were close to Halifax. They had all been 'overtaken on the left' by others more extreme than they. All their experience in debate was unavailing against the arguments of members like Boscawen, who argued that the King's proposals for limiting the powers of a Popish successor 'look like gold, but are leaf-gold when you touch them', and that Exclusion was the only practical solution. After many hours, in which we are told that the younger members gloried in the martyrdom of enforced fasting, the time came for a vote shortly after ten o'clock. The Exclusionists had won a previous vote about the introduction of candles by a majority of about two to one; now, as in accordance with the procedure of the time those in favour of the bill left their seats to be counted, the Noes saw in the flickering candle-light that they were going to be heavily outnumbered, and rose in their seats to give

---

[1] E. Cooke to Ormond, 10 May, *H.M.C. Ormond MSS.*, N.S. v. 89.
[2] *C.J.* ix. 619; Grey, vii. 228–36.

up the vote. The first name on the committee of thirteen which was instructed to prepare and introduce an Exclusion Bill was that of Shaftesbury's follower, Bennet.[1]

The vote was celebrated by a bonfire over against the Temple gate, which was planned by the members of the famous Green Ribbon Club who met in the neighbouring King's Head tavern at the corner of Chancery Lane. When the porter and servants of the Temple came to put out the fire, 'the gentlemen of the club' prevented them from doing so by threatening to draw their swords.[2] This was a deliberate demonstration; and its counterpart was the organization of a petition in the City, designed to thank Parliament for their vigorous prosecution of the Plot and promising to assist them with the 'lives and fortunes' of the signatories. Shaftesbury's City allies were active in promoting this in the Common Council: they included Sir Thomas Player, Alderman Pilkington (who was to be one of the most vehement City Whigs in the next few years), and the one-legged Francis Charlton, who frequently dined at the Earl's house and remained loyal to him when others fell away. This was a return to the policy pursued by Pym and Alderman Pennington in 1641, and its purpose was the same, namely to bring such a pressure of public opinion to bear that first the House of Lords and then the King would fall in with the demand of the House of Commons.[3]

That the Exclusion Bill would go through the Commons there could be no doubt. When the Bill received its first reading on 15 May, the House was thin—it was said, as a result of a dog match at Hampton Court and a horse match at Banstead Downs which took priority even over Exclusion!—but the attempts of the Court to delay the vote were swept aside.[4] Before the second reading in the following week the opposition brought opinion in the House to fever-heat again by an attack on Samuel Pepys, the Secretary to the Admiralty, and Sir Anthony Deane, the ship's architect who like Pepys had been patronized by the Duke of York. On behalf of a committee of enquiry, William Harbord reported to the House that one Colonel Scott had seen in the French Navy Office copies of maps and plans signed by Pepys; and Pepys's former butler, John James, then appeared at the bar of the House to give evidence about the diarist's alleged addiction to Popery, as shown by his intimacy with one Morelli, who had said mass at the Queen's Chapel. There had been psalm-singing, he said, and disputations about philosophy till three in the morning.

[1] *C.J.* ix. 620; Grey, vii. 236–60; Southwell to Ormond, 13 May, *H.M.C. Ormond MSS.*, N.S. iv. 511–12; E. Cooke to Ormond, 13 May, ibid. iv. 98.

[2] Southwell to Ormond, 17 May, ibid. iv. 514.

[3] Algernon Sidney to H. Savile, 19 May, *Letters . . . to the hon. Henry Savile*, p. 74; Van Beuningen, 23 May/2 June, Add. MSS. 17677, EE; Danby to the King, 21 May, Browning, ii. 82; Southwell to Ormond, 20, 24 May, *H.M.C. Ormond MSS.*, N.S. iv. 516, 517; Barrillon, 26 May/5 June.

[4] *C.J.* ix. 623; Grey, vii. 285–7; Cooke to Ormond, 15 May, op. cit. v. 102.

Pepys's indignant denials, his revelation that his butler had been caught in 'an amour with my housekeeper' 'at an unseasonable time of the night' and dismissed, and his assertion that he had shared with Morelli only a taste in music, were all of no avail. For Pepys this was a prelude to a journey to the Tower by way of the Traitors' Gate; and the suspicion of treason extended naturally to his master, the Duke of York.[1]

On the day after Shaftesbury or some other impresario had arranged for these 'revelations' to be made, the Exclusion Bill duly received its second reading. After one former prominent Country member, Clarges, had opposed the bill (painting a gloomy picture of the confusion which would result, and arguing that the 'condescensions' promised by the King would offer greater security), loud shouts of 'The Bill, the Bill!' cut short any further debate. This time the Court members stood their ground in the division, but none the less the motion for the bill's commitment was carried by 207 votes to 128. In order to assess the significance of this vote it is necessary to stress that one cannot recall any previous controversial issue in the reign of Charles II on which either side had managed to muster as many as two hundred votes[2]; and a majority of 79 was quite exceptional. This was a large number of members prepared to go to the length of declaring themselves publicly against the King's brother. Nor should too much be made of the large number of abstentions involved. The French ambassador declared that many of the abstainers were reserving their votes for the third reading, but it is doubtful whether he was right in thinking that they would then vote for the rejection of the bill: on the

---

[1] *C.J.* 626, 628–9; Grey, vii. 303–12, 315. The assumption made by Sir Arthur Bryant, *Samuel Pepys: The Years of Peril* (1935), chs. x, xi, is that the plot against Pepys was formed by Shaftesbury, but the evidence is insufficient to prove this conclusively. James later confessed that he had been first tempted by Colonel Mansell, a steward of Buckingham's, and that he had been present at a committee meeting at the Mitre Tavern in Fenchurch Street attended by Harbord, Sir John Hotham (James's godfather), Papillon, Mansell, Scott, and others (MSS. Rawlinson A 175, fos. 215, 224). It was Buckingham who recommended him to the Admiralty Commissioners, stating that James had been in his service. The adventurer Scott was also more closely connected with Buckingham than with Shaftesbury (cf. ibid. fo. 196 for his visits to the Duke in the Tower in 1677), and it is significant that Buckingham had appeared in the Lords for the first time this session on the previous Thursday (Cooke to Ormond, 20 May, *H.M.C. Ormond MSS.*, N.S. v. 108). This could have been Buckingham's attempt to return to the stage, in rivalry with Shaftesbury of whose leadership of the opposition he was jealous. When Scott landed at Dover on 29 Apr. 1679 he wrote to Shaftesbury as Lord President of the Council (MSS. Rawlinson A 188, fo. 139), but this does not prove complicity; and the dinners with the Earl of which he bragged at a later date (MSS. Rawlinson A 175, fo. 204) only prove that the Earl took him up, with other informers. From the Earl's point of view the most suspicious circumstance is that while in Paris in the winter of 1678–9 Scott had associated with the Earl's 'cousin', John Harrington, who was present there under the name of Mr. Benson on some mysterious mission (*H.M.C. Lindsey MSS.*, p. 404; small payments to 'my cousin at Paris' in accounts at Wimborne St. Giles). Whether or not Shaftesbury hatched the plot, it is likely enough that he helped to arrange that the 'evidence' against Pepys should appear in the House on the day fixed for the second reading of the Exclusion Bill. But the failure of the King's law officers to bring Pepys to trial was not Shaftesbury's doing.   [2] In 1641 204 members had voted for the attainder of Strafford.

contrary, the complete absence of the members for some counties, including such partisan members of the opposition as Francis Charlton, Sir Scrope Howe, and Richard Newport, suggests that an informal system of 'pairing' of neighbours may have operated. This was a decisive vote, which meant that the King must reckon that the bill would go through the Commons— if Parliament were allowed to remain in session.[1]

Among those who pressed the King to dissolve Parliament was the Earl of Danby, who from his prison in the Tower continued to pour a flood of advice on the political situation as he saw it, and urged that otherwise Shaftesbury and his 'instruments' would 'carry things beyond a possibility of being retrieved'. From their own standpoint Sunderland, Essex, and Halifax came round to the idea that at least a prorogation was necessary. For some time these three ministers had been holding consultations with Shaftesbury and Monmouth, but now they were perturbed by Shaftesbury's success and afraid that they would be swept helplessly along and left under the Earl's control; and accordingly they agreed with Sir William Temple that the possibility of a prorogation should be raised at the meeting of the Privy Council on 27 May. Charles for his part remained surprisingly cheerful among his difficulties, knowing by this time that he had a ready-made means of disposing of Parliament when he chose to do so.[2]

The King's salvation lay in the complications in which the impeachments of Danby and the five Catholic peers had become involved. Anxious as much to avoid an embarrassing trial as to stir up contention, Charles had sent Danby instructions to plead his pardon in bar of the impeachment, and Danby had reluctantly done so on 25 April, while still seeking to maintain that he was innocent and in no need of any pardon. It was inevitable that the House of Commons should deny the validity of a royal pardon which would stultify the whole impeachment procedure which they liked to use; and after several indignant debates the House resolved on 5 May to proceed in a body to the Lords and, on the ground that Danby's plea was invalid, to demand immediate judgement against him. Not only did they vote that the pardon was illegal, but they resolved that any counsel who maintained its validity before the Lords would be accounted a betrayer of the liberties of the commons of England.[3]

---

[1] *C.J.* ix. 626–7; Grey, vii. 313–14; Barrillon, 22 May/1 June; Van Beuningen, 23 May/ 2 June, Add. MSS. 17677, EE. My interpretation of the vote differs from that of Dr. J. R. Jones (*The First Whigs*, pp. 70–72). Dr. Jones argues that the result 'was only superficially a victory for the Whigs', and that 'Exclusion was rushed forward with insufficient preparation'. But it is difficult to believe that delay (which would mean maintaining the anti-Popish excitement consistently) was either desirable or necessary. The fact that a prorogation came within a week suggests what Charles's view of the matter was. Division lists are printed by D. Milne and A. Browning, *Bull. Inst. Hist. Res.* (1950), pp. 205–25, and K. Feiling, *History of the Tory Party* (1924), pp. 494–5.

[2] Danby to the King, 21 May, Browning, ii. 83; Temple, *Works*, i. 422–4; Reresby, p. 182.

[3] *L.J.* xiii. 537–40, 544–5, 552–3, 555–9, 562–5; *C.J.* ix. 602, 606, 611–12, 614–19; Grey, vii. 133–7, 152–7, 167–87, 199–213, 219–28; Browning, *Danby*, i. 333–7.

Many members of the opposition, like Cavendish, were aware of the danger that this would lead to a deadlock with the Upper House, where Danby's friends were numerous and unlikely to allow him to be condemned without trial. Shaftesbury, for his part, in May as in March cared less for revenge on Danby than for the prosecution of the Exclusion issue, and he cannot have relished the possibility that the tactics which he had used in *Shirley* v. *Fagg* to destroy Danby's programme in 1675 might now be employed to block his own in 1679. But whatever his misgivings, he had no choice but to follow the lead given by the opposition in the Commons. So far was he from being the unquestioned leader of a docile following, that had he tried to divert the Country members in the Commons from seeking to enforce their view about Danby's pardon, his efforts would have broken down on their insistence on their House's right to bring delinquent ministers to book by impeachment. And in any case, he had no desire to see the King's ministers freed from the threat of impeachment by royal pardons, and left dependent on royal favour rather than on pressure from Parliament; this would have deprived the opposition of an obvious weapon. Once the issue of the pardon had been raised, therefore, Shaftesbury had effectively no option but to assist his colleagues in the Lower House and hope that somehow enough pressure could be brought to bear upon the Lords to induce the Court majority there to give way.

On one point he was successful. When the Lords refused to agree to a Commons proposal for a joint committee of the two Houses to discuss the impeachment procedure, the Court's majority fell from roughly 2–1 on 8 May to a mere 54–52 (excluding proxies) on the 10th; and the twenty peers, including Shaftesbury, who signed a protest on the former date, rose to fifty on the latter, including many who normally voted with the Court. Not surprisingly, on the next day (the day on which Exclusion was debated in the Commons) the King found it inadvisable to make a stand on this 'punctilio', and the Lords reversed their previous vote and agreed to a joint committee, on which Shaftesbury was one of the Lords' twelve representatives. But this was only a minor victory, and the closeness of the voting on 10 May had served to emphasize a more substantial problem. On an occasion when the House had been almost evenly divided, sixteen of the bishops had voted with Danby's friends and only two had favoured a joint committee. If there were to be any chance of securing a verdict against Danby, 'the dead weight' would have to be removed from Danby's side of the scales.[1]

The question whether the bishops had a right to vote in capital cases had already been raised on 6 May, and was the subject of several debates in the following fortnight. There was much support for the general principle

---

[1] *L.J.* xiii. 559, 564–7; E. Cooke to Ormond, 10, 13 May, *H.M.C. Ormond MSS.*, N.S. v. 90–91, 97; Algernon Sidney to H. Savile, 12 May, *Letters . . . to the hon. Henry Savile*, pp. 62–63; *H.M.C. House of Lords MSS., 1678–88*, p. 50.

that bishops could not vote in 'cases of blood'; what was much more difficult was the problem whether they could vote on preliminary legal questions—such as the legality or otherwise of Danby's pardon. Shaftesbury maintained at considerable length that they could not. He sought to establish a distinction between temporal peers and spiritual ones, who did not sit by 'nobility of blood', and had not all the rights of peers—for instance, they were not tried by peers, and 'if bishops be not tried by the peers, why should peers be tried by bishops?' Furthermore, he chose for tactical purposes the unusual position of relying on canon law. Canon law, he argued, forbade them to 'sit on blood', 'and the canons hold except they be against the law of the land or the King's prerogative'. In support of these assertions he brought a great array of medieval and Tudor precedents, dating back to the Constitutions of Clarendon and the chronicles of Matthew Paris, whom he described as 'a good author and angry monk'. From such incidental remarks as this and from the readiness with which he coped with counter-precedents raised in support of the bishops—for instance, the verdict against Thomas Cromwell—we may conclude that Shaftesbury had some historical knowledge and was not merely presenting information which had been dug up for him by some antiquarian 'devil'. Naturally the precedents were conflicting, and it is doubtful whether the repeated attempts to wrest them to one side or the other had any effect on opinions which were really political and not legal. On 13 May the majority resolved that bishops had a right to remain in Court until 'the time came to vote "Guilty" or "Not Guilty"', and only twenty peers (including Halifax) joined Shaftesbury in recording a protest. When, however, the Commons refused to accept this, the bishops asked leave to withdraw from any part in the actual trial of the five Catholic peers, with liberty to enter a protest to safeguard their rights in the future; but this still left them free to take part in deciding preliminary questions in Danby's case, and when the House of Lords reaffirmed its decision on this, Shaftesbury could again muster only twenty-four peers to sign a protest.[1]

There were those who suspected that Shaftesbury had deliberately dragged out this dispute over the rights of the bishops in order to delay the trials,[2] possibly in order that there might be time for the Exclusion Bill to go through first, possibly because he was doubtful about the strength of the prosecution's case in the impeachments. But the attack on the bishops' voting rights fitted in too well with Shaftesbury's long-standing hostility to them and with his obvious desire to weaken the Court's strength in the Lords for it to be possible to dismiss it as a mere temporizing tactic. In any case the attack was a failure; it only served to demonstrate the weakness

---

[1] *L.J.* xiii. 555–6, 568, 570–7, 579–80, 586–7; notes on the debates in MSS. Carte 81, fos. 561–8; *H.M.C. House of Lords MSS., 1678–88*, pp. 31–36; *C.J.* ix. 622–3; Grey, vii. 278–85; Cooke to Ormond, 19 May, *H.M.C. Ormond MSS.*, N.S. v. 106–8.

[2] North, op. cit. p. 217.

of his position in the Lords, and to harden the resolve of his opponents not to give way to pressure from the Commons, whose attempt to insist on the elimination of the bishops was resented as an interference with a matter which concerned the peers alone. And a further procedural point completed the deadlock between the Houses. On 15 May the Lord Privy Seal, Anglesey, pressed for a day to be fixed for the trial of the five Roman Catholic peers whom Oates had accused of complicity in the Plot. Shaftesbury, however, while paying fulsome compliments to avoid alienating his old colleague, urged that it was vital to settle the matter of Danby's pardon first. 'The whole frame of government turned on that single thing. For if it could be, such a King might be that would thereby shelter all criminals from justice. . . .' But there was widespread support from the Court majority for the idea of giving priority to the trial of the Catholic peers, and even such as Essex argued that the crime of which they were accused was far more heinous than Danby's. By a majority of about four to one a date was fixed for the trial; but Sacheverell led the Commons in refusing to proceed until Danby's case had first been dealt with, and the bishops had been eliminated from all share in the proceedings. Underlying this course of action there was, as the French ambassador noticed, the opposition's fear that once the Catholic peers had been tried the King would be free to prorogue Parliament without being accused of doing so to prevent the Catholics from conviction. Nevertheless the Lords insisted, over the protest of Shaftesbury and twenty-three other peers, in planning to hold the trial of the five Catholics on 27 May; and the Commons retaliated by drawing up a long, tactlessly phrased and uncompromising complaint about the way in which the Lords had handled Danby's case from the beginning.[1]

This was Charles's opportunity. Now was the moment to free himself from Parliament; to avert the trials both of the Catholic peers and Danby; to block both the Exclusion Bill and the dangerous investigations which the Commons had begun into the payments made under Danby's regime to Court members of Parliament[2]; and to cut short the address which was being planned in the City.[3] Availing himself of the advice offered him at this point by Sunderland, Essex, and Halifax, but without informing the

---

[1] Cooke to Ormond, 15, 16 May, H.M.C. Ormond MSS., N.S. v. 101–2, 102–3; L.J. xiii. 575, 580–1, 586–7, 590–4; C.J. ix. 625, 630–3; Grey, vii. 292–303, 324–6, 336–43; Barrillon, 26 May/5 June; H.M.C. House of Lords MSS., 1678–88, pp. 34–35; Southwell to Ormond, op. cit. iv. 518–19. A Narrative and Reasons of the House of Commons why the Earl of Danby should be tried before the Five Lords in the Tower appeared in print: ibid. v. 119.

[2] On 23 May Sir Stephen Fox named 27 people to whom payments had been made from 'secret service' monies, and Charles Bertie, Danby's brother-in-law and Secretary to the Treasury, was under considerable pressure: C.J. ix. 629–31; Grey, vii. 315–24, 326–36. 'They say by Tuesday next [27th] they shall bring in a hundred more at least' in addition to the 27; Cooke to Ormond, 24 May, H.M.C. Ormond MSS., N.S. v. 112.

[3] Van Beuningen, 27 May/6 June, Add. MSS. 17677, EE; Barrillon, 29 May/8 June.

new Privy Council which he had solemnly promised to consult, Charles went to Westminster on 27 May. He found the five Catholic peers awaiting their trial in Westminster Hall among crowds of spectators, and learned that the House of Lords had reaffirmed their votes about the bishops by sixty-five votes to thirty-six. Pausing only to give the royal assent to one or two bills, Charles cut short all these proceedings by proroguing Parliament to 14 August, with a brief reference to the differences between the two Houses which had made this unfortunate step necessary. The session was at an end, and with it Shaftesbury's first attempt to pass an Exclusion Bill.[1]

There was one small consolation for the opposition. One of the few bills which received the royal assent was the famous Habeas Corpus Amendment Act, which they had vainly endeavoured to pass in several previous sessions of the Cavalier Parliament. The Act's purpose was to stop up some serious loopholes in the traditional *habeas corpus* procedure which protected the subject from arbitrary imprisonment at the hands of the executive. It had been possible to prevent prisoners from suing out the *habeas corpus* writ by committing them to custody at the beginning of the Long Vacation, by moving them about from prison to prison ahead of the writ, or by sending them to places like the Channel Islands or Tangier where the writ did not run. Such devices had not been frequently employed in the years before 1679—they would have created too much animus against an already unpopular and weak government—but it is not fanciful to think that but for the Act the *habeas corpus* procedure might well have been evaded in the period of reaction between 1681 and 1688. The best commentary on the need for the Act is that James II would have liked to repeal it. Since the bill had first been introduced in 1674 Charles's ministers had found it prudent to abandon arguments of principle, and to rely instead on difficulties over the legal technicalities involved to prevent the bill from being completed before the end of the current parliamentary session. In this session of 1679 there had been a long exchange of amendments and provisos between the two Houses, until on 26 May the House of Commons, deciding to abandon the details in order to secure the essentials, suddenly resolved to accept the Lords' latest amendments and asked for a 'free conference' with the Lords at which the bill could be returned to the Upper House. On the morning of 27 May, therefore, the Lords debated whether or not to grant the free conference requested. Some peers by this time were thoroughly ill-disposed to the Commons; others probably wanted to proceed with the trial of the Catholic peers; and others were glad of a pretext to wreck the bill. At all events the vote on this apparently trivial procedural matter was a close one, and there is no reason to question the contemporary story that the vote was settled by a fluke—or by downright

---

[1] *L.J.* xiii. 594–5; *H.M.C. House of Lords MSS., 1678–88*, pp. 40–41; Temple, *Works*, i. 424; Cooke to Ormond, 27 May, *H.M.C. Ormond MSS.*, N.S. v. 116.

cheating. As one very fat peer came to be counted, Lord Grey of Wark, the young opposition peer who was teller for the bill counted him as ten, 'as a jest at first', and then noticed that the teller, Lord Norris, 'being a man subject to vapours' was not paying attention. Grey therefore went on deliberately with his miscount, and the motion for a free conference was carried by 57 votes to 55 in a House which, according to the Journals, was attended only by 107 peers. In order to distract attention from this, Shaftesbury is said to have risen and made a long speech about nothing in particular, until so many peers had gone out and come in that the vote could not be questioned. After the free conference with the Commons it was Shaftesbury again who reported the Commons' acceptance of the disputed amendments, and the bill was just ready in time to receive the royal assent.[1]

Except that Shaftesbury had been concerned in an earlier conference between the two Houses[2] this is all that is known of his direct part in what is sometimes known as the 'Shaftesbury Act'—though of course he may have intervened in committee or behind the scenes in the discussions on the disputed amendments and provisos, as someone who certainly possessed the technical legal knowledge. If this is known as the 'Shaftesbury Act' it is not because it represented the accomplishment of some cherished private scheme of his own, but because, after the failure of several previous attempts to pass such a measure, it was the one solid legislative success of the party which he led during the Exclusion Parliaments. Yet the name is not entirely undeserved. The effect of the Act was to strengthen the liberties of the subject against arbitrary action by the monarch, and this was the cause to which Shaftesbury was devoting the last years of his life and the reason why he was determined to exclude James from the succession. If Shaftesbury's name was foremost in the more disagreeable side of the opposition's actions in the Exclusion crisis, it perhaps deserves to be remembered in connection with the opposition's one prominent achievement as well. It is certainly remarkable that the Whigs of the eighteenth and nineteenth centuries, who were distinctly ashamed of their first leader's memory, nevertheless attached his name to a measure of which they were proud because it strengthened one of the features which

---

[1] *L.J.* xiii. 594–5; *H.M.C. House of Lords MSS., 1678–88*, pp. 132–6; Shaftesbury Papers, VI A, 339; Burnet, ii. 263–4 (and cf. *Supplement*, pp. 351–2, for the story that Grey deliberately jumped from 24 to 35); Martyn, Kippis and Cooke, *Life of Shaftesbury*, ii. 221. For the significance of the Act, cf. Sir W. S. Holdsworth, *History of English Law* (1944 ed.), ix. 112–25; and Helen A. Nutting, 'The most wholesome law—the Habeas Corpus Act of 1679', in *Am. Hist. Rev.* (1960), pp. 527–43. In doubting the episode of the 'fat peer' Professor Nutting ignores the note in the Shaftesbury Papers, cited above. And I cannot accept her view that the act was 'no longer controversial' and 'not really a party measure' merely because in the political circumstances of 1679 the Court dared not directly oppose it. The narrowness of the majority strongly suggests that, to put it mildly, many courtiers were not enthusiastic about restricting the Executive's powers in this way.

[2] On 9 May (*L.J.* xiii. 561).

distinguished English political liberties from the unfree states on the continent.

When the Act was passed, however, it was only a small consolation for the failure to pass an Exclusion Bill. The high hopes which had followed on the dissolution at long last of the Cavalier Parliament had so far been disappointed; and in Shaftesbury's own words, things would have to be worse before they could be better. But time was not really on his side. The agitation on which he relied could not easily be maintained in being, especially when Parliament was not in session; and the problem how to keep unabated the fear of a Popish successor was to be his central pre-occupation for the next eighteen months. For the first five of these, until October 1679, he was in the curious position of serving as Lord President of Charles's Council while keeping going an agitation of which Charles strongly disapproved; and the impossibility of preserving such an anomalous situation must be the subject of the next chapter.

CHAPTER XXIV

SHAFTESBURY'S SECOND PERIOD OF OFFICE
(APRIL-OCTOBER 1679)

> Nature made him a perverse wight, whose nose
> Extracts the essence of his gouty toes;
> Double with head to tail he crawls apart:
> His body's th'emblem of his double heart.
>
> *The Cabal* (1679)

WHEN Charles prorogued Parliament on 27 May 1679, he deemed it prudent to double the guards at Whitehall. No rioting took place, but the unpopularity of the action was obvious enough. Obvious, too, was the fact that it was Charles's own action, taken without consulting the new Council by which only five weeks earlier he had promised to be guided. He excused himself by saying that if he had called the Council the matter would have leaked out and the Commons would have had time to pass some offensive votes; but the excuse was not a very convincing one, and stories that Monmouth had urged his father to consult the Council did his own popularity no harm. Some had always considered the Council as a transparent dodge, and the prorogation supported the view that it was not seriously intended to have any authority.[1]

This raised in an acute form the question whether Shaftesbury ought to continue as Lord President of the Council. Gossip had already reported that he was weary of an office in which he plainly had less of the King's confidence even than Danby, who was suspected of guiding the King from the Tower through his son, Lord Latimer (a Gentleman of the Bedchamber) and through the Earl of Bath (whose son was married to Danby's daughter). At the prorogation Shaftesbury's rage was expressed in public. In the House of Lords he said aloud that he would have the heads of those who had advised it. He told the King that there was no need for anyone to hold a candle to his face, 'for his intent was visible by his actions'. In these circumstances there seemed at first sight to be little point in Shaftesbury's continuing to hold office and a privy councillorship which would be only nominal. Charles urged him to remain, for his departure, especially if followed by others, would have been too obviously the end of the coalition

---

[1] Barrillon, 29 May/8 June; Southwell to Ormond, 27, 31 May, *H.M.C. Ormond MSS.*, N.S. iv. 518–19, 520. On the Saturday before Whitsuntide (7 June) papers were distributed in London inviting the apprentices 'to pull down the whore of Babylon' and go to Somerset House, St. James's, and Whitehall to demand justice against Danby, but the fact that no riot took place suggests that these papers were not the work of anyone in authority in the Whig party: *C.S.P.D. 1679–80*, p. 177; John Verney to Sir R. Verney, 12 June, *H.M.C. Seventh Report*, p. 472.

which had been the professed basis of the new Council. And Shaftesbury in the end did remain; but for very different reasons. What he told his friends in the City was that he would stay at Court 'only to be a tribune for the people there'. As Lord President he would at least be better informed about what was being transacted in the Council than he would as an isolated private citizen; the initiative would not pass entirely into the King's hands; and Shaftesbury might hope to influence some at least of the other members of the Council Board. Any seventeenth-century politician had a natural predisposition to stay in office if he possibly could; and Shaftesbury stayed.[1]

The Council over which he presided included old opponents whom he hated, like Lauderdale; others whom he despised, like the Lord Chancellor, Finch; allies upon whom he could rely, like Monmouth, and other former allies, like Halifax, over whom he was now losing any control that he might ever have had. If the spring of 1679 was a period in which he drew much closer to Monmouth, it was also a period in which any friendship with Halifax finally broke down.

For many years the two men had been relatives and political associates, but the relationship had never been a comfortable one. As Halifax's uncle by marriage, and twelve years his senior, Shaftesbury had been a party to his marriage settlement and to devices to protect his estates from Cromwell's decimation tax in 1655[2]; and the political outlooks of the two men were not, in general, greatly dissimilar. In spite of the attempts which some have made to assimilate Halifax into a Tory tradition, the fact remains that it was he, not Shaftesbury, who remarked that no man would use the hereditary principle to select his coachman; and his religious principles were far from being of an orthodox, Anglican kind. His outlook was coolly rational and entirely secular; and he had the same dislike as Shaftesbury of episcopal authority, of the Roman Catholic Church, and of James, Duke of York. On the face of it, therefore, the two men should have been able to co-operate; and when selecting them both for his new Council Charles had been more reluctant to admit Halifax, as being more rooted in his opposition. Yet uncle and nephew had never been easy with one another. Indeed the family relationship was not in fact as close as it sounds: Shaftesbury's first wife and Halifax's mother were both Coventrys, but both were long dead, and perhaps the relationship remained only to give Shaftesbury a seniority which Halifax was not disposed to concede. Halifax was not temperamentally fitted to be anyone's lieutenant. He was intensely conscious of his own intellectual powers, conscious that in abilities and qualifications he was in no way inferior to any of his

---

[1] Southwell to Ormond, 24 May, op. cit. iv. 517 (where 'Worcester' should probably read 'Winchester'); Temple, *Works*, i. 424–5; [Bonell] to Watts, 31 May, *H.M.C. Ormond MSS.*, v. 119; Danby to Bath, 3 June, Browning, *Danby*, ii. 87–88.

[2] The legal documents are in the Chatsworth MSS., at present unclassified.

contemporaries; and while affecting to despise the common craving for office and for honours, he resented the fact that these were vouchsafed to lesser men than he. Unlike Shaftesbury, almost twenty years after the Restoration he enjoyed no influential ministerial position; even his diplomatic mission to Louis XIV in 1672 had been rapidly superseded by that of Arlington and Buckingham. His frustrations found expression at first in destructive criticism of the government: he had a strong and genuine dislike of the policies and methods of Danby, and equally of the government's connection with Louis XIV—here he had a more European view of the dangers of French expansion than did Shaftesbury. But even while he opposed Danby's regime on these points, he did so more in the independent mood of his other uncle, Sir William Coventry, than in the more disciplined 'party' spirit of Shaftesbury. In his famous letters of February 1675 to the Earl of Carlisle[1] Shaftesbury had sneered at Halifax; in February 1677 Halifax had not joined Shaftesbury in arguing that Parliament was dissolved, and therefore had not shared his imprisonment in the Tower. Shaftesbury was usually able to charm those whom he wanted to charm, but in Halifax's case he either disdained to do so or was quite unsuccessful. In the spring of 1679 the lack of sympathy which these incidents indicated became something worse. The King's reconstitution of his Council, with Halifax as one of its members, and his promise to consent to effective limitations on a Popish successor, seemed to Halifax to provide a much better foundation for the future than Shaftesbury's policy of Exclusion. It looked as though such a policy would operate in the interests of William of Orange and Princess Mary, whom both on English and European grounds Halifax preferred as eventual successors to the Duke of Monmouth.

Halifax had no illusions about the King's steadfastness of purpose, but thought that there was at least a chance that he might be kept to the course which he had declared to Parliament. He had no very high opinion of Charles's abilities and thought like many others that he might be controlled. Danby, whom Halifax hated, was out of harm's way in the Tower, and the field was open. While continuing, therefore, to maintain his belief in the existence of a Popish Plot[2] and the need for measures against Catholics, Halifax decided against Exclusion. Charles, who had at first resisted Halifax's admission to his Council, soon saw the possibilities of the situation and gave him suitable encouragement.[3] And, although Halifax was never inclined to work in harness with anyone, it was useful to know that some of Charles's other advisers were thinking on similar lines, particularly about the need to draw closer to William of Orange.

One of these was another of Shaftesbury's nephews by marriage, the

---

[1] pp. 369–71 above.

[2] Halifax to H. Savile, 2/12 June, *Savile Correspondence*, ed. W. D. Cooper (Camden Society, 1857), p. 98.

[3] Southwell to Ormond, 3, 24 May, *H.M.C. Ormond MSS.*, N.S. iv. 509, 517.

Earl of Sunderland, who had by now, in spite of his relative inexperience, established himself as the more important of the two Secretaries of State. He was not by any means inclined to fill the minor role of his predecessor, Sir Joseph Williamson. Something of a gambler by temperament as well as tastes, he proposed to stake everything on enlisting William's aid. In foreign policy there would be a joint Anglo-Dutch guarantee of the Nijme-gen settlement, which would protect what was left of the Spanish Nether-lands from further French aggression. And if William could also be persuaded to come over to England, and perhaps even take a seat in the Privy Council and House of Lords, the presence of such an undoubted Protestant and lifelong opponent of France might serve to allay some of the popular fears about a Popish succession to the throne. William would attract the support of those who looked to a future when he and Mary would rule; and accordingly it would be possible to meet Parliament with some hope of harmony. Sunderland had hopes of gaining Charles's acquiescence in such a policy, even though experience had taught Charles that he could never rely on his nephew to follow his lead without question. Sunderland counted a good deal on the influence which the Duchess of Portsmouth had over the King: as a Papist and a Frenchwoman she was violently unpopular, and motives of self-preservation led her to ally with Sunderland in default of anyone better.[1] And Sunderland hoped to gain William's own acquiescence through the newly appointed ambassador at The Hague, Henry Sidney.[2] At the same time he found it expedient to keep up friendly relations with his uncle Shaftesbury, who, he thought, in the last resort could hardly oppose an anti-French policy.

Another who looked to William was Sidney's predecessor as envoy to the States-General, Sir William Temple. In the last five years Temple had become devoted to William as the bulwark of European liberties against French aggression, and William had reciprocated, giving his confidence to the handsome Englishman as he gave it only to a handful of confidants. Temple, like William, hoped that England could be brought into a European coalition against Louis XIV, when once the English domestic situation could be resolved; yet experience had given him an instinctive distrust of almost all English politicians (including the King), and for this reason, intelligent and reflective as he was, he shrank from the responsibility of accepting the second Secretaryship of State (in place of Henry Coventry) and plunging into the muddy waters of English politics. When matters did not go as he wanted, he was prone to seek for a refuge from the ills of the world in his gardens at Sheen, 'like a schoolboy broke up from school'. However in the spring of 1679 he was not yet completely dis-illusioned with Whitehall; and he was much more inclined to co-operate with Sunderland, Halifax, and Essex than with Shaftesbury. As a lover of

---

[1] *Diary of the Times of Charles the Second*, ed. R. W. Blencowe (1843), i. 15, 18–19.
[2] Ibid. i. 3–5, 13, 15–16, 19–21, 27, 29–30.

the Dutch he had an invincible detestation of the author of the *Delenda est Carthago* speech which he made no attempt to surmount by means of any social contacts; and he gave to Shaftesbury the responsibility for causing 'divisions and distractions, at a time that our union was so necessary to the affairs of Christendom abroad'.[1]

Finally, Essex also inclined to William in preference to the Duke of Monmouth. At this time his relations with Shaftesbury were cooler than they had been at one time: as the principal Commissioner of the Treasury he was making a genuine effort to cope with the financial problem by means of economies, and he was being too successful in this for Shaftesbury's liking—since success postponed the day when Charles would have to call Parliament.[2]

These four, Halifax, Sunderland, Essex, and Temple, were able for some time to achieve a measure of co-operation—the more so as they were all fearful of the ascendancy which Shaftesbury and Monmouth seemed to be acquiring. The Council over which Shaftesbury presided, in short, contained many strong personalities with their own ideas about the right course of action to be pursued. Apart from Monmouth, Russell and possibly Winchester, there was no one among the thirty-three members who shared his own determination to use the coming months to prepare for a new session of Parliament and a new Exclusion Bill. Shaftesbury was almost isolated, and his ill-temper was manifest in 'spiteful repartees' exchanged with Halifax.[3] And notwithstanding the large salary of £1,000 per annum with which the office of Lord President had been endowed, he was not permitted to earn this by engaging in many administrative duties. He was authorized to be present at all committees as he thought fit; he was specially nominated to the Council's Committee of Intelligence 'for the opening and considering all advices, as well foreign as domestic'[4]; and naturally he was also the leading member of the Council's Committee on Trade and Plantations, in which capacity he recommended the loan of two royal ships to transport Huguenots to his plantation in Carolina (where they would plant vineyards and olive trees and make silk),[5] signed a long report on Jamaica[6] and a letter to the colonists of Massachusetts mentioning the King's expectation 'that perfect freedom of conscience will be granted to all (except Papists)' and 'that all [colonial] laws repugnant to the laws of trade will be abolished'.[7] But all these were side-issues. More germane

---

[1] Temple, *Works*, i. 421, refers to a business meeting at Halifax's house, 'which was the only time I ever had anything to do, or so much as talk, with my Lord Shaftesbury, further than the council chamber'. Cf. also ibid. i. 438.

[2] Barrillon, 2/12 June.   [3] Temple, *Works*, i. 427.

[4] P.C. Reg. 2/68, fo. 5 (21 Apr.). Minutes of the Committee of Intelligence's business are in Add. MSS. 15643.

[5] *C.S.P. Col. America and West Indies, 1677–80*, pp. 321, 327, 336–7, 364, 455.

[6] Ibid. pp. 364–6.

[7] Ibid. pp. 377–8. Cf. pp. 386–8 for questions about Barbados, and pp. 390–1 for a 'form of government' for New Hampshire.

to Shaftesbury's main purpose was the review which the Council initiated of all the justices of the peace and deputy lieutenants, in order to ensure that these were 'fit persons' and 'known Protestants'. Shaftesbury himself was asked to propose a method for the review of J.P.s, and it was agreed that different members of the Council should examine the lists for different counties and make recommendations. Naturally Dorset fell to Shaftesbury, together with Winchester and Holles; and with various other colleagues it also fell to him to look at Cheshire, Leicestershire, Middlesex, Somerset, Sussex, Wiltshire, and Wales. It was inevitable that the definition of 'fit persons' should depend on party considerations, and plainly in Shaftesbury's eyes the whole object of the exercise was to fill the commissions with men of his own persuasion. Equally obviously Charles did all that he could to obstruct the exercise, whether by serious or by frivolous means. We are told that he would find some jocular reason for allowing a man of whom he approved to remain on the rolls, 'as that he was a good cocker, understood hunting, kept a good house, had good chines of beef, kept good fox hounds, or some such indifferent matter, which it was ridiculous to contradict or dispute upon'.[1] There were infinite possibilities for delay; but probably a more important reason for the failure ever to complete the review was the Council's preoccupation with more controversial issues, all of which had to be debated not as between colleagues but as between rivals with eyes on the need to justify themselves before public opinion and eventually before Parliament. In these debates Shaftesbury was almost always defeated, and yet contrived to build up his reputation as a 'tribune of the people' fighting for their interests among ministers who had been bought over by the Court. He could, for instance, join in urging on the King a declaration that James should not be permitted to return to England without the consent of the Council[2]; but the debates on this were interrupted by news from another quarter.

On 7 June an extraordinary meeting of the Council was held to discuss the news of the rebellion of the Scottish Covenanters. This was not as widespread, nor did it receive the same measure of aristocratic support, as the movement against the Scottish policy of Charles I in 1638, but it raised some of the same issues. A rebellion was a rebellion and would have to be suppressed, but how and by whom? It looked as though it would be beyond Lauderdale's capacity to suppress it unaided. So far as Shaftesbury was concerned, he had no connexions with the rebels themselves, but he was on good terms with some of the Scottish peers, such as Hamilton, who were hostile to Lauderdale and who looked to him much as their predecessors had done to Pym in 1640.[3] If the Covenanting rabble had to be

---

[1] P.C. Reg. 2/68, fos. 30, 42, 47–48 (12, 21 May); Add. MSS. 15643, fo. 2; R. North, *Examen* (1740), pp. 77–78.

[2] Barrillon, 9/19 June.

[3] Cf. J. R. Jones, 'The Scottish Constitutional Opposition in 1679', *Scottish Historical Review* (1958), pp. 37–41. In the Shaftesbury Papers, VI A, 338, there is an extremely

suppressed, it would suit Shaftesbury much better that this should be done by his friends rather than by Lauderdale; and memories of the Bishops' Wars suggested that it would be better still if the rebellion were not quickly crushed at all, so that Parliament had to be called. At the same time there was the further complicating factor that, in the Duke of York's absence, the obvious commander of any English expeditionary force would be the Duke of Monmouth.

Shaftesbury therefore began by arguing that the rebellion was simply one more piece of evidence of the misgovernment of Lauderdale, and Russell began a long speech in support. But when Lauderdale, who was present, offered to withdraw, the King merely said 'No, no, sit down, my Lord; this is not a place for addresses', and made it plain that he did not propose to dismiss the minister on whose firmness and brutality he had depended for so long in Scotland. This was one more indication that the concessions which Charles had proffered to the Commons in April did not represent any real change of heart; and Halifax and Temple were as resentful about it as Shaftesbury, and even contemplated resignation. Charles gave way to the extent of agreeing to meet a group of Scottish opposition peers who were in London, but he gave them no satisfaction, and insisted that English troops should aid the government's Scottish army. Both forces were to be put under Monmouth's command, and while so many English soldiers were away in Scotland Monmouth was also ordered to raise a special guard of two hundred gentlemen to attend on the King 'whenever His Majesty shall walk out of his palace'.[1]

It can easily be imagined that this last order, if it had been carried into effect, would not have been unacceptable to Shaftesbury, who might have been able to use such a guard under certain circumstances. But to other features of the royal policy he was opposed, to the extent, it was said, that at one point he and three or four other peers asked for leave to withdraw from the Council. He shared the opinion of those who argued that, if the advice of the Scottish nobles was taken, the rebels might be appeased without expense and without 'giving jealousy of raising a new army for an army's sake'; and he shared, or suggested, the scruples of political associates like Lord Grey of Wark, the teller in the Habeas Corpus Act division, who, in spite of his known intimacy with Monmouth,[2] laid down his commission in the Army because of a clause in the Treaty of Ripon of 1640 which forbade armies to enter either country without the consent of both the respective Parliaments. At the Council Board he urged the need to call

---

long and tedious letter from William Carstares to the Earl, but its tone does not suggest any special familiarity between the two men.

[1] Temple, *Works*, i. 426–8; P.C. Reg. 2/68, fos. 98–99, 103–4, 107; Barrillon, 9/19, 12/22 June; Sidney's Diary, i. 5; North, op. cit. pp. 79–80; Southwell to Ormond, 10 June, *H.M.C. Ormond MSS.*, N.S. iv. 522–3.

[2] It was widely supposed that he connived at his wife's liaison with Monmouth.

Parliament to discuss the situation, or at the least to issue a proclamation declaring that Parliament would be permitted on the date of 14 August to which it had been prorogued. The debate grew heated, and some one used the dread word 'Commonwealth', referring perhaps to Shaftesbury's support of it in 1653; whereupon 'Shaftesbury thought fit to speak to it in the King's presence, and said if the King so governed as that his estate might with safety be transmitted to his son, as it was by his father to him, and he might enjoy the known rights and liberties of the subjects, he would rather be under kingly government, but if he could not be satisfied of that he declared he was for a Commonwealth'.[1] The Council adjourned; but there were ways and means of mobilizing out-of-doors pressure. A monster petition was planned, for signature 'by many lords, gentlemen, and all the principal householders of the City of London': it called upon the King to put an end to all fears of a standing army and of war between English and Scottish Protestants by 'composing matters' in Scotland, permitting Parliament to meet on 14 August, bringing Danby and others to trial, and disbanding the Army. If the petition attracted enough signatories it was planned to send it to the Grand Juries in the counties for their signatures too. There can be no doubt that there was an organization behind this, and that the great Whig petitioning movement of six months later would have been anticipated but for the speedy collapse of the insurrection in Scotland.[2]

If the Covenanter rebellion had lasted for any appreciable length of time, Charles's position would have been considerably weakened and he would have been compelled to meet his Parliament; but unfortunately for Shaftesbury, the Duke of Monmouth was completely successful over the ill-trained and ill-armed rebels at the battle of Bothwell Bridge on 22 June. Monmouth won some plaudits for his leniency to the defeated, and his reputation as soldier, statesman and his father's favourite son was somewhat enhanced; but Lauderdale soon returned to power in Scotland, and any chance of the rebellion having the same effect on English politics as the Bishops' Wars by forcing the King to call Parliament was at an end. It was noticed that at this time Shaftesbury was 'ill pleased' with Monmouth's preference for military glory at the expense of the needs of the political situation; and when in 1682 Shaftesbury commented with exasperation that 'God had thrice put it into his (Monmouth's) power to

---

[1] John Speke to Hugh Speke, 14 June, *C.S.P.D. 1679–80*, p. 176; Southwell to Ormond, 14, 17 June, *H.M.C. Ormond MSS.*, N.S. iv. 523–4; Longford to Ormond, 14 June, ibid. v. 134; Bonell to Watts, 17 June, ibid. v. 136. It should be noted that the quotation from Shaftesbury's speech comes by way of 'a member of the Commons', who had it 'from Lord Shaftesbury's own mouth'; so that there may have been some exaggeration in the communication.

[2] Add. MSS. 15643, fo. 10 (Charles bringing a copy of the petition to the Committee of Intelligence, 21 June); Algernon Sidney to Henry Savile, 23, 30 June, *Letters . . . to the hon. Henry Savile*, pp. 112–14, 123; Dutch secretary, 27 June/7 July, Add. MSS. 17677, EE.

save England, and make himself the greatest man in Europe, but he had neglected the use of all those opportunities', this was one of the occasions to which he was referring.[1] Nothing came even of the proposal to raise a special regiment under Monmouth's command, because of Essex's opposition.[2]

As a result of the collapse of the rebellion and the economies which Essex and the other Treasury Commissioners were enforcing, Charles was left with sufficient elbow-room to decide whether or not Parliament should meet at the appointed date. He was quite determined that it should not. First he sounded out Barrillon privately in the Duchess of Portsmouth's apartments, to discover whether there was any hope of money from Louis XIV; but that wily diplomat, slapping his fat thighs with enjoyment, gave him no satisfaction, believing as he did that his master's interest lay in keeping England disordered and weak.[3] Characteristically James urged him to use the troops set free by the failure of the Covenanters 'for his protection and security', but Charles wisely rejected this advice to rule by armed force.[4] Instead he decided on dissolving Parliament and trying what a new one would be like. It could certainly be no worse than the old one from his point of view. Sunderland, Essex, Halifax, and Temple also hoped that a new Parliament would be more moderate and more manageable; and accordingly the King raised the matter in Council at Hampton Court on 3 July. The general opinion then was opposed to a dissolution; but when the Council met again a week later, the King opened the proceedings by declaring that he had decided to dissolve. Since he had unwisely neglected to warn natural supporters like Lord Chancellor Finch in advance, the result was that Finch opposed the idea, and was followed by many others. Shaftesbury was enabled to say that the dissolution was supported only by four members of the Board, and was decided on in defiance of the majority of the Council which he had promised to consult. He spoke himself 'in the amplest manner, and most tragical terms'. He made his rage obvious, and announced that he intended to have the heads of those who had advised it.[5]

Shaftesbury had become noticeably more ill-tempered of late, but it is possible that on this occasion his rage was synthetic. It had never been likely that Parliament would meet in the middle of August. A meeting in

---

[1] Marginal note in the original of Sidney's diary, Add. MSS. 32682, fo. 9; Ford Lord Grey, *Secret History of the Rye House Plot* . . . (1754), pp. 19–20.

[2] Essex to the King, 21 July, *C.S.P.D. 1679–80*, p. 201; Sunderland to Essex, [22] July, ibid, p. 202; Temple, *Works*, i. 428.

[3] Barrillon, 26 June/6 July. See Algernon Sidney to Henry Savile, 10/20 July, *Letters . . . to the hon. Henry Savile*, pp. 130–1, for a curious picture of Barrillon's habits in company. Barrillon's analysis of the situation is to be found in his despatch of 3/13 July.

[4] J. S. Clarke, *Life of James II* (1816), i. 563.

[5] Sidney Diary, pp. 16 (27 June), 21 (3 July), 24–25 (8, 10, 11 July), 26–27 (14 July); Temple, *Works*, i. 429–32; Southwell to Ormond, 10 July, *H.M.C. Ormond MSS.*, N.S. iv. 530–1; Longford to Arran, 12 July, MSS. Carte 232, fo. 49.

October would be quite satisfactory, especially if new elections in the meantime had confirmed the positions of the members who had been chosen in February. Moreover, the King's promise of 22 April to be guided by his new Council had been revealed as patently insincere, and other promises could be given their true value in future. And, most important of all, Halifax and his colleagues were discredited with any popular following they might once have had, while Shaftesbury stood out as the 'tribune of the people' protesting on their behalf against the repeated prorogations and dissolutions by which their wishes were evaded. The King contributed to this by choosing this precise moment to promote Halifax to an earldom—a title which the latter accepted in spite of his professed scorn for such honours. The division between the two men was now complete, Halifax answering Shaftesbury's anger with contempt. Shaftesbury alternately railed at and derided the triumvirate of Halifax, Essex, and Sunderland. He disliked Essex's assiduity at the Treasury: Sunderland he treated rather less harshly, and when the latter's crony Henry Sidney departed on his embassy to The Hague, Shaftesbury 'hoped I would make a good alliance between us and the Dutch, that we might be able to make some resistance to France'. As for the Prince of Orange, Shaftesbury grudgingly added, 'if he would continue a good Protestant, we would do him right'.[1]

On 18 July, the day after Shaftesbury made these remarks, the trial of Sir George Wakeman took place, and we must now turn back to look at the Earl's attitude to these Plot trials and the use that he hoped to make of them. This was indeed intimately bound up with his preparations for the next meeting of Parliament. If he was to make another attempt to secure Exclusion, he must in the meantime keep the pot of anti-Catholicism boiling, if possible with the addition of new fuel. One advantage to be derived from his position as Lord President of the Council was that other informers could approach him naturally in the secure knowledge that if their 'disclosures' were politically valuable they would receive a sympathetic hearing from someone in authority. Shaftesbury's enemies, of course, insinuated that the encouragement which he gave extended to direct subornation, but there is no reliable evidence that he engaged in such a dangerous practice.[2] It was in any case unnecessary, because

---

[1] Burnet, ii. 233; Southwell to Ormond, 5 July, *H.M.C. Ormond MSS.*, N.S. iv. 530; Ossory to Ormond, 8 July, ibid. v. 152; Sidney Diary, i. 28. Sidney was to tell William, from Sunderland, that Shaftesbury was 'a good tool to work with' (ibid. i. 29–30)—a remarkable illustration of Sunderland's self-confidence.

[2] Thomas Culpeper to Danby, 3 June, Add. MSS. 28049, fo. 54: 'This day Mr. Tonge [jun.] hath confessed that the Earl of Shaftesbury hath solicited him to bear false witness against your lordship, and that he hath threatened him for refusing to do the same.' But it is difficult to tell precisely what the 'solicitation' really amounted to, and in any case Tonge's career suggests that he was quite capable of false witness against Shaftesbury. Cf. also Lionel Anderson to Lady Chaworth, 1 June, Shaftesbury Papers, VI A, 341, and *Mr. Tho. Dangerfield's Particular Narrative* (1679), pp. 6–7, for the tale of a convicted

informers had their own reasons for coming forward without being suborned to do so. One such was a young Yorkshireman, Robert Bolron, who arrived in London to accuse his aged master, Sir Thomas Gascoigne, and others of plotting to kill the King. Shaftesbury passed him on to the Privy Council, who sent him back to Yorkshire along with orders for the arrest of all those against whom he had informed. It was only much later that it appeared that Bolron was, like Dugdale, a dishonest steward who wished both to revenge himself on his master and to have an alternative way of earning, or rather obtaining, a living. For the present he told his story 'so discreetly, that every body believes him'.[1] A second informer was Robert Jennison, a convert from Catholicism who came from a well-to-do country family in county Durham. He purported to confirm Oates's statement that the convicted Jesuit, Ireland, was in London plotting to kill the King in August 1678, and not in Staffordshire as numerous Catholic witnesses claimed. Since the seventeenth century was naïvely predisposed to believe that gentlemen of good family were trustworthy witnesses, this was useful support for Oates's general credibility; and Jennison was encouraged to extend his information about the Plot in depositions made to Shaftesbury's acquaintance, Edmund Warcup. It was not immediately obvious that Jennison's secret motive was to ruin his Jesuit brother Thomas by involving him in the Plot.[2] Then there was a third informer, John Fitzgerald, who approached Shaftesbury and asked for the King's pardon in return for the revelations he could make. Shaftesbury sent him to the Lord Mayor 'to have him provided for in the Compter, not as a prisoner but to secure him from harm, and that he should be well provided for with all things necessary'. Little was heard of Fitzgerald for some months; but at an appropriate moment in the following spring Shaftesbury was to make use of his information about a plot in Ireland.[3]

All this was grist for Shaftesbury's mill. But he was also attentive to the possibility that some of the Catholics who were put on trial for their lives to answer Titus Oates's accusations would, when found guilty, seek to buy their lives by turning King's evidence and providing information, or what passed for information, about the Plot. On one occasion this tactic had led him into embarrassment. On 22 May, shortly before the end of the last session, the Commons had asked the Lords to send back to the country

---

murderer, William Strode, who alleged that Shaftesbury, through 'one Johnson his man', had offered him money to join Bedloe in accusing the Catholic Lords in the Tower. Strode had been promised pardon for the murder by the Duchess of York's intercession. The truth in such episodes can never now be disentangled.

[1] P.C. Reg., 4 July; Southwell to Ormond, 5 July, *H.M.C. Ormond MSS.*, N.S. iv. 530; A. Sidney to H. Savile, *Letters . . . to the hon. Henry Savile*, pp. 131–2; *State Trials*, vii. 962–1043.

[2] John Speke to Hugh Speke, 21 June, *C.S.P.D. 1679–80*, p. 186; and see p. 543 below.

[3] *C.S.P.D. 1679–80*, pp. 197–8; *C.S.P.D. 1682*, pp. 65–66; and cf. pp. 570–1 below.

for execution several Catholics who had been convicted of being priests, and sentenced to death according to the old Elizabethan statute, but had been reprieved and brought to London for examination. Shaftesbury supported the Commons' request, saying that the reprieve 'had revived the spirits of the Papists', only for the Lord Chancellor to recall that it was Shaftesbury himself who had moved for the reprieve, 'whose authority was so great that, because he moved it, it was ordered, without any reason asked or given'. Shaftesbury escaped from this small difficulty by saying that 'if he had any fault it was tender-heartedness, an infirmity he could not help'. This remark has a singularly disagreeable ring about it, for to say the least tender-heartedness was not the most obvious of Shaftesbury's qualities. The House ordered that Oates, Bedloe and Dugdale should go to Newgate to see if they could recognize any of the priests as conspirators in the Plot.[1]

None of this group confessed anything, and after the prorogation the Privy Council promptly proceeded to send them back to their counties for execution, and make arrangements for the trial of the prisoners in Newgate against whom Oates and others had brought charges. This was not only Shaftesbury's doing, but that of most members of the Council, who thought that they had a duty to bring the prisoners to justice and demonstrate to the public their zeal for the prosecution of the guilty ones in the Plot. And when Sir William Temple objected to trying priests merely for being priests without a preliminary warning, it was Halifax who threatened to tell people that he was a Papist and affirmed 'that the plot must be handled as if it were true, whether it were so or not, in those points that were so generally believed by city and country as well as both houses'.[2] In the bloodshed that followed, Shaftesbury's guilt was no greater than that of others, except in so far as he had indirectly contributed more to the growth of an excitement which made it impossible for judge and jury to view the evidence dispassionately. As Lord President he had nothing directly to do with the prosecutions.

On 13 June five of the prisoners were found guilty of plotting sedition and the murder of the King. One of them, Fenwick, complained that the evidence of Oates, Bedloe, and Dugdale was only 'that they saw such and such letters. . . . All the evidence that is given, comes but to this; there is but saying and swearing.' But this just observation was answered by the Lord Chief Justice, Sir William Scroggs, who argued that 'all the evidence and all the testimony in all trials is by swearing'. Oates's credibility as a swearer survived the challenge of sixteen witnesses from St. Omer who declared that he was there on 24 April 1678 and not in London as he claimed. In a noisy and disorderly trial Scroggs summed up against the prisoners, gratuitously including a long diatribe on the subject of Sir

[1] Cooke to Ormond, 22 May, *H.M.C. Ormond MSS.*, N.S. v. 110; *C.J.* ix. 627; *L.J.* xiii. 583, 587.   [2] P.C. Reg., 28 May, 4 June; Barrillon, 9/19 June; Temple, *Works*, i. 426.

Edmund Berry Godfrey, on the theme that the Catholics who were prepared to kill Godfrey would be quite ready to kill the King. As one observer wrote in the privacy of his diary, 'the trial was the clearest thing ever was seen'.[1] Next day the Catholic lawyer, Richard Langhorn, suffered a similar fate.[2]

The five Jesuits were hanged, drawn, and quartered a week later, on 20 June. It was generally believed that this speed was the work of Shaftesbury, with the idea that the imminence of death would lead one of the five to save himself by accusing the Duke; but all the Council shared the responsibility for permitting the sentence to be carried out. On the day before it was to be carried out, Shaftesbury visited two of them, promising pardon if they would admit the existence of a conspiracy. But not only did the Jesuits decline to beg for their lives, they died with protestations of innocence which made some impression on the populace, to judge from the pamphlet controversy to which they gave rise. There was some justice in Burnet's observation that the disadvantages of relying on Oates and Bedloe, instead of concentrating on purely political arguments, were now to be seen, and that the executions were 'like the letting blood . . .which abates a fever'. Shaftesbury himself was alleged to have said 'that hanging so many on one occasion had been a mistake, because now that the popular mind was pacified, it would be impossible to stir it up again without a great expenditure of careful effort over a long period of time'. This was an exaggeration: the fears of Popery were not so easily ended; but the situation increased the temptation to encourage fresh informations.[3]

Richard Langhorn found the prospect of martyrdom less attractive, and on 18 June Shaftesbury and Essex, on behalf of the Council, paid him a visit in Newgate in the hope of eliciting a confession. On another occasion, according to Langhorn's supposed memoirs, Shaftesbury sent two persons 'to propose something to me in charity, for the saving of my life'. The condition required for this work of charity was 'a discovery of the plot and treason for which I stood condemned'. Langhorn would not do this, but agreed to make a discovery of Jesuit estates in the country, and with the King's aid his execution was respited for some days to allow him to do this. Shaftesbury was then said to have paid him a visit, in the course of which he offered to put Langhorn into 'as good a post, both as to honour and estate, as my own heart could wish' in return for 'a full discovery of the plot'. Fortunately for the Duke of York, Langhorn resisted the temptation, and eventually, vainly believing that he had been promised pardon for preparing his list of Jesuit estates, suffered the barbarous penalty for treason on 14 July.[4]

---

[1] *State Trials*, vii. 311–418; Sidney Diary, i. 8.   [2] *State Trials*, vii. 417–90.
[3] Ibid. vii. 491–501, 529–90; Burnet, ii. 229; J. Warner, *History of the English Persecution . . .* (Catholic Record Society, 1953), pp. 115, 263–4.
[4] Langhorn's Memoirs (which, however, are not necessarily reliable), in *State Trials*, vii. 516–17, 521; Yard to Williamson, 19 June, *C.S.P.D. 1679–80*, p. 183; A. Sidney to H. Savile, *Letters . . . to the hon. Henry Savile*, p. 111; Sidney Diary, pp. 17–18.

Shaftesbury would no doubt have said that his actions here were only his duty to ferret out conspiracy by the normal methods of his time, but the picture of these interviews, and the contrast between his violence and the King's vain attempts to save the victims, is not an attractive one. He was shown in a slightly better light in the case of the Benedictine monk Peter Caryll. Oates identified Caryll with 'Nicholas Blundell, the Jesuit, one of the principal conspirators, whom he had often seen laden with a sack full of fireballs', and with whom he claimed often to have slept in the same bed. Shaftesbury, who knew and recognized Caryll when he appeared before the Council, enquired: 'Since when has Caryll the Benedictine become Blundell the Jesuit?'; rescued him from the trial which was imminent; and quietly had him released when an opportunity presented itself. The Catholic Father Warner, who probably heard of this from Caryll, believed that Shaftesbury was sincerely friendly to him, perhaps because they were neighbours; but it was also true that Oates's reputation as a trustworthy witness escaped from further challenge as a result.[1] The incident did not prevent the Earl from continuing to patronize Oates, who dedicated to him *The Pope's Warehouse, or the Merchandise of the Whore of Rome*, published on 12 July.

The third of the trials of the summer of 1679, that of Sir George Wakeman, was by far the most important politically, because 'the truth is, that this was looked on as the Queen's trial, as well as Wakeman's'. In the trial of the first Jesuits, Bedloe had reflected on the Queen and in Langhorn's trial Monmouth's cook had incriminated one Signor Antonio, the Queen's confessor's man. It was certain that when Wakeman, the Queen's physician, was tried, the implication of the evidence of the prosecution witnesses would be that he had agreed to poison the King on behalf of Queen Catherine; Bedloe and Oates would in fact revive the charges which they had brought against her in November 1678. If Wakeman was convicted, the way would be open for the Exclusionists to threaten the Queen and press Charles to divorce her and remarry, in accordance with Shaftesbury's cherished project. This Charles was determined to prevent. At the Council Board he made plain his detestation of those who blemished her innocency and declared that he would not allow her to be unjustly scandalized; and he had Wakeman's trial postponed until he had made sure that Bedloe and Oates had nothing more to say than they had already said. When that was assured, he was confident that the prosecution's case was not strong enough, and the trial was allowed to take place on 18 July.[2]

It is not unlikely that Wakeman's friends were provided with facilities

---

[1] Warner, op. cit. p. 113.

[2] Burnet, ii. 231; *State Trials*, vii. 348–9, 443–5, 486; P.C. Reg. 2/68, fos. 98–99; Southwell to Ormond, 21, 24 June, *H.M.C. Ormond MSS.*, N.S. iv. 526, 527; Ossory to Ormond, 21, 24 June, ibid. v. 140, 144; A. Sidney to H. Savile, *Letters . . . to the hon. Henry Savile*, pp. 111–12.

for his defence which other prisoners at that date did not normally enjoy. Sir Philip Lloyd, one of the Clerks of the Council, was on hand to testify that when Oates had appeared before the Council on 31 [*sic*] September 1678 he had declared that he knew nothing more against Wakeman than one reference in a letter. Wakeman's cross-questioning of the witnesses was calm and confident; and Oates and Bedloe had not had the help of Shaftesbury or any other organizer to make their stories watertight. Lord Chief Justice Scroggs, who had never been on good terms with Shaftesbury and probably knew of the King's attitude to the case, had the common sense to see the weaknesses of the evidence, and the courage to draw the jury's attention to them and urge them to follow their consciences. His summing-up made it plain that although he had accepted the evidence of Oates and Bedloe in previous cases, he doubted them now. After an hour's absence the jury acquitted Wakeman, and the Queen was safe, as well as her doctor.[1]

This was a serious defeat for Shaftesbury. It blocked any plans that he had to bring pressure on Charles to divorce his Queen, and obliged him to fall back on the alternative solution of supporting Monmouth; and it might discredit the witnesses' 'evidence' of the existence of any Popish Plot. He and his party could only have recourse to the argument that Wakeman's acquittal was one more evidence of the failure of those in authority to do justice to the popular cause. Some circumstances aided him in this. On the day after the trial the Portuguese ambassador very foolishly paid a ceremonial visit to Chief Justice Scroggs to thank him for his behaviour in the trial, and this naturally encouraged the view that Scroggs had been influenced or corrupted.[2] With equal folly Wakeman dared to return to Court at Windsor, and when persuaded of his indiscretion made matters worse by leaving the country, which was interpreted as a sign of guilt. And Robert Jennison came to Shaftesbury's aid with new information about the Plot, in the course of which he said that the dead priest Ireland had told him in 1678 that it was an easy matter to poison the King, and that Sir George Wakeman might do it. Jennison swore to this (and to various charges against his brother, whom he accused of saying that 'if C R would not be R C he should not long be C R', and that both the five Catholic lords and Danby were in the plot) before Justice Warcup, who passed his deposition on to Shaftesbury for him to transmit to the Council. At the last Council meeting before the holidays Jennison's evidence was read, and the Lord President took the opportunity to criticize Sir Philip Lloyd's testimony at the trial, and to say that Scroggs's behaviour had been such that he was no longer fit to serve either King or nation. To this Charles calmly replied that if men had proceeded according to their consciences he knew no fault that they had done, and the matter passed off; but later in the same month Titus Oates impudently put in accusations

---

[1] *State Trials*, vii. 591–702. [2] Burnet, ii. 232.

against Lloyd and Scroggs, which it was expected would be followed up when Parliament met.[1]

The episode served to emphasize the gulf which lay between the King and the Lord President of his Council. The expectation that Shaftesbury would be satisfied once he had been taken back into office had long since been disappointed. Further, Charles was aware of meetings at Shaftesbury's house and that of his friend Francis Charlton, at which Monmouth was present, and also, coming late and in a hackney coach, the Earl of Bath. This was curious in that the Earl of Bath was the ally of Danby, who after some months in the Tower had evidently been tempted by the idea of seeking release by a bargain with the opposition. As his share of the bargain Danby would have revealed in the House of Lords how in February 1679 and on other occasions the Duke of York had urged the King to govern by armed force.[2] Charles probably had no detailed information about this, but it is clear that he knew that something was going on which was unpalatable to himself. Why he did not proceed to dismiss a councillor who was working in direct contradiction to his wishes is uncertain: it may be that he thought Shaftesbury could be kept under closer observation in the Council than out of it; or that he was waiting to see what the new elections would produce; or that he was waiting to see whether his negotiations for a French subsidy[3] would be successful, so that he need not call Parliament; or that he was waiting for a suitable opportunity to dismiss the Earl, without making him a martyr. Certainly he told a Cavalier that it would not be long before he parted with 'Russell and his party'; and there were rumours that Shaftesbury would be 'plainly admonished that it was better to have him a declared enemy out of his post than in it, and that he should resolve accordingly'. Shaftesbury on his side was thought to 'undervalue his station' and to be prepared for a dismissal which would enhance his popular reputation. Nothing happened; and on 19 August Shaftesbury left for his country estates, still Lord President of the Council. Behind him Danby and the Catholic peers remained in the Tower. One of them, Lord Bellasis, who suffered severely from rheumatism, had petitioned for liberty to go into the country, and Shaftesbury had at first supported his petition but had later refused to sign the warrant, and the other councillors, with

---

[1] K. Feiling and F. R. D. Needham, 'The Journals of Edmund Warcup, 1679–84', in *E.H.R.* (1925), p. 242; Add. MSS. 15643, fos. 12–13; MSS. Rawlinson A 135, fos. 558 sqq.; Southwell to Ormond, 9 Aug., *H.M.C. Ormond MSS.*, N.S. iv. 532–3; Longford to Ormond, 29 Aug., ibid. v. 193; Anna M. Crinò, *Il Popish Plot* (Rome, 1954), pp. 84–85.

[2] Cholmley to Earl of Arran, 24 Sept., MSS. Carte 39, fo. 68; Danby's memoranda printed by Browning, *Danby*, ii. 89–91. These last are undated, but I incline to connect them with Cholmley's letter above, which refers to August. Browning for no very definite reason places them after James's return to England in September (ibid. i. 341); but at no time then were Shaftesbury and Monmouth in London together, as Browning's narrative implies.

[3] Barrillon, 24 July/3 Aug., 21/31 Aug. Brown (p. 264) is mistaken in saying that agreement was reached.

one eye on the meeting of Parliament, had thereupon declined to take the responsibility.[1]

When Shaftesbury left for Dorset, indeed, everyone's eye was on the coming Parliament, and all the signs were that the elections which were just beginning would produce a House of Commons that was, in Henry Coventry's words, 'much the same as to the persons, but more the same as to the humour'.[2] Shaftesbury could expect to be able in October to resume where the previous Parliament had left off, though Sunderland and his friends still clung to the hope that William of Orange would come to their rescue from Shaftesbury's dominance. But almost before Shaftesbury reached Wimborne St. Giles, the situation was dramatically changed by the news that the King was ill. On 21 August he was indisposed; next day, aggravated by the doctors, the symptoms were more serious; and, in spite of the optimistic tone of the bulletins which Sunderland sent to the Lord Mayor to reassure the City of London, it became clear that there was a danger that Charles might die. 'Good God, what a change would such an accident make!' wrote the English ambassador in Paris, when he heard the news. 'The very thought of it frights me out of my wits.' Such crowds flocked to Windsor to find out the news for themselves that the Gentlemen of the Bedchamber were powerless to prevent the King's room from being invaded, and the Privy Councillors had to use their authority to prevent the King from being 'smothered' by the press of people.[3]

In this crisis several people thought it advisable secretly to warn the legal heir to the throne, the Duke of York, and advise him to come over from Brussels. The French soldier, Lord Faversham, did so; so too did Halifax and Essex, who were desperately afraid of a *coup* by Monmouth. Temple, who was left out of the secret, was 'spited to the heart', and his relations with Halifax and Essex were never the same again. Sunderland also seems to have written: it is not clear whether he wrote of his own volition or at the King's command, or indeed whether his invitation to James was explicit. At all events James lost no time in crossing the Channel, and on 2 September there was a touching reunion between the two brothers. By this time, however, Charles was well on the way to recovery, and Sunderland, Halifax and Essex were not so touched that they did not find James's presence embarrassing. None of them relished the prospect of explaining it to Parliament, and they joined in asking James to leave before it met. It suited the plans alike of the three peers and of James that the King should be asked to send Monmouth out of the country too.

---

[1] Ailesbury, *Memoirs* (1890), i. 40; Southwell to Ormond, 20 Aug., *H.M.C. Ormond MSS.*, N.S. iv. 535; Add. MSS. 15643, fo. 50 v.; Southwell to Ormond, 9 Aug., op. cit. iv. 532; Crinò, op. cit. p. 86.

[2] Coventry to Ormond, 2 Aug., *H.M.C. Ormond MSS.*, N.S. v. 166.

[3] Charles Hatton to L. Hatton, 26 Aug., *Hatton Correspondence*, i. 189–90; *C.S.P.D. 1679–80*, p. 224; Ranelagh to Conway, 27 Aug., ibid. pp. 226–7; H. Savile to Sidney, 1/11 Sept., Sidney Diary, i. 141; Lady Sunderland to Sidney, 2 Sept., ibid. i. 122–3.

And so, when James left the country on 25 September, he did so in the knowledge that Monmouth had departed for the Netherlands on the previous afternoon. James also carried with him, as part of his price for agreeing to leave, a private assurance that he would be permitted to change his place of exile from Brussels to Edinburgh; and possibly also a promise that Shaftesbury would be dismissed at the first suitable opportunity.[1]

Yet the King's recovery and James's departure did not restore the situation that had existed five weeks earlier. No one could now look at the succession question in the same way again. Previously Charles had enjoyed very good health, and it had been possible for some people to think that the problem of the succession was not an immediate one: Charles was not quite fifty, and provided that he could be protected from Popish plots, there had seemed no reason why he should not live to a ripe old age, and perhaps even outlive James. It would be much more difficult to evade or postpone a solution to the problem now, in the hope that it could be left to the working of time. But more than this, the episode had shown the strength of the position of the heir to the throne. When James arrived at Windsor, the courtiers flocked to pay their respects to the man who might soon be their King. 'Who goes for Windsor?' was the cynical question being asked in London. So many bended knees were offered to James, wrote one observer, 'that it's believed for 3 days last past [there] has been more kneeling within these walls, than in 4 months before'. Even some of Monmouth's retinue found it prudent to pay their respects to James. Amongst them Sir Thomas Armstrong, who had recently been discharged from all his employments at Court for his underhand intrigues in Monmouth's cause, approached James; but James showed his unforgiving nature by turning his back upon him. Even Titus Oates made ready to leave the Exclusionist ship should it seem about to founder. In private he asserted his willingness to repeat that the Duke was innocent of any part in the Plot; 'voluntarily did declare that it was not safe for the Duke to go out of England for that there were bills of high treason prepared against him and that in his absence there would be rogues enough found to accuse him though never so innocent (and said that Mr. Bedloe was a beast of that nature)'; and offered his 'utmost endeavours' to prepare a good reception for the Duke with the people. Shaftesbury's setting up of another candidate to the throne was a dishonest thing, Oates continued; and with tears in his eyes he asked for an interview with the Duke.[2]

---

[1] Barrillon, 4/14 Sept. (based on a conversation with James); Temple, *Works*, i. 437–8; Clarke, op. cit. i. 564–74; Sidney Diary, i. 176 (29 Oct.); Charles Hatton to L. Hatton, 2 Sept., *Hatton Correspondence*, i. 191–2; 'W.F.' to ?, 5 Sept., Coventry Papers at Longleat, vi, fo. 127; Sunderland to the Lord Mayor, 2 Sept., *C.S.P.D. 1679–80*, p. 234; [R. Yard] to [Lady] O'Brien, 25 Sept., ibid. p. 251; Barrillon, 15/25 Sept.; Southwell to Ormond, 20, 30 Sept., *H.M.C. Ormond MSS.*, N.S. iv. 535–6, 537.

[2] Charles Hatton, *loc. cit.*; Mountstevens to Sidney, 5 Sept., Add. MSS. 32680, fo. 119; MSS. Rawlinson A 136, fos. 253–5. It is possible that if James had granted the

The fact was that if James was proclaimed King, his favour would be the passport to office and fortune, and his frown could mean ruin. To many people, whatever their misgivings about the policies which James was likely to pursue, self-interest was likely to dictate the advisability of at least not opposing them. In short, the King's illness greatly sharpened the Exclusion crisis. Those who were determined to exclude the Duke of York were even more determined after this demonstration of the prestige at the disposal of a new monarch: 'limitations' made even more dubious sense. And it was far more difficult than before for well-meaning men to be neither for nor against Exclusion: a definite choice was being forced upon them.

All this while Shaftesbury had remained on his estates. Although it was rumoured that his friends had sent for him to come to London, he did not travel up to his house in Aldersgate Street until the day after James's departure.[1] We know nothing whatsoever about his plans and activities in this crucial period between 19 August and 26 September, when one would have expected him to return, either to take up his seat as Lord President of the Council or to keep in touch with Monmouth and his friends in London. Perhaps he felt sure that Charles would not die; perhaps he was afraid of being arrested, as some people expected[2]; perhaps he wished to wait until the situation was clearer; perhaps he was ill; but no correspondence survives to make it possible for us to do more than guess. Probably he was kept aware, if only through the usual newsletters, of the activities of his supporters in London, who printed the last Parliament's votes declaring James to be the cause of the Plot and ordering the bringing in of an Exclusion Bill, while one of them, Sir Thomas Player, won notoriety for two public speeches which called for the doubling of the City guards on account of the danger caused by the Duke's arrival, and complained that the Lord Mayor had promised to proclaim James if the King should die.[3] But such activities could not be very satisfactorily guided from a hundred miles' distance; and Shaftesbury's absence also meant that he was not on hand to give advice when Charles sent for Monmouth and ordered him to leave the country. Monmouth could not have been compelled to go, and we know that Shaftesbury thought him ill-advised to go, even though he gained some popularity by suffering in the cause—and paying his debts before he left.[4]

---

interview Oates might have used it later to accuse him of trying to tamper with the Plot evidence; but the natural interpretation of Oates's remarks is that he was genuinely trying to insure his own safety should James succeed.

[1] Newsletter of 1 Sept., *H.M.C. Lindsey MSS.*, p. 29; account-book at St. Giles House for Shaftesbury's payments on his journeys to and from London, with dates.

[2] Charles Hatton to L. Hatton, 13 Sept., *Hatton Correspondence*, i. 194.

[3] 'W.F.', Coventry Papers at Longleat, vol. vi, fo. 127; Taylor to L. Wharton, 11, 13 Sept., MSS. Carte 228, fos. 103, 105; Hatton as in previous note.

[4] Hatton, loc. cit.; R. Yard to [Williamson], 12 Sept., *C.S.P.D. 1679–80*, p. 240; newsletters, 18, 20 Sept., ibid. pp. 244, 245; Van Leeuwen, 19/29 Sept., Add. MSS. 17677, SSS.

There were many who thought that Shaftesbury's disgrace would follow closely upon Monmouth's, the more so as it was rumoured that Shaftesbury's party was planning to open the new parliamentary session with a direct attack on the Duke of York and the Queen.[1] But Charles took no action before he left to continue his convalescence at Newmarket, either because he wanted a little longer in which to think matters over, or because he did not want to identify Shaftesbury's cause with Monmouth's by dismissing them simultaneously. In the meantime the Earl made no attempt to conciliate the King; it was supposed indeed that he was not unwilling to be dismissed. He was busy making preparations for Parliament, sending word to his former fellow-prisoner Wharton to be present without fail on 30 October; and Titus Oates believed that the Earl intended then to impeach the Duke for high treason.[2]

At the beginning of October the King kept his promise to his brother, and sent him permission to move from exile in Flanders to Scotland. Somehow Shaftesbury heard rumours that James was to move before the other members of the Council, and before James received the news himself. He promptly called a special Sunday meeting of the Council at which he remarked that if it were true 'he did fear the Mass and Presbytery would make but a mad medley together', and urged the need for serious consideration in case the Duke had undertaken to move without permission. Since Secretary Coventry was unable to confirm the news, the Council broke up without adopting any resolution; but at the next meeting three days later the Council was officially informed, through Sunderland at Newmarket. Shaftesbury 'declared it was the worst counsel that ever was given His Majesty' and commented that it showed once again how useless was the official Council which the King had promised to consult. His rage was increased by the further news that James, instead of travelling to Scotland by sea as Charles had intended, had asked for leave to journey by land, and had come to London on 12 October. Next day Shaftesbury called for a further extraordinary meeting of the Council and 'proposed a free debate in relation to the journey to Scotland; but by agreement it was put off until the next Council day'.[3] For Shaftesbury, however, the next Council day never arrived. The moment had come for the King to dismiss him. For Charles it was embarrassing to have his Lord President calling extra-

---

[1] Van Leeuwen, loc. cit.; Charles Hatton to L. Hatton, 25 Sept., *Hatton Correspondence*, i. 197; Southwell to Ormond, 30 Sept., 4 Oct., *H.M.C. Ormond MSS.*, N.S. iv. 537–8, 539; Ossory to Ormond, 5 Oct., ibid. v. 218.

[2] Southwell to Ormond, 20 Sept., ibid. iv. 536; W. Taylor to Wharton, 3 Oct., MSS. Carte 228, fo. 161; K. Feiling and F. R. D. Needham, 'The Journals of Edmund Warcup, 1676–84', in *E.H.R.* (1925), p. 244.

[3] Southwell to Ormond, 7, 10, 18 Oct., *H.M.C. Ormond MSS.*, iv. 540–1, 542, 545; Sidney Diary, 7 Oct., i. 161–2; Sunderland to the Lords of the Admiralty, 7 Oct., *C.S.P.D. 1679–80*, p. 257; James to Prince of Orange, 14 Oct., *H.M.C. Foljambe MSS.*, p. 139.

ordinary meetings without his authority; and the subject of the debate was also embarrassing, for others besides Shaftesbury had misgivings about James's journey to Scotland, even if they did not express themselves as strongly, and there could be no certainty what the majority view would be. But Charles had also made another decision which made Shaftesbury's dismissal or resignation inevitable: he did not propose to meet his Parliament on 30 October. Its composition would be much the same as that of the last, and members would meet embittered by the dissolution and the expenses of re-election; the impeachment of James must be averted; and all hope of an Anglo-Dutch treaty, of William coming over, and of using these as a counterpoise to Shaftesbury, was at an end for this year. At the same time it looked as though a subsidy treaty with France was almost ready for signature, though the amount that it would yield would be meagre. It was highly desirable, and just possible, for Charles to rule without Parliament; and if he proposed to do so, it was better to dismiss Shaftesbury first than allow him to protest and resign.

No sooner had Charles returned to London, therefore, than on 14 October he instructed Sunderland to send word to Shaftesbury that his attendance at the Council table would no longer be required. Sunderland's letter was couched in terms which made it clear that he personally did not want a complete breach with his uncle; and on his side Shaftesbury accepted his dismissal with equanimity. He said that the letter needed no other answer than that he would give obedience to it; added that he was not surprised to be dismissed, when he had seen His Majesty 'advised to send away even a son with tears in his eyes'; and ended by saying 'that he knew not that he had ever disserved His Majesty, and that when His Majesty thought so too he should be still ready to attend his commands'. These were sentiments which, when reported, would do no harm to Shaftesbury 'out of doors'; nor would the decision which the King announced to his Council next day, namely that he would prorogue Parliament further from 30 October to 26 January.[1] Shaftesbury was in fact no less a public martyr than he would have been had he been dismissed at the same time as Monmouth, while Halifax had lost almost all the support which he had once possessed. Shaftesbury said jestingly that the cause of his nephew's illness was 'that Ormond lay heavy in his stomach, and he would never be well till he brought him up or down'; and with more accuracy, that Halifax was 'troubled in mind for having left his old friends and meddled in matters that run amiss and reflect dangerously upon him'. Certainly neither Halifax nor Essex had intended to uphold a regime in which the King ignored both Council and Parliament, while James ruled without any limitations in Scotland. They found themselves irritated misfits without influence, while Shaftesbury enjoyed the benefits of

---

[1] Sunderland to Shaftesbury, 14 Oct., *C.S.P.D. 1679–80*, p. 260; Southwell to Ormond, 18 Oct., *H.M.C. Ormond MSS.*, iv. 545.

consistent extremism and was more the leader of a 'party' than he had ever previously been.[1]

Shaftesbury's following was so large, that his dismissal had the same kind of epilogue as his earlier dismissal in 1673. The failure of the French subsidy negotiations and the excitement of the Meal Tub Plot[2] combined to give Charles second thoughts, and there were some about him who were prepared to make the unpromising effort to bring about a reconciliation between him and the Earl. One such was Edmund Warcup, the magistrate who had taken many of the recent depositions of the Plot witnesses. Warcup had served in Sir Anthony Ashley Cooper's regiment in 1660, and had later been Receiver of the Excise in Wiltshire and Dorset; but he was catholic in his acquaintanceships, and was able to converse freely with Danby as well as Shaftesbury, with James as well as Monmouth. On 2 November he had an hour's private conversation with King Charles in the royal bedchamber, mostly about Shaftesbury. Charles said that 'he had no unkindness for him, and that he well knew his abilities'; went on to say that he knew his own right to pardon, and the bishops' rights in judicial matters, but that if Shaftesbury would agree on these two points which had been the subject of dispute in the last sessions 'he [Shaftesbury] could rely on him'; and ordered Warcup to go to the Earl, 'sift him and bring his answer'. The implication was that if these two disputes were settled, it would be possible to call Parliament, and there would be the basis for an agreement.

Warcup received a friendly reception from the Earl, who was most ready to serve the King, and said he would be prepared to agree to Danby's banishment to evade the need to decide the legality of his pardon, and to some similar expedient in the matter of the bishops' rights. Shaftesbury further 'presented his duty' to the King and offered to wait upon him in that famous chamber of Chiffinch's to which so many people had been admitted by the backstairs. He even sent his friend Sir Paul Neile to make this offer to the King in addition to Warcup; and the King, while insisting that he was 'tenacious to the two points', fixed an appointment for three o'clock next day.

On that day, 5 November, Warcup dined at Thanet House with the Earl. 'The coach was appointed, the sword ready to put on' for the Earl's departure to Whitehall. The Countess, who was pathetically devoted to her husband, worried about his safety and irritated him: old age, illness, and stress were making him more ill-tempered every year. Then at the last minute Shaftesbury sent Sir Paule Neile to say that he would not go to the meeting. He said something about his not being safe because of the

---

[1] Southwell to Ormond, 18 Oct., *H.M.C. Ormond MSS.*, iv. 546–7; Cooke to Ormond, 18 Nov., ibid. v. 239–40; and for Halifax and Essex, cf. also the earlier letter of 30 Sept., ibid. iv. 538–9.

[2] See below, pp. 554 sqq.

Duchess of Portsmouth; but what weighed more with him was that Sunderland had visited him that morning and left him with the impression that the King was not really disposed to take his counsel on the things that mattered. Sunderland, for his part, would have welcomed his uncle's return to the ministry as one of the Commissioners for the Treasury, but Shaftesbury insisted that the King would have to leave the Queen and the Duke of York to Parliament, and Sunderland could hold out no hopes that Charles would be prepared to do this. What Shaftesbury told his friends, indeed, was that he had been offered the Treasurer's staff 'and to make all other the great officers such as he should like, but that his answer was he would never more enter the lists at Whitehall till it was resolved there should be excluded from thence the Queen, Duke, Duchess of Portsmouth, and every other Papist that were but an inch long'.[1]

This sounds like the language of a man who both was arrogant and over-estimated the strength of his opposition. But the fact was that it was far too late to 'paper over the cracks' in the way suggested. The differences between Charles and Shaftesbury were now quite irreconcilable, and any ministerial office which the Earl held would have been futile. Precisely because Charles was determined to stand by his wife and his brother, and because Shaftesbury had committed himself to attacking them, the duel must now go on until one was able to enforce his will upon the other. Shaftesbury hoped that when next Parliament met he would be able to force himself back into power on his own terms; but as events turned out, he had sat at the Council Board for the last time.

----

[1] 'The Journals of Edmund Warcup, 1676–84', ed. K. Feiling and F. R. D. Needham, in *E.H.R.* (1925), pp. 245–7 (2–7 Nov); Add. MSS. 32862, fo. 79 (original of Sidney Diary, 5 Nov.); Sidney Diary, pp. 181, 185 (6, 7, 12, 13 Nov.); Southwell to Ormond, 8, 11, 18 Nov., *H.M.C. Ormond MSS.*, N.S. iv. 557–9.

CHAPTER XXV

PETITIONERS AND ABHORRERS
(OCTOBER 1679–JULY 1680)

ON 21 October the Duke of York dined with the Artillery Company at Merchant Taylors' Hall. It was noticed that not more than 120 of the 600 Artillery men appeared to do honour to their guest at their annual feast, though courtiers tried to argue that these were 'the better sort of citizens'. Six days later, however, when James set out for Scotland, he was accompanied as far as Hatfield by the largest escort of courtiers in their coaches-and-six that had been seen for many years.[1] The two incidents together illustrate the polarization of political life which had taken place since the King's illness. Men were choosing, and were dividing into two camps more sharply separated from one another than at any time since the Restoration.

The historian has no means of counting heads to determine which of the two camps was the larger in the population as a whole. What he can say without fear of contradiction is that in the parliamentary classes the Exclusionists were by far the stronger. The elections of August, September and October had provided them with an overwhelming majority,[2] and, though the traditional means of exercising territorial influence had not been neglected, political issues had been much more prominent than was customary at election time. Pamphlets like the *Unanimous Club of Voters*, *England's Great Interest in the Choice of a New Parliament*, and *Sober and Seasonable Queries, humbly offered to all good Protestants in England, in order to a choice of the New Parliament* urged the electorate to choose members who were not pensioners of the Court or office-holders, or 'favourers of Popery', but 'men of good conscience and courage, thoroughly principled in the Protestant religion'. It is not misleading to describe these as party political literature, and to say, when due allowance has been made for the influence of landlords over tenants, that the results of the elections mirrored, however imperfectly, the movement of opinion in the electorate—not least when, on 7 October, the City of London chose the same four burgesses who had sat in the spring, 'with such a torrent as that there was neither poll nor dispute that could stand in their way'.[3]

Shaftesbury's problem was to keep his majority together, conscious and

---

[1] Newsletter in MSS. Carte 228, fo. 157; F. Gwyn to L. Conway, 1 Nov., *C.S.P.D. 1679–80*, p. 272; Van Leeuwen, 28 Oct./7 Nov., Add. MSS. 17677, EE; Sir Thomas Wharton to Ormond, 7 Nov., *H.M.C. Ormond MSS.*, v. 234–5.

[2] For an account of them, cf. J. R. Jones, *The First Whigs* (1961), pp. 92–106.

[3] Southwell to Ormond, 7 Oct., *H.M.C. Ormond MSS.*, N.S. iv. 541.

confident of its strength, and unshaken in its belief in Exclusion, until the day, sooner or later, when Charles had to allow the House to assemble. As it turned out, he had to concentrate on this for almost exactly twelve months from his dismissal, and it was by no means easy to keep opinion steadfast, in an age when there were no public meetings and no methods of mass communication. However, in his endeavours to keep his grip on public opinion (and thus on the members of the Commons, for it was characteristic of his policy to use the one in order to influence the other) Shaftesbury had, as has been noticed, the assistance of the authors of many of the news-sheets and pamphlets of the day, when there were still few Royalist writers to compete with them. How far they were directly guided and subsidized by the Earl, and how far they simply cashed in on a lucrative market with their literature, it is impossible to say with certainty. A manuscript copy of one pamphlet, *A Word in Season to all True Protestants*, with amendments perhaps made for the press, survives amongst the Shaftesbury Papers[1]; it covers a great deal of ground from the Catholic treatment of the Waldensians to their treatment of natives in the West Indies, and includes the suggestion that it would be right to resist an aggressively Popish King. The Court also believed that a Narrative about the Plot (appearing under the name of an informer who was on that account differentiated from other members of the clan of Smith by the sobriquet of 'Narrative' Smith) 'was written or at least reviewed by Shaftesbury'.[2] In mid-October there appeared one of the most lurid, and one of the most celebrated, of all, significantly entitled *An Appeal from the Country to the City for the preservation of His Majesty's person, liberty, property, and religion*. This called upon its readers to imagine 'the whole town in a flame . . . troops of papists ravishing your wives and your daughters, dashing your little children's brains out against the walls, plundering your houses, and cutting your own throats, by the name of heretic dogs. Then represent to yourselves the Tower playing off its cannon. . . . Also casting your eye towards Smithfield, imagine you see your father, or your mother . . . tied to a stake in the midst of flames. . . .' Having disposed of the whole family in this way, the author turned from these crudities to a kind of specious rationality, for instance in his argument about the futility of 'limitations'. This example of the creation of a wave of passionate feeling, at the cost of eventually producing a reaction from its violence, was attributed to Robert Ferguson 'the Plotter', who was to be at Shaftesbury's deathbed in exile; but the attribution is far from certain.[3] The

---

[1] XLIII, 63. [2] Southwell to Ormond, 18 Nov., op. cit. iv. 560.

[3] The pamphlet is conveniently printed in the *Parliamentary History*, iv, pp. xcv–cxii; cf. also J. Ferguson, *Robert Ferguson the Plotter* (1887), pp. 40–43; and *Domestick Intelligence*, 17 Oct., for the date of its appearance. Shaftesbury's friend Murray (above, pp. 413, 424–6) was taken into custody for being concerned in the distribution of 'the damned libels now in print against the government' (Longford to Arran, 18 Oct., MSS. Carte 243, fo. 398), but I have been unable to discover his fate.

government's proclamations offering rewards for hawkers who informed on booksellers and printers, and for booksellers and printers who informed on authors, were generally ineffective, and the scent is now too cold for us to hope to discover how such pamphlets came to be published.

In his efforts to keep the Plot before the public Shaftesbury received indirect assistance from the indiscretions of his opponents. Many Catholics, knowing that the Plot tales were the work of unprincipled adventurers out for rewards, hoped to induce them to deny their stories, and to say that they had been suborned to tell them, in return for greater rewards. In September there were hopes that Stephen Dugdale could be persuaded to 'turn about' in this way, and Mrs. Anne Price offered to bring him into the Duke of York's presence. Dugdale, however, promptly told Justice Warcup of this—and also two of Shaftesbury's associates, Hampden and Charlton—and stationed two witnesses where one of Mrs. Price's conferences with him could be overheard. All Mrs. Price's protestations that she had been 'trepanned', and that the first overtures had come not from her but from Dugdale, did not prevent her, and two companions, from being found guilty of tampering with the King's evidence; and for many people the belief was confirmed that Catholics were desperate people who would stick at nothing to conceal their plots. And it was precisely at this time that a far greater scandal broke, the so-called Meal Tub Plot.[1]

The most active and enthusiastic of the Catholics who hoped to prove that the 'Popish Plot' was really a 'Presbyterian plot' against the monarchy and the Roman Church was the famous midwife, Mrs. Elizabeth Cellier. She was no ordinary midwife: she seems to have come from a landed family, she was married to a French merchant (and thus had a measure of security that she might not otherwise have enjoyed) and her 'practice' was among the aristocratic Catholic families, such as those of the peers who lay in the Tower. Though far from being a saint, she had a convert's zeal for her faith, and at the risk of considerable unpopularity she had helped to relieve Catholic prisoners in Newgate and lodged the witnesses who had been brought over from St. Omer in June to try to show that Oates was a perjurer. She was as enthusiastically partisan as her Whig opponents, and just as unscrupulous in her readiness to employ any agents, however disreputable. From about the end of March 1679, she had employed a good-looking young man who passed under the name of Willoughby but whose real name was Thomas Dangerfield; he had a long criminal record which included robbery, forgery and coining. By September 1679 Mrs. Cellier was encouraging him in his claims to be engaged in ferreting out a 'Presbyterian Plot', until, by the agency of Lady Powis, the wife of

---

[1] 'The Journals of Edmund Warcup', ed. K. Feiling and F. R. D. Needham, in *E.H.R.* (1925), p. 243 (14 Sept.); Southwell to Ormond, 15 Oct., *H.M.C. Ormond MSS.*, N.S. iv. 544; *State Trials*, vii. 881–926. Dugdale swore that he had consulted Shaftesbury as well as Hampden and Charlton, but Shaftesbury was not in London in mid-September.

one of the lords in the Tower, and the Earl of Peterborough, the Groom of the Stole to the Duke of York, he was brought with his story to James. His tale of clubs and cabals about town, and plans for a rising of the opposition, including Monmouth and Shaftesbury, sufficiently impressed the credulous James that he gave him twenty guineas and passed him on to the King, who gave him forty.[1] Thus encouraged, Willoughby paid one or two visits to Shaftesbury's house (which was not difficult of access), picked up a couple of letters from the Earl's desk to prove his intimacy, and then proceeded to forge some treasonable papers which he laboriously arranged should be discovered where he had planted them, in the room of Colonel Roderick Mansell, a steward of Buckingham's and a well-known supporter of the opposition. Unfortunately the 'frame-up' was an obvious one, and Willoughby, or Dangerfield as he now proved to be, was committed to Newgate for forgery. There he found it best to seek safety by changing sides and confessing that he had been hired by others to bring false charges; and for good measure added that the Popish lords in the Tower had offered him £2000 to kill the King and £500 to kill the Earl of Shaftesbury. The discovery of papers similar to the forged letters in Mrs. Cellier's meal tub (which gave its name to the incident) and the catching of Lady Powis in a downright lie to the Council seemed to confirm the suspicions that there was a widespread plot to defame the opposition.[2]

The political consequences of the discovery of this 'Sham-Plot' were so obviously to Shaftesbury's advantage that some have even imagined that he planned Dangerfield's activities throughout. But this would have been a very risky course of action for both Shaftesbury and Dangerfield; and there is no solid evidence to set against the undoubted fact that Dangerfield had been maintained and employed by Mrs. Cellier for the previous six months. Moreover, it is impossible to square the dates of the movements of the principal personages involved with the hypothesis of a Machiavellian plan by Shaftesbury.[3]

---

[1] One wonders whether it was these 'revelations' of Dangerfield's that led the King to send Monmouth into exile.

[2] Add. MSS. 15643, fo. 16, for James's account to the Committee of Intelligence on 26 Oct.; Southwell to Ormond, 28 Oct., 1, 3 and 6 Nov., *H.M.C. Ormond MSS.*, N.S. iv. 552–6; Longford to Arran, 1 Nov., MSS. Carte 243, fo. 404; *C.S.P.D. 1680–1*, pp. 519–20; C. Hatton to Lord Hatton, 6 Nov., *Hatton Correspondence*, i. 202; *Domestick Intelligence*, 18 Nov. for some remarks by Shaftesbury; *Mr. Tho. Dangerfield's Particular Narrative* (1679) and *Second Narrative* (1680); Mansell's *Exact and True Narrative* (1680); Mrs. Cellier's *Malice Defeated* (1680) are some of the unreliable contemporary accounts. There is a not very satisfactory modern one in M. Petherick, *Restoration Rogues* (1951), pp. 183–263.

[3] Dangerfield must have seen the Duke of York and the King between 2 and 24 Sept. when Shaftesbury was out of London and unable to prompt him. The Shaftesbury Papers, VI A, 372, contain a begging letter from Dangerfield to the Earl, dated 15 Dec. 1681; but this only proves that at that date, like other informers, he looked to the Earl for patronage. The letter's tone does not suggest any special intimacy.

The incident strengthened the desire of some of Charles's councillors for a meeting of Parliament. Temple, Essex, and Halifax could not silently acquiesce in the King's failure to call it. All three had for some time been thoroughly discontented; all felt that they were being made tacitly responsible for policies of which they disapproved and on which they had not been consulted; all talked of retiring from the Council. On 9 November, when the Council was discussing ways of dealing with the Plot, Essex stood up to move that the Parliament should be allowed to meet, but the King cut him short.[1] In all probability Charles had never intended to meet Parliament in January, for he had promised his brother that he would be able to return to London then; but even if he had thought of breaking his promise, the Meal Tub Plot, with the added fervour that it had given to the opposition, would have made it impossible for him to do so. He did not immediately declare that in January there would be a further prorogation, but Henry Sidney, who had paid a visit from his embassy at The Hague, was instructed on his return to tell William of Orange why Parliament could not be permitted to meet. Charles said that he knew that they would impeach his brother; that the opposition 'would be glad to mutiny, and wanted only a head, which the Parliament would be'; that when the violence wore off he would be glad to meet his Parliament, but that until then he intended to live on his ordinary revenues and do what he could 'to satisfy his people'. (He did not add that talks with Barrillon about a subsidy might also yield something.) On the same evening as Charles said this, Essex resigned his commissionership of the Treasury: it was rumoured that he consulted Shaftesbury to see if he should not also leave the Council, but that the Earl had advised him to remain for the present. Essex's brother, Sir Henry Capel, Russell, and Cavendish were also known to be reluctant members of the Council. Unlike Essex, Capel, and Cavendish who were in a position to resume the relations with Shaftesbury which had been severed at the time of the first Exclusion Bill, there were others who scorned to do so and yet wished to indicate dissatisfaction: Temple, conscious that the King viewed with disfavour his intimacy with William, abdicated to his gardens at Sheen, and Halifax also did not attend the Council. Only Sunderland remained optimistic and prominent in the King's service, while two other 'chits', Hyde and Godolphin, served in the background.[2]

As a consequence Shaftesbury stood out more than ever on the political scene. His difficulty was that, in Charles's phrase, he lacked the 'head' which Parliament could provide; and he had no means of coercing Charles

---

[1] Sidney Diary, i. pp. 176–81 (1, 4, 5, 7 Nov.); Sidney to Prince of Orange, [11] Nov., ibid. i. 182–3; Chas. Hatton to L. Hatton, Hatton Correspondence, i. 202–3; Sir Robert Howard to Ormond, 12 Nov., H.M.C. Ormond MSS., N.S. v. 238.

[2] Sidney Diary, i. 187–90 (15, 16 Nov.): F. Gwyn to L. Conway, 18 Nov., C.S.P.D. 1679–80, p. 283; Southwell to Ormond, 18 Nov., H.M.C. Ormond MSS, N.S. iv. 558–60.

to call it. It was said that he had proposed that the members should meet immediately and act as an 'unofficial' council before the King summoned them officially to meet.[1] This plan was talked of more than once in the next two years, but it was never practicable because members could never be relied upon to participate in such an unconstitutional course of action. However, Shaftesbury had a different idea, but one which involved some organization. In the meantime, his supporters arranged the most lavish of all the grand pope-burnings to celebrate the anniversary of Queen Elizabeth's accession on 17 November, attended, it was said, by 200,000 people, the richer of whom paid a guinea for a place at a window or balcony on the procession's route through Cheapside and Fleet Street. The expenses of the bonfires and fireworks, which ran into hundreds of pounds, were paid by the members of the King's Head or Green Ribbon Club, a body whose political importance has been greatly exaggerated, but whose members could afford to subscribe to a demonstration of this sort; and because it was carefully organized and not a real expression of a general frenzy, the demonstrators, having made their point, went 'without confusion' to their beds afterwards.[2] A week later there was an opportunity for a demonstration of a slightly different kind, when Knox and Lane, the former of whom had been a servant in the Danby household, stood trial on a charge of trying in the previous winter to fix a charge of sodomy on Titus Oates and thus disable him, as a convicted felon, from giving evidence on the Plot. In the view of Scroggs and his colleagues on the bench, the case was crystal-clear, and the jury did not even retire before finding Knox and Lane guilty; but Shaftesbury seized the chance to make plain his own confidence in the repulsive Titus by attending the trial in person, along with Lords Howard of Escrick, Chandos, North, Grey of Wark, Kent, Huntingdon, and Herbert. If the opposition cause had been bound up with Oates's revelations before, it was now quite irrevocably tied to a belief in Oates's credibility as a witness.[3]

These same peers were dining together once a week in the Swan tavern in Fleet Street, and it was no secret that they intended to launch a mass movement to petition the King to allow Parliament to sit in January.[4] But

---

[1] Southwell to Ormond, 8 Nov., ibid. iv. 557.

[2] Cf. Longford to Arran, 18 Nov., MSS. Carte 232, fo. 61; Southwell to Ormond, 25 Nov., op. cit. iv. 561; Van Leeuwen, 18/28 Nov., Add. MSS. 17677, EE; O. W. Furley, 'The Pope-Burning Processions of the late Seventeenth Century', in *History* (1959), pp. 16–23; and see also J. R. Jones, 'The Green Ribbon Club', in *Durham University Journal* (1956), pp. 17–20 for the scaling down to size of this notorious club. See also Sheila Williams, 'The Pope-Burning Processions of 1679, 1680 and 1681', in *Journal of the Warburg and Courtauld Institutes* (1958), pp. 104–18.

[3] *State Trials*, vii. 763–812; Southwell to Ormond, 25 Nov., *H.M.C. Ormond MSS.*, iv. 560–1; Barrillon, 27 Nov./7 Dec.; W. Denton to Sir R. Verney, 27 Nov., *H.M.C. Seventh Report*, p. 495.

[4] Southwell to Ormond, 18, 25 Nov., op. cit. iv. 560, 561; newsletter of 2 Dec., *C.S.P.D. 1679–80*, pp. 290–1.

as an essential preliminary Shaftesbury decided to bring back the Duke of Monmouth from exile. That spoilt young man (who had been entertained by William of Orange with a warmth of which James disapproved) had earlier prepared himself for a long stay in Holland and had even sent for his hounds and hunting horses,[1] but on 25 November he left abruptly, having received letters from Shaftesbury. Late on the evening of the 27th he came privately to the house of Sir Edmund Berry Godfrey's brother Michael in Covent Garden, and in the early hours of the 28th he went on to his lodgings in the Cockpit. Within an hour of his arrival and while it was still dark the church bells were ringing and bonfires were being prepared. By eight o'clock copies of verses in his honour were being sold in the streets. That evening there were more bonfires than on any occasion since the Restoration—over 60 between Temple Bar and Charing Cross alone. The 'rabble' stopped even the Lord Chancellor's coach and would not let it pass until he cried 'God bless the Duke of Monmouth!'; while others they treated even less ceremoniously, telling them to drink the Duke's health in kennel water, or pay for better liquor. Obviously some advance preparations must have been made to give Monmouth this reception, and yet the general impression of contemporaries was that the popular rejoicing was genuine, and that he was now 'the idol of the people' in a way that he had never been before.

Next day Shaftesbury and several other persons of quality paid a formal visit to Monmouth to welcome him back to London (though there were those who suspected that the two men had met secretly before Monmouth showed himself). The King, however, was very far from welcoming his son in the same way; indeed, he acted with unwonted severity. He forbade Monmouth to come to Court, and ordered him to go beyond sea again. When Monmouth, no doubt under advice from Shaftesbury, refused, pleading that he had come over to clear himself from the accusation (made in the papers found in the Meal Tub) that he had been plotting rebellion, Charles went further. To make his anger plain, on 1 December he stripped Monmouth of his command of the Guards, the lucrative Mastership of the Horse, and all his other posts and pensions, and granted them to others. When Nell Gwyn tried to intercede for Monmouth, she met with 'a very flat and angry denial'. Previously there had been many who had supposed that although Charles in public had to set his face against his son's claims, secretly he would not be loth to be compelled to give way to them. There were still some who thought in this way, and that on some occasion when Monmouth was concealed in Nell Gwyn's closet and the King arrived, there would be a reconciliation; but they were deluding themselves. The incident left Monmouth clearly ranged with Shaftesbury against the King, and more closely identified with the Earl than ever before. He announced that, now he had been deprived of his

---

[1] *Domestick Intelligence*, 17 Oct.

own income, he would live on his wife's; he received the visits of Shaftesbury and his group of peers; and a pamphlet appeared, claiming to prove that his mother had been married to the King. Halifax was correspondingly scornful of the 'morrice-dance' which Shaftesbury had advised, and persistently urged the King to call Parliament and try to pass such 'limitations' on the power of a Popish successor as would deprive the opposition of its strongest argument.[1]

For very different reasons Shaftesbury too wanted Charles to meet his Parliament, and the moment had come to launch his great petitioning movement and demonstrate that public opinion was behind his demand. The use of petitions for such a purpose was by no means a novel technique. Pym and his allies in the City had used them in the years 1640 to 1642. A wave of addresses for a free Parliament had greeted Monk on his journey south in 1660. Charles II's government had thought it worthwhile to pass an Act in 1661 to prevent 'tumultuous petitioning', that is the presentation of such petitions by a body of more than ten people. Political petitions had been suggested on various occasions in the 1670s, most recently in June 1679, when the Covenanter rebellion had seemed to strengthen the case for calling in Parliament.[2] But although the famous petitions of December 1679 and January 1680 were not strictly original in conception, they required and received much more organization than any previous ones. Forms were printed, some of them for distribution in London, and some to be sent down into the counties, where gentlemen would go from parish to parish to collect signatures. Before the middle of January ten gentlemen from each county would bring their rolls up to London and present them formally to the King, with, it was hoped, so many signatures that Charles could not easily refuse them. Contemporaries were clear that the scheme sprang from the group of peers, including Shaftesbury, Grey of Wark, Howard of Escrick, Herbert of Cherbury, North, Huntingdon, Chandos, and Kent, who were meeting and dining together from the middle of November; and of these Shaftesbury was plainly the leader.[3]

The idea was that London should 'lead the dance', and on 1 December, Shaftesbury and seven other peers dined with the Lord Mayor, Sir Robert Clayton, to persuade him to call a Common Council of the City, which

---

[1] Sidney Diary, 25 Nov., i. 194–5; Négotiations de M. le Comte d'Avaux (Paris, 1754), i. 33; Newsletter, 2 Dec., C.S.P.D. 1679–80, pp. 295–6; Chas. Hatton to L. Hatton, 29 Nov., Hatton Correspondence, i. 203–5; Sir C. Lyttelton to Hatton, 29 Nov., ibid. pp. 205–6; E. Cooke to Ormond, 29 Nov., H.M.C. Ormond MSS., N.S. v. 244–5; H. Coventry to Ormond, 29 Nov., ibid. v. 244; Southwell to Ormond, 29 Nov./2 Dec., ibid. iv. 561–3; Barrillon, 1/11, 8/18 Dec.; J. Vernon to Arran, 2 Dec., MSS. Carte 39, fo. 87; Van Leeuwen, 5/15 Dec., Add. MSS. 17677, EE; Lady Sunderland to Sidney, 16 Dec., Sidney Diary, i. 207–8.   [2] p. 536.
[3] J. Ellwell to G. Treby (from Exeter), 27 Oct., H.M.C. Fitzherbert MSS., pp. 21–22; Southwell to Ormond, 18, 25 Nov., 6 Dec., H.M.C. Ormond MSS., N.S. iv. 560–1, 565; Barrillon, 1/11 Dec.

would adopt an official address to the King in addition to the mass petition which was planned. Unfortunately others were present at the dinner, including Lord Chief Justice Scroggs, whose summing-up in the Wakeman trial in July had so much angered the opposition. Shaftesbury drank his health, and while the meal lasted he and Scroggs conducted a polite conversation about the trial of Knox and Lane a week earlier[1]; but after grace an unpleasant scene followed. Lord Huntingdon called for a toast to Monmouth, whereupon Scroggs followed this by a health to the Duke of York; then all the noblemen, 'in a great scuffle', rose from the table to avoid drinking it, and went into another room. Scroggs followed and complained of the aspersions which the Earl had thrown upon his conduct of the Wakeman trial. Shaftesbury, who had remained much more sober than this judge, 'told him he was a plain spoken man and he liked him the better for it', and called for 'the old Lord Chief Justice's health!' When Scroggs obtusely asked whether Judge Hale was meant, Shaftesbury said no; but Judge Scroggs himself as he had been when in charge of the Plot trials before Wakeman's. The insinuation that something had happened to change Scroggs's attitude was hotly resented by him, even though the Earl agreed that he was satisfied the judge had received no money; and it was two or three hours before Scroggs left to sit on the bench, though the noblemen wanted to resume their business with the Lord Mayor.[2]

Listening to this exchange of insults, Sir Robert Clayton was confirmed in his reluctance to get involved. Although he was later abused by Dryden in *Absalom and Achitophel*, during his mayoralty at least his Whiggism was in fact of a very cautious kind. His sympathies may well have been with the opposition, but he was a rich man and the head of a wealthy corporation whose interests might not be well served by a clash with the King. It was preferable to keep out of trouble, to leave someone else to pull the chestnuts out of the fire, and to recall that in less than twelve months someone else would be Lord Mayor. This attitude was by no means confined to Clayton; it was shared by many of the wealthy Aldermen and all the Lord Mayors of these crisis years, and therefore the Whigs came to put more reliance upon the sheriffs in whose election they could have a louder voice. For the time being Clayton declined to call an emergency meeting of the Common Council.

So the 'breaking of the ice and the firing of the first beacon' was done by sixteen peers,[3] who, claiming to use their right as peers to offer advice to the King, signed a petition asking the King to meet his Parliament on the appointed day (26 January). To keep within the law of 1661, only nine

---

[1] p. 557 above.
[2] Charles Hatton to L. Hatton, 11 Dec., *Hatton Correspondence*, i. 207–10.
[3] Bedford, Say and Sele, Huntingdon, Clare, Stamford, Shaftesbury, Rockingham, Kent, Eure, Holles, North, Chandos, Grey, Howard of Escrick, Herbert of Cherbury, Delamere. Cf. *H.M.C. Hastings MSS.*, iv. 302.

of them, the most senior of whom was the Earl of Huntingdon, waited on the King to present the petition on his return from Chapel on Sunday, 7 December. While they waited for the King Shaftesbury joked with the courtiers who crowded round them, saying that his project would be an advantage to them in particular, 'for whereas they had now neither meat nor money they were to have both, and even new wenches too, in case the old ones would but give them leave'. When Huntingdon read out the petition Charles commented coldly that he wished everyone took as great care of the welfare of the nation as he did, and turned away to dinner. The sixteen who had committed themselves by signing the petition were not a large or a particularly prominent selection from the nobility, and it was significant that some whose sympathies lay with the petitioners' purpose yet had shrunk from participating. Bedford, who if he had gone with the nine to Whitehall would have been the senior earl present and on whom the responsibility of handing the petition to the King would have fallen, fell ill that morning; Wharton was persuaded neither to go nor even to sign, and was reduced to saying that 'his heart was with them, but neither hand nor foot', and in the time of these petitions many others would have said the same.[1]

This was not true to the same extent of those with less to lose. On 9 December petition forms appeared in London, and it became clear that there was a determined and organized attempt to obtain signatures, even by providing tables, petition forms, pen and ink, in the taverns. Once again, as on Monmouth's return, Charles reacted with a speed and forcefulness which he did not ordinarily display. He sent for the Lord Mayor and Aldermen to the Council Board and instructed them to punish the distributors of 'libels' and those who went about soliciting signatures. A royal proclamation forbade tumultuous petitions got up by 'evil-disposed persons' and tending to promote rebellion. And, over the almost unanimous opposition of his Privy Council, and to the anger especially of Essex and Temple, Charles ordered a second proclamation which announced that on 26 January Parliament could not be allowed to meet, but would be put off until November.[2]

Thus it was clear that the petitions would be vain, and that those who signed would risk at least the King's disfavour to little purpose. Nevertheless the petitions grew. The proclamation forbidding them was largely ignored, except by Whig pamphleteers who complained in print that it was illegal. The signatures were counted in tens of thousands. Inevitably apologists for the government, then or later, sought to belittle their significance. As in the case of all mass petitions in all periods, it was alleged

[1] Southwell to Ormond, 9 Dec., *H.M.C. Ormond MSS.*, N.S. iv. 566; W. Denton to Sir R. Verney, 8 Dec., *H.M.C. Seventh Report*, p. 496.

[2] *C.S.P.D. 1679–80*, pp. 307–9; Chas. Hatton to L. Hatton, 18 Dec., *Hatton Correspondence*, i. 211–13; Southwell to Ormond, 13 Dec., *H.M.C. Ormond MSS.*, N.S. iv. 567; Temple, *Works*, i. 441–3; Barrillon, 11/21 Dec.

that signatures were forged or obtained by bribery. Some signatures, it was said, looked like 'insects, crawling about' and on closer inspection proved to be merely the 'hieroglyphics of clowns' whose political opinions were naturally beneath contempt. It was pointed out 'how absurd it was for workmen, before even washing their hands, to plunge into these secrets of government, and give the King instructions as to when it was politic to hold a Parliament—as if they knew more about affairs of state than the King or his Council!' For the next two years government propaganda constantly insisted that only 'the rabble' signed and that men of substance were either indifferent ('for', said they, 'we are at ease, and why should we trouble ourselves?') or actively hostile; but it would be dangerous to accept this sociological analysis in the absence of evidence from which to check it. It was also said that many of the signatories were Dissenters, and, for instance, that 'in all the length from Temple Bar to Whitehall' it was impossible to produce 'on both sides of the way to the street (and those are known to be the best men) 20 that have subscribed excepting only such as are constant conventiclers'. Dissenters were certainly active, and the King issued orders on that account that at the annual elections all the City's Common Council men must take the anti-Puritan oaths and declarations prescribed by the Corporation Act of 1661, which had become disused. But it is impossible to be sure whether the proportion of Puritans amongst those who signed was as large as was alleged by Tory propagandists in order to warn off true Churchmen from the Whig cause.[1]

At all events, the petitions grew in spite of all official discouragements. Shaftesbury was optimistic that the nation was on his side, and that Charles would have to make an accommodation with Parliament. His own health was poor, and there were rumours that he might be arrested and tried by a court of thirty peers picked by the King, but he was confident, and ready to turn anything to political advantage, as when he loudly complained that James had been released from the anti-Catholic laws required of anyone entering the Scottish Council, and argued that this proved the futility of trying to tie down 'the supreme authority' by any Act of Parliament. By the New Year of 1680 he was sufficiently confident to visit Whitehall by night and make a proposal to the King: he would call off the demand both for exclusion and for limitations, if Charles would instead agree to divorce the Queen and marry a Protestant. He still hankered after this solution to the problem, apparently telling Monmouth that if the King had no children by his second marriage all those who had disobliged James by voting for the divorce would not dare to allow him to reign and would be compelled to unite behind Monmouth's claim. But the King had not been

---

[1] R. North, *Examen* (1740), pp. 542–4; Warner, *History of the English Persecution of Catholics and the Presbyterian Plot* (Catholic Record Society, 1953), ii. 322, 418 (cf. R. L'Estrange, *A Short Answer to a whole Litter of Libels* (1680), p. 5); newsletter in the Thynne Papers at Longleat, vol. xli, fos. 191–2; *C.S.P.D. 1679–80*, pp. 312–13.

sufficiently intimidated by the petitioning movement to accept this solution.[1]

The first of the monster petitions was presented to King Charles on 13 January by Sir Gilbert Gerrard, Shaftesbury's friend Francis Charlton, Oates, Bedloe and their lawyer, and two relatives of those terrible Cromwellians, Ireton and Desborough. The petition was in the name of the inhabitants of Westminster and Southwark, was a roll three hundred feet long, and was said to contain fifty or sixty thousand signatures, including those of Shaftesbury, Huntingdon, Grey, and Howard. The King gave Gerrard a very cold reception, saying that it was his own right and no one else's to judge when Parliament was called, and insultingly regretting that a man of Gerrard's name and family was 'at the head of such a rout'.[2] Nine days later when a petition signed by 30,000 Wiltshire names was presented by Thomas Thynne ('Tom of Ten Thousand', the wealthy owner of Longleat), Charles again criticized him as a traitor to his class, saying 'that he did not think a gentleman of his fortune and estate would have concerned himself in anything that looked so like a rebellion'. But when Charles gave a similar snub to Colonel Mildmay, saying that 'he remembered '40 and '41', Mildmay retorted that he remembered '59 and '60.[3]

There were some who thought that the total number of signatures was disappointing, but the government was never in a position to argue that the number of people who signed counter-addresses abhorring the petitions to the King was anything like as great. What the Court's propagandists did allege was that the magistrates and grand juries declined to participate in the petitions, for instance the Wiltshire one, and that these were the work of 'the factions' and the classes that did not count.[4] That this itself was something of a distortion is shown by the number of people who were turned out of offices and out of the commission of the peace in the purge which the government was making at this very time.[5] No doubt there were many others who abstained, not necessarily because they did not wish the King to call Parliament, but often because they had more to lose and did not

[1] Southwell to Ormond, 20, 23, 27 Dec., *H.M.C. Ormond MSS.*, N.S. iv. 568–9; newsletter, 1 Jan. 1680, *C.S.P.D. 1679–80*, p. 364 ('Many of the ringleaders of the sectaries have their pockets lined with petitions'); *Domestick Intelligence*, 23 Dec.; Barrillon, 11/21, 15/25 Dec., 5/15, 8/18, 15/25, 19/29 Jan.

[2] Sir Chas. Lyttelton to L. Hatton, 13 Jan., *Hatton Correspondence*, i. 215; Southwell to Ormond, 13 Jan., *H.M.C. Ormond MSS.*, N.S. iv. 573–4; Sunderland to Sidney, 13 Jan., *Sidney Diary*, i. 230; Van Leeuwen, 13/23 Jan., Add. MSS. 17677, EE; Barrillon, 15/25 Jan.

[3] Newsletter of 22 Jan., *C.S.P.D. 1679–80*, pp. 376–7; and of 24 Jan. in *H.M.C. Le Fleming MSS.*, p. 165; Chas. Hatton to L. Hatton, 27 Jan., *Hatton Correspondence*, i. 220.

[4] Burnet, ii. 248–9; newsletter of 17 Jan., in Thynne Papers at Longleat, vol. xli, fo. 190; letter of 23 Jan. to Sir R. Peyton, Coventry Papers at Longleat, vol. vi, fo. 230; *C.S.P.D. 1679–80*, p. 425.

[5] Southwell to Ormond, 13 Jan., *H.M.C. Ormond MSS.*, N.S. iv. 574; F. Gwyn to Ormond, 3, 17 Feb., ibid. v. 270, 276; *H.M.C. House of Lords MSS. 1678–88*, pp. 172 sqq.

wish to expose themselves to the King's disapproval by taking a definite line. Amongst them were many of the merchants who held office in the City of London, where the King just managed in the end to win a notable victory. In the first place the King had, as we have seen, sought to enforce the provisions of the Corporation Act in the December elections to the Common Council; then he urged the Lord Mayor to put off the Council's meeting. Clayton said that he could not do this any further, and appointed 20 January for the meeting; whereupon Charles declared (or so it was reported) that if the Council petitioned for the Parliament to meet, he would next day dissolve it, and, 'if a [civil] war ensued, he would declare they [the Council] had begun it'. Such language as this persuaded many to caution. About fifty members stayed away, and ten were excluded because they had not taken the prescribed oaths. The remainder of the Common Council were almost equally divided, but among the Aldermen fifteen were against, and only five (including the Lord Mayor) for petitioning the King, so that in total the motion was lost by about five votes.[1]

This was undoubtedly encouraging for the King, but his mind had long been made up that he would not meet Parliament, and no amount of petitioning, from the Common Council or anyone else, could have compelled him to change it. In that sense the great effort which had been made had ended in failure. In another sense, however, Shaftesbury had gained a considerable success. The vast number of signatures that had been received served to make his followers conscious of the great amount of support which they enjoyed, and which would not quickly disappear. Buoyed up by this knowledge, they could wait for some months in the expectation that sooner or later financial stringency, if nothing else, would force Charles to allow them to meet: an additional excise duty would expire at midsummer. And after all, the very fact that Charles dared not meet them was a proof positive of the strength which they had demonstrated.

On 26 January Charles prorogued Parliament, formally only until 15 April in case the international situation should worsen; but he made no secret that if all went well he intended a further prorogation until November. Two days later, having already sent yachts off to Scotland, he told his Council that he proposed to allow the Duke and Duchess of York to return. Possibly he would have postponed this had Monmouth obeyed his renewed command to leave the country; but that duke, inspired by Shaftesbury, replied that he would not go unless the Duchess of Portsmouth,

---

[1] Newsletter, 17 Jan., MSS. Carte 228, fo. 153; Southwell to Ormond, 17 Jan., *H.M.C. Ormond MSS.*, N.S. iv. 576, and 20 Jan., ibid. p. 574 (where the figures should probably read 86 and 88 instead of 66 and 68); Countess of Manchester to L. Hatton, *Hatton Correspondence*, i. 218; Lady Sunderland to Sidney and Mountstevens to the same, 23 Jan., in Sidney Diary, i. 247–8, 255. Many of these sources give slightly different figures. A newsletter of 22 Jan., *C.S.P.D. 1679–80*, p. 376, says that many of those who stayed away did so because they too were not legally qualified under the Corporation Act.

Lauderdale, and Sunderland were in the same yacht—much as he disliked their company. Though the rumours that Charles secretly did not dislike his son were difficult to kill—or, perhaps, because of them—Charles made his position clear by sending for James. In effect he was defying the opposition to do their worst; and Shaftesbury's reply was to appeal to some of the Privy Councillors to resign. At first he had thought that they ought to stay in office; now he had changed his mind and urged several of them to quit in a body. They might not again have so good an opportunity to leave on an important issue, he wrote to them; and 'if the Papists of whom the Duke of York is the manifest head shall attempt within few weeks to alter the religion and government by the assistance of the French whose forces and provisions are ready upon the coast next us, your lordships have continued as blind watchmen for us, and will never be received into the number of good Englishmen'. The only hope for the future was 'by the weight of the nation in a manner compelling us to take right counsels: to this end your lordships' going out together at this juncture extremely serves: and the sense of the body of the Protestants and sober men, made known to his Majesty by their addresses and petitions through the whole nation, will not a little contribute'. It was a good chance for them to redeem themselves from the unpopularity which had fallen upon them at the time of the dissolution in July 1679, and for them to avoid becoming stalking-horses for the Papists.[1]

This appeal, with its highly coloured reference to the possibility of a French invasion, was answered only by Russell, Cavendish, Powle, and Sir Henry Capel amongst the Privy Councillors. If Capel's brother, the Earl of Essex, received a copy, he chose to disregard it and to remain for the present a member of the Council. But it is significant that the last three names of the four who waited upon the King to ask for permission to retire were the names of members who had voted against the first Exclusion Bill in May 1679: they had begun to move back into the opposition camp. This was one more sign that the opposition was hardening.[2]

Charles accepted their resignation without any reluctance, and three weeks later welcomed his brother back to Whitehall. He instructed the Lord Mayor that within the City there were to be no demonstrations of joy, whether because he feared that there would be none, or because he feared that they might lead to disorder; but 'at this end of the town', that is, at the Whitehall end, the bells rang and the bonfires were said to be

---

[1] Printed by Christie, ii. 357–8, from a copy in the Shaftesbury Papers, VI A, 351. It is interesting to note that this letter contains instructions to the addressees to burn it in the presence of the messenger—a practice which the Whigs probably adopted on other occasions too, thus helping to account for the small quantity of their political correspondence which survives.

[2] Sir C. Lyttelton to L. Hatton, 31 Jan., *Hatton Correspondence*, i. 221; Southwell to Ormond, 31 Jan., *H.M.C. Ormond MSS.*, N.S. iv. 578; H. Coventry to Ormond, 3 Feb., ibid. v. 271.

numerous, underlining the cleavage between Court and City which was threatening to develop.[1] The King's hope was that time would bring a drop in the political temperature, and that it might lead to a weakening in the resolution of some of his opponents including Monmouth, who, having been deprived of all his offices, was dependent on the 'charity' of his wife.[2] No sooner had the Duke of York returned than a message was sent, it was said by the Duke's mediation, to Monmouth: if he would ask the King's pardon and 'live well' with the Duke he should be restored to his offices again. Monmouth told his associates that his answer had been that he would readily submit to the King, but would have nothing to do either with the Duke, or with the Duchess of Portsmouth.[3] But time might bring Monmouth to a different opinion; meanwhile Charles accepted Sunderland's advice to win favour with the public by enforcing the laws against Catholic recusants,[4] and by a foreign policy based on the idea of a Protestant coalition to guard against any further attempts by Louis XIV.

As we have seen,[5] Sunderland had long cherished the idea of using a Dutch alliance to counteract the Exclusionists' propaganda about the unsoundness of the government's Protestantism, and he had hoped to bring over William of Orange to draw support away from Monmouth and Shaftesbury: he was trying to follow the same line as Danby had done in 1677. But in 1679, although the policy had been backed by Halifax, Essex, and Temple as well as others, nothing had come of it. William had seriously considered coming to England, but after the King's illness had thought better of it and decided to keep away from trouble: later he had to defend himself to the King against the suspicion that he had connived at Monmouth's return to England in November, and this confirmed him in the idea that he had better avoid getting his fingers burnt.[6] And the States-General knew only too well that England's offers of an alliance were worthless without the moral and financial support of a Parliament which was not being permitted to assemble, and preferred to explore the possibilities

---

[1] Southwell to Ormond, 24 Feb., ibid. iv. 580; Sir Robert Reading to the Earl of Arran, 24 Feb., MSS. Carte 39, fo. 111.

[2] Reading to Arran, 'Candlemas Day', ibid. fo. 107. Reading thought that 'the charity of a lady' referred to the Duchess of Portsmouth, but the Duke's own wife, with her large estates, or his mistress, Lady Wentworth seems more probable.

[3] Burnet to Halifax [27 Feb.?], 'Some Unpublished Letters of Gilbert Burnet', ed. Miss H. C. Foxwell [Foxcroft], *Camden Miscellany XI* (1907), p. 10; cf. *True Domestick Intelligence*, 27 Feb.–2 Mar.; newsletter, 2 Mar. *H.M.C. Le Fleming MSS.*, p. 166; Sir R. Reading to Arran, 9 Mar., MSS. Carte 243, fo. 444.

[4] Francis Gwyn to Ormond, 28 Feb., 2 Mar., *H.M.C. Ormond MSS.*, N.S. v. 281, 284–5.

[5] p. 532 above; cf. J. P. Kenyon, *Robert Spencer Earl of Sunderland* (1958), pp. 35 sqq.

[6] Sidney Diary, 7, 18, 19 Sept. 1679, i. 130–1, 142–3; Barrillon, 8/18 Dec., John Verney to Sir R. Verney, 8 Dec., *H.M.C. Seventh Report*, p. 477; Godolphin to William, 14 Dec., *Archives de la Maison Orange-Nassau*, ed. Groen van Prinsterer (The Hague, 1861), II. v. 373–4; Southwell to Ormond, 20 Dec., *H.M.C. Ormond MSS.*, N.S. iv. 568. I propose to write elsewhere about William's attitude to Exclusion, more fully than would be appropriate in a biography of Shaftesbury.

of reaching an understanding with Louis XIV. So, just like Danby previously, Sunderland had been obliged instead to acquiesce in the King's approaches to Louis XIV for French money, in return for not calling his Parliament and for an attitude of vaguely benevolent neutrality to French designs on the Continent; but these negotiations too had dragged on first because Barrillon had offered an inadequate sum of money, then because he demanded an impossibly long interval before Parliament was allowed to meet, and finally because he declined to make a promise not to make the Franco-Dutch alliance which had always been Charles's bugbear. At the end of 1679 Charles had received a warning that he could not trust Louis; the French ambassador in The Hague allowed it to be known that he had had a letter from Barrillon in London, in which the latter claimed to have been told by Charles that England was trying to obstruct a Franco-Dutch alliance only in order to reach an agreement with France itself. A chorus of denials and lies followed, in which Charles insisted with righteous indignation that he had never contemplated any such thing, and from which he emerged with the conclusion that for the present he could not depend on Louis not to double-cross him.[1] The negotiations with Barrillon were hastily dropped, and in February 1680 Charles once more fell in with Sunderland's suggestion that he should try to construct a coalition against France. A succession of envoys departed to the Northern courts: Southwell to the Great Elector, others to Denmark and the smaller German states, each with instructions to consult with the Prince of Orange on the way. Privately Charles confided in Barrillon that he would not enter into any final commitments hostile to Louis, and James's sentiments were even more pro-French; but publicly, from February 1680 the government was committed to seek to construct a defensive alliance against France. The attempt, like the Triple Alliance of 1668, would warn Louis that it was unwise to undervalue Charles; it would certainly look well in the eyes of the public; and it could be dropped when convenient, should it no longer be necessary and should Louis offer greater inducements. Having set all this new policy in motion, on 10 March Charles was able to leave for his customary relaxation at Newmarket.[2]

Of all these complicated manoeuvrings between April 1679 and February 1680, Shaftesbury knew as much as had been divulged to the Privy Council, and no more. He knew that publicly the King favoured a Dutch alliance, and experience taught him that privately the King still hankered after French money to ease his financial difficulties. This put him in an awkward position. His own preferences are not in doubt. Although Ralph

---

[1] Barrillon's despatches, *passim*; J. Dalrymple, *Memoirs* (1773), ii. 243-4; Sunderland to Sidney, 1/11 Jan., in Sidney Diary, i. 219; Southwell to Ormond, 10 Jan., *H.M.C. Ormond MSS.*, N.S. iv. 572.

[2] Southwell to Ormond, 17 Feb., ibid. iv. 580; Southwell's instructions, S.P. 81/82, fos. 15-16; Sir Chas. Lyttelton to L. Hatton, 28 Feb., *Hatton Correspondence*, i. 221-2; Barrillon, 1/11, 4/14, 11/21 Mar.

Montagu (who believed that every man had his price, like himself) was constantly suggesting to Barrillon that Shaftesbury could be bought for France, that astute ambassador never thought it worth while to make the attempt, and reported in his despatches that the Earl was constantly talking against France.[1] It was natural for Shaftesbury to be well disposed in principle to the idea of a coalition against France, and in any case it would be politically impossible for him to come out in opposition to it; yet he could not believe that it was sincerely intended by Charles and James. Further, as he had written to his friends when urging them to leave the Privy Council at the end of January, 'the Dutch alliance is a thing in itself good and desirable, but as wholesome and nourishing meat, though good in itself, yet to a disordered stomach serves only to add to the disease, so with us if their alliance serve to raise money, men and ships for our mutual defence under the conduct of His Royal Highness it had been much better never made. Nothing is good but what tends to set things right at home, in the first place'.[2] And in relation to this priority, there was the danger that what Sunderland hoped for would come to pass, and that public attention might be diverted from the problem of the succession.

This train of thought combined with other circumstances to suggest that the time had come to pile more fuel on to the flames of popular excitement about the Plot. James's return in February, like his return in the previous September, had induced some people to adopt a distinctly cautious attitude. Not least among these was the 'Whig' Lord Mayor, Sir Robert Clayton, who with the Recorder, sheriffs, and eighteen aldermen waited on the Duke to congratulate him on his safe arrival, and make a virtue of the City's care to prevent any 'sedition'. On 8 March the King and Duke were magnificently entertained by the Lord Mayor, with an accompaniment of bells and bonfires and shouts of 'God bless the King, God bless the Duke!'—though some of the aldermen present replaced other toasts by a private one to the Duke of Monmouth. A week later, when Shaftesbury sent word to the Lord Mayor that he proposed to bring Monmouth and other peers for dinner—an obvious counter-demonstration—Clayton first agreed, then excused himself, and when pressed said that if Monmouth came in at one door he would go out at another. Clayton was frank about his reasons: 'it was absolutely the interest of the city to live fair and well with the Court and . . . so long as he had the honour to serve it as their chief magistrate, he would endeavour to keep it so.' While the City authorities were adopting this attitude in public (whatever their views in private), at Newmarket Lord Cavendish, after first neglecting to kiss James's hand, did so rather than be forbidden to come into the King's presence.[3]

---

[1] Barrillon, 21 Apr./1 May, 3/13 July 1679, 22 Dec./1 Jan. 1680.   [2] Christie, ii. 357–8.
[3] Newsletter, 26 Feb., *C.S.P.D. 1679–80*, pp. 399–400 and 9 Mar., *H.M.C. Le Fleming MSS.*, p. 166; Dowager Lady to Sunderland, 12 Mar., Sidney Diary, i. 301–2; Francis

Something had clearly to be done to maintain Whig agitation and to keep their party together. Some of the peers were still dining together weekly to keep in touch with one another, but there was an awkward situation at the meeting at Lord Wharton's on 17 March. Shaftesbury sneered at Lord North, who, having kissed the Duke's hand, was something of a renegade, and was in litigation with another member of the group, Lord Grey of Wark. 'There were other ways of getting an earldom', said Shaftesbury; whereupon North scored a point by saying that Shaftesbury had found them, not he.[1] There were obviously tensions within the group, and we cannot tell whether what Shaftesbury intended to do next was discussed among them; but before they met a week later Shaftesbury made a grand dramatic gesture. On the morning of 24 March he appeared before the Privy Council (presided over, in the King's absence, by Lord Radnor), asked that the clerks should be ordered to leave, and then behind the locked doors communicated to them information which he had received about a Plot in Ireland. A revolt of the Catholics with French assistance and inevitably an accompanying massacre of Protestants was spoken of: it was a bloodthirsty story, in an age in which, if people feared plots by English Catholics, they believed Irish ones to be capable of anything. The Privy Council took it all very seriously; they declined Shaftesbury's suggestion that a select committee should be appointed to investigate, rather than the whole Council, but they resolved to send promptly to the King and ask him to return to London. And Charles did so, cutting short his holiday and coming back to the capital on the 31st. It would not do to allow the opposition to say that the government had wilfully neglected to make proper inquiries into the Plot.[2]

The Duke of Ormond's friends in London had long been expecting that Shaftesbury would be responsible for some devilish plot against their patron. The two noblemen represented completely different political, religious, and social attitudes, and at least since the time of the Irish Cattle Act of 1666–7 there had been no love lost between them.[3] Over the years Shaftesbury had frequently hinted, or asserted, that under Ormond's

---

Gwyn to Ormond, 9 Mar., *H.M.C. Ormond MSS.*, N.S. v. 288; Barrillon, 11/21 Mar.; Ossory to Ormond, 15 Mar. op. cit. v. 291; Sir R. Reading to Arran, 20 Mar., MSS. Carte 39, fo. 127; Sir Chas. Lyttelton to L. Hatton, *Hatton Correspondence*, i. 224.

[1] Lyttelton, loc. cit.

[2] Newsletters, 25 Mar., 30 Mar., *C.S.P.D. 1679–80*, pp. 424, 426; H. Coventry to Ormond, 2 Apr., *H.M.C. Ormond MSS.*, N.S. v. 295; F. Gwyn to Ormond, 3 Apr., ibid. v. 296; *The True News, or Mercurius Anglicus*, 24–28 Mar.; Barrillon, 25 Mar./4 Apr., 1/11 Apr.; Bridgwater to Shaftesbury, 24 Mar., Christie, ii. 362–3; James to William, 29 Mar., *Archives de la Maison Orange-Nassau*, ed. Groen van Prinsterer (The Hague, 1861), II. v. 388; Godolphin to William, 2 Apr., ibid. pp. 389–90.

[3] pp. 187–90 above. I have been unable to confirm Miss Brown's statement (p. 268) that Shaftesbury had estates of his own in Ireland, though he was one of the trustees for the Irish estates of the regicide Robert Wallop, to whom the Earl of Southampton and he were related by marriage.

lord-lieutenancy the Irish government was too lenient to the Catholic majority of the population, and that the precarious English and Protestant ascendancy was in danger: Ormond's friends had never given the Earl credit for any sincerity in this, always believing that his motive was personal animosity and jealousy of his wealth and power. If, then, Danby, the Duke of York, and even the Queen were under attack, why should the Duke of Ormond escape? Ormond's correspondents sent over a stream of fears that attack was imminent, and Shaftesbury's famous speech about the 'little sister with no breasts' on 25 March 1679, had been interpreted as the prelude to one, and had excited an outburst from Ormond's hot-headed son Ossory.[1] Yet the attack had never come; Shaftesbury said that Ossory had misinterpreted his speech, and, acting on his friends' advice, Ormond had written to the Earl, congratulating him on his appointment as Lord President, and formally apologizing for his son's impulsiveness.[2] Shaftesbury had not replied, and from time to time criticisms of Ormond's administration by him had been reported, and there had even been rumours that if Parliament were allowed to meet, Ormond would be impeached[3]; but no direct attack (as distinct from sneers in private conversation) had materialized before the Irish Plot stories burst upon the public, nor did one materialize afterwards. The political advantage to be derived from the Irish Plot stories was not the downfall of Ormond. Desirable as that may well have been to Shaftesbury, an attack would have diverted attention from the person of the Duke of York, just as Danby's impeachment had done; and it was the ruin of James that Shaftesbury was pursuing with such single-mindedness. When he gave encouragement to Fitzgerald, Murphy, and the rest of the disreputable gang of Irish witnesses, it was their effect in keeping up the anti-Catholic feeling in England that counted.

The story that the ex-Franciscan friar John Fitzgerald told, when in 1682 it paid him to co-operate with the government, was that in June 1679 at Dunkirk he had met a Scots factor named Gilbert Spence, who showed him a letter from Shaftesbury saying that if he could find any persons who would 'help the confirming of the Plot' 'no encouragement should be wanting'. Seeing visions of fame and, what was more important, fortune ahead, Fitzgerald agreed to go to London, where Spence introduced him to the Earl (then Lord President), who heard his account and asked him to write it down. On reading it the Earl exclaimed that 'it is not so much as we knew before, and I thought you would have hinted something of the Duke of Ormond, who and the Duke of York and the Duke of Lauderdale are the three greatest enemies of these three

---

[1] pp. 510–11 above.

[2] Southwell to Ormond, 22 Apr. 1679, *H.M.C. Ormond MSS.*, N.S. iv. 505; Ormond to Shaftesbury, 25 Mar., Christie, ii. 337–8.

[3] E.g. Cooke to Ormond, 10 May 1679, *H.M.C. Ormond MSS.*, N.S. v. 88; Ossory to Ormond, 17 Aug., ibid. v. 184; Longford to Ormond, 29 Aug., ibid. v. 192–3; Ossory to Ormond, 23 Sept., ibid. v. 212.

nations . . .'. As Fitzgerald told the story in 1682, he had in effect been told to 'improve' his story—which he did with the aid of Israel Tonge and the planting of some forged papers in a wall in Ireland—but Fitzgerald's words must be treated with caution. They were certainly embellished with some abuse of the King of which Shaftesbury would scarcely have been guilty to a complete stranger; and in a historical court of law Fitzgerald's words are no more deserving of belief in 1682 than they were when he forged and lied in 1680. If Shaftesbury is charged with subornation the verdict must once again be one of 'not proven'; but once again it is also true that his agents, notably one William Hetherington, were active in seeking out informers in Ireland, bringing them over to England and encouraging them to give evidence—and that Shaftesbury was prepared to make use of anything. In the matter of the Irish witnesses the case is much blacker than in respect of Oates, Bedloe, and others who would no doubt have come forward without Shaftesbury to push them. Their credibility was less from the start to any thinking person: Henry Coventry, who had shown some indecision about Titus Oates, was quite clear that the Irish stories were a complete fabrication, designed for their effect on public opinion. Consequently a heavier responsibility lies on Shaftesbury for the death of Oliver Plunket, Archbishop of Armagh, than for that of Lord Stafford, even though Plunket's death may not have been contemplated at the beginning. The old proverb about the impossibility of touching pitch without being defiled applies; from 'adopting' Oates Shaftesbury had been led much further than he had originally intended to go.[1]

Fitzgerald had been known to the government for some time. He had given out that if sent back to Ireland he could make some important discoveries, but on the way, at Bristol, some suspicious letters were 'found' in his inn-room and he was brought back to London to account for them.[2] It was five days later that Shaftesbury made his dramatic appearance before the Council Board to announce that an extraordinary courier, Hetherington, had brought further news of impending revolt from four witnesses of quality and reputation in Ireland, especially one Murphy. The story reached the public that Shaftesbury urged speedy and effectual action, on the ground that one of the four had already been poisoned. The question was how this action was to be taken. Political observers supposed that Shaftesbury wanted the Irish witnesses sent for privately and examined in London, unknown to the Duke of Ormond, but that Laurence Hyde argued that this would be insulting to the King's chosen representative in Ireland, and that Henry Coventry went a good deal further in urging that the examination should be carried out in Dublin. If Shaftesbury's audacity were not restrained, he said, matters would fall into irremediable confusion; this talk of an Irish plot had been invented solely to cause a revolt in

---

[1] *C.S.P.D. 1682*, pp. 46, 65–66; *C.S.P.D. 1679–80*, pp. 197–8.
[2] Roger Morrice's Entering Book P (Dr. Williams's Library), 17 Mar. 1680, fo. 251.

England; and those who had 'discovered' it could not be believed since instead of addressing the King's ministers they had gone to a man who could only subsist in confusion and who counted on keeping up the division between the King and his people. The Lord Chancellor, Lord Radnor (Shaftesbury's successor as Lord President of the Council), Essex, and others, however, took the stories seriously, and supported the idea that the witnesses should be brought to London; and in the end the King, while scorning the plot, also decided to show that at least it should be probed to the bottom, though he would not hear of keeping it a secret from Ormond. Hetherington and John Fitzgerald were sent over to find their 'witnesses' and arrange for their transportation to London, while Ormond sent a series of sarcastic descriptions of them: there was Macnamara, who lay under a charge of horse-stealing; another, 'my Lord of Essex's tool'[1], was 'a silly drunken vagabond that cares not for hanging a month hence if in the meantime he may solace himself with brandy and tobacco'; and in general they were 'such creatures that no schoolboy would trust them with a design for the robbing of an orchard'.[2]

All this took time, but Shaftesbury's immediate objective had been achieved. The coffee-houses, which had been 'in a most languishing condition before', were now 'in heart again, and you never saw a more sensible alteration in the country after a great rain than this makes in some people's looks'.[3] Other topics of conversation also stimulated the consumption of coffee. Some misguided apprentices of Tory sympathies, led by one Alford, a bell-founder, but probably egged on by others for their own purposes, planned a demonstration for Whit Sunday (29 May) which would be a grand reply to the Pope-burnings: instead of the Pope, they would once again burn the Rump, and, with magnificent impartiality, destroy both the bawdy-houses and the Nonconformist conventicles. Since plans were on foot at the end of March, they inevitably leaked out, and some of the apprentices were examined by Sir William Waller, the unbalanced son of the Parliamentarian general, who as a magistrate had earned a certain notoriety by searching out Catholic books and crucifixes. When Waller brought these examinations to the Council they mentioned hopes that the Guards would join in the riot, and that Ormond's son Ossory would assist. On his own behalf and, he said, on Shaftesbury's, Waller waited on Ossory to say that neither of them had 'reflected upon' Ossory as the talk of the

---

[1] If Ormond and his friends were sure that Shaftesbury wished to ruin him, they were equally convinced that Essex wished to supplant him and recover his former post at Dublin. Shaftesbury, however, complained that after at first believing in the Irish plot Essex 'did of a sudden fall from it'; Burnet to Halifax, 17 April, 'Some Unpublished Letters of Gilbert Burnet', ed. H. C. Fox[croft], *Camden Miscellany XI*, p. 22.
[2] Barrillon, 5/15 Apr.; Bridgwater to Coventry, 1 Apr., Coventry Papers at Longleat, vol. vi, fo. 266; Ormond to Ossory, 10, 12, 27 Apr., *H.M.C. Ormond MSS.*, N.S. v. 299, 302, 312; and to Sir Cyril Wyche, 14 Apr., ibid. p. 303.
[3] Burnet to Halifax, 27 Mar., op. cit. p. 17.

town alleged; but no one believed that he was sincere in this. Forty eminent citizens asked the Lord Mayor to call a Common Council to discuss measures for the security of the City (which, if the meeting had taken place, might have included petitioning the King for a Parliament); notes were scattered (according to the French ambassador, by Shaftesbury's agency) which talked of a plot to murder the Earl, Waller, and another violent partisan, Sir Thomas Player; and on the eve of Easter Shaftesbury left London for a few days, professing to fear that a 'tumult' would be contrived during the holidays to kill him. 'This great value he puts upon himself, which is more than any body else does', wrote Sunderland's mother, when relating this story, but in fact he was now the Protestant hero for many Londoners.[1] That the opposition's fears of a coup by the Court were not altogether irrational was illustrated by the despatches of the French ambassador, who was prepared to acquit the King of any such intention but was not prepared to say the same for the Duke of York.

Pepys wrote sarcastically that 'there is hardly a day passes without some new plot discovered, or old one laughed at', and that the affair of the apprentices in which Ossory was mentioned 'administered mirth in abundance more . . . than the little Great Lord you mention ever intended either him or me'. But Pepys's scorn for 'the little Great Lord' (Shaftesbury) and 'little Justice Overdo' (Waller) was mistaken if it implied that the stories should not be taken seriously by the government, which found it advisable to commit Alford to Newgate, to ban all gatherings of apprentices on Sundays and holidays, and to allow the Lord Mayor to keep four companies of the trained-bands in readiness during the Easter days. The King, who suspected Waller of putting words into the mouth of one of the apprentices whom he had examined, found an early pretext to dismiss him; the Lord Mayor, Sir Robert Clayton, was induced to put off the motion for a Common Council; and as a mark of defiance Ossory was made a Privy Councillor.[2] But the fever of popular excitement had risen by another degree; and on 15 April it mounted still higher on the news that Arnold, the virulent Papist-hater from Monmouthshire who had stirred up the feelings of the Commons about the growth of Popery at the end of April 1678, had been set upon by some cut-throats. Arnold was not seriously hurt, and the circumstances were a little suspicious: some said that the attack was faked and even that the wounds were self-inflicted. Whatever the truth of this, the incident was immediately compared with

[1] F. Gwyn to Conway, 23 Mar., *C.S.P.D. 1679–80*, p. 422; newsletters, 25/30 Mar., ibid. 423–4, 426; Burnet to Halifax, as in previous note; Barrillon, 1/11, 8/18, 12/22 Apr., Gwyn to Ormond, 3 Apr., *H.M.C. Ormond MSS.*, N.S. v. 296; Ossory to Ormond, 3 Apr. ibid. 297; Mountstevens to Sidney, 2 Apr., Sidney Diary, ii. 22; Lady Sunderland to Sidney, 16 Apr., ibid. ii. 39.

[2] Pepys to 'Madam', 9 Apr., MSS. Rawlinson A 194, fos. 146ᵛ–7; Van Leeuwen, 2/12, 13/23 Apr. in Add. MSS. 17677, EE; Burnet to Halifax, 3 Apr., op. cit. p. 18; Barrillon, 8/18 Apr.; *H.M.C. Le Fleming MSS.*, p. 166; James to William, 16 Apr., Groen van Prinsterer, II. v. 393.

the murder of Sir Edmund Berry Godfrey, as acts of Popish revenge. 'Just as old sores had got some skin grown over them and the true old good nature of Englishmen and charity were returning, this business of Mr. Arnold makes them bleed afresh.'[1] On 17 April the Court's supporters tried a counter-move with the first of the 'abhorring' addresses, presented by Francis Wythens and Sir George Jeffreys on behalf of the inhabitants of Westminster. Other addresses 'abhorring' the petitions of the previous winter followed, but not only were they signed by fewer people; on the whole they seem to have attracted less attention. The initiative, for the time being, was with the opposition.

It was at this time that rumours began to spread more strongly than ever before, that the Duke of Monmouth was Charles's legitimate son. An open statement to this effect had appeared at the beginning of April in a pamphlet, *The Popish Massacre*, with whose production Dr. Tonge was concerned. The coffee-houses talked of a strange story that the former bishop of Durham, Cosin, had left a sealed paper in a Black Box in the hands of his son-in-law, Sir Gilbert Gerrard, with instructions that it was not to be opened until after the King's death, but that Gerrard 'had been of late wrought on to open it' and had found a certificate to the effect that Cosin had married Charles to Monmouth's mother. This was an obvious piece of political kite-flying. It cannot be taken as absolutely certain that Shaftesbury was directly responsible; it is just possible that this was the doing of Ralph Montagu (with whom the Earl was not on good terms[2]) or of Sir Thomas Armstrong or someone else in Monmouth's entourage. But Shaftesbury, Monmouth, and others were dining together, either with 'a club of gentlemen' at the Rummer in Queen Street or more privately at one another's houses,[3] and the story can hardly have come as a complete surprise to those present. There were rumours, which did not detract from his popularity, that Monmouth was to be summoned before the Council, and sent to the Tower; but the King wisely did not make his son any more of a martyr than he already was. Instead he contented himself with sending for Gerrard, forcing that gentleman to deny that he had ever seen a certificate of the kind described, and making a further solemn declaration of his own that he had never been married to Lucy Walter. Sir William Temple, coming back to town for the first time for a month, found that the Duke of York's levee was more crowded than he could ever remember it.[4]

---

[1] Cf. J. Pollock, *The Popish Plot* (1903), p. 396; *C.S.P.D. 1679–80*, p. 480; van Leeuwen, 20/30 Apr., Add. MSS. 17677, EE; Barrillon, 19/29 Apr., 22 Apr./2 May; Sir Robert Reading to Earl of Arran, 18 Apr., MSS. Carte 39, fo. 129; Burnet to Halifax, 17 Apr., op. cit. p. 22.

[2] Dowager Lady Sunderland to Sidney, 22 Mar., Sidney Diary, ii. 13.

[3] *Protestant Intelligence*, 2 Apr.; Reresby, p. 193.

[4] Information of Robert Bolron, 1 May, *C.S.P.D. 1679–80*, p. 460; newsletter, 6 May, ibid. p. 466; Burnet to Halifax, 3, 10 Apr., op. cit. pp. 19, 21; James to William, 16 Apr.,

Monmouth for his part continued to show himself in public every day to attract some support, and no declaration of the King's could scotch the story about the Black Box. More details were passed from mouth to mouth: it was said that when Monmouth's mother had been a prisoner in the Tower she had signed a petition to Cromwell as the wife of Charles Stuart, and that this piece of evidence came from Shaftesbury, who had then been in office. Certainly the information which reached the Marquis of Halifax in the country left him in no doubt that 'the little gentleman' had been consulted, and that statesman was full of gloomy forecasts of an impending civil war: he had recently promised to meet Sunderland at Althorp to discuss the situation, fully expecting that 'our small friend' would misrepresent this as a political deal.[1]

On 7 May, meanwhile, the little flock of Irish witnesses reached London, and were promptly examined before the Council, where they 'did not express themselves very intelligibly' in their Irish accents, and were instructed to send in their depositions in writing. Warned by past experience, however, the King ordered that no one should be given access to them to prompt them, that the depositions should be brought 'to a full point' with no places for later additions, and that nothing should be published until the report was complete. The result was that much, though not all, of their sting was drawn: and one, Murphy, declared specifically that he had never heard of any plot which was still in progress. Witnesses claimed to have seen treasonable letters of Plunket, the Catholic archbishop of Armagh, in 1673, but neither Ormond nor the Duke of York was incriminated, and so far as English politics were concerned the effect of the depositions was only to keep alive the general feeling that Catholics were dangerous and desperate plotters. In any case Shaftesbury could not hope to turn them to account while Parliament was not sitting, and at this point it was even being said that (in contrast to the petitioning movement of the winter) he did not want Parliament to meet until the King's financial position had worsened by the lapse of certain taxes which had been voted in earlier sessions, so that the King would be 'constrained into greater compliances'. This was still some way ahead, and in the meantime it was ordered that Plunket should be tried in Ireland and that the witnesses should be sent back there.[2]

---

3 May, *Archives de la Maison Orange-Nassau*, II, v. 393, 397; Daniel Finch to Sir J. Finch, 10 May, *H.M.C. Finch MSS.*, ii. 76; Charles Hatton to L. Hatton, 27 Apr., *Hatton Correspondence*, i. 225; Lionel Jenkins to William, 27 Apr., Foreign Entry Book, SP. 104/67, fo. 1; *C.S.P.D. 1679–80*, pp. 447 sqq.

[1] O. Klopp, *Der Fall des Hauses Stuart* (Vienna, 1875–88), ii. 256, n. 1; Barrillon, 3/13 May; Halifax to Tho. Thynne, later Viscount Weymouth, 6 May, Thynne Papers at Longleat, vol. xv, fo. 9.

[2] F. Gwyn to Ormond, 8 May, *H.M.C. Ormond MSS.*, N.S. v. 314–15; Jenkins to Sunderland, 7 May, *C.S.P.D. 1679–80*, p. 467, and to Ormond, 14 May, ibid. p. 478; Barrillon, 7/17 May; Sir R. Reading to Arran, 11 May, MSS. Carte 243, fo. 474.

At this point a further crisis suddenly loomed up, for the King, who was at Windsor, fell on 13 May into a second indisposition. This was less serious than his illness in August of the previous year, but serious enough to entail the sending of twice-daily bulletins to Whitehall and extra vigilance on the part of the Guards.[1] By the 18th it could be said that the King was well again and would probably continue so 'if he can be kept from fishing when a dog would not be abroad',[2] but in these few days the opposition had been forced to consider what they should do were the King to die. It so happened that on 17 May a formal meeting of Parliament was due, for although the King had declared that he would allow no session to be held until November, for reasons of foreign policy he was accomplishing this by a series of short prorogations and not by one long one. Had not the King been on the way to recovery by that time, the French ambassador reported, three hundred members of the Commons would have ignored the prorogation order and remained assembled. The leaders of the opposition met several times at Shaftesbury's house. All that we know of their deliberations comes from the confession of one of them, Lord Grey of Wark, after his capture by James II's forces following the Monmouth rebellion in 1685. Grey declared that plans were made for an armed rising in the City. According to his account, Shaftesbury told Monmouth, Russell, Sir Thomas Armstrong, and himself that he had consulted with 'many of the eminent men in the city, who were all willing to rise if the King died, provided the Duke of Monmouth, my Lord Russell and [Shaftesbury] would assist'; and one Major Manley reported on the enthusiasm of the seamen of Wapping. After many suggestions had been canvassed, it was agreed that if the King died they should rise in arms and declare for a Parliament to settle the succession. In the meantime Shaftesbury was to arrange for a messenger to ride between Windsor and London and keep them informed of the King's condition. All the conspirators were to lodge secretly in the City at night, and Shaftesbury recommended to Monmouth the house of Bateman, the surgeon who was to suffer for succouring Titus Oates in 1685; but the King's recovery put an end to all these plans.[3]

Now it is never safe to accept the uncorroborated evidence of an accomplice seeking to save his own life by 'confessions'; and moreover when Grey wrote the four conspirators whom he mentioned, Shaftesbury, Monmouth, Russell, and Sir Thomas Armstrong, were all dead and unable to contradict him. There is also the curious circumstance that Grey was quite unable to put a date to the King's illness, and to these events, which he thought might have occurred either just before or after the Oxford Parliament of 1681. Nevertheless it would have been only common prudence

---

[1] *C.S.P.D. 1679–80*, pp. 474 sqq.
[2] Lady Sunderland to Sidney, 18 May, Sidney Diary, ii. 57.
[3] Ford Lord Grey, *The Secret History of the Rye House Plot* (1754), pp. 3–6; Barrillon, 20/30 May, 10/20 June.

for the Whigs to consider what their position would be if the King died, and it cannot be called unlikely that they contemplated the possibility of 'rising in arms'. But what is much more doubtful, in 1680 as in the autumn of 1682, is whether the talk ever became a definite plan.

What is certain is that 15 May, in the middle of the King's illness, was the date of Robert Ferguson's pamphlet *Letter to a Person of Honour concerning the Black Box*. This was no common pamphlet: the author spoke with a certain authority. The Black Box, he ingeniously argued, was 'a mere romance' designed to throw ridicule on the idea of the King's marriage to Lucy Walter, and to prevent a proper inquiry into the evidence—for instance, into a letter which Charles had written in Oliver's time, superscribed 'To his wife'. In any case Parliament had often provided a successor to the throne, when the public interest required it, without regard to 'such punctilios' as legitimacy: Henry VII's descent had been through a bastard, but he was made legitimate by Parliament. And the real issue was whether the Duke of York's treasonable activities had not made his life forfeit. 'The countenancing the burning of London, the endeavouring to alter the limited monarchy into a despotic rule, and the combining with the papists in all the parts of the late plot, make him liable to the axe, while he is aspiring to the sceptre.' The author also referred to the Council meeting of the previous Wednesday, when, he said, the Duke's importunities had failed to induce the King to order a declaration in favour of James's right to succeed. This was untrue, but near enough to the truth to be plausible: what James had persistently desired, and the King had declined, was further inquiry into the Black Box stories and the punishment of those responsible for spreading them.[1]

This was far more outspoken than any previous advocacy of Monmouth's claims, and than any previous printed attack on James. And someone paid for the scattering of large numbers of copies on the Royal Exchange, and there was talk of a nation-wide distribution.[2] It is natural to suppose that Shaftesbury cannot have been unaware of this much closer confrontation between the claims of York and Monmouth, and yet the risks would be very great for anyone who committed himself to the latter's cause. When Charles recovered the relief was general, and it did not spring from a universal devotion to the King's person.

The supporters of both Dukes had time to make further preparations. Monmouth, continuing his advisers' policy of frequent public appearances in the City of London, dined there with more than forty lords and gentlemen, including Russell. Monmouth gave the toast, 'The King—and Magna Charta!' and Lord Howard of Escrick followed it with 'The confusion of all pretending Popish successors!'. Shaftesbury's presence was not mentioned; but some of the personal preparations which the

---

[1] *Somers Tracts* (1809–15), viii. 189–95; Burnet to Halifax, 15 May, op. cit. p. 28.
[2] Letter to Sir L. Jenkins, 21 May, *C.S.P.D. 1679–80*, p. 487.

recent crisis had led him to make were a little ominous. On 26 May he gave his consent to a deed granting additional jointure to the Countess of Shaftesbury. Coming at this point, the deed looks like an attempt to make the family estates safe from confiscation if the Earl were found guilty of treason. Behind the scenes he was also taking an active interest in the fortunes of the Irish witnesses who had been sent back to Dublin so that Plunket and others could be tried there. One witness, Edmund Murphy, he recommended in particular to an Irish ally of his, the Protestant Bishop of Meath. On 1 June, however, the good bishop wrote to Colonel Mansell at Westminster—the same Mansell who had been mixed up in the Meal Tub Plot—reporting that Murphy had unfortunately neglected to take out his pardon for the charge which his enemies were pressing against him of corresponding with the Irish agrarian malcontents commonly called Tories: could Mansell arrange this, with the aid of Shaftesbury, Essex, and Hetherington, 'who I hear is agent for those persons at Court?' Mansell was able to reply that the three would arrange it: Shaftesbury had been consulted; Essex, who believed in the reality of a Popish Plot in Ireland, would move for the pardon in Council, and Hetherington should not lack counsel to see that it was properly drafted, 'but I perceive money is not very plenty with Mr. H: great men's purse-strings [Shaftesbury's?] are very close drawn—that I am sure of.'[1]

Meanwhile James's supporters had induced the King on 2 June to make a renewed declaration, which was printed, that he had never been married to anyone but the Queen, with penalties for anyone who maintained the contrary.[2] On 11 June the Catholics won another success, when the 'Popish midwife', Mrs. Cellier, was acquitted of high treason and the principal witness against her, Dangerfield, was shown to be incapable of being a witness since he had been pilloried and convicted of felony; and twelve days later, when Lord Castlemaine was also acquitted, doubt was thrown on Oates's credibility, as well as Dangerfield's. For some people this reinforced the belief, derived from a partisan view of Sir George Wakeman's trial in the previous year, that the authorities, and especially Lord Chief Justice Scroggs, were determined, come what may, to frustrate the people's desire for justice on the nation's enemies; for others present it was a serious blow at the authority of the Plot witnesses.[3] And meanwhile the Earl of Sunderland, though he did not share James's viewpoint, was also having a partial success in his attempt to counter the Exclusionist propaganda by means of a popular Protestant foreign policy. The Great Elector of Brandenburg and other foreign princes had declined to take part in a defensive alliance, fearing to be exposed to the anger of France

---

[1] Burnet to Halifax, 29 May, op. cit. p. 31; Shaftesbury Papers, XLIII, 71; Bishop of Meath, 1 June, MSS. Carte 39, fo. 142; Mansell's reply, 15 June, ibid. fo. 146.

[2] C.S.P.D. 1679–80, p. 502.

[3] State Trials, vii. 1044–55, 1067–1112; Burnet to Halifax, 12 June, op. cit. pp. 34–35; Mansell to Bishop of Meath, 15 June, MSS. Carte 39, fo. 146.

without the security, which only the unanimity of King and Parliament could give, that England's participation would be effective; but Spain, being unable to incur any more French hostility than already existed, clutched at the chance of an ally who would guarantee her possessions in Flanders, even if it was only on paper, and on 10 June an Anglo-Spanish defensive treaty was signed at Windsor. On this Sunderland hoped to build. He proposed to send Temple into Spain, and he renewed his persistent invitations to William of Orange to come over and lend his prestige to the new foreign policy; and inside England he tried to use the treaty as an inducement to Halifax to return to Court and renew the co-operation which had broken down six months earlier. By the time Parliament met in November, it would be possible for Sunderland to prove by these positive actions that there was no secret conspiracy between the government and France.[1]

Privately Charles tried to explain away the treaty to Barrillon, and the opposition too belittled it as futile, insincere, a mere demonstration to see if Parliament would fall into the trap: with some reason they argued that if Charles really wanted to save Flanders, he should have intervened before Cambrai, Saint Omer, and Ypres were lost to France in 1677.[2] But while the opposition affected to scorn it, they were secretly perturbed. A visitor found Shaftesbury bad-tempered, as he was increasingly becoming with advancing age and ill-health. When Hampden called and held a whispered conversation with the Earl, the latter was heard to say, 'I am afraid this will fool the Parliament'.[3] Some great counter-stroke was necessary; but Shaftesbury had one ready.

First of all, a pamphlet answer to the King's declaration of 2 June was planned. This, the *Letter to a Person of Honour concerning the King's disavowing the having been married to the Duke of Monmouth's Mother*, declared that James had 'hectored' his brother into making that declaration —and illustrated the worthlessness of such declarations by pointing to James's own attempts in 1660 to disavow his marriage to Anne Hyde, with the worst possible reflections on her chastity. For good measure it was added that the King's declarations were not final—as for instance the Declaration of Breda, the declaration on the occasion of the Stop of the Exchequer, and the declaration in April 1679 that he would govern with the advice of his Council. None of these promises had been kept; and as for the King's taking Almighty God to witness, if his faith did not restrain him from his 'adulteries and promiscuous scatterings', why pay much attention to his oaths? In any case Monmouth could not be denied the right of every subject to try to prove his own legitimacy. Not content with this, the

---

[1] Southwell to Ormond, 17 May, *H.M.C. Ormond MSS.*, N.S. iv. 581–2; Sidney Diary, ii. 70, 74–76; Halifax to Tho. Thynne (later Weymouth), 21 June, Thynne Papers at Longleat, xv. fo. 33.   [2] Barrillon, 13/23, 17/27 June.

[3] Dowager Countess of Sunderland to Halifax, 20 June [Mary Berry], *Life of Lady Russell* (1819), pp. 338–9.

writer went on to make twenty-one charges against the Duke of York: against his Popery and the seduction of others to it; against his procuring "the chiefest places of strength in the nation . . . to be conferred upon known Papists'; against his promoting of arbitrary government and authorizing the burning of London; against his part in the Dutch wars as a means of dividing Protestants and, if successful, turning 'the victorious arms of the King upon the heretics of home and the patrons of English liberty'. 'He was consenting to and hath co-operated in the whole popish plot; for both his confessor [Bedingfield] and secretary [Coleman] did, with his knowledge and approbation, seal the resolves for the King's death'. The conclusion urged that Parliament must on the one hand examine Monmouth's birth, and on the other try the Duke of York for 'his manifold treasons and conspiracies against the King and kingdom'.[1]

But even before Parliament met, it would be possible to make a sensational gesture. On 21 June rumours spread that Shaftesbury and Lord Grey of Wark had entered an information against the Duke of York for recusancy, and that later some of the charges in the pamphlet would be fastened upon him. The grand jury of Middlesex would present James as a recusant on 26 June, at the same time as they submitted a further petition for the calling of Parliament.[2] Since the grand jury's sympathies were already known, there was little need to keep the attack a secret; rather a little expectation of a sensation would enhance it. When the day came, the Whigs, who included Shaftesbury, Grey, Huntingdon, Russell, Cavendish, Thomas Wharton, Thomas Thynne ('Tom of Ten Thousand'), and others, met in the Court of Requests, and apparently had a preliminary word with the grand jury (who were, according to the Secretary of State, 'of the inferior sort of gentry as juries commonly are'). Then they all went into the court-room, and the grand jury began by presenting their petition; whereupon Scroggs, who had been warned of what was afoot, read them a lecture about minding their own business and not interfering in matters of state, and then discharged them without any opportunity to make their present-ments. Shaftesbury made a second attempt on 30 June, only to be prevented again by the dismissal of the grand jury. The Earl told the judges that this was not according to law, but Justice Raymond replied that he thought he understood law as well as his lordship, and since the judge and not the Earl sat on the bench, he had the last word.[3]

[1] *Somers Tracts* (1809–15), viii. 197–208. This may have been the pamphlet for being concerned in distributing which Edmund Everard was imprisoned until October (P.C. Reg. 2/69, pp. 24, 132), but it must have been inspired by someone of more authority.

[2] Information of Robert Whitehall, 24 June, *C.S.P.D. 1679–80*, p. 525; newsletter, 22 June, ibid. 524; Barrillon, 24 June/4 July; James to William, 24 June, Groen van Prinsterer, *Archives de la Maison Orange-Nassau* (The Hague, 1858–62), II. v. 408.

[3] John Verney to Sir R. Verney, 30 June, 1 July, *H.M.C. Seventh Report*, p. 479; Jenkins to William, 29 June, Foreign Entry Book, S.P. 104/67; Barrillon, 28 June/8 July; Shaftesbury Papers, VI B, 420; Burnet to Halifax, 26 June, op. cit. p. 38; Temple, *Works*, i. 450; James to William, 27, 29 June, Groen van Prinsterer, op. cit. II. v. 56, 57.

Superficially Shaftesbury had been foiled, but in practice he had achieved his purpose. Everyone knew that the Duke of York had narrowly escaped being indicted as a recusant—and the Duchess of Portsmouth from being indicted as a public nuisance; and the echoes reverberated all round Europe. It was a deliberate insult to the King's brother and to the King's mistress, and everyone interpreted it as a gesture of supreme self-confidence on the part of the opposition, which portended ill for the future. It was clear that the King was as far as ever from having conciliated his subjects; and everyone drew the conclusion that in foreign affairs he counted for very little, because without backing.[1] No one would now contemplate joining the coalition which Sunderland had planned. Sunderland's whole foreign policy lay in ruins, and there would be nothing with which to counter the Exclusionist case when Parliament met in the autumn. *The Reasons for the Indictment of the Duke of York presented to the Grand Jury of Middlesex* were printed, and with that Shaftesbury could rest content. There was no need for him to make a further attempt to present the Duke of York to the sessions at Hicks's Hall on 8 July, as some had anticipated.[2] Even without that there was talk of James returning to Scotland, and Charles joined his brother's Protestant friends in urging him to change his religion as a means of avoiding the attacks upon him. Shaftesbury's reply to the news was uncompromising. 'If the Duke should go away, that is nothing: if he should take the oaths [under the terms of the Test Act], receive the sacrament, abjure transubstantiation, that is nothing.' Even if James had professed to change his religion, few would have believed him.[3]

The government gained some consolation from the conviction of Henry Carr, the author of the *Weekly Pacquet of Advice from Rome*, a periodical whose title makes any description of its contents unnecessary: Jeffreys, prosecuting, relied on the recent opinion of the judges that no person could expose to the public any news-books without licence from the King, and some of those present showed their annoyance at the prosecution by making even more noisy demonstrations than usual. Drastic reductions in the pensions of Oates and Bedloe, and the ending of those of Dugdale and Dangerfield, were further ministerial acts of defiance, careless of the effect which they might have on London opinion.[4] At this time London seems to have been as defiantly opposed to the government as at any time in these years of crisis, stimulated, no doubt, by Monmouth and others, to the number of fifty or sixty, who dined near the Exchange, and drank

---

[1] Cf. William to Jenkins, 16/26 July, J. Dalrymple, *Memoirs* (1773), ii. 302.

[2] John Verney to Sir R. Verney, 5, 8 July, *Verney MSS.*, loc. cit.; Dowager Countess of Sunderland to Halifax, 8 July [Mary Berry], op. cit. p. 355. It was said that the jury at these sessions was less favourable than that at Westminster, since it contained several holders of offices in the Chancery Court and elsewhere.

[3] Barrillon, 1/11, 19/29 July; Dowager Countess of Sunderland to Halifax, 19 July [Mary Berry], op. cit. p. 360.

[4] *State Trials*, vii. 1111–30; newsletter of 3 July, *C.S.P.D. 1679–80*, p. 536.

their toasts to 'The King and Magna Charta' and 'The confusion of all pretending Popish successors', with rules drawn up to avoid alienating Nonconformist opinion by too much conviviality : no one was to drink more than a pint of wine, or swear.[1] And the full extent of the Londoners' hostility to the government was shown in the election of the two sheriffs for the next twelve months. On midsummer day Slingsby Bethel, a notorious former Republican whose Republicanism was too much even for Russell, and Henry Cornish, another Puritan, had been elected, but they had not qualified under the Corporation Act by taking the Anglican sacrament. On 14 July a second election was held, and the claims of Bethel and Cornish were again pressed, care having been taken that this time they had taken the sacrament first. Perhaps because the attempt to indict the Duke of York had reminded people of the importance of the sheriffs' power to select juries, there was a furious contest, with scenes of more than usual disorder in which one of the existing sheriffs was alleged to have been 'taken by the throat and pummelled in the breast'. The Bishop of London, the Recorder, Sir George Jeffreys, and Chiffinch (a striking combination) employed their various methods against Bethel and Cornish, and the King tried to offer a short list of six acceptable to himself, from which the City might choose two; but all in vain. When it came to a poll, the voting was overwhelming. The Court contemplated declaring Bethel and Cornish ineligible, while Jeffreys characteristically recommended that the present sheriffs should declare the Court candidates elected, irrespective of the minor matter of the voting; but eventually, when Bethel and Cornish were elected by a majority of two to one, the Court prudently accepted the situation, consoling itself with the reflection that 'the men of estates were (most of them) of the right side', that, on a different matter, the aldermen voted by seventeen to four 'for that which was most for the King's service', and that 'the great men' in the counties would be indignant 'to see that the dregs of the people here in London oppose themselves to the sober part as they did in the beginning of the late troubles'.[2]

Shaftesbury had not waited for the final poll before leaving London for Dorset. No doubt he felt that he could rely on the weight of opinion—and on the 'overseers of the poll', Sir Thomas Player, Alderman Pilkington, and the Huguenot merchants Papillon and Dubois. More than ever before he stood out as the great hope of the opposition, and the butt of the

---

[1] Burnet to Halifax, 3 July, op. cit. p. 39.

[2] Mansell to the Bishop of Meath, 12, 17 July, MSS. Carte 39, fos. 158, 160; Jenkins to Ormond, 17 July, *H.M.C. Ormond MSS.*, N.S. v. 349; James to William, 13 July, *Archives de la Maison Orange-Nassau*, II. v. 59; Barrillon, 15/25 July; Jenkins to Bishop of London, 16 July, *C.S.P.D. 1679–80*, p. 557, and to Hyde or Godolphin, 17 July, ibid. pp. 558–9; newsletter, 18 July, ibid. pp. 560–1; Jenkins to Skelton, 19 July, ibid. p. 564; Dowager Countess of Sunderland, 19 July, [Mary Berry], op. cit. p. 360; Sir R. Reading to Arran, 22, 27 July, MSS. Carte 243, fo. 484; Jenkins to William, 23 and 27 July, S.P. 104/67, and to Sidney, 24 July, Sidney Diary, ii. 87.

Court's pamphleteers.[1] When he transmitted the request of his Irish ally, the Bishop of Meath, that Archbishop Plunket's trial should be moved from Dundalk to Dublin, the Council found it wisest to fall in with his view.[2] Barrillon recognised him as the leader of the malcontents, and tentatively suggested to his master that if he were bribed into the French service, nothing less than 100,000 francs would do; but, in terms that rule out the possibility that Shaftesbury had been bribed at any earlier date, he went on to add that it might be better to bribe Montagu and Monmouth and hope that they would be able to handle him.[3] This curious idea rested on the fact that Montagu was temporarily on better terms with Shaftesbury than before, while the Earl was constantly seen with Monmouth, dining with Lord Cavendish and 'Mistress Nelly' at Lady Orrery's and elsewhere. Even that unbending Republican, Algernon Sidney, who had railed at Shaftesbury and been railed at in return, found it advisable to bend sufficiently to get in touch with the Earl 'to know his mind'.[4] Everyone now watched to see what Shaftesbury would do; the more moderate leaders of the opposition had long ago been passed by. By means of the petitions, the encouragement of the Irish Plot, and finally the sensational attempt to indict the King's own brother, he had taken the lead in a party which was committed to extreme measures in support of Exclusion: those who had gone so far could hardly turn back now. The same process had driven others to 'abhor' the petitions and actions which might lead to a civil war over the succession, and to commit themselves in their own way. Over against one another, indeed, stood the groups which were soon to acquire the classic names of Whigs and Tories; but in July 1680 the former were confident, and the latter feared, that if the Commons were allowed to meet the Whigs would be very much the stronger.

[1] Cf. *A Letter to the Earl of Shaftesbury, this 9th of July, 1680. From Tom Tell-Troth, a downright Englishman*, Harleian Miscellany (1810), v. 572–5, and also *Tell-Truth's Answer to Tell-Troth's Letter . . .* (1680).

[2] Bishop of Meath to Mansell, 3 July, MSS. Carte 39, fo. 154; Mansell to the bishop, 12 July, ibid. fo. 158; Gwyn to Ormond, 24 July, *H.M.C. Ormond MSS.*, N.S. v. 352.

[3] 12/22 July.

[4] Dowager Countess of Sunderland to Halifax, 8, 19, 27 July [Mary Berry], op. cit. pp. 354, 357–8, 360, 365–8. In view of the charges of unchastity sometimes levelled against Shaftesbury, it is perhaps necessary to point out that the reference in the first of these letters to his 'making love to my Lady Orrery' is jocular.

CHAPTER XXVI

WHIGS AND TORIES
(JULY 1680 – JANUARY 1681)

WHEN Shaftesbury left London for Dorset on 21 July 1680, on what was to be his last visit to his well-loved country home, he was on the eve of his fifty-ninth birthday. By this time the persistent ill-health that he had suffered all his life had undermined his constitution, and to all appearances he was a bent old man, clinging on to life by sheer will-power and a resolve to keep going at all costs until his political objectives had been attained: Dryden could never understand why he did not take the obvious course and spend his last years at ease, enjoying the wealth that he had accumulated. An anonymous poet wrote in a poem called *The Cabal*:

> Nature made him a perverse wight, whose nose
> Extracts the essence of his gouty toes;
> Double with head to tail he crawls apart:
> His body's th'emblem of his double heart.

And another observer described him, with the pungent expression characteristic of the period, as 'a little limping peer—though crazy [i.e. in body] yet in action nimble and as busy as a bodylouse'.[1] His was an active mind in an ever more decrepit body. The strain showed itself in a growing ill-temper and propensity to extreme language, even though it would be dangerous to imagine that he uttered every remark that was attributed to him. The French ambassador reported that the Earl, hearing that the King spoke of him and his followers as seditious rebels, said aloud in company that they would keep within the laws, and still find means through the laws to send him packing out of the kingdom. It is a little difficult to suppose that Shaftesbury was speaking here about the King (as Barrillon thought) and much more likely that the reference was to the Duke of York; but nonetheless the statement was an extreme one. So too was his language about Ireland. 'What! Does Ireland, the snake which we have harboured in our bosom and warmed it then when it could scarcely live, think to give law to England? To give money to make the King independent of his people, to raise an army if they be so powerful!' And he went on to say that Strafford had lost his head, 'and he did not question but to see those who thought to bring England under the same tyranny my Lord of Strafford

---

[1] Extract from letter to the Bishop of Meath, 29 June, MSS. Carte 39, fo. 152. The reference was not intended to be uncomplimentary.

did to have the same fate'. The violence of his language indicated that he had abandoned any hope of a compromise and staked everything on complete success within the short time that remained to him.[1]

Yet before he embarked upon the last struggle there was the opportunity to refresh himself on his estates for six or seven weeks. Though he enjoyed far more support in the City of London than he did among his Dorset neighbours, he never forgot that he was a land-owner and head of a family, and even when he was in the capital he constantly sent instructions to his steward. In April 1680, amid his other preoccupations, he found time to promise his son Lord Ashley four or five hundred bricks to build 'a little wall' to allow the Ashleys' mare and colt to run with his own, and to arrange for a supply of cedar to wainscot part of their house at Martin, a few miles from Wimborne St. Giles. 'One good turn deserves another', he quoted; and in return asked his son to see that his miller had the grinding of Ashley's grist. 'My best blessing to yourself and your lady and your little ones. I rest, your affectionate father . . . '. On the way down to Dorset, he passed on to John Locke, who was travelling with him, an old country remedy for a horse's sore eye: the blowing of a powder into its eye; but Locke, who was apt to note down such suggestions without putting much trust in them, did not choose to employ such an old wives' remedy when his own horse's eye was sore.[2]

Locke had returned in the previous year from an absence in France which had lasted for nearly four years, and had soon been on as intimate terms with the Earl as before his departure. How far he was admitted into his patron's secret activities, and whether he performed any political services for him at this time, it is impossible to tell; but little glimpses of their correspondence when temporarily separated suggest both the closeness of their friendship and the probability that their general political sympathies were not very different. On 20 March 1680, we find the Earl writing to Locke in Somerset, thanking him for a Cheddar cheese and in jocular terms ending a sarcastic description of the political situation by recommending Locke to the protection of the Bishop of Bath and Wells 'whose strong beer is the only spiritual thing any Somersetshire gentleman knows'. This same letter announced the Earl's decision to take his beloved grandson, now nine years old, into his own household, and his longing to consult Locke about the boy's education. At the end of July Locke spent a week at Wimborne and no doubt saw the lad and gave his advice; and then on 5 August we find Locke back in London and sending his patron the current political gossip. 'I was told today by one who had it whispered to him as a very true and serious secret, viz., that my Lord Sunderland was to go

---

[1] Barrillon, 8/18 July; Netterville to the Earl of Longford, July, *H.M.C. Ormond MSS.*, N.S. v. 351.

[2] Shaftesbury to Ashley, 26 Apr., Shaftesbury Papers, VI A, 353; Locke's Journal, 23 July, 21 Aug. MSS., Locke, f. 4.

Lord Lieutenant of Ireland, the Duke [of York] to retire thither, and that the white staff [of the Lord Treasurer] would very speedily be sent to your lordship, and that the Duchess of Portsmouth was soliciting it with all her endeavours. This, though it be so extraordinary that it seems fit to be put amongst huntsmen's stories, and therefore I have desired Mr. Percival[1] to give it to you as you are returning from the chase, yet it is apt to make one reflect upon what is very much believed, that there must be a parliament; and in preparation thereunto there is already great striving amongst those who think themselves most in danger who shall be thrown to the dogs. And who can think it other than good court-breeding that might become a duke or a duchess[2] to strain courtesy in the case, and each desire to prefer the other as most deserving?'[3]

It will be gathered from this that whether or not Shaftesbury attended the hunt, his holiday in the country did not mean that his political preoccupations could ever be put out of his mind. News reached St. Giles House of the Duke of Monmouth, who had left London two days after him for a long progress to the West, staying with his political friends all the way. This was the equivalent for the West Country of Monmouth's showing himself to the Londoners and appealing for their support. Charles had sent him word that he was not to go, but he had replied, no doubt under Shaftesbury's inspiration, that he would go unless he received a written order to the contrary. As Monmouth had expected, no one dared sign such an order, and on 23 July he left for Reading, and thence went to Bath and Bristol. He then spent some days with 'Tom of Ten Thousand' at Longleat before journeying through Somerset and on to Exeter. Here he was entertained by Sir William Courtenay and conducted into the city by a crowd estimated at as many as 10,000 horse and 1500 foot, all 'in white waistcoats and white drawers'. The King had sent instructions that his son was to be ignored by the authorities, and Leoline Jenkins, the second Secretary of State, insisted that this order had been obeyed and that few people of consequence had turned out to cheer. The 'common people' flocked to see the Duke, Jenkins reported, but 'not one gent. in 40'. What measure of truth there was in this, it is impossible to say. It is possible that the alterations in the commission of the peace in the previous winter and the official warnings made people reluctant, whatever their secret sympathies, to risk exposing themselves to the royal disfavour unnecessarily; but Jenkins had a clear motive to pass round the idea, to his correspondents abroad particularly, that 'no one who mattered' appeared for the Duke.

---

[1] Shaftesbury's banker.
[2] I.e. York or Portsmouth.
[3] These two letters are printed by Christie, ii. 361–2 and 367–9. Cf. newsletters of 10 Aug., *C.S.P.D. 1679–80*, p. 597, and Thynne Papers at Longleat, xli, fo. 198, and Barrillon, 16/26 Aug. for the rumour that Shaftesbury was to be Lord Treasurer. Maurice Cranston, *John Locke* (1957) p. 195 n., misinterprets the reference to the white staff as being to the Secretaryship of State.

What is certain is that the crowds were large, and that from the point of view of numbers at least the perambulation was a success.[1]

It is likely that the whole of this expedition had been planned by Shaftesbury, and certain that he was satisfied with its success. In the middle of it, the news arrived of a royal proclamation, dated 26 August, and declaring that Parliament would meet on 21 October. Charles had decided that he could not postpone Parliament indefinitely, and as a gesture of defiance he had brought the session forward a little from November, when he had originally proposed to hold it. As a result Shaftesbury's friends in London sent for him to the capital 'his presence being necessary to be early here to prepare and consult upon proper applications and remedies'. And after a few days' delay the Earl duly arrived back at Thanet House on 11 September and began his consultations. Shortly afterwards he was laid low with an ague, and reduced to taking the Jesuits' powder (quinine) five times within twenty-four fours: his prejudice against Popery did not extend to refusing the aid of the Jesuits' medical discoveries. He was visited by Prince Rupert and others of the nobility who were anxious about his illness, and after a week during which the political observers found it important to report on it, they were able to say that he was recovering.[2]

When he struggled back to health (if it could ever be called that) one of his more immediate tasks was to see the Irish witnesses who were beginning to arrive in droves, convinced that with a Parliament in the offing their information was likely to be better rewarded than in Dublin. Fourteen of them arrived, ragged and almost barefoot, on 16 September, complaining that they had received no encouragement from the King's Lord Lieutenant and had had to steal on board ship in the night with no money except for three pounds with which they had been supplied by 'the good bishop of Meath (who is the only Protestant bishop in that kingdom)'. In London, they were 'treated' by Oates and supplied with new shoes, and a collection was arranged for them 'in a seditious coffee-house' and at a conventicle. On 27 September one of them waited on Shaftesbury to ask him for charity for them all, and the Earl prudently directed them to apply to the Council, promising however that if the Council would not give them

---

[1] Barrillon, 24 July/3 Aug., Mansell to Bishop of Meath, 24 July, MSS. Carte 39, fo. 168; Jenkins to L. C. J. North, 24 July, *C.S.P.D. 1679–80*, p. 570; newsletter, 10 Aug., ibid. p. 597; Jenkins to Bishop of Bath and Wells, 12 Aug., ibid. p. 600; R. F[erguson] to his wife, 14 Aug., ibid. p. 604; Jenkins to William, 24 Aug., Foreign Entry Book, S.P. 104/67; newsletter, 28 Aug., *C.S.P.D. 1679–80*, p. 624; Jenkins to William, 31 Aug., S.P. 104/67; van Citters, 10/20 Sept., Add. MSS. 17677, EE; Mansell to Bishop of Meath, 12 Sept., MSS. Carte 39, fo. 198; Jenkins to William, 7 Sept., S.P. 104/67; Roger Morrice's Entering Book P, Dr. Williams's Library, fo. 265; Sir C. Lyttelton to L. Hatton, 9 Sept., *Hatton Correspondence*, i. 235–6.

[2] *C.S.P.D. 1679–80*, p. 621; [? Mansell to Bishop of Meath], 31 Aug., MSS. Carte 39, fo. 192; [? Vernon] to Arran, 14 Sept., ibid. fo. 203; Lady Russell to Russell, 17 Sept., [? Mary Berry], *Life of Lady Russell* (1819), pp. 225–6; newsletter, 21 Sept., *C.S.P.D. 1680–1*, p. 34; Jenkins to Ormond, 25 Sept., *H.M.C. Ormond MSS.*, N.S. v. 433.

relief he would find a way to do so until Parliament met. In the meantime Hetherington was said to 'have the guiding of them', and their stories were husbanded until the beginning of the session.[1]

But the main topic of conversation at Thanet House was not the Irish witnesses, but the question whether the Duke of York would leave the country and the dissensions which his presence was causing amongst the King's own ministers. Many believed that the King would sacrifice his brother when Parliament met. The attempt to indict James as a recusant made it quite clear that he would be attacked, as James himself recognized; and if the Commons impeached him, the Lords would find it difficult to avoid sending him to the Tower, since in Danby's case in 1679 they had eventually admitted the principle that those impeached of high treason should be committed to custody. James wanted to brazen it out. Seeing a stag attack and kill some of the dogs which were hunting it, he remarked that that was precisely what he would be reduced to by the English—an observation on which some sinister interpretations were inevitably placed. When he dined with the Artillery Company in the City the populace gave him a distinctly cool reception, and by the end of September Barrillon's informants were saying that the King's brother could only be saved by a miracle.[2]

Amongst those who drew their own conclusions were the King's mistress, the Duchess of Portsmouth, and his most active minister, the Earl of Sunderland. In these summer months of 1680 the two were not collaborating with each other as closely as at other times, but each had reasons for negotiating with the opposition. Royal mistresses are rarely popular, and the Duchess knew that she was more hated than most as a Frenchwoman and a Papist. She knew that in the previous winter some members of Parliament had drawn up articles of impeachment against her in readiness for the next session; and the attempt in June to present her as a common nuisance had convinced her that her enemies meant business. She was no altruist, and had no intention of being ruined along with the Duke of York if she could make her own peace with the opposition. We have seen Locke sneering at the Duke and the Duchess as each strove to make the other the first to be thrown to the dogs, and reporting stories that the Duchess was soliciting the Lord Treasurer's staff for the Earl of Shaftesbury.[3] Whether or not the Duchess went to such lengths, there can be no doubt that she had parted from James, and that she met the Whig peer Lord Howard of Escrick. James was certain that through him she had

---

[1] [?Mansell], 31 Aug., as in previous note, and 14 Sept., ibid. fo. 200; Longford to Ormond, 18 Sept., *H.M.C. Ormond MSS.*, N.S. v. 431–2; Jenkins to Godolphin, 17, 18, 28 Sept., *C.S.P.D. 1680–1*, pp. 24, 25, 43.

[2] Longford to Arran, 24 Aug., MSS. Carte 243, fo. 506; James to William, 10, 19 Sept., *Archives de la Maison Orange-Nassau*, II. v. 418–19, 420; Barrillon, 6/16, 9/19 Sept., 27 Sept./7 Oct.; Mansell to Bishop of Meath, 16 Sept., MSS. Carte 39, fo. 204.

[3] p. 586 above.

'made her conditions with my Lord Shaftesbury and the factious party';
and it is possible that the thought crossed her mind that, if illegitimate
sons were being considered for the succession, her own son, the Duke of
Richmond, might come into the reckoning.[1]

Sunderland was not in the same danger of impeachment, but all his
attempts to find an alternative to Exclusion had failed. William of Orange
had shown himself reluctant to accept Sunderland's repeated and pressing
invitations to come over to England, and early in September he left on a
prolonged visit to the Duke of Zell and the Elector of Brandenburg.
Plainly he was reluctant to risk burning his fingers by intervening in
English politics: it was safer to stay aloof until the situation was clearer.[2]
Deprived of the possibility of William's presence, Sunderland also began
to suspect that in the last resort Charles would abandon his brother to the
Parliament: perhaps, indeed, Charles was simply waiting until he was in
such a hopelessly inferior position that he could honourably consent to
Exclusion, saying that he had no choice. If this was so, the policy of
prudence for Sunderland would be one of 'co-operating with the inevitable'
—and with Shaftesbury. At the beginning of September he and the Duchess
of Portsmouth made no bones about saying that it was not their fault that
James had not left the country; by the end of the month they were saying
that the King should not ruin himself for anyone's sake, and the general
conclusion was that if two people so close to the King were talking like
this, then Charles was not likely to defend James to the point of exposing
himself to 'going on his travels again'. As Shaftesbury recovered from his
ague, he found that everything seemed to be moving in the way that he
wanted, and he professed himself to be amazed that Parliament had been
summoned in these circumstances, when, he said, there was not the least
probability of their 'doing good to the King'.[3]

The last three weeks before the new session were full of behind-the-
scenes activity, and Thanet House must have been one of the busiest
places. On the one hand Shaftesbury was negotiating with Sunderland
and the Duchess of Portsmouth, and on the other he was discussing with
his supporters the tactics to be followed when Parliament met. In the
nature of things it is impossible to be certain what agreements (if any)
were reached, for it could not be expected that they would be committed
to paper. But in regard to the first set of negotiations, well-informed
observers like Barrillon (who through Ralph Montagu knew something

---

[1] Barrillon, 18/28 Dec. 1679, 19/29 Jan. 1680; Reading to Arran, Candlemas 1680,
MSS. Carte 39, fo. 107; Barrillon, 30 Aug./9 Sept.; Life of James II, ed. J. S. Clarke
(1816), i. 599–600; Burnet, Supplement, p. 137.

[2] Sidney Diary, 4, 16 July, ii. 78–79, 84; J. P. Kenyon, 'Charles II and William of
Orange in 1680', in Bull. Inst. Hist. Res. (1957), pp. 95–101; William to Jenkins, 3/13
Sept., J. Dalrymple, Memoirs (1773), ii. 303.

[3] Barrillon, 2/12 Sept., 27 Sept./7 Oct.; Jenkins to Godolphin, 30 Sept., C.S.P.D.
1680–1, p. 45.

of the opposition's activities) and Henry Sidney (who was close to Sunder-land) were sure that they were serious on both sides. According to Sidney, Shaftesbury, Monmouth, Russell and others had undertaken 'to do great matters for the King, if he will part with the Duke'; and Barrillon was told that Shaftesbury had said that if any concessions to the opposition were to be made, they should be made before the meeting of Parliament, when the House's excitement would be beyond control and it would be too late to propose any accommodation. It was widely rumoured that Monmouth had been received both by the King and by the Duchess of Portsmouth. Some said that Shaftesbury would be Lord Treasurer, while Monmouth recovered the Mastership of the Horse and other offices; this was the interpretation which was placed upon the Earl's reported statements that he did not at all want to do anything which would result in the diminution of the King's authority, still less anything that would create confusion or discord. Rather would he at every opportunity show himself one of the King's truest subjects; but, he said, with the exception that so far as in him lay he was trying to prevent the government from becoming arbitrary and to ensure that the Protestant religion should remain inviolate. But these words, however outwardly polite, really constituted a declaration of intransigence on the main point of Exclusion. If anyone was to weaken it would be the other side, and the story which reached the French ambassador was that Sunderland and the Duchess of Portsmouth had promised Shaftesbury and Monmouth that the King would grant all that Parliament asked, in return for supplies; that Parliament should give Charles power (like Henry VIII) to dispose of the succession by will; and that Monmouth, Shaftesbury and Russell should return to office. But nothing was ever heard in public of this idea of settling the succession; and all that can be said with certainty is that from the negotiations Shaftesbury conceived the hope that Sunderland and the Duchess would help to persuade the King to consent to Exclusion.[1]

In this expectation he planned his tactics for the session. But even now, two years after the beginning of the Exclusion crisis, although his abilities made him stand out head and shoulders in the opposition, he could not necessarily impose his wishes upon them. On some points there was a ready agreement. Having learned the lesson of the previous session, they would not again allow themselves to be diverted from their main purpose by pressing on with the immediate impeachment either of Danby or of the five Catholic peers; these trials, with the contentious issues of the validity of Danby's pardon and the right of the bishops to take part in them, would be put into cold storage so that the Commons could concentrate on the main

---

[1] Sidney to William, 7 Oct., *Archives de la Maison Orange-Nassau*, II. v. 423; Sidney Diary, 10 Oct., ii. 109; Barrillon, 4/14, 7/17, 14/24, 18/28 Oct., 25 Oct./4 Nov.; Burlington to Ormond, 12 Oct., *H.M.C. Ormond MSS.*, N.S. v. 445; Longford to Arran, 16 Oct., ibid. v. 454; van Citters, 5/15, 8/18 Oct., Add. MSS. 17677, SSS; Burnet, *Supplement*, pp. 136-7.

task of excluding the Duke of York. But there was some disagreement about the best way of doing this. Some, like Russell, wanted to impeach James of high treason and press the charges home. Shaftesbury wanted to content himself with passing an Exclusion Bill, which would be more moderate—and more likely to survive the opposition of the Lords and the King. It was probably for this reason, as much as the fact that the retiring sheriffs had packed the new grand juries with Royalist supporters,[1] that he made no further attempt to indict James as a recusant at the new quarter sessions in October. If James were to go into exile, an Exclusion Bill would do all that was necessary. But Russell and others hoped that James would stay in England, and were certain that if he were once arrested he would lose his head. For once Russell opposed the Earl, pointing out with a certain specious logic that James might not come back in the Earl's time, but that he and his friends were younger and had reason to fear James's vengeance.[2]

This problem was settled by James's departure for Scotland on the day before Parliament was due to meet. A faction among Charles's ministers had been pressing for James's return into exile for some time: it included Sunderland, Godolphin, Essex (who had been reconciled to Shaftesbury and had, it was said, been promised the Lord Lieutenancy of Ireland in return) and Halifax, whose love for Shaftesbury was no greater than it had been, but who liked James no more. James paid no heed to the representations of a deputation to him, but Charles lent an ear to them, and even when James suggested that this would serve to confirm some of Shaftesbury's taunting words about the King's 'instability', he permitted the Council to debate the matter. The alternative was a dissolution, and this was far too dangerous. Finally on 16 October the Privy Council, reversing a previous vote three days earlier, decided by 11 votes to 7 that James must go. Charles's paradoxical comment was that he must go, precisely because there were so many people who voted for him: his presence in London in such circumstances would be like a red rag to a bull, to moderates as well as extremists. Taught by his experience in Danby's case, Charles declined to give his brother a royal pardon, and contented himself with a verbal promise that he would not consent to any act of attainder against him. On 20 October he accompanied James down river; and that evening the courtiers, with their eyes keenly fixed on him, noticed that he was in a particularly good humour at the Duchess of Portsmouth's. James, Sunderland, and Shaftesbury, each from his different point of view, were justified in doubting whether Charles would really stand by his brother when the crisis came.[3]

---

[1] Jenkins to Godolphin, 30 Sept., 4, 6, 7 Oct., *C.S.P.D. 1680–1*, pp. 44, 50, 53, 54; Mansell to Bishop of Meath, MSS. Carte 39, fo. 214.   [2] Barrillon, 18/28 Oct.

[3] The struggle to get James to leave, and his unsuccessful resistance, can be followed in the *Life of James II*, i. 593–8; Temple, *Works*, i. 450–2; Sidney to William, 7, 19, 22 Oct.,

It was all the more urgent for the opposition to decide who should succeed if James could indeed be successfully excluded. Monmouth's chances had strengthened considerably since the last Parliament. His 'Western progress' in August and September had been deliberately designed to build up his popularity; and he had followed it up with visits to Oxford and to Hampshire. At Oxford the townsmen greeted him with shouts of 'God bless the Protestant Duke', and 'No York, no bishop, no university', and drank healths to the Protestant Duke and Magna Charta, and confusion to the Vice-Chancellor and the Bishop of Oxford, who wisely kept the undergraduates inside their colleges. All this contributed powerfully to the image of Monmouth as 'the Protestant Duke' in contrast to the Catholic one. Protestantism was the most convenient banner under which to fight, though the religion of the notorious rake Lord Lovelace, who rode about shouting that 'he was for a Protestant Duke, no Papist, and God damn him, he was for the Protestant religion', can only have been nominal: this was the most convenient way of subsuming into one slogan all the fears of those who hated the political, as well as the religious, policies for which James stood, and who looked to Monmouth as an alternative. It is not surprising that Monmouth refused offers from the Court that he could have his places back if he would go into temporary exile. When he returned to London on 13 October about forty coaches paid prompt calls upon him; and to build up support among the Londoners still further he promptly took a house in the City, in Bishopsgate Street.[1]

Yet there were many who had doubts about the justice of replacing the King's brother by his bastard, and who cast about for a different solution. It is significant that when the Queen fell ill there was an immediate comparison of the claims of two German princesses and the daughter of the Earl of Manchester as possible brides for the King; but the death of the Queen, which would have transformed the political situation, did not take place.[2] Of much more permanent importance were the claims of James's daughter, Mary, and her husband the Prince of Orange, to the succession. There were many who thought that if James was to be passed over, the claims of Mary and William were stronger and more reputable than those of Monmouth—even though the French ambassador in The Hague, D'Avaux, was insinuating to members of the House of Commons that

---

Groen van Prinsterer, II. v. 422–4, 430, 431; Sidney Diary, 11, 12, 13, 16, 19 Oct., ii. 109–10, 112–14; Barrillon, 14/24, 18/28, 21/31 Oct.; van Citters, 12/22, 15/25 Oct., Add. MSS., 17677, SSS; James to William, 12, 15, 19 Oct., Groen van Prinsterer, II. v. 426–8; Jenkins to William, 12 Oct., S.P. 104/67, fo. 14; Lyttelton to Hatton, 12, 14 Oct., Hatton Correspondence, i. 238–9; Gwyn to Ormond, 24 Oct., H.M.C. Ormond MSS., N.S. v. 459; Anna M. Crinò, Il Popish Plot (Rome, 1954), p. 135.

[1] Cooke to Ormond, 15 Oct., H.M.C. Ormond MSS., N.S. v. 449; Jenkins to Godolphin, 20, 21 Sept., C.S.P.D. 1680–1, pp. 31, 33; James to Mary, 23 Sept., Groen van Prinsterer, II. v. 421; Barrillon, 9/19, 20/30 Sept.; newsletter, 14 Oct., in Thynne Papers at Longleat, xli, fos. 219–20; newsletter, 16 Oct., C.S.P.D. 1680–1, p. 62.

[2] Crinò, op. cit. p. 133.

there was a secret understanding between William and his Stuart uncles.[1] So far as Shaftesbury was concerned, he found it prudent not to commit himself publicly to any one solution of the problem. He was commonly supposed to be in close association with Monmouth (though not with all the Duke's friends, such as Ralph Montagu), but there is no means of knowing whether he made any specific promises to him. He may still have been undecided, or he may have preferred to remain uncommitted; and in any case it was prudent to enlist the support of all factions of the opposition in the effort to declare James incapable of succeding, before he had to divide them by naming the successor.

This, then, was the situation when Charles at last met his Parliament on 21 October 1680. On the previous day Shaftesbury, Monmouth and some hundred members of both houses of Parliament had dined together at the Sun tavern behind the Exchange, and had deputed some of their number, and a joiner named College who was soon to earn notoriety, to search the cellars under the Parliament House for a new Gunpowder Plot.[2] For many members of the Commons particularly the day had come when they could release some of their pent-up frustrations. It was over a year since they had been elected, and in the interval many had seen themselves or their friends turned off the commission of the peace and out of the deputy-lieutenancies. Their mood, as they listened to the King's opening speech, can readily be imagined. When he promised to give them 'the fullest satisfaction your hearts can wish, for the security of the Protestant religion', there was loud applause; but Charles went on to amplify this by repeating his reservation in the last Parliament, that the remedies must be consistent with the preservation of the succession 'in its due and legal course of descent'. When the Commons were back in their own Chamber, they promptly elected Russell's nominee, William Williams, as Speaker, instead of waiting for a Privy Councillor to make an official nomination in the traditional way. Williams did not make the customary request for royal approval, but Charles, warned by his experience in March 1679, thought it best not to contest this choice.[3]

The opposition's next steps were as smoothly taken as this planned election of the Speaker. In the Lords they began by hurrying through a bill for regulating the trial of peers, aimed at depriving the King of the possibility of packing a court with selected lords to try a peer during a recess of Parliament. Shaftesbury did not appear in the House until the 23rd, when, having taken the oaths, he observed with a sneer that since the trial of Sir George Wakeman the Popish Plot had been looked upon as

---

[1] *Négotiations de M. le Comte D'Avaux* (Paris, 1754), i. 55–56.

[2] Luttrell, i. 57; S. Ellis to J. Ellis, 23 Oct., Add. MSS. 28930, fo. 186; *State Trials*, viii. 624.

[3] *L.J.* xiii. 610–11, 613; van Leeuwen and van Citters, 22 Oct./1 Nov., Add. MSS. 17677, EE; Longford to Ormond, 23 Oct., *H.M.C. Ormond MSS.*, N.S. v. 456–7; Barrillon, 25 Oct./4 Nov.

a pretended plot, while the sham (Meal Tub) Plot was believed; and moved
for a committee to receive information. The Court majority in the House
dared not refuse to set up a committee, or to address the King for a proclamation offering pardon to any Plot informer who came in within two
months. Charles detected a trap in this. He feared that such a proclamation
would tacitly concede that Parliament should remain in session for two
months while inquiries were pursued, and tried to evade it by extending
the offer of pardon for an indefinite period; but when this came to the
notice of the Commons, Titus, Boscawen, Bennet, and other members
protested that this gave unlimited freedom to traitors, and the King found
it prudent to beat a retreat and accept the two months' limitation.[1] In any
case since the last Parliament there had accumulated a considerable back-
log of new witnesses whose evidence the Plot committee, under Shaftesbury's guidance, proceeded to put before the Lords. One such was
Francisco de Feria, a Portuguese Jew, who said that he had first been
converted to Catholicism in 1675 in Antwerp by three of Sir George
Wakeman's sisters; that in 1678 he had become interpreter to the former
Portuguese ambassador in London, who had tried to get him to kill, first
Oates and Bedloe, and then Shaftesbury by throwing a 'hand-grenado'
into his coach; and that the ambassador, after Wakeman's acquittal, had
expressed his gratitude for Sir Philip Lloyd's evidence and Lord Chief
Justice Scroggs's conduct of the trial. If Wakeman's acquittal had cast
some doubt on the credibility of the Plot witnesses and freed Queen
Catherine of Braganza from the danger of being involved in the conviction of her physician, Feria's evidence counter-balanced this and reopened the possibility of an attack on the Queen in whose interests the
ambassador had obviously been acting. Secondly, Shaftesbury reported
from the Committee information from Arnold (once again) about Papists
in his native county of Monmouthshire, where, it was said, the magistrates
had declined to take any action because the sheriff's daughter was a Papist
and married to the agent of the Marquis of Worcester, one of the King's
Tory councillors. And, thirdly and taking up most of the Plot Committee's
time, was the investigation of the 'Irish Plot'. Before the opening of the
session Shaftesbury's agent Hetherington had petitioned the Council that
Archbishop Plunket should be brought over from Ireland to London for
his trial; and since the petition had been supported by the opinions of
legal luminaries like Pollexfen, Pemberton, and Sir William Jones, the
Council had found it advisable to agree to this. The result was that the
committee was confronted by a flock of rascally Irishmen, all offering
'evidence' in a brogue which was only partly intelligible; and a special sub-
committee, consisting of Shaftesbury, Essex, the Earl of Burlington and
Viscount Fauconberg, was appointed to go through the relevant papers,

---

[1] *L.J.* xiii. 614–17; Col. E. Vernon to Arran, 23 Oct., *H.M.C. Ormond MSS.*, N.S. v.
458; Barrillon, 25 Oct./4 Nov.; *C.J.* ix. 640, 642; Grey, vii. 354–7.

'and given permission to report direct to the House', with Shaftesbury as its spokesman.[1]

The Plot Committee's activities, and the statements of the succession of witnesses whom Shaftesbury brought from the committee to parade before the House of Lords, all served the purpose of heightening the tension in readiness for more important events, which would begin in the Lower House. Here too the first step was to raise the tension by some 'revelations' which would hint that the Duke of York had been directly involved in the Popish Plot, and not simply been the beneficiary intended by the Jesuits. In view of Titus Oates's explicit statements to the contrary in 1678, he could not be produced. William Bedloe's carefully staged remarks on his bed of sickness at Bristol in August, to the effect that he had seen letters at Rome proving James's guilt of 'all but what tended to the King's death', might have served the purpose, had not Bedloe's professions of his readiness to appear cheerfully before the Lord of Hosts been involuntarily translated into reality.[2] And so it was left to Thomas Dangerfield to appear before the Commons on 26 October, and, speaking 'with great ease, clearness and presence of mind', to say that he had been three times brought into James's presence by Lord Peterborough. James, he boldly declared, had proposed that he should kill the King, and given him twenty guineas in the meantime, while Peterborough had 'encouraged him to go on with it courageously'.[3]

It was a most improbable story, and in Lord Castlemaine's case four months earlier it had been shown that, as a convicted felon, Dangerfield was valueless as a witness in a law-court. It is noticeable that in the debate the opposition leaders carefully refrained from identifying themselves with any of Dangerfield's statements, and indeed they made no reference to them. But Russell moved, in an obviously prepared speech, that the House should 'consider the danger we are in, and provide such effectual means to secure the government and religion, and quiet the just fears and apprehensions of the people, and provide against a Popish successor'. In speeches which had equally obviously been concerted with Russell, Sir Henry Capel and Sir Francis Winnington supported his motion, lingering skilfully on what they knew were sore points with many members: the turning out of Whigs from the commission of the peace, the official discountenancing of the petitions for the calling of Parliament, the official approval of the addresses 'abhorring' those petitions, and the action of the judges in dismissing the grand juries in June before the Duke of York

---

[1] *L.J.* xiii. 618–32; *H.M.C. House of Lords MSS. 1678–88*, pp. 145–6, 163, 167–8, 170, 207–8, 219, 252; Barrillon, 1/11 Nov.; Jenkins to Godolphin, 6 Oct., *C.S.P.D. 1680–1*, p. 53; Longford to Ormond, 30 Oct., 2 Nov., *H.M.C. Ormond MSS.*, N.S. v. 468, 474–5; Arran to Ormond, 30 Oct., ibid. v. 470; newsletter, 2 Nov., *C.S.P.D. 1680–1*, p. 76.

[2] *Lives of the Norths*, ed. A. Jessop (1890), i. 157–62.

[3] Longford to Ormond, 26 Oct., *H.M.C. Ormond MSS.*, N.S. v. 461–2; Jenkins, 26 Oct., *C.S.P.D. 1680–1*, p. 68.

could be indicted as a recusant. Russell's motion was carried *nemine contradicente*. Next day Laurence Hyde and Sir Leoline Jenkins tried a counter-attack on behalf of the Court, by drawing attention to the weaknesses in Dangerfield's evidence, and, without anyone going to the latter's defence, it was agreed that his written evidence be left sealed up in the Speaker's custody. But the House then proceeded to agree 'that it is the undoubted right of the subjects of England to petition the King for the calling and sitting of Parliament, and redressing of grievances', and in a few days to expel Sir Francis Wythens, the M.P. for Westminster, who had been prominent in managing the Westminster address of April 1680, 'abhorring' petitions. This looks like a piece of spite on the part of the majority in the Commons; but it must be remembered that many honestly thought that petitioning was a true liberty of Englishmen (and most of all petitioning that an elected Parliament should be allowed to meet), and believed that opponents of the right to petition were betrayers of the liberties of England. More vindictive was the expulsion of Sir Robert Cann, M.P. for Bristol, for allegedly saying that there was no Popish Plot, but a Presbyterian Plot. Here a sincere indignation merged into a determination to intimidate those who did not share the view of the majority.[1]

Not all this was necessarily part of a 'master plan' controlled by Shaftesbury. One observer commented on the tendency of those members who were new to Parliament 'to herd together', and to pay no attention to many of the old leaders of the Country Party, other than Russell, Titus, Harbord, Winnington, and Bennet.[2] Many were not very amenable to 'party discipline' and were liable to be carried away in the heat of the moment. But the House's resolution on 30 October that each day's Votes of the House should be printed fits in well with Shaftesbury's constant desire to get the maximum publicity for the opposition's proceedings in Parliament, in his endeavour to enlist 'out of doors' support. On the same day Russell suggested that a date be fixed to consider the prevention of a Popish successor, and Dugdale told the House that a Jesuit had told him that the Duke of York had promised Coleman that 'order should be taken to keep Godfrey from doing any hurt, which in a few days was performed by his death'.[3] It was no wonder that King Charles was unusually bad-tempered at this time, and that the Duchess of Portsmouth cried all one Sunday.[4] Monmouth, however, was at the height of his expectations. He had removed the baton sinister from the arms upon his coach, was preceded into the Parliament House by numbers of gentlemen walking bareheaded, and

---

[1] *C.J.* ix. 640–43; Grey, vii. 357–91; Clarke, op. cit. i. 601–3.

[2] Longford to Ormond, 30 Oct., *H.M.C. Ormond MSS.*, N.S. v. 467.

[3] *C.J.* ix. 643; Grey, vii. 391–3; *Letters of the Hon. Algernon Sydney to the Hon. Henry Savile* (1742), pp. 165–6 (31 Oct.).

[4] Sidney Diary, 22, 24, 27, 28 Oct., ii. 114, 116.

when he attended the Lord Mayor's Feast 'was received with wonderful acclamations by the rabble below and the gallants above in the windows'.[1] The ever-optimistic Sir Leoline Jenkins wrote cheerfully to William of Orange that 'it is certain the major part of the House are honest worthy persons and men of great estates: if they follow their own judgement all things are safe'[2]; but his fellow-Secretary of State Sunderland was more realistic and appealed frantically to William to come over, and use his influence, not to divert the Exclusion Bill, but to thwart Monmouth and preserve his own interests by persuading the King to give way in the clash which was imminent over the Bill.[3]

The crisis was now at hand. The Exclusion Bill was rushed through the House of Commons in precisely nine days, beginning on 2 November, when Shaftesbury's friend Russell began by moving a repetition of the motion of 27 April 1679, 'that the Duke of York being a Papist, and the hopes of his coming such to the Crown, hath given the greatest countenance and encouragement to the present designs and conspiracies of the Papists against the King and the Protestant religion'. It was William Harbord who elaborated on this, referred to Coleman's letters and the recent evidence of Dangerfield and Dugdale, deduced that 'till the Papists see that the Duke cannot be King, the King's life will be in danger', and moved for an Exclusion Bill. The attempts of Court spokesmen to argue that Exclusion would mean civil war, that Scotland and Ireland might not accept it, that the Duke might die first, that a grand committee should investigate 'expedients', and that James's right was indefeasible, were all swept away, and in the end, with only one member daring to shout No, and others leaving to avoid the vote, the House resolved that an Exclusion Bill be brought in, and appointed Russell and eighteen others to draw it up. They wasted no time. In two days Russell introduced the bill, and it received its first reading. Sir Leoline Jenkins, an honest, dull supporter of the established order, pluckily opposed the bill, on the grounds that it was inconsistent with the oath of allegiance which all had taken to the King, 'his heirs and successors', that it reduced England to an elective monarchy, and increased the danger of a civil war. Most of all, 'when God gives us a King in his wrath, it is not in our power to change him; we cannot require any qualifications; we must take him as he is'. The Exclusionists were not disposed to accept this philosophy that James was God-given, and in the 400 members present there were not enough supporters of James

[1] Christopher Ph[ilipson] to D. [Fleming], 23 Oct., 6 Nov., *H.M.C. Le Fleming MSS.*, pp. 172, 174; Sidney to Savile, 31 Oct., op. cit. p. 165; S. Ellis to J. Ellis, 30 Oct., Add. MSS. 28930, fo. 188; O. Klopp, *Der Fall des Hauses Stuart* (*Vienna, 1875–88*), ii. 293–4.
[2] S.P. 104/67, fo. 16.
[3] This is my reading of the evidence in Sidney Diary, 31 Oct., 3, 4 Nov., ii. 120–1 and Add. MSS. 32681, fo. 79; Lady Sunderland to Sidney, [5] Nov., ibid. fo. 69; Sunderland to William, 1 Nov., Groen van Prinsterer, II. v. 435–6; Godolphin to William, 1 Nov., ibid.

to force a vote.[1] Two more days, and there came the second reading, preceded by an account by the plot informer Jennison to maintain the required heat of indignation.

At this point a difficulty arose. It was noticed that, unlike the Exclusion Bill of 1679, this bill did not provide that the crown should descend as though James were naturally dead, that is, to his children; it simply said that James should be excluded and left open the question whether, if he were disabled from the succession, anyone could inherit through him. The opponents of Exclusion insisted that the succession could not thus be left uncertain, counting on a split between the supporters of Monmouth to whose advantage the vagueness of the bill would be, and those of Princess Mary and her husband, William of Orange, who wanted the interests of the Prince and Princess safeguarded, and were joined by Sir William Hickman and other allies of Halifax. After a debate (in which one or two members like Titus argued, significantly, against the nomination of a successor in the bill, because the possibility of Charles's remarriage must not be ruled out) the House eventually accepted the obvious compromise and instructed that the bill be amended in committee, so that the exclusion should extend to the person of the Duke of York only. It was Shaftesbury's friend, Russell, who on 8 November moved the proviso in committee, to the effect that if James survived the King, the crown should 'descend to such person . . . as should inherit the same, in case the Duke were dead'. This was a satisfactory compromise. Monmouth's supporters had failed to carry the original wording of the bill, which might have implied the exclusion of James's children along with James; the supporters of Mary and William had failed to get them named as successors in the bill. Monmouth's supporters could still hope for a later bill declaring that he was Charles's legitimate son and his heir; the supporters of Mary and William could maintain that in the meantime their claims were better. The cracks in the unity of the Exclusionists were papered over, and the bill went forward.[2] An attempt at a diversion by the King, who sent a message once again to accept any remedies 'provided they be such as may consist with preserving the succession of the Crown in its due and legal course of descent' and urging the House to turn its attention to the prosecution of the Plot, had no effect; and on 11 November, after the clerks had been made to sit up all night to engross it, the third reading took place. After a debate one feature of which was the way in which former opponents of Exclusion like Sir Henry Capel, Sir Francis Winnington and Cavendish spoke strongly in favour of it as the only means of protecting posterity from Popery,

[1] *C.J.* ix. 645–6; Grey, vii. 395–413, 418–21; Clarke, op. cit. i. 603–7; Cooke to Ormond, 2 Nov., *H.M.C. Ormond MSS.*, N.S. v. 475; van Leeuwen and van Citters, 5/15 Nov., Add. MSS. 17677, SSS.

[2] *C.J.* ix. 647–8; Grey, vii. 425–30, 431–3; Barrillon, 8/18 Nov., 11/21 Nov. Some writers imply that Russell's proviso was a compromise worked out behind the scenes, but it embodied the instruction of the House to its committee on 6 Nov.

slavery and bloodshed, the courtiers dared not even challenge a division. Just nine days after the House had resolved that an Exclusion Bill be introduced, Russell was ordered to take the completed bill up to the House of Lords.[1]

Russell and a few colleagues duly did so, only to find that the Lords had already adjourned for the day.[2] Next day they could have made another attempt, but they did not do so. At this late stage, when everything appeared to be going so well, it suddenly became probable that the bill could get no further; and a belated reconsideration was necessary.

During all these debates Shaftesbury had probably done much to arrange the bill's smooth progress, without serious interruptions or digressions. Not all the Exclusionists admired and followed him without question, but it was no accident that his close friend and ally Russell was so prominent. The very smoothness of the operation, with only the slight delay over the second reading, implied a leadership which, since Russell himself scarcely had the required qualities, could have come from no one but the Earl. All this had been done in the expectation that the Commons' overwhelmingly strong front would demoralize the opposition of the House of Lords and the King, and that the two latter estates of Parliament could be reluctantly induced to accept Exclusion, as they had accepted Strafford's attainder in 1641. Suddenly it became clear that this expectation could not be immediately fulfilled.

Shaftesbury had been busily continuing his efforts to produce the right atmosphere in the Lords. On 4 November he had reported from the committee on the Irish plot, and Murphy and his colleagues incriminated Archbishop Plunket and others, and complained bitterly of being discouraged from giving information by the Lord Lieutenant of Ireland, the Duke of Ormond. But the House found Murphy so unintelligible when he spoke at the bar that he had to be allowed simply to swear a written examination; and the peers were not impressed either by that or the evidence of the other witnesses.[3] On 9 November, Lord Conway, not the subtlest of politicians, made an astonishingly accurate forecast of the majority by which the peers would throw out the bill when it reached them. At the most thirty would vote for the bill, and fifty temporal peers, plus the bishops, would be against it.[4] There remained the possibility that the King might be persuaded to use his influence to reverse this majority, and it was widely believed that Sunderland had promised the Exclusionists that he would be able to do this. So too had the Duchess of Portsmouth,

[1] *C.J.* ix. 648–51; Grey, vii. 433, 439–59; Jenkins to William, 9 Nov., Groen van Prinsterer, II. v. 437–8; S. Ellis to J. Ellis, 7 [really 9] Nov., Add. MSS. 28930, fo. 191; Jenkins to William, 12 Nov., SP.. 104/67, fo. 17ᵛ.

[2] Barrillon, 11/21 Nov.

[3] *L.J.* xiii. 633–54; Arran to Ormond, 6, 9 Nov., *H.M.C. Ormond MSS.*, N.S. v. 477, 484; Barrillon, 8/18 Nov.

[4] Conway to Ormond, 9 Nov., *H.M.C. Ormond MSS.*, N.S. v. 486.

who in return had been left unmolested. The Exclusionists believed that
Charles would weaken, give way to the inevitable, and encourage the Lords
to do the same, as in 1641 and on other more recent occasions; and even
Tories feared that Charles would desert his friends. There was a story that
Charles had privately consented to the bill, and that a man had been sent
to the bishops to prepare them for it, and to swing their votes in favour of a
measure which would bring about 'a good correspondence' between the two
Houses and therefore be acceptable to the King. But on 9 November (over
Sunderland's opposition) the King killed this story by sending the message
to the Commons referred to previously,[1] in which he reaffirmed that he
would accept all remedies *provided that* the succession was preserved 'in
its due and legal course of descent'. A few optimists among the Exclusionists argued that Charles would have to say this in any case, even if in secret
he wished his hand to be forced. But to the discerning it was clear that, so
far from persuading a reluctant House of Lords to accept the bill, Charles
intended to encourage them to throw it out at the very first reading.[2]

Contrary to expectation, Charles had held firm to his brother, Sunderland
was unable to keep his bargain with the Whigs, and the Exclusion Bill,
instead of continuing its triumphant progress, was going to be thrown out.
Not surprisingly, Russell and his friends refrained from carrying the bill
to the Lords for a few days, while Shaftesbury cast about for a way of
bringing more pressure to bear. The Lord Mayor, Sir Patience Ward
(whose political views were more extreme than those of his predecessor
Clayton), called a Common Council which agreed on an address to the King,
thanking him for allowing Parliament to meet and for his care of the
Protestant religion, and asking him to accept his Parliament's advice.
Charles's reply was unusually brusque: He did not need to be reminded
of the needs of Protestantism by petitions and addresses, he said; and he
went on to tell the City's deputation that they were meddling in things
that were not their concern, and warned them to beware of incendiaries
who endeavoured to make divisions between him and his people. After
this failure, there were still some members who hoped that something
would turn up and rescue the bill, and there were rumours of a new witness
who would serve their turn; but by 15 November it was impossible to
hold back any longer, and an imposing deputation led by Russell and
including the Lord Mayor (by virtue of his seat in the Commons) carried
the bill up to the Lords to meet its fate.[3]

Just before the crowd of M.P.s reached the Upper House, they were

---

[1] p. 598 above.

[2] Christopher Philipson to D. F[leming], 6 Nov., *H.M.C. Le Fleming MSS.*, pp. 173–4;
Roger Morrice, 6 Nov., Entering Book P (Dr. Williams's Library), fo. 276; Barrillon,
11/21 Nov.; Reresby, 7 Nov., p. 202; Clarke, op. cit. i. 614–15; J. Macpherson, *Original
Papers* (1776), i. 107.

[3] Barrillon, 15/25, 18/28 Nov.; Jenkins to William, 12 Nov., S.P. 104/67, fos. 17ᵛ–18;
Longford to Ormond, 13 Nov., *H.M.C. Ormond MSS.*, N.S. v. 487; Grey, vii. 475–6.

preceded by two lords who reported that there was a man at the door 'who had the most desperate treason to reveal that ever was heard within those walls'. This was none other than Thomas Dangerfield, produced at the right moment in accordance with Shaftesbury's well-known technique of using an informer to supply the prologue to a critical debate. His information was substantially that which he had presented to the Commons on 26 October, and which the Lords had not yet heard. He spoke of interviews, which with Lord Peterborough's aid he had had with the Duke of York in the autumn of 1679. In the first of these, he said, James had spoken with approval of the 'Sham' or 'Meal Tub' plot to frame the 'Presbyterian' opposition; in the second James had been concerned at Dangerfield's initial refusal to kill the King, but when Dangerfield offered to attempt it if James personally ordered it, James had given him twenty guineas. Further, Dangerfield went on, for good measure, he had heard that Lord Peterborough had carried to Lord Chief Justice Scroggs a letter which contributed powerfully to Sir George Wakeman's acquittal. It was all very ingenious, but it all fell very flat, and by declining to commit Peterborough to custody the House made plain its disbelief of the witness, and in advance its attitude to Exclusion.

Probably between Dangerfield's appearance and the debate on it,[1] Russell and a crowd of his colleagues presented the bill, as they did so raising a 'great hum' which was answered by 'the lords of the party'. The debate which followed lasted until ten or eleven o'clock at night, but long before the November darkness descended and the candles were brought in the eventual outcome was certain. That the Exclusionists were on the defensive is shown by the argument which was used, that at least the bill should not be rejected immediately, but should be allowed to go into committee so that the Lords could see whether agreement could be reached on an amended version. But Charles was determined not to allow any delay which might foster the belief that he was not wholeheartedly opposed to the bill, and he was determined to kill it that very day. He had his dinner and supper brought to a neighbouring room, and apart from brief retirements to eat these meals he remained present throughout the debate, and made his wishes plain to the bishops and to the peers whom he had created since 1661. His presence, towering by the fire and deterring any waverers, was probably more effective in procuring the bill's rejection than all the fifteen or sixteen speeches that were made by Halifax. Yet Halifax, who had returned from the country in September determined that the problem of the succession must be dealt with by 'limitations' and not by the more extreme remedy of Exclusion,[2] attracted great attention by his speeches.

---

[1] It is clear from the other sources that the order of events given in *L.J.* is wrong. (Cf. n. 2, p. 602.)

[2] For Halifax's attitude, cf. Halifax to Sir Tho. Thynne, 5 Oct., Thynne Papers at Longleat, xv. fo. 13; Burnet, ii. 256–7.

Not only was he a former member of the 'Country Party' who had turned against them, but his arguments helped to make the courtiers feel that they would have, not only the better of the vote as expected, but the better of the argument. The surviving notes of the debate are too scrappy to enable us to judge whether Halifax did indeed win the debating duel: it appears that, apart from personal attacks on his uncle for his 'many changes' and the argument that civil war would follow, he laid some weight on the idea that if the bill were passed the Exclusionists would then go on to demand that only long-standing opponents of the Duke like themselves could be trusted with office. When at last the vote was taken, the bill was thrown out by 63 to 30. The peers with titles created before the Civil War were almost evenly divided, but all the bishops present, and an overwhelming majority of the lay peers created by Charles II since 1661 and the great officers of state voted against the bill. Very few courtiers voted for the bill, except for Anglesey (frightened because Dangerfield had referred to him) and Sunderland, who tried in this way to keep his bargain with the opposition, at the cost of losing the King's favour. Amongst those who voted for the bill was naturally Monmouth, who had been primed with a discreet speech about the dangers to his dear father's life which led Charles to remark, loudly and bitterly, 'The kiss of Judas!'[1] But Buckingham was ill, and took the opportunity to say that he had always had a poor opinion of Shaftesbury's leadership.[2]

The peers went out one by one into the darkness of the Palace Yard, and clambered into their coaches to disperse to their various mansions. The great Exclusion Bill on which the opposition had staked everything was no more. It remained to be seen whether there was any alternative, or whether another attempt could be made.

It is noteworthy that the bill's rejection was not followed by any rioting. Charles was afraid that something might have taken place, and sent to the Lord Mayor to try to prevent the annual Pope-burning on the anniversary of Queen Elizabeth's accession, which fell only two days after the vote; the Lord Mayor replied that it would be as easy to stop the tide from flowing under London Bridge, but guaranteed that there would be no disorders. Charles thought it prudent to station guards at Somerset House in readiness to oppose any movement from the City on Whitehall, but they were not called upon to take any action. The London Whigs had no plans for

---

[1] J. P. Kenyon (*Sunderland*, p. 66) is mistaken in saying that this remark referred to Sunderland (Barrillon, 18/28 Nov.).

[2] *L.J.* xiii. 665–71; *H.M.C. House of Lords MSS. 1678–88*, pp. 195–7; E. S. de Beer, 'The House of Lords in the Parliament of 1680', in *Bull. Inst. Hist. Res.* (1943–5), pp. 22–37; Barrillon, 18/28 Nov.; Clarke, op. cit. ii. 615–18; S. Ellis to J. Ellis, 16 Nov., Add. MSS. 28930, fo. 203; Longford to Ormond, 16 Nov., *H.M.C. Ormond MSS.*, N.S. v. 490; Gwyn to Ormond, 16 Nov., ibid. v. 488; Jenkins to Middleton, 15 Nov., *C.S.P.D. 1680–1*, p. 86; J. Verney to Sir R. Verney, *H.M.C. Seventh Report*, p. 479; Burnet, ii. 259.

any street-fighting, and the night passed off with plenty of noise, but no blows.[1]

The Whigs in the House of Commons were equally unprovided with any plan for constitutional action. When the House met on the day after the bill's rejection, the members sat looking at one another without speaking for nearly half an hour, before Sir John Hotham successfully moved an adjournment until next day to give time for consideration. That afternoon many members dined in the City, including a particularly 'great club' at the Sun tavern. But in all the heated conversations no solution could be found. Having committed themselves to the principle of Exclusion, they were now in an impasse, since by the rules of parliamentary procedure the bill could not be reintroduced in the same session even if a favourable situation could be manufactured.[2]

In the House of Lords, however, there were some proposals to be debated. Thanks probably to the influence of Halifax, the peers had followed their rejection of Exclusion by resolving to discuss the alternative of Limitations —'heads for the effectual securing of the Protestant religion'. Three suggestions attracted special attention. Essex proposed for the King's benefit a Bill of Association similar to that passed in 1585 to protect Queen Elizabeth from assassination at the hands of Papists; and a sub-committee which included Shaftesbury was appointed to draft it. Halifax, determined to show that his 'limitations' policy was no sham, proposed a bill to banish the Duke of York for five years, unless Charles died first. But Shaftesbury laughed at this as something that was unlikely to be carried into effect. Instead he said that since the best way of protecting the state and the Protestant religion had been rejected, there was only one way to remedy the misfortunes which might befall England from the peril of having a Popish king. This was to divorce the King and remarry him to a Protestant who might give him children. Clarendon, he asserted, had known beforehand that the Infanta would be barren, and had made the marriage so that his own grandchildren might succeed; and in other Christian kingdoms barrenness was a sufficient reason for divorce. In the course of the debates Shaftesbury explained that he had no intention to disturb the legitimate order of succession, and that he did not believe anyone had; and that was why he was proposing a divorce.

This remark, if it was correctly reported by the French ambassador, sounds a little odd, since superficially a divorce would be a defeat for the Duke of Monmouth, with whose cause everyone associated the Earl at this time. There is one possible Machiavellian explanation: if the Lords had rejected Exclusion, and if the King were now to reject a divorce (as he

---

[1] Barrillon, 18/28 Nov., 22 Nov./2 Dec.

[2] *C.J.* ix. 655; Grey, viii. 4 (misdated 17 Nov.); Anon., 16 Nov., *H.M.C. Portland MSS.* viii. 15; Barrillon, 18/28 Nov.; Anon. to the King, 17 Nov., *C.S.P.D. 1680–1*, pp. 86–87; Jenkins to Sidney, 16 Nov., S.P. 104/68, p. 18; Clarke, op. cit. i. 619; S. Ellis to J. Ellis, 16 Nov., Add. MSS. 28930, fo. 203.

had done before), then Monmouth's legitimization would be the only way left for those who wanted to keep James out. Alternatively, if Charles did agree to a divorce, Monmouth might be contented with a Regency for a Prince of Wales, or the command of the armed forces which would be needed to prevent James from contesting the situation. It was a nice decision for the King to have to make; but his opposition to a divorce was as unmistakable as his opposition to Exclusion. That night after dinner he had a nap in the Queen's room, instead of in the Duchess of Portsmouth's as he usually did; and he went from one peer to another to stifle the project at birth if he could.[1]

Halifax was as vehement in his opposition to a divorce as he had been to Exclusion. He attacked it as being based only on personal self-interest, hinting not only at Shaftesbury and Monmouth but at the Duchess of Portsmouth, whose hopes for her own son the Duke of Richmond—or even hopes that she herself might be Charles's second Queen—he suggested were at the bottom of all this. Shaftesbury impatiently retorted that no doubt Halifax did not believe that the Duke of York was a Catholic, since he was so warmly opposing all the reasonable precautions that the nation wanted to take against him; to which Halifax in turn replied that he had known the Duke's religion long ago, when Shaftesbury had been putting the Great Seal to the Declaration of Indulgence in the Papists' favour, and had been working for the break-up of the Triple Alliance. The vehemence of this interchange may be contrasted with a lighter interlude later in the debate. A peer pointed out that if the King did remarry he still might not have children. Whereupon Shaftesbury pointed at Charles, who was standing in his usual position by the fireplace, and said: 'Can we doubt when we look at the King that he is capable of getting children? He is only fifty. I know people who are more than sixty and would have no difficulty in getting them!' Whoever this was aimed at, the whole House began to laugh, and the King with the rest.[2]

When the House of Lords went into committee to resume this debate on 23 November, Shaftesbury was absent, suffering from 'gout' in his shoulder, and the peers resolved to postpone the discussion until he was back in his place; but when he appeared next day he declined to press the matter of the divorce, even though he said that he considered it the best remedy for the situation, and surprised everyone by moving that all the expedients proposed should be laid on the table for the time being.[3] The truth was that after a period of some uncertainty Shaftesbury had come

---

[1] *L.J.* xiii. 672, 674; *H.M.C. House of Lords MSS., 1678–88*, pp. 209, 211; Barrillon, 18/28 Nov.; Longford to Ormond, 16 Nov., *H.M.C. Ormond MSS.*, N.S. v. 490; Cooke to Ormond, 20 Nov., ibid. v. 497; Clarke, op. cit. i. 618–19; Macpherson, op. cit. i. 108–9; Lady Sunderland to Sidney, 16 Nov., Sidney Diary, ii. 126.   [2] Barrillon, 22 Nov./2 Dec.

[3] Barrillon, ibid. and 29 Nov./9 Dec.; *L.J.* xiii. 684; Longford to Ormond, 23 Nov., *H.M.C. Ormond MSS.*, N.S. v. 499; Cooke to Ormond, 24 Nov., ibid. v. 505; Dowager Lady Sunderland to Sidney, 25 Nov., Sidney Diary, ii. 136; Clarke, op. cit. i. 635.

round to the point of view that ultimately the combined effect of popular and parliamentary pressure and financial stringency would be to force Charles to yield to Exclusion. He was firmly convinced that any policy merely of limiting the power of a Popish successor would be ineffective, and that discussion of such proposals would only be a waste of time since there could be no guarantee that Charles would in the end accept them; and that this attitude was justified is shown by the reassurances that Charles was sending privately to William, to the effect that the expedients being discussed in the Lords were not his own proposals, that he was not committed to them, and could reject or accept them as he thought fit, and that he would take care of the royal prerogatives.[1] In spite of the defeat which had been sustained on 15 November, it still seemed to Shaftesbury simplest and safest to try to force Exclusion through.

According to the confession which Lord Grey of Wark made after Monmouth's rebellion in 1685, Shaftesbury said in the privacy of Thanet House that it would be the Whigs' own fault if they did not obtain the Exclusion Bill. All thinking men, he continued, looked upon its rejection as the King's work, and believed him to be 'in all parts of the Popish Plot except the murder of himself, which he [Shaftesbury] did not think was intended, knowing the Papists were well assured of his zeal to their religion'. The Whigs had made a great mistake in acting as a screen between the King and the House of Commons, and Shaftesbury repented his own part in this, and suggested that Monmouth, Russell and others should take up arms, when the King would comply with the desires of his people in Parliament 'and sacrifice a hundred brothers rather than hazard his crown'. According to Grey's account in 1685, he, Monmouth and Russell often heard such talk from Shaftesbury but gave it no serious attention. All this cannot be accepted as fact without corroboration, but it is not improbable that some wild talk did take place between the Whigs in their cups at Thanet House. Having said this, one must also go on immediately to say that any such talk was only hot air, and that Shaftesbury proceeded to rely, not on armed pressure on the King, but on the pressure which could be exerted by a House of Commons which remained obstinate in its attitude.[2]

Within two days of the throwing out of the Exclusion Bill, the Commons were called upon to debate the King's request for money to maintain the garrison at Tangier, and Hampden made plain what was in the minds of many members when he spoke of 'coming to a plain bargain'. An address was prepared which said that the House could not come to any resolution about money until members had first been secured from 'the power of Popish persons and counsels', and listed their complaints about the favour

---

[1] Van Leeuwen to William, 7/17 December, Groen van Prinsterer, II. v. 452–3.

[2] Ford Lord Grey, *The Secret History of the Rye House Plot* (1754), pp. 1–3. Contrast Ferguson's complaint that Shaftesbury restrained the extremists at this time: J. Ferguson, *Ferguson the Plotter* (1887), p. 411.

shown to Popery in recent years.[1] While the members waited for financial difficulties to have the requisite effect, they proceeded to lay about them recklessly against anyone whose activities had, in their view, favoured the cause of Popery. Inevitably they began with an attack on Halifax for advising the dissolution of the Parliament of 1679 and obstructing the passage of the Exclusion Bill, and they addressed the King for Halifax's removal from his counsels. They went on to attack Seymour and a number of people involved in the so-called 'abhorring' addresses which members strongly resented. It should not, however, be lightly assumed that Shaftesbury was behind these attacks. Indeed he and Russell specifically disowned any responsibility for the address against Halifax, and, lest this be thought hypocritical, it may be added that while Russell spoke strongly in the debate on Tangier, he remained silent while Halifax was being discussed. The truth was that the House was slipping out of control. Some of those who were new to the House were prone to dislike the advice of the older leaders of the 'Country Party' and to prefer the more extreme courses advocated by others like Ralph Montagu. Shaftesbury himself was reported as saying that 'he does no more understand the House of Commons than he does the Court'. For some time his part was less to prompt and lead the Commons than to try to turn whatever they chose to do to his own account. At least their actions might serve to convince the King that no compromise was possible, and help to persuade him to bow before the storm.[2]

A similar effect might be expected from the trial of Lord Stafford, which filled everyone's attention at the end of November. The five Catholic peers whom Oates had accused had languished in the Tower for two years without ever being brought to judgement and might have remained there much longer, in prison but otherwise unmolested, but for the King's message of 9 November, which reminded the Commons of the need to expedite matters relating to Popery and the Plot, instead of concentrating on the Exclusion Bill. It so happened that on that morning a new witness named Turberville, a man who had Dorsetshire and Glamorgan connexions, was due to appear at the bar of the House, and his 'evidence' was directed principally against Stafford, at a time when the case against the five together had been weakened by the death of Bedloe. As a natural consequence the House, led by Boscawen and Hampden, singled out Stafford to be prosecuted first, and, at their instance, on 12 November fixed his trial for the 30th.[3]

---

[1] Grey, viii. 5–21, 99–106; C.J. ix. 655, 665–7; Clarke, op. cit. i. 620–2. For the King's cool reception of the address, see Cooke to Ormond, 30 Nov., H.M.C. Ormond MSS. N.S. v. 511.

[2] Grey, viii. 21–35, 38–99; anon., H.M.C. Portland MSS., viii. 15–19; C.J. ix. 655–64; Dowager Lady Sunderland to Sidney, 25 Nov., Sidney Diary, ii. 134–5.

[3] C.J. ix. 649–50, 652; Grey, vii. 435–45; Roger Morrice, Entering Book P, fo. 275 (9 Nov.); L.J. xiii. 662–3.

It has sometimes been said that Stafford was deliberately selected by the Whigs because on account of his age and infirmities he was the least likely to be able to defend himself effectively against his accusers, and, when on trial for his life, 'might squeak'. But this is doubtful, not only because the coincidence of the King's message and Turberville's evidence could not have been arranged, but because Stafford was not in fact the most infirm of the five peers. Lord Arundel was over seventy; Lord Bellasis, who was in his sixties, was so crippled by gout that in 1679 he had been unable to appear at the bar of the Lords to put in his plea. What was much more important was that thanks to Dugdale the 'evidence' was 'strongest' against Stafford even before Turberville's appearance, which seemed to clinch it. It was also of some significance that Stafford was a man with many relatives among the peers—and few friends. He was disliked at Court and even among his fellow-Catholics; he was known to have been dissatisfied with the King's bounty to him at the Restoration, and if any peer was involved in a Plot to kill the King, he seemed the most likely. Courtiers like Seymour were not the only ones to believe that the case against Stafford was a strong one. In the same breath as King Charles described Oates and Bedloe as rascals, he remarked that the evidence against Stafford was strong, and that he might not be innocent. To single out Stafford was natural and not a Machiavellian plot. Curiously enough, this choice was something of an embarrassment to Shaftesbury, and something of a relief to Charles. So far as the Earl was concerned, he was likely to be reminded of his conversations with Stafford in 1675 about a possible combination to force the dissolution of Danby's Anglican Parliament. So far as the King was concerned, it was infinitely preferable to have Stafford facing death rather than his colleague, Lord Arundel of Wardour. For—a fact which has been generally overlooked—Lord Arundel had a dreadful secret in his possession. In 1670 he had signed the Secret Treaty of Dover; and Charles would have had some uneasy moments, fearing that he might seek to buy his life by revealing the 'Catholic clauses' in that treaty.[1]

The failure of the Exclusion Bill effectively destroyed any chance of mercy for Stafford from the Whigs. A reaffirmation of the 'reality' of a Popish Plot was politically vital for the Whigs, and fatal to Stafford. Many thought from the beginning that his only chance of escape was a confession.[2] It was in this situation that the trial began on 30 November. Until 7 December Westminster Hall was once again the scene of a man's fight

---

[1] Clarke, op. cit. i. 635–6; R. North, *Examen* (1740), pp. 217–18; Reresby, p. 206; Burnet, ii. 269; Conway to Ormond, 9 Nov., *H.M.C. Ormond MSS.*, N.S. v. 485–6; Barrillon, 11/21 Nov. for Charles's remark. North's account is a good example of his unreliability: not only does he talk of Stafford 'almost idolizing' Charles 'for his continual favour and bounty towards him', but he says that Stafford was condemned only by a small majority, and (p. 220) that the other peers were set free during the next recess.

[2] Cooke to Ormond, 25 Nov., op. cit. v. 505.

against the efforts of his political enemies to put him to death by due process of law. Crowds thronged the Hall to see it. Charles, in whose name the Courts normally acted in the Hall, was for once present, but in a private capacity in a special box of his own. The Duchess of Portsmouth dispensed sweetmeats to the members of the Commons who stood near to her, seeking in this way to divert possible hostility to the King's Catholic mistress. The foreign ambassadors in London also had places allocated, from which they could watch the curious spectacle of charges being brought against an English peer in the name of the people of England. Everyone of note was present, either as accuser (if he were a member of the Commons in whose name the impeachment took place), or as judge (if a lay peer) or as spectator.

Shaftesbury himself took no particularly prominent part in the trial. Indeed it had been noticed with some surprise that he had excused himself from the joint committee of Lords and Commons which settled the procedure to be adopted.[1] The bishops had agreed to abstain from being present, so that there was no possibility of a dispute over the rights of spiritual peers, such as had bedevilled the last Parliament. The prosecution in the name of the Commons was in the safe hands of skilled lawyers, including a former Attorney-General and Solicitor-General, Sir William Jones and Sir Francis Winnington, who had apparently come over to the Whigs in the last two years without entering into any special intimacy with the Earl. It is possible that there had been some preliminary consultation about the way in which the prosecution was to open by a general proof of the existence of a Plot, which some had questioned. 'Many were so ignorant that they would not think it; many were so unwise they would not believe it; some so ill that they would not favour it; and some so much worse that they did foster it; but all of them in not believing it, gave strength to the conspiracy and the treason.' So spoke Serjeant Maynard, quoting Cicero on Catiline; and followed it up with a history of Catholic atrocities, including Philip II's alleged murder of his own son, no less, for being a Protestant. Lest the moral should pass unobserved, Winnington stressed that the Plot was based on hopes of a Popish successor, and the first witness, 'Narrative' Smith, claimed to have seen in Rome letters from Coleman about support for the Plot from the Duke of York and the Queen. It is possible that Shaftesbury may have been consulted about this, for it had an obvious connexion with the political objective of the Exclusionists; but the pressing of the particular charges against Stafford, which followed, could be left to the skill of the lawyers, with Shaftesbury a supposedly impartial judge, weighing the evidence of the prisoner's guilt. Whether out of genuine compassion or out of a desire not to appear to press too hardly on the prisoner, on 1 December he encouraged Stafford to apply for an adjournment for two days—a concession of which he refused to

---

[1] Cooke to Ormond, 27 Nov., ibid. v. 506; *L.J.* xiii. 692.

avail himself—and next day he helped to cut short the proceedings when Stafford must have been more tired and under more strain than his judges. For the rest, in the House he denounced Stafford's legal argument that he should be set free because the Parliament which had first accused him had been dissolved—putting forward the constitutional doctrine that by the laws of England Parliament should not be ended until its business had been completed—and back in Westminster Hall he prevented Stafford from having access to an original letter which might just possibly have cast doubt on Dugdale's credit as a witness.

If one were to consider the seven days of the trial by themselves, and not as the culmination of an agitation which Shaftesbury had helped to foster, then one could say that Shaftesbury's guilt was no greater than that of the other fifty-four peers who voted for Stafford's guilt. For political reasons he wanted the prisoner to be convicted, but the evidence could be left to itself to produce this result, without any further manipulation. Certainly most contemporaries—not merely Whigs, but Tories like the correspondents of Ormond—thought that Stafford's defence was weak. Printed accounts suggest that in the early days of the trial Stafford made some effective points against the perjurers who were swearing his life away; but often they were inaudible, and the Lord High Steward had to go halfway towards him to hear his questions. As the days passed the old man went to pieces under the strain of conducting his own defence, and he was reduced to helpless tears and even a feeble argument that he could not be found guilty because he had not raised his right arm when pleading. Charles's own doubts had resolved into a belief in Stafford's innocence, but, whether he found it prudent not to intervene in a trial or whether he thought that the voting on the Exclusion Bill would be repeated without intervention from him, he did nothing to whip up support as he had done on the earlier occasion. Unprejudiced observers were sure that Stafford would be convicted, and deservedly so; and when on 7 December the time came for each peer in turn to voice his opinion, 'Guilty' or 'Not Guilty', and Charles in his box ticked off the votes as they spoke, he heard to his chagrin that Stafford was found guilty by 55 votes to 31. This was an almost exact reversal of the voting on the Exclusion Bill—and what was more, the majority included the Lord Chancellor (Nottingham), seven Bedchamber men, and four out of five Howards in the Lords. Although it has been suggested that some were intimidated, and that others voted against Stafford to reduce the odium which they had incurred by voting against Exclusion, the simplest and the best explanation of this reversal of the majority of only three weeks earlier, and the one which contemporaries accepted, was a widespread belief that there was a Popish Plot, and that the witnesses had proved Stafford's participation in it.[1]

---

[1] *State Trials*, vii. 1293–1559; *L.J.* xiii. 696–706; Cooke to Ormond, 30 Nov., 1, 2, 3, 4, 7 Dec., *H.M.C. Ormond MSS.*, N.S. v. 512, 514–15, 518; Burlington to Ormond, 4

As such the result of the trial was a great Whig victory, which could become the basis for further political action to exclude the Popish successor in whose interest the Catholics were supposed to have conspired. It mattered comparatively little that Stafford did not 'squeak'. Appear before the Lords he did, after a conversation with Burnet in the Tower, in which he hinted that he could discover many things 'more material than any thing that was yet known', and after the Lords had sent word that they would intercede for his pardon in return for 'a full and ingenuous discovery'; but at the bar of the House he spoke, not of plots to kill the King, but of conversations with Shaftesbury a few years earlier in which the Earl had tried to persuade him to combine in bringing about the dissolution of the Cavalier Parliament and the election of a new one which would be more favourable to non-Anglicans. This was obviously a debating point, designed to make mischief, and not a confession, and Shaftesbury was able successfully to move that the House should hear him no further. Shaftesbury evidently thought that Burnet had planned his discomfiture in co-operation with Halifax, and railed at that well-meaning but officious clergyman in consequence.[1] Perhaps the opposition's irritation at the incident partly influenced some of them in both Houses to object to the King's decision to commute the barbarous sentence of hanging, drawing, and quartering, which was the lot of commoners found guilty of treason, in favour of the beheading which was the privilege of noblemen. But the objections of such as Russell to this commutation were not simply the result of vindictiveness, as has sometimes been supposed; underneath lay the legal question whether, if the King might commute the penalty, he might not be able to pardon too, as in Danby's case. Eventually, Sir William Jones and the lawyers decided that there was no danger of this, the objections were withdrawn, and Stafford went to the block on Tower Hill on 29 December.[2]

There can be no doubt that Charles, though he had no liking for Stafford and no intention of risking anything for him, deeply resented the shameful political necessity (as he saw it) of having to agree to the death of a man of whose innocence he was now convinced. His face had revealed this to onlookers at the time of the Lords' vote. Equally there could be no doubt that Charles believed Shaftesbury to be indirectly responsible, and that he would lose no opportunity of avenging Stafford's death upon him. The

Dec., ibid. v. 518; Arran to Ormond, 4, 7 Dec., ibid. v. 519, 521; Longford to Ormond, 4 Dec., ibid. v. 520; S. Ellis to J. Ellis, 4 Dec., Add. MSS. 28930, fo. 212; Countess of Manchester to Lady Hatton, 7 Dec., *Hatton Correspondence*, i. 242; Barrillon, 6/16, 9/19 Dec.; Crinò, pp. 148–9.

[1] Burnet, ii. 276–8; Longford to Ormond, 18 Dec., op. cit. v. 529; *L.J.* xiii. 721; *H.M.C. House of Lords MSS. 1678–88*, pp. 43–44.

[2] *L.J.* xiii. 724; Grey, viii. 209–10; Barrillon, 23 Dec./2 Jan.; Clarke, op. cit. i. 639: Those who criticize Russell for vindictiveness should note that in 1681 Charles rejected Mrs. Fitzharris's plea that her husband should not be quartered. This has been generally overlooked, although Charles had no constitutional reason, such as Russell had, for preserving the barbarity of the punishment.

stakes were getting higher; and at the same time one possible safeguard against a reaction failed to materialize for Shaftesbury. A bill had been introduced to regulate the trial of peers when Parliament was not sitting, and when, according to existing practice, the King could select what peers he chose to try one of their number; it would have hindered the packing of such a court by providing that at least fifty-one peers be summoned, at least thirty-five should appear, and any twelve might be peremptorily challenged by the prisoner. The bill passed safely through the Lords, but here, ironically, the limitations of Shaftesbury's control over the Commons made themselves apparent. The Commons were always jealous of the special privileges of the peers, and aggrieved by their rejection of Exclusion; many were afraid that the bill would make it difficult to bring a peer to justice, and others demanded that if the bill were to be accepted, the peers should at the same time give up their right to bring actions of *scandalum magnatum* against commoners who insulted them. The resulting deadlock was never resolved before the end of the session, and the consequence was that twelve months later Shaftesbury, fearing to be tried by a packed court of Tory peers, had to rely on a packed *Ignoramus* jury to free him; and in another twelve months, losing the benefit of an *Ignoramus* jury, he had to flee the country.[1]

In December 1680, however, such possibilities did not affect Shaftesbury's self-confidence, which had recovered from the temporary setback of the rejection of the Exclusion Bill. The Stafford trial had reaffirmed the widespread belief in the existence of a Plot; the King's financial problems had received no relief, and there seemed a strong possibility that he might in the end give way to the heavy pressure on him, and abandon his brother. It seemed that the Whigs had an ally at Court in the Duchess of Portsmouth, who not only bestowed her sweets and gracious looks on the members of the Commons, but opened her doors to Shaftesbury himself: the Earl jestingly bragged of it, and some Whigs disapproved of a speech which Cavendish made against her, though others, like Essex, were scandalized at this and argued that a Popish mistress was still Popish even if she did favour Exclusion. It was also noticed that Sunderland, though he had voted for Exclusion, still retained his Secretaryship of State; and a letter procured by Sunderland's ally Henry Sidney in his embassy at The Hague made plain the Dutch hopes that the King would agree with his Parliament. With all these signs in his favour, Shaftesbury had some justification for believing that if he could hold the opposition together a little longer, he would reach his objective.[2]

---

[1] *C.J.* ix. 654, 680–1; Grey, vii. 472–4, viii. 171–5; Jenkins to Prince of Orange, 17 Dec., Groen van Prinsterer, II. v. 459; *H.M.C. House of Lords MSS. 1678–88*, pp. 127, 157; *L.J.* xiii. 721; Barrillon, 20/30 Dec.

[2] Clarke, op. cit. i. 640–6; Barrillon, 9/19, 20/30 Dec.; S.P. 84/216, fos. 98–101 (printed as *An Intimation of the Deputies of the States-General, in a late discourse with Mr. Sidney*).

With this in mind, on 21 December he and some allies in the Lords launched an attack on a number of James's supporters who held high office and who, they maintained, should be removed. Monmouth, Salisbury and Essex attacked Laurence Hyde, the first Commissioner of the Treasury and James's brother-in-law, and secondly Col. Legge, governor of the important garrison at Portsmouth which might secure communications with France. Shaftesbury followed, alluding to a man who had two brothers who were marshals of France, and who openly declared his attachment to the Duke of York: this was the Frenchman, Lord Duras, Earl of Feversham. Shaftesbury went on to repeat a declaration that he had made earlier, that he would not be satisfied until there was not a single Papist left at White-hall, and ended by saying that the noise which was being made on the mountains [i.e. in the Lords] might not be heard, but that answering echoes would come from the valleys, and that the commons of England would make themselves heard, however carefully people tried not to listen to them.[1]

Two days later, on the 23rd, Shaftesbury had an opportunity to be even more emphatic when the Lords debated a speech which the King had made to both Houses on the 15th. In answer to the King's request that Parliament should give some assistance to his foreign policy and for the defence of Tangier, and in reply to the King's offer once again to concur 'in any remedies which might consist with preserving the succession of the Crown in its due and legal course of descent', Shaftesbury, Essex and Salisbury spoke vehemently against James, and laid it down that no agreement between King and people was possible unless Charles agreed to his brother's exclusion.[2] A printed version of Shaftesbury's speech appeared within a few days under the title *A Speech lately made by a noble peer of the realm.* That this pamphlet was a version of Shaftesbury's speech is clear from the way in which it repeated some of the striking phrases noted by people who heard him in the Lords—for instance a reference to the King's mistress (not the Duchess of Portsmouth, but she of Mazarin) as Sempronia in the conspiracy of Catiline; the peroration is also clearly recognizable. It is likely that the pamphlet as a whole was more sharply phrased than the speech, and that this was why the Lords later ordered it to be burnt by the hangman though they had not interrupted Shaftesbury as he spoke; but there can be no doubt that it represented his views when he was freed from the possibility of being called to order by the House.[3]

[1] Barrillon, 23 Dec./2 Jan.; Jenkins to William, 21 Dec., Groen van Prinsterer, II. v. 460; Clarke, op. cit. i. 647; Macpherson, *Original Papers* (1776), i. 112.

[2] *L.J.* xiii. 727; Barrillon, 23 Dec./2 Jan., 27 Dec./6 Jan.

[3] When asked about it in the Lords, Shaftesbury did not disown it, 'but said he believed he might say some such thing': Luttrell, i. 62. Barrillon on the other hand (3/13 Jan.) reported that Shaftesbury disowned it, but that he distributed copies of it, and that the few changes from the speech as delivered were of little consequence. Cf. also *L.J.* xiii. 729, 734.

He began by repeating a precedent cited earlier, and urged that a wise prince would follow the example of Henry IV and 'when he hath need of his people, will rather "part with his family and counsellors, than displease them" '. He denied that an earlier reference had been to 'the chargeable ladies at court', 'but if I must speak of them, I shall say as the prophet did to King Saul, "What means the bleating of this kind of cattle?" And I hope the King will make me the same answer, "That he reserved them for sacrifice, and means to deliver them up to please his people." For there must be (in plain English), my Lords, a change; we must neither have popish wife, nor popish favourite, nor popish mistress, nor popish counsellor at court, or any new convert. . . . In this time of distress I humbly advise our Prince would take the same course that the Duke of Savoy did, to suffer neither strangers nor ambassadors to stay above some few weeks in his country. . . .' Having thus dealt out threats to Queen Catherine, Portsmouth, Mazarin, and Barrillon, he came to the main argument of his speech. Taking up Sunderland's hint that if the King were sure of supplies, Parliament need not doubt his compliance in what they asked, and that otherwise the King would fall into the worst plight of all and have a people with no confidence in him, Shaftesbury said that this line of thought was not enough. 'My lords, it is a very hard thing to say, "that we cannot trust the King"; and that we have already been deceived so often, that we see plainly the apprehensions of discontent in the people is no argument at Court. And though our Prince be in himself an excellent person, that the people have the greatest inclinations imaginable to love; yet we must say he is such an one, "as no story affords us a parallel of". . . .' Charles had scorned the Plot which was 'plainly headed by the Duke, his interest and his design', had permitted James to get into a strong position, had lent himself to 'the cutting short of parliaments' and everything that James wanted; and even now when James had been sent away and Charles had offered to accept 'expedients', 'in the meanwhile where is this Duke, that the King and both Houses have declared unanimously thus dangerous? Why, he is in Scotland raising of forces upon the terra firma, that can enter dry-foot upon us, without hazard of winds or seas, the very place he should be in to raise a party there, to be ready when from hence he shall have notice: so that this being the case, where is the trust? We all think the business is so ripe, that they have the garrisons, the arms, the ammunition, the seas and soldiery all in their hands; they want but one good sum of money to set up and crown the work, and then they shall have no more need of the people . . . this I know, and must boldly say it, and plainly, That the nation is betrayed if upon any terms we part with our money till we are sure the King is ours; have what laws you will, and what conditions you will, they will be of no use but waste paper before Easter, if the Court has money to set up for popery and arbitrary designs in the meanwhile.' Parliament must first be satisfied that it could trust the King, that is by his assent to Exclusion, before it voted money; on the other hand, 'The hour that the King shall satisfy the people, that what we give is not to make us slaves and papists, he may have what he will.' All these frank statements of his distrust of the King were uttered as Charles stood by the fireplace, listening as was his wont; and Shaftesbury boldly and bluntly ended his speech by saying: '. . . we know who hears, and I am glad of this, "that your lordships have dealt so honourably and so clearly in the King's presence and in the King's hearing", that he cannot say he wants a "right state of things"; he hath it before him, and may take council as he thinks fit.'[1]

All this was as highly coloured as it was outspoken, and it was easy for Tory spokesmen to draw attention to the question-begging phrases in it, such as 'the people' and 'the Court', and to enquire what was the evidence for the deeply laid conspiracy in which James was said to have engaged and to which Charles was alleged to have wittingly or unwittingly lent himself. The speech was an exaggeration. Yet it was not completely wide of the mark. Though James may have had no detailed, consistent, and formed plans, the logic of the policy of firmness towards Parliament which he pressed upon Charles was not very different from what Shaftesbury indicated. And when in 1685 a House of Commons did vote an ample revenue to James II, the upshot was precisely the army on Hounslow Heath, the dismissal of Parliament, and the 'popery and arbitrary designs' which Shaftesbury had feared.

It was all very well for Shaftesbury to make it plain 'on the mountains' that Exclusion should precede any grant of supplies, but, as he saw, it was the 'echoes from the valleys' of the Commons that mattered. For a time they were all that could be desired. The King's speech of 15 December, asking for assistance, had been followed there by a motion from Cavendish calling for a bill to provide for an Association in support of a Protestant heir and the exclusion from office of any who would not join it. William Harbord further proposed a bill for the banishment of all prominent Papists. Among those who supported both propositions were, curiously, both Sir William Hickman, a follower of Halifax's, and Sir William Cooper, who was a close friend and probably a relative of Shaftesbury's, and who argued that the most prominent Papist of all must be banished with the rest. It was resolved that both bills should be prepared, although some doubts were expressed whether it would be possible to draft the Association Bill in such a way that the Lords could not reject it on the technical point that it was a mere repetition of the Exclusion Bill rejected in this same session. Three days later Hampden moved that the Commons should answer the King's speech with an address declaring that the House could

---

[1] Printed in Christie, ii, pp. cii–cvi, and in *Parliamentary History*, iv, pp. cxi–cxiv. For a Tory reply, see *A Letter from Scotland, Written occasionally upon the Speech made by a Noble Peer of the Realm. By a better Protestant than the Author of it, though a Servant to His Royal Highness* (printed ibid. pp. cxix–cxii); and cf. North, op. cit. p. 89.

see no safety without the exclusion of the Duke, and an Association to guarantee it; and he threw in demands that the judges, the deputy lieu-tenants, and justices of the peace, and the naval captains must be 'well affected to the Protestant religion'. If these things were granted, the House would then be ready to supply money to defend Tangier and to support alliances with Protestant powers. Hampden was seconded by Russell and Sir William Jones in speeches which appear to have followed a previously concerted line; and there was general support for such an address, though not all the speakers were as melodramatic as the ex-Cromwellian Colonel Birch, who declared that 'Till this [Exclusion] Bill pass, I am afraid when the King goes to bed, to hear sad news of him by morning'. An address reiterating the case for Exclusion, urging the King to assent to Exclusion, Association, and the other demands, and making plain that only then would the House vote supplies, was duly presented to the King on 21 December, and finally, in the consciousness of work well done, the House adjourned on Christmas Eve for a few days of festivities.[1]

In all this the Whigs had maintained their unity quite well; but during these Christmas holidays there were some awkward developments from Shaftesbury's point of view. Believing that it was possible to make a bargain with the King, some of the Whigs entered into negotiations, probably through Sunderland and the Duchess of Portsmouth. The idea was that the King would agree to the Exclusion Bill in return for a vote of money, and (in the words of James's sneer) 'many of the heads of the party like the prudent Steward in the Gospel had the grace not to forget themselves' and expected to be given office as part of the settlement. Foremost of these was inevitably Ralph Montagu, the biggest self-seeker of all; but Russell, abandoning his usual willingness to follow Shaftesbury's lead, seems to have joined Montagu, and from their houses in Southampton Place the group were known as 'the Southamptons'. Monmouth (now, as often, at least as close to Montagu as to Shaftesbury) was also involved, as were the lawyers Jones and Winnington. It was rumoured that Russell would be given command of the key garrison at Portsmouth, Jones would become Lord Chief Justice and Silas Titus one of the two secretaries of State, with Montagu presumably as the other since this was the office on which he had long set his heart. Rumour had it that the bargain was on the point of being made, and that the question outstanding was merely the exact amount of money that the King could expect. Barrillon reported the rumours to his master, and the Dutch ambassador to William of Orange—on whom the possibility that Exclusion would come to pass had such an effect that at last he began seriously to contemplate the idea of coming over to look after his interests.

It is likely enough that Charles deliberately allowed such rumours to

---

[1] *C.J.* ix. 679–80, 683–6; Grey, viii. 147–8, 153–71, 186–201; *H.M.C. Beaufort MSS.* pp. 98–100.

leak out in the hope that they would split 'the Southamptons' from Shaftesbury. The group had planned that the Earl should become Lord Treasurer, 'thinking it dangerous to leave him out'; but, again to use James's sneering words, 'he (good man) as soon as he heard of it, fell into a mighty passion they should think him capable of sacrificing the public good to his private interest'. Clearer-sighted than Russell, and less blinded by self-interest than Montagu, Shaftesbury could see the trap. He was determined to see Exclusion safely passed before giving any money in return; and the talk of office threatened to divide the leaders from the rank and file in the Commons. Angrily he made plain his opposition to the scheme, and it promptly collapsed. When the Commons met again on 30 December, some of those who had been mentioned in the rumours felt compelled to vie with one another in proposing a resolution against members of the Commons accepting office without the express consent of the House. 'Lead us not into temptation', said Titus piously, and the rest agreed.[1]

The deadlock was now complete. On 4 January 1681, the King sent his official reply to the address which had been presented to him by the Commons on 21 December. He repeated his determination not to agree to Exclusion, and recommended all other means for the preservation of the Protestant religion, in which he would readily concur. In the course of the message he remarked that he was confirmed in his opinion against the Exclusion Bill by the judgement of the Lords, who had rejected it. This immediately led Russell to talk of 'setting a brand upon' those who had advised the King to send such a message, but the House did not proceed with this until it had had three days for thought. Then the son of that Sir George Booth who had rebelled against the Commonwealth in 1659 led the way in moving that the House should insist on Exclusion as the only remedy, and should 'put a brand upon them who have dissuaded the King from complying with our advice, and have divided the King from the country'; and Russell seconded him. The attacks on individual ministers which followed have generally been represented as the wild, reckless blows of a House which had lost all self-control and was hitting out regardless of the consequences, but this is a mistake. The attacks were not thoughtless even if the constitutional doctrine which was implied was not the conventional one. They sprang from the theory that the wishes of the representatives of the people were being thwarted by the influence of 'persons near the King' who were 'interested for the Duke'. The King's reference to the Lords' rejection of the bill was dismissed with the comment (by

[1] Barrillon, 27 Dec./6 Jan., 30 Dec./9 Jan., 3/13, 6/16 Jan.; Sidney Diary, 27 Dec., ii. 148; Sidney to Sunderland, 28 Dec., ibid. pp. 149–51; Clarke, op. cit. i. 649–50; Gwyn to Ormond, 1 Jan., *H.M.C. Ormond MSS.*, N.S. v. 541–2; Jenkins to William, 31 Dec., Groen van Prinsterer, II. v. 466–7, and to Sidney, 31 Dec., S.P. 104/68, fo. 22ᵛ; R. Morrice, Entering Book P (Dr. Williams's Library), 30 Dec., fos. 288–9; Grey, viii. 222–5; *C.J.* ix. 695–6.

Leveson Gower) that 'if the Lords had been left to themselves, they would have passed this Bill as well as we'. Reading between the lines of such speeches it is possible to detect that for some members at least the references to 'persons near the King' were simply the parliamentary expression of a desire that the King himself should accept the policy of the Commons—in which case the Lords would, it was felt, present little difficulty. For these, and for those less astute members who really believed in the evil group at Court, the best way of bringing it home was to make it unpleasant, risky, and unpopular for any minister to serve the King who did not support the Commons' policy of Exclusion. Accordingly, after Sir Henry Capel had drawn attention to the fact that no alternative bill had been offered by the Court, and the House had voted its insistence on Exclusion, Capel led the attack on Halifax, and Russell proceeded to name Clarendon's second son, Laurence Hyde, who was reduced to tears by the imputation that he was a promoter of Popery. After this some of the rank and file in the House took the bit between their teeth, and in the heated atmosphere of a late night sitting passed votes against the Marquis of Worcester, the second Earl of Clarendon, and Lord Feversham; and some of the Whig leaders had difficulty in diverting them from an attack on the Duchess of Portsmouth, whom the leaders still regarded as a possible ally. In each case it was voted to address the King for the removal of the offending Privy Councillor.[1]

Two days earlier, in pursuance of proceedings begun before Christmas, the House had voted to send up to the Lords articles of impeachment against Lord Chief Justice Scroggs and to order a committee to bring in similar impeachments against three other judges, North, Jones and Weston. All these could reasonably be accused of partiality (that is, the wrong kind of partiality from the Whigs' point of view) in their statements from the Bench, and notably in their attempts to hinder the petitioning which the Whigs conceived to be a right of the subject[2]; what some members plainly felt uneasy about was the attempt to stretch the accusations against Scroggs so that they amounted to high treason.[3] Taken together, these attacks on his ministers and judges gave Charles at once a motive and the excuse that he needed for getting rid of his Parliament. Though the Lords refused to commit Scroggs to custody or even to suspend him from his judicial office (with Shaftesbury mustering only twenty-one peers in support of his protest),[4] the King could not risk his ministers being affected by the danger of being 'branded' in this way; he had to come to their assistance. Moreover, there were nasty signs that at long last Shaftesbury was bringing the cauldron of the Irish Plot to the boil. The Lords' Plot committee, sitting usually under the chairmanship either of Shaftesbury

---

[1] *C.J.* ix. 699, 702; Grey, viii. 234–7, 260–85; *H.M.C. Beaufort MSS.* pp. 108–15; Barrillon, 6/16, 10/20 Jan.; Arran to Ormond, 25 Jan., *H.M.C. Ormond MSS.*, N.S. v. 563.   [2] See the report made to the House on 23 Dec. in *C.J.* ix. 688–92.
[3] Grey, viii. 205–11, 233–4, 237–50.   [4] *L.J.* xiii. 736–8.

or of Essex, had completed its examination of the swarm of Irish witnesses, and on 4 January the House (reluctant as it was to follow Shaftesbury's lead in other matters) readily voted their belief that for several years there had been a plot in Ireland to massacre the English and subvert the Protestant religion, and asked the Commons for their concurrence.[1] It was impossible to tell whether this might be developed into an attack on the Duke of Ormond or turned in some new and unforeseeable way against the Duke of York. And so on 10 January he went down to Parliament and ended the session.[2]

In so doing he incidentally put an end to some bills of importance. One of these was the bill for regulating the trial of peers, which would have done something to safeguard Shaftesbury from the danger of being put on trial for his life by a Court packed by the King. Useful bills had also been begun to ensure the sitting of frequent Parliaments; to provide for the judges to hold office *quam diu se bene gesserint* instead of being dismissable at the King's pleasure; and to prevent the extortion of exorbitant fines.[3] But much more important was the lapse of a series of measures designed to relieve Dissenters. The Whig politicians, though not themselves Dissenters, were tolerantly disposed towards them and conscious that they were often, not the only, but the most zealous opponents of Popery. The long-standing desire which such as Shaftesbury had had to obtain some indulgence for them was reinforced by the obvious political advantages of forming a Protestant Front against the common enemy. The difficulty was that there were different ideas about the form which this Front should take. On one measure, a bill for the repeal of the savage Elizabethan Act of 1593 against sectaries, they did agree, and it passed both Houses. In addition, the Commons had given leave for a bill to be brought in 'for uniting His Majesty's Protestant subjects', that is, by comprehension; but the support for this was decidedly lukewarm, and after two months it had still not passed the House.[4] The Lords, on the other hand, had appointed a committee to discuss the possibilities of discontinuing prosecutions for recusancy against Dissenters, and from this Shaftesbury reported the committee's preference for proceeding, not by an Address to the King as Anglesey had originally contemplated, but by a bill. The preamble spoke of 'the disuniting the Protestant interest in a time when Papists are designing and practising the ruin of our religion', and the remedy proposed was that Dissenters prosecuted under the necessary laws should be discharged if they subscribed the anti-Catholic declaration in the Test Act

---

[1] *L.J.* xiii. 731–5; *C.J.* ix. 699, 701; Grey, viii. 251–8; *H.M.C. Beaufort MSS.*, pp. 106–8; Sir John Davis to Ormond, 1 Jan., *H.M.C. Ormond MSS.*, N.S. v. 543. For the activities of Hetherington and Murphy at this time, cf. Ormond to Arran, 6 Jan., ibid. v. 545.   [2] *L.J.* xiii. 742.   [3] *C.J.* ix. 682–3, 696; Grey, viii. 226–9.
[4] *C.J.* ix. 645, 660–1, 681, 687; Grey, vii. 414, viii. 201–4; *H.M.C. Beaufort MSS.* pp. 101–2; *From Uniformity to Unity*, ed. G. F. Nuttall and O. Chadwick (1962), pp. 223–30.

of 1678. To Shaftesbury's chagrin the bill was weakened by the insistence of the bishops and Court lords that Dissenters should take the oath of allegiance as well, so that Quakers, being unable to swear, would be deprived of any benefit. With this proviso the bill eventually passed the House and was sent down to the Commons, but by this time the Commons had begun a bill of their own for the same purpose.[1]

If the session had lasted a month longer a Toleration Bill might have emerged which would have been placed to the credit of Shaftesbury and the Whigs instead of that of the Revolution settlement. As it was, the only bill which was ready on 10 January was that for the repeal of the Act of 1593, and Charles quietly ordered the Clerk not to present it, so that he had neither to assent to it nor reject it. In this way the bill was literally, if unconstitutionally lost.[2] This was quite contrary to the sentiments which Charles had expressed in his Declaration of Indulgence of 1672, but he had always thought of indulgence for Nonconformists mainly as a cover for indulgence to Catholics, and was not now going to leave his Catholic friends in isolation. Nor was he disposed to make any concessions to supporters of Exclusion. In December, indeed, he had ordered the Secretary of State, Jenkins, to remind the Lord Mayor to enforce the provisions of the Corporation Act in the elections to the Common Council, so that his opponents should be excluded[3]; and he already had in mind the propaganda line which was to be adopted by Sir Roger L'Estrange, that all good Anglicans should rally to the defence of Church and King against the plottings of Puritan ex-rebels. The famous nicknames of 'Whig' and 'Tory' which were to become firmly attached to the two parties in the course of 1681 would imply not only contrasting policies towards the succession, but contrasting outlooks on the problem of the policy to be pursued towards Dissent.

---

[1] H.M.C. House of Lords MSS. 1678–88, pp. 202–5; L.J. xiii. 709, 711, 713–15, 717–19, 722, 724, 727–8; Roger Morrice, Entering Book P (Dr. Williams's Library), fo. 286; Macpherson, op. cit. i. 112; C.J. ix. 681, 687, 695; Grey, viii. 214–18.

[2] Cf. p. 633 below.　　　　　　　　　　　　　[3] C.S.P.D. 1680–1, p. 104; cf. also p. 102.

CHAPTER XXVII

THE OXFORD PARLIAMENT
(JANUARY-JULY 1681)

THE first reactions to the ending of the session on 10 January 1681 were feelings of some uncertainty. On several occasions there had been Whig talk of the Commons foiling Charles's use of his prerogative of prorogation or dissolution by adjourning to the City and continuing to sit there,[1] and the government was well aware of this. On the other hand, in the circumstances the Exclusionists needed a *short* prorogation for procedural reasons so that they could re-introduce the Exclusion Bill in a new session. Realizing this, Charles did not bring the session to an end with a dissolution, but with a prorogation until 20 January which the Whigs obviously would have to accept. The first of the resolutions which they rushed through in the Commons before Black Rod could reach them was to the effect that whosoever advised His Majesty to prorogue this Parliament *to any other purpose than in order to the passing of an Exclusion Bill* was a betrayer of the King and the Protestant religion, and so on; and when, at the bar of the Lords, they heard that the prorogation was to be only for ten days, there was loud applause. There were even some at Court who were afraid that it was a deliberate expedient to permit of the re-introduction of the Bill, and with the Englishman's customary willingness to bet on anything possible, wagers were made.[2] In the City, Whig supporters such as Clayton (whose views had become more radical since he had given up the Mayoralty), Player, Dubois, and Michael Godfrey persuaded the Lord Mayor to call a Common Council, which agreed upon an address to the King, representing the sitting of Parliament as 'the only means under heaven to preserve King and nation'. In less than a week some of the members from the West were able to present similar petitions from far-away Exeter and Devon which were said to contain 4,000 and 6,000 signatures—remarkably fast work by any standards, even allowing for the inevitable exaggeration.[3]

The King was able to tell them in reply that it was now too late. On 18 January, having gained the few days that he needed, he announced his decision to dissolve Parliament and summon a new one to Oxford on 21 March.

---

[1] See, for instance, Jenkins to Godolphin, 4 Oct., 1680, *C.S.P.D. 1680–1*, p. 50.

[2] *C.J.* ix. 703–4; Grey, viii. 289–90; Luttrell, i. 62; van Leeuwen and van Citters, 11/21 Jan., Add. MSS. 17677, FF; Barrillon, 10/20 Jan.; Arran to Ormond, 10 Jan., *H.M.C. Ormond MSS.*, N.S. v. 549; Reresby, p. 209.

[3] Newsletter, 15 Jan., MSS. Carte 222, fos. 232–3; *Vox Patriae* (1681); Anna M. Crinò, *Il Popish Plot* (Rome, 1954), pp. 157–8; newsletter, 18 Jan., *C.S.P.D. 1680–1*, pp. 137–8.

This was not a new idea springing from the cunning brain of Charles II. Danby had suggested that Parliament should meet in some other place than London eighteen months earlier,[1] and before the session of October 1680 there had been rumours of an adjournment to Oxford.[2] The purpose of such a move was not simply to exchange the Whiggish atmosphere of London for a Royalist one at Oxford—for the City of Oxford was as Whiggish as the University was Tory—but to ensure that the King would be free from the danger of mob intervention, and able to dissolve Parliament when he chose without the possibility of the House of Commons adjourning to the Guildhall and appealing to the Londoners. That Charles was very much on his guard against the possibility of an armed rising in London is shown by the notes of the commander of his guards, the Earl of Craven: '1. How to pass the troops to the Tower, if the City oppose. . . .' On the afternoon of 21 February, it was noticed that the great guns on Tower Hill were moved within the walls of the Tower.[3]

At Oxford, then, Charles would be free from the danger that the deliberations would be affected by rioting such as he could remember had taken place forty years earlier, in those far-off days of 1641. That he was not contemplating surrender was also shown by some striking dismissals from his Privy Council. The Earl of Salisbury made the first move when the King prevented him from opposing the dissolution of the old Parliament at the Council Board: when the Earl asked leave to withdraw, Charles answered that he could not make any request that would be more easily granted, and ordered his name to be struck out of the Council Book. Amongst other dismissals were those of Essex and Temple, who had still been, nominally at least, his councillors; but the most sensational departure was that of Sunderland, who had hitherto been allowed to retain his Secretaryship in spite of his vote for Exclusion. The reason why he had been allowed to retain office, though without influence, cannot be established with certainty: it may have been the simple one that it would be difficult to find anyone who would pay the customary purchase price for the office, with the additional price of certain hostility from the Commons; or it may have been because Charles hesitated to dismiss a minister whose foreign policy he knew to be acceptable to William, and thus possibly alienate his nephew. Whatever the reason, when Charles finally dismissed him it caused a sensation, for this time there was no arrangement by which his successor, Lord Conway, should repay Sunderland the £6,000 which he had paid his predecessor for the Secretaryship.[4]

---

[1] Memorandum printed by J. Pollock, *The Popish Plot* (1903), p. 391.

[2] Jenkins to Godolphin, 5 Oct., *C.S.P.D. 1680–1*, p. 52; Barrillon, 7/17 Oct.

[3] *C.S.P.D. 1680–1*, p. 166; Luttrell, i. 68.

[4] Gwyn to Ormond, 18 Jan., *H.M.C. Ormond MSS.*, N.S. v. 555; Lady Sunderland to Sidney, 25 Jan., in Sidney Diary, ii. 165; Barrillon, 27 Jan./6 Feb. For other theories about the delay in dismissing Sunderland, cf. J. P. Kenyon, *Robert Spencer, Earl of Sunderland* (1958), p. 69, and J. R. Jones, *The First Whigs* (1961), p. 141 n.

In all this Charles was encouraged by the growing signs that at long last Louis XIV might be willing to come to his aid. Since the Treaty of Nijmegen Louis had found it more convenient, safer, and cheaper to rely on the domestic differences of Englishmen to produce English neutrality, rather than on subsidizing Charles; and Barrillon had been supplied with money to ingratiate himself with leading members of the opposition. But by the beginning of 1681 this policy began to look inadequate from Louis's point of view. Barrillon might have friendly relations with Ralph Montagu and others who were sweetened by gifts or the prospect of them, but he was not in touch with the most prominent Whig, Shaftesbury, whose sentiments were outspokenly hostile to France; and Louis concluded from Barrillon's despatches that in the next few months either Shaftesbury would win, or, in order to keep him out, Charles would propose that in the next reign the Prince of Orange should become Regent for James. Charles seems to have encouraged rumours to this effect, and their result, if not their purpose, was to lead Louis to the conclusion that it would be best for him to intervene and help Charles out of his difficulties. At about the New Year Barrillon was authorized to offer Charles 500,000 écus (£120,000) per annum for three years in return for his promise not to call Parliament, and the talks continued intermittently through January and February, with ever-increasing prospects of success, until in mid-March a verbal treaty was agreed on (for Charles would not sign anything) which by giving £375,000 in the next three years freed Charles from the need to ask Parliament for money. The sum was not large, but, in accordance with the principle enunciated later by Mr. Micawber, it made the difference between misery and happiness.[1]

Behind the scenes, therefore, Charles's position was improving and Shaftesbury's deteriorating, unknown to him, as the crisis approached. Superficially the King's need for money seemed to be one of the strongest reasons why the majority in the House of Commons should be able to enforce its will in the next Parliament—unless Charles tried, with the aid of his guards, to employ coercion. Of this possibility there was a good deal of talk in Whig circles. How much of the talk was serious, and how much of it had only propagandist aims, it is difficult to be sure. But just as Charles proposed to summon Parliament to Oxford in order to escape possible pressure from the Londoners and to prevent the Commons falling back upon them in the event of a dissolution, so many of the Whigs in their turn feared that the choice of Oxford—an unusual, inconvenient, and expensive choice—must have some sinister purpose. In the week after the royal proclamation was issued there was much discontent, and Whig members immediately began to talk of going to Oxford well attended.[2]

---

[1] Barrillon, 3/13 Jan., 6/16 Jan., 24 Jan./3 Feb., 3/13, 14/24 Feb., 21 Feb./3 Mar., 10/20, 14/24, 17/27 Mar.; J. S. Clarke, Life of James II (1816), i. 659–60, 664–5.

[2] Newsletter, 20 Jan., C.S.P.D. 1680–1, p. 139; Barrillon, 24 Jan./3 Feb.

On 25 January a petition, signed by sixteen peers, was presented to the King by Essex, Shaftesbury, Salisbury, and others. At Oxford, it said, 'neither Lords or Commons can be in safety, but will be daily exposed to the swords of the Papists and their adherents, of whom too many are crept into your Majesty's guards, the liberty of speaking . . . thereby destroyed . . . the straightness of the place noways admits of such a concourse of persons as now follows every Parliament, and the witnesses which are necessary to give evidence [upon the Commons' impeachments] can neither bear the charge of going thither nor trust themselves under the protection of a Parliament, that is itself evidently under the power of guards and soldiers.' They therefore asked that Parliament might sit in its usual place at Westminster.[1]

The peers can have had no expectation that their request would be granted, and attempts to organize a similar petition in the City were no more successful.[2] In the course of February members of the grand jury tried a different tack in the Court of King's Bench, suggesting that the regiments of guards which the King had raised since the Restoration, not being sanctioned by any Act of Parliament, were unconstitutional[3]; but this too had petered out. Knowing as we do that the King made no actual attempt at a *coup* at Oxford, we are tempted to dismiss all this as Whig propaganda; but in 1681 there were still those, like Shaftesbury, who could remember the attempt to arrest the Five Members in 1642, and suspicions that a similar plan might be behind the move to Oxford were neither completely feigned nor completely unnatural. Indeed two witnesses, neither of them very trustworthy it is true, declared that Shaftesbury contemplated refusing to go to Oxford, and leading a rising in London instead. One of these was the informer Turberville, who told Justice Warcup at the coffee-house on 3 February of an alleged conversation with the Earl that morning. The Earl had spoken of raising men; Turberville had offered 'to head any men to his lordship's design'; the Earl thanked him, but 'found the damned city to flag and fall off. His lordship further said he was sure of Wapping and Southwark and all that way, but the citizens were for peace, and flow off, and would not rise.' If we reflect that Shaftesbury was unlikely to have committed himself thus far to an informer of Turberville's stamp, what are we to think of the evidence of Lord Grey, who was certainly high in the Whig counsels? In his confession in 1685

---

[1] *Vox Patriae*, pp. 5–7; *Somers Tracts* (1811), viii. 282–3; *C.S.P.D. 1680–1*, pp. 146–7.

[2] Jenkins to William, 28 Jan., Groen van Prinsterer, II. v. 474; Jenkins to Ormond, 1 Feb., *H.M.C. Ormond MSS.*, N.S. v. 570; newsletter, 5 Feb., MSS. Carte 222, fo. 244; *Vox Patriae*, pp. 8–9.

[3] Jenkins to H. Savile, 7 Feb., *Savile Correspondence*, pp. 181–2, and to Ormond, 8, 12 Feb., op. cit. v. 575, 579; Luttrell, i. 67; Barrillon, 7/17 Feb. After the prorogation on 10 Jan. some of the Whigs had asked the Lord Mayor to see that companies of the guards on their way to relieve the Tower garrison were not permitted to march through the City; newsletter, 15 Jan., MSS. Carte 222, fos. 232–3.

Grey declared that Monmouth summoned him to town and told him that Shaftesbury, Macclesfield, Russell, and himself had decided to stay in London, instead of going to Oxford, because 'they were all well assured, the King did design to secure us at Oxford'. Two days later, Grey declared, Shaftesbury repeated this to him, 'and added further, that he had bestirred himself in the city, and was well assured of several thousand there, whenever the Duke of Monmouth, my Lord Russell, and himself, appeared with their swords in their hands, and brisk boys they were too'. In London the peers would be safe; at Oxford the House of Commons would either 'frighten the King into a compliance' or, if he tried to dissolve them, would adjourn to London, 'where we should be ready to stand by them'. But, Grey said, after a few days they thought better of all this, because of the difficulty which the Commons might have in getting back to the Guildhall through the King's guards, and decided that it was better to go to Oxford, taking as many friends as possible to protect them and to enable them to sit on after a dissolution.[1]

The chronology of all this is left very uncertain, and it must also be remembered that in 1685 Grey had every incentive to embroider his story in such a way as to save himself and those friends who were still alive at the expense of those, like Shaftesbury, Monmouth, and Russell, who were dead and beyond James II's reach. Nor is his evidence strictly independent of Turberville's, since when he wrote he knew what Turberville had sworn in Shaftesbury's trial and knew that he was expected to confirm it. Evidently Grey's confession must be taken with a good supply of salt. It remains possible that this was one of the courses of action which Shaftesbury considered, and discarded. Certainly he cannot have contemplated it very long or very systematically, because by the end of January he was making serious inquiries about accommodation for himself and his friends at Oxford.[2]

This was likely to be a difficult problem, even though the King had directed that 'the younger sort of students' should retire from the University and 'dispose of themselves as may best suit with their private conveniences'. Christ Church, Merton, and Corpus Christi Colleges had been set apart for the King and Queen and their courts, and Arlington as Lord Chamberlain provided suitable lodging for the foreign ambassadors.[3] But this did not mean that the rest of Oxford would be available to all comers. The other colleges, with their Royalist and Anglican traditions, would not be keen to accommodate Shaftesbury and the Whigs, who however proposed to come with an even larger following than normally

---

[1] 'The Journals of Edmund Warcup', by K. Feiling and F. R. G. Needham, in *E.H.R.* (1925), pp. 249–50; Grey, *The Secret History of the Rye House Plot* (1754), pp. 5–10.

[2] Dr. Bury to Locke, 2 Feb., MSS. Locke, c. 4, fo. 214.

[3] King to the University of Oxford, 25 Jan., *Life and Times of Anthony Wood*, ed. A. Clark (1892), ii. 513–14.

attended English peers. It was not an easy commission with which Shaftesbury entrusted his friend John Locke, in co-operation with Monmouth's secretary Vernon.

Rousing himself from an indisposition at his friend Tyrrell's house at Oakley, Locke returned immediately to Oxford to use his knowledge of the city and university in the Earl's service. At first, it seems, he had been asked to approach the Whig Alderman Wright to secure a house for Shaftesbury's 'family'; then there had been talk of finding a college for the Whigs to share—possibly the Earl's own college, Exeter; but in the end the Earl had directed Locke and Vernon to arrange lodgings with Dr. Wallis, the famous ex-Parliamentarian mathematician who had decoded Charles I's ciphers after the battle of Naseby, and was now Savilian Professor of Geometry. His house was 'in the lane between the Schools and New College, near in the midway betwixt them, as quiet a place as any in the town'. Locke inspected all the furniture, measured all the rooms, and approved them; he found two possible stables for the eleven horses that the Earl would bring, and a coach-house, and reported to his patron. All this was to the satisfaction of the Earl, who merely expressed a preference for a stable in which he could find his own hay and oats instead of having them provided; he did not care where the stables were or whether the coach and horses were together, for he was not contemplating having to make a hurried departure. He would bring his own bed and bedding, would need a pallet bed in his room for one footman, a bed in 'the little parlour' for two of his 'gentlemen-servants', and a bed in the little kitchen for his other footman. The second storey would be occupied by Lord Grey and his four servants. The Whigs would all dine in Wallis's college, Balliol—where indeed some of them had an 'allotment' of rooms; and to Balliol, after the session, Shaftesbury, Monmouth, Grey, and eleven persons presented a massive gilt bowl with a cover in gratitude for the facilities afforded to them.[1]

Locke's good offices were used not only in the mundane matter of arranging accommodation, but in more directly political preparations too. Shaftesbury asked him to intervene in the Oxfordshire election, where four 'very worthy men' (i.e. all Whigs) were causing one another expense by putting up against one another, and Shaftesbury thought that 'those that deserved well in the last Parliament ought in right to have the preference'; but as it turned out only one would stand down, and a poll had to be held to decide which two of the other three should be elected.[2]

---

[1] Locke to Shaftesbury, 6 Feb. 1681, Christie, ii. 392–8 (I am indebted to Mr. E. S. de Beer, for a transcript of the original, now in the Forster collection at the Victoria and Albert Museum, MSS. 363, 472); Shaftesbury to Locke, 8 Feb., Christie, ii. 398–9, 19 Feb., ibid. ii. 399–400; and 22 Feb., MSS. Locke c. 7, fo. 78; H. W. Carless Davis, *A History of Balliol College* (revised edn. 1963), pp. 295–6. The original bowl was melted down, but eight half-pint tankards made from it are still in use in the College buttery.

[2] Letter of 19 Feb., loc. cit.; Jones, op. cit. pp. 165–6.

Naturally this was by no means the only election in which Shaftesbury was interested. In his native Dorset, where his friend Thomas Freke acted as Whig manager and was himself re-elected as knight of the shire, he assisted with letters in support of Whig candidates. But if he was not without honour in his own country, he was far from being able to command universal support. In the borough of Shaftesbury from which he derived his title his letter on behalf of a candidate, Henry Whitaker, who did not engage in 'treating' was unsuccessful, though his client Thomas Bennet was elected to the other seat.[1] A little way across the Wiltshire border in the borough of Downton, where he himself had stood in the elections to the Long Parliament, his letters endeavouring to persuade the voters against one of the retiring members, Maurice Buckland, were in vain. Not much further across the Hampshire border lay Christchurch, which the Earl of Clarendon regarded as 'my own borough'. Shaftesbury, the Earl of Huntingdon, and other peers wrote to the Mayor to urge the exclusion of the two previous members (one of whom was Sir Thomas Clarges, a former prominent member of the Country Party who had, however, declared against Exclusion). Instead Shaftesbury and his colleagues recommended Thomas Hooper (who was later outlawed for his part in the Monmouth Rebellion) and John Ayloffe, who some years earlier had won some notoriety by putting a wooden shoe and a chaplet in the Speaker's chair as symbols of the Popish and French forces against which they were struggling, and who two or three years later was to be executed as a Rye House plotter. This intervention in what the Earl of Clarendon regarded as 'his own borough' caused him some uneasiness, but in the end the influence of the lord of the manor prevailed and the Whig candidates were defeated.[2]

In spite of such checks in particular places, the result of the elections as a whole was an emphatic re-affirmation of the elections of 1679. Nor will it do to suggest (as has sometimes been done) that the result was gained by aristocratic manipulation of rotten or pocket boroughs. A study of the returns shows that it is impossible to differentiate between county seats and boroughs, between larger borough seats and smaller ones; Whigs were predominant in all categories of seat, and Tory complaints were less of aristocratic influence (which Tories regarded as perfectly legitimate, as at Christchurch) than of the fact that 'the common unthinking people have a voice equal to a man of the best estate.'[3] The Court never had any hope of the House of Commons being differently composed from the last,[4] and there is no good ground for supposing either that the House was not

---

[1] *Pythouse Papers*, ed. W. A. Day (1879), pp. 89–90, 95.

[2] Clarendon to [? Jenkins], 13 Feb., *C.S.P.D. 1680–1*, pp. 164–6.

[3] *Ailesbury Memoirs*, i. 59–60.

[4] Cf. Duke of York to Col. Legge, 2/12 Feb., *H.M.C. Dartmouth MSS.*, i. 57; William to Jenkins, 1/11 Feb., J. Dalrymple, *Memoirs* . . . (1773), ii. 310; Jenkins to H. Savile, 7 Feb., *Savile Correspondence*, p. 182.

representative of the electorate as it existed, or that it would have been greatly different under any more democratic system.[1]

Not content with securing the election of a majority in the House, the Whigs also procured from the electorates the famous addresses of instructions to their Members of Parliament, intended to drive home the idea that Exclusion was the demand of 'the people'. These addresses were not identical either in wording or in content, but the similarities are so great as to make it plain that the main ideas were planned, and probable that Shaftesbury approved them if he did not originate them. As in the case of the petitioning movement of 1679–80, Londoners began it and others followed within a few days; in many cases copies were sent from the counties to London to be printed in *Protestant Domestic Intelligence*, and later collected in *Vox Patriae*. All the addresses contained prominently thanks to members for their endeavours in the last Parliament and instructions to them not to grant money in the next until provision had been made for the exclusion of a Popish successor. All this is obvious; what commentators have not generally noticed is that this was probably not simply a reiteration of a past demand, but a rejection in advance of 'expedients' which were being mooted. In past Parliaments Charles had professed his readiness to agree to any limitations on the power of a Popish successor but had not made any positive proposals of his own. Now, however, there was talk about an expedient by which, after James's succession, either his Protestant daughter, the Princess of Orange, or her husband should become Regent or 'Protector'.[2] As a result of the addresses members were committed in advance to agree to nothing short of the full demand for James's exclusion from the throne—although, be it noted, no single address specified who should succeed instead, so that the supporters of Monmouth and those of Mary and William could still co-operate. The addresses also commonly included demands for annual, or at least frequent Parliaments, to escape from the King's use of his prerogatives of prorogation and dissolution; and sometimes there were demands for the repeal of the Act of 1593 against sectaries, and for the reform of abuses in the electoral system.[3]

---

[1] The account of these elections by Dr. Jones, op. cit. pp. 159–73, supersedes the remarks of M. Dorothy George, 'Elections and Electioneering, 1679–81', in *E.H.R.* (1930), pp. 552–78, which are not based on such intensive research, and are neither consistent nor free from prejudice.

[2] Cf. Sunderland to H. Sidney, 4 Feb., Add. MSS. 32681, fo. 157; Jenkins to William, 18 Jan., Groen van Prinsterer, II. v. 472; loc. cit., p. 626 n. 4; Temple to Sidney, [15] Feb., Sidney Diary, ii. 177–8.

[3] Dr. Jones (op. cit. pp. 166, 169) refers to some draft instructions in the Shaftesbury Papers, VI B, 399, (Christie, ii, pp. cxi–cxii) as a model to be followed in the shires, and as 'Locke's draft', but this view of Locke's authorship seems to go further than the evidence will permit. The document belongs to the next century (*pace* Brown, p. 333) and although it bears the endorsement 'The original of this wrote in Mr. Lock's own hand', this may imply only that the copyist took it from Locke, who may in turn have copied it from elsewhere, for interest's sake. Locke's Journal (MSS. Locke, f. 5) shows that he left London

Taken together, these addresses represented a continuation of the efforts made by Shaftesbury and the Whigs in the petitioning movement of 1679–80 to mobilize 'out of doors' support to put pressure on the King, and to make propagandist use of the claim to represent the just demands of 'the people' as against a clique at Court. For the propaganda battle was now being waged much more fiercely than ever before in the news-sheets and pamphlets.

The Character of a Popish Successor, and what England may expect from such a one, humbly offered to the consideration of both Houses of Parliament appointed to meet at Oxford ... appeared, probably from the pen of Elkanah Settle, and set out once again the case for Exclusion. James's religion, he argued, was not simply a matter of his private devotions which need not affect the public. A Catholic prince must by his religion try to make his people Catholic. In answer to the argument that a Popish King might be restricted by potent laws, he asked: 'Who shall call this King to question for breaking these laws, if he has the power and will to do it?' It would be like building the hedge to fence in the cuckoo. A King of England was not like a Stadholder or a Doge. 'What monarch will be so unnatural to his own blood, so ill a defender, and so weak a champion for the royal dignity he wears, as to sign and ratify' laws which would 'render the Imperial Majesty of England but a pageant, a mere puppet upon a wire'? The writer suggested therefore, the taking out of 'one link out of the whole chain of succession'—a man who, having been converted to Catholicism, was anyway technically guilty of high treason under the terms of the Act of 1581. Parliament would be justified in disabling him; Parliament had varied the succession in Tudor times, when incidentally Elizabeth, though at one time declared illegitimate, had reigned and England had never been 'more blest'. (If the reference to the taking out of 'one link' might appeal to the supporters of William and Mary, this last sentence obviously encouraged those of Monmouth.) In the last resort the Crown was not like a country estate to be passed down to a Catholic heir and become his property, nor was the doctrine of passive obedience valid when 'the very essence of a Popish successor is the greatest plot upon England since the Creation'.

Whether or not Shaftesbury read all this before it appeared in print, these arguments admirably represented his case at this time—probably rather better than did Henry Nevile's *Plato Redivivus*, which was exciting interest at the same time and as an abstract political treatise had a more lasting value in the next century, but was less directly concerned with the immediate political situation and indeed did not favour Monmouth's claims.[1] And the next step of Shaftesbury and his supporters was formally

---

on 13 Jan., before the dissolution, and it is unlikely that his pen was used at Oakley or Oxford to draft what Shaftesbury or any Whig could easily have done at Thanet House.

[1] Crinò, op. cit. p. 166.

to indict the Duke of York of recusancy at the Old Bailey on 26 February. The Grand Jury, which consisted of Whigs, found a true bill, and counsel on the Duke's behalf was reduced to asking for a delay until Easter week before James was declared convicted.[1]

That this attempt attracted far less attention than the original ones was partly due to the appearance of another Plot informer, whose activities were the last factor in the political situation. This was Edmund Fitzharris, who was apprehended by order of the Council on an information of the Whig zealot Sir William Waller on 27 February, was sent to Newgate on a charge of high treason two days later, and began to seek to buy a pardon by providing information about the Plot in the course of the next week.

Fitzharris's case is in its way as intriguing and obscure as the death of Sir Edmund Berry Godfrey. He was perhaps the least hateful of the informers, not simply because no man's death lies at his door, but because, unlike Oates, Bedloe, and others he possessed qualities which went some way to compensate for his lying. He was above all pathetically devoted to his wife and small children, whom he was too poor to keep in the station to which he thought that they were entitled, and there is an element of tragedy in his ruin. One has the impression of an ordinary, weak-willed, not over-intelligent man, who in his efforts to turn a dishonest penny was caught up in events which were too much for him and very soon passed out of his control. But he was certainly a liar, and the difficulty is to know which of the many stories that he told was nearest the truth. Space forbids an exhaustive discussion of all the problems involved; what follows will be directed to the effects of the Fitzharris case upon the political situation and consequently upon Shaftesbury's own fortunes.[2]

Fitzharris came from an Irish family whose past services to the Royal cause entitled him, or so he thought, to some reward. He hung about the Court, and claimed to have been employed to obtain from members of the opposition copies of proposed articles of impeachment against the Duchess of Portsmouth.[3] In the process he had gained some reward, and some acquaintance with the Duchess, her maid, Mrs. Wall, some of the opposition, and possibly the French ambassador. Some time before Sunderland's dismissal, with the participation of Mrs. Wall and the knowledge of the King, he was given money 'for Lord Howard'[4] and apparently told to use this in an attempt to win over that Whig peer; the record of Lord

---

[1] Newsletters, 1, 8 Mar., MSS. Carte 222, fos. 258–9, 266.

[2] Dr. Jones has promised to deal with this case at some future date. In the meantime there is only the inadequate account in R. Petherick, *Restoration Rogues* (1950), pp. 264–324.

[3] These must have been the articles of which Barrillon sent a copy to his master with his despatch of 19/29 Jan. 1680; cf. also [Sir Robert Reading?] to Arran, Candlemas 1680, MSS. Carte 39, fo. 107.

[4] Fitzharris's statements here are supported by the King's remark, recorded in 'The Journals of Edmund Warcup', by K. Feiling and F. R. D. Needham, in *E.H.R.* (1925), p. 252 (entry for 8 Apr. 1681).

Howard of Escrick, 'a man of wit and learning, bold and poor', was such as to suggest that, in spite of his long record of opposition, dating back to Anabaptist days under the Commonwealth, he might be amenable to bribery,[1] and Fitzharris frequented his house in the village of Knightsbridge. Then he engaged in intrigues with an old acquaintance of his, named Everard, whom he had known since 1665, and sought to persuade him to write and distribute a pamphlet, *The True Englishman speaking plain English*, arguing that Charles was fully as guilty as James, and that the English should 'rise, and move as one man', and making other extremely seditious remarks; there would be a reward, he said, from the French ambassador, who was anxious to stir up as much disorder as he could. But Everard put Sir William Waller and the Plot witness Smith in hiding places where they could overhear his conversation with Fitzharris, and when they had heard all that they wanted to hear, they arrested Fitzharris and carried him before the Council, where all agreed that he was, in the staid Jenkins's words, 'a very naughty man'. Since the draft pamphlet was there for all to see, with amendments in Fitzharris's handwriting, the case was black against him, and he was committed to Newgate on a charge of high treason.

So far this Everard-Fitzharris business seemed a fairly run-of-the-mill minor Popish Plot case. But in prison Fitzharris was visited by the Whig sheriffs of London, Cornish, and Bethel, and to them he offered, or was induced to offer, to make a 'confession' of matters much more serious than the treasonable pamphlet. He appeared before the King on 7 March, and to make sure that his confession should not be concealed, the sheriffs arranged that the former Lord Mayor, Sir Robert Clayton, and the Recorder, Sir George Treby, should visit him three days later to take down his information. It was sensational. Apart from relating conversations which implied that a plot to establish Catholicism went back at least to 1672, he said that in April 1679 Montecuculi, the envoy of the Duke of Modena (father of the Duchess of York) had offered him £10,000 to kill the King; adding, that 'after that time, there should be no more Parliaments in England; and that the Duke of York was privy to all these designs'. The Queen was also implicated; and for good measure Fitzharris threw in the information that in April 1680 a priest named Kelly had confessed to him that he had been concerned in Godfrey's murder, which had taken place as Prance described, and according to the Duke's servant, du Puy, 'was consulted at Windsor'.

The straightforward interpretation of all this is that Fitzharris had tried to earn a reward from the King by entrapping Everard (and possibly Howard and others on whom copies of the libel could be planted), had

---

[1] For Howard and his activities against the government in 1672–4, see my *William of Orange and the English Opposition 1672–4* (1953), *passim*. As is well-known, he turned King's evidence against Russell and others in the Rye House Plot trials.

been foiled by Everard's superior cunning, and had frantically tried to escape from the charge of treason by following the example of many others and making himself an indispensable Plot witness. A more far-fetched interpretation would be that Fitzharris, Everard, and possibly Howard and others concocted the whole episode from start to finish in a way which they thought would make Fitzharris's final confession more credible, in the expectation that rewards would be forthcoming from the Whigs. Since there is no evidence that Shaftesbury and Fitzharris knew one another, there is no need to pursue the question here. What was important was the political use to which the information could be put. Too late, Charles sent the prisoner to the Tower where the Whigs would not be able to get at him again; and decided that, unlike previous informers, Fitzharris should not receive a pardon in return for his information. Fitzharris was in fact to be kept incommunicado until he could be tried and permanently silenced by being put to death. Equally obviously it became the objective of the Whigs to prevent this by getting him into the hands of the House of Commons, and this they hoped to do by impeaching him.[1]

All this was an additional reason, if one were needed, why the King should not allow the Oxford Parliament to remain in session for long. But for the sake of public opinion he had to go through the motions of meeting it, so that he could say that he had offered to consider 'expedients', but that the Commons would not listen and be reasonable. Ironically it was Shaftesbury's old partner in the proprietorship of Carolina, the Earl of Craven, whom Charles left behind in command of all the troops for securing the peace and quiet of London and Westminster, and suppressing any 'tumultuous meetings' with which the civil authorities could not, or would not, cope. Having taken these precautions and arranged to be accompanied by a large force of guards, with other troops quartered along the road to secure their return, Charles left for Oxford, accompanied by the Queen, the Duchess of Portsmouth, and Nell Gwynn, and was able to spend a day relaxing at the Burford races before returning to Oxford on the 18th.[2]

On Friday and Saturday, 18 and 19 March, the town began to fill with members of Parliament—and with their attendants; for these came in large numbers, some of them well armed. This was probably less in genuine fear of a *coup* than to obtain some propaganda advantage from insinuating

---

[1] For the unfolding of the case, see newsletters, 27 Feb., 5, 12 Mar., MSS. Carte 222, fos. 258, 268; newsletter in *C.S.P.D. 1680–1*, pp. 194–5; Gwyn to Ormond, 8 Mar., *H.M.C. Ormond MSS.*, N.S. v. 603–4; Fitzharris's libel in *Parliamentary History*, iv, pp. cxxiii–cxxviii; Barrillon, 7/17 Mar.; *C.J.* ix. 709–10; Arran to Ormond, 12 Mar., op. cit. v. 609.

[2] King to Craven, 9 Mar., *C.S.P.D. 1680–1*, p. 204; Clarke, i. 667; Prideaux to Ellis, 17 Mar., *Letters of Humphrey Prideaux to J. Ellis*, ed. E. M. Thompson (Camden Society, 1875), pp. 82–83; Anthony Wood, ed. A. Clark (1892), ii. 524–7; Luttrell, i. 71.

the existence of danger; but if so it was a tactic which recoiled upon them, for it formed the basis of equally unfounded Tory allegations that there had been a Whig plan for a *coup*. It was noticed that many people wore ribbons in their hats, with the slogan 'No Popery, no Slavery', woven into them; and the 'Protestant Joiner', Stephen College, had the task of distributing appropriate pamphlets and cartoons, showing the Tories and 'tantivies' (or hunting squires) riding the Church to Rome, accompanied by a barking Towzer (L'Estrange), and James, half Irishman and half-devil, with the latter half setting fire to London. All this implied some organization, though whether the notorious 'Green Ribbon Club' was really the body responsible is very doubtful. The climax of it all was the entry into Oxford of Shaftesbury. The Earl had left London with the Earls of Stamford and Salisbury, and attended by 'about two hundred persons well armed and mounted'; as a mark of his sympathy for Dissenters he stayed with a Quaker at Wycombe on Friday night; and on Saturday, he reached Oxford, not in a coach but on horseback 'with holsters and pistols before him, attended with a great many horsemen well armed and coaches'. That night there was a minor alarm when the chimney of his apartment caught fire; but otherwise everything went off peaceably, though Tories commented rancorously because the Whig faction insisted on sitting separately in St. Mary's next day.[1]

On Monday, 21 March, the peers and members of the Commons congregated in the Geometry School to hear the King open this new Parliament. In order to keep the events of this Parliament in a proper perspective it must be appreciated that no one expected it to last for very long. Shaftesbury's own forecast had been that it would last for three weeks.[2] It was expected that the King would put forward an 'expedient' as a compromise; that this expedient would be rejected; and that the King would either give way to get the money he needed, in which case it would adjourn to its more convenient home at Westminster to pass the necessary Acts, or he would hang on, dissolve Parliament, and make a further attempt in the autumn. What was unexpected about the famous dissolution was simply that it came after one week, and not after three.

To some members of the Commons the King's opening speech seemed to be 'an excellent gracious one'; 'all the rest' thought it 'a subtle crafty one'. To posterity the latter description seems the more appropriate. Charles talked of encouraging England's allies, when his secret negotiation with France was almost complete; he talked of 'the further prosecution of the plot . . . the providing a more speedy conviction of recusants, and if it be practicable, the ridding ourselves quite of all of that party that have any

---

[1] Newsletter, 22 Mar., MSS. Carte 222, fo. 272; Crinò, p. 171; Latimer to Danby, 20 Mar., *H.M.C. Lindsey MSS.* p. 423; *Protestant Oxford Intelligence*, 17–21 Mar.; *True Protestant Mercury*, 19–23 Mar.; Ailesbury, *Memoirs* (1890), i. 54–55; R. North, *Lives of the Norths* (ed. A. Jessopp, 1890), iii. 159.

[2] Feiling and Needham, op. cit. (6 Feb.) p. 250; cf. Barrillon, 3/13 Mar.

considerable authority and interest amongst them', when he had no real desire of any of these; and his final request that the Commons should 'make the laws of the land your rule, because I am resolved they shall be mine' contrasts with his later breach of the Triennial Act. But the kernel of his speech was the passage in which, while repeating his refusal to depart from the succession, 'to remove all reasonable fears that may arise from the possibility of a Popish successor coming to the crown, if means can be found that in such a case the administration of the government may remain in Protestant hands', he offered to 'hearken to any such expedient'. The offer was extremely vague; it was extremely insincere, in view of the conditions which were being privately agreed with Barrillon; it was made in the expectation that it would be rejected; but it served the purpose of doing something to conciliate William of Orange and his English supporters, such as Halifax and Sir Thomas Littleton, when an immediate dissolution might have driven them into opposition.[1]

The Whigs in the Commons responded by re-electing their former Speaker, William Williams; and by repeating their former decision that all their Votes be printed—a resolution which was seconded by Shaftesbury's relative, Sir William Cooper; Secretary Jenkins in reply complained 'it is a sort of appeal to the people', but that was precisely the point. In Winnington's words, 'I think it not natural, nor rational, that the people, who sent us hither, should not be informed of our actions'. Sir Nicholas Carew followed by moving for the Exclusion Bill on which members' instructions insisted; and although the House responded only by fixing Saturday the 26th to consider means for the security of the Protestant religion and the safety of the King's person, thus giving room for expedients to be proposed by those who favoured them, it was fairly clear that the Exclusionists only agreed to this in the expectation that they could easily out-debate and out-vote their opponents. The crisis would soon be reached.[2]

In the meantime Shaftesbury had set the ball rolling in the Lords by moving for an inquiry into the reasons why the Bill for the relief of Dissenters by the repeal of the Act of 1593, which had passed both Houses in the last session, had not been presented for the royal assent; and the Clerk of the Parliaments had been obliged to say that the King himself had ordered him not to present it.[3] This could have been embarrassing to the King had he really been concerned about the possibility of harmonious co-operation with Parliament; as it was, it mattered little. Of

---

[1] *L.J.* xiii. 745–6; Cooke to Ormond, 24 Mar., *H.M.C. Ormond MSS.*, N.S. v. 619; Gwyn to Ormond, 25 Mar., ibid. vi. 8.

[2] *L.J.* xiii. 748–9; *C.J.* ix. 708; Grey, viii. 292–9; *The Debates in the House of Commons assembled at Oxford* (1681); [Hoskins] to Stringer, 26 Mar., Shaftesbury Papers, VI A, 360 (mistakenly printed by Christie as 'Locke's letter', ii, pp. cxii–cxv); Cooke to Ormond, 25 Mar., *H.M.C. Ormond MSS.*, N.S. vi. 5.

[3] *L.J.* xiii. 748, 751; [Hoskins] to Stringer, loc. cit. ii. cxiii; Latimer to Danby, 23 Mar., *H.M.C. Lindsey MSS.*, p. 425.

much more significance were three conversations which Shaftesbury and Charles had during this week, in the course of their fencing with one another. On 21 March Essex and Shaftesbury had waited upon the King to kiss his hand and 'humbly to present to His Majesty the state of affairs touching Fitzharris'; we can only surmise the nature of their request and the King's refusal to give them satisfaction.[1] On the morning of the 24th Shaftesbury tried a different method of sounding out the King. As the peers chatted before the opening of the sitting, Shaftesbury went up to a group of them and announced that he had received in an anonymous letter an 'expedient' which would 'comply with the King's speech, and satisfy the people too'; but the King must see it first, and Shaftesbury had not leave to approach him. So the Marquis of Worcester carried the letter to the King. When Charles read it, he found that in about six lines, it advocated settling the Crown upon the Duke of Monmouth.

'Ay marry', said Charles, 'here is an expedient indeed, if one would trample over all laws of God and man.' Shaftesbury, who had followed Worcester to the King, eagerly seized his chance to enquire, 'Sire, will you give me leave to make it as lawful as we can?' If Charles gave him leave to introduce a bill, the imputation of 'trampling on the laws of man' could easily be removed. But this gave Charles an opportunity to declare his resolve to hold firm. 'Whoever goes about such things can be no better than knaves; by the grace of God I will stick to that that is law, and maintain the Church as it is now established, and not be of a religion that can make all things lawful, as I know Presbytery can. . . .' He went on to attack Presbyterianism and to proclaim his own determination to stand by the Church of England, however few people would stand by him. 'I am not like others that the older they grow the fearfuller they are.' Shaftesbury did not attempt to defend Presbyterianism; instead he merely reiterated his constant attitude that 'no Church nor clergy were but would impose upon the government' if given the opportunity, and this allowed Charles to repeat his belief that the monarchy and the Church of England 'must march together.'

One does not need a reminder of Charles's death-bed admission to the Church of Rome within four years of these high-sounding words to realize that they were less an expression of personal belief than a propagandist declaration, designed to rally support both inside the House and outside it. Within twenty-four hours a version of the conversation had been prepared for publication. Shaftesbury had come as near as he ever did to committing himself to Monmouth's cause; Charles had uncompromisingly refused it, in terms calculated to appeal to all Anglicans who

---

[1] *The Protestant Oxford Intelligence*, 21–24 Mar. On 24 Mar. Fitzharris told the Lieutenant of the Tower that he would say no more about Godfrey's murder 'till he was sent for to Oxford by the Parliament'; information of Thomas Hawley, 12 Apr., *C.S.P.D. 1680–1*, p. 238.

believed in the divine right of hereditary succession, to all others who disliked the legitimization of a bastard, and to all who looked to William and Mary to provide the ultimate solution.[1]

The next day there was a third and more light-hearted conversation between Charles and Shaftesbury, when Charles 'to entertain himself' called the Earl and in his turn asked whether no other expedient could be found instead of Exclusion. Shaftesbury answered No, and said that the whole nation seemed to be of his opinion. Charles replied by suggesting private talks, to which each should bring two companions; Shaftesbury agreed, and suggested for the meeting-place the lodgings of the Lord Chamberlain, Lord Arlington. Charles asked 'Why there above all places?', and was told, 'first, that it was the most indifferent [neutral] place in the world, because my Lord Chamberlain was neither good Protestant nor good Catholic; and next, because there was the best wine, which was the only good thing that could be had from their meeting.'[2] This was Shaftesbury's way of being as uncompromising as Charles had been on the previous day. They would meet on one occasion more, when the superficially polite tone of this conversation would be finally stripped away.

After these two confrontations, in which each made clear his refusal to give way, it was a foregone conclusion that nothing could come of the session. As Shaftesbury said, it was indeed an unfortunate moment for Danby to petition for bail. This was one of the now rare occasions on which Halifax agreed with him, for that statesman clung to the hope that an expedient would be accepted by the Commons.[3] It was a forlorn hope. On Friday, 26 March, the Commons heard Sir William Waller, Sir George Treby, and Sir Robert Clayton on the subject of Fitzharris, and resolved that he be impeached; and precisely because it was known that this would be unwelcome to the King and his ministers, it was facetiously proposed that Secretary Jenkins should carry the impeachment up to the Lords, and this was insisted upon, over the wretched Secretary's protests.[4] Next day, when the appointed time came to discuss 'the security of the Protestant

---

[1] Marquis of Worcester to the Marchioness, 25 Mar., H.M.C. Beaufort MSS., pp. 83–84; Barrillon, 28 Mar./7 Apr.; Cooke to Ormond, 26 Mar., H.M.C. Ormond MSS., N.S. vi. 8; The Earl of Shaftesbury's Expedient for Settling the Nation, discoursed with His Majesty in the House of Peers at Oxford, March the 24th, 1680–1 (ending with the words 'This was done yesterday in the House of Lords'). Miss Foxcroft, Life of Halifax (1898), i. 290, has been misled by Cooke's letter into thinking that Shaftesbury's idea was to make Monmouth, not King, but Regent instead of the Prince of Orange, as in the 'expedient' which was to be broached on the 26th; but the other sources agree and are likely to be better informed than Cooke.

[2] Cooke to Ormond, 25 [and 26] Mar., H.M.C. Ormond MSS., N.S. vi. 6–7. Since the letter refers to the Exclusion debate of the 26th as taking place 'just now', the concluding part of this letter must have been written on that day. The writer says that the conversation took place 'yesterday', and I interpret this as being the 25th; in this I differ from Miss Brown (p. 280), who interprets it as the conclusion of the previous talk on Monmouth.

[3] L.J. xiii. 752; Latimer to Danby, 24 Mar., H.M.C. Lindsey MSS., pp. 426–7.

[4] C.J. ix. 709–10; Grey, viii. 303–9; newsletter, C.S.P.D. 1680–1, p. 225.

religion, and the safety of the King's person', Sir Robert Clayton (less inhibited as a member than he had been as Lord Mayor) and Lord Russell began by moving for Exclusion, both of them claiming to discharge a trust imposed upon them by the addresses of their respective electors. Nothing but Exclusion would do. It was Sir Thomas Littleton, like Halifax a former leader of the Country Party, who put forward Halifax's solution, that after Charles's death James be allowed to retain the title of King, but in perpetual exile, while Princess Mary and her husband exercised a Regency in his name. But it was easy for Sir William Jones and others to show the practical objections to such a futile compromise: the birth of a son to James would make the situation impossibly uncertain; James would be as unlikely to accept this solution as to accept Exclusion, and 'if you allow the Duke the name of the King, it will imply a right'. It was hardly common sense to stop at a point where the Duke was excluded from everything but the name of King; indeed, 'it is less evil or injustice to take away from him both the crown and power than to leave him of both but the name'. If he was to be kept out, it was sensible to exclude him from both. Finally, a regency might mean an impossible strain on the conscience of James's daughter Mary, and there could be no guarantee that she would accept it. In the end the supporters of the expedient did not even force a division, and the House resolved that an Exclusion Bill be brought in.[1]

At this point the House learned that the Lords had refused to agree to the impeachment of Fitzharris, and had decided that he must be tried by the ordinary process of the common law. In the vote Shaftesbury mustered the same number of peers—thirty—as had voted for Exclusion, and no more, while all the fourteen bishops present and about fifty lay peers took Charles's view; and about the usual number of peers—twenty—signed a Protest in the Journals under Shaftesbury's leadership.[2] The King's majority in the upper House was impregnable. It was small consolation that the Commons resolved that the Lords' refusal was a denial of justice and a violation of the constitution of Parliaments; that it was 'an obstruction to the further discovery of the Popish Plot'; and that any inferior court proceeding against Fitzharris would be guilty of a breach of privilege.

On this Saturday night observers from both parties were forecasting that there would be a prorogation or a dissolution on Monday.[3] But the timing of it was a tricky matter, for Charles was afraid that his opponents might try to defy him and sit on. Whether this was a real danger is very

---

[1] C.J. ix. 711; Grey, viii. 309–32; Debates in the House of Commons assembled at Oxford (1681); 'The Heads of the Expedient proposed to the Parliament at Oxford . . .', Add. MSS. 38847, fo. 83; Hyde to William, 29 Mar., Groen van Prinsterer, II. v. 490–1; Conway to William, 29 Mar., ibid. 493; Cooke, loc. cit. p. 635, n. 2.

[2] L.J. xiii. 755; H.M.C. House of Lords MSS. 1678–88, pp. 272–3; Cooke, loc. cit.; Marquis of Worcester to the Marchioness, 28 Mar., H.M.C. Beaufort MSS., p. 85.

[3] Cooke to Ormond, 26 Mar., H.M.C. Ormond MSS., N.S. vi. 8; Sir E. Harley to Lady Harley, 26 Mar., H.M.C. Portland MSS., iii. 369.

doubtful. One of the Whigs, Lord Grey, who lodged in Dr. Wallis's house with Shaftesbury, 'confessed' in 1685 that on the Sunday Shaftesbury, Monmouth, Essex, Salisbury, and himself had agreed that the deadlock which now existed between the two Houses must lead to a dissolution 'in four or five days'; and that they resolved to stay in the Lords if members of the Commons kept their word to do the same, 'but we thought it inconvenient to propose it to many of them till the time'. Their gentlemen and servants with their sympathizers among the townspeople would be able to resist any attempt by the King to evict them by force.[1] This is plausible, but it must be remembered that Grey naturally told James what he expected to hear, and what could safely be told without incriminating anyone still alive; there is no corroboration for it, and certainly no plans were in readiness when the time came. Once again, one must say that this course of action may possibly have been talked of, but there is no good evidence that it had become a formed plan.

At all events, Charles decided to play his celebrated farce, in order to give his opponents as little notice as possible of his intention to dissolve. On Saturday the Commons, complaining of their lack of room in their present quarters, had asked the King to fit out the Sheldonian Theatre for them. Charles readily agreed, was free with his opinion about the work which was needed, went among the workmen, and entertained himself and the Court with talk about the Commons' new accommodation and how wonderful it would be. When Monday came, Charles went to the House of Lords in his ordinary clothes as his custom was; but he had caused his robes to be sent separately in a sedan. He slipped out for a moment, put on his robes, and re-entered to address his Parliament. The Commons came tumbling up the narrow stair from their chamber; and Charles, with the briefest of remarks, dissolved them. The last Parliament that either Charles or Shaftesbury was to see was over. Charles had a hasty mouthful of something to eat, gave orders that the post should be delayed until evening, left for Windsor early in the afternoon, and went on to London early next day.[2]

According to Grey, Shaftesbury and some other peers stayed in the Lords on the pretext of signing their protest against the vote on Fitzharris,[3] but their friends in the Commons did not respond to the suggestion that they should sit on. But to be effective such a step would have had to be taken immediately, formally, and by a majority; and it could not be

---

[1] *Secret History of the Rye House Plot* (1754), pp. 10–13.

[2] *C.J.* ix. 710, 712; North, op. cit. p. 104; Grey, viii. 338–40; *L.J.* xiii. 757; Sir Cyril Wyche to Ormond, 29 Mar., *H.M.C. Ormond MSS.*, N.S. vi. 21; *Life and Times of Anthony Wood*, ed. A. Clark (1892), ii. 532; Ailesbury, *Memoirs* (1890), i. 56–57; van Citters, 28 Mar./7 Apr., Add. MSS. 17677, FF; Barrillon, 31 Mar./10 Apr.

[3] This appears in *L.J.* in Saturday's proceedings, but it is possible that the formal signatures had to be entered on Monday when the clerks had prepared their record for Saturday.

suddenly improvised. Many members dispersed from Oxford with as much haste as the King; possibly there were equally unjustified fears of a *coup* on both sides. Shaftesbury himself was in no hurry to leave. Only on Good Friday, 1 April did he leave Dr. Wallis's lodgings, pay his servant at Balliol ten shillings, and leave by coach for London. That evening he was back in Aldersgate, and on Easter Sunday he was in his place at the parish church of St. Botolph, very much to the relief of the Countess of Shaftesbury, who had been terrified by rumours that her beloved husband had been impeached at Oxford.[1]

One of the most striking features of the situation is that the news of the dissolution was received in London with some discontent, but no demonstrations and above all no rioting.[2] The discontent was a controlled discontent—not the kind which was likely to vent itself in an outburst of passionate fury, irrespective of the wishes of its leaders. Of course, there had been prorogations and dissolutions before—and new Parliaments; and although to our hindsight there is an air of finality about this particular dissolution, to contemporaries it was by no means clear that Charles had parted with Parliament for good. No one knew that with the aid of economies at Court and French subsidies Charles would be able to dispense with his Commons; and even before people left Oxford the expectation was voiced that there would soon be new elections, possibly for a Parliament in October or November.[3] It was some time before these expectations were disappointed.

On 5 April the Whig peers and former M.P.s held one of their periodical meetings over a meal at the Sun tavern. Monmouth was away, attending the races at Northampton with the Earl of Sunderland,[4] but otherwise most of the leaders congregated in the City. The difficulty was to find something positive to do. There was the old tactic of persuading the Common Council of London to petition for a Parliament, and Lords Bedford and Salisbury waited several times on the Lord Mayor, Sir Patience Ward, to ask him to call a meeting; but the Lord Mayor was too ill to leave his house, or feigned to be.[5] Another possibility might be to make use of the proceedings at the Old Bailey on the indictment of recusancy against the Duke of York; the Court had planned to evade this by using a writ of certiorari to remove it to the King's Bench. Oates (who had laid the information) and his counsel nearly caught the Duke's counsel by

---

[1] Grey, *Secret History*, pp. 13–14; accounts in the muniment room at Wimborne St. Giles; *The Loyal Protestant and True Domestick Intelligence*, 5 Apr.; Lady Russell to L. Russell, c. 24 Mar., [Mary Berry], *Life of Lady Russell* (1819), p. 241.

[2] Cf. Barrillon, 31 Mar./10 Apr.

[3] Arran to Ormond, 28 Mar., *H.M.C. Ormond MSS.*, N.S. vi. 9; cf. newsletter, 16 Apr., MSS. Carte 222, fo. 286; Barrillon, 18/28 Apr.

[4] Feiling and Needham, op. cit. p. 252; *Loyal Protestant and True Domestick Intelligence*, 16 Apr.

[5] [Jenkins?] to William, 1 Apr., S.P. 104/67, fo. 30; Gwyn to Ormond, 5 Apr., *H.M.C. Ormond MSS.*, N.S. vi. 27.

surprise when they raised objections to what was normally only a legal formality; but by means of an adjournment the Duke's counsel were able to answer these objections, and the prosecution lapsed.[1] Very little was left. No further informers dared to come forward to confess knowledge of a Plot, because in the case of Fitzharris Charles had made plain that he would grant no further pardons for treason or misprision of it. The truth was that the initiative had suddenly passed to the King, and the Whigs were on the defensive.

Charles began by launching his own propaganda offensive. On 8 April he issued a Declaration to explain why he had dissolved his last two Parliaments. It recited what the King considered to be their unreasonable behaviour in refusing to accept anything but Exclusion, making indiscriminate and unjustified attacks on his ministers and judges, and sending him addresses which were more like the Remonstrances of pre-Civil War days; assured his people that this should not make him 'out of love with Parliaments', for he was resolved to have frequent ones [sic]; and ended with an appeal to the loyalty 'of all those who consider the rise and progress of the late troubles and confessions, and desire to preserve their country from a relapse, and who cannot but remember that religion, liberty and property were all lost and gone when the monarchy was shaken off, and could never be revived till that was restored'. Whoever drafted it, it was a skilful production; and Charles had facilities for distributing it even greater than those open to the Whigs. He wrote to the archbishops directing them to arrange for the Declaration to be read from all pulpits[2]; Crown and Church would indeed 'march together'. At the same time L'Estrange's *Observator* began to appear regularly to present the Court and Tory case to the public at intervals of a few days. Flatman's *Heraclitus Ridens* had been doing this since February, but L'Estrange's attacks on Whigs and Dissenters were more effective, though the Whigs tried to dismiss him contemptuously as a yapping dog whom they christened 'Towzer'. He was less successful in putting forward positive ideas of his own than in puncturing Whig propaganda on Sir Edmund Berry Godfrey and other themes; but in this last task he was every effective. He was a better journalist than those, such as 'Dick Implement' (Richard Janeway), who wrote periodically on the other side; he had a lively style and a sense of humour, and he had the journalist's supreme virtue of being easy to read. The Whigs tried to fight back, with several pamphlet replies to the Declaration[3] in which Shaftesbury may or may not have had a hand; but

---

[1] Luttrell, i. 73; Clarke, op. cit. i. 675; newsletter, 9 Apr., MSS. Carte 222, fo. 282.
[2] *C.S.P.D. 1680–1*, p. 237.
[3] See especially Sir William Jones's powerful reply, *A Just and Modest Vindication of the Proceedings of the Two last Parliaments* . . . (printed in *Parliamentary History*, iv, pp. cxxxiii–clxxiv); *A Letter from a Person of Quality to his friend concerning His Majesty's late Declaration*, in *State Tracts* (1689), pp. 187–92; and cf. *Observations upon a late Libel, called A Letter from a Person of Quality* . . . and *His Majesty's Declaration Defended in a Letter to a Friend* for some interesting debating replies in turn from the Tories.

their printers and publishers worked in the knowledge that they were marked men who would be seized if the slightest pretext presented itself. On 15 April, for instance, Francis Smith was committed to Newgate on a charge of high treason, because a witness alleged that he had said 'he would never leave printing and writing till this kingdom was brought to a free state'.[1]

The King's Declaration elicited a flood of addresses to thank him. These may be regarded as the Tory counterpart of the Whig instructions to members of Parliament in February. If the Whigs had published theirs in *Vox Patriae* the Tories printed theirs in *Vox Angliae*. What makes them difficult to evaluate is that many of them came from the very same places. Whig pamphleteers made great play with this, arguing that parliamentary elections were the real test of a borough's opinions, and suggesting by implication that the King should submit to this test.[2] As against this, the addresses have sometimes been accepted at their face value and used as an argument for the 'unrepresentativeness' of the Oxford Parliament, and the worthlessness of the instructions to members.[3] A third guess might be that some places which had elected Whig members thought it prudent to hedge their bets now that Exclusion, however desirable, seemed further off than ever, and thus ward off possible harm to the interests of their borough. But all that one can really be sure of is that almost everywhere signatories could be found for both Whig and Tory addresses, and that to the end of his reign Charles did not choose to inquire which party was the more powerful in the electorate.

For all petitioners and addressers, the City of London was the greatest prize. On 28 April in the Court of Aldermen a number of Tories presented a petition 'signed by about 2000 hands and collected in 12 hours'. Whilst this was being debated, Sir Thomas Player, Sheriff Bethel and the two Huguenot merchants Papillon and Dubois presented a counter-petition and asked that both should be referred to a Common Council, which might petition for a Parliament. The Aldermen prudently decided against this, and both parties 'were wished to go home and love one another', but this they could scarcely be expected to do.[4] It is in this context of a developing struggle for superiority in the City that we must consider Shaftesbury's

---

[1] Gwyn to Ormond, 16 Apr., *H.M.C. Ormond MSS.*, N.S. vi. 35. Smith was bailed on 1 June: Luttrell, i. 92.

[2] For the best of these critiques, see *An Impartial Account of the nature and tendency of the late Addresses* (28 June 1681). Miss Brown (p. 283) says that judging by the style this 'may well be attributed to Shaftesbury's pen', but the stylistic argument is vague and inconclusive. It is, however, interesting to note that the author mentions the worthlessness of the addresses made to Richard Cromwell on his accession to the Proctectorate, which Anthony Ashley Cooper could well remember. If he did not write it, he may have suggested some of the arguments.

[3] M. Dorothy George, 'Elections and Electioneering, 1679–81', in *E.H.R.* (1930), esp. pp. 575, 577.

[4] Newsletter, 30 Apr., MSS. Carte 222, fos. 294–5; *C.S.P.D. 1680–1*, pp. 256–7.

admission as a freeman of the Skinners' Company on 3 May. It was not a new idea: in the previous December Sheriff Bethel had proposed giving the freedom of the City to Buckingham, and it was said that if the Aldermen had agreed to this, the other Sheriff, Cornish, would have proposed Shaftesbury, and the two might have been elected aldermen, sheriffs, and even to the mayoralty.[1] Though the Aldermen evaded it on that occasion, on 4 March Buckingham became a freeman of the Merchant Taylors' Company[2] (without this in itself attracting much attention, since Buckingham was so much a spent force that he did not even go to Oxford), and, the precedent thus having been established, Shaftesbury's turn came two months later. On 4 May Major Manley 'signified that the Right Honourable the Earl of Shaftesbury would do the Company the honour to take his freedom of this Society'; and the Court of Assistants readily agreed.

The Skinners' Company was chosen in preference to others, not because the names of the livery companies still possessed any connexion with the trade, but because Whigs had more influence in its counsels than in those of most Companies. Manley was said by Grey to be employed by Shaftesbury to sound out opinion in London and among the 'brisk boys' of Wapping. A much more important figure in the Company was Alderman Pilkington, the most committed Whig alderman in the Court. Without surprise one discovers that after Shaftesbury's acquittal in November 1681 the Company ordered that Shaftesbury, Lord Herbert and Francis Charlton should have their freedoms presented them 'in boxes of silver, fairly gilt, and the Company's arms engrossed thereon, as a testimony of the Company's respects to them for the honour they have done the Company in coming into their Society'.[3]

The action served to encourage the Whigs in the City, and possibly facilitated Shaftesbury's intrigues there with Pilkington and others. No record of their conversations survives; but it is safe to assume that he was consulted about everything that followed in the City. The first objective was to get the petitions of 28 April submitted to a Common Council, and their own version adopted. The King tried to block this move by directing the Lord Mayor to ban the meeting of the Common Council, as it might lead to 'some disturbance or disorder'; but the Mayor, Sir Patience Ward, pleaded that after his recent illness there was too much City business waiting to be transacted, and the most that he could do, out of regard for the King's letter, would be to put off the meeting for a day or two. To Secretary Jenkins the Mayor was polite but firm when he added that the Common Council could not be deterred from petitioning considering 'the

---

[1] Clarke, op. cit. p. 651; J. Macpherson, *Original Papers* (1776), i. 112. There is, however, abundant evidence that the two noblemen were not on as good terms as these rumours would imply.

[2] Newsletter, 5 Mar., MSS. Carte 222, fo. 264; Luttrell, i. 69.

[3] J. F. Wadmore, *Some Account of the Worshipful Company of Skinners* (1902), pp. 46, 197.

fears or rather the terrors and amazements' that all good men were under for the King's life and for their religion, 'dearer to them than their lives'. The King retaliated by appointing a new City lieutenancy, an honour from which the Lord Mayor and other Whigs were omitted, while Sir George Jeffreys, the City's ex-Recorder, and other loyalists were included. He then sent to the Lord Mayor and Aldermen, ordering them to send the two petitions of 28 April to him. This the Lord Mayor and the other Whigs evaded by so arranging matters that the attendance at the Court of Alder-men fell one short of the quorum. All this time Jenkins was frantically active in whipping up support for the King, keeping in touch with Charles at Windsor by constant letters to his fellow-Secretary, Lord Conway; and the result of his efforts was seen on 13 May, when the Common Council finally met. The Common Council decided to address the King for a Parliament as the Whigs wanted, but only by 91 votes (84 Common Councilmen and 7 Aldermen) to 77 (66 Common Councilmen and 11 Aldermen). The Whigs had polled more Aldermen than in previous votes, but their overall majority was less than might have been hoped for; and the King could congratulate himself as he snubbed first Sir Robert Clayton and Sir George Treby, and then the Lord Mayor and Alderman: the Lord Chancellor on his behalf reprimanded them for presenting a paper in the name of the City when it was against the sense of the Court of Aldermen and 'the better part' of the City. He made it plain that anyone engaging in such unwelcome activities could be certain of the King's strong displeasure and the withdrawal of his favour.[1]

Even in the City there were signs that the Whig tide might be beginning to ebb. At the same time there were rumours of some impending defections from the ranks of the Whigs. Lord Macclesfield made his submission to the King, and waited on him as Gentleman of the Bedchamber. There was also much speculation about the position of Lord Howard of Escrick, whose dealings with Fitzharris had been decidedly equivocal, and who had failed to sign the Protest of the opposition peers on 26 March. Some time in April Howard met the King at the lodgings of the Duchess of Portsmouth, and there were rumours that his reward for going over to the Court was to be the treasurership of Ireland. Hard words passed between him and Shaftesbury in public.[2] And thirdly, there were even rumours that the Duke of Monmouth might take up the part of the prodigal son, much to

---

[1] Conway to Jenkins, 7 May, C.S.P.D. 1680–1, p. 266; and 8 May, ibid. p. 267; Jenkins to Conway, 9 May, ibid. pp. 268–70; Luttrell, i. 83; King to L. Mayor and Aldermen, 11 May, C.S.P.D. 1680–1, p. 271; Jenkins to Conway, 11 May, ibid. pp. 271–2; Conway to Jenkins, 12 May, ibid. pp. 272–3; L. Mayor to Jenkins, 12 May, ibid. p. 273; Sir T. Bludworth to Jenkins, 12 May, ibid.; Jenkins to Conway, 12 May, ibid. p. 274; notes by Jenkins, ibid. pp. 275–6; Jenkins to Bludworth, 14 May, ibid. p. 278; newsletter, 14 May, ibid. pp. 278–80; heads of the address, ibid. pp. 283–4; account of the vote, ibid. p. 680; newsletters, 14, 17, 21 May, MSS. Carte 222, fos. 302–3, 305, 307.

[2] Newsletters, 23, 26 Apr., MSS. Carte 222, fos. 290, 292; Feiling and Needham, op. cit. p. 253; Luttrell, i. 77.

the distaste of his father's younger brother, who feared that he 'would be brought home again, before he left eating husks, or even the company of the swine'. The Duchess of Portsmouth would certainly have liked this, knowing that her past activities had aroused James's dislike; and in Secretary Jenkins's words, for Monmouth 'the supplies come now but slowly on', and he was feeling the effects of deprivation of Court office. On 12 April orders were issued for the payment of £4,000 to Monmouth from the Excise money due to be paid into the Exchequer that week.[1]

If the position of some of the peers seemed to be in doubt, there was every reason for some of the Plot informers to waver. Already before the Oxford Parliament Edmund Warcup, the magistrate who had taken the informations of many of them, had veered away from Shaftesbury and towards the Court. His knowledge of the political underworld was valuable; in February and March 1681, he had seen the King and some of his ministers several times, and had been ordered £1,500 by privy seal, and he was soon found proclaiming that he 'would know no secrets, but as a justice do my duty'.[2] At about the same time some of the Irish witnesses, who had flocked to London in too large numbers to be lavishly rewarded by the opposition, began to consider that there might be greater gains to be made from the government by giving evidence that they had been suborned to give false information; and in February the first of them had begun to accuse William Hetherington, the man who had brought so many of them from Ireland, of instigating them to swear falsely against the Queen, the Duke of York, and the Duke of Ormond.[3] The Portuguese, Francisco da Feria, in consultation with Warcup, swore against one of his fellow-informers.[4] All such people were given an added incentive by the King's categorical refusal to give Fitzharris a pardon in return for his confession or to allow him to pass into the hands of Parliament, and by the dissolution. The rewards of the informer's trade were declining, and the dangers increasing. It looked as though the Whigs might be unable to provide protection, and as though a supply of the right kind of false evidence to the government might be both safer and more profitable.

Within a fortnight of the dissolution the Irish witnesses were quarrelling over money which Hetherington was alleged to have received for their benefit. Some of the Whig citizens composed their differences, arranged for the collection of small sums of money (two to six pounds) from tradesmen, and appointed one John Rouse to dole out the money in driblets of £5, or ten shillings per week, or the like. Rouse's attention was drawn to

---

[1] James to Col. Legge, 17/27 Apr., in Campana de Cavelli, *Les Derniers Stuarts* (Paris, 1871), i. 359; Clarke, op. cit. i. 675–6; *C.T.B. 1681–5*, pt. i, p. 103; Jenkins to Ormond, 23 Apr., *H.M.C. Ormond MSS.*, N.S. vi. 40.

[2] Feiling and Needham, 12 Mar., op. cit. p. 251.

[3] Newsletter, 15 Feb., *C.S.P.D. 1680–1*, pp. 169–70; Gwyn to Ormond, 12, 26 Feb., *H.M.C. Ormond MSS.*, N.S. v. 579–80, 590; Arran to Ormond, 12, 15 Feb., ibid. pp. 581, 582; Conway to Ormond, n.d., ibid. p. 602.   [4] *C.S.P.D. 1680–1*, pp. 219–22.

the special plight of Mrs. Fitzharris, and he was advised by Major Manley to go for help to Shaftesbury, 'who had promised to improve his interest with other lords to advance some money for the witnesses'. At Thanet House Shaftesbury stressed the need to look after Mrs. Fitzharris 'because she had many children to provide for', promised some money, and suggested that the Whig peers might promise £10 each.[1] From such a store the witnesses would not starve to death, but they could only eke out a precarious living, and there were some who preferred to turn on Hetherington and hope for reward from the government. On 14 May one Owen O'Callaghan deposed that Hetherington had offered £10 in cash and undertaken to procure him £100 per year from Parliament if he would swear against the Queen, the Duke of York, Ormond, and others, had said that nothing would oblige the Parliament more than to swear that the Queen was the author of the plot, and had declared that he would 'instruct' O'Callaghan what to swear against them; but, O'Callaghan reported, he had told Hetherington that 'he had a soul to be saved', and had declined. Within a week another Irish witness, David Fitzgerald, had marshalled no less than twelve of his compatriots to make similar depositions, and had been heard to say 'that he could have as many witnesses as he pleased from Ireland to forswear themselves for 2s. 6d. each'. Hetherington was arrested, bailed by a friendly J.P., and re-committed with two others, Macnamara and 'Dennis the Friar', to Newgate on charges of treasonable words and subornation. When they asked for bail, the Lord Chief Justice would not take sureties of less than £15,000. The effect of all this on other informants can easily be imagined.[2]

In this context the fate of Fitzharris was a matter of crucial importance. If he were condemned to death the flight of the witnesses from the Whigs to the King would be accelerated. Not only would no new ones come forward, but those 'in the trade' could be expected to swear that they had been suborned by the Whigs. The case of Fitzharris would then be a trial of strength between Charles and Shaftesbury, in which Charles would do his utmost to see that Fitzharris was put to death, while Shaftesbury did all that he could to protect him. But in that case Shaftesbury would start at a considerable disadvantage, since it was agreed on all hands that Fitzharris had written a libel of a treasonable character, and even a jury packed by Whig sheriffs would have to recognize this.

From the end of April until the beginning of June, the Whigs, under Shaftesbury's inspiration, fought a long delaying action. Sheriff Bethel prepared a grand jury which seemed to the courtiers nothing but 'a club

---

[1] Rouse's examination by Jenkins, 9 July, Shaftesbury Papers, XLIII, 63. Cf. the information of Colonel Rich, 27 May, C.S.P.D. 1680–1, pp. 295–6.

[2] Arran to Ormond, 16 Apr., 10, 17, 21, 24 May, H.M.C. Ormond MSS., N.S. vi. 36, 61, 64, 68, 70; information of Owen O'Callaghan, 14 May, C.S.P.D. 1680–1, pp. 276–7; newsletter, 24 May, ibid. p. 293; newsletter, 28 May, MSS. Carte 222, fo. 312; Luttrell, i. 89–90.

of malcontents'; amongst its four Whig members was the Earl's kinsman, Sir William Cooper. The Lord Chief Justice, Pemberton, to whom Charles had just given his office, replied by putting the Attorney-General's indictment of Fitzharris before another section of the Middlesex grand jury, the foreman of which was Michael Godfrey, the brother of the murdered justice. Since the Whig tactics were to lay great emphasis on Fitzharris's supposed knowledge of the murder, this was embarrassing, and Michael Godfrey tried to excuse himself; but Pemberton overrode his scruples. Then the first witness, Sir William Waller, asked whether he could safely give evidence, in view of the votes which the House of Commons had passed about the case at Oxford; and Godfrey and two of the jurymen followed suit, and asked whether they could safely take cognizance of the indictment. Pemberton adjourned the case to consult his colleagues, and ruled next day that it was the grand jury's duty, under the terms of their oath, to proceed. Thereupon Michael Godfrey asked that, before the jury proceeded on the indictment, Fitzharris might be summoned and questioned about Sir Edmund Berry Godfrey's death; the judge replied that the time for this would be after his arraignment. Their excuses thus evaded, the grand jury reluctantly found a 'true bill', and the first stage was completed.[1]

On the last day of April Fitzharris was brought to the King's Bench bar, and arraigned. After the Lord Chief Justice had declined to allow him to be first interrogated about the Godfrey murder, and after Fitzharris had complained that he had seen no one for ten weeks, his wife (about whose welfare Shaftesbury had been so solicitous) managed to slip him a written plea, to the effect that since he had been impeached by the Commons he ought to be tried in that way, and not by the King's Bench. This was a point of law on which Fitzharris was entitled to the aid of counsel, and a whole platoon of Whig lawyers who were conveniently present, including Williams (the Speaker of the last two Parliaments), Wallop, Winnington, Pollexfen and eventually Jones and Treby, were given four days in order to prepare a case. The moment then came at which the judge had promised to allow Fitzharris to speak about Godfrey. But here Mrs. Fitzharris, fearing that a 'confession' might lead, not to a pardon, but to further charges based on the prisoner's admissions, cried out a warning to 'speak only to little things', and her husband, clutching at her advice, missed what might, as it turned out, have been his best chance.[2]

Since the Lord Chief Justice rejected counsel's demands for more time and a copy of the indictment, saying significantly that these requests were only 'ad captandum populum, that you may say you are hardly used', 4 May

[1] Gwyn to Ormond, 12 Apr., *H.M.C. Ormond MSS.*, N.S. vi. 31; van Citters, 14/24 Apr., Add. MSS. 17677, FF; Jenkins to Ormond, 30 Apr., op. cit. vi. 51–52; *State Trials*, viii. 247–9; *The Arraignment and Plea of Edward Fitzharris* (1681).

[2] *State Trials*, viii. 250–4.

was the important day, and the King's Bench court was filled with nota-bilities. Shaftesbury, Essex, Salisbury, Grey, and other Whigs were on the floor to lend their patronage to the prisoner's cause; the 'loyalists' were above in the gallery for the trial of strength. After long technical wrangles the Lord Chief Justice grudgingly allowed the defence three more days to complete their case; and then Fitzharris, having been able to consult his Whig advisers since his last appearance, asked for a private interview with the Lord Chief Justice, the Whigs Essex and Salisbury, the Lord Mayor, and Sir Robert Clayton, 'to discover something' about Godfrey'. But now it was too late; the judges blocked the request on the ground that Fitzharris had been given every opportunity on 30 April, and had said very little to the purpose. Afterwards the Whigs tried to retrieve the situation. Shaftesbury could not intervene directly himself; but Essex and Salisbury wrote and asked for the King's permission to see the prisoner in accordance with his request. Charles parried this by having the letter read in Council, and then ordering that the King's Bench judges should examine him, without the intervention of anyone else, in a way which would be 'unquestionably legal and to the public satisfaction of all good men'. An interrogation of this kind was not what Fitzharris wanted, and he declined to speak.[1]

On 7 May the crowd in court was so great that the Attorney-General fainted away, and when revived complained that 'he was more like to die than the prisoners'. Shaftesbury and all those, except Monmouth, who had signed the Protest in the Lords on 26 March, were there, with many members of the Commons. Jeffreys, on behalf of the Crown, remarked with characteristic roughness that he hoped the court would not be 'bugbeared out of their opinions', and was hissed through the Hall for his pains. A curiosity about the legal arguments was that Fitzharris's counsel tried to take advantage of the ruling in Shaftesbury's own case, when the court declined to interfere with his committal by the Lords on the ground that it had no jurisdiction to enquire into proceedings in Parliament.[2] The Lord Chief Justice took some days to consider the matter, but he and three of his four colleagues found a technical reason for deciding against Fitz-harris without incurring too much risk from any future House of Commons: the defence plea, they said, did not establish that the matter of the impeach-ment was the same as that of the present indictment. Having given his ruling, Pemberton denied Fitzharris the opportunity for which he asked, of 'ending his confession', and fixed the trial for 9 June.[3]

---

[1] *State Trials*, viii. 254–81; 'I.H.', 4 May, *H.M.C. Various MSS.* (13), p. 172; newsletter, 5 May, *C.S.P.D. 1680–1*, p. 263; Salisbury and Essex to [Jenkins], 5 May, ibid. p. 264; Jenkins's reply, 5 May, and Jenkins to L. C. J. Pemberton, loc. cit.; newsletter, 10 May, MSS. Carte 222, fo. 300.

[2] *State Trials*, viii. 281–326; 'Mr. H.' to [Major John Braman], 10 May, *C.S.P.D. 1680–1*, p. 270; Luttrell, i. 80; *An Account of the Proceedings and Arguments of the Counsel on both sides, concerning the Plea of Mr. Fitzharris . . . (1681)*.

[3] *State Trials*, viii. 326–30; Luttrell, i. 82; *The Proceedings about Mr. Fitzharris . . .*; Terriesi, 16/26 May, in Crinò, p. 186.

As Fitzharris passed through Westminster Hall, bystanders called out to him 'Courage! The people of England are for you!'[1] But it was very doubtful whether 'the people of England' could be of any assistance, when Fitzharris had already confessed to the treasonable libel of which he was accused, and which was extant with amendments in his own handwriting. Somehow a diversion had to be created; and this could best be done by laying stress on Fitzharris's supposed knowledge of the Godfrey murder. On 16 May that section of the Middlesex Grand Jury which had Sir William Roberts as its foreman and Sir William Cooper as his right-hand man ('men well known for their principles') asked that Fitzharris be brought before them, and the judges found it prudent to agree, though they would not allow his examination to be private. In public Fitzharris now seized his chance to say that Godfrey's murder had been contrived at Windsor by the Duke of York, the Queen, the Earl of Danby, and others; special stress was laid on Danby's supposed part in it, for the tactical reason that if he was involved Fitzharris would have to be preserved as an indispensable witness until after Danby had been brought to trial, if that day ever dawned. The Grand Jury obliged by finding a true bill against Danby; and then Shaftesbury got up and asked that Fitzharris be examined about the Great Fire of London, 'saying, He did believe he might be able to give a very sensible account thereof, and also of a particular design to burn his [Shaftesbury's] house'. This was not simply a matter of keeping up anti-Papist hysteria; the Great Fire was a matter in which a Grand Jury sitting in Westminster Hall might legitimately take a keen interest, and which might therefore lead to an additional diversion. But the judges on the bench found reasons for arguing that the present grand jury was not the appropriate place to examine it, and the matter passed off.[2]

What was now needed was a second witness to 'corroborate' Fitzharris's tale of the Godfrey murder, and it could be expected that one would conveniently present himself. As a matter of fact, there were two who appeared hoping for a substantial reward in return for 'the true story'. One of these, James Magrath, another of the 'tribe of the Mack Shams', tried to back the government horse, and relate how Godfrey had committed suicide, and how his brothers had faked a murder in order to prevent his property from being confiscated; but he was not a good enough liar, broke down under questioning, and confessed that he knew the notorious 'Popish midwife', Mrs. Cellier, so that his 'evidence', which would have been invaluable to the Catholics and the King, fell to pieces.[3] The other was prepared to support the Whigs, and confirm what Fitzharris had said;

[1] Barrillon, 12/22 May.
[2] Newsletter, 17 May, MSS. Carte 222, fo. 307; *Impartial Protestant Mercury*, 16–19 May; Terriesi, 16/26 May, 23 May/2 June, Crinò, op. cit. pp. 188–9.
[3] *C.S.P.D. 1680–1*, pp. 293–4; Luttrell, i. 90; van Citters, 27 May/6 June, Add. MSS. 17677, FF; Sir John Hobart to W. Windham, 31 May, *H.M.C. Beaufort MSS.*, etc., p. 185; cf. *State Trials*, viii. 1390–1.

but he dared not come forward until he was sure of a royal pardon for having concealed what he proposed to confess. Through a disreputable friend named Ivy this stranger approached Shaftesbury, who treated the matter with great caution. He refused to hear what the man had to say except in the presence of two witnesses, on the ground that 'No man could know a knave from an honest man by his face', and 'that he did not know but he [the stranger] might be a trepan and impostor'. But eventually he professed to be convinced, and agreed to seek for a royal pardon so that the man could give his information without incriminating himself. He approached the Lord Chancellor and the judges and desired them to intercede with the King for a pardon for an unnamed person. He dared not name him in advance lest Charles should arrest the man and prosecute him along with Fitzharris. Quite naturally Charles declined to give a blank pardon of this sort.[1]

For some days the City was full of rumours about the identity of this mysterious stranger; it was even said that he was a Protestant earl. In reality his name was Haines—he was yet another of the 'tribe of the Mack Shams' and had been a solicitor for various Catholics—and his evidence was probably more impressive in rumour than it would have been had he been able to give it in person and in public. It may have encouraged some Whig optimists to believe that the King's 'cabinet council' was seriously debating the possibility of calling another Parliament.[2] But Charles remained quietly firm. Godfrey's brothers tried through counsel to persuade the judges in the King's Bench court to join them in petitioning for a pardon for a person who could make a full discovery of Sir Edmund's murder; but the judges declined. And finally, on 8 June, Shaftesbury, Salisbury, Kent, and Essex asked to speak to the King 'to reveal matters concerning the good of his state', but Charles's infuriating reply was that he was too busy to hear them, but would willingly listen to them at Windsor if they came next day. Since next day was the day fixed for Fitzharris's trial, he knew that they would not come; nor did they.[3]

In the meantime the Lord Mayor had declined to accept the suggestion of ten eminent citizens that he should call a Common Council, which might petition the King to allow Fitzharris to be examined about the Great Fire of London before he was put on trial.[4] All these activities had served

[1] *True Protestant Mercury*, 21–25 May, 28 May–1 June; Stephen College's evidence at his trial, *State Trials*, viii. 679–80; Gwyn to Ormond, 24 May, *H.M.C. Ormond MSS.*, N.S. vi. 70; informations of Lewis and Rich, [26?] and 27 May, *C.S.P.D. 1680–1*, pp. 294–6; newsletter, 31 May, MSS. Carte 222, fo. 314; memorandum by Danby, 27 May, Add. MSS. 28042, fo. 85ᵛ; newsletter, 2 June, *C.S.P.D. 1680–1*, p. 303. See also Add. MSS. 28043, fo. 61, for the story which reached Danby that Haines had been entreated by Mrs. Fitzharris, and incited by her solicitor Whittaker, to swear against him.

[2] Hobart, loc. cit. p. 647, n. 3; newsletter, 4 June, *C.S.P.D. 1680–1*, pp. 305–6.

[3] Newsletter, 6, 9 June, ibid. pp. 309, 311–12; Luttrell, i. 94; Terriesi, 13/23 June, in Crinò, op. cit. pp. 193–4; Barrillon, 9/19 June.

[4] Newsletters, 4 June, pp. 305–7; Anon., 4 June, *H.M.C. Ormond MSS.*, N.S. vi. 74.

to keep excitement at fever-pitch, and thus to prevent the Whigs from disintegrating; but they had done nothing to help Fitzharris, whose day of reckoning was now at hand. And in the process, in spite of his caution, Shaftesbury had become involved with Irishmen who would soon turn on him and endeavour to swear his own life away.

On 9 June Shaftesbury was one of a phalanx of Whig peers and commoners who congregated to see the trial. Whether he had been present in court on the previous day, when the evidence of a crowd of Irish witnesses, some at least of whom he had patronized, served to convict Archbishop Plunket of treason, it is impossible to say. Politically the verdict in the Fitzharris case was much more important; if he were put to death the Whigs would lose a valuable informer, and risk the loss of the mob of Irishmen who had been encouraged to come over. The Whig sheriffs had done what they could; they had packed the jury, and given it a foreman, Thomas Johnson, who had been responsible for giving Monmouth and his fellow-Whigs a dinner at Wapping six months previously.[1] But that was the limit of what they could do, since the law did not allow the prisoner the assistance of counsel unless a point of law had to be argued. Fitzharris's wife had arranged for some witnesses to be subpoenaed, notably the Duchess of Portsmouth and Mrs. Wall, her maid, and Fitzharris, taking the cue, tried to show that in what he had done he had been employed, through them, by the King, to ferret out treasonable activities by the opposition; but the witnesses and the King's lawyers, having had notice of this defence tactic, had prepared for it and were able to block the unskilled Fitzharris's examination of them. Though it was clear that at some time in the past Fitzharris had received money from the King for some purpose, it could not be proved that this was the explanation of the libel, and there was nothing solid to set against the evidence of two Clerks to the Council, that Fitzharris had acknowledged the handwriting of the libel to be his own before the Board. The foreman of the jury tried to raise doubts about the propriety of finding a verdict in view of the Commons' vote to impeach the prisoner; but the Lord Chief Justice swept these aside, and after retiring for only half an hour the jury, Whig as it was, found the prisoner guilty.[2]

Fitzharris was left with three weeks to live, during which he was naturally under strong temptation to try to earn a pardon by declaring that his statements had all been false, and had been induced by the persuasions of the Whig sheriffs and others who had visited him in prison in March. It was not in fact likely that the King would give his pardon in return for such a confession, since it would have been open for the Whigs to argue

---

[1] Macpherson, op. cit. i. 121; cf. Jenkins to Prince of Orange, 14 Dec. 1680, Groen van Prinsterer, II. v. 459; Barrillon, 16/26 Dec.

[2] C.S.P.D. 1680–1, pp. 336–8; C.S.P.D. Jan.-June 1683, pp. 217–19; State Trials, viii. 330–93; The Trial and Condemnation of Edw. Fitzharris (1681); Luttrell, i. 95.

that it was a false confession falsely sworn to save the prisoner's life, and the King could not have been sure that Fitzharris himself would not repudiate it when his life was safe. But it was natural for the Fitzharrises to clutch at straws; and even when the doomed man lost hope, he was pathetically concerned to do what was best for his wife and children. Which was the more likely to support them, the government or the opposition, if the right kind of statement was made? The wretched pair, caught in the trap that Fitzharris had dug for himself, struggled helplessly to free themselves; and the document that Mrs. Fitzharris later signed, describing the days after her husband's conviction, is a moving story of human suffering.[1] In her agony of mind, it was suggested to her by her friend, Mrs. Whittaker, and maid, Mrs. Peacock, that Lord Howard of Escrick might be the true author of the libel of which her husband had been accused; and, realizing that this might help her husband, she replied that she had 'always thought so'. Edward Whittaker, who was solicitor to her as to many Whig protégés, wrote this to the Lord Chancellor. Her reward was that, when visiting her husband in the Tower that night, she was arrested, with her maid, and accused of high treason or misprision of it; and the highly respectable Secretary Jenkins, behaving in precisely the same way as Shaftesbury and the Plot Committee had done to prisoners, told her: 'You must either make an end of your confession, or else go to prison.' Told by Seymour that her husband had sworn against Howard, she too swore against him; and Howard was duly arrested, charged with treason, and sent to the Tower.[2] This was distinctly useful to the King; yet it did not soften his attitude to Fitzharris. On 15 June the Lord Chief Justice pronounced the usual barbarous sentence which applied to traitors; Fitzharris's pleas that it would be prejudicial to the King's service if sentence should pass before he had 'made an end of the evidence he had given in' against Howard were of no avail. Next day Fitzharris asked the Under-Lieutenant of the Tower to tell the King that in return for the commutation of his punishment to transportation he would reveal who had persuaded him to accuse the Queen, Duke of York, and Danby.[3]

For the reasons indicated above, the King could not bargain; and the interesting fact is that Fitzharris did not seek further to save himself by volunteering information, true or false, against Shaftesbury. Only his dying statement on the scaffold could now be of value; for there was still a predisposition to believe that, however contradictory and untrustworthy

---

[1] Copy in Shaftesbury Papers, XLIII, 63. I am inclined to accept this graphic document as genuine, in spite of its provenance, except for the last paragraph which seems to have been added at someone's instigation, asserting that Fitzharris maintained his accusations against the Queen, Duke, and Danby to the last.

[2] *C.S.P.D. 1680-1*, pp. 312-15; Gwyn to Ormond, 11 June, *H.M.C. Ormond MSS.*, N.S. vi. 80; Burnet, ii. 293-4.

[3] *State Trials*, viii. 391-3; Marquis of Worcester to Marchioness, 16 June, *H.M.C. Beaufort MSS.*, p. 86; Barrillon, 20/30 June; Luttrell, i. 99.

a man's previous statements might have been, he could be expected to tell the truth when he was about to go to meet his Maker. Fitzharris's execution was fixed for 1 July, and on the previous day his wife's petition that the quartering of his body which was part of the sentence might be respited, was rejected by the King. Everyone waited; a story reached Danby (at second-hand) that Mrs. Whittaker visited Mrs. Fitzharris on the day before the execution, bearing a message from Shaftesbury that she should have £300 which had been promised her husband, if she persuaded him to accuse nobody on the scaffold. But in the end, feebly cunning to the last, Fitzharris tried to have it both ways. On the one hand, he left with the Tower's chaplain, Mr. Hawkins, a 'confession' implicating Howard, and also accusing the Whig sheriffs of having prompted him to swear against the Queen, the Duke, and Danby. On the other hand he wrote letters privately to his wife, saying that these were falsehoods only said to save his life. On the morning of 1 July, having signed both these statements, he was led out to Tyburn, along with a very different victim, Archbishop Plunket. No last-minute pardon came as a reward for his 'confession'; and Fitzharris's muddled life was ended.[1]

It is unnecessary here to describe the long controversy which followed about the genuineness or otherwise of Fitzharris's statement. What mattered was that the King had succeeded in putting to death an informer whom the House of Commons, the Whig peers, and the sheriffs had tried to preserve for their own political purposes. Other informers drew their own conclusions, that it was prudent to look to their own safety; and the King was emboldened to fly at higher game. Within twenty-four hours of Fitzharris's execution, Shaftesbury himself passed through the Traitors' Gate and became a prisoner in the Tower from which Fitzharris had just gone to his death.

---

[1] Newsletter, 2 July, *C.S.P.D. 1680–1*, pp. 340–1; Danby to ?, 5 July, *H.M.C. Lindsey MSS.*, p. 436; *State Trials*, viii. 394–426; Burnet, ii. 294–5; *No Protestant Plot* (1681), pp. 19–20; *Observator*, no. 69 (9 Nov. 1681).

CHAPTER XXVIII

UNDER THREAT OF DEATH
(JULY-NOVEMBER 1681)

Have you not lately heard of Lords sent to the Tower,
Who 'gainst the Popish plotters, seem'd men of chiefest power;
But now they're got into the Plot, and all their power in vain,
For the Plot is rent and torn, and will never be mended again,
'Tis rent and torn, and torn and rent, and rent and torn in twain,
For the Plot is rent and torn, and will never be mended again.
    A Song of the New Plot, to the Tune of *Joan's Placket is Torn*.

And now the Court intended to set the witnesses against all the hot party;
which was plainly murder in them, who believed them false witnesses, and yet
made use of them to destroy others.   *Burnet.*

SHAFTESBURY'S arrest was no great surprise. No sooner had Lord
Howard of Escrick been arrested than it was rumoured that there were
warrants for the apprehension of others of the so-called 'Protestant'
lords; and some of Howard's own party, knowing only too well his
propensity for saving himself at the expense of others, were afraid that he
would allow himself to be used to fix crimes on his colleagues. As it happened, on this occasion Howard remained calm, confident that the evidence
against him did not amount to anything and that he did not need to turn
King's evidence.[1] But there were others, less scrupulous, who were
prepared to supply the government with the 'evidence' which was obviously
needed for political purposes, and all through the month of June the
government's agents had been busy getting into touch with them. In
what follows it is difficult to draw any moral distinction between their
activities and those of people like William Hetherington who had procured
'evidence' to suit Shaftesbury's political purposes; though it must be added
that it should not be necessarily supposed that King Charles was aware of
everything that was done and promised in his name, any more than
Shaftesbury had been.

We have already seen that even before Fitzharris's conviction many of
the informers had shown a disposition to approach the government, and
to turn and rend one another. Amongst them had been Everard, whose
method of seeking to approach the King had been by way of Shaftesbury's
former ally, Justice Warcup. Shaftesbury had temporarily reconciled

---

[1] Luttrell, i. 99, 101; Barrillon, 23 June/3 July, 27 June/7 July; newsletter, 21 June,
C.S.P.D. *1680–1*, pp. 321–2; Sawyer to Jenkins, 22 June, ibid. p. 325; newsletter,
25 June, ibid. p. 331.

Everard and Oates to prevent this, but on 2 June Warcup took Everard to Windsor, and the informer had a long conversation with the King in private.[1] But the Irish witnesses were an even more fertile field, being at once poor, quarrelsome, and certainly not hindered by any thoughts of loyalty to those who had brought them over from Dublin; and the possibilities of getting some of them to acknowledge that they had been suborned were apparent. On 20 June Warcup took one of them, David Fitzgerald, to Windsor, and Fitzgerald earned the King's commendation and thanks for undertaking to provide some of his compatriots to accuse Shaftesbury of subornation. They were the more eager because, now that they had successfully given evidence against Archbishop Plunket, there was no reason why they should be permitted to remain in London, and the Attorney-General was busy sorting out those who should be sent back to Ireland. Warcup was active, meeting them at taverns, hearing their evidence and arranging for the payment of their 'allowances'; he was promised £300 from the Treasury to help on the good work, and £50 was awarded to Fitzgerald.[2]

Those who could not be won by financial inducements might be brought in by threats, and an obvious target here was the man Bryan Haines whom Shaftesbury had tried to produce as a witness to the murder of Sir Edmund Berry Godfrey. On 20 June a warrant was issued for his arrest on charges of high treason and other crimes, and before he could get away overseas he was found at a house in the City. After a chase across the roof-tops in which the City constables declined to assist the King's messengers he was caught, and on the 25th wrote abjectly to the King, saying that he had 'exteriorly complied' with the wishes of the opposition in order to ingratiate himself into their favour, and was 'capable to render . . . very beneficial service'. As an earnest of this he offered evidence against John Rouse, the servant of Sir Thomas Player whose task it had been to dole out Whig allowances to the informers, and against the 'Protestant joiner', Stephen College. Both were committed to the Tower on charges of treason, though at College's trial in August evidence was produced that a week previously College too had been offered a government bribe.[3]

Thus Haines and Ivy, John and Dennis Macnamara, David Fitzgerald and Brian Dennis were all lined up against the Earl; and to them were added Stephen Dugdale, to whom Laurence Hyde ordered a supply of £100 from the Treasury, and Turberville—both of them leading witnesses against Stafford only six months earlier, and anxious to insure themselves

[1] 'Journals of Edmund Warcup', 17 Apr., 4 May, 2 June, ed. by K. Feiling and F. R. D. Needham, in E.H.R. (1925), p. 253.

[2] Luttrell, i. 92; Rich to Jenkins, n.d., C.S.P.D. 1680–1, p. 312; Feiling and Needham, op. cit., 20, 28, 29, 30 June, 3 July, pp. 255–6; Sawyer's report, 23 June, C.S.P.D. 1680–1, pp. 326–7. Cf. also the information of John Zeal in Shaftesbury Papers, XLIII, 63. Though Zeal was as untrustworthy as any other informer, his story of attempts to suborn him against the Earl is so circumstantial that it is difficult to disbelieve it entirely.

[3] C.S.P.D. 1680–1, pp. 321, 332; John Ellis, 2 July, H.M.C. Ormond MSS., N.S. vi. 89–90; Haines to the King, 25 June, C.S.P.D. 1680–1, p. 329; State Trials, viii. 630–2.

against, or even profit from, a Tory reaction.[1] In the King's eyes they were all perjurers, but he considered it legitimate to make use of them to revenge himself upon Shaftesbury, and retort the Earl's own methods upon him.

The activities of such as Warcup and Fitzgerald to collect this 'evidence' did not pass unnoticed by the Whigs; indeed, one or two of the informers offered to disclose the conspiracy against the Earl, if they could be sure of more money for doing so than the Court had offered to corrupt them. Some suggested that it would be safest for the Earl to go over to Holland until Parliament met; the fiery Scots Nonconformist preacher and pamphleteer, Robert Ferguson, who has gone down to history under the name of 'Ferguson the Plotter', and who was becoming steadily closer to the Earl in these years, urged him to go to the Council and demand justice before his enemies had completed their preparations; others talked of an action of *scandalum magnatum* by the Earl against Fitzgerald. But Shaftesbury adopted none of these courses. He waited, calmly confident that he could demonstrate the worthlessness of any evidence that was brought against him; and, anticipating that his papers might be seized, he saw to it that nothing incriminating should be found at Thanet House.[2]

On 1 July, with Fitzharris safely out of the way, the time had come for the King to take action. That evening a warrant was signed for Shaftesbury's arrest on a charge of high treason, and a second warrant ordered Francis Gwyn, one of the Clerks of the Council, to seize the Earl's papers, seal them, and bring them before the Privy Council at Whitehall at 9 a.m. next day. Early on 2 July Charles left Windsor for Whitehall, and while he rode Gwyn and the Serjeant-at-Arms went to Aldersgate. The Earl was wakened at six and told that he was under arrest. He took the news calmly, gave Gwyn his keys and told him where his closets were, and waited while Gwyn impounded the papers which he found in them and in 'a great hair trunk'. When the Serjeant-at-Arms urged him to eat something before he appeared before the King and Council, the Earl replied that 'he had no stomach to eat unless he could get a roast Irishman'; to which some replied that none would have been more fitting than Fitzharris, and that if it had been a day earlier his lordship might have overtaken him at Tyburn.[3]

It was about eleven before Shaftesbury was brought into the Council room, to stand for the last time at the Board over which he had once presided. The King's tall figure was present, much older now than when Shaftesbury had greeted him in Holland twenty-one years earlier, and more forbidding. Many of the politicians with whom or against whom he had fought were there: Arlington and Nottingham; his nephew Halifax; Monk's

---

[1] Feiling and Needham, 30 June, op. cit. p. 256; Rich to Archbishop Sancroft, 21 June (two) and 23 June, MSS. Tanner 36, fos. 55, 56, 60.

[2] Zeal's account, Shaftesbury Papers, XLIII, 63, fo. 15; J. Ferguson, *Ferguson the Plotter* (1887), pp. 413–14; *Loyal Protestant and True Domestick Intelligence*, 28 June.

[3] *C.S.P.D. 1680–1*, p. 339; Gwyn's evidence at the trial, *State Trials*, viii. 780; anon., 2 July, MSS. Carte 39, fo. 382.

son Albemarle and both Clarendon's sons; and amongst the others, curiously, three of Shaftesbury's business partners, Rupert, Craven, and Sir Thomas Chicheley. He knew well all those before whom he stood as a prisoner, with the Clerks of the Council excluded. He defended himself against the charges that Lord Chancellor Nottingham brought against him: he had always been steadfast to His Majesty's interest, though in some things his judgment led him to take different measures from those advocated by some more near to His Majesty; and he hoped that the councillors did not think him capable of dealing with Irishmen and Papists to subvert the government—if he did such things he was fitter for Bedlam than prison. He seems also to have asked to be confronted with the witnesses, and to have argued that the charges against him were too vague and ill-defined; certainly the judges were called in to discuss some such legal point as this. But, as he probably expected, his defence was in vain. Three members of the Council, Rupert, Radnor, and Fauconberg, withdrew to avoid signing the warrant for his committal to the Tower, and Chicheley, as being his partner and relative by marriage, asked to go too; but at that point the King exclaimed 'Sign it one and all, sign it one and all!' and the seventeen who were there all did so. In the meantime Titus Oates arrived at Whitehall, gained access to the Earl and asked him how he came into 'Lob's pound', to which Shaftesbury made no reply. Not in the least disconcerted, Oates promised to visit him in the Tower and pray with him; and ministered to his physical needs by sending for a bottle of Madeira, some ale, and a couple of chickens, upon which Shaftesbury dined in the lobby of the Council chamber, with Oates saying grace. It cannot have been a very convivial occasion.[1]

Contemporaries noticed that, just as Shaftesbury had been brought to Whitehall from his house in the City by a mere two messengers without molestation, so his committal to the Tower was not accompanied by any popular expressions of discontent.[2] But the absence of rioting did not imply any lack of excitement. For the next five months the condemnation or acquittal of Shaftesbury would be the objective of every politician. There were rumours that others might follow him to the Tower—Monmouth, Essex, Salisbury, Sir Thomas Player, and others were all mentioned[3]; but Shaftesbury's head was the one that the King wanted, and for this prize he and the Whigs waged what the French ambassador called *une guerre de chicane*.

On the evening of the day on which the Earl passed through the Traitor's

---

[1] P.C. Reg. 2/69, fo. 315; Shaftesbury Papers, VI A, 363; Arran to Ormond, 2 July, *H.M.C. Ormond MSS.*, N.S. vi. 89; John Ellis, 2 July, ibid. vi. 90–91; Marquis of Worcester to Marchioness, 2 July, *H.M.C. Beaufort MSS.*, p. 86; Barrillon, 4/14 July; Roger Morrice, Ent. Bk. P. (Dr. Williams's Library), fos. 309–11 (2 July); Luttrell, i. 105–6.

[2] Barrillon, loc. cit.; Earl of Yarmouth to Edward L'Estrange, 5 July, *H.M.C. Seventh Report*, p. 533.

[3] R. Mulys to [?], 2 July, *H.M.C. Ormond MSS.*, N.S. vi. 91; Luttrell, i. 106; Anna M. Crinò, *Il Popish Plot* (Rome, 1954), p. 205.

Gate, he was visited by Monmouth and Montagu; but thereafter the King ordered that Shaftesbury and Howard should be kept close prisoners, separate from one another, and with no one but wives and children and 'necessary attendants' allowed access to them. Even the Earl's brother George was permitted to see him only in the presence and hearing of the Lieutenant of the Tower, and Whigs commented that this was severer treatment than that accorded to the four Popish peers whom Oates had accused with Stafford, and who were freely visited.[1] The result was something very far short of solitary confinement, and it is a fact, for instance, that three days after entry to the Tower it was possible to arrange for the mortgage of the guns manufactured under Prince Rupert's patent, together with the cedar wood and all 'indoor goods, utensils and household stuffs' at Thanet House, to his bankers, Peter Percival and Stephen Evans, in security for a debt of £2,489.[2] But the main burden of the preparations would inevitably have to be left to Shaftesbury's servants and friends, and his ever-faithful steward, Thomas Stringer, set to work, no doubt with the aid of the cash gained from the mortgage, to collect evidence that the Irish witnesses had been tampered with. The solicitor, Hoskins, and a secretary, Samuel Wilson, also set to work; and so too did John Locke, who paid fees to counsel and for the searching of records.[3]

On 6 July Shaftesbury and Howard almost took the government by surprise, by petitioning at the Old Bailey, under the *habeas corpus* procedure, for either bail or speedy trial. The Attorney-General, taken unawares, had to take advantage of the Court's willingness to postpone consideration of the matter for forty-eight hours.[4] The move was generally interpreted as an expression of Shaftesbury's confidence in his innocence, and his friends professed to be not greatly worried about him.[5] The evidence of the Irish witnesses they regarded as worthless; and the King's hopes that it might be supplemented from Shaftesbury's own papers were disappointed when the Earl's sealed trunks were opened by a committee of Council, with Samuel Wilson and Henry Starkey present as the Earl's representatives. Apart from an anonymous Association which the government was later able to wrest to some propagandist use, nothing was found which would remotely corroborate a charge of treason.[6]

There remained the possibility that a jury of the Earl's peers, suitably hand-picked by the King and presided over by a hostile Lord High Steward, might nevertheless allow its political prejudices to supplement

---

[1] Shaftesbury Papers, VI A, 363; P.C. Reg. 2/69, f. 320; Luttrell, i. 106.

[2] Shaftesbury Papers, VI B, 101.

[3] Cf. Shaftesbury Papers, XLIII, 63; MSS. Locke, f. 5; Luttrell, i. 107.

[4] Luttrell, i. 106; *Life of James II*, ed. J. S. Clarke (1816), i. 689; Jenkins to the Attorney-General, 6 July, *C.S.P.D. 1680–1*, p. 347; Stringer's notes in Shaftesbury Papers, VI A, 364.   [5] Barrillon, 7/17 July.

[6] Jenkins to Thos. Cheke, 5 July, *C.S.P.D. 1680–1*, p. 346; Blathwayt's evidence at the trial, *State Trials*, viii. 780.

the deficiencies of the evidence, give credit to the witnesses, and find Shaftesbury guilty. This was the contingency which had been foreseen by the Whig peers in 1680, when they had introduced a bill to regulate the trial of peers; but that bill had not been completed, and the composition of any Court which tried Shaftesbury remained entirely for the King to determine. For this reason there had even been rumours that the Earl would renounce his peerage, so that he could be tried by an ordinary jury of commoners.[1] This doubtful expedient had not been tried, and consequently the Earl might have to depend on the fairness of the peers whom the King appointed; but first his case would have to go before a grand jury of Londoners, and only if they found a true bill, indicating the existence of a *prima facie* case, would the charge proceed for trial by a court of peers. Now the grand jury would be nominated by the sheriffs, who were strongly Whig; indeed on 24 June the Court candidates had been ignominiously defeated at the annual elections by Common Hall of the next pair of sheriffs, who would take up office in September. Cornish and Bethel would then be replaced by an equally partisan pair in Alderman Pilkington (the leading Whig alderman, and a fellow-member with Shaftesbury in the Skinners' Company) and Benjamin Shute. Never had so many persons 'of rank and quality' been present at an election, the political importance of which was patent to all. The Tories had their excuses ready; they acknowledged that Pilkington came at the head of the poll, but complained that Shute's majority over the Tory was the result either of the votes of the *vraie canaille*, or of 'foul play', including the use of Whig polling-clerks. It seems difficult to explain away a majority of 2,245 to 1,266 in this way; but in any case the result was that the Whigs were assured of control over the nomination of grand juries in London and Middlesex until September 1682.[2]

This did not mean that Shaftesbury's safety could be absolutely guaranteed from the beginning, for a grand jury composed of Whigs had none the less found a true bill against Fitzharris, and Fitzharris had duly died as a traitor. But on 8 July the time came for a grand jury to examine the case against Stephen College, the 'Protestant joiner'. Six witnesses, including Dugdale, Smith, Haines, and the two Macnamaras who were all to depose against Shaftesbury, swore that College had talked of seizing the King, either in London where 1,500 barrels of powder and 100,000 arms had been prepared, or in Oxford, and that he had described the King as being 'as great a Papist in his heart as the Duke' and guilty both of firing the City and of ordering the murder of Sir Edmund Berry Godfrey. In the course of the evidence they declared that College had spoken to them on Shaftesbury's behalf. After four hours of debate the jury decided

---

[1] Barrillon, 23 June/3 July.

[2] Newsletter, 25 June, *C.S.P.D. 1680–1*, pp. 329–30; anon., 29 June, ibid. pp. 333–5; Jenkins to Savile, 27 June, *Savile Correspondence* (Camden Society, 1858), p. 203.

TT

that the evidence was worthless—and decided correctly, even though one has to add that the verdict might well have been the same even if the evidence had been a good deal stronger. When the jury brought in their verdict of *Ignoramus*, at a signal given from a gallery two loud shouts resounded through the Old Bailey courtroom, for the implications were immediately obvious. Indeed the Bench had to turn immediately to Shaftesbury's petition under the *habeas corpus* procedure for bail or a speedy trial. The Earls of Salisbury, Clare, Essex, and Macclesfield, Lords Grey and Russell, Ralph Montagu and Sir Scrope Howe, who were all in court, offered themselves as sureties, and talked of Shaftesbury's poor health; but the judges declared that they had no jurisdiction in the matter, since the Tower was not within their commission of oyer and terminer. Shaftesbury would have to wait in the Tower until the next term in the King's Bench—and the next legal term there would not begin until the middle of October.[1]

The Court's supporters complained bitterly of the verdict. The foreman of the jury, John Wilmore, was, they said, 'a professed fanatic', and the members were all poor tradesmen[2] who had no business to be on the jury. There was indeed some propaganda advantage to be gained from this, and from suggesting that the grand jury's action in preventing a prisoner accused of treason by six witnesses from going forward for trial did not augur any great zeal for the King's safety. Moreover in this *guerre de chicane* there was a new trick which the King could employ. College was not released; instead there would be another attempt to indict him, this time at Oxford, where it was alleged that his treason had been partly committed at the time of the Parliament there. And the worthy Secretary of State, Leoline Jenkins, wrote to the Lord Lieutenant, Lord Norris, to pass on the King's order 'to have all the care you possibly can that there be a good, honest, substantial grand jury' consisting of 'men rightly principled for the Church and the King'. Some of the righteous condemnations of the Whig Ignoramus juries have overlooked that the King was quite prepared to take similar counter-measures. Next day the judges for the Oxford circuit were instructed both to be present 'and assisting each other on the Crown side' when College was tried; the letter goes on to talk of 'the fairness and solemnity' of the proceedings and the King's devotion to the law, but this would be more impressive did one not recall that in a little more than two years Jeffreys was to be Lord Chief Justice. When the

---

[1] W. Longueville to L. Hatton, 9 July, *Hatton Correspondence* (Camden Society, 1888), ii. 2–3; Arran to Ormond, 9 July, *H.M.C. Ormond MSS.*, N.S. vi. 95; J. Ellis to [Ormond], 9 July, ibid. vi. 95–96; Barrillon, 11/21 July; Roger Morrice's Entering Book P (Dr. Williams's Library), 9 July, fo. 311.

[2] Their names and professions were later printed in *The Two Associations* (1681), p. 8. They include a strong-waterman, a tailor, an upholster (*sic*), a confectioner, a brasier, a carpenter, three apothecaries, etc. Cf. J. Ellis to Ormond, 12 July, op. cit. vi. 98, and van Citters, 15/25 July, Add. MSS. 17677, FF.

grand jury met, it included such 'eminent persons' as a member of the Bertie family, ever closely affiliated to Danby. A true bill was duly found, after the Attorney-General and Solicitor-General had been shut up with the jury; and Judge Raymond was quoted as saying that such a lord lieutenant as Norris, such a sheriff and such a grand jury 'would keep the King's crown fast on his head'.[1]

College's trial would come on at Oxford in mid-August. In the meantime Shaftesbury's nephew, Halifax, and Jenkins instructed Justice Warcup to review the evidence against the Earl, to see if in his case too there would be a basis for transferring it to Oxford.[2] Warcup was by no means loth to do his best to bring his former superior to the block; along with Richard Graham, Principal of Clifford's Inn, he claimed to have spent ten hours at a sitting going through the relevant papers. The two of them and a solicitor named Burton (whom Burnet, much as he disliked Shaftesbury, described with Graham as 'fitter men to have served in a court of inquisition than in a legal government') tried to entice some of the informers who had frequented Thanet House to give further evidence of treasonable remarks by the Earl, hinting what would be acceptable. On the Earl's side the faithful Stringer and other members devoted themselves to securing evidence from the informers that government agents had tried to suborn them: the informers must have been in some perplexity to know what to do for the best. Among those who claimed to have been 'tampered with' were John Zeal, William Lewis, Edmund Everard, Lawrence Mowbray and Robert Bolron.[3]

Meanwhile both sides were involved in a violent pamphlet controversy which focused directly on Shaftesbury's person and began within ten days of his commitment to the Tower. *A Brief Account of the Designs which the Papists have had against the Earl of Shaftesbury, occasioned by his commitment*, written in tones reminiscent of Stringer, talked of his past loyalty to the King—'nor is there a nobleman or gentleman within the King's dominions, to whose influence His Majesty doth more owe his peaceable and happy Restoration, and the successful administration of his affairs for many years together, than to this wise and noble Peer'. The Earl would not have 'withdrawn himself from meddling in the affairs of his country . . . but that he could not concur in designs which he conceived tended to the ruin of these kingdoms. . . . His faithful and unwearied cares and endeavours to obviate the formidable growth of France, and to prevent the re-establishment of Popery in these nations . . . may be thought the occasion of all the

---

[1] Jenkins to Norris, 11 July, *C.S.P.D. 1680–1*, p. 353, and to the judges, 12 July, ibid. p. 354, and to Norris, 26 July, ibid. p. 375; Luttrell, i. 110.

[2] Feiling and Needham, op. cit. 18 July, p. 257.

[3] Warcup to Jenkins, 2 Aug., *C.S.P.D. 1680–1*, p. 387; Burnet, ii. 298; Shaftesbury Papers XLIII, 63; J. Ellis to Ormond, 26 July, *H.M.C. Ormond MSS.*, N.S. vi. 110–11; Everard's information in S.P. Car. II. 416, no. 81; newsletter, 11 Aug., *C.S.P.D. 1680–1*, pp. 397–9; Mowbray's information, 25 Aug., ibid. pp. 418–19; Bolron's information, 25 Aug., ibid. p. 419; and cf. below, p. 663.

slanders which have been cast upon him. . . .' He had discovered the Duke of York's conversion and 'close correspondency' with Louis XIV long before the publication of Coleman's letters, and consequently had been victimized by dismissal from the Chancellorship, tempted by bribes, threatened with impeachment, vilified by 'that mercenary scribbler', Marchamont Needham,[1] and been the subject of assassination plots, as Feria, Dangerfield, and Prance had testified. The present charges were based on 'those few fellows, who besides their being Irish-men, are also Papists'; and the writer showed his inside knowledge by declaring that when Shaftesbury had appealed to the Council Board to know whether any believed the depositions against him, none had spoken. His arrest was described as the culmination of a Popish plot against him.

This piece laid itself open to *A Civil Correction of a Saucy Impudent Pamphlet, lately published, entitled, A Brief Account* . . ., possibly by L'Estrange.[2] This 'correction' scored some telling points, answering his opponent's panegyric on the Earl's loyalty by referring to his record in the Civil War, dragging up the old charge of 'breaking the Triple League' and 'shutting up' the exchequer, and above all pointing out that the Irish witnesses whose truthfulness was now impugned had quite recently been cherished by the Earl: Haines was 'his old friend and acquaintance' for whom the Earl had asked a pardon 'under the title of a man of quality and unquestionable reputation'. This was indeed the weakest point in Shaftesbury's position, and it was not fully defended even by the more skilful writer of *Some Modest Reflections upon the Commitment of the Earl of Shaftesbury*.[3] The argument here was that Shaftesbury would not be likely to confide in people like College, who had not the requisite ability or estates; that the idea of an armed attack on the King at Oxford was lunatic, and there was no evidence of it either before, during, or after the Parliament; that the witnesses had given their evidence at College's trial as though they had learned it by heart, and were suspiciously well off. It was even insinuated that some of the witnesses, when privately examined by College's grand jury, had confessed to being hired to do it. But in any case, the writer prudently observed, even if 'some rash and unadvised words' were proved against College, this would prove nothing against Shaftesbury.

The 'newspapers' such as *Heraclitus Ridens* and the *Observator* joined in the fray. But there were also writers who prided themselves on their

---

[1] That is, in the *Pacquet of Advice and Animadversions . . . to the Men of Shaftesbury* (1677). See above, p. 415.

[2] See also *An Answer to a Paper, Entitled, A Brief Account* . . ., which is more moderate in tone. On page 3 the writer describes the author of the *Brief Account* as 'a great Traveller': did he believe Locke, who had spent the years 1675–9 in France, to be the author?

[3] Miss Brown (p. 287) suggests that the pamphlet (which is conveniently available in *Somers Tracts*, 1812, viii. 295–300) 'bears the marks of the Earl's style'. This is not impossible, but not conclusive, more especially as the Earl seems to have been closely imprisoned in the few days between his arrest and the pamphlet's appearance on 12 July.

ability to write verse, or at least doggerel. Dryden's *Absalom and Achitophel*, which appeared in November, was by no means the first or the most violent of the poems which tried to pour ridicule upon Shaftesbury. There was, for instance, *An Excellent New Ballad, of the Plotting Head. To the Tune of How Unhappy is Phillis in Love. Or, Let Oliver now be Forgot*:

> Ah little Pate!
> Politick Pate!
> Which for treason at last, will be fixt on a gate.

This pleasant little ballad, like many others, refers to its butt as 'Tony'. It contains only a brief allusion to 'thy tap of sedition', but from now on the versifiers played more and more on the tap which still drained matter from the Earl's side. *Sejanus: or the Popular Favourite, now in his solitude, and sufferings. Written for the Consolation of E.S. the Famous Bromigen Protestant, in Bonds, and Imprisonment, for the Good Old Cause* was a more ambitious poem (though its curious title raised the question who was Tiberius) which contained a particularly scurrilous attack.

> . . . From's liquid corp (*sic*), distils a floating gore,
> And the whole carcase, makes one putrid sore.
> The better to emit this flowing sap,
> His belly carries still a silver tap,
> Through which black treason, all its dregs doth strain
> At once, both excrements, of guts, and brain. . . .

And so on, for some 170 lines. On such a battlefield it is always much easier to attack than to defend, and Shaftesbury's supporters were fewer and less effective, although we do find *An Elogy against occasion requires upon the Earl of Shaftesbury*, which begins an attack on the witnesses impressively as follows:

> At the West-End of th' Universal frame,
> A place there lies, which some a land mis-name;
> An excrement of world, called Nature's sink,
> A Mass of undrained mire, quag, bog, and stink,
> Ireland yclep'd. . . .

While Shaftesbury's enemies and defenders were so busy, and the latest rumours and scrawls passed from one citizen to another in the City, how was the 'little toad' (as his former protégé, Haines, called him[1]) faring in the Tower? Behind the walls of the ancient fortress there was now a very mixed collection of prisoners, including, besides Shaftesbury and Howard, the four remaining Catholic peers who had been accused by Oates in 1678, and the Earl's old rival Danby, who had been fretting impotently there for over two years. This did not mean that there were frequent meetings

---

[1] *State Trials*, viii. 633.

between them all; there was room and to spare in the Tower, even for noblemen with their servants. Shaftesbury's friends complained bitterly that he was treated rather more harshly than the Papists in the matter of visitors, and this seems to have been true at least in the early stages. Only servants were supposed to come to him, and even Titus Oates was refused permission to come and give 'spiritual consolation'. But Shaftesbury would survive that particular deprivation, and he was not totally cut off from the outside world. Danby at least thought that 'many who are very ill do come to Ld. Shaf: under pretence of being his servants who are not really so'. Certainly he was able to arrange, for instance, for the sale of many of his horses: he proposed to raise at least £767 in ready cash while retaining his Arabian stallion. It is likely enough that other messages passed.[1]

A more serious discouragement was probably the state of his health. He petitioned the King for 'the liberty of the Tower for the recovery of his health', and Charles would permit him only to 'take the air in his coach with his wife and servants', with a warder constantly in attendance to see that no one else had access to him. But it rapidly became clear that something more was necessary if Shaftesbury was not to be martyred. At the beginning of August rumours of ill-health were multiplied. 'Gout' was followed by a fever, and Sir John Micklethwaite, one of the King's physicians, who attended upon him, expressed the view that if the prisoner were left in his present quarters he would be in great danger: the house was 'so close, if a man were in the best of health, that he would be starved in it'. The Catholic Earl of Powis had previously been moved from it for the same reason. Accordingly the Lieutenant of the Tower, fearing that his prisoner would die on him and that he would get the popular blame, on his own responsibility arranged for the Earl to have a lodging at Sir Jonas Moore's, the Surveyor of the Ordnance, 'who has a great house to himself and very cool this hot weather'.[2]

There, still within the walls of the fortress, Shaftesbury was less uncomfortable and his fever abated. It was probably about this time, in his enforced leisure, that he began writing his memoirs, the surviving portions of which (relating to his youth before the Civil War and to the events of 1659–60) are of such quality as to make the loss of the rest doubly disappointing, both as history and as literature.[3] But Shaftesbury as always was more preoccupied with the present, and with what was going on beyond his prison walls. It was curious, and of some significance, that the Prince of Orange, who had paid his last visit to England during Shaftesbury's last imprisonment, paid another at the beginning of this month of August, and Shaftesbury like the rest could speculate about its meaning. In fact

[1] J. Ellis to Ormond, 26 July, *H.M.C. Ormond MSS.*, N.S. vi. 111; Danby, 14 July, Add. MSS. 28043, fo. 61ᵛ ; Christie, ii. 418–19.

[2] P.C. Register 2/69, p. 324 (14 July); Luttrell, i. 116; *True Protestant Mercury*, 13–17 Aug.; *Impartial Protestant Mercury*, 16–19 Aug.; Cheke to [Jenkins], 16 Aug., *C.S.P.D. 1680–1*, p. 405.   [3] Christie, i, Appendix, pp. iii–xxiv and 195–9.

the visit was markedly less successful than the previous one, when William had gained a wife; it was a mark of the King's growing confidence in the strength of his position that he both resisted all William's attempts to influence his foreign policy and forbade him to dine with the opposition —and William thought it wisest to comply and return home to Holland, frustrated.

Charles now told the French ambassador that he hoped to re-establish his authority, but that this could only be done by cutting off some heads. Shaftesbury's head was naturally the one principally aimed at—his down-fall would cow the others[1]—but Stephen College must go first, as a re-hearsal for his master. On 17 August he appeared at Oxford, charged with high treason in that at the time of the Parliament in March he did 'prepare arms, and warlike offensive habiliments to wage war against our said sovereign lord the King'; 'declare, that it was purposely designed to seize the person of our said sovereign lord the King at Oxford'; and made various remarks about the King, which were alleged to be seditious. The evidence of the witnesses (Dugdale, Smith, Haines, Turberville, and others) consisted almost entirely of the remarks which College was alleged to have made to them, together with assertions that he was the author of a silly scurrilous ballad, *The Raree Show*, with accompanying woodcuts which were coarsely uncomplimentary to the King and Duke. It was also shown that College had distributed the famous blue ribbons with the motto 'No Popery, No Slavery': these were presumably the alleged 'warlike offensive habiliments'. As evidence of a plot to wage war against the King it amounted to very little. For College a series of witnesses, including Oates, spoke against the character of the prosecution witnesses, Bolron and Mowbray declared that attempts had been made to hire them to give false evidence against both Shaftesbury and College, and Everard brought an accusation of this kind against Justice Warcup. It availed College nothing. In the early hours of the 18th, after a retirement of half an hour, the jury returned to the oppressive court-room and found him guilty. On the last day of the month College went to his death, having resisted the efforts of the Dean of Gloucester, the chaplain appointed 'to do the gracious offices of charity', to persuade him to 'penitence' and a revelation of all that he knew. The good Dean had no commission to offer a pardon in return for a confession: a pardon would not be deserved 'unless he at the same time show a way that full proofs may be come by'. It was suggested that he might tell how letters addressed to the Earl were sent to his house and from whom they came.[2]

---

[1] Barrillon, 15/25 Aug. Contrast, however, Halifax to H. Savile, 11 Aug., in *Savile Correspondence*, p. 216.

[2] *State Trials*, viii. 563–724; *The Arraignment, Trial and Condemnation of Stephen College* (1681); R. North, *Lives of the Norths* (ed. A. Jessopp, 1890), i. 188–9; Jenkins to Bishop of Oxford, 22, 29 Aug., *C.S.P.D. 1680–1*, pp. 413, 423–4; College's Declaration, 24 Aug., ibid. pp. 416–17.

All this was in its way fully as scandalous as any of the Popish Plot trials, but it was a great success for the King. *Have you any work for a COOPER?* was the title of a piece of doggerel which suggested that, after the Joiner, the Cooper would be the next to be 'exalted'. Not only had College been put to death, but the Plot informers had been shown divided amongst themselves, some arguing that others were hired perjurers; in the eyes of many the Plot bubble was now pricked. From Shaftesbury's point of view the trial did not encourage him to submit to a similar one in the expectation that he would receive unbiased treatment; his supporters could feel fully justified in packing the grand jury with members who would reject the evidence of such disreputable witnesses. Members of Shaftesbury's household had done what they could to organize College's defence; Stringer and Wilson had mobilized the defence witnesses and prepared instructions which the Whig publisher Aaron Smith and Henry Starkey (both certainly in the Shaftesbury entourage) had vainly tried to pass to College before the trial.[1] They would now have to do what they could for their master.

How far the Earl was able personally to direct their activities it is impossible to say. He does seem to have been able somehow to obtain counsel's opinion that grand juries could only deal with facts in their own county (so that remarks alleged to have been made in London could not be the basis of charges at Oxford), and also that it would be possible for him to bring an action against Warcup and others for endeavouring to suborn witnesses against a peer, in which damages of £20,000 would not be vexatious or oppressive. This last was the counter-attack which he was meditating at the end of August, and it was a serious one for his opponents in that if it were allowed to reach a London jury it might be successful in inflicting both punitive damages and discredit upon the King's agents and witnesses. Appropriate 'informations' were obtained from both Bolron and Mowbray. Further, at the sessions due to open at the Old Bailey on 31 August it was proposed again to move for a writ of *habeas corpus* and this time to argue the point of law which had been raised in the last attempt in July.[2]

In the meantime there was said to be confidence at Court that there was enough evidence against 'my Lord Erycespelas' to hang a hundred lords as guilty as he,[3] but it had proved impossible to find legal grounds for putting the evidence before a docile grand jury at Oxford. An attempt by the Tory justices of the peace of the county of Middlesex to claim that, by

---

[1] *State Trials*, viii. 572 sqq.; North, loc. cit.; Shaftesbury Papers, XLIII, 63, and VI B, 433; Sir J. Jennings to Jenkins, 31 Aug., *C.S.P.D. 1680–1*, p. 428.

[2] Shaftesbury Papers, VI A, 368, VI B, 434, XLIII, 63; *C.S.P.D. 1680–1*, pp. 418–19; newsletter, 30 Aug., ibid. pp. 424–5.

[3] J. Brydall to Dr. Nalson, 31 Aug., MSS. Tanner 36, fo. 106. The disease of erysipelas was formerly known as 'St Anthony's fire'.

virtue of an old statute of 3 Henry VIII, they had power to reform a grand
jury nominated by the sheriff (Bethel) and strike out those who were disqualified, for instance by virtue of not being Anglicans, failed before the
resistance of Bethel and his under-sheriff, Goodenough, and the reluctance
of the judges who were consulted.[1] Accordingly the King had to give up
any hope that he had had of finding a favourable jury at the Old Bailey,
and content himself with blocking Shaftesbury's moves. When Shaftesbury
and some others moved for their writ of *habeas corpus* so that they could be
either tried or bailed, the bench at the Old Bailey again refused to take
cognizance of it and referred the prisoners to the Court of King's Bench,
where the session would not begin until October; and they refused to
accept the indictment of Warcup and his accomplices for conspiracy to
suborn, on the ground that the indictments had been drawn up without
the Attorney-General's knowledge, and that such a procedure might
invalidate all manner of evidence for the King in any criminal proceedings
of any kind.[2] At the same time the immensely superior resources at the
government's disposal for purposes of intimidation were demonstrated
by a series of measures against their enemies. Wilmore, the foreman of
the London grand jury which had dared to bring in the first Ignoramus
verdict in College's favour had been arrested some time ago; now Oates was
at last dismissed from his quarters at Whitehall and deprived of his
allowance; and Bolron, who had given evidence to discredit the prosecution
witnesses at Oxford, was himself arrested. He promptly saved himself by
turning King's evidence. In this deposition, which was 'voluntary and
free', he alleged that Shaftesbury's agent Murray had first of all taken his
informations to Shaftesbury and promised that he should be 'well considered' by the Earl; that he had received, from Aaron Smith and Oates's
man, £10 and expenses for going to College's trial and agreeing to swear
what Everard dictated; and that Smith, Everard, and Murray told him
that what they did was by the Earl's direction and through the agency of
Ayloffe and Harrington. Bolron was promptly absorbed into the number
of witnesses against Shaftesbury. All these actions together, which the
government would hardly have dared to take six months earlier, showed
the King's increasing self-confidence, and some people drew their conclusions. The Earl of Huntingdon, who had previously signed petitions
and protests with Shaftesbury and had presented the petition of 6 December 1679 to the King, absented himself from the Old Bailey when
Shaftesbury's case came on there; he sent a fulsome apology, pleading

---

[1] Newsletter, 30 Aug., *C.S.P.D. 1680–1*, p. 426; Barrillon, 29 Aug./8 Sept.; van
Citters, 30 Aug./9 Sept., Add. MSS. 17677, FF; Arran to Ormond, 27 Aug., *H.M.C.
Ormond MSS.*, N.S. vi. 141.

[2] Newsletter, 1 Sept., *H.M.C. Kenyon MSS.*, pp. 128–9; Luttrell, i. 121; Barrillon,
1/11, 5/15 Sept.; Longford to Ormond, 3 Sept. op. cit. vi. 144–5; Stringer's account
(written however after Shaftesbury's death) in Shaftesbury Papers, VI A, 364, fos. 5–6,
9–22.

indisposition, but seven weeks later he kissed the King's hand and was received back into favour, to the disgust of his former associates.[1]

As the autumn days became shorter there was a curious outburst of rumours that the apparent political deadlock would be resolved by the King calling a new Parliament. The flow of Tory addresses still continued, and might be interpreted as an indication that a new House of Commons might be more tractable than the last. It was even rumoured that Halifax, in the interests of William of Orange and Anglo-Dutch co-operation in Europe, was suggesting a fresh political start on the basis of a simultaneous amnesty to the Catholic peers, Danby, and Shaftesbury; so little was it thought that the Oxford Parliament would be the last one of the reign. It is possible that some people knew that the King had ordered the payment of £500 from the proceeds of the hearth money tax to help keep the wolf from his beloved son Monmouth's door, and that this was the basis of the rumour; but if so, it was a mistake, for there was no weakening of Charles's fundamental resolve to make no political concessions and to call no Parliament.[2]

At this same period, however, there were some signs of a temporary weakening in Shaftesbury's resolve. At one moment we catch a glimpse of him jesting at the expense of the judges, who were, he said 'run off their legs': others that would 'carry the prerogative higher' must replace them, and he suggested Jeffreys, Wythens (whom the Commons had rebuked), and Scroggs, junior. But this was a grim jest for a prisoner accused of treason; and so was the question which he transmitted privately to Sir William Jones, wanting to know what would happen if a person lawfully indicted refused to plead—Jones giving him the doubtful consolation that his fate would be the same as if he were found guilty, since there was at least no pressing to death in a case of treason.[3] Plainly Shaftesbury was still concerned with the possibility that the King would find some means of indicting him before a grand jury other than the London one on which he could depend, and then before a court of hostile peers. Or, even if the worst did not come to the worst, there was the only slightly less unattractive possibility that the King might find means of continuing to evade bringing him to any trial, and simply keep him permanently imprisoned in the Tower. He was now sixty, and his health, though better than it had been, was still not good[4]; the possibility of a winter in the Tower might well daunt him. Whatever happened, his political rôle in the future would be

---

[1] Bolron, 1 Sept., C.S.P.D. 1680–1, pp. 431–2; newsletter, 6 Sept., ibid. p. 439; Huntingdon to Stringer, 1 Sept. (copy), Shaftesbury Papers, VI B, 400; Longford to Ormond, 18 [really 20] Oct., H.M.C. Ormond MSS., N.S. vi. 204; C.S.P.D. 1680–1, pp. 545–6.

[2] Barrillon, 12/22 Sept., 21 Sept./1 Oct.; Longford to Ormond, 24 Sept., op. cit. vi. 165–6; anon. to Jenkins, 27 Sept., C.S.P.D. 1680–1, p. 473; H. Guy to [the Auditor of the Receipt], 10 Sept., Cal. Tr. Bks. 1681–5, pt. i, p. 269.

[3] Jenkins to Conway, 19 Sept., C.S.P.D. 1680–1, p. 457; Shaftesbury Papers, VI A, 370.

[4] Cf. Lady Russell to Russell, 2 Oct., in [Mary Berry], Life of Lady Russell (1819), p. 249.

limited. Some such reasoning may have led to the *ballon d'essai* which he now proceeded to fly.

On 28 September, one of the gentlemen of his household, named Shepherd, brought a paper from Shaftesbury to the Lord Chamberlain, who was none other than his old associate, the Earl of Arlington—the one person at Court whom he might use as an intermediary with the King. In the paper Shaftesbury offered to do three things, if he were released. He would go to his house in the country and live there; he would go to 'some parts beyond the seas'; and he would go to his plantation in Carolina. His business and health, he said, required him to stay at Wimborne St. Giles, and he offered to give up Thanet House to remove 'all occasions of jealousy' about his activities there. If he were required to go 'beyond sea' he would expect a pardon, to prevent his enemies from manufacturing more evidence when his back was turned; but beyond sea, and in Carolina, not only would he be far removed from jealousy, but he would be helping to extend the King's dominions and increase the yield of his customs. To this he added a rather startling request for £3,000 which he said the King had often promised him, 'for making the house [Exeter House] fit for the Seals' when he became Lord Chancellor in 1672. Perhaps the explanation for this impertinence is that he thought Charles might jump at the chance of being rid of him at the price; at all events he suggested that if he were supplied with this sum, he could be ready for the journey to Carolina within two or three months, and would need a convoy and a captain whom he could trust. To discuss this, he offered to 'come to the King alone, without the interposition of the angry and the mighty'.[1]

Arlington duly took a suitable opportunity at Newmarket to broach the matter to the King. Charles asked to see Shaftesbury's letter and Arlington reluctantly went beyond his instructions and showed it, so that Hyde, glancing over, was able to memorize the contents and help to spread them later for propagandist purposes. Charles at first said that he would consider it and return an answer in four or five days—and possibly his hesitation was genuine; but when Arlington said that he was in honour bound to return the petition immediately if it was not granted, Charles handed it back and said that he would leave Shaftesbury to the law. Later he told courtiers that if the request had come from anyone else, he would have granted it, but that he knew Shaftesbury, if released, would say that the conditions had been extorted from him and were legally valueless. There were those who thought that even so the petition should have been granted in order to make Shaftesbury distrusted by his party; but some advantage was extracted even from spreading the story, and the Whig journalists were reduced to some desperate shifts in order to explain away

---

[1] MSS. Clar. 88, fo. 5. Roger Morrice later wrote that Lady Shaftesbury, Shepherd, and Locke took the letter to Arlington without any other friends being consulted (Entering Book P, Dr. Williams's Library, fo. 319, 13 Dec. 1681).

their leader's letter as some kind of attempt to exculpate himself from malicious accusations of disloyalty to the King.[1]

On the day after this little episode at Newmarket, the King enjoyed a triumph of a different kind at London, with the election of Sir John Moore as the new Lord Mayor. Moore was the alderman 'next to the chair'; as an ex-Nonconformist himself who was thought to have conformed to the Church only to qualify for office, he enjoyed naturally the support of many Dissenters; so that he had many natural voters, and when the Whigs woke up to the fact that he was politically unreliable, and was indeed being strongly supported by the Court, it was too late for them to coalesce round a rival. The Whig vote was split between two candidates, Sir John Shorter and Sir Thomas Gold,[2] and with the advantage of being the senior alderman, and not a man with a partisan Tory record, Moore finished at the top of the poll. In spite of all the efforts of Sheriff Pilkington, he had to be declared Lord Mayor. As the Court had foreseen, though Moore was not a party man he was much more amenable to government pressure than his predecessors had been: he was 'flexible and faint-hearted', and his cautious attitude to the responsibilities of his position was confirmed by resentment at the Whig opposition to his election. There would be a marked difference between his lukewarmness (at best) and the Whiggery of his predecessor, Sir Patience Ward.[3]

Here, however, the King's success stopped, and in the next two months the Whigs rallied. To some extent they may have been encouraged by the persistence of rumours that Parliament would be called at the end of September. This was the time when Louis XIV had just won his most striking gains from the *chambres de réunion* policy, for Strasbourg and Casale had been occupied and Luxemburg was seriously threatened; surely Charles II would have to do something to halt these French advances.[4] But more important was that in the martyred Shaftesbury, whose trial was approaching, there was an obvious rallying-point, and that by virtue of the sheriffs' power to nominate the grand jury, there was every

[1] Morrice, loc. cit.; Jenkins to Ormond, 8 Oct., *H.M.C. Ormond MSS.*, N.S. vi. 182; Arran to Ormond, 8 Oct., ibid.; Longford to Ormond, 9, 11 Oct. ibid. pp. 184, 187–8; same to same, 15 Sept. [really Oct.], ibid. 154; Sir C. Lyttelton to L. Hatton, 11 Oct., *Hatton Correspondence*, ii. 8; *True Protestant Mercury*, 8–12 Oct.; van Citters, 14/24 Oct., Add. MSS. 17677, FF; Luttrell, i. 136.

[2] There was, however, a theory that the King or the Court of Aldermen was entitled to choose from the top two candidates in the poll. The existence of this theory certainly made it necessary for the Whigs to nominate two candidates in 1682 (see below, p. 704), and may have accounted for the nomination of two in 1681.

[3] Jenkins to Conway, 19, 27–28 Sept., *C.S.P.D. 1680–1*, pp. 457, 473, 474–5; Jenkins to L. Chancellor, 29 Sept., ibid. pp. 475–6; Jenkins to Conway, 30 Sept., ibid. pp. 479–80; newsletter, 1 Oct., ibid. pp. 484–5; Burnet, ii. 335.

[4] Jenkins to Conway, 4 Oct., *C.S.P.D. 1680–1*, pp. 490–1; Longford to Ormond, 9 Oct., *H.M.C. Ormond MSS.*, N.S. vi. 184; newsletter, 11 Oct., *C.S.P.D. 1680–1*, p. 507; T. Venn to R. Newcourt, 15 Oct., ibid. pp. 514–15; Van Beuningen to Prince of Orange, 21/31 Oct., *Correspondentie van Willem III en van Bentinck*, ed. N. Japikse (The Hague, 1935), II. ii. 413–14.

likelihood that Shaftesbury's trial would end in a Whig victory. For the new Lord Mayor had no power to influence the sheriffs if they chose to pack the jury, and although some courtiers had hoped that Sheriffs Pilkington and Shute would be more impartial, the Westminster panel,[1] the names of which were revealed at the beginning of October, had the Earl's intimate 'lame Charlton' as its foreman, and Russell, Ralph Montagu and Tom Thynne among the members. All the efforts of Sir George Jeffreys to pick out of the fifty names thirteen or fifteen 'tolerably honest men' ended in failure, and a conference between Halifax, Hyde, and Lord Chief Justice Pemberton could provide no solution; it was obvious that any grand jury in London would be similar.[2]

To counteract this the King's agents were still working to collect further 'evidence', with which to make the case against Shaftesbury so strong that no grand jury could be shameless enough to avoid sending him for trial by his peers. Fresh witnesses were required, who were not, like the ex-Plot informers who had given evidence against College, open to accusations of perjury from their former colleagues. One such presented himself in John Booth, a former servant of Lord Eure in Yorkshire. The Earl's faithful Stringer later accused Booth of forgery, fraud, simony, perjury, murder, and clipping and coining. Whether or not this impressive catalogue of crime was accurate, Booth was certainly in prison when he offered his information. It was none the less welcome to Justice Warcup and his employers; and what was more, Booth offered to secure still more valuable information from a fellow-prisoner, Captain Henry Wilkinson, who had been offered the command of one of Shaftesbury's ships bound for Carolina, but now lay in prison for debt. How this was to rebound against the government we shall see later. In the meantime there was the possibility of intimidating Shaftesbury's own servants. For some time a watch had been kept on the activities of the Earl's secretary, Samuel Wilson, and all kinds of seditious talk had been reported: not only had he talked about 'our design' and 'prosecuting God's cause', but he had spoken disrespectfully of the King: 'Don't you know the reply Oliver made, Give him a shoulder of mutton and a whore and that's all he cares for?' On 10 October a warrant was issued for his arrest. Two days later he smuggled out from his prison a letter for his brother. Every scrap of a small piece of paper is filled (paper, pen, and ink being officially denied him). Part of the letter contains an account of his questioning by four privy councillors, Jenkins, Halifax, Hyde and Conway. He was first asked whether he had treated with one Brownrig to give evidence for College at Oxford, and whether he had offered him or anyone money for doing so. When he had denied

---

[1] The sheriffs were responsible for nominating the grand juries in the three hundreds of Middlesex, including Westminster, as well as in London.

[2] Newsletter, 3 Oct., *H.M.C. Various* (Throckmorton MSS.), p. 173; Jenkins to Conway, 6, 8 Oct., *C.S.P.D. 1680–1*, pp. 496, 500; newsletters, 11, 13, 15 Oct., ibid. pp. 507, 509–11, 517; Longford to Ormond, 11 Oct., *H.M.C. Ormond MSS.*, N.S. vi. 188.

this, 'Did you never speak slightly of the King, and say that he deserved to be seized and that you would assist in it?' He was further asked if he 'knew of none that had bought arms, and commissioned themselves to go to Oxford with that intent?'

These questions were intended to elicit replies which would fit in with the evidence which Booth and Wilkinson were expected to produce, and help to prove that Shaftesbury had been concerned in a plot to seize the King at the time of the Oxford Parliament. A servant less devoted to his master might have yielded to the temptation to save himself and perhaps earn reward. But the whole letter to his brother breathed a remarkable loyalty to his master and his cause. 'Tell Mr. Stringer that I look upon it as a fishing for somewhat against my Lord who I wish to God nobody would design him more hurt than I who cannot in the least accuse him of any crime. See and make it your business to know the sense of the City and honest men and particularly of our family, viz. Mr. Stringer, Mr. Locke, Mr. Shepherd etc. . . .' The letter goes on to give instructions for action to be taken against those whom Wilson suspected of swearing against him; but the details are less important than the apparent community of feeling in this 'family' of devoted followers. None of his intimates betrayed him during his lifetime. And it is worthy of note that John Locke is clearly regarded as one of the circle, helping to free his master and his fellow-servant: he was to be asked to visit Wilson's enemies as well as to help comfort his father and mother. Another friend of both Locke and Wilson, Edward Clarke, said here to be 'a milliner in Fleet Street', was also arrested and also gave nothing away.[1]

Not only were these arrests of no use to the government, but in this same week a powerful Whig pamphlet appeared, *No Protestant Plot: or, The Present pretended Conspiracy of Protestants against the King and Government, discovered to be a Conspiracy of the Papists against the King and his Protestant Subjects*. Some thought that Shaftesbury himself was the author; Ferguson later laid claim to it; John Locke's enemies at Oxford, probably mistakenly, saw the philosopher's hand in it.[2] Its purpose was to justify in advance an *Ignoramus* verdict from the grand jury, on the lines suggested in the title. Others besides Papists were struck at, however. Notably it was suggested that in the past seven years Shaftesbury had always shown more deference to the King than had 'a certain Gentleman that now glories in having the chief superintendency of his affairs'; and although it was often observed that apostates in religion were the greatest

---

[1] [Dr. Butler] to Jenkins, 20 Sept., *C.S.P.D. 1680–1*, pp. 458–9; Sir James Hayes to Jenkins, 24 Sept., ibid. p. 466; T. Taylor to B. Herne, 1, 4, 5 Oct., ibid. pp. 483–4, 489, 492; Hayes's information, 11 Oct., ibid. pp. 504–5; Wilson's examination, 12 Oct., ibid. pp. 507–8; his letter in Shaftesbury Papers, XLIII, 63; Longford to Ormond, 15 Oct., *H.M.C. Ormond MSS.*, N.S. vi. 154–5; Luttrell, i. 141.

[2] Newsletter, 13 Oct.; H. Prideaux to J. Ellis, 25 Oct., *Letters of Humphrey Prideaux . . .*, ed. E. M. Thompson (Camden Society, 1875), p. 115.

persecutors, 'I never heard till now, but men might see reasons to change measures in politics, without being for sacrificing those that cannot shift about to the several points of the State-compass, as the wind of Court-favour may happen to sit.' This was a vicious dig at the Earl's enemy Halifax. In general, the writer argued, the talk of a Protestant plot against the King did not make sense, because Protestants would be fools as well as knaves to conspire, knowing what they could expect from a Popish successor. 'Such as expect preferment and wealth from the next heir, may be tempted to disloyalty to the regnant Prince', not the Whigs. It was nothing but Shaftesbury's zeal for the King that had made him enemies, and the more hostile the French, the Papists, and the supporters of the Duke were to him, the more it was in the King's interest to protect him. Page after page was then devoted to attacks against the witnesses. It was ridiculous to suppose that Shaftesbury would confide in such people, and significant that no Church of England or 'fanatic' witnesses had been found, 'only a few fellows of no religion (and most of whom have not bread to eat but what they get by being the King's evidence)'. The whole business was 'of the same stamp' as Mrs. Cellier's plot in 1679. The denial to Shaftesbury of the right, which had been permitted to Coleman and the Jesuits, to confront the witnesses against him at the Council Board before being consigned to the Tower was suspicious, and so was the refusal to permit the indictment of these witnesses for subornation: 'an honest jury' would bear in mind that the charges against them had not been left for trial. There were attacks on Warcup and David Fitzgerald, allegations that they had attempted to suborn evidence with promises of reward in the names of Halifax, Seymour, and Jenkins, and allegations that some of the witnesses themselves had admitted that it was all a put-up job.

Though the King tried to counteract this by summoning first Warcup and Fitzgerald, and then the witnesses themselves, before the Council, and getting them to swear that what they had done was 'to discharge their conscience, and not upon any consideration of reward, promise, or expectation of gain',[1] the pamphlet made a considerable stir at a time when the King would find it difficult to postpone the trial any further. Though Tory journalists like Nathaniel Thompson still talked of the possibility of moving the trial to Oxford, courtiers who were better informed were already saying that the best to be hoped for was that the witnesses might be presented in open court, so that 'the world may be witnesses of their perjury in case they [the jury] do not find the Bill'; and the King was talking self-righteously of his resolve to allow the benefit of the law to his subjects, though he himself 'was the only man in England that now could not have the benefit of the law, by the practice of the fanatic party'.[2]

---

[1] *The Loyal Protestant and True Domestick Intelligence*, 15 Oct.

[2] Ibid.; Longford to Ormond, 15 Oct., and 15 Sept. [really Oct.], 25 Oct., *H.M.C. Ormond MSS.*, N.S. vi. 154, 155, 208.

At the Old Bailey on 17 October, two members of the grand jury were turned away on the ground that they had been convicted of attending Dissenting conventicles; it was said others were also 'fanatics', but had thoughtfully provided themselves with certificates of occasional attendance at their parish churches. After a lengthy altercation the sheriffs submitted to the exclusion of the two, knowing that they could rely on the others, and so it proved. After petitions by Shaftesbury, Howard, Wilmore, Whittaker, and Wilson for bail or a speedy trial had been rejected once again on the ground that it was a King's Bench matter, John Rouse, the man who had been responsible for paying small sums to the Irish witnesses, was brought up on a charge of treason. Eight witnesses, six of whom were also due to swear against Shaftesbury, deposed to various uncomplimentary and vaguely rebellious remarks by Rouse; and then, apparently only after some hours of discussion, the grand jury (some of whom were accused by the witnesses of being present when the remarks were made!) brought in a verdict of *Ignoramus*. When the judges expressed their surprise, the foreman bluntly replied 'That that was their verdict, and they had satisfied their own consciences, and conceived they were not bound to shew any reasons for it'. Rouse had to be set free; and the King declared to all and sundry, including the foreign ambassadors: 'It is a hard case that I am the last man to have law and justice in the whole nation.'[1] Whether his indignation was real or synthetic with a propagandist aim it is difficult to say, but he certainly repeated it at every opportunity. When he attended the Lord Mayor's banquet at the Guildhall he was reported as saying that with the assistance of 'the honest part of the City (for he believed all honest and rich men would be of his side) he did not doubt but to be too hard for those who were factious only for faction sake, and would perjure themselves only to mischief him, who was willing to afford the benefit of the law to all his subjects, though he was the only man in England could not have it himself'.[2]

On the first day of term in the King's Bench, 24 October, Shaftesbury and his fellow-prisoners again petitioned for trial or bail, and were told in reply that if there had been no prosecution before the last day of term, bail would be granted. Various last-minute expedients for securing a grand jury by means other than through the sheriffs were considered by the King and his ministers; some suggested that a commission of oyer and terminer might be sent to Westminster, where the Bailiff was 'well affected' to the government. The Bailiff, it was said, would have to return the jury, 'and the persons to be returned depend for the most part on His Majesty's

---

[1] *A Particular Account of the Proceedings at the Old Bailey, the 17 and 18 of this instant October* (1681); Longford to Ormond, 18 Oct., op. cit. vi. 197–8; J. Ellis to Ormond, 18 Oct., ibid. p. 199; Shaftesbury's petition in Shaftesbury Papers, XLIII, 63; Stringer's 'Short Account of the late great Earl of Shaftesbury's case', ibid. VI A, 364, fos. 7–8; *Loyal Protestant and True Domestick Intelligence*, 20 Oct.; van Citters, 21/31 Oct., Add. MSS. 17677, SSS; Barrillon, 20/30 Oct.; Reresby, p. 234.

[2] Longford to Ormond, 29 Oct., *H.M.C. Ormond MSS.*, N.S. vi. 212.

family, the church of Westminster and the Exchequer'. The judges spent some time considering whether such a right of the Bailiff could be established from King John's charters to the Abbot of Westminster and the City of London, but decided that it was doubtful and that anyway Shaftesbury could not be tried in Westminster because no legally valid evidence lay against him there.[1] Behind the scenes Halifax felt that since in these circumstances Shaftesbury was bound to be acquitted in any case, it was best to let him go as 'an act of mercy and legality' rather than in triumph; but in public the ministers maintained their unity, so that the Whig pamphleteers were able to say 'From Hell, Hyde, Halifax, deliver us'.[2] Finally it was decided that the evidence against Shaftesbury should be set out in court, and then if the jury refused to find the bill, his lordship would, in Charles's characteristic metaphor, 'go off with a bottle at his tail'. The usual annual commission of oyer and terminer was issued, to be opened in the Old Bailey on 24 November.[3]

For some years November had invariably been a month of great political excitement. It was the season of bonfires, which could be turned into political demonstrations by varying the effigies which were paraded and then installed on top of the pyres. On 5 November the boys of Westminster School burnt 'Jack Presbyter' on their bonfire; on 17 November, the anniversary of Queen Elizabeth's accession, the Whig procession which started from Whitechapel, by way of Chancery Lane and Holborn to Smithfield (where Monmouth and Grey were present), included in one pageant three Irishmen in a pillory, with the word *Suborner* inscribed over one and *Suborned* over the other two, and in another the Pope 'with a "towser" between his legs', Towser being Sir Roger L'Estrange, the author of the *Observator*.[4] The propaganda battle was fought with many different weapons. In pursuance of its efforts to identify its opponents with 'Jack Presbyter', the government issued orders for the enforcement of the penal laws against Dissenters. The Dutch ambassador thought that the intention was to use discretion and persecute only those who were stirring up trouble for the government; be that as it may, eleven Nonconformists on whom subpoenas were served in the week before Shaftesbury's trial would have been liable to penalties of £4,840 had a jury been

---

[1] Newsletter, 25 Oct., *C.S.P.D. 1680–1*, p. 534; 'Narrative for the Privy Council', 18 Oct., ibid. pp. 520–1; Longford to Ormond, 29 Oct., *H.M.C. Ormond MSS.*, N.S. vi. 211; Clarke, op. cit. i. 713–14. Longford, 1, 5, 8 Nov., *H.M.C. Ormond MSS.*, N.S. vi. 215, 217, 220 says that the Court had been led to believe that the sheriffs would after all return juries satisfactory to the King, but this is hard to believe.

[2] Reresby, p. 236 (6 Nov.); Barrillon, 5/15 Nov.; *Advice to the Painter . . . for limning to the Life the Witnesses against the Rt. Hon. Anthony, Earl of Shaftesbury* (early Dec. 1681).

[3] Longford to Ormond, 15 Nov., *H.M.C. Ormond MSS.*, N.S. vi. 229; E. Cooke to Ormond, 12 Nov., ibid. vi. 223–4; Marquis of Worcester to Marchioness, 12 Nov., *H.M.C. Beaufort MSS.*, p. 87; and cf. Burnet, ii. 300.

[4] Luttrell, i. 142; newsletter, 21 Dec. [really Nov.], *H.M.C. Various MSS.* (13), pp. 174–5.

UU

willing to convict them.[1] In these days probably the greatest literary piece of propaganda of all, *Absalom and Achitophel*, appeared on the Court side and won the applause of the discerning[2]; but at first it probably had less impact than a pamphlet, *The Information of Capt. Hen. Wilkinson*, which Shaftesbury and his friends had reserved for this juncture.

Captain Henry Wilkinson was a veteran soldier who had been originally selected in February 1681 by the proprietors of Carolina to act as governor of that portion of the colony which lay on the Albemarle River,[3] but before he could leave the country he was thrown into prison for debt. In the pamphlet which he wrote, or which was written on his behalf, he told the following story. On 8 October, precisely when the government was desperately looking round for fresh, untainted evidence, he had been visited in prison by one Walter Baines, who suggested that he must know much of Shaftesbury's designs against the King; if Wilkinson were prepared to discover them, he (Baines) had an interest with the Treasury solicitor, Graham, and with Lord Hyde. Three days later a fellow-prisoner, John Booth (to whose alleged criminal record reference has already been made)[4] was more specific. Wilkinson might have £500 a year settled upon him, or £10,000 in cash, whichever he preferred, if he would 'discover' what he knew. Wilkinson replied that although he had been with Shaftesbury on the night before the Earl's arrest he knew nothing of any designs; but on each of the next four days Baines and Booth visited him again, making liberal use of the names of Halifax, Hyde, and Graham, and finally making plain what he was expected to say. He had waited upon Shaftesbury out of town when he left for the Oxford Parliament, and was expected to say that, should the King not agree to the Exclusion Bill and bills for the relief of Dissenters, he was to be compelled to do so. On the last visit Booth said that the reason why Wilkinson's evidence was so urgently needed was that so far there were only Irish witnesses against the Earl, but unlike them Wilkinson was not 'blemished in my credit'. Finally, on 15 October, Wilkinson was taken to Whitehall and questioned by the King in person. Charles said he knew well the services Wilkinson had performed in the Army both for him and his father, and promised to 'consider me for my sufferings', while insisting that this kindness 'was not with a design to invite me to speak a word but truth itself'. When Wilkinson insisted that he knew nothing of any plot, Charles 'seemed to wonder at' it, and left him to be examined, equally fruitlessly, by five privy councillors and Lord Chief Justice Pemberton.

In this Plot period it is always difficult for the historian to establish

---

[1] Van Citters and van Beuningen, 15/25 Nov., Add. MSS. 17677, FF; William Sherman, 28 Nov., *C.S.P.D. 1680–1*, p. 592.

[2] Cf. the newsletter, p. 673, n. 4 above, and Lyttelton to L. Hatton, 22 Nov., *Hatton Correspondence*, ii. 10.

[3] See his instructions, *C.S.P. Col. America and West Indies, 1681–5*, pp. 14–15.

[4] p. 669 above.

which was the suborner and which the suborned; and certainly Booth and Baines tried to answer the accusations by saying that, so far from trying to entrap Wilkinson, they had been entrapped by him, and the Tories maintained that it was 'a manifest trepan of the Earl's'. But to the present writer the long, circumstantial account rings true, and it is not easy to find any flaws in it. Nor was Wilkinson rewarded for what he had done (or not done). There is in the Shaftesbury Papers a letter, dated September 1682, describing how Wilkinson and his family were still in prison and in want, with debts of £1,200 and their honesty unrewarded. No one contested that Wilkinson's past was infinitely more respectable than that of Booth; and so it seems probable that the latter was in fact trying to earn a living by bringing to the government the kind of 'information' that he knew it wanted. To the careful reader this does not necessarily mean that Halifax, Hyde, and Graham, still less the King, were accomplices in an attempt at subornation; but for people who were predisposed to believe the worst of the ministry, it was easy to 'read between the lines'. Amongst those who did so was Burnet, who was not normally well disposed to Shaftesbury. So too did many of the London public, among them no doubt the members of the grand jury.[1]

Two days before the trial all seats in the Old Bailey court-room had been bespoken,[2] and each side had completed its preparations. Sheriff Pilkington was reported to have said 'There is work cut out for us' on receiving the official writ to return a jury for the commission of oyer and terminer,[3] and the work had been done well from the Whig point of view. The foreman was Sir Samuel Barnardiston, a member of a well-known Puritan and Parliamentarian family in Suffolk, whose opposition to the Crown went back to 1640, and who had since become a well-known figure in the East India Company. Amongst the members was the Huguenot Thomas Papillon, whose record of opposition also dated back to the 1640s, and who was, again like Barnardiston, a director of the East India Company and a former Exclusionist member of Parliament. John Dubois, another Huguenot merchant and Exclusionist member, was to be Papillon's colleague in the elections for the shrievalty in 1682.[4] Michael Godfrey's name speaks for itself. The names of the other jurymen are less well known to posterity, though they must have been well known to contemporaries if we are to credit the assertion that the jurymen together were worth a million

---

[1] In addition to Wilkinson's printed information, see the last pages of Stringer's notes, Shaftesbury Papers, VI B, 404, for Booth's record; ibid. XLIII, 63 for the letter of Sept. 1682; Add. MSS. 41803, fos. 15–21; Burnet, ii. 298; Warcup's paper, *C.S.P.D. 1680–1*, p. 574; and for some Tory views of the information, see Longford to Ormond, 15 Nov., *H.M.C. Ormond MSS.*, N.S. vi. 229; *Observator*, 22 and 26 Nov. There is no evidence to support Roger North's guesswork, *Examen* (1740), pp. 119–20. Cf. the obvious flaws in Booth's own evidence, pp. 678, 680 below.

[2] Charles Bertie to Viscount Campden, 22 Nov., *H.M.C. Rutland MSS.*, ii. 60.

[3] *C.S.P.D. 1680–1*, pp. 573–4.

[4] See below, p. 699 sqq.

pounds.[1] On this last figure, however, some fallacious conclusions have been based: it has been inferred that the Whigs were a party of plutocrats. This misses the point. Previously Tory propaganda, commenting on the juries which had brought in *Ignoramus* verdicts in College's case in July and Rouse's in October, had stressed that these were common tradesmen, inconsiderable people[2]: all the well-to-do, respectable people supported the government, and only 'the rabble' and Dissenters, those without a property stake in the maintenance of law and order, favoured Exclusion. The composition of Shaftesbury's jury was intended to disprove this, and it would be just as unwise for the historian to derive any social analysis from it as it would for him to rely on the earlier juries—if not more so. Further, the jurymen must be substantial people with sufficient experience and knowledge of the law to be able to stand up to the bullying which was to be expected from Lord Chief Justice Pemberton and the other judges on the bench. To aid them, the jurymen were primed with all the information about the witnesses which had been laboriously collected by Stringer and others in collaboration. A notebook survives, consisting of fifty-nine pages of questions to be put to the witnesses 'in case the witnesses are examined publicly in court': it is even possible that there was a copy for each juror.[3]

Before the trial even opened, the populace made its opinions known, mobbing and jeering at the witnesses for 'perjured rogues' as they met at the Fountain tavern, with Titus Oates and his servants encouraging 'the rabble' and giving them wine. One of the witnesses, Dugdale, slipped away, not daring to give evidence. The rest survived the jostling and reached the court-room, only to find that 'a great rabble' had found an entrance and was rude enough to hiss them at the witness-stand. (Even poor Secretary Jenkins suffered from this.) The more fashionable members of the audience included Monmouth, Essex, Russell, Montagu and Armstrong, all lending their patronage to Shaftesbury's cause.[4] Since this was only a preliminary indictment before the grand jury and not a final trial before his peers, the Earl himself was not present; he remained in the Tower, playing cards with his wife, while his fate was being discussed.

Lord Chief Justice Pemberton opened the proceedings with a long harangue on the treason law, emphasizing that under the Act of 1661 words were treasonable if they signified any design to restrain the King's liberty or imprison him. He added that what the jury had to consider was only whether there was a *prima facie* ground for calling the prisoner to account; it was not necessary to hold such a strict enquiry as did a petty jury. The jurors had, he said, a double obligation to do right, as patriotic Englishmen and by virtue of their oath, if they had two witnesses to treasonable words.

---

[1] Cf. the annotated list, S.P. Car. II. 417, nos. 112, 113.
[2] Cf. above, pp. 658, 672.   [3] Shaftesbury Papers, XLIII, 63.
[4] John Smith's account, 12 Apr. 1682, *C.S.P.D. 1682*, pp. 162–3; Longford to Ormond, 26 Nov., *H.M.C. Ormond MSS.*, N.S. vi. 236.

The King's counsel, Sir Francis Wythens, then moved that the evidence be heard in open court, and the Lord Chief Justice upheld this 'so that it may not be hereafter in the mouths of any ill-minded persons abroad, to scatter any mistakes or untruths up and down'; the propagandist uses of the trial were in everyone's mind. The jury demurred on the ground that their oath bound them to 'keep the King's secrets', and Papillon impudently pointed out that public examination of treason cases was against the King's own interest in that it revealed all the evidence before the main trial and gave the defence time to prepare to prejudice the King's witnesses. The Lord Chief Justice conceded that private examination was customary, but said that this was only a matter of convenience. Sarcastically he complimented the jury on their care for the King's interests, but said that it was open to the King's counsel to please themselves in the matter. Foreman Barnardiston gave way to this ruling under protest. Sheriff Pilkington then intervened to suggest that at least the witnesses should be kept out of court and brought in for separate examination, but, rather remarkably, the Lord Chief Justice refused to make any such order.[1]

After these preliminary skirmishes, the indictment was read. It accused Shaftesbury of saying, on 18 March 1681, that he and his associates were determined to compel the King to accept the Exclusion Bill and the bills for the relief of Dissenters, and that armed men had been prepared, under the command of Capt. Wilkinson, and of whom John Booth was to be one. The Earl was further accused of having declared that the King was as deserving of deposition as Richard II; that he (the Earl) 'could never desist, until he had brought this kingdom of England into a commonwealth without a King', like Holland; 'and further . . . that our now sovereign lord the King was a man of an unfaithful heart, and not worthy to be trusted, and not fit to rule and govern, being false, unjust, and cruel to his people, and that if he would not be governed by his people, they . . . our said sovereign lord the King would depose . . .'.

After these edifying remarks had been read out, it turned out that the first piece of evidence related to something not mentioned in the indictment. A paper was produced, which it was alleged had been taken from Shaftesbury's closet at the time of his arrest, put into a velvet bag, and later taken out in the presence of his servants, Wilson and Starkey. It was a draft Association, such as had been more than once mooted in both Houses of Parliament, in imitation of the Elizabethan Association against

---

[1] The account of the trial in *State Trials*, viii. 759–842, is based on the 'authorized' narrative. *The Proceedings against the right honourable the Earl of Shaftesbury . . . as they were taken by an impartial hand, and faithfully transmitted to every unbiased reader. With sufficient reasons to justify the Grand Jury in bringing in the Bill Ignoramus* (1681), by 'Philonomus', does not conflict in any important point. There is a copy in Shaftesbury Papers, VI A, 374. Papillon later said that there were mistakes in the official narrative, which however the Whigs had not thought it worth while to correct (ibid., 379). There are also two shorter summaries, *An Account at Large of the Proceedings at the Sessions House in the Old Bailey . . .* and *The Proceedings at the Sessions House. . . .*

Mary, Queen of Scots in 1585, without any question that it had been treasonable; and Shaftesbury had sat on a sub-committee of the Lords which was instructed to draft one. The draft was very similar to a proposal discussed in general terms in the House of Commons on 15 December 1680.[1] It described the stimulus given to Popish plotters by their expectations of the Duke of York's succession to the throne, complained of the Duke's influence as indicated by the number of his dependants in office and by the untimely prorogations and dissolutions, argued that Mary Tudor's reign had 'proved the wisest laws to be of little force to keep out popery and tyranny under a Popish prince', and described how an Exclusion bill had been rejected; therefore an Association was proposed, in which all the participants would undertake, not only to protect the Protestant religion and the King's royal person against plots, but 'by all lawful means, and by force of arms if need so require' to prevent James or any Papist from succeeding. For this purpose they would undertake to obey the orders of 'this present Parliament' (that of 1680) while it was sitting, or those of the majority of subscribers to the Association if Parliament were prorogued or dissolved.

The foreman of the jury took care to establish that this draft, which was not in the Earl's handwriting, was both undated and unsigned. John Booth then gave evidence that he had first been introduced to Shaftesbury by Captain Wilkinson, whom he had known for twenty years, in January 1681 on business connected with Carolina. In Wilkinson's company he visited the Earl 'four or five times' and heard him express his discontent, until finally the Earl told him he had organized fifty men, under Wilkinson's command, who, if there was any attempt on the Whigs by the King's guards at Oxford, would be summoned there to purge the guards and the privy councillors, and bring the King to London. Booth confessed that he had agreed to be one of the fifty and had provided himself with horse and arms; during the Oxford Parliament Wilkinson had met him in London and told him that he expected a summons to Oxford any day, but the sudden dissolution had made the plan ineffective. The story was both uncorroborated and far-fetched: how fifty men waiting in London could have intervened effectively at Oxford (where the King's guards were much more numerous) it is not easy to see.

There followed a succession of witnesses who deposed to treasonable remarks which Shaftesbury was alleged to have made. Turberville, who had given evidence for him against Lord Stafford, now declared that the Earl had said that 'were it not for his guards, we would quickly go down to Whitehall, and obtain what terms we thought fit. His lordship said, that the rabble were all of that side, especially the people about Wapping and Aldersgate Street; and the rich men of the city would vote for elections;

---

[1] *L.J.* xiii. 674, 694; *H.M.C. House of Lords MSS. 1678–88*, pp. 210–11; *C.J.* ix. 680; Grey, viii. 153–71.

but they could not expect they should stand by them in case there should be any disturbance, for they valued their riches more than their cause.' John ('Narrative') Smith said that the Earl had spoken 'very irreverently and slightly of the King', as weak, inconstant, and 'of no firm and settled resolution'; the Earl had asserted that the King was 'as well satisfied with the coming in of popery as ever the Duke of York was', that he had endeavoured to stifle the Plot, and was taking 'the very same steps that his father followed when he was led by his Popish Queen, and the poor man doth not see his danger'; and the Earl had maintained that if the King offered any violence to the Oxford Parliament it would be lawful to oppose him in arms. Bryan Haines described how the Earl had promised him a pardon in order to enable him to accuse Danby of the murder of Sir Edmund Berry Godfrey; 'and if he doth not grant it, we will raise the whole kingdom against him'; on another occasion the Earl had declared that the Duke of Buckingham had as great a right to the Crown, by virtue of his mother's descent from 'one of the Edwards'. John Macnamara, Dennis Macnamara, and Edward Ivy added their quota; and finally Bernard Dennis described how, in the gallery of Thanet House, 'walking very slowly', the Earl had urged him to 'speak more home and positive' against the Queen and Duke of York, in return for promises of church preferment; and had asked Dennis to have the three or four hundred Dennises in Ireland in readiness 'to assist the commonwealth of England; for we do really intend to have England under a commonwealth and no crown' like Holland; 'and, says he, we will extirpate the King, and all his family as near as we can'.

After the last witness had spoken, Papillon asked whether the indictment was based on the treason act of 1351 or (as the Lord Chief Justice's opening remarks had seemed to imply) on that of 1661. This was a shrewd question, for under the provisions of the latter Act prosecutions for uttering treasonable words had to be made within six months, and this would disqualify all of them. The Lord Chief Justice hastily answered that the indictment was based on both acts. The jury then asked whether any of the witnesses had been indicted or not, and Pemberton directed that the credibility of witnesses was a matter for the petty jury, and not for this one, for then the King could in his turn produce witnesses to defend their credibility. Papillon protested: 'If we are not left to consider the credibility of the witnesses, we cannot satisfy our consciences', but Pemberton insisted that the grand jury could take into account nothing but the evidence against the prisoner, and anything that they knew of their own knowledge. On this note the jury withdrew to consider what questions they wished to put to their witnesses, and to eat. In the meantime the witnesses, who retired to an eating-house to refresh themselves, were very rudely treated by what the Tories called 'the rabble'; and the story went that they were sent an eel-pie, which when opened was found to contain 'eight ropes wrap'd up like eels' from which the obvious moral could be drawn. The sheriffs had to send a guard to bring them back safely into court.[1]

Here the witnesses' sufferings were by no means at an end, for they had to undergo a severe cross-examination before running the gauntlet of the crowds again. Secretary Jenkins was the first to be questioned: he was asked whether the Association had been read and debated in the Commons. 'I heard such a thing spoke of; but at the reading of it I was not present, to the best of my remembrance', he said, fumblingly. On this and minor points he was curiously indefinite: 'I do not know'; 'I do not remember precisely'; 'I cannot tell truly'. Booth was asked whether he knew any other of the fifty men alleged to have enlisted under Captain Wilkinson, and had to admit weakly that he 'never directly conversed with any other'.[2] Turberville, when questioned by Sir Samuel Barnardiston, said that (although he claimed to have had intimate conversations with the Earl of Shaftesbury) he knew none of the Earl's servants except one, Mr. Shepherd. When asked by Papillon about a petition to the Common Council of London in which Turberville had declared that he was being tempted to witness against his conscience, Turberville said that the petition had been drawn up by order of College, and he himself signed it but did not read it. Haines was vague about the date of the conversations with the Earl which he had mentioned in his evidence: 'I cannot keep an almanack in my head.' Dennis Macnamara was equally vague about an interview which had taken place, he said, at 'the latter end of March or the beginning of April'; this was the informer's stock device of mentioning two months in order to gain the maximum amount of elbow-room in which to cope with any counter-evidence produced by the defence. All in all, the witnesses fared very badly before some very shrewdly organized questioning on Shaftesbury's behalf. It is true that they had to answer under very discouraging circumstances, for the Whig partisans made a great deal of noise which it was beyond the power of the Lord Chief Justice to quell. As Booth and Turberville finished their evidence, they appealed for the court's protection against being 'knocked on the head'; and it was no great comfort that for this purpose they were handed over to the loving care of Sheriff Pilkington.

It came as no surprise when at the end of the proceedings the grand jury brought in their famous *Ignoramus* verdict. There can be no doubt that the implication that the Crown's evidence was worthless was correct; there was no convincing proof here of any intention to use force against the king, the treasonable words were out of date, and the witnesses were

---

[1] *Advice to the Painter . . . for Limning to the Life the Witnesses against the Rt. Hon. Anthony, Earl of Shaftesbury (1681)*; Longford to Ormond, 26 Nov., *H.M.C. Ormond MSS.*, N.S. vi. 237.

[2] Later Wilkinson issued a challenge, publicly offering a reward to anyone who came forward to say that he had sold Booth a horse, as Booth alleged. The reward was never claimed. (*Somers Tracts* (1812), viii. 305 n.)

people whom the court itself believed to have given perjured evidence in the past. The question remains whether the grand jury should have taken it upon itself to say so, or whether it should not have accepted the evidence of these witnesses as justifying investigation before a petty jury—a jury of peers whom the King would nominate, under the presidency of a Lord High Steward whom the King would also select. But no sooner has the question been posed in these terms than it is seen to be hopelessly un-realistic. The Whigs could take no other course of action than the one they did, and it can hardly be said that it resulted in a miscarriage of justice. It is of course possible that, had the evidence against Shaftesbury been much stronger than it actually was, the verdict would still have been one of *Ignoramus*; but this possibility does not alter the facts of the situation as they were, and the inadequacy of the case actually presented.

No less significant than the verdict itself was the popular reception of it in London. No doubt many of the bonfires that night and next day were organized and paid for by Whig leaders, but nevertheless the applause cannot be dismissed as merely synthetic. Indeed the Tory propagandists did not do so; they preferred to regard it as the work of what Roger North later elegantly described as 'a rattleheaded scum of the *Canaglia*', and there-fore beneath contempt. In the court the 'hollowing and shouting' lasted for half an hour, and the witnesses were sent away in two coaches attended by a guard and followed by a 'rabble' of more than six hundred men, 'very tumultously, and with very ill language', until they got to the Savoy 'where they alighted and would have been in danger of being torn in pieces if the doors had not been shut and well guarded'. Late that night bands of people (one of them led by John Harrington, Shaftesbury's kinsman, with sword drawn) roamed the streets shouting 'No Popish Successor, No York, A Monmouth, A Buckingham, and God bless the Earl of Shaftesbury'. Sheriff Shute was observed telling people to 'Shout, boys, shout'; and some of the officers of the Tower, making their way back to Tower Gate, had to struggle through crowds clamouring for money for the bonfires and to drink Shaftesbury's health. Indeed the noise was positively embarrassing, in that it later gave the King grounds for represent-ing it as a riot and basing an attack on the City's charter upon it. Yet riot in the true sense of the word there was none. There was no destruction of property, still less an attempt to turn the popular exaltation in support of an armed *coup*.[1]

On 28 November Shaftesbury and his fellow-prisoners appeared in the Court of King's Bench to ask for immediate release. When the Attorney-General opposed this, the Earl began a speech which sneered at the Irish

---

[1] Longford, loc. cit.; Barrillon, 28 Nov./8 Dec.; L'Estrange, 25 Nov., *C.S.P.D. 1680–1*, pp. 583–4; G. Evans to Jenkins, 26 Nov., ibid. pp. 588–9; newsletter, 26 Nov., ibid. p. 591; Charles Bertie to Ctess of Rutland, 24 Nov., *H.M.C. Rutland MSS.*, ii. 61; [de la Fontaine] to same, ibid.; North, op. cit. p. 114.

witnesses and boasted of the *Ignoramus* verdict; but the Lord Chief Justice cut him short, told him he must not reflect on the King's evidence, and warned him that on another occasion an ignoramus verdict in London had been reversed in another county and the defendant executed. Shaftesbury was, however, conceded bail, on his own surety of £3,000 and those of Russell, Montagu, Sir William Cooper, Sir John Sydenham, and Francis Charlton for £1,500. Monmouth also offered himself as a surety, and the fact that the court declined to accept him did not save him from the King's indignation on that account.[1]

On the King's instructions the Lord Mayor now took elaborate precautions to prevent any popular demonstration to celebrate the Earl's return home. There were to be no bonfires, and no bell-ringing. The constables were put on double watch and ordered to go from house to house warning all the inhabitants to keep in their children and servants so that they could take part in no bonfires or 'tumults'. Six companies of the lieutenancy were to be on guard, to walk the rounds, and be in readiness to assist, if required. Shaftesbury and the Whigs made no attempt to counter these precautions. The Earl went by water from the King's Bench at Westminster to Paul's Wharf, and thence quietly home to Thanet House in the Lieutenant of the Tower's coach. Yet, as the French ambassador noticed, the very fact that the ban on bonfires had been necessary drew as much attention to Shaftesbury's position as the bonfires themselves could have done.[2]

A story became current that when he left the Tower Shaftesbury told the Lieutenant, 'There, tailor, is your groat, and that is all your due'. In fact the 'groat' was a substantial one. Captain Cheke's fee was £100; and the use of Sir Jonas Moore's house for fifteen weeks cost £60, and there was £10 for the Porter of the Tower. Even more substantial, however, were the payments made to Stringer, which between 18 August and 9 December totalled £599 19s. 7d. What proportion of this had been spent in connexion with the Earl's defence we have no means of knowing: but it must have been an expensive triumph.[3]

Yet a triumph it certainly was. The King was quoted as saying that he did not care sixpence whether the bill against Shaftesbury was found or not[4]; but no one really believed this. The Earl's arrest had been intended to be a prelude to his execution, and the Earl was now released to resume his position at the head of a party which evidently still commanded much

[1] Longford to Ormond, 29 Nov., *H.M.C. Ormond MSS.*, N.S. vi. 242; *An Account at Large* . . . (1681); *The Proceedings at the King's Bench Bar at Westminster* (1681); Luttrell, i. 147, 150; Barrillon, 5/15 Dec.

[2] Lord Mayor to Jenkins, 28 Nov., *C.S.P.D. 1680–1*, p. 592; Jenkins to H. Savile, 29 Nov., *Savile Correspondence*, p. 246; Sir C. Lyttelton to L. Hatton, 29 Nov., *Hatton Correspondence*, ii. 10; Barrillon, 1/11 Dec.

[3] Ailesbury, *Memoirs* (1890), ii. 377; accounts at Wimborne St. Giles.

[4] Newsletter, 24 Nov., *H.M.C. Various MSS.* (13), p. 174.

support in London. He could afford to savour his triumph, as he dined with Sheriff Pilkington at the Skinners' Hall,[1] and as his supporters prepared the famous medal, showing the Earl on one side and on the other the sun emerging from clouds over the Tower, with the word *Laetamur* and the date, 24 November 1681.

[1] *Impartial Protestant Mercury*, 13–16 Dec.

CHAPTER XXIX

THE FIGHT FOR THE CITY
(NOVEMBER 1681-SEPTEMBER 1682)

Did you not hear of a Peer that was tried?
> *With a fa, la, la, la, la.*

That looks like a cask with a tap in his side;
> *With a fa, la, la, la, la.*

This Noble Peer to the bar was called;
The witnesses swore, but the foreman out-bawled;
> *With a fa, la, la, la, la. . . .*

. . . The witnesses for the King swore plain;
But had they been so many again;
The jury before such truths received,
Nor them, nor St. Peter they would have believed . . .

But had it been a Popish Lord;
One witness then had served in a word;
They had not then enquired so far;
But found it, and never have stept from the bar.

If by this law the Charter be lost;
Will Tony's estate repay the cost?
The boys will then find out the cheat,
And De Witt the old cannibal in his retreat.

They'll curse that pate that studied to bring
Plague to the country, and ruin to th' King;
Divested thus of 'Chitophel's pride,
They'll do him that justice which juries denied.

Ignoramus Justice

Methinks a little, old, uncertain, quaking, stooping gentleman should make but a sorry champion in any cause.

Heraclitus Ridens

SHAFTESBURY'S acquittal seemed to have brought the political situation into a deadlock. On the one hand the King had failed to kill his enemy, and though some of the witnesses anticipated that a second attempt, as in College's case, would be made at Oxford,[1] no one in authority thought that this would be practicable. On the other hand Shaftesbury and his followers could make no progress with Exclusion or anything else until a Parliament was allowed to meet.

[1] Cf. John Smith's account, *C.S.P.D. 1682–3*, p. 163.

There were those who anticipated that Parliament would be summoned in February or March 1682, possibly at Oxford. Since the Restoration few years had passed without a Parliament, and another could be expected soon in the normal course of events. Few realized that the King's financial position was now healthy enough to enable him to dispense with it. And the international situation seemed to demand it. In the course of his attempts to make further territorial acquisitions by mere threats in the cold war which had operated since the Treaty of Nijmegen, Louis XIV had occupied Strasbourg and was now blockading Luxemburg. In view of the widespread desire of Englishmen to oppose French expansion in the years 1674 to 1678 and their pressure on Charles to intervene, it seemed unlikely that Charles dare remain unmoved by this latest blatant aggression. Indeed in June 1680, at the height of Sunderland's anti-French policy, he had signed a treaty with Spain; and since then he had promised the Dutch (or had led them to believe that he had promised) to call Parliament rather than allow Louis to continue. Within the ministry Halifax especially advocated another attempt to meet Parliament in the expectation that it might be more amenable than before to appeals for support of a policy of co-operation with William of Orange and Spain. Such well-informed people as Sir Robert Southwell thought that after the failure to kill Shaftesbury there was a real possibility of a compromise between the King and the opposition; in return for being allowed to meet, the latter would give up Exclusion, and be content with the King's assurances, and there would be an act of oblivion for all past offences, possibly after the four Catholic lords in the Tower had first been tried. For some time the Dutch ambassadors, who probably knew Halifax well, were optimistic about such a settlement, which would bring with it the means to force Louis's armies back.[1]

However in spite of the talk it is certain that Charles himself faced the possibility with the greatest reluctance. He had no wish to lose the three years' subsidy which Louis had promised last March in return for a fortress for which he cared little; indeed, on 21 November he had privately suggested that Louis might get Luxemburg, with its fortifications razed, provided that he held off for four months and allowed provisions into the town in the meantime. Meeting Parliament was a doubtful pleasure at any time, and, as Barrillon observed, there was still no guarantee that a new House of Commons would be more Tory than the last, and the popular enthusiasm for Shaftesbury's acquittal pointed the other way; nor did Charles's *quo warranto* policy, to which reference will be made shortly, make it a

[1] Van Citters and van Beuningen, 29 Nov./9 Dec., Add. MSS. 17677, FF; newsletter, 1 Dec., *C.S.P.D. 1680–1*, p. 599; Southwell to Ormond, 3 Dec., *H.M.C. Ormond MSS.*, N.S. iv. 591; Longford to Ormond, 3, 6, Dec., ibid. vi. 244, 249; Halifax to Prince of Orange, 2 Dec., *Archives de la Maison Orange-Nassau*, ed. Groen van Prinsterer (The Hague, 1858–62), II. v. 534; Hyde to same, 2 Dec., ibid. II. v. 536; Preston to Sir D. Fleming, 6 Dec., *H.M.C. Le Fleming MSS.*, p. 184.

propitious moment at which to hold elections.[1] Barrillon rightly thought
that a Parliament was most unlikely. At the same time, Charles was not
strong enough to ignore public opinion, the wishes of Halifax and other
ministers, and his dangerous nephew William. As usual in such a situation,
Charles fell back on a complicated game of manoeuvre, pretending to
threaten to call Parliament if Louis did not give way. Over a period of
three months the rumours alternately grew stronger and died away, while
in the Privy Council Halifax and Hyde opposed one another on the
question.[2] On 21 January 1682, Halifax argued before the committee of
foreign affairs in favour of a forward foreign policy, after which 'we may
safely have a Parliament, and just before that must secure Shaftesbury'.[3]
On what pretext this would have been done we do not know. But by the
end of February even the optimistic Dutch ambassador had decided that
the wisest policy for William was *à mauvais jeu faire bonne mine*; and in
March the last faint chance of a Parliament disappeared with the news that
Louis had withdrawn his forces from before Luxemburg. Privately Louis
told Charles that he had done this at the latter's request, and that he would
refer his claims to Charles's arbitration; in reality William's success in
persuading the States of Holland to vote for 8,000 men to assist Spain
had made it plain that Luxemburg could not be won without actual
fighting. In any case, the international situation became clearer, and the
Whig hopes dwindled correspondingly.[4]

In the meantime Charles had initiated policies of his own, which he
intended should break the deadlock in his favour. By a combination of
propaganda and pressure he hoped to destroy the Whig stronghold in the
City of London. If he could get control of the Whig headquarters there,
he could break up their political organization, suppress their pamphlets,
and muzzle them; if he could manage to nominate the sheriffs, and through
them control the grand juries, Shaftesbury and the other Whig leaders
would lie at his mercy.

The propaganda offensive took different forms. *The Observator*,
Heraclitus Ridens, and the writers of doggerel ballads like *Ignoramus
Justice* (quoted at the head of this chapter) could stress the alleged injustice
of a packed grand jury's throwing out a charge of treason which was
backed by so many witnesses. But more important than the evidence of the

---

[1] Barrillon, 15/25 Dec.
[2] Longford to Ormond, 24, 27 Dec., *H.M.C. Ormond MSS.*, N.S. vi. 274, 282;
Barrillon, 2/12, 5/15, 9/19, 16/26 Jan., Sidney Diary, 11 Jan., ii. 227; Newsletter, 12 Jan.,
C.S.P.D. 1682, p. 24; Van Beuningen to Prince of Orange, 17/27 Jan., 31 Jan./10 Feb.,
Correspondentie van Willem III en van Bentinck, ed. N. Japikse (The Hague, 1927–37),
II. ii. 425–6, 433–5; Reresby, pp. 248–9; *Life of James II*, ed. J. S. Clarke (1816), ii.
720–3.
[3] Christie, ii, pp. cxviii–cxxii (misdated 21 June 1681).
[4] Van Beuningen to William, 24 Feb./6 Mar., Japikse, op. cit. II. ii. 450–2; Longford
to Ormond, 21 Mar., *H.M.C. Ormond MSS.*, N.S. vi. 349–50; Jenkins to Ormond,
21 Mar., ibid. p. 352.

latter, for propaganda purposes, was the draft Association which was produced in court. As evidence in a law-court this was valueless—it was unsigned, undated, not in Shaftesbury's hand, and based on a proposal debated in the House of Commons—but it could be turned to good political use. It had spoken of using 'force of arms if need so require' to prevent the succession of James. This played into the hands of the Tory pamphleteers who repeated what the Whigs called 'the cuckow-like tune' of ''41 is come again'; the spectre of imminent civil war was raised. Just three weeks after the trial *The Two Associations* was advertised in the official *London Gazette*. This pamphlet printed side by side an Association subscribed by Parliamentarian members of the Commons in 1643, and that found in Shaftesbury's closet, followed by the names of the grand jury which had found a true bill against Danby on Fitzharris's sole evidence, and those of the three which had returned *Ignoramus* in the cases of College, Rouse, and Shaftesbury. Within another month the first of a wave of addresses from Tories abhorring the Association were arriving. Some of these were certainly contrived; those from the justices of the peace in different counties reflected only the way in which the commissions had been packed with the right kind of people, and cannot be termed representative in any way.[1] But the discomfort of the Whigs was shown by the efforts which they made to argue that it had not been conclusively shown that the Association had actually come from Shaftesbury's closet; the suggestion was that it was a forgery.

Among a variety of other attacks, some more scurrilous than others, we may notice as one of the more readable *Grimalkin: or the Rebel Cat: a novel* which appeared at this time. This purported to be a story of the attempt of the Cat to replace King Lion by his bastard son the Leopard. Under the guise of the Cat Shaftesbury was described as 'a subtle, sly, shifting creature, and whose activity in climbing is well-known, no less than its dexterity in shifting upon every fall, so as in every toss and revolution of fortune, it hath been found to light upon its feet'. There were references to Shaftesbury's using the Leopard (Monmouth) as his 'cat's foot', to his 'caterwauling', to the cat's connexion with witches ('Rebellion is as the sin of witch-craft'), to 'his *Cat*ilineship', and to the cat's nine lives, with the rather confused conclusion that 'where other creatures have not fail'd duely to go to pot, this hath been ever sure to save his bacon'. Of more permanent literary value was Dryden's poem, *The Medal*, which appeared in February 1682 and was significantly more extreme in its language than *Absalom and Achitophel* had been in the previous November. It is unnecessary to say more of such well-known verses here than to remind the reader of the story that the theme of *The Medal* had been suggested to Dryden by none other than King Charles.[2]

[1] *C.S.P.D. 1682*, p. 19; Reresby, pp. 246–7 (17 and 18 Jan.); Burnet, ii. 301–2.
[2] *Spence's Anecdotes*, ed. S. W. Singer (1820), pp. 171–2.

The aim of all this was to destroy the loyalty of the Whig rank and file to their leader by portraying him as an unprincipled intriguer who was leading them into rebellion. Simultaneously other forms of more direct pressure were being applied. Orders were repeated for the enforcement of the penal laws against Dissenters, and the Lord Mayor was ordered to suppress all conventicles. Certainly in London accused Dissenters could be freed by more *Ignoramus* verdicts; but Dissenters could be persecuted in other ways which not even a Whig grand jury could block. Customs house officers were dismissed; and by the most delicate touch of all, it was laid down at the Middlesex quarter sessions that weekly poor relief payments should be made in the parish church immediately after morning service, so that those absent without excuse should lose their allowance for the week.[1] London Dissenters were to be made to feel the consequences of supporting the Whig cause, particularly in local elections. And finally, the same lesson was to be brought home to all Londoners by means of the famous *quo warranto* proceedings against the City's charter. On the day after Shaftesbury's acquittal the King had ordered the Attorney-General to investigate whether the sheriffs' failure to suppress the disorders during and after the trial did not constitute a ground for action against them, and to 'take into consideration the abuses of the franchises of the City of London'. On 21 December 1681, the *quo warranto* writ was delivered to Sheriff Pilkington by Graham, who reported that the sheriff's oral reply was 'in such words as were not very handsome'. It was not until June 1683, five months after Shaftesbury's death, that Charles secured the legal judgement that he wanted (having in the meantime demonstrated what his devotion to the law amounted to by promoting Saunders, who had advised him in the early stages of the case, to be the Lord Chief Justice who would decide it). But the threat hung over the London Whigs from December 1681 onwards; unless they could somehow defend their case the City would lose all its privileges, not least that of electing its sheriffs.[2]

In this same month of December the Tories were able to congratulate themselves on the results of the annual elections to the Common Council of the City. By Jenkins's own confession the decisive factor here was pressure from the Aldermen, who were naturally wealthy and conservative and had never, in a majority, favoured the opposition. Where the alderman of the ward was, in Jenkins's phrase, 'honest', the Whigs were thrown out and 'honest' men put in their places. However the result was achieved, it was a matter of satisfaction to the Court and of disappointment to the Whigs that ten of the Earl's *Ignoramus* jury and also Wilmore were excluded.

[1] Van Citters and van Beuningen, 9/19 Dec., 1681, Add. MSS. 17677, FF; newsletter, 10 Dec., *C.S.P.D. 1680–1*, pp. 610–11; Longford to Ormond, 17 Dec., *H.M.C. Ormond MSS.*, N.S. vi. 264; newsletter, 10 Jan., *C.S.P.D. 1682*, p. 20; cf. ibid. pp. 24–27, 59.

[2] P.C. Reg. 2/69, p. 411; Jenkins to Ormond, 26 Nov. 1681, *H.M.C. Ormond MSS.*, N.S. vi. 238; Longford to Ormond, 3, 13, 24 Dec., ibid. vi. 244, 257–8, 273; Barrillon, 15/25 Dec.; newsletter, 29 Dec., *C.S.P.D. 1680–1*, p. 651.

Jenkins's calculation was that a Tory deficit of 14 had been converted into a majority of 20. It is possible that he was over-confident here, for when in March 1682 there was talk of an address abhorring the Association, and of a counter-petition for the summoning of a Parliament, both parties shrank from putting it to the test. The Common Council was evenly divided, and therefore useless for propaganda purposes. It remained to be seen what would happen at the elections of the sheriffs and Lord Mayor in 1682.[1]

From all this it is apparent that Shaftesbury and his followers were now on the defensive; they could only try to keep out the attacks which the King was making, and hope that sooner or later there would be a Parliament. Immediately after his release, it is true, Shaftesbury had attempted to take his revenge on those who had built up the case against him. He entered actions against Graham, the Treasury Solicitor, and others for suborning witnesses against him, claiming punitive damages of £20,000 from each. Another action of *scandalum magnatum* was begun against a mercer named Craddock, who had said that Shaftesbury was a traitor and he was ready to prove it: when Craddock appeared in court on 17 December, prepared to make his statement good, the Earl found it best to allow himself to be non-suited, but he made another attempt later. An attempt was even made to serve a writ on Justice Warcup as he sat on the bench; and other actions of *scandalum magnatum* were begun inevitably against Booth and Baines, while the Macnamaras suffered ten actions for debt in addition.[2] But apart from these demonstrations that giving evidence against him might bring more loss than profit to the witnesses, and his dinner at the Skinners' Hall, Shaftesbury remained quietly at Thanet House, meditating on his future course of action and recuperating from the effects of his imprisonment. If *Heraclitus Ridens* is to be believed, there was a report that 'the King of Poland' (as Shaftesbury had been nicknamed, from his alleged desire to make England, like Poland, an elective monarchy) was ill in December[3]; and in studying his behaviour from now onwards it has to be remembered that he was constantly ailing, stooping, and supported by a stick. It is impossible to judge how far his mental faculties became impaired by this persistent ill-health.

Away in Edinburgh the Duke of York was prepared to believe that the

---

[1] Longford, 24 Dec., loc. cit.; Jenkins to Savile, 22 Dec., S.P. 104/188; *C.S.P.D. 1680–1*, pp. 636–8; *Loyal Protestant and Truce Domestick Intelligence* (Nath. Thompson), 22 Dec.; Reresby, 5 Jan., p. 244; Longford to Ormond, 21 Jan., 4, 11 Mar., 1682, op. cit. vi. 298, 335–6, 341–2.

[2] Longford to Ormond, 29 Nov., 6 Dec., ibid. vi. 242, 250; Jenkins to Ormond, 17 Dec., ibid. vi. 268; newsletters, 8, 10, 22 Dec., *C.S.P.D. 1680–1*, pp. 607, 611–12, 639–40; newsletter, 15 Dec., *H.M.C. Various MSS.* (13), p. 174; Booth to Jenkins, 12 Dec., *C.S.P.D. 1680–1*, p. 613; van Citters and van Beuningen, 23 Dec./2 Jan., Add. MSS. 17677, FF; Macnamara to Jenkins, 2 Jan., 1682, *C.S.P.D. 1682*, pp. 1, 27; Dennis to the King, n.d., ibid. p. 22.

[3] *Heraclitus Ridens*, 13 Dec.

Duchess of Portsmouth was working hard to reconcile the King and Monmouth, and was seeing Shaftesbury for the purpose; and even that Halifax was having 'private conferences' with Shaftesbury.[1] But James was too ready to believe that these two were capable of betraying him, and there is no confirmation that his fears were justified. One person whom the Earl did see privately in January 1682 was the Dutch ambassador, Van Beuningen. Shaftesbury approached him, using the pretext that the Dutchman had been making enquiries about the iron guns in which the Earl and Prince Rupert were interested.[2] Van Beuningen consulted two ministers before agreeing, but when the meeting had taken place he reported to the Prince of Orange that Shaftesbury had not trusted him sufficiently to say anything worth passing on.[3] At other times one must imagine Shaftesbury conferring privately with Alderman Pilkington and his City allies, and with the eighteen 'Protestant lords' who still followed him and the Duke of Monmouth. One or two of this group of peers had fallen off—Huntingdon's defection was followed by that of Delamere, who kissed the King's hand early in the New Year—but the rest kept in touch with one another, and were secretly reinforced in these weeks by the arrival in London of the Earl of Argyll. Argyll had been imprisoned by James in Edinburgh on a trumped-up charge of treason and leasing-making; and had been found guilty by a jury consisting largely of his enemies (as Shaftesbury's would have done, if the grand jury had found a true bill) and sentenced to death. James and Charles later professed that they had never intended to execute him, but Argyll, whose father had been executed in 1661, wisely put no trust in the leniency of a Stuart, escaped disguised as his step-daughter's lackey, and fled to London, where he went into hiding and, it may be safely presumed, into contact with Shaftesbury.[4]

Very little emerged, however, from these private consultations. The City Whigs were no doubt preoccupied with the defence of their charter, which the Common Council put into the hands of four Aldermen (including two Whig ex-Lord Mayors, Clayton and Ward, and one Whig ex-sheriff, Cornish) and eight commoners (including Sir Thomas Player and four members of Shaftesbury's jury).[5] We catch one authentic glimpse of the Earl himself, gravely answering the collectors of money for the building of St. Paul's to the effect 'that he would do any thing for the security of the Protestant religion, but he knew not what Paul's might come to'.[6] In the new legal term the Earl appeared to answer to his bail, and finally on

[1] Clarke, op. cit. i. 723; James to Col. Legge, 12 Jan. [1682], *H.M.C. Dartmouth MSS.*, i. 44; but cf. Roger Morrice's Entering Book P, fo. 325.

[2] p. 229-30 above.

[3] Van Beuningen to William, 24 Jan./3 Feb., 31 Jan./10 Feb., Japikse, op. cit. II. ii. 430-1, 435; Barrillon, 9/19 Feb.

[4] Longford to Ormond, 21 Jan., *H.M.C. Ormond MSS.*, N.S. vi. 298; newsletter, 7 Jan., *C.S.P.D. 1682*, p. 11; cf. Barrillon, 23 Jan./2 Feb., for Montagu's offer to arrange an interview with Argyll.   [5] Luttrell, i. 158.   [6] *Heraclitus Ridens*, 24 Jan.

13 February 1682, the very last day of the term, the prosecution against him was completely dropped.[1]

There were those who suspected that Shaftesbury's restless brain was occupied with the preparation of two Whig pamphlets which appeared in this month of February. One of these, *The Third Part of No Protestant Plot*, was a massive continuation in no less than 151 pages of a first part which had appeared in October,[2] and a second in January. Obviously no pamphlet on that scale could appear without considerable financial support and much organization to enable the printing to be done in secrecy. The pamphlet set out in more detail than before the Whig thesis of a Roman Catholic plot dating back at least to 1660 and favoured by James and influential people at Court: in order to free themselves from the discovery of the Plot in 1678 the Papists had tried to foist a sham plot on the Protestants, and the prosecution of Shaftesbury was part of this. Page after page ridicules the character of the witnesses, the absurdity of the statements attributed to the Earl and his supposed plan, by a body of men of whom only one, Booth, had been found, to seize the King at Oxford. The Association was defended, the conduct of the trial criticized, and seven pages on Argyll's case added in conclusion. Some certainly found the pamphlet an effective polemic.[3] *A Letter from a Person of Quality to his Friend, about Abhorrers and Addressors, etc.*[4] purported to be an answer to a letter from a friend who was afraid of not being thought a loyal subject, or a good son of the Church, if he did not join in an address abhorring the Association. It contains the following interesting analysis of the Tory Addressers:

As for your gentlemen of quality and estate, that you find generally go these highways, and call it the support of the monarchy and the church; when you consider how many of them have been secretly converted to the Romish faith, and remain as yet church-papists; how many of them gape after honours and preferments from the court; how many the power and dominion in their own country, and the retaining the office of deputy-lieutenant, or justice of the peace, does enslave; and how many the sordid and vile education they have had under the clergy does corrupt, you will not wonder that the yeoman and plain countryman hath kept his senses, when the greatest part of the nobility and gentry have lost theirs.

Up to a point this corroborates the frequent statements by Jenkins and other Court spokesmen that only 'inconsiderable' people were Whig. A study of the composition of the Exclusion Parliaments would certainly not bear this out. But there was clearly a tendency for those with most to lose, and those most dependent on royal favour for preferment, to be less radical at a time when the King's star seemed to be in the ascendant. The

---

[1] Roger Morrice's Entering Book P, fo. 324, 24 Jan.; newsletter, 16 Feb., *C.S.P.D. 1682*, p. 82.

[2] Cf. pp. 670–1 above. Miss Brown (p. 289) is mistaken in attributing the Third Part to Oct. 1681, as the references to Argyll will show.

[3] Cf. Van Beuningen to William, 24 Feb./6 Mar., Japikse op. cit. II. ii. 452.

[4] Printed in *Somers Tracts* (1809–15), viii. 319–22.

pamphlet quoted the names of members of the Oxford Parliament who had then been Exclusionists, but had since found it prudent to sign Addresses thanking the King for sending the Parliament packing. The analysis is that of an embittered man who fears that the support which he has in the past had from the well-to-do classes is slipping away from him. Such people, he argued, would play into the hands of a Popish prince who could use his control of preferment in the church, in national, and in local government to undermine Protestantism. As for the Association, if it had really been found in Shaftesbury's closet, and if the Crown's legal advisers had thought it treasonable, why had they not included it in his indictment? There was 'no proof that he ever saw it, read it, or conferred with any about it'. It was all part of an attempt to turn a Popish plot into a Protestant one.

This led to a rapid exchange of fire by the pamphleteers beginning with *A Letter from a Friend to a Person of Quality in Answer to a Letter from a Person of Quality to his Friend* in L'Estrange's style. This was addressed to 'My Lord', and plainly assumed that the Earl had written the first *Letter*. It made some shrewd debating points about the Earl's indiscriminate attacks on his opponents, and on 'churchmen' as crypto-Papists, and tried to turn his social analysis back against him. 'For a person of quality to set up clouted shoes for the oracles of law and government, turn the nobility and gentry to school in Bedlam, and reprobate the very religion of the Church of England [is] in effect, an appeal from the Privy Council to the Bear-garden. What, with submission, could a Masaniello or a Wat Tyler have said more?'[1]

While this skirmish was taking place in London, events in Newmarket were going far to justify the social analysis in the *Letter from a Person of Quality*. Now that the prospect of having to face a Parliament had finally receded, Charles felt able to allow his brother to return from exile. When James landed at Yarmouth on 10 March he received an enthusiastic welcome, and at Newmarket there were not beds enough for all those who flocked to greet him. In the City of London a majority of the conservatively minded Court of Aldermen wanted to send a resolution of congratulation to the Duke, and the Whig minority was able to obstruct it only by withdrawing, so that there was no longer a quorum.[2]

---

[1] Cf. also the *Observator*, 1 Mar.; *The Addresses importing an Abhorrence of an Association . . . laid open and detected, in a Letter to a Friend; A Second Return to the Letter of a Noble Peer . . .* (dated Newmarket, 16 Mar.); and *A Reply to the Second Return . . . (Somers Tracts*, viii. 337–43). This last attacked Halifax as the supposed author of the *Letter from a Friend* and the *Second Return*, while denying that Shaftesbury was the author of the original *Letter from a Person of Quality . . .*; it is criticized in turn in the *Observator* of 26 April, which refers also to *A Modest Account of the Present Posture of Affairs in England with particular reference to the Earl of Shaftesbury's case*, and a *Vindication of him from two Pretended Letters of a Noble Peer*.

[2] Newsletters, 14, 16 Mar., *C.S.P.D. 1682*, pp. 124, 128; Longford to Ormond, 16 [? really 18], 21 Mar., *H.M.C. Ormond MSS.*, N.S. vi. 347, 351; *Heraclitus Ridens*, 21 Mar.; Reresby, p. 259; Barrillon, 23 Mar./2 Apr.

Something would have to be done in reply, the more so as the Whigs now knew the disappointing news that Louis had given up his blockade of Luxemburg, so there was a no longer any possibility that Charles would be compelled to call Parliament to discuss the international situation.[1] The 'restless spirits', as Jenkins called them, proceeded to draw attention to themselves by holding dinner-parties, an activity which no one could describe as illegal. On 17 March Shaftesbury, Monmouth, Essex, Howard of Escrick, Grey, and others all dined with Sheriff Pilkington, and some ten days later with the other sheriff, Shute. Further, it was customary for the Lord Mayor to keep open house for aristocratic visitors, and to prevent the Whigs from inviting themselves to dinner with him and thus appearing to receive 'caresses or countenance' from the Lord Mayor the King sent him positive instructions not to entertain them—too late, however, for the Whig peers had already dined with Sir John Moore. On 6 April the Whigs dined again with Pilkington, while the Tories this time dined with the Lord Mayor.[2]

Apart from the self-advertisement which the Whigs gained in this way, it is possible that the Lord Mayor was sounded about the problem who the next sheriffs should be. Here the Whigs had a scheme planned in support of one Hawkins, a scrivener. Alderman Sir Thomas Allen wrote to the Lord Mayor asking for leave to resign for reasons of ill-health; at the next Court of Aldermen they were ready to vote for Hawkins as a replacement, and when elected he would, by a rule of the Corporation, necessarily become one of the sheriffs for the year 1682–3. The Tory propagandists ascribed the idea to 'the Oracle', one of their sneering names for Shaftesbury. But the Oracle had not seen far enough into the future: 'the Aldermen of the Royal Club', seeing what was on foot, in their turn adopted the tactic of walking out of the Court to leave no quorum. At the adjourned meeting the King's supporters had rallied their forces and were ready to put by Hawkins and vote for an 'honest man', only to be foiled in their turn when another letter from Allen was produced, saying that he had benefited to such an extent from the country air that he hoped still to be serviceable to the City.[3]

The King and his advisers had up their sleeves a device of their own for prearranging the result of the elections to the shrievalty at midsummer, but the Lord Mayor had first to be 'prepared' 'for such a one as the King shall recommend to him'. In the meantime, on 8 April James Duke of York returned to the capital from which he had been driven eighteen months earlier before the Parliament of 1680. Now there was no Parliament

[1] Van Beuningen to William, 24 Apr./3 Apr., Japikse, op. cit. II. ii. 475.

[2] Jenkins to Ormond, 25 Mar., op. cit. vi. 353; Luttrell, i. 172, 176; Jenkins to the Lord Mayor, 31 Mar., C.S.P.D. 1682, p. 147; anon. to Jenkins, n.d., ibid. pp. 149–50; newsletter, 6 Apr., H.M.C. Various MSS. (13), p. 176.

[3] Conway to Jenkins, 3 Apr., C.S.P.D. 1682, p. 150; Longford to Arran, 9 Apr., MSS. Carte 232, fos. 99–100; Heraclitus Ridens, 11 Apr.

in the offing, and from some at least there was an enthusiastic welcome. The Lord Mayor and most of the Aldermen (including, some said, Sir Robert Clayton[1]) but not the sheriffs went to St. James's to congratulate him. In the neighbourhood of Whitehall and St. James's there were numerous bonfires, with ceremonial burnings of the Association, of the Exclusion Bill, of old wigs, and even of effigies of Shaftesbury himself, who now shared the fate formerly meted out to Popish guys. In the City, however, it was observed that there was markedly less rejoicing than there had been on the 'Feast of St. Ignoramus, or the Nineteen Consciences'; and in Aldersgate Street itself, where eight or ten bonfires had celebrated the Earl's acquittal, only one burned now.[2] Sheriff Pilkington was said to have expressed his feelings with more force than prudence, and James boldly brought an accusation of *scandalum magnatum* against him: he accused Pilkington of saying that he (the Duke) had fired the City of London in 1666 and had now come out of Scotland to put the whole kingdom in a flame, and in his turn claimed vindictive damages of £100,000 —with every prospect of success since such actions could be tried outside London.[3]

There followed a curious rivalry between the organizers of dinners for the two parties. On 20 April the annual feast of the Artillery Company was held at Merchant Taylors' Hall, with James as the principal guest. Inside the Hall there was a throng of the well-to-do to greet the Duke and pay their guineas; outside the Hall, some newsletters spoke of 'acclamations of the people', others scornfully of half a dozen paid boys crying 'God bless him' and running after the coach. More important was the total failure of the corresponding Whig dinner. This had originally been fixed for the same day, but the Whigs had thought it prudent to postpone it for twenty-four hours. Eight hundred of them had contributed a guinea each, and tickets had been printed inviting them, as 'loyal Protestant nobility, gentry, clergy, and citizens', to show their thanksgiving for the preservation of the King from Popish Plots, 'and for the preserving and improving mutual love and charity among such as are sensible thereof', to meet at St. Michael's Church, Cornhill, to hear a sermon, and to proceed to the Haberdashers' Hall or Goldsmiths' Hall for a feast, with Monmouth's coach being cheered on its way. However when all the preparations had been made the King peremptorily forbade it, on the grounds that only he as supreme head of the Church could order public fasts and thanksgivings. The Lord Mayor and Aldermen were ordered to prevent the dinner from

---

[1] So Longford; Barrillon said the opposite, loc. cit. below.

[2] Van Citters and van Beuningen, 11/21, 14/24 Apr., Add. MSS. 17677, FF; Barrillon, 10/20 Apr.; Longford to Ormond, 11 Apr., MSS. Carte 216, fo. 29; *Heraclitus Ridens*, 18 Apr.

[3] Longford to Arran, 20 May, MSS. Carte 216, fo. 47; newsletter, 22 June, *C.S.P.D. 1682*, p. 261, for the failure of the Deputy Coroner to serve the writ on Pilkington for a month.

being held, as being an unlawful assembly, and four companies of the trained bands were stationed to support the constables in seeing that the order was carried out. All this was abundant evidence of the King's confidence, and it was a sign of the weakness of their position (though not of weakness in the City) that the Whigs found it prudent to obey. To disobey the King's order would have been a peculiar way of thanking God for his preservation, but also any failure of the City authorities to carry it out might have strengthened the King's case in the *quo warranto* proceedings. So the food which had been prepared was distributed to the poor and the prisons, and the banquet abandoned. It was a heavy defeat, which attracted a good deal of ridicule from the Tories. The writer of *Heraclitus Ridens*, reporting that Shaftesbury had resolved to be there if he had to be carried in a litter, sneered that ''Twould have been a great temptation to see the little idol set up at the upper end of the table, like Puss in her majesty, with his blind votaries about him hanging upon his lips, from whence they expect nothing less than oracles concerning the present posture of affairs, in which yet, by his successless managements, one would think he had no more knowledge than they'.[1]

Within three months Shaftesbury suffered another reverse, with the failure of his actions of *scandalum magnatum*. The defendants had the benefit of the finest array of legal talent at the government's disposal, and by their advice, on 3 May, the first day of the new legal term, Craddock, the first of the defendants, moved to be allowed a jury out of London and consequently not nominated by Whig sheriffs. The affidavits which his counsel produced in support of this request very reasonably argued that Shaftesbury had considerable influence in London, that he was free of the Skinners' Company, of which Sheriff Pilkington was master, and that there was great intimacy between the Earl and the sheriffs; consequently defendant believed that he could not have an impartial trial in London. It was argued that there were precedents for a change of venue in cases of *scandalum magnatum*. On the Earl's side, after a few days' notice, it was argued that the action should be tried where the words complained of had been uttered, and that a nobleman had the privilege of bringing such an action wherever he wished. But the Lord Chief Justice found for the defendant, and offered the Earl the choice of bringing the action in any county he wished, other than London and Middlesex; to which Shaftesbury sulkily replied that since so many counties had reflected upon him in their addresses against the Association, he could expect no justice from them, and that he would withdraw his action rather than have it tried

[1] Newsletter, 20 Apr., *C.S.P.D. 1682*, pp. 173–4; Luttrell, i. 179–80; van Citters and van Beuningen, 18/28 Apr., 21 Apr./1 May, Add. MSS. 17677, FF: Barrillon, 24 Apr./4 May; Viscountess Campden to Viscount Campden, 20 Apr., *H.M.C. Rutland MSS.*, ii. 69; *Heraclitus Ridens*, 25 Apr.

elsewhere than in what he thought the proper place. Evidently he could
not risk the possibility of an unfavourable verdict. The Lord Chief Justice
took the opportunity of saying that this proved the justice of his decision
to allow the trial to be moved out of London. The other defendants all
made similar motions, that of the solicitor Graham being supported by the
Attorney-General, the Solicitor-General, Sir George Jeffreys, Sir Francis
Wythens, and Roger North; and Shaftesbury again had to withdraw,
impotently remarking that 'he doubted not but a time would come, that
he should have justice, and that this cause would be heard'.[1]

It is not surprising that some of Monmouth's cronies thought that the
time had come to investigate the possibility of a reconciliation between
him and his father, and that they must take advantage of the Duke of
York's brief absence to fetch his wife back from Scotland. The French
ambassador came to suspect that the King's illegitimate daughter, the
Countess of Sussex, was active in seeking to promote a reconciliation, and
that behind her was the egregious Ralph Montagu, never anxious to be
out of office if by any sacrifice of principle or colleague he could get in.
The King's fondness, in spite of everything, for Monmouth was well
known and might be the best passport back to favour from the wilderness
of opposition. What is certain is that one of Monmouth's companions,
Major Holmes, had conversations both with Lord Conway and with the
King, and that these turned out badly because Holmes represented that his
master was ready and willing to submit to the King and to beg pardon
upon his knees for any offence that he had given, but that he would rather
die than be reconciled or submit to the Duke of York. At this Charles was
furious—or, possibly, took care to be angrier than he really was in order
to make plain that nothing short of complete submission by his opponents
would do. At all events he talked of 'making a distinction between the
sheep and the goats', said that 'he had the Black Box still in his head', and
ordered all his servants and all who expected his favour not to visit
Monmouth or have any communication with him or his associates. Monmouth on his own side disowned having sent any message to the King,
pointed out that to expect to achieve a reconciliation in the way suggested
would have been incredibly foolish, and, possibly at Shaftesbury's instigation, took care to pick a quarrel with Halifax, whom he accused of being
responsible for the ban on communication with him, although in reality
Halifax hoped against hope for a restoration of national harmony, was no
believer in intransigence and certainly no rabid supporter of the Duke of
York. In this way Monmouth removed all suspicion that he was deserting
the Whigs; and, to make assurance doubly sure, at a dinner at the Earl of

---

[1] Warcup, 1 Mar., *C.S.P.D. 1682*, pp. 104–6; Longford to Arran, 13 May, MSS.
Carte 216, fo. 41; Luttrell, i. 183, 185–6, 190; van Citters and van Beuningen, 12/22 May,
Add. MSS. 17677, FF; Sir W. Galloway to L. Preston, 7 Aug., *H.M.C. Seventh Report*,
p. 372; newsletter, 16 May, *C.S.P.D. 1682*, p. 210; *Observator*, 17 May.

Bedford's the Whig leaders gave one another promises that they would not make separate terms for themselves with the King.[1]

Thus the ranks were closed for the elections of the London sheriffs, which were due at Midsummer, and on which the Whigs' protection from prosecution, by means of *Ignoramus* juries, depended. The government fired its first shot on 18 May, having completed its 'preparation' of the Lord Mayor by that time. It was assumed by all parties that if the election were left to a straight vote by the members of the livery companies meeting in Common Hall, Tory candidates would have no chance; but the government had at its disposal a possible device with which to frustrate the electoral procedure. There was an old custom by which the Lord Mayor could nominate one of the two sheriffs, by drinking to him at a public banquet; and if the man selected in this way did not avoid his responsibility by paying his fine (as had apparently frequently happened in by-gone days, when the procedure seems to have been used as a means of raising funds from reluctant merchants) his name was submitted to the Common Hall for formal confirmation only. The practice had been abandoned during the Commonwealth period when it was obviously not in accord with current political ideas. It was revived between 1663 and 1674, when objections were raised, as a result of which it lapsed until 1680 when Sir Robert Clayton as Lord Mayor had drunk to a nonentity named Hockenhull whom he favoured, and had been foiled. In 1681, possibly as a result of collusion with the Whig Lord Mayor, Sir Patience Ward, Sheriff Pilkington took an opportunity to declare that in his view he owed his election to the votes of the Common Hall and not to the nomination of the Lord Mayor[2]; and no one formally challenged this view of the controversy which had occurred in 1680. Now, on 18 May 1682, at 'the bridge house feast' Sir John Moore formally drank to Dudley North, the brother of the Lord Chief Justice of the Common Pleas, and obviously a Tory. At midsummer it would have to be decided whether this method of nomination was valid in general, and also whether in particular cases the Common Hall possessed the power to refuse to confirm the Lord Mayor's choice. But if the Lord Mayor held firm the Tories could hardly lose, since he and the Tory majority on the Court of Aldermen could return North to the Exchequer Court as legally elected; and the Court's verdict would hardly go against the King's wishes. If the worst came to the worst, it would take months for the Whigs to challenge it, and in the meantime there would be a Tory sheriff to counterbalance a Whig one elected by the Common Hall.[3]

---

[1] Barrillon, 15/25 May, 22 May/1 June, 25 May/4 June, 29 May/8 June, 1/11, 19/29 June; Jenkins to Viscount Preston, 15/25 May, S.P. 104/188; Longford to Arran, 16 May, MSS. Carte 232, fo. 105, and 20 May, ibid. 216, fo. 47, and 27 May, ibid. 232, fo. 109; Sir Cyril Wyche to Arran, 23 May, ibid. 216, fo. 53.

[2] Newsletter, 25 June 1681, *C.S.P.D. 1680–1*, p. 330. Cf. R. R. Sharpe, *London and the Kingdom* (1894), ii. 469–72.

[3] Luttrell, i. 186; Longford to Arran, 20 May, MSS. Carte 216, fo. 47.

Before the day came there was a brief alarm when the King caught a chill, and to over-heated imaginations a Popish succession again seemed imminent. This gave a particular zest to the celebrations of the King's birthday on 29 May, when the two parties vied with one another to show their patriotism by bonfires, and Macclesfield won the day for the opposition with his use of trumpets and kettledrums.[1] The Whigs also had the satisfaction of seeing Danby, who had now been in prison for over three years, fail in another attempt to get bail: the judges ruled, as they had done in Shaftesbury's case in 1677, that they had no power to interfere with a committal by Parliament, and the fact that in his vain speech Danby quoted Shaftesbury's earlier arguments no doubt gave the latter a certain wry pleasure.[2]

But there was little else to give the Whigs any pleasure. Even Titus Oates's brother Samuel was secretly giving information to the government about the activities of their clubs: interestingly enough, he distinguished between those who followed Shaftesbury's leadership (formerly at the Angel and now at the Nag's Head, Cheapside) and the remnants who still followed Buckingham (at the Salutation in Lombard Street); the former, Oates said, criticized the latter for their relations with the French.[3] On 15 June the Tories were able to crow over a victory in a by-election in Shaftesbury's own ward of Aldersgate, when their candidates were successful by over fifty votes. This was not such a complete reversal as it might appear, since the dead alderman, Sir Thomas Bludworth, had also been a friend of the government; but the conclusion was that support for the Crown, in the Earl's own neighbourhood, was increasing. Secretary Jenkins was also confident of the strength of the King's case in the *quo warranto* proceedings, when the City put in their plea on 13 June, and was hopeful that in the Michaelmas term the King would be able to seize the City franchises into his own hands. On 20 June, when one of the priests, Kearney, who had been accused of plotting to assassinate the King, stood trial in the Court of King's Bench, Oates and Jennison did not even appear to give evidence in support of their earlier depositions, and Kearney was acquitted.[4] There was even a curious rumour that Shaftesbury had been served with a writ *Ne exeat Regnum*, to prevent him from fleeing into exile.[5] It looked as though only the outbreak of a European war could come to the rescue of the Whigs: if Spain, the Dutch, and the Emperor were at war with Louis

---

[1] Barrillon, 29 May/8 June, 1/11 June; van Citters and van Beuningen, 2/12 June, Add. MSS. 17677, FF.

[2] *An account of the coming up of the Earl of Danby from the Tower of London to the Court of King's Bench* (1682), pp. 4–5.

[3] *C.S.P.D. 1682*, pp. 236–8.

[4] Luttrell, i. 194; van Citters and van Beuningen, 16/26 June, Add. MSS. 17677, FF; *Heraclitus Ridens*, 20 June; Jenkins to Arran, 17 June, MSS. Carte 216, fo. 79; newsletter, 22 June, *C.S.P.D. 1682*, p. 261.

[5] *The Loyal Protestant and True Domestick Intelligence*, 3 June.

XIV, Charles would find it difficult to maintain his neutrality and to refrain from calling Parliament, and the Whigs were still confident that they could carry a general election, if only there were one. But nothing occurred to halt the decline in the political fortunes of the Whigs.[1]

Nevertheless there was no thought of weakening and conceding to the government the election of one of the sheriffs; the Whigs were determined somehow to elect both, and had selected as their candidates Papillon and Dubois, the two Huguenot merchants who had served on Shaftesbury's jury.[2] The choice may have been designed to rally the Dissenters who were still being harassed by the authorities; when others might be seeking compromise, there was little incentive for Nonconformists to do so. If the Whigs had their plans ready, so too had the King: on the evening before the election the Lord Mayor and two or three aldermen were summoned to Whitehall to receive their instructions. Next day at the Guildhall Moore tried to insist that the assembled liverymen were to confirm Dudley North and to elect one other: he was shouted down, and after he had withdrawn the sheriffs proceeded to arrange a poll for two places between four candidates, Papillon and Dubois for the Whigs, and North and Box for the Tories. The matter then resolved itself into a dispute over who was to conduct the poll. The Lord Mayor, returning to the hustings, tried to adjourn the meeting, but was badly jostled out of the hall, and the sheriffs allowed the poll to continue for some time before declaring that it was their intention 'to act nothing but what was just and honest', and also adjourned the poll for a few days, when it would be continued or the result declared. All this time Shaftesbury had not been present—it is likely that his health would no longer permit him to stand a long and crowded meeting—but two of Monmouth's friends, Grey and Armstrong, were in one of the balconies encouraging their supporters. The King's response was to send the two sheriffs to the Tower: they were sent through Cheapside and by the Exchange attended by only four of the Beefeaters—a clear challenge to the Whigs to rescue them if they dared. Wisely the sheriffs' supporters left them to avail themselves of their legal liberties, and by suing for their *habeas corpus* obtain bail; but from henceforth they would be under the shadow of prosecution for encouraging a riot.[3]

The Whigs were not daunted, however, calculating that the indignation of their followers would be increased and not abated by this attempt to

[1] Barrillon, 15/25, 19/29 June; van Citters and van Beuningen, 20/30 June, Add. MSS. 17677, FF; Longford to Arran, 17 June, MSS. Carte 232, fo. 119.

[2] Newsletter, 10 June, C.S.P.D. *1682*, p. 244.

[3] Jenkins to Lord Mayor, 23 June, C.S.P.D. *1682*, p. 263; narrative of the proceedings at the Guildhall, ibid. pp. 263–4; E. Parker to Jenkins, 24 June, ibid. p. 265; Longford to Arran, 23 [really 24], 27 June, MSS. Carte 216, fos. 84, 86; Barrillon, 29 June/9 July. Cf. the later trial of Pilkington et al. in *State Trials*, ix. 187–298; and for a Tory view of the dispute and its aftermath, see Roger North, *Examen* (1740), pp. 595–617. See also R. R. Sharpe, *London and the Kingdom* (1894), ii. 479–90.

punish the two sheriffs for doing what they maintained was their duty. In this they were probably correct, but in the end it availed them nothing. The Lord Mayor was ordered by the King to insist on his right to choose a sheriff, and to conduct the election himself. On the appointed day, 5 July, the wretched Sir John Moore, who in his year of office had had a more harassing time than is given to most Lord Mayors, pleaded a sudden indisposition, and sent the Recorder to adjourn the Court; but the wily Recorder, the Whig Sir George Treby, gave the message in the form of a request and not an order. The sheriffs put the request to the meeting; it was greeted with loud shouts of no; the sheriffs concluded the poll begun on 24 June and declared the result: Papillon 2,754 votes, Dubois 2,709, Box 1,609, North 1,557. But their triumph was short-lived. After hearing legal arguments about his right to adjourn the meeting the Lord Mayor on 7 July declined to declare Papillon and Dubois elected; on 13 July an Order in Council directed that the proceedings should be begun afresh; on 14 July the Lord Mayor directed the Common Serjeant to call upon those in favour of confirming North's election to hold up their hands, and when 'above 1000 hands' were lifted up, declared North elected; and then on 15 July the Lord Mayor's officers held one poll as between Papillon, Dubois and Box at one end of the hall, while the sheriffs held another poll of their own between all four candidates at the other. Inevitably Box came top of the former poll with 1,244 votes, and Papillon and Dubois at the head of the latter, with 2,487 and 2,481 votes; but equally inevitably it was Box whom the Lord Mayor declared to be elected in conjunction with North. The sheriffs declared in favour of Papillon and Dubois, but had no means of enforcing it on the Court of Aldermen. Thus the obvious wishes of a majority of the liverymen were flouted, and instead of having to contend with one Tory sheriff, the Whigs were now disastrously confronted with two. The contest of trickery had been won decisively by the government.[1]

Shaftesbury still had two and a half months left before the new sheriffs would take up their office, and the responsibility of nominating grand juries, and his supporters did not immediately abandon all hope of reversing the Lord Mayor's decision about the election. Seventeen of them brought actions in the law-courts; and on 18 July there was the first of a series of petitions calling upon the Lord Mayor and Aldermen to recognize Papillon and Dubois as the rightful sheriffs. But the legal actions were on very doubtful ground, and in any case would take months to complete; and the Lord Mayor now maintained a firm front, having after some vacillations decided that he had gone too far to draw back from his identification with the

---

[1] Jenkins's notes, 2 July, *C.S.P.D. 1682*, pp. 280–1; Barrillon, 3/13 July; Longford to Arran, 4 July, MSS. Carte 216, fo. 94, and 8, 15 July, ibid. 232, fos. 121–2, 123–4; Luttrell, i. 203, 206; Order in Council, 13 July, and Jenkins's notes, 14 July, *C.S.P.D. 1682*, pp. 292–3; newsletter, ibid. pp. 294–5; van Citters and van Beuningen, 7/17, 14/24, 18/28 July, Add. MSS. 17677, FF.

government's cause. A more serious possibility was that Box would fine off rather than take up what would clearly be a very embarrassing office; it was said that he had scruples about the propriety of becoming sheriff after such a dubious and controversial election.[1] In that case the whole matter of the election would have to be reopened; but it would be foolish to depend on this, and more foolish to depend on a new election ending differently from the last. Shaftesbury and his fellow-peers had to consider their position very carefully.

The Earl of Salisbury's reaction was to prepare to accompany his wife to take the waters at Bourbon, and thence to Montpellier. The Marquis of Winchester, returning from such a stay in France, kissed the hands of the King and the Duke of York, and was officially forgiven for the past.[2] The Duke of Monmouth, meeting the Duke of York by chance in Hyde Park for the first time for nearly three years, stopped his coach, stood up, and made a low bow, which James returned; and another spate of rumours about a possible reconciliation followed. Some thought that, in spite of their quarrel three months earlier, Halifax favoured it, in the interests of national harmony and co-operation with the Confederates against Louis XIV; more certainly, the indulgent Duchess of Monmouth was active to help her faithless, but ever charming husband.[3] There was talk even of his restoration to the Mastership of the Horse; and rumour had it that Essex and Montagu and others were making conditions for themselves too. Most important of all, the Earl of Shaftesbury brought himself to send a message to his hated enemy, the Duke of York. The terms have not come down to us; James's biographers tell us only that the Earl sued for pardon, that the message was 'something ambiguous', and that it included an insinuation that the Duchess of Portsmouth was planning to make her son, the Duke of Richmond, Prince of Wales. James's reply, we are told, was that if the Earl would make his submission to the King and give convincing proofs of a true conversion, he would willingly take him by the hand; for if his greatest enemy became a loyal and dutiful subject to the King, he would easily overlook the injuries done to himself, and forgive them.

There the matter rested; for Shaftesbury made no approach to the King. Charles's private comment was that if Monmouth had submitted he would willingly have received him, but that so far as Shaftesbury was concerned, he would not do him that injury; for as long as the Earl remained with 'the other party', he was 'the noble patriot of his country, the Protestant Lord',

---

[1] Conway to Jenkins, 18 July, C.S.P.D. 1682, p. 304; Henry Crispe to Jenkins [18 July], ibid.; memorandum, ibid. p. 305; Longford to Arran, 21 July, MSS. Carte 216, fo. 117; newsletter, 27 July, C.S.P.D. 1682, pp. 315–16.

[2] Van Citters and van Beuningen, 4/14 Aug., 25 Aug./4 Sept., Add. MSS. 17677, FF.

[3] Sir W. Stewart to Arran, 12 Aug., MSS. Carte 216, fo. 141; Barrillon, 24 Aug./3 Sept., 28 Aug./7 Sept., 4/14 Sept.; Ormond to Primate Boyle, 25 Aug., H.M.C. Ormond MSS., N.S. vi. 430; F. Gwyn to Lord Conway, 26 Aug., Rawdon Papers, ed. Rev. E. Berwick (1819), p. 276; Longford to Arran, 29 Aug., MSS. Carte 216, fo. 155.

but if he came in, he would be 'the false and popish traitorous Lord Shaftesbury'. The fact was that there was no political need for Charles to be forgiving, and he certainly had not the inclination. Shaftesbury for his part may have made the approach in a moment of despair after the election of Tory sheriffs, but many could not credit that his desire for pardon was sincere, and saw it as a tactical move. Some regarded it as an attempt to make trouble between James and the Duchess of Portsmouth; but the most plausible interpretation was that the Whig leaders, faced with the end of the *Ignoramus* juries, were being prodigal in promises of submission, and even of money subsidies, to persuade the King to call a Parliament which would pass a general act of indemnity. When such a Parliament was in existence, and such an act had once been passed, the opposition would recover some freedom of action. But whatever Halifax thought in his ignorance of Charles's bargain with Louis XIV, Charles knew that he had no need to make concessions.[1]

It did not take the hard core of the opposition long to realize the futility of any hopes of a compromise and a Parliament, and they reverted rapidly to their earlier intransigence. Monmouth was induced to disavow the activities of his Duchess, and to demonstrate his disavowal publicly by going ahead with an earlier plan for a semi-royal 'progress' into Cheshire.[2] Whether or not this was intended as a prelude to a rebellion will be discussed in the next chapter; in the meantime it is sufficient to say that it was certainly an act of defiance, and that in the first three weeks of September reports of Monmouth's enthusiastic welcome there flowed into London, and served to encourage the Whigs in their last-ditch struggle against the installation of Tory sheriffs.

Resisting all the persuasions of the government, Box had finally decided to pay his fine rather than accept such an unpopular task. At this point the Whigs had a difficult tactical decision to make. They might either accept North as one sheriff, and join in a poll for the other with very good chances of success, while making a protest about the rights of the Common Hall for future use; or they might take the view that Papillon and Dubois had been legally elected in July and that a further poll would be unnecessary and indeed invalid. It was the latter course that they adopted, when on 5 September, in reply to a further petition to the Court of Aldermen, the Lord Mayor announced that Box had fined off and that a new Common Hall would be necessary. They would abide by their view of their rights, albeit at the cost of almost certain defeat. Whether this was the course advocated by Shaftesbury from his house in Aldersgate Street,

---

[1] Clarke, op. cit. i. 734–5; J. Macpherson, *Original Papers* (1776), i. 136; Barrillon, 14/24 Aug.; Sir C. Lyttelton to L. Hatton, 14 Aug., 5 Sept., *Hatton Correspondence*, ed. E. M. Thompson (Camden Society, 1878), ii. 17, 18–19; J. Brydall, 13 Sept., MSS. Tanner 35, fos. 91–92; Longford to Arran, 2 Sept., MSS. Carte 216, fo. 157.

[2] Clarke, op. cit. i. 737.

or whether the City Whigs took the bit between their teeth, it is impossible to say. Certainly the fight would be resumed on the same positions as in July; and, in pursuance of the custom whereby, when a member of a livery company was elected sheriff, he was chosen as master of that company, the Mercers chose Papillon in preference to North, and the Weavers chose Dubois.[1]

On 12 and 14 September the Court of Aldermen received further petitions from the Whigs, calling for a declaration that Papillon and Dubois had been rightfully elected, with Tory counter-petitions; but all the organization involved in this was futile, and elicited only that a poll would be held on the 19th and that the law would judge between the Lord Mayor, with the majority of the Aldermen, and any who disagreed. When the day came the Lord Mayor ordered the Common Serjeant to ask those who were for Mr. Rich ('an honest and stout gentleman' on confidential terms with Secretary Jenkins) to hold up their hands. 'At least 500' (according to a Tory estimate) did so; the negative was not put, and the Lord Mayor declared Rich to be sheriff. The two existing sheriffs protested, claiming that theirs was the responsibility of conducting the election and they had not yet decided whether to hold a poll or not since Papillon and Dubois had already been legally chosen; and eventually, in defiance of the Lord Mayor, did hold a poll 'for their confirmation' and declared them sheriffs with 2,082 votes. But all this earned them was a summons to attend the Council, and a requirement to give bail to answer an information of a riot in the next legal term. And finally, when the time came to swear in Rich and North on 28 September, and the Mercers' Company arranged for its members to accompany Papillon to the Guildhall and present him for office, they found two companies of militia guarding the gates. A determined body of rioters might well have swept two companies away, but the Whigs' protest was characteristically orderly to the last. Papillon laid his hand on the Bible to be sworn but removed it when required to do so by the Lord Mayor, and the ex-sheriff Shute would not accept the suggestion that he should refuse to deliver up his gaol to his successors. The Tory sheriffs were duly sworn in, with a sermon on Titus iii, 1: 'Put them in mind to be subject to principalities and powers, to obey magistrates, to be ready to every good work.'[2]

The principalities and powers also had their own way over the election of a new Lord Mayor. Here again the new man was chosen in defiance of the clearly expressed wishes of the electorate of freemen of the livery

---

[1] Luttrell, i. 217–18; van Citters and van Beuningen, 8/18 Sept., Add. MSS. 17677, FF.

[2] John Brydall, 13 Sept., MSS. Tanner 35, fo. 91; Luttrell, i. 218–24; van Citters and van Beuningen, 12/22 Sept., 22 Sept./2 Oct., Add. MSS. 17677, FF; Longford to Arran, 19, 23, 30 Sept., MSS. Carte 216, fos. 173–4, 181, 191; newsletters, 19, 21, 29 Sept., C.S.P.D. 1682, pp. 412, 417, 441; Sir John Moore to Jenkins, 26 Sept., ibid. p. 430; Israel Fielding to Arran, 30 Sept., MSS. Carte 232, fo. 125; O. Wynne to L. Preston, 28 Sept., H.M.C. Seventh Report, p. 358.

companies. The alderman 'nearest the chair', Sir William Pritchard, was a Tory; and—a more important factor than mere seniority—the Court of Aldermen had the right to choose either of the two candidates at the top of the poll, so that *two* Whigs, not one, would have to beat him for one of them to claim the mayoralty. Even if this should happen, the government had long since decided to lay claim to a right to approve, or disapprove, of the City's choice, and in the event of a candidate of whom the King disapproved, to continue the present Lord Mayor for a further twelve months. The dice were loaded against the Whigs from the start. But their organization made one last supreme effort, which enjoyed a remarkable measure of success. When the result of the poll was revealed on 4 October, the two Whig candidates, Gold and Cornish, had 2,289 and 2,258 votes respectively, while Sir William Pritchard had 2,233 and a second Tory, Henry Tulse, only 236. Whereas the Tories had been able to plump for one candidate the Whigs had had to divide their votes evenly between two, in order to keep Pritchard in third place. The Tories, consoling themselves with the thought that the Whigs made out their numbers 'by the rascality and meanness of the people' while their own party was made up of 'the substantiallest and ablest citizens', proceeded to cook the books. Scrutineers were appointed to examine the poll-books and see whether all the voters had been properly qualified. The Whigs complained that some who were not liverymen had voted, that some had voted on behalf of absentees, and that some had been made liverymen improperly (particularly in the Stationers' Company, always closely dependent on the government); and a few Tory votes were struck out on this account. But more Whig votes were disqualified as being those of Quakers, excommunicates, and Dissenters who had not taken the oaths prescribed; and the Tory votes of the Musicians were allowed although they had never voted before. On 24 October the revised figures were given: Pritchard, 2,138; Gold 2,124; Cornish, 2,093; and next day Pritchard was declared Lord Mayor over the usual vain Whig protests. As a Tory observer wrote: 'the King has mastered this great beast the City'.[1]

But Shaftesbury had not waited for this last débâcle. On the day after the new sheriffs had been sworn in, and a few days before the term of the previously selected grand juries was brought to an unusually premature end, he had left Thanet House for the last time, and had gone into hiding.

---

[1] Notes by Jenkins, 16 July, *C.S.P.D. 1682*, p. 303; Ormond to Primate Boyle, 26 Sept., *H.M.C. Ormond MSS.*, N.S. vi. 451–2; newsletters, 29 Sept., 5, 7, 14 Oct., *C.S.P.D. 1682*, pp. 441–2, 453, 461–2, 475–6; Longford to Arran, 30 Sept., 3, 7, 17, 21, 24, 28 Oct., MSS. Carte 216, fos. 191, 195, 202, 216, 218–20, 222, 228; Jenkins to Arran, 17 Oct., MSS. Carte 216, fo. 212; Crispe's report, ibid. fo. 214; Crispe to Jenkins, 21 Oct., *C.S.P.D. 1682*, pp. 486–7; Barrillon, 4/14 Oct., 30 Oct./9 Nov., 2/12 Nov.; Luttrell, i. 226–7.

CHAPTER XXX

THE LAST CAMPAIGN
(SEPTEMBER 1682-JANUARY 1683)

> Who would not be a Tory
> When the Loyal are call'd so,
> And a Whig is known,
> To be the Nation's mortal foe;
> So a Tory I will be, will be, will be,
> And a Tory I will be.

Fanatick Zeal, or a Looking Glass for the Whigs

WHILE all these events had been taking place in the City, Shaftesbury had scarcely been noticed out of doors. If he did direct his party's operations, he did so from the seclusion of Thanet House, where his ruined health compelled him to lead a physically inactive life. Nor can we glimpse much of him from his correspondence, which for obvious reasons was destroyed. Two papers do survive, reminding us that even as a semi-invalid in Aldersgate Street he still preserved his interest in his country estates and in his grandchildren. One is a letter from a servant, acknowledging his lordship's instructions about the proportion of land under arable farming, and about the management of his hundreds of sheep; sending a hamper of wine; and reporting that, God be thanked, the grandchildren were now well recovered from the measles, and would shortly return from Martin to school at Winchester. The second is a memorandum of Shaftesbury's own for his steward at Wimborne St. Giles, relating to a replanning of fields and tenancies, in which the tenants were expected to co-operate without argument. To the last he remained the country landlord, even when circumstances compelled him to remain in London.[1]

Another continuing interest, which indeed revived more strongly in 1682 than for some years past, was in his darling project of Carolina. In the northern colony on the Albemarle river it was clear by now that the proprietors' authority counted for little, and that such prosperity as the settlers enjoyed was the result of their own rough efforts and the flouting of the Navigation laws. There had indeed been a highly embarrassing rebellion against a deputy governor's injudicious use of his authority,

[1] Shaftesbury Papers, VI A, 380, 381.

which Shaftesbury had had to explain away to the Privy Council's committee of trade and plantations.[1] Further south the accounts of his servant Andrew Percival for the Earl's own St. Giles plantation were beginning to show a profit, mainly from the trade in skins with the Indians, until the colonists of Charles Town made war on the Westoe tribe. But this was the period when the settlers were ordered to move to the new site between the Ashley and Cooper rivers,[2] and in conjunction with this a renewed attempt was made by Shaftesbury and his colleagues to attract more people to the colony. A new governor, Joseph Moreton, took over some West Countrymen, and perhaps even more important was the arrival of a number of Huguenots.[3] But, beginning in the spring of 1682, the proprietors had embarked upon a more ambitious programme to promote emigration from both England and Scotland. Samuel Wilson, who had succeeded Locke as their secretary—the same who had been arrested in October 1681 and released along with his master—wrote a pamphlet *Account of the Province of Carolina in America* which is one of the more important sources for the early history of the colony, although naturally it does not err in the direction of underestimating its natural advantages. On 21 March 1682, the six remaining proprietors or their representatives, Shaftesbury, Craven, the Earl of Bath (on behalf of Carteret), Sir Peter Colleton, Mr. Thomas Archdale (who had taken over Berkeley's share), and Mr. Vivian (on behalf of the Duke of Albemarle) met at the Carolina coffee-house in Birching Lane to answer enquiries. The Whig news-sheet *The True Protestant Mercury* gave the meeting plenty of publicity, and announced that the proprietors intended to meet at the same coffee-house every Tuesday morning at eleven o'clock. At least one shipload of emigrants sailed, at the beginning of September, and next month the *True Protestant Mercury* referred to letters reporting from Carolina that the colony was flourishing, and that the Huguenots had developed the cultivation of olives, wine, silk, and cotton. Another ship was then about to sail. A number of Scotsmen of some note were interested in the prospects. Since they belonged to opposition groups, the government came to suspect that their interest in Carolina was a blind for more sinister schemes of rebellion in Britain; but in fact a number of Scotsmen, led by Lord Cardross, did emigrate to Carolina in the winter of 1682-3.[4]

Along with all this promotion of emigration went the usual stream of

---

[1] *C.S.P. Col. America and West Indies, 1677–80*, pp. 477–83, 590–1, 635; ibid. *1681–5*, pp. 14–15.

[2] See p. 249 above.

[3] It is possible that the glimpses we get of agents of Shaftesbury's at Paris are attributable to Carolina business rather than to political activities. See for instance Murray's visit in August 1682, when he seems to have talked to Huguenots (who were being harassed in these years immediately previous to the revocation of the Edict of Nantes) and not to Louis XIV's ministers: Preston to Jenkins, 17/27 Aug., *C.S.P.D. 1682*, p. 346; Everard to Jenkins, 12 Sept., ibid. p. 390.

[4] *True Protestant Mercury*, 18–22 Mar. 1682, 2–6 Sept., 14–18 Oct., 21 Oct.

instructions to Carolina. A letter to the agent on his private plantation, Andrew Percival, discussed the possibilities of the Indian trade, in which the Earl was interested in partnership with Colleton and Dr. Henry Woodward; Percival was to send accounts, and to bear in mind that since the trading goods sent from England had 'run the risks of the sea' it would be reasonable to expect forty per cent profit on their value. Evidently the goods shipped back from Carolina were mainly furs and skins obtained by barter from the Indians, but Shaftesbury refers also to two shiploads of cedar-wood which had arrived, and which at 3s. per foot would yield £438; and he speaks with particular approval of the whale fishing which Percival had been developing. Other instructions, this time from the Earl and his co-proprietors (including the aged Earl of Craven, whom the King commissioned on 21 April to command all troops in London and suppress any Whig tumults), went to the governor and Council in Charles Town. They made no departure from the principles laid down earlier for the plantation. Two further sets of the *Fundamental Constitutions* were sent; and an attempt was made to insist on favourable treatment of the Indians. No one was to take up land within two miles of an Indian settlement; and those who did take up land near settlements were to help the Indians to fence their corn so that the pigs and cattle of the English did not damage it—'For we conceive that the Indians will be of great use to the English'. But the fact that these not altogether consistent instructions were necessary suggests that the settlers, separated by thousands of miles of ocean from the proprietors, did not feel obliged to adhere too strictly to the proprietors' policies.[1]

From all this it is plain that Shaftesbury was not idle; he had plenty of legitimate business and family interests to occupy him. It is possible that, had he been willing to restrict himself to them and to give up all political activities, perhaps retiring tactfully to his country estates, he might have been left alone by the government in these, the last months of his life. But, in spite of his petition to the King in September 1681, and his more recent offer of submission to James, he was not the kind of person who could draw back from politics after a lifetime of involvement in them: it was partly because he realized this that Charles had made no pretence of accepting his offers. We must now discuss, therefore, whether Shaftesbury devoted his last months to the planning of a rebellion, as the 'Rye House Plotters' later suggested.

Here it will be necessary to make a distinction between considering the possibility of a rebellion and making definite plans to organize it. In what follows it will be argued that it is very likely that the possibility of a rising

[1] Shaftesbury Papers, VII, 505; *C.S.P. Col. America and West Indies, 1681–5*, pp. 229–30, 231, 234, 242. For this period in the life of the colony, cf. E. McCrady, *History of South Carolina under the Proprietary Government, 1670–1719* (New York, 1897), pp. 180–96.

was examined, but that there is no good evidence that in Shaftesbury's lifetime matters went beyond that stage.

To consider a rebellion was both natural and logical. There was no reason why Shaftesbury should feel any compunction about it, believing as he did that a Popish succession was something to be prevented if at all possible. He had never been a believer in the doctrine of passive obedience which was being enunciated from every Anglican pulpit. After all, he had already fought against his king in one civil war, and had never admitted that he was wrong to do so. In the debates on Danby's Test in 1675 he had openly maintained that in certain circumstances it could be right for a subject to resist his monarch. Given that conviction, it was arguable that by 1682 such circumstances existed. In the last three Parliaments the desire of a majority (indeed, a considerable majority) of the elected representatives of the people to pass an Exclusion Bill had been frustrated. It was apparent that no further Parliament was likely to be allowed to meet in the near future, and it was not difficult for Shaftesbury to guess that the reason why Charles was able to dispense with a Parliament was money provided by the Catholic, authoritarian Louis XIV. It was plain that Charles was not on good terms with his nephew William of Orange, and natural to conclude from a review of the political scene, international and domestic, that Charles and Louis were secretly co-operating with one another, and that the results of this co-operation were not likely to favour either political liberty or religious toleration. Since Parliament was not allowed to meet, there were no constitutional means of stating the case or of making any protest. By blatant trickery Charles had managed to insinuate his own nominees as Lord Mayor and sheriffs of London, and to make his control permanent he was adopting the *quo warranto* procedure to have the City's age-old charter declared invalid. The same procedure could be adopted in the provincial boroughs; in any case, the King had already interfered in some places, for instance to impose his own Recorder upon Northampton,[1] and the deputy-lieutenancies and commissions of justices of the peace were filled by his appointment. Dissenters were also being increasingly persecuted in England as they were in France: on 21 October Richard Baxter, who had been left unmolested for many years, was arrested at his house in Bloomsbury for contravening the provisions of the Five Mile Act.[2] And, most sinister of all, the Duke of York was back at Court, in the strong position normally appropriate to the heir to the throne who will shortly have complete control of all patronage.

Such a train of thought led logically to a consideration of the use of force to redress the position, since no constitutional means were available. Moreover, it could also be argued that the longer action was postponed, the more the political situation was likely to deteriorate. With every day

---

[1] *C.S.P.D. 1682*, pp. 207, 244.   [2] Luttrell, i. 230.

the King's position grew stronger, as it became clearer that no Parliament would be permitted to meet and exercise any pressure upon him.

So resistance must be envisaged; and yet a sober appraisal of the situation immediately showed at what a disadvantage the Whigs would stand, in comparison with the Parliamentarians in 1642. Scotland and Ireland, then in rebellion, were in 1682 firmly under the King's control. The Navy, organized by James's protégé Samuel Pepys and officered by nominees of James and Pepys, could certainly not be relied upon to support any rising. The King had also taken every care to appoint loyal officers to command the key garrisons and magazines, in the Tower, at Hull, Portsmouth, Plymouth, and elsewhere, and, taking into consideration that the Lord Lieutenants and deputy lieutenants who controlled the county armouries were also Tories, there would be no easy means of securing supplies of weapons and ammunition. Though it was true that many country-houses had their stock of fowling pieces and other weapons used in the Civil War, a trained military commander like Monmouth might well shrink from the improvisation which would be necessary to collect them, to supply them with powder, and to train men to use them in battle. In 1685 Monmouth did make the attempt, and the inadequacy of the weapons at the disposal of his troops played a substantial part in his failure; but without the two ships which brought him over from Amsterdam, and which carried a cargo of weapons and ammunition, his rebellion would never have got under way at all. In short, a rebellion was not something which could be suddenly conjured up by a few country gentry at a signal from their leader. And finally, unlike Pym, Shaftesbury was not backed by a Parliament in being at Westminster, capable of giving orders and in control of the central machinery of government and taxation. All in all, even if his cause would be a popular one, Shaftesbury's means for waging a civil war would be incomparably weaker than Pym's. Unless, that is, he were to throw confusion into the ranks of the Tories by first staging an armed *coup* to seize the persons of the King and his brother.

It can be taken as certain that all these elements of the situation were present to the minds of the Whig leaders in 1682. But no strictly contemporary evidence of their discussions survives—it was not the kind of discussion that one carries on by correspondence—and all that is known of it comes from the confessions of those taken prisoner after the so-called 'Rye House Plot' in 1683 and after the Monmouth rebellion in 1685.[1]

---

[1] I do not differentiate Ferguson's manuscript 'Concerning the Rye House Business' (printed by J. Ferguson, *Ferguson the Plotter* (1887), pp. 409–37) from other confessions in this respect, although the precise circumstances in which it was written can only be conjectured. It was evidently written 'on this side' (i.e. in Holland) between the failure of Monmouth's rebellion and William's expedition in 1688. Ferguson was not a prisoner when he wrote it, but the fact that it was not printed suggests that it was written privately to exculpate himself. His attempt to put all the blame on Shaftesbury cannot easily be reconciled with the contemporary evidence of his admiration for the Earl.

But these confessions were not the truth, the whole truth, and nothing but the truth; they were not acts of complete contrition, nor were they objectively intended for the enlightenment of posterity. They were intended to lighten the load on the writer, and on his living friends, by putting as much of the responsibility as possible on the dead, and especially on Shaftesbury, of whom it was known that Charles and James were prepared to believe anything. The kind of story which the government needed for its political purposes was well known, and could easily be provided, with the aid of the type of hearsay statements which Oates and his friends had used. In many cases the writers had the advantage of knowing what had previously been deposed by others, so that repetition of a statement does not necessarily afford proof of its truth, and the inconsistencies are often more significant than the similarities.

Such a confession was that of Ford, Lord Grey of Wark, to which reference has previously been made. It was signed by Grey when he was a prisoner on 16 October 1685, helped him to avoid the consequences of his part in Monmouth's rebellion, and was printed long afterwards, in 1754, as *The Secret History of the Rye House Plot*. Apart from the kind of 'evidence' supplied by the informers at Shaftesbury's trial, it is the only source which suggests that Shaftesbury had contemplated a rising before 1682. Grey alleged that Shaftesbury had considered one first at the time of the King's second illness (misdating this as February 1681, instead of May 1680), again after the defeat of the Exclusion Bill in November 1680, and again shortly before and during the Oxford Parliament of 1681. All these stories were plausible; all obligingly confirmed what the government already suspected and what its propagandists had been saying; all consisted entirely of reported conversations with people who were dead when Grey wrote; all were vague about dates and totally lacking in any objective evidence in support of them.[1]

Grey's story then went on to describe how in the summer of 1682 there were secret meetings between Shaftesbury and the Earl of Argyll, who was hiding in London after his escape from execution in Scotland.[2] Grey had been told (he claimed) that Argyll had asked for £30,000 to enable him to make preparations for a rebellion in Scotland, but that these proposals had ended in nothing. Such statements had earlier been made by some of those involved in the Rye House Plot in 1683, and could have been copied from them. Grey's statement by itself is of little value; but there is another source which describes messages and two meetings between the two Earls about a joint rising in England and Scotland. This is the notorious Robert Ferguson, 'the Plotter', of whose intimacy with Shaftesbury in these last months of his life something will be said below. According to Ferguson,

[1] Cf. pp. 576, 605, 623–4, 637 above.
[2] He stayed part of the time with the informer Edward Everard: *C.S.P.D. 1682*, p. 327.

the proposals broke down on the earls' suspicion of one another—Shaftes-bury had never had anything in common with the stiff Presbyterian, Argyll—and on the impossibility of getting the English Whigs to subscribe. There is nothing improbable in all this, nor in Ferguson's conclusion about the episode: 'So that all the issue and effect of this transaction between those two Earls served only to discover, what little preparation, notwithstanding all the fears and dangers men pretended to be in . . . had been made for relieving themselves by forcible means, and what small probability there was of bringing the grandees of the party into union of councils and endeavours for vindicating the rights and liberties of their countries.'[1]

So far clearly there had been nothing but talk. Both Grey and Ferguson, however, agreed that the episode of the Duke of Monmouth's visit to Cheshire in September 1682 marked a stage further on the road; but whereas Ferguson declared that Monmouth had promised Shaftesbury to 'draw his sword' immediately should he get a favourable reception in Cheshire, and that Monmouth did not keep his promise because he had no money or arms or correspondence with other parts of the kingdom, Grey's story was that the progress was only exploratory. It is difficult to believe that Ferguson was right, and that there was already a clearly informed intention to begin a rising in Cheshire. An insurrection without preparation, without arms or money, would have no better fortune than that of Sir George Booth in the same area in 1659—a revolt which Shaftesbury could well remember. Grey's account was that while Monmouth went to Cheshire to consult with Lord Macclesfield, Sir George Booth himself (now Lord Delamere), and their sons, Shaftesbury and Russell would confer with the leading men of the party in the City, about a possible rising; Russell should also sound Sir William Courtenay, Sir Francis Rowles, Sir Walter Young, Sir Francis Drake, Mr. Freke, and other West Country gentry. Grey added that he himself was asked to go to Essex, but refused; and Monmouth obtained a promise of 1,500 men from the Taunton neighbour-hood from John Trenchard.[2]

Like Monmouth's previous progresses to the West Country, Chichester, Northampton, and elsewhere, his journey to Cheshire was very successful in eliciting enthusiastic demonstrations of support. The statements of Secretary Jenkins's correspondents that he was cheered only by 'the rabble' and by Dissenters may be heavily discounted.[3] On his return southwards on 20 September, he was arrested at Stafford for causing a riot at Chester. He sent his companion Sir Thomas Armstrong on post-haste to London, and by this means there was a writ of *habeas corpus* ready for his release

---

[1] Grey, *Secret History*, pp. 14–15; Ferguson's MS. printed in Ferguson, op. cit. pp. 414–16.

[2] Ferguson, op. cit. pp. 417–18; Grey, op. cit. pp. 16–18.

[3] *C.S.P.D. 1682*, esp. pp. 383, 387–90.

when the Duke arrived in London on the 23rd. He was visited by all his Whig friends, including Shaftesbury, Russell, and Grey; was stiffened by their encouragement to refuse to give security against a breach of the peace; was re-arrested, again applied for his *habeas corpus* and, this time giving his bail, was again released.[1]

So much is clear. But in his narrative of these events Grey added that when Armstrong rode ahead in such haste to London, he carried with him a private message for Shaftesbury, Russell, and Grey, which was delivered to the Earl as he sat in his garden in the September sunshine. The message said that Monmouth had been warmly welcomed by the gentry of Cheshire, that when he had been arrested they had offered 'to draw their swords and rise instantly', but that he had declined to do so without the Earl's approval and had sent ahead to know whether he should come to London or escape to Cheshire 'and rise there'. 'My Lord Shaftesbury replied, the Duke of Monmouth was an unfortunate man, for God had thrice put it into his power to save England, and make himself the greatest man in Europe; but he had neglected the use of all those opportunities; one was in Scotland [in June 1679], when he was general, the other in the West [in August 1680], and now in Cheshire.' Undoubtedly, if an unplanned rising could have any chance of success, this moment when Monmouth's popularity had been demonstrated, and when the City was indignant about its sheriffs, was the best chance of success; but it would have been a hare-brained scheme even then.

That evening (Grey related) he, Shaftesbury, and Russell met at the latter's house. Shaftesbury is then said to have related the results of his consultations in the afternoon with 'many of the most considerable men' in the City, who were all of the opinion that Monmouth should return into Cheshire and lead a rising, in which they would join if Russell would lead them; and the Earl supported this view, claiming that he had 'several thousands' at his command in Wapping, ready to support Russell. But Russell said that his friends were divided in their opinions, and that the peers had not yet heard from their friends in the West, had no arms, ammunition, or money collected, and had no Declaration prepared to appeal to the public; and Russell complained that Shaftesbury had talked as though his men favoured a Commonwealth, while he himself 'thought the English government the best in the world'. Shaftesbury 'argued for some time with great heat with my Lord Russell', but in the end Grey had to leave, to go and meet Monmouth and tell him that his friends could not agree. Shaftesbury followed Grey out, and urged him to lie to Monmouth, and say that all his friends advised him to go back into Cheshire; but Grey refused, to Shaftesbury's anger.

Grey describes one further meeting with the Earl, Monmouth, and

---

[1] Longford to Arran, 23, 26 Sept., MSS. Carte 216, fos. 181, 189–90; Luttrell, i. 222; Sjt. Ramsey's memoranda, *C.S.P.D. 1682*, p. 429.

Russell at Thanet House, at which the Earl confessed that he had wanted to cheat Monmouth, and urged that now that Cheshire was out of the question they must depend solely upon a rising in London. When Russell asked why there was such a hurry when they had not completed their inquiries in the West, and urged Shaftesbury to have a little patience, and not let his fears carry him away, so as to ruin both himself and his friends, Shaftesbury retorted, 'in the greatest passion I ever saw', that patience would be their destruction because the preparations that he had made would inevitably be discovered; so he would 'stand upon his own legs' and act by himself. The conversation ended with Monmouth rallying Shaftesbury on his 'invisible army', and the Earl departing in anger, having first said that he would see the ten thousand men at Whitehall gates before he was many days older. And that, said Grey, was the last occasion on which he saw the Earl. He might have added that in the next two months he had preoccupations of his own, culminating in his appearance in court to answer the famous charge of having abducted his sister-in-law.[1]

Before he was many days older the new Tory sheriffs had been sworn in, and Shaftesbury left his house in Aldersgate and went into hiding. His absence was noticed almost immediately, but there were conflicting reports about where he had gone. Some said that he had fled to Holland, and that he had been seen in Rotterdam and Amsterdam; others said that he had gone to Hamburg; others that he had only retired into the country. But those who thought that he was still in London, 'the best lurking place in Europe', were right. He seems to have hidden first at the house of a merchant named Watson, the corner house in Wood Street, where a lodging was obtained for him in the name of 'Mr. Tucker'; later he spent a week at the house of Robert Ferguson, and finally settled with a sea-captain named Tracy in Goodman's Fields at Wapping.[2]

Concealment by itself did not mean that Shaftesbury was engaged in conspiracy. Others besides himself had found it advisable to keep out of harm's way for a time—Bristol in 1663, Buckingham in 1667, Danby in 1679, Argyll only recently. In each case they had been unmolested. And the King, whose great pleasure at the news was obvious, did not issue a warrant for his arrest. Some courtiers, indeed, saw in Shaftesbury's disappearance a trick: he might have 'stepped aside' with the intention of reappearing 'to the confusion of his enemies and the joy and mirth of his friends'.[3] What in fact was Shaftesbury doing in the seven or eight weeks

---

[1] Grey, op. cit. pp. 18–27.

[2] Barrillon, 4/14 Oct.; Longford to Arran, 7, 10, 21 Oct., MSS. Carte 216, fos. 202, 204, 218; Conway to Jenkins, 7, 11, 14, 19 Oct., *C.S.P.D. 1682*, pp. 455, 466, 471, 483; Luttrell, i. 228; *The Loyal Protestant and True Domestick Intelligence*, 7, 10, 17 Oct.; Robert Blayney's examination in Sprat, *Copies of the Informations and Original Papers relating to the Proof of the Horrid Conspiracy against the Late King . . .* (1685), p. 24; *C.S.P.D. 1682*, pp. 79, 91, 111; Ferguson, op. cit. p. 422.

[3] Conway to Jenkins, 7 Oct., as in previous note; Ormond to Primate Boyle, 10 Oct., *H.M.C. Ormond MSS.*, N.S. vi. 463.

before he decided to take refuge in Holland? On this point our sources are completely inconsistent with one another.

In disentangling them it is best to begin with the stories told by William, Lord Howard of Escrick. That nobleman's long career of conspiracy, dating back to the Commonwealth, reached its climax six months after Shaftesbury's death in the summer of 1683 when he found himself incriminated in the confessions of those who were accused of plotting to kill Charles at the Rye House in March of that year. Howard had been in trouble many times before, and in the Tower more than once; but on this occasion his neck was really in danger. His first reaction was to hide in a chimney. There, after four hours, he was discovered, and taken before the Council. Told that his life was concerned, he said that 'if any expedient can be chalked out, that he may do His Majesty service and take care of his own preservation, he will be glad of it'. The result was the most far-reaching of the confessions with which he had always escaped trouble by the skin of his teeth; it was responsible for the deaths of Russell, Algernon Sidney, and, less directly, that of Essex. Here we shall be concerned only with his remarks about Shaftesbury.[1]

Howard's story begins after the Earl had gone into hiding at the beginning of October 1682. There is no suggestion from any quarter that Howard had been involved in any discussions about a rising in September. He was not trusted: his propensities for confession were well known, his relations with the Duchess of Portsmouth had been shown to be somewhat equivocal in the Fitzharris case, and his stay in the Tower at the same time as Shaftesbury had not fully regained the Earl's confidence. However on 30 October, he said, he found himself summoned to the Earl's hiding-place in Wood Street by one of his dependants, Colonel Walcot. There the Earl described how not only himself, but Howard and 'all honest men in England' could not feel safe after the sheriffs had been obtruded upon the City; therefore he had made preparations for 'ten thousand brisk boys', aided by 1,000 or 1,200 horse who were to be 'drawn insensibly into town from several adjacent parts', to make themselves masters of the City and attack the guards at Whitehall. The only hindrance was the 'backwardness' of Monmouth and Russell, who had failed in their promise to co-operate in a simultaneous rising in the West and in Cheshire; but he proposed that Howard and Grey should raise Essex, while Herbert and Col. Rumsey assisted him in the City, 'together with very many eminent citizens who desired to have their names spared till the time of action'.

Howard went on to describe how he acted as an intermediary to bring

---

[1] Various versions of the story exist, incorporating embellishments which were not always consistent. See the minutes of the proceedings before the Council, 9, 10 July 1683, *C.S.P.D. July–Sept. 1683*, pp. 80, 90; Sprat, op. cit. pp. 67–73 (Howard's information, with Supplement); *State Trials*, ix. 602–11 (evidence at Russell trial, 1683) and 1065–73 (evidence at Hampden trial, 1684). Sprat was said to have admitted that James altered various passages before they were printed in his book: *State Trials*, ix. 364–5.

Shaftesbury and Monmouth together again. Next day at Moor Park Monmouth denied that he and Russell had made any such agreement with the Earl, and said that the Earl 'had withdrawn himself from them and acted upon separate councils of his own grounded . . . upon the hasty conceptions of some hot-headed men, who might lead him into some untimely undertaking, which in all probability would prove fatal to himself and all the party'. To prevent this, Monmouth asked Howard to arrange a meeting, and next day, Thursday, 5 October,[1] Howard urged Shaftesbury to agree. But Shaftesbury (so Howard said) retorted that Monmouth's recent dilatoriness must proceed from a secret agreement between him and his father, that England's liberties could only be secured under a Commonwealth, and that for these reasons he was determined no longer to wait for the Duke, but to rely on 'an honest brisk party in the City'. Two days later Shaftesbury did agree to a meeting with Monmouth and Russell on Sunday the 8th, when the shops would be shut and Shaftesbury could go back to his home through quiet streets. But on Sunday morning Shaftesbury excused himself, on the ground that he was not safe, and must remove to another lodging. From other more strictly contemporary sources we hear of a 'consult' of Whig leaders taking place elsewhere on that week-end, at Lord Essex's house at Cassiobury in Hertfordshire. Since Essex later admitted that he and Lord Salisbury had met Shaftesbury on some occasion in these weeks, it is possible that Shaftesbury attended this 'consult' instead of the meeting planned by Howard, and that in this way he returned for the last time secretly to the house at Cassiobury where he had once lived with his father and stepmother, over fifty years earlier before the Civil War broke upon England. But since the 'consult' figures in none of the confessions, it remains wrapped in impenetrable secrecy.[2]

Howard's story was that he never saw Shaftesbury again after 7 October, but that through others he heard of plans for a rising by Shaftesbury, Monmouth, and Russell. We are not told how they were supposed to have patched up their quarrel, but that the rising was fixed first for the time of the King's return from Newmarket (i.e. 21 October); that at Monmouth's instigation it was postponed for a fortnight; that then 2 November was made 'a day peremptory'; and finally that it was put off until that well-known Protestant occasion, the anniversary of Queen Elizabeth's accession, 17 November. In the meantime, he said, he heard 'dark hints' from various people 'of striking at the head, of shortening the work by removing two persons', from which he concluded that there was some design on the lives of the King and the Duke of York; 'but when and where, and by whom, and in what manner and place this was to be acted, I never saw'. So at

---

[1] Howard's information (Sprat, p. 68) says 'Thursday the 3rd or 4th of October'. From internal evidence it is clear that this should read Thursday, 5 Oct.

[2] Israel Fielding to Arran, 10, 14 Oct., MSS. Carte 216, fos. 206, 208; Burnet, ii. 351; cf. also minutes of Walcot's confession, 8 July 1683, *C.S.P.D. July–Sept. 1683*, p. 72.

least he said in his first information: later he 'remembered' rather more, and asserted his suspicions, or rather more than suspicions, that Monmouth and Grey expected the attempt on the royal brothers to be made on the day of their return from Newmarket.

At this point we are brought up against the alleged activities of a group of non-aristocratic members of Shaftesbury's entourage. The first of these was Colonel John Rumsey. Rumsey was the nephew of Sir Thomas Morgan a former Cromwellian Major-General who had come to terms with the Restoration. Before 1660 Rumsey had only been a cornet in the army of the Commonwealth, but when the remains of the Ironsides were shipped off to Portugal to fight in the war of independence against Spain he rose to the rank of lieutenant-colonel. On his return from Lisbon he was recommended to Clarendon and obtained a post in the customs at Bristol which he later sold for £600. At what point he became acquainted with Shaftesbury we cannot tell, but by 1670 he was taking part in the latter's mining enterprises. Other Whigs later claimed that they had never liked him, but reading between the lines it is possible to detect that this was because he was entirely in Shaftesbury's service. Yet this does not mean that he was a penniless desperado, hired as a bodyguard for the Earl: on the contrary, we find him lending the Earl £800.[1]

Colonel Thomas Walcot was an older man, of some fifty-seven years of age, who during the civil war had been lieutenant to Edmund Ludlow, the uncompromising Republican who even after twenty years of exile in Switzerland remained a bogeyman of the English Royalists. Like others in the Cromwellian armies, he was able to buy lands in Ireland on easy terms and after the Restoration he settled in his house at Limerick, where he was in trouble with the authorities in 1672. Precisely when or in what circumstances he came into Shaftesbury's orbit is not known, but from what follows it is plain that in the last months of the Earl's life he was one of the closest to him. His dying confession to the chaplain of Newgate in July 1683 had an unmistakable Puritan stamp about it; he denied that he had done anything with any prospect of 'earthly advantage' to himself, and said that he had stood only for liberty of conscience and to preserve 'the people's liberties now in hazard'. There is no reason to doubt this description of his motives, and he is best regarded as a Puritan who had never been reconciled to the Restoration.[2]

Thirdly there was Robert Ferguson, 'Ferguson the Plotter', to whom some reference has been made. Tall and stooping, with a 'lean and hungry look' and a pronounced Scottish accent, he was a Nonconformist preacher— his letters are steeped in Puritan phraseology—but his real importance

---

[1] T. Maynard to [Clarendon], 29 Jan./8 Feb. 1667, MSS. Clar. 85, fos. 44–45; accounts at Wimborne St. Giles; Burnet, ii. 357.

[2] Certificate by Samuel Smith, 18 July 1683, C.S.P.D. July-Sept. 1683, pp. 154–5; Orrery to Danby, 12 Sept. 1672, Egerton MSS., 3327 (unfoliated).

was as a pamphleteer. He is the probable author of the Black Box pamphlet of 1679, the *Appeal from the Country to the City* (1680) and *No Protestant Plot* (1681), and was in the autumn of 1682 engaged in preparing a continuation of Marvell's *Growth of Popery*. But in spite of the extreme language he used, and the vehemence of his arguments, his career was lacking in consistency. There was always something restless and unstable about him. Devoted to Shaftesbury at the end of 1682 but dissatisfied with the Earl's bequest to him, he attached himself to Monmouth and denigrated the Earl. Coming over with William of Orange's expedition in 1688 but even more dissatisfied with his reward after the Revolution, he became a non-juror and Jacobite, and ended his days repenting the activities of his earlier career. It is difficult to imagine him being content under any government. His fellow-Scotsman Burnet strongly disliked him as 'a hot and bold man, whose spirit was naturally turned to plotting' and who was always 'setting on some to mischief'. Burnet also claimed to have private knowledge of Ferguson's dishonesty: Ferguson was deeply attached to his wife and large family, and at some points in his hazardous course he had difficulty in providing for them by honest means. As a Plotter, in spite of his nickname, he was uniformly unsuccessful. His genius lay rather in survival when others were caught and perished on the scaffold; perhaps the most remarkable fact about this remarkable man was that he died in his bed in a ripe old age. His value to Shaftesbury resided in the facility of his pen.[1]

Others in the circle, but not so close to the Earl, were Goodenough, another plotter who had joined in Du Moulin's intrigues in 1673, and who as under-sheriff to Pilkington and Shute had helped to arrange the *Ignoramus* juries—his knowledge of the City was valuable[2]—and Robert West, a barrister of the Middle Temple, 'a witty and active man, full of talk, and believed to be a determined atheist'.[3] The group sometimes met in West's chambers and at other times at the home of Thomas Shepherd, a wine-merchant in Abchurch lane who was probably related to Shaftesbury's gentleman servant, Anthony Shepherd.

At the end of June 1683 (five months after Shaftesbury's death) Rumsey, Walcot, and West were all arrested after a London oilman, Josiah Keeling, had handed in an information about an alleged plan to kill the King and the Duke of York on their return from Newmarket in the previous March. The story was that a one-eyed man named Rumbold and a few companions had bought a Rye House near the Newmarket to London road, from which they intended to waylay Charles and James; but they had been foiled

---

[1] Ferguson, op. cit. *passim*, and esp. pp. 385–6 for a list of the pamphlets to which he laid claim; Burnet, ii. 358.

[2] Haley, *William of Orange and the English Opposition, 1672–4* (1953), pp. 59, 195, 198–200; Jenkins to Conway, 8 Oct. 1681, *C.S.P.D. 1680–1*, p. 500; Burnet, loc. cit.

[3] Burnet, ii. 357.

because an accidental fire in the cramped quarters at Newmarket led the royal brothers to leave earlier than had been expected. As usual the story was based on reported conversations rather than on more concrete evidence. Since the Rye House Plot occurred or failed to occur two months after Shaftesbury's death, it is unnecessary here to examine the problem of its authenticity. What are of interest are the statements which Rumsey, Walcot, West, and Howard of Escrick made, when arrested, about events in the previous autumn and during Shaftesbury's lifetime. For all four realized that, as associates of Shaftesbury, they were all marked men; that something sinister had been talked of in October and November 1682, but that the King would need an additional witness in the Rye House prosecutions, and that their only chance of escape was to be that witness. Before Walcot was arrested, indeed, he wrote to Secretary Jenkins offering to surrender voluntarily, to provide extra details of the conspiracy and if necessary to go to Holland to investigate the activities of the exiles there.[1] Faced with an embarrassment of choice, the King decided to use West and Howard of Escrick (after his ordeal in the chimney) to convict the more dangerous Rumsey and Walcot, and Russell, Essex, and Algernon Sidney[2] amongst the Whig leaders; but confessions were also accepted from Romsey and Walcot.

In so far as these related not to the Rye House Plot proper, but to the previous October and November, they referred both to talk about a revolt and to talk about intercepting the King on his return from Newmarket; but it is noticeable that they were in a position to say considerably more about the former. Rumsey, for instance, said that the dead Shaftesbury had told him that in the event of an insurrection his post was to be at Bristol; but of an assassination plot at the time, all he knew was what he had been told by West. All that West claimed to know about both was what he had heard from Ferguson, one Francis Shute, and Walcot: he produced a little more each time that he was examined, sometimes contradicting what he had said earlier. Walcot admitted knowledge of proposals for an insurrection, but denied knowing anything about a plot to kill the King. Howard's stories about the latter were apt to vary: at one time, as we have seen, he said he had 'dark hints' from Walcot, Goodenough, West, and Ferguson; at another he quoted Monmouth as saying that he had seriously considered 'falling upon the King at Newmarket with 40 or 50 men' and described the allegedly suspicious behaviour of Monmouth, Grey, and Sir Thomas Armstrong on the day of the King's return to London; at Russell's trial he (Howard) swore that he passed on Walcot's hints to Monmouth, who promptly put a stop to any attempt on the King's

---

[1] Sprat, op. cit. p. 86.

[2] The evidence against Essex and Sidney related entirely to events after Shaftesbury's flight, and consequently will not be referred to here. Sidney and Shaftesbury were at no time on good terms.

person. All this cancels itself out as worthless. We are left with the story of Ferguson, who did not tell it as a prisoner under duress, but nevertheless in an evident attempt to exculpate himself to some unknown person in the reign of James II. Ferguson's view was that Shaftesbury did have the idea of 'an enterprise to be made upon the person of the King and his brother' and that it sprang from the Earl's dissatisfaction at Monmouth's failure to rise in Cheshire; such an enterprise would require neither the help of Monmouth, nor the large sum of money and magazine of arms which a rising would need. Ferguson claimed that, having heard of such a tale from someone he chose not to name, he confronted Shaftesbury ('to whom I could at all time make my own access') with it, and the Earl told him 'that he was resolved to try, whether it was not possible to save and deliver the nation by a few, seeing as there was no hope of effecting it by united councils and a combined strength'. But, if Ferguson is to believed, he was convinced that Shaftesbury's real reason for such a plot was not anything that Monmouth had failed to do, but 'partly a disgust of monarchy, of which he was grown weary' and partly that the preparations for an insurrection would be both expensive and liable to discovery before they were complete; and so Shaftesbury was putting his faith in an assault by a small number of men and deliberately trying to destroy Monmouth's credit. Ferguson added that, having failed to divert Shaftesbury from his resolve, he told Monmouth about the plot; that they pressed on with schemes for revolt to try to divert Shaftesbury from the idea of assassination; that Ferguson got possession of the money intended to supply horses and arms for the attempt and prevented it being used; and, in contrast to Howard, that on the day of the King's return to London, he persuaded Monmouth and Armstrong to be prepared to cope with any attempt that Shaftesbury made.[1]

The picture of Ferguson the Plotter remaining aloof from the plot for which others blamed him, and acting instead as the innocent guardian angel of Monmouth (who was his hero when he wrote), is an impressive one, but it would be dangerous to put much reliance upon it. What emerges clearly from all this evidence about talk of a possible attempt on the King's life is that even if it is credible it was only talk. Even supposing that Shaftesbury did make the remarks quoted by Ferguson, he did nothing to ensure that the *coup* took place, and there is no indication at all of what would have followed on the King's death or capture, and the precise political use to which it would have been put. All this a politician like Shaftesbury would surely have had to work out; and since there is no sign that he did, the likelihood is that at the most there was some wild talk in

---

[1] For the examinations of Rumsey and West, see Sprat, op. cit. pp. 12–48; for West, cf. also Add. MSS. 38847, fos. 88–121; for Walcot, see Sprat, op. cit. p. 87, *C.S.P.D. July–Sept. 1683*, pp. 70, 72 and *State Trials*, ix. 450, 550–5; for Howard, as in p. 714, n. 1; and Ferguson, op. cit. pp. 418–27.

moments of frustration. Whatever view is taken of the Rye House Plot of March 1683, the evidence that a similar plan existed in October 1682 under Shaftesbury's inspiration is far too slender to accept.

With the King's return to Whitehall on 21 October even any wild talk about intercepting him on his way from Newmarket would have to stop until he made his next journey. There remained the possibility of continuing to talk about a possible rising. According to the confessions, this went on for at least another fortnight, especially at a meeting at the house of the wine-merchant Shepherd, the evidence about which played a big part some months later in the conviction of Lord Russell. Curiously enough none of those who gave evidence, either in court or in writing, was able to remember the precise date of the meeting. Grey (writing, it is true, three years later) fell back on the old plot informers' formula of saying that a meeting was held 'either at the end of October or the beginning of November', followed by a second meeting 'next week' three or four days before the date of 19 November fixed for the rising. Shepherd said only that there was a meeting at his house 'some time before my Lord Shaftesbury went into Holland', followed by a 'next meeting'. Rumsey said that there was a meeting about the beginning of November, and was frankly uncertain whether there was one meeting or two—a remarkable uncertainty on a matter which did more to kill Russell than anything else.[1] Ferguson mentioned one meeting and gave no date to it. Howard knew nothing about it, not being sufficiently trusted to be invited to attend. If the witnesses were vague about the date of the meeting or meetings, they were equally untrustworthy about what happened there, and disagreed on the question, crucial to Russell, whether he or Rumsey arrived first, and thus whether Russell was present at the treasonable part of the discussion.

Fortunately there is no doubt that a meeting took place, since Russell admitted it; and equally there can be no doubt that the original reason which Russell gave for his presence, namely that he had been invited to taste some sherry, was not the true one, since he himself later admitted that he had been invited there by Monmouth in order to restrain Shaftesbury and 'some hot men' who would ruin everything if they were not prevented. In the paper which he handed to the sheriffs Russell accepted that he was guilty of misprision of treason in not revealing what he had heard to the government, while denying that he himself had concurred in any treasonable plan.[2] At the least, therefore, there was a meeting at which some reckless talk took place.

According to Lord Grey there was a first meeting attended by himself, Armstrong, Monmouth, Russell, Rumsey, Shepherd, and Ferguson. Shaftesbury was not present, but Ferguson (who however maintained a

[1] Rumsey to the Earl of Rochester, n.d., Sprat, op. cit. p. 20.
[2] State Trials, ix. 691–3.

discreet silence about this in his own account) conveyed the Earl's views on the situation. The Earl claimed that he, Monmouth, Russell, and Grey had agreed to combine in raising insurrections; urged that since then he had done his own part in the City, at great risk to himself unless something was now done quickly; and appealed for their assistance, otherwise he would act without them. Monmouth and Russell replied (Grey said) that they would willingly join if the Earl's support was strong enough, but that 'they had often heard of my Lord's ten thousand brisk boys, but did not know where to find them', and wanted some information about them and their arms. Ferguson's answer was that Shaftesbury had fifteen or sixteen gentlemen of his acquaintance in and about the City (whom however he did not name) who had undertaken to bring a total of 5,000 men into action; that the Earl himself had purchased several cannon[1] and three field carriages which had been buried in the meantime; and that they must fix a date. Grey continued that all present agreed to do this, and settled on Sunday week, 19 November, since on a Sunday men might be taken, unnoticed among people returning home through crowded streets, to their posts where they would be armed. A detailed account of the dispositions was added, including, for instance, the shipping of men in lighters from Lambeth to Westminster to attack the King's forces in the rear; everything was laid down, except the source of the arms and lighters and how they were to be brought together. In the meantime Sir William Courtenay was to be informed in the West, and Trenchard, who had introduced one of the Exclusion Bills, was to go down to Taunton to plan a simultaneous rising there: Trenchard when told, although very sanguine previously, 'showed more fear than ever I saw in any man before or since',[2] but could not do less than go. In none of these details was Shaftesbury consulted.

In the following week, Grey went on, they met to discuss the rising which was fixed for Sunday. The same group were present, Shaftesbury apparently not showing enough interest, if Grey is to be believed, to attend now that the others had accepted his policy and were within a few days of a rebellion. Monmouth opened by reporting to Russell and the others on the positions of the King's guards, saying that he had found them in a 'careless posture'; but then he cast a damper on the proceedings by saying that Trenchard could not be ready in Taunton in less than a fortnight or three weeks. After a long discussion they decided to postpone the rising, and meet again in ten or fourteen days; Rumsey reported this to Shaftesbury, who took it as a sign that their intentions were not serious, and fled the country; and although the other conspirators had in fact

---

[1] Can this be a reference to the 'great guns' which Shaftesbury still had on his hands from his partnership with Rupert?

[2] Those defeated in the Monmouth Rebellion had a grudge against Trenchard for his alleged cowardice then.

intended to go ahead with the rising they now had to abandon it, since
Shaftesbury alone was familiar with the organization in the City. The
implication would be that Monmouth had done nothing to get acquainted
with the subordinates whom he was due to command in two or three days.[1]

In this, the most circumstantial of the narratives, Grey provided James II
in 1685 with what James wanted to find: namely, much more detailed
evidence of Monmouth's sinister aims than any witness had previously
supplied, and confirmation of Russell's firm complicity, which some had
questioned after his execution. On some points its implausibility has
already been suggested. Ferguson's emphasis was entirely different: he had
been co-operating, not with Shaftesbury but with Monmouth, in an attempt
to divert the former from his assassination plot; he had never trusted
Rumsey, who was only present at the 'consult' to spy for the Earl; and the
news from Trenchard really had caused them to abandon their plans.
Rumsey, who had been the first to give evidence about the 'consult' in
1683, insisted that Russell had been present throughout the discussion of
an attack on the guards and the proposed rising; Russell said that this
discussion had been only hypothetical, that he had opposed it, and knew
nothing of any plan to rise on 19 November. Several times, he said, he had
heard an attack on the guards 'mentioned, as a thing might easily be done,
but never consented to as fit to be done'. This statement of the facts was
accepted by Burnet, who supposed a discussion between Rumsey, arguing
that a surprise attack would be feasible, and Armstrong, who had commanded the guards, arguing against it. 'This', Burnet thought, 'was no
consultation what was to be done, but what might have been done'.[2]

At all events, no rising did take place on 19 November 1682; and the
time has now come to summarize all these conflicting stories of plans for
one, to assess what they amounted to, and to define Shaftesbury's part in
this. We may first of all take it for granted that there was some talk about
the possibility of a rebellion; this was a natural outcome of the political
situation, and both Russell and Walcot, on trial for their lives, admitted
hearing it. Secondly, all the different accounts, unreliable as they are in
detail, agree that Shaftesbury was the most vehement supporter of the
idea of a rebellion, while Monmouth, Russell, Grey, and others all at
times showed reluctance. This was something that could safely be alleged
by any liar when Shaftesbury was dead and people were prepared to believe
any villainy of him. Shaftesbury had the most obvious motive for suggesting
rebellion: he had already been in danger of conviction for treason once,
and another attempt to pin a charge on him was probable, when others
might think that their turn was a long way off and might never come.
Shaftesbury was the oldest of them all, and if he was to see any of his
political hopes achieved he could not afford to wait long; he might also
argue plausibly that the Tory reaction was so pronounced that the longer

action was postponed, the less its prospects of success were likely to be. It is logical, therefore, to suppose that Shaftesbury could naturally have pressed more for an insurrection than others, and there is a little evidence, more reliable than that on which we have drawn, to suggest that he did. Burnet recorded that 'Lord Shaftesbury had one meeting with the Earls of Essex and Salisbury before he went out of England. Fear, anger, and disappointment had wrought so much on him, that Lord Essex told me he was much broke in his thoughts; his notions were wild and impracticable: and he was glad he was gone out of England: but that he had done them already a great deal of mischief, and would have done more if he had stayed.' This conversation between Burnet and Essex must have taken place in December 1682, when Essex could not reveal the nature of Shaftesbury's 'wild and impracticable notions'. Many years later, after Burnet's *History* had been published, one who had been in Shaftesbury's household in 1682 wrote, under the pseudonym of Philoicus, *A Vindication of the Character and Actions of the Rt. Honble. late Earl of Shaftesbury. . . .* The author of this was concerned to argue that Shaftesbury's notions were not 'wild and impracticable'; he did this by quoting Shaftesbury as saying that rebellion was justifiable, by alleging that the other Whigs differed from him not over the morality but over the practicability of it, and by contending that the eventual deaths of Russell, Essex, and Monmouth showed that he was right and they were wrong.[1]

If, however, the likelihood is that Shaftesbury advocated a rebellion, the available evidence is inadequate to sustain a belief that anything was in existence which could be called a plan for a rising at any date. Against the interested and inconsistent accounts of the informers must be set the plain fact of the absence of concrete evidence of, for instance, the collection of money, arms, powder, and horses. West quoted an interesting observation of Ferguson's 'which he used to repeat often for our encouragement. Says he, It is a wonderful thing to me that the insurrection intended in November, which was imparted to twenty thousand people at least, and many women, was never discovered.'[2] It is so wonderful as to be incredible that no inkling of a plan intended in November reached the government until the Rye House plotters were arrested in the following June.[3] One piece of evidence alone might give us pause: in the Shaftesbury Papers, there is an undated list of the gentry of Dorset and Somerset, with marks opposite each name to indicate their political sympathies, in the Earl's hand. It bears a later endorsement by Stringer, 'I suppose for the design

---

[1] Burnet, ii. 351; Shaftesbury Papers, XVII, 18, pp. 33–35.

[2] Add. MSS. 38847, fo. 100ᵛ.

[3] Roger Morrice, Entering Book P (Dr. Williams's Library), fo. 340, says that on 21 Oct. two worthless Plot informers, Mowbray and Zeal, swore that 40,000 men were to be put in arms on 17 Nov. But the date of 19 Nov. was not fixed on according to Rumsey, Grey, and the rest, until the beginning of Nov. No one seems to have paid attention to Mowbray and Zeal, who had been proved liars many times before.

of defending our liberties in 1682'.[1] But even if a sinister interpretation were to be placed upon this, it cannot be taken necessarily to imply more than a weighing of possible support; it falls far short of an actual plan to rebel.

Certainly by mid-November Shaftesbury had to abandon, temporarily at least, all hope of achieving anything, whether by constitutional or unconstitutional means. The government was now in full control. From all the pulpits the duty of obedience to the monarch and the Church established by divine authority was being preached; and even aspirants for licenses to keep public-houses had to produce certificates that they frequented divine service in the parish church, had taken the sacrament there and were 'in all things conformable to the government as now by law established in church and state'. 'Some hundreds of the ordinary sort of people' who tried to celebrate the anniversary of Gunpowder Plot in the noisy manner to which they had grown accustomed, with shouts of 'A Monmouth, No York', were roughly handled by the trained bands and their leaders committed to prison.[2] It was significant that on 13 November L'Estrange's *Observator* turned from its habitual attacks on Whigs and Dissenters to assault the 'Trimmers'; not even a 'middle way' would do. Shortly afterwards the Whig news-sheets were silenced, and the publication of all except the *London Gazette* and *Observator* was banned. A London jury, selected this time by Tory sheriffs, found against Shaftesbury's friend Alderman Pilkington on a charge of *scandalum magnatum* brought by the Duke of York, and the vindictively ruinous fine of £100,000 was imposed upon him. The *quo warranto* proceedings against the City's charter were slowly moving forward, and the citizens received an indication of what was intended when their compatriots in Norwich were induced 'voluntarily' to surrender their own charter and to present to the King a petition for a new one, in which Charles was asked to reserve to himself the right to approve not only their mayor and sheriff but their aldermen and common-council men. And in the meantime, to make sure that the aldermanic election in the Fleet Street ward went the right way, the Bishop of London was instructed to get his clergy to mobilize their parishioners, and every alehouse-keeper and coffeeman was required to be present at the ward moot 'to vote for such men as are right to the King and government, as they shall expect licences for the year ensuing'.[3]

The time had come for Shaftesbury to flee the country, to wait and plan

---

[1] Shaftesbury Papers, VI B, 447. On 3 Oct. 1683 the justices of Essex reported information that just after the dissolution of the Oxford Parliament of 1681 one John Rotherham, jun. had been employed by Stringer to draw up a list of all the gentlemen in the country. Rotherham admitted this and said that Stringer had told him that a friend of his was 'making a catalogue of all the gentry and their families throughout England'. (*C.S.P.D. Oct. 1683–Apr. 1684*, p. 9.)

[2] Newsletter, 19 Oct., *C.S.P.D. 1682*, p. 485; ibid. pp. 528–30.

[3] Van Beuningen, 24 Nov./4 Dec., Add. MSS. 17677, FF; Luttrell, i. 236; *C.S.P.D. 1682*, pp. 557, 572.

to fight another day. From the day of his disappearance from Thanet House, it had been rumoured that he had been preparing to depart. Since then the government's agents had done little to seek him out, but this state of affairs was unlikely to last; and as a matter of fact on 26 November Lord Hyde instructed the Earl's former subordinate, Warcup, to consult solicitor Graham about the possibility of basing a new indictment upon the Association, which, as we have seen, had not been mentioned in the earlier one. A fortnight later Lord Chief Justice North told the King in Council that the Association was at least a fineable misdemeanour; and Shaftesbury's servant Stringer was actually arrested on a charge of seditious libel.[1] Shaftesbury had done well not to wait until then.

Before leaving he completed his preparations for the possibility of his death abroad in the near future. He had to provide both for the repayment of his debts and for the disposal of his estates to the advantage of his widow and his favourite eldest grandchild.

From a note of money to be paid by the Earl's trustees which Thomas Stringer drew up in the following year it is clear that already in the two years between May 1680 and July 1682 Shaftesbury's need for ready money had led him to incur debts of over £7,600 to six people. On 18 May 1680 he had borrowed £1,000 from a London apothecary, Mr. Samuel Stringer (presumably a relative of Thomas's), and the loan had since been renewed; and on 25 March 1681, at the time of the Oxford Parliament, he had borrowed £800 from Colonel Rumsey and a further £820 from his kinsman Wallop. On 5 July 1681, when he had just been committed to the Tower, he mortgaged the 'great guns' manufactured under Prince Rupert's patent, together with some cedar-wood and timber and all his personal property at Thanet House to his bankers, Peter Percival and Stephen Evans, in security for a debt of £2,489; and on 20 July 1682, for the better security for the repayment of this sum, he had agreed to an indenture granting to the two partners the whole of his landed property in eight English counties and in Carolina for a term of ninety-nine years. Since Shaftesbury's property was worth far more than the sum indicated and the size of the security was plainly unnecessary, I interpret this as a collusive arrangement designed to guard against possible confiscation of his estates by nominally mortgaging it all to friends. On 20 May 1682, he borrowed £1,000 from Sir Benjamin Ayliff and his partners: here too an originally limited security of fee-farm rents was extended on 4 September 1682, to include the whole of his lands in England and Carolina. And finally, on 22 July he borrowed £1,000 from Sir Philip Meadows—a sum which became £1,500 at some unknown date, possibly 30 September 1682, when once again a limited

---

[1] Warcup, 26 Nov., 12 Dec., 'Journals of Edmund Warcup', ed. K. Feiling and F. R. D. Needham, in E.H.R. (1925), p. 258; John Verney to Sir R. Verney, 27 Nov., H.M.C. Seventh Report, p. 480; C.S.P.D. 1682, pp. 537, 564; Life and Times of Anthony Wood, ed. A. Clark (1894), iii. 33. The charge against Stringer must have been dropped, but I have been unable to discover any details.

security was extended to the whole of his estates, so that these figured in three different mortgages.[1]

Adding in a few small debts, Stringer calculated in 1683 that principals of £8,589 were awaiting repayment.[2] It was an appreciable sum, but far from being a crippling one when one considers it against annual rents from the Shaftesbury estates of £3,000 per annum or more. Their total capital value must have been far in excess of £8,589; and it may be added that an inventory of February 1683 valued the stock and goods on the Earl's estates at £2,728 and his household goods, excluding paintings, at £1,516, while Stringer asserted that at one time £2,100 was offered for the Earl's personal plantation in Carolina. Again, an unknown proportion of the £8,589 undoubtedly represented ready cash, not spent but available for emergencies.

It was not so much the amount of the Earl's debts that presented a problem, as his son's unreliability in money matters. During the last years of his life, indeed, Shaftesbury and his Countess had become seriously estranged from Lord and Lady Ashley. Weakness of health and character had led Ashley to become more and more dependent on his wife, rather than on his father, and this had probably been accentuated after the Ashleys' departure from Wimborne St. Giles to establish a separate household at Martin. It is likely that Lady Ashley resented her father-in-law's propensity to regulate everything—even her children's education; while on his side Shaftesbury was exasperated by their incapacity and feared both that his own widow would be unjustly treated and that the family estates which he hoped to pass to his grandson would be wasted. Stringer's sympathies lay with the Earl and Countess rather than the younger generation, and his description of the situation[3] may well be too one-sided; but what took place after the Earl's death seems to justify his fears, for his

---

[1] These details are taken from the uncatalogued papers in the Muniment Room in St. Giles House: Stringer's accounts recording receipt of the moneys; his note of the money to be paid by the trustees; and a memorandum of 2 May 1693 recording Lord Ashley's repayment of the combined Ayliff and Meadows debts to the latter. For the mortgage of the great guns, cf. Shaftesbury Papers (P.R.O.), XLVI B, 101, 102.

[2] His grand total of £9,724 included accumulated interest of £635 and £500 owing to the Dowager Countess. It should be added, however, that in another document, probably drawn up for the Countess's lawyer Samuel Eyre, Stringer calculated rather differently. He spoke of collusive judgements obtained by him against the Earl in Michaelmas term, 1682, for £22,000 in the Court of Exchequer, £9,000 in King's Bench and £9,000 in Common Pleas. These, Stringer said, were intended to indemnify him from any danger incurred by allowing himself to be bound with the Earl for the latter's debts, which, he went on, amounted to £16,800 of which £13,600 was still outstanding. But there are no details in Stringer's surviving accounts and papers to corroborate this figure rather than the careful estimate of £9,724, and I am inclined to believe that he may have inflated the amount of the Earl's debts in the interests of the Countess's case in *Shaftesbury* v. *Shaftesbury*.

[3] Recorded in a long document of 74 pages drawn up to instruct the Dowager Countess's lawyer, Samuel Eyre, in the case of *Shaftesbury* v. *Shaftesbury*, and to be found in a bundle with that label in the Muniment Room at St. Giles House.

son both treated the Dowager very badly and allowed himself to be swindled out of large sums by a dishonest steward.

Already in May 1680, when the King's second illness had demonstrated the uncertainty of the political situation, Shaftesbury had taken certain steps to deal with the problem of the fate of his estates after his death. In regard to some of them his hands were tied. His grandfather, Sir Anthony Ashley, had settled many of them on Sir John Cooper and his heirs male, and these would pass down automatically to his son. Other lands formed his wife's jointure and would go safely to her; while a third section would be governed correspondingly by the terms of the settlement made on Lord and Lady Ashley at the time of their marriage, and could not be prevented from passing to them. But there were some other estates, and these, by a series of documents dated 25, 26 and 27 May 1680, Shaftesbury had devised to his kinsman and political associate, Sir William Cooper, John Hoskins of the Inner Temple, Edward Clarke, and Thomas Stringer, as trustees, first for his own use, then for that of Lady Shaftesbury, then for his small grandson Anthony, and only lastly to Lord Ashley. At the same time he prepared a further deed granting to the same trustees all his personal estate and his property in Carolina and the Bahamas, in trust to pay his creditors, to pay £500 to Lady Shaftesbury and to invest the rest for her use.[1]

Now, on 11 November 1682, he caused this last deed to be executed, so that he could depart with an easier mind. Events after his death were to show that the arrangements that he had made were not absolutely watertight; like so many who are adept at business in their lifetime, he could not regulate everything that would happen after his death. In particular there was a long and squalid dispute between his widow and his son and daughter-in-law over the question whether his debts should be paid from his personal estate (and therefore by the Dowager Countess) or from the landed estates which descended to his son and which had been used as security for them; and inevitably other causes of dispute were introduced too. But his widow was enabled to live out her last years in reasonable material comfort, with an income of over £2,000 per annum, if in considerable mental dejection; and his grandson, when he succeeded as third Earl of Shaftesbury, though he had ample reason to complain of the mismanagement and dishonesty of his father's servants, was not a poor man.

Shaftesbury was now ready to leave. Evidently he still had in his hands a substantial proportion of the money that he had borrowed, in the form of ready cash; and he also took with him some of his and his wife's

---

[1] This paragraph is distilled from a mass of deeds and documents in the Muniment Room. Since many of the legal documents are collusive, and since they were in any case the subject of legal argument in *Shaftesbury* v. *Shaftesbury*, I cannot be sure that I have avoided error, but I believe the main lines of my interpretation to be correct.

jewellery. His destination would obviously be the Dutch Republic. Not only was it near at hand, so that he could quickly hear the English news and instruct his supporters, but, as many refugees had found since 1660, the looseness of its constitution, combined with a tradition of toleration of dissident elements, enabled exiles to settle there without much molestation from the authorities. Charles and James would no doubt press William of Orange to do what he could, but, even if William was compliant, his authority in the great merchant city of Amsterdam, with its jealous independence, was limited. From Amsterdam, too, he would be able to return speedily when the political situation changed in England; and the fact that he made no arrangements for his wife to follow him across the North Sea strongly suggests that he was optimistic that his exile would be brief. But many of his servants he did propose to take with him; and along with members of his household like Anthony Shepherd, John Wheelock, and John Gray, there travelled both Colonel Thomas Walcot and the Reverend Mr. Robert Ferguson.[1] Ferguson left behind him as a parting shot a pamphlet *Second Part of the Growth of Popery*, and L'Estrange was probably right in suspecting that 'some touches in it betray the E. of S. had a sight of it' before it appeared.[2] If Ferguson is to be believed, he left from one door at the precise moment when a royal messenger was entering by another to arrest him; but not, apparently, before he had borrowed money from Shaftesbury's friend Francis Charlton.[3]

The exact date of Shaftesbury's departure is not known; it was successfully kept in the deepest secrecy to prevent any possible interception by the English government. Probably some time after 20 November he took leave of his wife in a last fond interview. According to a servant who was present at their parting, and described it forty years later, the Earl was serene and composed, as he calmly bade farewell to the wife who had shared his life for more than a quarter of a century. It was a tradition in the household that Shaftesbury went to Harwich in the disguise of a Presbyterian minister, and when this disguise seemed in danger of being penetrated, he jestingly told his staid servant Wheelock to divert the attention of the maid at the place where he was staying by making love to her. But there was no truth in the anecdote. It would have been too dangerous for a man in poor health and well known to the general public to attempt the journey to Harwich to travel by the packet boat; and it was much safer for Captain Tracy, at whose house in Wapping he had been hiding, to find a small boat nearby. Tracy made a bargain with Robert

---

[1] According to van Citters (26 June/6 July 1683, Add. MSS. 17677, FF) Rumsey went too; but since he was not mentioned, like the rest, in Shaftesbury's will it seems possible that van Citters confused him with Walcot.

[2] King to Jenkins, 13 Nov., *C.S.P.D. 1682*, p. 537; *Observator*, 1, 4 Dec.; Clark, *Life and Times of Anthony Wood*, iii. L32–33; 'Estrange to Jenkins, 6 Dec., *C.S.P.D. 1682*, pp. 563–4. Ferguson's denial of authorship to his wife, 19 Dec., ibid. p. 582, is not necessarily to be believed.   [3] Ferguson, op. cit. p. 429; Charlton in *C.S.P.D. July-Sept. 1683*, p. 255.

Locke (no relation of John, as far as is known), master of the *Hare*, and Locke received £35 for taking Shaftesbury over to the Brill.[1]

Some time before 26 November, therefore, there landed at the Brill a small party which included a 'sickly infirm man', passing under the name of Johnson. He was in Rotterdam, lodging on the new haven there with an English merchant named Washington, by 28 November, when Ferguson wrote home to his wife. The story which belatedly reached the deluded English ambassador at The Hague, Thomas Chudleigh, was that he had sought the protection of the magistrates there and had hired a house. But Amsterdam was the real destination; he had friends there who were preparing to receive him—many of them connected with the Brownist Church there.[2] They included Israel Hayes, Francis Prince, and, most important, Abraham Kick, a merchant at whose house the regicides were said once to have lodged, and whose papers, if they survived, would tell us much about the radical opposition to Charles II over twenty years and more. Sir William Waller, the fanatical Puritan magistrate who had been the scourge of London Catholics, had preceded the Earl into exile and was there to receive him on 2 December.[3]

At first Shaftesbury stayed at an ordinary in the Warnstraat, eating in public there, though it was noticed that a valet tasted everything before he drank. On 5 December he was visited by William Carr, an impudent adventurer who had been in the Dutch service a decade earlier during the Anglo-Dutch war of 1672–4, but who since then had been trying to ingratiate himself again with the English government. Suppressing his anger at the appearance of such an obvious spy, Shaftesbury drank politely to him, and spoke sadly of the death of his old partner Prince Rupert a few days earlier; but Carr elicited no information of any importance. Five days later, probably seeking greater privacy from such unwelcome visitors, the Earl moved to lodge with Abraham Kick on the Gelderskai. One informant of the English ambassador told him that the Earl had taken a noble house on the new Heerengracht; another related that the Earl had wanted to rent the whole of Monsieur Feron's ordinary for twelve months, but that negotiations broke down at the last moment when Shaftesbury insisted on a clause that if a Parliament met before the end of the twelve months, the lease should end with his own departure. In the meantime he deposited a large sum of money (which wild rumours put as high as £30,000)

[1] 'A Vindication of the Character and Actions of the Rt. Honble. the late Earl of Shaftesbury', by Philoicus, Shaftesbury Papers, XVII, 18; Brown, p. 301; Locke's examination, 21 July 1683, *C.S.P.D. July-Sept. 1683*, pp. 181–2.

[2] Cf. W. Carr to Skelton, 12/22 July, 30 Aug./9 Sept., 1681, Add. MSS. 37981, fos. 58, 68.

[3] Marquis of Worcester to the Marchioness, 27 Nov., *H.M.C. Beaufort MSS.*, p. 87; Conway to Chudleigh, 28 Nov., *Despatches of Thomas Plott and Thomas Chudleigh*, ed. F. A. Middlebush (The Hague, 1926), p. 180; Chudleigh to Conway, 5/15 Dec., ibid. p. 188; Ezekiel Everest, 19 June 1684, *C.S.P.D. Oct. 1683–Apr. 1684*, p. 223; Ferguson to his wife, 28 Nov., Ferguson, op. cit. pp. 93–94; Carr to Jenkins, 8/18 Dec., P.R.O., S.P. 84/217, fo. 144.

in the bank, and more modestly invested £590 with Francis Prince for the purchase of pepper.[1]

From all this the reader will deduce the English government's anxiety to know what its great enemy was doing across the sea. As soon as he was reported to be in Holland the King sent orders to his ambassador to let the Prince of Orange know 'that his Majesty is most assured that His Highness will not give any countenance or protection to the Earl of Shaftesbury or suffer any of his family to have communication with him, knowing how highly obnoxious and disaffected his Lordship is to the King and the government'. William 'earnestly' gave the necessary assurances, to the Duke of York's great satisfaction. But there remained the possibility that through members of the States-General and the Amsterdam regents Shaftesbury might be able to influence Dutch attitudes towards England, and Charles was indignant to learn that Shaftesbury had asked for protection from the Amsterdam authorities and had been made a burgher there. This last report was premature; the truth seems to be that the regents of Amsterdam were polite both to him and to Chudleigh and Carr when the latter made representations to them—and that in practice Shaftesbury was allowed to remain there unmolested.[2]

We catch glimpses of the Earl limping along the Amsterdam streets, supported on the one side by Sir William Waller and on the other by Ferguson; while at other times he and Ferguson were said to be hard at work drawing up memoranda for the States-General, urging upon them the need for co-operation to secure the Reformed faith from the plots of the Papists. This last was the guess of one Marsal, the nephew of a former Savoyard ambassador in London who had since struggled to earn a living by teaching languages in Holland, and had scraped up some acquaintance with Waller. In pursuit of his desire, he said, to do useful service for England, he proceeded to write a series of letters to the Archbishop of Canterbury about the activities of the Shaftesbury circle in Amsterdam. Not much reliance can be placed on his guesses about the nature of Shaftesbury's political activities, for he was never as well informed as he claimed to be, but it is possible to glean a little more from him than we might otherwise know about Shaftesbury's last illness. For on 29 December he was able to report that for the past three days Shaftesbury had been ill with what he described as gout in the stomach, since a distressing symptom

---

[1] Carr, loc. cit.; Chudleigh to Conway, 12/22, 19/29 Dec., Middlebush, op. cit. pp. 196–7, 201–2; Marsal to the Archbishop of Canterbury, 22 Dec./1 Jan., S.P. 84/217, fos. 156–7; Hughes's report of Bampfield's discourses, ibid. p. 242; newsletter, 13 Jan., *H.M.C. Egmont MSS.*, ii. 126.

[2] Conway to Chudleigh, 30 Nov., 15 Dec., Middlebush, op. cit. pp. 180–1, 199; Chudleigh to Conway, 8/18, 12/22, 19/29 Dec., ibid. pp. 192–3, 196–7, 201–2; Duke of York to William, 18 Dec., *C.S.P.D. 1682*, p. 581; Barrillon, 11/21 Dec.; Carr, loc. cit. p. 729, n. 3; 'Philoicus' in Shaftesbury Papers, XVII, 18, p. 39; Marsal to the Archbishop of Canterbury, 29 Dec./8 Jan., S.P. 84/217, fo. 159; newsletter, 13 Jan., *H.M.C. Egmont MSS.*, ii. 126.

was his inability to keep down any food. In actual fact the illness was connected with a stoppage of the discharge from his side which had been drained for the past twenty-five years. He could not consult the doctors who had been familiar with his condition for so long, and the Dutch doctors could not help him.[1]

Weak as he was, Shaftesbury could not hold out for long against his inability to take nourishment. For a time Ferguson retained his customary optimism, and after about a week the Earl rallied, only to relapse again into a worse condition than before. On 17 January, realizing that he was dying, Shaftesbury made his will. As we have seen, he had already made his arrangements for the disposal of his property in England and America, but he still had a few provisions to make for what he had with him in Holland, and some small legacies to bequeath to those around him. He began by expressing the desire that his body should be taken back to England by his servant Anthony Shepherd and buried with his ancestors at Wimborne St. Giles. Then he gave to his 'dear, virtuous, loving and faithful wife', whom he made his sole executrix, all the jewellery that he had deposited with the Amsterdam merchant, Francis Prince. Prince was given £10 to buy himself a ring, and asked to make up his accounts with Kick about the pepper in which Shaftesbury had invested, and to sell it to the best advantage of his widow. Finally, from the monies in his hands Prince was asked to pay £10 to the Earl's 'worthy friend' Thomas Walcot to buy a ring; £40 to the Earl's other 'worthy friend', Mr. Robert Ferguson; £80 to Shepherd; £60, and all his wearing apparel, to John Wheelock; and £40 each to his servant John Gray and his coachman, Daniel Dale.[2]

It was said that Shaftesbury had sent for his wife and son, no doubt to urge harmony upon them; but if any message was indeed sent there was no time for an answer. He was so weak that he could hardly make himself heard to those who ministered to him. Even soup did not suit his stomach, and he could not sleep. Day and night he lay there, always with his eyes open. But he was calm and composed, and there was no sign of any regrets about the past; indeed he was reported as saying to the merchant Thomas Dare who had witnessed his will, that whatever his enemies claimed, he had had no other aim than to serve his country and to preserve its liberty.[3] On Saturday, 20 January, he seemed a little better, and was able to get a little rest, but it proved to be the last rally. That night it fell to Ferguson

---

[1] Hughes's report of Bampfield's discourses, S.P. 84/217, fo. 242; Marsal to the Archbishop, 22 Dec./1 Jan., 29 Dec./8 Jan., n.d., and 23 Jan./2 Feb., ibid. fos. 157, 158–9, 190, 197.

[2] Ferguson to his wife, 29 Dec., 5, 12, 16 Jan., Ferguson, op. cit. pp. 99, 101, 102; Shaftesbury's will printed by Christie, ii. 458–9.

[3] Marsal, 19/29 Jan., S.P. 84/217, fos. 193–4; Hughes's report of Bampfield's discourses, ibid. fo. 242; newsletter, 6 Feb., MSS. Carte 72, fo. 832; and cf. a pamphlet obviously written either by Ferguson or someone else who was present by the death-bed, *A brief Account of many memorable Passages of the Life and Death of the Earl of Shaftesbury*, in *Harleian Miscellany* (1810), v. 372–3.

to take his turn by the bedside, and twenty-five years later, in his Jacobite days, Ferguson gave his description of their last conversation. Ferguson took occasion to talk about Shaftesbury's soul and the other world, and the need for repentance and faith in the Lord Jesus who came into the world to die for sinners and to reconcile them to God. In reply, if Ferguson is to be believed, Shaftesbury declared himself to be a professed Arian, 'saying that he believed Jesus Christ to be the first creature that God made, and that by him He (God) made the world, rejecting the doctrine of satisfaction by Jesus Christ's death'. Another version of the conversation, also derived from Ferguson, has it that the Earl 'talked all over Arianism and Socinianism, which notions he confessed he imbibed from Mr. Locke and his tenth chapter of "Human Understanding" '.[1]

Next morning, Sunday, 21 January 1683, at about half-past eleven, Shaftesbury sat up on his bed, drank some broth, and said that he felt a little better. But death then came quite suddenly. Ferguson, hastily summoned to the scene, found him in his last agonies and speechless. They gave him cordial, and Ferguson lifted up his pillow so that he could receive it the more easily; but he gulped and died immediately in the arms of John Wheelock.[2]

'Lord Shaftesbury is gone to answer in another world for all the villainies and treasons he committed in this.' So wrote ambassador Chudleigh with great satisfaction. But Shaftesbury's servants, who had nursed him with devotion, mourned his loss deeply. Even Robert Ferguson, writing the news to his wife, talked sorrowfully of the Earl's 'fatherly love and care'; it was not until some months later that he began to talk of Shaftesbury's 'ingratitude' at leaving him only £40, and later still that he claimed that his real loyalty had always been to Monmouth and not to the extremism of his patron.[3]

In view of Shaftesbury's desire, expressed in his will, that his body should be returned to his native Wimborne St. Giles for burial, his servants wrote away for instructions, and in the meantime caused the corpse to be embalmed. It was dressed in his usual clothes, with 'a very fine new wig', and placed in a wooden case shaped like a coffin with a glass over the face.

[1] Bodleian Library, MSS. Smith 141, fo. 65, and Rawlinson D 824, fo. 64; Thomas Cherry to Thomas Hearne, 25 July 1706, *Letters addressed to Thomas Hearne*, ed. F. Ouvry, 1874, p. 9. I am not so sure as Professor von Leyden (*John Locke: Essays on the Law of Nature*, 1954, p. 67) that the reference to the tenth chapter of Book IV of the *Essay on Human Understanding* shows that this chapter must have been written before 1683; it seems to me that the reference may have been tacked on by Ferguson or Cherry in 1706 by a natural retrospective association of ideas. That Shaftesbury and Locke had talked over these problems, however, there is no reason to doubt.

[2] Ferguson, loc. cit. in previous note; Marsal, 19/29 Jan., 23 Jan./2 Feb., S.P. 84/217, fos. 193–4, 197–8; Abraham Kick to Lady Shaftesbury, 22 Jan., Shaftesbury Papers, VII, 506; Francis Prince to Lady Shaftesbury, 26 Jan./5 Feb., ibid. VI A, 387.

[3] Chudleigh to Conway, 23 Jan./2 Feb., Add. MSS. 41809, fo. 13; Ferguson to his wife, [23 Jan.?], *C.S.P.D. 1682*, pp. 23–24; Forbes, 10 July, *C.S.P.D. July–Sept. 1683*, p. 90; Abraham Kick and Prince, as in previous note.

Someone then took the decision to make the statesman's corpse available to public view, and some were curious enough to come and inspect it as it lay there, 'with a very smiling countenance' which caused a silly rumour that the Earl was not really dead.[1]

In England one of the first to hear the news was the Earl's old friend, John Locke. Locke had not seen the Earl in London after the latter's departure from Thanet House at the end of September, and therefore can hardly have been involved in the Earl's last consultations before fleeing the country; certainly he did not, like Ferguson, feel driven to share the Earl's exile. But when Locke heard of Shaftesbury's death, though he himself was ill in bed at Clapham and 'the circumstances I was in both of body and mind made me very uncapable of advising in such an occasion of this', he thought it incumbent on him to write back to Amsterdam his impression that it would be best to ship the body, not to London, but to Poole, the nearest port to Wimborne St. Giles. This impression was endorsed by the Earl's kinsman, friend, and trustee, Sir William Cooper, at St. Giles House; and accordingly the little group at Amsterdam chartered an English pink, the *Elizabeth*. Shepherd, Wheelock, and Gray travelled with the body; Ferguson, Walcot, Waller, and the others remained behind, 'fearing the English air or laws would not very well agree with men of their constitutions'. It was a wise precaution, for when the ship arrived in Poole harbour, flying its mourning flag and streamers with the dead man's arms, it was promptly searched by the authorities for both persons and papers—but in vain.[2]

The widow's grief could not be measured, but the cost of the funeral was recorded to the last penny. Of the £424 19s. 3d. some £309 was spent on black cloth for the mourners; it is a sum which contrasts oddly with the £10 of largesse which was given to the poor at Poole, with £1 to the parson and poor at Wimborne so that they might remember the dead with gratitude. So that the dead man might sleep more appropriately and comfortably, £5 forfeiture was paid for a breach of the Act for burying in woollen; and last of all, there was £2 10s. for 'making and bricking up the grave, it being arched over'.[3]

Amongst the mourners to whom the Countess gave three yards of black cloth was Mr. John Locke, who arrived at St. Giles on 25 February to pay his last respects to his former patron. Next day he read from Cicero's *De Natura Deorum*, and the entry in his diary records extracts from that and from a *Traité des Fièvres*. There follows the brief, laconic entry,' E. Shaftesbury buried'. It has the absolute finality of the bricking-up of the grave.

---

[1] Marsal, 5/15 Feb., S.P. 84/217, fos. 208–9; newsletter, 10 Feb., MSS. Carte 222, fo. 318.

[2] Locke to Hoskins or Stringer, 26 Jan., Victoria and Albert Museum, Forster collection, MS. 363 (I am indebted to Mr. E. S. de Beer for a transcript of this letter); W. Cooper to Stringer, 30 Jan., Christie, ii. 459–60; Kick to Lady Shaftesbury, 16/26 Feb., Shaftesbury Papers, VI A, 387; *Loyal Protestant and True Domestick Intelligence*, 22 Feb., 1, 8 Mar.

[3] Shaftesbury Papers, XLIII, p. 27.

CHAPTER XXXI

CONCLUSION

> Of these the false Achitophel was first,
> A name to all succeeding ages curst . . .
> Dryden

> . . . Haec non Sepulchri ornamenta, sed Viri.
> Quippe quae nec Majoribus debuit nec favori.
> Comitate, acumine, suadela, consilio, animo, constantia, fide,
> Vix Parem alibi invenias, Superiorem certe nullibi.
> Libertatis Civilis, Ecclesiasticae,
> Propugnator strenuus, indefessus.
> Vitae publicis commodis impensae memoriam et laudes,
> Stante libertate, numquam obliterabit
> Tempus edax, nec edacior Invidia.
> Servo pecori inutilia, invisa magna exempla.
> Locke's epitaph for Shaftesbury[1]

ON 6 April 1683, John Locke left the house at which he had so often been the Earl's guest; and at approximately the same date the Dowager left too, and the second Earl and his countess arrived to take possession, and to quarrel with her over the dead man's property. Soon the new generation was installed, and the first Earl's personality was a rapidly fading memory. Some who had been close to the Earl cherished his memory: 'mournful Margaret Shaftesbury' (as his widow was still signing herself to her step-son in 1688) was as devoted in death as she had been in life; his steward Stringer and other servants resisted all temptation to blacken his reputation or to forget him, when it might have been more worldly-wise to do so; Locke himself never lost his early admiration for the Earl's ability. 'He lost no opportunity of speaking of it, and that in a manner which sufficiently showed he spoke from his heart.'[2] The few who knew him intimately remembered his charm, his kindness, his wit, and his generosity, and in their memory was compounded both affection and respect.

Yet in the political situation of 1683 this feeling had to be muted. Admiration for Shaftesbury had been possible at the time of his triumphant acquittal a year earlier, when the Medal had been struck; it was much more unfashionable now, and would do no good to those who expressed it. It was thought worthy of comment that his aristocratic relations by his

---

[1] *Works* (1823), ix. 281.
[2] Ibid. x. 167 (from The Character of Mr. Locke, by Mr. Peter Coste).

first (Coventry) marriage, Lords Halifax, Coventry, and Plymouth, observed the convention of going into mourning for him. The Duke of York told William of Orange that the Whigs themselves did not regret his death, because his extremism had harmed their cause; and the Duke of Ormond added that for this very reason the government itself did not regard the Earl's death as an advantage—'so that his departure (whither God knows) is neither lamented by his friends nor rejoiced at by his enemies'.[1]

Amongst the scribblers who seized the chance to profit from the occasion of the death of so prominent a political figure, the panegyrists[2] were heavily outnumbered by the detractors. Freed from the possibility of any charge of *scandalum magnatum* in the event of Shaftesbury's return, they spared no blow, in prose or in doggerel.

> My Tap is run; then Baxter tell me why
> Should not the good, the great Potapskie die?

These opening words of *The Last Will and Testament of Anthony, King of Poland* strike the characteristic note of scurrilous abuse of Shaftesbury for the abscess which was supposedly the result of fornication, and for his imagined devotion to an elective monarchy like that of Poland. The same poem ends with an equally elegant 'Epitaph upon his Bowels':—

> Ye Mortal Whigs for Death prepare,
> For Mighty Tapski's Guts lie here,
> Will his great Name keep sweet, d'y' think?
> For certainly his Entrails stink . . ."

And so on, *ad infinitum* and *ad nauseam*.[3] In answer to such effusions, an anonymous Whig propagandist, writing under the pseudonym of Philanax Misopappas (Lover of the King, Hater of the Pope), compiled a panegyric called *Rawleigh Redivivus*; but this was overtaken by the revelations of the so-called Rye House Plot in the summer of 1683. There might be room for argument about the guilt of some of those implicated by the informers;

---

[1] Sir Chas. Lyttelton to L. Hatton, *Hatton Correspondence*, ed. E. M. Thompson (Camden Society, 1878), ii. 22; James to William, 2 Feb., *C.S.P.D. Jan.-June 1683*, p. 40; T. Carte, *Life of Ormond* (1861), v. 165.

[2] See, for instance, *A Brief Account of many memorable Passages of the Life and Death of the Earl of Shaftesbury . . .* (*Harleian Miscellany*, 1810, v. 372–3); *An Essay upon the Earl of Shaftesbury's Death* (*Poems on Affairs of State*, 1697, pp. 134–6); *An Elegy on the Rt. Hon. Anthony Earl of Shaftesbury* (1683).

[3] Cf. also *Dagon's Fall* (printed in *Political Ballads of the Seventeenth and Eighteenth Centuries*, ed. W. W. Wilkins, 1860, i. 249–52; in the British Museum under the title of *The Whigs' Lamentations for the Death of Anthony King of Poland*); *A Supplement to the Last Will and Testament of Anthony Earl of Shaftesbury* (1683); *An Elogy on the Death of (the much to be lamented) Anthony King of Poland* (1683) ('Wretch of 3 names farewell!'); and *Shaftesbury's Farewell; or, The New Association* (printed in the *Roxburgh Ballads*, ed. J. W. Ebsworth, v. (1885), 239–40.) *Memoirs of the Life of Anthony late Earl of Shaftesbury* (1683) and *Great News from Poland* (1683) are prose works.

but the name of Shaftesbury was blackened freely as that of a man whose malevolent influence had inspired plans for assassination and rebellion even after his own death.

Shaftesbury's friends could boast neither of his success nor of his martyrdom. There could be no doubt that in the year 1683 in which he died the royal authority was more extensive than it had ever been at any time during the reign; Parliament was not summoned, opposition was muzzled, and everything was being prepared for a peaceful Popish succession. No martyrdom compensated for this. The death of an old man on his sick-bed after the briefest of exiles did not excite the same sympathy as did the deaths of Russell and Monmouth on a public scaffold. Moreover, these same deaths together with the suicide of Essex removed those of Shaftesbury's closest associates who might ultimately have helped to rehabilitate him; and when the Whigs once more came on to the political scene in 1689 their salvation was the work of William of Orange with whom Shaftesbury had had little to do. Titus Oates, being still alive, might be shamefacedly rewarded with a pension; his dead patron was an embarrassing skeleton in the cupboard, best left there in obscurity if possible, as one who had done more harm than good, and as the general scapegoat for the excesses of the Exclusion crisis. The Shaftesbury family itself could do little against the general trend. The Earl's widow, devoted as she might be, was little regarded in comparison with Lady Russell, and was at odds with the second Earl who was a political nonentity. The third Earl, the favourite grandson, was devoted to his grandfather's memory, but ill-health restricted his participation in politics to little more than the exercise of his influence at local elections. In the eighteenth century the Shaftesburys never occupied the same place in the Whig oligarchy as did the Russells, the Cavendishes, and other Revolution families; and the first Earl never occupied the same place in the ruling Whig tradition.

Shaftesbury's reputation also suffered from the fact that none of his contemporaries who wrote their memoirs of the period for the benefit of posterity was either a close friend or even shared his political standpoint. It was not only that Tories like L'Estrange and Roger North painted his activities during the Popish Plot in the blackest possible colours; but even a Whig apologist for the Revolution settlement like Bishop Burnet rejoiced that Exclusion had come through the intervention of William of Orange and not in the manner and by the methods that Shaftesbury had envisaged. Burnet and Shaftesbury had the same dislike for James II, but the *History of My Own Time* defended the events of 1688 rather than those of 1678–81. The two men were plainly antipathetic to one another: Burnet disliked Shaftesbury's unorthodoxy and even anti-clericalism, and also what he took to be the Earl's vanity but may have been his reaction to Burnet's officiousness and inquisitiveness. Burnet was certainly in no position to interpret the Earl's complicated personality to his readers. Nor was Shaftesbury likely to gain a better hearing from Sir William Temple. Temple's conviction that the best hope for Europe's safety from Louis XIV lay in co-operation between English and Dutch was not likely to make him well disposed to the author of the *Delenda est Carthago* speech. Pre-occupied with the international situation as he was, Temple regarded Shaftesbury in later years as a dangerous incendiary, fostering internal disharmony and thus hindering the possibility that England might play her proper part in an anti-French coalition; and his hopes were placed in William of Orange, to whom Shaftesbury was always distinctly cool. Temple's personal acquaintance with Shaftesbury was even less intimate than Burnet's had been; writing of the year 1679, he refers proudly to a meeting with Shaftesbury at Lord Halifax's house as 'the only time I ever had any thing to do, or so much as talk, with my Lord Shaftesbury, further than the council chamber'.[1]

If the memoir-writers were hard on Shaftesbury, it is also true that the balance was never redressed by the publication of his own writings and correspondence. Strafford and Cromwell, Clarendon and Danby, Halifax and Walpole, left enough personal records behind for it to be possible to see events through their eyes; not all their records were published, but at least the manuscripts have become available to the historian. Nothing comparable is there for the biographer of Shaftesbury to examine. No other of the great political figures of the seventeenth century, with the exception of Pym, has left so little behind him. W. D. Christie published a handful of letters, a few short and formal speeches, and an autobiographi-cal fragment about his youth. The Shaftesbury Papers in the Public Record Office are voluminous but largely formal, and the amount in them which throws any light on the workings of his mind is almost insignificant. He has to be viewed almost entirely through the observations of others.

All these circumstances have combined to enable Dryden's famous character-sketch to hold almost unchallenged sway over men's minds. It is safe to say that for any reader of Dryden's poem the name of Shaftesbury immediately calls to mind the lines on Achitophel. They are the work of a poet of genius and a dramatist of talent; they form an apparently careful and coherent delineation of character; they are apparently consistent with the 'plain facts' of Shaftesbury's changes of political affiliation and his patronage of Titus Oates. Against them Christie's laudatory biography, though a very considerable scholarly achievement when it was published in 1871, struggled largely in vain. Historians in the Whig tradition followed Macaulay in repudiating Shaftesbury as first a member of the most corrupt administration and then a member of the most violent opposition of the century; apologists for the Stuarts continued to concentrate their fire upon him.

Christie did, however, draw attention to one aspect of Shaftesbury's

[1] *Works*, iv. 421.

career which seemed to count in his favour.[1] Amongst the primary documentary sources to which he obtained access was a large amount of the private correspondence of John Locke; and he was able to argue that the friendship of so renowned an apostle of the civil and religious liberty which the later nineteenth century cherished must have been creditable to Shaftesbury. A little over twenty years ago the Lovelace collection of Locke's papers was deposited in the Bodleian Library and became generally available to scholars; and the renewed interest in Locke which this has stimulated has led inevitably to further stress being laid upon the significance of the relationship between the great thinker and the practical politician who was his patron.[2] Historians had long been aware, for instance, of the two men's collaboration over the *Fundamental Constitutions* of Carolina, and of Locke's preparations for the Oxford Parliament of 1681; but the recent trend has been to emphasize far more the importance of the period between 1667 and 1675, when Locke was a member of Shaftesbury's 'family' at Exeter House, in the development of his philosophical, religious, political, and economic thinking, and in the drafting of it on paper. Mr. Laslett has gone further, and has argued strongly that both the *Treatises of Civil Government* were first written, not as a retrospective justification of the Revolution of 1688, but as an 'Exclusionist tract' in support of Shaftesbury.[3]

This is not the place to set out in detail the complicated arguments about the dating of the *Two Treatises*. It is sufficient here to say that much of Mr. Laslett's argument is directed to proving that some at least of Locke's attack on Filmer must have been written between his return from France in the spring of 1679 and the time when he read the new edition of Filmer which appeared early in 1680. If this is so—and it appears probable, though not certain—we are left with the awkward problem of explaining why a book which was begun in 1679 did not appear before the Exclusion crisis subsided. Such lack of urgency does not suggest that the book can have figured very prominently in Shaftesbury's plans; nor, if it was begun in 1679 when the Whigs still hoped to achieve their aims by constitutional means, can it have been intended as an anticipatory defence for the rebellion which Shaftesbury has been accused of planning in 1682. In any case its length would surely have unfitted it for that purpose, which would have been served better by something from the pen of Ferguson.

The likelihood therefore seems to be that the book was begun in 1679, and that it was prompted by the political controversies to which Filmer's doctrines had given rise; it attacked the Tory doctrine of patriarchal

---

[1] Cf. also Ranke, *History of England*, trans. Sir R. Lodge (1875), iv. 166.

[2] See, for instance, Mr. Laslett's edition of the *Two Treatises of Government* (1960), pp. 25–37, and Mr. Maurice Cranston's biography of Locke (1957), chs. 8–12, 14–16.

[3] Op. cit. pp. 45–66; and cf. the article, 'The English Revolution and Locke's Two Treatises of Government', in *Cambridge Historical Journal* (1956), pp. 40–55.

authority and fitted in with the Whig desire to exclude the Papist heir by hereditary succession; and the theme could have been suggested by Shaftesbury; but the evidence is never likely to enable us to make a categorical statement. Equally we shall never know the extent to which Locke was admitted into the Earl's detailed political planning and the number of occasions on which he met Titus Oates at Thanet House. The historian cannot describe the conversations which the Earl and Locke must have enjoyed on matters of politics and religion, or define the extent to which Shaftesbury helped the other to clarify his ideas and encouraged him to set them down. But it can scarcely be doubted that Locke shared his patron's general political outlook. After all, he was not a merely abstract thinker, confined to some academic ivory tower of his own. He had practical tasks to perform for his patron as Lord Chancellor, as President of the Council of Trade and Plantations, as proprietor of Carolina; he bustled about to find lodgings for Shaftesbury at Oxford, and also to help arrange his defence against charges of high treason later in the same year. Although he was of an excessively timid disposition, he was not exaggerating his danger when in 1683 he chose to go into exile: he was a marked man in the eyes of authority, and identified with the arch-villain, Shaftesbury. He was both a realist and sufficiently intimate with Shaftesbury not to be under any illusions about him; and yet he always retained his admiration for him, when he had no need to do so and when others fell away.

If this is so, it follows that one must treat seriously the claim which Locke made for Shaftesbury, in the draft epitaph printed at the head of this chapter, that he was a 'vigorous and indefatigable champion of civil and ecclesiastical liberty'. In the words of the most recent writer on *The First Whigs*, 'Later generations disowned Shaftesbury, but they did not repudiate the principles on which the case for Exclusion, as well as the Revolution, rested—that political power should reside with those who possessed the greatest weight in society, and that in the last resort sovereignty rests with the people, the interests of the nation taking precedence over those of the Crown.'[1] It will be noticed that this is a carefully limited claim, which uses once again the question-begging term 'the people'. Shaftesbury was no democrat, if by that one means a believer in universal suffrage; he was not even a Leveller; and he upheld the political and social privileges of the aristocracy. One must not, it is true, attach too much significance to the oligarchic provisions of the pamphlet *Some Observations concerning the Regulating of Elections for Parliament, found among the Earl of Shaftesbury's Papers after his Death*, which was printed in 1689, and would have raised the forty-shilling franchise and required a property qualification of £10,000 for members of Parliament; these observations have often been treated as though they were Shaftesbury's

---

[1] J. R. Jones (1961), p. 217.

own,[1] but, particularly when one considers how few of the surviving Shaftesbury Papers were written by him, the mere fact that this document was found amongst them does not prove his authorship, and there are good reasons for doubting it.[2] But there is more convincing evidence elsewhere of his opposition to democracy, for instance in his remark to Evelyn that he would support the principle of monarchy 'to his last breath, as having seen and felt the misery of being under a mechanic tyranny'[3]; no return to the Barebones Parliament for him. On numerous occasions he had been a stickler for the privileges of the House of Lords. Yet at the same time he was undoubtedly a believer in parliamentary government; in all his political changes he never attached himself to any regime which set itself firmly against frequent parliaments, and in his last years he worked with those who even clamoured for annual ones. Once a measure of parliamentary sovereignty had been gained, once the principle that government should be based on the consent of 'the people' had been accepted, then sooner or later the conception of what constituted 'the people' would be capable of being broadened. And it is just possible that this broadening might have taken place a little more quickly if Shaftesbury had been victorious. He had, after all, made a deliberate appeal for the 'out of doors' support of a wider public opinion than that of the normal politically conscious classes.

Similarly Shaftesbury was 'on the side of the future' in the matter of religious toleration, though here too the liberality which he favoured was considerably limited in comparison with the toleration to which we are nowadays accustomed. Even where Dissenters were concerned he did not believe in complete religious equality: he believed in an established church, based on tithes and not on voluntary contributions, and he supported the Test Act of 1673 which restricted office to those who took the sacraments of this established church. But he did not believe in an exclusive or a persecuting Church, and he was tolerant of unorthodox views because his own were unorthodox. He favoured both freedom of conscience and

[1] E.g. by A. Browning, *English Historical Documents* (1953), pp. 211–16; and by Dr. Jones, op. cit. p. 213 n.

[2] For instance, the writer chooses as his example of the way in which the over-representation of some shires has led to the passing of acts 'to the prejudice of the whole body of the people, merely to advance the gains and advantage of some particular places', the agitation by the western counties for the passing of the Irish Cattle Act in 1666–7; but Shaftesbury had strongly supported that agitation. Again, the writer says, 'To me it seems extremely irregular to see the unfledged youth make his first advances into the world in the quality of a burgess for Parliament', and suggests a minimum age of 40. Since Shaftesbury had himself entered the Commons as an 'unfledged youth' of 18, and had procured a seat for his son at the same age, he would hardly have written this. Some passages in the pamphlet, such as that referring to the writs of *quo warranto*, must have been written after his death; and, for what the argument from style is worth, the whole does not seem to me to be in Shaftesbury's. The pamphlet is printed in full in the *Somers Tracts* (1812), viii. 396–403.

[3] Evelyn, iv. 328.

freedom of worship for Dissenters. Had he triumphed in 1681 it is likely that the Toleration Act of 1689 would have been anticipated, and even possible that in return for their political support the Test Act would have become a dead letter, like the Corporation Act. The more extreme sects like the Quakers would have benefited with the rest. So far as the Catholics were concerned, Shaftesbury has naturally gone down to history as their vehement opponent, and certainly he had no sympathy with their religious point of view at any time in his life. Yet it has to be remembered that in 1662 and 1672 he was prepared to support Declarations of Indulgence which made practical concessions to Catholics as well as to Dissenters. It was only when Catholicism presented a serious political danger in the person of the heir to the throne that Shaftesbury came out strongly against it and countenanced what was in effect persecution. It is curious to reflect how through the apparently favourable but really unlucky dynastic accident that the heir to the throne was a Papist the fortunes of Catholics were in the end held back when they might have hoped for the peaceful development of a practical indulgence. The possibility that Catholics might not merely be quietly indulged but be permitted to aim at supremacy under an arbitrary-minded king like James had to be prevented, and Shaftesbury took the lead in this.

In the political and religious policies which he favoured, Shaftesbury was then, within limits, progressive. In the same way his colonial and commercial ideas were on the whole enlightened, but he was no believer in any sort of social equality. Ranke, viewing him with possibly greater objectivity than English historians bound up in English party conflicts, wrote that he 'seized the ideas which had the greatest future', and in another passage: 'He started from the conception of tolerance, as Locke had done: Locke's principles are those of Shaftesbury; their friendship rested, like all true friendships in men of mature years, upon a community of ideas. However much the phases vary in which Shaftesbury appears, through all there runs, if we may so say, one single liberal principle logically pursued. . . . He may be regarded as the principal founder of that great party which, in opposition to the prerogative and to uniformity, has inscribed upon its banner political freedom and religious tolerance.'[1] But, probably with the prerogative Declaration of Indulgence in mind, Ranke thought that religious toleration was more important to him than parliamentary government, and there were times when he plainly considered the possibility that in Shaftesbury's mind both might be a means to political advancement rather than true principles sincerely held.

This brings us to discuss the first of the two gravest charges which are commonly levelled at him—the charge that he was resolved 'to ruin or to rule the state', that his objective was the exercise of power and that it was immaterial to him on what basis it rested. Superficially this motivation

[1] *History of England*, trans. Sir R. Lodge (1875), iii. 520, iv. 166–7.

seems the easy explanation for his numerous changes of political party—
from Royalist to Parliamentarian in the Civil War, from membership of
the Barebones Parliament and Cromwell's Council of State to opposition
to the Protectorate and eventual Royalism, from service of Charles II to
opposition to him. Contemporary Tory propagandists like L'Estrange
made great play with the idea that these shifts demonstrated Shaftesbury's
basic insincerity and that no sensible person could be advised to place any
reliance in him. Charles himself is said to have nicknamed him 'Little
Sincerity' (though sincerity was not the most obvious of his own attributes)
and others called him 'the Dorsetshire eel' (*Dorsettensis anguilla*), 'because
he could wriggle out of anyone's grasp'.[1]

With such estimates of Shaftesbury's record the Whig Burnet was
fully in agreement: 'by his changing sides so often it was very visible how
little he was to be depended on.' But at the same time Burnet was astonished
to discover that Shaftesbury himself was completely insensitive to such
criticisms: indeed, 'he was not ashamed to reckon up the many turns he had
made; and he valued himself on the doing it at the properest season, and in
the best manner'.[2] Burnet threw up his hands in horror and disgust at
such cynical 'meanness or levity'. But was Shaftesbury in fact demonstrating a cynicism which would have been not only morally reprehensible but
impolitic as well? Or was he in effect saying that 'what Shaftesbury thinks
today, England thinks tomorrow', that the right course both for Shaftesbury and for England might vary with the political circumstances of the
day, and that he had no regrets about any of the past choices that he had
made?

There is no simple answer to this problem. It would be unwise to underestimate a politician's urge for power or his instinct for survival at any
time, and a historian who claimed that even in normal times these motives
did not influence a politician to make any compromising manoeuvres
would be foolish indeed. Shaftesbury's times were far from being normal.
In the general political instability only extreme supporters of Divine
Right monarchy and extreme Republicans could adopt the attitude of
undeviating loyalty to a party even if it entailed exile or martyrdom. For
the great majority political life was not a matter of attaching oneself to one
or other of two clearly defined parties and devoting one's career to it;
rather it was a question of constantly revising one's attitude in the confusion
of rapidly changing circumstances and deciding what course of action and
what affiliations were most likely to further one's general objectives,
public and personal. In the case of Shaftesbury it has been argued in the
earlier chapters of this book that there was a logical political argument
for a believer in parliamentary government and religious liberty making

[1] J. Warner, *History of the English Persecution of the Catholics and the Presbyterian Plot*,
ed. J. A. Birrell for the Catholic Record Society (1953), i. 27, 183.
[2] Burnet, i. 174 and *Supplement*, p. 59.

the changes that he did at particular times, in 1644, in 1653–4, in 1659–60, and in 1673, because the changes seemed most likely to further the ideals in which he believed. In all these periods he made decisions which involved the loss of office or of the possibility of office. In 1644 his move to the Parliamentarians lost him his estates, the chance of a peerage, and the advantages of trading on his Coventry connexions. In 1654 and 1659 he preferred opposition to the possibility of serving the governments of the Commonwealth, so that he was nearly 39 when he gained his first minor ministerial office, that of Chancellor of the Exchequer. In 1673 his conduct led to his dismissal from the highest office of all, that of Lord Chancellor. Equally in 1667 he did not join in the general rush to hunt down Clarendon, and endangered his prospects; and in and after 1673 he rejected various opportunities to return to office which a more unprincipled man might have accepted. While it is theoretically possible that in some of these cases he might have been sacrificing advancement in the present for the sake of more brilliant prospects in the future, this is hardly the record of a man whose aim was power and office at all costs; it differs markedly from the career of a Sunderland, creeping back to office under different regimes.

Most significant of all is the fact that the very Tory propagandists who dwelt most on Shaftesbury's alleged insincerity and unreliability tried to combine this with arguing or implying that under all his surface changes he was a man of the opposition, even a Republican, at heart. The 'insincerity' to which they really objected was that of his ministerial period between 1660–73, when he had simulated a devotion to the King which he did not feel. Here Roger North may be taken to speak for many of his fellow-Tories:

Another token is, that his Lordship, from the time he was openly determined that way, shewed a remarkable constancy and perseverance in the same steps of opposition to the Court; not lightly, or as for humour, but desperately and bloodily against the King, his family and government during all the rest of his life. And no means served, as, I believe, many, and very considerable, and some notoriously, were used, to quiet him; but all would not do. He was not, like the Party volant, waiting for proffers to determine him. . . . In place or out of place, he moved not the least from his purpose, or cast an eye towards returning into the interest of the Crown, upon any emergence that happened either of favour or displeasure. Therefore he was not a person so given to change as many thought when they nicknamed him my Lord Shiftsbury: his changes were, as Caesar's, only *mutando rationem belli*.[1]

For North and his fellow-Tories, in the last ten years of his life the natural malignity towards government which had always been present but partially concealed was once more fully revealed. This may be taken as an acknowledgement of consistency of principle of a sort: it is the 'vigorous

---

[1] North, *Examen* (1740), p. 42.

and indefatigable champion of civil and ecclesiastical liberty' viewed from the other side.

The second charge against Shaftesbury concerns not the sincerity of his motives but the unscrupulousness of his methods. The burden of this charge may be to some extent reduced but by no means removed. It is not the case that he prompted Titus Oates and his fellow-informers to say what they did say; nor that everything done or said or written by any Whig during the Popish Plot was done or said or written by puppets at his direction; nor necessarily that he contemplated from the beginning the possibility that innocent people might have to die for his political purposes; nor that he can be blamed entirely for the verdicts of juries under the guidance of judges and legal officers who were, after all, appointed by the King. He is rather to be censured for yielding to the temptation to use Oates's disclosures to solve the problem of a desperate political situation, as it appeared to him. In the summer of 1678 the King had substantial armed forces in being, Parliament seemed helpless, and the heir to the throne stood for everything that was objectionable to Shaftesbury; there was a 'Popish Plot' of a sort in that Catholics were indulged for the moment and hoping for more in the next reign. It is easy to see why Shaftesbury decided first to make use of the excitement generated by Oates to press for Exclusion and then, when hindered by the King's delaying tactics, to avail himself of the willingness of others to come forward with new stories which would keep public opinion at that fever-pitch that would alone serve to bring pressure to bear upon the House of Lords and the King for their consent to the Bill. Anyone with a suitable tale could be presented at the appropriate moment to the Council, to the House of Commons, or to the House of Lords; and if the tale involved accusations, then truth or falsehood, guilt or innocence, could be sifted by the appointed process of law. It is easy to see where such a slippery slope would lead in a crisis which was not quickly settled, but prolonged over three years.

It should be remembered that even if Shaftesbury had remained on his Dorset estates, silent and inactive, in 1678, the excitement in London would have been little less. Oates's story, Coleman's letters, the murder of Sir Edmund Berry Godfrey, and Ralph Montagu's revelation of Danby's secret negotiations with Louis XIV would have had the same effect on public opinion. The idea of the Exclusion of a Popish successor would have occurred to others in the Country Party (if indeed it had not occurred to them previously) and there is no reason to suppose that they would have acted differently in regard to Oates and any other informers who came forward. Neither the Exclusion crisis itself nor the more objectionable techniques employed can be regarded as though they were the creation of Shaftesbury, as the evil genius of the Whigs manipulating them as his puppets and leading them to eventual disgrace and disaster. What he did was rather to lend them the prestige of his name, the inspiration of his leadership, the impetus of his immense organizing ability, and the assistance of his tactical skill, so that the crisis was much more prolonged and the Exclusionists came nearer to success than they would have done under a lesser man. And even as it was, there were times, as in March 1679, when Shaftesbury was rather carried along by his followers than able to lead them like a flock of sheep as and where he wished them to go; and amongst them were people, like Montagu, Algernon Sidney, Sir William Jones, and others, who accepted his influence in the Country Party only with considerable unwillingness and acted in their own way whenever they thought it good. Equally the evidence does not permit us to assume that everything done by men like Hetherington to procure informers or everything done by men like Harbord and Scott to hound Pepys was necessarily done at Shaftesbury's direct instigation.

For these reasons it would be unwise to regard Shaftesbury as a peculiarly bad man, leading a flock of comparatively innocent sheep to a destruction which they would not otherwise have incurred. Nevertheless it would plainly be impossible to extenuate his conduct completely. No political leader can escape responsibility for what is done in his name, or for what, though possibly not directly planned by him, is at least the indirect consequence of his actions. Oates and his fellows benefited from his encouragement, and many would hardly have come forward without the prospect of his patronage. In the sense that there was no plot to assassinate the King, the perfectly legitimate political objective of Exclusion was based on a lie which in due time was bound to be revealed as such and the revelation of which helped to enable James to come to the throne in 1685 with greater powers than he would otherwise have possessed.

Such thoughts have led one authority to describe him as the 'Jekyll and Hyde' of English politics in the period.[1] He was a man of charm, intellect, courage, great constructive ability for which he never had a satisfactory outlet, and enlightened political and religious ideas which were on the whole in advance of his time; but in his methods he was very much a man of his age. Too much can be made of this contrast between relatively modern ideas and less than modern methods. Not all twentieth-century politicians have been scrupulously careful about the bogeys which they raise in order to mobilize public opinion behind their policies, although nowadays the penalties for the incidental victims are usually less barbaric than that of hanging, drawing, and quartering. The problem of the relationship between ends and means crops up in all ages; only forms and circumstances differ.

We return in conclusion to discuss the nature and extent of Shaftesbury's bequest to posterity. Superficially at least it was very little. When he lay on his death-bed in exile he could not boast of success in any of his enterprises, except possibly for the existence of a permanent, though still

[1] D. Ogg, *England in the Reign of Charles II* (1955), i. 330.

small, settlement in Carolina. Sometimes he is spoken of as the founder of one of the two great traditional parties, but the fortunes of the Whigs were low when he died, and certainly if one thinks in terms of a close-knit party organization there was little which the Whigs inherited from the Exclusion Parliaments when normal parliamentary life was resumed. Yet if one accepts a broader definition of Whiggery in terms of attitudes of mind and political habits, the case may be different. The gap in time between 1681 and 1689 was not great. All the members of the Convention Parliament had lived through the Exclusion crisis; many of them derived their first parliamentary experience from Parliaments under Shaftesbury's influence. They might think it undesirable to honour his memory, but they could not free themselves from their past experience. The Bill of Rights and the Toleration Act may be regarded as the taking up of Shaftesbury's work under different auspices; and in so far as Locke provided the theoretical justification for the Revolution settlement, the connexion with the earlier age was both personal and intellectual. It was Shaftesbury's function to transmit part of what he had taken over from the Parliamentarians of the Civil War to become part of the Whiggism of the eighteenth century, and of the liberalism of the nineteenth. He died while the people under his command were still in the wilderness; others would lead them into the promised land.

INDEX

Note: The abbreviation S. indicates Shaftesbury throughout